HEALTH CARE STATE RANKINGS
2007

Health Care in the 50 United States

Kathleen O'Leary Morgan and Scott Morgan, Editors

Morgan Quitno Press
© Copyright 2007, All Rights Reserved

512 East 9th Street, P.O. Box 1656
Lawrence, KS 66044-8656
USA
800-457-0742 or 785-841-3534
www.statestats.com
Fifteenth Edition

ISBN:
978-0-7401-1713-8
0-7401-1713-0
ISSN: 1065-1403

Health Care State Rankings 2007 sells for $59.95 ($6 shipping) and is only available in paper binding. For those who prefer ranking information tailored to a particular state, we also offer *Health Care State Perspectives*, state-specific reports for each of the 50 states. These individual guides provide information on a state's data and rank for each of the categories featured in the national *Health Care State Rankings* volume. Perspectives sell for $19 or $9.50 if ordered with *Health Care State Rankings*. If crime statistics are your interest, please ask about our annual *Crime State Rankings* ($59.95 paper). If you are interested in city and metropolitan crime data, we offer *City Crime Rankings* ($49.95 paper). For a general view of the states, please ask about our annual *State Rankings* reference book ($59.95 paper) or our new annual *State Trends* ($59.95 paper). Also available is *Education State Rankings*. This view of preK-12 education at the state level is $59.95. All of our books are available on CD-ROM in PDF format (same price as printed book) or with both PDF format and data sets in various database formats ($99.95). Shipping and handling is $6 per order. For information, please visit our website at www.statestats.com.

Fifteenth Edition
Printed in the United States of America
March 2007

PREFACE

A strong health care system is a major factor in the quality of life of every state and community. Along with good medical care and hospitals, citizens and leaders need to have access to straightforward, unbiased and reliable health care information. This newly revised, 15th edition of *Health Care State Rankings* provides a huge collection of relevant, user-friendly health care data for each of the 50 United States. Our books provide this information with no agenda other than to bring readers the most up-to-date and reliable collection of state health care facts possible.

Virtually every aspect of health care is addressed in *Health Care State Rankings 2007*. Births and reproductive health, deaths, disease, insurance and finance, health care providers, facilities and physical fitness are compared state-by-state. From the average cost of health insurance premiums to teen birth rates, *Health Care State Rankings 2007* is an essential information tool for researchers, librarians, community leaders and concerned citizens throughout the United States.

Important Notes About *Health Care State Rankings 2007*

Health Care State Rankings 2007 presents information from government and private sector sources in one user-friendly volume. Our goal is to translate complicated and often convoluted health care data into easy-to-understand, meaningful state comparisons. As we revise this volume each year, we reexamine each table, update most, delete others and add new tables of interest to our readers.

We make every effort to present the data in *Health Care State Rankings 2007* as simply and straightforwardly as possible. Source information and other pertinent footnotes are clearly shown at the bottom of each page. National totals, rates and percentages are prominently displayed at the top of each table. Every other line is shaded in gray for easier reading. In addition, numerous information-finding tools are provided: a thorough table of contents, table listings at the beginning of each chapter, a roster of sources with addresses and phone numbers, a detailed index and a chapter thumb index.

The numbers shown in *Health Care State Rankings* require no additional calculations to convert them from millions, thousands, etc. All states are ranked on a high to low basis, with any ties among the states listed alphabetically for a given ranking. Negative numbers are shown in parentheses "( )." For tables with national totals (as opposed to rates, per capitas, etc.) a separate column is included showing what percent of the national total each individual state's total represents. This column is headed by "% of USA." This percentage figure is particularly interesting when compared with a state's share of the nation's population for a particular year (see appendix.)

For those researchers needing information for just one state, our *Health Care State Perspective* series of publications fills the bill. These 21-page comb bound reports feature data and ranking information for an individual state, as reported in *Health Care State Rankings 2007*. (For example *California Health Care in Perspective* features information about the state of California only.) These serve as handy, quick reference guides for those who do not want to page through the entire *Health Care State Rankings* volume searching for information for their particular state. *Health Care State Perspectives* sell for $19. When purchased with a copy of *Health Care State Rankings 2007*, these handy quick reference guides are just $9.50. For additional information, please call us toll-free at 1-800-457-0742.

Other Books From Morgan Quitno Press

In addition to *Health Care State Rankings 2007*, our company offers five other annual rankings reference books. *State Rankings* is our original title, providing a general view of the states. Now in its 18th edition, *State Ranking 2007* provides easy-to-understand state comparisons in agriculture, transportation, government finance, health, crime, education, housing, energy and so much more. *Education State Rankings 2006-2007* takes an in-depth look at preK-12 education, comparing states in teachers' salaries, class sizes, per pupil spending, graduation rates and 400 other categories. *Crime State Rankings 2007* provides a huge collection of user-friendly state statistics regarding law enforcement personnel and expenditures, corrections, juvenile crime and delinquency, arrests and offenses. A companion volume, *City Crime Rankings,* compares crime in all metropolitan areas and cities of 75,000 or more population (approx. 370 cities). Numbers of crimes, crime rates and changes in crime rates over one and five years are presented for all major crime categories reported by the FBI. *State Trends* is the newest reference book in Morgan Quitno's collection. Now in its third edition, this volume has earned rave reviews for providing a quick and easy way to track important changes in the 50 United States. One, five, 10 and 20-year trends are measured for a wide variety of quality of life factors.

The information in all our books also is available on CD-ROM. These electronic editions provide a searchable PDF version of each book as well as the raw data in .dbf, Excel and ASCII formats. Additional information about all of our publications, including prices and ISBN numbers, is available online at www. morganquitno.com or by calling 1-800-457-0742.

Finally, we are so thankful for the many librarians, government and health care industry officials who help us understand and decipher data year after year. Thanks also to you, our readers, for helping us keep our books relevant and useful. Please continue to send your comments to information@morganquitno.com. We look forward to hearing from you.   - THE EDITORS

WHICH STATE IS HEALTHIEST?

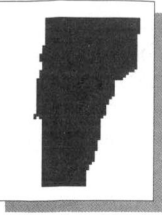

Vermont is on a healthy winning streak! For the fifth time in six years, Vermont is the nation's Healthiest State. The Green Mountain State has earned bragging rights to first place in Morgan Quitno's 15th annual Healthiest State Award due to its healthy population and access to affordable and reliable health care. Following Vermont were Minnesota, Massachusetts, Maine and New Hampshire.

At the opposite end of the rankings list, Louisiana slipped to last place, a position it last held in 2005. Joining Louisiana on the less healthy end of the rankings scale were New Mexico, Mississippi, Nevada and Florida.

Methodology

The Healthiest State designation is awarded based on 21 factors chosen from the 2007 edition of Morgan Quitno's annual reference book, *Health Care State Rankings.* These factors reflect access to health care providers, affordability of health care and a generally healthy population (see box below.)

The 21 factors selected for this year's

2007 HEALTHIEST STATE AWARD

RANK	STATE	SUM	06	RANK	STATE	SUM	06
1	Vermont	21.43	1	26	Montana	3.02	27
2	Minnesota	19.45	3	27	New York	0.97	31
3	Massachusetts	17.32	6	28	Colorado	0.44	32
4	Maine	16.25	4	29	Kentucky	0.18	26
5	New Hampshire	16.15	2	30	Wyoming	0.10	25
6	Nebraska	15.79	7	31	North Carolina	0.07	30
7	Iowa	15.20	5	32	Illinois	(0.11)	33
8	Utah	13.93	8	33	Indiana	(0.25)	28
9	Hawaii	13.89	10	34	Missouri	(0.42)	34
10	Kansas	12.69	12	35	Maryland	(0.71)	35
11	Rhode Island	12.17	13	36	Alaska	(4.71)	39
12	North Dakota	11.93	11	37	Arkansas	(5.59)	36
13	Connecticut	10.74	9	38	Tennessee	(7.01)	38
14	Washington	9.71	20	39	Delaware	(7.02)	37
15	Wisconsin	8.17	14	40	Alabama	(8.64)	42
16	New Jersey	8.04	16	41	Oklahoma	(9.48)	45
17	Oregon	6.77	15	42	Arizona	(10.17)	40
18	Virginia	5.73	21	43	Texas	(10.32)	46
19	California	5.46	19	44	Georgia	(10.78)	44
20	Ohio	5.41	24	45	South Carolina	(11.14)	42
21	Michigan	5.04	23	46	Florida	(13.05)	41
22	South Dakota	4.77	17	47	Nevada	(16.45)	47
23	Pennsylvania	4.71	29	48	Mississippi	(21.00)	50
24	Idaho	4.57	18	49	New Mexico	(21.18)	49
25	West Virginia	4.00	22	50	Louisiana	(23.65)	48

award remained unchanged from those used last year. The factors were divided into two groups: those that are "negative" for which a high ranking would be considered bad for a state, and those that are "positive" for which a high ranking would be considered good for a state. Rates for each of the 21 factors were processed through a formula that measures how a state compares to the national average for a given category. The positive and negative nature of each factor was taken into account as part of the formula. Once these computations were made, the factors then were weighted equally. These weighted scores then were added together to get a state's final score ("SUM" on the table above). This way, states are assessed based on how they stack up against the national average. The end result is that the farther below the national average a state's health ranking is, the lower (and less healthy) it ranks. The farther above the national average, the higher (and healthier) a state ranks. This same methodology is used for our Dangerous State and Safest/Dangerous City Awards.

The table above shows how each state fared in the 2007 Healthiest State Award as well as its placement in 2006. Our award always spurs some rousing debate among states. While our selection of factors clearly affects the final rankings, we believe that they provide a solid measurement of how states are faring in regard to health care.

Congratulations to Vermont for it's continuing success!

- THE EDITORS

POSITIVE (+) AND NEGATIVE (-) FACTORS CONSIDERED:
1. Births of Low Birthweight as a Percent of All Births (Table 14) -
2. Teenage Birth Rate (Table 33) -
3. Percent of Mothers Receiving Late or No Prenatal Care (Table 62) -
4. Age-Adjusted Death Rate (Table 90) -
5. Infant Mortality Rate (Table 96) -
6. Age-Adjusted Death Rate by Malignant Neoplasms (Table 156) -
7. Age-Adjusted Death Rate by Suicide (Table 180) -
8. Average Annual Family Coverage Health Insurance Premium (Table 237) -
9. Percent of Population Not Covered by Health Insurance (Table 241) -
10. Percent of Children Not Covered by Health Insurance (Table 245) -
11. Estimated Rate of New Cancer Cases (Table 324) -
12. AIDS Rate (Table 352) -
13. Sexually Transmitted Disease Rate (Table 386) -
14. Percent of Population Lacking Access to Primary Care (Table 411) -
15. Percent of Adults Who Are Binge Drinkers (Table 494) -
16. Percent of Adults Who Smoke (Table 495) -
17. Percent of Adults Obese (Table 502) -
18. Percent of Adults Who Do Not Exercise (Table 504) -
19. Beds in Community Hospitals per 100,000 Population (Table 197) +
20. Percent of Children Aged 19-35 Months Immunized (Table 381) +
21. Safety Belt Usage Rate (Table 513) +

TABLE OF CONTENTS

I. Births and Reproductive Health

1   Births in 2005
2   Birth Rate in 2005
3   Percent Change in Birth Rate: 1996 to 2005
4   Births in 2004
5   Birth Rate in 2004
6   Fertility Rate in 2005
7   Births to White Women in 2005
8   White Births as a Percent of All Births in 2005
9   Births to Black Women in 2005
10 Black Births as a Percent of All Births in 2005
11 Births to Hispanic Women in 2005
12 Hispanic Births as a Percent of All Births in 2005
13 Births of Low Birthweight in 2005
14 Births of Low Birthweight as a Percent of All Births in 2005
15 Births of Low Birthweight to White Women in 2005
16 Births of Low Birthweight to White Women as a Percent of All Births to White Women in 2005
17 Births of Low Birthweight to Black Women in 2005
18 Births of Low Birthweight to Black Women as a Percent of All Births to Black Women in 2005
19 Births of Low Birthweight to Hispanic Women in 2005
20 Births of Low Birthweight to Hispanic Women as a Percent of All Births to Hispanic Women in 2005
21 Births to Unmarried Women in 2005
22 Births to Unmarried Women as a Percent of All Births in 2005
23 Births to Unmarried White Women in 2005
24 Births to Unmarried White Women as a Percent of All Births to White Women in 2005
25 Births to Unmarried Black Women in 2005
26 Births to Unmarried Black Women as a Percent of All Births to Black Women in 2005
27 Births to Unmarried Hispanic Women in 2005
28 Births to Unmarried Hispanic Women as a Percent of All Births to Hispanic Women in 2005
29 Pregnancy Rate in 2003
30 Teenage Pregnancy Rate in 2003
31 Percent Change in Teenage Pregnancy Rate: 1999 to 2003
32 Births to Teenage Mothers in 2005
33 Teenage Birth Rate in 2005
34 Births to Teenage Mothers as a Percent of Births in 2005
35 Percent Change in Teenage Birth Rate: 2001 to 2005
36 Teenage Birth Rate in 2004
37 Births to White Teenage Mothers in 2005
38 White Teenage Birth Rate in 2005
39 Births to White Teenage Mothers as a Percent of White Births in 2005
40 Births to Black Teenage Mothers in 2005
41 Black Teenage Birth Rate in 2005
42 Births to Black Teenage Mothers as a Percent of Black Births in 2005
43 Births to Young Teenagers: 2002 to 2004
44 Young Teen Birthrate: 2002 to 2004
45 Births to Women 35 to 54 Years Old in 2004
46 Births to Women 35 to 54 Years Old as a Percent of All Births in 2004
47 Births by Vaginal Delivery in 2005
48 Percent of Births by Vaginal Delivery in 2005
49 Births by Cesarean Delivery in 2005
50 Percent of Births by Cesarean Delivery in 2005
51 Percent Change in Rate of Cesarean Births: 2001 to 2005
52 Twin Birth Rate: 2002-2004
53 Assisted Reproductive Technology Procedures in 2003
54 Infants Born from Assisted Reproductive Technology Procedures in 2003
55 Percent of Assisted Reproductive Technology Procedures that Resulted in Live Births in 2003
56 Percent of Total Live Births Resulting from Assisted Reproductive Technology Procedures in 2003
57 Percent of Assisted Reproductive Technology Procedure Infants Born in Multiple Birth Deliveries in 2003
58 Percent of Mothers Beginning Prenatal Care in First Trimester in 2004
59 Percent of White Mothers Beginning Prenatal Care in First Trimester in 2004

TABLE OF CONTENTS (continued)

60   Percent of Black Mothers Beginning Prenatal Care in First Trimester in 2004
61   Percent of Hispanic Mothers Beginning Prenatal Care in First Trimester in 2004
62   Percent of Mothers Receiving Late or No Prenatal Care in 2004
63   Percent of White Mothers Receiving Late or No Prenatal Care in 2004
64   Percent of Black Mothers Receiving Late or No Prenatal Care in 2004
65   Percent of Hispanic Mothers Receiving Late or No Prenatal Care in 2004

Abortions

66   Reported Legal Abortions in 2003
67   Percent Change in Reported Legal Abortions: 1999 to 2003
68   Reported Legal Abortions per 1,000 Live Births in 2003
69   Reported Legal Abortions per 1,000 Women Ages 15 to 44 in 2003
70   Percent of Legal Abortions Obtained by Out-Of-State Residents in 2003
71   Percent of Reported Legal Abortions that were First-Time Abortions: 2003
72   Percent of Reported Legal Abortions Obtained by White Women in 2003
73   Percent of Reported Legal Abortions Obtained by Black Women in 2003
74   Percent of Reported Legal Abortions Obtained by Hispanic Women in 2003
75   Percent of Reported Legal Abortions Obtained by Married Women in 2003
76   Percent of Reported Legal Abortions Obtained by Unmarried Women in 2003
77   Reported Legal Abortions Obtained by Teenagers in 2003
78   Percent of Reported Legal Abortions Obtained by Teenagers in 2003
79   Reported Legal Abortions Obtained by Teenagers 17 Years and Younger in 2003
80   Percent of Reported Legal Abortions Obtained by Teenagers 17 Years and Younger in 2003
81   Percent of Teenage Abortions Obtained by Teenagers 17 Years and Younger in 2003
82   Reported Legal Abortions Performed at 12 Weeks or Less of Gestation in 2003
83   Percent of Reported Legal Abortions Performed at 12 Weeks or Less of Gestation in 2003
84   Reported Legal Abortions Performed at or After 21 Weeks of Gestation in 2003
85   Percent of Reported Legal Abortions Performed at or After 21 Weeks of Gestation in 2003

II. Deaths

86   Deaths in 2005
87   Death Rate in 2005
88   Deaths in 2004
89   Death Rate in 2004
90   Age-Adjusted Death Rate in 2004
91   Percent Change in Death Rate: 1995 to 2004
92   Deaths in 2003
93   Death Rate in 2003
94   Age-Adjusted Death Rate in 2003
95   Infant Deaths in 2005
96   Infant Mortality Rate in 2005
97   Infant Deaths in 2003
98   Infant Mortality Rate in 2003
99   White Infant Deaths in 2003
100   White Infant Mortality Rate in 2003
101   Black Infant Deaths in 2003
102   Black Infant Mortality Rate in 2003
103   Neonatal Deaths in 2003
104   Neonatal Death Rate in 2003
105   White Neonatal Deaths in 2003
106   White Neonatal Death Rate in 2003
107   Black Neonatal Deaths in 2003
108   Black Neonatal Death Rate in 2003
109   Deaths by AIDS in 2003
110   Death Rate by AIDS in 2003
111   Age-Adjusted Death Rate by AIDS in 2003
112   Estimated Deaths by Cancer in 2007
113   Estimated Death Rate by Cancer in 2007
114   Age-Adjusted Death Rate by Cancer for Males in 2003
115   Age-Adjusted Death Rate by Cancer for Females in 2003

TABLE OF CONTENTS (continued)

116 Estimated Deaths by Brain Cancer in 2007
117 Estimated Death Rate by Brain Cancer in 2007
118 Estimated Deaths by Female Breast Cancer in 2007
119 Age-Adjusted Death Rate by Female Breast Cancer in 2003
120 Estimated Deaths by Colon and Rectum Cancer in 2007
121 Estimated Death Rate by Colon and Rectum Cancer in 2007
122 Estimated Deaths by Leukemia in 2007
123 Estimated Death Rate by Leukemia in 2007
124 Estimated Deaths by Liver Cancer in 2007
125 Estimated Death Rate by Liver Cancer in 2007
126 Estimated Deaths by Lung Cancer in 2007
127 Estimated Death Rate by Lung Cancer in 2007
128 Estimated Deaths by Non-Hodgkin's Lymphoma in 2007
129 Estimated Death Rate by Non-Hodgkin's Lymphoma in 2007
130 Estimated Deaths by Pancreatic Cancer in 2007
131 Estimated Death Rate by Pancreatic Cancer in 2007
132 Estimated Deaths by Prostate Cancer in 2007
133 Age-Adjusted Death Rate by Prostate Cancer in 2003
134 Estimated Deaths by Ovarian Cancer in 2007
135 Estimated Death Rate by Ovarian Cancer in 2007
136 Deaths by Alzheimer's Disease in 2003
137 Death Rate by Alzheimer's Disease in 2003
138 Age-Adjusted Death Rate by Alzheimer's Disease in 2003
139 Deaths by Cerebrovascular Diseases in 2003
140 Death Rate by Cerebrovascular Diseases in 2003
141 Age-Adjusted Death Rate by Cerebrovascular Diseases in 2003
142 Deaths by Chronic Liver Disease and Cirrhosis in 2003
143 Death Rate by Chronic Liver Disease and Cirrhosis in 2003
144 Age-Adjusted Death Rate by Chronic Liver Disease and Cirrhosis in 2003
145 Deaths by Chronic Lower Respiratory Diseases in 2003
146 Death Rate by Chronic Lower Respiratory Diseases in 2003
147 Age-Adjusted Death Rate by Chronic Lower Respiratory Diseases in 2003
148 Deaths by Diabetes Mellitus in 2003
149 Death Rate by Diabetes Mellitus in 2003
150 Age-Adjusted Death Rate by Diabetes Mellitus in 2003
151 Deaths by Diseases of the Heart in 2003
152 Death Rate by Diseases of the Heart in 2003
153 Age-Adjusted Death Rate by Diseases of the Heart in 2003
154 Deaths by Malignant Neoplasms in 2003
155 Death Rate by Malignant Neoplasms in 2003
156 Age-Adjusted Death Rate by Malignant Neoplasms in 2003
157 Deaths by Nephritis and Other Kidney Diseases in 2003
158 Death Rate by Nephritis and Other Kidney Diseases in 2003
159 Age-Adjusted Death Rate by Nephritis and Other Kidney Diseases in 2003
160 Deaths by Pneumonia and Influenza in 2003
161 Death Rate by Pneumonia and Influenza in 2003
162 Age-Adjusted Death Rate by Pneumonia and Influenza in 2003
163 Deaths by Injury in 2003
164 Death Rate by Injury in 2003
165 Age-Adjusted Death Rate by Injury in 2003
166 Deaths by Accidents in 2003
167 Death Rate by Accidents in 2003
168 Age-Adjusted Death Rate by Accidents in 2003
169 Deaths by Motor Vehicle Accidents in 2003
170 Death Rate by Motor Vehicle Accidents in 2003
171 Age-Adjusted Death Rate by Motor Vehicle Accidents in 2003
172 Deaths by Firearm Injury in 2003
173 Death Rate by Firearm Injury in 2003
174 Age-Adjusted Death Rate by Firearm Injury in 2003
175 Deaths by Homicide in 2003
176 Death Rate by Homicide in 2003
177 Age-Adjusted Death Rate by Homicide in 2003

TABLE OF CONTENTS (continued)

178 Deaths by Suicide in 2003
179 Death Rate by Suicide in 2003
180 Age-Adjusted Death Rate by Suicide in 2003
181 Alcohol-Induced Deaths in 2003
182 Death Rate by Alcohol-Induced Deaths in 2003
183 Age-Adjusted Death Rate by Alcohol-Induced Deaths in 2003
184 Occupational Fatalities in 2005
185 Occupational Fatality Rate in 2005

III. Facilities

186 Community Hospitals in 2005
187 Rate of Community Hospitals in 2005
188 Community Hospitals per 1,000 Square Miles in 2005
189 Community Hospitals in Urban Areas in 2005
190 Percent of Community Hospitals in Urban Areas in 2005
191 Community Hospitals in Rural Areas in 2005
192 Percent of Community Hospitals in Rural Areas in 2005
193 Nongovernment Not-For-Profit Hospitals in 2005
194 Investor-Owned (For-Profit) Hospitals in 2005
195 State and Local Government-Owned Hospitals in 2005
196 Beds in Community Hospitals in 2005
197 Rate of Beds in Community Hospitals in 2005
198 Average Number of Beds per Community Hospital in 2005
199 Admissions to Community Hospitals in 2005
200 Inpatient Days in Community Hospitals in 2005
201 Average Daily Census in Community Hospitals in 2005
202 Average Stay in Community Hospitals in 2005
203 Occupancy Rate in Community Hospitals in 2005
204 Outpatient Visits to Community Hospitals in 2005
205 Emergency Outpatient Visits to Community Hospitals in 2005
206 Surgical Operations in Community Hospitals in 2005
207 Medicare and Medicaid Certified Facilities in 2007
208 Medicare and Medicaid Certified Hospitals in 2007
209 Beds in Medicare and Medicaid Certified Hospitals in 2007
210 Medicare and Medicaid Certified Children's Hospitals in 2007
211 Beds in Medicare and Medicaid Certified Children's Hospitals in 2007
212 Medicare and Medicaid Certified Rehabilitation Hospitals in 2007
213 Beds in Medicare and Medicaid Certified Rehabilitation Hospitals in 2007
214 Medicare and Medicaid Certified Psychiatric Hospitals in 2007
215 Beds in Medicare and Medicaid Certified Psychiatric Hospitals in 2007
216 Medicare and Medicaid Certified Outpatient Surgery Centers in 2007
217 Medicare and Medicaid Certified Community Mental Health Centers in 2007
218 Medicare and Medicaid Certified Outpatient Physical Therapy Facilities in 2007
219 Medicare and Medicaid Certified Rural Health Clinics in 2007
220 Medicare and Medicaid Certified Home Health Agencies in 2007
221 Medicare and Medicaid Certified Hospices in 2007
222 Hospice Patients in Residential Facilities in 2007
223 Medicare and Medicaid Certified Nursing Care Facilities in 2007
224 Beds in Medicare and Medicaid Certified Nursing Care Facilities in 2007
225 Rate of Beds in Medicare and Medicaid Certified Nursing Care Facilities in 2007
226 Nursing Home Occupancy Rate in 2004
227 Nursing Home Resident Rate in 2004
228 Nursing Home Population in 2004
229 Health Care Establishments in 2004

IV. Finance

230 Average Medical Malpractice Payment in 2004
231 Percent of Private-Sector Establishments That Offer Health Insurance: 2004
232 Percent of Private-Sector Establishments with Fewer Than 50 Employees That Offer Health Insurance: 2004
233 Percent of Private-Sector Establishments with More Than 50 Employees That Offer Health Insurance: 2004

TABLE OF CONTENTS (continued)

234 Average Annual Single Coverage Health Insurance Premium per Enrolled Employee in 2004
235 Average Annual Employee Contribution for Single Coverage Health Insurance in 2004
236 Percent of Total Premiums for Single Coverage Health Insurance Paid by Employees in 2004
237 Average Annual Family Coverage Health Insurance Premium per Enrolled Employee in 2004
238 Average Annual Employee Contribution for Family Coverage Health Insurance in 2004
239 Percent of Total Premiums for Family Coverage Health Insurance Paid by Employees in 2004
240 Persons Not Covered by Health Insurance in 2005
241 Percent of Population Not Covered by Health Insurance in 2005
242 Numerical Change in Persons Uninsured: 2001 to 2005
243 Percent Change in Persons Uninsured: 2001 to 2005
244 Change in Percent of Population Uninsured: 2001 to 2005
245 Percent of Children Not Covered by Health Insurance in 2005
246 Persons Covered by Health Insurance in 2005
247 Percent of Population Covered by Health Insurance in 2005
248 Percent of Population Covered by Private Health Insurance in 2005
249 Percent of Population Covered by Employment-Based Health Insurance in 2005
250 Percent of Population Covered by Direct Purchase Health Insurance in 2005
251 Percent of Population Covered by Government Health Insurance in 2005
252 Percent of Population Covered by Military Health Care in 2005
253 Percent of Children Covered by Health Insurance in 2005
254 Percent of Children Covered by Private Health Insurance in 2005
255 Percent of Children Covered by Employment-Based Health Insurance in 2005
256 Percent of Children Covered by Direct Purchase Health Insurance in 2005
257 Percent of Children Covered by Government Health Insurance in 2005
258 Percent of Children Covered by Military Health Care in 2005
259 Percent of Children Covered by Medicaid in 2005
260 State Children's Health Insurance Program (SCHIP) Enrollment in 2005
261 Percent Change in State Children's Health Insurance Program (SCHIP) Enrollment: 2004 to 2005
262 Percent of Children Enrolled in State Children's Health Insurance Program (SCHIP) in 2005
263 Expenditures for State Children's Health Insurance Program (SCHIP) in 2005
264 Per Capita Expenditures for State Children's Health Insurance Program (SCHIP) in 2005
265 Expenditures per State Children's Health Insurance Program (SCHIP) Participant in 2005
266 Health Maintenance Organizations (HMOs) in 2006
267 Enrollees in Health Maintenance Organizations (HMOs) in 2006
268 Percent Change in Enrollees in Health Maintenance Organizations (HMOs): 2005 to 2006
269 Percent of Population Enrolled in Health Maintenance Organizations (HMOs) in 2006
270 Percent of Insured Population Enrolled in Health Maintenance Organizations (HMOs) in 2006
271 Medicare Enrollees in 2005
272 Percent Change in Medicare Enrollees: 2004 to 2005
273 Percent of Population Enrolled in Medicare in 2005
274 Enrollment in Medicare Prescription Drug Plans as of June 14, 2006
275 Percent of Population Enrolled in Medicare Prescription Drug Plans in 2006
276 Medicare Managed Care Enrollees in 2005
277 Percent of Medicare Enrollees in Managed Care Programs in 2005
278 Percent of Physicians Participating in Medicare in 2006
279 Medicare Program Payments in 2004
280 Per Capita Medicare Program Payments in 2004
281 Medicare Program Payments per Enrollee in 2004
282 Medicaid Enrollment in 2005
283 Percent of Population Enrolled in Medicaid in 2005
284 Medicaid Managed Care Enrollment in 2005
285 Percent of Medicaid Enrollees in Managed Care in 2005
286 Estimated Medicaid Expenditures in 2006
287 Estimated Per Capita Medicaid Expenditures in 2006
288 Estimated Medicaid Expenditures as a Percent of Total Expenditures in 2006
289 Percent Change in Medicaid Expenditures: 2005 to 2006
290 Medicaid Expenditures in 2005
291 Per Capita Medicaid Expenditures in 2005
292 Medicaid Expenditures per Beneficiary in 2005
293 Federal Medicaid Matching Fund Rate for 2007
294 State and Local Government Expenditures for Hospitals in 2004
295 Per Capita State and Local Government Expenditures for Hospitals in 2004
296 Percent of State and Local Government Expenditures Used for Hospitals in 2004

TABLE OF CONTENTS (continued)

297   State and Local Government Expenditures for Health Programs in 2004
298   Per Capita State and Local Government Expenditures for Health Programs in 2004
299   Percent of State and Local Government Expenditures Used for Health Programs in 2004
300   Estimated Tobacco Settlement Revenues in FY 2007
301   Personal Health Care Expenditures in 2004
302   Health Care Expenditures as a Percent of Gross State Product in 2004
303   Per Capita Personal Health Care Expenditures in 2004
304   Expenditures for Hospital Care in 2004
305   Percent of Total Personal Health Care Expenditures Spent on Hospital Care in 2004
306   Per Capita Expenditures for Hospital Care in 2004
307   Expenditures for Physician and Clinical Services in 2004
308   Percent of Total Personal Health Care Expenditures Spent on Physician and Clinical Services in 2004
309   Per Capita Expenditures for Physician and Clinical Services in 2004
310   Expenditures for Dental Services in 2004
311   Percent of Total Personal Health Care Expenditures Spent on Dental Services in 2004
312   Per Capita Expenditures for Dental Services in 2004
313   Expenditures for Other Professional Health Care Services in 2004
314   Percent of Total Personal Health Care Expenditures Spent on Other Professional Health Care Services in 2004
315   Per Capita Expenditures for Other Professional Health Care Services in 2004
316   Expenditures for Nursing Home Care in 2004
317   Percent of Total Personal Health Care Expenditures Spent on Nursing Home Care in 2004
318   Per Capita Expenditures for Nursing Home Care in 2004
319   Expenditures for Prescription Drugs in 2004
320   Percent of Total Personal Health Care Expenditures Spent Spent on Prescription Drugs in 2004
321   Per Capita Expenditures for Prescription Drugs in 2004
322   Projected National Health Care Expenditures in 2007

V. Incidence of Disease

323   Estimated New Cancer Cases in 2007
324   Estimated Rate of New Cancer Cases in 2007
325   Age-Adjusted Cancer Incidence Rates for Males in 2003
326   Age-Adjusted Cancer Incidence Rates for Females in 2003
327   Estimated New Cases of Bladder Cancer in 2007
328   Estimated Rate of New Bladder Cancer Cases in 2007
329   Estimated New Female Breast Cancer Cases in 2007
330   Age-Adjusted Incidence Rate of Female Breast Cancer Cases in 2003
331   Percent of Women 40 and Older Who Have Had a Mammogram in the Past Two Years: 2004
332   Estimated New Colon and Rectum Cancer Cases in 2007
333   Estimated Rate of New Colon and Rectum Cancer Cases in 2007
334   Percent of Adults Receiving Recent Sigmoidoscopy or Colonoscopy Exam: 2004
335   Estimated New Leukemia Cases in 2007
336   Estimated Rate of New Leukemia Cases in 2007
337   Estimated New Lung Cancer Cases in 2007
338   Estimated Rate of New Lung Cancer Cases in 2007
339   Estimated New Non-Hodgkin's Lymphoma Cases in 2007
340   Estimated Rate of New Non-Hodgkin's Lymphoma Cases in 2007
341   Estimated New Prostate Cancer Cases in 2007
342   Age-Adjusted Incidence Rate of Prostate Cancer Cases in 2003
343   Percent of Males Receiving Recent PSA Test for Prostate Cancer: 2004
344   Estimated New Skin Melanoma Cases in 2007
345   Estimated Rate of New Skin Melanoma Cases in 2007
346   Estimated New Cervical Cancer Cases in 2007
347   Estimated Rate of New Cervical Cancer Cases in 2007
348   Percent of Women 18 Years Old and Older Who Had a Pap Smear Within the Past Three Years: 2004
349   Estimated New Uterine Cancer Cases in 2007
350   Estimated Rate of New Uterine Cancer Cases in 2007
351   AIDS Cases Reported in 2005
352   AIDS Rate in 2005
353   AIDS Cases Reported Through December 2005
354   AIDS Cases in Children 12 Years and Younger Through December 2005
355   Chickenpox (Varicella) Cases Reported in 2006

TABLE OF CONTENTS (continued)

356 Chickenpox (Varicella) Rate in 2006
357 E-Coli Cases Reported in 2006
358 E-Coli Rate in 2006
359 Hepatitis A and B Cases Reported in 2006
360 Hepatitis A and B Rate in 2006
361 Legionellosis Cases Reported in 2006
362 Legionellosis Rate in 2006
363 Lyme Disease Cases in 2006
364 Lyme Disease Rate in 2006
365 Malaria Cases Reported in 2006
366 Malaria Rate in 2006
367 Meningococcal Infections Reported in 2006
368 Meningococcal Infection Rate in 2006
369 Rabies (Animal) Cases Reported in 2006
370 Rabies (Animal) Rate in 2006
371 Rocky Mountain Spotted Fever Cases Reported in 2006
372 Rocky Mountain Spotted Fever Rate in 2006
373 Salmonellosis Cases Reported in 2006
374 Salmonellosis Rate in 2006
375 Shigellosis Cases Reported in 2006
376 Shigellosis Rate in 2006
377 West Nile Virus Disease Cases Reported in 2006
378 West Nile Disease Rate in 2006
379 Whooping Cough (Pertussis) Cases Reported in 2006
380 Whooping Cough (Pertussis) Rate in 2006
381 Percent of Children Aged 19 to 35 Months Immunized in 2005
382 Percent of Children Aged 19 to 35 Months Fully Immunized in 2005
383 Percent of Adults Aged 65 Years and Older Who Received Flu Shots in 2005
384 Percent of Adults Aged 65 Years and Older Who Have Had a Pneumonia Vaccine: 2005
385 Sexually Transmitted Diseases in 2005
386 Sexually Transmitted Disease Rate in 2005
387 Chlamydia Cases Reported in 2005
388 Chlamydia Rate in 2005
389 Gonorrhea Cases Reported in 2005
390 Gonorrhea Rate in 2005
391 Syphilis Cases Reported in 2005
392 Syphilis Rate in 2005
393 Percent of Adults Who Have Asthma: 2005
394 Percent of Children Who Have Asthma: 2005
395 Percent of Adults Who Have Been Told They Have Arthritis: 2005
396 Percent of Adults Who Have Been Told They Have Diabetes: 2005
397 Percent of Adults Reporting Serious Psychological Distress: 2004

VI. Providers

398 Health Care Practitioners and Technicians in 2005
399 Rate of Health Care Practitioners and Technicians in 2005
400 Average Annual Wages of Health Care Practitioners and Technicians in 2005
401 Physicians in 2005
402 Rate of Physicians in 2005
403 Percent of Physicians Who Are Female: 2005
404 Percent of Physicians Under 35 Years Old in 2005
405 Percent of Physicians 65 Years Old and Older in 2005
406 Physicians in Patient Care in 2005
407 Rate of Physicians in Patient Care in 2005
408 Physicians in Primary Care in 2005
409 Rate of Physicians in Primary Care in 2005
410 Percent of Physicians in Primary Care in 2005
411 Percent of Population Lacking Access to Primary Care in 2006
412 Physicians in General/Family Practice in 2005
413 Rate of Physicians in General/Family Practice in 2005
414 Average Annual Wages of Family and General Practitioners in 2005

TABLE OF CONTENTS (continued)

415   Percent of Physicians Who Are Specialists in 2005
416   Physicians in Medical Specialties in 2005
417   Rate of Nonfederal Physicians in Medical Specialties in 2005
418   Physicians in Internal Medicine in 2005
419   Rate of Physicians in Internal Medicine in 2005
420   Physicians in Pediatrics in 2005
421   Rate of Physicians in Pediatrics in 2005
422   Physicians in Surgical Specialties in 2005
423   Rate of Physicians in Surgical Specialties in 2005
424   Average Annual Wages of Surgeons in 2005
425   Physicians in General Surgery in 2005
426   Rate of Physicians in General Surgery in 2005
427   Physicians in Obstetrics and Gynecology in 2005
428   Rate of Physicians in Obstetrics and Gynecology in 2005
429   Physicians in Ophthalmology in 2005
430   Rate of Physicians in Ophthalmology in 2005
431   Physicians in Orthopedic Surgery in 2005
432   Rate of Physicians in Orthopedic Surgery in 2005
433   Physicians in Plastic Surgery in 2005
434   Rate of Physicians in Plastic Surgery in 2005
435   Physicians in Other Specialties in 2005
436   Rate of Physicians in Other Specialties in 2005
437   Physicians in Anesthesiology in 2005
438   Rate of Physicians in Anesthesiology in 2005
439   Physicians in Psychiatry in 2005
440   Rate of Physicians in Psychiatry in 2005
441   Percent of Population Lacking Access to Mental Health Care in 2006
442   International Medical School Graduates in 2005
443   International Medical School Graduates as a Percent of Physicians in 2005
444   Osteopathic Physicians in 2006
445   Rate of Osteopathic Physicians in 2006
446   Podiatrists in 2005
447   Rate of Podiatrists in 2005
448   Average Annual Wages of Podiatrists in 2005
449   Doctors of Chiropractic in 2005
450   Rate of Doctors of Chiropractic in 2005
451   Average Annual Wages of Chiropractors in 2005
452   Physician Assistants in Clinical Practice in 2007
453   Rate of Physician Assistants in Clinical Practice in 2007
454   Average Annual Wages of Physician Assistants in 2005
455   Registered Nurses in 2005
456   Rate of Registered Nurses in 2005
457   Average Annual Wages of Registered Nurses in 2005
458   Licensed Practical and Licensed Vocational Nurses in 2005
459   Rate of Licensed Practical and Licensed Vocational Nurses in 2005
460   Average Annual Wages of Licensed Practical and Licensed Vocational Nurses in 2005
461   Physical Therapists in 2005
462   Rate of Physical Therapists in 2005
463   Average Annual Wages of Physical Therapists in 2005
464   Dentists in 2004
465   Rate of Dentists in 2004
466   Average Annual Wages of Dentists in 2005
467   Percent of Population Lacking Access to Dental Care in 2006
468   Pharmacists in 2005
469   Rate of Pharmacists in 2005
470   Average Annual Wages of Pharmacists in 2005
471   Optometrists in 2005
472   Rate of Optometrists in 2005
473   Average Annual Wages of Optometrists in 2005
474   Emergency Medical Technicians and Paramedics in 2005
475   Rate of Emergency Medical Technicians and Paramedics in 2005
476   Average Annual Wages of Emergency Medical Technicians and Paramedics in 2005

TABLE OF CONTENTS (continued)

477   Employment in Health Care Support Industries in 2005
478   Rate of Employees in Health Care Support Industries in 2005
479   Average Annual Wages of Employees in Health Care Support Industries in 2005

VII. Physical Fitness

480   Users of Exercise Equipment in 2005
481   Participants in Golf in 2005
482   Participants in Running/Jogging in 2005
483   Participants in Swimming in 2005
484   Participants in Tennis in 2005
485   Alcohol Consumption in 2004
486   Adult Per Capita Alcohol Consumption in 2004
487   Apparent Beer Consumption in 2004
488   Adult Per Capita Beer Consumption in 2004
489   Wine Consumption in 2004
490   Adult Per Capita Wine Consumption in 2004
491   Distilled Spirits Consumption in 2004
492   Adult Per Capita Distilled Spirits Consumption in 2004
493   Percent of Adults Who Do Not Drink Alcohol: 2005
494   Percent of Adults Who Are Binge Drinkers: 2005
495   Percent of Adults Who Smoke: 2005
496   Percent of Men Who Smoke: 2005
497   Percent of Women Who Smoke: 2005
498   Percent of Adults Who are Former Smokers: 2005
499   Percent of Adults Who Have Never Smoked: 2005
500   Percent of Population Who are Illicit Drug Users: 2004
501   Percent of Adults Overweight: 2005
502   Percent of Adults Obese: 2005
503   Percent of Adults Overweight or Obese: 2005
504   Percent of Adults Who Do Not Exercise: 2005
505   Percent of Adults Who Exercise Vigorously: 2005
506   Percent of Adults Who are Disabled: 2005
507   Percent of Adults with High Blood Pressure: 2005
508   Percent of Adults with High Cholesterol: 2005
509   Percent of Adults Who Have Visited a Dentist or Dental Clinic: 2004
510   Percent of Adults 65 Years Old and Older Who Have Lost All Their Natural Teeth: 2004
511   Percent of Adults Who Average Five or More Servings of Fruits and Vegetables Each Day: 2005
512   Percent of Adults Rating Their Health as Fair or Poor in 2005
513   Safety Belt Usage Rate in 2006

VIII. Appendix

A-1   Population in 2006
A-2   Population in 2005
A-3   Male Population in 2005
A-4   Female Population in 2005

IX. Sources

X. Index

I. BIRTHS AND REPRODUCTIVE HEALTH

1   Births in 2005
2   Birth Rate in 2005
3   Percent Change in Birth Rate: 1996 to 2005
4   Births in 2004
5   Birth Rate in 2004
6   Fertility Rate in 2005
7   Births to White Women in 2005
8   White Births as a Percent of All Births in 2005
9   Births to Black Women in 2005
10 Black Births as a Percent of All Births in 2005
11 Births to Hispanic Women in 2005
12 Hispanic Births as a Percent of All Births in 2005
13 Births of Low Birthweight in 2005
14 Births of Low Birthweight as a Percent of All Births in 2005
15 Births of Low Birthweight to White Women in 2005
16 Births of Low Birthweight to White Women as a Percent of All Births to White Women in 2005
17 Births of Low Birthweight to Black Women in 2005
18 Births of Low Birthweight to Black Women as a Percent of All Births to Black Women in 2005
19 Births of Low Birthweight to Hispanic Women in 2005
20 Births of Low Birthweight to Hispanic Women as a Percent of All Births to Hispanic Women in 2005
21 Births to Unmarried Women in 2005
22 Births to Unmarried Women as a Percent of All Births in 2005
23 Births to Unmarried White Women in 2005
24 Births to Unmarried White Women as a Percent of All Births to White Women in 2005
25 Births to Unmarried Black Women in 2005
26 Births to Unmarried Black Women as a Percent of All Births to Black Women in 2005
27 Births to Unmarried Hispanic Women in 2005
28 Births to Unmarried Hispanic Women as a Percent of All Births to Hispanic Women in 2005
29 Pregnancy Rate in 2003
30 Teenage Pregnancy Rate in 2003
31 Percent Change in Teenage Pregnancy Rate: 1999 to 2003
32 Births to Teenage Mothers in 2005
33 Teenage Birth Rate in 2005
34 Births to Teenage Mothers as a Percent of Births in 2005
35 Percent Change in Teenage Birth Rate: 2001 to 2005
36 Teenage Birth Rate in 2004
37 Births to White Teenage Mothers in 2005
38 White Teenage Birth Rate in 2005
39 Births to White Teenage Mothers as a Percent of White Births in 2005
40 Births to Black Teenage Mothers in 2005
41 Black Teenage Birth Rate in 2005
42 Births to Black Teenage Mothers as a Percent of Black Births in 2005
43 Births to Young Teenagers: 2002 to 2004
44 Young Teen Birthrate: 2002 to 2004
45 Births to Women 35 to 54 Years Old in 2004
46 Births to Women 35 to 54 Years Old as a Percent of All Births in 2004
47 Births by Vaginal Delivery in 2005
48 Percent of Births by Vaginal Delivery in 2005
49 Births by Cesarean Delivery in 2005
50 Percent of Births by Cesarean Delivery in 2005
51 Percent Change in Rate of Cesarean Births: 2001 to 2005
52 Twin Birth Rate: 2002-2004
53 Assisted Reproductive Technology Procedures in 2003
54 Infants Born from Assisted Reproductive Technology Procedures in 2003
55 Percent of Assisted Reproductive Technology Procedures that Resulted in Live Births in 2003
56 Percent of Total Live Births Resulting from Assisted Reproductive Technology Procedures in 2003
57 Percent of Assisted Reproductive Technology Procedure Infants Born in Multiple Birth Deliveries in 2003
58 Percent of Mothers Beginning Prenatal Care in First Trimester in 2004
59 Percent of White Mothers Beginning Prenatal Care in First Trimester in 2004
60 Percent of Black Mothers Beginning Prenatal Care in First Trimester in 2004
61 Percent of Hispanic Mothers Beginning Prenatal Care in First Trimester in 2004

I. BIRTHS AND REPRODUCTIVE HEALTH
(CONTINUED)

62   Percent of Mothers Receiving Late or No Prenatal Care in 2004
63   Percent of White Mothers Receiving Late or No Prenatal Care in 2004
64   Percent of Black Mothers Receiving Late or No Prenatal Care in 2004
65   Percent of Hispanic Mothers Receiving Late or No Prenatal Care in 2004

Abortions

66   Reported Legal Abortions in 2003
67   Percent Change in Reported Legal Abortions: 1999 to 2003
68   Reported Legal Abortions per 1,000 Live Births in 2003
69   Reported Legal Abortions per 1,000 Women Ages 15 to 44 in 2003
70   Percent of Legal Abortions Obtained by Out-Of-State Residents in 2003
71   Percent of Reported Legal Abortions that were First-Time Abortions: 2003
72   Percent of Reported Legal Abortions Obtained by White Women in 2003
73   Percent of Reported Legal Abortions Obtained by Black Women in 2003
74   Percent of Reported Legal Abortions Obtained by Hispanic Women in 2003
75   Percent of Reported Legal Abortions Obtained by Married Women in 2003
76   Percent of Reported Legal Abortions Obtained by Unmarried Women in 2003
77   Reported Legal Abortions Obtained by Teenagers in 2003
78   Percent of Reported Legal Abortions Obtained by Teenagers in 2003
79   Reported Legal Abortions Obtained by Teenagers 17 Years and Younger in 2003
80   Percent of Reported Legal Abortions Obtained by Teenagers 17 Years and Younger in 2003
81   Percent of Teenage Abortions Obtained by Teenagers 17 Years and Younger in 2003
82   Reported Legal Abortions Performed at 12 Weeks or Less of Gestation in 2003
83   Percent of Reported Legal Abortions Performed at 12 Weeks or Less of Gestation in 2003
84   Reported Legal Abortions Performed at or After 21 Weeks of Gestation in 2003
85   Percent of Reported Legal Abortions Performed at or After 21 Weeks of Gestation in 2003

Births in 2005

National Total = 4,140,419 Live Births*

ALPHA ORDER

RANK	STATE	BIRTHS	% of USA
24	Alabama	60,447	1.5%
47	Alaska	10,463	0.3%
13	Arizona	96,231	2.3%
34	Arkansas	39,196	0.9%
1	California	549,626	13.3%
22	Colorado	68,963	1.7%
31	Connecticut	41,717	1.0%
44	Delaware	11,648	0.3%
4	Florida	226,280	5.5%
8	Georgia	142,256	3.4%
40	Hawaii	17,925	0.4%
38	Idaho	23,062	0.6%
5	Illinois	179,061	4.3%
14	Indiana	87,282	2.1%
33	Iowa	39,312	0.9%
32	Kansas	39,893	1.0%
26	Kentucky	56,385	1.4%
23	Louisiana	61,005	1.5%
42	Maine	14,113	0.3%
19	Maryland	74,986	1.8%
18	Massachusetts	76,920	1.9%
9	Michigan	127,799	3.1%
21	Minnesota	70,969	1.7%
30	Mississippi	42,398	1.0%
17	Missouri	78,619	1.9%
45	Montana	11,602	0.3%
37	Nebraska	26,148	0.6%
35	Nevada	37,258	0.9%
41	New Hampshire	14,426	0.3%
11	New Jersey	113,700	2.7%
36	New Mexico	28,834	0.7%
3	New York	246,354	5.9%
10	North Carolina	123,118	3.0%
48	North Dakota	8,393	0.2%
6	Ohio	148,916	3.6%
27	Oklahoma	51,746	1.2%
29	Oregon	45,937	1.1%
7	Pennsylvania	145,584	3.5%
43	Rhode Island	12,680	0.3%
25	South Carolina	57,728	1.4%
46	South Dakota	11,457	0.3%
16	Tennessee	81,743	2.0%
2	Texas	385,963	9.3%
28	Utah	51,554	1.2%
50	Vermont	6,475	0.2%
12	Virginia	104,592	2.5%
15	Washington	82,705	2.0%
39	West Virginia	20,838	0.5%
20	Wisconsin	70,978	1.7%
49	Wyoming	7,239	0.2%

RANK ORDER

RANK	STATE	BIRTHS	% of USA
1	California	549,626	13.3%
2	Texas	385,963	9.3%
3	New York	246,354	5.9%
4	Florida	226,280	5.5%
5	Illinois	179,061	4.3%
6	Ohio	148,916	3.6%
7	Pennsylvania	145,584	3.5%
8	Georgia	142,256	3.4%
9	Michigan	127,799	3.1%
10	North Carolina	123,118	3.0%
11	New Jersey	113,700	2.7%
12	Virginia	104,592	2.5%
13	Arizona	96,231	2.3%
14	Indiana	87,282	2.1%
15	Washington	82,705	2.0%
16	Tennessee	81,743	2.0%
17	Missouri	78,619	1.9%
18	Massachusetts	76,920	1.9%
19	Maryland	74,986	1.8%
20	Wisconsin	70,978	1.7%
21	Minnesota	70,969	1.7%
22	Colorado	68,963	1.7%
23	Louisiana	61,005	1.5%
24	Alabama	60,447	1.5%
25	South Carolina	57,728	1.4%
26	Kentucky	56,385	1.4%
27	Oklahoma	51,746	1.2%
28	Utah	51,554	1.2%
29	Oregon	45,937	1.1%
30	Mississippi	42,398	1.0%
31	Connecticut	41,717	1.0%
32	Kansas	39,893	1.0%
33	Iowa	39,312	0.9%
34	Arkansas	39,196	0.9%
35	Nevada	37,258	0.9%
36	New Mexico	28,834	0.7%
37	Nebraska	26,148	0.6%
38	Idaho	23,062	0.6%
39	West Virginia	20,838	0.5%
40	Hawaii	17,925	0.4%
41	New Hampshire	14,426	0.3%
42	Maine	14,113	0.3%
43	Rhode Island	12,680	0.3%
44	Delaware	11,648	0.3%
45	Montana	11,602	0.3%
46	South Dakota	11,457	0.3%
47	Alaska	10,463	0.3%
48	North Dakota	8,393	0.2%
49	Wyoming	7,239	0.2%
50	Vermont	6,475	0.2%
	District of Columbia	7,893	0.2%

Source: U.S. Department of Health and Human Services, National Center for Health Statistics
    "National Vital Statistics Reports" (Preliminary Report, November 2006, http://www.cdc.gov/nchs/births.htm)
*Preliminary data by state of residence.

Birth Rate in 2005

National Rate = 14.0 Live Births per 1,000 Population*

ALPHA ORDER

RANK	STATE	RATE
31	Alabama	13.3
5	Alaska	15.8
3	Arizona	16.2
18	Arkansas	14.1
8	California	15.2
11	Colorado	14.8
44	Connecticut	11.9
22	Delaware	13.8
39	Florida	12.7
6	Georgia	15.7
18	Hawaii	14.1
4	Idaho	16.1
20	Illinois	14.0
21	Indiana	13.9
31	Iowa	13.3
14	Kansas	14.5
28	Kentucky	13.5
28	Louisiana	13.5
49	Maine	10.7
30	Maryland	13.4
43	Massachusetts	12.0
40	Michigan	12.6
22	Minnesota	13.8
14	Mississippi	14.5
26	Missouri	13.6
42	Montana	12.4
10	Nebraska	14.9
7	Nevada	15.4
48	New Hampshire	11.0
35	New Jersey	13.0
9	New Mexico	15.0
37	New York	12.8
16	North Carolina	14.2
33	North Dakota	13.2
35	Ohio	13.0
13	Oklahoma	14.6
40	Oregon	12.6
46	Pennsylvania	11.7
45	Rhode Island	11.8
26	South Carolina	13.6
11	South Dakota	14.8
25	Tennessee	13.7
2	Texas	16.9
1	Utah	20.9
50	Vermont	10.4
22	Virginia	13.8
33	Washington	13.2
47	West Virginia	11.5
37	Wisconsin	12.8
16	Wyoming	14.2

RANK ORDER

RANK	STATE	RATE
1	Utah	20.9
2	Texas	16.9
3	Arizona	16.2
4	Idaho	16.1
5	Alaska	15.8
6	Georgia	15.7
7	Nevada	15.4
8	California	15.2
9	New Mexico	15.0
10	Nebraska	14.9
11	Colorado	14.8
11	South Dakota	14.8
13	Oklahoma	14.6
14	Kansas	14.5
14	Mississippi	14.5
16	North Carolina	14.2
16	Wyoming	14.2
18	Arkansas	14.1
18	Hawaii	14.1
20	Illinois	14.0
21	Indiana	13.9
22	Delaware	13.8
22	Minnesota	13.8
22	Virginia	13.8
25	Tennessee	13.7
26	Missouri	13.6
26	South Carolina	13.6
28	Kentucky	13.5
28	Louisiana	13.5
30	Maryland	13.4
31	Alabama	13.3
31	Iowa	13.3
33	North Dakota	13.2
33	Washington	13.2
35	New Jersey	13.0
35	Ohio	13.0
37	New York	12.8
37	Wisconsin	12.8
39	Florida	12.7
40	Michigan	12.6
40	Oregon	12.6
42	Montana	12.4
43	Massachusetts	12.0
44	Connecticut	11.9
45	Rhode Island	11.8
46	Pennsylvania	11.7
47	West Virginia	11.5
48	New Hampshire	11.0
49	Maine	10.7
50	Vermont	10.4
	District of Columbia	14.3

Source: U.S. Department of Health and Human Services, National Center for Health Statistics
"National Vital Statistics Reports" (Preliminary Report, November 2006, http://www.cdc.gov/nchs/births.htm)
*Preliminary data by state of residence.

Percent Change in Birth Rate: 1996 to 2005

National Percent Change = 4.8% Decrease*

ALPHA ORDER

RANK	STATE	PERCENT CHANGE
36	Alabama	(6.3)
29	Alaska	(4.2)
31	Arizona	(4.7)
24	Arkansas	(2.8)
47	California	(10.1)
9	Colorado	1.4
50	Connecticut	(12.5)
18	Delaware	(1.4)
27	Florida	(3.8)
10	Georgia	1.3
40	Hawaii	(9.0)
5	Idaho	2.5
45	Illinois	(9.7)
24	Indiana	(2.8)
6	Iowa	2.3
7	Kansas	2.1
16	Kentucky	(0.7)
46	Louisiana	(10.0)
26	Maine	(3.6)
33	Maryland	(5.0)
41	Massachusetts	(9.1)
43	Michigan	(9.4)
13	Minnesota	0.7
28	Mississippi	(4.0)
18	Missouri	(1.4)
12	Montana	0.8
2	Nebraska	5.7
34	Nevada	(5.5)
49	New Hampshire	(12.0)
41	New Jersey	(9.1)
35	New Mexico	(5.7)
48	New York	(11.7)
16	North Carolina	(0.7)
8	North Dakota	1.5
30	Ohio	(4.4)
3	Oklahoma	4.3
38	Oregon	(7.4)
32	Pennsylvania	(4.9)
39	Rhode Island	(7.8)
18	South Carolina	(1.4)
4	South Dakota	3.5
18	Tennessee	(1.4)
23	Texas	(2.3)
15	Utah	(0.5)
44	Vermont	(9.6)
14	Virginia	0.0
37	Washington	(6.4)
11	West Virginia	0.9
22	Wisconsin	(1.5)
1	Wyoming	8.4

RANK ORDER

RANK	STATE	PERCENT CHANGE
1	Wyoming	8.4
2	Nebraska	5.7
3	Oklahoma	4.3
4	South Dakota	3.5
5	Idaho	2.5
6	Iowa	2.3
7	Kansas	2.1
8	North Dakota	1.5
9	Colorado	1.4
10	Georgia	1.3
11	West Virginia	0.9
12	Montana	0.8
13	Minnesota	0.7
14	Virginia	0.0
15	Utah	(0.5)
16	Kentucky	(0.7)
16	North Carolina	(0.7)
18	Delaware	(1.4)
18	Missouri	(1.4)
18	South Carolina	(1.4)
18	Tennessee	(1.4)
22	Wisconsin	(1.5)
23	Texas	(2.3)
24	Arkansas	(2.8)
24	Indiana	(2.8)
26	Maine	(3.6)
27	Florida	(3.8)
28	Mississippi	(4.0)
29	Alaska	(4.2)
30	Ohio	(4.4)
31	Arizona	(4.7)
32	Pennsylvania	(4.9)
33	Maryland	(5.0)
34	Nevada	(5.5)
35	New Mexico	(5.7)
36	Alabama	(6.3)
37	Washington	(6.4)
38	Oregon	(7.4)
39	Rhode Island	(7.8)
40	Hawaii	(9.0)
41	Massachusetts	(9.1)
41	New Jersey	(9.1)
43	Michigan	(9.4)
44	Vermont	(9.6)
45	Illinois	(9.7)
46	Louisiana	(10.0)
47	California	(10.1)
48	New York	(11.7)
49	New Hampshire	(12.0)
50	Connecticut	(12.5)

| | District of Columbia | (7.1) |

Source: Morgan Quitno Press using data from U.S. Department of Health and Human Services
"National Vital Statistics Reports" (Preliminary Report, November 2006, http://www.cdc.gov/nchs/births.htm)
"Monthly Vital Statistics Report" (Vol. 47, No. 4, October 7, 1998)
*By state of residence.

Births in 2004

National Total = 4,112,052 Live Births*

ALPHA ORDER

RANK	STATE	BIRTHS	% of USA
24	Alabama	59,510	1.4%
47	Alaska	10,338	0.3%
13	Arizona	93,663	2.3%
33	Arkansas	38,573	0.9%
1	California	544,843	13.2%
22	Colorado	68,503	1.7%
31	Connecticut	42,095	1.0%
45	Delaware	11,369	0.3%
4	Florida	218,053	5.3%
8	Georgia	138,849	3.4%
40	Hawaii	18,281	0.4%
38	Idaho	22,532	0.5%
5	Illinois	180,778	4.4%
14	Indiana	87,142	2.1%
34	Iowa	38,438	0.9%
32	Kansas	39,669	1.0%
26	Kentucky	55,720	1.4%
23	Louisiana	65,369	1.6%
42	Maine	13,944	0.3%
19	Maryland	74,628	1.8%
17	Massachusetts	78,484	1.9%
9	Michigan	129,776	3.2%
20	Minnesota	70,624	1.7%
30	Mississippi	42,827	1.0%
18	Missouri	77,765	1.9%
44	Montana	11,519	0.3%
37	Nebraska	26,332	0.6%
35	Nevada	35,200	0.9%
41	New Hampshire	14,565	0.4%
11	New Jersey	115,253	2.8%
36	New Mexico	28,384	0.7%
3	New York	249,947	6.1%
10	North Carolina	119,847	2.9%
48	North Dakota	8,189	0.2%
6	Ohio	148,954	3.6%
27	Oklahoma	51,306	1.2%
29	Oregon	45,678	1.1%
7	Pennsylvania	144,748	3.5%
43	Rhode Island	12,779	0.3%
25	South Carolina	56,590	1.4%
46	South Dakota	11,338	0.3%
16	Tennessee	79,642	1.9%
2	Texas	381,293	9.3%
28	Utah	50,670	1.2%
50	Vermont	6,599	0.2%
12	Virginia	103,933	2.5%
15	Washington	81,747	2.0%
39	West Virginia	20,880	0.5%
21	Wisconsin	70,146	1.7%
49	Wyoming	6,807	0.2%

RANK ORDER

RANK	STATE	BIRTHS	% of USA
1	California	544,843	13.2%
2	Texas	381,293	9.3%
3	New York	249,947	6.1%
4	Florida	218,053	5.3%
5	Illinois	180,778	4.4%
6	Ohio	148,954	3.6%
7	Pennsylvania	144,748	3.5%
8	Georgia	138,849	3.4%
9	Michigan	129,776	3.2%
10	North Carolina	119,847	2.9%
11	New Jersey	115,253	2.8%
12	Virginia	103,933	2.5%
13	Arizona	93,663	2.3%
14	Indiana	87,142	2.1%
15	Washington	81,747	2.0%
16	Tennessee	79,642	1.9%
17	Massachusetts	78,484	1.9%
18	Missouri	77,765	1.9%
19	Maryland	74,628	1.8%
20	Minnesota	70,624	1.7%
21	Wisconsin	70,146	1.7%
22	Colorado	68,503	1.7%
23	Louisiana	65,369	1.6%
24	Alabama	59,510	1.4%
25	South Carolina	56,590	1.4%
26	Kentucky	55,720	1.4%
27	Oklahoma	51,306	1.2%
28	Utah	50,670	1.2%
29	Oregon	45,678	1.1%
30	Mississippi	42,827	1.0%
31	Connecticut	42,095	1.0%
32	Kansas	39,669	1.0%
33	Arkansas	38,573	0.9%
34	Iowa	38,438	0.9%
35	Nevada	35,200	0.9%
36	New Mexico	28,384	0.7%
37	Nebraska	26,332	0.6%
38	Idaho	22,532	0.5%
39	West Virginia	20,880	0.5%
40	Hawaii	18,281	0.4%
41	New Hampshire	14,565	0.4%
42	Maine	13,944	0.3%
43	Rhode Island	12,779	0.3%
44	Montana	11,519	0.3%
45	Delaware	11,369	0.3%
46	South Dakota	11,338	0.3%
47	Alaska	10,338	0.3%
48	North Dakota	8,189	0.2%
49	Wyoming	6,807	0.2%
50	Vermont	6,599	0.2%
	District of Columbia	7,933	0.2%

*Source: U.S. Department of Health and Human Services, National Center for Health Statistics
"National Vital Statistics Reports" (Vol. 55, No. 1, September 29, 2006)*
Final data by state of residence.

Birth Rate in 2004

National Rate = 14.0 Live Births per 1,000 Population*

ALPHA ORDER

RANK	STATE	RATE
33	Alabama	13.1
5	Alaska	15.8
3	Arizona	16.3
19	Arkansas	14.0
7	California	15.2
10	Colorado	14.9
44	Connecticut	12.0
24	Delaware	13.7
41	Florida	12.5
6	Georgia	15.7
15	Hawaii	14.5
4	Idaho	16.2
18	Illinois	14.2
19	Indiana	14.0
34	Iowa	13.0
15	Kansas	14.5
28	Kentucky	13.4
15	Louisiana	14.5
49	Maine	10.6
28	Maryland	13.4
43	Massachusetts	12.2
38	Michigan	12.8
23	Minnesota	13.8
12	Mississippi	14.8
25	Missouri	13.5
42	Montana	12.4
8	Nebraska	15.1
8	Nevada	15.1
48	New Hampshire	11.2
31	New Jersey	13.2
10	New Mexico	14.9
34	New York	13.0
19	North Carolina	14.0
37	North Dakota	12.9
34	Ohio	13.0
14	Oklahoma	14.6
39	Oregon	12.7
46	Pennsylvania	11.7
45	Rhode Island	11.8
25	South Carolina	13.5
13	South Dakota	14.7
25	Tennessee	13.5
2	Texas	17.0
1	Utah	21.2
49	Vermont	10.6
22	Virginia	13.9
31	Washington	13.2
47	West Virginia	11.5
39	Wisconsin	12.7
28	Wyoming	13.4

RANK ORDER

RANK	STATE	RATE
1	Utah	21.2
2	Texas	17.0
3	Arizona	16.3
4	Idaho	16.2
5	Alaska	15.8
6	Georgia	15.7
7	California	15.2
8	Nebraska	15.1
8	Nevada	15.1
10	Colorado	14.9
10	New Mexico	14.9
12	Mississippi	14.8
13	South Dakota	14.7
14	Oklahoma	14.6
15	Hawaii	14.5
15	Kansas	14.5
15	Louisiana	14.5
18	Illinois	14.2
19	Arkansas	14.0
19	Indiana	14.0
19	North Carolina	14.0
22	Virginia	13.9
23	Minnesota	13.8
24	Delaware	13.7
25	Missouri	13.5
25	South Carolina	13.5
25	Tennessee	13.5
28	Kentucky	13.4
28	Maryland	13.4
28	Wyoming	13.4
31	New Jersey	13.2
31	Washington	13.2
33	Alabama	13.1
34	Iowa	13.0
34	New York	13.0
34	Ohio	13.0
37	North Dakota	12.9
38	Michigan	12.8
39	Oregon	12.7
39	Wisconsin	12.7
41	Florida	12.5
42	Montana	12.4
43	Massachusetts	12.2
44	Connecticut	12.0
45	Rhode Island	11.8
46	Pennsylvania	11.7
47	West Virginia	11.5
48	New Hampshire	11.2
49	Maine	10.6
49	Vermont	10.6
	District of Columbia	14.3

Source: U.S. Department of Health and Human Services, National Center for Health Statistics
      "National Vital Statistics Reports" (Vol. 55, No. 1, September 29, 2006)
*Final data by state of residence.

Fertility Rate in 2005

National Rate = 66.7 Live Births per 1,000 Women 15 to 44 Years Old*

ALPHA ORDER

RANK ORDER

RANK	STATE	RATE	RANK	STATE	RATE
33	Alabama	63.5	1	Utah	90.4
5	Alaska	75.4	2	Arizona	79.2
2	Arizona	79.2	3	Texas	77.7
16	Arkansas	69.1	4	Idaho	77.4
11	California	71.4	5	Alaska	75.4
17	Colorado	68.8	6	Nevada	74.5
45	Connecticut	58.7	7	South Dakota	73.4
26	Delaware	65.1	8	Hawaii	72.9
22	Florida	65.6	9	New Mexico	72.8
15	Georgia	70.0	10	Nebraska	72.1
8	Hawaii	72.9	11	California	71.4
4	Idaho	77.4	12	Wyoming	71.3
21	Illinois	66.4	13	Oklahoma	70.8
19	Indiana	67.3	14	Kansas	70.4
23	Iowa	65.4	15	Georgia	70.0
14	Kansas	70.4	16	Arkansas	69.1
30	Kentucky	64.7	17	Colorado	68.8
37	Louisiana	62.6	18	Mississippi	67.8
48	Maine	53.6	19	Indiana	67.3
36	Maryland	62.8	20	North Carolina	67.2
46	Massachusetts	56.1	21	Illinois	66.4
41	Michigan	61.0	22	Florida	65.6
27	Minnesota	65.0	23	Iowa	65.4
18	Mississippi	67.8	24	North Dakota	65.3
27	Missouri	65.0	25	Virginia	65.2
34	Montana	63.3	26	Delaware	65.1
10	Nebraska	72.1	27	Minnesota	65.0
6	Nevada	74.5	27	Missouri	65.0
49	New Hampshire	53.4	29	Tennessee	64.9
32	New Jersey	63.8	30	Kentucky	64.7
9	New Mexico	72.8	31	South Carolina	64.5
42	New York	60.3	32	New Jersey	63.8
20	North Carolina	67.2	33	Alabama	63.5
24	North Dakota	65.3	34	Montana	63.3
35	Ohio	63.2	35	Ohio	63.2
13	Oklahoma	70.8	36	Maryland	62.8
40	Oregon	61.6	37	Louisiana	62.6
43	Pennsylvania	58.8	38	Washington	62.1
47	Rhode Island	55.6	39	Wisconsin	61.7
31	South Carolina	64.5	40	Oregon	61.6
7	South Dakota	73.4	41	Michigan	61.0
29	Tennessee	64.9	42	New York	60.3
3	Texas	77.7	43	Pennsylvania	58.8
1	Utah	90.4	43	West Virginia	58.8
50	Vermont	51.0	45	Connecticut	58.7
25	Virginia	65.2	46	Massachusetts	56.1
38	Washington	62.1	47	Rhode Island	55.6
43	West Virginia	58.8	48	Maine	53.6
39	Wisconsin	61.7	49	New Hampshire	53.4
12	Wyoming	71.3	50	Vermont	51.0
				District of Columbia	59.2

Source: U.S. Department of Health and Human Services, National Center for Health Statistics
  "National Vital Statistics Reports" (Preliminary Report, November 2006, http://www.cdc.gov/nchs/births.htm)
*Preliminary data by state of residence.

Births to White Women in 2005

National Total = 3,231,783 Live Births to White Women*

ALPHA ORDER

RANK	STATE	BIRTHS	% of USA
26	Alabama	41,247	1.3%
48	Alaska	6,537	0.2%
11	Arizona	83,163	2.6%
33	Arkansas	30,798	1.0%
1	California	445,665	13.8%
17	Colorado	62,875	1.9%
32	Connecticut	33,985	1.1%
45	Delaware	8,199	0.3%
4	Florida	161,497	5.0%
9	Georgia	91,165	2.8%
50	Hawaii	5,044	0.2%
38	Idaho	22,112	0.7%
5	Illinois	138,991	4.3%
13	Indiana	75,808	2.3%
28	Iowa	36,605	1.1%
31	Kansas	35,123	1.1%
22	Kentucky	50,398	1.6%
30	Louisiana	35,498	1.1%
41	Maine	13,508	0.4%
24	Maryland	43,326	1.3%
18	Massachusetts	62,453	1.9%
8	Michigan	100,142	3.1%
21	Minnesota	57,827	1.8%
37	Mississippi	23,047	0.7%
16	Missouri	64,730	2.0%
43	Montana	9,931	0.3%
36	Nebraska	23,236	0.7%
34	Nevada	30,665	0.9%
40	New Hampshire	13,578	0.4%
12	New Jersey	82,617	2.6%
35	New Mexico	24,120	0.7%
3	New York	170,026	5.3%
10	North Carolina	89,650	2.8%
46	North Dakota	7,196	0.2%
6	Ohio	120,914	3.7%
27	Oklahoma	39,991	1.2%
25	Oregon	41,576	1.3%
7	Pennsylvania	116,580	3.6%
42	Rhode Island	10,691	0.3%
29	South Carolina	36,109	1.1%
44	South Dakota	9,263	0.3%
19	Tennessee	61,405	1.9%
2	Texas	327,419	10.1%
23	Utah	48,930	1.5%
49	Vermont	6,273	0.2%
14	Virginia	74,351	2.3%
15	Washington	67,921	2.1%
39	West Virginia	19,936	0.6%
20	Wisconsin	60,466	1.9%
47	Wyoming	6,771	0.2%

RANK ORDER

RANK	STATE	BIRTHS	% of USA
1	California	445,665	13.8%
2	Texas	327,419	10.1%
3	New York	170,026	5.3%
4	Florida	161,497	5.0%
5	Illinois	138,991	4.3%
6	Ohio	120,914	3.7%
7	Pennsylvania	116,580	3.6%
8	Michigan	100,142	3.1%
9	Georgia	91,165	2.8%
10	North Carolina	89,650	2.8%
11	Arizona	83,163	2.6%
12	New Jersey	82,617	2.6%
13	Indiana	75,808	2.3%
14	Virginia	74,351	2.3%
15	Washington	67,921	2.1%
16	Missouri	64,730	2.0%
17	Colorado	62,875	1.9%
18	Massachusetts	62,453	1.9%
19	Tennessee	61,405	1.9%
20	Wisconsin	60,466	1.9%
21	Minnesota	57,827	1.8%
22	Kentucky	50,398	1.6%
23	Utah	48,930	1.5%
24	Maryland	43,326	1.3%
25	Oregon	41,576	1.3%
26	Alabama	41,247	1.3%
27	Oklahoma	39,991	1.2%
28	Iowa	36,605	1.1%
29	South Carolina	36,109	1.1%
30	Louisiana	35,498	1.1%
31	Kansas	35,123	1.1%
32	Connecticut	33,985	1.1%
33	Arkansas	30,798	1.0%
34	Nevada	30,665	0.9%
35	New Mexico	24,120	0.7%
36	Nebraska	23,236	0.7%
37	Mississippi	23,047	0.7%
38	Idaho	22,112	0.7%
39	West Virginia	19,936	0.6%
40	New Hampshire	13,578	0.4%
41	Maine	13,508	0.4%
42	Rhode Island	10,691	0.3%
43	Montana	9,931	0.3%
44	South Dakota	9,263	0.3%
45	Delaware	8,199	0.3%
46	North Dakota	7,196	0.2%
47	Wyoming	6,771	0.2%
48	Alaska	6,537	0.2%
49	Vermont	6,273	0.2%
50	Hawaii	5,044	0.2%
	District of Columbia	2,425	0.1%

Source: U.S. Department of Health and Human Services, National Center for Health Statistics
"National Vital Statistics Reports" (Preliminary Report, November 2006, http://www.cdc.gov/nchs/births.htm)
*Preliminary data by state of residence. By race of mother.

White Births as a Percent of All Births in 2005

National Percent = 78.1% of Live Births*

ALPHA ORDER				RANK ORDER		
RANK	STATE	PERCENT		RANK	STATE	PERCENT
43	Alabama	68.2		1	Vermont	96.9
46	Alaska	62.5		2	Idaho	95.9
15	Arizona	86.4		3	Maine	95.7
32	Arkansas	78.6		3	West Virginia	95.7
29	California	81.1		5	Utah	94.9
9	Colorado	91.2		6	New Hampshire	94.1
25	Connecticut	81.5		7	Wyoming	93.5
41	Delaware	70.4		8	Iowa	93.1
39	Florida	71.4		9	Colorado	91.2
44	Georgia	64.1		10	Oregon	90.5
50	Hawaii	28.1		11	Kentucky	89.4
2	Idaho	95.9		12	Nebraska	88.9
34	Illinois	77.6		13	Kansas	88.0
14	Indiana	86.9		14	Indiana	86.9
8	Iowa	93.1		15	Arizona	86.4
13	Kansas	88.0		16	North Dakota	85.7
11	Kentucky	89.4		17	Montana	85.6
47	Louisiana	58.2		18	Wisconsin	85.2
3	Maine	95.7		19	Texas	84.8
48	Maryland	57.8		20	Rhode Island	84.3
27	Massachusetts	81.2		21	New Mexico	83.7
33	Michigan	78.4		22	Missouri	82.3
25	Minnesota	81.5		22	Nevada	82.3
49	Mississippi	54.4		24	Washington	82.1
22	Missouri	82.3		25	Connecticut	81.5
17	Montana	85.6		25	Minnesota	81.5
12	Nebraska	88.9		27	Massachusetts	81.2
22	Nevada	82.3		27	Ohio	81.2
6	New Hampshire	94.1		29	California	81.1
38	New Jersey	72.7		30	South Dakota	80.9
21	New Mexico	83.7		31	Pennsylvania	80.1
42	New York	69.0		32	Arkansas	78.6
37	North Carolina	72.8		33	Michigan	78.4
16	North Dakota	85.7		34	Illinois	77.6
27	Ohio	81.2		35	Oklahoma	77.3
35	Oklahoma	77.3		36	Tennessee	75.1
10	Oregon	90.5		37	North Carolina	72.8
31	Pennsylvania	80.1		38	New Jersey	72.7
20	Rhode Island	84.3		39	Florida	71.4
45	South Carolina	62.6		40	Virginia	71.1
30	South Dakota	80.9		41	Delaware	70.4
36	Tennessee	75.1		42	New York	69.0
19	Texas	84.8		43	Alabama	68.2
5	Utah	94.9		44	Georgia	64.1
1	Vermont	96.9		45	South Carolina	62.6
40	Virginia	71.1		46	Alaska	62.5
24	Washington	82.1		47	Louisiana	58.2
3	West Virginia	95.7		48	Maryland	57.8
18	Wisconsin	85.2		49	Mississippi	54.4
7	Wyoming	93.5		50	Hawaii	28.1

District of Columbia	30.7

Source: Morgan Quitno Press using data from U.S. Dept. of Health and Human Services, Nat'l Center for Health Statistics "National Vital Statistics Reports" (Preliminary Report, November 2006, http://www.cdc.gov/nchs/births.htm)
*Preliminary data by state of residence. By race of mother.

Births to Black Women in 2005

National Total = 632,625 Live Births to Black Women*

ALPHA ORDER					RANK ORDER			
RANK	STATE	BIRTHS	% of USA		RANK	STATE	BIRTHS	% of USA
18	Alabama	18,137	2.9%		1	Florida	56,520	8.9%
42	Alaska	424	0.1%		2	New York	54,358	8.6%
29	Arizona	3,648	0.6%		3	Georgia	45,818	7.2%
22	Arkansas	7,470	1.2%		4	Texas	44,088	7.0%
5	California	32,410	5.1%		5	California	32,410	5.1%
32	Colorado	3,123	0.5%		6	Illinois	30,733	4.9%
25	Connecticut	5,279	0.8%		7	North Carolina	28,441	4.5%
33	Delaware	2,911	0.5%		8	Maryland	26,491	4.2%
1	Florida	56,520	8.9%		9	Ohio	24,233	3.8%
3	Georgia	45,818	7.2%		10	Louisiana	24,109	3.8%
40	Hawaii	487	0.1%		11	Virginia	22,916	3.6%
45	Idaho	146	0.0%		12	Pennsylvania	22,886	3.6%
6	Illinois	30,733	4.9%		13	Michigan	22,480	3.6%
20	Indiana	9,885	1.6%		14	South Carolina	20,376	3.2%
35	Iowa	1,507	0.2%		15	New Jersey	19,967	3.2%
31	Kansas	3,125	0.5%		16	Mississippi	18,660	2.9%
26	Kentucky	5,085	0.8%		17	Tennessee	18,484	2.9%
10	Louisiana	24,109	3.8%		18	Alabama	18,137	2.9%
43	Maine	265	0.0%		19	Missouri	11,686	1.8%
8	Maryland	26,491	4.2%		20	Indiana	9,885	1.6%
21	Massachusetts	8,805	1.4%		21	Massachusetts	8,805	1.4%
13	Michigan	22,480	3.6%		22	Arkansas	7,470	1.2%
23	Minnesota	6,897	1.1%		23	Minnesota	6,897	1.1%
16	Mississippi	18,660	2.9%		24	Wisconsin	6,796	1.1%
19	Missouri	11,686	1.8%		25	Connecticut	5,279	0.8%
50	Montana	62	0.0%		26	Kentucky	5,085	0.8%
34	Nebraska	1,719	0.3%		27	Oklahoma	4,817	0.8%
30	Nevada	3,206	0.5%		28	Washington	4,228	0.7%
44	New Hampshire	233	0.0%		29	Arizona	3,648	0.6%
15	New Jersey	19,967	3.2%		30	Nevada	3,206	0.5%
39	New Mexico	538	0.1%		31	Kansas	3,125	0.5%
2	New York	54,358	8.6%		32	Colorado	3,123	0.5%
7	North Carolina	28,441	4.5%		33	Delaware	2,911	0.5%
47	North Dakota	130	0.0%		34	Nebraska	1,719	0.3%
9	Ohio	24,233	3.8%		35	Iowa	1,507	0.2%
27	Oklahoma	4,817	0.8%		36	Rhode Island	1,286	0.2%
37	Oregon	1,010	0.2%		37	Oregon	1,010	0.2%
12	Pennsylvania	22,886	3.6%		38	West Virginia	708	0.1%
36	Rhode Island	1,286	0.2%		39	New Mexico	538	0.1%
14	South Carolina	20,376	3.2%		40	Hawaii	487	0.1%
46	South Dakota	143	0.0%		41	Utah	484	0.1%
17	Tennessee	18,484	2.9%		42	Alaska	424	0.1%
4	Texas	44,088	7.0%		43	Maine	265	0.0%
41	Utah	484	0.1%		44	New Hampshire	233	0.0%
48	Vermont	78	0.0%		45	Idaho	146	0.0%
11	Virginia	22,916	3.6%		46	South Dakota	143	0.0%
28	Washington	4,228	0.7%		47	North Dakota	130	0.0%
38	West Virginia	708	0.1%		48	Vermont	78	0.0%
24	Wisconsin	6,796	1.1%		49	Wyoming	63	0.0%
49	Wyoming	63	0.0%		50	Montana	62	0.0%
						District of Columbia	5,268	0.8%

Source: U.S. Department of Health and Human Services, National Center for Health Statistics
"National Vital Statistics Reports" (Preliminary Report, November 2006, http://www.cdc.gov/nchs/births.htm)
Preliminary data by state of residence. By race of mother.

Black Births as a Percent of All Births in 2005

National Percent = 15.3% of Live Births*

ALPHA ORDER

RANK ORDER

RANK	STATE	PERCENT		RANK	STATE	PERCENT
6	Alabama	30.0		1	Mississippi	44.0
35	Alaska	4.1		2	Louisiana	39.5
36	Arizona	3.8		3	Maryland	35.3
13	Arkansas	19.1		3	South Carolina	35.3
32	California	5.9		5	Georgia	32.2
34	Colorado	4.5		6	Alabama	30.0
20	Connecticut	12.7		7	Delaware	25.0
7	Delaware	25.0		7	Florida	25.0
7	Florida	25.0		9	North Carolina	23.1
5	Georgia	32.2		10	Tennessee	22.6
39	Hawaii	2.7		11	New York	22.1
49	Idaho	0.6		12	Virginia	21.9
16	Illinois	17.2		13	Arkansas	19.1
23	Indiana	11.3		14	Michigan	17.6
36	Iowa	3.8		14	New Jersey	17.6
30	Kansas	7.8		16	Illinois	17.2
28	Kentucky	9.0		17	Ohio	16.3
2	Louisiana	39.5		18	Pennsylvania	15.7
41	Maine	1.9		19	Missouri	14.9
3	Maryland	35.3		20	Connecticut	12.7
21	Massachusetts	11.4		21	Massachusetts	11.4
14	Michigan	17.6		21	Texas	11.4
25	Minnesota	9.7		23	Indiana	11.3
1	Mississippi	44.0		24	Rhode Island	10.1
19	Missouri	14.9		25	Minnesota	9.7
50	Montana	0.5		26	Wisconsin	9.6
31	Nebraska	6.6		27	Oklahoma	9.3
29	Nevada	8.6		28	Kentucky	9.0
43	New Hampshire	1.6		29	Nevada	8.6
14	New Jersey	17.6		30	Kansas	7.8
41	New Mexico	1.9		31	Nebraska	6.6
11	New York	22.1		32	California	5.9
9	North Carolina	23.1		33	Washington	5.1
44	North Dakota	1.5		34	Colorado	4.5
17	Ohio	16.3		35	Alaska	4.1
27	Oklahoma	9.3		36	Arizona	3.8
40	Oregon	2.2		36	Iowa	3.8
18	Pennsylvania	15.7		38	West Virginia	3.4
24	Rhode Island	10.1		39	Hawaii	2.7
3	South Carolina	35.3		40	Oregon	2.2
45	South Dakota	1.2		41	Maine	1.9
10	Tennessee	22.6		41	New Mexico	1.9
21	Texas	11.4		43	New Hampshire	1.6
47	Utah	0.9		44	North Dakota	1.5
45	Vermont	1.2		45	South Dakota	1.2
12	Virginia	21.9		45	Vermont	1.2
33	Washington	5.1		47	Utah	0.9
38	West Virginia	3.4		47	Wyoming	0.9
26	Wisconsin	9.6		49	Idaho	0.6
47	Wyoming	0.9		50	Montana	0.5

District of Columbia   66.7

Source: Morgan Quitno Press using data from U.S. Dept. of Health and Human Services, Nat'l Center for Health Statistics
"National Vital Statistics Reports" (Preliminary Report, November 2006, http://www.cdc.gov/nchs/births.htm)
*Preliminary data by state of residence. By race of mother.

Births to Hispanic Women in 2005

National Total = 982,862 Live Births to Hispanic Women*

ALPHA ORDER				RANK ORDER			
RANK	STATE	BIRTHS	% of USA	RANK	STATE	BIRTHS	% of USA
32	Alabama	3,987	0.4%	1	California	283,600	28.9%
43	Alaska	780	0.1%	2	Texas	191,492	19.5%
6	Arizona	42,883	4.4%	3	Florida	60,082	6.1%
31	Arkansas	4,037	0.4%	4	New York	57,436	5.8%
1	California	283,600	28.9%	5	Illinois	43,449	4.4%
9	Colorado	21,798	2.2%	6	Arizona	42,883	4.4%
21	Connecticut	8,005	0.8%	7	New Jersey	27,952	2.8%
40	Delaware	1,654	0.2%	8	Georgia	22,001	2.2%
3	Florida	60,082	6.1%	9	Colorado	21,798	2.2%
8	Georgia	22,001	2.2%	10	North Carolina	19,529	2.0%
36	Hawaii	2,792	0.3%	11	New Mexico	15,825	1.6%
34	Idaho	3,493	0.4%	12	Washington	15,019	1.5%
5	Illinois	43,449	4.4%	13	Nevada	14,056	1.4%
20	Indiana	8,054	0.8%	14	Virginia	13,064	1.3%
35	Iowa	3,117	0.3%	15	Pennsylvania	12,189	1.2%
26	Kansas	6,127	0.6%	16	Massachusetts	10,119	1.0%
38	Kentucky	2,509	0.3%	17	Oregon	9,175	0.9%
39	Louisiana	1,947	0.2%	18	Maryland	8,689	0.9%
47	Maine	183	0.0%	19	Michigan	8,614	0.9%
18	Maryland	8,689	0.9%	20	Indiana	8,054	0.8%
16	Massachusetts	10,119	1.0%	21	Connecticut	8,005	0.8%
19	Michigan	8,614	0.9%	22	Utah	7,565	0.8%
28	Minnesota	5,515	0.6%	23	Tennessee	7,005	0.7%
41	Mississippi	1,170	0.1%	24	Oklahoma	6,273	0.6%
30	Missouri	4,275	0.4%	25	Wisconsin	6,240	0.6%
45	Montana	397	0.0%	26	Kansas	6,127	0.6%
33	Nebraska	3,858	0.4%	27	Ohio	6,098	0.6%
13	Nevada	14,056	1.4%	28	Minnesota	5,515	0.6%
44	New Hampshire	523	0.1%	29	South Carolina	4,994	0.5%
7	New Jersey	27,952	2.8%	30	Missouri	4,275	0.4%
11	New Mexico	15,825	1.6%	31	Arkansas	4,037	0.4%
4	New York	57,436	5.8%	32	Alabama	3,987	0.4%
10	North Carolina	19,529	2.0%	33	Nebraska	3,858	0.4%
48	North Dakota	180	0.0%	34	Idaho	3,493	0.4%
27	Ohio	6,098	0.6%	35	Iowa	3,117	0.3%
24	Oklahoma	6,273	0.6%	36	Hawaii	2,792	0.3%
17	Oregon	9,175	0.9%	37	Rhode Island	2,559	0.3%
15	Pennsylvania	12,189	1.2%	38	Kentucky	2,509	0.3%
37	Rhode Island	2,559	0.3%	39	Louisiana	1,947	0.2%
29	South Carolina	4,994	0.5%	40	Delaware	1,654	0.2%
46	South Dakota	392	0.0%	41	Mississippi	1,170	0.1%
23	Tennessee	7,005	0.7%	42	Wyoming	829	0.1%
2	Texas	191,492	19.5%	43	Alaska	780	0.1%
22	Utah	7,565	0.8%	44	New Hampshire	523	0.1%
50	Vermont	73	0.0%	45	Montana	397	0.0%
14	Virginia	13,064	1.3%	46	South Dakota	392	0.0%
12	Washington	15,019	1.5%	47	Maine	183	0.0%
49	West Virginia	174	0.0%	48	North Dakota	180	0.0%
25	Wisconsin	6,240	0.6%	49	West Virginia	174	0.0%
42	Wyoming	829	0.1%	50	Vermont	73	0.0%
					District of Columbia	1,086	0.1%

Source: U.S. Department of Health and Human Services, National Center for Health Statistics
   "National Vital Statistics Reports" (Preliminary Report, November 2006, http://www.cdc.gov/nchs/births.htm)
*Preliminary data by state of residence. By race of mother. Persons of Hispanic origin may be of any race.

Hispanic Births as a Percent of All Births in 2005

National Percent = 23.7% of Live Births*

ALPHA ORDER				RANK ORDER		
RANK	STATE	PERCENT		RANK	STATE	PERCENT
38	Alabama	6.6		1	New Mexico	54.9
36	Alaska	7.5		2	California	51.6
4	Arizona	44.6		3	Texas	49.6
28	Arkansas	10.3		4	Arizona	44.6
2	California	51.6		5	Nevada	37.7
6	Colorado	31.6		6	Colorado	31.6
13	Connecticut	19.2		7	Florida	26.6
22	Delaware	14.2		8	New Jersey	24.6
7	Florida	26.6		9	Illinois	24.3
17	Georgia	15.5		10	New York	23.3
16	Hawaii	15.6		11	Rhode Island	20.2
19	Idaho	15.1		12	Oregon	20.0
9	Illinois	24.3		13	Connecticut	19.2
29	Indiana	9.2		14	Washington	18.2
34	Iowa	7.9		15	North Carolina	15.9
18	Kansas	15.4		16	Hawaii	15.6
40	Kentucky	4.4		17	Georgia	15.5
45	Louisiana	3.2		18	Kansas	15.4
48	Maine	1.3		19	Idaho	15.1
26	Maryland	11.6		20	Nebraska	14.8
23	Massachusetts	13.2		21	Utah	14.7
37	Michigan	6.7		22	Delaware	14.2
35	Minnesota	7.8		23	Massachusetts	13.2
46	Mississippi	2.8		24	Virginia	12.5
39	Missouri	5.4		25	Oklahoma	12.1
43	Montana	3.4		26	Maryland	11.6
20	Nebraska	14.8		27	Wyoming	11.5
5	Nevada	37.7		28	Arkansas	10.3
42	New Hampshire	3.6		29	Indiana	9.2
8	New Jersey	24.6		30	Wisconsin	8.8
1	New Mexico	54.9		31	South Carolina	8.7
10	New York	23.3		32	Tennessee	8.6
15	North Carolina	15.9		33	Pennsylvania	8.4
47	North Dakota	2.1		34	Iowa	7.9
41	Ohio	4.1		35	Minnesota	7.8
25	Oklahoma	12.1		36	Alaska	7.5
12	Oregon	20.0		37	Michigan	6.7
33	Pennsylvania	8.4		38	Alabama	6.6
11	Rhode Island	20.2		39	Missouri	5.4
31	South Carolina	8.7		40	Kentucky	4.4
43	South Dakota	3.4		41	Ohio	4.1
32	Tennessee	8.6		42	New Hampshire	3.6
3	Texas	49.6		43	Montana	3.4
21	Utah	14.7		43	South Dakota	3.4
49	Vermont	1.1		45	Louisiana	3.2
24	Virginia	12.5		46	Mississippi	2.8
14	Washington	18.2		47	North Dakota	2.1
50	West Virginia	0.8		48	Maine	1.3
30	Wisconsin	8.8		49	Vermont	1.1
27	Wyoming	11.5		50	West Virginia	0.8
					District of Columbia	13.8

Source: Morgan Quitno Press using data from U.S. Dept. of Health and Human Services, Nat'l Center for Health Statistics
"National Vital Statistics Reports" (Preliminary Report, November 2006, http://www.cdc.gov/nchs/births.htm)
*Preliminary data by state of residence. By race of mother. Persons of Hispanic origin may be of any race.

Births of Low Birthweight in 2005

National Total = 339,514 Live Births*

ALPHA ORDER					RANK ORDER			
RANK	STATE	BIRTHS	% of USA		RANK	STATE	BIRTHS	% of USA
18	Alabama	6,468	1.9%		1	California	37,924	11.2%
47	Alaska	638	0.2%		2	Texas	32,035	9.4%
17	Arizona	6,640	2.0%		3	New York	20,447	6.0%
30	Arkansas	3,488	1.0%		4	Florida	19,686	5.8%
1	California	37,924	11.2%		5	Illinois	15,220	4.5%
20	Colorado	6,345	1.9%		6	Georgia	13,372	3.9%
31	Connecticut	3,337	1.0%		7	Ohio	12,956	3.8%
41	Delaware	1,107	0.3%		8	Pennsylvania	11,938	3.5%
4	Florida	19,686	5.8%		9	North Carolina	11,327	3.3%
6	Georgia	13,372	3.9%		10	Michigan	10,607	3.1%
40	Hawaii	1,470	0.4%		11	New Jersey	9,323	2.7%
39	Idaho	1,545	0.5%		12	Virginia	8,577	2.5%
5	Illinois	15,220	4.5%		13	Tennessee	7,766	2.3%
14	Indiana	7,244	2.1%		14	Indiana	7,244	2.1%
34	Iowa	2,830	0.8%		15	Louisiana	6,894	2.0%
33	Kansas	2,872	0.8%		16	Maryland	6,824	2.0%
23	Kentucky	5,131	1.5%		17	Arizona	6,640	2.0%
15	Louisiana	6,894	2.0%		18	Alabama	6,468	1.9%
44	Maine	960	0.3%		19	Missouri	6,368	1.9%
16	Maryland	6,824	2.0%		20	Colorado	6,345	1.9%
21	Massachusetts	6,077	1.8%		21	Massachusetts	6,077	1.8%
10	Michigan	10,607	3.1%		22	South Carolina	5,888	1.7%
27	Minnesota	4,613	1.4%		23	Kentucky	5,131	1.5%
25	Mississippi	5,003	1.5%		24	Washington	5,045	1.5%
19	Missouri	6,368	1.9%		25	Mississippi	5,003	1.5%
45	Montana	766	0.2%		26	Wisconsin	4,968	1.5%
38	Nebraska	1,830	0.5%		27	Minnesota	4,613	1.4%
32	Nevada	3,092	0.9%		28	Oklahoma	4,140	1.2%
42	New Hampshire	1,010	0.3%		29	Utah	3,506	1.0%
11	New Jersey	9,323	2.7%		30	Arkansas	3,488	1.0%
36	New Mexico	2,451	0.7%		31	Connecticut	3,337	1.0%
3	New York	20,447	6.0%		32	Nevada	3,092	0.9%
9	North Carolina	11,327	3.3%		33	Kansas	2,872	0.8%
49	North Dakota	537	0.2%		34	Iowa	2,830	0.8%
7	Ohio	12,956	3.8%		35	Oregon	2,802	0.8%
28	Oklahoma	4,140	1.2%		36	New Mexico	2,451	0.7%
35	Oregon	2,802	0.8%		37	West Virginia	1,980	0.6%
8	Pennsylvania	11,938	3.5%		38	Nebraska	1,830	0.5%
43	Rhode Island	976	0.3%		39	Idaho	1,545	0.5%
22	South Carolina	5,888	1.7%		40	Hawaii	1,470	0.4%
46	South Dakota	756	0.2%		41	Delaware	1,107	0.3%
13	Tennessee	7,766	2.3%		42	New Hampshire	1,010	0.3%
2	Texas	32,035	9.4%		43	Rhode Island	976	0.3%
29	Utah	3,506	1.0%		44	Maine	960	0.3%
50	Vermont	401	0.1%		45	Montana	766	0.2%
12	Virginia	8,577	2.5%		46	South Dakota	756	0.2%
24	Washington	5,045	1.5%		47	Alaska	638	0.2%
37	West Virginia	1,980	0.6%		48	Wyoming	623	0.2%
26	Wisconsin	4,968	1.5%		49	North Dakota	537	0.2%
48	Wyoming	623	0.2%		50	Vermont	401	0.1%
						District of Columbia	876	0.3%

Source: Morgan Quitno Press using data from U.S. Dept. of Health and Human Services, Nat'l Center for Health Statistics
   "Births: Preliminary data for 2005"
*Preliminary data by state of residence. Births of less than 2,500 grams (5 pounds 8 ounces).

Births of Low Birthweight as a Percent of All Births in 2005

National Percent = 8.2% of Live Births*

ALPHA ORDER				RANK ORDER		
RANK	STATE	PERCENT		RANK	STATE	PERCENT
3	Alabama	10.7		1	Mississippi	11.8
48	Alaska	6.1		2	Louisiana	11.3
38	Arizona	6.9		3	Alabama	10.7
13	Arkansas	8.9		4	South Carolina	10.2
38	California	6.9		5	Delaware	9.5
9	Colorado	9.2		5	Tennessee	9.5
29	Connecticut	8.0		5	West Virginia	9.5
5	Delaware	9.5		8	Georgia	9.4
14	Florida	8.7		9	Colorado	9.2
8	Georgia	9.4		9	North Carolina	9.2
24	Hawaii	8.2		11	Kentucky	9.1
42	Idaho	6.7		11	Maryland	9.1
17	Illinois	8.5		13	Arkansas	8.9
19	Indiana	8.3		14	Florida	8.7
33	Iowa	7.2		14	Ohio	8.7
33	Kansas	7.2		16	Wyoming	8.6
11	Kentucky	9.1		17	Illinois	8.5
2	Louisiana	11.3		17	New Mexico	8.5
40	Maine	6.8		19	Indiana	8.3
11	Maryland	9.1		19	Michigan	8.3
31	Massachusetts	7.9		19	Nevada	8.3
19	Michigan	8.3		19	New York	8.3
45	Minnesota	6.5		19	Texas	8.3
1	Mississippi	11.8		24	Hawaii	8.2
28	Missouri	8.1		24	New Jersey	8.2
43	Montana	6.6		24	Pennsylvania	8.2
35	Nebraska	7.0		24	Virginia	8.2
19	Nevada	8.3		28	Missouri	8.1
35	New Hampshire	7.0		29	Connecticut	8.0
24	New Jersey	8.2		29	Oklahoma	8.0
17	New Mexico	8.5		31	Massachusetts	7.9
19	New York	8.3		32	Rhode Island	7.7
9	North Carolina	9.2		33	Iowa	7.2
46	North Dakota	6.4		33	Kansas	7.2
14	Ohio	8.7		35	Nebraska	7.0
29	Oklahoma	8.0		35	New Hampshire	7.0
48	Oregon	6.1		35	Wisconsin	7.0
24	Pennsylvania	8.2		38	Arizona	6.9
32	Rhode Island	7.7		38	California	6.9
4	South Carolina	10.2		40	Maine	6.8
43	South Dakota	6.6		40	Utah	6.8
5	Tennessee	9.5		42	Idaho	6.7
19	Texas	8.3		43	Montana	6.6
40	Utah	6.8		43	South Dakota	6.6
47	Vermont	6.2		45	Minnesota	6.5
24	Virginia	8.2		46	North Dakota	6.4
48	Washington	6.1		47	Vermont	6.2
5	West Virginia	9.5		48	Alaska	6.1
35	Wisconsin	7.0		48	Oregon	6.1
16	Wyoming	8.6		48	Washington	6.1
					District of Columbia	11.1

Source: U.S. Department of Health and Human Services, National Center for Health Statistics
"Births: Preliminary data for 2005"
*Preliminary data by state of residence. Births of less than 2,500 grams (5 pounds 8 ounces).

Births of Low Birthweight to White Women in 2005

National Total = 232,688 Live Births*

ALPHA ORDER

ALPHA ORDER

RANK ORDER

RANK	STATE	BIRTHS	% of USA		RANK	STATE	BIRTHS	% of USA
22	Alabama	3,547	1.5%		1	California	28,077	12.1%
49	Alaska	379	0.2%		2	Texas	24,556	10.6%
14	Arizona	5,489	2.4%		3	New York	12,242	5.3%
33	Arkansas	2,341	1.0%		4	Florida	11,789	5.1%
1	California	28,077	12.1%		5	Illinois	9,868	4.2%
13	Colorado	5,533	2.4%		6	Ohio	9,310	4.0%
31	Connecticut	2,413	1.0%		7	Pennsylvania	8,510	3.7%
44	Delaware	615	0.3%		8	Michigan	6,910	3.0%
4	Florida	11,789	5.1%		9	North Carolina	6,724	2.9%
10	Georgia	6,382	2.7%		10	Georgia	6,382	2.7%
50	Hawaii	333	0.1%		11	New Jersey	5,866	2.5%
39	Idaho	1,459	0.6%		12	Indiana	5,837	2.5%
5	Illinois	9,868	4.2%		13	Colorado	5,533	2.4%
12	Indiana	5,837	2.5%		14	Arizona	5,489	2.4%
29	Iowa	2,526	1.1%		15	Virginia	5,205	2.2%
32	Kansas	2,353	1.0%		16	Tennessee	5,035	2.2%
19	Kentucky	4,385	1.9%		17	Massachusetts	4,684	2.0%
26	Louisiana	3,017	1.3%		18	Missouri	4,531	1.9%
40	Maine	919	0.4%		19	Kentucky	4,385	1.9%
25	Maryland	3,076	1.3%		20	Washington	3,939	1.7%
17	Massachusetts	4,684	2.0%		21	Wisconsin	3,809	1.6%
8	Michigan	6,910	3.0%		22	Alabama	3,547	1.5%
23	Minnesota	3,470	1.5%		23	Minnesota	3,470	1.5%
36	Mississippi	1,959	0.8%		24	Utah	3,278	1.4%
18	Missouri	4,531	1.9%		25	Maryland	3,076	1.3%
43	Montana	636	0.3%		26	Louisiana	3,017	1.3%
38	Nebraska	1,510	0.6%		27	Oklahoma	2,959	1.3%
34	Nevada	2,269	1.0%		28	South Carolina	2,780	1.2%
41	New Hampshire	910	0.4%		29	Iowa	2,526	1.1%
11	New Jersey	5,866	2.5%		30	Oregon	2,453	1.1%
35	New Mexico	2,050	0.9%		31	Connecticut	2,413	1.0%
3	New York	12,242	5.3%		32	Kansas	2,353	1.0%
9	North Carolina	6,724	2.9%		33	Arkansas	2,341	1.0%
47	North Dakota	453	0.2%		34	Nevada	2,269	1.0%
6	Ohio	9,310	4.0%		35	New Mexico	2,050	0.9%
27	Oklahoma	2,959	1.3%		36	Mississippi	1,959	0.8%
30	Oregon	2,453	1.1%		37	West Virginia	1,874	0.8%
7	Pennsylvania	8,510	3.7%		38	Nebraska	1,510	0.6%
42	Rhode Island	780	0.3%		39	Idaho	1,459	0.6%
28	South Carolina	2,780	1.2%		40	Maine	919	0.4%
45	South Dakota	602	0.3%		41	New Hampshire	910	0.4%
16	Tennessee	5,035	2.2%		42	Rhode Island	780	0.3%
2	Texas	24,556	10.6%		43	Montana	636	0.3%
24	Utah	3,278	1.4%		44	Delaware	615	0.3%
48	Vermont	383	0.2%		45	South Dakota	602	0.3%
15	Virginia	5,205	2.2%		46	Wyoming	589	0.3%
20	Washington	3,939	1.7%		47	North Dakota	453	0.2%
37	West Virginia	1,874	0.8%		48	Vermont	383	0.2%
21	Wisconsin	3,809	1.6%		49	Alaska	379	0.2%
46	Wyoming	589	0.3%		50	Hawaii	333	0.1%
						District of Columbia	170	0.1%

Source: Morgan Quitno Press using data from U.S. Dept. of Health and Human Services, Nat'l Center for Health Statistics
"Births: Preliminary data for 2005"
*Preliminary data by state of residence. Births of less than 2,500 grams (5 pounds 8 ounces).

Births of Low Birthweight to White Women
as a Percent of All Births to White Women in 2005
National Percent = 7.2% of Live Births to White Women*

ALPHA ORDER

RANK ORDER

RANK	STATE	PERCENT	RANK	STATE	PERCENT
5	Alabama	8.6	1	West Virginia	9.4
49	Alaska	5.8	2	Colorado	8.8
37	Arizona	6.6	3	Kentucky	8.7
13	Arkansas	7.6	3	Wyoming	8.7
43	California	6.3	5	Alabama	8.6
2	Colorado	8.8	6	Louisiana	8.5
24	Connecticut	7.1	6	Mississippi	8.5
14	Delaware	7.5	6	New Mexico	8.5
20	Florida	7.3	9	Tennessee	8.2
28	Georgia	7.0	10	Indiana	7.7
37	Hawaii	6.6	10	Ohio	7.7
37	Idaho	6.6	10	South Carolina	7.7
24	Illinois	7.1	13	Arkansas	7.6
10	Indiana	7.7	14	Delaware	7.5
31	Iowa	6.9	14	Massachusetts	7.5
34	Kansas	6.7	14	North Carolina	7.5
3	Kentucky	8.7	14	Texas	7.5
6	Louisiana	8.5	18	Nevada	7.4
33	Maine	6.8	18	Oklahoma	7.4
24	Maryland	7.1	20	Florida	7.3
14	Massachusetts	7.5	20	Pennsylvania	7.3
31	Michigan	6.9	20	Rhode Island	7.3
47	Minnesota	6.0	23	New York	7.2
6	Mississippi	8.5	24	Connecticut	7.1
28	Missouri	7.0	24	Illinois	7.1
42	Montana	6.4	24	Maryland	7.1
40	Nebraska	6.5	24	New Jersey	7.1
18	Nevada	7.4	28	Georgia	7.0
34	New Hampshire	6.7	28	Missouri	7.0
24	New Jersey	7.1	28	Virginia	7.0
6	New Mexico	8.5	31	Iowa	6.9
23	New York	7.2	31	Michigan	6.9
14	North Carolina	7.5	33	Maine	6.8
43	North Dakota	6.3	34	Kansas	6.7
10	Ohio	7.7	34	New Hampshire	6.7
18	Oklahoma	7.4	34	Utah	6.7
48	Oregon	5.9	37	Arizona	6.6
20	Pennsylvania	7.3	37	Hawaii	6.6
20	Rhode Island	7.3	37	Idaho	6.6
10	South Carolina	7.7	40	Nebraska	6.5
40	South Dakota	6.5	40	South Dakota	6.5
9	Tennessee	8.2	42	Montana	6.4
14	Texas	7.5	43	California	6.3
34	Utah	6.7	43	North Dakota	6.3
46	Vermont	6.1	43	Wisconsin	6.3
28	Virginia	7.0	46	Vermont	6.1
49	Washington	5.8	47	Minnesota	6.0
1	West Virginia	9.4	48	Oregon	5.9
43	Wisconsin	6.3	49	Alaska	5.8
3	Wyoming	8.7	49	Washington	5.8
				District of Columbia	7.0

Source: U.S. Department of Health and Human Services, National Center for Health Statistics
        "Births: Preliminary data for 2005"
*Preliminary data by state of residence. Births of less than 2,500 grams (5 pounds 8 ounces).

Births of Low Birthweight to Black Women in 2005

National Total = 86,037 Live Births*

RANK	STATE	BIRTHS	% of USA
16	Alabama	2,811	3.3%
40	Alaska	59	0.1%
30	Arizona	456	0.5%
21	Arkansas	1,076	1.3%
7	California	4,019	4.7%
28	Colorado	468	0.5%
25	Connecticut	692	0.8%
31	Delaware	428	0.5%
1	Florida	7,235	8.4%
3	Georgia	6,506	7.6%
41	Hawaii	50	0.1%
NA	Idaho**	NA	NA
5	Illinois	4,610	5.4%
20	Indiana	1,325	1.5%
35	Iowa	187	0.2%
32	Kansas	409	0.5%
27	Kentucky	681	0.8%
8	Louisiana	3,785	4.4%
44	Maine	24	0.0%
9	Maryland	3,364	3.9%
22	Massachusetts	960	1.1%
11	Michigan	3,282	3.8%
24	Minnesota	724	0.8%
13	Mississippi	3,004	3.5%
19	Missouri	1,659	1.9%
NA	Montana**	NA	NA
34	Nebraska	225	0.3%
28	Nevada	468	0.5%
43	New Hampshire	26	0.0%
18	New Jersey	2,496	2.9%
39	New Mexico	79	0.1%
2	New York	6,523	7.6%
6	North Carolina	4,124	4.8%
NA	North Dakota**	NA	NA
10	Ohio	3,296	3.8%
26	Oklahoma	684	0.8%
37	Oregon	114	0.1%
12	Pennsylvania	3,021	3.5%
36	Rhode Island	135	0.2%
14	South Carolina	2,995	3.5%
NA	South Dakota**	NA	NA
17	Tennessee	2,588	3.0%
4	Texas	6,128	7.1%
42	Utah	48	0.1%
NA	Vermont**	NA	NA
15	Virginia	2,865	3.3%
33	Washington	406	0.5%
38	West Virginia	94	0.1%
23	Wisconsin	917	1.1%
NA	Wyoming**	NA	NA

RANK	STATE	BIRTHS	% of USA
1	Florida	7,235	8.4%
2	New York	6,523	7.6%
3	Georgia	6,506	7.6%
4	Texas	6,128	7.1%
5	Illinois	4,610	5.4%
6	North Carolina	4,124	4.8%
7	California	4,019	4.7%
8	Louisiana	3,785	4.4%
9	Maryland	3,364	3.9%
10	Ohio	3,296	3.8%
11	Michigan	3,282	3.8%
12	Pennsylvania	3,021	3.5%
13	Mississippi	3,004	3.5%
14	South Carolina	2,995	3.5%
15	Virginia	2,865	3.3%
16	Alabama	2,811	3.3%
17	Tennessee	2,588	3.0%
18	New Jersey	2,496	2.9%
19	Missouri	1,659	1.9%
20	Indiana	1,325	1.5%
21	Arkansas	1,076	1.3%
22	Massachusetts	960	1.1%
23	Wisconsin	917	1.1%
24	Minnesota	724	0.8%
25	Connecticut	692	0.8%
26	Oklahoma	684	0.8%
27	Kentucky	681	0.8%
28	Colorado	468	0.5%
28	Nevada	468	0.5%
30	Arizona	456	0.5%
31	Delaware	428	0.5%
32	Kansas	409	0.5%
33	Washington	406	0.5%
34	Nebraska	225	0.3%
35	Iowa	187	0.2%
36	Rhode Island	135	0.2%
37	Oregon	114	0.1%
38	West Virginia	94	0.1%
39	New Mexico	79	0.1%
40	Alaska	59	0.1%
41	Hawaii	50	0.1%
42	Utah	48	0.1%
43	New Hampshire	26	0.0%
44	Maine	24	0.0%
NA	Idaho**	NA	NA
NA	Montana**	NA	NA
NA	North Dakota**	NA	NA
NA	South Dakota**	NA	NA
NA	Vermont**	NA	NA
NA	Wyoming**	NA	NA
	District of Columbia	690	0.8%

Source: Morgan Quitno Press using data from U.S. Dept. of Health and Human Services, Nat'l Center for Health Statistics
   "Births: Preliminary data for 2005"
*Preliminary data by state of residence. Births of less than 2,500 grams (5 pounds 8 ounces).
**Not available. Fewer than 20 births of low birthweight to black women.

Births of Low Birthweight to Black Women as a Percent of All Births to Black Women in 2005
National Percent = 13.6% of Live Births to Black Women*

RANK	STATE	PERCENT
3	Alabama	15.5
17	Alaska	13.9
30	Arizona	12.5
12	Arkansas	14.4
33	California	12.4
4	Colorado	15.0
25	Connecticut	13.1
6	Delaware	14.7
28	Florida	12.8
13	Georgia	14.2
41	Hawaii	10.3
NA	Idaho**	NA
4	Illinois	15.0
21	Indiana	13.4
33	Iowa	12.4
25	Kansas	13.1
21	Kentucky	13.4
2	Louisiana	15.7
44	Maine	9.1
29	Maryland	12.7
38	Massachusetts	10.9
9	Michigan	14.6
39	Minnesota	10.5
1	Mississippi	16.1
13	Missouri	14.2
NA	Montana**	NA
25	Nebraska	13.1
9	Nevada	14.6
37	New Hampshire	11.2
30	New Jersey	12.5
6	New Mexico	14.7
35	New York	12.0
11	North Carolina	14.5
NA	North Dakota**	NA
19	Ohio	13.6
13	Oklahoma	14.2
36	Oregon	11.3
24	Pennsylvania	13.2
39	Rhode Island	10.5
6	South Carolina	14.7
NA	South Dakota**	NA
16	Tennessee	14.0
17	Texas	13.9
42	Utah	9.9
NA	Vermont**	NA
30	Virginia	12.5
43	Washington	9.6
23	West Virginia	13.3
20	Wisconsin	13.5
NA	Wyoming**	NA

RANK	STATE	PERCENT
1	Mississippi	16.1
2	Louisiana	15.7
3	Alabama	15.5
4	Colorado	15.0
4	Illinois	15.0
6	Delaware	14.7
6	New Mexico	14.7
6	South Carolina	14.7
9	Michigan	14.6
9	Nevada	14.6
11	North Carolina	14.5
12	Arkansas	14.4
13	Georgia	14.2
13	Missouri	14.2
13	Oklahoma	14.2
16	Tennessee	14.0
17	Alaska	13.9
17	Texas	13.9
19	Ohio	13.6
20	Wisconsin	13.5
21	Indiana	13.4
21	Kentucky	13.4
23	West Virginia	13.3
24	Pennsylvania	13.2
25	Connecticut	13.1
25	Kansas	13.1
25	Nebraska	13.1
28	Florida	12.8
29	Maryland	12.7
30	Arizona	12.5
30	New Jersey	12.5
30	Virginia	12.5
33	California	12.4
33	Iowa	12.4
35	New York	12.0
36	Oregon	11.3
37	New Hampshire	11.2
38	Massachusetts	10.9
39	Minnesota	10.5
39	Rhode Island	10.5
41	Hawaii	10.3
42	Utah	9.9
43	Washington	9.6
44	Maine	9.1
NA	Idaho**	NA
NA	Montana**	NA
NA	North Dakota**	NA
NA	South Dakota**	NA
NA	Vermont**	NA
NA	Wyoming**	NA
	District of Columbia	13.1

Source: U.S. Department of Health and Human Services, National Center for Health Statistics
   "Births: Preliminary data for 2005"
*Preliminary data by state of residence. Births of less than 2,500 grams (5 pounds 8 ounces).
**Not available. Fewer than 20 births of low birthweight to black women.

Births of Low Birthweight to Hispanic Women in 2005

National Total = 67,817 Live Births*

ALPHA ORDER RANK	STATE	BIRTHS	% of USA	RANK ORDER RANK	STATE	BIRTHS	% of USA
31	Alabama	287	0.4%	1	California	17,583	25.9%
43	Alaska	42	0.1%	2	Texas	14,362	21.2%
6	Arizona	2,787	4.1%	3	New York	4,480	6.6%
30	Arkansas	291	0.4%	4	Florida	4,206	6.2%
1	California	17,583	25.9%	5	Illinois	2,911	4.3%
8	Colorado	1,896	2.8%	6	Arizona	2,787	4.1%
17	Connecticut	664	1.0%	7	New Jersey	2,013	3.0%
40	Delaware	119	0.2%	8	Colorado	1,896	2.8%
4	Florida	4,206	6.2%	9	New Mexico	1,329	2.0%
10	Georgia	1,298	1.9%	10	Georgia	1,298	1.9%
34	Hawaii	243	0.4%	11	North Carolina	1,230	1.8%
35	Idaho	227	0.3%	12	Pennsylvania	1,048	1.5%
5	Illinois	2,911	4.3%	13	Nevada	970	1.4%
20	Indiana	540	0.8%	14	Washington	916	1.4%
37	Iowa	190	0.3%	15	Massachusetts	850	1.3%
28	Kansas	355	0.5%	16	Virginia	797	1.2%
38	Kentucky	176	0.3%	17	Connecticut	664	1.0%
39	Louisiana	136	0.2%	18	Maryland	626	0.9%
NA	Maine**	NA	NA	19	Michigan	560	0.8%
18	Maryland	626	0.9%	20	Indiana	540	0.8%
15	Massachusetts	850	1.3%	21	Utah	537	0.8%
19	Michigan	560	0.8%	22	Oregon	523	0.8%
29	Minnesota	309	0.5%	23	Ohio	439	0.6%
42	Mississippi	60	0.1%	24	Oklahoma	420	0.6%
32	Missouri	269	0.4%	24	Tennessee	420	0.6%
45	Montana	32	0.0%	26	Wisconsin	399	0.6%
33	Nebraska	251	0.4%	27	South Carolina	360	0.5%
13	Nevada	970	1.4%	28	Kansas	355	0.5%
44	New Hampshire	39	0.1%	29	Minnesota	309	0.5%
7	New Jersey	2,013	3.0%	30	Arkansas	291	0.4%
9	New Mexico	1,329	2.0%	31	Alabama	287	0.4%
3	New York	4,480	6.6%	32	Missouri	269	0.4%
11	North Carolina	1,230	1.8%	33	Nebraska	251	0.4%
NA	North Dakota**	NA	NA	34	Hawaii	243	0.4%
23	Ohio	439	0.6%	35	Idaho	227	0.3%
24	Oklahoma	420	0.6%	36	Rhode Island	223	0.3%
22	Oregon	523	0.8%	37	Iowa	190	0.3%
12	Pennsylvania	1,048	1.5%	38	Kentucky	176	0.3%
36	Rhode Island	223	0.3%	39	Louisiana	136	0.2%
27	South Carolina	360	0.5%	40	Delaware	119	0.2%
NA	South Dakota**	NA	NA	41	Wyoming	68	0.1%
24	Tennessee	420	0.6%	42	Mississippi	60	0.1%
2	Texas	14,362	21.2%	43	Alaska	42	0.1%
21	Utah	537	0.8%	44	New Hampshire	39	0.1%
NA	Vermont**	NA	NA	45	Montana	32	0.0%
16	Virginia	797	1.2%	NA	Maine**	NA	NA
14	Washington	916	1.4%	NA	North Dakota**	NA	NA
NA	West Virginia**	NA	NA	NA	South Dakota**	NA	NA
26	Wisconsin	399	0.6%	NA	Vermont**	NA	NA
41	Wyoming	68	0.1%	NA	West Virginia**	NA	NA
					District of Columbia	78	0.1%

Source: Morgan Quitno Press using data from U.S. Dept. of Health and Human Services, Nat'l Center for Health Statistics
   "Births: Preliminary data for 2005"
*Preliminary data by state of residence. Births of less than 2,500 grams (5 pounds 8 ounces). Hispanic can be of any race.
**Not available. Fewer than 20 births of low birthweight to Hispanic women.

Births of Low Birthweight to Hispanic Women as a Percent of All Births to Hispanic Women in 2005
National Percent = 6.9% of Live Births to Hispanic Women*

<table>
<tr><td colspan="3">ALPHA ORDER</td><td colspan="3">RANK ORDER</td></tr>
<tr><td>RANK</td><td>STATE</td><td>PERCENT</td><td>RANK</td><td>STATE</td><td>PERCENT</td></tr>
<tr><td>13</td><td>Alabama</td><td>7.2</td><td>1</td><td>Colorado</td><td>8.7</td></tr>
<tr><td>44</td><td>Alaska</td><td>5.4</td><td>1</td><td>Hawaii</td><td>8.7</td></tr>
<tr><td>28</td><td>Arizona</td><td>6.5</td><td>1</td><td>Rhode Island</td><td>8.7</td></tr>
<tr><td>13</td><td>Arkansas</td><td>7.2</td><td>4</td><td>Pennsylvania</td><td>8.6</td></tr>
<tr><td>35</td><td>California</td><td>6.2</td><td>5</td><td>Massachusetts</td><td>8.4</td></tr>
<tr><td>1</td><td>Colorado</td><td>8.7</td><td>5</td><td>New Mexico</td><td>8.4</td></tr>
<tr><td>7</td><td>Connecticut</td><td>8.3</td><td>7</td><td>Connecticut</td><td>8.3</td></tr>
<tr><td>13</td><td>Delaware</td><td>7.2</td><td>8</td><td>Wyoming</td><td>8.2</td></tr>
<tr><td>21</td><td>Florida</td><td>7.0</td><td>9</td><td>Montana</td><td>8.1</td></tr>
<tr><td>40</td><td>Georgia</td><td>5.9</td><td>10</td><td>New York</td><td>7.8</td></tr>
<tr><td>1</td><td>Hawaii</td><td>8.7</td><td>11</td><td>New Hampshire</td><td>7.5</td></tr>
<tr><td>28</td><td>Idaho</td><td>6.5</td><td>11</td><td>Texas</td><td>7.5</td></tr>
<tr><td>25</td><td>Illinois</td><td>6.7</td><td>13</td><td>Alabama</td><td>7.2</td></tr>
<tr><td>25</td><td>Indiana</td><td>6.7</td><td>13</td><td>Arkansas</td><td>7.2</td></tr>
<tr><td>36</td><td>Iowa</td><td>6.1</td><td>13</td><td>Delaware</td><td>7.2</td></tr>
<tr><td>41</td><td>Kansas</td><td>5.8</td><td>13</td><td>Maryland</td><td>7.2</td></tr>
<tr><td>21</td><td>Kentucky</td><td>7.0</td><td>13</td><td>New Jersey</td><td>7.2</td></tr>
<tr><td>21</td><td>Louisiana</td><td>7.0</td><td>13</td><td>Ohio</td><td>7.2</td></tr>
<tr><td>NA</td><td>Maine**</td><td>NA</td><td>13</td><td>South Carolina</td><td>7.2</td></tr>
<tr><td>13</td><td>Maryland</td><td>7.2</td><td>20</td><td>Utah</td><td>7.1</td></tr>
<tr><td>5</td><td>Massachusetts</td><td>8.4</td><td>21</td><td>Florida</td><td>7.0</td></tr>
<tr><td>28</td><td>Michigan</td><td>6.5</td><td>21</td><td>Kentucky</td><td>7.0</td></tr>
<tr><td>43</td><td>Minnesota</td><td>5.6</td><td>21</td><td>Louisiana</td><td>7.0</td></tr>
<tr><td>45</td><td>Mississippi</td><td>5.1</td><td>24</td><td>Nevada</td><td>6.9</td></tr>
<tr><td>33</td><td>Missouri</td><td>6.3</td><td>25</td><td>Illinois</td><td>6.7</td></tr>
<tr><td>9</td><td>Montana</td><td>8.1</td><td>25</td><td>Indiana</td><td>6.7</td></tr>
<tr><td>28</td><td>Nebraska</td><td>6.5</td><td>25</td><td>Oklahoma</td><td>6.7</td></tr>
<tr><td>24</td><td>Nevada</td><td>6.9</td><td>28</td><td>Arizona</td><td>6.5</td></tr>
<tr><td>11</td><td>New Hampshire</td><td>7.5</td><td>28</td><td>Idaho</td><td>6.5</td></tr>
<tr><td>13</td><td>New Jersey</td><td>7.2</td><td>28</td><td>Michigan</td><td>6.5</td></tr>
<tr><td>5</td><td>New Mexico</td><td>8.4</td><td>28</td><td>Nebraska</td><td>6.5</td></tr>
<tr><td>10</td><td>New York</td><td>7.8</td><td>32</td><td>Wisconsin</td><td>6.4</td></tr>
<tr><td>33</td><td>North Carolina</td><td>6.3</td><td>33</td><td>Missouri</td><td>6.3</td></tr>
<tr><td>NA</td><td>North Dakota**</td><td>NA</td><td>33</td><td>North Carolina</td><td>6.3</td></tr>
<tr><td>13</td><td>Ohio</td><td>7.2</td><td>35</td><td>California</td><td>6.2</td></tr>
<tr><td>25</td><td>Oklahoma</td><td>6.7</td><td>36</td><td>Iowa</td><td>6.1</td></tr>
<tr><td>42</td><td>Oregon</td><td>5.7</td><td>36</td><td>Virginia</td><td>6.1</td></tr>
<tr><td>4</td><td>Pennsylvania</td><td>8.6</td><td>36</td><td>Washington</td><td>6.1</td></tr>
<tr><td>1</td><td>Rhode Island</td><td>8.7</td><td>39</td><td>Tennessee</td><td>6.0</td></tr>
<tr><td>13</td><td>South Carolina</td><td>7.2</td><td>40</td><td>Georgia</td><td>5.9</td></tr>
<tr><td>NA</td><td>South Dakota**</td><td>NA</td><td>41</td><td>Kansas</td><td>5.8</td></tr>
<tr><td>39</td><td>Tennessee</td><td>6.0</td><td>42</td><td>Oregon</td><td>5.7</td></tr>
<tr><td>11</td><td>Texas</td><td>7.5</td><td>43</td><td>Minnesota</td><td>5.6</td></tr>
<tr><td>20</td><td>Utah</td><td>7.1</td><td>44</td><td>Alaska</td><td>5.4</td></tr>
<tr><td>NA</td><td>Vermont**</td><td>NA</td><td>45</td><td>Mississippi</td><td>5.1</td></tr>
<tr><td>36</td><td>Virginia</td><td>6.1</td><td>NA</td><td>Maine**</td><td>NA</td></tr>
<tr><td>36</td><td>Washington</td><td>6.1</td><td>NA</td><td>North Dakota**</td><td>NA</td></tr>
<tr><td>NA</td><td>West Virginia**</td><td>NA</td><td>NA</td><td>South Dakota**</td><td>NA</td></tr>
<tr><td>32</td><td>Wisconsin</td><td>6.4</td><td>NA</td><td>Vermont**</td><td>NA</td></tr>
<tr><td>8</td><td>Wyoming</td><td>8.2</td><td>NA</td><td>West Virginia**</td><td>NA</td></tr>
</table>

District of Columbia   7.2

Source: U.S. Department of Health and Human Services, National Center for Health Statistics
    "Births: Preliminary data for 2005"

*Preliminary data by state of residence. Births of less than 2,500 grams (5 pounds 8 ounces). Hispanic can be of any race.
**Not available. Fewer than 20 births of low birthweight to Hispanic women.

Births to Unmarried Women in 2005

National Total = 1,523,674 Live Births*

RANK	STATE	BIRTHS	% of USA
23	Alabama	21,580	1.4%
47	Alaska	3,767	0.2%
11	Arizona	41,476	2.7%
29	Arkansas	15,757	1.0%
1	California	196,216	12.9%
28	Colorado	18,689	1.2%
34	Connecticut	13,433	0.9%
41	Delaware	5,160	0.3%
3	Florida	96,848	6.4%
7	Georgia	57,329	3.8%
39	Hawaii	6,489	0.4%
40	Idaho	5,281	0.3%
5	Illinois	66,432	4.4%
13	Indiana	35,087	2.3%
35	Iowa	12,776	0.8%
33	Kansas	13,643	0.9%
27	Kentucky	20,073	1.3%
17	Louisiana	29,038	1.9%
42	Maine	4,940	0.3%
18	Maryland	27,745	1.8%
21	Massachusetts	23,153	1.5%
10	Michigan	45,752	3.0%
24	Minnesota	21,078	1.4%
25	Mississippi	20,987	1.4%
16	Missouri	29,718	2.0%
45	Montana	4,003	0.3%
37	Nebraska	8,080	0.5%
31	Nevada	15,164	1.0%
46	New Hampshire	3,938	0.3%
12	New Jersey	35,816	2.4%
32	New Mexico	14,648	1.0%
4	New York	95,339	6.3%
9	North Carolina	47,277	3.1%
48	North Dakota	2,703	0.2%
6	Ohio	57,928	3.8%
26	Oklahoma	20,233	1.3%
30	Oregon	15,251	1.0%
8	Pennsylvania	52,847	3.5%
43	Rhode Island	4,793	0.3%
20	South Carolina	25,169	1.7%
44	South Dakota	4,147	0.3%
15	Tennessee	32,861	2.2%
2	Texas	145,122	9.5%
36	Utah	8,713	0.6%
50	Vermont	2,091	0.1%
14	Virginia	33,679	2.2%
19	Washington	25,556	1.7%
38	West Virginia	7,606	0.5%
22	Wisconsin	23,068	1.5%
49	Wyoming	2,374	0.2%

RANK	STATE	BIRTHS	% of USA
1	California	196,216	12.9%
2	Texas	145,122	9.5%
3	Florida	96,848	6.4%
4	New York	95,339	6.3%
5	Illinois	66,432	4.4%
6	Ohio	57,928	3.8%
7	Georgia	57,329	3.8%
8	Pennsylvania	52,847	3.5%
9	North Carolina	47,277	3.1%
10	Michigan	45,752	3.0%
11	Arizona	41,476	2.7%
12	New Jersey	35,816	2.4%
13	Indiana	35,087	2.3%
14	Virginia	33,679	2.2%
15	Tennessee	32,861	2.2%
16	Missouri	29,718	2.0%
17	Louisiana	29,038	1.9%
18	Maryland	27,745	1.8%
19	Washington	25,556	1.7%
20	South Carolina	25,169	1.7%
21	Massachusetts	23,153	1.5%
22	Wisconsin	23,068	1.5%
23	Alabama	21,580	1.4%
24	Minnesota	21,078	1.4%
25	Mississippi	20,987	1.4%
26	Oklahoma	20,233	1.3%
27	Kentucky	20,073	1.3%
28	Colorado	18,689	1.2%
29	Arkansas	15,757	1.0%
30	Oregon	15,251	1.0%
31	Nevada	15,164	1.0%
32	New Mexico	14,648	1.0%
33	Kansas	13,643	0.9%
34	Connecticut	13,433	0.9%
35	Iowa	12,776	0.8%
36	Utah	8,713	0.6%
37	Nebraska	8,080	0.5%
38	West Virginia	7,606	0.5%
39	Hawaii	6,489	0.4%
40	Idaho	5,281	0.3%
41	Delaware	5,160	0.3%
42	Maine	4,940	0.3%
43	Rhode Island	4,793	0.3%
44	South Dakota	4,147	0.3%
45	Montana	4,003	0.3%
46	New Hampshire	3,938	0.3%
47	Alaska	3,767	0.2%
48	North Dakota	2,703	0.2%
49	Wyoming	2,374	0.2%
50	Vermont	2,091	0.1%
	District of Columbia	4,381	0.3%

Source: Morgan Quitno Press using data from U.S. Dept. of Health and Human Services, Nat'l Center for Health Statistics
"Births: Preliminary data for 2005"
*Preliminary data by state of residence.

Births to Unmarried Women as a Percent of All Births in 2005

National Percent = 36.8% of Live Births*

RANK	STATE	PERCENT
28	Alabama	35.7
26	Alaska	36.0
6	Arizona	43.1
10	Arkansas	40.2
28	California	35.7
48	Colorado	27.1
39	Connecticut	32.2
4	Delaware	44.3
7	Florida	42.8
9	Georgia	40.3
24	Hawaii	36.2
49	Idaho	22.9
20	Illinois	37.1
10	Indiana	40.2
36	Iowa	32.5
33	Kansas	34.2
30	Kentucky	35.6
3	Louisiana	47.6
31	Maine	35.0
21	Maryland	37.0
45	Massachusetts	30.1
27	Michigan	35.8
46	Minnesota	29.7
2	Mississippi	49.5
17	Missouri	37.8
32	Montana	34.5
43	Nebraska	30.9
8	Nevada	40.7
47	New Hampshire	27.3
42	New Jersey	31.5
1	New Mexico	50.8
15	New York	38.7
16	North Carolina	38.4
39	North Dakota	32.2
14	Ohio	38.9
13	Oklahoma	39.1
34	Oregon	33.2
23	Pennsylvania	36.3
17	Rhode Island	37.8
5	South Carolina	43.6
24	South Dakota	36.2
10	Tennessee	40.2
19	Texas	37.6
50	Utah	16.9
38	Vermont	32.3
39	Virginia	32.2
43	Washington	30.9
22	West Virginia	36.5
36	Wisconsin	32.5
35	Wyoming	32.8

RANK	STATE	PERCENT
1	New Mexico	50.8
2	Mississippi	49.5
3	Louisiana	47.6
4	Delaware	44.3
5	South Carolina	43.6
6	Arizona	43.1
7	Florida	42.8
8	Nevada	40.7
9	Georgia	40.3
10	Arkansas	40.2
10	Indiana	40.2
10	Tennessee	40.2
13	Oklahoma	39.1
14	Ohio	38.9
15	New York	38.7
16	North Carolina	38.4
17	Missouri	37.8
17	Rhode Island	37.8
19	Texas	37.6
20	Illinois	37.1
21	Maryland	37.0
22	West Virginia	36.5
23	Pennsylvania	36.3
24	Hawaii	36.2
24	South Dakota	36.2
26	Alaska	36.0
27	Michigan	35.8
28	Alabama	35.7
28	California	35.7
30	Kentucky	35.6
31	Maine	35.0
32	Montana	34.5
33	Kansas	34.2
34	Oregon	33.2
35	Wyoming	32.8
36	Iowa	32.5
36	Wisconsin	32.5
38	Vermont	32.3
39	Connecticut	32.2
39	North Dakota	32.2
39	Virginia	32.2
42	New Jersey	31.5
43	Nebraska	30.9
43	Washington	30.9
45	Massachusetts	30.1
46	Minnesota	29.7
47	New Hampshire	27.3
48	Colorado	27.1
49	Idaho	22.9
50	Utah	16.9

	District of Columbia	55.5

Source: U.S. Department of Health and Human Services, National Center for Health Statistics
    "Births: Preliminary data for 2005"
*Preliminary data by state of residence.

Births to Unmarried White Women in 2005

National Total = 1,025,475 Live Births*

ALPHA ORDER

ALPHA ORDER

RANK	STATE	BIRTHS	% of USA
34	Alabama	8,662	0.8%
49	Alaska	1,556	0.2%
8	Arizona	33,931	3.3%
32	Arkansas	9,794	1.0%
1	California	163,559	16.0%
19	Colorado	16,348	1.6%
33	Connecticut	9,618	0.9%
43	Delaware	3,034	0.3%
3	Florida	57,331	5.6%
12	Georgia	26,073	2.5%
50	Hawaii	1,362	0.1%
39	Idaho	4,953	0.5%
5	Illinois	41,558	4.1%
10	Indiana	27,139	2.6%
27	Iowa	11,311	1.1%
29	Kansas	10,958	1.1%
21	Kentucky	16,228	1.6%
30	Louisiana	10,223	1.0%
40	Maine	4,741	0.5%
28	Maryland	11,308	1.1%
18	Massachusetts	16,987	1.7%
9	Michigan	29,542	2.9%
22	Minnesota	14,457	1.4%
38	Mississippi	6,338	0.6%
14	Missouri	20,260	2.0%
44	Montana	2,840	0.3%
37	Nebraska	6,436	0.6%
25	Nevada	11,867	1.2%
41	New Hampshire	3,788	0.4%
13	New Jersey	22,059	2.2%
26	New Mexico	11,433	1.1%
4	New York	54,068	5.3%
11	North Carolina	26,178	2.6%
48	North Dakota	1,893	0.2%
6	Ohio	38,934	3.8%
24	Oklahoma	13,357	1.3%
23	Oregon	13,720	1.3%
7	Pennsylvania	34,275	3.3%
42	Rhode Island	3,688	0.4%
31	South Carolina	10,183	1.0%
45	South Dakota	2,492	0.2%
16	Tennessee	18,913	1.8%
2	Texas	115,251	11.2%
35	Utah	7,927	0.8%
47	Vermont	2,039	0.2%
17	Virginia	18,439	1.8%
15	Washington	20,173	2.0%
36	West Virginia	7,037	0.7%
20	Wisconsin	16,326	1.6%
46	Wyoming	2,085	0.2%

RANK ORDER

RANK	STATE	BIRTHS	% of USA
1	California	163,559	16.0%
2	Texas	115,251	11.2%
3	Florida	57,331	5.6%
4	New York	54,068	5.3%
5	Illinois	41,558	4.1%
6	Ohio	38,934	3.8%
7	Pennsylvania	34,275	3.3%
8	Arizona	33,931	3.3%
9	Michigan	29,542	2.9%
10	Indiana	27,139	2.6%
11	North Carolina	26,178	2.6%
12	Georgia	26,073	2.5%
13	New Jersey	22,059	2.2%
14	Missouri	20,260	2.0%
15	Washington	20,173	2.0%
16	Tennessee	18,913	1.8%
17	Virginia	18,439	1.8%
18	Massachusetts	16,987	1.7%
19	Colorado	16,348	1.6%
20	Wisconsin	16,326	1.6%
21	Kentucky	16,228	1.6%
22	Minnesota	14,457	1.4%
23	Oregon	13,720	1.3%
24	Oklahoma	13,357	1.3%
25	Nevada	11,867	1.2%
26	New Mexico	11,433	1.1%
27	Iowa	11,311	1.1%
28	Maryland	11,308	1.1%
29	Kansas	10,958	1.1%
30	Louisiana	10,223	1.0%
31	South Carolina	10,183	1.0%
32	Arkansas	9,794	1.0%
33	Connecticut	9,618	0.9%
34	Alabama	8,662	0.8%
35	Utah	7,927	0.8%
36	West Virginia	7,037	0.7%
37	Nebraska	6,436	0.6%
38	Mississippi	6,338	0.6%
39	Idaho	4,953	0.5%
40	Maine	4,741	0.5%
41	New Hampshire	3,788	0.4%
42	Rhode Island	3,688	0.4%
43	Delaware	3,034	0.3%
44	Montana	2,840	0.3%
45	South Dakota	2,492	0.2%
46	Wyoming	2,085	0.2%
47	Vermont	2,039	0.2%
48	North Dakota	1,893	0.2%
49	Alaska	1,556	0.2%
50	Hawaii	1,362	0.1%
	District of Columbia	313	0.0%

Source: Morgan Quitno Press using data from U.S. Dept. of Health and Human Services, Nat'l Center for Health Statistics
"Births: Preliminary data for 2005"
*Preliminary data by state of residence. By race of mother.

Births to Unmarried White Women
as a Percent of All Births to White Women in 2005
National Percent = 31.7% of Live Births*

ALPHA ORDER

RANK	STATE	PERCENT
49	Alabama	21.0
47	Alaska	23.8
2	Arizona	40.8
17	Arkansas	31.8
5	California	36.7
44	Colorado	26.0
32	Connecticut	28.3
4	Delaware	37.0
7	Florida	35.5
30	Georgia	28.6
38	Hawaii	27.0
48	Idaho	22.4
24	Illinois	29.9
6	Indiana	35.8
21	Iowa	30.9
20	Kansas	31.2
15	Kentucky	32.2
29	Louisiana	28.8
10	Maine	35.1
43	Maryland	26.1
37	Massachusetts	27.2
26	Michigan	29.5
45	Minnesota	25.0
36	Mississippi	27.5
19	Missouri	31.3
30	Montana	28.6
35	Nebraska	27.7
3	Nevada	38.7
34	New Hampshire	27.9
41	New Jersey	26.7
1	New Mexico	47.4
17	New York	31.8
28	North Carolina	29.2
42	North Dakota	26.3
15	Ohio	32.2
12	Oklahoma	33.4
13	Oregon	33.0
27	Pennsylvania	29.4
11	Rhode Island	34.5
33	South Carolina	28.2
40	South Dakota	26.9
22	Tennessee	30.8
9	Texas	35.2
50	Utah	16.2
14	Vermont	32.5
46	Virginia	24.8
25	Washington	29.7
8	West Virginia	35.3
38	Wisconsin	27.0
22	Wyoming	30.8

RANK ORDER

RANK	STATE	PERCENT
1	New Mexico	47.4
2	Arizona	40.8
3	Nevada	38.7
4	Delaware	37.0
5	California	36.7
6	Indiana	35.8
7	Florida	35.5
8	West Virginia	35.3
9	Texas	35.2
10	Maine	35.1
11	Rhode Island	34.5
12	Oklahoma	33.4
13	Oregon	33.0
14	Vermont	32.5
15	Kentucky	32.2
15	Ohio	32.2
17	Arkansas	31.8
17	New York	31.8
19	Missouri	31.3
20	Kansas	31.2
21	Iowa	30.9
22	Tennessee	30.8
22	Wyoming	30.8
24	Illinois	29.9
25	Washington	29.7
26	Michigan	29.5
27	Pennsylvania	29.4
28	North Carolina	29.2
29	Louisiana	28.8
30	Georgia	28.6
30	Montana	28.6
32	Connecticut	28.3
33	South Carolina	28.2
34	New Hampshire	27.9
35	Nebraska	27.7
36	Mississippi	27.5
37	Massachusetts	27.2
38	Hawaii	27.0
38	Wisconsin	27.0
40	South Dakota	26.9
41	New Jersey	26.7
42	North Dakota	26.3
43	Maryland	26.1
44	Colorado	26.0
45	Minnesota	25.0
46	Virginia	24.8
47	Alaska	23.8
48	Idaho	22.4
49	Alabama	21.0
50	Utah	16.2

	District of Columbia	12.9

Source: U.S. Department of Health and Human Services, National Center for Health Statistics
   "Births: Preliminary data for 2005"
Preliminary data by state of residence. By race of mother.

Births to Unmarried Black Women in 2005

National Total = 436,511 Live Births*

ALPHA ORDER

RANK	STATE	BIRTHS	% of USA
18	Alabama	12,750	2.9%
40	Alaska	217	0.0%
28	Arizona	2,251	0.5%
21	Arkansas	5,744	1.3%
6	California	20,645	4.7%
33	Colorado	1,649	0.4%
26	Connecticut	3,563	0.8%
32	Delaware	2,052	0.5%
1	Florida	37,812	8.7%
3	Georgia	30,606	7.0%
42	Hawaii	133	0.0%
46	Idaho	44	0.0%
5	Illinois	23,972	5.5%
20	Indiana	7,681	1.8%
35	Iowa	1,100	0.3%
29	Kansas	2,241	0.5%
25	Kentucky	3,727	0.9%
8	Louisiana	18,419	4.2%
43	Maine	95	0.0%
11	Maryland	15,842	3.6%
23	Massachusetts	5,265	1.2%
12	Michigan	15,241	3.5%
24	Minnesota	4,049	0.9%
15	Mississippi	14,368	3.3%
19	Missouri	8,951	2.1%
50	Montana	27	0.0%
34	Nebraska	1,167	0.3%
31	Nevada	2,203	0.5%
44	New Hampshire	91	0.0%
17	New Jersey	13,018	3.0%
39	New Mexico	321	0.1%
2	New York	36,855	8.4%
7	North Carolina	19,624	4.5%
48	North Dakota	34	0.0%
9	Ohio	18,344	4.2%
27	Oklahoma	3,531	0.8%
37	Oregon	654	0.1%
10	Pennsylvania	17,416	4.0%
36	Rhode Island	832	0.2%
13	South Carolina	14,773	3.4%
45	South Dakota	56	0.0%
16	Tennessee	13,475	3.1%
4	Texas	28,349	6.5%
41	Utah	188	0.0%
49	Vermont	32	0.0%
14	Virginia	14,529	3.3%
30	Washington	2,215	0.5%
38	West Virginia	535	0.1%
22	Wisconsin	5,593	1.3%
47	Wyoming	41	0.0%

RANK ORDER

RANK	STATE	BIRTHS	% of USA
1	Florida	37,812	8.7%
2	New York	36,855	8.4%
3	Georgia	30,606	7.0%
4	Texas	28,349	6.5%
5	Illinois	23,972	5.5%
6	California	20,645	4.7%
7	North Carolina	19,624	4.5%
8	Louisiana	18,419	4.2%
9	Ohio	18,344	4.2%
10	Pennsylvania	17,416	4.0%
11	Maryland	15,842	3.6%
12	Michigan	15,241	3.5%
13	South Carolina	14,773	3.4%
14	Virginia	14,529	3.3%
15	Mississippi	14,368	3.3%
16	Tennessee	13,475	3.1%
17	New Jersey	13,018	3.0%
18	Alabama	12,750	2.9%
19	Missouri	8,951	2.1%
20	Indiana	7,681	1.8%
21	Arkansas	5,744	1.3%
22	Wisconsin	5,593	1.3%
23	Massachusetts	5,265	1.2%
24	Minnesota	4,049	0.9%
25	Kentucky	3,727	0.9%
26	Connecticut	3,563	0.8%
27	Oklahoma	3,531	0.8%
28	Arizona	2,251	0.5%
29	Kansas	2,241	0.5%
30	Washington	2,215	0.5%
31	Nevada	2,203	0.5%
32	Delaware	2,052	0.5%
33	Colorado	1,649	0.4%
34	Nebraska	1,167	0.3%
35	Iowa	1,100	0.3%
36	Rhode Island	832	0.2%
37	Oregon	654	0.1%
38	West Virginia	535	0.1%
39	New Mexico	321	0.1%
40	Alaska	217	0.0%
41	Utah	188	0.0%
42	Hawaii	133	0.0%
43	Maine	95	0.0%
44	New Hampshire	91	0.0%
45	South Dakota	56	0.0%
46	Idaho	44	0.0%
47	Wyoming	41	0.0%
48	North Dakota	34	0.0%
49	Vermont	32	0.0%
50	Montana	27	0.0%
	District of Columbia	4,025	0.9%

Source: Morgan Quitno Press using data from U.S. Dept. of Health and Human Services, Nat'l Center for Health Statistics
 "Births: Preliminary data for 2005"
*Preliminary data by state of residence. By race of mother.

Births to Unmarried Black Women
as a Percent of All Births to Black Women in 2005
National Percent = 69.0% of Live Births*

ALPHA ORDER

RANK	STATE	PERCENT
18	Alabama	70.3
41	Alaska	51.1
34	Arizona	61.7
5	Arkansas	76.9
32	California	63.7
39	Colorado	52.8
24	Connecticut	67.5
17	Delaware	70.5
25	Florida	66.9
26	Georgia	66.8
49	Hawaii	27.3
48	Idaho	30.1
2	Illinois	78.0
3	Indiana	77.7
13	Iowa	73.0
16	Kansas	71.7
11	Kentucky	73.3
7	Louisiana	76.4
47	Maine	35.8
35	Maryland	59.8
35	Massachusetts	59.8
22	Michigan	67.8
38	Minnesota	58.7
4	Mississippi	77.0
6	Missouri	76.6
42	Montana	43.5
21	Nebraska	67.9
20	Nevada	68.7
45	New Hampshire	39.1
27	New Jersey	65.2
37	New Mexico	59.7
22	New York	67.8
19	North Carolina	69.0
50	North Dakota	26.2
9	Ohio	75.7
11	Oklahoma	73.3
29	Oregon	64.8
8	Pennsylvania	76.1
30	Rhode Island	64.7
15	South Carolina	72.5
44	South Dakota	39.2
14	Tennessee	72.9
31	Texas	64.3
46	Utah	38.8
43	Vermont	41.0
33	Virginia	63.4
40	Washington	52.4
10	West Virginia	75.5
1	Wisconsin	82.3
28	Wyoming	65.1

RANK ORDER

RANK	STATE	PERCENT
1	Wisconsin	82.3
2	Illinois	78.0
3	Indiana	77.7
4	Mississippi	77.0
5	Arkansas	76.9
6	Missouri	76.6
7	Louisiana	76.4
8	Pennsylvania	76.1
9	Ohio	75.7
10	West Virginia	75.5
11	Kentucky	73.3
11	Oklahoma	73.3
13	Iowa	73.0
14	Tennessee	72.9
15	South Carolina	72.5
16	Kansas	71.7
17	Delaware	70.5
18	Alabama	70.3
19	North Carolina	69.0
20	Nevada	68.7
21	Nebraska	67.9
22	Michigan	67.8
22	New York	67.8
24	Connecticut	67.5
25	Florida	66.9
26	Georgia	66.8
27	New Jersey	65.2
28	Wyoming	65.1
29	Oregon	64.8
30	Rhode Island	64.7
31	Texas	64.3
32	California	63.7
33	Virginia	63.4
34	Arizona	61.7
35	Maryland	59.8
35	Massachusetts	59.8
37	New Mexico	59.7
38	Minnesota	58.7
39	Colorado	52.8
40	Washington	52.4
41	Alaska	51.1
42	Montana	43.5
43	Vermont	41.0
44	South Dakota	39.2
45	New Hampshire	39.1
46	Utah	38.8
47	Maine	35.8
48	Idaho	30.1
49	Hawaii	27.3
50	North Dakota	26.2
	District of Columbia	76.4

Source: U.S. Department of Health and Human Services, National Center for Health Statistics
   "Births: Preliminary data for 2005"
*Preliminary data by state of residence. By race of mother.

Births to Unmarried Hispanic Women in 2005

National Total = 470,791 Live Births*

ALPHA ORDER

RANK	STATE	BIRTHS	% of USA
39	Alabama	857	0.2%
43	Alaska	294	0.1%
5	Arizona	23,371	5.0%
32	Arkansas	1,801	0.4%
1	California	129,889	27.6%
10	Colorado	8,981	1.9%
17	Connecticut	5,011	1.1%
38	Delaware	1,025	0.2%
4	Florida	27,217	5.8%
8	Georgia	10,318	2.2%
36	Hawaii	1,321	0.3%
35	Idaho	1,327	0.3%
6	Illinois	20,291	4.3%
19	Indiana	4,381	0.9%
34	Iowa	1,481	0.3%
26	Kansas	2,984	0.6%
37	Kentucky	1,244	0.3%
40	Louisiana	728	0.2%
47	Maine	79	0.0%
18	Maryland	4,449	0.9%
15	Massachusetts	6,456	1.4%
21	Michigan	3,652	0.8%
28	Minnesota	2,802	0.6%
41	Mississippi	589	0.1%
30	Missouri	2,069	0.4%
46	Montana	173	0.0%
31	Nebraska	1,817	0.4%
14	Nevada	6,873	1.5%
44	New Hampshire	246	0.1%
7	New Jersey	15,597	3.3%
11	New Mexico	8,973	1.9%
3	New York	36,070	7.7%
9	North Carolina	10,136	2.2%
49	North Dakota	63	0.0%
23	Ohio	3,421	0.7%
27	Oklahoma	2,898	0.6%
20	Oregon	4,193	0.9%
12	Pennsylvania	7,460	1.6%
33	Rhode Island	1,538	0.3%
29	South Carolina	2,242	0.5%
45	South Dakota	194	0.0%
22	Tennessee	3,538	0.8%
2	Texas	82,533	17.5%
25	Utah	3,003	0.6%
50	Vermont	25	0.0%
16	Virginia	6,153	1.3%
13	Washington	6,909	1.5%
48	West Virginia	76	0.0%
24	Wisconsin	3,045	0.6%
42	Wyoming	400	0.1%

RANK ORDER

RANK	STATE	BIRTHS	% of USA
1	California	129,889	27.6%
2	Texas	82,533	17.5%
3	New York	36,070	7.7%
4	Florida	27,217	5.8%
5	Arizona	23,371	5.0%
6	Illinois	20,291	4.3%
7	New Jersey	15,597	3.3%
8	Georgia	10,318	2.2%
9	North Carolina	10,136	2.2%
10	Colorado	8,981	1.9%
11	New Mexico	8,973	1.9%
12	Pennsylvania	7,460	1.6%
13	Washington	6,909	1.5%
14	Nevada	6,873	1.5%
15	Massachusetts	6,456	1.4%
16	Virginia	6,153	1.3%
17	Connecticut	5,011	1.1%
18	Maryland	4,449	0.9%
19	Indiana	4,381	0.9%
20	Oregon	4,193	0.9%
21	Michigan	3,652	0.8%
22	Tennessee	3,538	0.8%
23	Ohio	3,421	0.7%
24	Wisconsin	3,045	0.6%
25	Utah	3,003	0.6%
26	Kansas	2,984	0.6%
27	Oklahoma	2,898	0.6%
28	Minnesota	2,802	0.6%
29	South Carolina	2,242	0.5%
30	Missouri	2,069	0.4%
31	Nebraska	1,817	0.4%
32	Arkansas	1,801	0.4%
33	Rhode Island	1,538	0.3%
34	Iowa	1,481	0.3%
35	Idaho	1,327	0.3%
36	Hawaii	1,321	0.3%
37	Kentucky	1,244	0.3%
38	Delaware	1,025	0.2%
39	Alabama	857	0.2%
40	Louisiana	728	0.2%
41	Mississippi	589	0.1%
42	Wyoming	400	0.1%
43	Alaska	294	0.1%
44	New Hampshire	246	0.1%
45	South Dakota	194	0.0%
46	Montana	173	0.0%
47	Maine	79	0.0%
48	West Virginia	76	0.0%
49	North Dakota	63	0.0%
50	Vermont	25	0.0%
	District of Columbia	725	0.2%

Source: Morgan Quitno Press using data from U.S. Dept. of Health and Human Services, Nat'l Center for Health Statistics
"Births: Preliminary data for 2005"
*Preliminary data by state of residence. Hispanic can be of any race.

Births to Unmarried Hispanic Women
as a Percent of All Births to Hispanic Women in 2005
National Percent = 47.9% of Live Births*

ALPHA ORDER				RANK ORDER		
RANK	STATE	PERCENT		RANK	STATE	PERCENT
50	Alabama	21.5		1	Massachusetts	63.8
46	Alaska	37.7		2	New York	62.8
10	Arizona	54.5		3	Connecticut	62.6
37	Arkansas	44.6		4	Delaware	62.0
33	California	45.8		5	Pennsylvania	61.2
43	Colorado	41.2		6	Rhode Island	60.1
3	Connecticut	62.6		7	New Mexico	56.7
4	Delaware	62.0		8	Ohio	56.1
35	Florida	45.3		9	New Jersey	55.8
29	Georgia	46.9		10	Arizona	54.5
25	Hawaii	47.3		11	Indiana	54.4
45	Idaho	38.0		12	North Carolina	51.9
30	Illinois	46.7		13	Maryland	51.2
11	Indiana	54.4		14	Minnesota	50.8
24	Iowa	47.5		15	Tennessee	50.5
21	Kansas	48.7		16	Mississippi	50.3
17	Kentucky	49.6		17	Kentucky	49.6
47	Louisiana	37.4		18	South Dakota	49.5
40	Maine	43.2		19	Nevada	48.9
13	Maryland	51.2		20	Wisconsin	48.8
1	Massachusetts	63.8		21	Kansas	48.7
42	Michigan	42.4		22	Missouri	48.4
14	Minnesota	50.8		23	Wyoming	48.3
16	Mississippi	50.3		24	Iowa	47.5
22	Missouri	48.4		25	Hawaii	47.3
38	Montana	43.6		26	Nebraska	47.1
26	Nebraska	47.1		26	Virginia	47.1
19	Nevada	48.9		28	New Hampshire	47.0
28	New Hampshire	47.0		29	Georgia	46.9
9	New Jersey	55.8		30	Illinois	46.7
7	New Mexico	56.7		31	Oklahoma	46.2
2	New York	62.8		32	Washington	46.0
12	North Carolina	51.9		33	California	45.8
48	North Dakota	35.0		34	Oregon	45.7
8	Ohio	56.1		35	Florida	45.3
31	Oklahoma	46.2		36	South Carolina	44.9
34	Oregon	45.7		37	Arkansas	44.6
5	Pennsylvania	61.2		38	Montana	43.6
6	Rhode Island	60.1		38	West Virginia	43.6
36	South Carolina	44.9		40	Maine	43.2
18	South Dakota	49.5		41	Texas	43.1
15	Tennessee	50.5		42	Michigan	42.4
41	Texas	43.1		43	Colorado	41.2
44	Utah	39.7		44	Utah	39.7
49	Vermont	34.2		45	Idaho	38.0
26	Virginia	47.1		46	Alaska	37.7
32	Washington	46.0		47	Louisiana	37.4
38	West Virginia	43.6		48	North Dakota	35.0
20	Wisconsin	48.8		49	Vermont	34.2
23	Wyoming	48.3		50	Alabama	21.5
					District of Columbia	66.8

Source: U.S. Department of Health and Human Services, National Center for Health Statistics
"Births: Preliminary data for 2005"
Preliminary data by state of residence. Hispanic can be of any race.

Pregnancy Rate in 2003

National Rate = 69.0 Births and Abortions per 1,000 Women 15-49 Years Old*

ALPHA ORDER

RANK	STATE	RATE
35	Alabama	62.5
12	Alaska	71.1
5	Arizona	75.9
25	Arkansas	65.4
NA	California**	NA
19	Colorado	67.6
30	Connecticut	64.0
8	Delaware	74.5
5	Florida	75.9
9	Georgia	73.9
10	Hawaii	73.4
21	Idaho	67.3
14	Illinois	70.3
32	Indiana	63.7
36	Iowa	61.6
5	Kansas	75.9
44	Kentucky	56.8
24	Louisiana	65.6
47	Maine	50.6
39	Maryland	60.5
30	Massachusetts	64.0
32	Michigan	63.7
27	Minnesota	65.2
34	Mississippi	63.0
41	Missouri	59.8
37	Montana	61.3
15	Nebraska	69.8
3	Nevada	79.2
NA	New Hampshire**	NA
16	New Jersey	69.7
11	New Mexico	72.5
4	New York	77.2
13	North Carolina	70.6
40	North Dakota	60.2
28	Ohio	65.1
22	Oklahoma	67.0
23	Oregon	66.9
38	Pennsylvania	60.9
17	Rhode Island	67.8
42	South Carolina	59.6
29	South Dakota	64.1
26	Tennessee	65.3
2	Texas	80.6
1	Utah	86.0
46	Vermont	53.0
20	Virginia	67.5
18	Washington	67.7
NA	West Virginia**	NA
43	Wisconsin	58.8
45	Wyoming	54.1

RANK ORDER

RANK	STATE	RATE
1	Utah	86.0
2	Texas	80.6
3	Nevada	79.2
4	New York	77.2
5	Arizona	75.9
5	Florida	75.9
5	Kansas	75.9
8	Delaware	74.5
9	Georgia	73.9
10	Hawaii	73.4
11	New Mexico	72.5
12	Alaska	71.1
13	North Carolina	70.6
14	Illinois	70.3
15	Nebraska	69.8
16	New Jersey	69.7
17	Rhode Island	67.8
18	Washington	67.7
19	Colorado	67.6
20	Virginia	67.5
21	Idaho	67.3
22	Oklahoma	67.0
23	Oregon	66.9
24	Louisiana	65.6
25	Arkansas	65.4
26	Tennessee	65.3
27	Minnesota	65.2
28	Ohio	65.1
29	South Dakota	64.1
30	Connecticut	64.0
30	Massachusetts	64.0
32	Indiana	63.7
32	Michigan	63.7
34	Mississippi	63.0
35	Alabama	62.5
36	Iowa	61.6
37	Montana	61.3
38	Pennsylvania	60.9
39	Maryland	60.5
40	North Dakota	60.2
41	Missouri	59.8
42	South Carolina	59.6
43	Wisconsin	58.8
44	Kentucky	56.8
45	Wyoming	54.1
46	Vermont	53.0
47	Maine	50.6
NA	California**	NA
NA	New Hampshire**	NA
NA	West Virginia**	NA

District of Columbia   80.9

Source: Morgan Quitno Press using data from US Dept of Health & Human Serv's, Centers for Disease Control-Prevention
"Abortion Surveillance-United States, 2003" (Morbidity and Mortality Weekly Report, Vol. 55, No. SS-11, 11/24/06)
*The sum of live births and legal induced abortions per 1,000 women aged 15-49 years old. Births by state of residence, abortions by state of occurrence. Miscarriages are not included in these rates. National rate includes only states reporting abortions and births.
**Not available.

Teenage Pregnancy Rate in 2003

National Rate = 59.2 Births and Abortions per 1,000 Women 15-19 Years Old*

ALPHA ORDER				RANK ORDER		
RANK	STATE	RATE		RANK	STATE	RATE
13	Alabama	66.5		1	New Mexico	81.3
24	Alaska	53.5		2	Texas	78.5
5	Arizona	72.2		3	Nevada	75.6
6	Arkansas	71.5		4	Georgia	72.5
NA	California**	NA		5	Arizona	72.2
20	Colorado	55.9		6	Arkansas	71.5
32	Connecticut	46.7		7	Mississippi	71.3
8	Delaware	70.5		8	Delaware	70.5
NA	Florida**	NA		9	Tennessee	69.8
4	Georgia	72.5		10	North Carolina	68.3
18	Hawaii	58.0		11	Louisiana	68.2
35	Idaho	43.0		12	Oklahoma	66.7
NA	Illinois**	NA		13	Alabama	66.5
26	Indiana	52.6		14	New York	64.1
36	Iowa	42.5		15	Kansas	62.1
15	Kansas	62.1		16	South Carolina	61.2
21	Kentucky	55.3		17	Rhode Island	60.3
11	Louisiana	68.2		18	Hawaii	58.0
43	Maine	35.5		19	Ohio	56.3
NA	Maryland**	NA		20	Colorado	55.9
34	Massachusetts	46.1		21	Kentucky	55.3
28	Michigan	49.6		22	Washington	54.5
42	Minnesota	38.7		23	Virginia	53.7
7	Mississippi	71.3		24	Alaska	53.5
27	Missouri	50.3		25	Oregon	53.4
29	Montana	48.9		26	Indiana	52.6
30	Nebraska	47.7		27	Missouri	50.3
3	Nevada	75.6		28	Michigan	49.6
NA	New Hampshire**	NA		29	Montana	48.9
31	New Jersey	46.9		30	Nebraska	47.7
1	New Mexico	81.3		31	New Jersey	46.9
14	New York	64.1		32	Connecticut	46.7
10	North Carolina	68.3		33	Pennsylvania	46.3
41	North Dakota	39.1		34	Massachusetts	46.1
19	Ohio	56.3		35	Idaho	43.0
12	Oklahoma	66.7		36	Iowa	42.5
25	Oregon	53.4		37	Wyoming	41.6
33	Pennsylvania	46.3		38	Wisconsin	41.4
17	Rhode Island	60.3		39	Utah	41.0
16	South Carolina	61.2		40	South Dakota	40.7
40	South Dakota	40.7		41	North Dakota	39.1
9	Tennessee	69.8		42	Minnesota	38.7
2	Texas	78.5		43	Maine	35.5
39	Utah	41.0		44	Vermont	34.1
44	Vermont	34.1		NA	California**	NA
23	Virginia	53.7		NA	Florida**	NA
22	Washington	54.5		NA	Illinois**	NA
NA	West Virginia**	NA		NA	Maryland**	NA
38	Wisconsin	41.4		NA	New Hampshire**	NA
37	Wyoming	41.6		NA	West Virginia**	NA

District of Columbia	143.9

Source: Morgan Quitno Press using data from US Dept of Health & Human Serv's, Centers for Disease Control-Prevention "Abortion Surveillance-United States, 2003" (Morbidity and Mortality Weekly Report, Vol. 55, No. SS-11, 11/24/06)
The sum of live births and legal induced abortions per 1,000 women aged 15-19 years old. Births by state of residence, abortions by state of occurrence. Miscarriages are not included in these rates. National rate includes only states reporting abortions and births.
**Not available.*

Percent Change in Teenage Pregnancy Rate: 1999 to 2003

National Percent Change = 13.1% Decrease*

ALPHA ORDER				RANK ORDER		
RANK	**STATE**	**PERCENT CHANGE**		**RANK**	**STATE**	**PERCENT CHANGE**
35	Alabama	(17.1)		1	Colorado	(0.4)
NA	Alaska**	NA		2	Wyoming	(0.5)
21	Arizona	(11.6)		3	North Dakota	(1.0)
18	Arkansas	(11.4)		4	New Mexico	(1.6)
NA	California**	NA		5	South Dakota	(6.4)
1	Colorado	(0.4)		6	Montana	(8.3)
41	Connecticut	(22.8)		6	Nevada	(8.3)
37	Delaware	(17.5)		8	Michigan	(8.8)
NA	Florida**	NA		9	Nebraska	(9.0)
34	Georgia	(17.0)		10	Rhode Island	(9.3)
29	Hawaii	(15.6)		11	Louisiana	(9.8)
12	Idaho	(10.2)		12	Idaho	(10.2)
NA	Illinois**	NA		12	Wisconsin	(10.2)
31	Indiana	(16.0)		14	Mississippi	(10.5)
15	Iowa	(10.7)		15	Iowa	(10.7)
30	Kansas	(15.7)		16	Texas	(10.9)
26	Kentucky	(13.5)		17	Massachusetts	(11.3)
11	Louisiana	(9.8)		18	Arkansas	(11.4)
36	Maine	(17.4)		18	Missouri	(11.4)
NA	Maryland**	NA		18	Utah	(11.4)
17	Massachusetts	(11.3)		21	Arizona	(11.6)
8	Michigan	(8.8)		22	Ohio	(11.8)
23	Minnesota	(12.0)		23	Minnesota	(12.0)
14	Mississippi	(10.5)		24	Pennsylvania	(12.3)
18	Missouri	(11.4)		25	Tennessee	(13.0)
6	Montana	(8.3)		26	Kentucky	(13.5)
9	Nebraska	(9.0)		27	Virginia	(14.9)
6	Nevada	(8.3)		28	South Carolina	(15.4)
NA	New Hampshire**	NA		29	Hawaii	(15.6)
40	New Jersey	(21.0)		30	Kansas	(15.7)
4	New Mexico	(1.6)		31	Indiana	(16.0)
38	New York	(19.7)		32	North Carolina	(16.9)
32	North Carolina	(16.9)		32	Washington	(16.9)
3	North Dakota	(1.0)		34	Georgia	(17.0)
22	Ohio	(11.8)		35	Alabama	(17.1)
NA	Oklahoma**	NA		36	Maine	(17.4)
42	Oregon	(25.9)		37	Delaware	(17.5)
24	Pennsylvania	(12.3)		38	New York	(19.7)
10	Rhode Island	(9.3)		39	Vermont	(20.9)
28	South Carolina	(15.4)		40	New Jersey	(21.0)
5	South Dakota	(6.4)		41	Connecticut	(22.8)
25	Tennessee	(13.0)		42	Oregon	(25.9)
16	Texas	(10.9)		NA	Alaska**	NA
18	Utah	(11.4)		NA	California**	NA
39	Vermont	(20.9)		NA	Florida**	NA
27	Virginia	(14.9)		NA	Illinois**	NA
32	Washington	(16.9)		NA	Maryland**	NA
NA	West Virginia**	NA		NA	New Hampshire**	NA
12	Wisconsin	(10.2)		NA	Oklahoma**	NA
2	Wyoming	(0.5)		NA	West Virginia**	NA
					District of Columbia	(25.4)

Source: Morgan Quitno Press using data from US Dept of Health & Human Serv's, Centers for Disease Control-Prevention "Abortion Surveillance-United States, 2003" (Morbidity and Mortality Weekly Report, Vol. 55, No. SS-11, 11/24/06)
*The sum of live births and legal induced abortions per 1,000 women aged 15-19 years old. Births by state of residence, abortions by state of occurrence. Miscarriages are not included in these rates. National rate includes only states reporting abortions and births.
**Not available.

Births to Teenage Mothers in 2005

National Total = 422,323 Live Births*

ALPHA ORDER					RANK ORDER			
RANK	STATE		BIRTHS	% of USA	RANK	STATE	BIRTHS	% of USA
17	Alabama		7,919	1.9%	1	Texas	52,105	12.3%
46	Alaska		1,046	0.2%	2	California	50,566	12.0%
10	Arizona		12,029	2.8%	3	Florida	24,665	5.8%
27	Arkansas		5,723	1.4%	4	Illinois	17,369	4.1%
2	California		50,566	12.0%	5	New York	17,245	4.1%
23	Colorado		6,758	1.6%	6	Georgia	16,786	4.0%
36	Connecticut		2,837	0.7%	7	Ohio	15,785	3.7%
41	Delaware		1,246	0.3%	8	North Carolina	14,159	3.4%
3	Florida		24,665	5.8%	9	Pennsylvania	13,103	3.1%
6	Georgia		16,786	4.0%	10	Arizona	12,029	2.8%
40	Hawaii		1,488	0.4%	11	Michigan	12,013	2.8%
39	Idaho		2,029	0.5%	12	Tennessee	10,954	2.6%
4	Illinois		17,369	4.1%	13	Indiana	9,601	2.3%
13	Indiana		9,601	2.3%	14	Virginia	8,890	2.1%
34	Iowa		3,342	0.8%	15	Missouri	8,727	2.1%
31	Kansas		4,109	1.0%	16	Louisiana	8,297	2.0%
21	Kentucky		6,823	1.6%	17	Alabama	7,919	1.9%
16	Louisiana		8,297	2.0%	18	South Carolina	7,620	1.8%
44	Maine		1,115	0.3%	19	New Jersey	6,936	1.6%
25	Maryland		6,374	1.5%	20	Washington	6,865	1.6%
29	Massachusetts		4,615	1.1%	21	Kentucky	6,823	1.6%
11	Michigan		12,013	2.8%	22	Oklahoma	6,779	1.6%
28	Minnesota		4,826	1.1%	23	Colorado	6,758	1.6%
24	Mississippi		6,614	1.6%	24	Mississippi	6,614	1.6%
15	Missouri		8,727	2.1%	25	Maryland	6,374	1.5%
42	Montana		1,207	0.3%	26	Wisconsin	6,104	1.4%
38	Nebraska		2,170	0.5%	27	Arkansas	5,723	1.4%
33	Nevada		3,949	0.9%	28	Minnesota	4,826	1.1%
47	New Hampshire		851	0.2%	29	Massachusetts	4,615	1.1%
19	New Jersey		6,936	1.6%	30	New Mexico	4,556	1.1%
30	New Mexico		4,556	1.1%	31	Kansas	4,109	1.0%
5	New York		17,245	4.1%	32	Oregon	4,042	1.0%
8	North Carolina		14,159	3.4%	33	Nevada	3,949	0.9%
49	North Dakota		663	0.2%	34	Iowa	3,342	0.8%
7	Ohio		15,785	3.7%	35	Utah	3,093	0.7%
22	Oklahoma		6,779	1.6%	36	Connecticut	2,837	0.7%
32	Oregon		4,042	1.0%	37	West Virginia	2,480	0.6%
9	Pennsylvania		13,103	3.1%	38	Nebraska	2,170	0.5%
43	Rhode Island		1,129	0.3%	39	Idaho	2,029	0.5%
18	South Carolina		7,620	1.8%	40	Hawaii	1,488	0.4%
45	South Dakota		1,088	0.3%	41	Delaware	1,246	0.3%
12	Tennessee		10,954	2.6%	42	Montana	1,207	0.3%
1	Texas		52,105	12.3%	43	Rhode Island	1,129	0.3%
35	Utah		3,093	0.7%	44	Maine	1,115	0.3%
50	Vermont		434	0.1%	45	South Dakota	1,088	0.3%
14	Virginia		8,890	2.1%	46	Alaska	1,046	0.2%
20	Washington		6,865	1.6%	47	New Hampshire	851	0.2%
37	West Virginia		2,480	0.6%	48	Wyoming	804	0.2%
26	Wisconsin		6,104	1.4%	49	North Dakota	663	0.2%
48	Wyoming		804	0.2%	50	Vermont	434	0.1%
						District of Columbia	852	0.2%

Source: Morgan Quitno Press using data from U.S. Dept. of Health and Human Services, Nat'l Center for Health Statistics
"Births: Preliminary data for 2005"
*Preliminary estimates of live births to women 15 to 19 years old by state of residence.

Teenage Birth Rate in 2005

National Rate = 41.2 Live Births per 1,000 Women 15 to 19 Years Old*

ALPHA ORDER

RANK	STATE	RATE
10	Alabama	50.7
28	Alaska	37.6
5	Arizona	59.2
4	Arkansas	59.9
25	California	39.2
19	Colorado	43.3
47	Connecticut	23.5
15	Delaware	44.8
19	Florida	43.3
8	Georgia	53.4
29	Hawaii	36.4
26	Idaho	38.0
24	Illinois	39.4
18	Indiana	43.6
35	Iowa	32.8
22	Kansas	42.0
13	Kentucky	49.8
12	Louisiana	50.0
45	Maine	24.5
37	Maryland	32.3
48	Massachusetts	22.2
34	Michigan	33.0
44	Minnesota	26.3
3	Mississippi	62.4
21	Missouri	43.1
30	Montana	35.9
32	Nebraska	34.6
11	Nevada	50.5
50	New Hampshire	18.0
46	New Jersey	23.6
1	New Mexico	62.7
43	New York	26.8
14	North Carolina	49.3
42	North Dakota	29.8
23	Ohio	39.6
7	Oklahoma	55.0
33	Oregon	33.4
40	Pennsylvania	30.8
38	Rhode Island	31.7
9	South Carolina	51.9
27	South Dakota	37.7
6	Tennessee	55.7
1	Texas	62.7
36	Utah	32.5
49	Vermont	19.5
31	Virginia	34.9
39	Washington	31.6
16	West Virginia	43.9
40	Wisconsin	30.8
17	Wyoming	43.7

RANK ORDER

RANK	STATE	RATE
1	New Mexico	62.7
1	Texas	62.7
3	Mississippi	62.4
4	Arkansas	59.9
5	Arizona	59.2
6	Tennessee	55.7
7	Oklahoma	55.0
8	Georgia	53.4
9	South Carolina	51.9
10	Alabama	50.7
11	Nevada	50.5
12	Louisiana	50.0
13	Kentucky	49.8
14	North Carolina	49.3
15	Delaware	44.8
16	West Virginia	43.9
17	Wyoming	43.7
18	Indiana	43.6
19	Colorado	43.3
19	Florida	43.3
21	Missouri	43.1
22	Kansas	42.0
23	Ohio	39.6
24	Illinois	39.4
25	California	39.2
26	Idaho	38.0
27	South Dakota	37.7
28	Alaska	37.6
29	Hawaii	36.4
30	Montana	35.9
31	Virginia	34.9
32	Nebraska	34.6
33	Oregon	33.4
34	Michigan	33.0
35	Iowa	32.8
36	Utah	32.5
37	Maryland	32.3
38	Rhode Island	31.7
39	Washington	31.6
40	Pennsylvania	30.8
40	Wisconsin	30.8
42	North Dakota	29.8
43	New York	26.8
44	Minnesota	26.3
45	Maine	24.5
46	New Jersey	23.6
47	Connecticut	23.5
48	Massachusetts	22.2
49	Vermont	19.5
50	New Hampshire	18.0

District of Columbia   63.4

Source: Morgan Quitno Press using data from U.S. Dept. of Health and Human Services, Nat'l Center for Health Statistics
      "Births: Preliminary data for 2005"
*Preliminary data by state of residence.

Births to Teenage Mothers as a Percent of Births in 2005

National Percent = 10.2% of Live Births*

<table>
<tr><td colspan="3">ALPHA ORDER</td><td colspan="3">RANK ORDER</td></tr>
<tr><td>RANK</td><td>STATE</td><td>PERCENT</td><td>RANK</td><td>STATE</td><td>PERCENT</td></tr>
<tr><td>8</td><td>Alabama</td><td>13.1</td><td>1</td><td>New Mexico</td><td>15.8</td></tr>
<tr><td>24</td><td>Alaska</td><td>10.0</td><td>2</td><td>Mississippi</td><td>15.6</td></tr>
<tr><td>10</td><td>Arizona</td><td>12.5</td><td>3</td><td>Arkansas</td><td>14.6</td></tr>
<tr><td>3</td><td>Arkansas</td><td>14.6</td><td>4</td><td>Louisiana</td><td>13.6</td></tr>
<tr><td>29</td><td>California</td><td>9.2</td><td>5</td><td>Texas</td><td>13.5</td></tr>
<tr><td>25</td><td>Colorado</td><td>9.8</td><td>6</td><td>Tennessee</td><td>13.4</td></tr>
<tr><td>44</td><td>Connecticut</td><td>6.8</td><td>7</td><td>South Carolina</td><td>13.2</td></tr>
<tr><td>19</td><td>Delaware</td><td>10.7</td><td>8</td><td>Alabama</td><td>13.1</td></tr>
<tr><td>18</td><td>Florida</td><td>10.9</td><td>8</td><td>Oklahoma</td><td>13.1</td></tr>
<tr><td>13</td><td>Georgia</td><td>11.8</td><td>10</td><td>Arizona</td><td>12.5</td></tr>
<tr><td>38</td><td>Hawaii</td><td>8.3</td><td>11</td><td>Kentucky</td><td>12.1</td></tr>
<tr><td>32</td><td>Idaho</td><td>8.8</td><td>12</td><td>West Virginia</td><td>11.9</td></tr>
<tr><td>26</td><td>Illinois</td><td>9.7</td><td>13</td><td>Georgia</td><td>11.8</td></tr>
<tr><td>17</td><td>Indiana</td><td>11.0</td><td>14</td><td>North Carolina</td><td>11.5</td></tr>
<tr><td>35</td><td>Iowa</td><td>8.5</td><td>15</td><td>Missouri</td><td>11.1</td></tr>
<tr><td>23</td><td>Kansas</td><td>10.3</td><td>15</td><td>Wyoming</td><td>11.1</td></tr>
<tr><td>11</td><td>Kentucky</td><td>12.1</td><td>17</td><td>Indiana</td><td>11.0</td></tr>
<tr><td>4</td><td>Louisiana</td><td>13.6</td><td>18</td><td>Florida</td><td>10.9</td></tr>
<tr><td>41</td><td>Maine</td><td>7.9</td><td>19</td><td>Delaware</td><td>10.7</td></tr>
<tr><td>35</td><td>Maryland</td><td>8.5</td><td>20</td><td>Nevada</td><td>10.6</td></tr>
<tr><td>48</td><td>Massachusetts</td><td>6.0</td><td>20</td><td>Ohio</td><td>10.6</td></tr>
<tr><td>28</td><td>Michigan</td><td>9.4</td><td>22</td><td>Montana</td><td>10.4</td></tr>
<tr><td>44</td><td>Minnesota</td><td>6.8</td><td>23</td><td>Kansas</td><td>10.3</td></tr>
<tr><td>2</td><td>Mississippi</td><td>15.6</td><td>24</td><td>Alaska</td><td>10.0</td></tr>
<tr><td>15</td><td>Missouri</td><td>11.1</td><td>25</td><td>Colorado</td><td>9.8</td></tr>
<tr><td>22</td><td>Montana</td><td>10.4</td><td>26</td><td>Illinois</td><td>9.7</td></tr>
<tr><td>38</td><td>Nebraska</td><td>8.3</td><td>27</td><td>South Dakota</td><td>9.5</td></tr>
<tr><td>20</td><td>Nevada</td><td>10.6</td><td>28</td><td>Michigan</td><td>9.4</td></tr>
<tr><td>50</td><td>New Hampshire</td><td>5.9</td><td>29</td><td>California</td><td>9.2</td></tr>
<tr><td>47</td><td>New Jersey</td><td>6.1</td><td>30</td><td>Pennsylvania</td><td>9.0</td></tr>
<tr><td>1</td><td>New Mexico</td><td>15.8</td><td>31</td><td>Rhode Island</td><td>8.9</td></tr>
<tr><td>43</td><td>New York</td><td>7.0</td><td>32</td><td>Idaho</td><td>8.8</td></tr>
<tr><td>14</td><td>North Carolina</td><td>11.5</td><td>32</td><td>Oregon</td><td>8.8</td></tr>
<tr><td>41</td><td>North Dakota</td><td>7.9</td><td>34</td><td>Wisconsin</td><td>8.6</td></tr>
<tr><td>20</td><td>Ohio</td><td>10.6</td><td>35</td><td>Iowa</td><td>8.5</td></tr>
<tr><td>8</td><td>Oklahoma</td><td>13.1</td><td>35</td><td>Maryland</td><td>8.5</td></tr>
<tr><td>32</td><td>Oregon</td><td>8.8</td><td>35</td><td>Virginia</td><td>8.5</td></tr>
<tr><td>30</td><td>Pennsylvania</td><td>9.0</td><td>38</td><td>Hawaii</td><td>8.3</td></tr>
<tr><td>31</td><td>Rhode Island</td><td>8.9</td><td>38</td><td>Nebraska</td><td>8.3</td></tr>
<tr><td>7</td><td>South Carolina</td><td>13.2</td><td>38</td><td>Washington</td><td>8.3</td></tr>
<tr><td>27</td><td>South Dakota</td><td>9.5</td><td>41</td><td>Maine</td><td>7.9</td></tr>
<tr><td>6</td><td>Tennessee</td><td>13.4</td><td>41</td><td>North Dakota</td><td>7.9</td></tr>
<tr><td>5</td><td>Texas</td><td>13.5</td><td>43</td><td>New York</td><td>7.0</td></tr>
<tr><td>48</td><td>Utah</td><td>6.0</td><td>44</td><td>Connecticut</td><td>6.8</td></tr>
<tr><td>46</td><td>Vermont</td><td>6.7</td><td>44</td><td>Minnesota</td><td>6.8</td></tr>
<tr><td>35</td><td>Virginia</td><td>8.5</td><td>46</td><td>Vermont</td><td>6.7</td></tr>
<tr><td>38</td><td>Washington</td><td>8.3</td><td>47</td><td>New Jersey</td><td>6.1</td></tr>
<tr><td>12</td><td>West Virginia</td><td>11.9</td><td>48</td><td>Massachusetts</td><td>6.0</td></tr>
<tr><td>34</td><td>Wisconsin</td><td>8.6</td><td>48</td><td>Utah</td><td>6.0</td></tr>
<tr><td>15</td><td>Wyoming</td><td>11.1</td><td>50</td><td>New Hampshire</td><td>5.9</td></tr>
<tr><td></td><td></td><td></td><td></td><td>District of Columbia</td><td>10.8</td></tr>
</table>

Source: U.S. Department of Health and Human Services, National Center for Health Statistics
   "Births: Preliminary data for 2005"
*Preliminary data. Live births to women 15 to 19 years old by state of residence.

Percent Change in Teenage Birth Rate: 2001 to 2005

National Percent Change = 9.1% Decrease*

ALPHA ORDER

RANK	STATE	PERCENT CHANGE
36	Alabama	(12.3)
5	Alaska	(0.3)
26	Arizona	(9.3)
21	Arkansas	(6.7)
38	California	(13.3)
14	Colorado	(5.3)
48	Connecticut	(20.1)
22	Delaware	(7.1)
35	Florida	(12.2)
36	Georgia	(12.3)
41	Hawaii	(14.4)
18	Idaho	(6.4)
45	Illinois	(16.7)
23	Indiana	(7.6)
6	Iowa	(0.6)
7	Kansas	(2.3)
9	Kentucky	(3.1)
39	Louisiana	(13.5)
28	Maine	(9.6)
44	Maryland	(15.4)
32	Massachusetts	(11.2)
33	Michigan	(11.3)
15	Minnesota	(5.7)
18	Mississippi	(6.4)
20	Missouri	(6.5)
4	Montana	0.8
11	Nebraska	(3.9)
30	Nevada	(10.5)
40	New Hampshire	(14.3)
49	New Jersey	(21.1)
8	New Mexico	(2.8)
50	New York	(21.4)
31	North Carolina	(10.7)
2	North Dakota	9.6
17	Ohio	(6.2)
13	Oklahoma	(5.2)
46	Oregon	(18.3)
25	Pennsylvania	(8.3)
43	Rhode Island	(15.2)
28	South Carolina	(9.6)
3	South Dakota	1.6
12	Tennessee	(4.6)
15	Texas	(5.7)
42	Utah	(14.9)
47	Vermont	(18.4)
34	Virginia	(11.4)
27	Washington	(9.5)
10	West Virginia	(3.5)
24	Wisconsin	(7.8)
1	Wyoming	13.2

RANK ORDER

RANK	STATE	PERCENT CHANGE
1	Wyoming	13.2
2	North Dakota	9.6
3	South Dakota	1.6
4	Montana	0.8
5	Alaska	(0.3)
6	Iowa	(0.6)
7	Kansas	(2.3)
8	New Mexico	(2.8)
9	Kentucky	(3.1)
10	West Virginia	(3.5)
11	Nebraska	(3.9)
12	Tennessee	(4.6)
13	Oklahoma	(5.2)
14	Colorado	(5.3)
15	Minnesota	(5.7)
15	Texas	(5.7)
17	Ohio	(6.2)
18	Idaho	(6.4)
18	Mississippi	(6.4)
20	Missouri	(6.5)
21	Arkansas	(6.7)
22	Delaware	(7.1)
23	Indiana	(7.6)
24	Wisconsin	(7.8)
25	Pennsylvania	(8.3)
26	Arizona	(9.3)
27	Washington	(9.5)
28	Maine	(9.6)
28	South Carolina	(9.6)
30	Nevada	(10.5)
31	North Carolina	(10.7)
32	Massachusetts	(11.2)
33	Michigan	(11.3)
34	Virginia	(11.4)
35	Florida	(12.2)
36	Alabama	(12.3)
36	Georgia	(12.3)
38	California	(13.3)
39	Louisiana	(13.5)
40	New Hampshire	(14.3)
41	Hawaii	(14.4)
42	Utah	(14.9)
43	Rhode Island	(15.2)
44	Maryland	(15.4)
45	Illinois	(16.7)
46	Oregon	(18.3)
47	Vermont	(18.4)
48	Connecticut	(20.1)
49	New Jersey	(21.1)
50	New York	(21.4)

District of Columbia | (15.4)

Source: Morgan Quitno Press using data from U.S. Dept. of Health and Human Services, Nat'l Center for Health Statistics "Births: Preliminary data for 2005" and "National Vital Statistics Reports" (Vol. 51, No. 2, December 18, 2002)
Preliminary data by state of residence. Births to women aged 15 to 19 years old.

Teenage Birth Rate in 2004

National Rate = 41.1 Live Births per 1,000 Women 15 to 19 Years Old*

RANK	STATE	RATE
9	Alabama	52.4
25	Alaska	38.9
5	Arizona	60.1
4	Arkansas	60.3
24	California	39.5
15	Colorado	43.9
45	Connecticut	24.4
17	Delaware	43.5
21	Florida	42.4
8	Georgia	53.4
29	Hawaii	36.1
26	Idaho	38.6
23	Illinois	40.2
17	Indiana	43.5
38	Iowa	31.6
22	Kansas	40.7
13	Kentucky	49.2
6	Louisiana	56.2
46	Maine	24.3
37	Maryland	32.4
48	Massachusetts	22.3
33	Michigan	34.1
44	Minnesota	26.7
2	Mississippi	61.9
19	Missouri	43.4
31	Montana	35.8
30	Nebraska	35.9
12	Nevada	51.1
50	New Hampshire	18.2
47	New Jersey	24.1
3	New Mexico	60.8
43	New York	26.9
14	North Carolina	48.8
42	North Dakota	27.2
27	Ohio	38.5
7	Oklahoma	55.6
35	Oregon	33.3
40	Pennsylvania	30.5
36	Rhode Island	32.9
10	South Carolina	52.1
27	South Dakota	38.5
10	Tennessee	52.1
1	Texas	62.6
34	Utah	34.0
49	Vermont	20.9
32	Virginia	35.2
39	Washington	31.3
16	West Virginia	43.8
41	Wisconsin	30.2
20	Wyoming	42.7

RANK	STATE	RATE
1	Texas	62.6
2	Mississippi	61.9
3	New Mexico	60.8
4	Arkansas	60.3
5	Arizona	60.1
6	Louisiana	56.2
7	Oklahoma	55.6
8	Georgia	53.4
9	Alabama	52.4
10	South Carolina	52.1
10	Tennessee	52.1
12	Nevada	51.1
13	Kentucky	49.2
14	North Carolina	48.8
15	Colorado	43.9
16	West Virginia	43.8
17	Delaware	43.5
17	Indiana	43.5
19	Missouri	43.4
20	Wyoming	42.7
21	Florida	42.4
22	Kansas	40.7
23	Illinois	40.2
24	California	39.5
25	Alaska	38.9
26	Idaho	38.6
27	Ohio	38.5
27	South Dakota	38.5
29	Hawaii	36.1
30	Nebraska	35.9
31	Montana	35.8
32	Virginia	35.2
33	Michigan	34.1
34	Utah	34.0
35	Oregon	33.3
36	Rhode Island	32.9
37	Maryland	32.4
38	Iowa	31.6
39	Washington	31.3
40	Pennsylvania	30.5
41	Wisconsin	30.2
42	North Dakota	27.2
43	New York	26.9
44	Minnesota	26.7
45	Connecticut	24.4
46	Maine	24.3
47	New Jersey	24.1
48	Massachusetts	22.3
49	Vermont	20.9
50	New Hampshire	18.2
	District of Columbia	66.7

Source: U.S. Department of Health and Human Services, National Center for Health Statistics
"National Vital Statistics Reports" (Vol. 55, No. 1, September 29, 2006)
Final data by state of residence.

Births to White Teenage Mothers in 2005

National Total = 297,324 Live Births*

ALPHA ORDER

RANK ORDER

RANK	STATE	BIRTHS	% of USA		RANK	STATE	BIRTHS	% of USA
20	Alabama	4,496	1.5%		1	Texas	43,874	14.8%
47	Alaska	477	0.2%		2	California	43,675	14.7%
7	Arizona	10,063	3.4%		3	Florida	15,019	5.1%
22	Arkansas	4,035	1.4%		4	Illinois	10,980	3.7%
2	California	43,675	14.7%		5	Ohio	10,882	3.7%
15	Colorado	6,099	2.1%		6	New York	10,542	3.5%
37	Connecticut	2,107	0.7%		7	Arizona	10,063	3.4%
45	Delaware	722	0.2%		8	Georgia	9,117	3.1%
3	Florida	15,019	5.1%		9	North Carolina	8,427	2.8%
8	Georgia	9,117	3.1%		10	Pennsylvania	8,277	2.8%
50	Hawaii	328	0.1%		11	Indiana	7,732	2.6%
38	Idaho	1,924	0.6%		12	Michigan	7,611	2.6%
4	Illinois	10,980	3.7%		13	Tennessee	7,123	2.4%
11	Indiana	7,732	2.6%		14	Missouri	6,408	2.2%
32	Iowa	2,965	1.0%		15	Colorado	6,099	2.1%
29	Kansas	3,372	1.1%		16	Kentucky	5,846	2.0%
16	Kentucky	5,846	2.0%		17	Washington	5,502	1.9%
28	Louisiana	3,443	1.2%		18	Virginia	5,205	1.8%
40	Maine	1,081	0.4%		19	Oklahoma	4,719	1.6%
34	Maryland	2,686	0.9%		20	Alabama	4,496	1.5%
27	Massachusetts	3,497	1.2%		21	New Jersey	4,213	1.4%
12	Michigan	7,611	2.6%		22	Arkansas	4,035	1.4%
31	Minnesota	3,180	1.1%		23	Wisconsin	3,991	1.3%
35	Mississippi	2,673	0.9%		24	New Mexico	3,835	1.3%
14	Missouri	6,408	2.2%		25	Oregon	3,700	1.2%
42	Montana	834	0.3%		26	South Carolina	3,683	1.2%
39	Nebraska	1,719	0.6%		27	Massachusetts	3,497	1.2%
30	Nevada	3,189	1.1%		28	Louisiana	3,443	1.2%
43	New Hampshire	828	0.3%		29	Kansas	3,372	1.1%
21	New Jersey	4,213	1.4%		30	Nevada	3,189	1.1%
24	New Mexico	3,835	1.3%		31	Minnesota	3,180	1.1%
6	New York	10,542	3.5%		32	Iowa	2,965	1.0%
9	North Carolina	8,427	2.8%		33	Utah	2,887	1.0%
48	North Dakota	461	0.2%		34	Maryland	2,686	0.9%
5	Ohio	10,882	3.7%		35	Mississippi	2,673	0.9%
19	Oklahoma	4,719	1.6%		36	West Virginia	2,333	0.8%
25	Oregon	3,700	1.2%		37	Connecticut	2,107	0.7%
10	Pennsylvania	8,277	2.8%		38	Idaho	1,924	0.6%
41	Rhode Island	887	0.3%		39	Nebraska	1,719	0.6%
26	South Carolina	3,683	1.2%		40	Maine	1,081	0.4%
46	South Dakota	648	0.2%		41	Rhode Island	887	0.3%
13	Tennessee	7,123	2.4%		42	Montana	834	0.3%
1	Texas	43,874	14.8%		43	New Hampshire	828	0.3%
33	Utah	2,887	1.0%		44	Wyoming	724	0.2%
49	Vermont	427	0.1%		45	Delaware	722	0.2%
18	Virginia	5,205	1.8%		46	South Dakota	648	0.2%
17	Washington	5,502	1.9%		47	Alaska	477	0.2%
36	West Virginia	2,333	0.8%		48	North Dakota	461	0.2%
23	Wisconsin	3,991	1.3%		49	Vermont	427	0.1%
44	Wyoming	724	0.2%		50	Hawaii	328	0.1%
						District of Columbia	29	0.0%

Source: Morgan Quitno Press using data from U.S. Dept. of Health and Human Services, Nat'l Center for Health Statistics
"Births: Preliminary data for 2005"
*Preliminary estimates of live births to women 15 to 19 years old by state of residence.

White Teenage Birth Rate in 2005

National Rate = 36.9 Births per 1,000 White Teenage Women*

ALPHA ORDER

RANK ORDER

RANK	STATE	RATE		RANK	STATE	RATE
11	Alabama	44.3		1	New Mexico	64.5
37	Alaska	24.7		2	Texas	64.0
3	Arizona	58.0		3	Arizona	58.0
4	Arkansas	54.7		4	Arkansas	54.7
13	California	43.1		5	Nevada	49.5
14	Colorado	42.9		5	Oklahoma	49.5
44	Connecticut	20.9		7	Georgia	47.8
23	Delaware	36.1		7	Kentucky	47.8
24	Florida	35.3		9	Tennessee	47.4
7	Georgia	47.8		10	Mississippi	47.2
50	Hawaii	17.6		11	Alabama	44.3
21	Idaho	37.3		12	West Virginia	43.4
27	Illinois	32.3		13	California	43.1
18	Indiana	40.0		14	Colorado	42.9
29	Iowa	30.6		15	North Carolina	42.7
19	Kansas	38.4		16	Wyoming	41.3
7	Kentucky	47.8		17	South Carolina	40.9
22	Louisiana	36.3		18	Indiana	40.0
38	Maine	24.5		19	Kansas	38.4
43	Maryland	22.1		20	Missouri	37.8
46	Massachusetts	19.6		21	Idaho	37.3
36	Michigan	26.2		22	Louisiana	36.3
46	Minnesota	19.6		23	Delaware	36.1
10	Mississippi	47.2		24	Florida	35.3
20	Missouri	37.8		25	Oregon	33.1
34	Montana	27.7		26	Ohio	32.6
30	Nebraska	29.9		27	Illinois	32.3
5	Nevada	49.5		28	Utah	32.2
49	New Hampshire	18.0		29	Iowa	30.6
48	New Jersey	19.0		30	Nebraska	29.9
1	New Mexico	64.5		31	Washington	29.2
42	New York	22.7		32	Rhode Island	28.6
15	North Carolina	42.7		32	Virginia	28.6
41	North Dakota	22.8		34	Montana	27.7
26	Ohio	32.6		35	South Dakota	26.3
5	Oklahoma	49.5		36	Michigan	26.2
25	Oregon	33.1		37	Alaska	24.7
39	Pennsylvania	23.2		38	Maine	24.5
32	Rhode Island	28.6		39	Pennsylvania	23.2
17	South Carolina	40.9		40	Wisconsin	22.9
35	South Dakota	26.3		41	North Dakota	22.8
9	Tennessee	47.4		42	New York	22.7
2	Texas	64.0		43	Maryland	22.1
28	Utah	32.2		44	Connecticut	20.9
45	Vermont	19.7		45	Vermont	19.7
32	Virginia	28.6		46	Massachusetts	19.6
31	Washington	29.2		46	Minnesota	19.6
12	West Virginia	43.4		48	New Jersey	19.0
40	Wisconsin	22.9		49	New Hampshire	18.0
16	Wyoming	41.3		50	Hawaii	17.6

District of Columbia 5.8

Source: Morgan Quitno Press using data from U.S. Dept. of Health and Human Services, Nat'l Center for Health Statistics
"Births: Preliminary data for 2005"
*Preliminary data. Live births to women age 15 to 19 years old by state of residence. Rates calculated using
Census 2005 estimates for females ages 15 to 19 years old in the category of "White Alone or in Combination."

Births to White Teenage Mothers as a Percent of White Births in 2005

National Percent = 9.2% of White Live Births*

RANK	STATE	PERCENT
10	Alabama	10.9
35	Alaska	7.3
4	Arizona	12.1
3	Arkansas	13.1
17	California	9.8
18	Colorado	9.7
43	Connecticut	6.2
25	Delaware	8.8
22	Florida	9.3
15	Georgia	10.0
41	Hawaii	6.5
26	Idaho	8.7
32	Illinois	7.9
13	Indiana	10.2
29	Iowa	8.1
20	Kansas	9.6
7	Kentucky	11.6
18	Louisiana	9.7
31	Maine	8.0
43	Maryland	6.2
48	Massachusetts	5.6
33	Michigan	7.6
49	Minnesota	5.5
7	Mississippi	11.6
16	Missouri	9.9
27	Montana	8.4
34	Nebraska	7.4
12	Nevada	10.4
46	New Hampshire	6.1
50	New Jersey	5.1
1	New Mexico	15.9
43	New York	6.2
21	North Carolina	9.4
42	North Dakota	6.4
23	Ohio	9.0
5	Oklahoma	11.8
24	Oregon	8.9
36	Pennsylvania	7.1
28	Rhode Island	8.3
13	South Carolina	10.2
37	South Dakota	7.0
7	Tennessee	11.6
2	Texas	13.4
47	Utah	5.9
39	Vermont	6.8
37	Virginia	7.0
29	Washington	8.1
6	West Virginia	11.7
40	Wisconsin	6.6
11	Wyoming	10.7

RANK	STATE	PERCENT
1	New Mexico	15.9
2	Texas	13.4
3	Arkansas	13.1
4	Arizona	12.1
5	Oklahoma	11.8
6	West Virginia	11.7
7	Kentucky	11.6
7	Mississippi	11.6
7	Tennessee	11.6
10	Alabama	10.9
11	Wyoming	10.7
12	Nevada	10.4
13	Indiana	10.2
13	South Carolina	10.2
15	Georgia	10.0
16	Missouri	9.9
17	California	9.8
18	Colorado	9.7
18	Louisiana	9.7
20	Kansas	9.6
21	North Carolina	9.4
22	Florida	9.3
23	Ohio	9.0
24	Oregon	8.9
25	Delaware	8.8
26	Idaho	8.7
27	Montana	8.4
28	Rhode Island	8.3
29	Iowa	8.1
29	Washington	8.1
31	Maine	8.0
32	Illinois	7.9
33	Michigan	7.6
34	Nebraska	7.4
35	Alaska	7.3
36	Pennsylvania	7.1
37	South Dakota	7.0
37	Virginia	7.0
39	Vermont	6.8
40	Wisconsin	6.6
41	Hawaii	6.5
42	North Dakota	6.4
43	Connecticut	6.2
43	Maryland	6.2
43	New York	6.2
46	New Hampshire	6.1
47	Utah	5.9
48	Massachusetts	5.6
49	Minnesota	5.5
50	New Jersey	5.1
	District of Columbia	1.2

Source: U.S. Department of Health and Human Services, National Center for Health Statistics
  "Births: Preliminary data for 2005"
*Preliminary data. Live births to women 15 to 19 years old by state of residence.

Births to Black Teenage Mothers in 2005

National Total = 106,281 Live Births*

RANK	STATE	BIRTHS	% of USA
17	Alabama	3,392	3.2%
41	Alaska	52	0.0%
28	Arizona	598	0.6%
21	Arkansas	1,643	1.5%
10	California	4,537	4.3%
33	Colorado	465	0.4%
27	Connecticut	707	0.7%
32	Delaware	495	0.5%
1	Florida	9,213	8.7%
3	Georgia	7,468	7.0%
42	Hawaii	34	0.0%
NA	Idaho**	NA	NA
5	Illinois	6,270	5.9%
20	Indiana	1,868	1.8%
35	Iowa	298	0.3%
29	Kansas	581	0.5%
25	Kentucky	895	0.8%
8	Louisiana	4,725	4.4%
43	Maine	24	0.0%
15	Maryland	3,550	3.3%
24	Massachusetts	898	0.8%
11	Michigan	4,181	3.9%
26	Minnesota	855	0.8%
13	Mississippi	3,844	3.6%
19	Missouri	2,185	2.1%
NA	Montana**	NA	NA
34	Nebraska	321	0.3%
30	Nevada	551	0.5%
NA	New Hampshire**	NA	NA
18	New Jersey	2,676	2.5%
39	New Mexico	90	0.1%
4	New York	6,360	6.0%
6	North Carolina	5,233	4.9%
NA	North Dakota**	NA	NA
7	Ohio	4,774	4.5%
23	Oklahoma	930	0.9%
37	Oregon	154	0.1%
9	Pennsylvania	4,646	4.4%
36	Rhode Island	170	0.2%
12	South Carolina	3,851	3.6%
NA	South Dakota**	NA	NA
14	Tennessee	3,734	3.5%
2	Texas	7,627	7.2%
40	Utah	69	0.1%
NA	Vermont**	NA	NA
16	Virginia	3,506	3.3%
31	Washington	529	0.5%
38	West Virginia	140	0.1%
22	Wisconsin	1,577	1.5%
NA	Wyoming**	NA	NA

RANK	STATE	BIRTHS	% of USA
1	Florida	9,213	8.7%
2	Texas	7,627	7.2%
3	Georgia	7,468	7.0%
4	New York	6,360	6.0%
5	Illinois	6,270	5.9%
6	North Carolina	5,233	4.9%
7	Ohio	4,774	4.5%
8	Louisiana	4,725	4.4%
9	Pennsylvania	4,646	4.4%
10	California	4,537	4.3%
11	Michigan	4,181	3.9%
12	South Carolina	3,851	3.6%
13	Mississippi	3,844	3.6%
14	Tennessee	3,734	3.5%
15	Maryland	3,550	3.3%
16	Virginia	3,506	3.3%
17	Alabama	3,392	3.2%
18	New Jersey	2,676	2.5%
19	Missouri	2,185	2.1%
20	Indiana	1,868	1.8%
21	Arkansas	1,643	1.5%
22	Wisconsin	1,577	1.5%
23	Oklahoma	930	0.9%
24	Massachusetts	898	0.8%
25	Kentucky	895	0.8%
26	Minnesota	855	0.8%
27	Connecticut	707	0.7%
28	Arizona	598	0.6%
29	Kansas	581	0.5%
30	Nevada	551	0.5%
31	Washington	529	0.5%
32	Delaware	495	0.5%
33	Colorado	465	0.4%
34	Nebraska	321	0.3%
35	Iowa	298	0.3%
36	Rhode Island	170	0.2%
37	Oregon	154	0.1%
38	West Virginia	140	0.1%
39	New Mexico	90	0.1%
40	Utah	69	0.1%
41	Alaska	52	0.0%
42	Hawaii	34	0.0%
43	Maine	24	0.0%
NA	Idaho**	NA	NA
NA	Montana**	NA	NA
NA	New Hampshire**	NA	NA
NA	North Dakota**	NA	NA
NA	South Dakota**	NA	NA
NA	Vermont**	NA	NA
NA	Wyoming**	NA	NA

District of Columbia 817 0.8%

Source: Morgan Quitno Press using data from U.S. Dept. of Health and Human Services, Nat'l Center for Health Statistics "Births: Preliminary data for 2005"

Preliminary data. Estimated live births to women 15 to 19 years old by state of residence.

**Not available. Fewer than 20 births to black teenage women.*

Black Teenage Birth Rate in 2005

National Rate = 62.2 Births per 1,000 Black Teenage Women*

ALPHA ORDER			RANK ORDER		
RANK	STATE	RATE	RANK	STATE	RATE
23	Alabama	63.9	1	Wisconsin	92.1
42	Alaska	34.1	2	Tennessee	84.4
26	Arizona	55.1	3	Nebraska	83.1
4	Arkansas	80.9	4	Arkansas	80.9
39	California	37.8	5	Mississippi	79.8
30	Colorado	50.7	6	Iowa	79.7
36	Connecticut	41.8	7	Ohio	77.4
18	Delaware	66.8	8	Pennsylvania	76.6
15	Florida	69.6	9	Indiana	73.9
22	Georgia	64.0	10	Kansas	73.0
43	Hawaii	20.7	10	Minnesota	73.0
NA	Idaho**	NA	12	Illinois	72.5
12	Illinois	72.5	13	Missouri	70.7
9	Indiana	73.9	14	South Carolina	70.0
6	Iowa	79.7	15	Florida	69.6
10	Kansas	73.0	16	Louisiana	68.9
19	Kentucky	64.6	17	Oklahoma	67.3
16	Louisiana	68.9	18	Delaware	66.8
41	Maine	35.0	19	Kentucky	64.6
29	Maryland	51.6	20	North Carolina	64.1
34	Massachusetts	44.3	20	Texas	64.1
24	Michigan	62.8	22	Georgia	64.0
10	Minnesota	73.0	23	Alabama	63.9
5	Mississippi	79.8	24	Michigan	62.8
13	Missouri	70.7	25	Nevada	62.3
NA	Montana**	NA	26	Arizona	55.1
3	Nebraska	83.1	27	West Virginia	54.4
25	Nevada	62.3	28	Virginia	54.2
NA	New Hampshire**	NA	29	Maryland	51.6
32	New Jersey	48.3	30	Colorado	50.7
40	New Mexico	36.6	30	Rhode Island	50.7
33	New York	44.6	32	New Jersey	48.3
20	North Carolina	64.1	33	New York	44.6
NA	North Dakota**	NA	34	Massachusetts	44.3
7	Ohio	77.4	35	Washington	43.0
17	Oklahoma	67.3	36	Connecticut	41.8
37	Oregon	40.1	37	Oregon	40.1
8	Pennsylvania	76.6	38	Utah	39.6
30	Rhode Island	50.7	39	California	37.8
14	South Carolina	70.0	40	New Mexico	36.6
NA	South Dakota**	NA	41	Maine	35.0
2	Tennessee	84.4	42	Alaska	34.1
20	Texas	64.1	43	Hawaii	20.7
38	Utah	39.6	NA	Idaho**	NA
NA	Vermont**	NA	NA	Montana**	NA
28	Virginia	54.2	NA	New Hampshire**	NA
35	Washington	43.0	NA	North Dakota**	NA
27	West Virginia	54.4	NA	South Dakota**	NA
1	Wisconsin	92.1	NA	Vermont**	NA
NA	Wyoming**	NA	NA	Wyoming**	NA
				District of Columbia	101.0

Source: Morgan Quitno Press using data from U.S. Dept. of Health and Human Services, Nat'l Center for Health Statistics
   "Births: Preliminary data for 2005"
*Preliminary data. Live births to women age 15 to 19 years old by state of residence. Rates calculated using
Census 2005 estimates for females ages 15 to 19 years old in the category of "Black Alone or in Combination."
**Insufficient number of births for a reliable figure.

Births to Black Teenage Mothers as a Percent of Black Births in 2005

National Percent = 16.8% of Black Live Births*

ALPHA ORDER

RANK	STATE	PERCENT
14	Alabama	18.7
39	Alaska	12.3
25	Arizona	16.4
2	Arkansas	22.0
32	California	14.0
30	Colorado	14.9
33	Connecticut	13.4
23	Delaware	17.0
26	Florida	16.3
26	Georgia	16.3
43	Hawaii	7.0
NA	Idaho**	NA
4	Illinois	20.4
12	Indiana	18.9
7	Iowa	19.8
17	Kansas	18.6
20	Kentucky	17.6
10	Louisiana	19.6
42	Maine	9.1
33	Maryland	13.4
41	Massachusetts	10.2
17	Michigan	18.6
38	Minnesota	12.4
3	Mississippi	20.6
14	Missouri	18.7
NA	Montana**	NA
14	Nebraska	18.7
22	Nevada	17.2
NA	New Hampshire**	NA
33	New Jersey	13.4
24	New Mexico	16.7
40	New York	11.7
19	North Carolina	18.4
NA	North Dakota**	NA
9	Ohio	19.7
11	Oklahoma	19.3
29	Oregon	15.2
5	Pennsylvania	20.3
36	Rhode Island	13.2
12	South Carolina	18.9
NA	South Dakota**	NA
6	Tennessee	20.2
21	Texas	17.3
31	Utah	14.3
NA	Vermont**	NA
28	Virginia	15.3
37	Washington	12.5
7	West Virginia	19.8
1	Wisconsin	23.2
NA	Wyoming**	NA

RANK ORDER

RANK	STATE	PERCENT
1	Wisconsin	23.2
2	Arkansas	22.0
3	Mississippi	20.6
4	Illinois	20.4
5	Pennsylvania	20.3
6	Tennessee	20.2
7	Iowa	19.8
7	West Virginia	19.8
9	Ohio	19.7
10	Louisiana	19.6
11	Oklahoma	19.3
12	Indiana	18.9
12	South Carolina	18.9
14	Alabama	18.7
14	Missouri	18.7
14	Nebraska	18.7
17	Kansas	18.6
17	Michigan	18.6
19	North Carolina	18.4
20	Kentucky	17.6
21	Texas	17.3
22	Nevada	17.2
23	Delaware	17.0
24	New Mexico	16.7
25	Arizona	16.4
26	Florida	16.3
26	Georgia	16.3
28	Virginia	15.3
29	Oregon	15.2
30	Colorado	14.9
31	Utah	14.3
32	California	14.0
33	Connecticut	13.4
33	Maryland	13.4
33	New Jersey	13.4
36	Rhode Island	13.2
37	Washington	12.5
38	Minnesota	12.4
39	Alaska	12.3
40	New York	11.7
41	Massachusetts	10.2
42	Maine	9.1
43	Hawaii	7.0
NA	Idaho**	NA
NA	Montana**	NA
NA	New Hampshire**	NA
NA	North Dakota**	NA
NA	South Dakota**	NA
NA	Vermont**	NA
NA	Wyoming**	NA
	District of Columbia	15.5

Source: U.S. Department of Health and Human Services, National Center for Health Statistics
   "Births: Preliminary data for 2005"

*Preliminary data. Live births to women 15 to 19 years old by state of residence.
**Not available. Fewer than 20 births to black teenage women.

Births to Young Teenagers: 2002 to 2004

National Total = 20,757 Live Births*

<u>ALPHA ORDER</u>

RANK	STATE	BIRTHS	% of USA
15	Alabama	504	2.4%
43	Alaska	40	0.2%
11	Arizona	612	2.9%
23	Arkansas	325	1.6%
2	California	2,150	10.4%
24	Colorado	321	1.5%
34	Connecticut	126	0.6%
39	Delaware	67	0.3%
3	Florida	1,188	5.7%
4	Georgia	934	4.5%
41	Hawaii	56	0.3%
42	Idaho	49	0.2%
5	Illinois	890	4.3%
20	Indiana	377	1.8%
35	Iowa	90	0.4%
33	Kansas	144	0.7%
22	Kentucky	326	1.6%
10	Louisiana	618	3.0%
48	Maine	19	0.1%
17	Maryland	405	2.0%
31	Massachusetts	171	0.8%
12	Michigan	605	2.9%
29	Minnesota	199	1.0%
14	Mississippi	523	2.5%
19	Missouri	390	1.9%
47	Montana	21	0.1%
38	Nebraska	73	0.4%
30	Nevada	182	0.9%
50	New Hampshire	3	0.0%
21	New Jersey	331	1.6%
28	New Mexico	225	1.1%
7	New York	797	3.8%
6	North Carolina	844	4.1%
46	North Dakota	23	0.1%
8	Ohio	732	3.5%
25	Oklahoma	311	1.5%
32	Oregon	153	0.7%
9	Pennsylvania	668	3.2%
40	Rhode Island	57	0.3%
18	South Carolina	403	1.9%
44	South Dakota	29	0.1%
13	Tennessee	546	2.6%
1	Texas	2,947	14.2%
36	Utah	87	0.4%
49	Vermont	8	0.0%
16	Virginia	463	2.2%
27	Washington	260	1.3%
37	West Virginia	86	0.4%
26	Wisconsin	283	1.4%
45	Wyoming	25	0.1%

<u>RANK ORDER</u>

RANK	STATE	BIRTHS	% of USA
1	Texas	2,947	14.2%
2	California	2,150	10.4%
3	Florida	1,188	5.7%
4	Georgia	934	4.5%
5	Illinois	890	4.3%
6	North Carolina	844	4.1%
7	New York	797	3.8%
8	Ohio	732	3.5%
9	Pennsylvania	668	3.2%
10	Louisiana	618	3.0%
11	Arizona	612	2.9%
12	Michigan	605	2.9%
13	Tennessee	546	2.6%
14	Mississippi	523	2.5%
15	Alabama	504	2.4%
16	Virginia	463	2.2%
17	Maryland	405	2.0%
18	South Carolina	403	1.9%
19	Missouri	390	1.9%
20	Indiana	377	1.8%
21	New Jersey	331	1.6%
22	Kentucky	326	1.6%
23	Arkansas	325	1.6%
24	Colorado	321	1.5%
25	Oklahoma	311	1.5%
26	Wisconsin	283	1.4%
27	Washington	260	1.3%
28	New Mexico	225	1.1%
29	Minnesota	199	1.0%
30	Nevada	182	0.9%
31	Massachusetts	171	0.8%
32	Oregon	153	0.7%
33	Kansas	144	0.7%
34	Connecticut	126	0.6%
35	Iowa	90	0.4%
36	Utah	87	0.4%
37	West Virginia	86	0.4%
38	Nebraska	73	0.4%
39	Delaware	67	0.3%
40	Rhode Island	57	0.3%
41	Hawaii	56	0.3%
42	Idaho	49	0.2%
43	Alaska	40	0.2%
44	South Dakota	29	0.1%
45	Wyoming	25	0.1%
46	North Dakota	23	0.1%
47	Montana	21	0.1%
48	Maine	19	0.1%
49	Vermont	8	0.0%
50	New Hampshire	3	0.0%
	District of Columbia	71	0.3%

Source: Morgan Quitno Press using data from U.S. Dept of Health & Human Services, National Center for Health Statistics "Table W-206A Live Births by Marital Status, Age and Race of Mother" (2002, 2003 and 2004)
*Final data. Births to 10 to 14 years old during the three years of 2002 to 2004 by state of residence.

Young Teen Birthrate: 2002 to 2004

National Rate = 0.7 Live Births per 1,000 10 to 14 Year Old Females*

ALPHA ORDER

RANK	STATE	RATE
5	Alabama	1.1
24	Alaska	0.5
7	Arizona	1.0
3	Arkansas	1.2
24	California	0.5
16	Colorado	0.7
42	Connecticut	0.3
13	Delaware	0.8
16	Florida	0.7
7	Georgia	1.0
24	Hawaii	0.5
42	Idaho	0.3
16	Illinois	0.7
21	Indiana	0.6
42	Iowa	0.3
24	Kansas	0.5
13	Kentucky	0.8
2	Louisiana	1.3
NA	Maine**	NA
16	Maryland	0.7
42	Massachusetts	0.3
24	Michigan	0.5
34	Minnesota	0.4
1	Mississippi	1.6
16	Missouri	0.7
47	Montana	0.2
34	Nebraska	0.4
13	Nevada	0.8
NA	New Hampshire**	NA
34	New Jersey	0.4
5	New Mexico	1.1
34	New York	0.4
7	North Carolina	1.0
34	North Dakota	0.4
21	Ohio	0.6
10	Oklahoma	0.9
34	Oregon	0.4
24	Pennsylvania	0.5
24	Rhode Island	0.5
10	South Carolina	0.9
34	South Dakota	0.4
10	Tennessee	0.9
3	Texas	1.2
42	Utah	0.3
NA	Vermont**	NA
21	Virginia	0.6
34	Washington	0.4
24	West Virginia	0.5
24	Wisconsin	0.5
24	Wyoming	0.5

RANK ORDER

RANK	STATE	RATE
1	Mississippi	1.6
2	Louisiana	1.3
3	Arkansas	1.2
3	Texas	1.2
5	Alabama	1.1
5	New Mexico	1.1
7	Arizona	1.0
7	Georgia	1.0
7	North Carolina	1.0
10	Oklahoma	0.9
10	South Carolina	0.9
10	Tennessee	0.9
13	Delaware	0.8
13	Kentucky	0.8
13	Nevada	0.8
16	Colorado	0.7
16	Florida	0.7
16	Illinois	0.7
16	Maryland	0.7
16	Missouri	0.7
21	Indiana	0.6
21	Ohio	0.6
21	Virginia	0.6
24	Alaska	0.5
24	California	0.5
24	Hawaii	0.5
24	Kansas	0.5
24	Michigan	0.5
24	Pennsylvania	0.5
24	Rhode Island	0.5
24	West Virginia	0.5
24	Wisconsin	0.5
24	Wyoming	0.5
34	Minnesota	0.4
34	Nebraska	0.4
34	New Jersey	0.4
34	New York	0.4
34	North Dakota	0.4
34	Oregon	0.4
34	South Dakota	0.4
34	Washington	0.4
42	Connecticut	0.3
42	Idaho	0.3
42	Iowa	0.3
42	Massachusetts	0.3
42	Utah	0.3
47	Montana	0.2
NA	Maine**	NA
NA	New Hampshire**	NA
NA	Vermont**	NA

District of Columbia 1.6

Source: Morgan Quitno Press using data from U.S. Dept of Health & Human Services, National Center for Health Statistics "Table W-206A Live Births by Marital Status, Age and Race of Mother" (2002, 2003 and 2004)
Final data. Births to 10 to 14 years old during the three years of 2002 to 2004 by state of residence.
***Insufficient data for a reliable rate.*

Births to Women 35 to 54 Years Old in 2004

National Total = 585,407 Live Births*

ALPHA ORDER

RANK	STATE	BIRTHS	% of USA
28	Alabama	5,385	0.9%
45	Alaska	1,379	0.2%
17	Arizona	10,790	1.8%
38	Arkansas	2,923	0.5%
1	California	93,723	16.0%
18	Colorado	10,295	1.8%
20	Connecticut	9,565	1.6%
44	Delaware	1,620	0.3%
4	Florida	31,748	5.4%
12	Georgia	16,901	2.9%
35	Hawaii	3,085	0.5%
41	Idaho	2,200	0.4%
5	Illinois	27,721	4.7%
21	Indiana	9,076	1.6%
32	Iowa	4,253	0.7%
31	Kansas	4,420	0.8%
27	Kentucky	5,448	0.9%
26	Louisiana	5,819	1.0%
42	Maine	1,950	0.3%
14	Maryland	14,197	2.4%
8	Massachusetts	18,468	3.2%
10	Michigan	17,330	3.0%
16	Minnesota	10,807	1.8%
34	Mississippi	3,213	0.5%
22	Missouri	8,523	1.5%
46	Montana	1,332	0.2%
36	Nebraska	3,054	0.5%
30	Nevada	4,493	0.8%
39	New Hampshire	2,705	0.5%
6	New Jersey	25,391	4.3%
37	New Mexico	2,925	0.5%
2	New York	50,132	8.6%
13	North Carolina	14,431	2.5%
49	North Dakota	871	0.1%
9	Ohio	18,309	3.1%
33	Oklahoma	4,223	0.7%
24	Oregon	6,174	1.1%
7	Pennsylvania	22,847	3.9%
40	Rhode Island	2,310	0.4%
25	South Carolina	6,001	1.0%
47	South Dakota	1,162	0.2%
23	Tennessee	7,968	1.4%
3	Texas	41,440	7.1%
29	Utah	4,558	0.8%
48	Vermont	1,117	0.2%
11	Virginia	17,057	2.9%
15	Washington	12,392	2.1%
43	West Virginia	1,787	0.3%
19	Wisconsin	9,673	1.7%
50	Wyoming	601	0.1%

RANK ORDER

RANK	STATE	BIRTHS	% of USA
1	California	93,723	16.0%
2	New York	50,132	8.6%
3	Texas	41,440	7.1%
4	Florida	31,748	5.4%
5	Illinois	27,721	4.7%
6	New Jersey	25,391	4.3%
7	Pennsylvania	22,847	3.9%
8	Massachusetts	18,468	3.2%
9	Ohio	18,309	3.1%
10	Michigan	17,330	3.0%
11	Virginia	17,057	2.9%
12	Georgia	16,901	2.9%
13	North Carolina	14,431	2.5%
14	Maryland	14,197	2.4%
15	Washington	12,392	2.1%
16	Minnesota	10,807	1.8%
17	Arizona	10,790	1.8%
18	Colorado	10,295	1.8%
19	Wisconsin	9,673	1.7%
20	Connecticut	9,565	1.6%
21	Indiana	9,076	1.6%
22	Missouri	8,523	1.5%
23	Tennessee	7,968	1.4%
24	Oregon	6,174	1.1%
25	South Carolina	6,001	1.0%
26	Louisiana	5,819	1.0%
27	Kentucky	5,448	0.9%
28	Alabama	5,385	0.9%
29	Utah	4,558	0.8%
30	Nevada	4,493	0.8%
31	Kansas	4,420	0.8%
32	Iowa	4,253	0.7%
33	Oklahoma	4,223	0.7%
34	Mississippi	3,213	0.5%
35	Hawaii	3,085	0.5%
36	Nebraska	3,054	0.5%
37	New Mexico	2,925	0.5%
38	Arkansas	2,923	0.5%
39	New Hampshire	2,705	0.5%
40	Rhode Island	2,310	0.4%
41	Idaho	2,200	0.4%
42	Maine	1,950	0.3%
43	West Virginia	1,787	0.3%
44	Delaware	1,620	0.3%
45	Alaska	1,379	0.2%
46	Montana	1,332	0.2%
47	South Dakota	1,162	0.2%
48	Vermont	1,117	0.2%
49	North Dakota	871	0.1%
50	Wyoming	601	0.1%
	District of Columbia	1,615	0.3%

Source: Morgan Quitno Press using data from U.S. Dept of Health & Human Services, National Center for Health Statistics
   "Table W-206A Live Births by Marital Status, Age and Race of Mother" (2004)
*Final data by state of residence.

Births to Women 35 to 54 Years Old as a Percent of All Births in 2004

National Percent = 14.2% of Live Births*

ALPHA ORDER

RANK	STATE	PERCENT		RANK	STATE	PERCENT
43	Alabama	9.0		1	Massachusetts	23.5
23	Alaska	13.3		2	Connecticut	22.7
30	Arizona	11.5		3	New Jersey	22.0
49	Arkansas	7.6		4	New York	20.1
8	California	17.2		5	Maryland	19.0
16	Colorado	15.0		6	New Hampshire	18.6
2	Connecticut	22.7		7	Rhode Island	18.1
18	Delaware	14.2		8	California	17.2
17	Florida	14.6		9	Hawaii	16.9
26	Georgia	12.2		9	Vermont	16.9
9	Hawaii	16.9		11	Virginia	16.4
41	Idaho	9.8		12	Pennsylvania	15.8
13	Illinois	15.3		13	Illinois	15.3
37	Indiana	10.4		13	Minnesota	15.3
31	Iowa	11.1		15	Washington	15.2
31	Kansas	11.1		16	Colorado	15.0
41	Kentucky	9.8		17	Florida	14.6
45	Louisiana	8.9		18	Delaware	14.2
19	Maine	14.0		19	Maine	14.0
5	Maryland	19.0		20	Wisconsin	13.8
1	Massachusetts	23.5		21	Oregon	13.5
22	Michigan	13.4		22	Michigan	13.4
13	Minnesota	15.3		23	Alaska	13.3
50	Mississippi	7.5		24	Nevada	12.8
33	Missouri	11.0		25	Ohio	12.3
28	Montana	11.6		26	Georgia	12.2
28	Nebraska	11.6		27	North Carolina	12.0
24	Nevada	12.8		28	Montana	11.6
6	New Hampshire	18.6		28	Nebraska	11.6
3	New Jersey	22.0		30	Arizona	11.5
38	New Mexico	10.3		31	Iowa	11.1
4	New York	20.1		31	Kansas	11.1
27	North Carolina	12.0		33	Missouri	11.0
35	North Dakota	10.6		34	Texas	10.9
25	Ohio	12.3		35	North Dakota	10.6
48	Oklahoma	8.2		35	South Carolina	10.6
21	Oregon	13.5		37	Indiana	10.4
12	Pennsylvania	15.8		38	New Mexico	10.3
7	Rhode Island	18.1		39	South Dakota	10.2
35	South Carolina	10.6		40	Tennessee	10.0
39	South Dakota	10.2		41	Idaho	9.8
40	Tennessee	10.0		41	Kentucky	9.8
34	Texas	10.9		43	Alabama	9.0
43	Utah	9.0		43	Utah	9.0
9	Vermont	16.9		45	Louisiana	8.9
11	Virginia	16.4		46	Wyoming	8.8
15	Washington	15.2		47	West Virginia	8.6
47	West Virginia	8.6		48	Oklahoma	8.2
20	Wisconsin	13.8		49	Arkansas	7.6
46	Wyoming	8.8		50	Mississippi	7.5

RANK ORDER

District of Columbia 20.4

Source: Morgan Quitno Press using data from U.S. Dept of Health & Human Services, National Center for Health Statistics
"Table W-206A Live Births by Marital Status, Age and Race of Mother" (2004)
*Final data by state of residence.

Births by Vaginal Delivery in 2005

National Total = 2,890,012 Live Births*

ALPHA ORDER

RANK	STATE	BIRTHS	% of USA
23	Alabama	41,225	1.4%
47	Alaska	8,161	0.3%
11	Arizona	72,462	2.5%
34	Arkansas	26,849	0.9%
1	California	383,089	13.3%
21	Colorado	51,998	1.8%
32	Connecticut	28,201	1.0%
46	Delaware	8,165	0.3%
4	Florida	147,308	5.1%
8	Georgia	99,010	3.4%
40	Hawaii	13,336	0.5%
38	Idaho	17,850	0.6%
5	Illinois	127,491	4.4%
14	Indiana	62,668	2.2%
30	Iowa	28,816	1.0%
31	Kansas	28,364	1.0%
27	Kentucky	37,270	1.3%
26	Louisiana	38,494	1.3%
42	Maine	10,119	0.4%
22	Maryland	51,665	1.8%
20	Massachusetts	52,152	1.8%
9	Michigan	90,993	3.1%
19	Minnesota	53,014	1.8%
33	Mississippi	27,516	1.0%
17	Missouri	55,269	1.9%
44	Montana	8,609	0.3%
37	Nebraska	18,591	0.6%
35	Nevada	25,745	0.9%
41	New Hampshire	10,387	0.4%
12	New Jersey	72,427	2.5%
36	New Mexico	22,433	0.8%
3	New York	168,752	5.8%
10	North Carolina	87,044	3.0%
48	North Dakota	6,177	0.2%
6	Ohio	107,071	3.7%
28	Oklahoma	34,929	1.2%
29	Oregon	33,258	1.2%
7	Pennsylvania	103,656	3.6%
43	Rhode Island	8,851	0.3%
25	South Carolina	38,851	1.3%
45	South Dakota	8,581	0.3%
16	Tennessee	56,321	1.9%
2	Texas	260,139	9.0%
24	Utah	40,418	1.4%
50	Vermont	4,798	0.2%
13	Virginia	71,750	2.5%
15	Washington	59,713	2.1%
39	West Virginia	13,732	0.5%
18	Wisconsin	54,156	1.9%
49	Wyoming	5,458	0.2%

RANK ORDER

RANK	STATE	BIRTHS	% of USA
1	California	383,089	13.3%
2	Texas	260,139	9.0%
3	New York	168,752	5.8%
4	Florida	147,308	5.1%
5	Illinois	127,491	4.4%
6	Ohio	107,071	3.7%
7	Pennsylvania	103,656	3.6%
8	Georgia	99,010	3.4%
9	Michigan	90,993	3.1%
10	North Carolina	87,044	3.0%
11	Arizona	72,462	2.5%
12	New Jersey	72,427	2.5%
13	Virginia	71,750	2.5%
14	Indiana	62,668	2.2%
15	Washington	59,713	2.1%
16	Tennessee	56,321	1.9%
17	Missouri	55,269	1.9%
18	Wisconsin	54,156	1.9%
19	Minnesota	53,014	1.8%
20	Massachusetts	52,152	1.8%
21	Colorado	51,998	1.8%
22	Maryland	51,665	1.8%
23	Alabama	41,225	1.4%
24	Utah	40,418	1.4%
25	South Carolina	38,851	1.3%
26	Louisiana	38,494	1.3%
27	Kentucky	37,270	1.3%
28	Oklahoma	34,929	1.2%
29	Oregon	33,258	1.2%
30	Iowa	28,816	1.0%
31	Kansas	28,364	1.0%
32	Connecticut	28,201	1.0%
33	Mississippi	27,516	1.0%
34	Arkansas	26,849	0.9%
35	Nevada	25,745	0.9%
36	New Mexico	22,433	0.8%
37	Nebraska	18,591	0.6%
38	Idaho	17,850	0.6%
39	West Virginia	13,732	0.5%
40	Hawaii	13,336	0.5%
41	New Hampshire	10,387	0.4%
42	Maine	10,119	0.4%
43	Rhode Island	8,851	0.3%
44	Montana	8,609	0.3%
45	South Dakota	8,581	0.3%
46	Delaware	8,165	0.3%
47	Alaska	8,161	0.3%
48	North Dakota	6,177	0.2%
49	Wyoming	5,458	0.2%
50	Vermont	4,798	0.2%
	District of Columbia	5,478	0.2%

Source: Morgan Quitno Press using data from U.S. Dept. of Health and Human Services, Nat'l Center for Health Statistics "Births: Preliminary data for 2005"

Preliminary estimates by state of residence.

Percent of Births by Vaginal Delivery in 2005

National Percent = 69.8% of Live Births*

ALPHA ORDER

RANK	STATE	PERCENT
39	Alabama	68.2
2	Alaska	78.0
8	Arizona	75.3
37	Arkansas	68.5
31	California	69.7
6	Colorado	75.4
41	Connecticut	67.6
29	Delaware	70.1
47	Florida	65.1
32	Georgia	69.6
11	Hawaii	74.4
4	Idaho	77.4
22	Illinois	71.2
20	Indiana	71.8
15	Iowa	73.3
25	Kansas	71.1
45	Kentucky	66.1
50	Louisiana	63.1
21	Maine	71.7
34	Maryland	68.9
40	Massachusetts	67.8
22	Michigan	71.2
10	Minnesota	74.7
48	Mississippi	64.9
28	Missouri	70.3
12	Montana	74.2
25	Nebraska	71.1
33	Nevada	69.1
18	New Hampshire	72.0
49	New Jersey	63.7
3	New Mexico	77.8
37	New York	68.5
27	North Carolina	70.7
14	North Dakota	73.6
19	Ohio	71.9
42	Oklahoma	67.5
16	Oregon	72.4
22	Pennsylvania	71.2
30	Rhode Island	69.8
44	South Carolina	67.3
9	South Dakota	74.9
34	Tennessee	68.9
43	Texas	67.4
1	Utah	78.4
13	Vermont	74.1
36	Virginia	68.6
17	Washington	72.2
46	West Virginia	65.9
5	Wisconsin	76.3
6	Wyoming	75.4

RANK ORDER

RANK	STATE	PERCENT
1	Utah	78.4
2	Alaska	78.0
3	New Mexico	77.8
4	Idaho	77.4
5	Wisconsin	76.3
6	Colorado	75.4
6	Wyoming	75.4
8	Arizona	75.3
9	South Dakota	74.9
10	Minnesota	74.7
11	Hawaii	74.4
12	Montana	74.2
13	Vermont	74.1
14	North Dakota	73.6
15	Iowa	73.3
16	Oregon	72.4
17	Washington	72.2
18	New Hampshire	72.0
19	Ohio	71.9
20	Indiana	71.8
21	Maine	71.7
22	Illinois	71.2
22	Michigan	71.2
22	Pennsylvania	71.2
25	Kansas	71.1
25	Nebraska	71.1
27	North Carolina	70.7
28	Missouri	70.3
29	Delaware	70.1
30	Rhode Island	69.8
31	California	69.7
32	Georgia	69.6
33	Nevada	69.1
34	Maryland	68.9
34	Tennessee	68.9
36	Virginia	68.6
37	Arkansas	68.5
37	New York	68.5
39	Alabama	68.2
40	Massachusetts	67.8
41	Connecticut	67.6
42	Oklahoma	67.5
43	Texas	67.4
44	South Carolina	67.3
45	Kentucky	66.1
46	West Virginia	65.9
47	Florida	65.1
48	Mississippi	64.9
49	New Jersey	63.7
50	Louisiana	63.1

District of Columbia   69.4

Source: Morgan Quitno Press using data from U.S. Dept. of Health and Human Services, Nat'l Center for Health Statistics
     "Births: Preliminary data for 2005"
*Preliminary data by state of residence.

Births by Cesarean Delivery in 2005

National Total = 1,250,407 Live Cesarean Births*

ALPHA ORDER				RANK ORDER			
RANK	STATE	BIRTHS	% of USA	RANK	STATE	BIRTHS	% of USA
21	Alabama	19,222	1.5%	1	California	166,537	13.3%
47	Alaska	2,302	0.2%	2	Texas	125,824	10.1%
16	Arizona	23,769	1.9%	3	Florida	78,972	6.3%
31	Arkansas	12,347	1.0%	4	New York	77,602	6.2%
1	California	166,537	13.3%	5	Illinois	51,570	4.1%
25	Colorado	16,965	1.4%	6	Georgia	43,246	3.5%
29	Connecticut	13,516	1.1%	7	Pennsylvania	41,928	3.4%
44	Delaware	3,483	0.3%	8	Ohio	41,845	3.3%
3	Florida	78,972	6.3%	9	New Jersey	41,273	3.3%
6	Georgia	43,246	3.5%	10	Michigan	36,806	2.9%
40	Hawaii	4,589	0.4%	11	North Carolina	36,074	2.9%
39	Idaho	5,212	0.4%	12	Virginia	32,842	2.6%
5	Illinois	51,570	4.1%	13	Tennessee	25,422	2.0%
15	Indiana	24,614	2.0%	14	Massachusetts	24,768	2.0%
35	Iowa	10,496	0.8%	15	Indiana	24,614	2.0%
32	Kansas	11,529	0.9%	16	Arizona	23,769	1.9%
22	Kentucky	19,115	1.5%	17	Missouri	23,350	1.9%
20	Louisiana	22,511	1.8%	18	Maryland	23,321	1.9%
42	Maine	3,994	0.3%	19	Washington	22,992	1.8%
18	Maryland	23,321	1.9%	20	Louisiana	22,511	1.8%
14	Massachusetts	24,768	2.0%	21	Alabama	19,222	1.5%
10	Michigan	36,806	2.9%	22	Kentucky	19,115	1.5%
24	Minnesota	17,955	1.4%	23	South Carolina	18,877	1.5%
28	Mississippi	14,882	1.2%	24	Minnesota	17,955	1.4%
17	Missouri	23,350	1.9%	25	Colorado	16,965	1.4%
45	Montana	2,993	0.2%	26	Wisconsin	16,822	1.3%
36	Nebraska	7,557	0.6%	27	Oklahoma	16,817	1.3%
33	Nevada	11,513	0.9%	28	Mississippi	14,882	1.2%
41	New Hampshire	4,039	0.3%	29	Connecticut	13,516	1.1%
9	New Jersey	41,273	3.3%	30	Oregon	12,679	1.0%
38	New Mexico	6,401	0.5%	31	Arkansas	12,347	1.0%
4	New York	77,602	6.2%	32	Kansas	11,529	0.9%
11	North Carolina	36,074	2.9%	33	Nevada	11,513	0.9%
48	North Dakota	2,216	0.2%	34	Utah	11,136	0.9%
8	Ohio	41,845	3.3%	35	Iowa	10,496	0.8%
27	Oklahoma	16,817	1.3%	36	Nebraska	7,557	0.6%
30	Oregon	12,679	1.0%	37	West Virginia	7,106	0.6%
7	Pennsylvania	41,928	3.4%	38	New Mexico	6,401	0.5%
43	Rhode Island	3,829	0.3%	39	Idaho	5,212	0.4%
23	South Carolina	18,877	1.5%	40	Hawaii	4,589	0.4%
46	South Dakota	2,876	0.2%	41	New Hampshire	4,039	0.3%
13	Tennessee	25,422	2.0%	42	Maine	3,994	0.3%
2	Texas	125,824	10.1%	43	Rhode Island	3,829	0.3%
34	Utah	11,136	0.9%	44	Delaware	3,483	0.3%
50	Vermont	1,677	0.1%	45	Montana	2,993	0.2%
12	Virginia	32,842	2.6%	46	South Dakota	2,876	0.2%
19	Washington	22,992	1.8%	47	Alaska	2,302	0.2%
37	West Virginia	7,106	0.6%	48	North Dakota	2,216	0.2%
26	Wisconsin	16,822	1.3%	49	Wyoming	1,781	0.1%
49	Wyoming	1,781	0.1%	50	Vermont	1,677	0.1%
					District of Columbia	2,415	0.2%

Source: Morgan Quitno Press using data from U.S. Dept. of Health and Human Services, Nat'l Center for Health Statistics
   "Births: Preliminary data for 2005"
*Preliminary estimates by state of residence.

Percent of Births by Cesarean Delivery in 2005

National Percent = 30.2% of Live Births*

ALPHA ORDER

RANK ORDER

RANK	STATE	PERCENT		RANK	STATE	PERCENT
12	Alabama	31.8		1	Louisiana	36.9
49	Alaska	22.0		2	New Jersey	36.3
43	Arizona	24.7		3	Mississippi	35.1
13	Arkansas	31.5		4	Florida	34.9
20	California	30.3		5	West Virginia	34.1
44	Colorado	24.6		6	Kentucky	33.9
10	Connecticut	32.4		7	South Carolina	32.7
22	Delaware	29.9		8	Texas	32.6
4	Florida	34.9		9	Oklahoma	32.5
19	Georgia	30.4		10	Connecticut	32.4
40	Hawaii	25.6		11	Massachusetts	32.2
47	Idaho	22.6		12	Alabama	31.8
27	Illinois	28.8		13	Arkansas	31.5
31	Indiana	28.2		13	New York	31.5
36	Iowa	26.7		15	Virginia	31.4
25	Kansas	28.9		16	Maryland	31.1
6	Kentucky	33.9		16	Tennessee	31.1
1	Louisiana	36.9		18	Nevada	30.9
30	Maine	28.3		19	Georgia	30.4
16	Maryland	31.1		20	California	30.3
11	Massachusetts	32.2		21	Rhode Island	30.2
27	Michigan	28.8		22	Delaware	29.9
41	Minnesota	25.3		23	Missouri	29.7
3	Mississippi	35.1		24	North Carolina	29.3
23	Missouri	29.7		25	Kansas	28.9
39	Montana	25.8		25	Nebraska	28.9
25	Nebraska	28.9		27	Illinois	28.8
18	Nevada	30.9		27	Michigan	28.8
33	New Hampshire	28.0		27	Pennsylvania	28.8
2	New Jersey	36.3		30	Maine	28.3
48	New Mexico	22.2		31	Indiana	28.2
13	New York	31.5		32	Ohio	28.1
24	North Carolina	29.3		33	New Hampshire	28.0
37	North Dakota	26.4		34	Washington	27.8
32	Ohio	28.1		35	Oregon	27.6
9	Oklahoma	32.5		36	Iowa	26.7
35	Oregon	27.6		37	North Dakota	26.4
27	Pennsylvania	28.8		38	Vermont	25.9
21	Rhode Island	30.2		39	Montana	25.8
7	South Carolina	32.7		40	Hawaii	25.6
42	South Dakota	25.1		41	Minnesota	25.3
16	Tennessee	31.1		42	South Dakota	25.1
8	Texas	32.6		43	Arizona	24.7
50	Utah	21.6		44	Colorado	24.6
38	Vermont	25.9		44	Wyoming	24.6
15	Virginia	31.4		46	Wisconsin	23.7
34	Washington	27.8		47	Idaho	22.6
5	West Virginia	34.1		48	New Mexico	22.2
46	Wisconsin	23.7		49	Alaska	22.0
44	Wyoming	24.6		50	Utah	21.6
					District of Columbia	30.6

Source: U.S. Department of Health and Human Services, National Center for Health Statistics
    "Births: Preliminary data for 2005"
*Preliminary data by state of residence.

Percent Change in Rate of Cesarean Births: 2001 to 2005

National Percent Change = 23.8% Increase*

ALPHA ORDER

RANK ORDER

RANK	STATE	PERCENT CHANGE		RANK	STATE	PERCENT CHANGE
48	Alabama	15.2		1	Vermont	45.5
46	Alaska	16.4		2	Connecticut	33.3
25	Arizona	23.5		3	Florida	32.2
49	Arkansas	14.1		4	Oregon	31.4
36	California	20.7		5	Nevada	30.4
15	Colorado	25.5		6	Ohio	29.5
2	Connecticut	33.3		7	Kentucky	29.4
45	Delaware	17.3		8	Illinois	29.1
3	Florida	32.2		9	West Virginia	28.2
19	Georgia	25.1		10	Virginia	27.6
11	Hawaii	27.4		11	Hawaii	27.4
35	Idaho	20.9		12	Massachusetts	26.8
8	Illinois	29.1		13	New Jersey	25.6
34	Indiana	21.0		13	Utah	25.6
47	Iowa	15.6		15	Colorado	25.5
33	Kansas	21.4		15	Oklahoma	25.5
7	Kentucky	29.4		17	Rhode Island	25.3
26	Louisiana	23.4		18	Pennsylvania	25.2
44	Maine	17.4		19	Georgia	25.1
29	Maryland	22.4		19	North Dakota	25.1
12	Massachusetts	26.8		21	Missouri	24.3
27	Michigan	23.1		22	Wisconsin	24.1
37	Minnesota	19.9		23	Texas	24.0
42	Mississippi	18.2		24	South Carolina	23.9
21	Missouri	24.3		25	Arizona	23.5
39	Montana	19.4		26	Louisiana	23.4
37	Nebraska	19.9		27	Michigan	23.1
5	Nevada	30.4		28	Washington	23.0
31	New Hampshire	21.7		29	Maryland	22.4
13	New Jersey	25.6		29	Wyoming	22.4
39	New Mexico	19.4		31	New Hampshire	21.7
32	New York	21.6		32	New York	21.6
43	North Carolina	17.7		33	Kansas	21.4
19	North Dakota	25.1		34	Indiana	21.0
6	Ohio	29.5		35	Idaho	20.9
15	Oklahoma	25.5		36	California	20.7
4	Oregon	31.4		37	Minnesota	19.9
18	Pennsylvania	25.2		37	Nebraska	19.9
17	Rhode Island	25.3		39	Montana	19.4
24	South Carolina	23.9		39	New Mexico	19.4
50	South Dakota	9.1		41	Tennessee	18.7
41	Tennessee	18.7		42	Mississippi	18.2
23	Texas	24.0		43	North Carolina	17.7
13	Utah	25.6		44	Maine	17.4
1	Vermont	45.5		45	Delaware	17.3
10	Virginia	27.6		46	Alaska	16.4
28	Washington	23.0		47	Iowa	15.6
9	West Virginia	28.2		48	Alabama	15.2
22	Wisconsin	24.1		49	Arkansas	14.1
29	Wyoming	22.4		50	South Dakota	9.1

District of Columbia   22.4

Source: Morgan Quitno Press using data from U.S. Dept. of Health and Human Services, Nat'l Center for Health Statistics "Births: Preliminary data for 2005" and "National Vital Statistics Reports" (Vol. 51, No. 2, December 18, 2002)
*Preliminary data by state of residence.

Twin Birth Rate: 2002-2004

National Rate = 31.6 Twins Born per 1,000 Live Births*

ALPHA ORDER

RANK	STATE	RATE
20	Alabama	31.8
47	Alaska	26.4
47	Arizona	26.4
39	Arkansas	28.6
42	California	28.2
27	Colorado	31.0
3	Connecticut	40.5
8	Delaware	35.5
36	Florida	29.5
23	Georgia	31.4
43	Hawaii	28.1
35	Idaho	29.6
8	Illinois	35.5
21	Indiana	31.7
15	Iowa	32.9
30	Kansas	30.4
31	Kentucky	30.3
28	Louisiana	30.8
17	Maine	32.7
5	Maryland	37.3
1	Massachusetts	45.2
10	Michigan	34.0
13	Minnesota	33.1
24	Mississippi	31.3
19	Missouri	32.4
38	Montana	28.9
22	Nebraska	31.6
40	Nevada	28.3
7	New Hampshire	36.0
2	New Jersey	41.3
50	New Mexico	23.8
6	New York	36.1
24	North Carolina	31.3
18	North Dakota	32.5
12	Ohio	33.3
46	Oklahoma	26.9
34	Oregon	29.7
15	Pennsylvania	32.9
4	Rhode Island	38.3
26	South Carolina	31.2
29	South Dakota	30.5
33	Tennessee	30.1
44	Texas	27.7
49	Utah	26.1
11	Vermont	33.8
14	Virginia	33.0
37	Washington	29.0
40	West Virginia	28.3
31	Wisconsin	30.3
45	Wyoming	27.0

RANK ORDER

RANK	STATE	RATE
1	Massachusetts	45.2
2	New Jersey	41.3
3	Connecticut	40.5
4	Rhode Island	38.3
5	Maryland	37.3
6	New York	36.1
7	New Hampshire	36.0
8	Delaware	35.5
8	Illinois	35.5
10	Michigan	34.0
11	Vermont	33.8
12	Ohio	33.3
13	Minnesota	33.1
14	Virginia	33.0
15	Iowa	32.9
15	Pennsylvania	32.9
17	Maine	32.7
18	North Dakota	32.5
19	Missouri	32.4
20	Alabama	31.8
21	Indiana	31.7
22	Nebraska	31.6
23	Georgia	31.4
24	Mississippi	31.3
24	North Carolina	31.3
26	South Carolina	31.2
27	Colorado	31.0
28	Louisiana	30.8
29	South Dakota	30.5
30	Kansas	30.4
31	Kentucky	30.3
31	Wisconsin	30.3
33	Tennessee	30.1
34	Oregon	29.7
35	Idaho	29.6
36	Florida	29.5
37	Washington	29.0
38	Montana	28.9
39	Arkansas	28.6
40	Nevada	28.3
40	West Virginia	28.3
42	California	28.2
43	Hawaii	28.1
44	Texas	27.7
45	Wyoming	27.0
46	Oklahoma	26.9
47	Alaska	26.4
47	Arizona	26.4
49	Utah	26.1
50	New Mexico	23.8
	District of Columbia	31.9

Source: U.S. Department of Health and Human Services, National Center for Health Statistics
"National Vital Statistics Reports" (Vol. 55, No. 1, September 29, 2006)
*Final data by state of residence. Number of live births in twin deliveries.

Assisted Reproductive Technology Procedures in 2003

National Total = 121,210 Procedures*

ALPHA ORDER

RANK	STATE	PROCEDURES	% of USA
37	Alabama	461	0.4%
49	Alaska	110	0.1%
19	Arizona	1,754	1.4%
47	Arkansas	135	0.1%
1	California	15,911	13.1%
20	Colorado	1,580	1.3%
14	Connecticut	2,689	2.2%
38	Delaware	460	0.4%
7	Florida	5,101	4.2%
13	Georgia	2,767	2.3%
32	Hawaii	645	0.5%
40	Idaho	352	0.3%
4	Illinois	8,676	7.2%
18	Indiana	1,935	1.6%
23	Iowa	1,026	0.8%
30	Kansas	746	0.6%
25	Kentucky	924	0.8%
31	Louisiana	656	0.5%
44	Maine	175	0.1%
9	Maryland	3,963	3.3%
3	Massachusetts	8,813	7.3%
12	Michigan	3,232	2.7%
16	Minnesota	2,138	1.8%
39	Mississippi	452	0.4%
22	Missouri	1,304	1.1%
48	Montana	118	0.1%
27	Nebraska	783	0.6%
34	Nevada	623	0.5%
33	New Hampshire	637	0.5%
5	New Jersey	8,299	6.8%
42	New Mexico	203	0.2%
2	New York	15,534	12.8%
15	North Carolina	2,161	1.8%
43	North Dakota	191	0.2%
11	Ohio	3,394	2.8%
35	Oklahoma	570	0.5%
28	Oregon	781	0.6%
8	Pennsylvania	4,653	3.8%
29	Rhode Island	771	0.6%
26	South Carolina	899	0.7%
45	South Dakota	166	0.1%
24	Tennessee	959	0.8%
6	Texas	5,843	4.8%
36	Utah	555	0.5%
46	Vermont	160	0.1%
10	Virginia	3,631	3.0%
17	Washington	2,057	1.7%
41	West Virginia	284	0.2%
21	Wisconsin	1,323	1.1%
50	Wyoming	40	0.0%

RANK ORDER

RANK	STATE	PROCEDURES	% of USA
1	California	15,911	13.1%
2	New York	15,534	12.8%
3	Massachusetts	8,813	7.3%
4	Illinois	8,676	7.2%
5	New Jersey	8,299	6.8%
6	Texas	5,843	4.8%
7	Florida	5,101	4.2%
8	Pennsylvania	4,653	3.8%
9	Maryland	3,963	3.3%
10	Virginia	3,631	3.0%
11	Ohio	3,394	2.8%
12	Michigan	3,232	2.7%
13	Georgia	2,767	2.3%
14	Connecticut	2,689	2.2%
15	North Carolina	2,161	1.8%
16	Minnesota	2,138	1.8%
17	Washington	2,057	1.7%
18	Indiana	1,935	1.6%
19	Arizona	1,754	1.4%
20	Colorado	1,580	1.3%
21	Wisconsin	1,323	1.1%
22	Missouri	1,304	1.1%
23	Iowa	1,026	0.8%
24	Tennessee	959	0.8%
25	Kentucky	924	0.8%
26	South Carolina	899	0.7%
27	Nebraska	783	0.6%
28	Oregon	781	0.6%
29	Rhode Island	771	0.6%
30	Kansas	746	0.6%
31	Louisiana	656	0.5%
32	Hawaii	645	0.5%
33	New Hampshire	637	0.5%
34	Nevada	623	0.5%
35	Oklahoma	570	0.5%
36	Utah	555	0.5%
37	Alabama	461	0.4%
38	Delaware	460	0.4%
39	Mississippi	452	0.4%
40	Idaho	352	0.3%
41	West Virginia	284	0.2%
42	New Mexico	203	0.2%
43	North Dakota	191	0.2%
44	Maine	175	0.1%
45	South Dakota	166	0.1%
46	Vermont	160	0.1%
47	Arkansas	135	0.1%
48	Montana	118	0.1%
49	Alaska	110	0.1%
50	Wyoming	40	0.0%
	District of Columbia	552	0.5%

Source: U.S. Department of Health and Human Services, Centers for Disease Control and Prevention
"Assisted Reproductive Technology, 2003" (Morbidity and Mortality Weekly Report, Vol. 55, No. SS-04, 05/26/06)
*By patient's residence. Does not include 1,662 procedures for patients with residences outside the U.S. Assisted reproductive technology (ART) includes treatments in which both eggs and sperm are handled in the laboratory. In 2003, 74% of ART treatments were freshly fertilized embryos using the patient's eggs, 14% were thawed embryos using the patient's eggs, 8% were freshly fertilized embryos from donor eggs and 4% were thawed embryos from donor eggs.

Infants Born from Assisted Reproductive Technology Procedures in 2003

National Total = 48,050 Live Births*

ALPHA ORDER

RANK ORDER

RANK	STATE	BIRTHS	% of USA
40	Alabama	157	0.3%
49	Alaska	52	0.1%
19	Arizona	862	1.8%
46	Arkansas	63	0.1%
1	California	6,199	12.9%
18	Colorado	883	1.8%
14	Connecticut	1,003	2.1%
39	Delaware	181	0.4%
7	Florida	2,054	4.3%
13	Georgia	1,183	2.5%
38	Hawaii	191	0.4%
36	Idaho	207	0.4%
4	Illinois	2,957	6.2%
20	Indiana	737	1.5%
23	Iowa	492	1.0%
28	Kansas	335	0.7%
24	Kentucky	466	1.0%
34	Louisiana	238	0.5%
47	Maine	61	0.1%
10	Maryland	1,380	2.9%
5	Massachusetts	2,912	6.1%
12	Michigan	1,356	2.8%
15	Minnesota	971	2.0%
37	Mississippi	206	0.4%
21	Missouri	555	1.2%
45	Montana	72	0.1%
30	Nebraska	294	0.6%
33	Nevada	265	0.6%
35	New Hampshire	226	0.5%
3	New Jersey	3,379	7.0%
42	New Mexico	120	0.2%
2	New York	5,823	12.1%
16	North Carolina	930	1.9%
43	North Dakota	95	0.2%
9	Ohio	1,398	2.9%
32	Oklahoma	269	0.6%
27	Oregon	413	0.9%
8	Pennsylvania	1,575	3.3%
31	Rhode Island	285	0.6%
26	South Carolina	435	0.9%
44	South Dakota	73	0.2%
24	Tennessee	466	1.0%
6	Texas	2,731	5.7%
29	Utah	305	0.6%
48	Vermont	57	0.1%
11	Virginia	1,359	2.8%
17	Washington	914	1.9%
41	West Virginia	126	0.3%
22	Wisconsin	531	1.1%
50	Wyoming	29	0.1%

RANK	STATE	BIRTHS	% of USA
1	California	6,199	12.9%
2	New York	5,823	12.1%
3	New Jersey	3,379	7.0%
4	Illinois	2,957	6.2%
5	Massachusetts	2,912	6.1%
6	Texas	2,731	5.7%
7	Florida	2,054	4.3%
8	Pennsylvania	1,575	3.3%
9	Ohio	1,398	2.9%
10	Maryland	1,380	2.9%
11	Virginia	1,359	2.8%
12	Michigan	1,356	2.8%
13	Georgia	1,183	2.5%
14	Connecticut	1,003	2.1%
15	Minnesota	971	2.0%
16	North Carolina	930	1.9%
17	Washington	914	1.9%
18	Colorado	883	1.8%
19	Arizona	862	1.8%
20	Indiana	737	1.5%
21	Missouri	555	1.2%
22	Wisconsin	531	1.1%
23	Iowa	492	1.0%
24	Kentucky	466	1.0%
24	Tennessee	466	1.0%
26	South Carolina	435	0.9%
27	Oregon	413	0.9%
28	Kansas	335	0.7%
29	Utah	305	0.6%
30	Nebraska	294	0.6%
31	Rhode Island	285	0.6%
32	Oklahoma	269	0.6%
33	Nevada	265	0.6%
34	Louisiana	238	0.5%
35	New Hampshire	226	0.5%
36	Idaho	207	0.4%
37	Mississippi	206	0.4%
38	Hawaii	191	0.4%
39	Delaware	181	0.4%
40	Alabama	157	0.3%
41	West Virginia	126	0.3%
42	New Mexico	120	0.2%
43	North Dakota	95	0.2%
44	South Dakota	73	0.2%
45	Montana	72	0.1%
46	Arkansas	63	0.1%
47	Maine	61	0.1%
48	Vermont	57	0.1%
49	Alaska	52	0.1%
50	Wyoming	29	0.1%
	District of Columbia	171	0.4%

Source: U.S. Department of Health and Human Services, Centers for Disease Control and Prevention
"Assisted Reproductive Technology, 2003" (Morbidity and Mortality Weekly Report, Vol. 55, No. SS-04, 05/26/06)
*By patient's residence. Does not include 706 births to patients with residences outside the U.S. Assisted reproductive technology (ART) includes treatments in which both eggs and sperm are handled in the laboratory. In 2003, 74% of ART treatments were freshly fertilized embryos using the patient's eggs, 14% were thawed embryos using the patient's eggs, 8% were freshly fertilized embryos from donor eggs and 4% were thawed embryos from donor eggs.

54

Percent of Assisted Reproductive Technology Procedures that Resulted in Live Births in 2003
National Percent = 29.1%*

ALPHA ORDER

RANK	STATE	PERCENT
49	Alabama	24.5
21	Alaska	32.7
16	Arizona	33.6
11	Arkansas	34.8
32	California	28.6
5	Colorado	40.1
35	Connecticut	28.0
34	Delaware	28.3
31	Florida	29.6
25	Georgia	31.1
50	Hawaii	21.7
4	Idaho	41.5
46	Illinois	25.3
40	Indiana	27.0
10	Iowa	35.1
19	Kansas	33.1
9	Kentucky	35.6
46	Louisiana	25.3
44	Maine	25.7
43	Maryland	26.3
45	Massachusetts	25.5
30	Michigan	29.7
12	Minnesota	34.6
22	Mississippi	32.1
23	Missouri	31.5
3	Montana	44.1
42	Nebraska	26.7
27	Nevada	30.7
39	New Hampshire	27.3
28	New Jersey	30.1
2	New Mexico	44.3
37	New York	27.6
26	North Carolina	30.9
12	North Dakota	34.6
29	Ohio	29.9
14	Oklahoma	34.2
7	Oregon	36.9
48	Pennsylvania	25.1
37	Rhode Island	27.6
8	South Carolina	35.7
24	South Dakota	31.3
15	Tennessee	33.9
17	Texas	33.4
6	Utah	39.8
41	Vermont	26.9
36	Virginia	27.9
18	Washington	33.2
19	West Virginia	33.1
32	Wisconsin	28.6
1	Wyoming	52.5

RANK ORDER

RANK	STATE	PERCENT
1	Wyoming	52.5
2	New Mexico	44.3
3	Montana	44.1
4	Idaho	41.5
5	Colorado	40.1
6	Utah	39.8
7	Oregon	36.9
8	South Carolina	35.7
9	Kentucky	35.6
10	Iowa	35.1
11	Arkansas	34.8
12	Minnesota	34.6
12	North Dakota	34.6
14	Oklahoma	34.2
15	Tennessee	33.9
16	Arizona	33.6
17	Texas	33.4
18	Washington	33.2
19	Kansas	33.1
19	West Virginia	33.1
21	Alaska	32.7
22	Mississippi	32.1
23	Missouri	31.5
24	South Dakota	31.3
25	Georgia	31.1
26	North Carolina	30.9
27	Nevada	30.7
28	New Jersey	30.1
29	Ohio	29.9
30	Michigan	29.7
31	Florida	29.6
32	California	28.6
32	Wisconsin	28.6
34	Delaware	28.3
35	Connecticut	28.0
36	Virginia	27.9
37	New York	27.6
37	Rhode Island	27.6
39	New Hampshire	27.3
40	Indiana	27.0
41	Vermont	26.9
42	Nebraska	26.7
43	Maryland	26.3
44	Maine	25.7
45	Massachusetts	25.5
46	Illinois	25.3
46	Louisiana	25.3
48	Pennsylvania	25.1
49	Alabama	24.5
50	Hawaii	21.7
	District of Columbia	23.4

Source: Morgan Quitno Press using data from US Dept of Health & Human Serv's, Centers for Disease Control-Prevention
"Assisted Reproductive Technology, 2003" (Morbidity and Mortality Weekly Report, Vol. 55, No. SS-04, 05/26/06)
*By patient's residence. Assisted reproductive technology (ART) includes treatments in which both eggs and sperm are handled in the laboratory. In 2003, 74% of ART treatments were freshly fertilized embryos using the patient's eggs, 14% were thawed embryos using the patient's eggs, 8% were freshly fertilized embryos from donor eggs and 4% were thawed embryos from donor eggs.

Percent of Total Live Births Resulting from Assisted Reproductive Technology Procedures in 2003
National Percent = 1.2% of Live Births*

ALPHA ORDER

RANK	STATE	PERCENT
49	Alabama	0.3
42	Alaska	0.5
22	Arizona	0.9
50	Arkansas	0.2
15	California	1.1
11	Colorado	1.3
3	Connecticut	2.3
7	Delaware	1.6
20	Florida	1.0
22	Georgia	0.9
15	Hawaii	1.1
22	Idaho	0.9
7	Illinois	1.6
22	Indiana	0.9
11	Iowa	1.3
29	Kansas	0.8
29	Kentucky	0.8
45	Louisiana	0.4
45	Maine	0.4
6	Maryland	1.8
1	Massachusetts	3.6
20	Michigan	1.0
10	Minnesota	1.4
42	Mississippi	0.5
35	Missouri	0.7
38	Montana	0.6
15	Nebraska	1.1
29	Nevada	0.8
7	New Hampshire	1.6
2	New Jersey	2.9
45	New Mexico	0.4
3	New York	2.3
29	North Carolina	0.8
14	North Dakota	1.2
22	Ohio	0.9
42	Oklahoma	0.5
22	Oregon	0.9
15	Pennsylvania	1.1
5	Rhode Island	2.2
29	South Carolina	0.8
35	South Dakota	0.7
38	Tennessee	0.6
35	Texas	0.7
38	Utah	0.6
22	Vermont	0.9
11	Virginia	1.3
15	Washington	1.1
38	West Virginia	0.6
29	Wisconsin	0.8
45	Wyoming	0.4

RANK ORDER

RANK	STATE	PERCENT
1	Massachusetts	3.6
2	New Jersey	2.9
3	Connecticut	2.3
3	New York	2.3
5	Rhode Island	2.2
6	Maryland	1.8
7	Delaware	1.6
7	Illinois	1.6
7	New Hampshire	1.6
10	Minnesota	1.4
11	Colorado	1.3
11	Iowa	1.3
11	Virginia	1.3
14	North Dakota	1.2
15	California	1.1
15	Hawaii	1.1
15	Nebraska	1.1
15	Pennsylvania	1.1
15	Washington	1.1
20	Florida	1.0
20	Michigan	1.0
22	Arizona	0.9
22	Georgia	0.9
22	Idaho	0.9
22	Indiana	0.9
22	Ohio	0.9
22	Oregon	0.9
22	Vermont	0.9
29	Kansas	0.8
29	Kentucky	0.8
29	Nevada	0.8
29	North Carolina	0.8
29	South Carolina	0.8
29	Wisconsin	0.8
35	Missouri	0.7
35	South Dakota	0.7
35	Texas	0.7
38	Montana	0.6
38	Tennessee	0.6
38	Utah	0.6
38	West Virginia	0.6
42	Alaska	0.5
42	Mississippi	0.5
42	Oklahoma	0.5
45	Louisiana	0.4
45	Maine	0.4
45	New Mexico	0.4
45	Wyoming	0.4
49	Alabama	0.3
50	Arkansas	0.2

District of Columbia 2.2

Source: Morgan Quitno Press using data from US Dept of Health & Human Serv's, Centers for Disease Control-Prevention
"Assisted Reproductive Technology, 2003" (Morbidity and Mortality Weekly Report, Vol. 55, No. SS-04, 05/26/06)
"National Vital Statistics Reports" (Vol. 54, No. 2, September 8, 2005)
*By patient's residence. Does not include births or procedures to patients with residences outside the U.S. Assisted reproductive technology (ART) includes treatments in which both eggs and sperm are handled in the laboratory (i.e. in vitro fertilization and related procedures).

Percent of Assisted Reproductive Technology Procedure Infants Born in Multiple Birth Deliveries in 2003
National Percent = 51.3% of Assisted Reproductive Technology Births*

ALPHA ORDER

RANK	STATE	PERCENT
23	Alabama	52.9
6	Alaska	57.7
2	Arizona	58.8
33	Arkansas	50.8
30	California	51.6
12	Colorado	55.0
45	Connecticut	48.3
19	Delaware	53.6
32	Florida	51.0
25	Georgia	52.7
23	Hawaii	52.9
11	Idaho	55.1
39	Illinois	50.1
14	Indiana	54.8
26	Iowa	52.6
37	Kansas	50.4
8	Kentucky	56.2
4	Louisiana	58.0
27	Maine	52.5
46	Maryland	47.6
50	Massachusetts	44.5
13	Michigan	54.9
48	Minnesota	46.1
9	Mississippi	55.8
44	Missouri	48.8
16	Montana	54.2
20	Nebraska	53.4
17	Nevada	54.0
49	New Hampshire	46.0
33	New Jersey	50.8
40	New Mexico	50.0
35	New York	50.5
20	North Carolina	53.4
5	North Dakota	57.9
29	Ohio	51.8
22	Oklahoma	53.2
1	Oregon	59.3
41	Pennsylvania	49.7
35	Rhode Island	50.5
38	South Carolina	50.3
7	South Dakota	57.5
3	Tennessee	58.2
15	Texas	54.7
27	Utah	52.5
47	Vermont	47.4
41	Virginia	49.7
43	Washington	49.0
30	West Virginia	51.6
18	Wisconsin	53.7
10	Wyoming	55.2

RANK ORDER

RANK	STATE	PERCENT
1	Oregon	59.3
2	Arizona	58.8
3	Tennessee	58.2
4	Louisiana	58.0
5	North Dakota	57.9
6	Alaska	57.7
7	South Dakota	57.5
8	Kentucky	56.2
9	Mississippi	55.8
10	Wyoming	55.2
11	Idaho	55.1
12	Colorado	55.0
13	Michigan	54.9
14	Indiana	54.8
15	Texas	54.7
16	Montana	54.2
17	Nevada	54.0
18	Wisconsin	53.7
19	Delaware	53.6
20	Nebraska	53.4
20	North Carolina	53.4
22	Oklahoma	53.2
23	Alabama	52.9
23	Hawaii	52.9
25	Georgia	52.7
26	Iowa	52.6
27	Maine	52.5
27	Utah	52.5
29	Ohio	51.8
30	California	51.6
30	West Virginia	51.6
32	Florida	51.0
33	Arkansas	50.8
33	New Jersey	50.8
35	New York	50.5
35	Rhode Island	50.5
37	Kansas	50.4
38	South Carolina	50.3
39	Illinois	50.1
40	New Mexico	50.0
41	Pennsylvania	49.7
41	Virginia	49.7
43	Washington	49.0
44	Missouri	48.8
45	Connecticut	48.3
46	Maryland	47.6
47	Vermont	47.4
48	Minnesota	46.1
49	New Hampshire	46.0
50	Massachusetts	44.5

District of Columbia   46.8

Source: U.S. Department of Health and Human Services, Centers for Disease Control and Prevention
    "Assisted Reproductive Technology, 2003" (Morbidity and Mortality Weekly Report, Vol. 55, No. SS-04, 05/26/06)
*By patient's residence. Includes births and procedures to patients with residences outside the U.S. Assisted reproductive technology (ART) includes treatments in which both eggs and sperm are handled in the laboratory (i.e. in vitro fertilization and related procedures).

Percent of Mothers Beginning Prenatal Care in First Trimester in 2004

National Percent = 83.9% of Mothers*

ALPHA ORDER

RANK	STATE	PERCENT
22	Alabama	84.0
32	Alaska	80.7
39	Arizona	76.3
27	Arkansas	82.3
9	California	87.1
34	Colorado	80.2
8	Connecticut	87.2
20	Delaware	85.1
NA	Florida**	NA
24	Georgia	83.9
29	Hawaii	81.8
NA	Idaho**	NA
16	Illinois	85.5
31	Indiana	80.8
5	Iowa	88.4
10	Kansas	86.5
NA	Kentucky**	NA
16	Louisiana	85.5
4	Maine	88.5
27	Maryland	82.3
3	Massachusetts	89.6
13	Michigan	85.9
11	Minnesota	86.3
21	Mississippi	84.4
6	Missouri	88.2
25	Montana	83.2
26	Nebraska	82.9
40	Nevada	75.0
NA	New Hampshire**	NA
36	New Jersey	79.1
41	New Mexico	69.4
NA	New York**	NA
22	North Carolina	84.0
14	North Dakota	85.7
7	Ohio	87.8
37	Oklahoma	78.1
33	Oregon	80.5
NA	Pennsylvania**	NA
1	Rhode Island	90.0
NA	South Carolina**	NA
38	South Dakota	77.9
NA	Tennessee**	NA
29	Texas	81.8
35	Utah	80.0
1	Vermont	90.0
15	Virginia	85.6
NA	Washington**	NA
12	West Virginia	86.0
18	Wisconsin	85.3
19	Wyoming	85.2

RANK ORDER

RANK	STATE	PERCENT
1	Rhode Island	90.0
1	Vermont	90.0
3	Massachusetts	89.6
4	Maine	88.5
5	Iowa	88.4
6	Missouri	88.2
7	Ohio	87.8
8	Connecticut	87.2
9	California	87.1
10	Kansas	86.5
11	Minnesota	86.3
12	West Virginia	86.0
13	Michigan	85.9
14	North Dakota	85.7
15	Virginia	85.6
16	Illinois	85.5
16	Louisiana	85.5
18	Wisconsin	85.3
19	Wyoming	85.2
20	Delaware	85.1
21	Mississippi	84.4
22	Alabama	84.0
22	North Carolina	84.0
24	Georgia	83.9
25	Montana	83.2
26	Nebraska	82.9
27	Arkansas	82.3
27	Maryland	82.3
29	Hawaii	81.8
29	Texas	81.8
31	Indiana	80.8
32	Alaska	80.7
33	Oregon	80.5
34	Colorado	80.2
35	Utah	80.0
36	New Jersey	79.1
37	Oklahoma	78.1
38	South Dakota	77.9
39	Arizona	76.3
40	Nevada	75.0
41	New Mexico	69.4
NA	Florida**	NA
NA	Idaho**	NA
NA	Kentucky**	NA
NA	New Hampshire**	NA
NA	New York**	NA
NA	Pennsylvania**	NA
NA	South Carolina**	NA
NA	Tennessee**	NA
NA	Washington**	NA

District of Columbia   77.8

Source: U.S. Department of Health and Human Services, National Center for Health Statistics
"National Vital Statistics Reports" (Vol. 55, No. 1, September 29, 2006)
*Final data by state of residence.
**Not available.

Percent of White Mothers Beginning Prenatal Care in First Trimester in 2004

National Percent = 88.9% of White Mothers*

ALPHA ORDER

RANK	STATE	PERCENT
15	Alabama	90.1
32	Alaska	85.4
26	Arizona	87.2
32	Arkansas	85.4
6	California	90.7
30	Colorado	86.2
2	Connecticut	92.3
16	Delaware	90.0
NA	Florida**	NA
12	Georgia	90.3
34	Hawaii	85.2
NA	Idaho**	NA
5	Illinois	90.8
35	Indiana	84.3
16	Iowa	90.0
19	Kansas	89.8
NA	Kentucky**	NA
4	Louisiana	91.5
21	Maine	88.9
13	Maryland	90.2
3	Massachusetts	92.2
19	Michigan	89.8
9	Minnesota	90.4
7	Mississippi	90.6
13	Missouri	90.2
28	Montana	86.4
31	Nebraska	86.0
37	Nevada	83.8
NA	New Hampshire**	NA
24	New Jersey	88.4
41	New Mexico	76.5
NA	New York**	NA
9	North Carolina	90.4
22	North Dakota	88.7
18	Ohio	89.9
40	Oklahoma	82.3
36	Oregon	84.0
NA	Pennsylvania**	NA
1	Rhode Island	92.5
NA	South Carolina**	NA
39	South Dakota	83.4
NA	Tennessee**	NA
25	Texas	88.2
38	Utah	83.7
9	Vermont	90.4
8	Virginia	90.5
NA	Washington**	NA
28	West Virginia	86.4
22	Wisconsin	88.7
27	Wyoming	87.0

RANK ORDER

RANK	STATE	PERCENT
1	Rhode Island	92.5
2	Connecticut	92.3
3	Massachusetts	92.2
4	Louisiana	91.5
5	Illinois	90.8
6	California	90.7
7	Mississippi	90.6
8	Virginia	90.5
9	Minnesota	90.4
9	North Carolina	90.4
9	Vermont	90.4
12	Georgia	90.3
13	Maryland	90.2
13	Missouri	90.2
15	Alabama	90.1
16	Delaware	90.0
16	Iowa	90.0
18	Ohio	89.9
19	Kansas	89.8
19	Michigan	89.8
21	Maine	88.9
22	North Dakota	88.7
22	Wisconsin	88.7
24	New Jersey	88.4
25	Texas	88.2
26	Arizona	87.2
27	Wyoming	87.0
28	Montana	86.4
28	West Virginia	86.4
30	Colorado	86.2
31	Nebraska	86.0
32	Alaska	85.4
32	Arkansas	85.4
34	Hawaii	85.2
35	Indiana	84.3
36	Oregon	84.0
37	Nevada	83.8
38	Utah	83.7
39	South Dakota	83.4
40	Oklahoma	82.3
41	New Mexico	76.5
NA	Florida**	NA
NA	Idaho**	NA
NA	Kentucky**	NA
NA	New Hampshire**	NA
NA	New York**	NA
NA	Pennsylvania**	NA
NA	South Carolina**	NA
NA	Tennessee**	NA
NA	Washington**	NA

District of Columbia 91.8

Source: U.S. Department of Health and Human Services, National Center for Health Statistics
"National Vital Statistics Reports" (Vol. 55, No. 1, September 29, 2006)
*Final data by state of residence.
**Not available.

Percent of Black Mothers Beginning Prenatal Care in First Trimester in 2004

National Percent = 76.5% of Black Mothers*

ALPHA ORDER

RANK ORDER

RANK	STATE	PERCENT	RANK	STATE	PERCENT
21	Alabama	77.2	1	Montana	93.6
3	Alaska	85.2	2	Hawaii	87.4
17	Arizona	77.8	3	Alaska	85.2
26	Arkansas	76.1	4	California	83.5
4	California	83.5	5	Wyoming	83.3
33	Colorado	72.0	6	Rhode Island	82.4
19	Connecticut	77.4	7	Delaware	81.7
7	Delaware	81.7	8	North Dakota	81.1
NA	Florida**	NA	9	Massachusetts	80.4
12	Georgia	79.4	9	Missouri	80.4
2	Hawaii	87.4	11	Maine	80.2
NA	Idaho**	NA	12	Georgia	79.4
28	Illinois	74.2	13	Virginia	79.0
37	Indiana	68.5	14	Ohio	78.6
24	Iowa	76.3	15	Texas	78.4
16	Kansas	78.3	16	Kansas	78.3
NA	Kentucky**	NA	17	Arizona	77.8
19	Louisiana	77.4	18	Mississippi	77.6
11	Maine	80.2	19	Connecticut	77.4
27	Maryland	74.7	19	Louisiana	77.4
9	Massachusetts	80.4	21	Alabama	77.2
34	Michigan	71.9	22	Wisconsin	76.9
29	Minnesota	74.0	23	North Carolina	76.5
18	Mississippi	77.6	24	Iowa	76.3
9	Missouri	80.4	25	West Virginia	76.2
1	Montana	93.6	26	Arkansas	76.1
31	Nebraska	72.5	27	Maryland	74.7
36	Nevada	68.8	28	Illinois	74.2
NA	New Hampshire**	NA	29	Minnesota	74.0
40	New Jersey	63.3	30	Oregon	73.6
38	New Mexico	66.9	31	Nebraska	72.5
NA	New York**	NA	32	Oklahoma	72.2
23	North Carolina	76.5	33	Colorado	72.0
8	North Dakota	81.1	34	Michigan	71.9
14	Ohio	78.6	35	Vermont	71.7
32	Oklahoma	72.2	36	Nevada	68.8
30	Oregon	73.6	37	Indiana	68.5
NA	Pennsylvania**	NA	38	New Mexico	66.9
6	Rhode Island	82.4	39	South Dakota	63.6
NA	South Carolina**	NA	40	New Jersey	63.3
39	South Dakota	63.6	41	Utah	60.5
NA	Tennessee**	NA	NA	Florida**	NA
15	Texas	78.4	NA	Idaho**	NA
41	Utah	60.5	NA	Kentucky**	NA
35	Vermont	71.7	NA	New Hampshire**	NA
13	Virginia	79.0	NA	New York**	NA
NA	Washington**	NA	NA	Pennsylvania**	NA
25	West Virginia	76.2	NA	South Carolina**	NA
22	Wisconsin	76.9	NA	Tennessee**	NA
5	Wyoming	83.3	NA	Washington**	NA
				District of Columbia	72.8

Source: U.S. Department of Health and Human Services, National Center for Health Statistics
   "National Vital Statistics Reports" (Vol. 55, No. 1, September 29, 2006)
*Final data by state of residence.
**Not available.

Percent of Hispanic Mothers Beginning Prenatal Care in First Trimester in 2004

National Percent = 77.5% of Hispanic Mothers*

<table>
<thead>
<tr><th colspan="3">ALPHA ORDER</th><th colspan="3">RANK ORDER</th></tr>
<tr><th>RANK</th><th>STATE</th><th>PERCENT</th><th>RANK</th><th>STATE</th><th>PERCENT</th></tr>
</thead>
<tbody>
<tr><td>41</td><td>Alabama</td><td>53.4</td><td>1</td><td>Rhode Island</td><td>87.5</td></tr>
<tr><td>13</td><td>Alaska</td><td>78.1</td><td>2</td><td>California</td><td>85.0</td></tr>
<tr><td>33</td><td>Arizona</td><td>67.1</td><td>3</td><td>Louisiana</td><td>84.3</td></tr>
<tr><td>24</td><td>Arkansas</td><td>71.7</td><td>4</td><td>Massachusetts</td><td>82.3</td></tr>
<tr><td>2</td><td>California</td><td>85.0</td><td>5</td><td>Illinois</td><td>80.3</td></tr>
<tr><td>29</td><td>Colorado</td><td>69.7</td><td>6</td><td>Hawaii</td><td>80.2</td></tr>
<tr><td>20</td><td>Connecticut</td><td>75.6</td><td>6</td><td>Montana</td><td>80.2</td></tr>
<tr><td>30</td><td>Delaware</td><td>69.5</td><td>8</td><td>Missouri</td><td>80.0</td></tr>
<tr><td>NA</td><td>Florida**</td><td>NA</td><td>9</td><td>Wyoming</td><td>79.3</td></tr>
<tr><td>26</td><td>Georgia</td><td>70.6</td><td>10</td><td>Ohio</td><td>79.0</td></tr>
<tr><td>6</td><td>Hawaii</td><td>80.2</td><td>11</td><td>North Dakota</td><td>78.8</td></tr>
<tr><td>NA</td><td>Idaho**</td><td>NA</td><td>12</td><td>Michigan</td><td>78.6</td></tr>
<tr><td>5</td><td>Illinois</td><td>80.3</td><td>13</td><td>Alaska</td><td>78.1</td></tr>
<tr><td>40</td><td>Indiana</td><td>62.6</td><td>14</td><td>Maine</td><td>77.8</td></tr>
<tr><td>19</td><td>Iowa</td><td>76.6</td><td>15</td><td>Mississippi</td><td>77.6</td></tr>
<tr><td>21</td><td>Kansas</td><td>72.7</td><td>16</td><td>Texas</td><td>77.3</td></tr>
<tr><td>NA</td><td>Kentucky**</td><td>NA</td><td>17</td><td>West Virginia</td><td>77.2</td></tr>
<tr><td>3</td><td>Louisiana</td><td>84.3</td><td>18</td><td>Vermont</td><td>76.8</td></tr>
<tr><td>14</td><td>Maine</td><td>77.8</td><td>19</td><td>Iowa</td><td>76.6</td></tr>
<tr><td>38</td><td>Maryland</td><td>64.1</td><td>20</td><td>Connecticut</td><td>75.6</td></tr>
<tr><td>4</td><td>Massachusetts</td><td>82.3</td><td>21</td><td>Kansas</td><td>72.7</td></tr>
<tr><td>12</td><td>Michigan</td><td>78.6</td><td>22</td><td>Wisconsin</td><td>72.0</td></tr>
<tr><td>27</td><td>Minnesota</td><td>69.9</td><td>23</td><td>Virginia</td><td>71.8</td></tr>
<tr><td>15</td><td>Mississippi</td><td>77.6</td><td>24</td><td>Arkansas</td><td>71.7</td></tr>
<tr><td>8</td><td>Missouri</td><td>80.0</td><td>25</td><td>Nebraska</td><td>70.9</td></tr>
<tr><td>6</td><td>Montana</td><td>80.2</td><td>26</td><td>Georgia</td><td>70.6</td></tr>
<tr><td>25</td><td>Nebraska</td><td>70.9</td><td>27</td><td>Minnesota</td><td>69.9</td></tr>
<tr><td>35</td><td>Nevada</td><td>64.6</td><td>27</td><td>North Carolina</td><td>69.9</td></tr>
<tr><td>NA</td><td>New Hampshire**</td><td>NA</td><td>29</td><td>Colorado</td><td>69.7</td></tr>
<tr><td>34</td><td>New Jersey</td><td>66.5</td><td>30</td><td>Delaware</td><td>69.5</td></tr>
<tr><td>32</td><td>New Mexico</td><td>67.6</td><td>31</td><td>Oregon</td><td>69.3</td></tr>
<tr><td>NA</td><td>New York**</td><td>NA</td><td>32</td><td>New Mexico</td><td>67.6</td></tr>
<tr><td>27</td><td>North Carolina</td><td>69.9</td><td>33</td><td>Arizona</td><td>67.1</td></tr>
<tr><td>11</td><td>North Dakota</td><td>78.8</td><td>34</td><td>New Jersey</td><td>66.5</td></tr>
<tr><td>10</td><td>Ohio</td><td>79.0</td><td>35</td><td>Nevada</td><td>64.6</td></tr>
<tr><td>35</td><td>Oklahoma</td><td>64.6</td><td>35</td><td>Oklahoma</td><td>64.6</td></tr>
<tr><td>31</td><td>Oregon</td><td>69.3</td><td>35</td><td>Utah</td><td>64.6</td></tr>
<tr><td>NA</td><td>Pennsylvania**</td><td>NA</td><td>38</td><td>Maryland</td><td>64.1</td></tr>
<tr><td>1</td><td>Rhode Island</td><td>87.5</td><td>39</td><td>South Dakota</td><td>63.2</td></tr>
<tr><td>NA</td><td>South Carolina**</td><td>NA</td><td>40</td><td>Indiana</td><td>62.6</td></tr>
<tr><td>39</td><td>South Dakota</td><td>63.2</td><td>41</td><td>Alabama</td><td>53.4</td></tr>
<tr><td>NA</td><td>Tennessee**</td><td>NA</td><td>NA</td><td>Florida**</td><td>NA</td></tr>
<tr><td>16</td><td>Texas</td><td>77.3</td><td>NA</td><td>Idaho**</td><td>NA</td></tr>
<tr><td>35</td><td>Utah</td><td>64.6</td><td>NA</td><td>Kentucky**</td><td>NA</td></tr>
<tr><td>18</td><td>Vermont</td><td>76.8</td><td>NA</td><td>New Hampshire**</td><td>NA</td></tr>
<tr><td>23</td><td>Virginia</td><td>71.8</td><td>NA</td><td>New York**</td><td>NA</td></tr>
<tr><td>NA</td><td>Washington**</td><td>NA</td><td>NA</td><td>Pennsylvania**</td><td>NA</td></tr>
<tr><td>17</td><td>West Virginia</td><td>77.2</td><td>NA</td><td>South Carolina**</td><td>NA</td></tr>
<tr><td>22</td><td>Wisconsin</td><td>72.0</td><td>NA</td><td>Tennessee**</td><td>NA</td></tr>
<tr><td>9</td><td>Wyoming</td><td>79.3</td><td>NA</td><td>Washington**</td><td>NA</td></tr>
</tbody>
</table>

District of Columbia   68.6

Source: U.S. Department of Health and Human Services, National Center for Health Statistics
   "National Vital Statistics Reports" (Vol. 55, No. 1, September 29, 2006)
*Final data by state of residence. Persons of Hispanic origin may be of any race.
**Not available.

Percent of Mothers Receiving Late or No Prenatal Care in 2004

National Percent = 3.6% of Mothers*

<u>ALPHA ORDER</u>

RANK	STATE	PERCENT
16	Alabama	3.7
6	Alaska	4.5
2	Arizona	7.5
10	Arkansas	4.4
30	California	2.6
6	Colorado	4.5
38	Connecticut	1.9
18	Delaware	3.6
NA	Florida**	NA
12	Georgia	4.0
16	Hawaii	3.7
NA	Idaho**	NA
28	Illinois	2.7
12	Indiana	4.0
35	Iowa	2.2
30	Kansas	2.6
NA	Kentucky**	NA
23	Louisiana	2.9
39	Maine	1.6
15	Maryland	3.9
35	Massachusetts	2.2
22	Michigan	3.0
33	Minnesota	2.3
28	Mississippi	2.7
33	Missouri	2.3
23	Montana	2.9
20	Nebraska	3.3
3	Nevada	7.3
NA	New Hampshire**	NA
4	New Jersey	4.7
1	New Mexico	8.3
NA	New York**	NA
23	North Carolina	2.9
27	North Dakota	2.8
32	Ohio	2.4
4	Oklahoma	4.7
11	Oregon	4.1
NA	Pennsylvania**	NA
40	Rhode Island	1.5
NA	South Carolina**	NA
12	South Dakota	4.0
NA	Tennessee**	NA
6	Texas	4.5
6	Utah	4.5
40	Vermont	1.5
19	Virginia	3.4
NA	Washington**	NA
37	West Virginia	2.1
23	Wisconsin	2.9
21	Wyoming	3.1

<u>RANK ORDER</u>

RANK	STATE	PERCENT
1	New Mexico	8.3
2	Arizona	7.5
3	Nevada	7.3
4	New Jersey	4.7
4	Oklahoma	4.7
6	Alaska	4.5
6	Colorado	4.5
6	Texas	4.5
6	Utah	4.5
10	Arkansas	4.4
11	Oregon	4.1
12	Georgia	4.0
12	Indiana	4.0
12	South Dakota	4.0
15	Maryland	3.9
16	Alabama	3.7
16	Hawaii	3.7
18	Delaware	3.6
19	Virginia	3.4
20	Nebraska	3.3
21	Wyoming	3.1
22	Michigan	3.0
23	Louisiana	2.9
23	Montana	2.9
23	North Carolina	2.9
23	Wisconsin	2.9
27	North Dakota	2.8
28	Illinois	2.7
28	Mississippi	2.7
30	California	2.6
30	Kansas	2.6
32	Ohio	2.4
33	Minnesota	2.3
33	Missouri	2.3
35	Iowa	2.2
35	Massachusetts	2.2
37	West Virginia	2.1
38	Connecticut	1.9
39	Maine	1.6
40	Rhode Island	1.5
40	Vermont	1.5
NA	Florida**	NA
NA	Idaho**	NA
NA	Kentucky**	NA
NA	New Hampshire**	NA
NA	New York**	NA
NA	Pennsylvania**	NA
NA	South Carolina**	NA
NA	Tennessee**	NA
NA	Washington**	NA
	District of Columbia	6.0

*Source: U.S. Department of Health and Human Services, National Center for Health Statistics
"National Vital Statistics Reports" (Vol. 55, No. 1, September 29, 2006)*
Final data by state of residence. "Late" means care begun in third trimester.
**Not available.*

Percent of White Mothers Receiving Late or No Prenatal Care in 2004

National Percent = 2.2% of White Mothers*

ALPHA ORDER

RANK ORDER

RANK	STATE	PERCENT	RANK	STATE	PERCENT
31	Alabama	1.7	1	New Mexico	5.5
4	Alaska	3.5	2	Nevada	4.3
8	Arizona	3.1	3	Oklahoma	3.7
7	Arkansas	3.2	4	Alaska	3.5
21	California	1.9	5	Utah	3.4
11	Colorado	2.8	6	Oregon	3.3
40	Connecticut	1.2	7	Arkansas	3.2
18	Delaware	2.0	8	Arizona	3.1
NA	Florida**	NA	9	Hawaii	3.0
15	Georgia	2.3	10	Indiana	2.9
9	Hawaii	3.0	11	Colorado	2.8
NA	Idaho**	NA	12	Texas	2.6
33	Illinois	1.5	12	Wyoming	2.6
10	Indiana	2.9	14	Nebraska	2.5
21	Iowa	1.9	15	Georgia	2.3
29	Kansas	1.8	15	New Jersey	2.3
NA	Kentucky**	NA	15	Wisconsin	2.3
36	Louisiana	1.4	18	Delaware	2.0
32	Maine	1.6	18	Michigan	2.0
21	Maryland	1.9	18	West Virginia	2.0
33	Massachusetts	1.5	21	California	1.9
18	Michigan	2.0	21	Iowa	1.9
36	Minnesota	1.4	21	Maryland	1.9
36	Mississippi	1.4	21	Montana	1.9
29	Missouri	1.8	21	North Dakota	1.9
21	Montana	1.9	21	Ohio	1.9
14	Nebraska	2.5	21	South Dakota	1.9
2	Nevada	4.3	21	Virginia	1.9
NA	New Hampshire**	NA	29	Kansas	1.8
15	New Jersey	2.3	29	Missouri	1.8
1	New Mexico	5.5	31	Alabama	1.7
NA	New York**	NA	32	Maine	1.6
33	North Carolina	1.5	33	Illinois	1.5
21	North Dakota	1.9	33	Massachusetts	1.5
21	Ohio	1.9	33	North Carolina	1.5
3	Oklahoma	3.7	36	Louisiana	1.4
6	Oregon	3.3	36	Minnesota	1.4
NA	Pennsylvania**	NA	36	Mississippi	1.4
41	Rhode Island	1.0	36	Vermont	1.4
NA	South Carolina**	NA	40	Connecticut	1.2
21	South Dakota	1.9	41	Rhode Island	1.0
NA	Tennessee**	NA	NA	Florida**	NA
12	Texas	2.6	NA	Idaho**	NA
5	Utah	3.4	NA	Kentucky**	NA
36	Vermont	1.4	NA	New Hampshire**	NA
21	Virginia	1.9	NA	New York**	NA
NA	Washington**	NA	NA	Pennsylvania**	NA
18	West Virginia	2.0	NA	South Carolina**	NA
15	Wisconsin	2.3	NA	Tennessee**	NA
12	Wyoming	2.6	NA	Washington**	NA

District of Columbia 2.2

Source: U.S. Department of Health and Human Services, National Center for Health Statistics
    "National Vital Statistics Reports" (Vol. 55, No. 1, September 29, 2006)
*Final data by state of residence. "Late" means care begun in third trimester.
**Not available.

Percent of Black Mothers Receiving Late or No Prenatal Care in 2004

National Percent = 5.7% of Black Mothers*

ALPHA ORDER

RANK	STATE	PERCENT
28	Alabama	4.5
NA	Alaska**	NA
7	Arizona	6.9
7	Arkansas	6.9
32	California	3.5
9	Colorado	6.8
28	Connecticut	4.5
30	Delaware	4.3
NA	Florida**	NA
21	Georgia	5.0
NA	Hawaii**	NA
NA	Idaho**	NA
13	Illinois	6.3
4	Indiana	7.6
16	Iowa	5.3
25	Kansas	4.8
NA	Kentucky**	NA
21	Louisiana	5.0
NA	Maine**	NA
11	Maryland	6.4
15	Massachusetts	5.5
5	Michigan	7.1
19	Minnesota	5.2
31	Mississippi	4.0
25	Missouri	4.8
NA	Montana**	NA
14	Nebraska	5.8
2	Nevada	10.6
NA	New Hampshire**	NA
2	New Jersey	10.6
5	New Mexico	7.1
NA	New York**	NA
27	North Carolina	4.7
NA	North Dakota**	NA
24	Ohio	4.9
11	Oklahoma	6.4
9	Oregon	6.8
NA	Pennsylvania**	NA
33	Rhode Island	3.3
NA	South Carolina**	NA
NA	South Dakota**	NA
NA	Tennessee**	NA
16	Texas	5.3
1	Utah	17.3
NA	Vermont**	NA
21	Virginia	5.0
NA	Washington**	NA
16	West Virginia	5.3
20	Wisconsin	5.1
NA	Wyoming**	NA

RANK ORDER

RANK	STATE	PERCENT
1	Utah	17.3
2	Nevada	10.6
2	New Jersey	10.6
4	Indiana	7.6
5	Michigan	7.1
5	New Mexico	7.1
7	Arizona	6.9
7	Arkansas	6.9
9	Colorado	6.8
9	Oregon	6.8
11	Maryland	6.4
11	Oklahoma	6.4
13	Illinois	6.3
14	Nebraska	5.8
15	Massachusetts	5.5
16	Iowa	5.3
16	Texas	5.3
16	West Virginia	5.3
19	Minnesota	5.2
20	Wisconsin	5.1
21	Georgia	5.0
21	Louisiana	5.0
21	Virginia	5.0
24	Ohio	4.9
25	Kansas	4.8
25	Missouri	4.8
27	North Carolina	4.7
28	Alabama	4.5
28	Connecticut	4.5
30	Delaware	4.3
31	Mississippi	4.0
32	California	3.5
33	Rhode Island	3.3
NA	Alaska**	NA
NA	Florida**	NA
NA	Hawaii**	NA
NA	Idaho**	NA
NA	Kentucky**	NA
NA	Maine**	NA
NA	Montana**	NA
NA	New Hampshire**	NA
NA	New York**	NA
NA	North Dakota**	NA
NA	Pennsylvania**	NA
NA	South Carolina**	NA
NA	South Dakota**	NA
NA	Tennessee**	NA
NA	Vermont**	NA
NA	Washington**	NA
NA	Wyoming**	NA

District of Columbia   8.0

Source: U.S. Department of Health and Human Services, National Center for Health Statistics
"National Vital Statistics Reports" (Vol. 55, No. 1, September 29, 2006)
*Final data by state of residence. "Late" means care begun in third trimester.
**Insufficient data or not available.

Percent of Hispanic Mothers Receiving Late or No Prenatal Care in 2004

National Percent = 5.4% of Hispanic Mothers*

ALPHA ORDER

RANK	STATE	PERCENT
1	Alabama	21.2
21	Alaska	5.7
2	Arizona	11.1
10	Arkansas	8.3
31	California	3.1
12	Colorado	7.3
31	Connecticut	3.1
4	Delaware	9.9
NA	Florida**	NA
8	Georgia	8.6
35	Hawaii	3.0
NA	Idaho**	NA
31	Illinois	3.1
7	Indiana	8.9
25	Iowa	4.4
20	Kansas	5.8
NA	Kentucky**	NA
31	Louisiana	3.1
NA	Maine**	NA
14	Maryland	7.2
29	Massachusetts	3.6
25	Michigan	4.4
23	Minnesota	5.2
11	Mississippi	7.4
30	Missouri	3.3
NA	Montana**	NA
17	Nebraska	6.5
3	Nevada	10.5
NA	New Hampshire**	NA
16	New Jersey	6.9
6	New Mexico	9.1
NA	New York**	NA
22	North Carolina	5.6
NA	North Dakota**	NA
27	Ohio	4.2
14	Oklahoma	7.2
18	Oregon	6.2
NA	Pennsylvania**	NA
36	Rhode Island	2.1
NA	South Carolina**	NA
5	South Dakota	9.6
NA	Tennessee**	NA
19	Texas	5.9
9	Utah	8.5
NA	Vermont**	NA
12	Virginia	7.3
NA	Washington**	NA
NA	West Virginia**	NA
24	Wisconsin	5.1
27	Wyoming	4.2

RANK ORDER

RANK	STATE	PERCENT
1	Alabama	21.2
2	Arizona	11.1
3	Nevada	10.5
4	Delaware	9.9
5	South Dakota	9.6
6	New Mexico	9.1
7	Indiana	8.9
8	Georgia	8.6
9	Utah	8.5
10	Arkansas	8.3
11	Mississippi	7.4
12	Colorado	7.3
12	Virginia	7.3
14	Maryland	7.2
14	Oklahoma	7.2
16	New Jersey	6.9
17	Nebraska	6.5
18	Oregon	6.2
19	Texas	5.9
20	Kansas	5.8
21	Alaska	5.7
22	North Carolina	5.6
23	Minnesota	5.2
24	Wisconsin	5.1
25	Iowa	4.4
25	Michigan	4.4
27	Ohio	4.2
27	Wyoming	4.2
29	Massachusetts	3.6
30	Missouri	3.3
31	California	3.1
31	Connecticut	3.1
31	Illinois	3.1
31	Louisiana	3.1
35	Hawaii	3.0
36	Rhode Island	2.1
NA	Florida**	NA
NA	Idaho**	NA
NA	Kentucky**	NA
NA	Maine**	NA
NA	Montana**	NA
NA	New Hampshire**	NA
NA	New York**	NA
NA	North Dakota**	NA
NA	Pennsylvania**	NA
NA	South Carolina**	NA
NA	Tennessee**	NA
NA	Vermont**	NA
NA	Washington**	NA
NA	West Virginia**	NA

District of Columbia   5.9

Source: U.S. Department of Health and Human Services, National Center for Health Statistics
"National Vital Statistics Reports" (Vol. 55, No. 1, September 29, 2006)
*Final data by state of residence. "Late" means care begun in third trimester.
**Insufficient data or not available.*

Reported Legal Abortions in 2003

Reporting States' Total = 848,163 Abortions*

ALPHA ORDER

RANK ORDER

RANK	STATE	ABORTIONS	% of USA		RANK	STATE	ABORTIONS	% of USA
21	Alabama	10,979	1.3%		1	New York	124,957	14.7%
42	Alaska	1,806	0.2%		2	Florida	88,247	10.4%
24	Arizona	10,316	1.2%		3	Texas	79,166	9.3%
33	Arkansas	5,408	0.6%		4	Illinois	42,247	5.0%
NA	California**	NA	NA		5	Pennsylvania	36,908	4.4%
25	Colorado	9,852	1.2%		6	Ohio	35,319	4.2%
17	Connecticut	12,404	1.5%		7	Georgia	34,363	4.1%
34	Delaware	4,178	0.5%		8	New Jersey	32,762	3.9%
2	Florida	88,247	10.4%		9	North Carolina	31,006	3.7%
7	Georgia	34,363	4.1%		10	Michigan	29,540	3.5%
38	Hawaii	3,608	0.4%		11	Virginia	26,437	3.1%
45	Idaho	911	0.1%		12	Massachusetts	25,741	3.0%
4	Illinois	42,247	5.0%		13	Washington	25,084	3.0%
20	Indiana	11,458	1.4%		14	Tennessee	17,610	2.1%
30	Iowa	5,916	0.7%		15	Minnesota	14,091	1.7%
18	Kansas	11,600	1.4%		16	Oregon	12,622	1.5%
37	Kentucky	3,621	0.4%		17	Connecticut	12,404	1.5%
22	Louisiana	10,642	1.3%		18	Kansas	11,600	1.4%
40	Maine	2,550	0.3%		19	Maryland	11,485	1.4%
19	Maryland	11,485	1.4%		20	Indiana	11,458	1.4%
12	Massachusetts	25,741	3.0%		21	Alabama	10,979	1.3%
10	Michigan	29,540	3.5%		22	Louisiana	10,642	1.3%
15	Minnesota	14,091	1.7%		23	Wisconsin	10,557	1.2%
36	Mississippi	3,753	0.4%		24	Arizona	10,316	1.2%
27	Missouri	8,350	1.0%		25	Colorado	9,852	1.2%
41	Montana	2,213	0.3%		26	Nevada	9,323	1.1%
35	Nebraska	3,990	0.5%		27	Missouri	8,350	1.0%
26	Nevada	9,323	1.1%		28	Oklahoma	6,644	0.8%
NA	New Hampshire**	NA	NA		29	South Carolina	6,573	0.8%
8	New Jersey	32,762	3.9%		30	Iowa	5,916	0.7%
31	New Mexico	5,832	0.7%		31	New Mexico	5,832	0.7%
1	New York	124,957	14.7%		32	Rhode Island	5,538	0.7%
9	North Carolina	31,006	3.7%		33	Arkansas	5,408	0.6%
44	North Dakota	1,354	0.2%		34	Delaware	4,178	0.5%
6	Ohio	35,319	4.2%		35	Nebraska	3,990	0.5%
28	Oklahoma	6,644	0.8%		36	Mississippi	3,753	0.4%
16	Oregon	12,622	1.5%		37	Kentucky	3,621	0.4%
5	Pennsylvania	36,908	4.4%		38	Hawaii	3,608	0.4%
32	Rhode Island	5,538	0.7%		39	Utah	3,576	0.4%
29	South Carolina	6,573	0.8%		40	Maine	2,550	0.3%
46	South Dakota	819	0.1%		41	Montana	2,213	0.3%
14	Tennessee	17,610	2.1%		42	Alaska	1,806	0.2%
3	Texas	79,166	9.3%		43	Vermont	1,679	0.2%
39	Utah	3,576	0.4%		44	North Dakota	1,354	0.2%
43	Vermont	1,679	0.2%		45	Idaho	911	0.1%
11	Virginia	26,437	3.1%		46	South Dakota	819	0.1%
13	Washington	25,084	3.0%		47	Wyoming	7	0.0%
NA	West Virginia**	NA	NA		NA	California**	NA	NA
23	Wisconsin	10,557	1.2%		NA	New Hampshire**	NA	NA
47	Wyoming	7	0.0%		NA	West Virginia**	NA	NA
						District of Columbia	5,121	0.6%

Source: U.S. Department of Health and Human Services, Centers for Disease Control and Prevention
  "Abortion Surveillance-United States, 2003" (Morbidity and Mortality Weekly Report, Vol. 55, No. SS-11, 11/24/06)
*By state of occurrence. Total is for reporting states only.
**Not reported.

Percent Change in Reported Legal Abortions: 1999 to 2003

National Percent Change = 2.6% Decrease*

ALPHA ORDER

RANK	STATE	PERCENT CHANGE
41	Alabama	(17.3)
NA	Alaska**	NA
27	Arizona	(4.2)
31	Arkansas	(6.0)
NA	California**	NA
1	Colorado	96.4
28	Connecticut	(4.3)
43	Delaware	(19.0)
9	Florida	5.1
13	Georgia	3.8
42	Hawaii	(18.1)
9	Idaho	5.1
34	Illinois	(8.0)
30	Indiana	(5.4)
20	Iowa	(3.1)
32	Kansas	(6.4)
44	Kentucky	(33.8)
37	Louisiana	(11.4)
9	Maine	5.1
14	Maryland	2.9
25	Massachusetts	(4.1)
4	Michigan	12.7
18	Minnesota	(1.8)
21	Mississippi	(3.2)
14	Missouri	2.9
37	Montana	(11.4)
39	Nebraska	(12.6)
2	Nevada	60.5
NA	New Hampshire**	NA
33	New Jersey	(6.7)
3	New Mexico	14.4
35	New York	(8.9)
22	North Carolina	(3.4)
16	North Dakota	0.7
29	Ohio	(4.6)
NA	Oklahoma**	NA
36	Oregon	(10.8)
7	Pennsylvania	7.0
5	Rhode Island	10.7
40	South Carolina	(14.5)
5	South Dakota	10.7
12	Tennessee	4.1
19	Texas	(1.9)
8	Utah	5.8
24	Vermont	(3.9)
22	Virginia	(3.4)
17	Washington	(1.7)
NA	West Virginia**	NA
25	Wisconsin	(4.1)
45	Wyoming	(93.6)

RANK ORDER

RANK	STATE	PERCENT CHANGE
1	Colorado	96.4
2	Nevada	60.5
3	New Mexico	14.4
4	Michigan	12.7
5	Rhode Island	10.7
5	South Dakota	10.7
7	Pennsylvania	7.0
8	Utah	5.8
9	Florida	5.1
9	Idaho	5.1
9	Maine	5.1
12	Tennessee	4.1
13	Georgia	3.8
14	Maryland	2.9
14	Missouri	2.9
16	North Dakota	0.7
17	Washington	(1.7)
18	Minnesota	(1.8)
19	Texas	(1.9)
20	Iowa	(3.1)
21	Mississippi	(3.2)
22	North Carolina	(3.4)
22	Virginia	(3.4)
24	Vermont	(3.9)
25	Massachusetts	(4.1)
25	Wisconsin	(4.1)
27	Arizona	(4.2)
28	Connecticut	(4.3)
29	Ohio	(4.6)
30	Indiana	(5.4)
31	Arkansas	(6.0)
32	Kansas	(6.4)
33	New Jersey	(6.7)
34	Illinois	(8.0)
35	New York	(8.9)
36	Oregon	(10.8)
37	Louisiana	(11.4)
37	Montana	(11.4)
39	Nebraska	(12.6)
40	South Carolina	(14.5)
41	Alabama	(17.3)
42	Hawaii	(18.1)
43	Delaware	(19.0)
44	Kentucky	(33.8)
45	Wyoming	(93.6)
NA	Alaska**	NA
NA	California**	NA
NA	New Hampshire**	NA
NA	Oklahoma**	NA
NA	West Virginia**	NA

District of Columbia   (30.5)

Source: Morgan Quitno Press using data from US Dept of Health & Human Serv's, Centers for Disease Control-Prevention
"Abortion Surveillance-United States, 2003" (Morbidity and Mortality Weekly Report, Vol. 55, No. SS-11, 11/24/06)
"Abortion Surveillance-United States, 1999" (Morbidity Mortality Weekly Report, Vol. 51, No. SS-9, 11/29/02)
*By state of occurrence. Percent change is only for states reporting in both years.
**Not reported.

Reported Legal Abortions per 1,000 Live Births in 2003

Reporting States' Ratio = 241 Abortions per 1,000 Live Births*

ALPHA ORDER

RANK	STATE	RATIO
26	Alabama	184
28	Alaska	179
40	Arizona	113
35	Arkansas	143
NA	California**	NA
36	Colorado	142
8	Connecticut	289
4	Delaware	369
3	Florida	416
15	Georgia	253
24	Hawaii	199
46	Idaho	42
18	Illinois	231
37	Indiana	133
31	Iowa	155
7	Kansas	294
45	Kentucky	66
30	Louisiana	164
26	Maine	184
33	Maryland	153
5	Massachusetts	321
19	Michigan	225
23	Minnesota	201
42	Mississippi	89
41	Missouri	108
25	Montana	194
32	Nebraska	154
10	Nevada	277
NA	New Hampshire**	NA
9	New Jersey	280
21	New Mexico	210
1	New York	509
12	North Carolina	262
29	North Dakota	170
17	Ohio	236
38	Oklahoma	130
11	Oregon	275
15	Pennsylvania	253
2	Rhode Island	419
39	South Carolina	118
43	South Dakota	74
20	Tennessee	223
21	Texas	210
44	Utah	72
14	Vermont	255
13	Virginia	261
6	Washington	312
NA	West Virginia**	NA
34	Wisconsin	151
NA	Wyoming**	NA

RANK ORDER

RANK	STATE	RATIO
1	New York	509
2	Rhode Island	419
3	Florida	416
4	Delaware	369
5	Massachusetts	321
6	Washington	312
7	Kansas	294
8	Connecticut	289
9	New Jersey	280
10	Nevada	277
11	Oregon	275
12	North Carolina	262
13	Virginia	261
14	Vermont	255
15	Georgia	253
15	Pennsylvania	253
17	Ohio	236
18	Illinois	231
19	Michigan	225
20	Tennessee	223
21	New Mexico	210
21	Texas	210
23	Minnesota	201
24	Hawaii	199
25	Montana	194
26	Alabama	184
26	Maine	184
28	Alaska	179
29	North Dakota	170
30	Louisiana	164
31	Iowa	155
32	Nebraska	154
33	Maryland	153
34	Wisconsin	151
35	Arkansas	143
36	Colorado	142
37	Indiana	133
38	Oklahoma	130
39	South Carolina	118
40	Arizona	113
41	Missouri	108
42	Mississippi	89
43	South Dakota	74
44	Utah	72
45	Kentucky	66
46	Idaho	42
NA	California**	NA
NA	New Hampshire**	NA
NA	West Virginia**	NA
NA	Wyoming**	NA

District of Columbia   672

Source: U.S. Department of Health and Human Services, Centers for Disease Control and Prevention
   "Abortion Surveillance-United States, 2003" (Morbidity and Mortality Weekly Report, Vol. 55, No. SS-11, 11/24/06)
*By state of occurrence. National figure is for reporting states only.
**Not reported.

Reported Legal Abortions per 1,000 Women Ages 15 to 44 in 2003

Reporting States' Rate = 16 Abortions per 1,000 Women Ages 15 to 44*

ALPHA ORDER

RANK	STATE	RATE
26	Alabama	12
23	Alaska	13
36	Arizona	9
30	Arkansas	10
NA	California**	NA
30	Colorado	10
11	Connecticut	17
3	Delaware	24
2	Florida	26
8	Georgia	18
20	Hawaii	14
46	Idaho	3
15	Illinois	16
36	Indiana	9
30	Iowa	10
5	Kansas	20
45	Kentucky	4
28	Louisiana	11
30	Maine	10
30	Maryland	10
8	Massachusetts	18
20	Michigan	14
23	Minnesota	13
43	Mississippi	6
40	Missouri	7
26	Montana	12
28	Nebraska	11
5	Nevada	20
NA	New Hampshire**	NA
8	New Jersey	18
17	New Mexico	15
1	New York	30
11	North Carolina	17
30	North Dakota	10
17	Ohio	15
36	Oklahoma	9
11	Oregon	17
17	Pennsylvania	15
3	Rhode Island	24
40	South Carolina	7
44	South Dakota	5
20	Tennessee	14
15	Texas	16
40	Utah	7
23	Vermont	13
11	Virginia	17
7	Washington	19
NA	West Virginia**	NA
36	Wisconsin	9
NA	Wyoming**	NA

RANK ORDER

RANK	STATE	RATE
1	New York	30
2	Florida	26
3	Delaware	24
3	Rhode Island	24
5	Kansas	20
5	Nevada	20
7	Washington	19
8	Georgia	18
8	Massachusetts	18
8	New Jersey	18
11	Connecticut	17
11	North Carolina	17
11	Oregon	17
11	Virginia	17
15	Illinois	16
15	Texas	16
17	New Mexico	15
17	Ohio	15
17	Pennsylvania	15
20	Hawaii	14
20	Michigan	14
20	Tennessee	14
23	Alaska	13
23	Minnesota	13
23	Vermont	13
26	Alabama	12
26	Montana	12
28	Louisiana	11
28	Nebraska	11
30	Arkansas	10
30	Colorado	10
30	Iowa	10
30	Maine	10
30	Maryland	10
30	North Dakota	10
36	Arizona	9
36	Indiana	9
36	Oklahoma	9
36	Wisconsin	9
40	Missouri	7
40	South Carolina	7
40	Utah	7
43	Mississippi	6
44	South Dakota	5
45	Kentucky	4
46	Idaho	3
NA	California**	NA
NA	New Hampshire**	NA
NA	West Virginia**	NA
NA	Wyoming**	NA

District of Columbia   36

Source: U.S. Department of Health and Human Services, Centers for Disease Control and Prevention
    "Abortion Surveillance-United States, 2003" (Morbidity and Mortality Weekly Report, Vol. 55, No. SS-11, 11/24/06)
By state of occurrence. National figure is for reporting states only.
Not reported.

Percent of Legal Abortions Obtained by Out-Of-State Residents in 2003

Reporting States' Percent = 8.5% of Abortions*

ALPHA ORDER

RANK	STATE	PERCENT
11	Alabama	15.0
41	Alaska	0.4
40	Arizona	1.6
10	Arkansas	15.3
NA	California**	NA
17	Colorado	9.9
33	Connecticut	3.8
4	Delaware	25.2
NA	Florida**	NA
14	Georgia	12.1
42	Hawaii	0.1
31	Idaho	4.4
20	Illinois	8.3
28	Indiana	4.6
NA	Iowa**	NA
1	Kansas	47.7
12	Kentucky	14.3
NA	Louisiana**	NA
37	Maine	3.0
6	Maryland	18.8
24	Massachusetts	5.3
36	Michigan	3.2
20	Minnesota	8.3
38	Mississippi	2.9
19	Missouri	8.8
16	Montana	10.6
9	Nebraska	15.6
23	Nevada	6.5
NA	New Hampshire**	NA
25	New Jersey	5.1
31	New Mexico	4.4
NA	New York**	NA
8	North Carolina	15.9
2	North Dakota	39.2
18	Ohio	8.9
28	Oklahoma	4.6
15	Oregon	11.6
28	Pennsylvania	4.6
NA	Rhode Island**	NA
34	South Carolina	3.7
7	South Dakota	17.0
5	Tennessee	20.5
35	Texas	3.6
22	Utah	6.7
13	Vermont	14.1
27	Virginia	4.8
25	Washington	5.1
NA	West Virginia**	NA
39	Wisconsin	2.2
3	Wyoming	28.6

RANK ORDER

RANK	STATE	PERCENT
1	Kansas	47.7
2	North Dakota	39.2
3	Wyoming	28.6
4	Delaware	25.2
5	Tennessee	20.5
6	Maryland	18.8
7	South Dakota	17.0
8	North Carolina	15.9
9	Nebraska	15.6
10	Arkansas	15.3
11	Alabama	15.0
12	Kentucky	14.3
13	Vermont	14.1
14	Georgia	12.1
15	Oregon	11.6
16	Montana	10.6
17	Colorado	9.9
18	Ohio	8.9
19	Missouri	8.8
20	Illinois	8.3
20	Minnesota	8.3
22	Utah	6.7
23	Nevada	6.5
24	Massachusetts	5.3
25	New Jersey	5.1
25	Washington	5.1
27	Virginia	4.8
28	Indiana	4.6
28	Oklahoma	4.6
28	Pennsylvania	4.6
31	Idaho	4.4
31	New Mexico	4.4
33	Connecticut	3.8
34	South Carolina	3.7
35	Texas	3.6
36	Michigan	3.2
37	Maine	3.0
38	Mississippi	2.9
39	Wisconsin	2.2
40	Arizona	1.6
41	Alaska	0.4
42	Hawaii	0.1
NA	California**	NA
NA	Florida**	NA
NA	Iowa**	NA
NA	Louisiana**	NA
NA	New Hampshire**	NA
NA	New York**	NA
NA	Rhode Island**	NA
NA	West Virginia**	NA

| | District of Columbia | 55.9 |

Source: U.S. Department of Health and Human Services, Centers for Disease Control and Prevention
    "Abortion Surveillance-United States, 2003" (Morbidity and Mortality Weekly Report, Vol. 55, No. SS-11, 11/24/06)
By state of occurrence. National figure is for reporting states only.
**Not reported.*

Percent of Reported Legal Abortions that were First-Time Abortions: 2003

Reporting States' Percent = 53.9% of Abortions*

ALPHA ORDER

RANK	STATE	PERCENT
9	Alabama	64.3
14	Alaska	61.5
NA	Arizona**	NA
13	Arkansas	62.0
NA	California**	NA
8	Colorado	64.6
NA	Connecticut**	NA
23	Delaware	55.8
NA	Florida**	NA
16	Georgia	60.5
18	Hawaii	57.9
4	Idaho	75.9
NA	Illinois**	NA
20	Indiana	57.4
10	Iowa	64.0
15	Kansas	61.1
26	Kentucky	55.1
NA	Louisiana**	NA
12	Maine	63.1
37	Maryland	29.6
35	Massachusetts	48.0
31	Michigan	51.7
21	Minnesota	56.7
7	Mississippi	66.2
22	Missouri	56.4
24	Montana	55.3
5	Nebraska	70.3
28	Nevada	53.6
NA	New Hampshire**	NA
11	New Jersey	63.7
NA	New Mexico**	NA
36	New York	43.9
34	North Carolina	49.6
2	North Dakota	85.9
NA	Ohio**	NA
1	Oklahoma	87.5
27	Oregon	54.5
25	Pennsylvania	55.2
28	Rhode Island	53.6
38	South Carolina	25.8
3	South Dakota	78.0
33	Tennessee	50.6
18	Texas	57.9
6	Utah	67.0
17	Vermont	60.3
32	Virginia	51.5
30	Washington	52.7
NA	West Virginia**	NA
NA	Wisconsin**	NA
NA	Wyoming**	NA

RANK ORDER

RANK	STATE	PERCENT
1	Oklahoma	87.5
2	North Dakota	85.9
3	South Dakota	78.0
4	Idaho	75.9
5	Nebraska	70.3
6	Utah	67.0
7	Mississippi	66.2
8	Colorado	64.6
9	Alabama	64.3
10	Iowa	64.0
11	New Jersey	63.7
12	Maine	63.1
13	Arkansas	62.0
14	Alaska	61.5
15	Kansas	61.1
16	Georgia	60.5
17	Vermont	60.3
18	Hawaii	57.9
18	Texas	57.9
20	Indiana	57.4
21	Minnesota	56.7
22	Missouri	56.4
23	Delaware	55.8
24	Montana	55.3
25	Pennsylvania	55.2
26	Kentucky	55.1
27	Oregon	54.5
28	Nevada	53.6
28	Rhode Island	53.6
30	Washington	52.7
31	Michigan	51.7
32	Virginia	51.5
33	Tennessee	50.6
34	North Carolina	49.6
35	Massachusetts	48.0
36	New York	43.9
37	Maryland	29.6
38	South Carolina	25.8
NA	Arizona**	NA
NA	California**	NA
NA	Connecticut**	NA
NA	Florida**	NA
NA	Illinois**	NA
NA	Louisiana**	NA
NA	New Hampshire**	NA
NA	New Mexico**	NA
NA	Ohio**	NA
NA	West Virginia**	NA
NA	Wisconsin**	NA
NA	Wyoming**	NA
	District of Columbia**	NA

Source: U.S. Department of Health and Human Services, Centers for Disease Control and Prevention
    "Abortion Surveillance-United States, 2003" (Morbidity and Mortality Weekly Report, Vol. 55, No. SS-11, 11/24/06)
*By state of occurrence. National figure is for reporting states only. Percent of abortions to women who had no previous abortions.
**Not reported.

Percent of Reported Legal Abortions Obtained by White Women in 2003

Reporting States' Percent = 53.2% of Abortions*

<u>ALPHA ORDER</u>

<u>RANK ORDER</u>

RANK	STATE	PERCENT	RANK	STATE	PERCENT
25	Alabama	45.5	1	Idaho	92.8
18	Alaska	57.7	2	Vermont	92.2
NA	Arizona**	NA	3	Oregon	84.3
17	Arkansas	57.9	4	Montana	82.7
NA	California**	NA	5	North Dakota	82.3
7	Colorado	77.4	6	Iowa	81.6
NA	Connecticut**	NA	7	Colorado	77.4
24	Delaware	49.6	8	Kentucky	72.2
NA	Florida**	NA	9	Texas	71.9
30	Georgia	40.1	10	Oklahoma	71.6
33	Hawaii	26.3	11	Kansas	71.3
1	Idaho	92.8	12	Wisconsin	69.5
NA	Illinois**	NA	13	Minnesota	64.5
14	Indiana	63.0	14	Indiana	63.0
6	Iowa	81.6	15	Ohio	58.7
11	Kansas	71.3	16	South Carolina	58.1
8	Kentucky	72.2	17	Arkansas	57.9
29	Louisiana	40.6	18	Alaska	57.7
NA	Maine**	NA	19	Missouri	56.7
32	Maryland	26.4	20	Pennsylvania	56.1
23	Massachusetts	51.4	21	Michigan	53.5
21	Michigan	53.5	22	Tennessee	52.8
13	Minnesota	64.5	23	Massachusetts	51.4
34	Mississippi	25.5	24	Delaware	49.6
19	Missouri	56.7	25	Alabama	45.5
4	Montana	82.7	26	Virginia	44.2
NA	Nebraska**	NA	27	North Carolina	43.9
NA	Nevada**	NA	28	New York**	41.3
NA	New Hampshire**	NA	29	Louisiana	40.6
31	New Jersey	30.9	30	Georgia	40.1
NA	New Mexico**	NA	31	New Jersey	30.9
28	New York**	41.3	32	Maryland	26.4
27	North Carolina	43.9	33	Hawaii	26.3
5	North Dakota	82.3	34	Mississippi	25.5
15	Ohio	58.7	NA	Arizona**	NA
10	Oklahoma	71.6	NA	California**	NA
3	Oregon	84.3	NA	Connecticut**	NA
20	Pennsylvania	56.1	NA	Florida**	NA
NA	Rhode Island**	NA	NA	Illinois**	NA
16	South Carolina	58.1	NA	Maine**	NA
NA	South Dakota**	NA	NA	Nebraska**	NA
22	Tennessee	52.8	NA	Nevada**	NA
9	Texas	71.9	NA	New Hampshire**	NA
NA	Utah**	NA	NA	New Mexico**	NA
2	Vermont	92.2	NA	Rhode Island**	NA
26	Virginia	44.2	NA	South Dakota**	NA
NA	Washington**	NA	NA	Utah**	NA
NA	West Virginia**	NA	NA	Washington**	NA
12	Wisconsin	69.5	NA	West Virginia**	NA
NA	Wyoming**	NA	NA	Wyoming**	NA

	District of Columbia	11.0

Source: U.S. Department of Health and Human Services, Centers for Disease Control and Prevention
  "Abortion Surveillance-United States, 2003" (Morbidity and Mortality Weekly Report, Vol. 55, No. SS-11, 11/24/06)
*By state of occurrence. Includes those of Hispanic ethnicity. National percent is for reporting states only.
**Not reported. New York's number is for New York City only.

Percent of Reported Legal Abortions Obtained by Black Women in 2003

Reporting States' Percent = 35.8% of Abortions*

ALPHA ORDER

RANK	STATE	PERCENT
4	Alabama	51.4
27	Alaska	6.4
NA	Arizona**	NA
16	Arkansas	35.6
NA	California**	NA
28	Colorado	5.9
NA	Connecticut**	NA
8	Delaware	43.3
NA	Florida**	NA
3	Georgia	55.3
30	Hawaii	3.4
33	Idaho	1.2
NA	Illinois**	NA
18	Indiana	27.4
26	Iowa	7.3
20	Kansas	23.3
24	Kentucky	19.6
5	Louisiana	49.9
NA	Maine**	NA
2	Maryland	57.0
23	Massachusetts	20.5
15	Michigan	37.6
22	Minnesota	20.8
1	Mississippi	73.6
14	Missouri	37.8
34	Montana	0.7
NA	Nebraska**	NA
NA	Nevada**	NA
NA	New Hampshire**	NA
10	New Jersey	42.2
NA	New Mexico**	NA
6	New York**	48.2
9	North Carolina	42.4
31	North Dakota	2.2
17	Ohio	35.3
25	Oklahoma	17.4
29	Oregon	5.8
12	Pennsylvania	39.0
NA	Rhode Island**	NA
13	South Carolina	38.9
NA	South Dakota**	NA
7	Tennessee	43.7
21	Texas	21.0
NA	Utah**	NA
32	Vermont	1.7
11	Virginia	40.9
NA	Washington**	NA
NA	West Virginia**	NA
19	Wisconsin	23.5
NA	Wyoming**	NA

RANK ORDER

RANK	STATE	PERCENT
1	Mississippi	73.6
2	Maryland	57.0
3	Georgia	55.3
4	Alabama	51.4
5	Louisiana	49.9
6	New York**	48.2
7	Tennessee	43.7
8	Delaware	43.3
9	North Carolina	42.4
10	New Jersey	42.2
11	Virginia	40.9
12	Pennsylvania	39.0
13	South Carolina	38.9
14	Missouri	37.8
15	Michigan	37.6
16	Arkansas	35.6
17	Ohio	35.3
18	Indiana	27.4
19	Wisconsin	23.5
20	Kansas	23.3
21	Texas	21.0
22	Minnesota	20.8
23	Massachusetts	20.5
24	Kentucky	19.6
25	Oklahoma	17.4
26	Iowa	7.3
27	Alaska	6.4
28	Colorado	5.9
29	Oregon	5.8
30	Hawaii	3.4
31	North Dakota	2.2
32	Vermont	1.7
33	Idaho	1.2
34	Montana	0.7
NA	Arizona**	NA
NA	California**	NA
NA	Connecticut**	NA
NA	Florida**	NA
NA	Illinois**	NA
NA	Maine**	NA
NA	Nebraska**	NA
NA	Nevada**	NA
NA	New Hampshire**	NA
NA	New Mexico**	NA
NA	Rhode Island**	NA
NA	South Dakota**	NA
NA	Utah**	NA
NA	Washington**	NA
NA	West Virginia**	NA
NA	Wyoming**	NA

| | District of Columbia | 72.6 |

Source: U.S. Department of Health and Human Services, Centers for Disease Control and Prevention
   "Abortion Surveillance-United States, 2003" (Morbidity and Mortality Weekly Report, Vol. 55, No. SS-11, 11/24/06)
*By state of occurrence. National percent is for reporting states only.
**Not reported. New York's number is for New York City only.

Percent of Reported Legal Abortions Obtained by Hispanic Women in 2003

Reporting States' Percent = 17.4%*

ALPHA ORDER

RANK	STATE	PERCENT
21	Alabama	2.4
11	Alaska	6.6
NA	Arizona**	NA
18	Arkansas	4.2
NA	California**	NA
5	Colorado	19.9
NA	Connecticut**	NA
8	Delaware	9.2
NA	Florida**	NA
14	Georgia	5.7
16	Hawaii	4.5
6	Idaho	12.1
NA	Illinois**	NA
12	Indiana	6.4
NA	Iowa**	NA
10	Kansas	7.5
25	Kentucky	0.1
NA	Louisiana**	NA
NA	Maine**	NA
NA	Maryland**	NA
NA	Massachusetts**	NA
NA	Michigan**	NA
15	Minnesota	5.5
24	Mississippi	0.6
22	Missouri	2.2
NA	Montana**	NA
NA	Nebraska**	NA
NA	Nevada**	NA
NA	New Hampshire**	NA
4	New Jersey	23.3
NA	New Mexico**	NA
2	New York	26.7
NA	North Carolina**	NA
25	North Dakota	0.1
20	Ohio	3.1
NA	Oklahoma**	NA
7	Oregon	10.4
13	Pennsylvania	6.0
NA	Rhode Island**	NA
17	South Carolina	4.3
NA	South Dakota**	NA
19	Tennessee	3.3
1	Texas	36.8
3	Utah	23.4
23	Vermont	1.2
NA	Virginia**	NA
NA	Washington**	NA
NA	West Virginia**	NA
9	Wisconsin	8.0
NA	Wyoming**	NA

RANK ORDER

RANK	STATE	PERCENT
1	Texas	36.8
2	New York	26.7
3	Utah	23.4
4	New Jersey	23.3
5	Colorado	19.9
6	Idaho	12.1
7	Oregon	10.4
8	Delaware	9.2
9	Wisconsin	8.0
10	Kansas	7.5
11	Alaska	6.6
12	Indiana	6.4
13	Pennsylvania	6.0
14	Georgia	5.7
15	Minnesota	5.5
16	Hawaii	4.5
17	South Carolina	4.3
18	Arkansas	4.2
19	Tennessee	3.3
20	Ohio	3.1
21	Alabama	2.4
22	Missouri	2.2
23	Vermont	1.2
24	Mississippi	0.6
25	Kentucky	0.1
25	North Dakota	0.1
NA	Arizona**	NA
NA	California**	NA
NA	Connecticut**	NA
NA	Florida**	NA
NA	Illinois**	NA
NA	Iowa**	NA
NA	Louisiana**	NA
NA	Maine**	NA
NA	Maryland**	NA
NA	Massachusetts**	NA
NA	Michigan**	NA
NA	Montana**	NA
NA	Nebraska**	NA
NA	Nevada**	NA
NA	New Hampshire**	NA
NA	New Mexico**	NA
NA	North Carolina**	NA
NA	Oklahoma**	NA
NA	Rhode Island**	NA
NA	South Dakota**	NA
NA	Virginia**	NA
NA	Washington**	NA
NA	West Virginia**	NA
NA	Wyoming**	NA

	District of Columbia	10.3

Source: U.S. Department of Health and Human Services, Centers for Disease Control and Prevention
   "Abortion Surveillance-United States, 2003" (Morbidity and Mortality Weekly Report, Vol. 55, No. SS-11, 11/24/06)
*By state of occurrence. National percent is for reporting states only. Hispanic can be of any race.
**Not reported.

Percent of Reported Legal Abortions Obtained by Married Women in 2003

Reporting States' Percent = 17.4% of Abortions*

RANK	STATE	PERCENT	RANK	STATE	PERCENT
32	Alabama	14.9	1	Idaho	26.1
7	Alaska	20.7	2	Utah	22.6
30	Arizona	15.2	3	Oregon	21.9
19	Arkansas	17.1	4	North Carolina	21.5
NA	California**	NA	5	Nevada	20.9
13	Colorado	18.5	5	Oklahoma	20.9
NA	Connecticut**	NA	7	Alaska	20.7
31	Delaware	15.1	8	Hawaii	20.2
NA	Florida**	NA	8	Texas	20.2
15	Georgia	18.1	10	Missouri	19.9
8	Hawaii	20.2	11	Vermont	19.7
1	Idaho	26.1	12	Kansas	18.9
22	Illinois	16.5	13	Colorado	18.5
34	Indiana	14.7	14	Minnesota	18.2
NA	Iowa**	NA	15	Georgia	18.1
12	Kansas	18.9	16	Tennessee	17.6
29	Kentucky	15.5	16	Virginia	17.6
NA	Louisiana**	NA	18	South Carolina	17.3
NA	Maine**	NA	19	Arkansas	17.1
23	Maryland	16.4	20	Massachusetts	16.8
20	Massachusetts	16.8	21	Ohio	16.7
35	Michigan	14.2	22	Illinois	16.5
14	Minnesota	18.2	23	Maryland	16.4
36	Mississippi	12.4	24	North Dakota	16.3
10	Missouri	19.9	24	Wisconsin	16.3
NA	Montana**	NA	26	Pennsylvania	16.0
NA	Nebraska**	NA	27	New Jersey	15.9
5	Nevada	20.9	27	New York**	15.9
NA	New Hampshire**	NA	29	Kentucky	15.5
27	New Jersey	15.9	30	Arizona	15.2
32	New Mexico	14.9	31	Delaware	15.1
27	New York**	15.9	32	Alabama	14.9
4	North Carolina	21.5	32	New Mexico	14.9
24	North Dakota	16.3	34	Indiana	14.7
21	Ohio	16.7	35	Michigan	14.2
5	Oklahoma	20.9	36	Mississippi	12.4
3	Oregon	21.9	NA	California**	NA
26	Pennsylvania	16.0	NA	Connecticut**	NA
NA	Rhode Island**	NA	NA	Florida**	NA
18	South Carolina	17.3	NA	Iowa**	NA
NA	South Dakota**	NA	NA	Louisiana**	NA
16	Tennessee	17.6	NA	Maine**	NA
8	Texas	20.2	NA	Montana**	NA
2	Utah	22.6	NA	Nebraska**	NA
11	Vermont	19.7	NA	New Hampshire**	NA
16	Virginia	17.6	NA	Rhode Island**	NA
NA	Washington**	NA	NA	South Dakota**	NA
NA	West Virginia**	NA	NA	Washington**	NA
24	Wisconsin	16.3	NA	West Virginia**	NA
NA	Wyoming**	NA	NA	Wyoming**	NA

District of Columbia   8.8

Source: U.S. Department of Health and Human Services, Centers for Disease Control and Prevention
    "Abortion Surveillance-United States, 2003" (Morbidity and Mortality Weekly Report, Vol. 55, No. SS-11, 11/24/06)
*By state of occurrence. National percent is for reporting states only.
**Not reported. New York's number is for New York City only.

Percent of Reported Legal Abortions Obtained by Unmarried Women in 2003

Reporting States' Percent = 79.9% of Abortions*

ALPHA ORDER			RANK ORDER		
RANK	STATE	PERCENT	RANK	STATE	PERCENT
6	Alabama	83.8	1	Mississippi	86.5
30	Alaska	74.0	2	Delaware	84.9
29	Arizona	75.8	3	Kentucky	84.5
14	Arkansas	81.7	3	Michigan	84.5
NA	California**	NA	5	Pennsylvania	84.0
27	Colorado	77.1	6	Alabama	83.8
NA	Connecticut**	NA	7	North Dakota	83.5
2	Delaware	84.9	7	Wisconsin	83.5
NA	Florida**	NA	9	New Jersey	83.0
19	Georgia	80.2	10	South Carolina	82.7
23	Hawaii	78.3	11	New Mexico	82.6
31	Idaho	73.7	12	Ohio	82.2
15	Illinois	81.0	13	New York**	82.1
21	Indiana	79.6	14	Arkansas	81.7
NA	Iowa**	NA	15	Illinois	81.0
15	Kansas	81.0	15	Kansas	81.0
3	Kentucky	84.5	15	Minnesota	81.0
NA	Louisiana**	NA	18	Tennessee	80.6
NA	Maine**	NA	19	Georgia	80.2
35	Maryland	68.8	20	Massachusetts	79.8
20	Massachusetts	79.8	21	Indiana	79.6
3	Michigan	84.5	22	Oklahoma	79.1
15	Minnesota	81.0	23	Hawaii	78.3
1	Mississippi	86.5	24	Missouri	78.2
24	Missouri	78.2	25	Texas	78.0
NA	Montana**	NA	26	Vermont	77.4
NA	Nebraska**	NA	27	Colorado	77.1
32	Nevada	73.5	28	Oregon	76.0
NA	New Hampshire**	NA	29	Arizona	75.8
9	New Jersey	83.0	30	Alaska	74.0
11	New Mexico	82.6	31	Idaho	73.7
13	New York**	82.1	32	Nevada	73.5
33	North Carolina	73.3	33	North Carolina	73.3
7	North Dakota	83.5	34	Virginia	70.2
12	Ohio	82.2	35	Maryland	68.8
22	Oklahoma	79.1	36	Utah	64.7
28	Oregon	76.0	NA	California**	NA
5	Pennsylvania	84.0	NA	Connecticut**	NA
NA	Rhode Island**	NA	NA	Florida**	NA
10	South Carolina	82.7	NA	Iowa**	NA
NA	South Dakota**	NA	NA	Louisiana**	NA
18	Tennessee	80.6	NA	Maine**	NA
25	Texas	78.0	NA	Montana**	NA
36	Utah	64.7	NA	Nebraska**	NA
26	Vermont	77.4	NA	New Hampshire**	NA
34	Virginia	70.2	NA	Rhode Island**	NA
NA	Washington**	NA	NA	South Dakota**	NA
NA	West Virginia**	NA	NA	Washington**	NA
7	Wisconsin	83.5	NA	West Virginia**	NA
NA	Wyoming**	NA	NA	Wyoming**	NA
			District of Columbia		90.7

Source: U.S. Department of Health and Human Services, Centers for Disease Control and Prevention
    "Abortion Surveillance-United States, 2003" (Morbidity and Mortality Weekly Report, Vol. 55, No. SS-11, 11/24/06)
By state of occurrence. National percent is for reporting states only.
***Not reported. New York's number is for New York City only.*

Reported Legal Abortions Obtained by Teenagers in 2003

Reporting States' Total = 121,304 Abortions Obtained by Teenagers*

ALPHA ORDER

RANK	STATE	ABORTIONS	% of USA
17	Alabama	1,992	1.6%
39	Alaska	385	0.3%
19	Arizona	1,898	1.6%
29	Arkansas	1,015	0.8%
NA	California**	NA	NA
22	Colorado	1,744	1.4%
13	Connecticut	2,475	2.0%
34	Delaware	662	0.5%
NA	Florida**	NA	NA
6	Georgia	5,438	4.5%
31	Hawaii	801	0.7%
42	Idaho	181	0.1%
NA	Illinois**	NA	NA
21	Indiana	1,828	1.5%
28	Iowa	1,064	0.9%
16	Kansas	2,071	1.7%
35	Kentucky	608	0.5%
20	Louisiana	1,870	1.5%
37	Maine	482	0.4%
NA	Maryland**	NA	NA
10	Massachusetts	4,555	3.8%
7	Michigan	5,173	4.3%
15	Minnesota	2,139	1.8%
33	Mississippi	690	0.6%
24	Missouri	1,336	1.1%
38	Montana	473	0.4%
32	Nebraska	719	0.6%
23	Nevada	1,519	1.3%
NA	New Hampshire**	NA	NA
5	New Jersey	5,928	4.9%
26	New Mexico	1,282	1.1%
1	New York	22,367	18.4%
8	North Carolina	4,904	4.0%
41	North Dakota	281	0.2%
4	Ohio	6,306	5.2%
25	Oklahoma	1,293	1.1%
14	Oregon	2,206	1.8%
3	Pennsylvania	6,514	5.4%
30	Rhode Island	989	0.8%
27	South Carolina	1,215	1.0%
43	South Dakota	169	0.1%
12	Tennessee	2,913	2.4%
2	Texas	11,050	9.1%
35	Utah	608	0.5%
40	Vermont	330	0.3%
11	Virginia	4,123	3.4%
9	Washington	4,805	4.0%
NA	West Virginia**	NA	NA
18	Wisconsin	1,918	1.6%
44	Wyoming	0	0.0%

RANK ORDER

RANK	STATE	ABORTIONS	% of USA
1	New York	22,367	18.4%
2	Texas	11,050	9.1%
3	Pennsylvania	6,514	5.4%
4	Ohio	6,306	5.2%
5	New Jersey	5,928	4.9%
6	Georgia	5,438	4.5%
7	Michigan	5,173	4.3%
8	North Carolina	4,904	4.0%
9	Washington	4,805	4.0%
10	Massachusetts	4,555	3.8%
11	Virginia	4,123	3.4%
12	Tennessee	2,913	2.4%
13	Connecticut	2,475	2.0%
14	Oregon	2,206	1.8%
15	Minnesota	2,139	1.8%
16	Kansas	2,071	1.7%
17	Alabama	1,992	1.6%
18	Wisconsin	1,918	1.6%
19	Arizona	1,898	1.6%
20	Louisiana	1,870	1.5%
21	Indiana	1,828	1.5%
22	Colorado	1,744	1.4%
23	Nevada	1,519	1.3%
24	Missouri	1,336	1.1%
25	Oklahoma	1,293	1.1%
26	New Mexico	1,282	1.1%
27	South Carolina	1,215	1.0%
28	Iowa	1,064	0.9%
29	Arkansas	1,015	0.8%
30	Rhode Island	989	0.8%
31	Hawaii	801	0.7%
32	Nebraska	719	0.6%
33	Mississippi	690	0.6%
34	Delaware	662	0.5%
35	Kentucky	608	0.5%
35	Utah	608	0.5%
37	Maine	482	0.4%
38	Montana	473	0.4%
39	Alaska	385	0.3%
40	Vermont	330	0.3%
41	North Dakota	281	0.2%
42	Idaho	181	0.1%
43	South Dakota	169	0.1%
44	Wyoming	0	0.0%
NA	California**	NA	NA
NA	Florida**	NA	NA
NA	Illinois**	NA	NA
NA	Maryland**	NA	NA
NA	New Hampshire**	NA	NA
NA	West Virginia**	NA	NA
	District of Columbia	985	0.8%

Source: U.S. Department of Health and Human Services, Centers for Disease Control and Prevention
    "Abortion Surveillance-United States, 2003" (Morbidity and Mortality Weekly Report, Vol. 55, No. SS-11, 11/24/06)
Nineteen years old and younger by state of occurrence. National total is for reporting states only.
**Not reported.*

Percent of Reported Legal Abortions Obtained by Teenagers in 2003

Reporting States' Percent = 17.3% of Abortions*

ALPHA ORDER

RANK	STATE	PERCENT	RANK	STATE	PERCENT
18	Alabama	18.1	1	Hawaii	22.2
4	Alaska	21.3	2	New Mexico	22.0
15	Arizona	18.4	3	Montana	21.4
13	Arkansas	18.8	4	Alaska	21.3
NA	California**	NA	5	North Dakota	20.8
26	Colorado	17.7	6	South Dakota	20.6
7	Connecticut	20.0	7	Connecticut	20.0
38	Delaware	15.8	8	Idaho	19.9
NA	Florida**	NA	9	Vermont	19.7
38	Georgia	15.8	10	Oklahoma	19.5
1	Hawaii	22.2	11	Washington	19.2
8	Idaho	19.9	12	Maine	18.9
NA	Illinois**	NA	13	Arkansas	18.8
36	Indiana	16.0	14	South Carolina	18.5
20	Iowa	18.0	15	Arizona	18.4
22	Kansas	17.9	15	Mississippi	18.4
33	Kentucky	16.8	17	Wisconsin	18.2
28	Louisiana	17.6	18	Alabama	18.1
12	Maine	18.9	18	New Jersey	18.1
NA	Maryland**	NA	20	Iowa	18.0
26	Massachusetts	17.7	20	Nebraska	18.0
30	Michigan	17.5	22	Kansas	17.9
42	Minnesota	15.2	22	New York	17.9
15	Mississippi	18.4	22	Ohio	17.9
36	Missouri	16.0	22	Rhode Island	17.9
3	Montana	21.4	26	Colorado	17.7
20	Nebraska	18.0	26	Massachusetts	17.7
35	Nevada	16.3	28	Louisiana	17.6
NA	New Hampshire**	NA	28	Pennsylvania	17.6
18	New Jersey	18.1	30	Michigan	17.5
2	New Mexico	22.0	30	Oregon	17.5
22	New York	17.9	32	Utah	17.0
38	North Carolina	15.8	33	Kentucky	16.8
5	North Dakota	20.8	34	Tennessee	16.5
22	Ohio	17.9	35	Nevada	16.3
10	Oklahoma	19.5	36	Indiana	16.0
30	Oregon	17.5	36	Missouri	16.0
28	Pennsylvania	17.6	38	Delaware	15.8
22	Rhode Island	17.9	38	Georgia	15.8
14	South Carolina	18.5	38	North Carolina	15.8
6	South Dakota	20.6	41	Virginia	15.6
34	Tennessee	16.5	42	Minnesota	15.2
43	Texas	14.0	43	Texas	14.0
32	Utah	17.0	44	Wyoming	0.0
9	Vermont	19.7	NA	California**	NA
41	Virginia	15.6	NA	Florida**	NA
11	Washington	19.2	NA	Illinois**	NA
NA	West Virginia**	NA	NA	Maryland**	NA
17	Wisconsin	18.2	NA	New Hampshire**	NA
44	Wyoming	0.0	NA	West Virginia**	NA

District of Columbia   19.2

Source: Morgan Quitno Press using data from US Dept of Health & Human Serv's, Centers for Disease Control-Prevention "Abortion Surveillance-United States, 2003" (Morbidity and Mortality Weekly Report, Vol. 55, No. SS-11, 11/24/06)
Nineteen years old and younger by state of occurrence. National percent is for reporting states only.
**Not reported.*

Reported Legal Abortions Obtained by Teenagers 17 Years and Younger in 2003

Reporting States' Total = 46,902 Abortions*

ALPHA ORDER

RANK ORDER

RANK	STATE	ABORTIONS	% of USA	RANK	STATE	ABORTIONS	% of USA
16	Alabama	787	1.7%	1	New York	9,428	20.1%
39	Alaska	166	0.4%	2	Texas	3,684	7.9%
21	Arizona	691	1.5%	3	New Jersey	2,521	5.4%
27	Arkansas	438	0.9%	4	Ohio	2,506	5.3%
NA	California**	NA	NA	5	Pennsylvania	2,401	5.1%
19	Colorado	704	1.5%	6	Georgia	2,218	4.7%
13	Connecticut	1,092	2.3%	7	Michigan	2,008	4.3%
32	Delaware	282	0.6%	8	Washington	1,894	4.0%
NA	Florida**	NA	NA	9	North Carolina	1,786	3.8%
6	Georgia	2,218	4.7%	10	Massachusetts	1,475	3.1%
30	Hawaii	354	0.8%	11	Virginia	1,386	3.0%
43	Idaho	50	0.1%	12	Tennessee	1,099	2.3%
NA	Illinois**	NA	NA	13	Connecticut	1,092	2.3%
22	Indiana	630	1.3%	14	Oregon	855	1.8%
28	Iowa	430	0.9%	15	Kansas	823	1.8%
15	Kansas	823	1.8%	16	Alabama	787	1.7%
35	Kentucky	256	0.5%	17	Minnesota	778	1.7%
20	Louisiana	697	1.5%	18	Wisconsin	737	1.6%
37	Maine	191	0.4%	19	Colorado	704	1.5%
NA	Maryland**	NA	NA	20	Louisiana	697	1.5%
10	Massachusetts	1,475	3.1%	21	Arizona	691	1.5%
7	Michigan	2,008	4.3%	22	Indiana	630	1.3%
17	Minnesota	778	1.7%	23	Nevada	585	1.2%
34	Mississippi	259	0.6%	24	South Carolina	560	1.2%
29	Missouri	428	0.9%	25	New Mexico	506	1.1%
38	Montana	189	0.4%	26	Oklahoma	477	1.0%
33	Nebraska	276	0.6%	27	Arkansas	438	0.9%
23	Nevada	585	1.2%	28	Iowa	430	0.9%
NA	New Hampshire**	NA	NA	29	Missouri	428	0.9%
3	New Jersey	2,521	5.4%	30	Hawaii	354	0.8%
25	New Mexico	506	1.1%	31	Rhode Island	307	0.7%
1	New York	9,428	20.1%	32	Delaware	282	0.6%
9	North Carolina	1,786	3.8%	33	Nebraska	276	0.6%
41	North Dakota	99	0.2%	34	Mississippi	259	0.6%
4	Ohio	2,506	5.3%	35	Kentucky	256	0.5%
26	Oklahoma	477	1.0%	36	Utah	219	0.5%
14	Oregon	855	1.8%	37	Maine	191	0.4%
5	Pennsylvania	2,401	5.1%	38	Montana	189	0.4%
31	Rhode Island	307	0.7%	39	Alaska	166	0.4%
24	South Carolina	560	1.2%	40	Vermont	119	0.3%
42	South Dakota	66	0.1%	41	North Dakota	99	0.2%
12	Tennessee	1,099	2.3%	42	South Dakota	66	0.1%
2	Texas	3,684	7.9%	43	Idaho	50	0.1%
36	Utah	219	0.5%	44	Wyoming	0	0.0%
40	Vermont	119	0.3%	NA	California**	NA	NA
11	Virginia	1,386	3.0%	NA	Florida**	NA	NA
8	Washington	1,894	4.0%	NA	Illinois**	NA	NA
NA	West Virginia**	NA	NA	NA	Maryland**	NA	NA
18	Wisconsin	737	1.6%	NA	New Hampshire**	NA	NA
44	Wyoming	0	0.0%	NA	West Virginia**	NA	NA
					District of Columbia	445	0.9%

Source: U.S. Department of Health and Human Services, Centers for Disease Control and Prevention
    "Abortion Surveillance-United States, 2003" (Morbidity and Mortality Weekly Report, Vol. 55, No. SS-11, 11/24/06)
*By state of occurrence. National total is for reporting states only.
**Not reported.

Percent of Reported Legal Abortions Obtained by Teenagers 17 Years and Younger in 2003
Reporting States' Percent = 6.6% of Abortions*

RANK	STATE	PERCENT
15	Alabama	7.2
2	Alaska	9.2
27	Arizona	6.7
7	Arkansas	8.1
NA	California**	NA
17	Colorado	7.1
3	Connecticut	8.8
27	Delaware	6.7
NA	Florida**	NA
29	Georgia	6.5
1	Hawaii	9.8
37	Idaho	5.5
NA	Illinois**	NA
37	Indiana	5.5
13	Iowa	7.3
17	Kansas	7.1
17	Kentucky	7.1
29	Louisiana	6.5
11	Maine	7.5
NA	Maryland**	NA
36	Massachusetts	5.7
25	Michigan	6.8
37	Minnesota	5.5
23	Mississippi	6.9
42	Missouri	5.1
5	Montana	8.5
23	Nebraska	6.9
32	Nevada	6.3
NA	New Hampshire**	NA
9	New Jersey	7.7
4	New Mexico	8.7
11	New York	7.5
35	North Carolina	5.8
13	North Dakota	7.3
17	Ohio	7.1
15	Oklahoma	7.2
25	Oregon	6.8
29	Pennsylvania	6.5
37	Rhode Island	5.5
5	South Carolina	8.5
7	South Dakota	8.1
33	Tennessee	6.2
43	Texas	4.7
34	Utah	6.1
17	Vermont	7.1
41	Virginia	5.2
10	Washington	7.6
NA	West Virginia**	NA
22	Wisconsin	7.0
44	Wyoming	0.0

RANK	STATE	PERCENT
1	Hawaii	9.8
2	Alaska	9.2
3	Connecticut	8.8
4	New Mexico	8.7
5	Montana	8.5
5	South Carolina	8.5
7	Arkansas	8.1
7	South Dakota	8.1
9	New Jersey	7.7
10	Washington	7.6
11	Maine	7.5
11	New York	7.5
13	Iowa	7.3
13	North Dakota	7.3
15	Alabama	7.2
15	Oklahoma	7.2
17	Colorado	7.1
17	Kansas	7.1
17	Kentucky	7.1
17	Ohio	7.1
17	Vermont	7.1
22	Wisconsin	7.0
23	Mississippi	6.9
23	Nebraska	6.9
25	Michigan	6.8
25	Oregon	6.8
27	Arizona	6.7
27	Delaware	6.7
29	Georgia	6.5
29	Louisiana	6.5
29	Pennsylvania	6.5
32	Nevada	6.3
33	Tennessee	6.2
34	Utah	6.1
35	North Carolina	5.8
36	Massachusetts	5.7
37	Idaho	5.5
37	Indiana	5.5
37	Minnesota	5.5
37	Rhode Island	5.5
41	Virginia	5.2
42	Missouri	5.1
43	Texas	4.7
44	Wyoming	0.0
NA	California**	NA
NA	Florida**	NA
NA	Illinois**	NA
NA	Maryland**	NA
NA	New Hampshire**	NA
NA	West Virginia**	NA

District of Columbia	8.7

Source: Morgan Quitno Press using data from US Dept of Health & Human Serv's, Centers for Disease Control-Prevention
"Abortion Surveillance-United States, 2003" (Morbidity and Mortality Weekly Report, Vol. 55, No. SS-11, 11/24/06)
*By state of occurrence. National percent is for reporting states only.
**Not reported.

Percent of Teenage Abortions Obtained
by Teenagers 17 Years and Younger in 2003
Reporting States' Percent = 38.7% of Teenage Abortions*

ALPHA ORDER

RANK ORDER

RANK	STATE	PERCENT		RANK	STATE	PERCENT
17	Alabama	39.5		1	South Carolina	46.1
5	Alaska	43.1		2	Hawaii	44.2
31	Arizona	36.4		3	Connecticut	44.1
4	Arkansas	43.2		4	Arkansas	43.2
NA	California**	NA		5	Alaska	43.1
11	Colorado	40.4		6	Delaware	42.6
3	Connecticut	44.1		7	New Jersey	42.5
6	Delaware	42.6		8	New York	42.2
NA	Florida**	NA		9	Kentucky	42.1
10	Georgia	40.8		10	Georgia	40.8
2	Hawaii	44.2		11	Colorado	40.4
43	Idaho	27.6		11	Iowa	40.4
NA	Illinois**	NA		13	Montana	40.0
37	Indiana	34.5		14	Kansas	39.7
11	Iowa	40.4		14	Ohio	39.7
14	Kansas	39.7		16	Maine	39.6
9	Kentucky	42.1		17	Alabama	39.5
28	Louisiana	37.3		17	New Mexico	39.5
16	Maine	39.6		19	Washington	39.4
NA	Maryland**	NA		20	South Dakota	39.1
40	Massachusetts	32.4		21	Michigan	38.8
21	Michigan	38.8		21	Oregon	38.8
31	Minnesota	36.4		23	Nevada	38.5
27	Mississippi	37.5		24	Nebraska	38.4
41	Missouri	32.0		24	Wisconsin	38.4
13	Montana	40.0		26	Tennessee	37.7
24	Nebraska	38.4		27	Mississippi	37.5
23	Nevada	38.5		28	Louisiana	37.3
NA	New Hampshire**	NA		29	Oklahoma	36.9
7	New Jersey	42.5		29	Pennsylvania	36.9
17	New Mexico	39.5		31	Arizona	36.4
8	New York	42.2		31	Minnesota	36.4
31	North Carolina	36.4		31	North Carolina	36.4
36	North Dakota	35.2		34	Vermont	36.1
14	Ohio	39.7		35	Utah	36.0
29	Oklahoma	36.9		36	North Dakota	35.2
21	Oregon	38.8		37	Indiana	34.5
29	Pennsylvania	36.9		38	Virginia	33.6
42	Rhode Island	31.0		39	Texas	33.3
1	South Carolina	46.1		40	Massachusetts	32.4
20	South Dakota	39.1		41	Missouri	32.0
26	Tennessee	37.7		42	Rhode Island	31.0
39	Texas	33.3		43	Idaho	27.6
35	Utah	36.0		44	Wyoming	0.0
34	Vermont	36.1		NA	California**	NA
38	Virginia	33.6		NA	Florida**	NA
19	Washington	39.4		NA	Illinois**	NA
NA	West Virginia**	NA		NA	Maryland**	NA
24	Wisconsin	38.4		NA	New Hampshire**	NA
44	Wyoming	0.0		NA	West Virginia**	NA

	District of Columbia	45.2

Source: Morgan Quitno Press using data from US Dept of Health & Human Serv's, Centers for Disease Control-Prevention "Abortion Surveillance-United States, 2003" (Morbidity and Mortality Weekly Report, Vol. 55, No. SS-11, 11/24/06)
*By state of occurrence. National percent is for reporting states only.
**Not reported.

Reported Legal Abortions Performed at 12 Weeks or Less of Gestation in 2003

Reporting States' Total = 584,711 Abortions*

ALPHA ORDER

RANK	STATE	ABORTIONS	% of USA
17	Alabama	9,558	1.6%
37	Alaska	1,703	0.3%
19	Arizona	8,624	1.5%
29	Arkansas	4,489	0.8%
NA	California**	NA	NA
21	Colorado	8,565	1.5%
13	Connecticut	10,924	1.9%
34	Delaware	2,758	0.5%
NA	Florida**	NA	NA
5	Georgia	29,552	5.1%
33	Hawaii	3,037	0.5%
40	Idaho	879	0.2%
NA	Illinois**	NA	NA
15	Indiana	10,697	1.8%
26	Iowa	5,480	0.9%
16	Kansas	9,810	1.7%
32	Kentucky	3,041	0.5%
20	Louisiana	8,609	1.5%
35	Maine	2,464	0.4%
NA	Maryland**	NA	NA
NA	Massachusetts**	NA	NA
6	Michigan	26,221	4.5%
12	Minnesota	12,637	2.2%
30	Mississippi	3,315	0.6%
23	Missouri	7,695	1.3%
36	Montana	1,888	0.3%
NA	Nebraska**	NA	NA
22	Nevada	8,209	1.4%
NA	New Hampshire**	NA	NA
7	New Jersey	26,173	4.5%
27	New Mexico	5,043	0.9%
1	New York	103,465	17.7%
8	North Carolina	25,375	4.3%
39	North Dakota	1,208	0.2%
4	Ohio	30,180	5.2%
25	Oklahoma	6,043	1.0%
14	Oregon	10,875	1.9%
3	Pennsylvania	32,772	5.6%
28	Rhode Island	4,924	0.8%
24	South Carolina	6,340	1.1%
41	South Dakota	779	0.1%
11	Tennessee	16,693	2.9%
2	Texas	69,631	11.9%
31	Utah	3,073	0.5%
38	Vermont	1,561	0.3%
9	Virginia	25,138	4.3%
10	Washington	22,076	3.8%
NA	West Virginia**	NA	NA
18	Wisconsin	8,902	1.5%
NA	Wyoming**	NA	NA

RANK ORDER

RANK	STATE	ABORTIONS	% of USA
1	New York	103,465	17.7%
2	Texas	69,631	11.9%
3	Pennsylvania	32,772	5.6%
4	Ohio	30,180	5.2%
5	Georgia	29,552	5.1%
6	Michigan	26,221	4.5%
7	New Jersey	26,173	4.5%
8	North Carolina	25,375	4.3%
9	Virginia	25,138	4.3%
10	Washington	22,076	3.8%
11	Tennessee	16,693	2.9%
12	Minnesota	12,637	2.2%
13	Connecticut	10,924	1.9%
14	Oregon	10,875	1.9%
15	Indiana	10,697	1.8%
16	Kansas	9,810	1.7%
17	Alabama	9,558	1.6%
18	Wisconsin	8,902	1.5%
19	Arizona	8,624	1.5%
20	Louisiana	8,609	1.5%
21	Colorado	8,565	1.5%
22	Nevada	8,209	1.4%
23	Missouri	7,695	1.3%
24	South Carolina	6,340	1.1%
25	Oklahoma	6,043	1.0%
26	Iowa	5,480	0.9%
27	New Mexico	5,043	0.9%
28	Rhode Island	4,924	0.8%
29	Arkansas	4,489	0.8%
30	Mississippi	3,315	0.6%
31	Utah	3,073	0.5%
32	Kentucky	3,041	0.5%
33	Hawaii	3,037	0.5%
34	Delaware	2,758	0.5%
35	Maine	2,464	0.4%
36	Montana	1,888	0.3%
37	Alaska	1,703	0.3%
38	Vermont	1,561	0.3%
39	North Dakota	1,208	0.2%
40	Idaho	879	0.2%
41	South Dakota	779	0.1%
NA	California**	NA	NA
NA	Florida**	NA	NA
NA	Illinois**	NA	NA
NA	Maryland**	NA	NA
NA	Massachusetts**	NA	NA
NA	Nebraska**	NA	NA
NA	New Hampshire**	NA	NA
NA	West Virginia**	NA	NA
NA	Wyoming**	NA	NA

District of Columbia 4,310 0.7%

Source: Morgan Quitno Press using data from US Dept of Health & Human Serv's, Centers for Disease Control-Prevention
"Abortion Surveillance-United States, 2003" (Morbidity and Mortality Weekly Report, Vol. 55, No. SS-11, 11/24/06)
*By state of occurrence. National total is for reporting states only.
**Not reported.

Percent of Reported Legal Abortions Performed
at 12 Weeks or Less of Gestation in 2003
Reporting States' Percent = 86.4% of Abortions*

ALPHA ORDER

RANK ORDER

RANK	STATE	PERCENT	RANK	STATE	PERCENT
23	Alabama	87.1	1	Maine	96.6
7	Alaska	94.3	2	Idaho	96.5
35	Arizona	83.6	2	South Carolina	96.5
36	Arkansas	83.0	4	South Dakota	95.1
NA	California**	NA	4	Virginia	95.1
24	Colorado	86.9	6	Tennessee	94.8
19	Connecticut	88.1	7	Alaska	94.3
41	Delaware	66.0	8	Indiana	93.4
NA	Florida**	NA	9	Vermont	93.0
27	Georgia	86.0	10	Iowa	92.6
33	Hawaii	84.2	11	Missouri	92.2
2	Idaho	96.5	12	Oklahoma	91.0
NA	Illinois**	NA	13	Minnesota	89.7
8	Indiana	93.4	14	North Dakota	89.2
10	Iowa	92.6	15	Rhode Island	88.9
31	Kansas	84.6	16	Michigan	88.8
34	Kentucky	84.0	16	Pennsylvania	88.8
39	Louisiana	80.9	18	Mississippi	88.3
1	Maine	96.6	19	Connecticut	88.1
NA	Maryland**	NA	19	Nevada	88.1
NA	Massachusetts**	NA	21	Texas	88.0
16	Michigan	88.8	21	Washington	88.0
13	Minnesota	89.7	23	Alabama	87.1
18	Mississippi	88.3	24	Colorado	86.9
11	Missouri	92.2	25	New Mexico	86.5
30	Montana	85.3	26	Oregon	86.2
NA	Nebraska**	NA	27	Georgia	86.0
19	Nevada	88.1	28	Utah	85.9
NA	New Hampshire**	NA	29	Ohio	85.4
40	New Jersey	79.9	30	Montana	85.3
25	New Mexico	86.5	31	Kansas	84.6
37	New York	82.8	32	Wisconsin	84.3
38	North Carolina	81.8	33	Hawaii	84.2
14	North Dakota	89.2	34	Kentucky	84.0
29	Ohio	85.4	35	Arizona	83.6
12	Oklahoma	91.0	36	Arkansas	83.0
26	Oregon	86.2	37	New York	82.8
16	Pennsylvania	88.8	38	North Carolina	81.8
15	Rhode Island	88.9	39	Louisiana	80.9
2	South Carolina	96.5	40	New Jersey	79.9
4	South Dakota	95.1	41	Delaware	66.0
6	Tennessee	94.8	NA	California**	NA
21	Texas	88.0	NA	Florida**	NA
28	Utah	85.9	NA	Illinois**	NA
9	Vermont	93.0	NA	Maryland**	NA
4	Virginia	95.1	NA	Massachusetts**	NA
21	Washington	88.0	NA	Nebraska**	NA
NA	West Virginia**	NA	NA	New Hampshire**	NA
32	Wisconsin	84.3	NA	West Virginia**	NA
NA	Wyoming**	NA	NA	Wyoming**	NA
			District of Columbia		84.2

Source: Morgan Quitno Press using data from US Dept of Health & Human Serv's, Centers for Disease Control-Prevention "Abortion Surveillance-United States, 2003" (Morbidity and Mortality Weekly Report, Vol. 55, No. SS-11, 11/24/06)
*By state of occurrence. National percent is for reporting states only.
**Not reported.

Reported Legal Abortions Performed at or After 21 Weeks of Gestation in 2003

Reporting States' Total = 9,383 Abortions*

ALPHA ORDER

RANK ORDER

RANK	STATE	ABORTIONS	% of USA		RANK	STATE	ABORTIONS	% of USA
18	Alabama	61	0.7%		1	New York	2,644	28.2%
37	Alaska	1	0.0%		2	Georgia	981	10.5%
15	Arizona	77	0.8%		3	Texas	910	9.7%
21	Arkansas	42	0.4%		4	New Jersey	874	9.3%
NA	California**	NA	NA		5	Ohio	696	7.4%
12	Colorado	229	2.4%		6	Kansas	561	6.0%
20	Connecticut	54	0.6%		7	Virginia	450	4.8%
30	Delaware	10	0.1%		8	Oregon	292	3.1%
NA	Florida**	NA	NA		9	Louisiana	275	2.9%
2	Georgia	981	10.5%		10	Pennsylvania	263	2.8%
23	Hawaii	27	0.3%		11	Michigan	244	2.6%
34	Idaho	4	0.0%		12	Colorado	229	2.4%
NA	Illinois**	NA	NA		13	Wisconsin	201	2.1%
40	Indiana	0	0.0%		14	Minnesota	124	1.3%
33	Iowa	5	0.1%		15	Arizona	77	0.8%
6	Kansas	561	6.0%		16	Washington	76	0.8%
19	Kentucky	59	0.6%		17	New Mexico	63	0.7%
9	Louisiana	275	2.9%		18	Alabama	61	0.7%
29	Maine	11	0.1%		19	Kentucky	59	0.6%
NA	Maryland**	NA	NA		20	Connecticut	54	0.6%
NA	Massachusetts**	NA	NA		21	Arkansas	42	0.4%
11	Michigan	244	2.6%		22	Nevada	33	0.4%
14	Minnesota	124	1.3%		23	Hawaii	27	0.3%
37	Mississippi	1	0.0%		23	Montana	27	0.3%
26	Missouri	19	0.2%		25	South Carolina	25	0.3%
23	Montana	27	0.3%		26	Missouri	19	0.2%
NA	Nebraska**	NA	NA		27	Rhode Island	12	0.1%
22	Nevada	33	0.4%		27	Tennessee	12	0.1%
NA	New Hampshire**	NA	NA		29	Maine	11	0.1%
4	New Jersey	874	9.3%		30	Delaware	10	0.1%
17	New Mexico	63	0.7%		31	North Carolina	8	0.1%
1	New York	2,644	28.2%		32	Oklahoma	7	0.1%
31	North Carolina	8	0.1%		33	Iowa	5	0.1%
40	North Dakota	0	0.0%		34	Idaho	4	0.0%
5	Ohio	696	7.4%		35	Utah	2	0.0%
32	Oklahoma	7	0.1%		35	Vermont	2	0.0%
8	Oregon	292	3.1%		37	Alaska	1	0.0%
10	Pennsylvania	263	2.8%		37	Mississippi	1	0.0%
27	Rhode Island	12	0.1%		37	South Dakota	1	0.0%
25	South Carolina	25	0.3%		40	Indiana	0	0.0%
37	South Dakota	1	0.0%		40	North Dakota	0	0.0%
27	Tennessee	12	0.1%		NA	California**	NA	NA
3	Texas	910	9.7%		NA	Florida**	NA	NA
35	Utah	2	0.0%		NA	Illinois**	NA	NA
35	Vermont	2	0.0%		NA	Maryland**	NA	NA
7	Virginia	450	4.8%		NA	Massachusetts**	NA	NA
16	Washington	76	0.8%		NA	Nebraska**	NA	NA
NA	West Virginia**	NA	NA		NA	New Hampshire**	NA	NA
13	Wisconsin	201	2.1%		NA	West Virginia**	NA	NA
NA	Wyoming**	NA	NA		NA	Wyoming**	NA	NA
						District of Columbia	0	0.0%

Source: U.S. Department of Health and Human Services, Centers for Disease Control and Prevention
 "Abortion Surveillance-United States, 2003" (Morbidity and Mortality Weekly Report, Vol. 55, No. SS-11, 11/24/06)
By state of occurrence. National total is for reporting states only.
***Not reported.*

Percent of Reported Legal Abortions Performed at or After
21 Weeks of Gestation in 2003
Reporting States' Percent = 1.4% of Abortions*

ALPHA ORDER

RANK ORDER

RANK	STATE	PERCENT
21	Alabama	0.6
31	Alaska	0.1
18	Arizona	0.7
16	Arkansas	0.8
NA	California**	NA
5	Colorado	2.3
22	Connecticut	0.4
28	Delaware	0.2
NA	Florida**	NA
2	Georgia	2.9
18	Hawaii	0.7
22	Idaho	0.4
NA	Illinois**	NA
38	Indiana	0.0
31	Iowa	0.1
1	Kansas	4.8
11	Kentucky	1.6
4	Louisiana	2.6
22	Maine	0.4
NA	Maryland**	NA
NA	Massachusetts**	NA
16	Michigan	0.8
15	Minnesota	0.9
38	Mississippi	0.0
28	Missouri	0.2
12	Montana	1.2
NA	Nebraska**	NA
22	Nevada	0.4
NA	New Hampshire**	NA
3	New Jersey	2.7
13	New Mexico	1.1
7	New York	2.1
38	North Carolina	0.0
38	North Dakota	0.0
8	Ohio	2.0
31	Oklahoma	0.1
5	Oregon	2.3
18	Pennsylvania	0.7
28	Rhode Island	0.2
22	South Carolina	0.4
31	South Dakota	0.1
31	Tennessee	0.1
13	Texas	1.1
31	Utah	0.1
31	Vermont	0.1
10	Virginia	1.7
27	Washington	0.3
NA	West Virginia**	NA
9	Wisconsin	1.9
NA	Wyoming**	NA

RANK	STATE	PERCENT
1	Kansas	4.8
2	Georgia	2.9
3	New Jersey	2.7
4	Louisiana	2.6
5	Colorado	2.3
5	Oregon	2.3
7	New York	2.1
8	Ohio	2.0
9	Wisconsin	1.9
10	Virginia	1.7
11	Kentucky	1.6
12	Montana	1.2
13	New Mexico	1.1
13	Texas	1.1
15	Minnesota	0.9
16	Arkansas	0.8
16	Michigan	0.8
18	Arizona	0.7
18	Hawaii	0.7
18	Pennsylvania	0.7
21	Alabama	0.6
22	Connecticut	0.4
22	Idaho	0.4
22	Maine	0.4
22	Nevada	0.4
22	South Carolina	0.4
27	Washington	0.3
28	Delaware	0.2
28	Missouri	0.2
28	Rhode Island	0.2
31	Alaska	0.1
31	Iowa	0.1
31	Oklahoma	0.1
31	South Dakota	0.1
31	Tennessee	0.1
31	Utah	0.1
31	Vermont	0.1
38	Indiana	0.0
38	Mississippi	0.0
38	North Carolina	0.0
38	North Dakota	0.0
NA	California**	NA
NA	Florida**	NA
NA	Illinois**	NA
NA	Maryland**	NA
NA	Massachusetts**	NA
NA	Nebraska**	NA
NA	New Hampshire**	NA
NA	West Virginia**	NA
NA	Wyoming**	NA

District of Columbia   0.0

Source: Morgan Quitno Press using data from US Dept of Health & Human Serv's, Centers for Disease Control-Prevention "Abortion Surveillance-United States, 2003" (Morbidity and Mortality Weekly Report, Vol. 55, No. SS-11, 11/24/06)
By state of occurrence. National percent is for reporting states only.
**Not reported.*

II. DEATHS

86   Deaths in 2005
87   Death Rate in 2005
88   Deaths in 2004
89   Death Rate in 2004
90   Age-Adjusted Death Rate in 2004
91   Percent Change in Death Rate: 1995 to 2004
92   Deaths in 2003
93   Death Rate in 2003
94   Age-Adjusted Death Rate in 2003
95   Infant Deaths in 2005
96   Infant Mortality Rate in 2005
97   Infant Deaths in 2003
98   Infant Mortality Rate in 2003
99   White Infant Deaths in 2003
100   White Infant Mortality Rate in 2003
101   Black Infant Deaths in 2003
102   Black Infant Mortality Rate in 2003
103   Neonatal Deaths in 2003
104   Neonatal Death Rate in 2003
105   White Neonatal Deaths in 2003
106   White Neonatal Death Rate in 2003
107   Black Neonatal Deaths in 2003
108   Black Neonatal Death Rate in 2003
109   Deaths by AIDS in 2003
110   Death Rate by AIDS in 2003
111   Age-Adjusted Death Rate by AIDS in 2003
112   Estimated Deaths by Cancer in 2007
113   Estimated Death Rate by Cancer in 2007
114   Age-Adjusted Death Rate by Cancer for Males in 2003
115   Age-Adjusted Death Rate by Cancer for Females in 2003
116   Estimated Deaths by Brain Cancer in 2007
117   Estimated Death Rate by Brain Cancer in 2007
118   Estimated Deaths by Female Breast Cancer in 2007
119   Age-Adjusted Death Rate by Female Breast Cancer in 2003
120   Estimated Deaths by Colon and Rectum Cancer in 2007
121   Estimated Death Rate by Colon and Rectum Cancer in 2007
122   Estimated Deaths by Leukemia in 2007
123   Estimated Death Rate by Leukemia in 2007
124   Estimated Deaths by Liver Cancer in 2007
125   Estimated Death Rate by Liver Cancer in 2007
126   Estimated Deaths by Lung Cancer in 2007
127   Estimated Death Rate by Lung Cancer in 2007
128   Estimated Deaths by Non-Hodgkin's Lymphoma in 2007
129   Estimated Death Rate by Non-Hodgkin's Lymphoma in 2007
130   Estimated Deaths by Pancreatic Cancer in 2007
131   Estimated Death Rate by Pancreatic Cancer in 2007
132   Estimated Deaths by Prostate Cancer in 2007
133   Age-Adjusted Death Rate by Prostate Cancer in 2003
134   Estimated Deaths by Ovarian Cancer in 2007
135   Estimated Death Rate by Ovarian Cancer in 2007
136   Deaths by Alzheimer's Disease in 2003
137   Death Rate by Alzheimer's Disease in 2003
138   Age-Adjusted Death Rate by Alzheimer's Disease in 2003
139   Deaths by Cerebrovascular Diseases in 2003
140   Death Rate by Cerebrovascular Diseases in 2003
141   Age-Adjusted Death Rate by Cerebrovascular Diseases in 2003
142   Deaths by Chronic Liver Disease and Cirrhosis in 2003
143   Death Rate by Chronic Liver Disease and Cirrhosis in 2003
144   Age-Adjusted Death Rate by Chronic Liver Disease and Cirrhosis in 2003
145   Deaths by Chronic Lower Respiratory Diseases in 2003
146   Death Rate by Chronic Lower Respiratory Diseases in 2003

II. DEATHS (Continued)

147   Age-Adjusted Death Rate by Chronic Lower Respiratory Diseases in 2003
148   Deaths by Diabetes Mellitus in 2003
149   Death Rate by Diabetes Mellitus in 2003
150   Age-Adjusted Death Rate by Diabetes Mellitus in 2003
151   Deaths by Diseases of the Heart in 2003
152   Death Rate by Diseases of the Heart in 2003
153   Age-Adjusted Death Rate by Diseases of the Heart in 2003
154   Deaths by Malignant Neoplasms in 2003
155   Death Rate by Malignant Neoplasms in 2003
156   Age-Adjusted Death Rate by Malignant Neoplasms in 2003
157   Deaths by Nephritis and Other Kidney Diseases in 2003
158   Death Rate by Nephritis and Other Kidney Diseases in 2003
159   Age-Adjusted Death Rate by Nephritis and Other Kidney Diseases in 2003
160   Deaths by Pneumonia and Influenza in 2003
161   Death Rate by Pneumonia and Influenza in 2003
162   Age-Adjusted Death Rate by Pneumonia and Influenza in 2003
163   Deaths by Injury in 2003
164   Death Rate by Injury in 2003
165   Age-Adjusted Death Rate by Injury in 2003
166   Deaths by Accidents in 2003
167   Death Rate by Accidents in 2003
168   Age-Adjusted Death Rate by Accidents in 2003
169   Deaths by Motor Vehicle Accidents in 2003
170   Death Rate by Motor Vehicle Accidents in 2003
171   Age-Adjusted Death Rate by Motor Vehicle Accidents in 2003
172   Deaths by Firearm Injury in 2003
173   Death Rate by Firearm Injury in 2003
174   Age-Adjusted Death Rate by Firearm Injury in 2003
175   Deaths by Homicide in 2003
176   Death Rate by Homicide in 2003
177   Age-Adjusted Death Rate by Homicide in 2003
178   Deaths by Suicide in 2003
179   Death Rate by Suicide in 2003
180   Age-Adjusted Death Rate by Suicide in 2003
181   Alcohol-Induced Deaths in 2003
182   Death Rate by Alcohol-Induced Deaths in 2003
183   Age-Adjusted Death Rate by Alcohol-Induced Deaths in 2003
184   Occupational Fatalities in 2005
185   Occupational Fatality Rate in 2005

Deaths in 2005

National Total = 2,431,828 Deaths*

ALPHA ORDER					RANK ORDER			
RANK	STATE	DEATHS	% of USA		RANK	STATE	DEATHS	% of USA
17	Alabama	47,150	1.9%		1	California	232,211	9.5%
50	Alaska	2,944	0.1%		2	Florida	170,050	7.0%
20	Arizona	45,654	1.9%		3	Texas	154,994	6.4%
31	Arkansas	28,227	1.2%		4	New York	154,147	6.3%
1	California	232,211	9.5%		5	Pennsylvania	128,401	5.3%
28	Colorado	29,563	1.2%		6	Ohio	108,088	4.4%
29	Connecticut	29,515	1.2%		7	Illinois	102,922	4.2%
45	Delaware	7,375	0.3%		8	Michigan	86,933	3.6%
2	Florida	170,050	7.0%		9	North Carolina	74,693	3.1%
11	Georgia	65,683	2.7%		10	New Jersey	71,955	3.0%
43	Hawaii	9,105	0.4%		11	Georgia	65,683	2.7%
40	Idaho	10,665	0.4%		12	Virginia	57,715	2.4%
7	Illinois	102,922	4.2%		13	Tennessee	57,129	2.3%
14	Indiana	54,874	2.3%		14	Indiana	54,874	2.3%
32	Iowa	27,875	1.1%		15	Missouri	54,692	2.2%
33	Kansas	24,774	1.0%		16	Massachusetts	53,447	2.2%
23	Kentucky	40,386	1.7%		17	Alabama	47,150	1.9%
22	Louisiana	42,012	1.7%		18	Wisconsin	46,699	1.9%
39	Maine	12,849	0.5%		19	Washington	45,951	1.9%
21	Maryland	44,044	1.8%		20	Arizona	45,654	1.9%
16	Massachusetts	53,447	2.2%		21	Maryland	44,044	1.8%
8	Michigan	86,933	3.6%		22	Louisiana	42,012	1.7%
24	Minnesota	37,461	1.5%		23	Kentucky	40,386	1.7%
30	Mississippi	29,257	1.2%		24	Minnesota	37,461	1.5%
15	Missouri	54,692	2.2%		25	South Carolina	37,167	1.5%
44	Montana	8,414	0.3%		26	Oklahoma	36,278	1.5%
36	Nebraska	14,882	0.6%		27	Oregon	31,120	1.3%
35	Nevada	18,562	0.8%		28	Colorado	29,563	1.2%
42	New Hampshire	9,985	0.4%		29	Connecticut	29,515	1.2%
10	New Jersey	71,955	3.0%		30	Mississippi	29,257	1.2%
37	New Mexico	14,788	0.6%		31	Arkansas	28,227	1.2%
4	New York	154,147	6.3%		32	Iowa	27,875	1.1%
9	North Carolina	74,693	3.1%		33	Kansas	24,774	1.0%
47	North Dakota	5,761	0.2%		34	West Virginia	20,649	0.8%
6	Ohio	108,088	4.4%		35	Nevada	18,562	0.8%
26	Oklahoma	36,278	1.5%		36	Nebraska	14,882	0.6%
27	Oregon	31,120	1.3%		37	New Mexico	14,788	0.6%
5	Pennsylvania	128,401	5.3%		38	Utah	13,356	0.5%
41	Rhode Island	10,042	0.4%		39	Maine	12,849	0.5%
25	South Carolina	37,167	1.5%		40	Idaho	10,665	0.4%
46	South Dakota	7,042	0.3%		41	Rhode Island	10,042	0.4%
13	Tennessee	57,129	2.3%		42	New Hampshire	9,985	0.4%
3	Texas	154,994	6.4%		43	Hawaii	9,105	0.4%
38	Utah	13,356	0.5%		44	Montana	8,414	0.3%
48	Vermont	4,889	0.2%		45	Delaware	7,375	0.3%
12	Virginia	57,715	2.4%		46	South Dakota	7,042	0.3%
19	Washington	45,951	1.9%		47	North Dakota	5,761	0.2%
34	West Virginia	20,649	0.8%		48	Vermont	4,889	0.2%
18	Wisconsin	46,699	1.9%		49	Wyoming	4,062	0.2%
49	Wyoming	4,062	0.2%		50	Alaska	2,944	0.1%
						District of Columbia	5,391	0.2%

Source: U.S. Department of Health and Human Services, National Center for Health Statistics
"National Vital Statistics Reports" (Vol. 54, No. 20, July 21, 2006)
*Provisional data for 12 months ending with December by state of residence.

Death Rate in 2005

National Rate = 820.2 Deaths per 100,000 Population*

ALPHA ORDER				RANK ORDER		
RANK	STATE	RATE		RANK	STATE	RATE
2	Alabama	1,036.6		1	West Virginia	1,138.3
50	Alaska	443.9		2	Alabama	1,036.6
38	Arizona	766.9		3	Pennsylvania	1,035.0
5	Arkansas	1,016.9		4	Oklahoma	1,023.8
47	California	642.3		5	Arkansas	1,016.9
48	Colorado	634.0		6	Mississippi	1,005.9
28	Connecticut	843.1		7	Maine	974.7
20	Delaware	876.2		8	Kentucky	967.9
10	Florida	957.0		9	Tennessee	959.2
44	Georgia	719.2		10	Florida	957.0
45	Hawaii	715.1		11	Missouri	943.3
41	Idaho	746.1		12	Ohio	942.3
31	Illinois	806.3		13	Iowa	940.0
21	Indiana	875.7		14	Rhode Island	935.4
13	Iowa	940.0		15	Louisiana	932.1
18	Kansas	901.5		16	South Dakota	908.8
8	Kentucky	967.9		17	North Dakota	907.8
15	Louisiana	932.1		18	Kansas	901.5
7	Maine	974.7		19	Montana	900.1
34	Maryland	788.0		20	Delaware	876.2
29	Massachusetts	830.8		21	Indiana	875.7
24	Michigan	860.7		22	South Carolina	875.1
42	Minnesota	730.7		23	North Carolina	861.3
6	Mississippi	1,005.9		24	Michigan	860.7
11	Missouri	943.3		25	Oregon	855.2
19	Montana	900.1		26	Nebraska	846.5
26	Nebraska	846.5		27	Wisconsin	844.8
36	Nevada	769.5		28	Connecticut	843.1
39	New Hampshire	764.1		29	Massachusetts	830.8
30	New Jersey	826.8		30	New Jersey	826.8
37	New Mexico	767.8		31	Illinois	806.3
33	New York	798.0		32	Wyoming	798.4
23	North Carolina	861.3		33	New York	798.0
17	North Dakota	907.8		34	Maryland	788.0
12	Ohio	942.3		35	Vermont	785.5
4	Oklahoma	1,023.8		36	Nevada	769.5
25	Oregon	855.2		37	New Mexico	767.8
3	Pennsylvania	1,035.0		38	Arizona	766.9
14	Rhode Island	935.4		39	New Hampshire	764.1
22	South Carolina	875.1		40	Virginia	763.0
16	South Dakota	908.8		41	Idaho	746.1
9	Tennessee	959.2		42	Minnesota	730.7
46	Texas	676.0		43	Washington	730.3
49	Utah	536.3		44	Georgia	719.2
35	Vermont	785.5		45	Hawaii	715.1
40	Virginia	763.0		46	Texas	676.0
43	Washington	730.3		47	California	642.3
1	West Virginia	1,138.3		48	Colorado	634.0
27	Wisconsin	844.8		49	Utah	536.3
32	Wyoming	798.4		50	Alaska	443.9

| | | | | | District of Columbia | 926.2 |

Source: Morgan Quitno Press using data from US Dept of Health & Human Services, National Center for Health Statistics
    "National Vital Statistics Reports" (Vol. 54, No. 20, July 21, 2006)
*Provisional data for 12 months ending with December by state of residence. Not age-adjusted.

Deaths in 2004

National Total = 2,398,343 Deaths*

ALPHA ORDER

RANK	STATE	DEATHS	% of USA
14	Alabama	46,111	1.9%
47	Alaska	3,049	0.1%
18	Arizona	43,172	1.8%
28	Arkansas	27,539	1.1%
NA	California**	NA	NA
26	Colorado	28,310	1.2%
25	Connecticut	29,289	1.2%
42	Delaware	7,153	0.3%
1	Florida	168,952	7.0%
8	Georgia	65,859	2.7%
40	Hawaii	9,038	0.4%
38	Idaho	10,044	0.4%
NA	Illinois**	NA	NA
12	Indiana	54,260	2.3%
29	Iowa	26,884	1.1%
30	Kansas	23,816	1.0%
20	Kentucky	38,668	1.6%
19	Louisiana	42,304	1.8%
36	Maine	12,405	0.5%
17	Maryland	43,224	1.8%
11	Massachusetts	54,546	2.3%
6	Michigan	85,160	3.6%
22	Minnesota	37,074	1.5%
27	Mississippi	27,870	1.2%
13	Missouri	53,933	2.2%
41	Montana	8,097	0.3%
33	Nebraska	14,648	0.6%
32	Nevada	17,864	0.7%
37	New Hampshire	10,110	0.4%
NA	New Jersey**	NA	NA
34	New Mexico	14,292	0.6%
3	New York	152,665	6.4%
7	North Carolina	72,383	3.0%
44	North Dakota	5,603	0.2%
5	Ohio	106,350	4.4%
23	Oklahoma	34,477	1.4%
24	Oregon	30,332	1.3%
4	Pennsylvania	127,630	5.3%
39	Rhode Island	9,767	0.4%
21	South Carolina	37,289	1.6%
43	South Dakota	6,839	0.3%
10	Tennessee	55,835	2.3%
2	Texas	153,031	6.4%
35	Utah	13,327	0.6%
45	Vermont	4,995	0.2%
9	Virginia	56,549	2.4%
16	Washington	44,820	1.9%
31	West Virginia	20,795	0.9%
15	Wisconsin	45,607	1.9%
46	Wyoming	3,950	0.2%

RANK ORDER

RANK	STATE	DEATHS	% of USA
1	Florida	168,952	7.0%
2	Texas	153,031	6.4%
3	New York	152,665	6.4%
4	Pennsylvania	127,630	5.3%
5	Ohio	106,350	4.4%
6	Michigan	85,160	3.6%
7	North Carolina	72,383	3.0%
8	Georgia	65,859	2.7%
9	Virginia	56,549	2.4%
10	Tennessee	55,835	2.3%
11	Massachusetts	54,546	2.3%
12	Indiana	54,260	2.3%
13	Missouri	53,933	2.2%
14	Alabama	46,111	1.9%
15	Wisconsin	45,607	1.9%
16	Washington	44,820	1.9%
17	Maryland	43,224	1.8%
18	Arizona	43,172	1.8%
19	Louisiana	42,304	1.8%
20	Kentucky	38,668	1.6%
21	South Carolina	37,289	1.6%
22	Minnesota	37,074	1.5%
23	Oklahoma	34,477	1.4%
24	Oregon	30,332	1.3%
25	Connecticut	29,289	1.2%
26	Colorado	28,310	1.2%
27	Mississippi	27,870	1.2%
28	Arkansas	27,539	1.1%
29	Iowa	26,884	1.1%
30	Kansas	23,816	1.0%
31	West Virginia	20,795	0.9%
32	Nevada	17,864	0.7%
33	Nebraska	14,648	0.6%
34	New Mexico	14,292	0.6%
35	Utah	13,327	0.6%
36	Maine	12,405	0.5%
37	New Hampshire	10,110	0.4%
38	Idaho	10,044	0.4%
39	Rhode Island	9,767	0.4%
40	Hawaii	9,038	0.4%
41	Montana	8,097	0.3%
42	Delaware	7,153	0.3%
43	South Dakota	6,839	0.3%
44	North Dakota	5,603	0.2%
45	Vermont	4,995	0.2%
46	Wyoming	3,950	0.2%
47	Alaska	3,049	0.1%
NA	California**	NA	NA
NA	Illinois**	NA	NA
NA	New Jersey**	NA	NA
	District of Columbia	5,432	0.2%

Source: U.S. Department of Health and Human Services, National Center for Health Statistics
    "National Vital Statistics Reports" (Vol. 54, No. 19, June 28, 2006)
Preliminary data by state of residence.
**Not available by state but are included in national total.*

Death Rate in 2004

National Rate = 816.7 Deaths per 100,000 Population*

ALPHA ORDER

RANK ORDER

RANK	STATE	RATE		RANK	STATE	RATE
3	Alabama	1,017.9		1	West Virginia	1,145.5
47	Alaska	465.2		2	Pennsylvania	1,028.8
37	Arizona	751.6		3	Alabama	1,017.9
4	Arkansas	1,000.5		4	Arkansas	1,000.5
NA	California**	NA		5	Oklahoma	978.5
45	Colorado	615.2		6	Florida	971.1
28	Connecticut	836.0		7	Mississippi	960.1
22	Delaware	861.4		8	Tennessee	946.2
6	Florida	971.1		9	Maine	941.7
39	Georgia	745.9		10	Missouri	937.2
43	Hawaii	715.7		11	Louisiana	936.8
42	Idaho	720.9		12	Kentucky	932.7
NA	Illinois**	NA		13	Ohio	928.1
21	Indiana	869.9		14	Iowa	909.9
14	Iowa	909.9		15	Rhode Island	903.8
20	Kansas	870.6		16	South Carolina	888.2
12	Kentucky	932.7		17	South Dakota	887.2
11	Louisiana	936.8		18	North Dakota	883.2
9	Maine	941.7		19	Montana	873.6
34	Maryland	777.7		20	Kansas	870.6
23	Massachusetts	850.1		21	Indiana	869.9
26	Michigan	842.1		22	Delaware	861.4
40	Minnesota	726.8		23	Massachusetts	850.1
7	Mississippi	960.1		24	North Carolina	847.5
10	Missouri	937.2		25	Oregon	843.8
19	Montana	873.6		26	Michigan	842.1
27	Nebraska	838.4		27	Nebraska	838.4
35	Nevada	765.1		28	Connecticut	836.0
33	New Hampshire	778.0		29	Wisconsin	827.9
NA	New Jersey**	NA		30	Vermont	803.8
38	New Mexico	750.9		31	New York	794.0
31	New York	794.0		32	Wyoming	779.8
24	North Carolina	847.5		33	New Hampshire	778.0
18	North Dakota	883.2		34	Maryland	777.7
13	Ohio	928.1		35	Nevada	765.1
5	Oklahoma	978.5		36	Virginia	758.0
25	Oregon	843.8		37	Arizona	751.6
2	Pennsylvania	1,028.8		38	New Mexico	750.9
15	Rhode Island	903.8		39	Georgia	745.9
16	South Carolina	888.2		40	Minnesota	726.8
17	South Dakota	887.2		41	Washington	722.5
8	Tennessee	946.2		42	Idaho	720.9
44	Texas	680.4		43	Hawaii	715.7
46	Utah	557.8		44	Texas	680.4
30	Vermont	803.8		45	Colorado	615.2
36	Virginia	758.0		46	Utah	557.8
41	Washington	722.5		47	Alaska	465.2
1	West Virginia	1,145.5		NA	California**	NA
29	Wisconsin	827.9		NA	Illinois**	NA
32	Wyoming	779.8		NA	New Jersey**	NA
					District of Columbia	981.4

Source: U.S. Department of Health and Human Services, National Center for Health Statistics
"National Vital Statistics Reports" (Vol. 54, No. 19, June 28, 2006)
Preliminary data by state of residence. Not age-adjusted.
**Not available by state but are included in national rate.*

Age-Adjusted Death Rate in 2004

National Rate = 801.0 Deaths per 100,000 Population*

RANK	STATE	RATE
2	Alabama	992.3
34	Alaska	749.5
31	Arizona	757.6
8	Arkansas	925.2
NA	California**	NA
40	Colorado	736.5
44	Connecticut	705.6
17	Delaware	824.7
28	Florida	763.3
8	Georgia	925.2
47	Hawaii	623.6
32	Idaho	754.7
NA	Illinois**	NA
14	Indiana	850.3
43	Iowa	728.9
23	Kansas	793.5
7	Kentucky	935.4
3	Louisiana	988.1
22	Maine	803.6
21	Maryland	805.8
37	Massachusetts	741.1
19	Michigan	812.6
46	Minnesota	692.0
1	Mississippi	998.2
13	Missouri	871.7
25	Montana	778.8
36	Nebraska	746.4
11	Nevada	877.9
29	New Hampshire	761.0
NA	New Jersey**	NA
26	New Mexico	778.5
41	New York	733.7
12	North Carolina	874.9
45	North Dakota	697.6
15	Ohio	848.5
6	Oklahoma	947.5
27	Oregon	778.1
18	Pennsylvania	814.5
38	Rhode Island	740.9
10	South Carolina	898.2
35	South Dakota	747.1
5	Tennessee	954.1
16	Texas	836.5
30	Utah	760.3
42	Vermont	730.9
20	Virginia	809.2
39	Washington	739.1
4	West Virginia	966.1
33	Wisconsin	749.9
24	Wyoming	788.5

RANK	STATE	RATE
1	Mississippi	998.2
2	Alabama	992.3
3	Louisiana	988.1
4	West Virginia	966.1
5	Tennessee	954.1
6	Oklahoma	947.5
7	Kentucky	935.4
8	Arkansas	925.2
8	Georgia	925.2
10	South Carolina	898.2
11	Nevada	877.9
12	North Carolina	874.9
13	Missouri	871.7
14	Indiana	850.3
15	Ohio	848.5
16	Texas	836.5
17	Delaware	824.7
18	Pennsylvania	814.5
19	Michigan	812.6
20	Virginia	809.2
21	Maryland	805.8
22	Maine	803.6
23	Kansas	793.5
24	Wyoming	788.5
25	Montana	778.8
26	New Mexico	778.5
27	Oregon	778.1
28	Florida	763.3
29	New Hampshire	761.0
30	Utah	760.3
31	Arizona	757.6
32	Idaho	754.7
33	Wisconsin	749.9
34	Alaska	749.5
35	South Dakota	747.1
36	Nebraska	746.4
37	Massachusetts	741.1
38	Rhode Island	740.9
39	Washington	739.1
40	Colorado	736.5
41	New York	733.7
42	Vermont	730.9
43	Iowa	728.9
44	Connecticut	705.6
45	North Dakota	697.6
46	Minnesota	692.0
47	Hawaii	623.6
NA	California**	NA
NA	Illinois**	NA
NA	New Jersey**	NA

District of Columbia   970.2

Source: U.S. Department of Health and Human Services, National Center for Health Statistics
"National Vital Statistics Reports" (Vol. 54, No. 19, June 28, 2006)
*Preliminary data by state of residence. Age-adjusted rates eliminate the distorting effects of the aging of the population. Rates based on the year 2000 standard population.
**Not available by state but are included in national rate.

Percent Change in Death Rate: 1995 to 2004

National Percent Change = 7.2% Decrease*

ALPHA ORDER

RANK	STATE	PERCENT CHANGE
5	Alabama	2.2
2	Alaska	10.0
45	Arizona	(10.3)
34	Arkansas	(6.9)
NA	California**	NA
40	Colorado	(7.8)
36	Connecticut	(7.1)
12	Delaware	(1.7)
44	Florida	(10.2)
41	Georgia	(8.0)
1	Hawaii	11.3
11	Idaho	(1.5)
NA	Illinois**	NA
26	Indiana	(5.3)
39	Iowa	(7.7)
33	Kansas	(6.7)
18	Kentucky	(3.2)
4	Louisiana	2.4
9	Maine	(0.5)
30	Maryland	(6.3)
34	Massachusetts	(6.9)
21	Michigan	(3.9)
46	Minnesota	(10.7)
22	Mississippi	(4.2)
42	Missouri	(8.3)
8	Montana	(0.3)
43	Nebraska	(10.1)
31	Nevada	(6.5)
18	New Hampshire	(3.2)
NA	New Jersey**	NA
6	New Mexico	0.9
47	New York	(14.5)
28	North Carolina	(6.1)
24	North Dakota	(5.2)
13	Ohio	(2.3)
14	Oklahoma	(2.4)
28	Oregon	(6.1)
16	Pennsylvania	(2.9)
37	Rhode Island	(7.4)
15	South Carolina	(2.7)
31	South Dakota	(6.5)
17	Tennessee	(3.1)
38	Texas	(7.6)
9	Utah	(0.5)
23	Vermont	(5.1)
24	Virginia	(5.2)
20	Washington	(3.8)
3	West Virginia	3.5
27	Wisconsin	(5.9)
7	Wyoming	0.7

RANK ORDER

RANK	STATE	PERCENT CHANGE
1	Hawaii	11.3
2	Alaska	10.0
3	West Virginia	3.5
4	Louisiana	2.4
5	Alabama	2.2
6	New Mexico	0.9
7	Wyoming	0.7
8	Montana	(0.3)
9	Maine	(0.5)
9	Utah	(0.5)
11	Idaho	(1.5)
12	Delaware	(1.7)
13	Ohio	(2.3)
14	Oklahoma	(2.4)
15	South Carolina	(2.7)
16	Pennsylvania	(2.9)
17	Tennessee	(3.1)
18	Kentucky	(3.2)
18	New Hampshire	(3.2)
20	Washington	(3.8)
21	Michigan	(3.9)
22	Mississippi	(4.2)
23	Vermont	(5.1)
24	North Dakota	(5.2)
24	Virginia	(5.2)
26	Indiana	(5.3)
27	Wisconsin	(5.9)
28	North Carolina	(6.1)
28	Oregon	(6.1)
30	Maryland	(6.3)
31	Nevada	(6.5)
31	South Dakota	(6.5)
33	Kansas	(6.7)
34	Arkansas	(6.9)
34	Massachusetts	(6.9)
36	Connecticut	(7.1)
37	Rhode Island	(7.4)
38	Texas	(7.6)
39	Iowa	(7.7)
40	Colorado	(7.8)
41	Georgia	(8.0)
42	Missouri	(8.3)
43	Nebraska	(10.1)
44	Florida	(10.2)
45	Arizona	(10.3)
46	Minnesota	(10.7)
47	New York	(14.5)
NA	California**	NA
NA	Illinois**	NA
NA	New Jersey**	NA

District of Columbia   (21.1)

Source: Morgan Quitno Press using data from US Dept of Health & Human Services, National Center for Health Statistics
"National Vital Statistics Reports" (Vol. 54, No. 19, June 28, 2006)
"Monthly Vital Statistics Report" (Vol. 46, No. 1(S)2, September 11, 1997)

*By state of residence. Not age-adjusted.
**Not available.

Deaths in 2003

National Total = 2,448,288 Deaths*

ALPHA ORDER

RANK	STATE	DEATHS	% of USA
17	Alabama	46,716	1.9%
50	Alaska	3,180	0.1%
21	Arizona	43,392	1.8%
32	Arkansas	27,918	1.1%
1	California	239,371	9.8%
29	Colorado	29,506	1.2%
28	Connecticut	29,627	1.2%
46	Delaware	7,070	0.3%
2	Florida	168,657	6.9%
11	Georgia	66,478	2.7%
43	Hawaii	8,978	0.4%
40	Idaho	10,380	0.4%
7	Illinois	105,325	4.3%
15	Indiana	55,968	2.3%
31	Iowa	28,062	1.1%
33	Kansas	24,593	1.0%
23	Kentucky	40,241	1.6%
22	Louisiana	42,719	1.7%
39	Maine	12,540	0.5%
20	Maryland	44,499	1.8%
14	Massachusetts	56,291	2.3%
8	Michigan	86,728	3.5%
25	Minnesota	37,620	1.5%
30	Mississippi	28,489	1.2%
16	Missouri	55,582	2.3%
44	Montana	8,467	0.3%
36	Nebraska	15,465	0.6%
35	Nevada	17,858	0.7%
42	New Hampshire	9,708	0.4%
9	New Jersey	73,689	3.0%
37	New Mexico	14,805	0.6%
3	New York	155,877	6.4%
10	North Carolina	73,459	3.0%
47	North Dakota	6,090	0.2%
6	Ohio	109,110	4.5%
26	Oklahoma	35,721	1.5%
27	Oregon	30,912	1.3%
5	Pennsylvania	129,769	5.3%
41	Rhode Island	10,039	0.4%
24	South Carolina	38,112	1.6%
45	South Dakota	7,132	0.3%
13	Tennessee	57,313	2.3%
4	Texas	154,870	6.3%
38	Utah	13,412	0.5%
48	Vermont	5,120	0.2%
12	Virginia	58,282	2.4%
19	Washington	45,920	1.9%
34	West Virginia	21,306	0.9%
18	Wisconsin	46,177	1.9%
49	Wyoming	4,172	0.2%

RANK ORDER

RANK	STATE	DEATHS	% of USA
1	California	239,371	9.8%
2	Florida	168,657	6.9%
3	New York	155,877	6.4%
4	Texas	154,870	6.3%
5	Pennsylvania	129,769	5.3%
6	Ohio	109,110	4.5%
7	Illinois	105,325	4.3%
8	Michigan	86,728	3.5%
9	New Jersey	73,689	3.0%
10	North Carolina	73,459	3.0%
11	Georgia	66,478	2.7%
12	Virginia	58,282	2.4%
13	Tennessee	57,313	2.3%
14	Massachusetts	56,291	2.3%
15	Indiana	55,968	2.3%
16	Missouri	55,582	2.3%
17	Alabama	46,716	1.9%
18	Wisconsin	46,177	1.9%
19	Washington	45,920	1.9%
20	Maryland	44,499	1.8%
21	Arizona	43,392	1.8%
22	Louisiana	42,719	1.7%
23	Kentucky	40,241	1.6%
24	South Carolina	38,112	1.6%
25	Minnesota	37,620	1.5%
26	Oklahoma	35,721	1.5%
27	Oregon	30,912	1.3%
28	Connecticut	29,627	1.2%
29	Colorado	29,506	1.2%
30	Mississippi	28,489	1.2%
31	Iowa	28,062	1.1%
32	Arkansas	27,918	1.1%
33	Kansas	24,593	1.0%
34	West Virginia	21,306	0.9%
35	Nevada	17,858	0.7%
36	Nebraska	15,465	0.6%
37	New Mexico	14,805	0.6%
38	Utah	13,412	0.5%
39	Maine	12,540	0.5%
40	Idaho	10,380	0.4%
41	Rhode Island	10,039	0.4%
42	New Hampshire	9,708	0.4%
43	Hawaii	8,978	0.4%
44	Montana	8,467	0.3%
45	South Dakota	7,132	0.3%
46	Delaware	7,070	0.3%
47	North Dakota	6,090	0.2%
48	Vermont	5,120	0.2%
49	Wyoming	4,172	0.2%
50	Alaska	3,180	0.1%
	District of Columbia	5,573	0.2%

Source: U.S. Department of Health and Human Services, National Center for Health Statistics "National Vital Statistics Reports" (Vol. 54, No. 13, April 19, 2006)
Final data by state of residence.

Death Rate in 2003

National Rate = 841.9 Deaths per 100,000 Population*

RANK	STATE	RATE
3	Alabama	1,038.0
50	Alaska	490.1
39	Arizona	777.5
4	Arkansas	1,024.2
47	California	674.6
48	Colorado	648.4
29	Connecticut	850.5
26	Delaware	864.8
6	Florida	991.0
40	Georgia	765.5
45	Hawaii	713.9
41	Idaho	759.7
31	Illinois	832.4
20	Indiana	903.3
14	Iowa	953.2
21	Kansas	903.0
9	Kentucky	977.2
15	Louisiana	950.1
12	Maine	960.4
35	Maryland	807.8
23	Massachusetts	875.0
27	Michigan	860.4
44	Minnesota	743.6
7	Mississippi	988.8
10	Missouri	974.4
18	Montana	922.7
22	Nebraska	889.2
36	Nevada	796.8
42	New Hampshire	753.9
28	New Jersey	853.0
37	New Mexico	789.8
34	New York	812.3
24	North Carolina	873.8
11	North Dakota	960.8
13	Ohio	954.1
5	Oklahoma	1,017.2
25	Oregon	868.4
2	Pennsylvania	1,049.4
17	Rhode Island	932.8
19	South Carolina	919.0
16	South Dakota	933.1
8	Tennessee	981.1
46	Texas	700.2
49	Utah	570.4
33	Vermont	827.0
38	Virginia	789.1
43	Washington	748.9
1	West Virginia	1,176.9
30	Wisconsin	843.8
32	Wyoming	832.3

RANK	STATE	RATE
1	West Virginia	1,176.9
2	Pennsylvania	1,049.4
3	Alabama	1,038.0
4	Arkansas	1,024.2
5	Oklahoma	1,017.2
6	Florida	991.0
7	Mississippi	988.8
8	Tennessee	981.1
9	Kentucky	977.2
10	Missouri	974.4
11	North Dakota	960.8
12	Maine	960.4
13	Ohio	954.1
14	Iowa	953.2
15	Louisiana	950.1
16	South Dakota	933.1
17	Rhode Island	932.8
18	Montana	922.7
19	South Carolina	919.0
20	Indiana	903.3
21	Kansas	903.0
22	Nebraska	889.2
23	Massachusetts	875.0
24	North Carolina	873.8
25	Oregon	868.4
26	Delaware	864.8
27	Michigan	860.4
28	New Jersey	853.0
29	Connecticut	850.5
30	Wisconsin	843.8
31	Illinois	832.4
32	Wyoming	832.3
33	Vermont	827.0
34	New York	812.3
35	Maryland	807.8
36	Nevada	796.8
37	New Mexico	789.8
38	Virginia	789.1
39	Arizona	777.5
40	Georgia	765.5
41	Idaho	759.7
42	New Hampshire	753.9
43	Washington	748.9
44	Minnesota	743.6
45	Hawaii	713.9
46	Texas	700.2
47	California	674.6
48	Colorado	648.4
49	Utah	570.4
50	Alaska	490.1

	District of Columbia	987.5

*Source: U.S. Department of Health and Human Services, National Center for Health Statistics
"National Vital Statistics Reports" (Vol. 54, No. 13, April 19, 2006)*
Final data by state of residence. Not age-adjusted.

Age-Adjusted Death Rate in 2003

National Rate = 832.7 Deaths per 100,000 Population*

ALPHA ORDER

RANK	STATE	RATE
3	Alabama	1,001.7
24	Alaska	829.8
34	Arizona	787.1
9	Arkansas	937.5
46	California	754.3
36	Colorado	784.3
48	Connecticut	734.6
22	Delaware	844.4
39	Florida	776.0
8	Georgia	946.4
50	Hawaii	649.3
30	Idaho	797.1
23	Illinois	834.5
14	Indiana	894.5
42	Iowa	768.4
26	Kansas	824.0
6	Kentucky	977.7
2	Louisiana	1,004.6
28	Maine	822.3
17	Maryland	852.9
38	Massachusetts	778.7
19	Michigan	850.5
49	Minnesota	713.0
1	Mississippi	1,014.0
13	Missouri	902.6
25	Montana	828.1
32	Nebraska	790.5
11	Nevada	924.5
47	New Hampshire	749.8
31	New Jersey	794.8
27	New Mexico	823.8
45	New York	760.1
12	North Carolina	905.8
43	North Dakota	766.6
15	Ohio	889.8
7	Oklahoma	974.3
29	Oregon	808.5
21	Pennsylvania	849.2
35	Rhode Island	786.9
10	South Carolina	934.8
32	South Dakota	790.5
5	Tennessee	982.2
16	Texas	855.7
37	Utah	782.3
44	Vermont	765.3
18	Virginia	850.9
40	Washington	775.9
4	West Virginia	994.9
41	Wisconsin	772.5
20	Wyoming	849.9

RANK ORDER

RANK	STATE	RATE
1	Mississippi	1,014.0
2	Louisiana	1,004.6
3	Alabama	1,001.7
4	West Virginia	994.9
5	Tennessee	982.2
6	Kentucky	977.7
7	Oklahoma	974.3
8	Georgia	946.4
9	Arkansas	937.5
10	South Carolina	934.8
11	Nevada	924.5
12	North Carolina	905.8
13	Missouri	902.6
14	Indiana	894.5
15	Ohio	889.8
16	Texas	855.7
17	Maryland	852.9
18	Virginia	850.9
19	Michigan	850.5
20	Wyoming	849.9
21	Pennsylvania	849.2
22	Delaware	844.4
23	Illinois	834.5
24	Alaska	829.8
25	Montana	828.1
26	Kansas	824.0
27	New Mexico	823.8
28	Maine	822.3
29	Oregon	808.5
30	Idaho	797.1
31	New Jersey	794.8
32	Nebraska	790.5
32	South Dakota	790.5
34	Arizona	787.1
35	Rhode Island	786.9
36	Colorado	784.3
37	Utah	782.3
38	Massachusetts	778.7
39	Florida	776.0
40	Washington	775.9
41	Wisconsin	772.5
42	Iowa	768.4
43	North Dakota	766.6
44	Vermont	765.3
45	New York	760.1
46	California	754.3
47	New Hampshire	749.8
48	Connecticut	734.6
49	Minnesota	713.0
50	Hawaii	649.3
	District of Columbia	982.3

Source: U.S. Department of Health and Human Services, National Center for Health Statistics
"National Vital Statistics Reports" (Vol. 54, No. 13, April 19, 2006)
Final data by state of residence. Age-adjusted rates eliminate the distorting effects of the aging of the population. Rates based on the year 2000 standard population.

Infant Deaths in 2005

National Total = 27,968 Infant Deaths*

ALPHA ORDER

RANK	STATE	DEATHS	% of USA
19	Alabama	546	2.0%
47	Alaska	54	0.2%
14	Arizona	667	2.4%
29	Arkansas	294	1.1%
1	California	2,800	10.0%
23	Colorado	451	1.6%
32	Connecticut	226	0.8%
42	Delaware	88	0.3%
3	Florida	1,633	5.8%
7	Georgia	1,108	4.0%
40	Hawaii	123	0.4%
38	Idaho	154	0.6%
5	Illinois	1,261	4.5%
13	Indiana	676	2.4%
35	Iowa	202	0.7%
30	Kansas	280	1.0%
28	Kentucky	367	1.3%
15	Louisiana	632	2.3%
41	Maine	97	0.3%
16	Maryland	602	2.2%
26	Massachusetts	395	1.4%
10	Michigan	1,014	3.6%
27	Minnesota	370	1.3%
22	Mississippi	465	1.7%
18	Missouri	580	2.1%
46	Montana	71	0.3%
39	Nebraska	149	0.5%
34	Nevada	210	0.8%
43	New Hampshire	75	0.3%
17	New Jersey	586	2.1%
36	New Mexico	177	0.6%
4	New York	1,499	5.4%
8	North Carolina	1,058	3.8%
48	North Dakota	53	0.2%
6	Ohio	1,208	4.3%
24	Oklahoma	422	1.5%
31	Oregon	265	0.9%
9	Pennsylvania	1,036	3.7%
45	Rhode Island	74	0.3%
20	South Carolina	516	1.8%
43	South Dakota	75	0.3%
12	Tennessee	737	2.6%
2	Texas	2,480	8.9%
32	Utah	226	0.8%
50	Vermont	39	0.1%
11	Virginia	760	2.7%
25	Washington	414	1.5%
37	West Virginia	169	0.6%
21	Wisconsin	468	1.7%
49	Wyoming	42	0.2%

RANK ORDER

RANK	STATE	DEATHS	% of USA
1	California	2,800	10.0%
2	Texas	2,480	8.9%
3	Florida	1,633	5.8%
4	New York	1,499	5.4%
5	Illinois	1,261	4.5%
6	Ohio	1,208	4.3%
7	Georgia	1,108	4.0%
8	North Carolina	1,058	3.8%
9	Pennsylvania	1,036	3.7%
10	Michigan	1,014	3.6%
11	Virginia	760	2.7%
12	Tennessee	737	2.6%
13	Indiana	676	2.4%
14	Arizona	667	2.4%
15	Louisiana	632	2.3%
16	Maryland	602	2.2%
17	New Jersey	586	2.1%
18	Missouri	580	2.1%
19	Alabama	546	2.0%
20	South Carolina	516	1.8%
21	Wisconsin	468	1.7%
22	Mississippi	465	1.7%
23	Colorado	451	1.6%
24	Oklahoma	422	1.5%
25	Washington	414	1.5%
26	Massachusetts	395	1.4%
27	Minnesota	370	1.3%
28	Kentucky	367	1.3%
29	Arkansas	294	1.1%
30	Kansas	280	1.0%
31	Oregon	265	0.9%
32	Connecticut	226	0.8%
32	Utah	226	0.8%
34	Nevada	210	0.8%
35	Iowa	202	0.7%
36	New Mexico	177	0.6%
37	West Virginia	169	0.6%
38	Idaho	154	0.6%
39	Nebraska	149	0.5%
40	Hawaii	123	0.4%
41	Maine	97	0.3%
42	Delaware	88	0.3%
43	New Hampshire	75	0.3%
43	South Dakota	75	0.3%
45	Rhode Island	74	0.3%
46	Montana	71	0.3%
47	Alaska	54	0.2%
48	North Dakota	53	0.2%
49	Wyoming	42	0.2%
50	Vermont	39	0.1%
	District of Columbia	74	0.3%

Source: U.S. Department of Health and Human Services, National Center for Health Statistics
   "National Vital Statistics Reports" (Vol. 54, No. 20, July 21, 2006)
*Provisional data for 12 months ending with December. Deaths under 1 year old by state of residence.

Infant Mortality Rate in 2005

National Rate = 6.8 Infant Deaths per 1,000 Live Births*

ALPHA ORDER

RANK ORDER

RANK	STATE	RATE	RANK	STATE	RATE
3	Alabama	9.1	1	Mississippi	11.0
42	Alaska	5.2	2	Louisiana	9.7
21	Arizona	6.9	3	Alabama	9.1
15	Arkansas	7.5	4	Tennessee	9.0
46	California	5.1	5	South Carolina	8.9
27	Colorado	6.5	6	North Carolina	8.6
41	Connecticut	5.4	7	Ohio	8.2
14	Delaware	7.6	7	West Virginia	8.2
17	Florida	7.2	9	Oklahoma	8.1
12	Georgia	7.8	10	Maryland	7.9
21	Hawaii	6.9	10	Michigan	7.9
25	Idaho	6.7	12	Georgia	7.8
20	Illinois	7.1	13	Indiana	7.7
13	Indiana	7.7	14	Delaware	7.6
42	Iowa	5.2	15	Arkansas	7.5
21	Kansas	6.9	16	Missouri	7.4
27	Kentucky	6.5	17	Florida	7.2
2	Louisiana	9.7	17	Pennsylvania	7.2
24	Maine	6.8	17	Virginia	7.2
10	Maryland	7.9	20	Illinois	7.1
46	Massachusetts	5.1	21	Arizona	6.9
10	Michigan	7.9	21	Hawaii	6.9
42	Minnesota	5.2	21	Kansas	6.9
1	Mississippi	11.0	24	Maine	6.8
16	Missouri	7.4	25	Idaho	6.7
31	Montana	6.3	26	Wisconsin	6.6
40	Nebraska	5.7	27	Colorado	6.5
37	Nevada	5.8	27	Kentucky	6.5
42	New Hampshire	5.2	27	South Dakota	6.5
46	New Jersey	5.1	30	Texas	6.4
33	New Mexico	6.2	31	Montana	6.3
35	New York	6.0	31	North Dakota	6.3
6	North Carolina	8.6	33	New Mexico	6.2
31	North Dakota	6.3	34	Vermont	6.1
7	Ohio	8.2	35	New York	6.0
9	Oklahoma	8.1	36	Rhode Island	5.9
37	Oregon	5.8	37	Nevada	5.8
17	Pennsylvania	7.2	37	Oregon	5.8
36	Rhode Island	5.9	37	Wyoming	5.8
5	South Carolina	8.9	40	Nebraska	5.7
27	South Dakota	6.5	41	Connecticut	5.4
4	Tennessee	9.0	42	Alaska	5.2
30	Texas	6.4	42	Iowa	5.2
50	Utah	4.4	42	Minnesota	5.2
34	Vermont	6.1	42	New Hampshire	5.2
17	Virginia	7.2	46	California	5.1
49	Washington	5.0	46	Massachusetts	5.1
7	West Virginia	8.2	46	New Jersey	5.1
26	Wisconsin	6.6	49	Washington	5.0
37	Wyoming	5.8	50	Utah	4.4

District of Columbia   10.2

Source: U.S. Department of Health and Human Services, National Center for Health Statistics
"National Vital Statistics Reports" (Vol. 54, No. 20, July 21, 2006)
*Provisional data for 12 months ending with December. Deaths under 1 year old by state of residence.

Infant Deaths in 2003

National Total = 28,025 Infant Deaths*

ALPHA ORDER

ALPHA ORDER

RANK	STATE	DEATHS	% of USA
19	Alabama	519	1.9%
45	Alaska	71	0.3%
18	Arizona	593	2.1%
28	Arkansas	327	1.2%
1	California	2,820	10.1%
24	Colorado	420	1.5%
33	Connecticut	230	0.8%
41	Delaware	107	0.4%
3	Florida	1,583	5.6%
7	Georgia	1,151	4.1%
40	Hawaii	136	0.5%
39	Idaho	138	0.5%
5	Illinois	1,412	5.0%
13	Indiana	661	2.4%
34	Iowa	215	0.8%
30	Kansas	262	0.9%
27	Kentucky	381	1.4%
17	Louisiana	606	2.2%
46	Maine	68	0.2%
15	Maryland	617	2.2%
26	Massachusetts	388	1.4%
8	Michigan	1,119	4.0%
29	Minnesota	324	1.2%
22	Mississippi	455	1.6%
16	Missouri	610	2.2%
43	Montana	78	0.3%
38	Nebraska	141	0.5%
35	Nevada	192	0.7%
48	New Hampshire	57	0.2%
13	New Jersey	661	2.4%
36	New Mexico	160	0.6%
4	New York	1,533	5.5%
10	North Carolina	972	3.5%
47	North Dakota	58	0.2%
6	Ohio	1,159	4.1%
25	Oklahoma	397	1.4%
31	Oregon	256	0.9%
9	Pennsylvania	1,070	3.8%
42	Rhode Island	88	0.3%
20	South Carolina	463	1.7%
44	South Dakota	74	0.3%
12	Tennessee	730	2.6%
2	Texas	2,484	8.9%
32	Utah	249	0.9%
50	Vermont	33	0.1%
11	Virginia	779	2.8%
23	Washington	451	1.6%
37	West Virginia	152	0.5%
21	Wisconsin	456	1.6%
49	Wyoming	39	0.1%

RANK ORDER

RANK	STATE	DEATHS	% of USA
1	California	2,820	10.1%
2	Texas	2,484	8.9%
3	Florida	1,583	5.6%
4	New York	1,533	5.5%
5	Illinois	1,412	5.0%
6	Ohio	1,159	4.1%
7	Georgia	1,151	4.1%
8	Michigan	1,119	4.0%
9	Pennsylvania	1,070	3.8%
10	North Carolina	972	3.5%
11	Virginia	779	2.8%
12	Tennessee	730	2.6%
13	Indiana	661	2.4%
13	New Jersey	661	2.4%
15	Maryland	617	2.2%
16	Missouri	610	2.2%
17	Louisiana	606	2.2%
18	Arizona	593	2.1%
19	Alabama	519	1.9%
20	South Carolina	463	1.7%
21	Wisconsin	456	1.6%
22	Mississippi	455	1.6%
23	Washington	451	1.6%
24	Colorado	420	1.5%
25	Oklahoma	397	1.4%
26	Massachusetts	388	1.4%
27	Kentucky	381	1.4%
28	Arkansas	327	1.2%
29	Minnesota	324	1.2%
30	Kansas	262	0.9%
31	Oregon	256	0.9%
32	Utah	249	0.9%
33	Connecticut	230	0.8%
34	Iowa	215	0.8%
35	Nevada	192	0.7%
36	New Mexico	160	0.6%
37	West Virginia	152	0.5%
38	Nebraska	141	0.5%
39	Idaho	138	0.5%
40	Hawaii	136	0.5%
41	Delaware	107	0.4%
42	Rhode Island	88	0.3%
43	Montana	78	0.3%
44	South Dakota	74	0.3%
45	Alaska	71	0.3%
46	Maine	68	0.2%
47	North Dakota	58	0.2%
48	New Hampshire	57	0.2%
49	Wyoming	39	0.1%
50	Vermont	33	0.1%
	District of Columbia	80	0.3%

Source: U.S. Department of Health and Human Services, National Center for Health Statistics
   "National Vital Statistics Reports" (Vol. 54, No. 13, April 19, 2006)
*Final data. Deaths under 1 year old by state of residence.

Infant Mortality Rate in 2003

National Rate = 6.9 Infant Deaths per 1,000 Live Births*

ALPHA ORDER

RANK	STATE	RATE
5	Alabama	8.7
23	Alaska	7.0
30	Arizona	6.5
5	Arkansas	8.7
44	California	5.2
33	Colorado	6.1
42	Connecticut	5.4
2	Delaware	9.4
18	Florida	7.5
7	Georgia	8.5
18	Hawaii	7.5
32	Idaho	6.3
14	Illinois	7.7
14	Indiana	7.7
39	Iowa	5.6
28	Kansas	6.6
24	Kentucky	6.9
3	Louisiana	9.3
47	Maine	4.9
10	Maryland	8.2
48	Massachusetts	4.8
7	Michigan	8.5
49	Minnesota	4.6
1	Mississippl	10.7
12	Missouri	7.9
25	Montana	6.8
42	Nebraska	5.4
37	Nevada	5.7
50	New Hampshire	4.0
37	New Jersey	5.7
35	New Mexico	5.8
34	New York	6.0
10	North Carolina	8.2
20	North Dakota	7.3
14	Ohio	7.7
13	Oklahoma	7.8
39	Oregon	5.6
20	Pennsylvania	7.3
26	Rhode Island	6.7
9	South Carolina	8.3
26	South Dakota	6.7
3	Tennessee	9.3
28	Texas	6.6
45	Utah	5.0
45	Vermont	5.0
14	Virginia	7.7
39	Washington	5.6
20	West Virginia	7.3
30	Wisconsin	6.5
35	Wyoming	5.8

RANK ORDER

RANK	STATE	RATE
1	Mississippi	10.7
2	Delaware	9.4
3	Louisiana	9.3
3	Tennessee	9.3
5	Alabama	8.7
5	Arkansas	8.7
7	Georgia	8.5
7	Michigan	8.5
9	South Carolina	8.3
10	Maryland	8.2
10	North Carolina	8.2
12	Missouri	7.9
13	Oklahoma	7.8
14	Illinois	7.7
14	Indiana	7.7
14	Ohio	7.7
14	Virginia	7.7
18	Florida	7.5
18	Hawaii	7.5
20	North Dakota	7.3
20	Pennsylvania	7.3
20	West Virginia	7.3
23	Alaska	7.0
24	Kentucky	6.9
25	Montana	6.8
26	Rhode Island	6.7
26	South Dakota	6.7
28	Kansas	6.6
28	Texas	6.6
30	Arizona	6.5
30	Wisconsin	6.5
32	Idaho	6.3
33	Colorado	6.1
34	New York	6.0
35	New Mexico	5.8
35	Wyoming	5.8
37	Nevada	5.7
37	New Jersey	5.7
39	Iowa	5.6
39	Oregon	5.6
39	Washington	5.6
42	Connecticut	5.4
42	Nebraska	5.4
44	California	5.2
45	Utah	5.0
45	Vermont	5.0
47	Maine	4.9
48	Massachusetts	4.8
49	Minnesota	4.6
50	New Hampshire	4.0

| | District of Columbia | 10.5 |

Source: U.S. Department of Health and Human Services, National Center for Health Statistics
 "National Vital Statistics Reports" (Vol. 54, No. 13, April 19, 2006)
*Final data. Deaths under 1 year old by state of residence.

White Infant Deaths in 2003

National Total = 18,440 Deaths*

ALPHA ORDER

RANK	STATE	DEATHS	% of USA
23	Alabama	267	1.4%
47	Alaska	37	0.2%
12	Arizona	488	2.6%
29	Arkansas	225	1.2%
1	California	2,130	11.6%
18	Colorado	348	1.9%
33	Connecticut	165	0.9%
44	Delaware	53	0.3%
4	Florida	911	4.9%
9	Georgia	541	2.9%
48	Hawaii	33	0.2%
37	Idaho	136	0.7%
5	Illinois	876	4.8%
11	Indiana	508	2.8%
32	Iowa	185	1.0%
30	Kansas	217	1.2%
20	Kentucky	321	1.7%
26	Louisiana	238	1.3%
41	Maine	65	0.4%
25	Maryland	242	1.3%
21	Massachusetts	292	1.6%
8	Michigan	692	3.8%
24	Minnesota	258	1.4%
34	Mississippi	161	0.9%
14	Missouri	432	2.3%
42	Montana	64	0.3%
39	Nebraska	111	0.6%
35	Nevada	147	0.8%
43	New Hampshire	55	0.3%
16	New Jersey	388	2.1%
38	New Mexico	127	0.7%
3	New York	919	5.0%
10	North Carolina	524	2.8%
45	North Dakota	48	0.3%
6	Ohio	803	4.4%
21	Oklahoma	292	1.6%
28	Oregon	228	1.2%
7	Pennsylvania	728	3.9%
40	Rhode Island	72	0.4%
31	South Carolina	212	1.1%
46	South Dakota	44	0.2%
15	Tennessee	426	2.3%
2	Texas	1,846	10.0%
27	Utah	231	1.3%
49	Vermont	32	0.2%
13	Virginia	442	2.4%
17	Washington	368	2.0%
36	West Virginia	138	0.7%
19	Wisconsin	328	1.8%
50	Wyoming	31	0.2%

RANK ORDER

RANK	STATE	DEATHS	% of USA
1	California	2,130	11.6%
2	Texas	1,846	10.0%
3	New York	919	5.0%
4	Florida	911	4.9%
5	Illinois	876	4.8%
6	Ohio	803	4.4%
7	Pennsylvania	728	3.9%
8	Michigan	692	3.8%
9	Georgia	541	2.9%
10	North Carolina	524	2.8%
11	Indiana	508	2.8%
12	Arizona	488	2.6%
13	Virginia	442	2.4%
14	Missouri	432	2.3%
15	Tennessee	426	2.3%
16	New Jersey	388	2.1%
17	Washington	368	2.0%
18	Colorado	348	1.9%
19	Wisconsin	328	1.8%
20	Kentucky	321	1.7%
21	Massachusetts	292	1.6%
21	Oklahoma	292	1.6%
23	Alabama	267	1.4%
24	Minnesota	258	1.4%
25	Maryland	242	1.3%
26	Louisiana	238	1.3%
27	Utah	231	1.3%
28	Oregon	228	1.2%
29	Arkansas	225	1.2%
30	Kansas	217	1.2%
31	South Carolina	212	1.1%
32	Iowa	185	1.0%
33	Connecticut	165	0.9%
34	Mississippi	161	0.9%
35	Nevada	147	0.8%
36	West Virginia	138	0.7%
37	Idaho	136	0.7%
38	New Mexico	127	0.7%
39	Nebraska	111	0.6%
40	Rhode Island	72	0.4%
41	Maine	65	0.4%
42	Montana	64	0.3%
43	New Hampshire	55	0.3%
44	Delaware	53	0.3%
45	North Dakota	48	0.3%
46	South Dakota	44	0.2%
47	Alaska	37	0.2%
48	Hawaii	33	0.2%
49	Vermont	32	0.2%
50	Wyoming	31	0.2%
	District of Columbia	15	0.1%

Source: U.S. Department of Health and Human Services, National Center for Health Statistics
"National Vital Statistics Reports" (Vol. 54, No. 13, April 19, 2006)
*Final data. Deaths of infants under 1 year old, exclusive of fetal deaths. Based on race of the mother.

White Infant Mortality Rate in 2003

National Rate = 5.7 White Infant Deaths per 1,000 White Live Births*

ALPHA ORDER

RANK	STATE	RATE
11	Alabama	6.5
28	Alaska	5.7
19	Arizona	6.2
1	Arkansas	7.6
40	California	4.9
30	Colorado	5.5
46	Connecticut	4.7
8	Delaware	6.7
27	Florida	5.8
24	Georgia	6.1
11	Hawaii	6.5
11	Idaho	6.5
19	Illinois	6.2
8	Indiana	6.7
37	Iowa	5.2
19	Kansas	6.2
11	Kentucky	6.5
17	Louisiana	6.4
40	Maine	4.9
34	Maryland	5.4
48	Massachusetts	4.4
8	Michigan	6.7
49	Minnesota	4.3
5	Mississippi	6.9
7	Missouri	6.8
11	Montana	6.5
45	Nebraska	4.8
36	Nevada	5.3
50	New Hampshire	4.0
47	New Jersey	4.5
30	New Mexico	5.5
38	New York	5.0
24	North Carolina	6.1
3	North Dakota	7.0
11	Ohio	6.5
2	Oklahoma	7.3
30	Oregon	5.5
19	Pennsylvania	6.2
17	Rhode Island	6.4
26	South Carolina	5.9
40	South Dakota	4.9
3	Tennessee	7.0
28	Texas	5.7
40	Utah	4.9
38	Vermont	5.0
19	Virginia	6.2
30	Washington	5.5
5	West Virginia	6.9
34	Wisconsin	5.4
40	Wyoming	4.9

RANK ORDER

RANK	STATE	RATE
1	Arkansas	7.6
2	Oklahoma	7.3
3	North Dakota	7.0
3	Tennessee	7.0
5	Mississippi	6.9
5	West Virginia	6.9
7	Missouri	6.8
8	Delaware	6.7
8	Indiana	6.7
8	Michigan	6.7
11	Alabama	6.5
11	Hawaii	6.5
11	Idaho	6.5
11	Kentucky	6.5
11	Montana	6.5
11	Ohio	6.5
17	Louisiana	6.4
17	Rhode Island	6.4
19	Arizona	6.2
19	Illinois	6.2
19	Kansas	6.2
19	Pennsylvania	6.2
19	Virginia	6.2
24	Georgia	6.1
24	North Carolina	6.1
26	South Carolina	5.9
27	Florida	5.8
28	Alaska	5.7
28	Texas	5.7
30	Colorado	5.5
30	New Mexico	5.5
30	Oregon	5.5
30	Washington	5.5
34	Maryland	5.4
34	Wisconsin	5.4
36	Nevada	5.3
37	Iowa	5.2
38	New York	5.0
38	Vermont	5.0
40	California	4.9
40	Maine	4.9
40	South Dakota	4.9
40	Utah	4.9
40	Wyoming	4.9
45	Nebraska	4.8
46	Connecticut	4.7
47	New Jersey	4.5
48	Massachusetts	4.4
49	Minnesota	4.3
50	New Hampshire	4.0
	District of Columbia**	NA

Source: U.S. Department of Health and Human Services, National Center for Health Statistics
    "National Vital Statistics Reports" (Vol. 54, No. 13, April 19, 2006)
Final data. Deaths of infants under 1 year old, exclusive of fetal deaths. Based on race of the mother.
**Not available, fewer than 20 white infant deaths.*

Black Infant Deaths in 2003

National Total = 8,402 Deaths*

ALPHA ORDER

ALPHA ORDER

RANK	STATE	DEATHS	% of USA
16	Alabama	252	3.0%
42	Alaska	5	0.1%
29	Arizona	48	0.6%
22	Arkansas	98	1.2%
7	California	408	4.9%
25	Colorado	60	0.7%
26	Connecticut	58	0.7%
28	Delaware	53	0.6%
1	Florida	646	7.7%
2	Georgia	593	7.1%
39	Hawaii	7	0.1%
45	Idaho	1	0.0%
5	Illinois	511	6.1%
20	Indiana	148	1.8%
34	Iowa	25	0.3%
31	Kansas	40	0.5%
27	Kentucky	57	0.7%
10	Louisiana	359	4.3%
45	Maine	1	0.0%
9	Maryland	361	4.3%
23	Massachusetts	81	1.0%
8	Michigan	392	4.7%
30	Minnesota	41	0.5%
15	Mississippi	283	3.4%
19	Missouri	168	2.0%
45	Montana	1	0.0%
35	Nebraska	23	0.3%
33	Nevada	35	0.4%
45	New Hampshire	1	0.0%
18	New Jersey	238	2.8%
39	New Mexico	7	0.1%
4	New York	547	6.5%
6	North Carolina	427	5.1%
43	North Dakota	3	0.0%
11	Ohio	348	4.1%
24	Oklahoma	69	0.8%
38	Oregon	10	0.1%
12	Pennsylvania	329	3.9%
37	Rhode Island	13	0.2%
17	South Carolina	248	3.0%
44	South Dakota	2	0.0%
14	Tennessee	293	3.5%
3	Texas	577	6.9%
39	Utah	7	0.1%
45	Vermont	1	0.0%
13	Virginia	307	3.7%
32	Washington	39	0.5%
36	West Virginia	14	0.2%
21	Wisconsin	102	1.2%
50	Wyoming	0	0.0%

RANK ORDER

RANK	STATE	DEATHS	% of USA
1	Florida	646	7.7%
2	Georgia	593	7.1%
3	Texas	577	6.9%
4	New York	547	6.5%
5	Illinois	511	6.1%
6	North Carolina	427	5.1%
7	California	408	4.9%
8	Michigan	392	4.7%
9	Maryland	361	4.3%
10	Louisiana	359	4.3%
11	Ohio	348	4.1%
12	Pennsylvania	329	3.9%
13	Virginia	307	3.7%
14	Tennessee	293	3.5%
15	Mississippi	283	3.4%
16	Alabama	252	3.0%
17	South Carolina	248	3.0%
18	New Jersey	238	2.8%
19	Missouri	168	2.0%
20	Indiana	148	1.8%
21	Wisconsin	102	1.2%
22	Arkansas	98	1.2%
23	Massachusetts	81	1.0%
24	Oklahoma	69	0.8%
25	Colorado	60	0.7%
26	Connecticut	58	0.7%
27	Kentucky	57	0.7%
28	Delaware	53	0.6%
29	Arizona	48	0.6%
30	Minnesota	41	0.5%
31	Kansas	40	0.5%
32	Washington	39	0.5%
33	Nevada	35	0.4%
34	Iowa	25	0.3%
35	Nebraska	23	0.3%
36	West Virginia	14	0.2%
37	Rhode Island	13	0.2%
38	Oregon	10	0.1%
39	Hawaii	7	0.1%
39	New Mexico	7	0.1%
39	Utah	7	0.1%
42	Alaska	5	0.1%
43	North Dakota	3	0.0%
44	South Dakota	2	0.0%
45	Idaho	1	0.0%
45	Maine	1	0.0%
45	Montana	1	0.0%
45	New Hampshire	1	0.0%
45	Vermont	1	0.0%
50	Wyoming	0	0.0%
	District of Columbia	65	0.8%

Source: U.S. Department of Health and Human Services, National Center for Health Statistics
  "National Vital Statistics Reports" (Vol. 54, No. 13, April 19, 2006)
*Final data. Deaths of infants under 1 year old, exclusive of fetal deaths. Based on race of the mother.

Black Infant Mortality Rate in 2003

National Rate = 14.0 Black Infant Deaths per 1,000 Black Live Births*

ALPHA ORDER

RANK	STATE	RATE
19	Alabama	14.1
NA	Alaska**	NA
16	Arizona	14.7
25	Arkansas	13.5
27	California	12.6
1	Colorado	20.4
32	Connecticut	11.2
3	Delaware	18.2
22	Florida	13.7
20	Georgia	13.8
NA	Hawaii**	NA
NA	Idaho**	NA
6	Illinois	16.2
7	Indiana	15.8
2	Iowa	19.4
17	Kansas	14.5
29	Kentucky	11.8
22	Louisiana	13.7
NA	Maine**	NA
18	Maryland	14.2
34	Massachusetts	9.4
5	Michigan	17.4
35	Minnesota	7.7
12	Mississippi	15.3
13	Missouri	15.1
NA	Montana**	NA
8	Nebraska	15.7
28	Nevada	12.1
NA	New Hampshire**	NA
29	New Jersey	11.8
NA	New Mexico**	NA
31	New York	11.4
8	North Carolina	15.7
NA	North Dakota**	NA
11	Ohio	15.4
14	Oklahoma	14.9
NA	Oregon**	NA
14	Pennsylvania	14.9
NA	Rhode Island**	NA
25	South Carolina	13.5
NA	South Dakota**	NA
4	Tennessee	18.0
20	Texas	13.8
NA	Utah**	NA
NA	Vermont**	NA
24	Virginia	13.6
33	Washington	9.7
NA	West Virginia**	NA
8	Wisconsin	15.7
NA	Wyoming**	NA

RANK ORDER

RANK	STATE	RATE
1	Colorado	20.4
2	Iowa	19.4
3	Delaware	18.2
4	Tennessee	18.0
5	Michigan	17.4
6	Illinois	16.2
7	Indiana	15.8
8	Nebraska	15.7
8	North Carolina	15.7
8	Wisconsin	15.7
11	Ohio	15.4
12	Mississippi	15.3
13	Missouri	15.1
14	Oklahoma	14.9
14	Pennsylvania	14.9
16	Arizona	14.7
17	Kansas	14.5
18	Maryland	14.2
19	Alabama	14.1
20	Georgia	13.8
20	Texas	13.8
22	Florida	13.7
22	Louisiana	13.7
24	Virginia	13.6
25	Arkansas	13.5
25	South Carolina	13.5
27	California	12.6
28	Nevada	12.1
29	Kentucky	11.8
29	New Jersey	11.8
31	New York	11.4
32	Connecticut	11.2
33	Washington	9.7
34	Massachusetts	9.4
35	Minnesota	7.7
NA	Alaska**	NA
NA	Hawaii**	NA
NA	Idaho**	NA
NA	Maine**	NA
NA	Montana**	NA
NA	New Hampshire**	NA
NA	New Mexico**	NA
NA	North Dakota**	NA
NA	Oregon**	NA
NA	Rhode Island**	NA
NA	South Dakota**	NA
NA	Utah**	NA
NA	Vermont**	NA
NA	West Virginia**	NA
NA	Wyoming**	NA

District of Columbia   12.4

Source: U.S. Department of Health and Human Services, National Center for Health Statistics
      "National Vital Statistics Reports" (Vol. 54, No. 13, April 19, 2006)
*Final data. Deaths of infants under 1 year old, exclusive of fetal deaths. Based on race of the mother.
**Not available, fewer than 20 black infant deaths.

Neonatal Deaths in 2003

National Total = 18,893 Deaths*

RANK	STATE	DEATHS	% of USA	RANK	STATE	DEATHS	% of USA
20	Alabama	312	1.7%	1	California	1,909	10.1%
48	Alaska	33	0.2%	2	Texas	1,649	8.7%
17	Arizona	392	2.1%	3	New York	1,073	5.7%
29	Arkansas	202	1.1%	4	Florida	1,024	5.4%
1	California	1,909	10.1%	5	Illinois	984	5.2%
23	Colorado	305	1.6%	6	Ohio	802	4.2%
33	Connecticut	160	0.8%	7	Pennsylvania	785	4.2%
41	Delaware	73	0.4%	8	Georgia	779	4.1%
4	Florida	1,024	5.4%	9	Michigan	777	4.1%
8	Georgia	779	4.1%	10	North Carolina	672	3.6%
37	Hawaii	95	0.5%	11	Virginia	542	2.9%
40	Idaho	82	0.4%	12	New Jersey	476	2.5%
5	Illinois	984	5.2%	13	Tennessee	472	2.5%
16	Indiana	435	2.3%	14	Maryland	442	2.3%
34	Iowa	135	0.7%	15	Missouri	441	2.3%
31	Kansas	176	0.9%	16	Indiana	435	2.3%
26	Kentucky	224	1.2%	17	Arizona	392	2.1%
18	Louisiana	374	2.0%	18	Louisiana	374	2.0%
43	Maine	55	0.3%	19	South Carolina	329	1.7%
14	Maryland	442	2.3%	20	Alabama	312	1.7%
24	Massachusetts	289	1.5%	20	Wisconsin	312	1.7%
9	Michigan	777	4.1%	22	Washington	306	1.6%
28	Minnesota	215	1.1%	23	Colorado	305	1.6%
25	Mississippi	248	1.3%	24	Massachusetts	289	1.5%
15	Missouri	441	2.3%	25	Mississippi	248	1.3%
45	Montana	43	0.2%	26	Kentucky	224	1.2%
36	Nebraska	96	0.5%	27	Oklahoma	223	1.2%
35	Nevada	116	0.6%	28	Minnesota	215	1.1%
46	New Hampshire	39	0.2%	29	Arkansas	202	1.1%
12	New Jersey	476	2.5%	30	Utah	181	1.0%
37	New Mexico	95	0.5%	31	Kansas	176	0.9%
3	New York	1,073	5.7%	32	Oregon	173	0.9%
10	North Carolina	672	3.6%	33	Connecticut	160	0.8%
44	North Dakota	45	0.2%	34	Iowa	135	0.7%
6	Ohio	802	4.2%	35	Nevada	116	0.6%
27	Oklahoma	223	1.2%	36	Nebraska	96	0.5%
32	Oregon	173	0.9%	37	Hawaii	95	0.5%
7	Pennsylvania	785	4.2%	37	New Mexico	95	0.5%
42	Rhode Island	66	0.3%	39	West Virginia	94	0.5%
19	South Carolina	329	1.7%	40	Idaho	82	0.4%
47	South Dakota	36	0.2%	41	Delaware	73	0.4%
13	Tennessee	472	2.5%	42	Rhode Island	66	0.3%
2	Texas	1,649	8.7%	43	Maine	55	0.3%
30	Utah	181	1.0%	44	North Dakota	45	0.2%
49	Vermont	30	0.2%	45	Montana	43	0.2%
11	Virginia	542	2.9%	46	New Hampshire	39	0.2%
22	Washington	306	1.6%	47	South Dakota	36	0.2%
39	West Virginia	94	0.5%	48	Alaska	33	0.2%
20	Wisconsin	312	1.7%	49	Vermont	30	0.2%
50	Wyoming	23	0.1%	50	Wyoming	23	0.1%
					District of Columbia	54	0.3%

Source: U.S. Department of Health and Human Services, National Center for Health Statistics
    "National Vital Statistics Reports" (Vol. 54, No. 13, April 19, 2006)
*Final data. Deaths of infants under 28 days, exclusive of fetal deaths.

Neonatal Death Rate in 2003

National Rate = 4.6 Deaths per 1,000 Live Births*

ALPHA ORDER

RANK	STATE	RATE
18	Alabama	5.2
47	Alaska	3.3
29	Arizona	4.3
12	Arkansas	5.4
42	California	3.5
26	Colorado	4.4
38	Connecticut	3.7
1	Delaware	6.4
21	Florida	4.8
8	Georgia	5.7
17	Hawaii	5.3
34	Idaho	3.8
12	Illinois	5.4
19	Indiana	5.0
42	Iowa	3.5
23	Kansas	4.5
31	Kentucky	4.1
7	Louisiana	5.8
33	Maine	4.0
3	Maryland	5.9
40	Massachusetts	3.6
3	Michigan	5.9
49	Minnesota	3.1
3	Mississippi	5.9
8	Missouri	5.7
34	Montana	3.8
38	Nebraska	3.7
42	Nevada	3.5
50	New Hampshire	2.7
31	New Jersey	4.1
45	New Mexico	3.4
30	New York	4.2
8	North Carolina	5.7
11	North Dakota	5.6
12	Ohio	5.4
26	Oklahoma	4.4
34	Oregon	3.8
12	Pennsylvania	5.4
19	Rhode Island	5.0
3	South Carolina	5.9
47	South Dakota	3.3
2	Tennessee	6.0
26	Texas	4.4
40	Utah	3.6
22	Vermont	4.6
12	Virginia	5.4
34	Washington	3.8
23	West Virginia	4.5
23	Wisconsin	4.5
45	Wyoming	3.4

RANK ORDER

RANK	STATE	RATE
1	Delaware	6.4
2	Tennessee	6.0
3	Maryland	5.9
3	Michigan	5.9
3	Mississippi	5.9
3	South Carolina	5.9
7	Louisiana	5.8
8	Georgia	5.7
8	Missouri	5.7
8	North Carolina	5.7
11	North Dakota	5.6
12	Arkansas	5.4
12	Illinois	5.4
12	Ohio	5.4
12	Pennsylvania	5.4
12	Virginia	5.4
17	Hawaii	5.3
18	Alabama	5.2
19	Indiana	5.0
19	Rhode Island	5.0
21	Florida	4.8
22	Vermont	4.6
23	Kansas	4.5
23	West Virginia	4.5
23	Wisconsin	4.5
26	Colorado	4.4
26	Oklahoma	4.4
26	Texas	4.4
29	Arizona	4.3
30	New York	4.2
31	Kentucky	4.1
31	New Jersey	4.1
33	Maine	4.0
34	Idaho	3.8
34	Montana	3.8
34	Oregon	3.8
34	Washington	3.8
38	Connecticut	3.7
38	Nebraska	3.7
40	Massachusetts	3.6
40	Utah	3.6
42	California	3.5
42	Iowa	3.5
42	Nevada	3.5
45	New Mexico	3.4
45	Wyoming	3.4
47	Alaska	3.3
47	South Dakota	3.3
49	Minnesota	3.1
50	New Hampshire	2.7

| | District of Columbia | 7.1 |

Source: U.S. Department of Health and Human Services, National Center for Health Statistics
"National Vital Statistics Reports" (Vol. 54, No. 13, April 19, 2006)
*Final data. Deaths of infants under 28 days, exclusive of fetal deaths.

White Neonatal Deaths in 2003

National Total = 12,495 Deaths*

ALPHA ORDER					RANK ORDER			
RANK	STATE		DEATHS	% of USA	RANK	STATE	DEATHS	% of USA
27	Alabama		152	1.2%	1	California	1,450	11.6%
49	Alaska		19	0.2%	2	Texas	1,237	9.9%
11	Arizona		336	2.7%	3	New York	646	5.2%
31	Arkansas		132	1.1%	4	Illinois	635	5.1%
1	California		1,450	11.6%	5	Florida	588	4.7%
17	Colorado		249	2.0%	6	Ohio	561	4.5%
32	Connecticut		123	1.0%	7	Pennsylvania	530	4.2%
45	Delaware		35	0.3%	8	Michigan	493	3.9%
5	Florida		588	4.7%	9	Georgia	364	2.9%
9	Georgia		364	2.9%	10	North Carolina	363	2.9%
47	Hawaii		26	0.2%	11	Arizona	336	2.7%
36	Idaho		81	0.6%	12	Indiana	331	2.6%
4	Illinois		635	5.1%	13	Missouri	311	2.5%
12	Indiana		331	2.6%	14	Virginia	308	2.5%
33	Iowa		117	0.9%	15	New Jersey	288	2.3%
30	Kansas		139	1.1%	16	Washington	263	2.1%
21	Kentucky		188	1.5%	17	Colorado	249	2.0%
28	Louisiana		147	1.2%	18	Tennessee	246	2.0%
40	Maine		53	0.4%	19	Wisconsin	233	1.9%
23	Maryland		172	1.4%	20	Massachusetts	218	1.7%
20	Massachusetts		218	1.7%	21	Kentucky	188	1.5%
8	Michigan		493	3.9%	22	Minnesota	180	1.4%
22	Minnesota		180	1.4%	23	Maryland	172	1.4%
37	Mississippi		79	0.6%	24	Utah	169	1.4%
13	Missouri		311	2.5%	25	Oklahoma	161	1.3%
42	Montana		37	0.3%	26	Oregon	159	1.3%
38	Nebraska		77	0.6%	27	Alabama	152	1.2%
34	Nevada		90	0.7%	28	Louisiana	147	1.2%
42	New Hampshire		37	0.3%	29	South Carolina	142	1.1%
15	New Jersey		288	2.3%	30	Kansas	139	1.1%
39	New Mexico		74	0.6%	31	Arkansas	132	1.1%
3	New York		646	5.2%	32	Connecticut	123	1.0%
10	North Carolina		363	2.9%	33	Iowa	117	0.9%
42	North Dakota		37	0.3%	34	Nevada	90	0.7%
6	Ohio		561	4.5%	35	West Virginia	86	0.7%
25	Oklahoma		161	1.3%	36	Idaho	81	0.6%
26	Oregon		159	1.3%	37	Mississippi	79	0.6%
7	Pennsylvania		530	4.2%	38	Nebraska	77	0.6%
40	Rhode Island		53	0.4%	39	New Mexico	74	0.6%
29	South Carolina		142	1.1%	40	Maine	53	0.4%
48	South Dakota		23	0.2%	40	Rhode Island	53	0.4%
18	Tennessee		246	2.0%	42	Montana	37	0.3%
2	Texas		1,237	9.9%	42	New Hampshire	37	0.3%
24	Utah		169	1.4%	42	North Dakota	37	0.3%
46	Vermont		29	0.2%	45	Delaware	35	0.3%
14	Virginia		308	2.5%	46	Vermont	29	0.2%
16	Washington		263	2.1%	47	Hawaii	26	0.2%
35	West Virginia		86	0.7%	48	South Dakota	23	0.2%
19	Wisconsin		233	1.9%	49	Alaska	19	0.2%
49	Wyoming		19	0.2%	49	Wyoming	19	0.2%
						District of Columbia	9	0.1%

Source: U.S. Department of Health and Human Services, National Center for Health Statistics
    "National Vital Statistics Reports" (Vol. 54, No. 13, April 19, 2006)
*Final data. Deaths of infants under 28 days, exclusive of fetal deaths. Based on race of the mother.

White Neonatal Death Rate in 2003

National Rate = 3.9 White Neonatal Deaths per 1,000 White Live Births*

<table>
<tr><td colspan="3">ALPHA ORDER</td><td colspan="3">RANK ORDER</td></tr>
<tr><th>RANK</th><th>STATE</th><th>RATE</th><th>RANK</th><th>STATE</th><th>RATE</th></tr>
<tr><td>33</td><td>Alabama</td><td>3.7</td><td>1</td><td>North Dakota</td><td>5.4</td></tr>
<tr><td>NA</td><td>Alaska**</td><td>NA</td><td>2</td><td>Hawaii</td><td>5.1</td></tr>
<tr><td>13</td><td>Arizona</td><td>4.3</td><td>3</td><td>Missouri</td><td>4.9</td></tr>
<tr><td>10</td><td>Arkansas</td><td>4.4</td><td>4</td><td>Michigan</td><td>4.8</td></tr>
<tr><td>40</td><td>California</td><td>3.3</td><td>5</td><td>Rhode Island</td><td>4.7</td></tr>
<tr><td>23</td><td>Colorado</td><td>3.9</td><td>6</td><td>Illinois</td><td>4.5</td></tr>
<tr><td>36</td><td>Connecticut</td><td>3.5</td><td>6</td><td>Ohio</td><td>4.5</td></tr>
<tr><td>10</td><td>Delaware</td><td>4.4</td><td>6</td><td>Pennsylvania</td><td>4.5</td></tr>
<tr><td>33</td><td>Florida</td><td>3.7</td><td>6</td><td>Vermont</td><td>4.5</td></tr>
<tr><td>17</td><td>Georgia</td><td>4.1</td><td>10</td><td>Arkansas</td><td>4.4</td></tr>
<tr><td>2</td><td>Hawaii</td><td>5.1</td><td>10</td><td>Delaware</td><td>4.4</td></tr>
<tr><td>23</td><td>Idaho</td><td>3.9</td><td>10</td><td>Indiana</td><td>4.4</td></tr>
<tr><td>6</td><td>Illinois</td><td>4.5</td><td>13</td><td>Arizona</td><td>4.3</td></tr>
<tr><td>10</td><td>Indiana</td><td>4.4</td><td>13</td><td>Virginia</td><td>4.3</td></tr>
<tr><td>40</td><td>Iowa</td><td>3.3</td><td>13</td><td>West Virginia</td><td>4.3</td></tr>
<tr><td>18</td><td>Kansas</td><td>4.0</td><td>16</td><td>North Carolina</td><td>4.2</td></tr>
<tr><td>30</td><td>Kentucky</td><td>3.8</td><td>17</td><td>Georgia</td><td>4.1</td></tr>
<tr><td>23</td><td>Louisiana</td><td>3.9</td><td>18</td><td>Kansas</td><td>4.0</td></tr>
<tr><td>18</td><td>Maine</td><td>4.0</td><td>18</td><td>Maine</td><td>4.0</td></tr>
<tr><td>23</td><td>Maryland</td><td>3.9</td><td>18</td><td>Oklahoma</td><td>4.0</td></tr>
<tr><td>40</td><td>Massachusetts</td><td>3.3</td><td>18</td><td>Tennessee</td><td>4.0</td></tr>
<tr><td>4</td><td>Michigan</td><td>4.8</td><td>18</td><td>Washington</td><td>4.0</td></tr>
<tr><td>46</td><td>Minnesota</td><td>3.0</td><td>23</td><td>Colorado</td><td>3.9</td></tr>
<tr><td>38</td><td>Mississippi</td><td>3.4</td><td>23</td><td>Idaho</td><td>3.9</td></tr>
<tr><td>3</td><td>Missouri</td><td>4.9</td><td>23</td><td>Louisiana</td><td>3.9</td></tr>
<tr><td>30</td><td>Montana</td><td>3.8</td><td>23</td><td>Maryland</td><td>3.9</td></tr>
<tr><td>40</td><td>Nebraska</td><td>3.3</td><td>23</td><td>South Carolina</td><td>3.9</td></tr>
<tr><td>40</td><td>Nevada</td><td>3.3</td><td>23</td><td>Texas</td><td>3.9</td></tr>
<tr><td>47</td><td>New Hampshire</td><td>2.7</td><td>23</td><td>Wisconsin</td><td>3.9</td></tr>
<tr><td>38</td><td>New Jersey</td><td>3.4</td><td>30</td><td>Kentucky</td><td>3.8</td></tr>
<tr><td>45</td><td>New Mexico</td><td>3.2</td><td>30</td><td>Montana</td><td>3.8</td></tr>
<tr><td>36</td><td>New York</td><td>3.5</td><td>30</td><td>Oregon</td><td>3.8</td></tr>
<tr><td>16</td><td>North Carolina</td><td>4.2</td><td>33</td><td>Alabama</td><td>3.7</td></tr>
<tr><td>1</td><td>North Dakota</td><td>5.4</td><td>33</td><td>Florida</td><td>3.7</td></tr>
<tr><td>6</td><td>Ohio</td><td>4.5</td><td>35</td><td>Utah</td><td>3.6</td></tr>
<tr><td>18</td><td>Oklahoma</td><td>4.0</td><td>36</td><td>Connecticut</td><td>3.5</td></tr>
<tr><td>30</td><td>Oregon</td><td>3.8</td><td>36</td><td>New York</td><td>3.5</td></tr>
<tr><td>6</td><td>Pennsylvania</td><td>4.5</td><td>38</td><td>Mississippi</td><td>3.4</td></tr>
<tr><td>5</td><td>Rhode Island</td><td>4.7</td><td>38</td><td>New Jersey</td><td>3.4</td></tr>
<tr><td>23</td><td>South Carolina</td><td>3.9</td><td>40</td><td>California</td><td>3.3</td></tr>
<tr><td>48</td><td>South Dakota</td><td>2.6</td><td>40</td><td>Iowa</td><td>3.3</td></tr>
<tr><td>18</td><td>Tennessee</td><td>4.0</td><td>40</td><td>Massachusetts</td><td>3.3</td></tr>
<tr><td>23</td><td>Texas</td><td>3.9</td><td>40</td><td>Nebraska</td><td>3.3</td></tr>
<tr><td>35</td><td>Utah</td><td>3.6</td><td>40</td><td>Nevada</td><td>3.3</td></tr>
<tr><td>6</td><td>Vermont</td><td>4.5</td><td>45</td><td>New Mexico</td><td>3.2</td></tr>
<tr><td>13</td><td>Virginia</td><td>4.3</td><td>46</td><td>Minnesota</td><td>3.0</td></tr>
<tr><td>18</td><td>Washington</td><td>4.0</td><td>47</td><td>New Hampshire</td><td>2.7</td></tr>
<tr><td>13</td><td>West Virginia</td><td>4.3</td><td>48</td><td>South Dakota</td><td>2.6</td></tr>
<tr><td>23</td><td>Wisconsin</td><td>3.9</td><td>NA</td><td>Alaska**</td><td>NA</td></tr>
<tr><td>NA</td><td>Wyoming**</td><td>NA</td><td>NA</td><td>Wyoming**</td><td>NA</td></tr>
<tr><td></td><td></td><td></td><td></td><td>District of Columbia**</td><td>NA</td></tr>
</table>

Source: U.S. Department of Health and Human Services, National Center for Health Statistics
    "National Vital Statistics Reports" (Vol. 54, No. 13, April 19, 2006)
*Final data. Deaths of infants under 28 days, exclusive of fetal deaths. Based on race of the mother.
**Not available. Fewer than 20 white neonatal deaths.

Black Neonatal Deaths in 2003

National Total = 5,640 Deaths*

ALPHA ORDER

RANK	STATE	DEATHS	% of USA
17	Alabama	160	2.8%
42	Alaska	2	0.0%
30	Arizona	31	0.5%
21	Arkansas	67	1.2%
7	California	265	4.7%
24	Colorado	48	0.9%
27	Connecticut	34	0.6%
26	Delaware	37	0.7%
1	Florida	419	7.4%
2	Georgia	399	7.1%
38	Hawaii	6	0.1%
45	Idaho	1	0.0%
5	Illinois	331	5.9%
20	Indiana	99	1.8%
35	Iowa	15	0.3%
29	Kansas	33	0.6%
27	Kentucky	34	0.6%
12	Louisiana	221	3.9%
45	Maine	1	0.0%
9	Maryland	259	4.6%
22	Massachusetts	61	1.1%
8	Michigan	263	4.7%
31	Minnesota	21	0.4%
16	Mississippi	163	2.9%
19	Missouri	121	2.1%
49	Montana	0	0.0%
34	Nebraska	16	0.3%
32	Nevada	20	0.4%
45	New Hampshire	1	0.0%
18	New Jersey	158	2.8%
38	New Mexico	6	0.1%
3	New York	379	6.7%
6	North Carolina	294	5.2%
42	North Dakota	2	0.0%
11	Ohio	235	4.2%
25	Oklahoma	44	0.8%
38	Oregon	6	0.1%
10	Pennsylvania	245	4.3%
36	Rhode Island	11	0.2%
15	South Carolina	185	3.3%
42	South Dakota	2	0.0%
13	Tennessee	219	3.9%
4	Texas	374	6.6%
38	Utah	6	0.1%
45	Vermont	1	0.0%
14	Virginia	212	3.8%
32	Washington	20	0.4%
37	West Virginia	8	0.1%
23	Wisconsin	60	1.1%
49	Wyoming	0	0.0%

RANK ORDER

RANK	STATE	DEATHS	% of USA
1	Florida	419	7.4%
2	Georgia	399	7.1%
3	New York	379	6.7%
4	Texas	374	6.6%
5	Illinois	331	5.9%
6	North Carolina	294	5.2%
7	California	265	4.7%
8	Michigan	263	4.7%
9	Maryland	259	4.6%
10	Pennsylvania	245	4.3%
11	Ohio	235	4.2%
12	Louisiana	221	3.9%
13	Tennessee	219	3.9%
14	Virginia	212	3.8%
15	South Carolina	185	3.3%
16	Mississippi	163	2.9%
17	Alabama	160	2.8%
18	New Jersey	158	2.8%
19	Missouri	121	2.1%
20	Indiana	99	1.8%
21	Arkansas	67	1.2%
22	Massachusetts	61	1.1%
23	Wisconsin	60	1.1%
24	Colorado	48	0.9%
25	Oklahoma	44	0.8%
26	Delaware	37	0.7%
27	Connecticut	34	0.6%
27	Kentucky	34	0.6%
29	Kansas	33	0.6%
30	Arizona	31	0.5%
31	Minnesota	21	0.4%
32	Nevada	20	0.4%
32	Washington	20	0.4%
34	Nebraska	16	0.3%
35	Iowa	15	0.3%
36	Rhode Island	11	0.2%
37	West Virginia	8	0.1%
38	Hawaii	6	0.1%
38	New Mexico	6	0.1%
38	Oregon	6	0.1%
38	Utah	6	0.1%
42	Alaska	2	0.0%
42	North Dakota	2	0.0%
42	South Dakota	2	0.0%
45	Idaho	1	0.0%
45	Maine	1	0.0%
45	New Hampshire	1	0.0%
45	Vermont	1	0.0%
49	Montana	0	0.0%
49	Wyoming	0	0.0%
	District of Columbia	45	0.8%

Source: U.S. Department of Health and Human Services, National Center for Health Statistics
"National Vital Statistics Reports" (Vol. 54, No. 13, April 19, 2006)
*Final data. Deaths of infants under 28 days, exclusive of fetal deaths. Based on race of the mother.

Black Neonatal Death Rate in 2003

National Rate = 9.4 Black Neonatal Deaths per 1,000 Black Live Births*

<u>ALPHA ORDER</u>

RANK	STATE	RATE
20	Alabama	8.9
NA	Alaska**	NA
14	Arizona	9.5
17	Arkansas	9.3
25	California	8.2
1	Colorado	16.3
31	Connecticut	6.6
3	Delaware	12.7
20	Florida	8.9
17	Georgia	9.3
NA	Hawaii**	NA
NA	Idaho**	NA
10	Illinois	10.5
9	Indiana	10.6
NA	Iowa**	NA
4	Kansas	11.9
29	Kentucky	7.0
24	Louisiana	8.4
NA	Maine**	NA
12	Maryland	10.2
28	Massachusetts	7.1
5	Michigan	11.7
33	Minnesota	3.9
23	Mississippi	8.8
7	Missouri	10.8
NA	Montana**	NA
NA	Nebraska**	NA
30	Nevada	6.9
NA	New Hampshire**	NA
27	New Jersey	7.8
NA	New Mexico**	NA
26	New York	7.9
7	North Carolina	10.8
NA	North Dakota**	NA
11	Ohio	10.4
14	Oklahoma	9.5
NA	Oregon**	NA
6	Pennsylvania	11.1
NA	Rhode Island**	NA
13	South Carolina	10.1
NA	South Dakota**	NA
2	Tennessee	13.5
20	Texas	8.9
NA	Utah**	NA
NA	Vermont**	NA
16	Virginia	9.4
32	Washington	5.0
NA	West Virginia**	NA
19	Wisconsin	9.2
NA	Wyoming**	NA

<u>RANK ORDER</u>

RANK	STATE	RATE
1	Colorado	16.3
2	Tennessee	13.5
3	Delaware	12.7
4	Kansas	11.9
5	Michigan	11.7
6	Pennsylvania	11.1
7	Missouri	10.8
7	North Carolina	10.8
9	Indiana	10.6
10	Illinois	10.5
11	Ohio	10.4
12	Maryland	10.2
13	South Carolina	10.1
14	Arizona	9.5
14	Oklahoma	9.5
16	Virginia	9.4
17	Arkansas	9.3
17	Georgia	9.3
19	Wisconsin	9.2
20	Alabama	8.9
20	Florida	8.9
20	Texas	8.9
23	Mississippi	8.8
24	Louisiana	8.4
25	California	8.2
26	New York	7.9
27	New Jersey	7.8
28	Massachusetts	7.1
29	Kentucky	7.0
30	Nevada	6.9
31	Connecticut	6.6
32	Washington	5.0
33	Minnesota	3.9
NA	Alaska**	NA
NA	Hawaii**	NA
NA	Idaho**	NA
NA	Iowa**	NA
NA	Maine**	NA
NA	Montana**	NA
NA	Nebraska**	NA
NA	New Hampshire**	NA
NA	New Mexico**	NA
NA	North Dakota**	NA
NA	Oregon**	NA
NA	Rhode Island**	NA
NA	South Dakota**	NA
NA	Utah**	NA
NA	Vermont**	NA
NA	West Virginia**	NA
NA	Wyoming**	NA

District of Columbia   8.6

*Source: U.S. Department of Health and Human Services, National Center for Health Statistics
"National Vital Statistics Reports" (Vol. 54, No. 13, April 19, 2006)*
*Final data. Deaths of infants under 28 days, exclusive of fetal deaths. Based on race of the mother.
**Not available. Fewer than 20 black neonatal deaths.*

Deaths by AIDS in 2003

National Total = 13,658 Deaths*

ALPHA ORDER

RANK	STATE	DEATHS	% of USA
18	Alabama	190	1.4%
46	Alaska	6	0.0%
21	Arizona	178	1.3%
30	Arkansas	72	0.5%
3	California	1,364	10.0%
27	Colorado	81	0.6%
20	Connecticut	187	1.4%
28	Delaware	80	0.6%
2	Florida	1,743	12.8%
5	Georgia	671	4.9%
38	Hawaii	21	0.2%
44	Idaho	11	0.1%
10	Illinois	436	3.2%
24	Indiana	113	0.8%
39	Iowa	20	0.1%
34	Kansas	51	0.4%
32	Kentucky	67	0.5%
11	Louisiana	392	2.9%
42	Maine	14	0.1%
7	Maryland	641	4.7%
17	Massachusetts	226	1.7%
15	Michigan	237	1.7%
33	Minnesota	52	0.4%
18	Mississippi	190	1.4%
23	Missouri	125	0.9%
47	Montana	5	0.0%
40	Nebraska	18	0.1%
29	Nevada	77	0.6%
40	New Hampshire	18	0.1%
5	New Jersey	671	4.9%
35	New Mexico	44	0.3%
1	New York	1,894	13.9%
9	North Carolina	456	3.3%
48	North Dakota	3	0.0%
16	Ohio	236	1.7%
26	Oklahoma	91	0.7%
25	Oregon	92	0.7%
8	Pennsylvania	469	3.4%
36	Rhode Island	31	0.2%
14	South Carolina	279	2.0%
48	South Dakota	3	0.0%
13	Tennessee	289	2.1%
4	Texas	1,013	7.4%
43	Utah	13	0.1%
45	Vermont	8	0.1%
12	Virginia	290	2.1%
22	Washington	146	1.1%
37	West Virginia	30	0.2%
31	Wisconsin	68	0.5%
48	Wyoming	3	0.0%

RANK ORDER

RANK	STATE	DEATHS	% of USA
1	New York	1,894	13.9%
2	Florida	1,743	12.8%
3	California	1,364	10.0%
4	Texas	1,013	7.4%
5	Georgia	671	4.9%
5	New Jersey	671	4.9%
7	Maryland	641	4.7%
8	Pennsylvania	469	3.4%
9	North Carolina	456	3.3%
10	Illinois	436	3.2%
11	Louisiana	392	2.9%
12	Virginia	290	2.1%
13	Tennessee	289	2.1%
14	South Carolina	279	2.0%
15	Michigan	237	1.7%
16	Ohio	236	1.7%
17	Massachusetts	226	1.7%
18	Alabama	190	1.4%
18	Mississippi	190	1.4%
20	Connecticut	187	1.4%
21	Arizona	178	1.3%
22	Washington	146	1.1%
23	Missouri	125	0.9%
24	Indiana	113	0.8%
25	Oregon	92	0.7%
26	Oklahoma	91	0.7%
27	Colorado	81	0.6%
28	Delaware	80	0.6%
29	Nevada	77	0.6%
30	Arkansas	72	0.5%
31	Wisconsin	68	0.5%
32	Kentucky	67	0.5%
33	Minnesota	52	0.4%
34	Kansas	51	0.4%
35	New Mexico	44	0.3%
36	Rhode Island	31	0.2%
37	West Virginia	30	0.2%
38	Hawaii	21	0.2%
39	Iowa	20	0.1%
40	Nebraska	18	0.1%
40	New Hampshire	18	0.1%
42	Maine	14	0.1%
43	Utah	13	0.1%
44	Idaho	11	0.1%
45	Vermont	8	0.1%
46	Alaska	6	0.0%
47	Montana	5	0.0%
48	North Dakota	3	0.0%
48	South Dakota	3	0.0%
48	Wyoming	3	0.0%
	District of Columbia	243	1.8%

Source: U.S. Department of Health and Human Services, National Center for Health Statistics
   "National Vital Statistics Reports" (Vol. 54, No. 13, April 19, 2006)
*AIDS is Acquired Immunodeficiency Syndrome. It is a specific group of diseases or conditions which are indicative
of severe immunosuppression related to infection with the Human Immunodeficiency Virus (HIV).

Death Rate by AIDS in 2003

National Rate = 4.7 Deaths per 100,000 Population*

ALPHA ORDER

RANK	STATE	RATE
14	Alabama	4.2
NA	Alaska**	NA
21	Arizona	3.2
23	Arkansas	2.6
16	California	3.8
32	Colorado	1.8
10	Connecticut	5.4
4	Delaware	9.8
2	Florida	10.2
7	Georgia	7.7
34	Hawaii	1.7
NA	Idaho**	NA
19	Illinois	3.4
32	Indiana	1.8
39	Iowa	0.7
31	Kansas	1.9
36	Kentucky	1.6
5	Louisiana	8.7
NA	Maine**	NA
1	Maryland	11.6
18	Massachusetts	3.5
26	Michigan	2.4
38	Minnesota	1.0
9	Mississippi	6.6
29	Missouri	2.2
NA	Montana**	NA
NA	Nebraska**	NA
19	Nevada	3.4
NA	New Hampshire**	NA
6	New Jersey	7.8
28	New Mexico	2.3
3	New York	9.9
10	North Carolina	5.4
NA	North Dakota**	NA
30	Ohio	2.1
23	Oklahoma	2.6
23	Oregon	2.6
16	Pennsylvania	3.8
22	Rhode Island	2.9
8	South Carolina	6.7
NA	South Dakota**	NA
12	Tennessee	4.9
13	Texas	4.6
NA	Utah**	NA
NA	Vermont**	NA
15	Virginia	3.9
26	Washington	2.4
34	West Virginia	1.7
37	Wisconsin	1.2
NA	Wyoming**	NA

RANK ORDER

RANK	STATE	RATE
1	Maryland	11.6
2	Florida	10.2
3	New York	9.9
4	Delaware	9.8
5	Louisiana	8.7
6	New Jersey	7.8
7	Georgia	7.7
8	South Carolina	6.7
9	Mississippi	6.6
10	Connecticut	5.4
10	North Carolina	5.4
12	Tennessee	4.9
13	Texas	4.6
14	Alabama	4.2
15	Virginia	3.9
16	California	3.8
16	Pennsylvania	3.8
18	Massachusetts	3.5
19	Illinois	3.4
19	Nevada	3.4
21	Arizona	3.2
22	Rhode Island	2.9
23	Arkansas	2.6
23	Oklahoma	2.6
23	Oregon	2.6
26	Michigan	2.4
26	Washington	2.4
28	New Mexico	2.3
29	Missouri	2.2
30	Ohio	2.1
31	Kansas	1.9
32	Colorado	1.8
32	Indiana	1.8
34	Hawaii	1.7
34	West Virginia	1.7
36	Kentucky	1.6
37	Wisconsin	1.2
38	Minnesota	1.0
39	Iowa	0.7
NA	Alaska**	NA
NA	Idaho**	NA
NA	Maine**	NA
NA	Montana**	NA
NA	Nebraska**	NA
NA	New Hampshire**	NA
NA	North Dakota**	NA
NA	South Dakota**	NA
NA	Utah**	NA
NA	Vermont**	NA
NA	Wyoming**	NA

| | District of Columbia | 43.1 |

Source: U.S. Department of Health and Human Services, National Center for Health Statistics
"National Vital Statistics Reports" (Vol. 54, No. 13, April 19, 2006)
*AIDS is Acquired Immunodeficiency Syndrome. It is a specific group of diseases or conditions which are indicative of severe immunosuppression related to infection with the Human Immunodeficiency Virus (HIV). Not age-adjusted.
**Insufficient data to determine a reliable rate.

Age-Adjusted Death Rate by AIDS in 2003

National Rate = 4.7 Deaths per 100,000 Population*

ALPHA ORDER

RANK	STATE	RATE
14	Alabama	4.3
NA	Alaska**	NA
18	Arizona	3.5
22	Arkansas	2.8
15	California	3.9
33	Colorado	1.8
11	Connecticut	5.1
3	Delaware	9.7
2	Florida	10.4
6	Georgia	7.7
34	Hawaii	1.7
NA	Idaho**	NA
18	Illinois	3.5
31	Indiana	1.9
39	Iowa	0.7
31	Kansas	1.9
36	Kentucky	1.6
5	Louisiana	9.1
NA	Maine**	NA
1	Maryland	11.1
21	Massachusetts	3.4
27	Michigan	2.3
38	Minnesota	1.0
8	Mississippi	7.0
29	Missouri	2.2
NA	Montana**	NA
NA	Nebraska**	NA
18	Nevada	3.5
NA	New Hampshire**	NA
7	New Jersey	7.4
26	New Mexico	2.4
4	New York	9.6
10	North Carolina	5.4
NA	North Dakota**	NA
30	Ohio	2.1
24	Oklahoma	2.7
25	Oregon	2.6
16	Pennsylvania	3.8
22	Rhode Island	2.8
9	South Carolina	6.8
NA	South Dakota**	NA
12	Tennessee	5.0
13	Texas	4.8
NA	Utah**	NA
NA	Vermont**	NA
16	Virginia	3.8
27	Washington	2.3
34	West Virginia	1.7
37	Wisconsin	1.2
NA	Wyoming**	NA

RANK ORDER

RANK	STATE	RATE
1	Maryland	11.1
2	Florida	10.4
3	Delaware	9.7
4	New York	9.6
5	Louisiana	9.1
6	Georgia	7.7
7	New Jersey	7.4
8	Mississippi	7.0
9	South Carolina	6.8
10	North Carolina	5.4
11	Connecticut	5.1
12	Tennessee	5.0
13	Texas	4.8
14	Alabama	4.3
15	California	3.9
16	Pennsylvania	3.8
16	Virginia	3.8
18	Arizona	3.5
18	Illinois	3.5
18	Nevada	3.5
21	Massachusetts	3.4
22	Arkansas	2.8
22	Rhode Island	2.8
24	Oklahoma	2.7
25	Oregon	2.6
26	New Mexico	2.4
27	Michigan	2.3
27	Washington	2.3
29	Missouri	2.2
30	Ohio	2.1
31	Indiana	1.9
31	Kansas	1.9
33	Colorado	1.8
34	Hawaii	1.7
34	West Virginia	1.7
36	Kentucky	1.6
37	Wisconsin	1.2
38	Minnesota	1.0
39	Iowa	0.7
NA	Alaska**	NA
NA	Idaho**	NA
NA	Maine**	NA
NA	Montana**	NA
NA	Nebraska**	NA
NA	New Hampshire**	NA
NA	North Dakota**	NA
NA	South Dakota**	NA
NA	Utah**	NA
NA	Vermont**	NA
NA	Wyoming**	NA

District of Columbia   43.3

Source: U.S. Department of Health and Human Services, National Center for Health Statistics
        "National Vital Statistics Reports" (Vol. 54, No. 13, April 19, 2006)
*AIDS is Acquired Immunodeficiency Syndrome. It is a specific group of diseases or conditions which are indicative
of severe immunosuppression related to infection with the Human Immunodeficiency Virus (HIV). Age-adjusted rates
based on the year 2000 standard population.
**Insufficient data to determine a reliable rate.

Estimated Deaths by Cancer in 2007

National Estimated Total = 559,650 Deaths

ALPHA ORDER

RANK	STATE	DEATHS	% of USA
21	Alabama	9,740	1.7%
50	Alaska	810	0.1%
20	Arizona	10,120	1.8%
31	Arkansas	6,240	1.1%
1	California	54,890	9.8%
29	Colorado	6,660	1.2%
28	Connecticut	6,990	1.2%
45	Delaware	1,810	0.3%
2	Florida	40,430	7.2%
11	Georgia	14,950	2.7%
43	Hawaii	2,260	0.4%
41	Idaho	2,370	0.4%
7	Illinois	23,870	4.3%
15	Indiana	12,730	2.3%
30	Iowa	6,510	1.2%
33	Kansas	5,290	0.9%
23	Kentucky	9,390	1.7%
22	Louisiana	9,550	1.7%
38	Maine	3,190	0.6%
19	Maryland	10,210	1.8%
13	Massachusetts	13,240	2.4%
8	Michigan	19,180	3.4%
24	Minnesota	9,380	1.7%
32	Mississippi	5,990	1.1%
16	Missouri	12,610	2.3%
44	Montana	1,920	0.3%
36	Nebraska	3,320	0.6%
34	Nevada	4,660	0.8%
40	New Hampshire	2,630	0.5%
9	New Jersey	17,140	3.1%
37	New Mexico	3,270	0.6%
3	New York	35,270	6.3%
10	North Carolina	16,880	3.0%
47	North Dakota	1,220	0.2%
6	Ohio	24,600	4.4%
26	Oklahoma	7,380	1.3%
27	Oregon	7,370	1.3%
5	Pennsylvania	29,140	5.2%
41	Rhode Island	2,370	0.4%
25	South Carolina	8,940	1.6%
46	South Dakota	1,600	0.3%
14	Tennessee	12,920	2.3%
4	Texas	34,170	6.1%
39	Utah	2,690	0.5%
48	Vermont	1,160	0.2%
12	Virginia	13,740	2.5%
17	Washington	11,370	2.0%
35	West Virginia	4,610	0.8%
18	Wisconsin	10,870	1.9%
49	Wyoming	980	0.2%

RANK ORDER

RANK	STATE	DEATHS	% of USA
1	California	54,890	9.8%
2	Florida	40,430	7.2%
3	New York	35,270	6.3%
4	Texas	34,170	6.1%
5	Pennsylvania	29,140	5.2%
6	Ohio	24,600	4.4%
7	Illinois	23,870	4.3%
8	Michigan	19,180	3.4%
9	New Jersey	17,140	3.1%
10	North Carolina	16,880	3.0%
11	Georgia	14,950	2.7%
12	Virginia	13,740	2.5%
13	Massachusetts	13,240	2.4%
14	Tennessee	12,920	2.3%
15	Indiana	12,730	2.3%
16	Missouri	12,610	2.3%
17	Washington	11,370	2.0%
18	Wisconsin	10,870	1.9%
19	Maryland	10,210	1.8%
20	Arizona	10,120	1.8%
21	Alabama	9,740	1.7%
22	Louisiana	9,550	1.7%
23	Kentucky	9,390	1.7%
24	Minnesota	9,380	1.7%
25	South Carolina	8,940	1.6%
26	Oklahoma	7,380	1.3%
27	Oregon	7,370	1.3%
28	Connecticut	6,990	1.2%
29	Colorado	6,660	1.2%
30	Iowa	6,510	1.2%
31	Arkansas	6,240	1.1%
32	Mississippi	5,990	1.1%
33	Kansas	5,290	0.9%
34	Nevada	4,660	0.8%
35	West Virginia	4,610	0.8%
36	Nebraska	3,320	0.6%
37	New Mexico	3,270	0.6%
38	Maine	3,190	0.6%
39	Utah	2,690	0.5%
40	New Hampshire	2,630	0.5%
41	Idaho	2,370	0.4%
41	Rhode Island	2,370	0.4%
43	Hawaii	2,260	0.4%
44	Montana	1,920	0.3%
45	Delaware	1,810	0.3%
46	South Dakota	1,600	0.3%
47	North Dakota	1,220	0.2%
48	Vermont	1,160	0.2%
49	Wyoming	980	0.2%
50	Alaska	810	0.1%
	District of Columbia	1,020	0.2%

Source: American Cancer Society
"Cancer Facts & Figures 2007" (Copyright 2007, American Cancer Society)

Estimated Death Rate by Cancer in 2007

National Estimated Rate = 186.9 Deaths per 100,000 Population*

ALPHA ORDER

RANK ORDER

RANK	STATE	RATE
14	Alabama	211.8
49	Alaska	120.9
43	Arizona	164.1
7	Arkansas	222.0
46	California	150.6
48	Colorado	140.1
23	Connecticut	199.4
13	Delaware	212.1
4	Florida	223.5
45	Georgia	159.7
41	Hawaii	175.8
44	Idaho	161.6
34	Illinois	186.0
21	Indiana	201.6
9	Iowa	218.3
28	Kansas	191.4
5	Kentucky	223.2
6	Louisiana	222.7
2	Maine	241.4
37	Maryland	181.8
18	Massachusetts	205.7
31	Michigan	190.0
38	Minnesota	181.5
17	Mississippi	205.8
10	Missouri	215.8
20	Montana	203.3
32	Nebraska	187.7
33	Nevada	186.7
22	New Hampshire	200.0
25	New Jersey	196.5
42	New Mexico	167.3
36	New York	182.7
29	North Carolina	190.6
27	North Dakota	191.9
11	Ohio	214.3
16	Oklahoma	206.2
24	Oregon	199.1
3	Pennsylvania	234.2
7	Rhode Island	222.0
15	South Carolina	206.9
19	South Dakota	204.6
12	Tennessee	213.9
47	Texas	145.4
50	Utah	105.5
35	Vermont	185.9
39	Virginia	179.8
40	Washington	177.8
1	West Virginia	253.5
26	Wisconsin	195.6
30	Wyoming	190.3

RANK	STATE	RATE
1	West Virginia	253.5
2	Maine	241.4
3	Pennsylvania	234.2
4	Florida	223.5
5	Kentucky	223.2
6	Louisiana	222.7
7	Arkansas	222.0
7	Rhode Island	222.0
9	Iowa	218.3
10	Missouri	215.8
11	Ohio	214.3
12	Tennessee	213.9
13	Delaware	212.1
14	Alabama	211.8
15	South Carolina	206.9
16	Oklahoma	206.2
17	Mississippi	205.8
18	Massachusetts	205.7
19	South Dakota	204.6
20	Montana	203.3
21	Indiana	201.6
22	New Hampshire	200.0
23	Connecticut	199.4
24	Oregon	199.1
25	New Jersey	196.5
26	Wisconsin	195.6
27	North Dakota	191.9
28	Kansas	191.4
29	North Carolina	190.6
30	Wyoming	190.3
31	Michigan	190.0
32	Nebraska	187.7
33	Nevada	186.7
34	Illinois	186.0
35	Vermont	185.9
36	New York	182.7
37	Maryland	181.8
38	Minnesota	181.5
39	Virginia	179.8
40	Washington	177.8
41	Hawaii	175.8
42	New Mexico	167.3
43	Arizona	164.1
44	Idaho	161.6
45	Georgia	159.7
46	California	150.6
47	Texas	145.4
48	Colorado	140.1
49	Alaska	120.9
50	Utah	105.5

District of Columbia — 175.4

Source: Morgan Quitno Press using data from American Cancer Society
    "Cancer Facts & Figures 2007" (Copyright 2007, American Cancer Society)
*Rates calculated using 2006 Census resident population estimates. Not age-adjusted.

Age-Adjusted Death Rate by Cancer for Males in 2003

National Rate = 243.7 Deaths per 100,000 Male Population*

ALPHA ORDER			RANK ORDER		
RANK	STATE	RATE	RANK	STATE	RATE
4	Alabama	282.2	1	Mississippi	298.4
28	Alaska	237.5	2	Kentucky	296.6
46	Arizona	211.3	3	Louisiana	296.1
7	Arkansas	275.4	4	Alabama	282.2
45	California	213.9	5	Tennessee	281.6
48	Colorado	208.1	6	South Carolina	276.6
39	Connecticut	228.5	7	Arkansas	275.4
18	Delaware	255.8	8	West Virginia	273.7
37	Florida	229.4	9	Indiana	268.0
10	Georgia	264.5	10	Georgia	264.5
49	Hawaii	192.5	11	North Carolina	263.8
44	Idaho	216.0	12	Ohio	261.9
16	Illinois	256.1	13	Oklahoma	260.8
9	Indiana	268.0	14	Maine	259.4
30	Iowa	237.2	15	Virginia	256.5
33	Kansas	235.2	16	Illinois	256.1
2	Kentucky	296.6	16	Missouri	256.1
3	Louisiana	296.1	18	Delaware	255.8
14	Maine	259.4	19	Pennsylvania	252.9
20	Maryland	252.5	20	Maryland	252.5
21	Massachusetts	249.1	21	Massachusetts	249.1
23	Michigan	247.4	22	Rhode Island	248.1
38	Minnesota	229.1	23	Michigan	247.4
1	Mississippi	298.4	24	New Hampshire	245.8
16	Missouri	256.1	25	Nevada	245.4
35	Montana	232.7	26	New Jersey	244.5
43	Nebraska	226.9	27	Texas	243.4
25	Nevada	245.4	28	Alaska	237.5
24	New Hampshire	245.8	28	Vermont	237.5
26	New Jersey	244.5	30	Iowa	237.2
47	New Mexico	210.7	31	Wisconsin	237.1
40	New York	228.0	32	South Dakota	236.6
11	North Carolina	263.8	33	Kansas	235.2
41	North Dakota	227.3	34	Oregon	234.7
12	Ohio	261.9	35	Montana	232.7
13	Oklahoma	260.8	36	Washington	232.0
34	Oregon	234.7	37	Florida	229.4
19	Pennsylvania	252.9	38	Minnesota	229.1
22	Rhode Island	248.1	39	Connecticut	228.5
6	South Carolina	276.6	40	New York	228.0
32	South Dakota	236.6	41	North Dakota	227.3
5	Tennessee	281.6	42	Wyoming	227.1
27	Texas	243.4	43	Nebraska	226.9
50	Utah	182.2	44	Idaho	216.0
28	Vermont	237.5	45	California	213.9
15	Virginia	256.5	46	Arizona	211.3
36	Washington	232.0	47	New Mexico	210.7
8	West Virginia	273.7	48	Colorado	208.1
31	Wisconsin	237.1	49	Hawaii	192.5
42	Wyoming	227.1	50	Utah	182.2

District of Columbia   299.1

Source: American Cancer Society
"Cancer Facts & Figures 2007" (Copyright 2007, American Cancer Society)
For 1999 to 2003. Age-adjusted to the 2000 U.S. standard population.

Age-Adjusted Death Rate by Cancer for Females in 2003

National Rate = 164.3 Deaths per 100,000 Female Population*

ALPHA ORDER

RANK	STATE	RATE
26	Alabama	165.3
25	Alaska	165.8
46	Arizona	148.3
23	Arkansas	167.0
42	California	155.3
47	Colorado	148.2
34	Connecticut	160.2
7	Delaware	175.6
43	Florida	154.2
27	Georgia	163.8
50	Hawaii	122.7
44	Idaho	151.6
10	Illinois	172.6
5	Indiana	176.2
38	Iowa	157.1
35	Kansas	159.3
2	Kentucky	182.0
3	Louisiana	181.1
4	Maine	178.8
11	Maryland	172.2
16	Massachusetts	171.0
20	Michigan	168.7
39	Minnesota	157.0
18	Mississippi	169.7
12	Missouri	171.8
30	Montana	163.2
40	Nebraska	156.8
5	Nevada	176.2
22	New Hampshire	167.6
9	New Jersey	175.0
48	New Mexico	142.9
32	New York	162.5
30	North Carolina	163.2
45	North Dakota	151.1
8	Ohio	175.2
21	Oklahoma	168.5
17	Oregon	170.2
14	Pennsylvania	171.2
14	Rhode Island	171.2
27	South Carolina	163.8
41	South Dakota	156.2
13	Tennessee	171.6
36	Texas	159.1
49	Utah	124.1
29	Vermont	163.3
19	Virginia	169.0
24	Washington	166.9
1	West Virginia	182.7
37	Wisconsin	158.9
33	Wyoming	160.9

RANK ORDER

RANK	STATE	RATE
1	West Virginia	182.7
2	Kentucky	182.0
3	Louisiana	181.1
4	Maine	178.8
5	Indiana	176.2
5	Nevada	176.2
7	Delaware	175.6
8	Ohio	175.2
9	New Jersey	175.0
10	Illinois	172.6
11	Maryland	172.2
12	Missouri	171.8
13	Tennessee	171.6
14	Pennsylvania	171.2
14	Rhode Island	171.2
16	Massachusetts	171.0
17	Oregon	170.2
18	Mississippi	169.7
19	Virginia	169.0
20	Michigan	168.7
21	Oklahoma	168.5
22	New Hampshire	167.6
23	Arkansas	167.0
24	Washington	166.9
25	Alaska	165.8
26	Alabama	165.3
27	Georgia	163.8
27	South Carolina	163.8
29	Vermont	163.3
30	Montana	163.2
30	North Carolina	163.2
32	New York	162.5
33	Wyoming	160.9
34	Connecticut	160.2
35	Kansas	159.3
36	Texas	159.1
37	Wisconsin	158.9
38	Iowa	157.1
39	Minnesota	157.0
40	Nebraska	156.8
41	South Dakota	156.2
42	California	155.3
43	Florida	154.2
44	Idaho	151.6
45	North Dakota	151.1
46	Arizona	148.3
47	Colorado	148.2
48	New Mexico	142.9
49	Utah	124.1
50	Hawaii	122.7

District of Columbia   187.8

Source: American Cancer Society
   "Cancer Facts & Figures 2007" (Copyright 2007, American Cancer Society)
For 1999 to 2003. Age-adjusted to the 2000 U.S. standard population.

Estimated Deaths by Brain Cancer in 2007

National Estimated Total = 12,740 Deaths

ALPHA ORDER

RANK	STATE	DEATHS	% of USA
22	Alabama	210	1.6%
NA	Alaska*	NA	NA
19	Arizona	250	2.0%
32	Arkansas	140	1.1%
1	California	1,460	11.5%
25	Colorado	190	1.5%
30	Connecticut	150	1.2%
NA	Delaware*	NA	NA
3	Florida	790	6.2%
13	Georgia	280	2.2%
NA	Hawaii*	NA	NA
38	Idaho	80	0.6%
7	Illinois	490	3.8%
13	Indiana	280	2.2%
28	Iowa	160	1.3%
32	Kansas	140	1.1%
30	Kentucky	150	1.2%
23	Louisiana	200	1.6%
38	Maine	80	0.6%
21	Maryland	230	1.8%
16	Massachusetts	270	2.1%
8	Michigan	450	3.5%
20	Minnesota	240	1.9%
28	Mississippi	160	1.3%
16	Missouri	270	2.1%
42	Montana	50	0.4%
35	Nebraska	90	0.7%
34	Nevada	100	0.8%
41	New Hampshire	70	0.5%
12	New Jersey	320	2.5%
38	New Mexico	80	0.6%
4	New York	720	5.7%
10	North Carolina	360	2.8%
NA	North Dakota*	NA	NA
6	Ohio	540	4.2%
27	Oklahoma	170	1.3%
23	Oregon	200	1.6%
5	Pennsylvania	560	4.4%
42	Rhode Island	50	0.4%
25	South Carolina	190	1.5%
42	South Dakota	50	0.4%
11	Tennessee	350	2.7%
2	Texas	840	6.6%
35	Utah	90	0.7%
NA	Vermont*	NA	NA
13	Virginia	280	2.2%
9	Washington	370	2.9%
35	West Virginia	90	0.7%
18	Wisconsin	260	2.0%
NA	Wyoming*	NA	NA

RANK ORDER

RANK	STATE	DEATHS	% of USA
1	California	1,460	11.5%
2	Texas	840	6.6%
3	Florida	790	6.2%
4	New York	720	5.7%
5	Pennsylvania	560	4.4%
6	Ohio	540	4.2%
7	Illinois	490	3.8%
8	Michigan	450	3.5%
9	Washington	370	2.9%
10	North Carolina	360	2.8%
11	Tennessee	350	2.7%
12	New Jersey	320	2.5%
13	Georgia	280	2.2%
13	Indiana	280	2.2%
13	Virginia	280	2.2%
16	Massachusetts	270	2.1%
16	Missouri	270	2.1%
18	Wisconsin	260	2.0%
19	Arizona	250	2.0%
20	Minnesota	240	1.9%
21	Maryland	230	1.8%
22	Alabama	210	1.6%
23	Louisiana	200	1.6%
23	Oregon	200	1.6%
25	Colorado	190	1.5%
25	South Carolina	190	1.5%
27	Oklahoma	170	1.3%
28	Iowa	160	1.3%
28	Mississippi	160	1.3%
30	Connecticut	150	1.2%
30	Kentucky	150	1.2%
32	Arkansas	140	1.1%
32	Kansas	140	1.1%
34	Nevada	100	0.8%
35	Nebraska	90	0.7%
35	Utah	90	0.7%
35	West Virginia	90	0.7%
38	Idaho	80	0.6%
38	Maine	80	0.6%
38	New Mexico	80	0.6%
41	New Hampshire	70	0.5%
42	Montana	50	0.4%
42	Rhode Island	50	0.4%
42	South Dakota	50	0.4%
NA	Alaska*	NA	NA
NA	Delaware*	NA	NA
NA	Hawaii*	NA	NA
NA	North Dakota*	NA	NA
NA	Vermont*	NA	NA
NA	Wyoming*	NA	NA
	District of Columbia*	NA	NA

Source: American Cancer Society
   "Cancer Facts & Figures 2007" (Copyright 2007, American Cancer Society)
*Fewer than 50 deaths.

Estimated Death Rate by Brain Cancer in 2007

National Estimated Rate = 4.3 Deaths per 100,000 Population*

ALPHA ORDER				RANK ORDER		
RANK	STATE	RATE		RANK	STATE	RATE
20	Alabama	4.6		1	South Dakota	6.4
NA	Alaska**	NA		2	Maine	6.1
30	Arizona	4.1		3	Tennessee	5.8
13	Arkansas	5.0		3	Washington	5.8
34	California	4.0		5	Idaho	5.5
34	Colorado	4.0		5	Mississippi	5.5
28	Connecticut	4.3		7	Iowa	5.4
NA	Delaware**	NA		7	Oregon	5.4
25	Florida	4.4		9	Montana	5.3
44	Georgia	3.0		9	New Hampshire	5.3
NA	Hawaii**	NA		11	Kansas	5.1
5	Idaho	5.5		11	Nebraska	5.1
37	Illinois	3.8		13	Arkansas	5.0
25	Indiana	4.4		14	West Virginia	4.9
7	Iowa	5.4		15	Louisiana	4.7
11	Kansas	5.1		15	Ohio	4.7
41	Kentucky	3.6		15	Oklahoma	4.7
15	Louisiana	4.7		15	Rhode Island	4.7
2	Maine	6.1		15	Wisconsin	4.7
30	Maryland	4.1		20	Alabama	4.6
29	Massachusetts	4.2		20	Minnesota	4.6
23	Michigan	4.5		20	Missouri	4.6
20	Minnesota	4.6		23	Michigan	4.5
5	Mississippi	5.5		23	Pennsylvania	4.5
20	Missouri	4.6		25	Florida	4.4
9	Montana	5.3		25	Indiana	4.4
11	Nebraska	5.1		25	South Carolina	4.4
34	Nevada	4.0		28	Connecticut	4.3
9	New Hampshire	5.3		29	Massachusetts	4.2
38	New Jersey	3.7		30	Arizona	4.1
30	New Mexico	4.1		30	Maryland	4.1
38	New York	3.7		30	New Mexico	4.1
30	North Carolina	4.1		30	North Carolina	4.1
NA	North Dakota**	NA		34	California	4.0
15	Ohio	4.7		34	Colorado	4.0
15	Oklahoma	4.7		34	Nevada	4.0
7	Oregon	5.4		37	Illinois	3.8
23	Pennsylvania	4.5		38	New Jersey	3.7
15	Rhode Island	4.7		38	New York	3.7
25	South Carolina	4.4		38	Virginia	3.7
1	South Dakota	6.4		41	Kentucky	3.6
3	Tennessee	5.8		41	Texas	3.6
41	Texas	3.6		43	Utah	3.5
43	Utah	3.5		44	Georgia	3.0
NA	Vermont**	NA		NA	Alaska**	NA
38	Virginia	3.7		NA	Delaware**	NA
3	Washington	5.8		NA	Hawaii**	NA
14	West Virginia	4.9		NA	North Dakota**	NA
15	Wisconsin	4.7		NA	Vermont**	NA
NA	Wyoming**	NA		NA	Wyoming**	NA
				District of Columbia**		NA

Source: Morgan Quitno Press using data from American Cancer Society
   "Cancer Facts & Figures 2007" (Copyright 2007, American Cancer Society)
*Rates calculated using 2006 Census resident population estimates. Not age-adjusted.
**Fewer than 50 deaths.

Estimated Deaths by Female Breast Cancer in 2007

National Estimated Total = 40,460 Deaths

<table>
<tr><td colspan="4">ALPHA ORDER</td><td colspan="4">RANK ORDER</td></tr>
<tr><td>RANK</td><td>STATE</td><td>DEATHS</td><td>% of USA</td><td>RANK</td><td>STATE</td><td>DEATHS</td><td>% of USA</td></tr>
<tr><td>22</td><td>Alabama</td><td>680</td><td>1.7%</td><td>1</td><td>California</td><td>4,130</td><td>10.2%</td></tr>
<tr><td>50</td><td>Alaska</td><td>50</td><td>0.1%</td><td>2</td><td>Florida</td><td>2,700</td><td>6.7%</td></tr>
<tr><td>21</td><td>Arizona</td><td>710</td><td>1.8%</td><td>3</td><td>New York</td><td>2,670</td><td>6.6%</td></tr>
<tr><td>31</td><td>Arkansas</td><td>410</td><td>1.0%</td><td>4</td><td>Texas</td><td>2,480</td><td>6.1%</td></tr>
<tr><td>1</td><td>California</td><td>4,130</td><td>10.2%</td><td>5</td><td>Pennsylvania</td><td>2,470</td><td>6.1%</td></tr>
<tr><td>27</td><td>Colorado</td><td>520</td><td>1.3%</td><td>6</td><td>Ohio</td><td>1,820</td><td>4.5%</td></tr>
<tr><td>29</td><td>Connecticut</td><td>490</td><td>1.2%</td><td>7</td><td>Illinois</td><td>1,740</td><td>4.3%</td></tr>
<tr><td>45</td><td>Delaware</td><td>120</td><td>0.3%</td><td>8</td><td>New Jersey</td><td>1,350</td><td>3.3%</td></tr>
<tr><td>2</td><td>Florida</td><td>2,700</td><td>6.7%</td><td>9</td><td>Michigan</td><td>1,320</td><td>3.3%</td></tr>
<tr><td>11</td><td>Georgia</td><td>1,120</td><td>2.8%</td><td>10</td><td>North Carolina</td><td>1,240</td><td>3.1%</td></tr>
<tr><td>43</td><td>Hawaii</td><td>130</td><td>0.3%</td><td>11</td><td>Georgia</td><td>1,120</td><td>2.8%</td></tr>
<tr><td>40</td><td>Idaho</td><td>180</td><td>0.4%</td><td>12</td><td>Virginia</td><td>1,100</td><td>2.7%</td></tr>
<tr><td>7</td><td>Illinois</td><td>1,740</td><td>4.3%</td><td>13</td><td>Massachusetts</td><td>890</td><td>2.2%</td></tr>
<tr><td>16</td><td>Indiana</td><td>860</td><td>2.1%</td><td>13</td><td>Tennessee</td><td>890</td><td>2.2%</td></tr>
<tr><td>31</td><td>Iowa</td><td>410</td><td>1.0%</td><td>15</td><td>Missouri</td><td>870</td><td>2.2%</td></tr>
<tr><td>33</td><td>Kansas</td><td>380</td><td>0.9%</td><td>16</td><td>Indiana</td><td>860</td><td>2.1%</td></tr>
<tr><td>23</td><td>Kentucky</td><td>600</td><td>1.5%</td><td>17</td><td>Maryland</td><td>830</td><td>2.1%</td></tr>
<tr><td>20</td><td>Louisiana</td><td>730</td><td>1.8%</td><td>18</td><td>Washington</td><td>770</td><td>1.9%</td></tr>
<tr><td>39</td><td>Maine</td><td>190</td><td>0.5%</td><td>18</td><td>Wisconsin</td><td>770</td><td>1.9%</td></tr>
<tr><td>17</td><td>Maryland</td><td>830</td><td>2.1%</td><td>20</td><td>Louisiana</td><td>730</td><td>1.8%</td></tr>
<tr><td>13</td><td>Massachusetts</td><td>890</td><td>2.2%</td><td>21</td><td>Arizona</td><td>710</td><td>1.8%</td></tr>
<tr><td>9</td><td>Michigan</td><td>1,320</td><td>3.3%</td><td>22</td><td>Alabama</td><td>680</td><td>1.7%</td></tr>
<tr><td>23</td><td>Minnesota</td><td>600</td><td>1.5%</td><td>23</td><td>Kentucky</td><td>600</td><td>1.5%</td></tr>
<tr><td>30</td><td>Mississippi</td><td>450</td><td>1.1%</td><td>23</td><td>Minnesota</td><td>600</td><td>1.5%</td></tr>
<tr><td>15</td><td>Missouri</td><td>870</td><td>2.2%</td><td>25</td><td>South Carolina</td><td>570</td><td>1.4%</td></tr>
<tr><td>43</td><td>Montana</td><td>130</td><td>0.3%</td><td>26</td><td>Oregon</td><td>530</td><td>1.3%</td></tr>
<tr><td>38</td><td>Nebraska</td><td>220</td><td>0.5%</td><td>27</td><td>Colorado</td><td>520</td><td>1.3%</td></tr>
<tr><td>34</td><td>Nevada</td><td>330</td><td>0.8%</td><td>28</td><td>Oklahoma</td><td>510</td><td>1.3%</td></tr>
<tr><td>40</td><td>New Hampshire</td><td>180</td><td>0.4%</td><td>29</td><td>Connecticut</td><td>490</td><td>1.2%</td></tr>
<tr><td>8</td><td>New Jersey</td><td>1,350</td><td>3.3%</td><td>30</td><td>Mississippi</td><td>450</td><td>1.1%</td></tr>
<tr><td>36</td><td>New Mexico</td><td>240</td><td>0.6%</td><td>31</td><td>Arkansas</td><td>410</td><td>1.0%</td></tr>
<tr><td>3</td><td>New York</td><td>2,670</td><td>6.6%</td><td>31</td><td>Iowa</td><td>410</td><td>1.0%</td></tr>
<tr><td>10</td><td>North Carolina</td><td>1,240</td><td>3.1%</td><td>33</td><td>Kansas</td><td>380</td><td>0.9%</td></tr>
<tr><td>48</td><td>North Dakota</td><td>90</td><td>0.2%</td><td>34</td><td>Nevada</td><td>330</td><td>0.8%</td></tr>
<tr><td>6</td><td>Ohio</td><td>1,820</td><td>4.5%</td><td>35</td><td>West Virginia</td><td>280</td><td>0.7%</td></tr>
<tr><td>28</td><td>Oklahoma</td><td>510</td><td>1.3%</td><td>36</td><td>New Mexico</td><td>240</td><td>0.6%</td></tr>
<tr><td>26</td><td>Oregon</td><td>530</td><td>1.3%</td><td>36</td><td>Utah</td><td>240</td><td>0.6%</td></tr>
<tr><td>5</td><td>Pennsylvania</td><td>2,470</td><td>6.1%</td><td>38</td><td>Nebraska</td><td>220</td><td>0.5%</td></tr>
<tr><td>42</td><td>Rhode Island</td><td>140</td><td>0.3%</td><td>39</td><td>Maine</td><td>190</td><td>0.5%</td></tr>
<tr><td>25</td><td>South Carolina</td><td>570</td><td>1.4%</td><td>40</td><td>Idaho</td><td>180</td><td>0.4%</td></tr>
<tr><td>46</td><td>South Dakota</td><td>100</td><td>0.2%</td><td>40</td><td>New Hampshire</td><td>180</td><td>0.4%</td></tr>
<tr><td>13</td><td>Tennessee</td><td>890</td><td>2.2%</td><td>42</td><td>Rhode Island</td><td>140</td><td>0.3%</td></tr>
<tr><td>4</td><td>Texas</td><td>2,480</td><td>6.1%</td><td>43</td><td>Hawaii</td><td>130</td><td>0.3%</td></tr>
<tr><td>36</td><td>Utah</td><td>240</td><td>0.6%</td><td>43</td><td>Montana</td><td>130</td><td>0.3%</td></tr>
<tr><td>46</td><td>Vermont</td><td>100</td><td>0.2%</td><td>45</td><td>Delaware</td><td>120</td><td>0.3%</td></tr>
<tr><td>12</td><td>Virginia</td><td>1,100</td><td>2.7%</td><td>46</td><td>South Dakota</td><td>100</td><td>0.2%</td></tr>
<tr><td>18</td><td>Washington</td><td>770</td><td>1.9%</td><td>46</td><td>Vermont</td><td>100</td><td>0.2%</td></tr>
<tr><td>35</td><td>West Virginia</td><td>280</td><td>0.7%</td><td>48</td><td>North Dakota</td><td>90</td><td>0.2%</td></tr>
<tr><td>18</td><td>Wisconsin</td><td>770</td><td>1.9%</td><td>49</td><td>Wyoming</td><td>60</td><td>0.1%</td></tr>
<tr><td>49</td><td>Wyoming</td><td>60</td><td>0.1%</td><td>50</td><td>Alaska</td><td>50</td><td>0.1%</td></tr>
<tr><td></td><td></td><td></td><td></td><td colspan="2">District of Columbia</td><td>80</td><td>0.2%</td></tr>
</table>

Source: American Cancer Society
"Cancer Facts & Figures 2007" (Copyright 2007, American Cancer Society)

Age-Adjusted Death Rate by Female Breast Cancer in 2003

National Rate = 26.0 Deaths per 100,000 Female Population*

ALPHA ORDER

RANK	STATE	RATE
18	Alabama	26.3
46	Alaska	23.0
39	Arizona	24.1
36	Arkansas	24.4
35	California	24.6
45	Colorado	23.4
27	Connecticut	25.3
10	Delaware	26.8
44	Florida	23.7
22	Georgia	25.7
50	Hawaii	18.3
34	Idaho	24.7
7	Illinois	27.8
13	Indiana	26.6
38	Iowa	24.3
22	Kansas	25.7
13	Kentucky	26.6
1	Louisiana	30.1
32	Maine	24.8
4	Maryland	27.9
20	Massachusetts	26.2
13	Michigan	26.6
36	Minnesota	24.4
4	Mississippi	27.9
12	Missouri	26.7
42	Montana	23.8
42	Nebraska	23.8
18	Nevada	26.3
25	New Hampshire	25.6
2	New Jersey	29.1
49	New Mexico	22.5
9	New York	27.0
25	North Carolina	25.6
32	North Dakota	24.8
3	Ohio	28.5
16	Oklahoma	26.4
22	Oregon	25.7
4	Pennsylvania	27.9
30	Rhode Island	25.0
10	South Carolina	26.8
40	South Dakota	24.0
16	Tennessee	26.4
31	Texas	24.9
46	Utah	23.0
21	Vermont	26.1
8	Virginia	27.6
40	Washington	24.0
27	West Virginia	25.3
29	Wisconsin	25.1
46	Wyoming	23.0

RANK ORDER

RANK	STATE	RATE
1	Louisiana	30.1
2	New Jersey	29.1
3	Ohio	28.5
4	Maryland	27.9
4	Mississippi	27.9
4	Pennsylvania	27.9
7	Illinois	27.8
8	Virginia	27.6
9	New York	27.0
10	Delaware	26.8
10	South Carolina	26.8
12	Missouri	26.7
13	Indiana	26.6
13	Kentucky	26.6
13	Michigan	26.6
16	Oklahoma	26.4
16	Tennessee	26.4
18	Alabama	26.3
18	Nevada	26.3
20	Massachusetts	26.2
21	Vermont	26.1
22	Georgia	25.7
22	Kansas	25.7
22	Oregon	25.7
25	New Hampshire	25.6
25	North Carolina	25.6
27	Connecticut	25.3
27	West Virginia	25.3
29	Wisconsin	25.1
30	Rhode Island	25.0
31	Texas	24.9
32	Maine	24.8
32	North Dakota	24.8
34	Idaho	24.7
35	California	24.6
36	Arkansas	24.4
36	Minnesota	24.4
38	Iowa	24.3
39	Arizona	24.1
40	South Dakota	24.0
40	Washington	24.0
42	Montana	23.8
42	Nebraska	23.8
44	Florida	23.7
45	Colorado	23.4
46	Alaska	23.0
46	Utah	23.0
46	Wyoming	23.0
49	New Mexico	22.5
50	Hawaii	18.3

District of Columbia   33.7

Source: American Cancer Society
   "Cancer Facts & Figures 2007" (Copyright 2007, American Cancer Society)
*For 1999 to 2003. Age-adjusted to the 2000 U.S. standard population.

Estimated Deaths by Colon and Rectum Cancer in 2007

National Estimated Total = 52,180 Deaths

ALPHA ORDER

RANK	STATE	DEATHS	% of USA
22	Alabama	880	1.7%
50	Alaska	70	0.1%
18	Arizona	970	1.9%
29	Arkansas	610	1.2%
1	California	5,230	10.0%
28	Colorado	630	1.2%
32	Connecticut	590	1.1%
44	Delaware	160	0.3%
2	Florida	3,530	6.8%
11	Georgia	1,340	2.6%
41	Hawaii	210	0.4%
43	Idaho	200	0.4%
6	Illinois	2,380	4.6%
13	Indiana	1,180	2.3%
31	Iowa	600	1.1%
33	Kansas	520	1.0%
23	Kentucky	860	1.6%
20	Louisiana	960	1.8%
38	Maine	280	0.5%
18	Maryland	970	1.9%
13	Massachusetts	1,180	2.3%
8	Michigan	1,750	3.4%
24	Minnesota	810	1.6%
29	Mississippi	610	1.2%
15	Missouri	1,170	2.2%
44	Montana	160	0.3%
36	Nebraska	350	0.7%
34	Nevada	490	0.9%
40	New Hampshire	220	0.4%
9	New Jersey	1,680	3.2%
37	New Mexico	320	0.6%
3	New York	3,350	6.4%
10	North Carolina	1,480	2.8%
47	North Dakota	120	0.2%
7	Ohio	2,350	4.5%
26	Oklahoma	720	1.4%
27	Oregon	640	1.2%
5	Pennsylvania	2,730	5.2%
41	Rhode Island	210	0.4%
25	South Carolina	790	1.5%
44	South Dakota	160	0.3%
16	Tennessee	1,160	2.2%
4	Texas	3,220	6.2%
39	Utah	240	0.5%
47	Vermont	120	0.2%
12	Virginia	1,320	2.5%
17	Washington	990	1.9%
35	West Virginia	480	0.9%
20	Wisconsin	960	1.8%
49	Wyoming	110	0.2%

RANK ORDER

RANK	STATE	DEATHS	% of USA
1	California	5,230	10.0%
2	Florida	3,530	6.8%
3	New York	3,350	6.4%
4	Texas	3,220	6.2%
5	Pennsylvania	2,730	5.2%
6	Illinois	2,380	4.6%
7	Ohio	2,350	4.5%
8	Michigan	1,750	3.4%
9	New Jersey	1,680	3.2%
10	North Carolina	1,480	2.8%
11	Georgia	1,340	2.6%
12	Virginia	1,320	2.5%
13	Indiana	1,180	2.3%
13	Massachusetts	1,180	2.3%
15	Missouri	1,170	2.2%
16	Tennessee	1,160	2.2%
17	Washington	990	1.9%
18	Arizona	970	1.9%
18	Maryland	970	1.9%
20	Louisiana	960	1.8%
20	Wisconsin	960	1.8%
22	Alabama	880	1.7%
23	Kentucky	860	1.6%
24	Minnesota	810	1.6%
25	South Carolina	790	1.5%
26	Oklahoma	720	1.4%
27	Oregon	640	1.2%
28	Colorado	630	1.2%
29	Arkansas	610	1.2%
29	Mississippi	610	1.2%
31	Iowa	600	1.1%
32	Connecticut	590	1.1%
33	Kansas	520	1.0%
34	Nevada	490	0.9%
35	West Virginia	480	0.9%
36	Nebraska	350	0.7%
37	New Mexico	320	0.6%
38	Maine	280	0.5%
39	Utah	240	0.5%
40	New Hampshire	220	0.4%
41	Hawaii	210	0.4%
41	Rhode Island	210	0.4%
43	Idaho	200	0.4%
44	Delaware	160	0.3%
44	Montana	160	0.3%
44	South Dakota	160	0.3%
47	North Dakota	120	0.2%
47	Vermont	120	0.2%
49	Wyoming	110	0.2%
50	Alaska	70	0.1%
	District of Columbia	100	0.2%

Source: American Cancer Society
"Cancer Facts & Figures 2007" (Copyright 2007, American Cancer Society)

Estimated Death Rate by Colon and Rectum Cancer in 2007

National Estimated Rate = 17.4 Deaths per 100,000 Population*

<u>ALPHA ORDER</u>

RANK	STATE	RATE
21	Alabama	19.1
49	Alaska	10.4
41	Arizona	15.7
4	Arkansas	21.7
44	California	14.3
48	Colorado	13.3
36	Connecticut	16.8
24	Delaware	18.7
17	Florida	19.5
44	Georgia	14.3
40	Hawaii	16.3
47	Idaho	13.6
26	Illinois	18.5
24	Indiana	18.7
11	Iowa	20.1
23	Kansas	18.8
10	Kentucky	20.4
2	Louisiana	22.4
6	Maine	21.2
30	Maryland	17.3
27	Massachusetts	18.3
30	Michigan	17.3
41	Minnesota	15.7
7	Mississippi	21.0
13	Missouri	20.0
35	Montana	16.9
14	Nebraska	19.8
16	Nevada	19.6
37	New Hampshire	16.7
18	New Jersey	19.3
39	New Mexico	16.4
29	New York	17.4
37	North Carolina	16.7
22	North Dakota	18.9
8	Ohio	20.5
11	Oklahoma	20.1
30	Oregon	17.3
3	Pennsylvania	21.9
15	Rhode Island	19.7
27	South Carolina	18.3
8	South Dakota	20.5
19	Tennessee	19.2
46	Texas	13.7
50	Utah	9.4
19	Vermont	19.2
30	Virginia	17.3
43	Washington	15.5
1	West Virginia	26.4
30	Wisconsin	17.3
5	Wyoming	21.4

<u>RANK ORDER</u>

RANK	STATE	RATE
1	West Virginia	26.4
2	Louisiana	22.4
3	Pennsylvania	21.9
4	Arkansas	21.7
5	Wyoming	21.4
6	Maine	21.2
7	Mississippi	21.0
8	Ohio	20.5
8	South Dakota	20.5
10	Kentucky	20.4
11	Iowa	20.1
11	Oklahoma	20.1
13	Missouri	20.0
14	Nebraska	19.8
15	Rhode Island	19.7
16	Nevada	19.6
17	Florida	19.5
18	New Jersey	19.3
19	Tennessee	19.2
19	Vermont	19.2
21	Alabama	19.1
22	North Dakota	18.9
23	Kansas	18.8
24	Delaware	18.7
24	Indiana	18.7
26	Illinois	18.5
27	Massachusetts	18.3
27	South Carolina	18.3
29	New York	17.4
30	Maryland	17.3
30	Michigan	17.3
30	Oregon	17.3
30	Virginia	17.3
30	Wisconsin	17.3
35	Montana	16.9
36	Connecticut	16.8
37	New Hampshire	16.7
37	North Carolina	16.7
39	New Mexico	16.4
40	Hawaii	16.3
41	Arizona	15.7
41	Minnesota	15.7
43	Washington	15.5
44	California	14.3
44	Georgia	14.3
46	Texas	13.7
47	Idaho	13.6
48	Colorado	13.3
49	Alaska	10.4
50	Utah	9.4

District of Columbia   17.2

Source: Morgan Quitno Press using data from American Cancer Society
"Cancer Facts & Figures 2007" (Copyright 2007, American Cancer Society)
*Rates calculated using 2006 Census resident population estimates. Not age-adjusted.

Estimated Deaths by Leukemia in 2007

National Estimated Total = 21,790 Deaths

ALPHA ORDER

RANK	STATE	DEATHS	% of USA
22	Alabama	350	1.6%
NA	Alaska*	NA	NA
19	Arizona	400	1.8%
31	Arkansas	240	1.1%
1	California	2,150	9.9%
27	Colorado	290	1.3%
29	Connecticut	270	1.2%
45	Delaware	70	0.3%
2	Florida	1,630	7.5%
11	Georgia	540	2.5%
42	Hawaii	80	0.4%
38	Idaho	120	0.6%
6	Illinois	990	4.5%
12	Indiana	510	2.3%
26	Iowa	310	1.4%
32	Kansas	230	1.1%
25	Kentucky	320	1.5%
23	Louisiana	330	1.5%
40	Maine	100	0.5%
21	Maryland	390	1.8%
14	Massachusetts	490	2.2%
8	Michigan	770	3.5%
19	Minnesota	400	1.8%
33	Mississippi	210	1.0%
18	Missouri	460	2.1%
42	Montana	80	0.4%
35	Nebraska	150	0.7%
34	Nevada	160	0.7%
40	New Hampshire	100	0.5%
9	New Jersey	680	3.1%
38	New Mexico	120	0.6%
4	New York	1,360	6.2%
10	North Carolina	610	2.8%
NA	North Dakota*	NA	NA
7	Ohio	950	4.4%
27	Oklahoma	290	1.3%
30	Oregon	260	1.2%
5	Pennsylvania	1,070	4.9%
42	Rhode Island	80	0.4%
23	South Carolina	330	1.5%
45	South Dakota	70	0.3%
17	Tennessee	480	2.2%
3	Texas	1,410	6.5%
36	Utah	130	0.6%
47	Vermont	50	0.2%
13	Virginia	500	2.3%
14	Washington	490	2.2%
36	West Virginia	130	0.6%
14	Wisconsin	490	2.2%
NA	Wyoming*	NA	NA

RANK ORDER

RANK	STATE	DEATHS	% of USA
1	California	2,150	9.9%
2	Florida	1,630	7.5%
3	Texas	1,410	6.5%
4	New York	1,360	6.2%
5	Pennsylvania	1,070	4.9%
6	Illinois	990	4.5%
7	Ohio	950	4.4%
8	Michigan	770	3.5%
9	New Jersey	680	3.1%
10	North Carolina	610	2.8%
11	Georgia	540	2.5%
12	Indiana	510	2.3%
13	Virginia	500	2.3%
14	Massachusetts	490	2.2%
14	Washington	490	2.2%
14	Wisconsin	490	2.2%
17	Tennessee	480	2.2%
18	Missouri	460	2.1%
19	Arizona	400	1.8%
19	Minnesota	400	1.8%
21	Maryland	390	1.8%
22	Alabama	350	1.6%
23	Louisiana	330	1.5%
23	South Carolina	330	1.5%
25	Kentucky	320	1.5%
26	Iowa	310	1.4%
27	Colorado	290	1.3%
27	Oklahoma	290	1.3%
29	Connecticut	270	1.2%
30	Oregon	260	1.2%
31	Arkansas	240	1.1%
32	Kansas	230	1.1%
33	Mississippi	210	1.0%
34	Nevada	160	0.7%
35	Nebraska	150	0.7%
36	Utah	130	0.6%
36	West Virginia	130	0.6%
38	Idaho	120	0.6%
38	New Mexico	120	0.6%
40	Maine	100	0.5%
40	New Hampshire	100	0.5%
42	Hawaii	80	0.4%
42	Montana	80	0.4%
42	Rhode Island	80	0.4%
45	Delaware	70	0.3%
45	South Dakota	70	0.3%
47	Vermont	50	0.2%
NA	Alaska*	NA	NA
NA	North Dakota*	NA	NA
NA	Wyoming*	NA	NA
	District of Columbia*	NA	NA

Source: American Cancer Society
  "Cancer Facts & Figures 2007" (Copyright 2007, American Cancer Society)
Fewer than 50 deaths.

Estimated Death Rate by Leukemia in 2007

National Estimated Rate = 7.3 Deaths per 100,000 Population*

ALPHA ORDER

RANK	STATE	RATE
24	Alabama	7.6
NA	Alaska**	NA
38	Arizona	6.5
6	Arkansas	8.5
45	California	5.9
42	Colorado	6.1
19	Connecticut	7.7
11	Delaware	8.2
2	Florida	9.0
46	Georgia	5.8
41	Hawaii	6.2
11	Idaho	8.2
19	Illinois	7.7
13	Indiana	8.1
1	Iowa	10.4
9	Kansas	8.3
24	Kentucky	7.6
19	Louisiana	7.7
24	Maine	7.6
36	Maryland	6.9
24	Massachusetts	7.6
24	Michigan	7.6
19	Minnesota	7.7
32	Mississippi	7.2
16	Missouri	7.9
6	Montana	8.5
6	Nebraska	8.5
40	Nevada	6.4
24	New Hampshire	7.6
18	New Jersey	7.8
42	New Mexico	6.1
34	New York	7.0
36	North Carolina	6.9
NA	North Dakota**	NA
9	Ohio	8.3
13	Oklahoma	8.1
34	Oregon	7.0
5	Pennsylvania	8.6
31	Rhode Island	7.5
24	South Carolina	7.6
2	South Dakota	9.0
16	Tennessee	7.9
44	Texas	6.0
47	Utah	5.1
15	Vermont	8.0
38	Virginia	6.5
19	Washington	7.7
33	West Virginia	7.1
4	Wisconsin	8.8
NA	Wyoming**	NA

RANK ORDER

RANK	STATE	RATE
1	Iowa	10.4
2	Florida	9.0
2	South Dakota	9.0
4	Wisconsin	8.8
5	Pennsylvania	8.6
6	Arkansas	8.5
6	Montana	8.5
6	Nebraska	8.5
9	Kansas	8.3
9	Ohio	8.3
11	Delaware	8.2
11	Idaho	8.2
13	Indiana	8.1
13	Oklahoma	8.1
15	Vermont	8.0
16	Missouri	7.9
16	Tennessee	7.9
18	New Jersey	7.8
19	Connecticut	7.7
19	Illinois	7.7
19	Louisiana	7.7
19	Minnesota	7.7
19	Washington	7.7
24	Alabama	7.6
24	Kentucky	7.6
24	Maine	7.6
24	Massachusetts	7.6
24	Michigan	7.6
24	New Hampshire	7.6
24	South Carolina	7.6
31	Rhode Island	7.5
32	Mississippi	7.2
33	West Virginia	7.1
34	New York	7.0
34	Oregon	7.0
36	Maryland	6.9
36	North Carolina	6.9
38	Arizona	6.5
38	Virginia	6.5
40	Nevada	6.4
41	Hawaii	6.2
42	Colorado	6.1
42	New Mexico	6.1
44	Texas	6.0
45	California	5.9
46	Georgia	5.8
47	Utah	5.1
NA	Alaska**	NA
NA	North Dakota**	NA
NA	Wyoming**	NA
	District of Columbia**	NA

Source: Morgan Quitno Press using data from American Cancer Society
   "Cancer Facts & Figures 2007" (Copyright 2007, American Cancer Society)
*Rates calculated using 2006 Census resident population estimates. Not age-adjusted.
**Fewer than 50 deaths.

Estimated Deaths by Liver Cancer in 2007

National Estimated Total = 16,780 Deaths

ALPHA ORDER

ALPHA ORDER

RANK ORDER

RANK	STATE	DEATHS	% of USA
20	Alabama	300	1.8%
NA	Alaska*	NA	NA
15	Arizona	330	2.0%
26	Arkansas	200	1.2%
1	California	2,270	13.5%
26	Colorado	200	1.2%
28	Connecticut	190	1.1%
NA	Delaware*	NA	NA
3	Florida	1,190	7.1%
14	Georgia	360	2.1%
36	Hawaii	110	0.7%
43	Idaho	50	0.3%
6	Illinois	650	3.9%
21	Indiana	290	1.7%
32	Iowa	140	0.8%
35	Kansas	120	0.7%
25	Kentucky	220	1.3%
15	Louisiana	330	2.0%
38	Maine	70	0.4%
22	Maryland	250	1.5%
11	Massachusetts	380	2.3%
8	Michigan	560	3.3%
23	Minnesota	240	1.4%
30	Mississippi	180	1.1%
15	Missouri	330	2.0%
NA	Montana*	NA	NA
38	Nebraska	70	0.4%
32	Nevada	140	0.8%
38	New Hampshire	70	0.4%
9	New Jersey	530	3.2%
32	New Mexico	140	0.8%
4	New York	1,090	6.5%
10	North Carolina	420	2.5%
NA	North Dakota*	NA	NA
7	Ohio	600	3.6%
30	Oklahoma	180	1.1%
28	Oregon	190	1.1%
5	Pennsylvania	790	4.7%
38	Rhode Island	70	0.4%
24	South Carolina	230	1.4%
NA	South Dakota*	NA	NA
15	Tennessee	330	2.0%
2	Texas	1,490	8.9%
38	Utah	70	0.4%
NA	Vermont*	NA	NA
13	Virginia	370	2.2%
11	Washington	380	2.3%
36	West Virginia	110	0.7%
19	Wisconsin	310	1.8%
NA	Wyoming*	NA	NA

RANK ORDER

RANK	STATE	DEATHS	% of USA
1	California	2,270	13.5%
2	Texas	1,490	8.9%
3	Florida	1,190	7.1%
4	New York	1,090	6.5%
5	Pennsylvania	790	4.7%
6	Illinois	650	3.9%
7	Ohio	600	3.6%
8	Michigan	560	3.3%
9	New Jersey	530	3.2%
10	North Carolina	420	2.5%
11	Massachusetts	380	2.3%
11	Washington	380	2.3%
13	Virginia	370	2.2%
14	Georgia	360	2.1%
15	Arizona	330	2.0%
15	Louisiana	330	2.0%
15	Missouri	330	2.0%
15	Tennessee	330	2.0%
19	Wisconsin	310	1.8%
20	Alabama	300	1.8%
21	Indiana	290	1.7%
22	Maryland	250	1.5%
23	Minnesota	240	1.4%
24	South Carolina	230	1.4%
25	Kentucky	220	1.3%
26	Arkansas	200	1.2%
26	Colorado	200	1.2%
28	Connecticut	190	1.1%
28	Oregon	190	1.1%
30	Mississippi	180	1.1%
30	Oklahoma	180	1.1%
32	Iowa	140	0.8%
32	Nevada	140	0.8%
32	New Mexico	140	0.8%
35	Kansas	120	0.7%
36	Hawaii	110	0.7%
36	West Virginia	110	0.7%
38	Maine	70	0.4%
38	Nebraska	70	0.4%
38	New Hampshire	70	0.4%
38	Rhode Island	70	0.4%
38	Utah	70	0.4%
43	Idaho	50	0.3%
NA	Alaska*	NA	NA
NA	Delaware*	NA	NA
NA	Montana*	NA	NA
NA	North Dakota*	NA	NA
NA	South Dakota*	NA	NA
NA	Vermont*	NA	NA
NA	Wyoming*	NA	NA
	District of Columbia*	NA	NA

Source: American Cancer Society
"Cancer Facts & Figures 2007" (Copyright 2007, American Cancer Society)
*Fewer than 50 deaths.

Estimated Death Rate by Liver Cancer in 2007

National Estimated Rate = 5.6 Deaths per 100,000 Population*

ALPHA ORDER			RANK ORDER		
RANK	**STATE**	**RATE**	**RANK**	**STATE**	**RATE**
7	Alabama	6.5	1	Hawaii	8.6
NA	Alaska**	NA	2	Louisiana	7.7
22	Arizona	5.4	3	New Mexico	7.2
4	Arkansas	7.1	4	Arkansas	7.1
10	California	6.2	5	Florida	6.6
39	Colorado	4.2	5	Rhode Island	6.6
22	Connecticut	5.4	7	Alabama	6.5
NA	Delaware**	NA	8	Pennsylvania	6.4
5	Florida	6.6	9	Texas	6.3
41	Georgia	3.8	10	California	6.2
1	Hawaii	8.6	10	Mississippi	6.2
42	Idaho	3.4	12	New Jersey	6.1
29	Illinois	5.1	13	West Virginia	6.0
35	Indiana	4.6	14	Massachusetts	5.9
33	Iowa	4.7	14	Washington	5.9
38	Kansas	4.3	16	Missouri	5.6
27	Kentucky	5.2	16	Nevada	5.6
2	Louisiana	7.7	16	New York	5.6
24	Maine	5.3	16	Wisconsin	5.6
37	Maryland	4.5	20	Michigan	5.5
14	Massachusetts	5.9	20	Tennessee	5.5
20	Michigan	5.5	22	Arizona	5.4
35	Minnesota	4.6	22	Connecticut	5.4
10	Mississippi	6.2	24	Maine	5.3
16	Missouri	5.6	24	New Hampshire	5.3
NA	Montana**	NA	24	South Carolina	5.3
40	Nebraska	4.0	27	Kentucky	5.2
16	Nevada	5.6	27	Ohio	5.2
24	New Hampshire	5.3	29	Illinois	5.1
12	New Jersey	6.1	29	Oregon	5.1
3	New Mexico	7.2	31	Oklahoma	5.0
16	New York	5.6	32	Virginia	4.8
33	North Carolina	4.7	33	Iowa	4.7
NA	North Dakota**	NA	33	North Carolina	4.7
27	Ohio	5.2	35	Indiana	4.6
31	Oklahoma	5.0	35	Minnesota	4.6
29	Oregon	5.1	37	Maryland	4.5
8	Pennsylvania	6.4	38	Kansas	4.3
5	Rhode Island	6.6	39	Colorado	4.2
24	South Carolina	5.3	40	Nebraska	4.0
NA	South Dakota**	NA	41	Georgia	3.8
20	Tennessee	5.5	42	Idaho	3.4
9	Texas	6.3	43	Utah	2.7
43	Utah	2.7	NA	Alaska**	NA
NA	Vermont**	NA	NA	Delaware**	NA
32	Virginia	4.8	NA	Montana**	NA
14	Washington	5.9	NA	North Dakota**	NA
13	West Virginia	6.0	NA	South Dakota**	NA
16	Wisconsin	5.6	NA	Vermont**	NA
NA	Wyoming**	NA	NA	Wyoming**	NA
				District of Columbia**	NA

Source: Morgan Quitno Press using data from American Cancer Society
    "Cancer Facts & Figures 2007" (Copyright 2007, American Cancer Society)
*Rates calculated using 2006 Census resident population estimates. Not age-adjusted.
**Fewer than 50 deaths.

Estimated Deaths by Lung Cancer in 2007

National Estimated Total = 160,390 Deaths

ALPHA ORDER

RANK	STATE	DEATHS	% of USA
18	Alabama	3,240	2.0%
50	Alaska	230	0.1%
23	Arizona	2,850	1.8%
27	Arkansas	2,220	1.4%
1	California	13,220	8.2%
32	Colorado	1,650	1.0%
30	Connecticut	1,860	1.2%
41	Delaware	580	0.4%
2	Florida	12,360	7.7%
10	Georgia	4,500	2.8%
43	Hawaii	530	0.3%
42	Idaho	570	0.4%
7	Illinois	6,690	4.2%
15	Indiana	3,800	2.4%
31	Iowa	1,750	1.1%
33	Kansas	1,530	1.0%
17	Kentucky	3,450	2.2%
20	Louisiana	3,020	1.9%
36	Maine	970	0.6%
21	Maryland	2,900	1.8%
16	Massachusetts	3,630	2.3%
8	Michigan	5,840	3.6%
25	Minnesota	2,460	1.5%
29	Mississippi	2,040	1.3%
14	Missouri	4,120	2.6%
44	Montana	520	0.3%
37	Nebraska	900	0.6%
35	Nevada	1,330	0.8%
38	New Hampshire	740	0.5%
11	New Jersey	4,380	2.7%
39	New Mexico	720	0.4%
4	New York	9,500	5.9%
9	North Carolina	5,150	3.2%
47	North Dakota	350	0.2%
6	Ohio	7,310	4.6%
26	Oklahoma	2,390	1.5%
28	Oregon	2,140	1.3%
5	Pennsylvania	7,780	4.9%
40	Rhode Island	640	0.4%
24	South Carolina	2,750	1.7%
46	South Dakota	420	0.3%
12	Tennessee	4,340	2.7%
3	Texas	9,920	6.2%
45	Utah	470	0.3%
47	Vermont	350	0.2%
13	Virginia	4,290	2.7%
19	Washington	3,170	2.0%
34	West Virginia	1,450	0.9%
22	Wisconsin	2,890	1.8%
49	Wyoming	260	0.2%

RANK ORDER

RANK	STATE	DEATHS	% of USA
1	California	13,220	8.2%
2	Florida	12,360	7.7%
3	Texas	9,920	6.2%
4	New York	9,500	5.9%
5	Pennsylvania	7,780	4.9%
6	Ohio	7,310	4.6%
7	Illinois	6,690	4.2%
8	Michigan	5,840	3.6%
9	North Carolina	5,150	3.2%
10	Georgia	4,500	2.8%
11	New Jersey	4,380	2.7%
12	Tennessee	4,340	2.7%
13	Virginia	4,290	2.7%
14	Missouri	4,120	2.6%
15	Indiana	3,800	2.4%
16	Massachusetts	3,630	2.3%
17	Kentucky	3,450	2.2%
18	Alabama	3,240	2.0%
19	Washington	3,170	2.0%
20	Louisiana	3,020	1.9%
21	Maryland	2,900	1.8%
22	Wisconsin	2,890	1.8%
23	Arizona	2,850	1.8%
24	South Carolina	2,750	1.7%
25	Minnesota	2,460	1.5%
26	Oklahoma	2,390	1.5%
27	Arkansas	2,220	1.4%
28	Oregon	2,140	1.3%
29	Mississippi	2,040	1.3%
30	Connecticut	1,860	1.2%
31	Iowa	1,750	1.1%
32	Colorado	1,650	1.0%
33	Kansas	1,530	1.0%
34	West Virginia	1,450	0.9%
35	Nevada	1,330	0.8%
36	Maine	970	0.6%
37	Nebraska	900	0.6%
38	New Hampshire	740	0.5%
39	New Mexico	720	0.4%
40	Rhode Island	640	0.4%
41	Delaware	580	0.4%
42	Idaho	570	0.4%
43	Hawaii	530	0.3%
44	Montana	520	0.3%
45	Utah	470	0.3%
46	South Dakota	420	0.3%
47	North Dakota	350	0.2%
47	Vermont	350	0.2%
49	Wyoming	260	0.2%
50	Alaska	230	0.1%
	District of Columbia	260	0.2%

Source: American Cancer Society
"Cancer Facts & Figures 2007" (Copyright 2007, American Cancer Society)

Estimated Death Rate by Lung Cancer in 2007

National Estimated Rate = 53.6 Deaths per 100,000 Population*

<table>
<tr><td colspan="3">ALPHA ORDER</td><td colspan="3">RANK ORDER</td></tr>
<tr><td>RANK</td><td>STATE</td><td>RATE</td><td>RANK</td><td>STATE</td><td>RATE</td></tr>
<tr><td>7</td><td>Alabama</td><td>70.4</td><td>1</td><td>Kentucky</td><td>82.0</td></tr>
<tr><td>49</td><td>Alaska</td><td>34.3</td><td>2</td><td>West Virginia</td><td>79.7</td></tr>
<tr><td>42</td><td>Arizona</td><td>46.2</td><td>3</td><td>Arkansas</td><td>79.0</td></tr>
<tr><td>3</td><td>Arkansas</td><td>79.0</td><td>4</td><td>Maine</td><td>73.4</td></tr>
<tr><td>47</td><td>California</td><td>36.3</td><td>5</td><td>Tennessee</td><td>71.9</td></tr>
<tr><td>48</td><td>Colorado</td><td>34.7</td><td>6</td><td>Missouri</td><td>70.5</td></tr>
<tr><td>31</td><td>Connecticut</td><td>53.1</td><td>7</td><td>Alabama</td><td>70.4</td></tr>
<tr><td>11</td><td>Delaware</td><td>68.0</td><td>7</td><td>Louisiana</td><td>70.4</td></tr>
<tr><td>10</td><td>Florida</td><td>68.3</td><td>9</td><td>Mississippi</td><td>70.1</td></tr>
<tr><td>40</td><td>Georgia</td><td>48.1</td><td>10</td><td>Florida</td><td>68.3</td></tr>
<tr><td>44</td><td>Hawaii</td><td>41.2</td><td>11</td><td>Delaware</td><td>68.0</td></tr>
<tr><td>45</td><td>Idaho</td><td>38.9</td><td>12</td><td>Oklahoma</td><td>66.8</td></tr>
<tr><td>32</td><td>Illinois</td><td>52.1</td><td>13</td><td>Ohio</td><td>63.7</td></tr>
<tr><td>16</td><td>Indiana</td><td>60.2</td><td>14</td><td>South Carolina</td><td>63.6</td></tr>
<tr><td>18</td><td>Iowa</td><td>58.7</td><td>15</td><td>Pennsylvania</td><td>62.5</td></tr>
<tr><td>26</td><td>Kansas</td><td>55.4</td><td>16</td><td>Indiana</td><td>60.2</td></tr>
<tr><td>1</td><td>Kentucky</td><td>82.0</td><td>17</td><td>Rhode Island</td><td>59.9</td></tr>
<tr><td>7</td><td>Louisiana</td><td>70.4</td><td>18</td><td>Iowa</td><td>58.7</td></tr>
<tr><td>4</td><td>Maine</td><td>73.4</td><td>19</td><td>North Carolina</td><td>58.1</td></tr>
<tr><td>34</td><td>Maryland</td><td>51.6</td><td>20</td><td>Michigan</td><td>57.8</td></tr>
<tr><td>22</td><td>Massachusetts</td><td>56.4</td><td>20</td><td>Oregon</td><td>57.8</td></tr>
<tr><td>20</td><td>Michigan</td><td>57.8</td><td>22</td><td>Massachusetts</td><td>56.4</td></tr>
<tr><td>41</td><td>Minnesota</td><td>47.6</td><td>23</td><td>New Hampshire</td><td>56.3</td></tr>
<tr><td>9</td><td>Mississippi</td><td>70.1</td><td>24</td><td>Vermont</td><td>56.1</td></tr>
<tr><td>6</td><td>Missouri</td><td>70.5</td><td>24</td><td>Virginia</td><td>56.1</td></tr>
<tr><td>27</td><td>Montana</td><td>55.0</td><td>26</td><td>Kansas</td><td>55.4</td></tr>
<tr><td>35</td><td>Nebraska</td><td>50.9</td><td>27</td><td>Montana</td><td>55.0</td></tr>
<tr><td>30</td><td>Nevada</td><td>53.3</td><td>27</td><td>North Dakota</td><td>55.0</td></tr>
<tr><td>23</td><td>New Hampshire</td><td>56.3</td><td>29</td><td>South Dakota</td><td>53.7</td></tr>
<tr><td>37</td><td>New Jersey</td><td>50.2</td><td>30</td><td>Nevada</td><td>53.3</td></tr>
<tr><td>46</td><td>New Mexico</td><td>36.8</td><td>31</td><td>Connecticut</td><td>53.1</td></tr>
<tr><td>39</td><td>New York</td><td>49.2</td><td>32</td><td>Illinois</td><td>52.1</td></tr>
<tr><td>19</td><td>North Carolina</td><td>58.1</td><td>33</td><td>Wisconsin</td><td>52.0</td></tr>
<tr><td>27</td><td>North Dakota</td><td>55.0</td><td>34</td><td>Maryland</td><td>51.6</td></tr>
<tr><td>13</td><td>Ohio</td><td>63.7</td><td>35</td><td>Nebraska</td><td>50.9</td></tr>
<tr><td>12</td><td>Oklahoma</td><td>66.8</td><td>36</td><td>Wyoming</td><td>50.5</td></tr>
<tr><td>20</td><td>Oregon</td><td>57.8</td><td>37</td><td>New Jersey</td><td>50.2</td></tr>
<tr><td>15</td><td>Pennsylvania</td><td>62.5</td><td>38</td><td>Washington</td><td>49.6</td></tr>
<tr><td>17</td><td>Rhode Island</td><td>59.9</td><td>39</td><td>New York</td><td>49.2</td></tr>
<tr><td>14</td><td>South Carolina</td><td>63.6</td><td>40</td><td>Georgia</td><td>48.1</td></tr>
<tr><td>29</td><td>South Dakota</td><td>53.7</td><td>41</td><td>Minnesota</td><td>47.6</td></tr>
<tr><td>5</td><td>Tennessee</td><td>71.9</td><td>42</td><td>Arizona</td><td>46.2</td></tr>
<tr><td>43</td><td>Texas</td><td>42.2</td><td>43</td><td>Texas</td><td>42.2</td></tr>
<tr><td>50</td><td>Utah</td><td>18.4</td><td>44</td><td>Hawaii</td><td>41.2</td></tr>
<tr><td>24</td><td>Vermont</td><td>56.1</td><td>45</td><td>Idaho</td><td>38.9</td></tr>
<tr><td>24</td><td>Virginia</td><td>56.1</td><td>46</td><td>New Mexico</td><td>36.8</td></tr>
<tr><td>38</td><td>Washington</td><td>49.6</td><td>47</td><td>California</td><td>36.3</td></tr>
<tr><td>2</td><td>West Virginia</td><td>79.7</td><td>48</td><td>Colorado</td><td>34.7</td></tr>
<tr><td>33</td><td>Wisconsin</td><td>52.0</td><td>49</td><td>Alaska</td><td>34.3</td></tr>
<tr><td>36</td><td>Wyoming</td><td>50.5</td><td>50</td><td>Utah</td><td>18.4</td></tr>
<tr><td></td><td></td><td></td><td></td><td>District of Columbia</td><td>44.7</td></tr>
</table>

Source: Morgan Quitno Press using data from American Cancer Society
"Cancer Facts & Figures 2007" (Copyright 2007, American Cancer Society)
*Rates calculated using 2006 Census resident population estimates. Not age-adjusted.

Estimated Deaths by Non-Hodgkin's Lymphoma in 2007

National Estimated Total = 18,660 Deaths

ALPHA ORDER

RANK	STATE	DEATHS	% of USA
20	Alabama	330	1.8%
NA	Alaska*	NA	NA
21	Arizona	320	1.7%
32	Arkansas	200	1.1%
1	California	1,830	9.8%
28	Colorado	240	1.3%
29	Connecticut	230	1.2%
45	Delaware	60	0.3%
2	Florida	1,300	7.0%
12	Georgia	470	2.5%
41	Hawaii	90	0.5%
40	Idaho	100	0.5%
6	Illinois	750	4.0%
14	Indiana	430	2.3%
25	Iowa	300	1.6%
30	Kansas	220	1.2%
26	Kentucky	290	1.6%
24	Louisiana	310	1.7%
38	Maine	110	0.6%
21	Maryland	320	1.7%
15	Massachusetts	420	2.3%
7	Michigan	660	3.5%
19	Minnesota	350	1.9%
33	Mississippi	170	0.9%
11	Missouri	500	2.7%
43	Montana	80	0.4%
38	Nebraska	110	0.6%
36	Nevada	130	0.7%
41	New Hampshire	90	0.5%
9	New Jersey	600	3.2%
37	New Mexico	120	0.6%
5	New York	1,030	5.5%
10	North Carolina	570	3.1%
NA	North Dakota*	NA	NA
8	Ohio	610	3.3%
31	Oklahoma	210	1.1%
17	Oregon	360	1.9%
4	Pennsylvania	1,140	6.1%
45	Rhode Island	60	0.3%
27	South Carolina	260	1.4%
43	South Dakota	80	0.4%
16	Tennessee	410	2.2%
3	Texas	1,160	6.2%
35	Utah	140	0.8%
47	Vermont	50	0.3%
17	Virginia	360	1.9%
13	Washington	440	2.4%
33	West Virginia	170	0.9%
21	Wisconsin	320	1.7%
NA	Wyoming*	NA	NA

RANK ORDER

RANK	STATE	DEATHS	% of USA
1	California	1,830	9.8%
2	Florida	1,300	7.0%
3	Texas	1,160	6.2%
4	Pennsylvania	1,140	6.1%
5	New York	1,030	5.5%
6	Illinois	750	4.0%
7	Michigan	660	3.5%
8	Ohio	610	3.3%
9	New Jersey	600	3.2%
10	North Carolina	570	3.1%
11	Missouri	500	2.7%
12	Georgia	470	2.5%
13	Washington	440	2.4%
14	Indiana	430	2.3%
15	Massachusetts	420	2.3%
16	Tennessee	410	2.2%
17	Oregon	360	1.9%
17	Virginia	360	1.9%
19	Minnesota	350	1.9%
20	Alabama	330	1.8%
21	Arizona	320	1.7%
21	Maryland	320	1.7%
21	Wisconsin	320	1.7%
24	Louisiana	310	1.7%
25	Iowa	300	1.6%
26	Kentucky	290	1.6%
27	South Carolina	260	1.4%
28	Colorado	240	1.3%
29	Connecticut	230	1.2%
30	Kansas	220	1.2%
31	Oklahoma	210	1.1%
32	Arkansas	200	1.1%
33	Mississippi	170	0.9%
33	West Virginia	170	0.9%
35	Utah	140	0.8%
36	Nevada	130	0.7%
37	New Mexico	120	0.6%
38	Maine	110	0.6%
38	Nebraska	110	0.6%
40	Idaho	100	0.5%
41	Hawaii	90	0.5%
41	New Hampshire	90	0.5%
43	Montana	80	0.4%
43	South Dakota	80	0.4%
45	Delaware	60	0.3%
45	Rhode Island	60	0.3%
47	Vermont	50	0.3%
NA	Alaska*	NA	NA
NA	North Dakota*	NA	NA
NA	Wyoming*	NA	NA
	District of Columbia*	NA	NA

Source: American Cancer Society
    "Cancer Facts & Figures 2007" (Copyright 2007, American Cancer Society)
*Fewer than 50 deaths.

Estimated Death Rate by Non-Hodgkin's Lymphoma in 2007

National Estimated Rate = 6.2 Deaths per 100,000 Population*

ALPHA ORDER

RANK	STATE	RATE
11	Alabama	7.2
NA	Alaska**	NA
41	Arizona	5.2
14	Arkansas	7.1
43	California	5.0
43	Colorado	5.0
25	Connecticut	6.6
15	Delaware	7.0
11	Florida	7.2
43	Georgia	5.0
15	Hawaii	7.0
20	Idaho	6.8
33	Illinois	5.8
20	Indiana	6.8
2	Iowa	10.1
9	Kansas	8.0
17	Kentucky	6.9
11	Louisiana	7.2
8	Maine	8.3
36	Maryland	5.7
26	Massachusetts	6.5
26	Michigan	6.5
20	Minnesota	6.8
33	Mississippi	5.8
6	Missouri	8.6
7	Montana	8.5
29	Nebraska	6.2
41	Nevada	5.2
20	New Hampshire	6.8
17	New Jersey	6.9
30	New Mexico	6.1
39	New York	5.3
28	North Carolina	6.4
NA	North Dakota**	NA
39	Ohio	5.3
32	Oklahoma	5.9
3	Oregon	9.7
5	Pennsylvania	9.2
37	Rhode Island	5.6
31	South Carolina	6.0
1	South Dakota	10.2
20	Tennessee	6.8
46	Texas	4.9
38	Utah	5.5
9	Vermont	8.0
47	Virginia	4.7
17	Washington	6.9
4	West Virginia	9.3
33	Wisconsin	5.8
NA	Wyoming**	NA

RANK ORDER

RANK	STATE	RATE
1	South Dakota	10.2
2	Iowa	10.1
3	Oregon	9.7
4	West Virginia	9.3
5	Pennsylvania	9.2
6	Missouri	8.6
7	Montana	8.5
8	Maine	8.3
9	Kansas	8.0
9	Vermont	8.0
11	Alabama	7.2
11	Florida	7.2
11	Louisiana	7.2
14	Arkansas	7.1
15	Delaware	7.0
15	Hawaii	7.0
17	Kentucky	6.9
17	New Jersey	6.9
17	Washington	6.9
20	Idaho	6.8
20	Indiana	6.8
20	Minnesota	6.8
20	New Hampshire	6.8
20	Tennessee	6.8
25	Connecticut	6.6
26	Massachusetts	6.5
26	Michigan	6.5
28	North Carolina	6.4
29	Nebraska	6.2
30	New Mexico	6.1
31	South Carolina	6.0
32	Oklahoma	5.9
33	Illinois	5.8
33	Mississippi	5.8
33	Wisconsin	5.8
36	Maryland	5.7
37	Rhode Island	5.6
38	Utah	5.5
39	New York	5.3
39	Ohio	5.3
41	Arizona	5.2
41	Nevada	5.2
43	California	5.0
43	Colorado	5.0
43	Georgia	5.0
46	Texas	4.9
47	Virginia	4.7
NA	Alaska**	NA
NA	North Dakota**	NA
NA	Wyoming**	NA
	District of Columbia**	NA

Source: Morgan Quitno Press using data from American Cancer Society
   "Cancer Facts & Figures 2007" (Copyright 2007, American Cancer Society)
*Rates calculated using 2006 Census resident population estimates. Not age-adjusted.
**Fewer than 50 deaths.

Estimated Deaths by Pancreatic Cancer in 2007

National Estimated Total = 33,370 Deaths

RANK	STATE	DEATHS	% of USA
22	Alabama	530	1.6%
50	Alaska	50	0.1%
20	Arizona	590	1.8%
32	Arkansas	310	0.9%
1	California	3,480	10.4%
28	Colorado	410	1.2%
25	Connecticut	480	1.4%
45	Delaware	100	0.3%
2	Florida	2,350	7.0%
12	Georgia	820	2.5%
39	Hawaii	170	0.5%
42	Idaho	140	0.4%
6	Illinois	1,480	4.4%
14	Indiana	740	2.2%
29	Iowa	390	1.2%
32	Kansas	310	0.9%
26	Kentucky	460	1.4%
22	Louisiana	530	1.6%
36	Maine	190	0.6%
19	Maryland	640	1.9%
11	Massachusetts	860	2.6%
8	Michigan	1,180	3.5%
21	Minnesota	550	1.6%
31	Mississippi	340	1.0%
17	Missouri	690	2.1%
44	Montana	110	0.3%
38	Nebraska	180	0.5%
34	Nevada	260	0.8%
41	New Hampshire	150	0.4%
9	New Jersey	1,070	3.2%
36	New Mexico	190	0.6%
3	New York	2,330	7.0%
10	North Carolina	980	2.9%
47	North Dakota	80	0.2%
7	Ohio	1,370	4.1%
30	Oklahoma	370	1.1%
27	Oregon	440	1.3%
5	Pennsylvania	1,780	5.3%
42	Rhode Island	140	0.4%
24	South Carolina	510	1.5%
45	South Dakota	100	0.3%
16	Tennessee	700	2.1%
4	Texas	2,010	6.0%
39	Utah	170	0.5%
48	Vermont	70	0.2%
13	Virginia	800	2.4%
14	Washington	740	2.2%
35	West Virginia	220	0.7%
18	Wisconsin	680	2.0%
49	Wyoming	60	0.2%

RANK	STATE	DEATHS	% of USA
1	California	3,480	10.4%
2	Florida	2,350	7.0%
3	New York	2,330	7.0%
4	Texas	2,010	6.0%
5	Pennsylvania	1,780	5.3%
6	Illinois	1,480	4.4%
7	Ohio	1,370	4.1%
8	Michigan	1,180	3.5%
9	New Jersey	1,070	3.2%
10	North Carolina	980	2.9%
11	Massachusetts	860	2.6%
12	Georgia	820	2.5%
13	Virginia	800	2.4%
14	Indiana	740	2.2%
14	Washington	740	2.2%
16	Tennessee	700	2.1%
17	Missouri	690	2.1%
18	Wisconsin	680	2.0%
19	Maryland	640	1.9%
20	Arizona	590	1.8%
21	Minnesota	550	1.6%
22	Alabama	530	1.6%
22	Louisiana	530	1.6%
24	South Carolina	510	1.5%
25	Connecticut	480	1.4%
26	Kentucky	460	1.4%
27	Oregon	440	1.3%
28	Colorado	410	1.2%
29	Iowa	390	1.2%
30	Oklahoma	370	1.1%
31	Mississippi	340	1.0%
32	Arkansas	310	0.9%
32	Kansas	310	0.9%
34	Nevada	260	0.8%
35	West Virginia	220	0.7%
36	Maine	190	0.6%
36	New Mexico	190	0.6%
38	Nebraska	180	0.5%
39	Hawaii	170	0.5%
39	Utah	170	0.5%
41	New Hampshire	150	0.4%
42	Idaho	140	0.4%
42	Rhode Island	140	0.4%
44	Montana	110	0.3%
45	Delaware	100	0.3%
45	South Dakota	100	0.3%
47	North Dakota	80	0.2%
48	Vermont	70	0.2%
49	Wyoming	60	0.2%
50	Alaska	50	0.1%
	District of Columbia	60	0.2%

Source: American Cancer Society
"Cancer Facts & Figures 2007" (Copyright 2007, American Cancer Society)

Estimated Death Rate by Pancreatic Cancer in 2007

National Estimated Rate = 11.1 Deaths per 100,000 Population*

ALPHA ORDER

RANK	STATE	RATE
28	Alabama	11.5
49	Alaska	7.5
43	Arizona	9.6
35	Arkansas	11.0
44	California	9.5
47	Colorado	8.6
3	Connecticut	13.7
20	Delaware	11.7
8	Florida	13.0
46	Georgia	8.8
5	Hawaii	13.2
44	Idaho	9.5
28	Illinois	11.5
20	Indiana	11.7
6	Iowa	13.1
32	Kansas	11.2
36	Kentucky	10.9
11	Louisiana	12.4
1	Maine	14.4
30	Maryland	11.4
4	Massachusetts	13.4
20	Michigan	11.7
37	Minnesota	10.6
20	Mississippi	11.7
18	Missouri	11.8
25	Montana	11.6
41	Nebraska	10.2
39	Nevada	10.4
30	New Hampshire	11.4
12	New Jersey	12.3
42	New Mexico	9.7
14	New York	12.1
34	North Carolina	11.1
10	North Dakota	12.6
16	Ohio	11.9
40	Oklahoma	10.3
16	Oregon	11.9
2	Pennsylvania	14.3
6	Rhode Island	13.1
18	South Carolina	11.8
9	South Dakota	12.8
25	Tennessee	11.6
47	Texas	8.6
50	Utah	6.7
32	Vermont	11.2
38	Virginia	10.5
25	Washington	11.6
14	West Virginia	12.1
13	Wisconsin	12.2
20	Wyoming	11.7

RANK ORDER

RANK	STATE	RATE
1	Maine	14.4
2	Pennsylvania	14.3
3	Connecticut	13.7
4	Massachusetts	13.4
5	Hawaii	13.2
6	Iowa	13.1
6	Rhode Island	13.1
8	Florida	13.0
9	South Dakota	12.8
10	North Dakota	12.6
11	Louisiana	12.4
12	New Jersey	12.3
13	Wisconsin	12.2
14	New York	12.1
14	West Virginia	12.1
16	Ohio	11.9
16	Oregon	11.9
18	Missouri	11.8
18	South Carolina	11.8
20	Delaware	11.7
20	Indiana	11.7
20	Michigan	11.7
20	Mississippi	11.7
20	Wyoming	11.7
25	Montana	11.6
25	Tennessee	11.6
25	Washington	11.6
28	Alabama	11.5
28	Illinois	11.5
30	Maryland	11.4
30	New Hampshire	11.4
32	Kansas	11.2
32	Vermont	11.2
34	North Carolina	11.1
35	Arkansas	11.0
36	Kentucky	10.9
37	Minnesota	10.6
38	Virginia	10.5
39	Nevada	10.4
40	Oklahoma	10.3
41	Nebraska	10.2
42	New Mexico	9.7
43	Arizona	9.6
44	California	9.5
44	Idaho	9.5
46	Georgia	8.8
47	Colorado	8.6
47	Texas	8.6
49	Alaska	7.5
50	Utah	6.7

District of Columbia	10.3

Source: Morgan Quitno Press using data from American Cancer Society
    "Cancer Facts & Figures 2007" (Copyright 2007, American Cancer Society)
*Rates calculated using 2006 Census resident population estimates. Not age-adjusted.

Estimated Deaths by Prostate Cancer in 2007

National Estimated Total = 27,050 Deaths

RANK	STATE	DEATHS	% of USA
22	Alabama	480	1.8%
NA	Alaska*	NA	NA
19	Arizona	520	1.9%
30	Arkansas	300	1.1%
1	California	3,040	11.2%
28	Colorado	330	1.2%
25	Connecticut	390	1.4%
47	Delaware	90	0.3%
2	Florida	2,180	8.1%
11	Georgia	630	2.3%
42	Hawaii	130	0.5%
39	Idaho	150	0.6%
7	Illinois	990	3.7%
13	Indiana	600	2.2%
26	Iowa	350	1.3%
34	Kansas	220	0.8%
29	Kentucky	310	1.1%
24	Louisiana	400	1.5%
36	Maine	180	0.7%
17	Maryland	540	2.0%
15	Massachusetts	560	2.1%
8	Michigan	850	3.1%
21	Minnesota	490	1.8%
31	Mississippi	290	1.1%
20	Missouri	510	1.9%
43	Montana	110	0.4%
37	Nebraska	170	0.6%
33	Nevada	230	0.9%
40	New Hampshire	140	0.5%
10	New Jersey	750	2.8%
35	New Mexico	200	0.7%
3	New York	1,630	6.0%
9	North Carolina	800	3.0%
46	North Dakota	100	0.4%
5	Ohio	1,350	5.0%
32	Oklahoma	280	1.0%
27	Oregon	340	1.3%
6	Pennsylvania	1,310	4.8%
43	Rhode Island	110	0.4%
23	South Carolina	420	1.6%
43	South Dakota	110	0.4%
16	Tennessee	550	2.0%
4	Texas	1,620	6.0%
40	Utah	140	0.5%
48	Vermont	80	0.3%
13	Virginia	600	2.2%
11	Washington	630	2.3%
38	West Virginia	160	0.6%
17	Wisconsin	540	2.0%
49	Wyoming	60	0.2%

RANK	STATE	DEATHS	% of USA
1	California	3,040	11.2%
2	Florida	2,180	8.1%
3	New York	1,630	6.0%
4	Texas	1,620	6.0%
5	Ohio	1,350	5.0%
6	Pennsylvania	1,310	4.8%
7	Illinois	990	3.7%
8	Michigan	850	3.1%
9	North Carolina	800	3.0%
10	New Jersey	750	2.8%
11	Georgia	630	2.3%
11	Washington	630	2.3%
13	Indiana	600	2.2%
13	Virginia	600	2.2%
15	Massachusetts	560	2.1%
16	Tennessee	550	2.0%
17	Maryland	540	2.0%
17	Wisconsin	540	2.0%
19	Arizona	520	1.9%
20	Missouri	510	1.9%
21	Minnesota	490	1.8%
22	Alabama	480	1.8%
23	South Carolina	420	1.6%
24	Louisiana	400	1.5%
25	Connecticut	390	1.4%
26	Iowa	350	1.3%
27	Oregon	340	1.3%
28	Colorado	330	1.2%
29	Kentucky	310	1.1%
30	Arkansas	300	1.1%
31	Mississippi	290	1.1%
32	Oklahoma	280	1.0%
33	Nevada	230	0.9%
34	Kansas	220	0.8%
35	New Mexico	200	0.7%
36	Maine	180	0.7%
37	Nebraska	170	0.6%
38	West Virginia	160	0.6%
39	Idaho	150	0.6%
40	New Hampshire	140	0.5%
40	Utah	140	0.5%
42	Hawaii	130	0.5%
43	Montana	110	0.4%
43	Rhode Island	110	0.4%
43	South Dakota	110	0.4%
46	North Dakota	100	0.4%
47	Delaware	90	0.3%
48	Vermont	80	0.3%
49	Wyoming	60	0.2%
NA	Alaska*	NA	NA
	District of Columbia	60	0.2%

Source: American Cancer Society
    "Cancer Facts & Figures 2007" (Copyright 2007, American Cancer Society)
*Fewer than 50 deaths.

Age-Adjusted Death Rate by Prostate Cancer in 2003

National Rate = 29.1 Deaths per 100,000 Male Population*

ALPHA ORDER

RANK	STATE	RATE
2	Alabama	36.9
41	Alaska	27.4
48	Arizona	25.5
9	Arkansas	31.9
46	California	26.4
33	Colorado	28.4
44	Connecticut	27.1
35	Delaware	28.3
49	Florida	24.5
5	Georgia	34.8
50	Hawaii	20.3
13	Idaho	31.1
15	Illinois	30.6
16	Indiana	30.5
19	Iowa	29.7
43	Kansas	27.2
18	Kentucky	29.9
4	Louisiana	34.9
31	Maine	28.8
12	Maryland	31.3
22	Massachusetts	29.4
22	Michigan	29.4
14	Minnesota	30.9
1	Mississippi	41.9
44	Missouri	27.1
21	Montana	29.6
47	Nebraska	26.2
32	Nevada	28.5
27	New Hampshire	29.3
33	New Jersey	28.4
27	New Mexico	29.3
37	New York	28.2
6	North Carolina	33.7
22	North Dakota	29.4
27	Ohio	29.3
40	Oklahoma	27.7
19	Oregon	29.7
30	Pennsylvania	29.2
41	Rhode Island	27.4
3	South Carolina	36.3
11	South Dakota	31.4
8	Tennessee	32.5
37	Texas	28.2
22	Utah	29.4
22	Vermont	29.4
7	Virginia	33.4
39	Washington	27.9
35	West Virginia	28.3
17	Wisconsin	30.4
10	Wyoming	31.8

RANK ORDER

RANK	STATE	RATE
1	Mississippi	41.9
2	Alabama	36.9
3	South Carolina	36.3
4	Louisiana	34.9
5	Georgia	34.8
6	North Carolina	33.7
7	Virginia	33.4
8	Tennessee	32.5
9	Arkansas	31.9
10	Wyoming	31.8
11	South Dakota	31.4
12	Maryland	31.3
13	Idaho	31.1
14	Minnesota	30.9
15	Illinois	30.6
16	Indiana	30.5
17	Wisconsin	30.4
18	Kentucky	29.9
19	Iowa	29.7
19	Oregon	29.7
21	Montana	29.6
22	Massachusetts	29.4
22	Michigan	29.4
22	North Dakota	29.4
22	Utah	29.4
22	Vermont	29.4
27	New Hampshire	29.3
27	New Mexico	29.3
27	Ohio	29.3
30	Pennsylvania	29.2
31	Maine	28.8
32	Nevada	28.5
33	Colorado	28.4
33	New Jersey	28.4
35	Delaware	28.3
35	West Virginia	28.3
37	New York	28.2
37	Texas	28.2
39	Washington	27.9
40	Oklahoma	27.7
41	Alaska	27.4
41	Rhode Island	27.4
43	Kansas	27.2
44	Connecticut	27.1
44	Missouri	27.1
46	California	26.4
47	Nebraska	26.2
48	Arizona	25.5
49	Florida	24.5
50	Hawaii	20.3

District of Columbia   49.2

Source: American Cancer Society
    "Cancer Facts & Figures 2007" (Copyright 2007, American Cancer Society)
*For 1999 to 2003. Age-adjusted to the 2000 U.S. standard population.

Estimated Deaths by Ovarian Cancer in 2007

National Estimated Total = 15,280 Deaths

RANK	STATE	DEATHS	% of USA
19	Alabama	290	1.9%
NA	Alaska*	NA	NA
18	Arizona	300	2.0%
33	Arkansas	140	0.9%
1	California	1,680	11.0%
24	Colorado	220	1.4%
28	Connecticut	190	1.2%
43	Delaware	50	0.3%
2	Florida	1,040	6.8%
11	Georgia	420	2.7%
43	Hawaii	50	0.3%
43	Idaho	50	0.3%
7	Illinois	620	4.1%
15	Indiana	350	2.3%
28	Iowa	190	1.2%
31	Kansas	150	1.0%
24	Kentucky	220	1.4%
24	Louisiana	220	1.4%
39	Maine	80	0.5%
21	Maryland	270	1.8%
14	Massachusetts	360	2.4%
8	Michigan	540	3.5%
22	Minnesota	250	1.6%
31	Mississippi	150	1.0%
16	Missouri	320	2.1%
40	Montana	60	0.4%
36	Nebraska	90	0.6%
35	Nevada	130	0.9%
40	New Hampshire	60	0.4%
9	New Jersey	490	3.2%
36	New Mexico	90	0.6%
3	New York	1,020	6.7%
10	North Carolina	450	2.9%
NA	North Dakota*	NA	NA
6	Ohio	650	4.3%
30	Oklahoma	170	1.1%
23	Oregon	230	1.5%
5	Pennsylvania	790	5.2%
40	Rhode Island	60	0.4%
24	South Carolina	220	1.4%
43	South Dakota	50	0.3%
16	Tennessee	320	2.1%
4	Texas	860	5.6%
36	Utah	90	0.6%
NA	Vermont*	NA	NA
12	Virginia	390	2.6%
13	Washington	370	2.4%
33	West Virginia	140	0.9%
19	Wisconsin	290	1.9%
NA	Wyoming*	NA	NA

RANK	STATE	DEATHS	% of USA
1	California	1,680	11.0%
2	Florida	1,040	6.8%
3	New York	1,020	6.7%
4	Texas	860	5.6%
5	Pennsylvania	790	5.2%
6	Ohio	650	4.3%
7	Illinois	620	4.1%
8	Michigan	540	3.5%
9	New Jersey	490	3.2%
10	North Carolina	450	2.9%
11	Georgia	420	2.7%
12	Virginia	390	2.6%
13	Washington	370	2.4%
14	Massachusetts	360	2.4%
15	Indiana	350	2.3%
16	Missouri	320	2.1%
16	Tennessee	320	2.1%
18	Arizona	300	2.0%
19	Alabama	290	1.9%
19	Wisconsin	290	1.9%
21	Maryland	270	1.8%
22	Minnesota	250	1.6%
23	Oregon	230	1.5%
24	Colorado	220	1.4%
24	Kentucky	220	1.4%
24	Louisiana	220	1.4%
24	South Carolina	220	1.4%
28	Connecticut	190	1.2%
28	Iowa	190	1.2%
30	Oklahoma	170	1.1%
31	Kansas	150	1.0%
31	Mississippi	150	1.0%
33	Arkansas	140	0.9%
33	West Virginia	140	0.9%
35	Nevada	130	0.9%
36	Nebraska	90	0.6%
36	New Mexico	90	0.6%
36	Utah	90	0.6%
39	Maine	80	0.5%
40	Montana	60	0.4%
40	New Hampshire	60	0.4%
40	Rhode Island	60	0.4%
43	Delaware	50	0.3%
43	Hawaii	50	0.3%
43	Idaho	50	0.3%
43	South Dakota	50	0.3%
NA	Alaska*	NA	NA
NA	North Dakota*	NA	NA
NA	Vermont*	NA	NA
NA	Wyoming*	NA	NA
	District of Columbia*	NA	NA

Source: American Cancer Society
"Cancer Facts & Figures 2007" (Copyright 2007, American Cancer Society)
*Fewer than 50 deaths.

Estimated Death Rate by Ovarian Cancer in 2007

National Estimated Rate = 10.2 Deaths per 100,000 Female Population*

ALPHA ORDER

RANK	STATE	RATE
6	Alabama	12.4
NA	Alaska**	NA
27	Arizona	10.1
32	Arkansas	9.9
39	California	9.3
34	Colorado	9.5
20	Connecticut	10.5
10	Delaware	11.6
11	Florida	11.5
40	Georgia	9.2
43	Hawaii	7.8
46	Idaho	7.0
34	Illinois	9.5
13	Indiana	11.0
4	Iowa	12.6
16	Kansas	10.9
23	Kentucky	10.4
34	Louisiana	9.5
8	Maine	11.8
38	Maryland	9.4
16	Massachusetts	10.9
20	Michigan	10.5
33	Minnesota	9.7
31	Mississippi	10.0
18	Missouri	10.8
2	Montana	12.8
27	Nebraska	10.1
13	Nevada	11.0
42	New Hampshire	9.0
13	New Jersey	11.0
40	New Mexico	9.2
25	New York	10.3
26	North Carolina	10.2
NA	North Dakota**	NA
12	Ohio	11.1
34	Oklahoma	9.5
4	Oregon	12.6
7	Pennsylvania	12.3
18	Rhode Island	10.8
27	South Carolina	10.1
2	South Dakota	12.8
20	Tennessee	10.5
44	Texas	7.5
45	Utah	7.3
NA	Vermont**	NA
27	Virginia	10.1
8	Washington	11.8
1	West Virginia	15.1
23	Wisconsin	10.4
NA	Wyoming**	NA

RANK ORDER

RANK	STATE	RATE
1	West Virginia	15.1
2	Montana	12.8
2	South Dakota	12.8
4	Iowa	12.6
4	Oregon	12.6
6	Alabama	12.4
7	Pennsylvania	12.3
8	Maine	11.8
8	Washington	11.8
10	Delaware	11.6
11	Florida	11.5
12	Ohio	11.1
13	Indiana	11.0
13	Nevada	11.0
13	New Jersey	11.0
16	Kansas	10.9
16	Massachusetts	10.9
18	Missouri	10.8
18	Rhode Island	10.8
20	Connecticut	10.5
20	Michigan	10.5
20	Tennessee	10.5
23	Kentucky	10.4
23	Wisconsin	10.4
25	New York	10.3
26	North Carolina	10.2
27	Arizona	10.1
27	Nebraska	10.1
27	South Carolina	10.1
27	Virginia	10.1
31	Mississippi	10.0
32	Arkansas	9.9
33	Minnesota	9.7
34	Colorado	9.5
34	Illinois	9.5
34	Louisiana	9.5
34	Oklahoma	9.5
38	Maryland	9.4
39	California	9.3
40	Georgia	9.2
40	New Mexico	9.2
42	New Hampshire	9.0
43	Hawaii	7.8
44	Texas	7.5
45	Utah	7.3
46	Idaho	7.0
NA	Alaska**	NA
NA	North Dakota**	NA
NA	Vermont**	NA
NA	Wyoming**	NA
	District of Columbia**	NA

*Source: Morgan Quitno Press using data from American Cancer Society
"Cancer Facts & Figures 2007" (Copyright 2007, American Cancer Society)*
Rates calculated using 2005 Census female population estimates. Not age-adjusted.
**Fewer than 50 deaths.*

135

Deaths by Alzheimer's Disease in 2003

National Total = 63,457 Deaths*

ALPHA ORDER

RANK	STATE	DEATHS	% of USA
20	Alabama	1,268	2.0%
50	Alaska	56	0.1%
11	Arizona	1,703	2.7%
33	Arkansas	552	0.9%
1	California	6,585	10.4%
26	Colorado	899	1.4%
31	Connecticut	612	1.0%
48	Delaware	147	0.2%
2	Florida	4,316	6.8%
13	Georgia	1,630	2.6%
47	Hawaii	161	0.3%
38	Idaho	355	0.6%
6	Illinois	2,626	4.1%
15	Indiana	1,515	2.4%
27	Iowa	887	1.4%
30	Kansas	781	1.2%
24	Kentucky	1,072	1.7%
22	Louisiana	1,184	1.9%
35	Maine	467	0.7%
28	Maryland	865	1.4%
14	Massachusetts	1,609	2.5%
9	Michigan	2,133	3.4%
21	Minnesota	1,243	2.0%
32	Mississippi	583	0.9%
19	Missouri	1,293	2.0%
44	Montana	235	0.4%
36	Nebraska	461	0.7%
41	Nevada	309	0.5%
43	New Hampshire	286	0.5%
12	New Jersey	1,636	2.6%
37	New Mexico	360	0.6%
10	New York	1,866	2.9%
8	North Carolina	2,145	3.4%
39	North Dakota	336	0.5%
5	Ohio	2,902	4.6%
29	Oklahoma	794	1.3%
23	Oregon	1,157	1.8%
4	Pennsylvania	2,952	4.7%
42	Rhode Island	303	0.5%
25	South Carolina	1,051	1.7%
45	South Dakota	174	0.3%
16	Tennessee	1,466	2.3%
3	Texas	4,015	6.3%
40	Utah	332	0.5%
46	Vermont	171	0.3%
16	Virginia	1,466	2.3%
7	Washington	2,380	3.8%
34	West Virginia	470	0.7%
18	Wisconsin	1,411	2.2%
49	Wyoming	142	0.2%

RANK ORDER

RANK	STATE	DEATHS	% of USA
1	California	6,585	10.4%
2	Florida	4,316	6.8%
3	Texas	4,015	6.3%
4	Pennsylvania	2,952	4.7%
5	Ohio	2,902	4.6%
6	Illinois	2,626	4.1%
7	Washington	2,380	3.8%
8	North Carolina	2,145	3.4%
9	Michigan	2,133	3.4%
10	New York	1,866	2.9%
11	Arizona	1,703	2.7%
12	New Jersey	1,636	2.6%
13	Georgia	1,630	2.6%
14	Massachusetts	1,609	2.5%
15	Indiana	1,515	2.4%
16	Tennessee	1,466	2.3%
16	Virginia	1,466	2.3%
18	Wisconsin	1,411	2.2%
19	Missouri	1,293	2.0%
20	Alabama	1,268	2.0%
21	Minnesota	1,243	2.0%
22	Louisiana	1,184	1.9%
23	Oregon	1,157	1.8%
24	Kentucky	1,072	1.7%
25	South Carolina	1,051	1.7%
26	Colorado	899	1.4%
27	Iowa	887	1.4%
28	Maryland	865	1.4%
29	Oklahoma	794	1.3%
30	Kansas	781	1.2%
31	Connecticut	612	1.0%
32	Mississippi	583	0.9%
33	Arkansas	552	0.9%
34	West Virginia	470	0.7%
35	Maine	467	0.7%
36	Nebraska	461	0.7%
37	New Mexico	360	0.6%
38	Idaho	355	0.6%
39	North Dakota	336	0.5%
40	Utah	332	0.5%
41	Nevada	309	0.5%
42	Rhode Island	303	0.5%
43	New Hampshire	286	0.5%
44	Montana	235	0.4%
45	South Dakota	174	0.3%
46	Vermont	171	0.3%
47	Hawaii	161	0.3%
48	Delaware	147	0.2%
49	Wyoming	142	0.2%
50	Alaska	56	0.1%
	District of Columbia	95	0.1%

Source: U.S. Department of Health and Human Services, National Center for Health Statistics "National Vital Statistics Reports" (Vol. 54, No. 13, April 19, 2006)

Final data by state of residence. A degenerative disease of the brain cells producing loss of memory and general intellectual impairment. It usually affects people over age 65. As the disease progresses, a variety of symptoms may become apparent, including confusion, irritability, and restlessness, as well as disorientation and impaired judgment and concentration.

Death Rate by Alzheimer's Disease in 2003

National Rate = 21.8 Deaths per 100,000 Population*

RANK	STATE	RATE
9	Alabama	28.2
50	Alaska	8.6
5	Arizona	30.5
34	Arkansas	20.3
41	California	18.6
36	Colorado	19.8
44	Connecticut	17.6
43	Delaware	18.0
20	Florida	25.4
40	Georgia	18.8
48	Hawaii	12.8
14	Idaho	26.0
33	Illinois	20.8
26	Indiana	24.5
6	Iowa	30.1
7	Kansas	28.7
14	Kentucky	26.0
13	Louisiana	26.3
3	Maine	35.8
45	Maryland	15.7
24	Massachusetts	25.0
32	Michigan	21.2
25	Minnesota	24.6
35	Mississippi	20.2
29	Missouri	22.7
18	Montana	25.6
12	Nebraska	26.5
47	Nevada	13.8
31	New Hampshire	22.2
39	New Jersey	18.9
38	New Mexico	19.2
49	New York	9.7
19	North Carolina	25.5
1	North Dakota	53.0
20	Ohio	25.4
30	Oklahoma	22.6
4	Oregon	32.5
27	Pennsylvania	23.9
9	Rhode Island	28.2
22	South Carolina	25.3
28	South Dakota	22.8
23	Tennessee	25.1
42	Texas	18.2
46	Utah	14.1
11	Vermont	27.6
36	Virginia	19.8
2	Washington	38.8
14	West Virginia	26.0
17	Wisconsin	25.8
8	Wyoming	28.3

RANK	STATE	RATE
1	North Dakota	53.0
2	Washington	38.8
3	Maine	35.8
4	Oregon	32.5
5	Arizona	30.5
6	Iowa	30.1
7	Kansas	28.7
8	Wyoming	28.3
9	Alabama	28.2
9	Rhode Island	28.2
11	Vermont	27.6
12	Nebraska	26.5
13	Louisiana	26.3
14	Idaho	26.0
14	Kentucky	26.0
14	West Virginia	26.0
17	Wisconsin	25.8
18	Montana	25.6
19	North Carolina	25.5
20	Florida	25.4
20	Ohio	25.4
22	South Carolina	25.3
23	Tennessee	25.1
24	Massachusetts	25.0
25	Minnesota	24.6
26	Indiana	24.5
27	Pennsylvania	23.9
28	South Dakota	22.8
29	Missouri	22.7
30	Oklahoma	22.6
31	New Hampshire	22.2
32	Michigan	21.2
33	Illinois	20.8
34	Arkansas	20.3
35	Mississippi	20.2
36	Colorado	19.8
36	Virginia	19.8
38	New Mexico	19.2
39	New Jersey	18.9
40	Georgia	18.8
41	California	18.6
42	Texas	18.2
43	Delaware	18.0
44	Connecticut	17.6
45	Maryland	15.7
46	Utah	14.1
47	Nevada	13.8
48	Hawaii	12.8
49	New York	9.7
50	Alaska	8.6
	District of Columbia	16.8

Source: U.S. Department of Health and Human Services, National Center for Health Statistics
"National Vital Statistics Reports" (Vol. 54, No. 13, April 19, 2006)
*Final data by state of residence. A degenerative disease of the brain cells producing loss of memory and general intellectual impairment. It usually affects people over age 65. As the disease progresses, a variety of symptoms may become apparent, including confusion, irritability, and restlessness, as well as disorientation and impaired judgment and concentration. Not age-adjusted.

Age-Adjusted Death Rate by Alzheimer's Disease in 2003

National Rate = 21.4 Deaths per 100,000 Population*

ALPHA ORDER

RANK ORDER

RANK	STATE	RATE	RANK	STATE	RATE
8	Alabama	27.6	1	Washington	39.9
22	Alaska	22.2	2	North Dakota	36.2
3	Arizona	31.6	3	Arizona	31.6
42	Arkansas	18.0	4	Wyoming	30.1
32	California	21.3	5	Maine	29.7
15	Colorado	25.9	6	Louisiana	29.1
48	Connecticut	13.9	7	Oregon	28.9
42	Delaware	18.0	8	Alabama	27.6
41	Florida	18.2	8	North Carolina	27.6
14	Georgia	26.0	10	South Carolina	27.3
49	Hawaii	11.4	11	Idaho	27.1
11	Idaho	27.1	12	Kentucky	27.0
39	Illinois	20.2	13	Tennessee	26.1
19	Indiana	23.9	14	Georgia	26.0
28	Iowa	21.6	15	Colorado	25.9
17	Kansas	24.3	16	Vermont	25.1
12	Kentucky	27.0	17	Kansas	24.3
6	Louisiana	29.1	18	Texas	24.2
5	Maine	29.7	19	Indiana	23.9
45	Maryland	17.3	20	Ohio	23.2
36	Massachusetts	20.7	21	Virginia	22.7
35	Michigan	20.8	22	Alaska	22.2
22	Minnesota	22.2	22	Minnesota	22.2
33	Mississippi	21.1	22	Montana	22.2
38	Missouri	20.3	22	New Hampshire	22.2
22	Montana	22.2	26	Wisconsin	22.0
27	Nebraska	21.7	27	Nebraska	21.7
40	Nevada	19.0	28	Iowa	21.6
22	New Hampshire	22.2	28	West Virginia	21.6
46	New Jersey	17.1	30	Oklahoma	21.5
34	New Mexico	20.9	31	Rhode Island	21.4
50	New York	8.8	32	California	21.3
8	North Carolina	27.6	33	Mississippi	21.1
2	North Dakota	36.2	34	New Mexico	20.9
20	Ohio	23.2	35	Michigan	20.8
30	Oklahoma	21.5	36	Massachusetts	20.7
7	Oregon	28.9	36	Utah	20.7
44	Pennsylvania	17.7	38	Missouri	20.3
31	Rhode Island	21.4	39	Illinois	20.2
10	South Carolina	27.3	40	Nevada	19.0
46	South Dakota	17.1	41	Florida	18.2
13	Tennessee	26.1	42	Arkansas	18.0
18	Texas	24.2	42	Delaware	18.0
36	Utah	20.7	44	Pennsylvania	17.7
16	Vermont	25.1	45	Maryland	17.3
21	Virginia	22.7	46	New Jersey	17.1
1	Washington	39.9	46	South Dakota	17.1
28	West Virginia	21.6	48	Connecticut	13.9
26	Wisconsin	22.0	49	Hawaii	11.4
4	Wyoming	30.1	50	New York	8.8
				District of Columbia	16.5

Source: U.S. Department of Health and Human Services, National Center for Health Statistics "National Vital Statistics Reports" (Vol. 54, No. 13, April 19, 2006)
Final data by state of residence. A degenerative disease of the brain cells producing loss of memory and general intellectual impairment. It usually affects people over age 65. As the disease progresses, a variety of symptoms may become apparent, including confusion, irritability, and restlessness, as well as disorientation and impaired judgment and concentration. Age-adjusted rates based on the year 2000 standard population.

138

Deaths by Cerebrovascular Diseases in 2003

National Total = 157,689 Deaths*

ALPHA ORDER

RANK	STATE	DEATHS	% of USA
19	Alabama	3,028	1.9%
50	Alaska	185	0.1%
27	Arizona	2,428	1.5%
28	Arkansas	2,107	1.3%
1	California	17,692	11.2%
31	Colorado	1,813	1.1%
30	Connecticut	1,828	1.2%
47	Delaware	407	0.3%
3	Florida	9,899	6.3%
10	Georgia	4,301	2.7%
41	Hawaii	752	0.5%
40	Idaho	762	0.5%
7	Illinois	6,909	4.4%
14	Indiana	3,627	2.3%
29	Iowa	2,081	1.3%
32	Kansas	1,758	1.1%
26	Kentucky	2,442	1.5%
24	Louisiana	2,526	1.6%
38	Maine	802	0.5%
21	Maryland	2,734	1.7%
17	Massachusetts	3,407	2.2%
8	Michigan	5,470	3.5%
23	Minnesota	2,550	1.6%
33	Mississippi	1,736	1.1%
16	Missouri	3,580	2.3%
42	Montana	576	0.4%
35	Nebraska	1,094	0.7%
36	Nevada	1,028	0.7%
44	New Hampshire	536	0.3%
11	New Jersey	3,966	2.5%
39	New Mexico	770	0.5%
5	New York	7,281	4.6%
9	North Carolina	5,203	3.3%
45	North Dakota	476	0.3%
6	Ohio	6,910	4.4%
25	Oklahoma	2,485	1.6%
22	Oregon	2,554	1.6%
4	Pennsylvania	8,261	5.2%
43	Rhode Island	565	0.4%
20	South Carolina	2,748	1.7%
45	South Dakota	476	0.3%
13	Tennessee	3,883	2.5%
2	Texas	10,303	6.5%
37	Utah	876	0.6%
48	Vermont	306	0.2%
12	Virginia	3,938	2.5%
15	Washington	3,595	2.3%
34	West Virginia	1,309	0.8%
18	Wisconsin	3,216	2.0%
49	Wyoming	253	0.2%

RANK ORDER

RANK	STATE	DEATHS	% of USA
1	California	17,692	11.2%
2	Texas	10,303	6.5%
3	Florida	9,899	6.3%
4	Pennsylvania	8,261	5.2%
5	New York	7,281	4.6%
6	Ohio	6,910	4.4%
7	Illinois	6,909	4.4%
8	Michigan	5,470	3.5%
9	North Carolina	5,203	3.3%
10	Georgia	4,301	2.7%
11	New Jersey	3,966	2.5%
12	Virginia	3,938	2.5%
13	Tennessee	3,883	2.5%
14	Indiana	3,627	2.3%
15	Washington	3,595	2.3%
16	Missouri	3,580	2.3%
17	Massachusetts	3,407	2.2%
18	Wisconsin	3,216	2.0%
19	Alabama	3,028	1.9%
20	South Carolina	2,748	1.7%
21	Maryland	2,734	1.7%
22	Oregon	2,554	1.6%
23	Minnesota	2,550	1.6%
24	Louisiana	2,526	1.6%
25	Oklahoma	2,485	1.6%
26	Kentucky	2,442	1.5%
27	Arizona	2,428	1.5%
28	Arkansas	2,107	1.3%
29	Iowa	2,081	1.3%
30	Connecticut	1,828	1.2%
31	Colorado	1,813	1.1%
32	Kansas	1,758	1.1%
33	Mississippi	1,736	1.1%
34	West Virginia	1,309	0.8%
35	Nebraska	1,094	0.7%
36	Nevada	1,028	0.7%
37	Utah	876	0.6%
38	Maine	802	0.5%
39	New Mexico	770	0.5%
40	Idaho	762	0.5%
41	Hawaii	752	0.5%
42	Montana	576	0.4%
43	Rhode Island	565	0.4%
44	New Hampshire	536	0.3%
45	North Dakota	476	0.3%
45	South Dakota	476	0.3%
47	Delaware	407	0.3%
48	Vermont	306	0.2%
49	Wyoming	253	0.2%
50	Alaska	185	0.1%
	District of Columbia	257	0.2%

Source: U.S. Department of Health and Human Services, National Center for Health Statistics
   "National Vital Statistics Reports" (Vol. 54, No. 13, April 19, 2006)
*Final data by state of residence. Cerebrovascular diseases include stroke and other disorders of the blood vessels of the brain.

Death Rate by Cerebrovascular Diseases in 2003

National Rate = 54.2 Deaths per 100,000 Population*

ALPHA ORDER

RANK	STATE	RATE
7	Alabama	67.3
50	Alaska	28.5
44	Arizona	43.5
1	Arkansas	77.3
36	California	49.9
47	Colorado	39.8
32	Connecticut	52.5
37	Delaware	49.8
25	Florida	58.2
39	Georgia	49.5
20	Hawaii	59.8
27	Idaho	55.8
28	Illinois	54.6
24	Indiana	58.5
6	Iowa	70.7
11	Kansas	64.5
21	Kentucky	59.3
26	Louisiana	56.2
17	Maine	61.4
38	Maryland	49.6
31	Massachusetts	53.0
29	Michigan	54.3
35	Minnesota	50.4
19	Mississippi	60.3
13	Missouri	62.8
13	Montana	62.8
12	Nebraska	62.9
42	Nevada	45.9
45	New Hampshire	41.6
42	New Jersey	45.9
46	New Mexico	41.1
48	New York	37.9
16	North Carolina	61.9
2	North Dakota	75.1
18	Ohio	60.4
5	Oklahoma	70.8
4	Oregon	71.7
8	Pennsylvania	66.8
32	Rhode Island	52.5
10	South Carolina	66.3
15	South Dakota	62.3
9	Tennessee	66.5
41	Texas	46.6
49	Utah	37.3
40	Vermont	49.4
30	Virginia	53.3
23	Washington	58.6
3	West Virginia	72.3
22	Wisconsin	58.8
34	Wyoming	50.5

RANK ORDER

RANK	STATE	RATE
1	Arkansas	77.3
2	North Dakota	75.1
3	West Virginia	72.3
4	Oregon	71.7
5	Oklahoma	70.8
6	Iowa	70.7
7	Alabama	67.3
8	Pennsylvania	66.8
9	Tennessee	66.5
10	South Carolina	66.3
11	Kansas	64.5
12	Nebraska	62.9
13	Missouri	62.8
13	Montana	62.8
15	South Dakota	62.3
16	North Carolina	61.9
17	Maine	61.4
18	Ohio	60.4
19	Mississippi	60.3
20	Hawaii	59.8
21	Kentucky	59.3
22	Wisconsin	58.8
23	Washington	58.6
24	Indiana	58.5
25	Florida	58.2
26	Louisiana	56.2
27	Idaho	55.8
28	Illinois	54.6
29	Michigan	54.3
30	Virginia	53.3
31	Massachusetts	53.0
32	Connecticut	52.5
32	Rhode Island	52.5
34	Wyoming	50.5
35	Minnesota	50.4
36	California	49.9
37	Delaware	49.8
38	Maryland	49.6
39	Georgia	49.5
40	Vermont	49.4
41	Texas	46.6
42	Nevada	45.9
42	New Jersey	45.9
44	Arizona	43.5
45	New Hampshire	41.6
46	New Mexico	41.1
47	Colorado	39.8
48	New York	37.9
49	Utah	37.3
50	Alaska	28.5

	District of Columbia	45.5

Source: U.S. Department of Health and Human Services, National Center for Health Statistics
    "National Vital Statistics Reports" (Vol. 54, No. 13, April 19, 2006)
*Final data by state of residence. Cerebrovascular diseases include stroke and other disorders of the blood vessels of the brain. Not age-adjusted.

Age-Adjusted Death Rate by Cerebrovascular Diseases in 2003

National Rate = 53.5 Deaths per 100,000 Population*

ALPHA ORDER

RANK	STATE	RATE
7	Alabama	65.1
11	Alaska	60.7
43	Arizona	44.4
1	Arkansas	69.6
21	California	56.8
37	Colorado	50.7
45	Connecticut	43.5
39	Delaware	49.0
46	Florida	43.4
8	Georgia	64.5
27	Hawaii	53.9
17	Idaho	58.8
26	Illinois	54.2
18	Indiana	57.7
30	Iowa	53.7
21	Kansas	56.8
12	Kentucky	60.4
12	Louisiana	60.4
36	Maine	51.5
31	Maryland	53.6
41	Massachusetts	45.6
32	Michigan	53.5
40	Minnesota	47.1
9	Mississippi	62.1
19	Missouri	57.2
25	Montana	55.1
27	Nebraska	53.9
20	Nevada	57.0
49	New Hampshire	41.8
47	New Jersey	42.2
44	New Mexico	43.7
50	New York	35.1
5	North Carolina	65.6
24	North Dakota	55.4
23	Ohio	55.7
4	Oklahoma	67.6
6	Oregon	65.4
35	Pennsylvania	51.7
48	Rhode Island	42.1
2	South Carolina	69.0
38	South Dakota	49.8
3	Tennessee	67.8
15	Texas	59.7
27	Utah	53.9
42	Vermont	44.9
16	Virginia	59.2
10	Washington	60.8
14	West Virginia	60.2
34	Wisconsin	52.3
33	Wyoming	53.0

RANK ORDER

RANK	STATE	RATE
1	Arkansas	69.6
2	South Carolina	69.0
3	Tennessee	67.8
4	Oklahoma	67.6
5	North Carolina	65.6
6	Oregon	65.4
7	Alabama	65.1
8	Georgia	64.5
9	Mississippi	62.1
10	Washington	60.8
11	Alaska	60.7
12	Kentucky	60.4
12	Louisiana	60.4
14	West Virginia	60.2
15	Texas	59.7
16	Virginia	59.2
17	Idaho	58.8
18	Indiana	57.7
19	Missouri	57.2
20	Nevada	57.0
21	California	56.8
21	Kansas	56.8
23	Ohio	55.7
24	North Dakota	55.4
25	Montana	55.1
26	Illinois	54.2
27	Hawaii	53.9
27	Nebraska	53.9
27	Utah	53.9
30	Iowa	53.7
31	Maryland	53.6
32	Michigan	53.5
33	Wyoming	53.0
34	Wisconsin	52.3
35	Pennsylvania	51.7
36	Maine	51.5
37	Colorado	50.7
38	South Dakota	49.8
39	Delaware	49.0
40	Minnesota	47.1
41	Massachusetts	45.6
42	Vermont	44.9
43	Arizona	44.4
44	New Mexico	43.7
45	Connecticut	43.5
46	Florida	43.4
47	New Jersey	42.2
48	Rhode Island	42.1
49	New Hampshire	41.8
50	New York	35.1

| | District of Columbia | 45.0 |

Source: U.S. Department of Health and Human Services, National Center for Health Statistics
   "National Vital Statistics Reports" (Vol. 54, No. 13, April 19, 2006)
*Final data by state of residence. Cerebrovascular diseases include stroke and other disorders of the blood vessels of the brain. Age-adjusted rates based on the year 2000 standard population.

Deaths by Chronic Liver Disease and Cirrhosis in 2003

National Total = 27,503 Deaths*

ALPHA ORDER

RANK	STATE	DEATHS	% of USA
19	Alabama	440	1.6%
48	Alaska	58	0.2%
13	Arizona	643	2.3%
33	Arkansas	220	0.8%
1	California	3,833	13.9%
23	Colorado	408	1.5%
30	Connecticut	319	1.2%
42	Delaware	102	0.4%
3	Florida	2,245	8.2%
12	Georgia	680	2.5%
46	Hawaii	78	0.3%
37	Idaho	127	0.5%
7	Illinois	1,041	3.8%
17	Indiana	479	1.7%
36	Iowa	200	0.7%
35	Kansas	204	0.7%
26	Kentucky	353	1.3%
25	Louisiana	356	1.3%
38	Maine	126	0.5%
20	Maryland	436	1.6%
15	Massachusetts	569	2.1%
8	Michigan	998	3.6%
27	Minnesota	341	1.2%
33	Mississippi	220	0.8%
22	Missouri	429	1.6%
40	Montana	111	0.4%
42	Nebraska	102	0.4%
31	Nevada	272	1.0%
41	New Hampshire	106	0.4%
9	New Jersey	774	2.8%
29	New Mexico	326	1.2%
4	New York	1,374	5.0%
10	North Carolina	749	2.7%
46	North Dakota	78	0.3%
6	Ohio	1,043	3.8%
27	Oklahoma	341	1.2%
24	Oregon	375	1.4%
5	Pennsylvania	1,169	4.3%
44	Rhode Island	94	0.3%
18	South Carolina	463	1.7%
45	South Dakota	80	0.3%
11	Tennessee	703	2.6%
2	Texas	2,309	8.4%
39	Utah	121	0.4%
48	Vermont	58	0.2%
14	Virginia	606	2.2%
16	Washington	568	2.1%
32	West Virginia	236	0.9%
21	Wisconsin	435	1.6%
50	Wyoming	55	0.2%

RANK ORDER

RANK	STATE	DEATHS	% of USA
1	California	3,833	13.9%
2	Texas	2,309	8.4%
3	Florida	2,245	8.2%
4	New York	1,374	5.0%
5	Pennsylvania	1,169	4.3%
6	Ohio	1,043	3.8%
7	Illinois	1,041	3.8%
8	Michigan	998	3.6%
9	New Jersey	774	2.8%
10	North Carolina	749	2.7%
11	Tennessee	703	2.6%
12	Georgia	680	2.5%
13	Arizona	643	2.3%
14	Virginia	606	2.2%
15	Massachusetts	569	2.1%
16	Washington	568	2.1%
17	Indiana	479	1.7%
18	South Carolina	463	1.7%
19	Alabama	440	1.6%
20	Maryland	436	1.6%
21	Wisconsin	435	1.6%
22	Missouri	429	1.6%
23	Colorado	408	1.5%
24	Oregon	375	1.4%
25	Louisiana	356	1.3%
26	Kentucky	353	1.3%
27	Minnesota	341	1.2%
27	Oklahoma	341	1.2%
29	New Mexico	326	1.2%
30	Connecticut	319	1.2%
31	Nevada	272	1.0%
32	West Virginia	236	0.9%
33	Arkansas	220	0.8%
33	Mississippi	220	0.8%
35	Kansas	204	0.7%
36	Iowa	200	0.7%
37	Idaho	127	0.5%
38	Maine	126	0.5%
39	Utah	121	0.4%
40	Montana	111	0.4%
41	New Hampshire	106	0.4%
42	Delaware	102	0.4%
42	Nebraska	102	0.4%
44	Rhode Island	94	0.3%
45	South Dakota	80	0.3%
46	Hawaii	78	0.3%
46	North Dakota	78	0.3%
48	Alaska	58	0.2%
48	Vermont	58	0.2%
50	Wyoming	55	0.2%
	District of Columbia	50	0.2%

Source: U.S. Department of Health and Human Services, National Center for Health Statistics
"National Vital Statistics Reports" (Vol. 54, No. 13, April 19, 2006)
*Final data by state of residence. Cirrhosis of the liver is characterized by the replacement of normal tissue with fibrous tissue and the loss of functional liver cells. It can result from alcohol abuse, nutritional deprivation, or infection especially by the hepatitis virus.

Death Rate by Chronic Liver Disease and Cirrhosis in 2003

National Rate = 9.5 Deaths per 100,000 Population*

ALPHA ORDER

RANK	STATE	RATE
17	Alabama	9.8
28	Alaska	8.9
9	Arizona	11.5
36	Arkansas	8.1
12	California	10.8
26	Colorado	9.0
24	Connecticut	9.2
4	Delaware	12.5
2	Florida	13.2
40	Georgia	7.8
48	Hawaii	6.2
22	Idaho	9.3
33	Illinois	8.2
41	Indiana	7.7
46	Iowa	6.8
43	Kansas	7.5
32	Kentucky	8.6
37	Louisiana	7.9
19	Maine	9.6
37	Maryland	7.9
30	Massachusetts	8.8
16	Michigan	9.9
47	Minnesota	6.7
42	Mississippi	7.6
43	Missouri	7.5
6	Montana	12.1
49	Nebraska	5.9
6	Nevada	12.1
33	New Hampshire	8.2
26	New Jersey	9.0
1	New Mexico	17.4
45	New York	7.2
28	North Carolina	8.9
5	North Dakota	12.3
25	Ohio	9.1
18	Oklahoma	9.7
13	Oregon	10.5
20	Pennsylvania	9.5
31	Rhode Island	8.7
10	South Carolina	11.2
13	South Dakota	10.5
8	Tennessee	12.0
15	Texas	10.4
50	Utah	5.1
21	Vermont	9.4
33	Virginia	8.2
22	Washington	9.3
3	West Virginia	13.0
37	Wisconsin	7.9
11	Wyoming	11.0

RANK ORDER

RANK	STATE	RATE
1	New Mexico	17.4
2	Florida	13.2
3	West Virginia	13.0
4	Delaware	12.5
5	North Dakota	12.3
6	Montana	12.1
6	Nevada	12.1
8	Tennessee	12.0
9	Arizona	11.5
10	South Carolina	11.2
11	Wyoming	11.0
12	California	10.8
13	Oregon	10.5
13	South Dakota	10.5
15	Texas	10.4
16	Michigan	9.9
17	Alabama	9.8
18	Oklahoma	9.7
19	Maine	9.6
20	Pennsylvania	9.5
21	Vermont	9.4
22	Idaho	9.3
22	Washington	9.3
24	Connecticut	9.2
25	Ohio	9.1
26	Colorado	9.0
26	New Jersey	9.0
28	Alaska	8.9
28	North Carolina	8.9
30	Massachusetts	8.8
31	Rhode Island	8.7
32	Kentucky	8.6
33	Illinois	8.2
33	New Hampshire	8.2
33	Virginia	8.2
36	Arkansas	8.1
37	Louisiana	7.9
37	Maryland	7.9
37	Wisconsin	7.9
40	Georgia	7.8
41	Indiana	7.7
42	Mississippi	7.6
43	Kansas	7.5
43	Missouri	7.5
45	New York	7.2
46	Iowa	6.8
47	Minnesota	6.7
48	Hawaii	6.2
49	Nebraska	5.9
50	Utah	5.1

District of Columbia   8.9

Source: U.S. Department of Health and Human Services, National Center for Health Statistics
    "National Vital Statistics Reports" (Vol. 54, No. 13, April 19, 2006)
*Final data by state of residence. Cirrhosis of the liver is characterized by the replacement of normal tissue with fibrous tissue and the loss of functional liver cells. It can result from alcohol abuse, nutritional deprivation, or infection especially by the hepatitis virus. Not age-adjusted.

Age-Adjusted Death Rate by Chronic Liver Disease and Cirrhosis in 2003

National Rate = 9.3 Deaths per 100,000 Population*

ALPHA ORDER			RANK ORDER		
RANK	STATE	RATE	RANK	STATE	RATE
21	Alabama	9.3	1	New Mexico	17.4
14	Alaska	10.5	2	Delaware	12.0
4	Arizona	11.9	2	Nevada	12.0
40	Arkansas	7.6	4	Arizona	11.9
7	California	11.5	5	Texas	11.8
18	Colorado	9.5	6	Tennessee	11.6
28	Connecticut	8.4	7	California	11.5
2	Delaware	12.0	7	North Dakota	11.5
9	Florida	11.4	9	Florida	11.4
25	Georgia	8.6	10	West Virginia	11.1
50	Hawaii	5.7	11	Montana	11.0
18	Idaho	9.5	12	South Carolina	10.8
28	Illinois	8.4	13	Wyoming	10.6
40	Indiana	7.6	14	Alaska	10.5
48	Iowa	6.3	15	South Dakota	10.1
43	Kansas	7.4	16	Oregon	10.0
30	Kentucky	8.3	17	Michigan	9.6
34	Louisiana	8.1	18	Colorado	9.5
32	Maine	8.2	18	Idaho	9.5
37	Maryland	7.8	20	Oklahoma	9.4
30	Massachusetts	8.3	21	Alabama	9.3
17	Michigan	9.6	22	Washington	9.2
47	Minnesota	6.6	23	North Carolina	8.8
39	Mississippi	7.7	24	Vermont	8.7
44	Missouri	7.2	25	Georgia	8.6
11	Montana	11.0	25	Ohio	8.6
49	Nebraska	5.8	27	New Jersey	8.5
2	Nevada	12.0	28	Connecticut	8.4
37	New Hampshire	7.8	28	Illinois	8.4
27	New Jersey	8.5	30	Kentucky	8.3
1	New Mexico	17.4	30	Massachusetts	8.3
45	New York	6.8	32	Maine	8.2
23	North Carolina	8.8	32	Pennsylvania	8.2
7	North Dakota	11.5	34	Louisiana	8.1
25	Ohio	8.6	34	Virginia	8.1
20	Oklahoma	9.4	36	Rhode Island	8.0
16	Oregon	10.0	37	Maryland	7.8
32	Pennsylvania	8.2	37	New Hampshire	7.8
36	Rhode Island	8.0	39	Mississippi	7.7
12	South Carolina	10.8	40	Arkansas	7.6
15	South Dakota	10.1	40	Indiana	7.6
6	Tennessee	11.6	40	Wisconsin	7.6
5	Texas	11.8	43	Kansas	7.4
45	Utah	6.8	44	Missouri	7.2
24	Vermont	8.7	45	New York	6.8
34	Virginia	8.1	45	Utah	6.8
22	Washington	9.2	47	Minnesota	6.6
10	West Virginia	11.1	48	Iowa	6.3
40	Wisconsin	7.6	49	Nebraska	5.8
13	Wyoming	10.6	50	Hawaii	5.7
				District of Columbia	8.7

Source: U.S. Department of Health and Human Services, National Center for Health Statistics
    "National Vital Statistics Reports" (Vol. 54, No. 13, April 19, 2006)
*Final data by state of residence. Cirrhosis of the liver is characterized by the replacement of normal tissue with fibrous tissue and the loss of functional liver cells. It can result from alcohol abuse, nutritional deprivation, or infection especially by the hepatitis virus. Age-adjusted rates based on the year 2000 standard population.

Deaths by Chronic Lower Respiratory Diseases in 2003

National Total = 126,382 Deaths*

ALPHA ORDER

RANK	STATE	DEATHS	% of USA
19	Alabama	2,434	1.9%
50	Alaska	147	0.1%
18	Arizona	2,560	2.0%
30	Arkansas	1,500	1.2%
1	California	13,448	10.6%
24	Colorado	1,931	1.5%
31	Connecticut	1,445	1.1%
45	Delaware	339	0.3%
2	Florida	9,087	7.2%
11	Georgia	3,254	2.6%
48	Hawaii	287	0.2%
39	Idaho	601	0.5%
7	Illinois	4,858	3.8%
10	Indiana	3,264	2.6%
29	Iowa	1,674	1.3%
32	Kansas	1,443	1.1%
20	Kentucky	2,391	1.9%
28	Louisiana	1,731	1.4%
38	Maine	782	0.6%
23	Maryland	1,986	1.6%
16	Massachusetts	2,765	2.2%
8	Michigan	4,472	3.5%
26	Minnesota	1,832	1.4%
33	Mississippi	1,394	1.1%
14	Missouri	2,939	2.3%
40	Montana	588	0.5%
37	Nebraska	894	0.7%
35	Nevada	1,173	0.9%
42	New Hampshire	531	0.4%
15	New Jersey	2,910	2.3%
36	New Mexico	936	0.7%
4	New York	6,709	5.3%
9	North Carolina	3,887	3.1%
46	North Dakota	302	0.2%
6	Ohio	5,927	4.7%
22	Oklahoma	2,160	1.7%
27	Oregon	1,819	1.4%
5	Pennsylvania	6,046	4.8%
43	Rhode Island	495	0.4%
25	South Carolina	1,913	1.5%
44	South Dakota	379	0.3%
12	Tennessee	3,067	2.4%
3	Texas	7,567	6.0%
41	Utah	569	0.5%
47	Vermont	301	0.2%
13	Virginia	2,983	2.4%
17	Washington	2,652	2.1%
34	West Virginia	1,296	1.0%
21	Wisconsin	2,299	1.8%
49	Wyoming	278	0.2%

RANK ORDER

RANK	STATE	DEATHS	% of USA
1	California	13,448	10.6%
2	Florida	9,087	7.2%
3	Texas	7,567	6.0%
4	New York	6,709	5.3%
5	Pennsylvania	6,046	4.8%
6	Ohio	5,927	4.7%
7	Illinois	4,858	3.8%
8	Michigan	4,472	3.5%
9	North Carolina	3,887	3.1%
10	Indiana	3,264	2.6%
11	Georgia	3,254	2.6%
12	Tennessee	3,067	2.4%
13	Virginia	2,983	2.4%
14	Missouri	2,939	2.3%
15	New Jersey	2,910	2.3%
16	Massachusetts	2,765	2.2%
17	Washington	2,652	2.1%
18	Arizona	2,560	2.0%
19	Alabama	2,434	1.9%
20	Kentucky	2,391	1.9%
21	Wisconsin	2,299	1.8%
22	Oklahoma	2,160	1.7%
23	Maryland	1,986	1.6%
24	Colorado	1,931	1.5%
25	South Carolina	1,913	1.5%
26	Minnesota	1,832	1.4%
27	Oregon	1,819	1.4%
28	Louisiana	1,731	1.4%
29	Iowa	1,674	1.3%
30	Arkansas	1,500	1.2%
31	Connecticut	1,445	1.1%
32	Kansas	1,443	1.1%
33	Mississippi	1,394	1.1%
34	West Virginia	1,296	1.0%
35	Nevada	1,173	0.9%
36	New Mexico	936	0.7%
37	Nebraska	894	0.7%
38	Maine	782	0.6%
39	Idaho	601	0.5%
40	Montana	588	0.5%
41	Utah	569	0.5%
42	New Hampshire	531	0.4%
43	Rhode Island	495	0.4%
44	South Dakota	379	0.3%
45	Delaware	339	0.3%
46	North Dakota	302	0.2%
47	Vermont	301	0.2%
48	Hawaii	287	0.2%
49	Wyoming	278	0.2%
50	Alaska	147	0.1%
	District of Columbia	137	0.1%

Source: U.S. Department of Health and Human Services, National Center for Health Statistics
"National Vital Statistics Reports" (Vol. 54, No. 13, April 19, 2006)
*Final data by state of residence. Chronic lower respiratory diseases are diseases of the lungs including bronchitis, emphysema and asthma. Includes allied conditions.

Death Rate by Chronic Lower Respiratory Diseases in 2003

National Rate = 43.5 Deaths per 100,000 Population*

ALPHA ORDER

RANK	STATE	RATE
9	Alabama	54.1
50	Alaska	22.7
28	Arizona	45.9
8	Arkansas	55.0
41	California	37.9
33	Colorado	42.4
35	Connecticut	41.5
35	Delaware	41.5
10	Florida	53.4
42	Georgia	37.5
49	Hawaii	22.8
30	Idaho	44.0
40	Illinois	38.4
12	Indiana	52.7
6	Iowa	56.9
11	Kansas	53.0
5	Kentucky	58.1
39	Louisiana	38.5
4	Maine	59.9
44	Maryland	36.1
32	Massachusetts	43.0
29	Michigan	44.4
43	Minnesota	36.2
23	Mississippi	48.4
16	Missouri	51.5
2	Montana	64.1
17	Nebraska	51.4
14	Nevada	52.3
37	New Hampshire	41.2
47	New Jersey	33.7
19	New Mexico	49.9
45	New York	35.0
25	North Carolina	46.2
24	North Dakota	47.6
15	Ohio	51.8
3	Oklahoma	61.5
18	Oregon	51.1
21	Pennsylvania	48.9
27	Rhode Island	46.0
26	South Carolina	46.1
20	South Dakota	49.6
13	Tennessee	52.5
46	Texas	34.2
48	Utah	24.2
22	Vermont	48.6
38	Virginia	40.4
31	Washington	43.3
1	West Virginia	71.6
34	Wisconsin	42.0
7	Wyoming	55.5

RANK ORDER

RANK	STATE	RATE
1	West Virginia	71.6
2	Montana	64.1
3	Oklahoma	61.5
4	Maine	59.9
5	Kentucky	58.1
6	Iowa	56.9
7	Wyoming	55.5
8	Arkansas	55.0
9	Alabama	54.1
10	Florida	53.4
11	Kansas	53.0
12	Indiana	52.7
13	Tennessee	52.5
14	Nevada	52.3
15	Ohio	51.8
16	Missouri	51.5
17	Nebraska	51.4
18	Oregon	51.1
19	New Mexico	49.9
20	South Dakota	49.6
21	Pennsylvania	48.9
22	Vermont	48.6
23	Mississippi	48.4
24	North Dakota	47.6
25	North Carolina	46.2
26	South Carolina	46.1
27	Rhode Island	46.0
28	Arizona	45.9
29	Michigan	44.4
30	Idaho	44.0
31	Washington	43.3
32	Massachusetts	43.0
33	Colorado	42.4
34	Wisconsin	42.0
35	Connecticut	41.5
35	Delaware	41.5
37	New Hampshire	41.2
38	Virginia	40.4
39	Louisiana	38.5
40	Illinois	38.4
41	California	37.9
42	Georgia	37.5
43	Minnesota	36.2
44	Maryland	36.1
45	New York	35.0
46	Texas	34.2
47	New Jersey	33.7
48	Utah	24.2
49	Hawaii	22.8
50	Alaska	22.7
	District of Columbia	24.3

Source: U.S. Department of Health and Human Services, National Center for Health Statistics
    "National Vital Statistics Reports" (Vol. 54, No. 13, April 19, 2006)
*Final data by state of residence. Chronic lower respiratory diseases are diseases of the lungs including bronchitis, emphysema and asthma. Includes allied conditions. Not age-adjusted.

Age-Adjusted Death Rate by Chronic Lower Respiratory Diseases in 2003

National Rate = 43.3 Deaths per 100,000 Population*

ALPHA ORDER

RANK ORDER

RANK	STATE	RATE		RANK	STATE	RATE
11	Alabama	51.8		1	Nevada	62.6
25	Alaska	46.1		2	West Virginia	59.0
26	Arizona	46.0		3	Oklahoma	58.6
14	Arkansas	49.9		4	Kentucky	58.2
31	California	43.5		5	Montana	58.0
7	Colorado	53.7		6	Wyoming	57.2
45	Connecticut	36.0		7	Colorado	53.7
36	Delaware	40.2		8	New Mexico	52.9
37	Florida	39.9		9	Indiana	52.5
16	Georgia	48.4		9	Tennessee	52.5
50	Hawaii	20.6		11	Alabama	51.8
21	Idaho	47.2		12	Maine	51.0
38	Illinois	39.1		13	Mississippi	50.1
9	Indiana	52.5		14	Arkansas	49.9
24	Iowa	46.4		15	Kansas	49.5
15	Kansas	49.5		16	Georgia	48.4
4	Kentucky	58.2		17	Oregon	48.3
35	Louisiana	41.1		18	North Carolina	48.2
12	Maine	51.0		18	Ohio	48.2
39	Maryland	39.0		20	Missouri	47.9
43	Massachusetts	38.5		21	Idaho	47.2
30	Michigan	44.3		22	South Carolina	46.8
46	Minnesota	35.6		23	Nebraska	46.7
13	Mississippi	50.1		24	Iowa	46.4
20	Missouri	47.9		25	Alaska	46.1
5	Montana	58.0		26	Arizona	46.0
23	Nebraska	46.7		26	Washington	46.0
1	Nevada	62.6		28	Vermont	45.5
34	New Hampshire	41.9		29	Virginia	44.5
49	New Jersey	31.5		30	Michigan	44.3
8	New Mexico	52.9		31	California	43.5
48	New York	32.9		32	Texas	43.4
18	North Carolina	48.2		33	South Dakota	42.7
41	North Dakota	38.8		34	New Hampshire	41.9
18	Ohio	48.2		35	Louisiana	41.1
3	Oklahoma	58.6		36	Delaware	40.2
17	Oregon	48.3		37	Florida	39.9
41	Pennsylvania	38.8		38	Illinois	39.1
43	Rhode Island	38.5		39	Maryland	39.0
22	South Carolina	46.8		40	Wisconsin	38.9
33	South Dakota	42.7		41	North Dakota	38.8
9	Tennessee	52.5		41	Pennsylvania	38.8
32	Texas	43.4		43	Massachusetts	38.5
47	Utah	34.7		43	Rhode Island	38.5
28	Vermont	45.5		45	Connecticut	36.0
29	Virginia	44.5		46	Minnesota	35.6
26	Washington	46.0		47	Utah	34.7
2	West Virginia	59.0		48	New York	32.9
40	Wisconsin	38.9		49	New Jersey	31.5
6	Wyoming	57.2		50	Hawaii	20.6

District of Columbia   24.2

Source: U.S. Department of Health and Human Services, National Center for Health Statistics
  "National Vital Statistics Reports" (Vol. 54, No. 13, April 19, 2006)
*Final data by state of residence. Chronic lower respiratory diseases are diseases of the lungs including bronchitis, emphysema and asthma. Includes allied conditions. Age-adjusted rates based on the year 2000 standard population.

Deaths by Diabetes Mellitus in 2003

National Total = 74,219 Deaths*

ALPHA ORDER

RANK	STATE	DEATHS	% of USA
20	Alabama	1,414	1.9%
50	Alaska	102	0.1%
25	Arizona	1,153	1.6%
28	Arkansas	884	1.2%
1	California	7,093	9.6%
31	Colorado	708	1.0%
34	Connecticut	665	0.9%
44	Delaware	239	0.3%
3	Florida	4,762	6.4%
14	Georgia	1,717	2.3%
47	Hawaii	202	0.3%
39	Idaho	358	0.5%
7	Illinois	3,044	4.1%
13	Indiana	1,731	2.3%
30	Iowa	727	1.0%
33	Kansas	676	0.9%
22	Kentucky	1,296	1.7%
12	Louisiana	1,740	2.3%
38	Maine	398	0.5%
18	Maryland	1,454	2.0%
19	Massachusetts	1,424	1.9%
8	Michigan	2,640	3.6%
23	Minnesota	1,276	1.7%
32	Mississippi	680	0.9%
15	Missouri	1,666	2.2%
42	Montana	261	0.4%
37	Nebraska	407	0.5%
40	Nevada	301	0.4%
41	New Hampshire	300	0.4%
9	New Jersey	2,484	3.3%
35	New Mexico	599	0.8%
4	New York	4,227	5.7%
10	North Carolina	2,388	3.2%
45	North Dakota	211	0.3%
6	Ohio	3,731	5.0%
26	Oklahoma	1,104	1.5%
27	Oregon	1,032	1.4%
5	Pennsylvania	3,732	5.0%
43	Rhode Island	252	0.3%
24	South Carolina	1,161	1.6%
46	South Dakota	203	0.3%
11	Tennessee	1,855	2.5%
2	Texas	5,668	7.6%
36	Utah	520	0.7%
48	Vermont	183	0.2%
16	Virginia	1,587	2.1%
17	Washington	1,509	2.0%
29	West Virginia	807	1.1%
21	Wisconsin	1,331	1.8%
49	Wyoming	138	0.2%

RANK ORDER

RANK	STATE	DEATHS	% of USA
1	California	7,093	9.6%
2	Texas	5,668	7.6%
3	Florida	4,762	6.4%
4	New York	4,227	5.7%
5	Pennsylvania	3,732	5.0%
6	Ohio	3,731	5.0%
7	Illinois	3,044	4.1%
8	Michigan	2,640	3.6%
9	New Jersey	2,484	3.3%
10	North Carolina	2,388	3.2%
11	Tennessee	1,855	2.5%
12	Louisiana	1,740	2.3%
13	Indiana	1,731	2.3%
14	Georgia	1,717	2.3%
15	Missouri	1,666	2.2%
16	Virginia	1,587	2.1%
17	Washington	1,509	2.0%
18	Maryland	1,454	2.0%
19	Massachusetts	1,424	1.9%
20	Alabama	1,414	1.9%
21	Wisconsin	1,331	1.8%
22	Kentucky	1,296	1.7%
23	Minnesota	1,276	1.7%
24	South Carolina	1,161	1.6%
25	Arizona	1,153	1.6%
26	Oklahoma	1,104	1.5%
27	Oregon	1,032	1.4%
28	Arkansas	884	1.2%
29	West Virginia	807	1.1%
30	Iowa	727	1.0%
31	Colorado	708	1.0%
32	Mississippi	680	0.9%
33	Kansas	676	0.9%
34	Connecticut	665	0.9%
35	New Mexico	599	0.8%
36	Utah	520	0.7%
37	Nebraska	407	0.5%
38	Maine	398	0.5%
39	Idaho	358	0.5%
40	Nevada	301	0.4%
41	New Hampshire	300	0.4%
42	Montana	261	0.4%
43	Rhode Island	252	0.3%
44	Delaware	239	0.3%
45	North Dakota	211	0.3%
46	South Dakota	203	0.3%
47	Hawaii	202	0.3%
48	Vermont	183	0.2%
49	Wyoming	138	0.2%
50	Alaska	102	0.1%
	District of Columbia	179	0.2%

Source: U.S. Department of Health and Human Services, National Center for Health Statistics
"National Vital Statistics Reports" (Vol. 54, No. 13, April 19, 2006)
*Final data by state of residence. A severe, chronic form of diabetes caused by insufficient production of insulin and resulting in abnormal metabolism of carbohydrates, fats, and proteins. The disease, which typically appears in childhood or adolescence, is characterized by increased sugar levels Mell the blood and urine, excessive thirst and frequent urination.

Death Rate by Diabetes Mellitus in 2003

National Rate = 25.5 Deaths per 100,000 Population*

RANK	STATE	RATE
9	Alabama	31.4
48	Alaska	15.7
43	Arizona	20.7
5	Arkansas	32.4
44	California	20.0
49	Colorado	15.6
46	Connecticut	19.1
14	Delaware	29.2
20	Florida	28.0
45	Georgia	19.8
47	Hawaii	16.1
26	Idaho	26.2
34	Illinois	24.1
22	Indiana	27.9
31	Iowa	24.7
30	Kansas	24.8
8	Kentucky	31.5
2	Louisiana	38.7
11	Maine	30.5
25	Maryland	26.4
39	Massachusetts	22.1
26	Michigan	26.2
29	Minnesota	25.2
35	Mississippi	23.6
14	Missouri	29.2
18	Montana	28.4
36	Nebraska	23.4
50	Nevada	13.4
38	New Hampshire	23.3
17	New Jersey	28.8
6	New Mexico	32.0
41	New York	22.0
18	North Carolina	28.4
3	North Dakota	33.3
4	Ohio	32.6
9	Oklahoma	31.4
16	Oregon	29.0
12	Pennsylvania	30.2
36	Rhode Island	23.4
20	South Carolina	28.0
24	South Dakota	26.6
7	Tennessee	31.8
28	Texas	25.6
39	Utah	22.1
13	Vermont	29.6
42	Virginia	21.5
32	Washington	24.6
1	West Virginia	44.6
33	Wisconsin	24.3
23	Wyoming	27.5

RANK	STATE	RATE
1	West Virginia	44.6
2	Louisiana	38.7
3	North Dakota	33.3
4	Ohio	32.6
5	Arkansas	32.4
6	New Mexico	32.0
7	Tennessee	31.8
8	Kentucky	31.5
9	Alabama	31.4
9	Oklahoma	31.4
11	Maine	30.5
12	Pennsylvania	30.2
13	Vermont	29.6
14	Delaware	29.2
14	Missouri	29.2
16	Oregon	29.0
17	New Jersey	28.8
18	Montana	28.4
18	North Carolina	28.4
20	Florida	28.0
20	South Carolina	28.0
22	Indiana	27.9
23	Wyoming	27.5
24	South Dakota	26.6
25	Maryland	26.4
26	Idaho	26.2
26	Michigan	26.2
28	Texas	25.6
29	Minnesota	25.2
30	Kansas	24.8
31	Iowa	24.7
32	Washington	24.6
33	Wisconsin	24.3
34	Illinois	24.1
35	Mississippi	23.6
36	Nebraska	23.4
36	Rhode Island	23.4
38	New Hampshire	23.3
39	Massachusetts	22.1
39	Utah	22.1
41	New York	22.0
42	Virginia	21.5
43	Arizona	20.7
44	California	20.0
45	Georgia	19.8
46	Connecticut	19.1
47	Hawaii	16.1
48	Alaska	15.7
49	Colorado	15.6
50	Nevada	13.4

	District of Columbia	31.7

Source: U.S. Department of Health and Human Services, National Center for Health Statistics
   "National Vital Statistics Reports" (Vol. 54, No. 13, April 19, 2006)
*Final data by state of residence. A severe, chronic form of diabetes caused by insufficient production of insulin and resulting in abnormal metabolism of carbohydrates, fats, and proteins. The disease, which typically appears in childhood or adolescence, is characterized by increased sugar levels in the blood and urine, excessive thirst and frequent urination. Not age-adjusted.

Age-Adjusted Death Rate by Diabetes Mellitus in 2003

National Rate = 25.3 Deaths per 100,000 Population*

ALPHA ORDER

RANK	STATE	RATE
10	Alabama	30.0
19	Alaska	27.3
42	Arizona	20.7
11	Arkansas	29.8
39	California	22.5
47	Colorado	19.0
48	Connecticut	16.7
13	Delaware	28.2
40	Florida	21.8
32	Georgia	24.3
50	Hawaii	14.5
16	Idaho	27.8
31	Illinois	24.4
17	Indiana	27.7
45	Iowa	20.0
35	Kansas	23.1
5	Kentucky	31.4
1	Louisiana	40.8
25	Maine	26.0
15	Maryland	27.9
45	Massachusetts	20.0
25	Michigan	26.0
29	Minnesota	24.7
33	Mississippi	24.1
21	Missouri	27.1
28	Montana	25.5
41	Nebraska	20.9
49	Nevada	15.0
34	New Hampshire	23.2
23	New Jersey	26.9
3	New Mexico	33.0
42	New York	20.7
12	North Carolina	29.2
24	North Dakota	26.8
8	Ohio	30.4
9	Oklahoma	30.2
21	Oregon	27.1
30	Pennsylvania	24.5
44	Rhode Island	20.2
14	South Carolina	28.0
36	South Dakota	22.9
4	Tennessee	31.5
5	Texas	31.4
7	Utah	31.2
20	Vermont	27.2
37	Virginia	22.8
27	Washington	25.8
2	West Virginia	36.9
38	Wisconsin	22.6
17	Wyoming	27.7

RANK ORDER

RANK	STATE	RATE
1	Louisiana	40.8
2	West Virginia	36.9
3	New Mexico	33.0
4	Tennessee	31.5
5	Kentucky	31.4
5	Texas	31.4
7	Utah	31.2
8	Ohio	30.4
9	Oklahoma	30.2
10	Alabama	30.0
11	Arkansas	29.8
12	North Carolina	29.2
13	Delaware	28.2
14	South Carolina	28.0
15	Maryland	27.9
16	Idaho	27.8
17	Indiana	27.7
17	Wyoming	27.7
19	Alaska	27.3
20	Vermont	27.2
21	Missouri	27.1
21	Oregon	27.1
23	New Jersey	26.9
24	North Dakota	26.8
25	Maine	26.0
25	Michigan	26.0
27	Washington	25.8
28	Montana	25.5
29	Minnesota	24.7
30	Pennsylvania	24.5
31	Illinois	24.4
32	Georgia	24.3
33	Mississippi	24.1
34	New Hampshire	23.2
35	Kansas	23.1
36	South Dakota	22.9
37	Virginia	22.8
38	Wisconsin	22.6
39	California	22.5
40	Florida	21.8
41	Nebraska	20.9
42	Arizona	20.7
42	New York	20.7
44	Rhode Island	20.2
45	Iowa	20.0
45	Massachusetts	20.0
47	Colorado	19.0
48	Connecticut	16.7
49	Nevada	15.0
50	Hawaii	14.5
	District of Columbia	32.2

Source: U.S. Department of Health and Human Services, National Center for Health Statistics
"National Vital Statistics Reports" (Vol. 54, No. 13, April 19, 2006)
*Final data by state of residence. A severe, chronic form of diabetes caused by insufficient production of insulin and resulting in abnormal metabolism of carbohydrates, fats, and proteins. The disease, which typically appears in childhood or adolescence, is characterized by increased sugar levels in the blood and urine, excessive thirst and frequent urination. Age-adjusted rates based on the year 2000 standard population.

Deaths by Diseases of the Heart in 2003

National Total = 685,089 Deaths*

RANK	STATE	DEATHS	% of USA
17	Alabama	13,150	1.9%
50	Alaska	626	0.1%
24	Arizona	10,887	1.6%
30	Arkansas	7,786	1.1%
1	California	68,864	10.1%
32	Colorado	6,499	0.9%
27	Connecticut	8,389	1.2%
44	Delaware	2,027	0.3%
3	Florida	48,141	7.0%
11	Georgia	17,188	2.5%
43	Hawaii	2,461	0.4%
42	Idaho	2,566	0.4%
7	Illinois	29,816	4.4%
14	Indiana	15,467	2.3%
29	Iowa	7,840	1.1%
33	Kansas	6,491	0.9%
21	Kentucky	11,319	1.7%
20	Louisiana	11,540	1.7%
38	Maine	3,106	0.5%
19	Maryland	12,164	1.8%
16	Massachusetts	14,634	2.1%
8	Michigan	26,010	3.8%
28	Minnesota	8,144	1.2%
26	Mississippi	8,683	1.3%
12	Missouri	16,410	2.4%
45	Montana	1,984	0.3%
36	Nebraska	3,954	0.6%
35	Nevada	4,599	0.7%
41	New Hampshire	2,725	0.4%
9	New Jersey	22,043	3.2%
37	New Mexico	3,402	0.5%
2	New York	55,276	8.1%
10	North Carolina	18,674	2.7%
47	North Dakota	1,632	0.2%
6	Ohio	30,667	4.5%
23	Oklahoma	11,061	1.6%
31	Oregon	7,049	1.0%
5	Pennsylvania	38,075	5.6%
40	Rhode Island	3,011	0.4%
25	South Carolina	9,510	1.4%
46	South Dakota	1,943	0.3%
13	Tennessee	15,919	2.3%
4	Texas	41,779	6.1%
39	Utah	3,018	0.4%
48	Vermont	1,349	0.2%
15	Virginia	14,756	2.2%
22	Washington	11,185	1.6%
34	West Virginia	6,186	0.9%
18	Wisconsin	12,479	1.8%
49	Wyoming	975	0.1%

RANK	STATE	DEATHS	% of USA
1	California	68,864	10.1%
2	New York	55,276	8.1%
3	Florida	48,141	7.0%
4	Texas	41,779	6.1%
5	Pennsylvania	38,075	5.6%
6	Ohio	30,667	4.5%
7	Illinois	29,816	4.4%
8	Michigan	26,010	3.8%
9	New Jersey	22,043	3.2%
10	North Carolina	18,674	2.7%
11	Georgia	17,188	2.5%
12	Missouri	16,410	2.4%
13	Tennessee	15,919	2.3%
14	Indiana	15,467	2.3%
15	Virginia	14,756	2.2%
16	Massachusetts	14,634	2.1%
17	Alabama	13,150	1.9%
18	Wisconsin	12,479	1.8%
19	Maryland	12,164	1.8%
20	Louisiana	11,540	1.7%
21	Kentucky	11,319	1.7%
22	Washington	11,185	1.6%
23	Oklahoma	11,061	1.6%
24	Arizona	10,887	1.6%
25	South Carolina	9,510	1.4%
26	Mississippi	8,683	1.3%
27	Connecticut	8,389	1.2%
28	Minnesota	8,144	1.2%
29	Iowa	7,840	1.1%
30	Arkansas	7,786	1.1%
31	Oregon	7,049	1.0%
32	Colorado	6,499	0.9%
33	Kansas	6,491	0.9%
34	West Virginia	6,186	0.9%
35	Nevada	4,599	0.7%
36	Nebraska	3,954	0.6%
37	New Mexico	3,402	0.5%
38	Maine	3,106	0.5%
39	Utah	3,018	0.4%
40	Rhode Island	3,011	0.4%
41	New Hampshire	2,725	0.4%
42	Idaho	2,566	0.4%
43	Hawaii	2,461	0.4%
44	Delaware	2,027	0.3%
45	Montana	1,984	0.3%
46	South Dakota	1,943	0.3%
47	North Dakota	1,632	0.2%
48	Vermont	1,349	0.2%
49	Wyoming	975	0.1%
50	Alaska	626	0.1%
	District of Columbia	1,630	0.2%

Source: U.S. Department of Health and Human Services, National Center for Health Statistics
"National Vital Statistics Reports" (Vol. 54, No. 13, April 19, 2006)
*Final data by state of residence.

Death Rate by Diseases of the Heart in 2003

National Rate = 235.6 Deaths per 100,000 Population*

ALPHA ORDER

RANK	STATE	RATE
5	Alabama	292.2
50	Alaska	96.5
40	Arizona	195.1
8	Arkansas	285.6
42	California	194.1
48	Colorado	142.8
22	Connecticut	240.8
21	Delaware	248.0
9	Florida	282.9
38	Georgia	197.9
39	Hawaii	195.7
44	Idaho	187.8
25	Illinois	235.6
20	Indiana	249.6
14	Iowa	266.3
23	Kansas	238.3
11	Kentucky	274.9
17	Louisiana	256.7
24	Maine	237.9
31	Maryland	220.8
28	Massachusetts	227.5
15	Michigan	258.0
47	Minnesota	161.0
4	Mississippi	301.4
7	Missouri	287.7
33	Montana	216.2
29	Nebraska	227.3
35	Nevada	205.2
34	New Hampshire	211.6
18	New Jersey	255.2
46	New Mexico	181.5
6	New York	288.0
30	North Carolina	222.1
16	North Dakota	257.5
13	Ohio	268.2
2	Oklahoma	315.0
37	Oregon	198.0
3	Pennsylvania	307.9
10	Rhode Island	279.8
26	South Carolina	229.3
19	South Dakota	254.2
12	Tennessee	272.5
43	Texas	188.9
49	Utah	128.3
32	Vermont	217.9
36	Virginia	199.8
45	Washington	182.4
1	West Virginia	341.7
27	Wisconsin	228.0
41	Wyoming	194.5

RANK ORDER

RANK	STATE	RATE
1	West Virginia	341.7
2	Oklahoma	315.0
3	Pennsylvania	307.9
4	Mississippi	301.4
5	Alabama	292.2
6	New York	288.0
7	Missouri	287.7
8	Arkansas	285.6
9	Florida	282.9
10	Rhode Island	279.8
11	Kentucky	274.9
12	Tennessee	272.5
13	Ohio	268.2
14	Iowa	266.3
15	Michigan	258.0
16	North Dakota	257.5
17	Louisiana	256.7
18	New Jersey	255.2
19	South Dakota	254.2
20	Indiana	249.6
21	Delaware	248.0
22	Connecticut	240.8
23	Kansas	238.3
24	Maine	237.9
25	Illinois	235.6
26	South Carolina	229.3
27	Wisconsin	228.0
28	Massachusetts	227.5
29	Nebraska	227.3
30	North Carolina	222.1
31	Maryland	220.8
32	Vermont	217.9
33	Montana	216.2
34	New Hampshire	211.6
35	Nevada	205.2
36	Virginia	199.8
37	Oregon	198.0
38	Georgia	197.9
39	Hawaii	195.7
40	Arizona	195.1
41	Wyoming	194.5
42	California	194.1
43	Texas	188.9
44	Idaho	187.8
45	Washington	182.4
46	New Mexico	181.5
47	Minnesota	161.0
48	Colorado	142.8
49	Utah	128.3
50	Alaska	96.5
	District of Columbia	288.8

Source: U.S. Department of Health and Human Services, National Center for Health Statistics
    "National Vital Statistics Reports" (Vol. 54, No. 13, April 19, 2006)
*Final data by state of residence. Not age-adjusted.

Age-Adjusted Death Rate by Diseases of the Heart in 2003

National Rate = 232.3 Deaths per 100,000 Population*

ALPHA ORDER

RANK	STATE	RATE
4	Alabama	281.7
46	Alaska	181.8
39	Arizona	198.3
10	Arkansas	258.4
25	California	219.8
48	Colorado	178.0
33	Connecticut	201.8
15	Delaware	243.1
27	Florida	212.7
12	Georgia	251.8
49	Hawaii	176.9
40	Idaho	197.0
20	Illinois	235.1
14	Indiana	246.3
30	Iowa	208.1
28	Kansas	212.5
5	Kentucky	275.9
6	Louisiana	274.2
34	Maine	200.6
19	Maryland	235.6
38	Massachusetts	198.4
11	Michigan	254.0
50	Minnesota	152.0
1	Mississippi	310.3
9	Missouri	262.9
43	Montana	190.7
41	Nebraska	196.9
16	Nevada	242.6
29	New Hampshire	210.8
21	New Jersey	234.8
42	New Mexico	191.5
8	New York	266.0
23	North Carolina	231.9
37	North Dakota	198.5
13	Ohio	247.9
2	Oklahoma	300.1
47	Oregon	181.6
17	Pennsylvania	241.8
24	Rhode Island	227.7
22	South Carolina	234.5
31	South Dakota	208.0
7	Tennessee	273.4
18	Texas	237.8
45	Utah	183.5
36	Vermont	199.3
26	Virginia	218.1
44	Washington	188.6
3	West Virginia	284.6
32	Wisconsin	205.1
35	Wyoming	199.5

RANK ORDER

RANK	STATE	RATE
1	Mississippi	310.3
2	Oklahoma	300.1
3	West Virginia	284.6
4	Alabama	281.7
5	Kentucky	275.9
6	Louisiana	274.2
7	Tennessee	273.4
8	New York	266.0
9	Missouri	262.9
10	Arkansas	258.4
11	Michigan	254.0
12	Georgia	251.8
13	Ohio	247.9
14	Indiana	246.3
15	Delaware	243.1
16	Nevada	242.6
17	Pennsylvania	241.8
18	Texas	237.8
19	Maryland	235.6
20	Illinois	235.1
21	New Jersey	234.8
22	South Carolina	234.5
23	North Carolina	231.9
24	Rhode Island	227.7
25	California	219.8
26	Virginia	218.1
27	Florida	212.7
28	Kansas	212.5
29	New Hampshire	210.8
30	Iowa	208.1
31	South Dakota	208.0
32	Wisconsin	205.1
33	Connecticut	201.8
34	Maine	200.6
35	Wyoming	199.5
36	Vermont	199.3
37	North Dakota	198.5
38	Massachusetts	198.4
39	Arizona	198.3
40	Idaho	197.0
41	Nebraska	196.9
42	New Mexico	191.5
43	Montana	190.7
44	Washington	188.6
45	Utah	183.5
46	Alaska	181.8
47	Oregon	181.6
48	Colorado	178.0
49	Hawaii	176.9
50	Minnesota	152.0

District of Columbia	287.3

Source: U.S. Department of Health and Human Services, National Center for Health Statistics
    "National Vital Statistics Reports" (Vol. 54, No. 13, April 19, 2006)
*Final data by state of residence. Age-adjusted rates based on the year 2000 standard population.

Deaths by Malignant Neoplasms in 2003

National Total = 556,902 Deaths*

ALPHA ORDER

RANK	STATE	DEATHS	% of USA
20	Alabama	9,812	1.8%
50	Alaska	735	0.1%
21	Arizona	9,627	1.7%
31	Arkansas	6,119	1.1%
1	California	54,319	9.8%
30	Colorado	6,417	1.2%
28	Connecticut	7,131	1.3%
45	Delaware	1,719	0.3%
2	Florida	39,404	7.1%
11	Georgia	14,032	2.5%
43	Hawaii	2,133	0.4%
42	Idaho	2,321	0.4%
7	Illinois	24,464	4.4%
14	Indiana	12,933	2.3%
29	Iowa	6,469	1.2%
33	Kansas	5,332	1.0%
23	Kentucky	9,378	1.7%
22	Louisiana	9,533	1.7%
37	Maine	3,120	0.6%
19	Maryland	10,292	1.8%
13	Massachusetts	13,551	2.4%
8	Michigan	19,713	3.5%
24	Minnesota	9,183	1.6%
32	Mississippi	5,960	1.1%
16	Missouri	12,354	2.2%
44	Montana	1,847	0.3%
36	Nebraska	3,339	0.6%
35	Nevada	4,138	0.7%
39	New Hampshire	2,485	0.4%
9	New Jersey	17,957	3.2%
38	New Mexico	3,103	0.6%
3	New York	36,238	6.5%
10	North Carolina	16,145	2.9%
47	North Dakota	1,334	0.2%
6	Ohio	25,076	4.5%
26	Oklahoma	7,338	1.3%
27	Oregon	7,232	1.3%
5	Pennsylvania	29,841	5.4%
41	Rhode Island	2,328	0.4%
25	South Carolina	8,512	1.5%
46	South Dakota	1,636	0.3%
15	Tennessee	12,613	2.3%
4	Texas	33,867	6.1%
40	Utah	2,444	0.4%
48	Vermont	1,210	0.2%
12	Virginia	13,781	2.5%
17	Washington	11,064	2.0%
34	West Virginia	4,610	0.8%
18	Wisconsin	10,648	1.9%
49	Wyoming	943	0.2%

RANK ORDER

RANK	STATE	DEATHS	% of USA
1	California	54,319	9.8%
2	Florida	39,404	7.1%
3	New York	36,238	6.5%
4	Texas	33,867	6.1%
5	Pennsylvania	29,841	5.4%
6	Ohio	25,076	4.5%
7	Illinois	24,464	4.4%
8	Michigan	19,713	3.5%
9	New Jersey	17,957	3.2%
10	North Carolina	16,145	2.9%
11	Georgia	14,032	2.5%
12	Virginia	13,781	2.5%
13	Massachusetts	13,551	2.4%
14	Indiana	12,933	2.3%
15	Tennessee	12,613	2.3%
16	Missouri	12,354	2.2%
17	Washington	11,064	2.0%
18	Wisconsin	10,648	1.9%
19	Maryland	10,292	1.8%
20	Alabama	9,812	1.8%
21	Arizona	9,627	1.7%
22	Louisiana	9,533	1.7%
23	Kentucky	9,378	1.7%
24	Minnesota	9,183	1.6%
25	South Carolina	8,512	1.5%
26	Oklahoma	7,338	1.3%
27	Oregon	7,232	1.3%
28	Connecticut	7,131	1.3%
29	Iowa	6,469	1.2%
30	Colorado	6,417	1.2%
31	Arkansas	6,119	1.1%
32	Mississippi	5,960	1.1%
33	Kansas	5,332	1.0%
34	West Virginia	4,610	0.8%
35	Nevada	4,138	0.7%
36	Nebraska	3,339	0.6%
37	Maine	3,120	0.6%
38	New Mexico	3,103	0.6%
39	New Hampshire	2,485	0.4%
40	Utah	2,444	0.4%
41	Rhode Island	2,328	0.4%
42	Idaho	2,321	0.4%
43	Hawaii	2,133	0.4%
44	Montana	1,847	0.3%
45	Delaware	1,719	0.3%
46	South Dakota	1,636	0.3%
47	North Dakota	1,334	0.2%
48	Vermont	1,210	0.2%
49	Wyoming	943	0.2%
50	Alaska	735	0.1%
	District of Columbia	1,122	0.2%

Source: U.S. Department of Health and Human Services, National Center for Health Statistics
"National Vital Statistics Reports" (Vol. 54, No. 13, April 19, 2006)
*Final data by state of residence. Neoplasms are abnormal tissue, tumors. Includes many cancers.

Death Rate by Malignant Neoplasms in 2003

National Rate = 191.5 Deaths per 100,000 Population*

ALPHA ORDER

RANK	STATE	RATE
9	Alabama	218.0
49	Alaska	113.3
41	Arizona	172.5
6	Arkansas	224.5
46	California	153.1
48	Colorado	141.0
23	Connecticut	204.7
17	Delaware	210.3
4	Florida	231.5
45	Georgia	161.6
43	Hawaii	169.6
42	Idaho	169.9
30	Illinois	193.3
19	Indiana	208.7
7	Iowa	219.7
26	Kansas	195.8
5	Kentucky	227.7
14	Louisiana	212.0
3	Maine	238.9
36	Maryland	186.8
15	Massachusetts	210.6
27	Michigan	195.6
39	Minnesota	181.5
21	Mississippi	206.9
10	Missouri	216.6
25	Montana	201.3
32	Nebraska	192.0
38	Nevada	184.6
31	New Hampshire	193.0
20	New Jersey	207.9
44	New Mexico	165.5
34	New York	188.8
32	North Carolina	192.0
16	North Dakota	210.5
8	Ohio	219.3
18	Oklahoma	209.0
24	Oregon	203.2
2	Pennsylvania	241.3
11	Rhode Island	216.3
22	South Carolina	205.2
13	South Dakota	214.0
12	Tennessee	215.9
46	Texas	153.1
50	Utah	103.9
28	Vermont	195.4
37	Virginia	186.6
40	Washington	180.4
1	West Virginia	254.6
29	Wisconsin	194.6
35	Wyoming	188.1

RANK ORDER

RANK	STATE	RATE
1	West Virginia	254.6
2	Pennsylvania	241.3
3	Maine	238.9
4	Florida	231.5
5	Kentucky	227.7
6	Arkansas	224.5
7	Iowa	219.7
8	Ohio	219.3
9	Alabama	218.0
10	Missouri	216.6
11	Rhode Island	216.3
12	Tennessee	215.9
13	South Dakota	214.0
14	Louisiana	212.0
15	Massachusetts	210.6
16	North Dakota	210.5
17	Delaware	210.3
18	Oklahoma	209.0
19	Indiana	208.7
20	New Jersey	207.9
21	Mississippi	206.9
22	South Carolina	205.2
23	Connecticut	204.7
24	Oregon	203.2
25	Montana	201.3
26	Kansas	195.8
27	Michigan	195.6
28	Vermont	195.4
29	Wisconsin	194.6
30	Illinois	193.3
31	New Hampshire	193.0
32	Nebraska	192.0
32	North Carolina	192.0
34	New York	188.8
35	Wyoming	188.1
36	Maryland	186.8
37	Virginia	186.6
38	Nevada	184.6
39	Minnesota	181.5
40	Washington	180.4
41	Arizona	172.5
42	Idaho	169.9
43	Hawaii	169.6
44	New Mexico	165.5
45	Georgia	161.6
46	California	153.1
46	Texas	153.1
48	Colorado	141.0
49	Alaska	113.3
50	Utah	103.9

	District of Columbia	198.8

Source: U.S. Department of Health and Human Services, National Center for Health Statistics
"National Vital Statistics Reports" (Vol. 54, No. 13, April 19, 2006)
*Final data by state of residence. Neoplasms are abnormal tissue, tumors. Includes many cancers. Not age-adjusted.

Age-Adjusted Death Rate by Malignant Neoplasms in 2003

National Rate = 190.1 Deaths per 100,000 Population*

ALPHA ORDER

RANK	STATE	RATE
7	Alabama	207.1
32	Alaska	186.4
45	Arizona	172.5
8	Arkansas	204.9
46	California	172.1
48	Colorado	169.2
35	Connecticut	183.0
14	Delaware	201.4
37	Florida	181.4
19	Georgia	196.5
49	Hawaii	154.8
41	Idaho	180.3
17	Illinois	197.1
6	Indiana	207.6
31	Iowa	187.3
33	Kansas	186.2
1	Kentucky	223.6
2	Louisiana	221.9
10	Maine	204.4
22	Maryland	195.0
23	Massachusetts	193.5
24	Michigan	193.4
39	Minnesota	181.0
5	Mississippi	211.1
13	Missouri	202.5
40	Montana	180.9
44	Nebraska	178.5
12	Nevada	202.6
26	New Hampshire	190.5
20	New Jersey	195.6
47	New Mexico	169.6
42	New York	178.7
21	North Carolina	195.4
43	North Dakota	178.6
9	Ohio	204.8
15	Oklahoma	199.1
25	Oregon	192.4
16	Pennsylvania	198.8
27	Rhode Island	190.2
11	South Carolina	203.3
28	South Dakota	189.6
3	Tennessee	212.2
34	Texas	185.6
50	Utah	144.1
38	Vermont	181.3
18	Virginia	196.9
29	Washington	188.8
4	West Virginia	211.8
35	Wisconsin	183.0
30	Wyoming	188.4

RANK ORDER

RANK	STATE	RATE
1	Kentucky	223.6
2	Louisiana	221.9
3	Tennessee	212.2
4	West Virginia	211.8
5	Mississippi	211.1
6	Indiana	207.6
7	Alabama	207.1
8	Arkansas	204.9
9	Ohio	204.8
10	Maine	204.4
11	South Carolina	203.3
12	Nevada	202.6
13	Missouri	202.5
14	Delaware	201.4
15	Oklahoma	199.1
16	Pennsylvania	198.8
17	Illinois	197.1
18	Virginia	196.9
19	Georgia	196.5
20	New Jersey	195.6
21	North Carolina	195.4
22	Maryland	195.0
23	Massachusetts	193.5
24	Michigan	193.4
25	Oregon	192.4
26	New Hampshire	190.5
27	Rhode Island	190.2
28	South Dakota	189.6
29	Washington	188.8
30	Wyoming	188.4
31	Iowa	187.3
32	Alaska	186.4
33	Kansas	186.2
34	Texas	185.6
35	Connecticut	183.0
35	Wisconsin	183.0
37	Florida	181.4
38	Vermont	181.3
39	Minnesota	181.0
40	Montana	180.9
41	Idaho	180.3
42	New York	178.7
43	North Dakota	178.6
44	Nebraska	178.5
45	Arizona	172.5
46	California	172.1
47	New Mexico	169.6
48	Colorado	169.2
49	Hawaii	154.8
50	Utah	144.1

	District of Columbia	199.7

Source: U.S. Department of Health and Human Services, National Center for Health Statistics
    "National Vital Statistics Reports" (Vol. 54, No. 13, April 19, 2006)
*Final data by state of residence. Neoplasms are abnormal tissue, tumors. Includes many cancers. Age-adjusted rates based on the year 2000 standard population.

Deaths by Nephritis and Other Kidney Diseases in 2003

National Total = 42,453 Deaths*

ALPHA ORDER

RANK	STATE	DEATHS	% of USA
17	Alabama	1,062	2.5%
50	Alaska	28	0.1%
27	Arizona	563	1.3%
29	Arkansas	526	1.2%
4	California	2,334	5.5%
32	Colorado	409	1.0%
25	Connecticut	567	1.3%
42	Delaware	130	0.3%
6	Florida	2,265	5.3%
10	Georgia	1,471	3.5%
44	Hawaii	123	0.3%
46	Idaho	97	0.2%
5	Illinois	2,297	5.4%
14	Indiana	1,235	2.9%
37	Iowa	241	0.6%
28	Kansas	531	1.3%
19	Kentucky	838	2.0%
16	Louisiana	1,065	2.5%
36	Maine	265	0.6%
24	Maryland	583	1.4%
12	Massachusetts	1,286	3.0%
9	Michigan	1,665	3.9%
23	Minnesota	654	1.5%
22	Mississippi	676	1.6%
15	Missouri	1,099	2.6%
45	Montana	101	0.2%
35	Nebraska	302	0.7%
31	Nevada	439	1.0%
40	New Hampshire	150	0.4%
8	New Jersey	1,696	4.0%
38	New Mexico	217	0.5%
3	New York	2,415	5.7%
11	North Carolina	1,387	3.3%
48	North Dakota	56	0.1%
7	Ohio	2,093	4.9%
26	Oklahoma	566	1.3%
33	Oregon	306	0.7%
1	Pennsylvania	3,013	7.1%
41	Rhode Island	149	0.4%
20	South Carolina	797	1.9%
43	South Dakota	124	0.3%
21	Tennessee	677	1.6%
2	Texas	2,678	6.3%
39	Utah	207	0.5%
49	Vermont	53	0.1%
13	Virginia	1,244	2.9%
34	Washington	304	0.7%
30	West Virginia	458	1.1%
18	Wisconsin	873	2.1%
47	Wyoming	57	0.1%

RANK ORDER

RANK	STATE	DEATHS	% of USA
1	Pennsylvania	3,013	7.1%
2	Texas	2,678	6.3%
3	New York	2,415	5.7%
4	California	2,334	5.5%
5	Illinois	2,297	5.4%
6	Florida	2,265	5.3%
7	Ohio	2,093	4.9%
8	New Jersey	1,696	4.0%
9	Michigan	1,665	3.9%
10	Georgia	1,471	3.5%
11	North Carolina	1,387	3.3%
12	Massachusetts	1,286	3.0%
13	Virginia	1,244	2.9%
14	Indiana	1,235	2.9%
15	Missouri	1,099	2.6%
16	Louisiana	1,065	2.5%
17	Alabama	1,062	2.5%
18	Wisconsin	873	2.1%
19	Kentucky	838	2.0%
20	South Carolina	797	1.9%
21	Tennessee	677	1.6%
22	Mississippi	676	1.6%
23	Minnesota	654	1.5%
24	Maryland	583	1.4%
25	Connecticut	567	1.3%
26	Oklahoma	566	1.3%
27	Arizona	563	1.3%
28	Kansas	531	1.3%
29	Arkansas	526	1.2%
30	West Virginia	458	1.1%
31	Nevada	439	1.0%
32	Colorado	409	1.0%
33	Oregon	306	0.7%
34	Washington	304	0.7%
35	Nebraska	302	0.7%
36	Maine	265	0.6%
37	Iowa	241	0.6%
38	New Mexico	217	0.5%
39	Utah	207	0.5%
40	New Hampshire	150	0.4%
41	Rhode Island	149	0.4%
42	Delaware	130	0.3%
43	South Dakota	124	0.3%
44	Hawaii	123	0.3%
45	Montana	101	0.2%
46	Idaho	97	0.2%
47	Wyoming	57	0.1%
48	North Dakota	56	0.1%
49	Vermont	53	0.1%
50	Alaska	28	0.1%
	District of Columbia	81	0.2%

Source: U.S. Department of Health and Human Services, National Center for Health Statistics
   "National Vital Statistics Reports" (Vol. 54, No. 13, April 19, 2006)
*Final data by state of residence. Includes nephrotic syndrome and nephrosis.

Death Rate by Nephritis and Other Kidney Diseases in 2003

National Rate = 14.6 Deaths per 100,000 Population*

ALPHA ORDER

RANK	STATE	RATE
4	Alabama	23.6
50	Alaska	4.3
39	Arizona	10.1
13	Arkansas	19.3
48	California	6.6
41	Colorado	9.0
23	Connecticut	16.3
27	Delaware	15.9
29	Florida	13.3
19	Georgia	16.9
40	Hawaii	9.8
47	Idaho	7.1
17	Illinois	18.2
9	Indiana	19.9
46	Iowa	8.2
12	Kansas	19.5
6	Kentucky	20.4
3	Louisiana	23.7
7	Maine	20.3
38	Maryland	10.6
8	Massachusetts	20.0
21	Michigan	16.5
30	Minnesota	12.9
5	Mississippi	23.5
13	Missouri	19.3
37	Montana	11.0
18	Nebraska	17.4
10	Nevada	19.6
33	New Hampshire	11.6
10	New Jersey	19.6
33	New Mexico	11.6
31	New York	12.6
21	North Carolina	16.5
42	North Dakota	8.8
16	Ohio	18.3
25	Oklahoma	16.1
44	Oregon	8.6
2	Pennsylvania	24.4
28	Rhode Island	13.8
15	South Carolina	19.2
24	South Dakota	16.2
33	Tennessee	11.6
32	Texas	12.1
42	Utah	8.8
44	Vermont	8.6
20	Virginia	16.8
49	Washington	5.0
1	West Virginia	25.3
26	Wisconsin	16.0
36	Wyoming	11.4

RANK ORDER

RANK	STATE	RATE
1	West Virginia	25.3
2	Pennsylvania	24.4
3	Louisiana	23.7
4	Alabama	23.6
5	Mississippi	23.5
6	Kentucky	20.4
7	Maine	20.3
8	Massachusetts	20.0
9	Indiana	19.9
10	Nevada	19.6
10	New Jersey	19.6
12	Kansas	19.5
13	Arkansas	19.3
13	Missouri	19.3
15	South Carolina	19.2
16	Ohio	18.3
17	Illinois	18.2
18	Nebraska	17.4
19	Georgia	16.9
20	Virginia	16.8
21	Michigan	16.5
21	North Carolina	16.5
23	Connecticut	16.3
24	South Dakota	16.2
25	Oklahoma	16.1
26	Wisconsin	16.0
27	Delaware	15.9
28	Rhode Island	13.8
29	Florida	13.3
30	Minnesota	12.9
31	New York	12.6
32	Texas	12.1
33	New Hampshire	11.6
33	New Mexico	11.6
33	Tennessee	11.6
36	Wyoming	11.4
37	Montana	11.0
38	Maryland	10.6
39	Arizona	10.1
40	Hawaii	9.8
41	Colorado	9.0
42	North Dakota	8.8
42	Utah	8.8
44	Oregon	8.6
44	Vermont	8.6
46	Iowa	8.2
47	Idaho	7.1
48	California	6.6
49	Washington	5.0
50	Alaska	4.3

District of Columbia	14.4

Source: U.S. Department of Health and Human Services, National Center for Health Statistics
    "National Vital Statistics Reports" (Vol. 54, No. 13, April 19, 2006)
*Final data by state of residence. Includes nephrotic syndrome and nephrosis.
Not age-adjusted.

Age-Adjusted Death Rate by Nephritis and Other Kidney Diseases in 2003

National Rate = 14.4 Deaths per 100,000 Population*

RANK	STATE	RATE
4	Alabama	22.7
43	Alaska	8.2
39	Arizona	10.2
15	Arkansas	17.5
46	California	7.5
36	Colorado	11.3
27	Connecticut	13.9
22	Delaware	15.5
40	Florida	10.0
5	Georgia	21.6
42	Hawaii	8.8
46	Idaho	7.5
12	Illinois	18.2
8	Indiana	19.7
49	Iowa	6.4
17	Kansas	17.4
7	Kentucky	20.5
1	Louisiana	25.2
19	Maine	17.1
36	Maryland	11.3
15	Massachusetts	17.5
21	Michigan	16.3
30	Minnesota	12.2
2	Mississippi	24.2
14	Missouri	17.6
41	Montana	9.7
25	Nebraska	15.1
3	Nevada	23.4
32	New Hampshire	11.7
12	New Jersey	18.2
30	New Mexico	12.2
32	New York	11.7
18	North Carolina	17.2
48	North Dakota	6.5
20	Ohio	16.9
23	Oklahoma	15.4
44	Oregon	8.0
10	Pennsylvania	19.2
36	Rhode Island	11.3
9	South Carolina	19.6
28	South Dakota	12.9
32	Tennessee	11.7
24	Texas	15.2
29	Utah	12.5
44	Vermont	8.0
11	Virginia	18.4
50	Washington	5.1
6	West Virginia	21.0
26	Wisconsin	14.3
32	Wyoming	11.7

RANK	STATE	RATE
1	Louisiana	25.2
2	Mississippi	24.2
3	Nevada	23.4
4	Alabama	22.7
5	Georgia	21.6
6	West Virginia	21.0
7	Kentucky	20.5
8	Indiana	19.7
9	South Carolina	19.6
10	Pennsylvania	19.2
11	Virginia	18.4
12	Illinois	18.2
12	New Jersey	18.2
14	Missouri	17.6
15	Arkansas	17.5
15	Massachusetts	17.5
17	Kansas	17.4
18	North Carolina	17.2
19	Maine	17.1
20	Ohio	16.9
21	Michigan	16.3
22	Delaware	15.5
23	Oklahoma	15.4
24	Texas	15.2
25	Nebraska	15.1
26	Wisconsin	14.3
27	Connecticut	13.9
28	South Dakota	12.9
29	Utah	12.5
30	Minnesota	12.2
30	New Mexico	12.2
32	New Hampshire	11.7
32	New York	11.7
32	Tennessee	11.7
32	Wyoming	11.7
36	Colorado	11.3
36	Maryland	11.3
36	Rhode Island	11.3
39	Arizona	10.2
40	Florida	10.0
41	Montana	9.7
42	Hawaii	8.8
43	Alaska	8.2
44	Oregon	8.0
44	Vermont	8.0
46	California	7.5
46	Idaho	7.5
48	North Dakota	6.5
49	Iowa	6.4
50	Washington	5.1

	District of Columbia	14.3

Source: U.S. Department of Health and Human Services, National Center for Health Statistics
    "National Vital Statistics Reports" (Vol. 54, No. 13, April 19, 2006)
*Final data by state of residence. Includes nephrotic syndrome and nephrosis.
Age-adjusted rates based on the year 2000 standard population.

Deaths by Pneumonia and Influenza in 2003

National Total = 65,163 Deaths*

ALPHA ORDER

RANK	STATE	DEATHS	% of USA
20	Alabama	1,157	1.8%
50	Alaska	60	0.1%
17	Arizona	1,286	2.0%
25	Arkansas	921	1.4%
1	California	8,185	12.6%
30	Colorado	810	1.2%
28	Connecticut	860	1.3%
48	Delaware	127	0.2%
5	Florida	2,996	4.6%
13	Georgia	1,687	2.6%
43	Hawaii	237	0.4%
39	Idaho	334	0.5%
6	Illinois	2,875	4.4%
16	Indiana	1,365	2.1%
23	Iowa	1,032	1.6%
32	Kansas	694	1.1%
22	Kentucky	1,033	1.6%
26	Louisiana	915	1.4%
40	Maine	327	0.5%
18	Maryland	1,175	1.8%
8	Massachusetts	2,019	3.1%
10	Michigan	1,941	3.0%
29	Minnesota	858	1.3%
31	Mississippi	758	1.2%
14	Missouri	1,604	2.5%
42	Montana	256	0.4%
36	Nebraska	435	0.7%
37	Nevada	410	0.6%
45	New Hampshire	204	0.3%
11	New Jersey	1,823	2.8%
38	New Mexico	369	0.6%
2	New York	5,335	8.2%
9	North Carolina	1,990	3.1%
46	North Dakota	189	0.3%
7	Ohio	2,330	3.6%
24	Oklahoma	949	1.5%
33	Oregon	632	1.0%
4	Pennsylvania	3,010	4.6%
41	Rhode Island	267	0.4%
27	South Carolina	907	1.4%
44	South Dakota	227	0.3%
12	Tennessee	1,814	2.8%
3	Texas	3,613	5.5%
35	Utah	453	0.7%
49	Vermont	116	0.2%
15	Virginia	1,559	2.4%
21	Washington	1,086	1.7%
34	West Virginia	536	0.8%
19	Wisconsin	1,165	1.8%
47	Wyoming	145	0.2%

RANK ORDER

RANK	STATE	DEATHS	% of USA
1	California	8,185	12.6%
2	New York	5,335	8.2%
3	Texas	3,613	5.5%
4	Pennsylvania	3,010	4.6%
5	Florida	2,996	4.6%
6	Illinois	2,875	4.4%
7	Ohio	2,330	3.6%
8	Massachusetts	2,019	3.1%
9	North Carolina	1,990	3.1%
10	Michigan	1,941	3.0%
11	New Jersey	1,823	2.8%
12	Tennessee	1,814	2.8%
13	Georgia	1,687	2.6%
14	Missouri	1,604	2.5%
15	Virginia	1,559	2.4%
16	Indiana	1,365	2.1%
17	Arizona	1,286	2.0%
18	Maryland	1,175	1.8%
19	Wisconsin	1,165	1.8%
20	Alabama	1,157	1.8%
21	Washington	1,086	1.7%
22	Kentucky	1,033	1.6%
23	Iowa	1,032	1.6%
24	Oklahoma	949	1.5%
25	Arkansas	921	1.4%
26	Louisiana	915	1.4%
27	South Carolina	907	1.4%
28	Connecticut	860	1.3%
29	Minnesota	858	1.3%
30	Colorado	810	1.2%
31	Mississippi	758	1.2%
32	Kansas	694	1.1%
33	Oregon	632	1.0%
34	West Virginia	536	0.8%
35	Utah	453	0.7%
36	Nebraska	435	0.7%
37	Nevada	410	0.6%
38	New Mexico	369	0.6%
39	Idaho	334	0.5%
40	Maine	327	0.5%
41	Rhode Island	267	0.4%
42	Montana	256	0.4%
43	Hawaii	237	0.4%
44	South Dakota	227	0.3%
45	New Hampshire	204	0.3%
46	North Dakota	189	0.3%
47	Wyoming	145	0.2%
48	Delaware	127	0.2%
49	Vermont	116	0.2%
50	Alaska	60	0.1%
	District of Columbia	87	0.1%

Source: U.S. Department of Health and Human Services, National Center for Health Statistics
"National Vital Statistics Reports" (Vol. 54, No. 13, April 19, 2006)
*Final data by state of residence.

Death Rate by Pneumonia and Influenza in 2003

National Rate = 22.4 Deaths per 100,000 Population*

ALPHA ORDER

RANK	STATE	RATE
14	Alabama	25.7
50	Alaska	9.2
25	Arizona	23.0
2	Arkansas	33.8
24	California	23.1
42	Colorado	17.8
20	Connecticut	24.7
49	Delaware	15.5
45	Florida	17.6
36	Georgia	19.4
39	Hawaii	18.8
21	Idaho	24.4
26	Illinois	22.7
27	Indiana	22.0
1	Iowa	35.1
15	Kansas	25.5
16	Kentucky	25.1
34	Louisiana	20.3
17	Maine	25.0
29	Maryland	21.3
3	Massachusetts	31.4
37	Michigan	19.3
46	Minnesota	17.0
13	Mississippi	26.3
9	Missouri	28.1
10	Montana	27.9
17	Nebraska	25.0
41	Nevada	18.3
48	New Hampshire	15.8
31	New Jersey	21.1
35	New Mexico	19.7
11	New York	27.8
23	North Carolina	23.7
5	North Dakota	29.8
33	Ohio	20.4
12	Oklahoma	27.0
42	Oregon	17.8
22	Pennsylvania	24.3
19	Rhode Island	24.8
28	South Carolina	21.9
6	South Dakota	29.7
4	Tennessee	31.1
47	Texas	16.3
37	Utah	19.3
40	Vermont	18.7
31	Virginia	21.1
44	Washington	17.7
7	West Virginia	29.6
29	Wisconsin	21.3
8	Wyoming	28.9

RANK ORDER

RANK	STATE	RATE
1	Iowa	35.1
2	Arkansas	33.8
3	Massachusetts	31.4
4	Tennessee	31.1
5	North Dakota	29.8
6	South Dakota	29.7
7	West Virginia	29.6
8	Wyoming	28.9
9	Missouri	28.1
10	Montana	27.9
11	New York	27.8
12	Oklahoma	27.0
13	Mississippi	26.3
14	Alabama	25.7
15	Kansas	25.5
16	Kentucky	25.1
17	Maine	25.0
17	Nebraska	25.0
19	Rhode Island	24.8
20	Connecticut	24.7
21	Idaho	24.4
22	Pennsylvania	24.3
23	North Carolina	23.7
24	California	23.1
25	Arizona	23.0
26	Illinois	22.7
27	Indiana	22.0
28	South Carolina	21.9
29	Maryland	21.3
29	Wisconsin	21.3
31	New Jersey	21.1
31	Virginia	21.1
33	Ohio	20.4
34	Louisiana	20.3
35	New Mexico	19.7
36	Georgia	19.4
37	Michigan	19.3
37	Utah	19.3
39	Hawaii	18.8
40	Vermont	18.7
41	Nevada	18.3
42	Colorado	17.8
42	Oregon	17.8
44	Washington	17.7
45	Florida	17.6
46	Minnesota	17.0
47	Texas	16.3
48	New Hampshire	15.8
49	Delaware	15.5
50	Alaska	9.2

	District of Columbia	15.4

Source: U.S. Department of Health and Human Services, National Center for Health Statistics
    "National Vital Statistics Reports" (Vol. 54, No. 13, April 19, 2006)
Final data by state of residence. Not age-adjusted.

161

Age-Adjusted Death Rate by Pneumonia and Influenza in 2003

National Rate = 22.0 Deaths per 100,000 Population*

ALPHA ORDER

RANK	STATE	RATE
16	Alabama	25.0
35	Alaska	20.5
19	Arizona	23.6
2	Arkansas	30.3
7	California	26.3
25	Colorado	22.5
36	Connecticut	20.1
48	Delaware	15.4
50	Florida	13.2
10	Georgia	25.6
45	Hawaii	16.9
13	Idaho	25.5
26	Illinois	22.3
29	Indiana	21.6
9	Iowa	25.7
28	Kansas	21.9
10	Kentucky	25.6
27	Louisiana	22.1
31	Maine	21.1
21	Maryland	23.1
6	Massachusetts	26.4
39	Michigan	19.0
48	Minnesota	15.4
5	Mississippi	27.2
14	Missouri	25.4
18	Montana	24.1
34	Nebraska	20.6
22	Nevada	23.0
46	New Hampshire	15.9
38	New Jersey	19.3
31	New Mexico	21.1
10	New York	25.6
15	North Carolina	25.2
30	North Dakota	21.2
40	Ohio	18.8
8	Oklahoma	25.8
46	Oregon	15.9
40	Pennsylvania	18.8
37	Rhode Island	19.5
22	South Carolina	23.0
24	South Dakota	22.8
1	Tennessee	31.7
33	Texas	20.9
4	Utah	27.4
44	Vermont	17.2
19	Virginia	23.6
43	Washington	18.3
17	West Virginia	24.8
42	Wisconsin	18.5
3	Wyoming	30.2

RANK ORDER

RANK	STATE	RATE
1	Tennessee	31.7
2	Arkansas	30.3
3	Wyoming	30.2
4	Utah	27.4
5	Mississippi	27.2
6	Massachusetts	26.4
7	California	26.3
8	Oklahoma	25.8
9	Iowa	25.7
10	Georgia	25.6
10	Kentucky	25.6
10	New York	25.6
13	Idaho	25.5
14	Missouri	25.4
15	North Carolina	25.2
16	Alabama	25.0
17	West Virginia	24.8
18	Montana	24.1
19	Arizona	23.6
19	Virginia	23.6
21	Maryland	23.1
22	Nevada	23.0
22	South Carolina	23.0
24	South Dakota	22.8
25	Colorado	22.5
26	Illinois	22.3
27	Louisiana	22.1
28	Kansas	21.9
29	Indiana	21.6
30	North Dakota	21.2
31	Maine	21.1
31	New Mexico	21.1
33	Texas	20.9
34	Nebraska	20.6
35	Alaska	20.5
36	Connecticut	20.1
37	Rhode Island	19.5
38	New Jersey	19.3
39	Michigan	19.0
40	Ohio	18.8
40	Pennsylvania	18.8
42	Wisconsin	18.5
43	Washington	18.3
44	Vermont	17.2
45	Hawaii	16.9
46	New Hampshire	15.9
46	Oregon	15.9
48	Delaware	15.4
48	Minnesota	15.4
50	Florida	13.2
	District of Columbia	15.2

Source: U.S. Department of Health and Human Services, National Center for Health Statistics
   "National Vital Statistics Reports" (Vol. 54, No. 13, April 19, 2006)
*Final data by state of residence. Age-adjusted rates based on the year 2000 standard population.

Deaths by Injury in 2003

National Total = 161,579 Deaths*

ALPHA ORDER

RANK	STATE	DEATHS	% of USA
21	Alabama	3,148	1.9%
46	Alaska	502	0.3%
12	Arizona	4,121	2.6%
30	Arkansas	1,964	1.2%
1	California	16,459	10.2%
23	Colorado	2,811	1.7%
35	Connecticut	1,484	0.9%
47	Delaware	411	0.3%
3	Florida	11,184	6.9%
10	Georgia	5,101	3.2%
43	Hawaii	592	0.4%
39	Idaho	871	0.5%
6	Illinois	5,935	3.7%
16	Indiana	3,409	2.1%
32	Iowa	1,563	1.0%
33	Kansas	1,560	1.0%
22	Kentucky	3,068	1.9%
17	Louisiana	3,349	2.1%
41	Maine	670	0.4%
20	Maryland	3,156	2.0%
25	Massachusetts	2,709	1.7%
9	Michigan	5,226	3.2%
26	Minnesota	2,557	1.6%
28	Mississippi	2,297	1.4%
14	Missouri	3,832	2.4%
40	Montana	765	0.5%
38	Nebraska	955	0.6%
34	Nevada	1,550	1.0%
43	New Hampshire	592	0.4%
15	New Jersey	3,422	2.1%
31	New Mexico	1,712	1.1%
5	New York	6,887	4.3%
7	North Carolina	5,384	3.3%
49	North Dakota	372	0.2%
8	Ohio	5,342	3.3%
27	Oklahoma	2,471	1.5%
29	Oregon	2,138	1.3%
4	Pennsylvania	7,103	4.4%
42	Rhode Island	623	0.4%
24	South Carolina	2,742	1.7%
45	South Dakota	525	0.3%
11	Tennessee	4,307	2.7%
2	Texas	12,365	7.7%
37	Utah	1,347	0.8%
50	Vermont	332	0.2%
13	Virginia	3,914	2.4%
18	Washington	3,311	2.0%
36	West Virginia	1,383	0.9%
19	Wisconsin	3,192	2.0%
48	Wyoming	402	0.2%

RANK ORDER

RANK	STATE	DEATHS	% of USA
1	California	16,459	10.2%
2	Texas	12,365	7.7%
3	Florida	11,184	6.9%
4	Pennsylvania	7,103	4.4%
5	New York	6,887	4.3%
6	Illinois	5,935	3.7%
7	North Carolina	5,384	3.3%
8	Ohio	5,342	3.3%
9	Michigan	5,226	3.2%
10	Georgia	5,101	3.2%
11	Tennessee	4,307	2.7%
12	Arizona	4,121	2.6%
13	Virginia	3,914	2.4%
14	Missouri	3,832	2.4%
15	New Jersey	3,422	2.1%
16	Indiana	3,409	2.1%
17	Louisiana	3,349	2.1%
18	Washington	3,311	2.0%
19	Wisconsin	3,192	2.0%
20	Maryland	3,156	2.0%
21	Alabama	3,148	1.9%
22	Kentucky	3,068	1.9%
23	Colorado	2,811	1.7%
24	South Carolina	2,742	1.7%
25	Massachusetts	2,709	1.7%
26	Minnesota	2,557	1.6%
27	Oklahoma	2,471	1.5%
28	Mississippi	2,297	1.4%
29	Oregon	2,138	1.3%
30	Arkansas	1,964	1.2%
31	New Mexico	1,712	1.1%
32	Iowa	1,563	1.0%
33	Kansas	1,560	1.0%
34	Nevada	1,550	1.0%
35	Connecticut	1,484	0.9%
36	West Virginia	1,383	0.9%
37	Utah	1,347	0.8%
38	Nebraska	955	0.6%
39	Idaho	871	0.5%
40	Montana	765	0.5%
41	Maine	670	0.4%
42	Rhode Island	623	0.4%
43	Hawaii	592	0.4%
43	New Hampshire	592	0.4%
45	South Dakota	525	0.3%
46	Alaska	502	0.3%
47	Delaware	411	0.3%
48	Wyoming	402	0.2%
49	North Dakota	372	0.2%
50	Vermont	332	0.2%
	District of Columbia	464	0.3%

Source: U.S. Department of Health and Human Services, National Center for Health Statistics (http://wonder.cdc.gov)

*By state of residence. Injury as used here includes Accidents (including motor vehicle), Suicides, Homicides and "Other" undetermined.

Death Rate by Injury in 2003

National Rate = 55.6 Deaths per 100,000 Population*

ALPHA ORDER

RANK	STATE	RATE
13	Alabama	69.9
5	Alaska	77.4
9	Arizona	73.9
11	Arkansas	72.0
45	California	46.4
21	Colorado	61.8
47	Connecticut	42.6
41	Delaware	50.2
18	Florida	65.8
23	Georgia	58.8
42	Hawaii	47.4
20	Idaho	63.7
43	Illinois	46.9
32	Indiana	55.0
36	Iowa	53.1
28	Kansas	57.3
7	Kentucky	74.5
7	Louisiana	74.5
39	Maine	51.2
28	Maryland	57.3
48	Massachusetts	42.2
38	Michigan	51.8
40	Minnesota	50.5
4	Mississippi	79.7
16	Missouri	67.0
2	Montana	83.3
32	Nebraska	55.0
14	Nevada	69.1
46	New Hampshire	45.9
49	New Jersey	39.6
1	New Mexico	91.1
50	New York	35.8
19	North Carolina	63.9
24	North Dakota	58.7
44	Ohio	46.7
12	Oklahoma	70.5
22	Oregon	60.0
27	Pennsylvania	57.4
26	Rhode Island	57.9
17	South Carolina	66.1
15	South Dakota	68.6
10	Tennessee	73.7
31	Texas	55.9
28	Utah	57.3
35	Vermont	53.6
36	Virginia	53.1
34	Washington	54.0
6	West Virginia	76.3
25	Wisconsin	58.3
3	Wyoming	80.1

RANK ORDER

RANK	STATE	RATE
1	New Mexico	91.1
2	Montana	83.3
3	Wyoming	80.1
4	Mississippi	79.7
5	Alaska	77.4
6	West Virginia	76.3
7	Kentucky	74.5
7	Louisiana	74.5
9	Arizona	73.9
10	Tennessee	73.7
11	Arkansas	72.0
12	Oklahoma	70.5
13	Alabama	69.9
14	Nevada	69.1
15	South Dakota	68.6
16	Missouri	67.0
17	South Carolina	66.1
18	Florida	65.8
19	North Carolina	63.9
20	Idaho	63.7
21	Colorado	61.8
22	Oregon	60.0
23	Georgia	58.8
24	North Dakota	58.7
25	Wisconsin	58.3
26	Rhode Island	57.9
27	Pennsylvania	57.4
28	Kansas	57.3
28	Maryland	57.3
28	Utah	57.3
31	Texas	55.9
32	Indiana	55.0
32	Nebraska	55.0
34	Washington	54.0
35	Vermont	53.6
36	Iowa	53.1
36	Virginia	53.1
38	Michigan	51.8
39	Maine	51.2
40	Minnesota	50.5
41	Delaware	50.2
42	Hawaii	47.4
43	Illinois	46.9
44	Ohio	46.7
45	California	46.4
46	New Hampshire	45.9
47	Connecticut	42.6
48	Massachusetts	42.2
49	New Jersey	39.6
50	New York	35.8
	District of Columbia	83.2

Source: U.S. Department of Health and Human Services, National Center for Health Statistics (http://wonder.cdc.gov)

By state of residence. Injury as used here includes Accidents (including motor vehicle), Suicides, Homicides and "Other" undetermined. Not age-adjusted.

Age-Adjusted Death Rate by Injury in 2003

National Rate = 55.2 Deaths per 100,000 Population*

ALPHA ORDER

RANK	STATE	RATE
14	Alabama	69.5
2	Alaska	83.8
7	Arizona	75.1
12	Arkansas	71.1
42	California	47.4
20	Colorado	64.3
47	Connecticut	40.3
38	Delaware	49.5
22	Florida	63.1
23	Georgia	61.8
45	Hawaii	45.1
18	Idaho	64.9
43	Illinois	46.8
29	Indiana	54.9
41	Iowa	48.5
28	Kansas	55.6
8	Kentucky	74.2
6	Louisiana	75.3
39	Maine	48.9
26	Maryland	57.4
48	Massachusetts	40.1
36	Michigan	51.4
40	Minnesota	48.8
4	Mississippi	80.8
17	Missouri	65.5
3	Montana	81.1
35	Nebraska	52.7
11	Nevada	71.2
46	New Hampshire	45.0
49	New Jersey	38.9
1	New Mexico	93.3
50	New York	34.8
19	North Carolina	64.5
34	North Dakota	53.5
44	Ohio	45.6
13	Oklahoma	70.4
25	Oregon	58.0
31	Pennsylvania	54.3
30	Rhode Island	54.4
15	South Carolina	66.5
16	South Dakota	66.0
10	Tennessee	73.5
24	Texas	58.8
20	Utah	64.3
37	Vermont	50.8
32	Virginia	53.9
33	Washington	53.6
9	West Virginia	73.9
27	Wisconsin	55.9
5	Wyoming	80.5

RANK ORDER

RANK	STATE	RATE
1	New Mexico	93.3
2	Alaska	83.8
3	Montana	81.1
4	Mississippi	80.8
5	Wyoming	80.5
6	Louisiana	75.3
7	Arizona	75.1
8	Kentucky	74.2
9	West Virginia	73.9
10	Tennessee	73.5
11	Nevada	71.2
12	Arkansas	71.1
13	Oklahoma	70.4
14	Alabama	69.5
15	South Carolina	66.5
16	South Dakota	66.0
17	Missouri	65.5
18	Idaho	64.9
19	North Carolina	64.5
20	Colorado	64.3
20	Utah	64.3
22	Florida	63.1
23	Georgia	61.8
24	Texas	58.8
25	Oregon	58.0
26	Maryland	57.4
27	Wisconsin	55.9
28	Kansas	55.6
29	Indiana	54.9
30	Rhode Island	54.4
31	Pennsylvania	54.3
32	Virginia	53.9
33	Washington	53.6
34	North Dakota	53.5
35	Nebraska	52.7
36	Michigan	51.4
37	Vermont	50.8
38	Delaware	49.5
39	Maine	48.9
40	Minnesota	48.8
41	Iowa	48.5
42	California	47.4
43	Illinois	46.8
44	Ohio	45.6
45	Hawaii	45.1
46	New Hampshire	45.0
47	Connecticut	40.3
48	Massachusetts	40.1
49	New Jersey	38.9
50	New York	34.8
	District of Columbia	80.1

Source: U.S. Department of Health and Human Services, National Center for Health Statistics
      (http://wonder.cdc.gov)
*By state of residence. Injury as used here includes Accidents (including motor vehicle), Suicides, Homicides and
"Other" undetermined. Age-adjusted rates based on the year 2000 standard population.

Deaths by Accidents in 2003

National Total = 109,277 Deaths*

ALPHA ORDER

RANK	STATE	DEATHS	% of USA
21	Alabama	2,179	2.0%
46	Alaska	321	0.3%
13	Arizona	2,697	2.5%
30	Arkansas	1,304	1.2%
1	California	10,471	9.6%
24	Colorado	1,806	1.7%
33	Connecticut	1,112	1.0%
47	Delaware	287	0.3%
3	Florida	7,919	7.2%
9	Georgia	3,528	3.2%
42	Hawaii	415	0.4%
39	Idaho	605	0.6%
6	Illinois	3,942	3.6%
20	Indiana	2,196	2.0%
32	Iowa	1,164	1.1%
34	Kansas	1,089	1.0%
17	Kentucky	2,270	2.1%
19	Louisiana	2,208	2.0%
41	Maine	516	0.5%
27	Maryland	1,432	1.3%
28	Massachusetts	1,421	1.3%
10	Michigan	3,324	3.0%
23	Minnesota	1,912	1.7%
26	Mississippi	1,656	1.5%
12	Missouri	2,786	2.5%
40	Montana	518	0.5%
38	Nebraska	696	0.6%
36	Nevada	911	0.8%
44	New Hampshire	405	0.4%
15	New Jersey	2,371	2.2%
31	New Mexico	1,227	1.1%
5	New York	4,708	4.3%
7	North Carolina	3,835	3.5%
48	North Dakota	282	0.3%
8	Ohio	3,757	3.4%
25	Oklahoma	1,748	1.6%
29	Oregon	1,401	1.3%
4	Pennsylvania	5,014	4.6%
45	Rhode Island	393	0.4%
22	South Carolina	1,941	1.8%
43	South Dakota	406	0.4%
11	Tennessee	3,004	2.7%
2	Texas	8,425	7.7%
37	Utah	702	0.6%
50	Vermont	235	0.2%
14	Virginia	2,644	2.4%
18	Washington	2,239	2.0%
35	West Virginia	1,004	0.9%
16	Wisconsin	2,345	2.1%
49	Wyoming	273	0.2%

RANK ORDER

RANK	STATE	DEATHS	% of USA
1	California	10,471	9.6%
2	Texas	8,425	7.7%
3	Florida	7,919	7.2%
4	Pennsylvania	5,014	4.6%
5	New York	4,708	4.3%
6	Illinois	3,942	3.6%
7	North Carolina	3,835	3.5%
8	Ohio	3,757	3.4%
9	Georgia	3,528	3.2%
10	Michigan	3,324	3.0%
11	Tennessee	3,004	2.7%
12	Missouri	2,786	2.5%
13	Arizona	2,697	2.5%
14	Virginia	2,644	2.4%
15	New Jersey	2,371	2.2%
16	Wisconsin	2,345	2.1%
17	Kentucky	2,270	2.1%
18	Washington	2,239	2.0%
19	Louisiana	2,208	2.0%
20	Indiana	2,196	2.0%
21	Alabama	2,179	2.0%
22	South Carolina	1,941	1.8%
23	Minnesota	1,912	1.7%
24	Colorado	1,806	1.7%
25	Oklahoma	1,748	1.6%
26	Mississippi	1,656	1.5%
27	Maryland	1,432	1.3%
28	Massachusetts	1,421	1.3%
29	Oregon	1,401	1.3%
30	Arkansas	1,304	1.2%
31	New Mexico	1,227	1.1%
32	Iowa	1,164	1.1%
33	Connecticut	1,112	1.0%
34	Kansas	1,089	1.0%
35	West Virginia	1,004	0.9%
36	Nevada	911	0.8%
37	Utah	702	0.6%
38	Nebraska	696	0.6%
39	Idaho	605	0.6%
40	Montana	518	0.5%
41	Maine	516	0.5%
42	Hawaii	415	0.4%
43	South Dakota	406	0.4%
44	New Hampshire	405	0.4%
45	Rhode Island	393	0.4%
46	Alaska	321	0.3%
47	Delaware	287	0.3%
48	North Dakota	282	0.3%
49	Wyoming	273	0.2%
50	Vermont	235	0.2%
	District of Columbia	233	0.2%

Source: U.S. Department of Health and Human Services, National Center for Health Statistics
"National Vital Statistics Reports" (Vol. 54, No. 13, April 19, 2006)
Final data by state of residence. Includes motor vehicle deaths, poisoning, falls, drowning and other accidents.

Death Rate by Accidents in 2003

National Rate = 37.6 Deaths per 100,000 Population*

ALPHA ORDER

RANK	STATE	RATE
13	Alabama	48.4
10	Alaska	49.5
14	Arizona	48.3
15	Arkansas	47.8
46	California	29.5
27	Colorado	39.7
42	Connecticut	31.9
38	Delaware	35.1
17	Florida	46.5
22	Georgia	40.6
39	Hawaii	33.0
20	Idaho	44.3
44	Illinois	31.2
37	Indiana	35.4
28	Iowa	39.5
25	Kansas	40.0
5	Kentucky	55.1
11	Louisiana	49.1
28	Maine	39.5
48	Maryland	26.0
50	Massachusetts	22.1
39	Michigan	33.0
33	Minnesota	37.8
2	Mississippi	57.5
12	Missouri	48.8
3	Montana	56.5
25	Nebraska	40.0
22	Nevada	40.6
43	New Hampshire	31.5
47	New Jersey	27.4
1	New Mexico	65.5
49	New York	24.5
18	North Carolina	45.6
19	North Dakota	44.5
41	Ohio	32.9
9	Oklahoma	49.8
30	Oregon	39.4
24	Pennsylvania	40.5
34	Rhode Island	36.5
16	South Carolina	46.8
7	South Dakota	53.1
8	Tennessee	51.4
31	Texas	38.1
45	Utah	29.9
32	Vermont	38.0
36	Virginia	35.8
34	Washington	36.5
4	West Virginia	55.5
21	Wisconsin	42.9
6	Wyoming	54.5

RANK ORDER

RANK	STATE	RATE
1	New Mexico	65.5
2	Mississippi	57.5
3	Montana	56.5
4	West Virginia	55.5
5	Kentucky	55.1
6	Wyoming	54.5
7	South Dakota	53.1
8	Tennessee	51.4
9	Oklahoma	49.8
10	Alaska	49.5
11	Louisiana	49.1
12	Missouri	48.8
13	Alabama	48.4
14	Arizona	48.3
15	Arkansas	47.8
16	South Carolina	46.8
17	Florida	46.5
18	North Carolina	45.6
19	North Dakota	44.5
20	Idaho	44.3
21	Wisconsin	42.9
22	Georgia	40.6
22	Nevada	40.6
24	Pennsylvania	40.5
25	Kansas	40.0
25	Nebraska	40.0
27	Colorado	39.7
28	Iowa	39.5
28	Maine	39.5
30	Oregon	39.4
31	Texas	38.1
32	Vermont	38.0
33	Minnesota	37.8
34	Rhode Island	36.5
34	Washington	36.5
36	Virginia	35.8
37	Indiana	35.4
38	Delaware	35.1
39	Hawaii	33.0
39	Michigan	33.0
41	Ohio	32.9
42	Connecticut	31.9
43	New Hampshire	31.5
44	Illinois	31.2
45	Utah	29.9
46	California	29.5
47	New Jersey	27.4
48	Maryland	26.0
49	New York	24.5
50	Massachusetts	22.1
	District of Columbia	41.3

Source: U.S. Department of Health and Human Services, National Center for Health Statistics
   "National Vital Statistics Reports" (Vol. 54, No. 13, April 19, 2006)
*Final data by state of residence. Includes motor vehicle deaths, poisoning, falls, drowning and other accidents.
Not age-adjusted.

Age-Adjusted Death Rate by Accidents in 2003

National Rate = 37.3 Deaths per 100,000 Population*

ALPHA ORDER

RANK	STATE	RATE
13	Alabama	47.9
3	Alaska	55.2
12	Arizona	49.4
16	Arkansas	46.7
45	California	30.4
22	Colorado	42.1
46	Connecticut	30.0
37	Delaware	34.8
19	Florida	44.1
20	Georgia	43.8
42	Hawaii	31.4
18	Idaho	45.0
43	Illinois	31.1
35	Indiana	35.3
36	Iowa	35.0
26	Kansas	38.4
4	Kentucky	55.0
10	Louisiana	49.8
28	Maine	37.8
48	Maryland	26.5
50	Massachusetts	20.6
40	Michigan	32.7
33	Minnesota	36.2
2	Mississippi	58.2
14	Missouri	47.4
6	Montana	54.4
28	Nebraska	37.8
21	Nevada	42.2
44	New Hampshire	31.0
47	New Jersey	26.8
1	New Mexico	67.2
49	New York	23.7
17	North Carolina	46.2
25	North Dakota	39.9
41	Ohio	31.9
11	Oklahoma	49.5
27	Oregon	37.9
30	Pennsylvania	37.7
39	Rhode Island	33.5
15	South Carolina	47.2
9	South Dakota	50.3
8	Tennessee	51.3
24	Texas	40.6
38	Utah	34.6
34	Vermont	35.8
31	Virginia	36.8
32	Washington	36.4
7	West Virginia	53.5
23	Wisconsin	40.7
5	Wyoming	54.9

RANK ORDER

RANK	STATE	RATE
1	New Mexico	67.2
2	Mississippi	58.2
3	Alaska	55.2
4	Kentucky	55.0
5	Wyoming	54.9
6	Montana	54.4
7	West Virginia	53.5
8	Tennessee	51.3
9	South Dakota	50.3
10	Louisiana	49.8
11	Oklahoma	49.5
12	Arizona	49.4
13	Alabama	47.9
14	Missouri	47.4
15	South Carolina	47.2
16	Arkansas	46.7
17	North Carolina	46.2
18	Idaho	45.0
19	Florida	44.1
20	Georgia	43.8
21	Nevada	42.2
22	Colorado	42.1
23	Wisconsin	40.7
24	Texas	40.6
25	North Dakota	39.9
26	Kansas	38.4
27	Oregon	37.9
28	Maine	37.8
28	Nebraska	37.8
30	Pennsylvania	37.7
31	Virginia	36.8
32	Washington	36.4
33	Minnesota	36.2
34	Vermont	35.8
35	Indiana	35.3
36	Iowa	35.0
37	Delaware	34.8
38	Utah	34.6
39	Rhode Island	33.5
40	Michigan	32.7
41	Ohio	31.9
42	Hawaii	31.4
43	Illinois	31.1
44	New Hampshire	31.0
45	California	30.4
46	Connecticut	30.0
47	New Jersey	26.8
48	Maryland	26.5
49	New York	23.7
50	Massachusetts	20.6

	District of Columbia	41.0

Source: U.S. Department of Health and Human Services, National Center for Health Statistics
    "National Vital Statistics Reports" (Vol. 54, No. 13, April 19, 2006)
*Final data by state of residence. Includes motor vehicle deaths, poisoning, falls, drowning and other accidents.
Age-adjusted rates based on the year 2000 standard population.

Deaths by Motor Vehicle Accidents in 2003

National Total = 44,757 Deaths*

ALPHA ORDER

RANK	STATE	DEATHS	% of USA
14	Alabama	1,069	2.4%
48	Alaska	119	0.3%
13	Arizona	1,097	2.5%
24	Arkansas	720	1.6%
1	California	4,465	10.0%
27	Colorado	707	1.6%
38	Connecticut	283	0.6%
45	Delaware	131	0.3%
3	Florida	3,248	7.3%
8	Georgia	1,432	3.2%
43	Hawaii	142	0.3%
38	Idaho	283	0.6%
7	Illinois	1,510	3.4%
17	Indiana	948	2.1%
32	Iowa	458	1.0%
31	Kansas	494	1.1%
19	Kentucky	940	2.1%
16	Louisiana	961	2.1%
42	Maine	201	0.4%
26	Maryland	709	1.6%
30	Massachusetts	529	1.2%
9	Michigan	1,390	3.1%
28	Minnesota	703	1.6%
20	Mississippi	898	2.0%
12	Missouri	1,225	2.7%
40	Montana	258	0.6%
36	Nebraska	307	0.7%
35	Nevada	371	0.8%
46	New Hampshire	130	0.3%
22	New Jersey	786	1.8%
33	New Mexico	435	1.0%
6	New York	1,573	3.5%
4	North Carolina	1,662	3.7%
47	North Dakota	121	0.3%
10	Ohio	1,348	3.0%
23	Oklahoma	721	1.6%
29	Oregon	543	1.2%
5	Pennsylvania	1,652	3.7%
49	Rhode Island	103	0.2%
18	South Carolina	946	2.1%
41	South Dakota	210	0.5%
11	Tennessee	1,308	2.9%
2	Texas	4,022	9.0%
36	Utah	307	0.7%
50	Vermont	74	0.2%
15	Virginia	1,009	2.3%
25	Washington	719	1.6%
34	West Virginia	402	0.9%
21	Wisconsin	888	2.0%
44	Wyoming	136	0.3%

RANK ORDER

RANK	STATE	DEATHS	% of USA
1	California	4,465	10.0%
2	Texas	4,022	9.0%
3	Florida	3,248	7.3%
4	North Carolina	1,662	3.7%
5	Pennsylvania	1,652	3.7%
6	New York	1,573	3.5%
7	Illinois	1,510	3.4%
8	Georgia	1,432	3.2%
9	Michigan	1,390	3.1%
10	Ohio	1,348	3.0%
11	Tennessee	1,308	2.9%
12	Missouri	1,225	2.7%
13	Arizona	1,097	2.5%
14	Alabama	1,069	2.4%
15	Virginia	1,009	2.3%
16	Louisiana	961	2.1%
17	Indiana	948	2.1%
18	South Carolina	946	2.1%
19	Kentucky	940	2.1%
20	Mississippi	898	2.0%
21	Wisconsin	888	2.0%
22	New Jersey	786	1.8%
23	Oklahoma	721	1.6%
24	Arkansas	720	1.6%
25	Washington	719	1.6%
26	Maryland	709	1.6%
27	Colorado	707	1.6%
28	Minnesota	703	1.6%
29	Oregon	543	1.2%
30	Massachusetts	529	1.2%
31	Kansas	494	1.1%
32	Iowa	458	1.0%
33	New Mexico	435	1.0%
34	West Virginia	402	0.9%
35	Nevada	371	0.8%
36	Nebraska	307	0.7%
36	Utah	307	0.7%
38	Connecticut	283	0.6%
38	Idaho	283	0.6%
40	Montana	258	0.6%
41	South Dakota	210	0.5%
42	Maine	201	0.4%
43	Hawaii	142	0.3%
44	Wyoming	136	0.3%
45	Delaware	131	0.3%
46	New Hampshire	130	0.3%
47	North Dakota	121	0.3%
48	Alaska	119	0.3%
49	Rhode Island	103	0.2%
50	Vermont	74	0.2%

| | District of Columbia | 64 | 0.1% |

Source: U.S. Department of Health and Human Services, National Center for Health Statistics
"National Vital Statistics Reports" (Vol. 54, No. 13, April 19, 2006)
*Final data by state of residence. These numbers are compiled from death certificates by the Centers for Disease Control and Prevention. They may differ from motor vehicle deaths collected by the U.S. Department of Transportation from other sources.

Death Rate by Motor Vehicle Accidents in 2003

National Rate = 15.4 Deaths per 100,000 Population*

ALPHA ORDER

RANK	STATE	RATE
6	Alabama	23.8
20	Alaska	18.3
17	Arizona	19.7
5	Arkansas	26.4
39	California	12.6
29	Colorado	15.5
50	Connecticut	8.1
27	Delaware	16.0
18	Florida	19.1
25	Georgia	16.5
44	Hawaii	11.3
14	Idaho	20.7
41	Illinois	11.9
31	Indiana	15.3
28	Iowa	15.6
22	Kansas	18.1
8	Kentucky	22.8
13	Louisiana	21.4
30	Maine	15.4
38	Maryland	12.9
48	Massachusetts	8.2
34	Michigan	13.8
33	Minnesota	13.9
1	Mississippi	31.2
12	Missouri	21.5
2	Montana	28.1
23	Nebraska	17.7
24	Nevada	16.6
45	New Hampshire	10.1
47	New Jersey	9.1
7	New Mexico	23.2
48	New York	8.2
16	North Carolina	19.8
18	North Dakota	19.1
42	Ohio	11.8
15	Oklahoma	20.5
31	Oregon	15.3
36	Pennsylvania	13.4
46	Rhode Island	9.6
8	South Carolina	22.8
3	South Dakota	27.5
10	Tennessee	22.4
21	Texas	18.2
37	Utah	13.1
40	Vermont	12.0
35	Virginia	13.7
43	Washington	11.7
11	West Virginia	22.2
26	Wisconsin	16.2
4	Wyoming	27.1

RANK ORDER

RANK	STATE	RATE
1	Mississippi	31.2
2	Montana	28.1
3	South Dakota	27.5
4	Wyoming	27.1
5	Arkansas	26.4
6	Alabama	23.8
7	New Mexico	23.2
8	Kentucky	22.8
8	South Carolina	22.8
10	Tennessee	22.4
11	West Virginia	22.2
12	Missouri	21.5
13	Louisiana	21.4
14	Idaho	20.7
15	Oklahoma	20.5
16	North Carolina	19.8
17	Arizona	19.7
18	Florida	19.1
18	North Dakota	19.1
20	Alaska	18.3
21	Texas	18.2
22	Kansas	18.1
23	Nebraska	17.7
24	Nevada	16.6
25	Georgia	16.5
26	Wisconsin	16.2
27	Delaware	16.0
28	Iowa	15.6
29	Colorado	15.5
30	Maine	15.4
31	Indiana	15.3
31	Oregon	15.3
33	Minnesota	13.9
34	Michigan	13.8
35	Virginia	13.7
36	Pennsylvania	13.4
37	Utah	13.1
38	Maryland	12.9
39	California	12.6
40	Vermont	12.0
41	Illinois	11.9
42	Ohio	11.8
43	Washington	11.7
44	Hawaii	11.3
45	New Hampshire	10.1
46	Rhode Island	9.6
47	New Jersey	9.1
48	Massachusetts	8.2
48	New York	8.2
50	Connecticut	8.1
	District of Columbia	11.3

Source: U.S. Department of Health and Human Services, National Center for Health Statistics
    "National Vital Statistics Reports" (Vol. 54, No. 13, April 19, 2006)
*Final data by state of residence. These numbers are compiled from death certificates by the Centers for Disease Control and Prevention. They may differ from motor vehicle deaths collected by the U.S. Department of Transportation from other sources. Not age-adjusted.

Age-Adjusted Death Rate by Motor Vehicle Accidents in 2003

National Rate = 15.3 Deaths per 100,000 Population*

ALPHA ORDER

RANK	STATE	RATE
6	Alabama	23.6
18	Alaska	19.1
16	Arizona	20.0
5	Arkansas	26.2
39	California	12.7
28	Colorado	15.6
48	Connecticut	8.2
26	Delaware	15.9
19	Florida	18.8
24	Georgia	16.8
44	Hawaii	11.1
14	Idaho	20.7
40	Illinois	11.9
29	Indiana	15.2
32	Iowa	14.9
22	Kansas	17.8
9	Kentucky	22.6
12	Louisiana	21.3
31	Maine	15.0
38	Maryland	12.9
50	Massachusetts	8.0
33	Michigan	13.7
33	Minnesota	13.7
1	Mississippi	31.3
13	Missouri	21.2
2	Montana	27.4
23	Nebraska	17.3
24	Nevada	16.8
45	New Hampshire	10.0
47	New Jersey	9.1
7	New Mexico	23.4
49	New York	8.1
17	North Carolina	19.8
21	North Dakota	18.2
41	Ohio	11.7
15	Oklahoma	20.4
30	Oregon	15.1
37	Pennsylvania	13.0
46	Rhode Island	9.3
8	South Carolina	22.7
3	South Dakota	27.2
10	Tennessee	22.2
20	Texas	18.4
36	Utah	13.6
43	Vermont	11.4
33	Virginia	13.7
41	Washington	11.7
11	West Virginia	21.7
26	Wisconsin	15.9
4	Wyoming	27.1

RANK ORDER

RANK	STATE	RATE
1	Mississippi	31.3
2	Montana	27.4
3	South Dakota	27.2
4	Wyoming	27.1
5	Arkansas	26.2
6	Alabama	23.6
7	New Mexico	23.4
8	South Carolina	22.7
9	Kentucky	22.6
10	Tennessee	22.2
11	West Virginia	21.7
12	Louisiana	21.3
13	Missouri	21.2
14	Idaho	20.7
15	Oklahoma	20.4
16	Arizona	20.0
17	North Carolina	19.8
18	Alaska	19.1
19	Florida	18.8
20	Texas	18.4
21	North Dakota	18.2
22	Kansas	17.8
23	Nebraska	17.3
24	Georgia	16.8
24	Nevada	16.8
26	Delaware	15.9
26	Wisconsin	15.9
28	Colorado	15.6
29	Indiana	15.2
30	Oregon	15.1
31	Maine	15.0
32	Iowa	14.9
33	Michigan	13.7
33	Minnesota	13.7
33	Virginia	13.7
36	Utah	13.6
37	Pennsylvania	13.0
38	Maryland	12.9
39	California	12.7
40	Illinois	11.9
41	Ohio	11.7
41	Washington	11.7
43	Vermont	11.4
44	Hawaii	11.1
45	New Hampshire	10.0
46	Rhode Island	9.3
47	New Jersey	9.1
48	Connecticut	8.2
49	New York	8.1
50	Massachusetts	8.0
	District of Columbia	11.1

Source: U.S. Department of Health and Human Services, National Center for Health Statistics
"National Vital Statistics Reports" (Vol. 54, No. 13, April 19, 2006)

*Final data by state of residence. These numbers are compiled from death certificates by the Centers for Disease
Control and Prevention. They may differ from motor vehicle deaths collected by the U.S. Department of
Transportation from other sources. Age-adjusted rates based on the year 2000 standard population.*

Deaths by Firearm Injury in 2003

National Total = 30,136 Deaths*

ALPHA ORDER

RANK ORDER

RANK	STATE	DEATHS	% of USA	RANK	STATE	DEATHS	% of USA
15	Alabama	765	2.5%	1	California	3,468	11.5%
41	Alaska	120	0.4%	2	Texas	2,432	8.1%
11	Arizona	849	2.8%	3	Florida	1,940	6.4%
27	Arkansas	413	1.4%	4	Pennsylvania	1,230	4.1%
1	California	3,468	11.5%	5	Georgia	1,173	3.9%
22	Colorado	501	1.7%	6	Illinois	1,146	3.8%
38	Connecticut	153	0.5%	7	North Carolina	1,055	3.5%
46	Delaware	65	0.2%	8	New York	1,034	3.4%
3	Florida	1,940	6.4%	9	Michigan	1,030	3.4%
5	Georgia	1,173	3.9%	10	Ohio	934	3.1%
49	Hawaii	37	0.1%	11	Arizona	849	2.8%
37	Idaho	164	0.5%	12	Louisiana	847	2.8%
6	Illinois	1,146	3.8%	13	Tennessee	837	2.8%
16	Indiana	696	2.3%	14	Virginia	811	2.7%
35	Iowa	208	0.7%	15	Alabama	765	2.5%
32	Kansas	304	1.0%	16	Indiana	696	2.3%
21	Kentucky	560	1.9%	17	Missouri	657	2.2%
12	Louisiana	847	2.8%	18	Maryland	648	2.2%
44	Maine	82	0.3%	19	South Carolina	593	2.0%
18	Maryland	648	2.2%	20	Washington	565	1.9%
36	Massachusetts	204	0.7%	21	Kentucky	560	1.9%
9	Michigan	1,030	3.4%	22	Colorado	501	1.7%
30	Minnesota	332	1.1%	23	Mississippi	477	1.6%
23	Mississippi	477	1.6%	24	Wisconsin	468	1.6%
17	Missouri	657	2.2%	25	New Jersey	458	1.5%
39	Montana	145	0.5%	26	Oklahoma	449	1.5%
40	Nebraska	134	0.4%	27	Arkansas	413	1.4%
29	Nevada	374	1.2%	28	Oregon	395	1.3%
42	New Hampshire	89	0.3%	29	Nevada	374	1.2%
25	New Jersey	458	1.5%	30	Minnesota	332	1.1%
31	New Mexico	326	1.1%	31	New Mexico	326	1.1%
8	New York	1,034	3.4%	32	Kansas	304	1.0%
7	North Carolina	1,055	3.5%	33	West Virginia	265	0.9%
47	North Dakota	58	0.2%	34	Utah	230	0.8%
10	Ohio	934	3.1%	35	Iowa	208	0.7%
26	Oklahoma	449	1.5%	36	Massachusetts	204	0.7%
28	Oregon	395	1.3%	37	Idaho	164	0.5%
4	Pennsylvania	1,230	4.1%	38	Connecticut	153	0.5%
50	Rhode Island	35	0.1%	39	Montana	145	0.5%
19	South Carolina	593	2.0%	40	Nebraska	134	0.4%
45	South Dakota	76	0.3%	41	Alaska	120	0.4%
13	Tennessee	837	2.8%	42	New Hampshire	89	0.3%
2	Texas	2,432	8.1%	42	Wyoming	89	0.3%
34	Utah	230	0.8%	44	Maine	82	0.3%
48	Vermont	48	0.2%	45	South Dakota	76	0.3%
14	Virginia	811	2.7%	46	Delaware	65	0.2%
20	Washington	565	1.9%	47	North Dakota	58	0.2%
33	West Virginia	265	0.9%	48	Vermont	48	0.2%
24	Wisconsin	468	1.6%	49	Hawaii	37	0.1%
42	Wyoming	89	0.3%	50	Rhode Island	35	0.1%
					District of Columbia	167	0.6%

Source: U.S. Department of Health and Human Services, National Center for Health Statistics
   "National Vital Statistics Reports" (Vol. 54, No. 13, April 19, 2006)
Final data by state of residence.

Death Rate by Firearm Injury in 2003

National Rate = 10.4 Deaths per 100,000 Population*

ALPHA ORDER

RANK	STATE	RATE
5	Alabama	17.0
2	Alaska	18.5
9	Arizona	15.2
9	Arkansas	15.2
31	California	9.8
25	Colorado	11.0
47	Connecticut	4.4
38	Delaware	8.0
21	Florida	11.4
15	Georgia	13.5
50	Hawaii	2.9
18	Idaho	12.0
35	Illinois	9.1
22	Indiana	11.2
41	Iowa	7.1
22	Kansas	11.2
14	Kentucky	13.6
1	Louisiana	18.8
44	Maine	6.3
19	Maryland	11.8
49	Massachusetts	3.2
28	Michigan	10.2
43	Minnesota	6.6
7	Mississippi	16.6
20	Missouri	11.5
8	Montana	15.8
40	Nebraska	7.7
6	Nevada	16.7
42	New Hampshire	6.9
46	New Jersey	5.3
4	New Mexico	17.4
45	New York	5.4
17	North Carolina	12.5
33	North Dakota	9.2
37	Ohio	8.2
16	Oklahoma	12.8
24	Oregon	11.1
29	Pennsylvania	9.9
48	Rhode Island	3.3
12	South Carolina	14.3
29	South Dakota	9.9
12	Tennessee	14.3
25	Texas	11.0
31	Utah	9.8
39	Vermont	7.8
25	Virginia	11.0
33	Washington	9.2
11	West Virginia	14.6
36	Wisconsin	8.6
3	Wyoming	17.8

RANK ORDER

RANK	STATE	RATE
1	Louisiana	18.8
2	Alaska	18.5
3	Wyoming	17.8
4	New Mexico	17.4
5	Alabama	17.0
6	Nevada	16.7
7	Mississippi	16.6
8	Montana	15.8
9	Arizona	15.2
9	Arkansas	15.2
11	West Virginia	14.6
12	South Carolina	14.3
12	Tennessee	14.3
14	Kentucky	13.6
15	Georgia	13.5
16	Oklahoma	12.8
17	North Carolina	12.5
18	Idaho	12.0
19	Maryland	11.8
20	Missouri	11.5
21	Florida	11.4
22	Indiana	11.2
22	Kansas	11.2
24	Oregon	11.1
25	Colorado	11.0
25	Texas	11.0
25	Virginia	11.0
28	Michigan	10.2
29	Pennsylvania	9.9
29	South Dakota	9.9
31	California	9.8
31	Utah	9.8
33	North Dakota	9.2
33	Washington	9.2
35	Illinois	9.1
36	Wisconsin	8.6
37	Ohio	8.2
38	Delaware	8.0
39	Vermont	7.8
40	Nebraska	7.7
41	Iowa	7.1
42	New Hampshire	6.9
43	Minnesota	6.6
44	Maine	6.3
45	New York	5.4
46	New Jersey	5.3
47	Connecticut	4.4
48	Rhode Island	3.3
49	Massachusetts	3.2
50	Hawaii	2.9

District of Columbia   29.6

Source: U.S. Department of Health and Human Services, National Center for Health Statistics
    "National Vital Statistics Reports" (Vol. 54, No. 13, April 19, 2006)
*Final data by state of residence. Not age-adjusted.

173

Age-Adjusted Death Rate by Firearm Injury in 2003

National Rate = 10.3 Deaths per 100,000 Population*

ALPHA ORDER

RANK	STATE	RATE
6	Alabama	16.9
1	Alaska	19.5
9	Arizona	15.3
10	Arkansas	15.1
32	California	9.8
23	Colorado	11.1
47	Connecticut	4.4
38	Delaware	7.9
23	Florida	11.1
14	Georgia	13.7
50	Hawaii	2.8
18	Idaho	12.2
34	Illinois	9.0
21	Indiana	11.3
41	Iowa	6.9
23	Kansas	11.1
15	Kentucky	13.4
2	Louisiana	18.8
44	Maine	6.0
19	Maryland	11.9
48	Massachusetts	3.1
29	Michigan	10.2
43	Minnesota	6.4
7	Mississippi	16.8
20	Missouri	11.4
8	Montana	15.5
39	Nebraska	7.6
5	Nevada	17.2
42	New Hampshire	6.7
45	New Jersey	5.4
3	New Mexico	17.6
46	New York	5.3
17	North Carolina	12.4
35	North Dakota	8.9
37	Ohio	8.1
16	Oklahoma	12.8
27	Oregon	10.7
30	Pennsylvania	9.9
48	Rhode Island	3.1
11	South Carolina	14.2
30	South Dakota	9.9
12	Tennessee	14.1
21	Texas	11.3
27	Utah	10.7
40	Vermont	7.5
26	Virginia	10.9
33	Washington	9.1
12	West Virginia	14.1
36	Wisconsin	8.4
4	Wyoming	17.5

RANK ORDER

RANK	STATE	RATE
1	Alaska	19.5
2	Louisiana	18.8
3	New Mexico	17.6
4	Wyoming	17.5
5	Nevada	17.2
6	Alabama	16.9
7	Mississippi	16.8
8	Montana	15.5
9	Arizona	15.3
10	Arkansas	15.1
11	South Carolina	14.2
12	Tennessee	14.1
12	West Virginia	14.1
14	Georgia	13.7
15	Kentucky	13.4
16	Oklahoma	12.8
17	North Carolina	12.4
18	Idaho	12.2
19	Maryland	11.9
20	Missouri	11.4
21	Indiana	11.3
21	Texas	11.3
23	Colorado	11.1
23	Florida	11.1
23	Kansas	11.1
26	Virginia	10.9
27	Oregon	10.7
27	Utah	10.7
29	Michigan	10.2
30	Pennsylvania	9.9
30	South Dakota	9.9
32	California	9.8
33	Washington	9.1
34	Illinois	9.0
35	North Dakota	8.9
36	Wisconsin	8.4
37	Ohio	8.1
38	Delaware	7.9
39	Nebraska	7.6
40	Vermont	7.5
41	Iowa	6.9
42	New Hampshire	6.7
43	Minnesota	6.4
44	Maine	6.0
45	New Jersey	5.4
46	New York	5.3
47	Connecticut	4.4
48	Massachusetts	3.1
48	Rhode Island	3.1
50	Hawaii	2.8

District of Columbia	26.9

Source: U.S. Department of Health and Human Services, National Center for Health Statistics
"National Vital Statistics Reports" (Vol. 54, No. 13, April 19, 2006)
*Final data by state of residence. Age-adjusted rates based on the year 2000 standard population.

Deaths by Homicide in 2003

National Total = 17,732 Homicides*

ALPHA ORDER

RANK ORDER

RANK	STATE	HOMICIDES	% of USA
16	Alabama	434	2.4%
39	Alaska	47	0.3%
13	Arizona	498	2.8%
24	Arkansas	195	1.1%
1	California	2,487	14.0%
27	Colorado	192	1.1%
33	Connecticut	107	0.6%
43	Delaware	25	0.1%
3	Florida	1,004	5.7%
6	Georgia	736	4.2%
44	Hawaii	20	0.1%
41	Idaho	33	0.2%
4	Illinois	966	5.4%
18	Indiana	347	2.0%
38	Iowa	50	0.3%
32	Kansas	121	0.7%
26	Kentucky	193	1.1%
9	Louisiana	602	3.4%
46	Maine	17	0.1%
11	Maryland	557	3.1%
30	Massachusetts	140	0.8%
8	Michigan	650	3.7%
31	Minnesota	130	0.7%
21	Mississippi	304	1.7%
20	Missouri	323	1.8%
40	Montana	37	0.2%
36	Nebraska	63	0.4%
28	Nevada	183	1.0%
44	New Hampshire	20	0.1%
17	New Jersey	423	2.4%
29	New Mexico	164	0.9%
5	New York	963	5.4%
10	North Carolina	598	3.4%
49	North Dakota	12	0.1%
12	Ohio	520	2.9%
22	Oklahoma	224	1.3%
34	Oregon	93	0.5%
7	Pennsylvania	676	3.8%
42	Rhode Island	29	0.2%
19	South Carolina	325	1.8%
47	South Dakota	16	0.1%
15	Tennessee	438	2.5%
2	Texas	1,525	8.6%
37	Utah	58	0.3%
49	Vermont	12	0.1%
14	Virginia	462	2.6%
23	Washington	219	1.2%
35	West Virginia	89	0.5%
24	Wisconsin	195	1.1%
47	Wyoming	16	0.1%

RANK	STATE	HOMICIDES	% of USA
1	California	2,487	14.0%
2	Texas	1,525	8.6%
3	Florida	1,004	5.7%
4	Illinois	966	5.4%
5	New York	963	5.4%
6	Georgia	736	4.2%
7	Pennsylvania	676	3.8%
8	Michigan	650	3.7%
9	Louisiana	602	3.4%
10	North Carolina	598	3.4%
11	Maryland	557	3.1%
12	Ohio	520	2.9%
13	Arizona	498	2.8%
14	Virginia	462	2.6%
15	Tennessee	438	2.5%
16	Alabama	434	2.4%
17	New Jersey	423	2.4%
18	Indiana	347	2.0%
19	South Carolina	325	1.8%
20	Missouri	323	1.8%
21	Mississippi	304	1.7%
22	Oklahoma	224	1.3%
23	Washington	219	1.2%
24	Arkansas	195	1.1%
24	Wisconsin	195	1.1%
26	Kentucky	193	1.1%
27	Colorado	192	1.1%
28	Nevada	183	1.0%
29	New Mexico	164	0.9%
30	Massachusetts	140	0.8%
31	Minnesota	130	0.7%
32	Kansas	121	0.7%
33	Connecticut	107	0.6%
34	Oregon	93	0.5%
35	West Virginia	89	0.5%
36	Nebraska	63	0.4%
37	Utah	58	0.3%
38	Iowa	50	0.3%
39	Alaska	47	0.3%
40	Montana	37	0.2%
41	Idaho	33	0.2%
42	Rhode Island	29	0.2%
43	Delaware	25	0.1%
44	Hawaii	20	0.1%
44	New Hampshire	20	0.1%
46	Maine	17	0.1%
47	South Dakota	16	0.1%
47	Wyoming	16	0.1%
49	North Dakota	12	0.1%
49	Vermont	12	0.1%
	District of Columbia	194	1.1%

Source: U.S. Department of Health and Human Services, National Center for Health Statistics "National Vital Statistics Reports" (Vol. 54, No. 13, April 19, 2006)
By state of residence. Includes legal intervention. Homicide data shown here are collected by the Centers for Disease Control and Prevention based on death certificates and differ from murder data collected by the F.B.I. from other sources.

Death Rate by Homicide in 2003

National Rate = 6.1 Deaths per 100,000 Population*

ALPHA ORDER

RANK ORDER

RANK	STATE	RATE	RANK	STATE	RATE
4	Alabama	9.6	1	Louisiana	13.4
12	Alaska	7.2	2	Mississippi	10.6
5	Arizona	8.9	3	Maryland	10.1
12	Arkansas	7.2	4	Alabama	9.6
15	California	7.0	5	Arizona	8.9
30	Colorado	4.2	6	New Mexico	8.7
35	Connecticut	3.1	7	Georgia	8.5
35	Delaware	3.1	8	Nevada	8.2
20	Florida	5.9	9	South Carolina	7.8
7	Georgia	8.5	10	Illinois	7.6
44	Hawaii	1.6	11	Tennessee	7.5
41	Idaho	2.4	12	Alaska	7.2
10	Illinois	7.6	12	Arkansas	7.2
22	Indiana	5.6	14	North Carolina	7.1
43	Iowa	1.7	15	California	7.0
29	Kansas	4.4	16	Texas	6.9
27	Kentucky	4.7	17	Michigan	6.4
1	Louisiana	13.4	17	Oklahoma	6.4
NA	Maine**	NA	19	Virginia	6.3
3	Maryland	10.1	20	Florida	5.9
42	Massachusetts	2.2	21	Missouri	5.7
17	Michigan	6.4	22	Indiana	5.6
38	Minnesota	2.6	23	Pennsylvania	5.5
2	Mississippi	10.6	24	New York	5.0
21	Missouri	5.7	25	New Jersey	4.9
31	Montana	4.0	25	West Virginia	4.9
32	Nebraska	3.6	27	Kentucky	4.7
8	Nevada	8.2	28	Ohio	4.5
44	New Hampshire	1.6	29	Kansas	4.4
25	New Jersey	4.9	30	Colorado	4.2
6	New Mexico	8.7	31	Montana	4.0
24	New York	5.0	32	Nebraska	3.6
14	North Carolina	7.1	32	Washington	3.6
NA	North Dakota**	NA	32	Wisconsin	3.6
28	Ohio	4.5	35	Connecticut	3.1
17	Oklahoma	6.4	35	Delaware	3.1
38	Oregon	2.6	37	Rhode Island	2.7
23	Pennsylvania	5.5	38	Minnesota	2.6
37	Rhode Island	2.7	38	Oregon	2.6
9	South Carolina	7.8	40	Utah	2.5
NA	South Dakota**	NA	41	Idaho	2.4
11	Tennessee	7.5	42	Massachusetts	2.2
16	Texas	6.9	43	Iowa	1.7
40	Utah	2.5	44	Hawaii	1.6
NA	Vermont**	NA	44	New Hampshire	1.6
19	Virginia	6.3	NA	Maine**	NA
32	Washington	3.6	NA	North Dakota**	NA
25	West Virginia	4.9	NA	South Dakota**	NA
32	Wisconsin	3.6	NA	Vermont**	NA
NA	Wyoming**	NA	NA	Wyoming**	NA

District of Columbia 34.4

Source: U.S. Department of Health and Human Services, National Center for Health Statistics "National Vital Statistics Reports" (Vol. 54, No. 13, April 19, 2006)

*By state of residence. Includes legal intervention. Homicide data shown here are collected by the Centers for Disease Control and Prevention based on death certificates and differ from murder data collected by the F.B.I. from other sources. Not age-adjusted.

**Insufficient data to determine a reliable rate.

Age-Adjusted Death Rate by Homicide in 2003

National Rate = 6.0 Deaths per 100,000 Population*

ALPHA ORDER

ALPHA ORDER

RANK	STATE	RATE
4	Alabama	9.7
14	Alaska	6.9
6	Arizona	8.7
12	Arkansas	7.3
15	California	6.8
31	Colorado	4.1
35	Connecticut	3.1
35	Delaware	3.1
19	Florida	6.2
7	Georgia	8.2
44	Hawaii	1.6
41	Idaho	2.4
10	Illinois	7.5
23	Indiana	5.6
43	Iowa	1.8
29	Kansas	4.4
27	Kentucky	4.7
1	Louisiana	13.3
NA	Maine**	NA
3	Maryland	10.2
42	Massachusetts	2.2
17	Michigan	6.5
39	Minnesota	2.5
2	Mississippi	10.6
21	Missouri	5.7
30	Montana	4.2
32	Nebraska	3.6
8	Nevada	8.1
45	New Hampshire	1.5
24	New Jersey	5.1
5	New Mexico	8.8
25	New York	5.0
13	North Carolina	7.0
NA	North Dakota**	NA
28	Ohio	4.6
18	Oklahoma	6.4
39	Oregon	2.5
21	Pennsylvania	5.7
37	Rhode Island	2.6
9	South Carolina	7.8
NA	South Dakota**	NA
10	Tennessee	7.5
16	Texas	6.7
37	Utah	2.6
NA	Vermont**	NA
19	Virginia	6.2
34	Washington	3.5
25	West Virginia	5.0
32	Wisconsin	3.6
NA	Wyoming**	NA

RANK ORDER

RANK	STATE	RATE
1	Louisiana	13.3
2	Mississippi	10.6
3	Maryland	10.2
4	Alabama	9.7
5	New Mexico	8.8
6	Arizona	8.7
7	Georgia	8.2
8	Nevada	8.1
9	South Carolina	7.8
10	Illinois	7.5
10	Tennessee	7.5
12	Arkansas	7.3
13	North Carolina	7.0
14	Alaska	6.9
15	California	6.8
16	Texas	6.7
17	Michigan	6.5
18	Oklahoma	6.4
19	Florida	6.2
19	Virginia	6.2
21	Missouri	5.7
21	Pennsylvania	5.7
23	Indiana	5.6
24	New Jersey	5.1
25	New York	5.0
25	West Virginia	5.0
27	Kentucky	4.7
28	Ohio	4.6
29	Kansas	4.4
30	Montana	4.2
31	Colorado	4.1
32	Nebraska	3.6
32	Wisconsin	3.6
34	Washington	3.5
35	Connecticut	3.1
35	Delaware	3.1
37	Rhode Island	2.6
37	Utah	2.6
39	Minnesota	2.5
39	Oregon	2.5
41	Idaho	2.4
42	Massachusetts	2.2
43	Iowa	1.8
44	Hawaii	1.6
45	New Hampshire	1.5
NA	Maine**	NA
NA	North Dakota**	NA
NA	South Dakota**	NA
NA	Vermont**	NA
NA	Wyoming**	NA
	District of Columbia	31.5

Source: U.S. Department of Health and Human Services, National Center for Health Statistics
   "National Vital Statistics Reports" (Vol. 54, No. 13, April 19, 2006)
*By state of residence. Includes legal intervention. Homicide data shown here are collected by the Centers for
Disease Control and Prevention based on death certificates and differ from murder data collected by the F.B.I. from
other sources. Age-adjusted rates based on the year 2000 standard population.
**Insufficient data to determine a reliable rate.

Deaths by Suicide in 2003

National Total = 31,484 Suicides*

RANK	STATE	SUICIDES	% of USA
22	Alabama	521	1.7%
44	Alaska	124	0.4%
11	Arizona	840	2.7%
30	Arkansas	374	1.2%
1	California	3,397	10.8%
16	Colorado	728	2.3%
36	Connecticut	272	0.9%
47	Delaware	94	0.3%
3	Florida	2,297	7.3%
9	Georgia	972	3.1%
43	Hawaii	131	0.4%
38	Idaho	217	0.7%
8	Illinois	1,011	3.2%
15	Indiana	736	2.3%
31	Iowa	352	1.1%
32	Kansas	347	1.1%
21	Kentucky	567	1.8%
27	Louisiana	461	1.5%
42	Maine	137	0.4%
24	Maryland	491	1.6%
29	Massachusetts	433	1.4%
7	Michigan	1,029	3.3%
23	Minnesota	497	1.6%
34	Mississippi	336	1.1%
17	Missouri	679	2.2%
39	Montana	180	0.6%
40	Nebraska	176	0.6%
28	Nevada	434	1.4%
41	New Hampshire	158	0.5%
20	New Jersey	588	1.9%
33	New Mexico	343	1.1%
5	New York	1,169	3.7%
10	North Carolina	955	3.0%
50	North Dakota	81	0.3%
6	Ohio	1,074	3.4%
25	Oklahoma	476	1.5%
19	Oregon	592	1.9%
4	Pennsylvania	1,340	4.3%
48	Rhode Island	84	0.3%
25	South Carolina	476	1.5%
46	South Dakota	102	0.3%
14	Tennessee	762	2.4%
2	Texas	2,363	7.5%
34	Utah	336	1.1%
49	Vermont	83	0.3%
12	Virginia	808	2.6%
13	Washington	803	2.6%
37	West Virginia	266	0.8%
18	Wisconsin	647	2.1%
45	Wyoming	109	0.3%

RANK	STATE	SUICIDES	% of USA
1	California	3,397	10.8%
2	Texas	2,363	7.5%
3	Florida	2,297	7.3%
4	Pennsylvania	1,340	4.3%
5	New York	1,169	3.7%
6	Ohio	1,074	3.4%
7	Michigan	1,029	3.3%
8	Illinois	1,011	3.2%
9	Georgia	972	3.1%
10	North Carolina	955	3.0%
11	Arizona	840	2.7%
12	Virginia	808	2.6%
13	Washington	803	2.6%
14	Tennessee	762	2.4%
15	Indiana	736	2.3%
16	Colorado	728	2.3%
17	Missouri	679	2.2%
18	Wisconsin	647	2.1%
19	Oregon	592	1.9%
20	New Jersey	588	1.9%
21	Kentucky	567	1.8%
22	Alabama	521	1.7%
23	Minnesota	497	1.6%
24	Maryland	491	1.6%
25	Oklahoma	476	1.5%
25	South Carolina	476	1.5%
27	Louisiana	461	1.5%
28	Nevada	434	1.4%
29	Massachusetts	433	1.4%
30	Arkansas	374	1.2%
31	Iowa	352	1.1%
32	Kansas	347	1.1%
33	New Mexico	343	1.1%
34	Mississippi	336	1.1%
34	Utah	336	1.1%
36	Connecticut	272	0.9%
37	West Virginia	266	0.8%
38	Idaho	217	0.7%
39	Montana	180	0.6%
40	Nebraska	176	0.6%
41	New Hampshire	158	0.5%
42	Maine	137	0.4%
43	Hawaii	131	0.4%
44	Alaska	124	0.4%
45	Wyoming	109	0.3%
46	South Dakota	102	0.3%
47	Delaware	94	0.3%
48	Rhode Island	84	0.3%
49	Vermont	83	0.3%
50	North Dakota	81	0.3%
	District of Columbia	36	0.1%

Source: U.S. Department of Health and Human Services, National Center for Health Statistics
"National Vital Statistics Reports" (Vol. 54, No. 13, April 19, 2006)
*Final data by state of residence.

Death Rate by Suicide in 2003

National Rate = 10.8 Deaths per 100,000 Population*

RANK	STATE	RATE
28	Alabama	11.6
4	Alaska	19.1
9	Arizona	15.1
13	Arkansas	13.7
42	California	9.6
7	Colorado	16.0
46	Connecticut	7.8
29	Delaware	11.5
15	Florida	13.5
32	Georgia	11.2
37	Hawaii	10.4
8	Idaho	15.9
45	Illinois	8.0
24	Indiana	11.9
23	Iowa	12.0
21	Kansas	12.7
12	Kentucky	13.8
38	Louisiana	10.3
36	Maine	10.5
44	Maryland	8.9
49	Massachusetts	6.7
39	Michigan	10.2
41	Minnesota	9.8
27	Mississippi	11.7
24	Missouri	11.9
2	Montana	19.6
40	Nebraska	10.1
3	Nevada	19.4
22	New Hampshire	12.3
48	New Jersey	6.8
5	New Mexico	18.3
50	New York	6.1
31	North Carolina	11.4
20	North Dakota	12.8
43	Ohio	9.4
14	Oklahoma	13.6
6	Oregon	16.6
34	Pennsylvania	10.8
46	Rhode Island	7.8
29	South Carolina	11.5
17	South Dakota	13.3
19	Tennessee	13.0
35	Texas	10.7
11	Utah	14.3
16	Vermont	13.4
33	Virginia	10.9
18	Washington	13.1
10	West Virginia	14.7
26	Wisconsin	11.8
1	Wyoming	21.7

RANK	STATE	RATE
1	Wyoming	21.7
2	Montana	19.6
3	Nevada	19.4
4	Alaska	19.1
5	New Mexico	18.3
6	Oregon	16.6
7	Colorado	16.0
8	Idaho	15.9
9	Arizona	15.1
10	West Virginia	14.7
11	Utah	14.3
12	Kentucky	13.8
13	Arkansas	13.7
14	Oklahoma	13.6
15	Florida	13.5
16	Vermont	13.4
17	South Dakota	13.3
18	Washington	13.1
19	Tennessee	13.0
20	North Dakota	12.8
21	Kansas	12.7
22	New Hampshire	12.3
23	Iowa	12.0
24	Indiana	11.9
24	Missouri	11.9
26	Wisconsin	11.8
27	Mississippi	11.7
28	Alabama	11.6
29	Delaware	11.5
29	South Carolina	11.5
31	North Carolina	11.4
32	Georgia	11.2
33	Virginia	10.9
34	Pennsylvania	10.8
35	Texas	10.7
36	Maine	10.5
37	Hawaii	10.4
38	Louisiana	10.3
39	Michigan	10.2
40	Nebraska	10.1
41	Minnesota	9.8
42	California	9.6
43	Ohio	9.4
44	Maryland	8.9
45	Illinois	8.0
46	Connecticut	7.8
46	Rhode Island	7.8
48	New Jersey	6.8
49	Massachusetts	6.7
50	New York	6.1

	District of Columbia	6.4

Source: U.S. Department of Health and Human Services, National Center for Health Statistics
    "National Vital Statistics Reports" (Vol. 54, No. 13, April 19, 2006)
Final data by state of residence. Not age-adjusted.

Age-Adjusted Death Rate by Suicide in 2003

National Rate = 10.8 Deaths per 100,000 Population*

ALPHA ORDER

RANK	STATE	RATE
30	Alabama	11.4
2	Alaska	20.4
10	Arizona	15.5
12	Arkansas	13.6
41	California	9.8
8	Colorado	16.1
47	Connecticut	7.5
30	Delaware	11.4
16	Florida	12.9
27	Georgia	11.6
37	Hawaii	10.1
6	Idaho	16.2
45	Illinois	8.0
22	Indiana	12.0
26	Iowa	11.7
20	Kansas	12.7
14	Kentucky	13.5
36	Louisiana	10.4
40	Maine	9.9
44	Maryland	8.9
49	Massachusetts	6.5
37	Michigan	10.1
42	Minnesota	9.7
23	Mississippi	11.9
25	Missouri	11.8
4	Montana	19.3
37	Nebraska	10.1
3	Nevada	20.1
23	New Hampshire	11.9
48	New Jersey	6.7
5	New Mexico	18.7
50	New York	5.9
32	North Carolina	11.3
21	North Dakota	12.4
43	Ohio	9.3
12	Oklahoma	13.6
6	Oregon	16.2
35	Pennsylvania	10.5
46	Rhode Island	7.6
29	South Carolina	11.5
14	South Dakota	13.5
19	Tennessee	12.8
33	Texas	11.2
9	Utah	15.6
16	Vermont	12.9
34	Virginia	10.9
16	Washington	12.9
11	West Virginia	14.1
27	Wisconsin	11.6
1	Wyoming	21.8

RANK ORDER

RANK	STATE	RATE
1	Wyoming	21.8
2	Alaska	20.4
3	Nevada	20.1
4	Montana	19.3
5	New Mexico	18.7
6	Idaho	16.2
6	Oregon	16.2
8	Colorado	16.1
9	Utah	15.6
10	Arizona	15.5
11	West Virginia	14.1
12	Arkansas	13.6
12	Oklahoma	13.6
14	Kentucky	13.5
14	South Dakota	13.5
16	Florida	12.9
16	Vermont	12.9
16	Washington	12.9
19	Tennessee	12.8
20	Kansas	12.7
21	North Dakota	12.4
22	Indiana	12.0
23	Mississippi	11.9
23	New Hampshire	11.9
25	Missouri	11.8
26	Iowa	11.7
27	Georgia	11.6
27	Wisconsin	11.6
29	South Carolina	11.5
30	Alabama	11.4
30	Delaware	11.4
32	North Carolina	11.3
33	Texas	11.2
34	Virginia	10.9
35	Pennsylvania	10.5
36	Louisiana	10.4
37	Hawaii	10.1
37	Michigan	10.1
37	Nebraska	10.1
40	Maine	9.9
41	California	9.8
42	Minnesota	9.7
43	Ohio	9.3
44	Maryland	8.9
45	Illinois	8.0
46	Rhode Island	7.6
47	Connecticut	7.5
48	New Jersey	6.7
49	Massachusetts	6.5
50	New York	5.9
	District of Columbia	6.2

Source: U.S. Department of Health and Human Services, National Center for Health Statistics
"National Vital Statistics Reports" (Vol. 54, No. 13, April 19, 2006)
*Final data by state of residence. Age-adjusted rates based on the year 2000 standard population.

Alcohol-Induced Deaths in 2003

National Total = 20,687 Deaths*

ALPHA ORDER

RANK	STATE	DEATHS	% of USA
30	Alabama	218	1.1%
38	Alaska	122	0.6%
9	Arizona	572	2.8%
35	Arkansas	138	0.7%
1	California	3,752	18.1%
11	Colorado	517	2.5%
31	Connecticut	184	0.9%
46	Delaware	66	0.3%
2	Florida	1,485	7.2%
12	Georgia	505	2.4%
50	Hawaii	31	0.1%
36	Idaho	135	0.7%
10	Illinois	568	2.7%
23	Indiana	330	1.6%
33	Iowa	167	0.8%
32	Kansas	173	0.8%
27	Kentucky	241	1.2%
29	Louisiana	227	1.1%
39	Maine	117	0.6%
25	Maryland	283	1.4%
18	Massachusetts	391	1.9%
5	Michigan	673	3.3%
24	Minnesota	304	1.5%
37	Mississippi	134	0.6%
22	Missouri	343	1.7%
41	Montana	109	0.5%
43	Nebraska	92	0.4%
26	Nevada	245	1.2%
42	New Hampshire	95	0.5%
16	New Jersey	439	2.1%
20	New Mexico	360	1.7%
4	New York	1,102	5.3%
7	North Carolina	611	3.0%
44	North Dakota	75	0.4%
8	Ohio	588	2.8%
28	Oklahoma	235	1.1%
13	Oregon	504	2.4%
14	Pennsylvania	490	2.4%
47	Rhode Island	65	0.3%
21	South Carolina	352	1.7%
45	South Dakota	70	0.3%
15	Tennessee	479	2.3%
3	Texas	1,168	5.6%
39	Utah	117	0.6%
48	Vermont	61	0.3%
18	Virginia	391	1.9%
6	Washington	629	3.0%
34	West Virginia	155	0.7%
17	Wisconsin	417	2.0%
49	Wyoming	60	0.3%

RANK ORDER

RANK	STATE	DEATHS	% of USA
1	California	3,752	18.1%
2	Florida	1,485	7.2%
3	Texas	1,168	5.6%
4	New York	1,102	5.3%
5	Michigan	673	3.3%
6	Washington	629	3.0%
7	North Carolina	611	3.0%
8	Ohio	588	2.8%
9	Arizona	572	2.8%
10	Illinois	568	2.7%
11	Colorado	517	2.5%
12	Georgia	505	2.4%
13	Oregon	504	2.4%
14	Pennsylvania	490	2.4%
15	Tennessee	479	2.3%
16	New Jersey	439	2.1%
17	Wisconsin	417	2.0%
18	Massachusetts	391	1.9%
18	Virginia	391	1.9%
20	New Mexico	360	1.7%
21	South Carolina	352	1.7%
22	Missouri	343	1.7%
23	Indiana	330	1.6%
24	Minnesota	304	1.5%
25	Maryland	283	1.4%
26	Nevada	245	1.2%
27	Kentucky	241	1.2%
28	Oklahoma	235	1.1%
29	Louisiana	227	1.1%
30	Alabama	218	1.1%
31	Connecticut	184	0.9%
32	Kansas	173	0.8%
33	Iowa	167	0.8%
34	West Virginia	155	0.7%
35	Arkansas	138	0.7%
36	Idaho	135	0.7%
37	Mississippi	134	0.6%
38	Alaska	122	0.6%
39	Maine	117	0.6%
39	Utah	117	0.6%
41	Montana	109	0.5%
42	New Hampshire	95	0.5%
43	Nebraska	92	0.4%
44	North Dakota	75	0.4%
45	South Dakota	70	0.3%
46	Delaware	66	0.3%
47	Rhode Island	65	0.3%
48	Vermont	61	0.3%
49	Wyoming	60	0.3%
50	Hawaii	31	0.1%
	District of Columbia	102	0.5%

Source: U.S. Department of Health and Human Services, National Center for Health Statistics
   (http://wonder.cdc.gov)
*By state of residence. Includes excessive blood level of alcohol, accidental poisoning by alcohol and the
following alcohol-related causes: psychoses, dependence syndrome, polyneuropathy, cardiomyopathy, gastritis,
chronic liver disease and cirrhosis. Excludes accidents, homicides and other causes indirectly related to alcohol use.

Death Rate by Alcohol-Induced Deaths in 2003

National Rate = 7.1 Deaths per 100,000 Population*

ALPHA ORDER

RANK ORDER

RANK	STATE	RATE		RANK	STATE	RATE
46	Alabama	4.8		1	New Mexico	19.2
2	Alaska	18.8		2	Alaska	18.8
10	Arizona	10.3		3	Oregon	14.1
40	Arkansas	5.1		4	Montana	11.9
9	California	10.6		4	Wyoming	11.9
7	Colorado	11.4		6	North Dakota	11.8
35	Connecticut	5.3		7	Colorado	11.4
20	Delaware	8.1		8	Nevada	10.9
16	Florida	8.7		9	California	10.6
32	Georgia	5.8		10	Arizona	10.3
50	Hawaii	2.5		10	Washington	10.3
12	Idaho	9.9		12	Idaho	9.9
48	Illinois	4.5		13	Vermont	9.8
35	Indiana	5.3		14	South Dakota	9.2
33	Iowa	5.7		15	Maine	8.9
26	Kansas	6.3		16	Florida	8.7
31	Kentucky	5.9		17	West Virginia	8.6
40	Louisiana	5.1		18	South Carolina	8.5
15	Maine	8.9		19	Tennessee	8.2
40	Maryland	5.1		20	Delaware	8.1
27	Massachusetts	6.1		21	Wisconsin	7.6
24	Michigan	6.7		22	New Hampshire	7.4
28	Minnesota	6.0		23	North Carolina	7.3
47	Mississippi	4.6		24	Michigan	6.7
28	Missouri	6.0		24	Oklahoma	6.7
4	Montana	11.9		26	Kansas	6.3
35	Nebraska	5.3		27	Massachusetts	6.1
8	Nevada	10.9		28	Minnesota	6.0
22	New Hampshire	7.4		28	Missouri	6.0
40	New Jersey	5.1		28	Rhode Island	6.0
1	New Mexico	19.2		31	Kentucky	5.9
33	New York	5.7		32	Georgia	5.8
23	North Carolina	7.3		33	Iowa	5.7
6	North Dakota	11.8		33	New York	5.7
40	Ohio	5.1		35	Connecticut	5.3
24	Oklahoma	6.7		35	Indiana	5.3
3	Oregon	14.1		35	Nebraska	5.3
49	Pennsylvania	4.0		35	Texas	5.3
28	Rhode Island	6.0		35	Virginia	5.3
18	South Carolina	8.5		40	Arkansas	5.1
14	South Dakota	9.2		40	Louisiana	5.1
19	Tennessee	8.2		40	Maryland	5.1
35	Texas	5.3		40	New Jersey	5.1
45	Utah	5.0		40	Ohio	5.1
13	Vermont	9.8		45	Utah	5.0
35	Virginia	5.3		46	Alabama	4.8
10	Washington	10.3		47	Mississippi	4.6
17	West Virginia	8.6		48	Illinois	4.5
21	Wisconsin	7.6		49	Pennsylvania	4.0
4	Wyoming	11.9		50	Hawaii	2.5
					District of Columbia	18.3

Source: U.S. Department of Health and Human Services, National Center for Health Statistics
    (http://wonder.cdc.gov)
*By state of residence. Includes excessive blood level of alcohol, accidental poisoning by alcohol and the following alcohol-related causes: psychoses, dependence syndrome, polyneuropathy, cardiomyopathy, gastritis, chronic liver disease and cirrhosis. Excludes accidents, homicides and other causes indirectly related to alcohol use. Not age-adjusted.

Age-Adjusted Death Rate by Alcohol-Induced Deaths in 2003

National Rate = 7.0 Deaths per 100,000 Population*

ALPHA ORDER

RANK	STATE	RATE
47	Alabama	4.6
1	Alaska	21.1
10	Arizona	10.7
44	Arkansas	4.8
7	California	11.1
4	Colorado	11.5
42	Connecticut	4.9
19	Delaware	7.6
16	Florida	8.0
28	Georgia	6.1
50	Hawaii	2.3
11	Idaho	10.1
48	Illinois	4.5
37	Indiana	5.3
36	Iowa	5.4
26	Kansas	6.3
34	Kentucky	5.6
39	Louisiana	5.1
18	Maine	7.7
41	Maryland	5.0
30	Massachusetts	5.8
24	Michigan	6.5
29	Minnesota	5.9
46	Mississippi	4.7
30	Missouri	5.8
8	Montana	11.0
37	Nebraska	5.3
9	Nevada	10.8
23	New Hampshire	6.6
44	New Jersey	4.8
2	New Mexico	18.9
35	New York	5.5
22	North Carolina	7.1
5	North Dakota	11.3
42	Ohio	4.9
24	Oklahoma	6.5
3	Oregon	13.5
49	Pennsylvania	3.7
32	Rhode Island	5.7
15	South Carolina	8.1
13	South Dakota	9.0
17	Tennessee	7.8
32	Texas	5.7
27	Utah	6.2
13	Vermont	9.0
39	Virginia	5.1
11	Washington	10.1
20	West Virginia	7.5
21	Wisconsin	7.3
5	Wyoming	11.3

RANK ORDER

RANK	STATE	RATE
1	Alaska	21.1
2	New Mexico	18.9
3	Oregon	13.5
4	Colorado	11.5
5	North Dakota	11.3
5	Wyoming	11.3
7	California	11.1
8	Montana	11.0
9	Nevada	10.8
10	Arizona	10.7
11	Idaho	10.1
11	Washington	10.1
13	South Dakota	9.0
13	Vermont	9.0
15	South Carolina	8.1
16	Florida	8.0
17	Tennessee	7.8
18	Maine	7.7
19	Delaware	7.6
20	West Virginia	7.5
21	Wisconsin	7.3
22	North Carolina	7.1
23	New Hampshire	6.6
24	Michigan	6.5
24	Oklahoma	6.5
26	Kansas	6.3
27	Utah	6.2
28	Georgia	6.1
29	Minnesota	5.9
30	Massachusetts	5.8
30	Missouri	5.8
32	Rhode Island	5.7
32	Texas	5.7
34	Kentucky	5.6
35	New York	5.5
36	Iowa	5.4
37	Indiana	5.3
37	Nebraska	5.3
39	Louisiana	5.1
39	Virginia	5.1
41	Maryland	5.0
42	Connecticut	4.9
42	Ohio	4.9
44	Arkansas	4.8
44	New Jersey	4.8
46	Mississippi	4.7
47	Alabama	4.6
48	Illinois	4.5
49	Pennsylvania	3.7
50	Hawaii	2.3

District of Columbia   18.2

Source: U.S. Department of Health and Human Services, National Center for Health Statistics
(http://wonder.cdc.gov)
*By state of residence. Includes excessive blood level of alcohol, accidental poisoning by alcohol and the following alcohol-related causes: psychoses, dependence syndrome, polyneuropathy, cardiomyopathy, gastritis, chronic liver disease and cirrhosis. Excludes accidents, homicides and other causes indirectly related to alcohol use. Age-adjusted rates based on the year 2000 standard population.

Occupational Fatalities in 2005

National Total = 5,702 Deaths*

RANK	STATE	DEATHS	% of USA
15	Alabama	128	2.2%
42	Alaska	29	0.5%
23	Arizona	99	1.7%
30	Arkansas	80	1.4%
2	California	453	7.9%
16	Colorado	125	2.2%
36	Connecticut	46	0.8%
48	Delaware	10	0.2%
3	Florida	404	7.1%
6	Georgia	200	3.5%
46	Hawaii	15	0.3%
41	Idaho	35	0.6%
7	Illinois	194	3.4%
12	Indiana	157	2.8%
26	Iowa	88	1.5%
29	Kansas	81	1.4%
18	Kentucky	122	2.1%
22	Louisiana	106	1.9%
46	Maine	15	0.3%
24	Maryland	95	1.7%
31	Massachusetts	75	1.3%
21	Michigan	110	1.9%
27	Minnesota	87	1.5%
19	Mississippi	111	1.9%
9	Missouri	183	3.2%
35	Montana	50	0.9%
40	Nebraska	36	0.6%
33	Nevada	57	1.0%
45	New Hampshire	18	0.3%
19	New Jersey	111	1.9%
39	New Mexico	44	0.8%
4	New York	239	4.2%
11	North Carolina	165	2.9%
44	North Dakota	22	0.4%
10	Ohio	168	2.9%
24	Oklahoma	95	1.7%
32	Oregon	65	1.1%
5	Pennsylvania	223	3.9%
50	Rhode Island	6	0.1%
14	South Carolina	133	2.3%
43	South Dakota	28	0.5%
13	Tennessee	139	2.4%
1	Texas	495	8.7%
34	Utah	54	0.9%
49	Vermont	7	0.1%
8	Virginia	186	3.3%
28	Washington	83	1.5%
36	West Virginia	46	0.8%
16	Wisconsin	125	2.2%
36	Wyoming	46	0.8%

RANK	STATE	DEATHS	% of USA
1	Texas	495	8.7%
2	California	453	7.9%
3	Florida	404	7.1%
4	New York	239	4.2%
5	Pennsylvania	223	3.9%
6	Georgia	200	3.5%
7	Illinois	194	3.4%
8	Virginia	186	3.3%
9	Missouri	183	3.2%
10	Ohio	168	2.9%
11	North Carolina	165	2.9%
12	Indiana	157	2.8%
13	Tennessee	139	2.4%
14	South Carolina	133	2.3%
15	Alabama	128	2.2%
16	Colorado	125	2.2%
16	Wisconsin	125	2.2%
18	Kentucky	122	2.1%
19	Mississippi	111	1.9%
19	New Jersey	111	1.9%
21	Michigan	110	1.9%
22	Louisiana	106	1.9%
23	Arizona	99	1.7%
24	Maryland	95	1.7%
24	Oklahoma	95	1.7%
26	Iowa	88	1.5%
27	Minnesota	87	1.5%
28	Washington	83	1.5%
29	Kansas	81	1.4%
30	Arkansas	80	1.4%
31	Massachusetts	75	1.3%
32	Oregon	65	1.1%
33	Nevada	57	1.0%
34	Utah	54	0.9%
35	Montana	50	0.9%
36	Connecticut	46	0.8%
36	West Virginia	46	0.8%
36	Wyoming	46	0.8%
39	New Mexico	44	0.8%
40	Nebraska	36	0.6%
41	Idaho	35	0.6%
42	Alaska	29	0.5%
43	South Dakota	28	0.5%
44	North Dakota	22	0.4%
45	New Hampshire	18	0.3%
46	Hawaii	15	0.3%
46	Maine	15	0.3%
48	Delaware	10	0.2%
49	Vermont	7	0.1%
50	Rhode Island	6	0.1%
	District of Columbia	12	0.2%

Source: U.S. Department of Labor, Bureau of Labor Statistics
"National Census of Fatal Occupational Injuries in 2005" (press release, August 10, 2006)
*Includes one fatality that occurred within the territorial boundaries of the United States but for which a state of incident could not be determined.

Occupational Fatality Rate in 2005

National Rate = 4.0 Deaths per 100,000 Workers*

ALPHA ORDER

RANK	STATE	RATE
10	Alabama	6.2
3	Alaska	9.2
31	Arizona	3.7
10	Arkansas	6.2
38	California	2.7
17	Colorado	5.2
38	Connecticut	2.7
44	Delaware	2.4
21	Florida	4.9
26	Georgia	4.6
44	Hawaii	2.4
21	Idaho	4.9
35	Illinois	3.2
17	Indiana	5.2
15	Iowa	5.6
13	Kansas	5.8
7	Kentucky	6.5
16	Louisiana	5.5
48	Maine	2.2
34	Maryland	3.4
46	Massachusetts	2.3
46	Michigan	2.3
36	Minnesota	3.1
4	Mississippi	9.0
8	Missouri	6.4
2	Montana	10.5
30	Nebraska	3.8
21	Nevada	4.9
43	New Hampshire	2.5
42	New Jersey	2.6
20	New Mexico	5.0
38	New York	2.7
29	North Carolina	4.0
9	North Dakota	6.3
37	Ohio	3.0
14	Oklahoma	5.7
31	Oregon	3.7
31	Pennsylvania	3.7
50	Rhode Island	1.1
5	South Carolina	6.9
6	South Dakota	6.7
19	Tennessee	5.1
25	Texas	4.7
27	Utah	4.4
49	Vermont	2.0
21	Virginia	4.9
38	Washington	2.7
12	West Virginia	6.0
28	Wisconsin	4.3
1	Wyoming	16.8

RANK ORDER

RANK	STATE	RATE
1	Wyoming	16.8
2	Montana	10.5
3	Alaska	9.2
4	Mississippi	9.0
5	South Carolina	6.9
6	South Dakota	6.7
7	Kentucky	6.5
8	Missouri	6.4
9	North Dakota	6.3
10	Alabama	6.2
10	Arkansas	6.2
12	West Virginia	6.0
13	Kansas	5.8
14	Oklahoma	5.7
15	Iowa	5.6
16	Louisiana	5.5
17	Colorado	5.2
17	Indiana	5.2
19	Tennessee	5.1
20	New Mexico	5.0
21	Florida	4.9
21	Idaho	4.9
21	Nevada	4.9
21	Virginia	4.9
25	Texas	4.7
26	Georgia	4.6
27	Utah	4.4
28	Wisconsin	4.3
29	North Carolina	4.0
30	Nebraska	3.8
31	Arizona	3.7
31	Oregon	3.7
31	Pennsylvania	3.7
34	Maryland	3.4
35	Illinois	3.2
36	Minnesota	3.1
37	Ohio	3.0
38	California	2.7
38	Connecticut	2.7
38	New York	2.7
38	Washington	2.7
42	New Jersey	2.6
43	New Hampshire	2.5
44	Delaware	2.4
44	Hawaii	2.4
46	Massachusetts	2.3
46	Michigan	2.3
48	Maine	2.2
49	Vermont	2.0
50	Rhode Island	1.1

District of Columbia 4.3

Source: Morgan Quitno Press using data from U.S. Department of Labor, Bureau of Labor Statistics
"National Census of Fatal Occupational Injuries in 2005" (press release, August 10, 2006)
*Based on employed civilian labor force.

III. FACILITIES

186   Community Hospitals in 2005
187   Rate of Community Hospitals in 2005
188   Community Hospitals per 1,000 Square Miles in 2005
189   Community Hospitals in Urban Areas in 2005
190   Percent of Community Hospitals in Urban Areas in 2005
191   Community Hospitals in Rural Areas in 2005
192   Percent of Community Hospitals in Rural Areas in 2005
193   Nongovernment Not-For-Profit Hospitals in 2005
194   Investor-Owned (For-Profit) Hospitals in 2005
195   State and Local Government-Owned Hospitals in 2005
196   Beds in Community Hospitals in 2005
197   Rate of Beds in Community Hospitals in 2005
198   Average Number of Beds per Community Hospital in 2005
199   Admissions to Community Hospitals in 2005
200   Inpatient Days in Community Hospitals in 2005
201   Average Daily Census in Community Hospitals in 2005
202   Average Stay in Community Hospitals in 2005
203   Occupancy Rate in Community Hospitals in 2005
204   Outpatient Visits to Community Hospitals in 2005
205   Emergency Outpatient Visits to Community Hospitals in 2005
206   Surgical Operations in Community Hospitals in 2005
207   Medicare and Medicaid Certified Facilities in 2007
208   Medicare and Medicaid Certified Hospitals in 2007
209   Beds in Medicare and Medicaid Certified Hospitals in 2007
210   Medicare and Medicaid Certified Children's Hospitals in 2007
211   Beds in Medicare and Medicaid Certified Children's Hospitals in 2007
212   Medicare and Medicaid Certified Rehabilitation Hospitals in 2007
213   Beds in Medicare and Medicaid Certified Rehabilitation Hospitals in 2007
214   Medicare and Medicaid Certified Psychiatric Hospitals in 2007
215   Beds in Medicare and Medicaid Certified Psychiatric Hospitals in 2007
216   Medicare and Medicaid Certified Outpatient Surgery Centers in 2007
217   Medicare and Medicaid Certified Community Mental Health Centers in 2007
218   Medicare and Medicaid Certified Outpatient Physical Therapy Facilities in 2007
219   Medicare and Medicaid Certified Rural Health Clinics in 2007
220   Medicare and Medicaid Certified Home Health Agencies in 2007
221   Medicare and Medicaid Certified Hospices in 2007
222   Hospice Patients in Residential Facilities in 2007
223   Medicare and Medicaid Certified Nursing Care Facilities in 2007
224   Beds in Medicare and Medicaid Certified Nursing Care Facilities in 2007
225   Rate of Beds in Medicare and Medicaid Certified Nursing Care Facilities in 2007
226   Nursing Home Occupancy Rate in 2004
227   Nursing Home Resident Rate in 2004
228   Nursing Home Population in 2004
229   Health Care Establishments in 2004

Community Hospitals in 2005

National Total = 4,936 Hospitals*

ALPHA ORDER

RANK	STATE	HOSPITALS	% of USA
20	Alabama	109	2.2%
47	Alaska	22	0.4%
30	Arizona	67	1.4%
26	Arkansas	85	1.7%
2	California	357	7.2%
29	Colorado	71	1.4%
42	Connecticut	36	0.7%
50	Delaware	6	0.1%
3	Florida	205	4.2%
8	Georgia	149	3.0%
45	Hawaii	25	0.5%
39	Idaho	39	0.8%
5	Illinois	191	3.9%
18	Indiana	113	2.3%
16	Iowa	116	2.4%
11	Kansas	131	2.7%
21	Kentucky	105	2.1%
13	Louisiana	128	2.6%
40	Maine	37	0.7%
36	Maryland	50	1.0%
27	Massachusetts	80	1.6%
9	Michigan	146	3.0%
10	Minnesota	133	2.7%
22	Mississippi	94	1.9%
15	Missouri	119	2.4%
34	Montana	54	1.1%
23	Nebraska	87	1.8%
43	Nevada	32	0.6%
44	New Hampshire	28	0.6%
27	New Jersey	80	1.6%
40	New Mexico	37	0.7%
4	New York	203	4.1%
17	North Carolina	115	2.3%
38	North Dakota	40	0.8%
7	Ohio	170	3.4%
19	Oklahoma	110	2.2%
32	Oregon	58	1.2%
5	Pennsylvania	191	3.9%
49	Rhode Island	11	0.2%
31	South Carolina	63	1.3%
35	South Dakota	52	1.1%
12	Tennessee	130	2.6%
1	Texas	415	8.4%
37	Utah	43	0.9%
48	Vermont	14	0.3%
23	Virginia	87	1.8%
25	Washington	86	1.7%
33	West Virginia	57	1.2%
14	Wisconsin	124	2.5%
46	Wyoming	24	0.5%

RANK ORDER

RANK	STATE	HOSPITALS	% of USA
1	Texas	415	8.4%
2	California	357	7.2%
3	Florida	205	4.2%
4	New York	203	4.1%
5	Illinois	191	3.9%
5	Pennsylvania	191	3.9%
7	Ohio	170	3.4%
8	Georgia	149	3.0%
9	Michigan	146	3.0%
10	Minnesota	133	2.7%
11	Kansas	131	2.7%
12	Tennessee	130	2.6%
13	Louisiana	128	2.6%
14	Wisconsin	124	2.5%
15	Missouri	119	2.4%
16	Iowa	116	2.4%
17	North Carolina	115	2.3%
18	Indiana	113	2.3%
19	Oklahoma	110	2.2%
20	Alabama	109	2.2%
21	Kentucky	105	2.1%
22	Mississippi	94	1.9%
23	Nebraska	87	1.8%
23	Virginia	87	1.8%
25	Washington	86	1.7%
26	Arkansas	85	1.7%
27	Massachusetts	80	1.6%
27	New Jersey	80	1.6%
29	Colorado	71	1.4%
30	Arizona	67	1.4%
31	South Carolina	63	1.3%
32	Oregon	58	1.2%
33	West Virginia	57	1.2%
34	Montana	54	1.1%
35	South Dakota	52	1.1%
36	Maryland	50	1.0%
37	Utah	43	0.9%
38	North Dakota	40	0.8%
39	Idaho	39	0.8%
40	Maine	37	0.7%
40	New Mexico	37	0.7%
42	Connecticut	36	0.7%
43	Nevada	32	0.6%
44	New Hampshire	28	0.6%
45	Hawaii	25	0.5%
46	Wyoming	24	0.5%
47	Alaska	22	0.4%
48	Vermont	14	0.3%
49	Rhode Island	11	0.2%
50	Delaware	6	0.1%
	District of Columbia	11	0.2%

Source: American Hospital Association (Chicago, IL)
    "Hospital Statistics" (2007 edition)
*Community hospitals are all nonfederal, short-term, general and special hospitals whose facilities and services are available to the public.

Rate of Community Hospitals in 2005

National Rate = 1.7 Community Hospitals per 100,000 Population*

<table>
<tr><td colspan="3">ALPHA ORDER</td><td colspan="3">RANK ORDER</td></tr>
<tr><th>RANK</th><th>STATE</th><th>RATE</th><th>RANK</th><th>STATE</th><th>RATE</th></tr>
<tr><td>18</td><td>Alabama</td><td>2.4</td><td>1</td><td>South Dakota</td><td>6.7</td></tr>
<tr><td>8</td><td>Alaska</td><td>3.3</td><td>2</td><td>North Dakota</td><td>6.3</td></tr>
<tr><td>43</td><td>Arizona</td><td>1.1</td><td>3</td><td>Montana</td><td>5.8</td></tr>
<tr><td>10</td><td>Arkansas</td><td>3.1</td><td>4</td><td>Nebraska</td><td>4.9</td></tr>
<tr><td>45</td><td>California</td><td>1.0</td><td>5</td><td>Kansas</td><td>4.8</td></tr>
<tr><td>31</td><td>Colorado</td><td>1.5</td><td>6</td><td>Wyoming</td><td>4.7</td></tr>
<tr><td>45</td><td>Connecticut</td><td>1.0</td><td>7</td><td>Iowa</td><td>3.9</td></tr>
<tr><td>50</td><td>Delaware</td><td>0.7</td><td>8</td><td>Alaska</td><td>3.3</td></tr>
<tr><td>40</td><td>Florida</td><td>1.2</td><td>9</td><td>Mississippi</td><td>3.2</td></tr>
<tr><td>29</td><td>Georgia</td><td>1.6</td><td>10</td><td>Arkansas</td><td>3.1</td></tr>
<tr><td>24</td><td>Hawaii</td><td>2.0</td><td>10</td><td>Oklahoma</td><td>3.1</td></tr>
<tr><td>15</td><td>Idaho</td><td>2.7</td><td>10</td><td>West Virginia</td><td>3.1</td></tr>
<tr><td>31</td><td>Illinois</td><td>1.5</td><td>13</td><td>Louisiana</td><td>2.8</td></tr>
<tr><td>26</td><td>Indiana</td><td>1.8</td><td>13</td><td>Maine</td><td>2.8</td></tr>
<tr><td>7</td><td>Iowa</td><td>3.9</td><td>15</td><td>Idaho</td><td>2.7</td></tr>
<tr><td>5</td><td>Kansas</td><td>4.8</td><td>16</td><td>Minnesota</td><td>2.6</td></tr>
<tr><td>17</td><td>Kentucky</td><td>2.5</td><td>17</td><td>Kentucky</td><td>2.5</td></tr>
<tr><td>13</td><td>Louisiana</td><td>2.8</td><td>18</td><td>Alabama</td><td>2.4</td></tr>
<tr><td>13</td><td>Maine</td><td>2.8</td><td>19</td><td>Tennessee</td><td>2.2</td></tr>
<tr><td>48</td><td>Maryland</td><td>0.9</td><td>19</td><td>Vermont</td><td>2.2</td></tr>
<tr><td>40</td><td>Massachusetts</td><td>1.2</td><td>19</td><td>Wisconsin</td><td>2.2</td></tr>
<tr><td>36</td><td>Michigan</td><td>1.4</td><td>22</td><td>Missouri</td><td>2.1</td></tr>
<tr><td>16</td><td>Minnesota</td><td>2.6</td><td>22</td><td>New Hampshire</td><td>2.1</td></tr>
<tr><td>9</td><td>Mississippi</td><td>3.2</td><td>24</td><td>Hawaii</td><td>2.0</td></tr>
<tr><td>22</td><td>Missouri</td><td>2.1</td><td>25</td><td>New Mexico</td><td>1.9</td></tr>
<tr><td>3</td><td>Montana</td><td>5.8</td><td>26</td><td>Indiana</td><td>1.8</td></tr>
<tr><td>4</td><td>Nebraska</td><td>4.9</td><td>26</td><td>Texas</td><td>1.8</td></tr>
<tr><td>38</td><td>Nevada</td><td>1.3</td><td>28</td><td>Utah</td><td>1.7</td></tr>
<tr><td>22</td><td>New Hampshire</td><td>2.1</td><td>29</td><td>Georgia</td><td>1.6</td></tr>
<tr><td>48</td><td>New Jersey</td><td>0.9</td><td>29</td><td>Oregon</td><td>1.6</td></tr>
<tr><td>25</td><td>New Mexico</td><td>1.9</td><td>31</td><td>Colorado</td><td>1.5</td></tr>
<tr><td>43</td><td>New York</td><td>1.1</td><td>31</td><td>Illinois</td><td>1.5</td></tr>
<tr><td>38</td><td>North Carolina</td><td>1.3</td><td>31</td><td>Ohio</td><td>1.5</td></tr>
<tr><td>2</td><td>North Dakota</td><td>6.3</td><td>31</td><td>Pennsylvania</td><td>1.5</td></tr>
<tr><td>31</td><td>Ohio</td><td>1.5</td><td>31</td><td>South Carolina</td><td>1.5</td></tr>
<tr><td>10</td><td>Oklahoma</td><td>3.1</td><td>36</td><td>Michigan</td><td>1.4</td></tr>
<tr><td>29</td><td>Oregon</td><td>1.6</td><td>36</td><td>Washington</td><td>1.4</td></tr>
<tr><td>31</td><td>Pennsylvania</td><td>1.5</td><td>38</td><td>Nevada</td><td>1.3</td></tr>
<tr><td>45</td><td>Rhode Island</td><td>1.0</td><td>38</td><td>North Carolina</td><td>1.3</td></tr>
<tr><td>31</td><td>South Carolina</td><td>1.5</td><td>40</td><td>Florida</td><td>1.2</td></tr>
<tr><td>1</td><td>South Dakota</td><td>6.7</td><td>40</td><td>Massachusetts</td><td>1.2</td></tr>
<tr><td>19</td><td>Tennessee</td><td>2.2</td><td>40</td><td>Virginia</td><td>1.2</td></tr>
<tr><td>26</td><td>Texas</td><td>1.8</td><td>43</td><td>Arizona</td><td>1.1</td></tr>
<tr><td>28</td><td>Utah</td><td>1.7</td><td>43</td><td>New York</td><td>1.1</td></tr>
<tr><td>19</td><td>Vermont</td><td>2.2</td><td>45</td><td>California</td><td>1.0</td></tr>
<tr><td>40</td><td>Virginia</td><td>1.2</td><td>45</td><td>Connecticut</td><td>1.0</td></tr>
<tr><td>36</td><td>Washington</td><td>1.4</td><td>45</td><td>Rhode Island</td><td>1.0</td></tr>
<tr><td>10</td><td>West Virginia</td><td>3.1</td><td>48</td><td>Maryland</td><td>0.9</td></tr>
<tr><td>19</td><td>Wisconsin</td><td>2.2</td><td>48</td><td>New Jersey</td><td>0.9</td></tr>
<tr><td>6</td><td>Wyoming</td><td>4.7</td><td>50</td><td>Delaware</td><td>0.7</td></tr>
<tr><td></td><td></td><td></td><td></td><td>District of Columbia</td><td>1.9</td></tr>
</table>

Source: Morgan Quitno Press using data from American Hospital Association (Chicago, IL)
    "Hospital Statistics" (2007 edition)
*Community hospitals are all nonfederal, short-term, general and special hospitals whose facilities and services are available to the public.

Community Hospitals per 1,000 Square Miles in 2005

National Rate = 1.3 Community Hospitals*

ALPHA ORDER

RANK ORDER

RANK	STATE	RATE	RANK	STATE	RATE
21	Alabama	2.1	1	New Jersey	9.2
50	Alaska**	0.0	2	Massachusetts	7.6
41	Arizona	0.6	3	Rhode Island	7.1
29	Arkansas	1.6	4	Connecticut	6.5
20	California	2.2	5	Pennsylvania	4.1
39	Colorado	0.7	6	Maryland	4.0
4	Connecticut	6.5	7	Ohio	3.8
17	Delaware	2.4	8	New York	3.7
10	Florida	3.1	9	Illinois	3.3
15	Georgia	2.5	10	Florida	3.1
19	Hawaii	2.3	10	Indiana	3.1
44	Idaho	0.5	10	Tennessee	3.1
9	Illinois	3.3	13	New Hampshire	3.0
10	Indiana	3.1	14	Kentucky	2.6
21	Iowa	2.1	15	Georgia	2.5
29	Kansas	1.6	15	Louisiana	2.5
14	Kentucky	2.6	17	Delaware	2.4
15	Louisiana	2.5	17	West Virginia	2.4
38	Maine	1.0	19	Hawaii	2.3
6	Maryland	4.0	20	California	2.2
2	Massachusetts	7.6	21	Alabama	2.1
32	Michigan	1.5	21	Iowa	2.1
32	Minnesota	1.5	21	North Carolina	2.1
26	Mississippi	1.9	24	South Carolina	2.0
28	Missouri	1.7	24	Virginia	2.0
46	Montana	0.4	26	Mississippi	1.9
37	Nebraska	1.1	26	Wisconsin	1.9
47	Nevada	0.3	28	Missouri	1.7
13	New Hampshire	3.0	29	Arkansas	1.6
1	New Jersey	9.2	29	Kansas	1.6
47	New Mexico	0.3	29	Oklahoma	1.6
8	New York	3.7	32	Michigan	1.5
21	North Carolina	2.1	32	Minnesota	1.5
41	North Dakota	0.6	32	Texas	1.5
7	Ohio	3.8	32	Vermont	1.5
29	Oklahoma	1.6	36	Washington	1.2
41	Oregon	0.6	37	Nebraska	1.1
5	Pennsylvania	4.1	38	Maine	1.0
3	Rhode Island	7.1	39	Colorado	0.7
24	South Carolina	2.0	39	South Dakota	0.7
39	South Dakota	0.7	41	Arizona	0.6
10	Tennessee	3.1	41	North Dakota	0.6
32	Texas	1.5	41	Oregon	0.6
44	Utah	0.5	44	Idaho	0.5
32	Vermont	1.5	44	Utah	0.5
24	Virginia	2.0	46	Montana	0.4
36	Washington	1.2	47	Nevada	0.3
17	West Virginia	2.4	47	New Mexico	0.3
26	Wisconsin	1.9	49	Wyoming	0.2
49	Wyoming	0.2	50	Alaska**	0.0

District of Columbia***   NA

Source: Morgan Quitno Press using data from American Hospital Association (Chicago, IL)
     "Hospital Statistics" (2007 edition)

*Based on land and water area figures. Community hospitals are nonfederal short-term general and other special hospitals, whose facilities and services are available to the public.

**Alaska has 22 community hospitals for its 663,267 square miles.

***The District of Columbia has 11 community hospitals for its 68 square miles.

Community Hospitals in Urban Areas in 2005

National Total = 2,927 Hospitals*

ALPHA ORDER

RANK	STATE	HOSPITALS	% of USA
17	Alabama	60	2.0%
47	Alaska	5	0.2%
21	Arizona	51	1.7%
27	Arkansas	35	1.2%
1	California	323	11.0%
27	Colorado	35	1.2%
30	Connecticut	31	1.1%
48	Delaware	4	0.1%
3	Florida	175	6.0%
9	Georgia	84	2.9%
41	Hawaii	13	0.4%
40	Idaho	14	0.5%
6	Illinois	127	4.3%
14	Indiana	72	2.5%
29	Iowa	32	1.1%
31	Kansas	30	1.0%
25	Kentucky	41	1.4%
11	Louisiana	78	2.7%
38	Maine	15	0.5%
24	Maryland	44	1.5%
11	Massachusetts	78	2.7%
8	Michigan	87	3.0%
22	Minnesota	50	1.7%
33	Mississippi	27	0.9%
16	Missouri	66	2.3%
45	Montana	6	0.2%
37	Nebraska	17	0.6%
36	Nevada	22	0.8%
42	New Hampshire	11	0.4%
10	New Jersey	80	2.7%
38	New Mexico	15	0.5%
4	New York	163	5.6%
19	North Carolina	56	1.9%
45	North Dakota	6	0.2%
7	Ohio	116	4.0%
23	Oklahoma	45	1.5%
32	Oregon	29	1.0%
5	Pennsylvania	143	4.9%
42	Rhode Island	11	0.4%
26	South Carolina	39	1.3%
44	South Dakota	10	0.3%
13	Tennessee	74	2.5%
2	Texas	266	9.1%
34	Utah	25	0.9%
49	Vermont	2	0.1%
18	Virginia	57	1.9%
20	Washington	52	1.8%
34	West Virginia	25	0.9%
15	Wisconsin	67	2.3%
49	Wyoming	2	0.1%

RANK ORDER

RANK	STATE	HOSPITALS	% of USA
1	California	323	11.0%
2	Texas	266	9.1%
3	Florida	175	6.0%
4	New York	163	5.6%
5	Pennsylvania	143	4.9%
6	Illinois	127	4.3%
7	Ohio	116	4.0%
8	Michigan	87	3.0%
9	Georgia	84	2.9%
10	New Jersey	80	2.7%
11	Louisiana	78	2.7%
11	Massachusetts	78	2.7%
13	Tennessee	74	2.5%
14	Indiana	72	2.5%
15	Wisconsin	67	2.3%
16	Missouri	66	2.3%
17	Alabama	60	2.0%
18	Virginia	57	1.9%
19	North Carolina	56	1.9%
20	Washington	52	1.8%
21	Arizona	51	1.7%
22	Minnesota	50	1.7%
23	Oklahoma	45	1.5%
24	Maryland	44	1.5%
25	Kentucky	41	1.4%
26	South Carolina	39	1.3%
27	Arkansas	35	1.2%
27	Colorado	35	1.2%
29	Iowa	32	1.1%
30	Connecticut	31	1.1%
31	Kansas	30	1.0%
32	Oregon	29	1.0%
33	Mississippi	27	0.9%
34	Utah	25	0.9%
34	West Virginia	25	0.9%
36	Nevada	22	0.8%
37	Nebraska	17	0.6%
38	Maine	15	0.5%
38	New Mexico	15	0.5%
40	Idaho	14	0.5%
41	Hawaii	13	0.4%
42	New Hampshire	11	0.4%
42	Rhode Island	11	0.4%
44	South Dakota	10	0.3%
45	Montana	6	0.2%
45	North Dakota	6	0.2%
47	Alaska	5	0.2%
48	Delaware	4	0.1%
49	Vermont	2	0.1%
49	Wyoming	2	0.1%
	District of Columbia	11	0.4%

Source: American Hospital Association (Chicago, IL)
"Hospital Statistics" (2007 edition)
*Community hospitals are all nonfederal, short-term, general and special hospitals whose facilities and services are available to the public. Urban is defined as any area inside a metropolitan statistical area as defined by the U.S. Office of Management and Budget.

Percent of Community Hospitals in Urban Areas in 2005

National Percent = 59.3% of Community Hospitals*

RANK	STATE	PERCENT
26	Alabama	55.0
44	Alaska	22.7
9	Arizona	76.1
33	Arkansas	41.2
4	California	90.5
30	Colorado	49.3
6	Connecticut	86.1
13	Delaware	66.7
7	Florida	85.4
24	Georgia	56.4
28	Hawaii	52.0
40	Idaho	35.9
14	Illinois	66.5
17	Indiana	63.7
42	Iowa	27.6
43	Kansas	22.9
38	Kentucky	39.0
19	Louisiana	60.9
35	Maine	40.5
5	Maryland	88.0
3	Massachusetts	97.5
21	Michigan	59.6
39	Minnesota	37.6
41	Mississippi	28.7
25	Missouri	55.5
49	Montana	11.1
45	Nebraska	19.5
11	Nevada	68.8
37	New Hampshire	39.3
1	New Jersey	100.0
35	New Mexico	40.5
8	New York	80.3
31	North Carolina	48.7
47	North Dakota	15.0
12	Ohio	68.2
34	Oklahoma	40.9
29	Oregon	50.0
10	Pennsylvania	74.9
1	Rhode Island	100.0
18	South Carolina	61.9
46	South Dakota	19.2
23	Tennessee	56.9
16	Texas	64.1
22	Utah	58.1
48	Vermont	14.3
15	Virginia	65.5
20	Washington	60.5
32	West Virginia	43.9
27	Wisconsin	54.0
50	Wyoming	8.3

RANK	STATE	PERCENT
1	New Jersey	100.0
1	Rhode Island	100.0
3	Massachusetts	97.5
4	California	90.5
5	Maryland	88.0
6	Connecticut	86.1
7	Florida	85.4
8	New York	80.3
9	Arizona	76.1
10	Pennsylvania	74.9
11	Nevada	68.8
12	Ohio	68.2
13	Delaware	66.7
14	Illinois	66.5
15	Virginia	65.5
16	Texas	64.1
17	Indiana	63.7
18	South Carolina	61.9
19	Louisiana	60.9
20	Washington	60.5
21	Michigan	59.6
22	Utah	58.1
23	Tennessee	56.9
24	Georgia	56.4
25	Missouri	55.5
26	Alabama	55.0
27	Wisconsin	54.0
28	Hawaii	52.0
29	Oregon	50.0
30	Colorado	49.3
31	North Carolina	48.7
32	West Virginia	43.9
33	Arkansas	41.2
34	Oklahoma	40.9
35	Maine	40.5
35	New Mexico	40.5
37	New Hampshire	39.3
38	Kentucky	39.0
39	Minnesota	37.6
40	Idaho	35.9
41	Mississippi	28.7
42	Iowa	27.6
43	Kansas	22.9
44	Alaska	22.7
45	Nebraska	19.5
46	South Dakota	19.2
47	North Dakota	15.0
48	Vermont	14.3
49	Montana	11.1
50	Wyoming	8.3

| | District of Columbia | 100.0 |

Source: Morgan Quitno Press using data from American Hospital Association (Chicago, IL)
"Hospital Statistics" (2007 edition)

Community hospitals are all nonfederal, short-term, general and special hospitals whose facilities and services are available to the public. Urban is defined as any area inside a metropolitan statistical area as defined by the U.S. Office of Management and Budget.

Community Hospitals in Rural Areas in 2005

National Total = 2,009 Hospitals*

ALPHA ORDER					RANK ORDER			
RANK	STATE		HOSPITALS	% of USA	RANK	STATE	HOSPITALS	% of USA
19	Alabama		49	2.4%	1	Texas	149	7.4%
39	Alaska		17	0.8%	2	Kansas	101	5.0%
41	Arizona		16	0.8%	3	Iowa	84	4.2%
17	Arkansas		50	2.5%	4	Minnesota	83	4.1%
26	California		34	1.7%	5	Nebraska	70	3.5%
25	Colorado		36	1.8%	6	Mississippi	67	3.3%
46	Connecticut		5	0.2%	7	Georgia	65	3.2%
47	Delaware		2	0.1%	7	Oklahoma	65	3.2%
30	Florida		30	1.5%	9	Illinois	64	3.2%
7	Georgia		65	3.2%	9	Kentucky	64	3.2%
42	Hawaii		12	0.6%	11	Michigan	59	2.9%
33	Idaho		25	1.2%	11	North Carolina	59	2.9%
9	Illinois		64	3.2%	13	Wisconsin	57	2.8%
23	Indiana		41	2.0%	14	Tennessee	56	2.8%
3	Iowa		84	4.2%	15	Ohio	54	2.7%
2	Kansas		101	5.0%	16	Missouri	53	2.6%
9	Kentucky		64	3.2%	17	Arkansas	50	2.5%
17	Louisiana		50	2.5%	17	Louisiana	50	2.5%
35	Maine		22	1.1%	19	Alabama	49	2.4%
45	Maryland		6	0.3%	20	Montana	48	2.4%
47	Massachusetts		2	0.1%	20	Pennsylvania	48	2.4%
11	Michigan		59	2.9%	22	South Dakota	42	2.1%
4	Minnesota		83	4.1%	23	Indiana	41	2.0%
6	Mississippi		67	3.3%	24	New York	40	2.0%
16	Missouri		53	2.6%	25	Colorado	36	1.8%
20	Montana		48	2.4%	26	California	34	1.7%
5	Nebraska		70	3.5%	26	North Dakota	34	1.7%
44	Nevada		10	0.5%	26	Washington	34	1.7%
39	New Hampshire		17	0.8%	29	West Virginia	32	1.6%
49	New Jersey		0	0.0%	30	Florida	30	1.5%
35	New Mexico		22	1.1%	30	Virginia	30	1.5%
24	New York		40	2.0%	32	Oregon	29	1.4%
11	North Carolina		59	2.9%	33	Idaho	25	1.2%
26	North Dakota		34	1.7%	34	South Carolina	24	1.2%
15	Ohio		54	2.7%	35	Maine	22	1.1%
7	Oklahoma		65	3.2%	35	New Mexico	22	1.1%
32	Oregon		29	1.4%	35	Wyoming	22	1.1%
20	Pennsylvania		48	2.4%	38	Utah	18	0.9%
49	Rhode Island		0	0.0%	39	Alaska	17	0.8%
34	South Carolina		24	1.2%	39	New Hampshire	17	0.8%
22	South Dakota		42	2.1%	41	Arizona	16	0.8%
14	Tennessee		56	2.8%	42	Hawaii	12	0.6%
1	Texas		149	7.4%	42	Vermont	12	0.6%
38	Utah		18	0.9%	44	Nevada	10	0.5%
42	Vermont		12	0.6%	45	Maryland	6	0.3%
30	Virginia		30	1.5%	46	Connecticut	5	0.2%
26	Washington		34	1.7%	47	Delaware	2	0.1%
29	West Virginia		32	1.6%	47	Massachusetts	2	0.1%
13	Wisconsin		57	2.8%	49	New Jersey	0	0.0%
35	Wyoming		22	1.1%	49	Rhode Island	0	0.0%
						District of Columbia	0	0.0%

Source: American Hospital Association (Chicago, IL)
        "Hospital Statistics" (2007 edition)

*Community hospitals are all nonfederal, short-term, general and special hospitals whose facilities and services are available to the public. Rural is defined as any area outside a metropolitan statistical area as defined by the U.S. Office of Management and Budget.

Percent of Community Hospitals in Rural Areas in 2005

National Percent = 40.7% of Community Hospitals*

ALPHA ORDER

RANK	STATE	PERCENT
25	Alabama	45.0
7	Alaska	77.3
42	Arizona	23.9
18	Arkansas	58.8
47	California	9.5
21	Colorado	50.7
45	Connecticut	13.9
38	Delaware	33.3
44	Florida	14.6
27	Georgia	43.6
23	Hawaii	48.0
11	Idaho	64.1
37	Illinois	33.5
34	Indiana	36.3
9	Iowa	72.4
8	Kansas	77.1
13	Kentucky	61.0
32	Louisiana	39.1
15	Maine	59.5
46	Maryland	12.0
48	Massachusetts	2.5
30	Michigan	40.4
12	Minnesota	62.4
10	Mississippi	71.3
26	Missouri	44.5
2	Montana	88.9
6	Nebraska	80.5
40	Nevada	31.3
14	New Hampshire	60.7
49	New Jersey	0.0
15	New Mexico	59.5
43	New York	19.7
20	North Carolina	51.3
4	North Dakota	85.0
39	Ohio	31.8
17	Oklahoma	59.1
22	Oregon	50.0
41	Pennsylvania	25.1
49	Rhode Island	0.0
33	South Carolina	38.1
5	South Dakota	80.8
28	Tennessee	43.1
35	Texas	35.9
29	Utah	41.9
3	Vermont	85.7
36	Virginia	34.5
31	Washington	39.5
19	West Virginia	56.1
24	Wisconsin	46.0
1	Wyoming	91.7

RANK ORDER

RANK	STATE	PERCENT
1	Wyoming	91.7
2	Montana	88.9
3	Vermont	85.7
4	North Dakota	85.0
5	South Dakota	80.8
6	Nebraska	80.5
7	Alaska	77.3
8	Kansas	77.1
9	Iowa	72.4
10	Mississippi	71.3
11	Idaho	64.1
12	Minnesota	62.4
13	Kentucky	61.0
14	New Hampshire	60.7
15	Maine	59.5
15	New Mexico	59.5
17	Oklahoma	59.1
18	Arkansas	58.8
19	West Virginia	56.1
20	North Carolina	51.3
21	Colorado	50.7
22	Oregon	50.0
23	Hawaii	48.0
24	Wisconsin	46.0
25	Alabama	45.0
26	Missouri	44.5
27	Georgia	43.6
28	Tennessee	43.1
29	Utah	41.9
30	Michigan	40.4
31	Washington	39.5
32	Louisiana	39.1
33	South Carolina	38.1
34	Indiana	36.3
35	Texas	35.9
36	Virginia	34.5
37	Illinois	33.5
38	Delaware	33.3
39	Ohio	31.8
40	Nevada	31.3
41	Pennsylvania	25.1
42	Arizona	23.9
43	New York	19.7
44	Florida	14.6
45	Connecticut	13.9
46	Maryland	12.0
47	California	9.5
48	Massachusetts	2.5
49	New Jersey	0.0
49	Rhode Island	0.0
	District of Columbia	0.0

Source: Morgan Quitno Press using data from American Hospital Association (Chicago, IL)
"Hospital Statistics" (2007 edition)
*Community hospitals are all nonfederal, short-term, general and special hospitals whose facilities and services are available to the public. Rural is defined as any area outside a metropolitan statistical area as defined by the U.S. Office of Management and Budget.

Nongovernment Not-For-Profit Hospitals in 2005

National Total = 2,958 Hospitals*

ALPHA ORDER

RANK	STATE	HOSPITALS	% of USA	RANK	STATE	HOSPITALS	% of USA
36	Alabama	31	1.0%	1	California	204	6.9%
45	Alaska	13	0.4%	2	New York	179	6.1%
29	Arizona	40	1.4%	3	Pennsylvania	165	5.6%
23	Arkansas	47	1.6%	4	Illinois	154	5.2%
1	California	204	6.9%	5	Texas	152	5.1%
34	Colorado	33	1.1%	6	Ohio	137	4.6%
32	Connecticut	34	1.1%	7	Michigan	124	4.2%
49	Delaware	6	0.2%	8	Wisconsin	118	4.0%
9	Florida	91	3.1%	9	Florida	91	3.1%
18	Georgia	59	2.0%	9	Minnesota	91	3.1%
42	Hawaii	17	0.6%	11	North Carolina	75	2.5%
45	Idaho	13	0.4%	12	New Jersey	74	2.5%
4	Illinois	154	5.2%	13	Kentucky	72	2.4%
19	Indiana	58	2.0%	14	Massachusetts	67	2.3%
21	Iowa	57	1.9%	15	Missouri	63	2.1%
19	Kansas	58	2.0%	16	Tennessee	62	2.1%
13	Kentucky	72	2.4%	16	Virginia	62	2.1%
35	Louisiana	32	1.1%	18	Georgia	59	2.0%
32	Maine	34	1.1%	19	Indiana	58	2.0%
22	Maryland	48	1.6%	19	Kansas	58	2.0%
14	Massachusetts	67	2.3%	21	Iowa	57	1.9%
7	Michigan	124	4.2%	22	Maryland	48	1.6%
9	Minnesota	91	3.1%	23	Arkansas	47	1.6%
38	Mississippi	29	1.0%	24	Nebraska	45	1.5%
15	Missouri	63	2.1%	25	Montana	44	1.5%
25	Montana	44	1.5%	25	South Dakota	44	1.5%
24	Nebraska	45	1.5%	27	Oregon	43	1.5%
47	Nevada	11	0.4%	28	Washington	42	1.4%
39	New Hampshire	24	0.8%	29	Arizona	40	1.4%
12	New Jersey	74	2.5%	29	North Dakota	40	1.4%
43	New Mexico	15	0.5%	31	Oklahoma	39	1.3%
2	New York	179	6.1%	32	Connecticut	34	1.1%
11	North Carolina	75	2.5%	32	Maine	34	1.1%
29	North Dakota	40	1.4%	34	Colorado	33	1.1%
6	Ohio	137	4.6%	35	Louisiana	32	1.1%
31	Oklahoma	39	1.3%	36	Alabama	31	1.0%
27	Oregon	43	1.5%	36	West Virginia	31	1.0%
3	Pennsylvania	165	5.6%	38	Mississippi	29	1.0%
47	Rhode Island	11	0.4%	39	New Hampshire	24	0.8%
40	South Carolina	23	0.8%	40	South Carolina	23	0.8%
25	South Dakota	44	1.5%	41	Utah	22	0.7%
16	Tennessee	62	2.1%	42	Hawaii	17	0.6%
5	Texas	152	5.1%	43	New Mexico	15	0.5%
41	Utah	22	0.7%	44	Vermont	14	0.5%
44	Vermont	14	0.5%	45	Alaska	13	0.4%
16	Virginia	62	2.1%	45	Idaho	13	0.4%
28	Washington	42	1.4%	47	Nevada	11	0.4%
36	West Virginia	31	1.0%	47	Rhode Island	11	0.4%
8	Wisconsin	118	4.0%	49	Delaware	6	0.2%
50	Wyoming	4	0.1%	50	Wyoming	4	0.1%
					District of Columbia	7	0.2%

RANK ORDER (right column header)

Source: American Hospital Association (Chicago, IL)
   "Hospital Statistics" (2007 edition)
*Nongovernment not-for-profit hospitals are a subset of community hospitals.

Investor-Owned (For-Profit) Hospitals in 2005

National Total = 868 Hospitals*

ALPHA ORDER

RANK	STATE	HOSPITALS	% of USA
6	Alabama	39	4.5%
37	Alaska	2	0.2%
12	Arizona	22	2.5%
11	Arkansas	23	2.6%
3	California	84	9.7%
23	Colorado	11	1.3%
41	Connecticut	1	0.1%
44	Delaware	0	0.0%
2	Florida	95	10.9%
7	Georgia	32	3.7%
44	Hawaii	0	0.0%
33	Idaho	3	0.3%
26	Illinois	8	0.9%
17	Indiana	19	2.2%
44	Iowa	0	0.0%
22	Kansas	12	1.4%
15	Kentucky	20	2.3%
4	Louisiana	45	5.2%
41	Maine	1	0.1%
37	Maryland	2	0.2%
24	Massachusetts	10	1.2%
28	Michigan	4	0.5%
41	Minnesota	1	0.1%
9	Mississippi	24	2.8%
15	Missouri	20	2.3%
44	Montana	0	0.0%
37	Nebraska	2	0.2%
19	Nevada	15	1.7%
28	New Hampshire	4	0.5%
28	New Jersey	4	0.5%
21	New Mexico	14	1.6%
37	New York	2	0.2%
26	North Carolina	8	0.9%
44	North Dakota	0	0.0%
24	Ohio	10	1.2%
8	Oklahoma	30	3.5%
33	Oregon	3	0.3%
9	Pennsylvania	24	2.8%
44	Rhode Island	0	0.0%
13	South Carolina	21	2.4%
33	South Dakota	3	0.3%
5	Tennessee	44	5.1%
1	Texas	139	16.0%
19	Utah	15	1.7%
44	Vermont	0	0.0%
13	Virginia	21	2.4%
28	Washington	4	0.5%
18	West Virginia	16	1.8%
28	Wisconsin	4	0.5%
33	Wyoming	3	0.3%

RANK ORDER

RANK	STATE	HOSPITALS	% of USA
1	Texas	139	16.0%
2	Florida	95	10.9%
3	California	84	9.7%
4	Louisiana	45	5.2%
5	Tennessee	44	5.1%
6	Alabama	39	4.5%
7	Georgia	32	3.7%
8	Oklahoma	30	3.5%
9	Mississippi	24	2.8%
9	Pennsylvania	24	2.8%
11	Arkansas	23	2.6%
12	Arizona	22	2.5%
13	South Carolina	21	2.4%
13	Virginia	21	2.4%
15	Kentucky	20	2.3%
15	Missouri	20	2.3%
17	Indiana	19	2.2%
18	West Virginia	16	1.8%
19	Nevada	15	1.7%
19	Utah	15	1.7%
21	New Mexico	14	1.6%
22	Kansas	12	1.4%
23	Colorado	11	1.3%
24	Massachusetts	10	1.2%
24	Ohio	10	1.2%
26	Illinois	8	0.9%
26	North Carolina	8	0.9%
28	Michigan	4	0.5%
28	New Hampshire	4	0.5%
28	New Jersey	4	0.5%
28	Washington	4	0.5%
28	Wisconsin	4	0.5%
33	Idaho	3	0.3%
33	Oregon	3	0.3%
33	South Dakota	3	0.3%
33	Wyoming	3	0.3%
37	Alaska	2	0.2%
37	Maryland	2	0.2%
37	Nebraska	2	0.2%
37	New York	2	0.2%
41	Connecticut	1	0.1%
41	Maine	1	0.1%
41	Minnesota	1	0.1%
44	Delaware	0	0.0%
44	Hawaii	0	0.0%
44	Iowa	0	0.0%
44	Montana	0	0.0%
44	North Dakota	0	0.0%
44	Rhode Island	0	0.0%
44	Vermont	0	0.0%
	District of Columbia	4	0.5%

Source: American Hospital Association (Chicago, IL)
   "Hospital Statistics" (2007 edition)
*Investor-owned (for-profit) hospitals are a subset of community hospitals.

State and Local Government-Owned Hospitals in 2005

National Total = 1,110 Hospitals*

ALPHA ORDER

RANK	STATE	HOSPITALS	% of USA
12	Alabama	39	3.5%
33	Alaska	7	0.6%
36	Arizona	5	0.5%
26	Arkansas	15	1.4%
2	California	69	6.2%
17	Colorado	27	2.4%
44	Connecticut	1	0.1%
45	Delaware	0	0.0%
22	Florida	19	1.7%
5	Georgia	58	5.2%
31	Hawaii	8	0.7%
19	Idaho	23	2.1%
16	Illinois	29	2.6%
13	Indiana	36	3.2%
4	Iowa	59	5.3%
3	Kansas	61	5.5%
27	Kentucky	13	1.2%
6	Louisiana	51	4.6%
40	Maine	2	0.2%
45	Maryland	0	0.0%
39	Massachusetts	3	0.3%
24	Michigan	18	1.6%
7	Minnesota	41	3.7%
7	Mississippi	41	3.7%
13	Missouri	36	3.2%
29	Montana	10	0.9%
10	Nebraska	40	3.6%
34	Nevada	6	0.5%
45	New Hampshire	0	0.0%
40	New Jersey	2	0.2%
31	New Mexico	8	0.7%
21	New York	22	2.0%
15	North Carolina	32	2.9%
45	North Dakota	0	0.0%
19	Ohio	23	2.1%
7	Oklahoma	41	3.7%
28	Oregon	12	1.1%
40	Pennsylvania	2	0.2%
45	Rhode Island	0	0.0%
22	South Carolina	19	1.7%
36	South Dakota	5	0.5%
18	Tennessee	24	2.2%
1	Texas	124	11.2%
34	Utah	6	0.5%
45	Vermont	0	0.0%
38	Virginia	4	0.4%
10	Washington	40	3.6%
29	West Virginia	10	0.9%
40	Wisconsin	2	0.2%
25	Wyoming	17	1.5%

RANK ORDER

RANK	STATE	HOSPITALS	% of USA
1	Texas	124	11.2%
2	California	69	6.2%
3	Kansas	61	5.5%
4	Iowa	59	5.3%
5	Georgia	58	5.2%
6	Louisiana	51	4.6%
7	Minnesota	41	3.7%
7	Mississippi	41	3.7%
7	Oklahoma	41	3.7%
10	Nebraska	40	3.6%
10	Washington	40	3.6%
12	Alabama	39	3.5%
13	Indiana	36	3.2%
13	Missouri	36	3.2%
15	North Carolina	32	2.9%
16	Illinois	29	2.6%
17	Colorado	27	2.4%
18	Tennessee	24	2.2%
19	Idaho	23	2.1%
19	Ohio	23	2.1%
21	New York	22	2.0%
22	Florida	19	1.7%
22	South Carolina	19	1.7%
24	Michigan	18	1.6%
25	Wyoming	17	1.5%
26	Arkansas	15	1.4%
27	Kentucky	13	1.2%
28	Oregon	12	1.1%
29	Montana	10	0.9%
29	West Virginia	10	0.9%
31	Hawaii	8	0.7%
31	New Mexico	8	0.7%
33	Alaska	7	0.6%
34	Nevada	6	0.5%
34	Utah	6	0.5%
36	Arizona	5	0.5%
36	South Dakota	5	0.5%
38	Virginia	4	0.4%
39	Massachusetts	3	0.3%
40	Maine	2	0.2%
40	New Jersey	2	0.2%
40	Pennsylvania	2	0.2%
40	Wisconsin	2	0.2%
44	Connecticut	1	0.1%
45	Delaware	0	0.0%
45	Maryland	0	0.0%
45	New Hampshire	0	0.0%
45	North Dakota	0	0.0%
45	Rhode Island	0	0.0%
45	Vermont	0	0.0%
	District of Columbia	0	0.0%

Source: American Hospital Association (Chicago, IL)
"Hospital Statistics" (2007 edition)
*State and local government-owned hospitals are a subset of community hospitals.

Beds in Community Hospitals in 2005

National Total = 802,311 Beds*

RANK	STATE	BEDS	% of USA
19	Alabama	15,486	1.9%
49	Alaska	1,393	0.2%
23	Arizona	11,767	1.5%
31	Arkansas	9,389	1.2%
1	California	70,192	8.7%
30	Colorado	9,620	1.2%
32	Connecticut	7,862	1.0%
48	Delaware	1,909	0.2%
4	Florida	51,174	6.4%
9	Georgia	25,015	3.1%
44	Hawaii	3,001	0.4%
43	Idaho	3,330	0.4%
6	Illinois	34,498	4.3%
14	Indiana	17,750	2.2%
28	Iowa	10,753	1.3%
29	Kansas	10,075	1.3%
20	Kentucky	14,891	1.9%
18	Louisiana	15,534	1.9%
40	Maine	3,526	0.4%
25	Maryland	11,404	1.4%
16	Massachusetts	16,213	2.0%
8	Michigan	26,214	3.3%
17	Minnesota	15,993	2.0%
22	Mississippi	12,753	1.6%
13	Missouri	19,146	2.4%
39	Montana	4,283	0.5%
33	Nebraska	7,566	0.9%
36	Nevada	4,685	0.6%
45	New Hampshire	2,843	0.4%
11	New Jersey	22,090	2.8%
41	New Mexico	3,505	0.4%
2	New York	63,068	7.9%
10	North Carolina	23,344	2.9%
42	North Dakota	3,494	0.4%
7	Ohio	33,250	4.1%
26	Oklahoma	10,814	1.3%
35	Oregon	6,515	0.8%
5	Pennsylvania	39,602	4.9%
46	Rhode Island	2,405	0.3%
24	South Carolina	11,458	1.4%
38	South Dakota	4,325	0.5%
12	Tennessee	20,578	2.6%
3	Texas	58,153	7.2%
37	Utah	4,555	0.6%
50	Vermont	1,358	0.2%
15	Virginia	17,483	2.2%
27	Washington	10,763	1.3%
34	West Virginia	7,243	0.9%
21	Wisconsin	14,458	1.8%
47	Wyoming	2,051	0.3%

RANK	STATE	BEDS	% of USA
1	California	70,192	8.7%
2	New York	63,068	7.9%
3	Texas	58,153	7.2%
4	Florida	51,174	6.4%
5	Pennsylvania	39,602	4.9%
6	Illinois	34,498	4.3%
7	Ohio	33,250	4.1%
8	Michigan	26,214	3.3%
9	Georgia	25,015	3.1%
10	North Carolina	23,344	2.9%
11	New Jersey	22,090	2.8%
12	Tennessee	20,578	2.6%
13	Missouri	19,146	2.4%
14	Indiana	17,750	2.2%
15	Virginia	17,483	2.2%
16	Massachusetts	16,213	2.0%
17	Minnesota	15,993	2.0%
18	Louisiana	15,534	1.9%
19	Alabama	15,486	1.9%
20	Kentucky	14,891	1.9%
21	Wisconsin	14,458	1.8%
22	Mississippi	12,753	1.6%
23	Arizona	11,767	1.5%
24	South Carolina	11,458	1.4%
25	Maryland	11,404	1.4%
26	Oklahoma	10,814	1.3%
27	Washington	10,763	1.3%
28	Iowa	10,753	1.3%
29	Kansas	10,075	1.3%
30	Colorado	9,620	1.2%
31	Arkansas	9,389	1.2%
32	Connecticut	7,862	1.0%
33	Nebraska	7,566	0.9%
34	West Virginia	7,243	0.9%
35	Oregon	6,515	0.8%
36	Nevada	4,685	0.6%
37	Utah	4,555	0.6%
38	South Dakota	4,325	0.5%
39	Montana	4,283	0.5%
40	Maine	3,526	0.4%
41	New Mexico	3,505	0.4%
42	North Dakota	3,494	0.4%
43	Idaho	3,330	0.4%
44	Hawaii	3,001	0.4%
45	New Hampshire	2,843	0.4%
46	Rhode Island	2,405	0.3%
47	Wyoming	2,051	0.3%
48	Delaware	1,909	0.2%
49	Alaska	1,393	0.2%
50	Vermont	1,358	0.2%
	District of Columbia	3,534	0.4%

Source: American Hospital Association (Chicago, IL)
"Hospital Statistics" (2007 edition)
All nonfederal short-term general and other special hospitals, whose facilities and services are available to the public. Includes beds in hospital and nursing home units.

Rate of Beds in Community Hospitals in 2005

National Rate = 271 Beds per 100,000 Population*

ALPHA ORDER					RANK ORDER		
RANK	STATE	RATE			RANK	STATE	RATE
13	Alabama	340			1	South Dakota	558
41	Alaska	210			2	North Dakota	551
44	Arizona	198			3	Montana	458
14	Arkansas	338			4	Mississippi	438
45	California	194			5	Nebraska	430
42	Colorado	206			6	Wyoming	403
37	Connecticut	225			7	West Virginia	399
36	Delaware	227			8	Kansas	367
21	Florida	288			9	Iowa	363
23	Georgia	274			10	Kentucky	357
33	Hawaii	236			11	Tennessee	346
34	Idaho	233			12	Louisiana	345
24	Illinois	270			13	Alabama	340
22	Indiana	283			14	Arkansas	338
9	Iowa	363			15	Missouri	330
8	Kansas	367			16	New York	327
10	Kentucky	357			17	Pennsylvania	319
12	Louisiana	345			18	Minnesota	312
27	Maine	267			19	Oklahoma	305
43	Maryland	204			20	Ohio	290
32	Massachusetts	252			21	Florida	288
29	Michigan	260			22	Indiana	283
18	Minnesota	312			23	Georgia	274
4	Mississippi	438			24	Illinois	270
15	Missouri	330			24	South Carolina	270
3	Montana	458			26	North Carolina	269
5	Nebraska	430			27	Maine	267
45	Nevada	194			28	Wisconsin	262
39	New Hampshire	218			29	Michigan	260
30	New Jersey	254			30	New Jersey	254
48	New Mexico	182			30	Texas	254
16	New York	327			32	Massachusetts	252
26	North Carolina	269			33	Hawaii	236
2	North Dakota	551			34	Idaho	233
20	Ohio	290			35	Virginia	231
19	Oklahoma	305			36	Delaware	227
49	Oregon	179			37	Connecticut	225
17	Pennsylvania	319			38	Rhode Island	224
38	Rhode Island	224			39	New Hampshire	218
24	South Carolina	270			39	Vermont	218
1	South Dakota	558			41	Alaska	210
11	Tennessee	346			42	Colorado	206
30	Texas	254			43	Maryland	204
47	Utah	183			44	Arizona	198
39	Vermont	218			45	California	194
35	Virginia	231			45	Nevada	194
50	Washington	171			47	Utah	183
7	West Virginia	399			48	New Mexico	182
28	Wisconsin	262			49	Oregon	179
6	Wyoming	403			50	Washington	171

District of Columbia 607

Source: Morgan Quitno Press using data from American Hospital Association (Chicago, IL)
    "Hospital Statistics" (2007 edition)
*All nonfederal short-term general and other special hospitals, whose facilities and services are available to the
public. Includes beds in hospital and nursing home units.

Average Number of Beds per Community Hospital in 2005

National Average = 163 Beds per Community Hospital*

ALPHA ORDER

RANK	STATE	BEDS
23	Alabama	142
50	Alaska	63
17	Arizona	176
35	Arkansas	110
12	California	197
27	Colorado	135
7	Connecticut	218
1	Delaware	318
4	Florida	250
18	Georgia	168
31	Hawaii	120
45	Idaho	85
15	Illinois	181
21	Indiana	157
42	Iowa	93
49	Kansas	77
23	Kentucky	142
30	Louisiana	121
40	Maine	95
5	Maryland	228
9	Massachusetts	203
16	Michigan	180
31	Minnesota	120
26	Mississippi	136
19	Missouri	161
48	Montana	79
43	Nebraska	87
22	Nevada	146
37	New Hampshire	102
3	New Jersey	276
40	New Mexico	95
2	New York	311
9	North Carolina	203
43	North Dakota	87
13	Ohio	196
38	Oklahoma	98
34	Oregon	112
8	Pennsylvania	207
6	Rhode Island	219
14	South Carolina	182
47	South Dakota	83
20	Tennessee	158
25	Texas	140
36	Utah	106
39	Vermont	97
11	Virginia	201
29	Washington	125
28	West Virginia	127
33	Wisconsin	117
45	Wyoming	85

RANK ORDER

RANK	STATE	BEDS
1	Delaware	318
2	New York	311
3	New Jersey	276
4	Florida	250
5	Maryland	228
6	Rhode Island	219
7	Connecticut	218
8	Pennsylvania	207
9	Massachusetts	203
9	North Carolina	203
11	Virginia	201
12	California	197
13	Ohio	196
14	South Carolina	182
15	Illinois	181
16	Michigan	180
17	Arizona	176
18	Georgia	168
19	Missouri	161
20	Tennessee	158
21	Indiana	157
22	Nevada	146
23	Alabama	142
23	Kentucky	142
25	Texas	140
26	Mississippi	136
27	Colorado	135
28	West Virginia	127
29	Washington	125
30	Louisiana	121
31	Hawaii	120
31	Minnesota	120
33	Wisconsin	117
34	Oregon	112
35	Arkansas	110
36	Utah	106
37	New Hampshire	102
38	Oklahoma	98
39	Vermont	97
40	Maine	95
40	New Mexico	95
42	Iowa	93
43	Nebraska	87
43	North Dakota	87
45	Idaho	85
45	Wyoming	85
47	South Dakota	83
48	Montana	79
49	Kansas	77
50	Alaska	63

District of Columbia — 321

Source: Morgan Quitno Press using data from American Hospital Association (Chicago, IL)
        "Hospital Statistics" (2007 edition)
*All nonfederal short-term general and other special hospitals, whose facilities and services are available to the public. Includes beds in hospital and nursing home units.

Admissions to Community Hospitals in 2005

National Total = 35,238,673 Admissions*

ALPHA ORDER

RANK	STATE	ADMISSIONS	% of USA
17	Alabama	706,442	2.0%
50	Alaska	51,022	0.1%
19	Arizona	664,595	1.9%
30	Arkansas	380,067	1.1%
1	California	3,434,221	9.7%
27	Colorado	417,338	1.2%
29	Connecticut	404,989	1.1%
45	Delaware	103,863	0.3%
4	Florida	2,371,397	6.7%
11	Georgia	961,195	2.7%
43	Hawaii	113,876	0.3%
40	Idaho	129,666	0.4%
6	Illinois	1,583,328	4.5%
16	Indiana	717,490	2.0%
31	Iowa	362,541	1.0%
33	Kansas	330,429	0.9%
22	Kentucky	617,969	1.8%
21	Louisiana	619,500	1.8%
39	Maine	151,303	0.4%
18	Maryland	679,838	1.9%
14	Massachusetts	799,653	2.3%
8	Michigan	1,198,076	3.4%
20	Minnesota	635,162	1.8%
28	Mississippi	414,373	1.2%
12	Missouri	836,179	2.4%
44	Montana	106,457	0.3%
37	Nebraska	214,240	0.6%
35	Nevada	240,596	0.7%
42	New Hampshire	117,468	0.3%
9	New Jersey	1,109,705	3.1%
38	New Mexico	171,547	0.5%
2	New York	2,537,762	7.2%
10	North Carolina	1,013,094	2.9%
47	North Dakota	87,485	0.2%
7	Ohio	1,511,171	4.3%
26	Oklahoma	456,759	1.3%
32	Oregon	336,173	1.0%
5	Pennsylvania	1,863,299	5.3%
41	Rhode Island	126,619	0.4%
25	South Carolina	528,122	1.5%
46	South Dakota	102,127	0.3%
13	Tennessee	829,247	2.4%
3	Texas	2,509,178	7.1%
36	Utah	222,985	0.6%
48	Vermont	51,430	0.1%
15	Virginia	780,063	2.2%
24	Washington	543,329	1.5%
34	West Virginia	291,936	0.8%
23	Wisconsin	611,669	1.7%
49	Wyoming	51,200	0.1%

RANK ORDER

RANK	STATE	ADMISSIONS	% of USA
1	California	3,434,221	9.7%
2	New York	2,537,762	7.2%
3	Texas	2,509,178	7.1%
4	Florida	2,371,397	6.7%
5	Pennsylvania	1,863,299	5.3%
6	Illinois	1,583,328	4.5%
7	Ohio	1,511,171	4.3%
8	Michigan	1,198,076	3.4%
9	New Jersey	1,109,705	3.1%
10	North Carolina	1,013,094	2.9%
11	Georgia	961,195	2.7%
12	Missouri	836,179	2.4%
13	Tennessee	829,247	2.4%
14	Massachusetts	799,653	2.3%
15	Virginia	780,063	2.2%
16	Indiana	717,490	2.0%
17	Alabama	706,442	2.0%
18	Maryland	679,838	1.9%
19	Arizona	664,595	1.9%
20	Minnesota	635,162	1.8%
21	Louisiana	619,500	1.8%
22	Kentucky	617,969	1.8%
23	Wisconsin	611,669	1.7%
24	Washington	543,329	1.5%
25	South Carolina	528,122	1.5%
26	Oklahoma	456,759	1.3%
27	Colorado	417,338	1.2%
28	Mississippi	414,373	1.2%
29	Connecticut	404,989	1.1%
30	Arkansas	380,067	1.1%
31	Iowa	362,541	1.0%
32	Oregon	336,173	1.0%
33	Kansas	330,429	0.9%
34	West Virginia	291,936	0.8%
35	Nevada	240,596	0.7%
36	Utah	222,985	0.6%
37	Nebraska	214,240	0.6%
38	New Mexico	171,547	0.5%
39	Maine	151,303	0.4%
40	Idaho	129,666	0.4%
41	Rhode Island	126,619	0.4%
42	New Hampshire	117,468	0.3%
43	Hawaii	113,876	0.3%
44	Montana	106,457	0.3%
45	Delaware	103,863	0.3%
46	South Dakota	102,127	0.3%
47	North Dakota	87,485	0.2%
48	Vermont	51,430	0.1%
49	Wyoming	51,200	0.1%
50	Alaska	51,022	0.1%
	District of Columbia	140,500	0.4%

Source: American Hospital Association (Chicago, IL)
   "Hospital Statistics" (2007 edition)
*Admissions to all nonfederal short-term general and other special hospitals, whose facilities and services are available to the public. Includes admissions to hospital and nursing home units.

Inpatient Days in Community Hospitals in 2005

National Total = 197,073,770 Inpatient Days*

RANK	STATE	DAYS	% of USA
18	Alabama	3,628,012	1.8%
50	Alaska	306,027	0.2%
24	Arizona	2,936,640	1.5%
32	Arkansas	2,002,721	1.0%
2	California	18,235,884	9.3%
30	Colorado	2,103,711	1.1%
29	Connecticut	2,312,197	1.2%
47	Delaware	639,855	0.3%
4	Florida	12,367,864	6.3%
9	Georgia	6,191,628	3.1%
40	Hawaii	853,247	0.4%
46	Idaho	645,598	0.3%
6	Illinois	8,258,893	4.2%
17	Indiana	3,763,741	1.9%
28	Iowa	2,323,346	1.2%
31	Kansas	2,070,956	1.1%
20	Kentucky	3,385,604	1.7%
19	Louisiana	3,404,395	1.7%
41	Maine	848,195	0.4%
22	Maryland	3,187,739	1.6%
15	Massachusetts	4,386,690	2.2%
8	Michigan	6,412,561	3.3%
16	Minnesota	4,020,255	2.0%
25	Mississippi	2,679,961	1.4%
14	Missouri	4,421,138	2.2%
38	Montana	1,023,301	0.5%
33	Nebraska	1,757,311	0.9%
36	Nevada	1,268,272	0.6%
45	New Hampshire	647,457	0.3%
11	New Jersey	5,925,414	3.0%
42	New Mexico	807,324	0.4%
1	New York	18,277,363	9.3%
10	North Carolina	6,089,400	3.1%
43	North Dakota	767,324	0.4%
7	Ohio	7,801,663	4.0%
27	Oklahoma	2,341,597	1.2%
35	Oregon	1,490,898	0.8%
5	Pennsylvania	10,170,812	5.2%
44	Rhode Island	684,067	0.3%
23	South Carolina	3,079,884	1.6%
37	South Dakota	1,027,776	0.5%
12	Tennessee	4,767,818	2.4%
3	Texas	13,101,744	6.6%
39	Utah	959,235	0.5%
49	Vermont	334,533	0.2%
13	Virginia	4,500,420	2.3%
26	Washington	2,481,368	1.3%
34	West Virginia	1,662,043	0.8%
21	Wisconsin	3,302,565	1.7%
48	Wyoming	421,352	0.2%

RANK	STATE	DAYS	% of USA
1	New York	18,277,363	9.3%
2	California	18,235,884	9.3%
3	Texas	13,101,744	6.6%
4	Florida	12,367,864	6.3%
5	Pennsylvania	10,170,812	5.2%
6	Illinois	8,258,893	4.2%
7	Ohio	7,801,663	4.0%
8	Michigan	6,412,561	3.3%
9	Georgia	6,191,628	3.1%
10	North Carolina	6,089,400	3.1%
11	New Jersey	5,925,414	3.0%
12	Tennessee	4,767,818	2.4%
13	Virginia	4,500,420	2.3%
14	Missouri	4,421,138	2.2%
15	Massachusetts	4,386,690	2.2%
16	Minnesota	4,020,255	2.0%
17	Indiana	3,763,741	1.9%
18	Alabama	3,628,012	1.8%
19	Louisiana	3,404,395	1.7%
20	Kentucky	3,385,604	1.7%
21	Wisconsin	3,302,565	1.7%
22	Maryland	3,187,739	1.6%
23	South Carolina	3,079,884	1.6%
24	Arizona	2,936,640	1.5%
25	Mississippi	2,679,961	1.4%
26	Washington	2,481,368	1.3%
27	Oklahoma	2,341,597	1.2%
28	Iowa	2,323,346	1.2%
29	Connecticut	2,312,197	1.2%
30	Colorado	2,103,711	1.1%
31	Kansas	2,070,956	1.1%
32	Arkansas	2,002,721	1.0%
33	Nebraska	1,757,311	0.9%
34	West Virginia	1,662,043	0.8%
35	Oregon	1,490,898	0.8%
36	Nevada	1,268,272	0.6%
37	South Dakota	1,027,776	0.5%
38	Montana	1,023,301	0.5%
39	Utah	959,235	0.5%
40	Hawaii	853,247	0.4%
41	Maine	848,195	0.4%
42	New Mexico	807,324	0.4%
43	North Dakota	767,324	0.4%
44	Rhode Island	684,067	0.3%
45	New Hampshire	647,457	0.3%
46	Idaho	645,598	0.3%
47	Delaware	639,855	0.3%
48	Wyoming	421,352	0.2%
49	Vermont	334,533	0.2%
50	Alaska	306,027	0.2%
	District of Columbia	995,971	0.5%

Source: American Hospital Association (Chicago, IL)
   "Hospital Statistics" (2007 edition)
*Inpatient days in all nonfederal short-term general and other special hospitals, whose facilities and services are available to the public. Includes days in hospital and nursing home units.

Average Daily Census in Community Hospitals in 2005

National Average = 539,928 Inpatients*

ALPHA ORDER				RANK ORDER		
RANK	STATE	INPATIENTS		RANK	STATE	INPATIENTS
18	Alabama	9,940		1	New York	50,075
50	Alaska	838		2	California	49,961
24	Arizona	8,046		3	Texas	35,895
32	Arkansas	5,487		4	Florida	33,885
2	California	49,961		5	Pennsylvania	27,865
30	Colorado	5,764		6	Illinois	22,627
29	Connecticut	6,335		7	Ohio	21,374
47	Delaware	1,753		8	Michigan	17,569
4	Florida	33,885		9	Georgia	16,963
9	Georgia	16,963		10	North Carolina	16,683
40	Hawaii	2,338		11	New Jersey	16,234
46	Idaho	1,769		12	Tennessee	13,063
6	Illinois	22,627		13	Virginia	12,330
17	Indiana	10,312		14	Missouri	12,113
28	Iowa	6,365		15	Massachusetts	12,018
31	Kansas	5,674		16	Minnesota	11,014
20	Kentucky	9,276		17	Indiana	10,312
19	Louisiana	9,327		18	Alabama	9,940
41	Maine	2,324		19	Louisiana	9,327
22	Maryland	8,734		20	Kentucky	9,276
15	Massachusetts	12,018		21	Wisconsin	9,048
8	Michigan	17,569		22	Maryland	8,734
16	Minnesota	11,014		23	South Carolina	8,438
25	Mississippi	7,342		24	Arizona	8,046
14	Missouri	12,113		25	Mississippi	7,342
38	Montana	2,804		26	Washington	6,798
33	Nebraska	4,815		27	Oklahoma	6,415
36	Nevada	3,475		28	Iowa	6,365
45	New Hampshire	1,774		29	Connecticut	6,335
11	New Jersey	16,234		30	Colorado	5,764
42	New Mexico	2,212		31	Kansas	5,674
1	New York	50,075		32	Arkansas	5,487
10	North Carolina	16,683		33	Nebraska	4,815
43	North Dakota	2,102		34	West Virginia	4,554
7	Ohio	21,374		35	Oregon	4,085
27	Oklahoma	6,415		36	Nevada	3,475
35	Oregon	4,085		37	South Dakota	2,816
5	Pennsylvania	27,865		38	Montana	2,804
44	Rhode Island	1,874		39	Utah	2,628
23	South Carolina	8,438		40	Hawaii	2,338
37	South Dakota	2,816		41	Maine	2,324
12	Tennessee	13,063		42	New Mexico	2,212
3	Texas	35,895		43	North Dakota	2,102
39	Utah	2,628		44	Rhode Island	1,874
49	Vermont	917		45	New Hampshire	1,774
13	Virginia	12,330		46	Idaho	1,769
26	Washington	6,798		47	Delaware	1,753
34	West Virginia	4,554		48	Wyoming	1,154
21	Wisconsin	9,048		49	Vermont	917
48	Wyoming	1,154		50	Alaska	838

District of Columbia   2,729

Source: Morgan Quitno Press using data from American Hospital Association (Chicago, IL) "Hospital Statistics" (2007 edition)

Average total of inpatients receiving care in all nonfederal short-term general and other special hospitals, whose facilities and services are available to the public. Excludes newborns.

Average Stay in Community Hospitals in 2005

National Average = 5.6 Days*

ALPHA ORDER

RANK	STATE	DAYS
41	Alabama	5.1
15	Alaska	6.0
48	Arizona	4.4
31	Arkansas	5.3
31	California	5.3
43	Colorado	5.0
19	Connecticut	5.7
14	Delaware	6.2
36	Florida	5.2
10	Georgia	6.4
6	Hawaii	7.5
43	Idaho	5.0
36	Illinois	5.2
36	Indiana	5.2
10	Iowa	6.4
12	Kansas	6.3
23	Kentucky	5.5
23	Louisiana	5.5
22	Maine	5.6
45	Maryland	4.7
23	Massachusetts	5.5
28	Michigan	5.4
12	Minnesota	6.3
8	Mississippi	6.5
31	Missouri	5.3
2	Montana	9.6
4	Nebraska	8.2
31	Nevada	5.3
23	New Hampshire	5.5
31	New Jersey	5.3
45	New Mexico	4.7
7	New York	7.2
15	North Carolina	6.0
3	North Dakota	8.8
36	Ohio	5.2
41	Oklahoma	5.1
48	Oregon	4.4
23	Pennsylvania	5.5
28	Rhode Island	5.4
17	South Carolina	5.8
1	South Dakota	10.1
19	Tennessee	5.7
36	Texas	5.2
50	Utah	4.3
8	Vermont	6.5
17	Virginia	5.8
47	Washington	4.6
19	West Virginia	5.7
28	Wisconsin	5.4
4	Wyoming	8.2

RANK ORDER

RANK	STATE	DAYS
1	South Dakota	10.1
2	Montana	9.6
3	North Dakota	8.8
4	Nebraska	8.2
4	Wyoming	8.2
6	Hawaii	7.5
7	New York	7.2
8	Mississippi	6.5
8	Vermont	6.5
10	Georgia	6.4
10	Iowa	6.4
12	Kansas	6.3
12	Minnesota	6.3
14	Delaware	6.2
15	Alaska	6.0
15	North Carolina	6.0
17	South Carolina	5.8
17	Virginia	5.8
19	Connecticut	5.7
19	Tennessee	5.7
19	West Virginia	5.7
22	Maine	5.6
23	Kentucky	5.5
23	Louisiana	5.5
23	Massachusetts	5.5
23	New Hampshire	5.5
23	Pennsylvania	5.5
28	Michigan	5.4
28	Rhode Island	5.4
28	Wisconsin	5.4
31	Arkansas	5.3
31	California	5.3
31	Missouri	5.3
31	Nevada	5.3
31	New Jersey	5.3
36	Florida	5.2
36	Illinois	5.2
36	Indiana	5.2
36	Ohio	5.2
36	Texas	5.2
41	Alabama	5.1
41	Oklahoma	5.1
43	Colorado	5.0
43	Idaho	5.0
45	Maryland	4.7
45	New Mexico	4.7
47	Washington	4.6
48	Arizona	4.4
48	Oregon	4.4
50	Utah	4.3

District of Columbia — 7.1

Source: American Hospital Association (Chicago, IL)
   "Hospital Statistics" (2007 edition)
*All nonfederal short-term general and other special hospitals, whose facilities and services are available to the public.

Occupancy Rate in Community Hospitals in 2005

National Rate = 67.3% of Community Hospital Beds Occupied*

ALPHA ORDER

RANK ORDER

RANK	STATE	PERCENT		RANK	STATE	PERCENT
26	Alabama	64.2		1	Delaware	91.8
38	Alaska	60.2		2	Connecticut	80.6
16	Arizona	68.4		3	New York	79.4
44	Arkansas	58.4		4	Hawaii	77.9
12	California	71.2		4	Rhode Island	77.9
41	Colorado	59.9		6	Maryland	76.6
2	Connecticut	80.6		7	Nevada	74.2
1	Delaware	91.8		8	Massachusetts	74.1
20	Florida	66.2		9	South Carolina	73.6
17	Georgia	67.8		10	New Jersey	73.5
4	Hawaii	77.9		11	North Carolina	71.5
50	Idaho	53.1		12	California	71.2
22	Illinois	65.6		13	Virginia	70.5
45	Indiana	58.1		14	Pennsylvania	70.4
43	Iowa	59.2		15	Minnesota	68.9
48	Kansas	56.3		16	Arizona	68.4
36	Kentucky	62.3		17	Georgia	67.8
40	Louisiana	60.0		18	Vermont	67.5
21	Maine	65.9		19	Michigan	67.0
6	Maryland	76.6		20	Florida	66.2
8	Massachusetts	74.1		21	Maine	65.9
19	Michigan	67.0		22	Illinois	65.6
15	Minnesota	68.9		23	Montana	65.5
47	Mississippi	57.6		24	South Dakota	65.1
29	Missouri	63.3		25	Ohio	64.3
23	Montana	65.5		26	Alabama	64.2
27	Nebraska	63.6		27	Nebraska	63.6
7	Nevada	74.2		28	Tennessee	63.5
35	New Hampshire	62.4		29	Missouri	63.3
10	New Jersey	73.5		30	Washington	63.2
31	New Mexico	63.1		31	New Mexico	63.1
3	New York	79.4		32	West Virginia	62.9
11	North Carolina	71.5		33	Oregon	62.7
38	North Dakota	60.2		34	Wisconsin	62.6
25	Ohio	64.3		35	New Hampshire	62.4
42	Oklahoma	59.3		36	Kentucky	62.3
33	Oregon	62.7		37	Texas	61.7
14	Pennsylvania	70.4		38	Alaska	60.2
4	Rhode Island	77.9		38	North Dakota	60.2
9	South Carolina	73.6		40	Louisiana	60.0
24	South Dakota	65.1		41	Colorado	59.9
28	Tennessee	63.5		42	Oklahoma	59.3
37	Texas	61.7		43	Iowa	59.2
46	Utah	57.7		44	Arkansas	58.4
18	Vermont	67.5		45	Indiana	58.1
13	Virginia	70.5		46	Utah	57.7
30	Washington	63.2		47	Mississippi	57.6
32	West Virginia	62.9		48	Kansas	56.3
34	Wisconsin	62.6		48	Wyoming	56.3
48	Wyoming	56.3		50	Idaho	53.1

District of Columbia   77.2

Source: Morgan Quitno Press using data from American Hospital Association (Chicago, IL)
    "Hospital Statistics" (2007 edition)
*Average daily census compared to number of community hospital beds.

Outpatient Visits to Community Hospitals in 2005

National Total = 584,428,736 Visits*

ALPHA ORDER

ALPHA ORDER

RANK	STATE	VISITS	% of USA
24	Alabama	7,547,202	1.3%
48	Alaska	1,666,617	0.3%
27	Arizona	6,776,451	1.2%
33	Arkansas	4,971,307	0.9%
2	California	49,032,480	8.4%
25	Colorado	7,378,106	1.3%
26	Connecticut	7,145,860	1.2%
46	Delaware	1,867,727	0.3%
8	Florida	22,298,310	3.8%
14	Georgia	13,803,079	2.4%
45	Hawaii	1,908,942	0.3%
41	Idaho	2,719,510	0.5%
6	Illinois	28,728,564	4.9%
13	Indiana	16,451,983	2.8%
18	Iowa	10,098,061	1.7%
30	Kansas	5,944,780	1.0%
22	Kentucky	8,859,077	1.5%
20	Louisiana	9,806,804	1.7%
36	Maine	4,299,499	0.7%
28	Maryland	6,750,277	1.2%
9	Massachusetts	18,865,165	3.2%
7	Michigan	26,149,516	4.5%
21	Minnesota	9,442,465	1.6%
37	Mississippi	4,093,476	0.7%
10	Missouri	17,213,164	2.9%
40	Montana	2,859,486	0.5%
38	Nebraska	3,890,404	0.7%
42	Nevada	2,613,654	0.4%
39	New Hampshire	3,782,042	0.6%
11	New Jersey	16,826,916	2.9%
35	New Mexico	4,714,377	0.8%
1	New York	51,538,293	8.8%
12	North Carolina	16,801,719	2.9%
47	North Dakota	1,863,437	0.3%
5	Ohio	31,350,391	5.4%
32	Oklahoma	5,411,491	0.9%
23	Oregon	7,973,209	1.4%
3	Pennsylvania	34,911,114	6.0%
43	Rhode Island	2,482,748	0.4%
31	South Carolina	5,826,452	1.0%
49	South Dakota	1,642,974	0.3%
17	Tennessee	11,666,319	2.0%
4	Texas	32,329,166	5.5%
34	Utah	4,799,076	0.8%
44	Vermont	2,476,668	0.4%
15	Virginia	13,299,267	2.3%
19	Washington	10,049,513	1.7%
29	West Virginia	6,115,745	1.0%
16	Wisconsin	12,726,534	2.2%
50	Wyoming	1,010,035	0.2%

RANK ORDER

RANK	STATE	VISITS	% of USA
1	New York	51,538,293	8.8%
2	California	49,032,480	8.4%
3	Pennsylvania	34,911,114	6.0%
4	Texas	32,329,166	5.5%
5	Ohio	31,350,391	5.4%
6	Illinois	28,728,564	4.9%
7	Michigan	26,149,516	4.5%
8	Florida	22,298,310	3.8%
9	Massachusetts	18,865,165	3.2%
10	Missouri	17,213,164	2.9%
11	New Jersey	16,826,916	2.9%
12	North Carolina	16,801,719	2.9%
13	Indiana	16,451,983	2.8%
14	Georgia	13,803,079	2.4%
15	Virginia	13,299,267	2.3%
16	Wisconsin	12,726,534	2.2%
17	Tennessee	11,666,319	2.0%
18	Iowa	10,098,061	1.7%
19	Washington	10,049,513	1.7%
20	Louisiana	9,806,804	1.7%
21	Minnesota	9,442,465	1.6%
22	Kentucky	8,859,077	1.5%
23	Oregon	7,973,209	1.4%
24	Alabama	7,547,202	1.3%
25	Colorado	7,378,106	1.3%
26	Connecticut	7,145,860	1.2%
27	Arizona	6,776,451	1.2%
28	Maryland	6,750,277	1.2%
29	West Virginia	6,115,745	1.0%
30	Kansas	5,944,780	1.0%
31	South Carolina	5,826,452	1.0%
32	Oklahoma	5,411,491	0.9%
33	Arkansas	4,971,307	0.9%
34	Utah	4,799,076	0.8%
35	New Mexico	4,714,377	0.8%
36	Maine	4,299,499	0.7%
37	Mississippi	4,093,476	0.7%
38	Nebraska	3,890,404	0.7%
39	New Hampshire	3,782,042	0.6%
40	Montana	2,859,486	0.5%
41	Idaho	2,719,510	0.5%
42	Nevada	2,613,654	0.4%
43	Rhode Island	2,482,748	0.4%
44	Vermont	2,476,668	0.4%
45	Hawaii	1,908,942	0.3%
46	Delaware	1,867,727	0.3%
47	North Dakota	1,863,437	0.3%
48	Alaska	1,666,617	0.3%
49	South Dakota	1,642,974	0.3%
50	Wyoming	1,010,035	0.2%
	District of Columbia	1,649,284	0.3%

Source: American Hospital Association (Chicago, IL)
    "Hospital Statistics" (2007 edition)
*All nonfederal short-term general and other special hospitals, whose facilities and services are available to the public. Includes emergency and other visits.

Emergency Outpatient Visits to Community Hospitals in 2005

National Total = 114,750,874 Visits*

ALPHA ORDER

RANK	STATE	VISITS	% of USA
21	Alabama	2,085,573	1.8%
45	Alaska	326,528	0.3%
22	Arizona	2,050,938	1.8%
30	Arkansas	1,263,822	1.1%
1	California	9,483,972	8.3%
27	Colorado	1,502,264	1.3%
28	Connecticut	1,452,412	1.3%
44	Delaware	330,570	0.3%
4	Florida	6,895,641	6.0%
10	Georgia	3,683,883	3.2%
43	Hawaii	336,483	0.3%
41	Idaho	509,964	0.4%
7	Illinois	5,021,453	4.4%
16	Indiana	2,594,196	2.3%
33	Iowa	1,118,233	1.0%
34	Kansas	959,699	0.8%
17	Kentucky	2,238,194	2.0%
20	Louisiana	2,147,600	1.9%
37	Maine	728,701	0.6%
18	Maryland	2,160,010	1.9%
14	Massachusetts	2,866,187	2.5%
8	Michigan	4,177,255	3.6%
25	Minnesota	1,717,155	1.5%
26	Mississippi	1,665,894	1.5%
15	Missouri	2,617,778	2.3%
46	Montana	311,144	0.3%
40	Nebraska	554,269	0.5%
38	Nevada	712,484	0.6%
39	New Hampshire	621,217	0.5%
11	New Jersey	3,078,419	2.7%
36	New Mexico	742,439	0.6%
3	New York	7,639,381	6.7%
9	North Carolina	3,784,070	3.3%
47	North Dakota	263,489	0.2%
5	Ohio	5,593,421	4.9%
29	Oklahoma	1,428,028	1.2%
31	Oregon	1,216,163	1.1%
6	Pennsylvania	5,379,119	4.7%
42	Rhode Island	454,840	0.4%
24	South Carolina	1,739,487	1.5%
49	South Dakota	222,415	0.2%
12	Tennessee	3,062,336	2.7%
2	Texas	8,206,013	7.2%
35	Utah	803,394	0.7%
48	Vermont	256,116	0.2%
13	Virginia	2,891,314	2.5%
19	Washington	2,150,665	1.9%
32	West Virginia	1,163,861	1.0%
23	Wisconsin	1,965,535	1.7%
50	Wyoming	218,686	0.2%

RANK ORDER

RANK	STATE	VISITS	% of USA
1	California	9,483,972	8.3%
2	Texas	8,206,013	7.2%
3	New York	7,639,381	6.7%
4	Florida	6,895,641	6.0%
5	Ohio	5,593,421	4.9%
6	Pennsylvania	5,379,119	4.7%
7	Illinois	5,021,453	4.4%
8	Michigan	4,177,255	3.6%
9	North Carolina	3,784,070	3.3%
10	Georgia	3,683,883	3.2%
11	New Jersey	3,078,419	2.7%
12	Tennessee	3,062,336	2.7%
13	Virginia	2,891,314	2.5%
14	Massachusetts	2,866,187	2.5%
15	Missouri	2,617,778	2.3%
16	Indiana	2,594,196	2.3%
17	Kentucky	2,238,194	2.0%
18	Maryland	2,160,010	1.9%
19	Washington	2,150,665	1.9%
20	Louisiana	2,147,600	1.9%
21	Alabama	2,085,573	1.8%
22	Arizona	2,050,938	1.8%
23	Wisconsin	1,965,535	1.7%
24	South Carolina	1,739,487	1.5%
25	Minnesota	1,717,155	1.5%
26	Mississippi	1,665,894	1.5%
27	Colorado	1,502,264	1.3%
28	Connecticut	1,452,412	1.3%
29	Oklahoma	1,428,028	1.2%
30	Arkansas	1,263,822	1.1%
31	Oregon	1,216,163	1.1%
32	West Virginia	1,163,861	1.0%
33	Iowa	1,118,233	1.0%
34	Kansas	959,699	0.8%
35	Utah	803,394	0.7%
36	New Mexico	742,439	0.6%
37	Maine	728,701	0.6%
38	Nevada	712,484	0.6%
39	New Hampshire	621,217	0.5%
40	Nebraska	554,269	0.5%
41	Idaho	509,964	0.4%
42	Rhode Island	454,840	0.4%
43	Hawaii	336,483	0.3%
44	Delaware	330,570	0.3%
45	Alaska	326,528	0.3%
46	Montana	311,144	0.3%
47	North Dakota	263,489	0.2%
48	Vermont	256,116	0.2%
49	South Dakota	222,415	0.2%
50	Wyoming	218,686	0.2%
	District of Columbia	358,164	0.3%

Source: American Hospital Association (Chicago, IL)
"Hospital Statistics" (2007 edition)
*All nonfederal short-term general and other special hospitals, whose facilities and services are available to the public.

Surgical Operations in Community Hospitals in 2005

National Total = 27,542,858 Surgical Operations*

ALPHA ORDER

RANK	STATE	OPERATIONS	% of USA
18	Alabama	566,110	2.1%
49	Alaska	59,246	0.2%
25	Arizona	403,933	1.5%
32	Arkansas	267,478	1.0%
1	California	2,190,702	8.0%
27	Colorado	324,606	1.2%
28	Connecticut	313,485	1.1%
43	Delaware	93,286	0.3%
5	Florida	1,487,427	5.4%
10	Georgia	856,880	3.1%
45	Hawaii	85,254	0.3%
42	Idaho	105,267	0.4%
8	Illinois	1,113,641	4.0%
16	Indiana	628,253	2.3%
23	Iowa	451,077	1.6%
33	Kansas	264,980	1.0%
19	Kentucky	554,203	2.0%
26	Louisiana	389,621	1.4%
38	Maine	161,326	0.6%
20	Maryland	545,786	2.0%
12	Massachusetts	729,347	2.6%
7	Michigan	1,118,865	4.1%
21	Minnesota	505,429	1.8%
34	Mississippi	262,386	1.0%
17	Missouri	609,104	2.2%
48	Montana	69,991	0.3%
36	Nebraska	203,013	0.7%
37	Nevada	168,196	0.6%
41	New Hampshire	125,969	0.5%
14	New Jersey	699,343	2.5%
39	New Mexico	133,939	0.5%
2	New York	1,927,762	7.0%
9	North Carolina	889,464	3.2%
47	North Dakota	70,622	0.3%
6	Ohio	1,220,824	4.4%
30	Oklahoma	303,803	1.1%
29	Oregon	311,776	1.1%
4	Pennsylvania	1,551,732	5.6%
40	Rhode Island	130,027	0.5%
22	South Carolina	484,586	1.8%
44	South Dakota	87,193	0.3%
15	Tennessee	639,570	2.3%
3	Texas	1,793,956	6.5%
35	Utah	245,034	0.9%
46	Vermont	70,919	0.3%
11	Virginia	738,177	2.7%
24	Washington	428,671	1.6%
31	West Virginia	286,165	1.0%
13	Wisconsin	727,004	2.6%
50	Wyoming	40,366	0.1%

RANK ORDER

RANK	STATE	OPERATIONS	% of USA
1	California	2,190,702	8.0%
2	New York	1,927,762	7.0%
3	Texas	1,793,956	6.5%
4	Pennsylvania	1,551,732	5.6%
5	Florida	1,487,427	5.4%
6	Ohio	1,220,824	4.4%
7	Michigan	1,118,865	4.1%
8	Illinois	1,113,641	4.0%
9	North Carolina	889,464	3.2%
10	Georgia	856,880	3.1%
11	Virginia	738,177	2.7%
12	Massachusetts	729,347	2.6%
13	Wisconsin	727,004	2.6%
14	New Jersey	699,343	2.5%
15	Tennessee	639,570	2.3%
16	Indiana	628,253	2.3%
17	Missouri	609,104	2.2%
18	Alabama	566,110	2.1%
19	Kentucky	554,203	2.0%
20	Maryland	545,786	2.0%
21	Minnesota	505,429	1.8%
22	South Carolina	484,586	1.8%
23	Iowa	451,077	1.6%
24	Washington	428,671	1.6%
25	Arizona	403,933	1.5%
26	Louisiana	389,621	1.4%
27	Colorado	324,606	1.2%
28	Connecticut	313,485	1.1%
29	Oregon	311,776	1.1%
30	Oklahoma	303,803	1.1%
31	West Virginia	286,165	1.0%
32	Arkansas	267,478	1.0%
33	Kansas	264,980	1.0%
34	Mississippi	262,386	1.0%
35	Utah	245,034	0.9%
36	Nebraska	203,013	0.7%
37	Nevada	168,196	0.6%
38	Maine	161,326	0.6%
39	New Mexico	133,939	0.5%
40	Rhode Island	130,027	0.5%
41	New Hampshire	125,969	0.5%
42	Idaho	105,267	0.4%
43	Delaware	93,286	0.3%
44	South Dakota	87,193	0.3%
45	Hawaii	85,254	0.3%
46	Vermont	70,919	0.3%
47	North Dakota	70,622	0.3%
48	Montana	69,991	0.3%
49	Alaska	59,246	0.2%
50	Wyoming	40,366	0.1%
	District of Columbia	107,064	0.4%

Source: American Hospital Association (Chicago, IL)
"Hospital Statistics" (2007 edition)
Includes inpatient and outpatient surgeries.

Medicare and Medicaid Certified Facilities in 2007

National Total = 260,611 Facilities*

ALPHA ORDER

RANK	STATE	FACILITIES	% of USA
18	Alabama	4,458	1.7%
48	Alaska	606	0.2%
20	Arizona	4,236	1.6%
32	Arkansas	2,819	1.1%
1	California	24,346	9.4%
28	Colorado	3,453	1.3%
30	Connecticut	3,260	1.3%
47	Delaware	877	0.3%
3	Florida	17,636	6.8%
9	Georgia	8,020	3.1%
44	Hawaii	979	0.4%
40	Idaho	1,307	0.5%
6	Illinois	11,105	4.3%
11	Indiana	6,684	2.6%
27	Iowa	3,904	1.5%
29	Kansas	3,360	1.3%
24	Kentucky	4,179	1.6%
16	Louisiana	5,574	2.2%
39	Maine	1,318	0.5%
19	Maryland	4,378	1.7%
17	Massachusetts	4,619	1.8%
8	Michigan	8,493	3.3%
26	Minnesota	4,092	1.6%
31	Mississippi	3,117	1.2%
13	Missouri	6,259	2.4%
43	Montana	1,004	0.4%
35	Nebraska	2,237	0.9%
38	Nevada	1,575	0.6%
41	New Hampshire	1,168	0.5%
12	New Jersey	6,474	2.5%
37	New Mexico	1,686	0.7%
4	New York	12,505	4.8%
10	North Carolina	7,767	3.0%
46	North Dakota	881	0.3%
5	Ohio	11,918	4.6%
22	Oklahoma	4,197	1.6%
33	Oregon	2,802	1.1%
7	Pennsylvania	9,986	3.9%
45	Rhode Island	953	0.4%
23	South Carolina	4,193	1.6%
42	South Dakota	1,153	0.4%
14	Tennessee	5,841	2.3%
2	Texas	24,068	9.3%
36	Utah	1,704	0.7%
49	Vermont	577	0.2%
15	Virginia	5,619	2.2%
25	Washington	4,143	1.6%
34	West Virginia	2,273	0.9%
21	Wisconsin	4,213	1.6%
50	Wyoming	532	0.2%

RANK ORDER

RANK	STATE	FACILITIES	% of USA
1	California	24,346	9.4%
2	Texas	24,068	9.3%
3	Florida	17,636	6.8%
4	New York	12,505	4.8%
5	Ohio	11,918	4.6%
6	Illinois	11,105	4.3%
7	Pennsylvania	9,986	3.9%
8	Michigan	8,493	3.3%
9	Georgia	8,020	3.1%
10	North Carolina	7,767	3.0%
11	Indiana	6,684	2.6%
12	New Jersey	6,474	2.5%
13	Missouri	6,259	2.4%
14	Tennessee	5,841	2.3%
15	Virginia	5,619	2.2%
16	Louisiana	5,574	2.2%
17	Massachusetts	4,619	1.8%
18	Alabama	4,458	1.7%
19	Maryland	4,378	1.7%
20	Arizona	4,236	1.6%
21	Wisconsin	4,213	1.6%
22	Oklahoma	4,197	1.6%
23	South Carolina	4,193	1.6%
24	Kentucky	4,179	1.6%
25	Washington	4,143	1.6%
26	Minnesota	4,092	1.6%
27	Iowa	3,904	1.5%
28	Colorado	3,453	1.3%
29	Kansas	3,360	1.3%
30	Connecticut	3,260	1.3%
31	Mississippi	3,117	1.2%
32	Arkansas	2,819	1.1%
33	Oregon	2,802	1.1%
34	West Virginia	2,273	0.9%
35	Nebraska	2,237	0.9%
36	Utah	1,704	0.7%
37	New Mexico	1,686	0.7%
38	Nevada	1,575	0.6%
39	Maine	1,318	0.5%
40	Idaho	1,307	0.5%
41	New Hampshire	1,168	0.5%
42	South Dakota	1,153	0.4%
43	Montana	1,004	0.4%
44	Hawaii	979	0.4%
45	Rhode Island	953	0.4%
46	North Dakota	881	0.3%
47	Delaware	877	0.3%
48	Alaska	606	0.2%
49	Vermont	577	0.2%
50	Wyoming	532	0.2%
	District of Columbia	643	0.2%

Source: U.S. Department of Health and Human Services, Centers for Medicare and Medicaid Services OSCAR Report 10 (January 22, 2007)

*Certified by CMS to participate in the Medicare/Medicaid programs. All provider groups including hospitals, home health agencies, rural health centers, community mental health centers, nursing facilities, outpatient physical therapy facilities, hospices and laboratories. National total does not include 1,420 certified facilities in U.S. territories.

Medicare and Medicaid Certified Hospitals in 2007

National Total = 6,116 Hospitals*

ALPHA ORDER

RANK	STATE	HOSPITALS	% of USA
19	Alabama	129	2.1%
47	Alaska	24	0.4%
27	Arizona	102	1.7%
26	Arkansas	104	1.7%
2	California	421	6.9%
30	Colorado	90	1.5%
42	Connecticut	45	0.7%
50	Delaware	10	0.2%
4	Florida	240	3.9%
10	Georgia	178	2.9%
46	Hawaii	27	0.4%
39	Idaho	49	0.8%
8	Illinois	213	3.5%
11	Indiana	160	2.6%
20	Iowa	128	2.1%
11	Kansas	160	2.6%
21	Kentucky	120	2.0%
5	Louisiana	238	3.9%
42	Maine	45	0.7%
34	Maryland	64	1.0%
23	Massachusetts	114	1.9%
9	Michigan	180	2.9%
15	Minnesota	147	2.4%
22	Mississippi	115	1.9%
17	Missouri	141	2.3%
34	Montana	64	1.0%
29	Nebraska	96	1.6%
41	Nevada	46	0.8%
44	New Hampshire	30	0.5%
25	New Jersey	109	1.8%
37	New Mexico	52	0.9%
3	New York	242	4.0%
18	North Carolina	134	2.2%
38	North Dakota	50	0.8%
7	Ohio	219	3.6%
14	Oklahoma	153	2.5%
36	Oregon	59	1.0%
6	Pennsylvania	236	3.9%
48	Rhode Island	15	0.2%
31	South Carolina	78	1.3%
33	South Dakota	66	1.1%
13	Tennessee	154	2.5%
1	Texas	537	8.8%
40	Utah	48	0.8%
48	Vermont	15	0.2%
24	Virginia	113	1.8%
28	Washington	101	1.7%
32	West Virginia	68	1.1%
16	Wisconsin	144	2.4%
45	Wyoming	29	0.5%

RANK ORDER

RANK	STATE	HOSPITALS	% of USA
1	Texas	537	8.8%
2	California	421	6.9%
3	New York	242	4.0%
4	Florida	240	3.9%
5	Louisiana	238	3.9%
6	Pennsylvania	236	3.9%
7	Ohio	219	3.6%
8	Illinois	213	3.5%
9	Michigan	180	2.9%
10	Georgia	178	2.9%
11	Indiana	160	2.6%
11	Kansas	160	2.6%
13	Tennessee	154	2.5%
14	Oklahoma	153	2.5%
15	Minnesota	147	2.4%
16	Wisconsin	144	2.4%
17	Missouri	141	2.3%
18	North Carolina	134	2.2%
19	Alabama	129	2.1%
20	Iowa	128	2.1%
21	Kentucky	120	2.0%
22	Mississippi	115	1.9%
23	Massachusetts	114	1.9%
24	Virginia	113	1.8%
25	New Jersey	109	1.8%
26	Arkansas	104	1.7%
27	Arizona	102	1.7%
28	Washington	101	1.7%
29	Nebraska	96	1.6%
30	Colorado	90	1.5%
31	South Carolina	78	1.3%
32	West Virginia	68	1.1%
33	South Dakota	66	1.1%
34	Maryland	64	1.0%
34	Montana	64	1.0%
36	Oregon	59	1.0%
37	New Mexico	52	0.9%
38	North Dakota	50	0.8%
39	Idaho	49	0.8%
40	Utah	48	0.8%
41	Nevada	46	0.8%
42	Connecticut	45	0.7%
42	Maine	45	0.7%
44	New Hampshire	30	0.5%
45	Wyoming	29	0.5%
46	Hawaii	27	0.4%
47	Alaska	24	0.4%
48	Rhode Island	15	0.2%
48	Vermont	15	0.2%
50	Delaware	10	0.2%
	District of Columbia	14	0.2%

Source: U.S. Department of Health and Human Services, Centers for Medicare and Medicaid Services OSCAR Database (January 22, 2007)

*Certified by CMS to participate in the Medicare/Medicaid programs. Excludes licensed facilities that do not accept federal funding and facilities managed by the Department of Veterans Affairs. National total does not include 64 certified hospitals in U.S. territories.

Beds in Medicare and Medicaid Certified Hospitals in 2007

National Total = 927,520 Beds*

ALPHA ORDER

RANK ORDER

RANK	STATE	BEDS	% of USA		RANK	STATE	BEDS	% of USA
17	Alabama	19,725	2.1%		1	California	80,715	8.7%
49	Alaska	1,506	0.2%		2	New York	70,276	7.6%
24	Arizona	14,322	1.5%		3	Texas	66,482	7.2%
31	Arkansas	10,512	1.1%		4	Florida	56,905	6.1%
1	California	80,715	8.7%		5	Illinois	45,077	4.9%
28	Colorado	12,089	1.3%		6	Ohio	44,520	4.8%
32	Connecticut	10,312	1.1%		7	Pennsylvania	36,191	3.9%
47	Delaware	2,261	0.2%		8	New Jersey	30,206	3.3%
4	Florida	56,905	6.1%		9	Michigan	28,941	3.1%
11	Georgia	24,976	2.7%		10	North Carolina	25,448	2.7%
46	Hawaii	2,718	0.3%		11	Georgia	24,976	2.7%
44	Idaho	3,288	0.4%		12	Tennessee	24,554	2.6%
5	Illinois	45,077	4.9%		13	Missouri	23,589	2.5%
18	Indiana	18,973	2.0%		14	Louisiana	21,747	2.3%
29	Iowa	11,738	1.3%		15	Virginia	20,681	2.2%
30	Kansas	11,405	1.2%		16	Massachusetts	19,844	2.1%
20	Kentucky	17,281	1.9%		17	Alabama	19,725	2.1%
14	Louisiana	21,747	2.3%		18	Indiana	18,973	2.0%
39	Maine	4,194	0.5%		19	Wisconsin	17,982	1.9%
21	Maryland	15,815	1.7%		20	Kentucky	17,281	1.9%
16	Massachusetts	19,844	2.1%		21	Maryland	15,815	1.7%
9	Michigan	28,941	3.1%		22	Minnesota	15,730	1.7%
22	Minnesota	15,730	1.7%		23	Oklahoma	14,837	1.6%
26	Mississippi	13,040	1.4%		24	Arizona	14,322	1.5%
13	Missouri	23,589	2.5%		25	Washington	13,579	1.5%
45	Montana	3,011	0.3%		26	Mississippi	13,040	1.4%
35	Nebraska	6,470	0.7%		27	South Carolina	12,580	1.4%
36	Nevada	5,782	0.6%		28	Colorado	12,089	1.3%
41	New Hampshire	3,526	0.4%		29	Iowa	11,738	1.3%
8	New Jersey	30,206	3.3%		30	Kansas	11,405	1.2%
38	New Mexico	4,932	0.5%		31	Arkansas	10,512	1.1%
2	New York	70,276	7.6%		32	Connecticut	10,312	1.1%
10	North Carolina	25,448	2.7%		33	West Virginia	9,260	1.0%
43	North Dakota	3,297	0.4%		34	Oregon	7,433	0.8%
6	Ohio	44,520	4.8%		35	Nebraska	6,470	0.7%
23	Oklahoma	14,837	1.6%		36	Nevada	5,782	0.6%
34	Oregon	7,433	0.8%		37	Utah	5,121	0.6%
7	Pennsylvania	36,191	3.9%		38	New Mexico	4,932	0.5%
40	Rhode Island	3,657	0.4%		39	Maine	4,194	0.5%
27	South Carolina	12,580	1.4%		40	Rhode Island	3,657	0.4%
42	South Dakota	3,378	0.4%		41	New Hampshire	3,526	0.4%
12	Tennessee	24,554	2.6%		42	South Dakota	3,378	0.4%
3	Texas	66,482	7.2%		43	North Dakota	3,297	0.4%
37	Utah	5,121	0.6%		44	Idaho	3,288	0.4%
48	Vermont	1,808	0.2%		45	Montana	3,011	0.3%
15	Virginia	20,681	2.2%		46	Hawaii	2,718	0.3%
25	Washington	13,579	1.5%		47	Delaware	2,261	0.2%
33	West Virginia	9,260	1.0%		48	Vermont	1,808	0.2%
19	Wisconsin	17,982	1.9%		49	Alaska	1,506	0.2%
50	Wyoming	1,474	0.2%		50	Wyoming	1,474	0.2%
						District of Columbia	4,332	0.5%

Source: U.S. Department of Health and Human Services, Centers for Medicare and Medicaid Services
OSCAR Database (January 22, 2007)
*Beds in hospitals certified by CMS to participate in the Medicare/Medicaid programs. Excludes licensed facilities that do not accept federal funding and facilities managed by the Department of Veterans Affairs. National total does not include 11,426 beds in U.S. territories.

Medicare and Medicaid Certified Children's Hospitals in 2007

National Total = 80 Hospitals*

ALPHA ORDER					RANK ORDER			
RANK	STATE	HOSPITALS	% of USA		RANK	STATE	HOSPITALS	% of USA
9	Alabama	2	2.5%		1	California	10	12.5%
34	Alaska	0	0.0%		2	Texas	8	10.0%
9	Arizona	2	2.5%		3	Ohio	7	8.8%
20	Arkansas	1	1.3%		4	Pennsylvania	6	7.5%
1	California	10	12.5%		5	Minnesota	3	3.8%
20	Colorado	1	1.3%		5	Missouri	3	3.8%
20	Connecticut	1	1.3%		5	Virginia	3	3.8%
20	Delaware	1	1.3%		5	Wisconsin	3	3.8%
9	Florida	2	2.5%		9	Alabama	2	2.5%
9	Georgia	2	2.5%		9	Arizona	2	2.5%
20	Hawaii	1	1.3%		9	Florida	2	2.5%
34	Idaho	0	0.0%		9	Georgia	2	2.5%
9	Illinois	2	2.5%		9	Illinois	2	2.5%
20	Indiana	1	1.3%		9	Maryland	2	2.5%
34	Iowa	0	0.0%		9	Massachusetts	2	2.5%
20	Kansas	1	1.3%		9	Nebraska	2	2.5%
34	Kentucky	0	0.0%		9	Oklahoma	2	2.5%
20	Louisiana	1	1.3%		9	Tennessee	2	2.5%
34	Maine	0	0.0%		9	Washington	2	2.5%
9	Maryland	2	2.5%		20	Arkansas	1	1.3%
9	Massachusetts	2	2.5%		20	Colorado	1	1.3%
20	Michigan	1	1.3%		20	Connecticut	1	1.3%
5	Minnesota	3	3.8%		20	Delaware	1	1.3%
34	Mississippi	0	0.0%		20	Hawaii	1	1.3%
5	Missouri	3	3.8%		20	Indiana	1	1.3%
34	Montana	0	0.0%		20	Kansas	1	1.3%
9	Nebraska	2	2.5%		20	Louisiana	1	1.3%
34	Nevada	0	0.0%		20	Michigan	1	1.3%
34	New Hampshire	0	0.0%		20	New Jersey	1	1.3%
20	New Jersey	1	1.3%		20	New Mexico	1	1.3%
20	New Mexico	1	1.3%		20	New York	1	1.3%
20	New York	1	1.3%		20	South Dakota	1	1.3%
34	North Carolina	0	0.0%		20	Utah	1	1.3%
34	North Dakota	0	0.0%		34	Alaska	0	0.0%
3	Ohio	7	8.8%		34	Idaho	0	0.0%
9	Oklahoma	2	2.5%		34	Iowa	0	0.0%
34	Oregon	0	0.0%		34	Kentucky	0	0.0%
4	Pennsylvania	6	7.5%		34	Maine	0	0.0%
34	Rhode Island	0	0.0%		34	Mississippi	0	0.0%
34	South Carolina	0	0.0%		34	Montana	0	0.0%
20	South Dakota	1	1.3%		34	Nevada	0	0.0%
9	Tennessee	2	2.5%		34	New Hampshire	0	0.0%
2	Texas	8	10.0%		34	North Carolina	0	0.0%
20	Utah	1	1.3%		34	North Dakota	0	0.0%
34	Vermont	0	0.0%		34	Oregon	0	0.0%
5	Virginia	3	3.8%		34	Rhode Island	0	0.0%
9	Washington	2	2.5%		34	South Carolina	0	0.0%
34	West Virginia	0	0.0%		34	Vermont	0	0.0%
5	Wisconsin	3	3.8%		34	West Virginia	0	0.0%
34	Wyoming	0	0.0%		34	Wyoming	0	0.0%
						District of Columbia	1	1.3%

Source: U.S. Department of Health and Human Services, Centers for Medicare and Medicaid Services
   OSCAR Database (January 22, 2007)
*Certified by CMS to participate in the Medicare/Medicaid programs. National total does not include one facility in U.S. territories. Excludes licensed facilities that do not accept federal funding and facilities managed by the Department of Veterans Affairs.

Beds in Medicare and Medicaid Certified Children's Hospitals in 2007

National Total = 12,217 Beds*

ALPHA ORDER

RANK	STATE	BEDS	% of USA
7	Alabama	424	3.5%
34	Alaska	0	0.0%
17	Arizona	250	2.0%
13	Arkansas	280	2.3%
1	California	1,665	13.6%
16	Colorado	253	2.1%
26	Connecticut	129	1.1%
27	Delaware	97	0.8%
7	Florida	424	3.5%
5	Georgia	469	3.8%
20	Hawaii	201	1.6%
34	Idaho	0	0.0%
10	Illinois	339	2.8%
33	Indiana	20	0.2%
34	Iowa	0	0.0%
31	Kansas	34	0.3%
34	Kentucky	0	0.0%
20	Louisiana	201	1.6%
34	Maine	0	0.0%
25	Maryland	150	1.2%
9	Massachusetts	421	3.4%
19	Michigan	228	1.9%
10	Minnesota	339	2.8%
34	Mississippi	0	0.0%
6	Missouri	432	3.5%
34	Montana	0	0.0%
22	Nebraska	200	1.6%
34	Nevada	0	0.0%
34	New Hampshire	0	0.0%
30	New Jersey	74	0.6%
32	New Mexico	28	0.2%
29	New York	92	0.8%
34	North Carolina	0	0.0%
34	North Dakota	0	0.0%
3	Ohio	1,419	11.6%
24	Oklahoma	160	1.3%
34	Oregon	0	0.0%
4	Pennsylvania	810	6.6%
34	Rhode Island	0	0.0%
34	South Carolina	0	0.0%
28	South Dakota	96	0.8%
23	Tennessee	175	1.4%
2	Texas	1,494	12.2%
18	Utah	232	1.9%
34	Vermont	0	0.0%
12	Virginia	286	2.3%
14	Washington	276	2.3%
34	West Virginia	0	0.0%
14	Wisconsin	276	2.3%
34	Wyoming	0	0.0%

RANK ORDER

RANK	STATE	BEDS	% of USA
1	California	1,665	13.6%
2	Texas	1,494	12.2%
3	Ohio	1,419	11.6%
4	Pennsylvania	810	6.6%
5	Georgia	469	3.8%
6	Missouri	432	3.5%
7	Alabama	424	3.5%
7	Florida	424	3.5%
9	Massachusetts	421	3.4%
10	Illinois	339	2.8%
10	Minnesota	339	2.8%
12	Virginia	286	2.3%
13	Arkansas	280	2.3%
14	Washington	276	2.3%
14	Wisconsin	276	2.3%
16	Colorado	253	2.1%
17	Arizona	250	2.0%
18	Utah	232	1.9%
19	Michigan	228	1.9%
20	Hawaii	201	1.6%
20	Louisiana	201	1.6%
22	Nebraska	200	1.6%
23	Tennessee	175	1.4%
24	Oklahoma	160	1.3%
25	Maryland	150	1.2%
26	Connecticut	129	1.1%
27	Delaware	97	0.8%
28	South Dakota	96	0.8%
29	New York	92	0.8%
30	New Jersey	74	0.6%
31	Kansas	34	0.3%
32	New Mexico	28	0.2%
33	Indiana	20	0.2%
34	Alaska	0	0.0%
34	Idaho	0	0.0%
34	Iowa	0	0.0%
34	Kentucky	0	0.0%
34	Maine	0	0.0%
34	Mississippi	0	0.0%
34	Montana	0	0.0%
34	Nevada	0	0.0%
34	New Hampshire	0	0.0%
34	North Carolina	0	0.0%
34	North Dakota	0	0.0%
34	Oregon	0	0.0%
34	Rhode Island	0	0.0%
34	South Carolina	0	0.0%
34	Vermont	0	0.0%
34	West Virginia	0	0.0%
34	Wyoming	0	0.0%
	District of Columbia	243	2.0%

*Source: U.S. Department of Health and Human Services, Centers for Medicare and Medicaid Services
OSCAR Database (January 22, 2007)*

Certified by CMS to participate in the Medicare/Medicaid programs. National total does not include 215 beds in one facility in U.S. territories. Excludes licensed facilities that do not accept federal funding and facilities managed by the Department of Veterans Affairs.

Medicare and Medicaid Certified Rehabilitation Hospitals in 2007

National Total = 217 Hospitals*

ALPHA ORDER

RANK	STATE	HOSPITALS	% of USA
7	Alabama	7	3.2%
41	Alaska	0	0.0%
7	Arizona	7	3.2%
7	Arkansas	7	3.2%
11	California	6	2.8%
21	Colorado	3	1.4%
30	Connecticut	1	0.5%
41	Delaware	0	0.0%
4	Florida	14	6.5%
25	Georgia	2	0.9%
30	Hawaii	1	0.5%
30	Idaho	1	0.5%
19	Illinois	4	1.8%
7	Indiana	7	3.2%
41	Iowa	0	0.0%
19	Kansas	4	1.8%
11	Kentucky	6	2.8%
2	Louisiana	24	11.1%
30	Maine	1	0.5%
25	Maryland	2	0.9%
6	Massachusetts	8	3.7%
15	Michigan	5	2.3%
30	Minnesota	1	0.5%
41	Mississippi	0	0.0%
21	Missouri	3	1.4%
41	Montana	0	0.0%
30	Nebraska	1	0.5%
21	Nevada	3	1.4%
25	New Hampshire	2	0.9%
5	New Jersey	9	4.1%
15	New Mexico	5	2.3%
30	New York	1	0.5%
25	North Carolina	2	0.9%
41	North Dakota	0	0.0%
21	Ohio	3	1.4%
25	Oklahoma	2	0.9%
41	Oregon	0	0.0%
3	Pennsylvania	16	7.4%
30	Rhode Island	1	0.5%
15	South Carolina	5	2.3%
41	South Dakota	0	0.0%
11	Tennessee	6	2.8%
1	Texas	32	14.7%
30	Utah	1	0.5%
41	Vermont	0	0.0%
11	Virginia	6	2.8%
30	Washington	1	0.5%
15	West Virginia	5	2.3%
30	Wisconsin	1	0.5%
41	Wyoming	0	0.0%

RANK ORDER

RANK	STATE	HOSPITALS	% of USA
1	Texas	32	14.7%
2	Louisiana	24	11.1%
3	Pennsylvania	16	7.4%
4	Florida	14	6.5%
5	New Jersey	9	4.1%
6	Massachusetts	8	3.7%
7	Alabama	7	3.2%
7	Arizona	7	3.2%
7	Arkansas	7	3.2%
7	Indiana	7	3.2%
11	California	6	2.8%
11	Kentucky	6	2.8%
11	Tennessee	6	2.8%
11	Virginia	6	2.8%
15	Michigan	5	2.3%
15	New Mexico	5	2.3%
15	South Carolina	5	2.3%
15	West Virginia	5	2.3%
19	Illinois	4	1.8%
19	Kansas	4	1.8%
21	Colorado	3	1.4%
21	Missouri	3	1.4%
21	Nevada	3	1.4%
21	Ohio	3	1.4%
25	Georgia	2	0.9%
25	Maryland	2	0.9%
25	New Hampshire	2	0.9%
25	North Carolina	2	0.9%
25	Oklahoma	2	0.9%
30	Connecticut	1	0.5%
30	Hawaii	1	0.5%
30	Idaho	1	0.5%
30	Maine	1	0.5%
30	Minnesota	1	0.5%
30	Nebraska	1	0.5%
30	New York	1	0.5%
30	Rhode Island	1	0.5%
30	Utah	1	0.5%
30	Washington	1	0.5%
30	Wisconsin	1	0.5%
41	Alaska	0	0.0%
41	Delaware	0	0.0%
41	Iowa	0	0.0%
41	Mississippi	0	0.0%
41	Montana	0	0.0%
41	North Dakota	0	0.0%
41	Oregon	0	0.0%
41	South Dakota	0	0.0%
41	Vermont	0	0.0%
41	Wyoming	0	0.0%
	District of Columbia	1	0.5%

Source: U.S. Department of Health and Human Services, Centers for Medicare and Medicaid Services OSCAR Database (January 22, 2007)

Certified by CMS to participate in the Medicare/Medicaid programs. Excludes licensed facilities that do not accept federal funding and facilities managed by the Department of Veterans Affairs. National total does not include one certified hospital in U.S. territories.

Beds in Medicare and Medicaid Certified Rehabilitation Hospitals in 2007

National Total = 13,929 Beds*

ALPHA ORDER					RANK ORDER				
RANK	STATE		BEDS	% of USA	RANK	STATE		BEDS	% of USA
11	Alabama		364	2.6%	1	Texas		1,836	13.2%
41	Alaska		0	0.0%	2	Pennsylvania		1,431	10.3%
12	Arizona		363	2.6%	3	Florida		1,102	7.9%
7	Arkansas		485	3.5%	4	Massachusetts		1,040	7.5%
9	California		405	2.9%	5	New Jersey		776	5.6%
22	Colorado		226	1.6%	6	Louisiana		607	4.4%
37	Connecticut		60	0.4%	7	Arkansas		485	3.5%
41	Delaware		0	0.0%	8	Illinois		448	3.2%
3	Florida		1,102	7.9%	9	California		405	2.9%
27	Georgia		110	0.8%	10	Tennessee		370	2.7%
31	Hawaii		100	0.7%	11	Alabama		364	2.6%
38	Idaho		56	0.4%	12	Arizona		363	2.6%
8	Illinois		448	3.2%	13	Kentucky		328	2.4%
14	Indiana		324	2.3%	14	Indiana		324	2.3%
41	Iowa		0	0.0%	15	South Carolina		294	2.1%
19	Kansas		257	1.8%	16	Michigan		285	2.0%
13	Kentucky		328	2.4%	17	Virginia		273	2.0%
6	Louisiana		607	4.4%	18	West Virginia		270	1.9%
31	Maine		100	0.7%	19	Kansas		257	1.8%
28	Maryland		109	0.8%	20	North Carolina		233	1.7%
4	Massachusetts		1,040	7.5%	21	Missouri		232	1.7%
16	Michigan		285	2.0%	22	Colorado		226	1.6%
40	Minnesota		16	0.1%	23	New Mexico		212	1.5%
41	Mississippi		0	0.0%	24	Ohio		199	1.4%
21	Missouri		232	1.7%	25	Nevada		169	1.2%
41	Montana		0	0.0%	26	New Hampshire		130	0.9%
36	Nebraska		66	0.5%	27	Georgia		110	0.8%
25	Nevada		169	1.2%	28	Maryland		109	0.8%
26	New Hampshire		130	0.9%	29	Oklahoma		107	0.8%
5	New Jersey		776	5.6%	30	Washington		102	0.7%
23	New Mexico		212	1.5%	31	Hawaii		100	0.7%
39	New York		37	0.3%	31	Maine		100	0.7%
20	North Carolina		233	1.7%	33	Utah		84	0.6%
41	North Dakota		0	0.0%	34	Rhode Island		82	0.6%
24	Ohio		199	1.4%	35	Wisconsin		81	0.6%
29	Oklahoma		107	0.8%	36	Nebraska		66	0.5%
41	Oregon		0	0.0%	37	Connecticut		60	0.4%
2	Pennsylvania		1,431	10.3%	38	Idaho		56	0.4%
34	Rhode Island		82	0.6%	39	New York		37	0.3%
15	South Carolina		294	2.1%	40	Minnesota		16	0.1%
41	South Dakota		0	0.0%	41	Alaska		0	0.0%
10	Tennessee		370	2.7%	41	Delaware		0	0.0%
1	Texas		1,836	13.2%	41	Iowa		0	0.0%
33	Utah		84	0.6%	41	Mississippi		0	0.0%
41	Vermont		0	0.0%	41	Montana		0	0.0%
17	Virginia		273	2.0%	41	North Dakota		0	0.0%
30	Washington		102	0.7%	41	Oregon		0	0.0%
18	West Virginia		270	1.9%	41	South Dakota		0	0.0%
35	Wisconsin		81	0.6%	41	Vermont		0	0.0%
41	Wyoming		0	0.0%	41	Wyoming		0	0.0%
						District of Columbia		160	1.1%

Source: U.S. Department of Health and Human Services, Centers for Medicare and Medicaid Services
    OSCAR Database (January 22, 2007)
*Beds in hospitals certified by CMS to participate in the Medicare/Medicaid programs. Excludes licensed facilities
that do not accept federal funding and facilities managed by the Department of Veterans Affairs. National total
does not include 32 beds in U.S. territories.

Medicare and Medicaid Certified Psychiatric Hospitals in 2007

National Total = 479 Psychiatric Hospitals*

ALPHA ORDER

RANK	STATE	HOSPITALS	% of USA
17	Alabama	10	2.1%
41	Alaska	2	0.4%
26	Arizona	6	1.3%
14	Arkansas	11	2.3%
3	California	30	6.3%
26	Colorado	6	1.3%
25	Connecticut	7	1.5%
38	Delaware	3	0.6%
6	Florida	21	4.4%
11	Georgia	14	2.9%
48	Hawaii	1	0.2%
29	Idaho	5	1.0%
10	Illinois	15	3.1%
7	Indiana	20	4.2%
31	Iowa	4	0.8%
31	Kansas	4	0.8%
14	Kentucky	11	2.3%
2	Louisiana	34	7.1%
31	Maine	4	0.8%
21	Maryland	9	1.9%
8	Massachusetts	16	3.3%
17	Michigan	10	2.1%
26	Minnesota	6	1.3%
31	Mississippi	4	0.8%
11	Missouri	14	2.9%
41	Montana	2	0.4%
31	Nebraska	4	0.8%
31	Nevada	4	0.8%
41	New Hampshire	2	0.4%
8	New Jersey	16	3.3%
41	New Mexico	2	0.4%
4	New York	29	6.1%
23	North Carolina	8	1.7%
38	North Dakota	3	0.6%
11	Ohio	14	2.9%
21	Oklahoma	9	1.9%
41	Oregon	2	0.4%
5	Pennsylvania	22	4.6%
41	Rhode Island	2	0.4%
23	South Carolina	8	1.7%
48	South Dakota	1	0.2%
17	Tennessee	10	2.1%
1	Texas	35	7.3%
38	Utah	3	0.6%
48	Vermont	1	0.2%
17	Virginia	10	2.1%
29	Washington	5	1.0%
31	West Virginia	4	0.8%
14	Wisconsin	11	2.3%
41	Wyoming	2	0.4%

RANK ORDER

RANK	STATE	HOSPITALS	% of USA
1	Texas	35	7.3%
2	Louisiana	34	7.1%
3	California	30	6.3%
4	New York	29	6.1%
5	Pennsylvania	22	4.6%
6	Florida	21	4.4%
7	Indiana	20	4.2%
8	Massachusetts	16	3.3%
8	New Jersey	16	3.3%
10	Illinois	15	3.1%
11	Georgia	14	2.9%
11	Missouri	14	2.9%
11	Ohio	14	2.9%
14	Arkansas	11	2.3%
14	Kentucky	11	2.3%
14	Wisconsin	11	2.3%
17	Alabama	10	2.1%
17	Michigan	10	2.1%
17	Tennessee	10	2.1%
17	Virginia	10	2.1%
21	Maryland	9	1.9%
21	Oklahoma	9	1.9%
23	North Carolina	8	1.7%
23	South Carolina	8	1.7%
25	Connecticut	7	1.5%
26	Arizona	6	1.3%
26	Colorado	6	1.3%
26	Minnesota	6	1.3%
29	Idaho	5	1.0%
29	Washington	5	1.0%
31	Iowa	4	0.8%
31	Kansas	4	0.8%
31	Maine	4	0.8%
31	Mississippi	4	0.8%
31	Nebraska	4	0.8%
31	Nevada	4	0.8%
31	West Virginia	4	0.8%
38	Delaware	3	0.6%
38	North Dakota	3	0.6%
38	Utah	3	0.6%
41	Alaska	2	0.4%
41	Montana	2	0.4%
41	New Hampshire	2	0.4%
41	New Mexico	2	0.4%
41	Oregon	2	0.4%
41	Rhode Island	2	0.4%
41	Wyoming	2	0.4%
48	Hawaii	1	0.2%
48	South Dakota	1	0.2%
48	Vermont	1	0.2%
	District of Columbia	3	0.6%

*Source: U.S. Department of Health and Human Services, Centers for Medicare and Medicaid Services
OSCAR Database (January 22, 2007)*
*Certified by CMS to participate in the Medicare/Medicaid programs. Excludes licensed facilities that do not accept federal funding and facilities managed by the Department of Veterans Affairs. National total does not include four certified psychiatric hospitals in U.S. territories.

Beds in Medicare and Medicaid Certified Psychiatric Hospitals in 2007

National Total = 53,488 Beds*

ALPHA ORDER

RANK	STATE	BEDS	% of USA
26	Alabama	655	1.2%
45	Alaska	169	0.3%
31	Arizona	416	0.8%
21	Arkansas	939	1.8%
7	California	2,188	4.1%
25	Colorado	744	1.4%
19	Connecticut	1,081	2.0%
42	Delaware	237	0.4%
5	Florida	2,648	5.0%
11	Georgia	1,650	3.1%
49	Hawaii	88	0.2%
41	Idaho	243	0.5%
10	Illinois	1,694	3.2%
14	Indiana	1,333	2.5%
34	Iowa	350	0.7%
28	Kansas	561	1.0%
15	Kentucky	1,303	2.4%
9	Louisiana	1,718	3.2%
32	Maine	397	0.7%
8	Maryland	2,006	3.8%
12	Massachusetts	1,427	2.7%
18	Michigan	1,165	2.2%
27	Minnesota	614	1.1%
38	Mississippi	279	0.5%
20	Missouri	958	1.8%
43	Montana	194	0.4%
40	Nebraska	258	0.5%
35	Nevada	348	0.7%
36	New Hampshire	341	0.6%
3	New Jersey	3,103	5.8%
46	New Mexico	151	0.3%
1	New York	6,425	12.0%
6	North Carolina	2,233	4.2%
39	North Dakota	267	0.5%
17	Ohio	1,237	2.3%
29	Oklahoma	500	0.9%
37	Oregon	281	0.5%
2	Pennsylvania	3,535	6.6%
44	Rhode Island	177	0.3%
24	South Carolina	822	1.5%
48	South Dakota	133	0.2%
22	Tennessee	854	1.6%
4	Texas	2,848	5.3%
33	Utah	391	0.7%
47	Vermont	149	0.3%
23	Virginia	851	1.6%
16	Washington	1,283	2.4%
30	West Virginia	463	0.9%
13	Wisconsin	1,407	2.6%
50	Wyoming	82	0.2%

RANK ORDER

RANK	STATE	BEDS	% of USA
1	New York	6,425	12.0%
2	Pennsylvania	3,535	6.6%
3	New Jersey	3,103	5.8%
4	Texas	2,848	5.3%
5	Florida	2,648	5.0%
6	North Carolina	2,233	4.2%
7	California	2,188	4.1%
8	Maryland	2,006	3.8%
9	Louisiana	1,718	3.2%
10	Illinois	1,694	3.2%
11	Georgia	1,650	3.1%
12	Massachusetts	1,427	2.7%
13	Wisconsin	1,407	2.6%
14	Indiana	1,333	2.5%
15	Kentucky	1,303	2.4%
16	Washington	1,283	2.4%
17	Ohio	1,237	2.3%
18	Michigan	1,165	2.2%
19	Connecticut	1,081	2.0%
20	Missouri	958	1.8%
21	Arkansas	939	1.8%
22	Tennessee	854	1.6%
23	Virginia	851	1.6%
24	South Carolina	822	1.5%
25	Colorado	744	1.4%
26	Alabama	655	1.2%
27	Minnesota	614	1.1%
28	Kansas	561	1.0%
29	Oklahoma	500	0.9%
30	West Virginia	463	0.9%
31	Arizona	416	0.8%
32	Maine	397	0.7%
33	Utah	391	0.7%
34	Iowa	350	0.7%
35	Nevada	348	0.7%
36	New Hampshire	341	0.6%
37	Oregon	281	0.5%
38	Mississippi	279	0.5%
39	North Dakota	267	0.5%
40	Nebraska	258	0.5%
41	Idaho	243	0.5%
42	Delaware	237	0.4%
43	Montana	194	0.4%
44	Rhode Island	177	0.3%
45	Alaska	169	0.3%
46	New Mexico	151	0.3%
47	Vermont	149	0.3%
48	South Dakota	133	0.2%
49	Hawaii	88	0.2%
50	Wyoming	82	0.2%
	District of Columbia	292	0.5%

Source: U.S. Department of Health and Human Services, Centers for Medicare and Medicaid Services
    OSCAR Database (January 22, 2007)
*Beds in hospitals certified by CMS to participate in the Medicare/Medicaid programs. Excludes licensed facilities that do not accept federal funding and facilities managed by the Department of Veterans Affairs. National total does not include 903 beds in U.S. territories.

Medicare and Medicaid Certified Outpatient Surgery Centers in 2007

National Total = 4,700 Centers*

ALPHA ORDER					RANK ORDER			
RANK	STATE	CENTERS	% of USA		RANK	STATE	CENTERS	% of USA
36	Alabama	33	0.7%		1	California	632	13.4%
48	Alaska	8	0.2%		2	Florida	345	7.3%
10	Arizona	146	3.1%		3	Maryland	343	7.3%
21	Arkansas	59	1.3%		4	Texas	329	7.0%
1	California	632	13.4%		5	Georgia	233	5.0%
14	Colorado	97	2.1%		6	Washington	216	4.6%
33	Connecticut	40	0.9%		7	Pennsylvania	200	4.3%
37	Delaware	23	0.5%		8	New Jersey	190	4.0%
2	Florida	345	7.3%		9	Ohio	182	3.9%
5	Georgia	233	5.0%		10	Arizona	146	3.1%
46	Hawaii	11	0.2%		11	Tennessee	143	3.0%
25	Idaho	54	1.1%		12	Indiana	123	2.6%
13	Illinois	116	2.5%		13	Illinois	116	2.5%
12	Indiana	123	2.6%		14	Colorado	97	2.1%
38	Iowa	20	0.4%		15	Missouri	96	2.0%
21	Kansas	59	1.3%		16	New York	82	1.7%
35	Kentucky	34	0.7%		17	Louisiana	73	1.6%
17	Louisiana	73	1.6%		18	Oregon	72	1.5%
42	Maine	17	0.4%		19	Mississippi	64	1.4%
3	Maryland	343	7.3%		20	Michigan	60	1.3%
30	Massachusetts	42	0.9%		21	Arkansas	59	1.3%
20	Michigan	60	1.3%		21	Kansas	59	1.3%
29	Minnesota	45	1.0%		23	South Carolina	57	1.2%
19	Mississippi	64	1.4%		24	North Carolina	55	1.2%
15	Missouri	96	2.0%		25	Idaho	54	1.1%
44	Montana	15	0.3%		26	Oklahoma	52	1.1%
34	Nebraska	38	0.8%		27	Nevada	51	1.1%
27	Nevada	51	1.1%		28	Wisconsin	48	1.0%
38	New Hampshire	20	0.4%		29	Minnesota	45	1.0%
8	New Jersey	190	4.0%		30	Massachusetts	42	0.9%
38	New Mexico	20	0.4%		30	Utah	42	0.9%
16	New York	82	1.7%		30	Virginia	42	0.9%
24	North Carolina	55	1.2%		33	Connecticut	40	0.9%
41	North Dakota	19	0.4%		34	Nebraska	38	0.8%
9	Ohio	182	3.9%		35	Kentucky	34	0.7%
26	Oklahoma	52	1.1%		36	Alabama	33	0.7%
18	Oregon	72	1.5%		37	Delaware	23	0.5%
7	Pennsylvania	200	4.3%		38	Iowa	20	0.4%
49	Rhode Island	7	0.1%		38	New Hampshire	20	0.4%
23	South Carolina	57	1.2%		38	New Mexico	20	0.4%
44	South Dakota	15	0.3%		41	North Dakota	19	0.4%
11	Tennessee	143	3.0%		42	Maine	17	0.4%
4	Texas	329	7.0%		42	Wyoming	17	0.4%
30	Utah	42	0.9%		44	Montana	15	0.3%
50	Vermont	0	0.0%		44	South Dakota	15	0.3%
30	Virginia	42	0.9%		46	Hawaii	11	0.2%
6	Washington	216	4.6%		46	West Virginia	11	0.2%
46	West Virginia	11	0.2%		48	Alaska	8	0.2%
28	Wisconsin	48	1.0%		49	Rhode Island	7	0.1%
42	Wyoming	17	0.4%		50	Vermont	0	0.0%
						District of Columbia	4	0.1%

Source: U.S. Department of Health and Human Services, Centers for Medicare and Medicaid Services
    OSCAR Report 10 (January 22, 2007)
*Certified by CMS to participate in the Medicare/Medicaid programs. Excludes licensed facilities that do not accept federal funding and facilities managed by the Department of Veterans Affairs. National total does not include 26 certified outpatient surgery centers in U.S. territories. Also known as Ambulatory Surgical Centers.

Medicare and Medicaid Certified Community Mental Health Centers in 2007

National Total = 616 Centers*

ALPHA ORDER

RANK	STATE	CENTERS	% of USA
2	Alabama	59	9.6%
41	Alaska	0	0.0%
30	Arizona	3	0.5%
12	Arkansas	14	2.3%
7	California	20	3.2%
12	Colorado	14	2.3%
28	Connecticut	4	0.6%
41	Delaware	0	0.0%
1	Florida	137	22.2%
21	Georgia	9	1.5%
41	Hawaii	0	0.0%
41	Idaho	0	0.0%
19	Illinois	10	1.6%
23	Indiana	8	1.3%
27	Iowa	6	1.0%
21	Kansas	9	1.5%
18	Kentucky	11	1.8%
3	Louisiana	46	7.5%
41	Maine	0	0.0%
37	Maryland	1	0.2%
15	Massachusetts	13	2.1%
25	Michigan	7	1.1%
12	Minnesota	14	2.3%
25	Mississippi	7	1.1%
19	Missouri	10	1.6%
41	Montana	0	0.0%
37	Nebraska	1	0.2%
33	Nevada	2	0.3%
37	New Hampshire	1	0.2%
5	New Jersey	31	5.0%
10	New Mexico	15	2.4%
28	New York	4	0.6%
7	North Carolina	20	3.2%
41	North Dakota	0	0.0%
15	Ohio	13	2.1%
23	Oklahoma	8	1.3%
17	Oregon	12	1.9%
10	Pennsylvania	15	2.4%
41	Rhode Island	0	0.0%
30	South Carolina	3	0.5%
33	South Dakota	2	0.3%
9	Tennessee	16	2.6%
4	Texas	38	6.2%
33	Utah	2	0.3%
41	Vermont	0	0.0%
37	Virginia	1	0.2%
6	Washington	25	4.1%
33	West Virginia	2	0.3%
41	Wisconsin	0	0.0%
30	Wyoming	3	0.5%

RANK ORDER

RANK	STATE	CENTERS	% of USA
1	Florida	137	22.2%
2	Alabama	59	9.6%
3	Louisiana	46	7.5%
4	Texas	38	6.2%
5	New Jersey	31	5.0%
6	Washington	25	4.1%
7	California	20	3.2%
7	North Carolina	20	3.2%
9	Tennessee	16	2.6%
10	New Mexico	15	2.4%
10	Pennsylvania	15	2.4%
12	Arkansas	14	2.3%
12	Colorado	14	2.3%
12	Minnesota	14	2.3%
15	Massachusetts	13	2.1%
15	Ohio	13	2.1%
17	Oregon	12	1.9%
18	Kentucky	11	1.8%
19	Illinois	10	1.6%
19	Missouri	10	1.6%
21	Georgia	9	1.5%
21	Kansas	9	1.5%
23	Indiana	8	1.3%
23	Oklahoma	8	1.3%
25	Michigan	7	1.1%
25	Mississippi	7	1.1%
27	Iowa	6	1.0%
28	Connecticut	4	0.6%
28	New York	4	0.6%
30	Arizona	3	0.5%
30	South Carolina	3	0.5%
30	Wyoming	3	0.5%
33	Nevada	2	0.3%
33	South Dakota	2	0.3%
33	Utah	2	0.3%
33	West Virginia	2	0.3%
37	Maryland	1	0.2%
37	Nebraska	1	0.2%
37	New Hampshire	1	0.2%
37	Virginia	1	0.2%
41	Alaska	0	0.0%
41	Delaware	0	0.0%
41	Hawaii	0	0.0%
41	Idaho	0	0.0%
41	Maine	0	0.0%
41	Montana	0	0.0%
41	North Dakota	0	0.0%
41	Rhode Island	0	0.0%
41	Vermont	0	0.0%
41	Wisconsin	0	0.0%
	District of Columbia	0	0.0%

Source: U.S. Department of Health and Human Services, Centers for Medicare and Medicaid Services
   OSCAR Report 10 (January 22, 2007)

*Certified by CMS to participate in the Medicare/Medicaid programs. Excludes licensed facilities that do not accept federal funding and facilities managed by the Department of Veterans Affairs. National total does not include 13 certified mental health centers in U.S. territories.

Medicare and Medicaid Certified Outpatient Physical Therapy Facilities in 2007

National Total = 3,018 Facilities*

RANK	STATE	FACILITIES	% of USA
24	Alabama	40	1.3%
35	Alaska	15	0.5%
30	Arizona	28	0.9%
28	Arkansas	29	1.0%
4	California	176	5.8%
16	Colorado	54	1.8%
26	Connecticut	33	1.1%
37	Delaware	13	0.4%
1	Florida	389	12.9%
9	Georgia	108	3.6%
44	Hawaii	5	0.2%
39	Idaho	12	0.4%
10	Illinois	101	3.3%
18	Indiana	53	1.8%
25	Iowa	34	1.1%
33	Kansas	19	0.6%
11	Kentucky	97	3.2%
19	Louisiana	52	1.7%
34	Maine	17	0.6%
12	Maryland	92	3.0%
37	Massachusetts	13	0.4%
3	Michigan	248	8.2%
23	Minnesota	47	1.6%
21	Mississippi	48	1.6%
14	Missouri	70	2.3%
44	Montana	5	0.2%
41	Nebraska	11	0.4%
32	Nevada	22	0.7%
39	New Hampshire	12	0.4%
8	New Jersey	112	3.7%
27	New Mexico	30	1.0%
31	New York	27	0.9%
15	North Carolina	61	2.0%
48	North Dakota	2	0.1%
5	Ohio	134	4.4%
16	Oklahoma	54	1.8%
36	Oregon	14	0.5%
6	Pennsylvania	126	4.2%
46	Rhode Island	3	0.1%
20	South Carolina	50	1.7%
46	South Dakota	3	0.1%
13	Tennessee	84	2.8%
2	Texas	255	8.4%
43	Utah	7	0.2%
48	Vermont	2	0.1%
7	Virginia	120	4.0%
28	Washington	29	1.0%
42	West Virginia	10	0.3%
21	Wisconsin	48	1.6%
50	Wyoming	1	0.0%

RANK	STATE	FACILITIES	% of USA
1	Florida	389	12.9%
2	Texas	255	8.4%
3	Michigan	248	8.2%
4	California	176	5.8%
5	Ohio	134	4.4%
6	Pennsylvania	126	4.2%
7	Virginia	120	4.0%
8	New Jersey	112	3.7%
9	Georgia	108	3.6%
10	Illinois	101	3.3%
11	Kentucky	97	3.2%
12	Maryland	92	3.0%
13	Tennessee	84	2.8%
14	Missouri	70	2.3%
15	North Carolina	61	2.0%
16	Colorado	54	1.8%
16	Oklahoma	54	1.8%
18	Indiana	53	1.8%
19	Louisiana	52	1.7%
20	South Carolina	50	1.7%
21	Mississippi	48	1.6%
21	Wisconsin	48	1.6%
23	Minnesota	47	1.6%
24	Alabama	40	1.3%
25	Iowa	34	1.1%
26	Connecticut	33	1.1%
27	New Mexico	30	1.0%
28	Arkansas	29	1.0%
28	Washington	29	1.0%
30	Arizona	28	0.9%
31	New York	27	0.9%
32	Nevada	22	0.7%
33	Kansas	19	0.6%
34	Maine	17	0.6%
35	Alaska	15	0.5%
36	Oregon	14	0.5%
37	Delaware	13	0.4%
37	Massachusetts	13	0.4%
39	Idaho	12	0.4%
39	New Hampshire	12	0.4%
41	Nebraska	11	0.4%
42	West Virginia	10	0.3%
43	Utah	7	0.2%
44	Hawaii	5	0.2%
44	Montana	5	0.2%
46	Rhode Island	3	0.1%
46	South Dakota	3	0.1%
48	North Dakota	2	0.1%
48	Vermont	2	0.1%
50	Wyoming	1	0.0%
	District of Columbia	3	0.1%

Source: U.S. Department of Health and Human Services, Centers for Medicare and Medicaid Services
    OSCAR Report 10 (January 22, 2007)
Certified by CMS to participate in the Medicare/Medicaid programs. Excludes licensed facilities that do not accept federal funding and facilities managed by the Department of Veterans Affairs. National total does not include two certified outpatient physical therapy facilities in U.S. territories.

Medicare and Medicaid Certified Rural Health Clinics in 2007

National Total = 3,721 Rural Health Clinics*

ALPHA ORDER

RANK	STATE	CLINICS	% of USA
20	Alabama	64	1.7%
43	Alaska	4	0.1%
38	Arizona	13	0.3%
18	Arkansas	65	1.7%
3	California	250	6.7%
29	Colorado	47	1.3%
47	Connecticut	0	0.0%
47	Delaware	0	0.0%
7	Florida	152	4.1%
15	Georgia	99	2.7%
44	Hawaii	2	0.1%
28	Idaho	48	1.3%
4	Illinois	225	6.0%
25	Indiana	55	1.5%
9	Iowa	137	3.7%
5	Kansas	185	5.0%
10	Kentucky	129	3.5%
16	Louisiana	88	2.4%
32	Maine	41	1.1%
47	Maryland	0	0.0%
45	Massachusetts	1	0.0%
6	Michigan	160	4.3%
17	Minnesota	83	2.2%
8	Mississippi	145	3.9%
2	Missouri	312	8.4%
31	Montana	42	1.1%
12	Nebraska	120	3.2%
42	Nevada	6	0.2%
37	New Hampshire	15	0.4%
47	New Jersey	0	0.0%
39	New Mexico	12	0.3%
41	New York	9	0.2%
14	North Carolina	102	2.7%
18	North Dakota	65	1.7%
39	Ohio	12	0.3%
33	Oklahoma	39	1.0%
24	Oregon	56	1.5%
30	Pennsylvania	44	1.2%
45	Rhode Island	1	0.0%
13	South Carolina	103	2.8%
22	South Dakota	61	1.6%
25	Tennessee	55	1.5%
1	Texas	327	8.8%
35	Utah	17	0.5%
35	Vermont	17	0.5%
23	Virginia	57	1.5%
11	Washington	125	3.4%
21	West Virginia	63	1.7%
27	Wisconsin	49	1.3%
34	Wyoming	19	0.5%

RANK ORDER

RANK	STATE	CLINICS	% of USA
1	Texas	327	8.8%
2	Missouri	312	8.4%
3	California	250	6.7%
4	Illinois	225	6.0%
5	Kansas	185	5.0%
6	Michigan	160	4.3%
7	Florida	152	4.1%
8	Mississippi	145	3.9%
9	Iowa	137	3.7%
10	Kentucky	129	3.5%
11	Washington	125	3.4%
12	Nebraska	120	3.2%
13	South Carolina	103	2.8%
14	North Carolina	102	2.7%
15	Georgia	99	2.7%
16	Louisiana	88	2.4%
17	Minnesota	83	2.2%
18	Arkansas	65	1.7%
18	North Dakota	65	1.7%
20	Alabama	64	1.7%
21	West Virginia	63	1.7%
22	South Dakota	61	1.6%
23	Virginia	57	1.5%
24	Oregon	56	1.5%
25	Indiana	55	1.5%
25	Tennessee	55	1.5%
27	Wisconsin	49	1.3%
28	Idaho	48	1.3%
29	Colorado	47	1.3%
30	Pennsylvania	44	1.2%
31	Montana	42	1.1%
32	Maine	41	1.1%
33	Oklahoma	39	1.0%
34	Wyoming	19	0.5%
35	Utah	17	0.5%
35	Vermont	17	0.5%
37	New Hampshire	15	0.4%
38	Arizona	13	0.3%
39	New Mexico	12	0.3%
39	Ohio	12	0.3%
41	New York	9	0.2%
42	Nevada	6	0.2%
43	Alaska	4	0.1%
44	Hawaii	2	0.1%
45	Massachusetts	1	0.0%
45	Rhode Island	1	0.0%
47	Connecticut	0	0.0%
47	Delaware	0	0.0%
47	Maryland	0	0.0%
47	New Jersey	0	0.0%
	District of Columbia	0	0.0%

Source: U.S. Department of Health and Human Services, Centers for Medicare and Medicaid Services
    OSCAR Report 10 (January 22, 2007)
*Certified by CMS to participate in the Medicare/Medicaid programs. Excludes licensed facilities that do not accept federal funding and facilities managed by the Department of Veterans Affairs. There are no certified rural health centers in U.S. territories.

Medicare and Medicaid Certified Home Health Agencies in 2007

National Total = 8,773 Home Health Agencies*

ALPHA ORDER

RANK	STATE	AGENCIES	% of USA
18	Alabama	144	1.6%
48	Alaska	16	0.2%
27	Arizona	80	0.9%
15	Arkansas	174	2.0%
3	California	662	7.5%
19	Colorado	142	1.6%
26	Connecticut	84	1.0%
47	Delaware	17	0.2%
2	Florida	753	8.6%
25	Georgia	100	1.1%
49	Hawaii	14	0.2%
39	Idaho	48	0.5%
5	Illinois	428	4.9%
11	Indiana	196	2.2%
13	Iowa	180	2.1%
21	Kansas	136	1.6%
24	Kentucky	104	1.2%
8	Louisiana	224	2.6%
43	Maine	29	0.3%
37	Maryland	50	0.6%
23	Massachusetts	122	1.4%
6	Michigan	317	3.6%
9	Minnesota	214	2.4%
36	Mississippi	56	0.6%
16	Missouri	168	1.9%
41	Montana	37	0.4%
28	Nebraska	70	0.8%
31	Nevada	63	0.7%
42	New Hampshire	36	0.4%
37	New Jersey	50	0.6%
29	New Mexico	69	0.8%
12	New York	187	2.1%
16	North Carolina	168	1.9%
45	North Dakota	26	0.3%
4	Ohio	446	5.1%
10	Oklahoma	207	2.4%
33	Oregon	61	0.7%
6	Pennsylvania	317	3.6%
46	Rhode Island	21	0.2%
29	South Carolina	69	0.8%
40	South Dakota	42	0.5%
20	Tennessee	141	1.6%
1	Texas	1,754	20.0%
31	Utah	63	0.7%
50	Vermont	12	0.1%
14	Virginia	178	2.0%
35	Washington	60	0.7%
33	West Virginia	61	0.7%
22	Wisconsin	128	1.5%
44	Wyoming	27	0.3%

RANK ORDER

RANK	STATE	AGENCIES	% of USA
1	Texas	1,754	20.0%
2	Florida	753	8.6%
3	California	662	7.5%
4	Ohio	446	5.1%
5	Illinois	428	4.9%
6	Michigan	317	3.6%
6	Pennsylvania	317	3.6%
8	Louisiana	224	2.6%
9	Minnesota	214	2.4%
10	Oklahoma	207	2.4%
11	Indiana	196	2.2%
12	New York	187	2.1%
13	Iowa	180	2.1%
14	Virginia	178	2.0%
15	Arkansas	174	2.0%
16	Missouri	168	1.9%
16	North Carolina	168	1.9%
18	Alabama	144	1.6%
19	Colorado	142	1.6%
20	Tennessee	141	1.6%
21	Kansas	136	1.6%
22	Wisconsin	128	1.5%
23	Massachusetts	122	1.4%
24	Kentucky	104	1.2%
25	Georgia	100	1.1%
26	Connecticut	84	1.0%
27	Arizona	80	0.9%
28	Nebraska	70	0.8%
29	New Mexico	69	0.8%
29	South Carolina	69	0.8%
31	Nevada	63	0.7%
31	Utah	63	0.7%
33	Oregon	61	0.7%
33	West Virginia	61	0.7%
35	Washington	60	0.7%
36	Mississippi	56	0.6%
37	Maryland	50	0.6%
37	New Jersey	50	0.6%
39	Idaho	48	0.5%
40	South Dakota	42	0.5%
41	Montana	37	0.4%
42	New Hampshire	36	0.4%
43	Maine	29	0.3%
44	Wyoming	27	0.3%
45	North Dakota	26	0.3%
46	Rhode Island	21	0.2%
47	Delaware	17	0.2%
48	Alaska	16	0.2%
49	Hawaii	14	0.2%
50	Vermont	12	0.1%
	District of Columbia	22	0.3%

Source: U.S. Department of Health and Human Services, Centers for Medicare and Medicaid Services OSCAR Report 10 (January 22, 2007)

*Certified by CMS to participate in the Medicare/Medicaid programs. Excludes agencies that do not accept federal funding. National total does not include 55 certified home health agencies in U.S. territories. A home health agency provides health services to individuals in their homes for the purpose of promoting, maintaining or restoring health or maximizing the level of independence, while minimizing the effects of disability and illness.

Medicare and Medicaid Certified Hospices in 2007

National Total = 3,043 Hospices*

ALPHA ORDER

RANK	STATE	HOSPICES	% of USA
5	Alabama	118	3.9%
50	Alaska	5	0.2%
21	Arizona	56	1.8%
26	Arkansas	51	1.7%
2	California	196	6.4%
29	Colorado	46	1.5%
35	Connecticut	30	1.0%
48	Delaware	7	0.2%
31	Florida	42	1.4%
6	Georgia	111	3.6%
48	Hawaii	7	0.2%
32	Idaho	36	1.2%
8	Illinois	105	3.5%
14	Indiana	78	2.6%
16	Iowa	70	2.3%
23	Kansas	54	1.8%
37	Kentucky	27	0.9%
9	Louisiana	103	3.4%
40	Maine	19	0.6%
36	Maryland	28	0.9%
24	Massachusetts	53	1.7%
11	Michigan	95	3.1%
17	Minnesota	64	2.1%
7	Mississippi	108	3.5%
11	Missouri	95	3.1%
37	Montana	27	0.9%
33	Nebraska	33	1.1%
44	Nevada	14	0.5%
39	New Hampshire	21	0.7%
25	New Jersey	52	1.7%
30	New Mexico	44	1.4%
26	New York	51	1.7%
13	North Carolina	80	2.6%
43	North Dakota	15	0.5%
9	Ohio	103	3.4%
3	Oklahoma	144	4.7%
28	Oregon	48	1.6%
3	Pennsylvania	144	4.7%
47	Rhode Island	8	0.3%
19	South Carolina	58	1.9%
44	South Dakota	14	0.5%
20	Tennessee	57	1.9%
1	Texas	257	8.4%
18	Utah	59	1.9%
46	Vermont	10	0.3%
15	Virginia	73	2.4%
34	Washington	32	1.1%
41	West Virginia	18	0.6%
21	Wisconsin	56	1.8%
41	Wyoming	18	0.6%

RANK ORDER

RANK	STATE	HOSPICES	% of USA
1	Texas	257	8.4%
2	California	196	6.4%
3	Oklahoma	144	4.7%
3	Pennsylvania	144	4.7%
5	Alabama	118	3.9%
6	Georgia	111	3.6%
7	Mississippi	108	3.5%
8	Illinois	105	3.5%
9	Louisiana	103	3.4%
9	Ohio	103	3.4%
11	Michigan	95	3.1%
11	Missouri	95	3.1%
13	North Carolina	80	2.6%
14	Indiana	78	2.6%
15	Virginia	73	2.4%
16	Iowa	70	2.3%
17	Minnesota	64	2.1%
18	Utah	59	1.9%
19	South Carolina	58	1.9%
20	Tennessee	57	1.9%
21	Arizona	56	1.8%
21	Wisconsin	56	1.8%
23	Kansas	54	1.8%
24	Massachusetts	53	1.7%
25	New Jersey	52	1.7%
26	Arkansas	51	1.7%
26	New York	51	1.7%
28	Oregon	48	1.6%
29	Colorado	46	1.5%
30	New Mexico	44	1.4%
31	Florida	42	1.4%
32	Idaho	36	1.2%
33	Nebraska	33	1.1%
34	Washington	32	1.1%
35	Connecticut	30	1.0%
36	Maryland	28	0.9%
37	Kentucky	27	0.9%
37	Montana	27	0.9%
39	New Hampshire	21	0.7%
40	Maine	19	0.6%
41	West Virginia	18	0.6%
41	Wyoming	18	0.6%
43	North Dakota	15	0.5%
44	Nevada	14	0.5%
44	South Dakota	14	0.5%
46	Vermont	10	0.3%
47	Rhode Island	8	0.3%
48	Delaware	7	0.2%
48	Hawaii	7	0.2%
50	Alaska	5	0.2%
	District of Columbia	3	0.1%

Source: U.S. Department of Health and Human Services, Centers for Medicare and Medicaid Services
    OSCAR Report 10 (January 22, 2007)

*Certified by CMS to participate in the Medicare/Medicaid programs. Excludes licensed facilities that do not accept federal funding and facilities managed by the Department of Veterans Affairs. National total does not include 35 certified hospices in U.S. territories. An hospice provides specialized services for terminally ill people and their families.

Hospice Patients in Residential Facilities in 2007

National Total = 56,450 Patients*

ALPHA ORDER

RANK	STATE	PATIENTS	% of USA		RANK	STATE	PATIENTS	% of USA
24	Alabama	718	1.3%		1	Florida	11,924	21.1%
50	Alaska	3	0.0%		2	Texas	4,983	8.8%
27	Arizona	642	1.1%		3	Pennsylvania	3,899	6.9%
30	Arkansas	449	0.8%		4	Ohio	3,097	5.5%
5	California	2,780	4.9%		5	California	2,780	4.9%
23	Colorado	750	1.3%		6	North Carolina	2,079	3.7%
36	Connecticut	305	0.5%		7	Oklahoma	1,873	3.3%
38	Delaware	190	0.3%		8	Missouri	1,868	3.3%
1	Florida	11,924	21.1%		9	Georgia	1,863	3.3%
9	Georgia	1,863	3.3%		10	Illinois	1,656	2.9%
48	Hawaii	19	0.0%		11	Washington	1,548	2.7%
40	Idaho	141	0.2%		12	Massachusetts	1,263	2.2%
10	Illinois	1,656	2.9%		13	Indiana	1,204	2.1%
13	Indiana	1,204	2.1%		14	New York	992	1.8%
18	Iowa	898	1.6%		15	Virginia	983	1.7%
29	Kansas	504	0.9%		16	Oregon	930	1.6%
28	Kentucky	599	1.1%		17	Montana	907	1.6%
30	Louisiana	449	0.8%		18	Iowa	898	1.6%
20	Maine	814	1.4%		19	Nebraska	853	1.5%
34	Maryland	414	0.7%		20	Maine	814	1.4%
12	Massachusetts	1,263	2.2%		21	Wisconsin	776	1.4%
26	Michigan	644	1.1%		22	Minnesota	751	1.3%
22	Minnesota	751	1.3%		23	Colorado	750	1.3%
35	Mississippi	343	0.6%		24	Alabama	718	1.3%
8	Missouri	1,868	3.3%		25	New Jersey	655	1.2%
17	Montana	907	1.6%		26	Michigan	644	1.1%
19	Nebraska	853	1.5%		27	Arizona	642	1.1%
39	Nevada	142	0.3%		28	Kentucky	599	1.1%
44	New Hampshire	44	0.1%		29	Kansas	504	0.9%
25	New Jersey	655	1.2%		30	Arkansas	449	0.8%
41	New Mexico	132	0.2%		30	Louisiana	449	0.8%
14	New York	992	1.8%		32	South Carolina	428	0.8%
6	North Carolina	2,079	3.7%		33	Tennessee	424	0.8%
43	North Dakota	65	0.1%		34	Maryland	414	0.7%
4	Ohio	3,097	5.5%		35	Mississippi	343	0.6%
7	Oklahoma	1,873	3.3%		36	Connecticut	305	0.5%
16	Oregon	930	1.6%		37	Utah	251	0.4%
3	Pennsylvania	3,899	6.9%		38	Delaware	190	0.3%
49	Rhode Island	8	0.0%		39	Nevada	142	0.3%
32	South Carolina	428	0.8%		40	Idaho	141	0.2%
47	South Dakota	22	0.0%		41	New Mexico	132	0.2%
33	Tennessee	424	0.8%		42	West Virginia	96	0.2%
2	Texas	4,983	8.8%		43	North Dakota	65	0.1%
37	Utah	251	0.4%		44	New Hampshire	44	0.1%
46	Vermont	27	0.0%		45	Wyoming	30	0.1%
15	Virginia	983	1.7%		46	Vermont	27	0.0%
11	Washington	1,548	2.7%		47	South Dakota	22	0.0%
42	West Virginia	96	0.2%		48	Hawaii	19	0.0%
21	Wisconsin	776	1.4%		49	Rhode Island	8	0.0%
45	Wyoming	30	0.1%		50	Alaska	3	0.0%
						District of Columbia	15	0.0%

RANK ORDER

*Source: U.S. Department of Health and Human Services, Centers for Medicare and Medicaid Services
OSCAR Database (January 22, 2007)*

*Patients in facilities certified by CMS to participate in the Medicare/Medicaid programs. Excludes licensed facilities that do not accept federal funding and facilities managed by the Department of Veterans Affairs. National total does not include 54 patients in U.S. territories. A hospice provides specialized services for terminally ill people and their families.

Medicare and Medicaid Certified Nursing Care Facilities in 2007

National Total = 15,889 Nursing Care Facilities*

ALPHA ORDER

RANK	STATE	FACILITIES	% of USA
28	Alabama	231	1.5%
50	Alaska	15	0.1%
34	Arizona	136	0.9%
26	Arkansas	235	1.5%
1	California	1,281	8.1%
30	Colorado	210	1.3%
24	Connecticut	245	1.5%
47	Delaware	44	0.3%
6	Florida	682	4.3%
17	Georgia	360	2.3%
46	Hawaii	46	0.3%
43	Idaho	80	0.5%
4	Illinois	802	5.0%
9	Indiana	514	3.2%
10	Iowa	455	2.9%
18	Kansas	352	2.2%
21	Kentucky	293	1.8%
22	Louisiana	290	1.8%
36	Maine	113	0.7%
27	Maryland	233	1.5%
11	Massachusetts	453	2.9%
12	Michigan	424	2.7%
14	Minnesota	399	2.5%
31	Mississippi	202	1.3%
8	Missouri	519	3.3%
38	Montana	96	0.6%
29	Nebraska	225	1.4%
45	Nevada	47	0.3%
42	New Hampshire	82	0.5%
16	New Jersey	361	2.3%
44	New Mexico	73	0.5%
7	New York	655	4.1%
13	North Carolina	422	2.7%
41	North Dakota	83	0.5%
3	Ohio	957	6.0%
19	Oklahoma	333	2.1%
33	Oregon	138	0.9%
5	Pennsylvania	715	4.5%
40	Rhode Island	87	0.5%
32	South Carolina	175	1.1%
37	South Dakota	111	0.7%
20	Tennessee	325	2.0%
2	Texas	1,146	7.2%
39	Utah	93	0.6%
48	Vermont	41	0.3%
23	Virginia	278	1.7%
25	Washington	244	1.5%
35	West Virginia	131	0.8%
15	Wisconsin	398	2.5%
49	Wyoming	39	0.2%

RANK ORDER

RANK	STATE	FACILITIES	% of USA
1	California	1,281	8.1%
2	Texas	1,146	7.2%
3	Ohio	957	6.0%
4	Illinois	802	5.0%
5	Pennsylvania	715	4.5%
6	Florida	682	4.3%
7	New York	655	4.1%
8	Missouri	519	3.3%
9	Indiana	514	3.2%
10	Iowa	455	2.9%
11	Massachusetts	453	2.9%
12	Michigan	424	2.7%
13	North Carolina	422	2.7%
14	Minnesota	399	2.5%
15	Wisconsin	398	2.5%
16	New Jersey	361	2.3%
17	Georgia	360	2.3%
18	Kansas	352	2.2%
19	Oklahoma	333	2.1%
20	Tennessee	325	2.0%
21	Kentucky	293	1.8%
22	Louisiana	290	1.8%
23	Virginia	278	1.7%
24	Connecticut	245	1.5%
25	Washington	244	1.5%
26	Arkansas	235	1.5%
27	Maryland	233	1.5%
28	Alabama	231	1.5%
29	Nebraska	225	1.4%
30	Colorado	210	1.3%
31	Mississippi	202	1.3%
32	South Carolina	175	1.1%
33	Oregon	138	0.9%
34	Arizona	136	0.9%
35	West Virginia	131	0.8%
36	Maine	113	0.7%
37	South Dakota	111	0.7%
38	Montana	96	0.6%
39	Utah	93	0.6%
40	Rhode Island	87	0.5%
41	North Dakota	83	0.5%
42	New Hampshire	82	0.5%
43	Idaho	80	0.5%
44	New Mexico	73	0.5%
45	Nevada	47	0.3%
46	Hawaii	46	0.3%
47	Delaware	44	0.3%
48	Vermont	41	0.3%
49	Wyoming	39	0.2%
50	Alaska	15	0.1%
	District of Columbia	20	0.1%

Source: U.S. Department of Health and Human Services, Centers for Medicare and Medicaid Services
OSCAR Database (January 22, 2007)

*Certified by CMS to participate in the Medicare/Medicaid programs. Excludes licensed facilities that do not accept federal funding and facilities managed by the Department of Veterans Affairs. National total does not include 10 certified nursing facilities in U.S. territories.

Beds in Medicare and Medicaid Certified Nursing Care Facilities in 2007

National Total = 1,677,292 Beds*

ALPHA ORDER

RANK	STATE	BEADS	% of USA	RANK	STATE	BEDS	% of USA
24	Alabama	26,611	1.6%	1	California	122,555	7.3%
50	Alaska	705	0.0%	2	New York	120,799	7.2%
32	Arizona	16,312	1.0%	3	Texas	119,789	7.1%
26	Arkansas	24,366	1.5%	4	Illinois	97,530	5.8%
1	California	122,555	7.3%	5	Ohio	92,183	5.5%
29	Colorado	19,873	1.2%	6	Pennsylvania	88,279	5.3%
22	Connecticut	29,721	1.8%	7	Florida	81,821	4.9%
46	Delaware	4,485	0.3%	8	New Jersey	51,577	3.1%
7	Florida	81,821	4.9%	9	Missouri	50,860	3.0%
14	Georgia	39,910	2.4%	10	Massachusetts	49,745	3.0%
47	Hawaii	4,032	0.2%	11	Indiana	48,971	2.9%
44	Idaho	6,195	0.4%	12	Michigan	46,468	2.8%
4	Illinois	97,530	5.8%	13	North Carolina	43,225	2.6%
11	Indiana	48,971	2.9%	14	Georgia	39,910	2.4%
19	Iowa	32,893	2.0%	15	Wisconsin	38,398	2.3%
27	Kansas	23,299	1.4%	16	Tennessee	37,014	2.2%
25	Kentucky	25,535	1.5%	17	Louisiana	36,179	2.2%
17	Louisiana	36,179	2.2%	18	Minnesota	35,449	2.1%
40	Maine	7,329	0.4%	19	Iowa	32,893	2.0%
23	Maryland	29,002	1.7%	20	Virginia	31,036	1.9%
10	Massachusetts	49,745	3.0%	21	Oklahoma	30,110	1.8%
12	Michigan	46,468	2.8%	22	Connecticut	29,721	1.8%
18	Minnesota	35,449	2.1%	23	Maryland	29,002	1.7%
30	Mississippi	18,354	1.1%	24	Alabama	26,611	1.6%
9	Missouri	50,860	3.0%	25	Kentucky	25,535	1.5%
39	Montana	7,341	0.4%	26	Arkansas	24,366	1.5%
33	Nebraska	15,827	0.9%	27	Kansas	23,299	1.4%
45	Nevada	5,554	0.3%	28	Washington	22,379	1.3%
37	New Hampshire	7,818	0.5%	29	Colorado	19,873	1.2%
8	New Jersey	51,577	3.1%	30	Mississippi	18,354	1.1%
41	New Mexico	6,922	0.4%	31	South Carolina	17,991	1.1%
2	New York	120,799	7.2%	32	Arizona	16,312	1.0%
13	North Carolina	43,225	2.6%	33	Nebraska	15,827	0.9%
43	North Dakota	6,502	0.4%	34	Oregon	12,569	0.7%
5	Ohio	92,183	5.5%	35	West Virginia	10,924	0.7%
21	Oklahoma	30,110	1.8%	36	Rhode Island	8,866	0.5%
34	Oregon	12,569	0.7%	37	New Hampshire	7,818	0.5%
6	Pennsylvania	88,279	5.3%	38	Utah	7,809	0.5%
36	Rhode Island	8,866	0.5%	39	Montana	7,341	0.4%
31	South Carolina	17,991	1.1%	40	Maine	7,329	0.4%
42	South Dakota	6,701	0.4%	41	New Mexico	6,922	0.4%
16	Tennessee	37,014	2.2%	42	South Dakota	6,701	0.4%
3	Texas	119,789	7.1%	43	North Dakota	6,502	0.4%
38	Utah	7,809	0.5%	44	Idaho	6,195	0.4%
48	Vermont	3,431	0.2%	45	Nevada	5,554	0.3%
20	Virginia	31,036	1.9%	46	Delaware	4,485	0.3%
28	Washington	22,379	1.3%	47	Hawaii	4,032	0.2%
35	West Virginia	10,924	0.7%	48	Vermont	3,431	0.2%
15	Wisconsin	38,398	2.3%	49	Wyoming	3,049	0.2%
49	Wyoming	3,049	0.2%	50	Alaska	705	0.0%
					District of Columbia	2,999	0.2%

Source: U.S. Department of Health and Human Services, Centers for Medicare and Medicaid Services
OSCAR Database (January 22, 2007)
Beds in nursing care facilities certified by CMS to participate in the Medicare/Medicaid programs. National total does not include 413 beds in U.S. territories.

Rate of Beds in Medicare and Medicaid Certified Nursing Care Facilities in 2007

National Rate = 329 Beds per 1,000 Population 85 Years and Older*

ALPHA ORDER

RANK	STATE	RATE
17	Alabama	391
47	Alaska	180
48	Arizona	179
3	Arkansas	502
43	California	226
25	Colorado	334
22	Connecticut	344
32	Delaware	313
45	Florida	205
16	Georgia	398
50	Hawaii	146
40	Idaho	265
10	Illinois	428
6	Indiana	451
8	Iowa	436
15	Kansas	404
13	Kentucky	421
1	Louisiana	581
39	Maine	280
30	Maryland	325
21	Massachusetts	349
41	Michigan	252
22	Minnesota	344
6	Mississippi	451
4	Missouri	490
18	Montana	383
10	Nebraska	428
44	Nevada	216
26	New Hampshire	333
33	New Jersey	302
41	New Mexico	252
29	New York	327
24	North Carolina	339
19	North Dakota	379
12	Ohio	424
2	Oklahoma	545
49	Oregon	169
34	Pennsylvania	289
31	Rhode Island	322
38	South Carolina	283
20	South Dakota	359
9	Tennessee	429
5	Texas	465
36	Utah	286
35	Vermont	288
37	Virginia	285
46	Washington	202
26	West Virginia	333
26	Wisconsin	333
14	Wyoming	406

RANK ORDER

RANK	STATE	RATE
1	Louisiana	581
2	Oklahoma	545
3	Arkansas	502
4	Missouri	490
5	Texas	465
6	Indiana	451
6	Mississippi	451
8	Iowa	436
9	Tennessee	429
10	Illinois	428
10	Nebraska	428
12	Ohio	424
13	Kentucky	421
14	Wyoming	406
15	Kansas	404
16	Georgia	398
17	Alabama	391
18	Montana	383
19	North Dakota	379
20	South Dakota	359
21	Massachusetts	349
22	Connecticut	344
22	Minnesota	344
24	North Carolina	339
25	Colorado	334
26	New Hampshire	333
26	West Virginia	333
26	Wisconsin	333
29	New York	327
30	Maryland	325
31	Rhode Island	322
32	Delaware	313
33	New Jersey	302
34	Pennsylvania	289
35	Vermont	288
36	Utah	286
37	Virginia	285
38	South Carolina	283
39	Maine	280
40	Idaho	265
41	Michigan	252
41	New Mexico	252
43	California	226
44	Nevada	216
45	Florida	205
46	Washington	202
47	Alaska	180
48	Arizona	179
49	Oregon	169
50	Hawaii	146

	District of Columbia	310

Source: MQ Press using data from U.S. Dept of Health & Human Services, Centers for Medicare and Medicaid Services OSCAR Database (January 22, 2007)

*Beds in nursing care facilities certified by CMS to participate in the Medicare/Medicaid programs. National rate does not include beds or population in U.S. territories. Calculated using 2005 Census population estimate.

Nursing Home Occupancy Rate in 2004

National Rate = 82.7% of Beds in Nursing Homes Occupied

ALPHA ORDER

RANK	STATE	RATE
18	Alabama	88.2
36	Alaska	77.6
35	Arizona	79.1
44	Arkansas	73.0
30	California	83.3
33	Colorado	81.4
10	Connecticut	91.0
32	Delaware	81.8
19	Florida	88.1
12	Georgia	89.7
5	Hawaii	92.6
38	Idaho	76.7
40	Illinois	75.4
45	Indiana	72.8
38	Iowa	76.7
37	Kansas	77.5
24	Kentucky	86.7
43	Louisiana	74.9
6	Maine	92.3
25	Maryland	86.2
15	Massachusetts	88.5
28	Michigan	85.3
7	Minnesota	91.9
23	Mississippi	87.8
48	Missouri	68.8
42	Montana	75.1
31	Nebraska	81.9
29	Nevada	83.6
8	New Hampshire	91.4
22	New Jersey	88.0
27	New Mexico	85.7
3	New York	93.0
19	North Carolina	88.1
2	North Dakota	93.5
41	Ohio	75.2
49	Oklahoma	65.6
50	Oregon	64.8
11	Pennsylvania	90.6
9	Rhode Island	91.3
13	South Carolina	89.2
3	South Dakota	93.0
19	Tennessee	88.1
46	Texas	72.6
47	Utah	70.0
1	Vermont	93.9
16	Virginia	88.4
26	Washington	85.9
14	West Virginia	88.7
17	Wisconsin	88.3
34	Wyoming	81.1

RANK ORDER

RANK	STATE	RATE
1	Vermont	93.9
2	North Dakota	93.5
3	New York	93.0
3	South Dakota	93.0
5	Hawaii	92.6
6	Maine	92.3
7	Minnesota	91.9
8	New Hampshire	91.4
9	Rhode Island	91.3
10	Connecticut	91.0
11	Pennsylvania	90.6
12	Georgia	89.7
13	South Carolina	89.2
14	West Virginia	88.7
15	Massachusetts	88.5
16	Virginia	88.4
17	Wisconsin	88.3
18	Alabama	88.2
19	Florida	88.1
19	North Carolina	88.1
19	Tennessee	88.1
22	New Jersey	88.0
23	Mississippi	87.8
24	Kentucky	86.7
25	Maryland	86.2
26	Washington	85.9
27	New Mexico	85.7
28	Michigan	85.3
29	Nevada	83.6
30	California	83.3
31	Nebraska	81.9
32	Delaware	81.8
33	Colorado	81.4
34	Wyoming	81.1
35	Arizona	79.1
36	Alaska	77.6
37	Kansas	77.5
38	Idaho	76.7
38	Iowa	76.7
40	Illinois	75.4
41	Ohio	75.2
42	Montana	75.1
43	Louisiana	74.9
44	Arkansas	73.0
45	Indiana	72.8
46	Texas	72.6
47	Utah	70.0
48	Missouri	68.8
49	Oklahoma	65.6
50	Oregon	64.8

	District of Columbia	90.7

Source: U.S. Department of Health and Human Services, Centers for Medicare and Medicaid Services
"Health, United States, 2006" (www.cdc.gov/nchs/data/hus/hus06.pdf)

Nursing Home Resident Rate in 2004

National Rate = 296.8 Residents per 1,000 Population Age 85 and Older*

RANK	STATE	RATE
18	Alabama	355.2
47	Alaska	173.0
48	Arizona	151.0
15	Arkansas	370.6
43	California	206.3
31	Colorado	293.4
20	Connecticut	339.8
32	Delaware	287.4
44	Florida	191.7
10	Georgia	377.2
49	Hawaii	149.1
41	Idaho	211.1
16	Illinois	361.5
5	Indiana	386.7
7	Iowa	381.1
11	Kansas	375.3
8	Kentucky	381.0
1	Louisiana	473.9
36	Maine	274.6
29	Maryland	304.8
22	Massachusetts	335.1
39	Michigan	236.3
19	Minnesota	354.7
2	Mississippi	407.0
14	Missouri	371.3
28	Montana	307.8
12	Nebraska	372.8
46	Nevada	178.9
23	New Hampshire	327.3
37	New Jersey	274.3
40	New Mexico	235.3
25	New York	320.5
27	North Carolina	314.4
13	North Dakota	371.8
6	Ohio	385.6
4	Oklahoma	395.0
50	Oregon	117.4
34	Pennsylvania	278.4
24	Rhode Island	323.3
35	South Carolina	275.1
9	South Dakota	379.9
3	Tennessee	397.4
17	Texas	360.3
42	Utah	207.3
33	Vermont	282.3
38	Virginia	272.8
45	Washington	190.0
30	West Virginia	302.9
26	Wisconsin	318.3
21	Wyoming	336.6

RANK	STATE	RATE
1	Louisiana	473.9
2	Mississippi	407.0
3	Tennessee	397.4
4	Oklahoma	395.0
5	Indiana	386.7
6	Ohio	385.6
7	Iowa	381.1
8	Kentucky	381.0
9	South Dakota	379.9
10	Georgia	377.2
11	Kansas	375.3
12	Nebraska	372.8
13	North Dakota	371.8
14	Missouri	371.3
15	Arkansas	370.6
16	Illinois	361.5
17	Texas	360.3
18	Alabama	355.2
19	Minnesota	354.7
20	Connecticut	339.8
21	Wyoming	336.6
22	Massachusetts	335.1
23	New Hampshire	327.3
24	Rhode Island	323.3
25	New York	320.5
26	Wisconsin	318.3
27	North Carolina	314.4
28	Montana	307.8
29	Maryland	304.8
30	West Virginia	302.9
31	Colorado	293.4
32	Delaware	287.4
33	Vermont	282.3
34	Pennsylvania	278.4
35	South Carolina	275.1
36	Maine	274.6
37	New Jersey	274.3
38	Virginia	272.8
39	Michigan	236.3
40	New Mexico	235.3
41	Idaho	211.1
42	Utah	207.3
43	California	206.3
44	Florida	191.7
45	Washington	190.0
46	Nevada	178.9
47	Alaska	173.0
48	Arizona	151.0
49	Hawaii	149.1
50	Oregon	117.4

District of Columbia	299.2

Source: U.S. Department of Health and Human Services, Centers for Medicare and Medicaid Services
"Health, United States, 2006" (www.cdc.gov/nchs/data/hus/hus06.pdf)
*Number of nursing home residents (all ages) per 1,000 resident population 85 years of age and over.

Nursing Home Population in 2004

National Total = 1,442,503

ALPHA ORDER

ALPHA ORDER

RANK	STATE	POPULATION	% of USA
23	Alabama	23,504	1.6%
50	Alaska	606	0.0%
33	Arizona	12,971	0.9%
28	Arkansas	17,730	1.2%
2	California	106,020	7.3%
30	Colorado	16,326	1.1%
20	Connecticut	27,887	1.9%
46	Delaware	3,811	0.3%
7	Florida	72,759	5.0%
14	Georgia	35,935	2.5%
47	Hawaii	3,780	0.3%
44	Idaho	4,746	0.3%
6	Illinois	79,311	5.5%
11	Indiana	40,553	2.8%
21	Iowa	27,581	1.9%
26	Kansas	20,662	1.4%
24	Kentucky	22,491	1.6%
18	Louisiana	28,587	2.0%
38	Maine	6,891	0.5%
22	Maryland	25,222	1.7%
8	Massachusetts	45,619	3.2%
10	Michigan	41,369	2.9%
16	Minnesota	34,834	2.4%
31	Mississippi	16,129	1.1%
13	Missouri	37,274	2.6%
42	Montana	5,612	0.4%
32	Nebraska	13,389	0.9%
45	Nevada	4,294	0.3%
37	New Hampshire	7,110	0.5%
9	New Jersey	44,658	3.1%
40	New Mexico	6,311	0.4%
1	New York	113,402	7.9%
12	North Carolina	37,926	2.6%
41	North Dakota	6,103	0.4%
5	Ohio	80,370	5.6%
25	Oklahoma	21,453	1.5%
36	Oregon	8,203	0.6%
4	Pennsylvania	80,982	5.6%
35	Rhode Island	8,500	0.6%
29	South Carolina	16,352	1.1%
39	South Dakota	6,709	0.5%
17	Tennessee	33,271	2.3%
3	Texas	88,631	6.1%
43	Utah	5,327	0.4%
48	Vermont	3,240	0.2%
19	Virginia	27,982	1.9%
27	Washington	19,619	1.4%
34	West Virginia	9,856	0.7%
15	Wisconsin	35,344	2.5%
49	Wyoming	2,482	0.2%

RANK ORDER

RANK	STATE	POPULATION	% of USA
1	New York	113,402	7.9%
2	California	106,020	7.3%
3	Texas	88,631	6.1%
4	Pennsylvania	80,982	5.6%
5	Ohio	80,370	5.6%
6	Illinois	79,311	5.5%
7	Florida	72,759	5.0%
8	Massachusetts	45,619	3.2%
9	New Jersey	44,658	3.1%
10	Michigan	41,369	2.9%
11	Indiana	40,553	2.8%
12	North Carolina	37,926	2.6%
13	Missouri	37,274	2.6%
14	Georgia	35,935	2.5%
15	Wisconsin	35,344	2.5%
16	Minnesota	34,834	2.4%
17	Tennessee	33,271	2.3%
18	Louisiana	28,587	2.0%
19	Virginia	27,982	1.9%
20	Connecticut	27,887	1.9%
21	Iowa	27,581	1.9%
22	Maryland	25,222	1.7%
23	Alabama	23,504	1.6%
24	Kentucky	22,491	1.6%
25	Oklahoma	21,453	1.5%
26	Kansas	20,662	1.4%
27	Washington	19,619	1.4%
28	Arkansas	17,730	1.2%
29	South Carolina	16,352	1.1%
30	Colorado	16,326	1.1%
31	Mississippi	16,129	1.1%
32	Nebraska	13,389	0.9%
33	Arizona	12,971	0.9%
34	West Virginia	9,856	0.7%
35	Rhode Island	8,500	0.6%
36	Oregon	8,203	0.6%
37	New Hampshire	7,110	0.5%
38	Maine	6,891	0.5%
39	South Dakota	6,709	0.5%
40	New Mexico	6,311	0.4%
41	North Dakota	6,103	0.4%
42	Montana	5,612	0.4%
43	Utah	5,327	0.4%
44	Idaho	4,746	0.3%
45	Nevada	4,294	0.3%
46	Delaware	3,811	0.3%
47	Hawaii	3,780	0.3%
48	Vermont	3,240	0.2%
49	Wyoming	2,482	0.2%
50	Alaska	606	0.0%
	District of Columbia	2,779	0.2%

Source: U.S. Department of Health and Human Services, Centers for Medicare and Medicaid Services "Health, United States, 2006" (www.cdc.gov/nchs/data/hus/hus06.pdf)

Health Care Establishments in 2004

National Total = 587,306 Establishments*

RANK	STATE	ESTABLISH'S	% of USA
26	Alabama	7,570	1.3%
47	Alaska	1,468	0.2%
18	Arizona	11,191	1.9%
32	Arkansas	5,212	0.9%
1	California	75,894	12.9%
21	Colorado	9,998	1.7%
27	Connecticut	7,559	1.3%
45	Delaware	1,653	0.3%
4	Florida	40,002	6.8%
10	Georgia	15,155	2.6%
41	Hawaii	2,751	0.5%
40	Idaho	3,055	0.5%
6	Illinois	23,518	4.0%
17	Indiana	11,210	1.9%
30	Iowa	5,563	0.9%
31	Kansas	5,559	0.9%
25	Kentucky	7,946	1.4%
23	Louisiana	8,786	1.5%
39	Maine	3,235	0.6%
15	Maryland	11,772	2.0%
12	Massachusetts	13,238	2.3%
9	Michigan	20,414	3.5%
22	Minnesota	9,784	1.7%
35	Mississippi	4,214	0.7%
16	Missouri	11,450	1.9%
44	Montana	2,233	0.4%
38	Nebraska	3,364	0.6%
34	Nevada	4,339	0.7%
43	New Hampshire	2,322	0.4%
8	New Jersey	20,452	3.5%
37	New Mexico	3,380	0.6%
2	New York	41,850	7.1%
11	North Carolina	14,633	2.5%
49	North Dakota	1,186	0.2%
7	Ohio	22,032	3.8%
28	Oklahoma	7,304	1.2%
24	Oregon	8,353	1.4%
5	Pennsylvania	26,917	4.6%
42	Rhode Island	2,469	0.4%
29	South Carolina	6,784	1.2%
46	South Dakota	1,527	0.3%
19	Tennessee	10,616	1.8%
3	Texas	40,995	7.0%
33	Utah	4,912	0.8%
48	Vermont	1,436	0.2%
14	Virginia	12,642	2.2%
13	Washington	12,920	2.2%
36	West Virginia	3,710	0.6%
20	Wisconsin	10,135	1.7%
50	Wyoming	1,175	0.2%

RANK	STATE	ESTABLISH'S	% of USA
1	California	75,894	12.9%
2	New York	41,850	7.1%
3	Texas	40,995	7.0%
4	Florida	40,002	6.8%
5	Pennsylvania	26,917	4.6%
6	Illinois	23,518	4.0%
7	Ohio	22,032	3.8%
8	New Jersey	20,452	3.5%
9	Michigan	20,414	3.5%
10	Georgia	15,155	2.6%
11	North Carolina	14,633	2.5%
12	Massachusetts	13,238	2.3%
13	Washington	12,920	2.2%
14	Virginia	12,642	2.2%
15	Maryland	11,772	2.0%
16	Missouri	11,450	1.9%
17	Indiana	11,210	1.9%
18	Arizona	11,191	1.9%
19	Tennessee	10,616	1.8%
20	Wisconsin	10,135	1.7%
21	Colorado	9,998	1.7%
22	Minnesota	9,784	1.7%
23	Louisiana	8,786	1.5%
24	Oregon	8,353	1.4%
25	Kentucky	7,946	1.4%
26	Alabama	7,570	1.3%
27	Connecticut	7,559	1.3%
28	Oklahoma	7,304	1.2%
29	South Carolina	6,784	1.2%
30	Iowa	5,563	0.9%
31	Kansas	5,559	0.9%
32	Arkansas	5,212	0.9%
33	Utah	4,912	0.8%
34	Nevada	4,339	0.7%
35	Mississippi	4,214	0.7%
36	West Virginia	3,710	0.6%
37	New Mexico	3,380	0.6%
38	Nebraska	3,364	0.6%
39	Maine	3,235	0.6%
40	Idaho	3,055	0.5%
41	Hawaii	2,751	0.5%
42	Rhode Island	2,469	0.4%
43	New Hampshire	2,322	0.4%
44	Montana	2,233	0.4%
45	Delaware	1,653	0.3%
46	South Dakota	1,527	0.3%
47	Alaska	1,468	0.2%
48	Vermont	1,436	0.2%
49	North Dakota	1,186	0.2%
50	Wyoming	1,175	0.2%
	District of Columbia	1,423	0.2%

Source: U.S. Bureau of the Census
"County Business Patterns 2004 (NAICS)" (http://censtats.census.gov/cbpnaic/cbpnaic.shtml)
Includes establishments exempt from as well as subject to the federal income tax. Includes those establishments within the North American Industry Classification System (NAICS) classifications 621 (ambulatory health care services), 622 (hospitals) and 623 (nursing and residential care facilities). Does not include classification 624 (social assistance facilities).

IV. FINANCE

230 Average Medical Malpractice Payment in 2004
231 Percent of Private-Sector Establishments That Offer Health Insurance: 2004
232 Percent of Private-Sector Establishments with Fewer Than 50 Employees That Offer Health Insurance: 2004
233 Percent of Private-Sector Establishments with More Than 50 Employees That Offer Health Insurance: 2004
234 Average Annual Single Coverage Health Insurance Premium per Enrolled Employee in 2004
235 Average Annual Employee Contribution for Single Coverage Health Insurance in 2004
236 Percent of Total Premiums for Single Coverage Health Insurance Paid by Employees in 2004
237 Average Annual Family Coverage Health Insurance Premium per Enrolled Employee in 2004
238 Average Annual Employee Contribution for Family Coverage Health Insurance in 2004
239 Percent of Total Premiums for Family Coverage Health Insurance Paid by Employees in 2004
240 Persons Not Covered by Health Insurance in 2005
241 Percent of Population Not Covered by Health Insurance in 2005
242 Numerical Change in Persons Uninsured: 2001 to 2005
243 Percent Change in Persons Uninsured: 2001 to 2005
244 Change in Percent of Population Uninsured: 2001 to 2005
245 Percent of Children Not Covered by Health Insurance in 2005
246 Persons Covered by Health Insurance in 2005
247 Percent of Population Covered by Health Insurance in 2005
248 Percent of Population Covered by Private Health Insurance in 2005
249 Percent of Population Covered by Employment-Based Health Insurance in 2005
250 Percent of Population Covered by Direct Purchase Health Insurance in 2005
251 Percent of Population Covered by Government Health Insurance in 2005
252 Percent of Population Covered by Military Health Care in 2005
253 Percent of Children Covered by Health Insurance in 2005
254 Percent of Children Covered by Private Health Insurance in 2005
255 Percent of Children Covered by Employment-Based Health Insurance in 2005
256 Percent of Children Covered by Direct Purchase Health Insurance in 2005
257 Percent of Children Covered by Government Health Insurance in 2005
258 Percent of Children Covered by Military Health Care in 2005
259 Percent of Children Covered by Medicaid in 2005
260 State Children's Health Insurance Program (SCHIP) Enrollment in 2005
261 Percent Change in State Children's Health Insurance Program (SCHIP) Enrollment: 2004 to 2005
262 Percent of Children Enrolled in State Children's Health Insurance Program (SCHIP) in 2005
263 Expenditures for State Children's Health Insurance Program (SCHIP) in 2005
264 Per Capita Expenditures for State Children's Health Insurance Program (SCHIP) in 2005
265 Expenditures per State Children's Health Insurance Program (SCHIP) Participant in 2005
266 Health Maintenance Organizations (HMOs) in 2006
267 Enrollees in Health Maintenance Organizations (HMOs) in 2006
268 Percent Change in Enrollees in Health Maintenance Organizations (HMOs): 2005 to 2006
269 Percent of Population Enrolled in Health Maintenance Organizations (HMOs) in 2006
270 Percent of Insured Population Enrolled in Health Maintenance Organizations (HMOs) in 2006
271 Medicare Enrollees in 2005
272 Percent Change in Medicare Enrollees: 2004 to 2005
273 Percent of Population Enrolled in Medicare in 2005
274 Enrollment in Medicare Prescription Drug Plans as of June 14, 2006
275 Percent of Population Enrolled in Medicare Prescription Drug Plans in 2006
276 Medicare Managed Care Enrollees in 2005
277 Percent of Medicare Enrollees in Managed Care Programs in 2005
278 Percent of Physicians Participating in Medicare in 2006
279 Medicare Program Payments in 2004
280 Per Capita Medicare Program Payments in 2004
281 Medicare Program Payments per Enrollee in 2004
282 Medicaid Enrollment in 2005
283 Percent of Population Enrolled in Medicaid in 2005
284 Medicaid Managed Care Enrollment in 2005
285 Percent of Medicaid Enrollees in Managed Care in 2005
286 Estimated Medicaid Expenditures in 2006
287 Estimated Per Capita Medicaid Expenditures in 2006
288 Estimated Medicaid Expenditures as a Percent of Total Expenditures in 2006
289 Percent Change in Medicaid Expenditures: 2005 to 2006
290 Medicaid Expenditures in 2005

IV. FINANCE (Continued)

291 Per Capita Medicaid Expenditures in 2005
292 Medicaid Expenditures per Beneficiary in 2005
293 Federal Medicaid Matching Fund Rate for 2007
294 State and Local Government Expenditures for Hospitals in 2004
295 Per Capita State and Local Government Expenditures for Hospitals in 2004
296 Percent of State and Local Government Expenditures Used for Hospitals in 2004
297 State and Local Government Expenditures for Health Programs in 2004
298 Per Capita State and Local Government Expenditures for Health Programs in 2004
299 Percent of State and Local Government Expenditures Used for Health Programs in 2004
300 Estimated Tobacco Settlement Revenues in FY 2007
301 Personal Health Care Expenditures in 2004
302 Health Care Expenditures as a Percent of Gross State Product in 2004
303 Per Capita Personal Health Care Expenditures in 2004
304 Expenditures for Hospital Care in 2004
305 Percent of Total Personal Health Care Expenditures Spent on Hospital Care in 2004
306 Per Capita Expenditures for Hospital Care in 2004
307 Expenditures for Physician and Clinical Services in 2004
308 Percent of Total Personal Health Care Expenditures Spent on Physician and Clinical Services in 2004
309 Per Capita Expenditures for Physician and Clinical Services in 2004
310 Expenditures for Dental Services in 2004
311 Percent of Total Personal Health Care Expenditures Spent on Dental Services in 2004
312 Per Capita Expenditures for Dental Services in 2004
313 Expenditures for Other Professional Health Care Services in 2004
314 Percent of Total Personal Health Care Expenditures Spent on Other Professional Health Care Services in 2004
315 Per Capita Expenditures for Other Professional Health Care Services in 2004
316 Expenditures for Nursing Home Care in 2004
317 Percent of Total Personal Health Care Expenditures Spent on Nursing Home Care in 2004
318 Per Capita Expenditures for Nursing Home Care in 2004
319 Expenditures for Prescription Drugs in 2004
320 Percent of Total Personal Health Care Expenditures Spent Spent on Prescription Drugs in 2004
321 Per Capita Expenditures for Prescription Drugs in 2004
322 Projected National Health Care Expenditures in 2007

Average Medical Malpractice Payment in 2004

National Average = $298,460*

ALPHA ORDER

RANK	STATE	AVERAGE PAYMENT
15	Alabama	$346,279
48	Alaska	151,524
18	Arizona	324,558
27	Arkansas	295,465
45	California	185,746
21	Colorado	314,268
4	Connecticut	449,296
5	Delaware	430,490
35	Florida**	241,204
22	Georgia	312,392
3	Hawaii	457,755
17	Idaho	332,220
1	Illinois	516,529
31	Indiana**	274,316
2	Iowa	481,776
46	Kansas**	175,247
42	Kentucky	219,604
49	Louisiana**	139,746
9	Maine	385,403
14	Maryland	349,697
8	Massachusetts	401,886
50	Michigan	137,484
25	Minnesota	305,483
19	Mississippi	323,567
23	Missouri	311,882
32	Montana	272,637
43	Nebraska**	206,885
28	Nevada	291,095
20	New Hampshire	317,647
11	New Jersey	368,672
44	New Mexico**	200,046
7	New York	404,762
12	North Carolina	366,447
6	North Dakota	416,080
26	Ohio	304,287
38	Oklahoma	235,197
24	Oregon	310,527
16	Pennsylvania**	337,579
10	Rhode Island	370,834
36	South Carolina**	239,055
41	South Dakota	223,723
34	Tennessee	244,408
37	Texas	237,989
47	Utah	154,452
40	Vermont	225,570
30	Virginia	283,567
29	Washington	288,207
33	West Virginia	255,506
13	Wisconsin**	365,662
39	Wyoming	225,865

RANK ORDER

RANK	STATE	AVERAGE PAYMENT
1	Illinois	$516,529
2	Iowa	481,776
3	Hawaii	457,755
4	Connecticut	449,296
5	Delaware	430,490
6	North Dakota	416,080
7	New York	404,762
8	Massachusetts	401,886
9	Maine	385,403
10	Rhode Island	370,834
11	New Jersey	368,672
12	North Carolina	366,447
13	Wisconsin**	365,662
14	Maryland	349,697
15	Alabama	346,279
16	Pennsylvania**	337,579
17	Idaho	332,220
18	Arizona	324,558
19	Mississippi	323,567
20	New Hampshire	317,647
21	Colorado	314,268
22	Georgia	312,392
23	Missouri	311,882
24	Oregon	310,527
25	Minnesota	305,483
26	Ohio	304,287
27	Arkansas	295,465
28	Nevada	291,095
29	Washington	288,207
30	Virginia	283,567
31	Indiana**	274,316
32	Montana	272,637
33	West Virginia	255,506
34	Tennessee	244,408
35	Florida**	241,204
36	South Carolina**	239,055
37	Texas	237,989
38	Oklahoma	235,197
39	Wyoming	225,865
40	Vermont	225,570
41	South Dakota	223,723
42	Kentucky	219,604
43	Nebraska**	206,885
44	New Mexico**	200,046
45	California	185,746
46	Kansas**	175,247
47	Utah	154,452
48	Alaska	151,524
49	Louisiana**	139,746
50	Michigan	137,484

District of Columbia	408,865

*Source: U.S. Department of Health and Human Services, Bureau of Health Professions
"National Practitioner Data Bank, 2004 Annual Report" (http://www.npdb-hipdb.com/annualrpt.html)*
*National figure includes U.S. territories and U.S. Armed Forces locations overseas.
***The figures for these states have not been adjusted for payments by state compensation funds and other similar
funds. Average payments for these states understate the actual average amounts received by claimants.*

Percent of Private-Sector Establishments That Offer Health Insurance: 2004

National Percent = 55.1%

ALPHA ORDER

RANK	STATE	PERCENT
11	Alabama	60.9
43	Alaska	44.2
17	Arizona	56.1
47	Arkansas	42.4
22	California	54.3
26	Colorado	52.7
2	Connecticut	68.8
5	Delaware	63.9
31	Florida	51.3
29	Georgia	51.8
1	Hawaii	82.6
41	Idaho	45.8
18	Illinois	55.5
33	Indiana	50.6
36	Iowa	48.7
28	Kansas	52.5
15	Kentucky	58.3
42	Louisiana	45.3
34	Maine	49.7
4	Maryland	64.9
6	Massachusetts	63.2
12	Michigan	60.7
24	Minnesota	53.7
48	Mississippi	42.2
21	Missouri	54.6
50	Montana	38.4
44	Nebraska	44.0
19	Nevada	54.7
10	New Hampshire	62.1
7	New Jersey	63.0
38	New Mexico	47.9
13	New York	59.1
29	North Carolina	51.8
46	North Dakota	43.2
9	Ohio	62.5
44	Oklahoma	44.0
26	Oregon	52.7
3	Pennsylvania	65.0
14	Rhode Island	58.9
35	South Carolina	49.3
39	South Dakota	47.6
19	Tennessee	54.7
40	Texas	45.9
37	Utah	48.1
23	Vermont	53.8
8	Virginia	62.9
16	Washington	56.2
32	West Virginia	50.7
24	Wisconsin	53.7
49	Wyoming	41.3

RANK ORDER

RANK	STATE	PERCENT
1	Hawaii	82.6
2	Connecticut	68.8
3	Pennsylvania	65.0
4	Maryland	64.9
5	Delaware	63.9
6	Massachusetts	63.2
7	New Jersey	63.0
8	Virginia	62.9
9	Ohio	62.5
10	New Hampshire	62.1
11	Alabama	60.9
12	Michigan	60.7
13	New York	59.1
14	Rhode Island	58.9
15	Kentucky	58.3
16	Washington	56.2
17	Arizona	56.1
18	Illinois	55.5
19	Nevada	54.7
19	Tennessee	54.7
21	Missouri	54.6
22	California	54.3
23	Vermont	53.8
24	Minnesota	53.7
24	Wisconsin	53.7
26	Colorado	52.7
26	Oregon	52.7
28	Kansas	52.5
29	Georgia	51.8
29	North Carolina	51.8
31	Florida	51.3
32	West Virginia	50.7
33	Indiana	50.6
34	Maine	49.7
35	South Carolina	49.3
36	Iowa	48.7
37	Utah	48.1
38	New Mexico	47.9
39	South Dakota	47.6
40	Texas	45.9
41	Idaho	45.8
42	Louisiana	45.3
43	Alaska	44.2
44	Nebraska	44.0
44	Oklahoma	44.0
46	North Dakota	43.2
47	Arkansas	42.4
48	Mississippi	42.2
49	Wyoming	41.3
50	Montana	38.4

	District of Columbia	74.2

Source: U.S. Department of Health and Human Services, Agency for Healthcare Research and Quality
"Private-Sector Data by Firm Size and State" (Table II Series, Medical Expenditures Panel Survey)
(http://www.meps.ahrq.gov/mepsweb/survey_comp/Insurance.jsp)

Percent of Private-Sector Establishments with Fewer Than 50 Employees That Offer Health Insurance: 2004
National Percent = 41.9%

ALPHA ORDER

RANK ORDER

RANK	STATE	PERCENT		RANK	STATE	PERCENT
14	Alabama	46.8		1	Hawaii	76.6
43	Alaska	30.6		2	Connecticut	59.5
26	Arizona	39.0		3	New Jersey	54.3
44	Arkansas	29.2		4	Pennsylvania	53.3
18	California	42.4		5	Massachusetts	52.4
25	Colorado	39.9		6	Maryland	52.3
2	Connecticut	59.5		7	New Hampshire	51.0
9	Delaware	50.6		8	Rhode Island	50.8
30	Florida	37.4		9	Delaware	50.6
34	Georgia	34.8		10	New York	50.1
1	Hawaii	76.6		11	Michigan	48.2
38	Idaho	33.9		12	Virginia	48.1
18	Illinois	42.4		13	Ohio	47.8
40	Indiana	33.0		14	Alabama	46.8
36	Iowa	34.2		15	Kentucky	44.6
24	Kansas	40.9		16	Vermont	43.9
15	Kentucky	44.6		16	Washington	43.9
48	Louisiana	27.6		18	California	42.4
27	Maine	38.9		18	Illinois	42.4
6	Maryland	52.3		20	Minnesota	42.2
5	Massachusetts	52.4		21	Oregon	42.0
11	Michigan	48.2		22	Missouri	41.7
20	Minnesota	42.2		22	Wisconsin	41.7
50	Mississippi	24.0		24	Kansas	40.9
22	Missouri	41.7		25	Colorado	39.9
48	Montana	27.6		26	Arizona	39.0
41	Nebraska	32.7		27	Maine	38.9
29	Nevada	37.5		27	North Carolina	38.9
7	New Hampshire	51.0		29	Nevada	37.5
3	New Jersey	54.3		30	Florida	37.4
39	New Mexico	33.4		31	Utah	36.3
10	New York	50.1		32	South Dakota	35.9
27	North Carolina	38.9		33	West Virginia	35.0
42	North Dakota	31.1		34	Georgia	34.8
13	Ohio	47.8		35	Tennessee	34.6
44	Oklahoma	29.2		36	Iowa	34.2
21	Oregon	42.0		37	South Carolina	34.1
4	Pennsylvania	53.3		38	Idaho	33.9
8	Rhode Island	50.8		39	New Mexico	33.4
37	South Carolina	34.1		40	Indiana	33.0
32	South Dakota	35.9		41	Nebraska	32.7
35	Tennessee	34.6		42	North Dakota	31.1
47	Texas	27.8		43	Alaska	30.6
31	Utah	36.3		44	Arkansas	29.2
16	Vermont	43.9		44	Oklahoma	29.2
12	Virginia	48.1		44	Wyoming	29.2
16	Washington	43.9		47	Texas	27.8
33	West Virginia	35.0		48	Louisiana	27.6
22	Wisconsin	41.7		48	Montana	27.6
44	Wyoming	29.2		50	Mississippi	24.0

District of Columbia   62.0

Source: U.S. Department of Health and Human Services, Agency for Healthcare Research and Quality "Private-Sector Data by Firm Size and State" (Table II Series, Medical Expenditures Panel Survey) (http://www.meps.ahrq.gov/mepsweb/survey_comp/Insurance.jsp)

Percent of Private-Sector Establishments with More Than 50 Employees
That Offer Health Insurance: 2004
National Percent = 96.0%

ALPHA ORDER

RANK	STATE	PERCENT
21	Alabama	96.6
15	Alaska	97.7
42	Arizona	92.8
49	Arkansas	89.8
32	California	94.7
18	Colorado	96.8
18	Connecticut	96.8
39	Delaware	93.7
31	Florida	94.8
11	Georgia	97.9
5	Hawaii	98.7
28	Idaho	95.4
5	Illinois	98.7
7	Indiana	98.6
8	Iowa	98.3
27	Kansas	95.7
37	Kentucky	94.2
30	Louisiana	95.1
37	Maine	94.2
3	Maryland	99.3
1	Massachusetts	100.0
13	Michigan	97.8
20	Minnesota	96.7
40	Mississippi	92.9
24	Missouri	96.1
35	Montana	94.5
43	Nebraska	92.7
17	Nevada	97.0
2	New Hampshire	99.5
23	New Jersey	96.4
46	New Mexico	91.7
13	New York	97.8
40	North Carolina	92.9
26	North Dakota	95.8
11	Ohio	97.9
48	Oklahoma	90.4
32	Oregon	94.7
9	Pennsylvania	98.2
29	Rhode Island	95.3
35	South Carolina	94.5
34	South Dakota	94.6
4	Tennessee	99.0
44	Texas	92.5
50	Utah	88.5
21	Vermont	96.6
10	Virginia	98.0
16	Washington	97.5
47	West Virginia	91.1
25	Wisconsin	96.0
45	Wyoming	92.3

RANK ORDER

RANK	STATE	PERCENT
1	Massachusetts	100.0
2	New Hampshire	99.5
3	Maryland	99.3
4	Tennessee	99.0
5	Hawaii	98.7
5	Illinois	98.7
7	Indiana	98.6
8	Iowa	98.3
9	Pennsylvania	98.2
10	Virginia	98.0
11	Georgia	97.9
11	Ohio	97.9
13	Michigan	97.8
13	New York	97.8
15	Alaska	97.7
16	Washington	97.5
17	Nevada	97.0
18	Colorado	96.8
18	Connecticut	96.8
20	Minnesota	96.7
21	Alabama	96.6
21	Vermont	96.6
23	New Jersey	96.4
24	Missouri	96.1
25	Wisconsin	96.0
26	North Dakota	95.8
27	Kansas	95.7
28	Idaho	95.4
29	Rhode Island	95.3
30	Louisiana	95.1
31	Florida	94.8
32	California	94.7
32	Oregon	94.7
34	South Dakota	94.6
35	Montana	94.5
35	South Carolina	94.5
37	Kentucky	94.2
37	Maine	94.2
39	Delaware	93.7
40	Mississippi	92.9
40	North Carolina	92.9
42	Arizona	92.8
43	Nebraska	92.7
44	Texas	92.5
45	Wyoming	92.3
46	New Mexico	91.7
47	West Virginia	91.1
48	Oklahoma	90.4
49	Arkansas	89.8
50	Utah	88.5
	District of Columbia	98.6

Source: U.S. Department of Health and Human Services, Agency for Healthcare Research and Quality
"Private-Sector Data by Firm Size and State" (Table II Series, Medical Expenditures Panel Survey)
(http://www.meps.ahrq.gov/mepsweb/survey_comp/Insurance.jsp)

Average Annual Single Coverage Health Insurance Premium per Enrolled Employee in 2004
National Average = $3,705*

ALPHA ORDER

RANK	STATE	PREMIUM
44	Alabama	$3,414
1	Alaska	4,379
42	Arizona	3,438
48	Arkansas	3,250
39	California	3,534
27	Colorado	3,684
12	Connecticut	3,864
14	Delaware	3,830
16	Florida	3,807
47	Georgia	3,335
49	Hawaii	3,119
43	Idaho	3,429
20	Illinois	3,768
34	Indiana	3,586
35	Iowa	3,561
24	Kansas	3,711
38	Kentucky	3,542
40	Louisiana	3,485
4	Maine	4,116
23	Maryland	3,721
3	Massachusetts	4,141
8	Michigan	3,918
15	Minnesota	3,809
33	Mississippi	3,607
36	Missouri	3,559
28	Montana	3,680
22	Nebraska	3,725
10	Nevada	3,874
5	New Hampshire	4,084
9	New Jersey	3,882
45	New Mexico	3,401
13	New York	3,858
37	North Carolina	3,551
46	North Dakota	3,342
17	Ohio	3,782
30	Oklahoma	3,644
25	Oregon	3,706
29	Pennsylvania	3,671
2	Rhode Island	4,368
19	South Carolina	3,773
41	South Dakota	3,449
31	Tennessee	3,634
18	Texas	3,781
50	Utah	3,034
6	Vermont	4,074
11	Virginia	3,865
32	Washington	3,608
26	West Virginia	3,692
7	Wisconsin	3,927
21	Wyoming	3,761

RANK ORDER

RANK	STATE	PREMIUM
1	Alaska	$4,379
2	Rhode Island	4,368
3	Massachusetts	4,141
4	Maine	4,116
5	New Hampshire	4,084
6	Vermont	4,074
7	Wisconsin	3,927
8	Michigan	3,918
9	New Jersey	3,882
10	Nevada	3,874
11	Virginia	3,865
12	Connecticut	3,864
13	New York	3,858
14	Delaware	3,830
15	Minnesota	3,809
16	Florida	3,807
17	Ohio	3,782
18	Texas	3,781
19	South Carolina	3,773
20	Illinois	3,768
21	Wyoming	3,761
22	Nebraska	3,725
23	Maryland	3,721
24	Kansas	3,711
25	Oregon	3,706
26	West Virginia	3,692
27	Colorado	3,684
28	Montana	3,680
29	Pennsylvania	3,671
30	Oklahoma	3,644
31	Tennessee	3,634
32	Washington	3,608
33	Mississippi	3,607
34	Indiana	3,586
35	Iowa	3,561
36	Missouri	3,559
37	North Carolina	3,551
38	Kentucky	3,542
39	California	3,534
40	Louisiana	3,485
41	South Dakota	3,449
42	Arizona	3,438
43	Idaho	3,429
44	Alabama	3,414
45	New Mexico	3,401
46	North Dakota	3,342
47	Georgia	3,335
48	Arkansas	3,250
49	I lawaii	3,119
50	Utah	3,034

	District of Columbia	4,218

Source: U.S. Department of Health and Human Services, Agency for Healthcare Research and Quality "Private-Sector Data by Firm Size and State" (Table II Series, Medical Expenditures Panel Survey) (http://www.meps.ahrq.gov/mepsweb/survey_comp/Insurance.jsp)
Enrolled employees at private-sector establishments that offer health insurance coverage.

Average Annual Employee Contribution for
Single Coverage Health Insurance in 2004
National Average = $671*

ALPHA ORDER

RANK	STATE	PREMIUM
16	Alabama	$726
47	Alaska	535
29	Arizona	662
38	Arkansas	616
46	California	554
26	Colorado	677
9	Connecticut	773
22	Delaware	694
17	Florida	723
19	Georgia	716
50	Hawaii	311
25	Idaho	682
23	Illinois	693
32	Indiana	646
31	Iowa	653
3	Kansas	887
21	Kentucky	700
15	Louisiana	729
2	Maine	892
6	Maryland	804
4	Massachusetts	885
45	Michigan	558
10	Minnesota	759
36	Mississippi	637
34	Missouri	641
43	Montana	582
12	Nebraska	736
37	Nevada	620
1	New Hampshire	944
40	New Jersey	613
41	New Mexico	611
20	New York	714
27	North Carolina	674
35	North Dakota	638
24	Ohio	687
44	Oklahoma	575
48	Oregon	427
30	Pennsylvania	661
8	Rhode Island	794
14	South Carolina	731
18	South Dakota	722
5	Tennessee	854
28	Texas	663
39	Utah	614
11	Vermont	744
13	Virginia	735
48	Washington	427
42	West Virginia	600
7	Wisconsin	795
33	Wyoming	645

RANK ORDER

RANK	STATE	PREMIUM
1	New Hampshire	$944
2	Maine	892
3	Kansas	887
4	Massachusetts	885
5	Tennessee	854
6	Maryland	804
7	Wisconsin	795
8	Rhode Island	794
9	Connecticut	773
10	Minnesota	759
11	Vermont	744
12	Nebraska	736
13	Virginia	735
14	South Carolina	731
15	Louisiana	729
16	Alabama	726
17	Florida	723
18	South Dakota	722
19	Georgia	716
20	New York	714
21	Kentucky	700
22	Delaware	694
23	Illinois	693
24	Ohio	687
25	Idaho	682
26	Colorado	677
27	North Carolina	674
28	Texas	663
29	Arizona	662
30	Pennsylvania	661
31	Iowa	653
32	Indiana	646
33	Wyoming	645
34	Missouri	641
35	North Dakota	638
36	Mississippi	637
37	Nevada	620
38	Arkansas	616
39	Utah	614
40	New Jersey	613
41	New Mexico	611
42	West Virginia	600
43	Montana	582
44	Oklahoma	575
45	Michigan	558
46	California	554
47	Alaska	535
48	Oregon	427
48	Washington	427
50	Hawaii	311
	District of Columbia	634

Source: U.S. Department of Health and Human Services, Agency for Healthcare Research and Quality
  "Private-Sector Data by Firm Size and State" (Table II Series, Medical Expenditures Panel Survey)
  (http://www.meps.ahrq.gov/mepsweb/survey_comp/Insurance.jsp)
*Enrolled employees at private-sector establishments that offer health insurance coverage.

Percent of Total Premiums for Single Coverage
Health Insurance Paid by Employees in 2004
National Average = 18.1%*

ALPHA ORDER

RANK	STATE	PERCENT
8	Alabama	21.3
47	Alaska	12.2
19	Arizona	19.2
24	Arkansas	18.9
45	California	15.7
26	Colorado	18.4
13	Connecticut	20.0
32	Delaware	18.1
21	Florida	19.0
6	Georgia	21.5
50	Hawaii	10.0
14	Idaho	19.9
26	Illinois	18.4
33	Indiana	18.0
28	Iowa	18.3
1	Kansas	23.9
16	Kentucky	19.8
9	Louisiana	20.9
4	Maine	21.7
5	Maryland	21.6
7	Massachusetts	21.4
46	Michigan	14.2
14	Minnesota	19.9
37	Mississippi	17.7
33	Missouri	18.0
42	Montana	15.8
17	Nebraska	19.7
41	Nevada	16.0
3	New Hampshire	23.1
42	New Jersey	15.8
33	New Mexico	18.0
25	New York	18.5
21	North Carolina	19.0
20	North Dakota	19.1
30	Ohio	18.2
42	Oklahoma	15.8
49	Oregon	11.5
33	Pennsylvania	18.0
30	Rhode Island	18.2
18	South Carolina	19.4
9	South Dakota	20.9
2	Tennessee	23.5
38	Texas	17.5
11	Utah	20.2
28	Vermont	18.3
21	Virginia	19.0
48	Washington	11.8
40	West Virginia	16.3
11	Wisconsin	20.2
39	Wyoming	17.2

RANK ORDER

RANK	STATE	PERCENT
1	Kansas	23.9
2	Tennessee	23.5
3	New Hampshire	23.1
4	Maine	21.7
5	Maryland	21.6
6	Georgia	21.5
7	Massachusetts	21.4
8	Alabama	21.3
9	Louisiana	20.9
9	South Dakota	20.9
11	Utah	20.2
11	Wisconsin	20.2
13	Connecticut	20.0
14	Idaho	19.9
14	Minnesota	19.9
16	Kentucky	19.8
17	Nebraska	19.7
18	South Carolina	19.4
19	Arizona	19.2
20	North Dakota	19.1
21	Florida	19.0
21	North Carolina	19.0
21	Virginia	19.0
24	Arkansas	18.9
25	New York	18.5
26	Colorado	18.4
26	Illinois	18.4
28	Iowa	18.3
28	Vermont	18.3
30	Ohio	18.2
30	Rhode Island	18.2
32	Delaware	18.1
33	Indiana	18.0
33	Missouri	18.0
33	New Mexico	18.0
33	Pennsylvania	18.0
37	Mississippi	17.7
38	Texas	17.5
39	Wyoming	17.2
40	West Virginia	16.3
41	Nevada	16.0
42	Montana	15.8
42	New Jersey	15.8
42	Oklahoma	15.8
45	California	15.7
46	Michigan	14.2
47	Alaska	12.2
48	Washington	11.8
49	Oregon	11.5
50	Hawaii	10.0

District of Columbia   15.0

*Source: U.S. Department of Health and Human Services, Agency for Healthcare Research and Quality
"Private-Sector Data by Firm Size and State" (Table II Series, Medical Expenditures Panel Survey)
(http://www.meps.ahrq.gov/mepsweb/survey_comp/Insurance.jsp)*
Enrolled employees at private-sector establishments that offer health insurance coverage.

Average Annual Family Coverage Health Insurance Premium per Enrolled Employee in 2004
National Average = $10,006*

ALPHA ORDER				RANK ORDER		
RANK	STATE	PREMIUM		RANK	STATE	PREMIUM
40	Alabama	$9,322		1	New Jersey	$11,425
11	Alaska	10,361		2	New Hampshire	11,156
45	Arizona	8,979		3	Connecticut	11,035
49	Arkansas	8,383		4	Maine	10,823
36	California	9,557		5	Vermont	10,690
16	Colorado	10,228		6	Delaware	10,589
3	Connecticut	11,035		7	Massachusetts	10,559
6	Delaware	10,589		8	Tennessee	10,541
9	Florida	10,444		9	Florida	10,444
41	Georgia	9,317		10	New York	10,397
48	Hawaii	8,580		11	Alaska	10,361
46	Idaho	8,908		12	Illinois	10,357
12	Illinois	10,357		13	Minnesota	10,307
28	Indiana	9,869		14	North Carolina	10,241
39	Iowa	9,422		15	Virginia	10,230
37	Kansas	9,482		16	Colorado	10,228
27	Kentucky	9,887		17	Rhode Island	10,220
19	Louisiana	10,211		18	Washington	10,217
4	Maine	10,823		19	Louisiana	10,211
29	Maryland	9,855		20	Wisconsin	10,146
7	Massachusetts	10,559		21	Texas	10,110
30	Michigan	9,763		22	South Dakota	10,023
13	Minnesota	10,307		23	Pennsylvania	9,987
43	Mississippi	9,188		24	South Carolina	9,977
42	Missouri	9,212		25	Nevada	9,970
44	Montana	9,034		26	Oregon	9,906
33	Nebraska	9,606		27	Kentucky	9,887
25	Nevada	9,970		28	Indiana	9,869
2	New Hampshire	11,156		29	Maryland	9,855
1	New Jersey	11,425		30	Michigan	9,763
32	New Mexico	9,623		31	Wyoming	9,687
10	New York	10,397		32	New Mexico	9,623
14	North Carolina	10,241		33	Nebraska	9,606
50	North Dakota	7,800		34	West Virginia	9,592
35	Ohio	9,590		35	Ohio	9,590
38	Oklahoma	9,439		36	California	9,557
26	Oregon	9,906		37	Kansas	9,482
23	Pennsylvania	9,987		38	Oklahoma	9,439
17	Rhode Island	10,220		39	Iowa	9,422
24	South Carolina	9,977		40	Alabama	9,322
22	South Dakota	10,023		41	Georgia	9,317
8	Tennessee	10,541		42	Missouri	9,212
21	Texas	10,110		43	Mississippi	9,188
47	Utah	8,654		44	Montana	9,034
5	Vermont	10,690		45	Arizona	8,979
15	Virginia	10,230		46	Idaho	8,908
18	Washington	10,217		47	Utah	8,654
34	West Virginia	9,592		48	Hawaii	8,580
20	Wisconsin	10,146		49	Arkansas	8,383
31	Wyoming	9,687		50	North Dakota	7,800
					District of Columbia	11,742

Source: U.S. Department of Health and Human Services, Agency for Healthcare Research and Quality
"Private-Sector Data by Firm Size and State" (Table II Series, Medical Expenditures Panel Survey)
(http://www.meps.ahrq.gov/mepsweb/survey_comp/Insurance.jsp)
*Enrolled employees at private-sector establishments that offer health insurance coverage.

Average Annual Employee Contribution for
Family Coverage Health Insurance in 2004
National Average = $2,438*

ALPHA ORDER

RANK	STATE	PREMIUM
15	Alabama	$2,713
35	Alaska	2,286
38	Arizona	2,253
24	Arkansas	2,414
21	California	2,430
12	Colorado	2,768
36	Connecticut	2,274
29	Delaware	2,358
6	Florida	2,972
19	Georgia	2,599
28	Hawaii	2,368
33	Idaho	2,327
31	Illinois	2,351
44	Indiana	2,107
30	Iowa	2,353
25	Kansas	2,374
43	Kentucky	2,120
13	Louisiana	2,767
10	Maine	2,784
4	Maryland	2,988
10	Massachusetts	2,784
50	Michigan	1,770
37	Minnesota	2,270
3	Mississippi	3,027
22	Missouri	2,424
39	Montana	2,223
8	Nebraska	2,887
17	Nevada	2,677
1	New Hampshire	3,102
49	New Jersey	1,886
48	New Mexico	1,930
45	New York	2,090
5	North Carolina	2,980
42	North Dakota	2,191
40	Ohio	2,206
20	Oklahoma	2,595
27	Oregon	2,370
47	Pennsylvania	2,033
34	Rhode Island	2,309
14	South Carolina	2,752
26	South Dakota	2,373
2	Tennessee	3,063
9	Texas	2,788
23	Utah	2,417
18	Vermont	2,657
16	Virginia	2,705
7	Washington	2,892
46	West Virginia	2,088
41	Wisconsin	2,193
32	Wyoming	2,340

RANK ORDER

RANK	STATE	PREMIUM
1	New Hampshire	$3,102
2	Tennessee	3,063
3	Mississippi	3,027
4	Maryland	2,988
5	North Carolina	2,980
6	Florida	2,972
7	Washington	2,892
8	Nebraska	2,887
9	Texas	2,788
10	Maine	2,784
10	Massachusetts	2,784
12	Colorado	2,768
13	Louisiana	2,767
14	South Carolina	2,752
15	Alabama	2,713
16	Virginia	2,705
17	Nevada	2,677
18	Vermont	2,657
19	Georgia	2,599
20	Oklahoma	2,595
21	California	2,430
22	Missouri	2,424
23	Utah	2,417
24	Arkansas	2,414
25	Kansas	2,374
26	South Dakota	2,373
27	Oregon	2,370
28	Hawaii	2,368
29	Delaware	2,358
30	Iowa	2,353
31	Illinois	2,351
32	Wyoming	2,340
33	Idaho	2,327
34	Rhode Island	2,309
35	Alaska	2,286
36	Connecticut	2,274
37	Minnesota	2,270
38	Arizona	2,253
39	Montana	2,223
40	Ohio	2,206
41	Wisconsin	2,193
42	North Dakota	2,191
43	Kentucky	2,120
44	Indiana	2,107
45	New York	2,090
46	West Virginia	2,088
47	Pennsylvania	2,033
48	New Mexico	1,930
49	New Jersey	1,886
50	Michigan	1,770
	District of Columbia	2,653

Source: U.S. Department of Health and Human Services, Agency for Healthcare Research and Quality
"Private-Sector Data by Firm Size and State" (Table II Series, Medical Expenditures Panel Survey)
(http://www.meps.ahrq.gov/mepsweb/survey_comp/Insurance.jsp)
*Enrolled employees at private-sector establishments that offer health insurance coverage.

Percent of Total Premiums for Family Coverage
Health Insurance Paid by Employees in 2004
National Average = 24.4%*

ALPHA ORDER

RANK	STATE	PERCENT
4	Alabama	29.1
39	Alaska	22.1
27	Arizona	25.1
7	Arkansas	28.8
26	California	25.4
18	Colorado	27.1
45	Connecticut	20.6
38	Delaware	22.3
8	Florida	28.5
11	Georgia	27.9
14	Hawaii	27.6
24	Idaho	26.1
36	Illinois	22.7
44	Indiana	21.3
28	Iowa	25.0
28	Kansas	25.0
43	Kentucky	21.4
18	Louisiana	27.1
25	Maine	25.7
2	Maryland	30.3
21	Massachusetts	26.4
49	Michigan	18.1
40	Minnesota	22.0
1	Mississippi	32.9
23	Missouri	26.3
31	Montana	24.6
3	Nebraska	30.1
20	Nevada	26.9
13	New Hampshire	27.8
50	New Jersey	16.5
47	New Mexico	20.1
47	New York	20.1
4	North Carolina	29.1
10	North Dakota	28.1
35	Ohio	23.0
17	Oklahoma	27.5
33	Oregon	23.9
46	Pennsylvania	20.4
37	Rhode Island	22.6
14	South Carolina	27.6
34	South Dakota	23.7
4	Tennessee	29.1
14	Texas	27.6
11	Utah	27.9
30	Vermont	24.9
21	Virginia	26.4
9	Washington	28.3
41	West Virginia	21.8
42	Wisconsin	21.6
32	Wyoming	24.2

RANK ORDER

RANK	STATE	PERCENT
1	Mississippi	32.9
2	Maryland	30.3
3	Nebraska	30.1
4	Alabama	29.1
4	North Carolina	29.1
4	Tennessee	29.1
7	Arkansas	28.8
8	Florida	28.5
9	Washington	28.3
10	North Dakota	28.1
11	Georgia	27.9
11	Utah	27.9
13	New Hampshire	27.8
14	Hawaii	27.6
14	South Carolina	27.6
14	Texas	27.6
17	Oklahoma	27.5
18	Colorado	27.1
18	Louisiana	27.1
20	Nevada	26.9
21	Massachusetts	26.4
21	Virginia	26.4
23	Missouri	26.3
24	Idaho	26.1
25	Maine	25.7
26	California	25.4
27	Arizona	25.1
28	Iowa	25.0
28	Kansas	25.0
30	Vermont	24.9
31	Montana	24.6
32	Wyoming	24.2
33	Oregon	23.9
34	South Dakota	23.7
35	Ohio	23.0
36	Illinois	22.7
37	Rhode Island	22.6
38	Delaware	22.3
39	Alaska	22.1
40	Minnesota	22.0
41	West Virginia	21.8
42	Wisconsin	21.6
43	Kentucky	21.4
44	Indiana	21.3
45	Connecticut	20.6
46	Pennsylvania	20.4
47	New Mexico	20.1
47	New York	20.1
49	Michigan	18.1
50	New Jersey	16.5
	District of Columbia	22.6

Source: U.S. Department of Health and Human Services, Agency for Healthcare Research and Quality
   "Private-Sector Data by Firm Size and State" (Table II Series, Medical Expenditures Panel Survey)
      (http://www.meps.ahrq.gov/mepsweb/survey_comp/Insurance.jsp)
*Enrolled employees at private-sector establishments that offer health insurance coverage.

Persons Not Covered by Health Insurance in 2005

National Total = 46,577,000 Uninsured

ALPHA ORDER

RANK ORDER

RANK	STATE	UNINSURED	% of USA	RANK	STATE	UNINSURED	% of USA
21	Alabama	696,000	1.5%	1	California	6,961,000	14.9%
44	Alaska	117,000	0.3%	2	Texas	5,516,000	11.8%
11	Arizona	1,219,000	2.6%	3	Florida	3,703,000	8.0%
29	Arkansas	494,000	1.1%	4	New York	2,559,000	5.5%
1	California	6,961,000	14.9%	5	Illinois	1,802,000	3.9%
17	Colorado	788,000	1.7%	6	Georgia	1,709,000	3.7%
34	Connecticut	394,000	0.8%	7	Ohio	1,394,000	3.0%
46	Delaware	110,000	0.2%	8	North Carolina	1,371,000	2.9%
3	Florida	3,703,000	8.0%	9	New Jersey	1,324,000	2.8%
6	Georgia	1,709,000	3.7%	10	Pennsylvania	1,287,000	2.8%
45	Hawaii	116,000	0.2%	11	Arizona	1,219,000	2.6%
38	Idaho	222,000	0.5%	12	Michigan	1,133,000	2.4%
5	Illinois	1,802,000	3.9%	13	Virginia	1,011,000	2.2%
14	Indiana	871,000	1.9%	14	Indiana	871,000	1.9%
37	Iowa	251,000	0.5%	15	Washington	866,000	1.9%
36	Kansas	290,000	0.6%	16	Tennessee	836,000	1.8%
27	Kentucky	514,000	1.1%	17	Colorado	788,000	1.7%
19	Louisiana	767,000	1.6%	17	Maryland	788,000	1.7%
41	Maine	143,000	0.3%	19	Louisiana	767,000	1.6%
17	Maryland	788,000	1.7%	20	South Carolina	741,000	1.6%
24	Massachusetts	618,000	1.3%	21	Alabama	696,000	1.5%
12	Michigan	1,133,000	2.4%	22	Missouri	691,000	1.5%
30	Minnesota	431,000	0.9%	23	Oklahoma	647,000	1.4%
28	Mississippi	495,000	1.1%	24	Massachusetts	618,000	1.3%
22	Missouri	691,000	1.5%	25	Oregon	579,000	1.2%
40	Montana	162,000	0.3%	26	Wisconsin	534,000	1.1%
39	Nebraska	208,000	0.4%	27	Kentucky	514,000	1.1%
31	Nevada	425,000	0.9%	28	Mississippi	495,000	1.1%
42	New Hampshire	135,000	0.3%	29	Arkansas	494,000	1.1%
9	New Jersey	1,324,000	2.8%	30	Minnesota	431,000	0.9%
33	New Mexico	396,000	0.9%	31	Nevada	425,000	0.9%
4	New York	2,559,000	5.5%	32	Utah	420,000	0.9%
8	North Carolina	1,371,000	2.9%	33	New Mexico	396,000	0.9%
49	North Dakota	76,000	0.2%	34	Connecticut	394,000	0.8%
7	Ohio	1,394,000	3.0%	35	West Virginia	322,000	0.7%
23	Oklahoma	647,000	1.4%	36	Kansas	290,000	0.6%
25	Oregon	579,000	1.2%	37	Iowa	251,000	0.5%
10	Pennsylvania	1,287,000	2.8%	38	Idaho	222,000	0.5%
43	Rhode Island	125,000	0.3%	39	Nebraska	208,000	0.4%
20	South Carolina	741,000	1.6%	40	Montana	162,000	0.3%
47	South Dakota	95,000	0.2%	41	Maine	143,000	0.3%
16	Tennessee	836,000	1.8%	42	New Hampshire	135,000	0.3%
2	Texas	5,516,000	11.8%	43	Rhode Island	125,000	0.3%
32	Utah	420,000	0.9%	44	Alaska	117,000	0.3%
50	Vermont	73,000	0.2%	45	Hawaii	116,000	0.2%
13	Virginia	1,011,000	2.2%	46	Delaware	110,000	0.2%
15	Washington	866,000	1.9%	47	South Dakota	95,000	0.2%
35	West Virginia	322,000	0.7%	48	Wyoming	82,000	0.2%
26	Wisconsin	534,000	1.1%	49	North Dakota	76,000	0.2%
48	Wyoming	82,000	0.2%	50	Vermont	73,000	0.2%
					District of Columbia	73,000	0.2%

Source: U.S. Bureau of the Census
   "Health Insurance Coverage Status by State for All People: 2005"
   (http://ferret.bls.census.gov/macro/032006/health/h06_000.htm)

Percent of Population Not Covered by Health Insurance in 2005

National Percent = 15.7% of Population*

ALPHA ORDER

RANK	STATE	PERCENT
23	Alabama	14.3
10	Alaska	17.8
9	Arizona	18.1
13	Arkansas	17.2
5	California	18.8
14	Colorado	16.9
40	Connecticut	11.0
32	Delaware	12.7
3	Florida	19.6
11	Georgia	17.5
49	Hawaii	9.5
17	Idaho	16.5
24	Illinois	14.2
24	Indiana	14.2
48	Iowa	9.8
42	Kansas	10.9
30	Kentucky	13.6
6	Louisiana	18.7
45	Maine	10.4
26	Maryland	14.1
43	Massachusetts	10.7
37	Michigan	11.3
50	Minnesota	8.7
12	Mississippi	17.3
35	Missouri	11.9
6	Montana	18.7
36	Nebraska	11.4
8	Nevada	18.4
45	New Hampshire	10.4
21	New Jersey	14.5
2	New Mexico	21.1
28	New York	13.9
18	North Carolina	16.2
38	North Dakota	11.2
34	Ohio	12.0
4	Oklahoma	19.5
16	Oregon	16.7
38	Pennsylvania	11.2
40	Rhode Island	11.0
19	South Carolina	15.6
33	South Dakota	12.1
29	Tennessee	13.7
1	Texas	24.6
21	Utah	14.5
43	Vermont	10.7
30	Virginia	13.6
26	Washington	14.1
14	West Virginia	16.9
47	Wisconsin	10.3
20	Wyoming	15.2

RANK ORDER

RANK	STATE	PERCENT
1	Texas	24.6
2	New Mexico	21.1
3	Florida	19.6
4	Oklahoma	19.5
5	California	18.8
6	Louisiana	18.7
6	Montana	18.7
8	Nevada	18.4
9	Arizona	18.1
10	Alaska	17.8
11	Georgia	17.5
12	Mississippi	17.3
13	Arkansas	17.2
14	Colorado	16.9
14	West Virginia	16.9
16	Oregon	16.7
17	Idaho	16.5
18	North Carolina	16.2
19	South Carolina	15.6
20	Wyoming	15.2
21	New Jersey	14.5
21	Utah	14.5
23	Alabama	14.3
24	Illinois	14.2
24	Indiana	14.2
26	Maryland	14.1
26	Washington	14.1
28	New York	13.9
29	Tennessee	13.7
30	Kentucky	13.6
30	Virginia	13.6
32	Delaware	12.7
33	South Dakota	12.1
34	Ohio	12.0
35	Missouri	11.9
36	Nebraska	11.4
37	Michigan	11.3
38	North Dakota	11.2
38	Pennsylvania	11.2
40	Connecticut	11.0
40	Rhode Island	11.0
42	Kansas	10.9
43	Massachusetts	10.7
43	Vermont	10.7
45	Maine	10.4
45	New Hampshire	10.4
47	Wisconsin	10.3
48	Iowa	9.8
49	Hawaii	9.5
50	Minnesota	8.7

District of Columbia   13.5

Source: U.S. Bureau of the Census
  "Income, Poverty and Health Insurance Covered in the United States: 2005"
    (http://www.census.gov/prod/2006pubs/p60-231.pdf)
Three-year average for 2003 through 2005.

Numerical Change in Persons Uninsured: 2001 to 2005

National Change = 5,370,000 Increase

ALPHA ORDER				RANK ORDER		
RANK	STATE	UNINSURED		RANK	STATE	UNINSURED
19	Alabama	123,000		1	Florida	847,000
40	Alaska	17,000		2	Texas	556,000
4	Arizona	269,000		3	Georgia	333,000
27	Arkansas	66,000		4	Arizona	269,000
6	California	243,000		5	South Carolina	248,000
21	Colorado	101,000		6	California	243,000
28	Connecticut	48,000		7	Virginia	237,000
33	Delaware	37,000		8	New Jersey	215,000
1	Florida	847,000		9	North Carolina	204,000
3	Georgia	333,000		10	Tennessee	196,000
47	Hawaii	(1,000)		11	Pennsylvania	168,000
44	Idaho	12,000		12	Indiana	157,000
16	Illinois	126,000		13	Ohio	146,000
12	Indiana	157,000		14	Oregon	136,000
35	Iowa	35,000		15	Maryland	135,000
48	Kansas	(11,000)		16	Illinois	126,000
39	Kentucky	22,000		16	Missouri	126,000
49	Louisiana	(78,000)		18	Wisconsin	125,000
45	Maine	11,000		19	Alabama	123,000
15	Maryland	135,000		20	Michigan	105,000
22	Massachusetts	98,000		21	Colorado	101,000
20	Michigan	105,000		22	Massachusetts	98,000
32	Minnesota	39,000		23	West Virginia	88,000
34	Mississippi	36,000		24	Washington	86,000
16	Missouri	126,000		25	Utah	85,000
31	Montana	41,000		26	Nevada	81,000
28	Nebraska	48,000		27	Arkansas	66,000
26	Nevada	81,000		28	Connecticut	48,000
41	New Hampshire	16,000		28	Nebraska	48,000
8	New Jersey	215,000		30	Rhode Island	45,000
38	New Mexico	23,000		31	Montana	41,000
50	New York	(357,000)		32	Minnesota	39,000
9	North Carolina	204,000		33	Delaware	37,000
41	North Dakota	16,000		34	Mississippi	36,000
13	Ohio	146,000		35	Iowa	35,000
36	Oklahoma	27,000		36	Oklahoma	27,000
14	Oregon	136,000		37	South Dakota	26,000
11	Pennsylvania	168,000		38	New Mexico	23,000
30	Rhode Island	45,000		39	Kentucky	22,000
5	South Carolina	248,000		40	Alaska	17,000
37	South Dakota	26,000		41	New Hampshire	16,000
10	Tennessee	196,000		41	North Dakota	16,000
2	Texas	556,000		43	Vermont	15,000
25	Utah	85,000		44	Idaho	12,000
43	Vermont	15,000		45	Maine	11,000
7	Virginia	237,000		46	Wyoming	4,000
24	Washington	86,000		47	Hawaii	(1,000)
23	West Virginia	88,000		48	Kansas	(11,000)
18	Wisconsin	125,000		49	Louisiana	(78,000)
46	Wyoming	4,000		50	New York	(357,000)
					District of Columbia	3,000

Source: Morgan Quitno Press using data from U.S. Bureau of the Census
"Health Insurance Coverage Status by State for All People: 2001"
"Health Insurance Coverage Status by State for All People: 2005"
(http://ferret.bls.census.gov/macro/032006/health/h06_000.htm)

Percent Change in Persons Uninsured: 2001 to 2005

National Percent Change = 13.0% Increase

ALPHA ORDER

RANK	STATE	PERCENT CHANGE
21	Alabama	21.5
26	Alaska	17.0
13	Arizona	28.3
28	Arkansas	15.4
46	California	3.6
30	Colorado	14.7
31	Connecticut	13.9
2	Delaware	50.7
12	Florida	29.7
17	Georgia	24.2
47	Hawaii	(0.9)
42	Idaho	5.7
40	Illinois	7.5
20	Indiana	22.0
27	Iowa	16.2
48	Kansas	(3.7)
44	Kentucky	4.5
49	Louisiana	(9.2)
38	Maine	8.3
22	Maryland	20.7
24	Massachusetts	18.8
36	Michigan	10.2
37	Minnesota	9.9
39	Mississippi	7.8
19	Missouri	22.3
6	Montana	33.9
11	Nebraska	30.0
18	Nevada	23.5
32	New Hampshire	13.4
23	New Jersey	19.4
41	New Mexico	6.2
50	New York	(12.2)
25	North Carolina	17.5
14	North Dakota	26.7
33	Ohio	11.7
45	Oklahoma	4.4
7	Oregon	30.7
29	Pennsylvania	15.0
1	Rhode Island	56.3
3	South Carolina	50.3
4	South Dakota	37.7
8	Tennessee	30.6
34	Texas	11.2
16	Utah	25.4
15	Vermont	25.9
8	Virginia	30.6
35	Washington	11.0
5	West Virginia	37.6
8	Wisconsin	30.6
43	Wyoming	5.1

RANK ORDER

RANK	STATE	PERCENT CHANGE
1	Rhode Island	56.3
2	Delaware	50.7
3	South Carolina	50.3
4	South Dakota	37.7
5	West Virginia	37.6
6	Montana	33.9
7	Oregon	30.7
8	Tennessee	30.6
8	Virginia	30.6
8	Wisconsin	30.6
11	Nebraska	30.0
12	Florida	29.7
13	Arizona	28.3
14	North Dakota	26.7
15	Vermont	25.9
16	Utah	25.4
17	Georgia	24.2
18	Nevada	23.5
19	Missouri	22.3
20	Indiana	22.0
21	Alabama	21.5
22	Maryland	20.7
23	New Jersey	19.4
24	Massachusetts	18.8
25	North Carolina	17.5
26	Alaska	17.0
27	Iowa	16.2
28	Arkansas	15.4
29	Pennsylvania	15.0
30	Colorado	14.7
31	Connecticut	13.9
32	New Hampshire	13.4
33	Ohio	11.7
34	Texas	11.2
35	Washington	11.0
36	Michigan	10.2
37	Minnesota	9.9
38	Maine	8.3
39	Mississippi	7.8
40	Illinois	7.5
41	New Mexico	6.2
42	Idaho	5.7
43	Wyoming	5.1
44	Kentucky	4.5
45	Oklahoma	4.4
46	California	3.6
47	Hawaii	(0.9)
48	Kansas	(3.7)
49	Louisiana	(9.2)
50	New York	(12.2)

District of Columbia   4.3

Source: Morgan Quitno Press using data from U.S. Bureau of the Census
"Health Insurance Coverage Status by State for All People: 2001" and
"Health Insurance Coverage Status by State for All People: 2005"
(http://ferret.bls.census.gov/macro/032006/health/h06_000.htm)

Change in Percent of Population Uninsured: 2001 to 2005

National Percent Change = 8.3% Increase*

ALPHA ORDER				RANK ORDER		
RANK	STATE	PERCENT CHANGE		RANK	STATE	PERCENT CHANGE
32	Alabama	8.3		1	Rhode Island	52.8
40	Alaska	0.6		2	Missouri	35.2
42	Arizona	(1.6)		3	Delaware	33.7
19	Arkansas	14.7		4	Indiana	31.5
43	California	(2.1)		5	Pennsylvania	28.7
26	Colorado	11.9		6	Oregon	27.5
25	Connecticut	13.4		7	Tennessee	26.9
3	Delaware	33.7		8	Maryland	24.8
30	Florida	10.1		9	Massachusetts	23.0
20	Georgia	14.4		10	Iowa	22.5
43	Hawaii	(2.1)		11	Wisconsin	21.2
41	Idaho	0.0		12	West Virginia	19.0
37	Illinois	4.4		13	Nebraska	18.7
4	Indiana	31.5		14	South Carolina	17.3
10	Iowa	22.5		15	Montana	16.9
47	Kansas	(4.4)		16	South Dakota	16.3
36	Kentucky	4.6		17	New Jersey	16.0
48	Louisiana	(5.1)		18	New Hampshire	15.6
46	Maine	(2.8)		19	Arkansas	14.7
8	Maryland	24.8		20	Georgia	14.4
9	Massachusetts	23.0		21	Virginia	14.3
22	Michigan	14.1		22	Michigan	14.1
27	Minnesota	11.5		22	North Carolina	14.1
24	Mississippi	13.8		24	Mississippi	13.8
2	Missouri	35.2		25	Connecticut	13.4
15	Montana	16.9		26	Colorado	11.9
13	Nebraska	18.7		27	Minnesota	11.5
33	Nevada	7.0		28	Ohio	11.1
18	New Hampshire	15.6		29	Vermont	10.3
17	New Jersey	16.0		30	Florida	10.1
49	New Mexico	(9.1)		31	Oklahoma	8.9
50	New York	(12.0)		32	Alabama	8.3
22	North Carolina	14.1		33	Nevada	7.0
39	North Dakota	2.8		33	Texas	7.0
28	Ohio	11.1		35	Utah	6.6
31	Oklahoma	8.9		36	Kentucky	4.6
6	Oregon	27.5		37	Illinois	4.4
5	Pennsylvania	28.7		37	Washington	4.4
1	Rhode Island	52.8		39	North Dakota	2.8
14	South Carolina	17.3		40	Alaska	0.6
16	South Dakota	16.3		41	Idaho	0.0
7	Tennessee	26.9		42	Arizona	(1.6)
33	Texas	7.0		43	California	(2.1)
35	Utah	6.6		43	Hawaii	(2.1)
29	Vermont	10.3		45	Wyoming	(2.6)
21	Virginia	14.3		46	Maine	(2.8)
37	Washington	4.4		47	Kansas	(4.4)
12	West Virginia	19.0		48	Louisiana	(5.1)
11	Wisconsin	21.2		49	New Mexico	(9.1)
45	Wyoming	(2.6)		50	New York	(12.0)
					District of Columbia	(0.7)

Source: Morgan Quitno Press using data from U.S. Bureau of the Census
   "Health Insurance Coverage Status by State for All People: 2001" and
   "Income, Poverty and Health Insurance Covered in the United States: 2005"
   (http://www.census.gov/prod/2006pubs/p60-231.pdf)
*Based on three-year averages for 2003 through 2005 and 1999 through 2001.

Percent of Children Not Covered by Health Insurance in 2005

National Percent = 11.2% of Children*

ALPHA ORDER

RANK	STATE	PERCENT
46	Alabama	5.3
32	Alaska	8.1
4	Arizona	16.7
17	Arkansas	10.9
7	California	13.8
8	Colorado	13.6
31	Connecticut	8.2
9	Delaware	12.3
3	Florida	18.6
16	Georgia	11.3
44	Hawaii	5.7
13	Idaho	11.6
20	Illinois	10.4
22	Indiana	9.7
49	Iowa	4.9
40	Kansas	7.0
41	Kentucky	6.8
23	Louisiana	9.4
32	Maine	8.1
25	Maryland	9.1
50	Massachusetts	4.5
46	Michigan	5.3
42	Minnesota	6.2
15	Mississippi	11.4
37	Missouri	7.6
5	Montana	14.6
43	Nebraska	5.9
6	Nevada	14.4
44	New Hampshire	5.7
18	New Jersey	10.8
1	New Mexico	20.2
34	New York	8.0
12	North Carolina	11.9
24	North Dakota	9.3
34	Ohio	8.0
13	Oklahoma	11.6
21	Oregon	10.2
30	Pennsylvania	8.3
36	Rhode Island	7.7
19	South Carolina	10.7
29	South Dakota	8.6
25	Tennessee	9.1
2	Texas	19.2
9	Utah	12.3
46	Vermont	5.3
28	Virginia	9.0
25	Washington	9.1
39	West Virginia	7.2
38	Wisconsin	7.5
9	Wyoming	12.3

RANK ORDER

RANK	STATE	PERCENT
1	New Mexico	20.2
2	Texas	19.2
3	Florida	18.6
4	Arizona	16.7
5	Montana	14.6
6	Nevada	14.4
7	California	13.8
8	Colorado	13.6
9	Delaware	12.3
9	Utah	12.3
9	Wyoming	12.3
12	North Carolina	11.9
13	Idaho	11.6
13	Oklahoma	11.6
15	Mississippi	11.4
16	Georgia	11.3
17	Arkansas	10.9
18	New Jersey	10.8
19	South Carolina	10.7
20	Illinois	10.4
21	Oregon	10.2
22	Indiana	9.7
23	Louisiana	9.4
24	North Dakota	9.3
25	Maryland	9.1
25	Tennessee	9.1
25	Washington	9.1
28	Virginia	9.0
29	South Dakota	8.6
30	Pennsylvania	8.3
31	Connecticut	8.2
32	Alaska	8.1
32	Maine	8.1
34	New York	8.0
34	Ohio	8.0
36	Rhode Island	7.7
37	Missouri	7.6
38	Wisconsin	7.5
39	West Virginia	7.2
40	Kansas	7.0
41	Kentucky	6.8
42	Minnesota	6.2
43	Nebraska	5.9
44	Hawaii	5.7
44	New Hampshire	5.7
46	Alabama	5.3
46	Michigan	5.3
46	Vermont	5.3
49	Iowa	4.9
50	Massachusetts	4.5

District of Columbia | 6.9

Source: U.S. Bureau of the Census
    "Health Insurance Coverage Status" (http://www.census.gov/hhes/www/hlthins/historic/hihistt5.html)
*Children under 18 years old.

Persons Covered by Health Insurance in 2005

National Total = 247,257,000 Insured

ALPHA ORDER

RANK	STATE	INSURED	% of USA
23	Alabama	3,828,000	1.5%
49	Alaska	542,000	0.2%
19	Arizona	4,828,000	2.0%
33	Arkansas	2,266,000	0.9%
1	California	28,979,000	11.7%
22	Colorado	3,853,000	1.6%
27	Connecticut	3,093,000	1.3%
45	Delaware	734,000	0.3%
4	Florida	14,183,000	5.7%
10	Georgia	7,335,000	3.0%
42	Hawaii	1,163,000	0.5%
39	Idaho	1,221,000	0.5%
6	Illinois	10,806,000	4.4%
15	Indiana	5,270,000	2.1%
30	Iowa	2,657,000	1.1%
31	Kansas	2,405,000	1.0%
24	Kentucky	3,539,000	1.4%
26	Louisiana	3,321,000	1.3%
40	Maine	1,177,000	0.5%
20	Maryland	4,781,000	1.9%
13	Massachusetts	5,710,000	2.3%
8	Michigan	8,848,000	3.6%
21	Minnesota	4,699,000	1.9%
32	Mississippi	2,359,000	1.0%
17	Missouri	5,019,000	2.0%
44	Montana	767,000	0.3%
36	Nebraska	1,558,000	0.6%
35	Nevada	2,023,000	0.8%
41	New Hampshire	1,166,000	0.5%
9	New Jersey	7,401,000	3.0%
37	New Mexico	1,542,000	0.6%
3	New York	16,463,000	6.7%
11	North Carolina	7,190,000	2.9%
47	North Dakota	550,000	0.2%
7	Ohio	9,940,000	4.0%
29	Oklahoma	2,859,000	1.2%
28	Oregon	3,049,000	1.2%
5	Pennsylvania	10,994,000	4.4%
43	Rhode Island	929,000	0.4%
25	South Carolina	3,439,000	1.4%
46	South Dakota	673,000	0.3%
16	Tennessee	5,031,000	2.0%
2	Texas	17,304,000	7.0%
34	Utah	2,104,000	0.9%
48	Vermont	549,000	0.2%
12	Virginia	6,443,000	2.6%
14	Washington	5,384,000	2.2%
38	West Virginia	1,477,000	0.6%
18	Wisconsin	4,913,000	2.0%
50	Wyoming	428,000	0.2%

RANK ORDER

RANK	STATE	INSURED	% of USA
1	California	28,979,000	11.7%
2	Texas	17,304,000	7.0%
3	New York	16,463,000	6.7%
4	Florida	14,183,000	5.7%
5	Pennsylvania	10,994,000	4.4%
6	Illinois	10,806,000	4.4%
7	Ohio	9,940,000	4.0%
8	Michigan	8,848,000	3.6%
9	New Jersey	7,401,000	3.0%
10	Georgia	7,335,000	3.0%
11	North Carolina	7,190,000	2.9%
12	Virginia	6,443,000	2.6%
13	Massachusetts	5,710,000	2.3%
14	Washington	5,384,000	2.2%
15	Indiana	5,270,000	2.1%
16	Tennessee	5,031,000	2.0%
17	Missouri	5,019,000	2.0%
18	Wisconsin	4,913,000	2.0%
19	Arizona	4,828,000	2.0%
20	Maryland	4,781,000	1.9%
21	Minnesota	4,699,000	1.9%
22	Colorado	3,853,000	1.6%
23	Alabama	3,828,000	1.5%
24	Kentucky	3,539,000	1.4%
25	South Carolina	3,439,000	1.4%
26	Louisiana	3,321,000	1.3%
27	Connecticut	3,093,000	1.3%
28	Oregon	3,049,000	1.2%
29	Oklahoma	2,859,000	1.2%
30	Iowa	2,657,000	1.1%
31	Kansas	2,405,000	1.0%
32	Mississippi	2,359,000	1.0%
33	Arkansas	2,266,000	0.9%
34	Utah	2,104,000	0.9%
35	Nevada	2,023,000	0.8%
36	Nebraska	1,558,000	0.6%
37	New Mexico	1,542,000	0.6%
38	West Virginia	1,477,000	0.6%
39	Idaho	1,221,000	0.5%
40	Maine	1,177,000	0.5%
41	New Hampshire	1,166,000	0.5%
42	Hawaii	1,163,000	0.5%
43	Rhode Island	929,000	0.4%
44	Montana	767,000	0.3%
45	Delaware	734,000	0.3%
46	South Dakota	673,000	0.3%
47	North Dakota	550,000	0.2%
48	Vermont	549,000	0.2%
49	Alaska	542,000	0.2%
50	Wyoming	428,000	0.2%
	District of Columbia	467,000	0.2%

Source: U.S. Bureau of the Census
"Health Insurance Coverage Status by State for All People: 2005"
(http://ferret.bls.census.gov/macro/032006/health/h06_000.htm)

Percent of Population Covered by Health Insurance in 2005

National Percent = 84.3% of Population

ALPHA ORDER				RANK ORDER		
RANK	STATE	PERCENT		RANK	STATE	PERCENT
28	Alabama	85.7		1	Minnesota	91.3
41	Alaska	82.2		2	Hawaii	90.5
42	Arizona	81.9		3	Iowa	90.2
38	Arkansas	82.8		4	Wisconsin	89.7
46	California	81.2		5	Maine	89.6
36	Colorado	83.1		5	New Hampshire	89.6
10	Connecticut	89.0		7	Massachusetts	89.3
19	Delaware	87.3		7	Vermont	89.3
48	Florida	80.4		9	Kansas	89.1
40	Georgia	82.5		10	Connecticut	89.0
2	Hawaii	90.5		10	Rhode Island	89.0
34	Idaho	83.5		12	North Dakota	88.8
26	Illinois	85.8		12	Pennsylvania	88.8
26	Indiana	85.8		14	Michigan	88.7
3	Iowa	90.2		15	Nebraska	88.6
9	Kansas	89.1		16	Missouri	88.1
20	Kentucky	86.4		17	Ohio	88.0
44	Louisiana	81.3		18	South Dakota	87.9
5	Maine	89.6		19	Delaware	87.3
24	Maryland	85.9		20	Kentucky	86.4
7	Massachusetts	89.3		20	Virginia	86.4
14	Michigan	88.7		22	Tennessee	86.3
1	Minnesota	91.3		23	New York	86.1
39	Mississippi	82.7		24	Maryland	85.9
16	Missouri	88.1		24	Washington	85.9
44	Montana	81.3		26	Illinois	85.8
15	Nebraska	88.6		26	Indiana	85.8
43	Nevada	81.6		28	Alabama	85.7
5	New Hampshire	89.6		29	New Jersey	85.5
29	New Jersey	85.5		29	Utah	85.5
49	New Mexico	78.9		31	Wyoming	84.8
23	New York	86.1		32	South Carolina	84.4
33	North Carolina	83.8		33	North Carolina	83.8
12	North Dakota	88.8		34	Idaho	83.5
17	Ohio	88.0		35	Oregon	83.3
47	Oklahoma	80.5		36	Colorado	83.1
35	Oregon	83.3		36	West Virginia	83.1
12	Pennsylvania	88.8		38	Arkansas	82.8
10	Rhode Island	89.0		39	Mississippi	82.7
32	South Carolina	84.4		40	Georgia	82.5
18	South Dakota	87.9		41	Alaska	82.2
22	Tennessee	86.3		42	Arizona	81.9
50	Texas	75.4		43	Nevada	81.6
29	Utah	85.5		44	Louisiana	81.3
7	Vermont	89.3		44	Montana	81.3
20	Virginia	86.4		46	California	81.2
24	Washington	85.9		47	Oklahoma	80.5
36	West Virginia	83.1		48	Florida	80.4
4	Wisconsin	89.7		49	New Mexico	78.9
31	Wyoming	84.8		50	Texas	75.4
					District of Columbia	86.5

Source: Morgan Quitno Press using data from U.S. Bureau of the Census
"Income, Poverty and Health Insurance Covered in the United States: 2005"
(http://www.census.gov/prod/2006pubs/p60-231.pdf)
*Three-year average for 2003 through 2005.

Percent of Population Covered by Private Health Insurance in 2005

National Percent = 67.7% of Population*

ALPHA ORDER

RANK	STATE	PERCENT
35	Alabama	65.3
46	Alaska	60.9
47	Arizona	59.1
43	Arkansas	62.2
44	California	62.1
19	Colorado	71.5
7	Connecticut	76.4
23	Delaware	71.3
42	Florida	62.4
45	Georgia	62.0
13	Hawaii	73.5
26	Idaho	69.6
18	Illinois	71.9
25	Indiana	71.1
2	Iowa	79.9
5	Kansas	77.0
29	Kentucky	68.5
39	Louisiana	62.7
33	Maine	66.5
15	Maryland	72.8
12	Massachusetts	74.0
10	Michigan	74.5
1	Minnesota	80.7
50	Mississippi	56.4
19	Missouri	71.5
36	Montana	65.2
9	Nebraska	74.7
27	Nevada	68.9
3	New Hampshire	79.0
11	New Jersey	74.2
49	New Mexico	57.5
32	New York	67.4
34	North Carolina	66.0
4	North Dakota	77.2
16	Ohio	72.7
41	Oklahoma	62.5
28	Oregon	68.8
8	Pennsylvania	76.2
19	Rhode Island	71.5
37	South Carolina	63.6
14	South Dakota	73.2
37	Tennessee	63.6
48	Texas	58.5
23	Utah	71.3
29	Vermont	68.5
17	Virginia	72.3
22	Washington	71.4
39	West Virginia	62.7
6	Wisconsin	76.9
31	Wyoming	68.1

RANK ORDER

RANK	STATE	PERCENT
1	Minnesota	80.7
2	Iowa	79.9
3	New Hampshire	79.0
4	North Dakota	77.2
5	Kansas	77.0
6	Wisconsin	76.9
7	Connecticut	76.4
8	Pennsylvania	76.2
9	Nebraska	74.7
10	Michigan	74.5
11	New Jersey	74.2
12	Massachusetts	74.0
13	Hawaii	73.5
14	South Dakota	73.2
15	Maryland	72.8
16	Ohio	72.7
17	Virginia	72.3
18	Illinois	71.9
19	Colorado	71.5
19	Missouri	71.5
19	Rhode Island	71.5
22	Washington	71.4
23	Delaware	71.3
23	Utah	71.3
25	Indiana	71.1
26	Idaho	69.6
27	Nevada	68.9
28	Oregon	68.8
29	Kentucky	68.5
29	Vermont	68.5
31	Wyoming	68.1
32	New York	67.4
33	Maine	66.5
34	North Carolina	66.0
35	Alabama	65.3
36	Montana	65.2
37	South Carolina	63.6
37	Tennessee	63.6
39	Louisiana	62.7
39	West Virginia	62.7
41	Oklahoma	62.5
42	Florida	62.4
43	Arkansas	62.2
44	California	62.1
45	Georgia	62.0
46	Alaska	60.9
47	Arizona	59.1
48	Texas	58.5
49	New Mexico	57.5
50	Mississippi	56.4

District of Columbia   63.1

Source: U.S. Bureau of the Census
    "Health Insurance Coverage Status" (http://www.census.gov/hhes/www/hlthins/historic/hihistt4.html)
*Private health insurance is coverage by a health plan provided through an employer or union or purchased by an individual from a private health insurance company.

Percent of Population Covered by
Employment-Based Health Insurance in 2005
National Percent = 59.5% of Population*

ALPHA ORDER

RANK	STATE	PERCENT
30	Alabama	58.6
38	Alaska	55.9
45	Arizona	52.5
46	Arkansas	52.4
44	California	52.9
22	Colorado	62.1
4	Connecticut	67.6
11	Delaware	65.9
43	Florida	53.0
37	Georgia	56.1
4	Hawaii	67.6
29	Idaho	59.5
15	Illinois	64.7
18	Indiana	63.2
7	Iowa	66.9
17	Kansas	63.6
19	Kentucky	62.7
41	Louisiana	54.6
33	Maine	57.8
10	Maryland	66.2
8	Massachusetts	66.8
6	Michigan	67.4
3	Minnesota	68.2
50	Mississippi	49.2
25	Missouri	61.8
48	Montana	50.9
19	Nebraska	62.7
22	Nevada	62.1
1	New Hampshire	70.3
2	New Jersey	68.3
48	New Mexico	50.9
28	New York	60.2
34	North Carolina	57.2
26	North Dakota	61.3
12	Ohio	65.7
41	Oklahoma	54.6
32	Oregon	58.2
14	Pennsylvania	65.2
16	Rhode Island	64.3
35	South Carolina	56.6
36	South Dakota	56.2
40	Tennessee	54.8
46	Texas	52.4
21	Utah	62.2
27	Vermont	60.4
13	Virginia	65.4
24	Washington	62.0
31	West Virginia	58.3
9	Wisconsin	66.7
39	Wyoming	55.7

RANK ORDER

RANK	STATE	PERCENT
1	New Hampshire	70.3
2	New Jersey	68.3
3	Minnesota	68.2
4	Connecticut	67.6
4	Hawaii	67.6
6	Michigan	67.4
7	Iowa	66.9
8	Massachusetts	66.8
9	Wisconsin	66.7
10	Maryland	66.2
11	Delaware	65.9
12	Ohio	65.7
13	Virginia	65.4
14	Pennsylvania	65.2
15	Illinois	64.7
16	Rhode Island	64.3
17	Kansas	63.6
18	Indiana	63.2
19	Kentucky	62.7
19	Nebraska	62.7
21	Utah	62.2
22	Colorado	62.1
22	Nevada	62.1
24	Washington	62.0
25	Missouri	61.8
26	North Dakota	61.3
27	Vermont	60.4
28	New York	60.2
29	Idaho	59.5
30	Alabama	58.6
31	West Virginia	58.3
32	Oregon	58.2
33	Maine	57.8
34	North Carolina	57.2
35	South Carolina	56.6
36	South Dakota	56.2
37	Georgia	56.1
38	Alaska	55.9
39	Wyoming	55.7
40	Tennessee	54.8
41	Louisiana	54.6
41	Oklahoma	54.6
43	Florida	53.0
44	California	52.9
45	Arizona	52.5
46	Arkansas	52.4
46	Texas	52.4
48	Montana	50.9
48	New Mexico	50.9
50	Mississippi	49.2

District of Columbia — 55.1

Source: U.S. Bureau of the Census
"Health Insurance Coverage Status" (http://www.census.gov/hhes/www/hlthins/historic/hihistt4.html)
Employment-based health insurance is private insurance coverage offered through one's own employment or a relative's. It may be offered by an employer or by a union.

Percent of Population Covered by Direct Purchase Health Insurance in 2005

National Percent = 9.1% of Population*

ALPHA ORDER

RANK ORDER

RANK	STATE	PERCENT		RANK	STATE	PERCENT
39	Alabama	7.3		1	South Dakota	19.0
50	Alaska	5.3		2	North Dakota	16.2
36	Arizona	7.4		3	Montana	14.3
16	Arkansas	10.3		4	Iowa	13.7
16	California	10.3		4	Wyoming	13.7
18	Colorado	10.0		6	Kansas	13.6
15	Connecticut	10.7		7	Nebraska	13.1
48	Delaware	5.8		8	Minnesota	12.5
14	Florida	11.2		9	Idaho	12.0
44	Georgia	6.9		10	Missouri	11.7
31	Hawaii	8.3		11	Oregon	11.6
9	Idaho	12.0		11	Wisconsin	11.6
31	Illinois	8.3		13	Pennsylvania	11.4
23	Indiana	9.1		14	Florida	11.2
4	Iowa	13.7		15	Connecticut	10.7
6	Kansas	13.6		16	Arkansas	10.3
44	Kentucky	6.9		16	California	10.3
25	Louisiana	8.8		18	Colorado	10.0
26	Maine	8.7		19	North Carolina	9.9
34	Maryland	7.7		20	Washington	9.7
44	Massachusetts	6.9		21	New Hampshire	9.6
43	Michigan	7.0		22	Tennessee	9.2
8	Minnesota	12.5		23	Indiana	9.1
24	Mississippi	9.0		24	Mississippi	9.0
10	Missouri	11.7		25	Louisiana	8.8
3	Montana	14.3		26	Maine	8.7
7	Nebraska	13.1		26	Utah	8.7
39	Nevada	7.3		26	Vermont	8.7
21	New Hampshire	9.6		26	Virginia	8.7
41	New Jersey	7.2		30	Oklahoma	8.4
47	New Mexico	6.0		31	Hawaii	8.3
33	New York	8.0		31	Illinois	8.3
19	North Carolina	9.9		33	New York	8.0
2	North Dakota	16.2		34	Maryland	7.7
36	Ohio	7.4		35	Rhode Island	7.5
30	Oklahoma	8.4		36	Arizona	7.4
11	Oregon	11.6		36	Ohio	7.4
13	Pennsylvania	11.4		36	South Carolina	7.4
35	Rhode Island	7.5		39	Alabama	7.3
36	South Carolina	7.4		39	Nevada	7.3
1	South Dakota	19.0		41	New Jersey	7.2
22	Tennessee	9.2		42	Texas	7.1
42	Texas	7.1		43	Michigan	7.0
26	Utah	8.7		44	Georgia	6.9
26	Vermont	8.7		44	Kentucky	6.9
26	Virginia	8.7		44	Massachusetts	6.9
20	Washington	9.7		47	New Mexico	6.0
48	West Virginia	5.8		48	Delaware	5.8
11	Wisconsin	11.6		48	West Virginia	5.8
4	Wyoming	13.7		50	Alaska	5.3

District of Columbia 7.8

Source: U.S. Bureau of the Census
    "Health Insurance Coverage Status" (http://www.census.gov/hhes/www/hlthins/historic/hihistt4.html)
*Direct-purchase health insurance is private insurance coverage though a plan purchased by an individual from a private company.

250

Percent of Population Covered by Government Health Insurance in 2005

National Percent = 27.3% of Population*

ALPHA ORDER

RANK ORDER

RANK	STATE	PERCENT	RANK	STATE	PERCENT
7	Alabama	33.1	1	Maine	35.4
7	Alaska	33.1	1	Mississippi	35.4
14	Arizona	30.4	3	New Mexico	34.2
11	Arkansas	31.6	4	West Virginia	33.8
27	California	26.9	5	Vermont	33.7
49	Colorado	20.4	6	Tennessee	33.5
43	Connecticut	24.1	7	Alabama	33.1
22	Delaware	28.3	7	Alaska	33.1
16	Florida	29.6	9	Hawaii	32.6
25	Georgia	27.2	10	Oklahoma	32.0
9	Hawaii	32.6	11	Arkansas	31.6
41	Idaho	24.4	12	New York	30.8
42	Illinois	24.3	13	Kentucky	30.5
44	Indiana	24.0	14	Arizona	30.4
38	Iowa	25.4	15	Rhode Island	29.9
34	Kansas	26.1	16	Florida	29.6
13	Kentucky	30.5	16	North Carolina	29.6
21	Louisiana	28.5	18	Montana	29.4
1	Maine	35.4	18	South Carolina	29.4
40	Maryland	24.6	20	South Dakota	28.8
27	Massachusetts	26.9	21	Louisiana	28.5
33	Michigan	26.4	22	Delaware	28.3
46	Minnesota	22.6	23	Wyoming	27.6
1	Mississippi	35.4	24	Missouri	27.5
24	Missouri	27.5	25	Georgia	27.2
18	Montana	29.4	26	Oregon	27.1
34	Nebraska	26.1	27	California	26.9
45	Nevada	23.7	27	Massachusetts	26.9
47	New Hampshire	21.9	27	Pennsylvania	26.9
50	New Jersey	20.0	30	Washington	26.7
3	New Mexico	34.2	31	Virginia	26.6
12	New York	30.8	32	Ohio	26.5
16	North Carolina	29.6	33	Michigan	26.4
39	North Dakota	25.3	34	Kansas	26.1
32	Ohio	26.5	34	Nebraska	26.1
10	Oklahoma	32.0	34	Wisconsin	26.1
26	Oregon	27.1	37	Texas	25.7
27	Pennsylvania	26.9	38	Iowa	25.4
15	Rhode Island	29.9	39	North Dakota	25.3
18	South Carolina	29.4	40	Maryland	24.6
20	South Dakota	28.8	41	Idaho	24.4
6	Tennessee	33.5	42	Illinois	24.3
37	Texas	25.7	43	Connecticut	24.1
48	Utah	21.2	44	Indiana	24.0
5	Vermont	33.7	45	Nevada	23.7
31	Virginia	26.6	46	Minnesota	22.6
30	Washington	26.7	47	New Hampshire	21.9
4	West Virginia	33.8	48	Utah	21.2
34	Wisconsin	26.1	49	Colorado	20.4
23	Wyoming	27.6	50	New Jersey	20.0
				District of Columbia	33.2

Source: U.S. Bureau of the Census
"Health Insurance Coverage Status" (http://www.census.gov/hhes/www/hlthins/historic/hihistt4.html)
*Includes Medicaid, Medicare, State Children's Health Insurance Program (SCHIP) and military health care.

Percent of Population Covered by Military Health Care in 2005

National Percent = 3.8% of Population*

RANK	STATE	PERCENT
18	Alabama	5.2
1	Alaska	12.7
32	Arizona	3.7
9	Arkansas	6.0
37	California	2.9
20	Colorado	5.0
43	Connecticut	2.2
28	Delaware	4.1
16	Florida	5.5
17	Georgia	5.3
2	Hawaii	10.6
35	Idaho	3.2
43	Illinois	2.2
40	Indiana	2.7
30	Iowa	3.8
24	Kansas	4.6
25	Kentucky	4.5
34	Louisiana	3.3
13	Maine	5.6
19	Maryland	5.1
47	Massachusetts	1.9
42	Michigan	2.3
46	Minnesota	2.0
20	Mississippi	5.0
37	Missouri	2.9
8	Montana	6.4
11	Nebraska	5.9
13	Nevada	5.6
30	New Hampshire	3.8
49	New Jersey	1.5
12	New Mexico	5.8
50	New York	1.2
20	North Carolina	5.0
13	North Dakota	5.6
41	Ohio	2.4
5	Oklahoma	7.2
37	Oregon	2.9
47	Pennsylvania	1.9
36	Rhode Island	3.1
27	South Carolina	4.2
7	South Dakota	6.5
9	Tennessee	6.0
26	Texas	4.4
33	Utah	3.5
28	Vermont	4.1
3	Virginia	9.9
4	Washington	7.3
23	West Virginia	4.9
45	Wisconsin	2.1
6	Wyoming	7.1

RANK	STATE	PERCENT
1	Alaska	12.7
2	Hawaii	10.6
3	Virginia	9.9
4	Washington	7.3
5	Oklahoma	7.2
6	Wyoming	7.1
7	South Dakota	6.5
8	Montana	6.4
9	Arkansas	6.0
9	Tennessee	6.0
11	Nebraska	5.9
12	New Mexico	5.8
13	Maine	5.6
13	Nevada	5.6
13	North Dakota	5.6
16	Florida	5.5
17	Georgia	5.3
18	Alabama	5.2
19	Maryland	5.1
20	Colorado	5.0
20	Mississippi	5.0
20	North Carolina	5.0
23	West Virginia	4.9
24	Kansas	4.6
25	Kentucky	4.5
26	Texas	4.4
27	South Carolina	4.2
28	Delaware	4.1
28	Vermont	4.1
30	Iowa	3.8
30	New Hampshire	3.8
32	Arizona	3.7
33	Utah	3.5
34	Louisiana	3.3
35	Idaho	3.2
36	Rhode Island	3.1
37	California	2.9
37	Missouri	2.9
37	Oregon	2.9
40	Indiana	2.7
41	Ohio	2.4
42	Michigan	2.3
43	Connecticut	2.2
43	Illinois	2.2
45	Wisconsin	2.1
46	Minnesota	2.0
47	Massachusetts	1.9
47	Pennsylvania	1.9
49	New Jersey	1.5
50	New York	1.2

| | District of Columbia | 1.8 |

Source: U.S. Bureau of the Census
   "Health Insurance Coverage Status" (http://www.census.gov/hhes/www/hlthins/historic/hihistt4.html)
*Includes CHAMPUS (Comprehensive Health and Medical Plan for Uniformed Services)/Tricare, Veterans and military health care.

Percent of Children Covered by Health Insurance in 2005

National Percent = 88.8% of Children*

ALPHA ORDER

RANK ORDER

RANK	STATE	PERCENT
3	Alabama	94.7
18	Alaska	91.9
47	Arizona	83.3
34	Arkansas	89.1
44	California	86.2
43	Colorado	86.4
20	Connecticut	91.8
40	Delaware	87.7
48	Florida	81.4
35	Georgia	88.7
6	Hawaii	94.3
37	Idaho	88.4
31	Illinois	89.6
29	Indiana	90.3
2	Iowa	95.1
11	Kansas	93.0
10	Kentucky	93.2
28	Louisiana	90.6
18	Maine	91.9
24	Maryland	90.9
1	Massachusetts	95.5
3	Michigan	94.7
9	Minnesota	93.8
36	Mississippi	88.6
14	Missouri	92.4
46	Montana	85.4
8	Nebraska	94.1
45	Nevada	85.6
6	New Hampshire	94.3
33	New Jersey	89.2
50	New Mexico	79.8
16	New York	92.0
39	North Carolina	88.1
27	North Dakota	90.7
16	Ohio	92.0
37	Oklahoma	88.4
30	Oregon	89.8
21	Pennsylvania	91.7
15	Rhode Island	92.3
32	South Carolina	89.3
22	South Dakota	91.4
24	Tennessee	90.9
49	Texas	80.8
40	Utah	87.7
3	Vermont	94.7
23	Virginia	91.0
24	Washington	90.9
12	West Virginia	92.8
13	Wisconsin	92.5
40	Wyoming	87.7

RANK	STATE	PERCENT
1	Massachusetts	95.5
2	Iowa	95.1
3	Alabama	94.7
3	Michigan	94.7
3	Vermont	94.7
6	Hawaii	94.3
6	New Hampshire	94.3
8	Nebraska	94.1
9	Minnesota	93.8
10	Kentucky	93.2
11	Kansas	93.0
12	West Virginia	92.8
13	Wisconsin	92.5
14	Missouri	92.4
15	Rhode Island	92.3
16	New York	92.0
16	Ohio	92.0
18	Alaska	91.9
18	Maine	91.9
20	Connecticut	91.8
21	Pennsylvania	91.7
22	South Dakota	91.4
23	Virginia	91.0
24	Maryland	90.9
24	Tennessee	90.9
24	Washington	90.9
27	North Dakota	90.7
28	Louisiana	90.6
29	Indiana	90.3
30	Oregon	89.8
31	Illinois	89.6
32	South Carolina	89.3
33	New Jersey	89.2
34	Arkansas	89.1
35	Georgia	88.7
36	Mississippi	88.6
37	Idaho	88.4
37	Oklahoma	88.4
39	North Carolina	88.1
40	Delaware	87.7
40	Utah	87.7
40	Wyoming	87.7
43	Colorado	86.4
44	California	86.2
45	Nevada	85.6
46	Montana	85.4
47	Arizona	83.3
48	Florida	81.4
49	Texas	80.8
50	New Mexico	79.8

	District of Columbia	93.1

Source: U.S. Bureau of the Census
   "Health Insurance Coverage Status" (http://www.census.gov/hhes/www/hlthins/historic/hihistt5.html)
*Children under 18 covered by either private or government health insurance.

Percent of Children Covered by Private Health Insurance in 2005

National Percent = 65.4% of Children*

ALPHA ORDER			RANK ORDER		
RANK	STATE	PERCENT	RANK	STATE	PERCENT
31	Alabama	65.1	1	New Hampshire	81.6
42	Alaska	60.0	2	Minnesota	80.8
46	Arizona	57.9	3	Iowa	77.4
41	Arkansas	61.0	4	Massachusetts	76.1
44	California	59.5	5	Nebraska	75.6
14	Colorado	72.0	6	Connecticut	75.4
6	Connecticut	75.4	7	Wisconsin	75.3
24	Delaware	68.3	8	New Jersey	74.9
43	Florida	59.6	9	North Dakota	74.6
45	Georgia	58.2	10	Michigan	74.2
16	Hawaii	71.7	11	Kansas	73.4
22	Idaho	69.1	12	Nevada	72.4
20	Illinois	70.4	13	Maryland	72.3
26	Indiana	67.6	14	Colorado	72.0
3	Iowa	77.4	15	Virginia	71.8
11	Kansas	73.4	16	Hawaii	71.7
30	Kentucky	65.5	17	Pennsylvania	71.3
35	Louisiana	63.9	18	Ohio	71.0
36	Maine	63.7	19	Utah	70.5
13	Maryland	72.3	20	Illinois	70.4
4	Massachusetts	76.1	21	South Dakota	70.1
10	Michigan	74.2	22	Idaho	69.1
2	Minnesota	80.8	23	Rhode Island	68.4
49	Mississippi	52.1	24	Delaware	68.3
25	Missouri	67.8	25	Missouri	67.8
34	Montana	64.4	26	Indiana	67.6
5	Nebraska	75.6	26	Washington	67.6
12	Nevada	72.4	28	Oregon	67.5
1	New Hampshire	81.6	29	New York	65.7
8	New Jersey	74.9	30	Kentucky	65.5
50	New Mexico	50.1	31	Alabama	65.1
29	New York	65.7	32	Wyoming	64.9
37	North Carolina	63.6	33	Tennessee	64.6
9	North Dakota	74.6	34	Montana	64.4
18	Ohio	71.0	35	Louisiana	63.9
47	Oklahoma	57.7	36	Maine	63.7
28	Oregon	67.5	37	North Carolina	63.6
17	Pennsylvania	71.3	38	West Virginia	63.4
23	Rhode Island	68.4	39	Vermont	63.0
40	South Carolina	61.4	40	South Carolina	61.4
21	South Dakota	70.1	41	Arkansas	61.0
33	Tennessee	64.6	42	Alaska	60.0
48	Texas	53.9	43	Florida	59.6
19	Utah	70.5	44	California	59.5
39	Vermont	63.0	45	Georgia	58.2
15	Virginia	71.8	46	Arizona	57.9
26	Washington	67.6	47	Oklahoma	57.7
38	West Virginia	63.4	48	Texas	53.9
7	Wisconsin	75.3	49	Mississippi	52.1
32	Wyoming	64.9	50	New Mexico	50.1

District of Columbia   49.6

Source: U.S. Bureau of the Census
    "Health Insurance Coverage Status" (http://www.census.gov/hhes/www/hlthins/historic/hihistt5.html)
*Children under 18. Private health insurance is coverage by a health plan provided through an employer or union or purchased by an individual from a private health insurance company.

Percent of Children Covered by Employment-Based Health Insurance in 2005

National Percent = 60.5% of Children*

ALPHA ORDER

RANK	STATE	PERCENT
26	Alabama	62.2
40	Alaska	56.6
45	Arizona	53.0
41	Arkansas	55.8
47	California	52.8
20	Colorado	64.8
6	Connecticut	71.0
18	Delaware	65.8
43	Florida	54.3
44	Georgia	54.2
13	Hawaii	67.6
32	Idaho	60.2
17	Illinois	66.6
23	Indiana	62.9
4	Iowa	71.7
19	Kansas	65.5
24	Kentucky	62.6
38	Louisiana	57.5
34	Maine	58.9
14	Maryland	67.3
5	Massachusetts	71.3
7	Michigan	70.4
2	Minnesota	73.8
49	Mississippi	47.9
31	Missouri	60.5
42	Montana	55.1
9	Nebraska	70.1
10	Nevada	69.4
1	New Hampshire	77.0
3	New Jersey	71.9
49	New Mexico	47.9
28	New York	61.1
39	North Carolina	57.3
11	North Dakota	67.9
15	Ohio	67.2
46	Oklahoma	52.9
33	Oregon	59.4
16	Pennsylvania	67.0
22	Rhode Island	64.0
37	South Carolina	57.8
30	South Dakota	60.6
29	Tennessee	60.7
48	Texas	50.1
21	Utah	64.4
34	Vermont	58.9
11	Virginia	67.9
25	Washington	62.4
27	West Virginia	61.4
8	Wisconsin	70.2
36	Wyoming	58.5

RANK ORDER

RANK	STATE	PERCENT
1	New Hampshire	77.0
2	Minnesota	73.8
3	New Jersey	71.9
4	Iowa	71.7
5	Massachusetts	71.3
6	Connecticut	71.0
7	Michigan	70.4
8	Wisconsin	70.2
9	Nebraska	70.1
10	Nevada	69.4
11	North Dakota	67.9
11	Virginia	67.9
13	Hawaii	67.6
14	Maryland	67.3
15	Ohio	67.2
16	Pennsylvania	67.0
17	Illinois	66.6
18	Delaware	65.8
19	Kansas	65.5
20	Colorado	64.8
21	Utah	64.4
22	Rhode Island	64.0
23	Indiana	62.9
24	Kentucky	62.6
25	Washington	62.4
26	Alabama	62.2
27	West Virginia	61.4
28	New York	61.1
29	Tennessee	60.7
30	South Dakota	60.6
31	Missouri	60.5
32	Idaho	60.2
33	Oregon	59.4
34	Maine	58.9
34	Vermont	58.9
36	Wyoming	58.5
37	South Carolina	57.8
38	Louisiana	57.5
39	North Carolina	57.3
40	Alaska	56.6
41	Arkansas	55.8
42	Montana	55.1
43	Florida	54.3
44	Georgia	54.2
45	Arizona	53.0
46	Oklahoma	52.9
47	California	52.8
48	Texas	50.1
49	Mississippi	47.9
49	New Mexico	47.9

District of Columbia   44.6

Source: U.S. Bureau of the Census
    "Health Insurance Coverage Status" (http://www.census.gov/hhes/www/hlthins/historic/hihistt5.html)
*Children under 18. Employment-based health insurance is private insurance coverage offered through one's own employment or a relative's. It may be offered by an employer or by a union.

Percent of Children Covered by Direct Purchase Health Insurance in 2005

National Percent = 5.5% of Children*

ALPHA ORDER

RANK	STATE	PERCENT
45	Alabama	3.3
33	Alaska	4.4
24	Arizona	5.3
16	Arkansas	6.2
9	California	7.6
10	Colorado	7.5
25	Connecticut	5.2
47	Delaware	2.7
14	Florida	6.7
29	Georgia	4.9
25	Hawaii	5.2
2	Idaho	10.2
37	Illinois	4.1
18	Indiana	5.9
12	Iowa	7.0
11	Kansas	7.1
46	Kentucky	2.9
15	Louisiana	6.3
38	Maine	4.0
21	Maryland	5.5
40	Massachusetts	3.7
39	Michigan	3.9
7	Minnesota	8.0
31	Mississippi	4.5
3	Missouri	9.1
4	Montana	9.0
17	Nebraska	6.1
41	Nevada	3.6
20	New Hampshire	5.6
44	New Jersey	3.5
50	New Mexico	1.8
27	New York	5.1
19	North Carolina	5.7
8	North Dakota	7.9
47	Ohio	2.7
30	Oklahoma	4.7
5	Oregon	8.9
31	Pennsylvania	4.5
36	Rhode Island	4.2
41	South Carolina	3.6
1	South Dakota	12.1
33	Tennessee	4.4
33	Texas	4.4
12	Utah	7.0
41	Vermont	3.6
21	Virginia	5.5
27	Washington	5.1
49	West Virginia	2.1
21	Wisconsin	5.5
6	Wyoming	8.1

RANK ORDER

RANK	STATE	PERCENT
1	South Dakota	12.1
2	Idaho	10.2
3	Missouri	9.1
4	Montana	9.0
5	Oregon	8.9
6	Wyoming	8.1
7	Minnesota	8.0
8	North Dakota	7.9
9	California	7.6
10	Colorado	7.5
11	Kansas	7.1
12	Iowa	7.0
12	Utah	7.0
14	Florida	6.7
15	Louisiana	6.3
16	Arkansas	6.2
17	Nebraska	6.1
18	Indiana	5.9
19	North Carolina	5.7
20	New Hampshire	5.6
21	Maryland	5.5
21	Virginia	5.5
21	Wisconsin	5.5
24	Arizona	5.3
25	Connecticut	5.2
25	Hawaii	5.2
27	New York	5.1
27	Washington	5.1
29	Georgia	4.9
30	Oklahoma	4.7
31	Mississippi	4.5
31	Pennsylvania	4.5
33	Alaska	4.4
33	Tennessee	4.4
33	Texas	4.4
36	Rhode Island	4.2
37	Illinois	4.1
38	Maine	4.0
39	Michigan	3.9
40	Massachusetts	3.7
41	Nevada	3.6
41	South Carolina	3.6
41	Vermont	3.6
44	New Jersey	3.5
45	Alabama	3.3
46	Kentucky	2.9
47	Delaware	2.7
47	Ohio	2.7
49	West Virginia	2.1
50	New Mexico	1.8
	District of Columbia	3.4

Source: U.S. Bureau of the Census
  "Health Insurance Coverage Status" (http://www.census.gov/hhes/www/hlthins/historic/hihistt5.html)
*Children under 18. Direct-purchase health insurance is private insurance coverage though a plan purchased by an individual from a private company.

Percent of Children Covered by Government Health Insurance in 2005

National Percent = 29.7% of Children*

ALPHA ORDER

RANK	STATE	PERCENT
5	Alabama	40.8
1	Alaska	45.9
22	Arizona	31.3
4	Arkansas	41.3
20	California	31.6
45	Colorado	20.6
46	Connecticut	19.8
33	Delaware	27.5
30	Florida	27.6
10	Georgia	36.7
12	Hawaii	34.9
39	Idaho	24.7
43	Illinois	23.6
26	Indiana	28.3
37	Iowa	25.3
29	Kansas	27.8
11	Kentucky	35.2
15	Louisiana	33.4
9	Maine	37.6
36	Maryland	26.3
43	Massachusetts	23.6
30	Michigan	27.6
49	Minnesota	17.6
3	Mississippi	44.1
23	Missouri	30.8
41	Montana	24.6
26	Nebraska	28.3
47	Nevada	18.2
50	New Hampshire	17.2
48	New Jersey	17.9
6	New Mexico	40.3
15	New York	33.4
21	North Carolina	31.4
39	North Dakota	24.7
35	Ohio	26.6
8	Oklahoma	39.7
28	Oregon	28.0
33	Pennsylvania	27.5
17	Rhode Island	32.7
13	South Carolina	34.0
24	South Dakota	29.8
14	Tennessee	33.6
18	Texas	32.0
42	Utah	23.9
2	Vermont	44.8
30	Virginia	27.6
19	Washington	31.8
6	West Virginia	40.3
38	Wisconsin	24.9
25	Wyoming	29.1

RANK ORDER

RANK	STATE	PERCENT
1	Alaska	45.9
2	Vermont	44.8
3	Mississippi	44.1
4	Arkansas	41.3
5	Alabama	40.8
6	New Mexico	40.3
6	West Virginia	40.3
8	Oklahoma	39.7
9	Maine	37.6
10	Georgia	36.7
11	Kentucky	35.2
12	Hawaii	34.9
13	South Carolina	34.0
14	Tennessee	33.6
15	Louisiana	33.4
15	New York	33.4
17	Rhode Island	32.7
18	Texas	32.0
19	Washington	31.8
20	California	31.6
21	North Carolina	31.4
22	Arizona	31.3
23	Missouri	30.8
24	South Dakota	29.8
25	Wyoming	29.1
26	Indiana	28.3
26	Nebraska	28.3
28	Oregon	28.0
29	Kansas	27.8
30	Florida	27.6
30	Michigan	27.6
30	Virginia	27.6
33	Delaware	27.5
33	Pennsylvania	27.5
35	Ohio	26.6
36	Maryland	26.3
37	Iowa	25.3
38	Wisconsin	24.9
39	Idaho	24.7
39	North Dakota	24.7
41	Montana	24.6
42	Utah	23.9
43	Illinois	23.6
43	Massachusetts	23.6
45	Colorado	20.6
46	Connecticut	19.8
47	Nevada	18.2
48	New Jersey	17.9
49	Minnesota	17.6
50	New Hampshire	17.2

| | District of Columbia | 48.9 |

Source: U.S. Bureau of the Census
    "Health Insurance Coverage Status" (http://www.census.gov/hhes/www/hlthins/historic/hihistt5.html)
*Children under 18. Includes Medicaid, Medicare, State Children's Health Insurance Program (SCHIP) and military health care.

Percent of Children Covered by Military Health Care in 2005

National Percent = 3.1% of Children*

ALPHA ORDER

RANK ORDER

RANK	STATE	PERCENT		RANK	STATE	PERCENT
20	Alabama	3.9		1	Alaska	16.1
1	Alaska	16.1		2	Hawaii	13.7
34	Arizona	2.2		3	Virginia	11.2
14	Arkansas	4.5		4	Washington	7.5
31	California	2.3		5	Oklahoma	7.0
10	Colorado	5.0		6	Wyoming	5.7
43	Connecticut	1.2		7	Nebraska	5.6
20	Delaware	3.9		7	North Dakota	5.6
19	Florida	4.0		9	South Dakota	5.5
11	Georgia	4.9		10	Colorado	5.0
2	Hawaii	13.7		11	Georgia	4.9
41	Idaho	1.7		12	Maine	4.8
38	Illinois	1.9		13	Tennessee	4.7
45	Indiana	1.0		14	Arkansas	4.5
27	Iowa	3.2		15	Montana	4.4
25	Kansas	3.5		16	Mississippi	4.2
20	Kentucky	3.9		16	Nevada	4.2
30	Louisiana	2.4		18	Texas	4.1
12	Maine	4.8		19	Florida	4.0
23	Maryland	3.8		20	Alabama	3.9
46	Massachusetts	0.9		20	Delaware	3.9
48	Michigan	0.8		20	Kentucky	3.9
50	Minnesota	0.5		23	Maryland	3.8
16	Mississippi	4.2		23	North Carolina	3.8
35	Missouri	2.1		25	Kansas	3.5
15	Montana	4.4		25	West Virginia	3.5
7	Nebraska	5.6		27	Iowa	3.2
16	Nevada	4.2		28	New Mexico	3.1
42	New Hampshire	1.6		29	Vermont	3.0
46	New Jersey	0.9		30	Louisiana	2.4
28	New Mexico	3.1		31	California	2.3
49	New York	0.7		31	Rhode Island	2.3
23	North Carolina	3.8		31	South Carolina	2.3
7	North Dakota	5.6		34	Arizona	2.2
40	Ohio	1.8		35	Missouri	2.1
5	Oklahoma	7.0		35	Utah	2.1
37	Oregon	2.0		37	Oregon	2.0
44	Pennsylvania	1.1		38	Illinois	1.9
31	Rhode Island	2.3		38	Wisconsin	1.9
31	South Carolina	2.3		40	Ohio	1.8
9	South Dakota	5.5		41	Idaho	1.7
13	Tennessee	4.7		42	New Hampshire	1.6
18	Texas	4.1		43	Connecticut	1.2
35	Utah	2.1		44	Pennsylvania	1.1
29	Vermont	3.0		45	Indiana	1.0
3	Virginia	11.2		46	Massachusetts	0.9
4	Washington	7.5		46	New Jersey	0.9
25	West Virginia	3.5		48	Michigan	0.8
38	Wisconsin	1.9		49	New York	0.7
6	Wyoming	5.7		50	Minnesota	0.5

District of Columbia   0.6

Source: U.S. Bureau of the Census
    "Health Insurance Coverage Status" (http://www.census.gov/hhes/www/hlthins/historic/hihistt5.html)
*Children under 18. Includes CHAMPUS (Comprehensive Health and Medical Plan for Uniformed Services)/Tricare,
Veterans and military health care.

Percent of Children Covered by Medicaid in 2005

National Percent = 26.7% of Children*

ALPHA ORDER

RANK ORDER

RANK	STATE	PERCENT		RANK	STATE	PERCENT
5	Alabama	36.7		1	Vermont	42.3
10	Alaska	31.6		2	Mississippi	40.8
17	Arizona	29.6		3	Arkansas	38.1
3	Arkansas	38.1		4	New Mexico	37.4
18	California	29.3		5	Alabama	36.7
48	Colorado	15.8		6	West Virginia	35.7
44	Connecticut	18.5		7	Oklahoma	35.1
36	Delaware	22.7		8	Maine	33.6
29	Florida	23.7		9	New York	32.4
12	Georgia	31.4		10	Alaska	31.6
40	Hawaii	21.5		10	Kentucky	31.6
33	Idaho	23.3		12	Georgia	31.4
39	Illinois	21.9		13	Louisiana	30.9
21	Indiana	27.3		13	South Carolina	30.9
38	Iowa	22.0		15	Rhode Island	30.0
29	Kansas	23.7		15	Tennessee	30.0
10	Kentucky	31.6		17	Arizona	29.6
13	Louisiana	30.9		18	California	29.3
8	Maine	33.6		19	Missouri	28.8
35	Maryland	22.8		20	Texas	28.4
36	Massachusetts	22.7		21	Indiana	27.3
23	Michigan	26.8		22	Oregon	26.9
46	Minnesota	16.8		23	Michigan	26.8
2	Mississippi	40.8		24	North Carolina	26.7
19	Missouri	28.8		25	Pennsylvania	25.6
42	Montana	21.2		26	Ohio	25.1
34	Nebraska	23.0		27	Washington	24.5
50	Nevada	14.7		28	South Dakota	24.4
49	New Hampshire	15.7		29	Florida	23.7
45	New Jersey	17.0		29	Kansas	23.7
4	New Mexico	37.4		31	Wisconsin	23.6
9	New York	32.4		31	Wyoming	23.6
24	North Carolina	26.7		33	Idaho	23.3
43	North Dakota	19.4		34	Nebraska	23.0
26	Ohio	25.1		35	Maryland	22.8
7	Oklahoma	35.1		36	Delaware	22.7
22	Oregon	26.9		36	Massachusetts	22.7
25	Pennsylvania	25.6		38	Iowa	22.0
15	Rhode Island	30.0		39	Illinois	21.9
13	South Carolina	30.9		40	Hawaii	21.5
28	South Dakota	24.4		40	Utah	21.5
15	Tennessee	30.0		42	Montana	21.2
20	Texas	28.4		43	North Dakota	19.4
40	Utah	21.5		44	Connecticut	18.5
1	Vermont	42.3		45	New Jersey	17.0
47	Virginia	16.3		46	Minnesota	16.8
27	Washington	24.5		47	Virginia	16.3
6	West Virginia	35.7		48	Colorado	15.8
31	Wisconsin	23.6		49	New Hampshire	15.7
31	Wyoming	23.6		50	Nevada	14.7

District of Columbia   48.5

Source: U.S. Bureau of the Census
   "Health Insurance Coverage Status" (http://www.census.gov/hhes/www/hlthins/historic/hihistt5.html)
Children under 18 years old. Medicaid is a form of government insurance.

State Children's Health Insurance Program (SCHIP) Enrollment in 2005

National Total = 6,114,018 Children*

ALPHA ORDER

RANK ORDER

RANK	STATE	CHILDREN	% of USA	RANK	STATE	CHILDREN	% of USA
20	Alabama	81,856	1.3%	1	California	1,223,475	20.0%
36	Alaska	22,322	0.4%	2	New York	618,973	10.1%
19	Arizona	88,005	1.4%	3	Texas	526,406	8.6%
49	Arkansas	1,214	0.0%	4	Florida	384,801	6.3%
1	California	1,223,475	20.0%	5	Georgia	306,733	5.0%
24	Colorado	59,530	1.0%	6	Illinois	281,432	4.6%
37	Connecticut	22,289	0.4%	7	Ohio	216,495	3.5%
44	Delaware	10,354	0.2%	8	North Carolina	196,181	3.2%
4	Florida	384,801	6.3%	9	Pennsylvania	179,807	2.9%
5	Georgia	306,733	5.0%	10	Massachusetts	162,679	2.7%
39	Hawaii	20,602	0.3%	11	New Jersey	129,591	2.1%
38	Idaho	21,839	0.4%	12	Indiana	129,544	2.1%
6	Illinois	281,432	4.6%	13	Virginia	124,055	2.0%
12	Indiana	129,544	2.1%	14	Maryland	120,316	2.0%
28	Iowa	46,562	0.8%	15	Missouri	115,355	1.9%
27	Kansas	47,323	0.8%	16	Louisiana	109,150	1.8%
23	Kentucky	63,728	1.0%	17	Oklahoma	108,100	1.8%
16	Louisiana	109,150	1.8%	18	Michigan	89,257	1.5%
33	Maine	30,654	0.5%	19	Arizona	88,005	1.4%
14	Maryland	120,316	2.0%	20	Alabama	81,856	1.3%
10	Massachusetts	162,679	2.7%	21	South Carolina	80,646	1.3%
18	Michigan	89,257	1.5%	22	Mississippi	79,352	1.3%
48	Minnesota	5,076	0.1%	23	Kentucky	63,728	1.0%
22	Mississippi	79,352	1.3%	24	Colorado	59,530	1.0%
15	Missouri	115,355	1.9%	25	Wisconsin	57,165	0.9%
40	Montana	15,841	0.3%	26	Oregon	52,722	0.9%
29	Nebraska	44,706	0.7%	27	Kansas	47,323	0.8%
31	Nevada	39,316	0.6%	28	Iowa	46,562	0.8%
43	New Hampshire	11,892	0.2%	29	Nebraska	44,706	0.7%
11	New Jersey	129,591	2.1%	30	Utah	43,931	0.7%
35	New Mexico	24,310	0.4%	31	Nevada	39,316	0.6%
2	New York	618,973	10.1%	32	West Virginia	38,614	0.6%
8	North Carolina	196,181	3.2%	33	Maine	30,654	0.5%
47	North Dakota	5,725	0.1%	34	Rhode Island	27,144	0.4%
7	Ohio	216,495	3.5%	35	New Mexico	24,310	0.4%
17	Oklahoma	108,100	1.8%	36	Alaska	22,322	0.4%
26	Oregon	52,722	0.9%	37	Connecticut	22,289	0.4%
9	Pennsylvania	179,807	2.9%	38	Idaho	21,839	0.4%
34	Rhode Island	27,144	0.4%	39	Hawaii	20,602	0.3%
21	South Carolina	80,646	1.3%	40	Montana	15,841	0.3%
42	South Dakota	14,038	0.2%	41	Washington	15,547	0.3%
NA	Tennessee**	NA	NA	42	South Dakota	14,038	0.2%
3	Texas	526,406	8.6%	43	New Hampshire	11,892	0.2%
30	Utah	43,931	0.7%	44	Delaware	10,354	0.2%
45	Vermont	6,614	0.1%	45	Vermont	6,614	0.1%
13	Virginia	124,055	2.0%	46	Wyoming	6,120	0.1%
41	Washington	15,547	0.3%	47	North Dakota	5,725	0.1%
32	West Virginia	38,614	0.6%	48	Minnesota	5,076	0.1%
25	Wisconsin	57,165	0.9%	49	Arkansas	1,214	0.0%
46	Wyoming	6,120	0.1%	NA	Tennessee**	NA	NA
					District of Columbia	6,631	0.1%

Source: U.S. Department of Health and Human Services, Centers for Medicare and Medicaid Services
   "Children's Health Insurance Program Annual Enrollment Report"
Figures for fiscal year 2005. The State Children's Health Insurance Program (SCHIP) was created in 1997 to help states expand health insurance to children whose families earn too much to qualify for Medicaid, yet not enough to afford private health insurance.
**Not available.*

Percent Change in State Children's Health Insurance
Program (SCHIP) Enrollment: 2004 to 2005
National Percent Change = 0.2% Increase*

ALPHA ORDER

RANK ORDER

RANK	STATE	PERCENT CHANGE
30	Alabama	3.1
34	Alaska	1.6
37	Arizona	0.4
2	Arkansas	51.9
5	California	18.1
26	Colorado	4.0
26	Connecticut	4.0
36	Delaware	1.0
43	Florida	(8.3)
14	Georgia	9.5
18	Hawaii	7.1
7	Idaho	14.6
4	Illinois	20.3
1	Indiana	60.5
11	Iowa	11.8
19	Kansas	6.7
48	Kentucky	(32.6)
29	Louisiana	3.4
23	Maine	5.1
16	Maryland	7.9
41	Massachusetts	(2.3)
32	Michigan	1.9
21	Minnesota	6.1
42	Mississippi	(4.3)
49	Missouri	(34.5)
28	Montana	3.7
38	Nebraska	0.1
31	Nevada	2.1
15	New Hampshire	8.4
33	New Jersey	1.8
6	New Mexico	16.9
46	New York	(19.1)
10	North Carolina	12.5
12	North Dakota	11.4
40	Ohio	(1.7)
17	Oklahoma	7.3
9	Oregon	12.8
35	Pennsylvania	1.3
21	Rhode Island	6.1
19	South Carolina	6.7
24	South Dakota	4.8
NA	Tennessee**	NA
46	Texas	(19.1)
8	Utah	13.5
39	Vermont	(1.2)
3	Virginia	24.6
44	Washington	(8.6)
25	West Virginia	4.6
45	Wisconsin	(15.8)
13	Wyoming	10.8

RANK	STATE	PERCENT CHANGE
1	Indiana	60.5
2	Arkansas	51.9
3	Virginia	24.6
4	Illinois	20.3
5	California	18.1
6	New Mexico	16.9
7	Idaho	14.6
8	Utah	13.5
9	Oregon	12.8
10	North Carolina	12.5
11	Iowa	11.8
12	North Dakota	11.4
13	Wyoming	10.8
14	Georgia	9.5
15	New Hampshire	8.4
16	Maryland	7.9
17	Oklahoma	7.3
18	Hawaii	7.1
19	Kansas	6.7
19	South Carolina	6.7
21	Minnesota	6.1
21	Rhode Island	6.1
23	Maine	5.1
24	South Dakota	4.8
25	West Virginia	4.6
26	Colorado	4.0
26	Connecticut	4.0
28	Montana	3.7
29	Louisiana	3.4
30	Alabama	3.1
31	Nevada	2.1
32	Michigan	1.9
33	New Jersey	1.8
34	Alaska	1.6
35	Pennsylvania	1.3
36	Delaware	1.0
37	Arizona	0.4
38	Nebraska	0.1
39	Vermont	(1.2)
40	Ohio	(1.7)
41	Massachusetts	(2.3)
42	Mississippi	(4.3)
43	Florida	(8.3)
44	Washington	(8.6)
45	Wisconsin	(15.8)
46	New York	(19.1)
46	Texas	(19.1)
48	Kentucky	(32.6)
49	Missouri	(34.5)
NA	Tennessee**	NA

District of Columbia 8.8

Source: MQ Press using data from U.S. Dept of Health & Human Services, Centers for Medicare and Medicaid Services
  "Children's Health Insurance Program Annual Enrollment Report"
*Figures for fiscal years. The State Children's Health Insurance Program (SCHIP) was created in 1997 to help
states expand health insurance to children whose families earn too much to qualify for Medicaid, yet not enough to
afford private health insurance.
**Not available.

Percent of Children Enrolled in State Children's Health Insurance Program (SCHIP) in 2005
National Percent = 8.5% of Children 17 Years and Younger*

ALPHA ORDER				RANK ORDER		
RANK	STATE	PERCENT		RANK	STATE	PERCENT
23	Alabama	7.5		1	New York	13.6
5	Alaska	11.9		2	Georgia	13.0
36	Arizona	5.6		3	Oklahoma	12.7
49	Arkansas	0.2		4	California	12.6
4	California	12.6		5	Alaska	11.9
39	Colorado	5.0		6	Massachusetts	11.2
46	Connecticut	2.7		7	Maine	11.1
38	Delaware	5.3		7	Rhode Island	11.1
12	Florida	9.5		9	Mississippi	10.6
2	Georgia	13.0		10	Nebraska	10.4
26	Hawaii	6.9		11	West Virginia	10.1
35	Idaho	5.8		12	Florida	9.5
15	Illinois	8.7		12	Louisiana	9.5
19	Indiana	8.1		14	North Carolina	9.2
26	Iowa	6.9		15	Illinois	8.7
25	Kansas	7.0		16	Maryland	8.6
29	Kentucky	6.5		17	Missouri	8.4
12	Louisiana	9.5		18	Texas	8.3
7	Maine	11.1		19	Indiana	8.1
16	Maryland	8.6		20	South Carolina	7.9
6	Massachusetts	11.2		21	Ohio	7.8
45	Michigan	3.5		22	Montana	7.7
48	Minnesota	0.4		23	Alabama	7.5
9	Mississippi	10.6		23	South Dakota	7.5
17	Missouri	8.4		25	Kansas	7.0
22	Montana	7.7		26	Hawaii	6.9
10	Nebraska	10.4		26	Iowa	6.9
31	Nevada	6.3		28	Virginia	6.8
44	New Hampshire	3.9		29	Kentucky	6.5
33	New Jersey	6.0		30	Pennsylvania	6.4
39	New Mexico	5.0		31	Nevada	6.3
1	New York	13.6		32	Oregon	6.2
14	North Carolina	9.2		33	New Jersey	6.0
43	North Dakota	4.2		34	Utah	5.9
21	Ohio	7.8		35	Idaho	5.8
3	Oklahoma	12.7		36	Arizona	5.6
32	Oregon	6.2		37	Wyoming	5.4
30	Pennsylvania	6.4		38	Delaware	5.3
7	Rhode Island	11.1		39	Colorado	5.0
20	South Carolina	7.9		39	New Mexico	5.0
23	South Dakota	7.5		39	Vermont	5.0
NA	Tennessee**	NA		42	Wisconsin	4.4
18	Texas	8.3		43	North Dakota	4.2
34	Utah	5.9		44	New Hampshire	3.9
39	Vermont	5.0		45	Michigan	3.5
28	Virginia	6.8		46	Connecticut	2.7
47	Washington	1.0		47	Washington	1.0
11	West Virginia	10.1		48	Minnesota	0.4
42	Wisconsin	4.4		49	Arkansas	0.2
37	Wyoming	5.4		NA	Tennessee**	NA
					District of Columbia	5.9

Source: MQ Press using data from U.S. Dept of Health & Human Services, Centers for Medicare and Medicaid Services "Children's Health Insurance Program Annual Enrollment Report"
*Figures for fiscal year 2005. The State Children's Health Insurance Program (SCHIP) was created in 1997 to help states expand health insurance to children whose families earn too much to qualify for Medicaid, yet not enough to afford private health insurance. Calculated using 2005 Census estimates for 17 and younger for reporting states.
**Not available.

Expenditures for State Children's Health Insurance Program (SCHIP) in 2005

National Total = $5,044,800,000*

ALPHA ORDER

RANK	STATE	EXPENDITURES	% of USA
19	Alabama	$80,200,000	1.6%
37	Alaska	24,400,000	0.5%
9	Arizona	198,000,000	3.9%
25	Arkansas	63,000,000	1.2%
1	California	760,000,000	15.1%
31	Colorado	38,700,000	0.8%
40	Connecticut	20,500,000	0.4%
47	Delaware	6,400,000	0.1%
5	Florida	244,000,000	4.8%
8	Georgia	201,600,000	4.0%
42	Hawaii	13,000,000	0.3%
41	Idaho	16,600,000	0.3%
3	Illinois	320,200,000	6.3%
21	Indiana	76,100,000	1.5%
29	Iowa	40,800,000	0.8%
28	Kansas	43,100,000	0.9%
23	Kentucky	70,800,000	1.4%
16	Louisiana	109,900,000	2.2%
39	Maine	20,600,000	0.4%
13	Maryland	122,400,000	2.4%
14	Massachusetts	121,500,000	2.4%
11	Michigan	172,200,000	3.4%
22	Minnesota	71,500,000	1.4%
15	Mississippi	112,500,000	2.2%
17	Missouri	88,700,000	1.8%
43	Montana	12,800,000	0.3%
33	Nebraska	34,000,000	0.7%
36	Nevada	26,600,000	0.5%
46	New Hampshire	7,600,000	0.2%
7	New Jersey	204,900,000	4.1%
38	New Mexico	23,200,000	0.5%
2	New York	362,500,000	7.2%
6	North Carolina	211,000,000	4.2%
45	North Dakota	8,300,000	0.2%
10	Ohio	172,300,000	3.4%
24	Oklahoma	63,600,000	1.3%
32	Oregon	38,600,000	0.8%
12	Pennsylvania	140,900,000	2.8%
27	Rhode Island	56,400,000	1.1%
26	South Carolina	57,300,000	1.1%
44	South Dakota	11,900,000	0.2%
50	Tennessee	3,400,000	0.1%
4	Texas	287,700,000	5.7%
35	Utah	28,700,000	0.6%
49	Vermont	3,700,000	0.1%
20	Virginia	79,800,000	1.6%
30	Washington	40,300,000	0.8%
34	West Virginia	33,300,000	0.7%
18	Wisconsin	86,300,000	1.7%
48	Wyoming	5,700,000	0.1%

RANK ORDER

RANK	STATE	EXPENDITURES	% of USA
1	California	$760,000,000	15.1%
2	New York	362,500,000	7.2%
3	Illinois	320,200,000	6.3%
4	Texas	287,700,000	5.7%
5	Florida	244,000,000	4.8%
6	North Carolina	211,000,000	4.2%
7	New Jersey	204,900,000	4.1%
8	Georgia	201,600,000	4.0%
9	Arizona	198,000,000	3.9%
10	Ohio	172,300,000	3.4%
11	Michigan	172,200,000	3.4%
12	Pennsylvania	140,900,000	2.8%
13	Maryland	122,400,000	2.4%
14	Massachusetts	121,500,000	2.4%
15	Mississippi	112,500,000	2.2%
16	Louisiana	109,900,000	2.2%
17	Missouri	88,700,000	1.8%
18	Wisconsin	86,300,000	1.7%
19	Alabama	80,200,000	1.6%
20	Virginia	79,800,000	1.6%
21	Indiana	76,100,000	1.5%
22	Minnesota	71,500,000	1.4%
23	Kentucky	70,800,000	1.4%
24	Oklahoma	63,600,000	1.3%
25	Arkansas	63,000,000	1.2%
26	South Carolina	57,300,000	1.1%
27	Rhode Island	56,400,000	1.1%
28	Kansas	43,100,000	0.9%
29	Iowa	40,800,000	0.8%
30	Washington	40,300,000	0.8%
31	Colorado	38,700,000	0.8%
32	Oregon	38,600,000	0.8%
33	Nebraska	34,000,000	0.7%
34	West Virginia	33,300,000	0.7%
35	Utah	28,700,000	0.6%
36	Nevada	26,600,000	0.5%
37	Alaska	24,400,000	0.5%
38	New Mexico	23,200,000	0.5%
39	Maine	20,600,000	0.4%
40	Connecticut	20,500,000	0.4%
41	Idaho	16,600,000	0.3%
42	Hawaii	13,000,000	0.3%
43	Montana	12,800,000	0.3%
44	South Dakota	11,900,000	0.2%
45	North Dakota	8,300,000	0.2%
46	New Hampshire	7,600,000	0.2%
47	Delaware	6,400,000	0.1%
48	Wyoming	5,700,000	0.1%
49	Vermont	3,700,000	0.1%
50	Tennessee	3,400,000	0.1%
	District of Columbia	7,400,000	0.1%

Source: U.S. Department of Health and Human Services, Centers for Medicare and Medicaid Services
"Statement of Expenditures for the SCHIP Program" (CMS-21 Report)
*Federal and state expenditures for fiscal year 2005. National total does not include funds spent in U.S. territories. The State Children's Health Insurance Program (SCHIP) was created in 1997 to help states expand health insurance to children whose families earn too much to qualify for Medicaid, yet not enough to afford private health insurance.

Per Capita Expenditures for State Children's Health Insurance Program (SCHIP) in 2005
National Per Capita = $17.01*

ALPHA ORDER

RANK	STATE	PER CAPITA
18	Alabama	$17.63
3	Alaska	36.79
4	Arizona	33.26
9	Arkansas	22.70
12	California	21.02
44	Colorado	8.30
48	Connecticut	5.86
45	Delaware	7.60
29	Florida	13.73
10	Georgia	22.07
43	Hawaii	10.21
36	Idaho	11.61
5	Illinois	25.08
34	Indiana	12.14
28	Iowa	13.76
21	Kansas	15.68
20	Kentucky	16.97
6	Louisiana	24.38
22	Maine	15.63
11	Maryland	21.90
14	Massachusetts	18.89
19	Michigan	17.05
27	Minnesota	13.95
2	Mississippi	38.68
25	Missouri	15.30
30	Montana	13.69
13	Nebraska	19.34
40	Nevada	11.03
49	New Hampshire	5.82
8	New Jersey	23.54
35	New Mexico	12.05
15	New York	18.77
7	North Carolina	24.33
32	North Dakota	13.08
26	Ohio	15.02
17	Oklahoma	17.95
41	Oregon	10.61
38	Pennsylvania	11.36
1	Rhode Island	52.53
31	South Carolina	13.49
24	South Dakota	15.36
50	Tennessee	0.57
33	Texas	12.55
37	Utah	11.52
47	Vermont	5.94
42	Virginia	10.55
46	Washington	6.41
16	West Virginia	18.36
23	Wisconsin	15.61
39	Wyoming	11.20

RANK ORDER

RANK	STATE	PER CAPITA
1	Rhode Island	$52.53
2	Mississippi	38.68
3	Alaska	36.79
4	Arizona	33.26
5	Illinois	25.08
6	Louisiana	24.38
7	North Carolina	24.33
8	New Jersey	23.54
9	Arkansas	22.70
10	Georgia	22.07
11	Maryland	21.90
12	California	21.02
13	Nebraska	19.34
14	Massachusetts	18.89
15	New York	18.77
16	West Virginia	18.36
17	Oklahoma	17.95
18	Alabama	17.63
19	Michigan	17.05
20	Kentucky	16.97
21	Kansas	15.68
22	Maine	15.63
23	Wisconsin	15.61
24	South Dakota	15.36
25	Missouri	15.30
26	Ohio	15.02
27	Minnesota	13.95
28	Iowa	13.76
29	Florida	13.73
30	Montana	13.69
31	South Carolina	13.49
32	North Dakota	13.08
33	Texas	12.55
34	Indiana	12.14
35	New Mexico	12.05
36	Idaho	11.61
37	Utah	11.52
38	Pennsylvania	11.36
39	Wyoming	11.20
40	Nevada	11.03
41	Oregon	10.61
42	Virginia	10.55
43	Hawaii	10.21
44	Colorado	8.30
45	Delaware	7.60
46	Washington	6.41
47	Vermont	5.94
48	Connecticut	5.86
49	New Hampshire	5.82
50	Tennessee	0.57

District of Columbia 12.71

Source: MQ Press using data from U.S. Dept of Health & Human Services, Centers for Medicare and Medicaid Services "Statement of Expenditures for the SCHIP Program" (CMS-21 Report)

*Federal and state expenditures for fiscal year 2005. National figure does not include funds spent in U.S. territories. The State Children's Health Insurance Program (SCHIP) was created in 1997 to help states expand health insurance to children whose families earn too much to qualify for Medicaid, yet not enough to afford private health insurance.

Expenditures per State Children's Health Insurance Program (SCHIP) Participant in 2005
National Per Participant = $825*

ALPHA ORDER

RANK	STATE	PER PARTICIPANT
15	Alabama	$980
11	Alaska	1,093
2	Arizona	2,250
NA	Arkansas**	NA
41	California	621
36	Colorado	650
18	Connecticut	920
42	Delaware	618
39	Florida	634
34	Georgia	657
40	Hawaii	631
28	Idaho	760
9	Illinois	1,138
44	Indiana	587
20	Iowa	876
19	Kansas	911
10	Kentucky	1,111
14	Louisiana	1,007
33	Maine	672
13	Maryland	1,017
29	Massachusetts	747
4	Michigan	1,929
NA	Minnesota**	NA
8	Mississippi	1,418
26	Missouri	769
23	Montana	808
27	Nebraska	761
32	Nevada	677
38	New Hampshire	639
5	New Jersey	1,581
16	New Mexico	954
45	New York	586
12	North Carolina	1,076
7	North Dakota	1,450
24	Ohio	796
43	Oklahoma	588
30	Oregon	732
25	Pennsylvania	784
3	Rhode Island	2,078
31	South Carolina	711
22	South Dakota	848
NA	Tennessee**	NA
47	Texas	547
35	Utah	653
46	Vermont	559
37	Virginia	643
1	Washington	2,592
21	West Virginia	862
6	Wisconsin	1,510
17	Wyoming	931

RANK ORDER

RANK	STATE	PER PARTICIPANT
1	Washington	$2,592
2	Arizona	2,250
3	Rhode Island	2,078
4	Michigan	1,929
5	New Jersey	1,581
6	Wisconsin	1,510
7	North Dakota	1,450
8	Mississippi	1,418
9	Illinois	1,138
10	Kentucky	1,111
11	Alaska	1,093
12	North Carolina	1,076
13	Maryland	1,017
14	Louisiana	1,007
15	Alabama	980
16	New Mexico	954
17	Wyoming	931
18	Connecticut	920
19	Kansas	911
20	Iowa	876
21	West Virginia	862
22	South Dakota	848
23	Montana	808
24	Ohio	796
25	Pennsylvania	784
26	Missouri	769
27	Nebraska	761
28	Idaho	760
29	Massachusetts	747
30	Oregon	732
31	South Carolina	711
32	Nevada	677
33	Maine	672
34	Georgia	657
35	Utah	653
36	Colorado	650
37	Virginia	643
38	New Hampshire	639
39	Florida	634
40	Hawaii	631
41	California	621
42	Delaware	618
43	Oklahoma	588
44	Indiana	587
45	New York	586
46	Vermont	559
47	Texas	547
NA	Arkansas**	NA
NA	Minnesota**	NA
NA	Tennessee**	NA

District of Columbia   1,116

Source: MQ Press using data from U.S. Dept of Health & Human Services, Centers for Medicare and Medicaid Services
"Statement of Expenditures for the SCHIP Program" (CMS-21 Report)
*For fiscal year 2005. National figure does not include expenditures in U.S. territories. The State Children's Health Insurance Program (SCHIP) was created in 1997 to help states expand health insurance to children whose families earn too much to qualify for Medicaid, yet not enough to afford private health insurance.
**Not available.

Health Maintenance Organizations (HMOs) in 2006

National Total = 451 HMOs*

ALPHA ORDER

RANK	STATE	HMOs	% of USA
50	Alabama	1	0.2%
39	Alaska	6	1.3%
13	Arizona	21	4.7%
34	Arkansas	7	1.6%
1	California	45	10.0%
21	Colorado	13	2.9%
21	Connecticut	13	2.9%
34	Delaware	7	1.6%
4	Florida	29	6.4%
19	Georgia	15	3.3%
45	Hawaii	4	0.9%
39	Idaho	6	1.3%
6	Illinois	25	5.5%
11	Indiana	22	4.9%
23	Iowa	12	2.7%
25	Kansas	11	2.4%
28	Kentucky	10	2.2%
25	Louisiana	11	2.4%
39	Maine	6	1.3%
17	Maryland	16	3.5%
17	Massachusetts	16	3.5%
3	Michigan	30	6.7%
15	Minnesota	17	3.8%
45	Mississippi	4	0.9%
6	Missouri	25	5.5%
45	Montana	4	0.9%
39	Nebraska	6	1.3%
25	Nevada	11	2.4%
34	New Hampshire	7	1.6%
23	New Jersey	12	2.7%
32	New Mexico	8	1.8%
2	New York	40	8.9%
31	North Carolina	9	2.0%
45	North Dakota	4	0.9%
8	Ohio	24	5.3%
28	Oklahoma	10	2.2%
9	Oregon	23	5.1%
11	Pennsylvania	22	4.9%
39	Rhode Island	6	1.3%
28	South Carolina	10	2.2%
34	South Dakota	7	1.6%
20	Tennessee	14	3.1%
4	Texas	29	6.4%
32	Utah	8	1.8%
14	Vermont	20	4.4%
34	Virginia	7	1.6%
15	Washington	17	3.8%
44	West Virginia	5	1.1%
9	Wisconsin	23	5.1%
45	Wyoming	4	0.9%

RANK ORDER

RANK	STATE	HMOs	% of USA
1	California	45	10.0%
2	New York	40	8.9%
3	Michigan	30	6.7%
4	Florida	29	6.4%
4	Texas	29	6.4%
6	Illinois	25	5.5%
6	Missouri	25	5.5%
8	Ohio	24	5.3%
9	Oregon	23	5.1%
9	Wisconsin	23	5.1%
11	Indiana	22	4.9%
11	Pennsylvania	22	4.9%
13	Arizona	21	4.7%
14	Vermont	20	4.4%
15	Minnesota	17	3.8%
15	Washington	17	3.8%
17	Maryland	16	3.5%
17	Massachusetts	16	3.5%
19	Georgia	15	3.3%
20	Tennessee	14	3.1%
21	Colorado	13	2.9%
21	Connecticut	13	2.9%
23	Iowa	12	2.7%
23	New Jersey	12	2.7%
25	Kansas	11	2.4%
25	Louisiana	11	2.4%
25	Nevada	11	2.4%
28	Kentucky	10	2.2%
28	Oklahoma	10	2.2%
28	South Carolina	10	2.2%
31	North Carolina	9	2.0%
32	New Mexico	8	1.8%
32	Utah	8	1.8%
34	Arkansas	7	1.6%
34	Delaware	7	1.6%
34	New Hampshire	7	1.6%
34	South Dakota	7	1.6%
34	Virginia	7	1.6%
39	Alaska	6	1.3%
39	Idaho	6	1.3%
39	Maine	6	1.3%
39	Nebraska	6	1.3%
39	Rhode Island	6	1.3%
44	West Virginia	5	1.1%
45	Hawaii	4	0.9%
45	Mississippi	4	0.9%
45	Montana	4	0.9%
45	North Dakota	4	0.9%
45	Wyoming	4	0.9%
50	Alabama	1	0.2%
	District of Columbia	11	2.4%

Source: Lance Wolkenbrod, Data Analyst
HealthLeaders - InterStudy (Nashville, TN)
As of January 2006. National total differs from past years for this table in that it reflects the total HMOs nationwide and does not count HMOs in more than one state as multiple HMOs. The total for all HMO programs by state is 713.

Enrollees in Health Maintenance Organizations (HMOs) in 2006

National Total = 72,302,165 Enrollees*

RANK	STATE	ENROLLEES	% of USA
40	Alabama	142,528	0.2%
50	Alaska	4	0.0%
10	Arizona	2,031,487	2.8%
43	Arkansas	96,294	0.1%
1	California	17,775,222	24.6%
18	Colorado	1,206,791	1.7%
20	Connecticut	1,100,188	1.5%
42	Delaware	130,810	0.2%
3	Florida	4,366,583	6.0%
17	Georgia	1,397,127	1.9%
27	Hawaii	596,490	0.8%
45	Idaho	41,974	0.1%
11	Illinois	1,940,465	2.7%
13	Indiana	1,613,999	2.2%
32	Iowa	341,713	0.5%
31	Kansas	404,884	0.6%
36	Kentucky	260,279	0.4%
30	Louisiana	431,722	0.6%
28	Maine	483,882	0.7%
12	Maryland	1,632,238	2.3%
5	Massachusetts	2,829,530	3.9%
7	Michigan	2,688,393	3.7%
24	Minnesota	682,123	0.9%
47	Mississippi	22,730	0.0%
21	Missouri	1,081,724	1.5%
46	Montana	37,917	0.1%
41	Nebraska	138,442	0.2%
26	Nevada	597,392	0.8%
34	New Hampshire	281,133	0.4%
9	New Jersey	2,131,175	2.9%
29	New Mexico	457,971	0.6%
2	New York	5,301,525	7.3%
23	North Carolina	854,301	1.2%
49	North Dakota	2,330	0.0%
8	Ohio	2,654,648	3.7%
37	Oklahoma	250,032	0.3%
22	Oregon	904,037	1.3%
4	Pennsylvania	3,347,362	4.6%
35	Rhode Island	269,548	0.4%
33	South Carolina	314,247	0.4%
44	South Dakota	58,434	0.1%
14	Tennessee	1,539,399	2.1%
6	Texas	2,765,712	3.8%
25	Utah	645,669	0.9%
39	Vermont	152,770	0.2%
15	Virginia	1,476,822	2.0%
19	Washington	1,149,200	1.6%
38	West Virginia	161,075	0.2%
16	Wisconsin	1,455,701	2.0%
48	Wyoming	10,340	0.0%

RANK	STATE	ENROLLEES	% of USA
1	California	17,775,222	24.6%
2	New York	5,301,525	7.3%
3	Florida	4,366,583	6.0%
4	Pennsylvania	3,347,362	4.6%
5	Massachusetts	2,829,530	3.9%
6	Texas	2,765,712	3.8%
7	Michigan	2,688,393	3.7%
8	Ohio	2,654,648	3.7%
9	New Jersey	2,131,175	2.9%
10	Arizona	2,031,487	2.8%
11	Illinois	1,940,465	2.7%
12	Maryland	1,632,238	2.3%
13	Indiana	1,613,999	2.2%
14	Tennessee	1,539,399	2.1%
15	Virginia	1,476,822	2.0%
16	Wisconsin	1,455,701	2.0%
17	Georgia	1,397,127	1.9%
18	Colorado	1,206,791	1.7%
19	Washington	1,149,200	1.6%
20	Connecticut	1,100,188	1.5%
21	Missouri	1,081,724	1.5%
22	Oregon	904,037	1.3%
23	North Carolina	854,301	1.2%
24	Minnesota	682,123	0.9%
25	Utah	645,669	0.9%
26	Nevada	597,392	0.8%
27	Hawaii	596,490	0.8%
28	Maine	483,882	0.7%
29	New Mexico	457,971	0.6%
30	Louisiana	431,722	0.6%
31	Kansas	404,884	0.6%
32	Iowa	341,713	0.5%
33	South Carolina	314,247	0.4%
34	New Hampshire	281,133	0.4%
35	Rhode Island	269,548	0.4%
36	Kentucky	260,279	0.4%
37	Oklahoma	250,032	0.3%
38	West Virginia	161,075	0.2%
39	Vermont	152,770	0.2%
40	Alabama	142,528	0.2%
41	Nebraska	138,442	0.2%
42	Delaware	130,810	0.2%
43	Arkansas	96,294	0.1%
44	South Dakota	58,434	0.1%
45	Idaho	41,974	0.1%
46	Montana	37,917	0.1%
47	Mississippi	22,730	0.0%
48	Wyoming	10,340	0.0%
49	North Dakota	2,330	0.0%
50	Alaska	4	0.0%
	District of Columbia	304,875	0.4%

Source: Lance Wolkenbrod, Data Analyst
    HealthLeaders - InterStudy (Nashville, TN)
*As of January 2006.

Percent Change in Enrollees in Health Maintenance Organizations (HMOs): 2005 to 2006
National Percent Change = 1.0% Increase*

RANK	STATE	PERCENT CHANGE
26	Alabama	(2.7)
NA	Alaska**	NA
1	Arizona	95.1
42	Arkansas	(21.5)
24	California	(0.8)
30	Colorado	(4.7)
37	Connecticut	(9.5)
39	Delaware	(10.4)
36	Florida	(7.9)
40	Georgia	(13.6)
16	Hawaii	7.5
21	Idaho	1.5
34	Illinois	(5.5)
8	Indiana	24.6
14	Iowa	12.1
10	Kansas	21.7
47	Kentucky	(37.5)
25	Louisiana	(1.0)
5	Maine	41.5
45	Maryland	(27.2)
11	Massachusetts	20.8
21	Michigan	1.5
48	Minnesota	(37.7)
49	Mississippi	(50.0)
38	Missouri	(10.2)
15	Montana	7.8
9	Nebraska	22.3
19	Nevada	4.6
28	New Hampshire	(3.7)
18	New Jersey	4.8
23	New Mexico	(0.2)
13	New York	12.3
17	North Carolina	5.9
44	North Dakota	(27.1)
6	Ohio	33.8
20	Oklahoma	2.6
27	Oregon	(3.1)
41	Pennsylvania	(18.1)
43	Rhode Island	(24.1)
33	South Carolina	(5.4)
30	South Dakota	(4.7)
2	Tennessee	84.1
32	Texas	(5.2)
7	Utah	27.7
4	Vermont	54.1
12	Virginia	13.3
46	Washington	(31.6)
3	West Virginia	65.0
35	Wisconsin	(7.0)
29	Wyoming	(4.1)

RANK	STATE	PERCENT CHANGE
1	Arizona	95.1
2	Tennessee	84.1
3	West Virginia	65.0
4	Vermont	54.1
5	Maine	41.5
6	Ohio	33.8
7	Utah	27.7
8	Indiana	24.6
9	Nebraska	22.3
10	Kansas	21.7
11	Massachusetts	20.8
12	Virginia	13.3
13	New York	12.3
14	Iowa	12.1
15	Montana	7.8
16	Hawaii	7.5
17	North Carolina	5.9
18	New Jersey	4.8
19	Nevada	4.6
20	Oklahoma	2.6
21	Idaho	1.5
21	Michigan	1.5
23	New Mexico	(0.2)
24	California	(0.8)
25	Louisiana	(1.0)
26	Alabama	(2.7)
27	Oregon	(3.1)
28	New Hampshire	(3.7)
29	Wyoming	(4.1)
30	Colorado	(4.7)
30	South Dakota	(4.7)
32	Texas	(5.2)
33	South Carolina	(5.4)
34	Illinois	(5.5)
35	Wisconsin	(7.0)
36	Florida	(7.9)
37	Connecticut	(9.5)
38	Missouri	(10.2)
39	Delaware	(10.4)
40	Georgia	(13.6)
41	Pennsylvania	(18.1)
42	Arkansas	(21.5)
43	Rhode Island	(24.1)
44	North Dakota	(27.1)
45	Maryland	(27.2)
46	Washington	(31.6)
47	Kentucky	(37.5)
48	Minnesota	(37.7)
49	Mississippi	(50.0)
NA	Alaska**	NA

	District of Columbia	36.2

Source: Morgan Quitno Press using data from Lance Wolkenbrod, Data Analyst
    HealthLeaders - InterStudy (Nashville, TN)
*As of January 2006. National figure does not include enrollees in U.S. territories.
**Not applicable.

Percent of Population Enrolled in Health Maintenance Organizations (HMOs) in 2006
National Percent = 24.4% Enrolled in HMOs*

ALPHA ORDER

RANK	STATE	PERCENT
45	Alabama	3.1
50	Alaska	0.0
5	Arizona	34.2
44	Arkansas	3.5
1	California	49.2
13	Colorado	25.9
6	Connecticut	31.3
28	Delaware	15.5
19	Florida	24.5
29	Georgia	15.4
2	Hawaii	46.8
46	Idaho	2.9
30	Illinois	15.2
15	Indiana	25.7
34	Iowa	11.5
31	Kansas	14.8
42	Kentucky	6.2
36	Louisiana	9.5
4	Maine	36.6
7	Maryland	29.1
3	Massachusetts	44.2
10	Michigan	26.6
32	Minnesota	13.3
48	Mississippi	0.8
26	Missouri	18.6
43	Montana	4.1
38	Nebraska	7.9
18	Nevada	24.7
24	New Hampshire	21.5
21	New Jersey	24.4
22	New Mexico	23.7
8	New York	27.5
35	North Carolina	9.8
49	North Dakota	0.4
23	Ohio	23.2
41	Oklahoma	7.0
17	Oregon	24.8
9	Pennsylvania	26.9
16	Rhode Island	25.0
40	South Carolina	7.4
39	South Dakota	7.5
14	Tennessee	25.8
33	Texas	12.1
12	Utah	26.1
19	Vermont	24.5
25	Virginia	19.5
27	Washington	18.3
37	West Virginia	8.9
11	Wisconsin	26.3
47	Wyoming	2.0

RANK ORDER

RANK	STATE	PERCENT
1	California	49.2
2	Hawaii	46.8
3	Massachusetts	44.2
4	Maine	36.6
5	Arizona	34.2
6	Connecticut	31.3
7	Maryland	29.1
8	New York	27.5
9	Pennsylvania	26.9
10	Michigan	26.6
11	Wisconsin	26.3
12	Utah	26.1
13	Colorado	25.9
14	Tennessee	25.8
15	Indiana	25.7
16	Rhode Island	25.0
17	Oregon	24.8
18	Nevada	24.7
19	Florida	24.5
19	Vermont	24.5
21	New Jersey	24.4
22	New Mexico	23.7
23	Ohio	23.2
24	New Hampshire	21.5
25	Virginia	19.5
26	Missouri	18.6
27	Washington	18.3
28	Delaware	15.5
29	Georgia	15.4
30	Illinois	15.2
31	Kansas	14.8
32	Minnesota	13.3
33	Texas	12.1
34	Iowa	11.5
35	North Carolina	9.8
36	Louisiana	9.5
37	West Virginia	8.9
38	Nebraska	7.9
39	South Dakota	7.5
40	South Carolina	7.4
41	Oklahoma	7.0
42	Kentucky	6.2
43	Montana	4.1
44	Arkansas	3.5
45	Alabama	3.1
46	Idaho	2.9
47	Wyoming	2.0
48	Mississippi	0.8
49	North Dakota	0.4
50	Alaska	0.0

| | District of Columbia | 55.4 |

Source: Lance Wolkenbrod, Data Analyst
      HealthLeaders - InterStudy (Nashville, TN)
*As of January 2006.

Percent of Insured Population Enrolled in
Health Maintenance Organizations (HMOs) in 2006
National Percent = 28.5% of Insured are Enrolled in HMOs*

ALPHA ORDER

RANK ORDER

RANK	STATE	PERCENT		RANK	STATE	PERCENT
45	Alabama	3.7		1	California	61.3
50	Alaska	0.0		2	Hawaii	51.3
4	Arizona	42.1		3	Massachusetts	49.6
44	Arkansas	4.2		4	Arizona	42.1
1	California	61.3		5	Maine	41.1
9	Colorado	31.3		6	Connecticut	35.6
6	Connecticut	35.6		7	Maryland	34.1
30	Delaware	17.8		8	New York	32.2
10	Florida	30.8		9	Colorado	31.3
28	Georgia	19.0		10	Florida	30.8
2	Hawaii	51.3		11	Utah	30.7
46	Idaho	3.4		12	Indiana	30.6
29	Illinois	18.0		12	Tennessee	30.6
12	Indiana	30.6		14	Michigan	30.4
35	Iowa	12.9		14	Pennsylvania	30.4
31	Kansas	16.8		16	New Mexico	29.7
42	Kentucky	7.4		16	Oregon	29.7
34	Louisiana	13.0		18	Wisconsin	29.6
5	Maine	41.1		19	Nevada	29.5
7	Maryland	34.1		20	Rhode Island	29.0
3	Massachusetts	49.6		21	New Jersey	28.8
14	Michigan	30.4		22	Vermont	27.8
33	Minnesota	14.5		23	Ohio	26.7
48	Mississippi	1.0		24	New Hampshire	24.1
26	Missouri	21.6		25	Virginia	22.9
43	Montana	4.9		26	Missouri	21.6
39	Nebraska	8.9		27	Washington	21.3
19	Nevada	29.5		28	Georgia	19.0
24	New Hampshire	24.1		29	Illinois	18.0
21	New Jersey	28.8		30	Delaware	17.8
16	New Mexico	29.7		31	Kansas	16.8
8	New York	32.2		32	Texas	16.0
36	North Carolina	11.9		33	Minnesota	14.5
49	North Dakota	0.4		34	Louisiana	13.0
23	Ohio	26.7		35	Iowa	12.9
40	Oklahoma	8.7		36	North Carolina	11.9
16	Oregon	29.7		37	West Virginia	10.9
14	Pennsylvania	30.4		38	South Carolina	9.1
20	Rhode Island	29.0		39	Nebraska	8.9
38	South Carolina	9.1		40	Oklahoma	8.7
40	South Dakota	8.7		40	South Dakota	8.7
12	Tennessee	30.6		42	Kentucky	7.4
32	Texas	16.0		43	Montana	4.9
11	Utah	30.7		44	Arkansas	4.2
22	Vermont	27.8		45	Alabama	3.7
25	Virginia	22.9		46	Idaho	3.4
27	Washington	21.3		47	Wyoming	2.4
37	West Virginia	10.9		48	Mississippi	1.0
18	Wisconsin	29.6		49	North Dakota	0.4
47	Wyoming	2.4		50	Alaska	0.0
					District of Columbia	65.3

Source: Morgan Quitno Press using data from Lance Wolkenbrod, Data Analyst
    HealthLeaders - InterStudy (Nashville, TN)
*As of January 2006. Calculated using estimated number of insured as of 2005 from the U.S. Census Bureau.

Medicare Enrollees in 2005

National Total = 42,499,593 Enrollees*

ALPHA ORDER					RANK ORDER			
RANK	STATE	ENROLLEES	% of USA		RANK	STATE	ENROLLEES	% of USA
20	Alabama	755,209	1.8%		1	California	4,200,640	9.9%
50	Alaska	51,866	0.1%		2	Florida	3,045,775	7.2%
19	Arizona	793,632	1.9%		3	New York	2,775,996	6.5%
31	Arkansas	472,341	1.1%		4	Texas	2,544,917	6.0%
1	California	4,200,640	9.9%		5	Pennsylvania	2,131,836	5.0%
29	Colorado	522,334	1.2%		6	Ohio	1,753,737	4.1%
28	Connecticut	525,380	1.2%		7	Illinois	1,690,970	4.0%
45	Delaware	127,798	0.3%		8	Michigan	1,482,713	3.5%
2	Florida	3,045,775	7.2%		9	North Carolina	1,277,358	3.0%
11	Georgia	1,038,955	2.4%		10	New Jersey	1,227,306	2.9%
42	Hawaii	181,711	0.4%		11	Georgia	1,038,955	2.4%
40	Idaho	192,314	0.5%		12	Virginia	992,718	2.3%
7	Illinois	1,690,970	4.0%		13	Massachusetts	970,528	2.3%
16	Indiana	905,272	2.1%		14	Tennessee	921,715	2.2%
30	Iowa	489,637	1.2%		15	Missouri	912,404	2.1%
33	Kansas	401,878	0.9%		16	Indiana	905,272	2.1%
23	Kentucky	678,427	1.6%		17	Wisconsin	825,935	1.9%
25	Louisiana	610,147	1.4%		18	Washington	821,369	1.9%
39	Maine	235,359	0.6%		19	Arizona	793,632	1.9%
22	Maryland	694,546	1.6%		20	Alabama	755,209	1.8%
13	Massachusetts	970,528	2.3%		21	Minnesota	697,522	1.6%
8	Michigan	1,482,713	3.5%		22	Maryland	694,546	1.6%
21	Minnesota	697,522	1.6%		23	Kentucky	678,427	1.6%
32	Mississippi	454,305	1.1%		24	South Carolina	650,941	1.5%
15	Missouri	912,404	2.1%		25	Louisiana	610,147	1.4%
44	Montana	148,004	0.3%		26	Oklahoma	541,496	1.3%
37	Nebraska	261,439	0.6%		27	Oregon	539,849	1.3%
35	Nevada	296,805	0.7%		28	Connecticut	525,380	1.2%
41	New Hampshire	191,793	0.5%		29	Colorado	522,334	1.2%
10	New Jersey	1,227,306	2.9%		30	Iowa	489,637	1.2%
36	New Mexico	266,869	0.6%		31	Arkansas	472,341	1.1%
3	New York	2,775,996	6.5%		32	Mississippi	454,305	1.1%
9	North Carolina	1,277,358	3.0%		33	Kansas	401,878	0.9%
47	North Dakota	103,774	0.2%		34	West Virginia	355,386	0.8%
6	Ohio	1,753,737	4.1%		35	Nevada	296,805	0.7%
26	Oklahoma	541,496	1.3%		36	New Mexico	266,869	0.6%
27	Oregon	539,849	1.3%		37	Nebraska	261,439	0.6%
5	Pennsylvania	2,131,836	5.0%		38	Utah	237,093	0.6%
43	Rhode Island	172,352	0.4%		39	Maine	235,359	0.6%
24	South Carolina	650,941	1.5%		40	Idaho	192,314	0.5%
46	South Dakota	124,937	0.3%		41	New Hampshire	191,793	0.5%
14	Tennessee	921,715	2.2%		42	Hawaii	181,711	0.4%
4	Texas	2,544,917	6.0%		43	Rhode Island	172,352	0.4%
38	Utah	237,093	0.6%		44	Montana	148,004	0.3%
48	Vermont	96,354	0.2%		45	Delaware	127,798	0.3%
12	Virginia	992,718	2.3%		46	South Dakota	124,937	0.3%
18	Washington	821,369	1.9%		47	North Dakota	103,774	0.2%
34	West Virginia	355,386	0.8%		48	Vermont	96,354	0.2%
17	Wisconsin	825,935	1.9%		49	Wyoming	70,961	0.2%
49	Wyoming	70,961	0.2%		50	Alaska	51,866	0.1%
						District of Columbia	73,256	0.2%

Source: U.S. Department of Health and Human Services, Centers for Medicare and Medicaid Services
    "2006 Data Compendium" (http://www.cms.hhs.gov/DataCompendium/)
Includes aged and disabled enrollees. Total includes 963,714 enrollees in Puerto Rico and other outlying areas, foreign countries or whose address is unknown.

Percent Change in Medicare Enrollees: 2004 to 2005

National Percent Change = 1.8% Increase

ALPHA ORDER

RANK ORDER

RANK	STATE	PERCENT CHANGE	RANK	STATE	PERCENT CHANGE
16	Alabama	3.0	1	Arizona	5.3
9	Alaska	3.7	2	Idaho	4.5
1	Arizona	5.3	2	South Carolina	4.5
21	Arkansas	2.5	4	Georgia	4.4
34	California	1.4	4	Utah	4.4
14	Colorado	3.2	6	New Mexico	4.2
46	Connecticut	0.1	7	Delaware	3.9
7	Delaware	3.9	7	Texas	3.9
24	Florida	2.2	9	Alaska	3.7
4	Georgia	4.4	10	North Carolina	3.5
25	Hawaii	2.1	11	Nevada	3.4
2	Idaho	4.5	11	Tennessee	3.4
41	Illinois	0.8	13	Washington	3.3
29	Indiana	1.8	14	Colorado	3.2
39	Iowa	1.0	15	New Hampshire	3.1
36	Kansas	1.2	16	Alabama	3.0
17	Kentucky	2.8	17	Kentucky	2.8
50	Louisiana	(3.0)	17	Oregon	2.8
27	Maine	1.9	17	Virginia	2.8
34	Maryland	1.4	17	Wyoming	2.8
45	Massachusetts	0.2	21	Arkansas	2.5
38	Michigan	1.1	21	Vermont	2.5
32	Minnesota	1.5	23	Oklahoma	2.4
27	Mississippi	1.9	24	Florida	2.2
29	Missouri	1.8	25	Hawaii	2.1
25	Montana	2.1	25	Montana	2.1
40	Nebraska	0.9	27	Maine	1.9
11	Nevada	3.4	27	Mississippi	1.9
15	New Hampshire	3.1	29	Indiana	1.8
46	New Jersey	0.1	29	Missouri	1.8
6	New Mexico	4.2	31	South Dakota	1.6
48	New York	(0.1)	32	Minnesota	1.5
10	North Carolina	3.5	32	Wisconsin	1.5
41	North Dakota	0.8	34	California	1.4
41	Ohio	0.8	34	Maryland	1.4
23	Oklahoma	2.4	36	Kansas	1.2
17	Oregon	2.8	36	West Virginia	1.2
44	Pennsylvania	0.6	38	Michigan	1.1
49	Rhode Island	(0.4)	39	Iowa	1.0
2	South Carolina	4.5	40	Nebraska	0.9
31	South Dakota	1.6	41	Illinois	0.8
11	Tennessee	3.4	41	North Dakota	0.8
7	Texas	3.9	41	Ohio	0.8
4	Utah	4.4	44	Pennsylvania	0.6
21	Vermont	2.5	45	Massachusetts	0.2
17	Virginia	2.8	46	Connecticut	0.1
13	Washington	3.3	46	New Jersey	0.1
36	West Virginia	1.2	48	New York	(0.1)
32	Wisconsin	1.5	49	Rhode Island	(0.4)
17	Wyoming	2.8	50	Louisiana	(3.0)

District of Columbia (1.0)

Source: MQ Press using data from U.S. Dept of Health & Human Services, Centers for Medicare and Medicaid Services "2006 Data Compendium" (http://www.cms.hhs.gov/DataCompendium/)
*Includes aged and disabled enrollees. National rate includes enrollees in Puerto Rico and other outlying areas, foreign countries or whose address is unknown.

Percent of Population Enrolled in Medicare in 2005

National Percent = 14.0% of Population*

ALPHA ORDER

RANK	STATE	PERCENT
6	Alabama	16.6
50	Alaska	7.8
39	Arizona	13.4
5	Arkansas	17.0
45	California	11.6
47	Colorado	11.2
22	Connecticut	15.0
20	Delaware	15.2
4	Florida	17.1
46	Georgia	11.5
32	Hawaii	14.2
37	Idaho	13.5
40	Illinois	13.2
30	Indiana	14.4
7	Iowa	16.5
28	Kansas	14.6
8	Kentucky	16.3
37	Louisiana	13.5
2	Maine	17.8
43	Maryland	12.4
20	Massachusetts	15.2
26	Michigan	14.7
36	Minnesota	13.6
14	Mississippi	15.6
13	Missouri	15.7
12	Montana	15.8
23	Nebraska	14.9
44	Nevada	12.3
28	New Hampshire	14.6
33	New Jersey	14.1
35	New Mexico	13.8
30	New York	14.4
26	North Carolina	14.7
8	North Dakota	16.3
17	Ohio	15.3
17	Oklahoma	15.3
25	Oregon	14.8
3	Pennsylvania	17.2
11	Rhode Island	16.0
17	South Carolina	15.3
10	South Dakota	16.1
15	Tennessee	15.5
48	Texas	11.1
49	Utah	9.6
15	Vermont	15.5
41	Virginia	13.1
41	Washington	13.1
1	West Virginia	19.6
23	Wisconsin	14.9
34	Wyoming	13.9

RANK ORDER

RANK	STATE	PERCENT
1	West Virginia	19.6
2	Maine	17.8
3	Pennsylvania	17.2
4	Florida	17.1
5	Arkansas	17.0
6	Alabama	16.6
7	Iowa	16.5
8	Kentucky	16.3
8	North Dakota	16.3
10	South Dakota	16.1
11	Rhode Island	16.0
12	Montana	15.8
13	Missouri	15.7
14	Mississippi	15.6
15	Tennessee	15.5
15	Vermont	15.5
17	Ohio	15.3
17	Oklahoma	15.3
17	South Carolina	15.3
20	Delaware	15.2
20	Massachusetts	15.2
22	Connecticut	15.0
23	Nebraska	14.9
23	Wisconsin	14.9
25	Oregon	14.8
26	Michigan	14.7
26	North Carolina	14.7
28	Kansas	14.6
28	New Hampshire	14.6
30	Indiana	14.4
30	New York	14.4
32	Hawaii	14.2
33	New Jersey	14.1
34	Wyoming	13.9
35	New Mexico	13.8
36	Minnesota	13.6
37	Idaho	13.5
37	Louisiana	13.5
39	Arizona	13.4
40	Illinois	13.2
41	Virginia	13.1
41	Washington	13.1
43	Maryland	12.4
44	Nevada	12.3
45	California	11.6
46	Georgia	11.5
47	Colorado	11.2
48	Texas	11.1
49	Utah	9.6
50	Alaska	7.8

	District of Columbia	13.3

Source: U.S. Department of Health and Human Services, Centers for Medicare and Medicaid Services
"2006 Data Compendium" (http://www.cms.hhs.gov/DataCompendium/)
*Includes aged and disabled enrollees. National rate includes only residents of the 50 states and the District of Columbia.

Enrollment in Medicare Prescription Drug Plans as of June 14, 2006

National Total = 32,838,292 Enrollees*

ALPHA ORDER

RANK	STATE	ENROLLEES	% of USA
19	Alabama	620,300	1.9%
50	Alaska	40,882	0.1%
17	Arizona	646,016	2.0%
31	Arkansas	366,160	1.1%
1	California	3,553,569	10.8%
26	Colorado	436,966	1.3%
29	Connecticut	396,574	1.2%
45	Delaware	102,827	0.3%
2	Florida	2,417,835	7.4%
11	Georgia	830,178	2.5%
40	Hawaii	155,619	0.5%
41	Idaho	143,236	0.4%
7	Illinois	1,304,950	4.0%
16	Indiana	682,533	2.1%
30	Iowa	375,187	1.1%
33	Kansas	292,476	0.9%
23	Kentucky	529,557	1.6%
25	Louisiana	472,339	1.4%
39	Maine	182,511	0.6%
20	Maryland	550,276	1.7%
13	Massachusetts	757,745	2.3%
8	Michigan	1,152,174	3.5%
21	Minnesota	547,376	1.7%
32	Mississippi	355,901	1.1%
15	Missouri	716,709	2.2%
44	Montana	110,260	0.3%
37	Nebraska	208,040	0.6%
35	Nevada	237,440	0.7%
43	New Hampshire	129,763	0.4%
10	New Jersey	929,400	2.8%
36	New Mexico	220,449	0.7%
4	New York	1,976,663	6.0%
9	North Carolina	1,048,553	3.2%
47	North Dakota	83,538	0.3%
6	Ohio	1,403,438	4.3%
27	Oklahoma	422,848	1.3%
28	Oregon	407,940	1.2%
5	Pennsylvania	1,475,883	4.5%
42	Rhode Island	136,797	0.4%
24	South Carolina	516,364	1.6%
46	South Dakota	98,529	0.3%
14	Tennessee	747,024	2.3%
3	Texas	2,066,504	6.3%
38	Utah	187,051	0.6%
48	Vermont	74,238	0.2%
12	Virginia	781,412	2.4%
18	Washington	622,721	1.9%
34	West Virginia	280,413	0.9%
22	Wisconsin	540,639	1.6%
49	Wyoming	52,765	0.2%

RANK ORDER

RANK	STATE	ENROLLEES	% of USA
1	California	3,553,569	10.8%
2	Florida	2,417,835	7.4%
3	Texas	2,066,504	6.3%
4	New York	1,976,663	6.0%
5	Pennsylvania	1,475,883	4.5%
6	Ohio	1,403,438	4.3%
7	Illinois	1,304,950	4.0%
8	Michigan	1,152,174	3.5%
9	North Carolina	1,048,553	3.2%
10	New Jersey	929,400	2.8%
11	Georgia	830,178	2.5%
12	Virginia	781,412	2.4%
13	Massachusetts	757,745	2.3%
14	Tennessee	747,024	2.3%
15	Missouri	716,709	2.2%
16	Indiana	682,533	2.1%
17	Arizona	646,016	2.0%
18	Washington	622,721	1.9%
19	Alabama	620,300	1.9%
20	Maryland	550,276	1.7%
21	Minnesota	547,376	1.7%
22	Wisconsin	540,639	1.6%
23	Kentucky	529,557	1.6%
24	South Carolina	516,364	1.6%
25	Louisiana	472,339	1.4%
26	Colorado	436,966	1.3%
27	Oklahoma	422,848	1.3%
28	Oregon	407,940	1.2%
29	Connecticut	396,574	1.2%
30	Iowa	375,187	1.1%
31	Arkansas	366,160	1.1%
32	Mississippi	355,901	1.1%
33	Kansas	292,476	0.9%
34	West Virginia	280,413	0.9%
35	Nevada	237,440	0.7%
36	New Mexico	220,449	0.7%
37	Nebraska	208,040	0.6%
38	Utah	187,051	0.6%
39	Maine	182,511	0.6%
40	Hawaii	155,619	0.5%
41	Idaho	143,236	0.4%
42	Rhode Island	136,797	0.4%
43	New Hampshire	129,763	0.4%
44	Montana	110,260	0.3%
45	Delaware	102,827	0.3%
46	South Dakota	98,529	0.3%
47	North Dakota	83,538	0.3%
48	Vermont	74,238	0.2%
49	Wyoming	52,765	0.2%
50	Alaska	40,882	0.1%
	District of Columbia	58,154	0.2%

Source: U.S. Department of Health and Human Services, Centers for Medicare and Medicaid Services
"Part D Enrollment Data" (http://www.cms.hhs.gov/PrescriptionDrugCovGenIn/02_EnrollmentData.asp)
*Press release dated June 14, 2006. National total includes 391,570 enrollees in U.S. territories.

Percent of Population Enrolled in Medicare Prescription Drug Plans in 2006

National Percent = 10.8%*

ALPHA ORDER

ALPHA ORDER

RANK	STATE	PERCENT
3	Alabama	13.5
50	Alaska	6.1
34	Arizona	10.5
6	Arkansas	13.0
42	California	9.7
46	Colorado	9.2
26	Connecticut	11.3
16	Delaware	12.0
4	Florida	13.4
47	Georgia	8.9
15	Hawaii	12.1
40	Idaho	9.8
35	Illinois	10.2
30	Indiana	10.8
8	Iowa	12.6
32	Kansas	10.6
8	Kentucky	12.6
28	Louisiana	11.0
2	Maine	13.8
40	Maryland	9.8
20	Massachusetts	11.8
25	Michigan	11.4
32	Minnesota	10.6
13	Mississippi	12.2
12	Missouri	12.3
24	Montana	11.7
20	Nebraska	11.8
45	Nevada	9.5
39	New Hampshire	9.9
31	New Jersey	10.7
26	New Mexico	11.3
35	New York	10.2
20	North Carolina	11.8
5	North Dakota	13.1
13	Ohio	12.2
20	Oklahoma	11.8
28	Oregon	11.0
17	Pennsylvania	11.9
7	Rhode Island	12.8
17	South Carolina	11.9
8	South Dakota	12.6
11	Tennessee	12.4
48	Texas	8.8
49	Utah	7.3
17	Vermont	11.9
35	Virginia	10.2
42	Washington	9.7
1	West Virginia	15.4
42	Wisconsin	9.7
35	Wyoming	10.2

RANK ORDER

RANK	STATE	PERCENT
1	West Virginia	15.4
2	Maine	13.8
3	Alabama	13.5
4	Florida	13.4
5	North Dakota	13.1
6	Arkansas	13.0
7	Rhode Island	12.8
8	Iowa	12.6
8	Kentucky	12.6
8	South Dakota	12.6
11	Tennessee	12.4
12	Missouri	12.3
13	Mississippi	12.2
13	Ohio	12.2
15	Hawaii	12.1
16	Delaware	12.0
17	Pennsylvania	11.9
17	South Carolina	11.9
17	Vermont	11.9
20	Massachusetts	11.8
20	Nebraska	11.8
20	North Carolina	11.8
20	Oklahoma	11.8
24	Montana	11.7
25	Michigan	11.4
26	Connecticut	11.3
26	New Mexico	11.3
28	Louisiana	11.0
28	Oregon	11.0
30	Indiana	10.8
31	New Jersey	10.7
32	Kansas	10.6
32	Minnesota	10.6
34	Arizona	10.5
35	Illinois	10.2
35	New York	10.2
35	Virginia	10.2
35	Wyoming	10.2
39	New Hampshire	9.9
40	Idaho	9.8
40	Maryland	9.8
42	California	9.7
42	Washington	9.7
42	Wisconsin	9.7
45	Nevada	9.5
46	Colorado	9.2
47	Georgia	8.9
48	Texas	8.8
49	Utah	7.3
50	Alaska	6.1

| | District of Columbia | 10.0 |

Source: MQ Press using data from U.S. Dept of Health and Human Services, Centers for Medicare and Medicaid Services "Part D Enrollment Data" (http://www.cms.hhs.gov/PrescriptionDrugCovGenIn/02_EnrollmentData.asp)
*Press release dated June 14, 2006. National percent does not include enrollees in U.S. territories. Calculated with 2006 population data.

Medicare Managed Care Enrollees in 2005

National Total = 5,891,211 Enrollees*

ALPHA ORDER

RANK	STATE	ENROLLEES	% of USA
21	Alabama	68,812	1.2%
44	Alaska	0	0.0%
7	Arizona	210,719	3.6%
43	Arkansas	55	0.0%
1	California	1,420,348	24.1%
10	Colorado	161,031	2.7%
19	Connecticut	70,279	1.2%
44	Delaware	0	0.0%
2	Florida	616,538	10.5%
33	Georgia	17,083	0.3%
23	Hawaii	60,174	1.0%
32	Idaho	17,318	0.3%
17	Illinois	83,764	1.4%
31	Indiana	18,200	0.3%
35	Iowa	7,143	0.1%
38	Kansas	2,575	0.0%
22	Kentucky	67,930	1.2%
18	Louisiana	75,384	1.3%
44	Maine	0	0.0%
25	Maryland	45,756	0.8%
9	Massachusetts	175,007	3.0%
29	Michigan	21,669	0.4%
14	Minnesota	109,519	1.9%
44	Mississippi	0	0.0%
11	Missouri	136,397	2.3%
42	Montana	135	0.0%
34	Nebraska	11,350	0.2%
16	Nevada	86,068	1.5%
39	New Hampshire	1,105	0.0%
15	New Jersey	96,925	1.6%
27	New Mexico	42,492	0.7%
3	New York	553,290	9.4%
20	North Carolina	70,205	1.2%
40	North Dakota	591	0.0%
5	Ohio	240,461	4.1%
26	Oklahoma	42,803	0.7%
8	Oregon	193,712	3.3%
4	Pennsylvania	525,006	8.9%
24	Rhode Island	58,113	1.0%
41	South Carolina	496	0.0%
44	South Dakota	0	0.0%
13	Tennessee	110,183	1.9%
6	Texas	226,030	3.8%
30	Utah	18,329	0.3%
44	Vermont	0	0.0%
37	Virginia	2,651	0.0%
12	Washington	131,129	2.2%
36	West Virginia	6,120	0.1%
28	Wisconsin	41,852	0.7%
44	Wyoming	0	0.0%

RANK ORDER

RANK	STATE	ENROLLEES	% of USA
1	California	1,420,348	24.1%
2	Florida	616,538	10.5%
3	New York	553,290	9.4%
4	Pennsylvania	525,006	8.9%
5	Ohio	240,461	4.1%
6	Texas	226,030	3.8%
7	Arizona	210,719	3.6%
8	Oregon	193,712	3.3%
9	Massachusetts	175,007	3.0%
10	Colorado	161,031	2.7%
11	Missouri	136,397	2.3%
12	Washington	131,129	2.2%
13	Tennessee	110,183	1.9%
14	Minnesota	109,519	1.9%
15	New Jersey	96,925	1.6%
16	Nevada	86,068	1.5%
17	Illinois	83,764	1.4%
18	Louisiana	75,384	1.3%
19	Connecticut	70,279	1.2%
20	North Carolina	70,205	1.2%
21	Alabama	68,812	1.2%
22	Kentucky	67,930	1.2%
23	Hawaii	60,174	1.0%
24	Rhode Island	58,113	1.0%
25	Maryland	45,756	0.8%
26	Oklahoma	42,803	0.7%
27	New Mexico	42,492	0.7%
28	Wisconsin	41,852	0.7%
29	Michigan	21,669	0.4%
30	Utah	18,329	0.3%
31	Indiana	18,200	0.3%
32	Idaho	17,318	0.3%
33	Georgia	17,083	0.3%
34	Nebraska	11,350	0.2%
35	Iowa	7,143	0.1%
36	West Virginia	6,120	0.1%
37	Virginia	2,651	0.0%
38	Kansas	2,575	0.0%
39	New Hampshire	1,105	0.0%
40	North Dakota	591	0.0%
41	South Carolina	496	0.0%
42	Montana	135	0.0%
43	Arkansas	55	0.0%
44	Alaska	0	0.0%
44	Delaware	0	0.0%
44	Maine	0	0.0%
44	Mississippi	0	0.0%
44	South Dakota	0	0.0%
44	Vermont	0	0.0%
44	Wyoming	0	0.0%
	District of Columbia	0	0.0%

*Source: U.S. Department of Health and Human Services, Centers for Medicare and Medicaid Services
"Medicare Managed Care Report"*
**As of September 2005. Includes M + C, Cost, Health Care Prepayment Plans (HCPP) and other demo plans.
National total includes 46,462 enrollees in the United Mine Workers' plan not shown separately by state.*

Percent of Medicare Enrollees in Managed Care Programs in 2005

National Percent = 15% of Medicare Enrollees*

ALPHA ORDER

RANK	STATE	PERCENT
21	Alabama	10
39	Alaska	0
7	Arizona	30
39	Arkansas	0
2	California	36
4	Colorado	34
16	Connecticut	14
39	Delaware	0
9	Florida	21
32	Georgia	2
2	Hawaii	36
21	Idaho	10
29	Illinois	5
32	Indiana	2
36	Iowa	1
39	Kansas	0
20	Kentucky	11
19	Louisiana	12
39	Maine	0
25	Maryland	8
11	Massachusetts	18
32	Michigan	2
14	Minnesota	17
39	Mississippi	0
15	Missouri	15
39	Montana	0
31	Nebraska	4
4	Nevada	34
36	New Hampshire	1
25	New Jersey	8
11	New Mexico	18
10	New York	20
28	North Carolina	6
36	North Dakota	1
16	Ohio	14
25	Oklahoma	8
1	Oregon	39
8	Pennsylvania	25
6	Rhode Island	33
39	South Carolina	0
39	South Dakota	0
18	Tennessee	13
23	Texas	9
23	Utah	9
39	Vermont	0
39	Virginia	0
11	Washington	18
32	West Virginia	2
29	Wisconsin	5
39	Wyoming	0

RANK ORDER

RANK	STATE	PERCENT
1	Oregon	39
2	California	36
2	Hawaii	36
4	Colorado	34
4	Nevada	34
6	Rhode Island	33
7	Arizona	30
8	Pennsylvania	25
9	Florida	21
10	New York	20
11	Massachusetts	18
11	New Mexico	18
11	Washington	18
14	Minnesota	17
15	Missouri	15
16	Connecticut	14
16	Ohio	14
18	Tennessee	13
19	Louisiana	12
20	Kentucky	11
21	Alabama	10
21	Idaho	10
23	Texas	9
23	Utah	9
25	Maryland	8
25	New Jersey	8
25	Oklahoma	8
28	North Carolina	6
29	Illinois	5
29	Wisconsin	5
31	Nebraska	4
32	Georgia	2
32	Indiana	2
32	Michigan	2
32	West Virginia	2
36	Iowa	1
36	New Hampshire	1
36	North Dakota	1
39	Alaska	0
39	Arkansas	0
39	Delaware	0
39	Kansas	0
39	Maine	0
39	Mississippi	0
39	Montana	0
39	South Carolina	0
39	South Dakota	0
39	Vermont	0
39	Virginia	0
39	Wyoming	0

| | District of Columbia | 0 |

Source: U.S. Department of Health and Human Services, Centers for Medicare and Medicaid Services
"Medicare Managed Care Report"
*As of September 2005. Includes M + C, Cost, Health Care Prepayment Plans (HCPP) and other demo plans.
National figure includes enrollees in the United Mine Workers' plan not shown separately by state.

Percent of Physicians Participating in Medicare in 2006

National Percent = 93.3% of Physicians Participate in Medicare*

ALPHA ORDER

RANK ORDER

RANK	STATE	PERCENT	RANK	STATE	PERCENT
7	Alabama	96.9	1	North Dakota	97.9
46	Alaska	90.0	2	Utah	97.8
36	Arizona	92.4	3	Michigan	97.7
12	Arkansas	96.4	3	Rhode Island	97.7
49	California	86.9	5	Kansas	97.0
37	Colorado	92.3	5	Pennsylvania	97.0
30	Connecticut	94.3	7	Alabama	96.9
16	Delaware	96.1	7	West Virginia	96.9
31	Florida	94.1	9	Ohio	96.7
35	Georgia	92.7	10	Washington	96.6
22	Hawaii	95.6	11	Wisconsin	96.5
46	Idaho	90.0	12	Arkansas	96.4
25	Illinois	94.9	12	Nebraska	96.4
14	Indiana	96.2	14	Indiana	96.2
23	Iowa	95.4	14	Nevada	96.2
5	Kansas	97.0	16	Delaware	96.1
24	Kentucky	95.1	17	Tennessee	96.0
32	Louisiana	93.6	18	Maryland	95.9
44	Maine	91.6	18	New Mexico	95.9
18	Maryland	95.9	18	North Carolina	95.9
42	Massachusetts	91.9	21	Oklahoma	95.7
3	Michigan	97.7	22	Hawaii	95.6
50	Minnesota	80.3	23	Iowa	95.4
41	Mississippi	92.0	24	Kentucky	95.1
28	Missouri	94.8	25	Illinois	94.9
33	Montana	93.3	25	South Carolina	94.9
12	Nebraska	96.4	25	Virginia	94.9
14	Nevada	96.2	28	Missouri	94.8
48	New Hampshire	89.4	29	Oregon	94.4
40	New Jersey	92.1	30	Connecticut	94.3
18	New Mexico	95.9	31	Florida	94.1
38	New York	92.2	32	Louisiana	93.6
18	North Carolina	95.9	33	Montana	93.3
1	North Dakota	97.9	34	South Dakota	92.9
9	Ohio	96.7	35	Georgia	92.7
21	Oklahoma	95.7	36	Arizona	92.4
29	Oregon	94.4	37	Colorado	92.3
5	Pennsylvania	97.0	38	New York	92.2
3	Rhode Island	97.7	38	Vermont	92.2
25	South Carolina	94.9	40	New Jersey	92.1
34	South Dakota	92.9	41	Mississippi	92.0
17	Tennessee	96.0	42	Massachusetts	91.9
45	Texas	91.5	43	Wyoming	91.7
2	Utah	97.8	44	Maine	91.6
38	Vermont	92.2	45	Texas	91.5
25	Virginia	94.9	46	Alaska	90.0
10	Washington	96.6	46	Idaho	90.0
7	West Virginia	96.9	48	New Hampshire	89.4
11	Wisconsin	96.5	49	California	86.9
43	Wyoming	91.7	50	Minnesota	80.3

			District of Columbia	92.7

Source: U.S. Department of Health and Human Services, Centers for Medicare and Medicaid Services
   "2006 Data Compendium" (http://www.cms.hhs.gov/DataCompendium/18_2006_Data_Compendium.asp)
As of January 1, 2006. Refers to Medicare Part B. Physicians include MDs, DOs, limited license practitioners and non-physician practitioners. National average is a weighted average based on state population.

Medicare Program Payments in 2004

National Total = $253,488,000,000*

RANK	STATE	BENEFITS	% of USA
18	Alabama	$4,705,000,000	1.9%
50	Alaska	333,000,000	0.1%
27	Arizona	3,526,000,000	1.4%
29	Arkansas	2,859,000,000	1.1%
1	California	20,809,000,000	8.2%
32	Colorado	2,395,000,000	0.9%
24	Connecticut	3,902,000,000	1.5%
41	Delaware	982,000,000	0.4%
2	Florida	20,133,000,000	7.9%
11	Georgia	6,641,000,000	2.6%
46	Hawaii	608,000,000	0.2%
42	Idaho	875,000,000	0.3%
6	Illinois	11,464,000,000	4.5%
14	Indiana	5,699,000,000	2.2%
30	Iowa	2,528,000,000	1.0%
31	Kansas	2,511,000,000	1.0%
21	Kentucky	4,159,000,000	1.6%
19	Louisiana	4,689,000,000	1.8%
37	Maine	1,320,000,000	0.5%
16	Maryland	5,416,000,000	2.1%
12	Massachusetts	6,367,000,000	2.5%
8	Michigan	10,763,000,000	4.2%
25	Minnesota	3,566,000,000	1.4%
28	Mississippi	3,286,000,000	1.3%
17	Missouri	5,278,000,000	2.1%
44	Montana	800,000,000	0.3%
35	Nebraska	1,530,000,000	0.6%
36	Nevada	1,451,000,000	0.6%
40	New Hampshire	1,133,000,000	0.4%
9	New Jersey	9,314,000,000	3.7%
39	New Mexico	1,180,000,000	0.5%
3	New York	18,090,000,000	7.1%
10	North Carolina	7,967,000,000	3.1%
47	North Dakota	558,000,000	0.2%
7	Ohio	10,887,000,000	4.3%
26	Oklahoma	3,538,000,000	1.4%
33	Oregon	2,128,000,000	0.8%
5	Pennsylvania	11,653,000,000	4.6%
43	Rhode Island	819,000,000	0.3%
22	South Carolina	4,110,000,000	1.6%
45	South Dakota	641,000,000	0.3%
15	Tennessee	5,687,000,000	2.2%
4	Texas	18,075,000,000	7.1%
38	Utah	1,292,000,000	0.5%
48	Vermont	547,000,000	0.2%
13	Virginia	5,714,000,000	2.3%
23	Washington	3,941,000,000	1.6%
34	West Virginia	2,098,000,000	0.8%
20	Wisconsin	4,521,000,000	1.8%
49	Wyoming	398,000,000	0.2%

RANK	STATE	BENEFITS	% of USA
1	California	$20,809,000,000	8.2%
2	Florida	20,133,000,000	7.9%
3	New York	18,090,000,000	7.1%
4	Texas	18,075,000,000	7.1%
5	Pennsylvania	11,653,000,000	4.6%
6	Illinois	11,464,000,000	4.5%
7	Ohio	10,887,000,000	4.3%
8	Michigan	10,763,000,000	4.2%
9	New Jersey	9,314,000,000	3.7%
10	North Carolina	7,967,000,000	3.1%
11	Georgia	6,641,000,000	2.6%
12	Massachusetts	6,367,000,000	2.5%
13	Virginia	5,714,000,000	2.3%
14	Indiana	5,699,000,000	2.2%
15	Tennessee	5,687,000,000	2.2%
16	Maryland	5,416,000,000	2.1%
17	Missouri	5,278,000,000	2.1%
18	Alabama	4,705,000,000	1.9%
19	Louisiana	4,689,000,000	1.8%
20	Wisconsin	4,521,000,000	1.8%
21	Kentucky	4,159,000,000	1.6%
22	South Carolina	4,110,000,000	1.6%
23	Washington	3,941,000,000	1.6%
24	Connecticut	3,902,000,000	1.5%
25	Minnesota	3,566,000,000	1.4%
26	Oklahoma	3,538,000,000	1.4%
27	Arizona	3,526,000,000	1.4%
28	Mississippi	3,286,000,000	1.3%
29	Arkansas	2,859,000,000	1.1%
30	Iowa	2,528,000,000	1.0%
31	Kansas	2,511,000,000	1.0%
32	Colorado	2,395,000,000	0.9%
33	Oregon	2,128,000,000	0.8%
34	West Virginia	2,098,000,000	0.8%
35	Nebraska	1,530,000,000	0.6%
36	Nevada	1,451,000,000	0.6%
37	Maine	1,320,000,000	0.5%
38	Utah	1,292,000,000	0.5%
39	New Mexico	1,180,000,000	0.5%
40	New Hampshire	1,133,000,000	0.4%
41	Delaware	982,000,000	0.4%
42	Idaho	875,000,000	0.3%
43	Rhode Island	819,000,000	0.3%
44	Montana	800,000,000	0.3%
45	South Dakota	641,000,000	0.3%
46	Hawaii	608,000,000	0.2%
47	North Dakota	558,000,000	0.2%
48	Vermont	547,000,000	0.2%
49	Wyoming	398,000,000	0.2%
50	Alaska	333,000,000	0.1%
	District of Columbia	600,000,000	0.2%

Source: U.S. Department of Health and Human Services, Centers for Medicare and Medicaid Services
"2006 Medicare and Medicaid Statistical Supplement" (http://cms.hhs.gov/MedicareMedicaidStatSupp)
*Figures for calendar year 2004. Includes payments to aged and disabled enrollees. Total does not include payments to beneficiaries in Puerto Rico and other outlying areas.

Per Capita Medicare Program Payments in 2004

National Per Capita = $863*

RANK	STATE	PER CAPITA		RANK	STATE	PER CAPITA
9	Alabama	$1,042		1	Delaware	$1,185
49	Alaska	507		2	Florida	1,159
44	Arizona	614		2	West Virginia	1,159
10	Arkansas	1,041		4	Mississippi	1,136
46	California	581		5	Connecticut	1,117
48	Colorado	521		6	New Jersey	1,074
5	Connecticut	1,117		7	Michigan	1,066
1	Delaware	1,185		8	Louisiana	1,043
2	Florida	1,159		9	Alabama	1,042
38	Georgia	743		10	Arkansas	1,041
50	Hawaii	483		11	Maine	1,005
41	Idaho	627		12	Kentucky	1,004
25	Illinois	902		12	Oklahoma	1,004
24	Indiana	916		14	Massachusetts	989
31	Iowa	856		15	South Carolina	980
22	Kansas	917		16	Maryland	975
12	Kentucky	1,004		17	Tennessee	966
8	Louisiana	1,043		18	Ohio	950
11	Maine	1,005		19	Pennsylvania	941
16	Maryland	975		20	New York	938
14	Massachusetts	989		21	North Carolina	934
7	Michigan	1,066		22	Kansas	917
39	Minnesota	700		22	Missouri	917
4	Mississippi	1,136		24	Indiana	916
22	Missouri	917		25	Illinois	902
30	Montana	864		26	Vermont	881
28	Nebraska	876		27	North Dakota	878
42	Nevada	622		28	Nebraska	876
29	New Hampshire	873		29	New Hampshire	873
6	New Jersey	1,074		30	Montana	864
43	New Mexico	621		31	Iowa	856
20	New York	938		32	South Dakota	832
21	North Carolina	934		33	Wisconsin	822
27	North Dakota	878		34	Texas	803
18	Ohio	950		35	Wyoming	787
12	Oklahoma	1,004		36	Virginia	765
45	Oregon	593		37	Rhode Island	759
19	Pennsylvania	941		38	Georgia	743
37	Rhode Island	759		39	Minnesota	700
15	South Carolina	980		40	Washington	635
32	South Dakota	832		41	Idaho	627
17	Tennessee	966		42	Nevada	622
34	Texas	803		43	New Mexico	621
47	Utah	534		44	Arizona	614
26	Vermont	881		45	Oregon	593
36	Virginia	765		46	California	581
40	Washington	635		47	Utah	534
2	West Virginia	1,159		48	Colorado	521
33	Wisconsin	822		49	Alaska	507
35	Wyoming	787		50	Hawaii	483

	District of Columbia	1,035

Source: MQ Press using data from U.S. Dept of Health & Human Services, Centers for Medicare and Medicaid Services "2006 Medicare and Medicaid Statistical Supplement" (http://cms.hhs.gov/MedicareMedicaidStatSupp)
*Figures for calendar year 2004. Includes payments to aged and disabled enrollees. National rate does not include payments or enrollees in Puerto Rico and other outlying areas.

Medicare Program Payments per Enrollee in 2004

National Rate = $7,148*

ALPHA ORDER				RANK ORDER		

RANK	STATE	PER ENROLLEE		RANK	STATE	PER ENROLLEE
19	Alabama	$6,915		1	Louisiana	$8,393
22	Alaska	6,737		2	New Jersey	8,264
31	Arizona	6,333		3	Maryland	8,247
32	Arkansas	6,236		4	Florida	8,243
11	California	7,447		5	Delaware	8,008
29	Colorado	6,466		6	New York	7,995
9	Connecticut	7,904		7	Massachusetts	7,927
5	Delaware	8,008		8	Texas	7,915
4	Florida	8,243		9	Connecticut	7,904
21	Georgia	6,767		10	Michigan	7,477
50	Hawaii	5,139		11	California	7,447
48	Idaho	5,255		12	Mississippi	7,389
15	Illinois	7,220		13	Pennsylvania	7,263
26	Indiana	6,550		14	Oklahoma	7,241
46	Iowa	5,436		15	Illinois	7,220
27	Kansas	6,541		16	Ohio	7,189
28	Kentucky	6,479		17	Rhode Island	7,131
1	Louisiana	8,393		18	Nevada	7,089
43	Maine	5,719		19	Alabama	6,915
3	Maryland	8,247		20	Tennessee	6,891
7	Massachusetts	7,927		21	Georgia	6,767
10	Michigan	7,477		22	Alaska	6,737
35	Minnesota	6,070		23	North Carolina	6,726
12	Mississippi	7,389		24	Missouri	6,717
24	Missouri	6,717		25	South Carolina	6,573
47	Montana	5,335		26	Indiana	6,550
33	Nebraska	6,157		27	Kansas	6,541
18	Nevada	7,089		28	Kentucky	6,479
34	New Hampshire	6,138		29	Colorado	6,466
2	New Jersey	8,264		30	West Virginia	6,408
44	New Mexico	5,464		31	Arizona	6,333
6	New York	7,995		32	Arkansas	6,236
23	North Carolina	6,726		33	Nebraska	6,157
45	North Dakota	5,456		34	New Hampshire	6,138
16	Ohio	7,189		35	Minnesota	6,070
14	Oklahoma	7,241		36	Virginia	6,031
37	Oregon	5,985		37	Oregon	5,985
13	Pennsylvania	7,263		38	Wisconsin	5,895
17	Rhode Island	7,131		39	Washington	5,884
25	South Carolina	6,573		40	Utah	5,862
49	South Dakota	5,214		41	Wyoming	5,825
20	Tennessee	6,891		42	Vermont	5,809
8	Texas	7,915		43	Maine	5,719
40	Utah	5,862		44	New Mexico	5,464
42	Vermont	5,809		45	North Dakota	5,456
36	Virginia	6,031		46	Iowa	5,436
39	Washington	5,884		47	Montana	5,335
30	West Virginia	6,408		48	Idaho	5,255
38	Wisconsin	5,895		49	South Dakota	5,214
41	Wyoming	5,825		50	Hawaii	5,139

District of Columbia 8,820

*Source: U.S. Department of Health and Human Services, Centers for Medicare and Medicaid Services
"2006 Medicare and Medicaid Statistical Supplement" (http://cms.hhs.gov/MedicareMedicaidStatSupp)*
**Figures for calendar year 2004. Includes payments to aged and disabled enrollees. National figure does not
include enrollees in managed care plans in the denominator used to calculate average payments. National rate
also does not include payments or enrollees in Puerto Rico and other outlying areas.*

Medicaid Enrollment in 2005

National Total = 45,654,725 Enrollees*

ALPHA ORDER

RANK ORDER

RANK	STATE	ENROLLEES	% of USA	RANK	STATE	ENROLLEES	% of USA
21	Alabama	819,256	1.8%	1	California	6,508,414	14.3%
47	Alaska	98,557	0.2%	2	New York	4,188,586	9.2%
13	Arizona	995,208	2.2%	3	Texas	2,770,069	6.1%
25	Arkansas	634,701	1.4%	4	Florida	2,308,886	5.1%
1	California	6,508,414	14.3%	5	Illinois	1,900,600	4.2%
32	Colorado	389,115	0.9%	6	Pennsylvania	1,731,139	3.8%
29	Connecticut	409,393	0.9%	7	Ohio	1,727,567	3.8%
43	Delaware	143,237	0.3%	8	Michigan	1,472,812	3.2%
4	Florida	2,308,886	5.1%	9	Georgia	1,411,908	3.1%
9	Georgia	1,411,908	3.1%	10	North Carolina	1,250,507	2.7%
39	Hawaii	203,090	0.4%	11	Tennessee	1,221,978	2.7%
42	Idaho	171,451	0.4%	12	Massachusetts	1,026,904	2.2%
5	Illinois	1,900,600	4.2%	13	Arizona	995,208	2.2%
17	Indiana	834,244	1.8%	14	Louisiana	991,931	2.2%
33	Iowa	327,308	0.7%	15	Missouri	883,441	1.9%
35	Kansas	282,597	0.6%	16	Washington	868,648	1.9%
23	Kentucky	708,203	1.6%	17	Indiana	834,244	1.8%
14	Louisiana	991,931	2.2%	18	South Carolina	832,727	1.8%
36	Maine	251,545	0.6%	19	New Jersey	831,122	1.8%
22	Maryland	717,040	1.6%	20	Wisconsin	820,948	1.8%
12	Massachusetts	1,026,904	2.2%	21	Alabama	819,256	1.8%
8	Michigan	1,472,812	3.2%	22	Maryland	717,040	1.6%
27	Minnesota	575,926	1.3%	23	Kentucky	708,203	1.6%
26	Mississippi	610,528	1.3%	24	Virginia	697,662	1.5%
15	Missouri	883,441	1.9%	25	Arkansas	634,701	1.4%
48	Montana	83,241	0.2%	26	Mississippi	610,528	1.3%
37	Nebraska	208,057	0.5%	27	Minnesota	575,926	1.3%
41	Nevada	173,658	0.4%	28	Oklahoma	571,969	1.3%
46	New Hampshire	108,719	0.2%	29	Connecticut	409,393	0.9%
19	New Jersey	831,122	1.8%	30	Oregon	408,457	0.9%
31	New Mexico	407,405	0.9%	31	New Mexico	407,405	0.9%
2	New York	4,188,586	9.2%	32	Colorado	389,115	0.9%
10	North Carolina	1,250,507	2.7%	33	Iowa	327,308	0.7%
50	North Dakota	54,312	0.1%	34	West Virginia	293,797	0.6%
7	Ohio	1,727,567	3.8%	35	Kansas	282,597	0.6%
28	Oklahoma	571,969	1.3%	36	Maine	251,545	0.6%
30	Oregon	408,457	0.9%	37	Nebraska	208,057	0.5%
6	Pennsylvania	1,731,139	3.8%	38	Utah	206,716	0.5%
40	Rhode Island	181,828	0.4%	39	Hawaii	203,090	0.4%
18	South Carolina	832,727	1.8%	40	Rhode Island	181,828	0.4%
45	South Dakota	126,886	0.3%	41	Nevada	173,658	0.4%
11	Tennessee	1,221,978	2.7%	42	Idaho	171,451	0.4%
3	Texas	2,770,069	6.1%	43	Delaware	143,237	0.3%
38	Utah	206,716	0.5%	44	Vermont	130,276	0.3%
44	Vermont	130,276	0.3%	45	South Dakota	126,886	0.3%
24	Virginia	697,662	1.5%	46	New Hampshire	108,719	0.2%
16	Washington	868,648	1.9%	47	Alaska	98,557	0.2%
34	West Virginia	293,797	0.6%	48	Montana	83,241	0.2%
20	Wisconsin	820,948	1.8%	49	Wyoming	61,871	0.1%
49	Wyoming	61,871	0.1%	50	North Dakota	54,312	0.1%
					District of Columbia	142,224	0.3%

Source: U.S. Department of Health and Human Services, Centers for Medicare and Medicaid Services "Medicaid Managed Care State Enrollment" (http://www.cms.hhs.gov/MedicaidDataSourcesGenInfo/)
Unduplicated enrollment as of December 31, 2005. National total includes 878,061 Medicaid enrollees in Puerto Rico and the Virgin Islands.

Percent of Population Enrolled in Medicaid in 2005

National Percent = 15.1% of Population*

ALPHA ORDER

RANK	STATE	PERCENT
10	Alabama	18.0
24	Alaska	14.9
15	Arizona	16.7
1	Arkansas	22.9
10	California	18.0
47	Colorado	8.3
38	Connecticut	11.7
12	Delaware	17.0
32	Florida	13.0
21	Georgia	15.5
19	Hawaii	16.0
36	Idaho	12.0
24	Illinois	14.9
31	Indiana	13.3
41	Iowa	11.0
42	Kansas	10.3
12	Kentucky	17.0
2	Louisiana	22.0
9	Maine	19.1
33	Maryland	12.8
19	Massachusetts	16.0
27	Michigan	14.6
39	Minnesota	11.2
5	Mississippi	21.0
22	Missouri	15.2
45	Montana	8.9
37	Nebraska	11.8
50	Nevada	7.2
47	New Hampshire	8.3
43	New Jersey	9.5
4	New Mexico	21.2
3	New York	21.7
28	North Carolina	14.4
46	North Dakota	8.6
23	Ohio	15.1
18	Oklahoma	16.1
39	Oregon	11.2
29	Pennsylvania	14.0
14	Rhode Island	16.9
8	South Carolina	19.6
16	South Dakota	16.4
7	Tennessee	20.5
35	Texas	12.1
47	Utah	8.3
6	Vermont	20.9
44	Virginia	9.2
30	Washington	13.8
17	West Virginia	16.2
24	Wisconsin	14.9
34	Wyoming	12.2

RANK ORDER

RANK	STATE	PERCENT
1	Arkansas	22.9
2	Louisiana	22.0
3	New York	21.7
4	New Mexico	21.2
5	Mississippi	21.0
6	Vermont	20.9
7	Tennessee	20.5
8	South Carolina	19.6
9	Maine	19.1
10	Alabama	18.0
10	California	18.0
12	Delaware	17.0
12	Kentucky	17.0
14	Rhode Island	16.9
15	Arizona	16.7
16	South Dakota	16.4
17	West Virginia	16.2
18	Oklahoma	16.1
19	Hawaii	16.0
19	Massachusetts	16.0
21	Georgia	15.5
22	Missouri	15.2
23	Ohio	15.1
24	Alaska	14.9
24	Illinois	14.9
24	Wisconsin	14.9
27	Michigan	14.6
28	North Carolina	14.4
29	Pennsylvania	14.0
30	Washington	13.8
31	Indiana	13.3
32	Florida	13.0
33	Maryland	12.8
34	Wyoming	12.2
35	Texas	12.1
36	Idaho	12.0
37	Nebraska	11.8
38	Connecticut	11.7
39	Minnesota	11.2
39	Oregon	11.2
41	Iowa	11.0
42	Kansas	10.3
43	New Jersey	9.5
44	Virginia	9.2
45	Montana	8.9
46	North Dakota	8.6
47	Colorado	8.3
47	New Hampshire	8.3
47	Utah	8.3
50	Nevada	7.2

District of Columbia   24.4

Source: MQ Press using data from U.S. Dept of Health & Human Services, Centers for Medicare and Medicaid Services
"Medicaid Managed Care State Enrollment" (http://www.cms.hhs.gov/MedicaidDataSourcesGenInfo/)
*Unduplicated enrollment as of December 31, 2005. National percent does not include recipients or population
in U.S. territories.

Medicaid Managed Care Enrollment in 2005

National Total = 29,250,215 Enrollees*

<ins>ALPHA ORDER</ins>					<ins>RANK ORDER</ins>			
RANK	STATE	ENROLLEES	% of USA		RANK	STATE	ENROLLEES	% of USA
21	Alabama	472,884	1.6%		1	California	3,282,341	11.2%
49	Alaska	0	0.0%		2	New York	2,563,617	8.8%
9	Arizona	888,801	3.0%		3	Texas	1,877,548	6.4%
18	Arkansas	527,234	1.8%		4	Pennsylvania	1,557,560	5.3%
1	California	3,282,341	11.2%		5	Florida	1,543,141	5.3%
25	Colorado	371,077	1.3%		6	Georgia	1,352,163	4.6%
28	Connecticut	302,061	1.0%		7	Michigan	1,307,910	4.5%
43	Delaware	108,795	0.4%		8	Tennessee	1,221,978	4.2%
5	Florida	1,543,141	5.3%		9	Arizona	888,801	3.0%
6	Georgia	1,352,163	4.6%		10	Washington	868,648	3.0%
34	Hawaii	162,394	0.6%		11	North Carolina	814,068	2.8%
38	Idaho	141,571	0.5%		12	Louisiana	735,339	2.5%
37	Illinois	148,900	0.5%		13	Kentucky	644,713	2.2%
16	Indiana	597,899	2.0%		14	Massachusetts	622,780	2.1%
29	Iowa	279,855	1.0%		15	Ohio	617,812	2.1%
36	Kansas	159,511	0.5%		16	Indiana	597,899	2.0%
13	Kentucky	644,713	2.2%		17	New Jersey	564,729	1.9%
12	Louisiana	735,339	2.5%		18	Arkansas	527,234	1.8%
33	Maine	163,385	0.6%		19	Maryland	486,691	1.7%
19	Maryland	486,691	1.7%		20	Oklahoma	479,168	1.6%
14	Massachusetts	622,780	2.1%		21	Alabama	472,884	1.6%
7	Michigan	1,307,910	4.5%		22	Virginia	438,709	1.5%
27	Minnesota	366,282	1.3%		23	Wisconsin	380,109	1.3%
45	Mississippi	67,702	0.2%		24	Missouri	379,759	1.3%
24	Missouri	379,759	1.3%		25	Colorado	371,077	1.3%
46	Montana	55,023	0.2%		26	Oregon	368,403	1.3%
32	Nebraska	168,784	0.6%		27	Minnesota	366,282	1.3%
35	Nevada	161,108	0.6%		28	Connecticut	302,061	1.0%
48	New Hampshire	2,305	0.0%		29	Iowa	279,855	1.0%
17	New Jersey	564,729	1.9%		30	New Mexico	244,934	0.8%
30	New Mexico	244,934	0.8%		31	Utah	188,079	0.6%
2	New York	2,563,617	8.8%		32	Nebraska	168,784	0.6%
11	North Carolina	814,068	2.8%		33	Maine	163,385	0.6%
47	North Dakota	31,120	0.1%		34	Hawaii	162,394	0.6%
15	Ohio	617,812	2.1%		35	Nevada	161,108	0.6%
20	Oklahoma	479,168	1.6%		36	Kansas	159,511	0.5%
26	Oregon	368,403	1.3%		37	Illinois	148,900	0.5%
4	Pennsylvania	1,557,560	5.3%		38	Idaho	141,571	0.5%
40	Rhode Island	126,225	0.4%		39	West Virginia	132,749	0.5%
42	South Carolina	118,893	0.4%		40	Rhode Island	126,225	0.4%
41	South Dakota	123,230	0.4%		41	South Dakota	123,230	0.4%
8	Tennessee	1,221,978	4.2%		42	South Carolina	118,893	0.4%
3	Texas	1,877,548	6.4%		43	Delaware	108,795	0.4%
31	Utah	188,079	0.6%		44	Vermont	84,995	0.3%
44	Vermont	84,995	0.3%		45	Mississippi	67,702	0.2%
22	Virginia	438,709	1.5%		46	Montana	55,023	0.2%
10	Washington	868,648	3.0%		47	North Dakota	31,120	0.1%
39	West Virginia	132,749	0.5%		48	New Hampshire	2,305	0.0%
23	Wisconsin	380,109	1.3%		49	Alaska	0	0.0%
49	Wyoming	0	0.0%		49	Wyoming	0	0.0%
						District of Columbia	91,732	0.3%

Source: U.S. Department of Health and Human Services, Centers for Medicare and Medicaid Services
"Medicaid Managed Care State Enrollment" (http://www.cms.hhs.gov/MedicaidDataSourcesGenInfo/)
*Unduplicated enrollment as of December 31, 2005. Enrollment in state health care reform programs that expand eligibility beyond traditional Medicaid standards. National total includes 855,501 Medicaid managed care enrollees in Puerto Rico.

Percent of Medicaid Enrollees in Managed Care in 2005

National Percent = 64.1% of Medicaid Enrollees*

ALPHA ORDER

RANK	STATE	PERCENT
37	Alabama	57.7
49	Alaska	0.0
11	Arizona	89.3
15	Arkansas	83.1
40	California	50.4
5	Colorado	95.4
21	Connecticut	73.8
19	Delaware	76.0
27	Florida	66.8
4	Georgia	95.8
18	Hawaii	80.0
16	Idaho	82.6
47	Illinois	7.8
22	Indiana	71.7
13	Iowa	85.5
39	Kansas	56.4
7	Kentucky	91.0
20	Louisiana	74.1
31	Maine	65.0
25	Maryland	67.9
35	Massachusetts	60.7
12	Michigan	88.8
32	Minnesota	63.6
46	Mississippi	11.1
43	Missouri	43.0
28	Montana	66.1
17	Nebraska	81.1
6	Nevada	92.8
48	New Hampshire	2.1
24	New Jersey	68.0
36	New Mexico	60.1
34	New York	61.2
30	North Carolina	65.1
38	North Dakota	57.3
44	Ohio	35.8
14	Oklahoma	83.8
9	Oregon	90.2
10	Pennsylvania	90.0
23	Rhode Island	69.4
45	South Carolina	14.3
3	South Dakota	97.1
1	Tennessee	100.0
26	Texas	67.8
7	Utah	91.0
29	Vermont	65.2
33	Virginia	62.9
1	Washington	100.0
42	West Virginia	45.2
41	Wisconsin	46.3
49	Wyoming	0.0

RANK ORDER

RANK	STATE	PERCENT
1	Tennessee	100.0
1	Washington	100.0
3	South Dakota	97.1
4	Georgia	95.8
5	Colorado	95.4
6	Nevada	92.8
7	Kentucky	91.0
7	Utah	91.0
9	Oregon	90.2
10	Pennsylvania	90.0
11	Arizona	89.3
12	Michigan	88.8
13	Iowa	85.5
14	Oklahoma	83.8
15	Arkansas	83.1
16	Idaho	82.6
17	Nebraska	81.1
18	Hawaii	80.0
19	Delaware	76.0
20	Louisiana	74.1
21	Connecticut	73.8
22	Indiana	71.7
23	Rhode Island	69.4
24	New Jersey	68.0
25	Maryland	67.9
26	Texas	67.8
27	Florida	66.8
28	Montana	66.1
29	Vermont	65.2
30	North Carolina	65.1
31	Maine	65.0
32	Minnesota	63.6
33	Virginia	62.9
34	New York	61.2
35	Massachusetts	60.7
36	New Mexico	60.1
37	Alabama	57.7
38	North Dakota	57.3
39	Kansas	56.4
40	California	50.4
41	Wisconsin	46.3
42	West Virginia	45.2
43	Missouri	43.0
44	Ohio	35.8
45	South Carolina	14.3
46	Mississippi	11.1
47	Illinois	7.8
48	New Hampshire	2.1
49	Alaska	0.0
49	Wyoming	0.0

District of Columbia   64.5

Source: MQ Press using data from U.S. Dept of Health & Human Services, Centers for Medicare and Medicaid Services "Medicaid Managed Care State Enrollment" (http://www.cms.hhs.gov/MedicaidDataSourcesGenInfo/)
Unduplicated enrollment as of December 31, 2005. Enrollment in state health care reform programs that expand eligibility beyond traditional Medicaid standards. National percent includes Medicaid enrollees in Puerto Rico and the Virgin Islands.

Estimated Medicaid Expenditures in 2006

National Total = $297,057,000,000*

ALPHA ORDER				RANK ORDER			
RANK	STATE	EXPENDITURES	% of USA	RANK	STATE	EXPENDITURES	% of USA
25	Alabama	$4,187,000,000	1.4%	1	California	$35,936,000,000	12.1%
43	Alaska	1,070,000,000	0.4%	2	New York	30,209,000,000	10.2%
23	Arizona	4,352,000,000	1.5%	3	Texas	17,702,000,000	6.0%
28	Arkansas	3,340,000,000	1.1%	4	Pennsylvania	17,622,000,000	5.9%
1	California	35,936,000,000	12.1%	5	Florida	14,706,000,000	5.0%
32	Colorado	2,697,000,000	0.9%	6	Ohio	13,439,000,000	4.5%
26	Connecticut	4,050,000,000	1.4%	7	Illinois	12,492,000,000	4.2%
45	Delaware	962,000,000	0.3%	8	North Carolina	9,035,000,000	3.0%
5	Florida	14,706,000,000	5.0%	9	New Jersey	8,943,000,000	3.0%
12	Georgia	6,926,000,000	2.3%	10	Michigan	8,566,000,000	2.9%
44	Hawaii	994,000,000	0.3%	11	Tennessee	8,299,000,000	2.8%
41	Idaho	1,134,000,000	0.4%	12	Georgia	6,926,000,000	2.3%
7	Illinois	12,492,000,000	4.2%	13	Massachusetts	6,898,000,000	2.3%
20	Indiana	4,593,000,000	1.5%	14	Washington	6,270,000,000	2.1%
31	Iowa	2,730,000,000	0.9%	15	Missouri	6,010,000,000	2.0%
36	Kansas	2,265,000,000	0.8%	16	Maryland	5,573,000,000	1.9%
22	Kentucky	4,467,000,000	1.5%	17	Minnesota	5,548,000,000	1.9%
19	Louisiana	4,766,000,000	1.6%	18	Virginia	4,773,000,000	1.6%
34	Maine	2,481,000,000	0.8%	19	Louisiana	4,766,000,000	1.6%
16	Maryland	5,573,000,000	1.9%	20	Indiana	4,593,000,000	1.5%
13	Massachusetts	6,898,000,000	2.3%	21	South Carolina	4,469,000,000	1.5%
10	Michigan	8,566,000,000	2.9%	22	Kentucky	4,467,000,000	1.5%
17	Minnesota	5,548,000,000	1.9%	23	Arizona	4,352,000,000	1.5%
27	Mississippi	3,622,000,000	1.2%	24	Wisconsin	4,351,000,000	1.5%
15	Missouri	6,010,000,000	2.0%	25	Alabama	4,187,000,000	1.4%
47	Montana	720,000,000	0.2%	26	Connecticut	4,050,000,000	1.4%
38	Nebraska	1,599,000,000	0.5%	27	Mississippi	3,622,000,000	1.2%
40	Nevada	1,215,000,000	0.4%	28	Arkansas	3,340,000,000	1.1%
42	New Hampshire	1,102,000,000	0.4%	29	Oklahoma	3,185,000,000	1.1%
9	New Jersey	8,943,000,000	3.0%	30	Oregon	3,145,000,000	1.1%
33	New Mexico	2,527,000,000	0.9%	31	Iowa	2,730,000,000	0.9%
2	New York	30,209,000,000	10.2%	32	Colorado	2,697,000,000	0.9%
8	North Carolina	9,035,000,000	3.0%	33	New Mexico	2,527,000,000	0.9%
49	North Dakota	529,000,000	0.2%	34	Maine	2,481,000,000	0.8%
6	Ohio	13,439,000,000	4.5%	35	West Virginia	2,284,000,000	0.8%
29	Oklahoma	3,185,000,000	1.1%	36	Kansas	2,265,000,000	0.8%
30	Oregon	3,145,000,000	1.1%	37	Rhode Island	1,720,000,000	0.6%
4	Pennsylvania	17,622,000,000	5.9%	38	Nebraska	1,599,000,000	0.5%
37	Rhode Island	1,720,000,000	0.6%	39	Utah	1,550,000,000	0.5%
21	South Carolina	4,469,000,000	1.5%	40	Nevada	1,215,000,000	0.4%
48	South Dakota	695,000,000	0.2%	41	Idaho	1,134,000,000	0.4%
11	Tennessee	8,299,000,000	2.8%	42	New Hampshire	1,102,000,000	0.4%
3	Texas	17,702,000,000	6.0%	43	Alaska	1,070,000,000	0.4%
39	Utah	1,550,000,000	0.5%	44	Hawaii	994,000,000	0.3%
46	Vermont	900,000,000	0.3%	45	Delaware	962,000,000	0.3%
18	Virginia	4,773,000,000	1.6%	46	Vermont	900,000,000	0.3%
14	Washington	6,270,000,000	2.1%	47	Montana	720,000,000	0.2%
35	West Virginia	2,284,000,000	0.8%	48	South Dakota	695,000,000	0.2%
24	Wisconsin	4,351,000,000	1.5%	49	North Dakota	529,000,000	0.2%
50	Wyoming	409,000,000	0.1%	50	Wyoming	409,000,000	0.1%
					District of Columbia**	NA	NA

Source: National Association of State Budget Officers
"2005 State Expenditure Report" (http://www.nasbo.org)
Estimates for fiscal year 2006.
**Not available.*

Estimated Per Capita Medicaid Expenditures in 2006

National Per Capita = $992*

ALPHA ORDER

RANK	STATE	PER CAPITA
28	Alabama	$910
3	Alaska	1,597
46	Arizona	706
11	Arkansas	1,188
24	California	986
49	Colorado	567
13	Connecticut	1,156
14	Delaware	1,127
37	Florida	813
44	Georgia	740
40	Hawaii	773
40	Idaho	773
26	Illinois	974
45	Indiana	727
27	Iowa	915
36	Kansas	819
18	Kentucky	1,062
15	Louisiana	1,112
1	Maine	1,877
23	Maryland	992
17	Massachusetts	1,072
33	Michigan	848
16	Minnesota	1,074
10	Mississippi	1,244
20	Missouri	1,029
42	Montana	762
29	Nebraska	904
50	Nevada	487
34	New Hampshire	838
21	New Jersey	1,025
8	New Mexico	1,293
4	New York	1,565
22	North Carolina	1,020
35	North Dakota	832
12	Ohio	1,171
30	Oklahoma	890
32	Oregon	850
6	Pennsylvania	1,416
2	Rhode Island	1,611
19	South Carolina	1,034
31	South Dakota	889
7	Tennessee	1,374
43	Texas	753
48	Utah	608
5	Vermont	1,443
47	Virginia	625
25	Washington	980
9	West Virginia	1,256
39	Wisconsin	783
38	Wyoming	794

RANK ORDER

RANK	STATE	PER CAPITA
1	Maine	$1,877
2	Rhode Island	1,611
3	Alaska	1,597
4	New York	1,565
5	Vermont	1,443
6	Pennsylvania	1,416
7	Tennessee	1,374
8	New Mexico	1,293
9	West Virginia	1,256
10	Mississippi	1,244
11	Arkansas	1,188
12	Ohio	1,171
13	Connecticut	1,156
14	Delaware	1,127
15	Louisiana	1,112
16	Minnesota	1,074
17	Massachusetts	1,072
18	Kentucky	1,062
19	South Carolina	1,034
20	Missouri	1,029
21	New Jersey	1,025
22	North Carolina	1,020
23	Maryland	992
24	California	986
25	Washington	980
26	Illinois	974
27	Iowa	915
28	Alabama	910
29	Nebraska	904
30	Oklahoma	890
31	South Dakota	889
32	Oregon	850
33	Michigan	848
34	New Hampshire	838
35	North Dakota	832
36	Kansas	819
37	Florida	813
38	Wyoming	794
39	Wisconsin	783
40	Hawaii	773
40	Idaho	773
42	Montana	762
43	Texas	753
44	Georgia	740
45	Indiana	727
46	Arizona	706
47	Virginia	625
48	Utah	608
49	Colorado	567
50	Nevada	487

District of Columbia** NA

Source: Morgan Quitno Press using data from National Association of State Budget Officers
   "2005 State Expenditure Report" (http://www.nasbo.org)
*Estimates for fiscal year 2006.
**Not available.

Estimated Medicaid Expenditures as a Percent of Total Expenditures in 2006

National Percent = 22.2%*

ALPHA ORDER

RANK	STATE	PERCENT
19	Alabama	21.3
48	Alaska	10.8
33	Arizona	18.4
32	Arkansas	18.7
29	California	19.5
37	Colorado	17.6
35	Connecticut	18.1
42	Delaware	15.1
17	Florida	22.5
16	Georgia	23.4
49	Hawaii	10.4
24	Idaho	20.7
8	Illinois	26.8
35	Indiana	18.1
25	Iowa	20.5
31	Kansas	19.2
28	Kentucky	20.2
4	Louisiana	31.6
1	Maine	34.7
25	Maryland	20.5
13	Massachusetts	24.5
25	Michigan	20.5
20	Minnesota	21.0
7	Mississippi	28.8
5	Missouri	30.2
41	Montana	15.4
38	Nebraska	17.5
44	Nevada	14.5
14	New Hampshire	24.3
20	New Jersey	21.0
18	New Mexico	22.0
6	New York	29.0
9	North Carolina	26.7
45	North Dakota	14.1
14	Ohio	24.3
34	Oklahoma	18.3
40	Oregon	15.5
3	Pennsylvania	32.1
10	Rhode Island	25.3
12	South Carolina	24.9
20	South Dakota	21.0
2	Tennessee	32.4
11	Texas	25.2
39	Utah	17.1
20	Vermont	21.0
43	Virginia	15.0
30	Washington	19.3
47	West Virginia	11.6
46	Wisconsin	13.0
50	Wyoming	7.4

RANK ORDER

RANK	STATE	PERCENT
1	Maine	34.7
2	Tennessee	32.4
3	Pennsylvania	32.1
4	Louisiana	31.6
5	Missouri	30.2
6	New York	29.0
7	Mississippi	28.8
8	Illinois	26.8
9	North Carolina	26.7
10	Rhode Island	25.3
11	Texas	25.2
12	South Carolina	24.9
13	Massachusetts	24.5
14	New Hampshire	24.3
14	Ohio	24.3
16	Georgia	23.4
17	Florida	22.5
18	New Mexico	22.0
19	Alabama	21.3
20	Minnesota	21.0
20	New Jersey	21.0
20	South Dakota	21.0
20	Vermont	21.0
24	Idaho	20.7
25	Iowa	20.5
25	Maryland	20.5
25	Michigan	20.5
28	Kentucky	20.2
29	California	19.5
30	Washington	19.3
31	Kansas	19.2
32	Arkansas	18.7
33	Arizona	18.4
34	Oklahoma	18.3
35	Connecticut	18.1
35	Indiana	18.1
37	Colorado	17.6
38	Nebraska	17.5
39	Utah	17.1
40	Oregon	15.5
41	Montana	15.4
42	Delaware	15.1
43	Virginia	15.0
44	Nevada	14.5
45	North Dakota	14.1
46	Wisconsin	13.0
47	West Virginia	11.6
48	Alaska	10.8
49	Hawaii	10.4
50	Wyoming	7.4
	District of Columbia**	NA

Source: National Association of State Budget Officers
    "2005 State Expenditure Report" (http://www.nasbo.org)
*Estimates for fiscal year 2006.
**Not available.

Percent Change in Medicaid Expenditures: 2005 to 2006

National Percent Change = 5.0% Increase*

ALPHA ORDER				RANK ORDER		
RANK	STATE	PERCENT		RANK	STATE	PERCENT
35	Alabama	3.1		1	Maine	18.2
32	Alaska	4.2		1	New Jersey	18.2
45	Arizona	(2.0)		3	Iowa	17.0
8	Arkansas	11.1		4	Oklahoma	16.5
12	California	9.0		5	Massachusetts	15.0
17	Colorado	7.5		6	Nebraska	11.7
12	Connecticut	9.0		7	Utah	11.3
29	Delaware	4.9		8	Arkansas	11.1
23	Florida	5.9		9	Virginia	10.8
18	Georgia	7.0		10	South Dakota	10.7
12	Hawaii	9.0		11	West Virginia	9.4
16	Idaho	7.7		12	California	9.0
25	Illinois	5.6		12	Connecticut	9.0
38	Indiana	1.8		12	Hawaii	9.0
3	Iowa	17.0		15	Maryland	7.9
30	Kansas	4.8		16	Idaho	7.7
28	Kentucky	5.1		17	Colorado	7.5
48	Louisiana	(5.9)		18	Georgia	7.0
1	Maine	18.2		18	Ohio	7.0
15	Maryland	7.9		20	North Carolina	6.4
5	Massachusetts	15.0		21	Nevada	6.0
43	Michigan	(1.4)		21	Vermont	6.0
31	Minnesota	4.4		23	Florida	5.9
41	Mississippi	(0.4)		23	Pennsylvania	5.9
49	Missouri	(8.4)		25	Illinois	5.6
26	Montana	5.4		26	Montana	5.4
6	Nebraska	11.7		27	New Mexico	5.2
21	Nevada	6.0		28	Kentucky	5.1
50	New Hampshire	(9.6)		29	Delaware	4.9
1	New Jersey	18.2		30	Kansas	4.8
27	New Mexico	5.2		31	Minnesota	4.4
37	New York	2.9		32	Alaska	4.2
20	North Carolina	6.4		33	Rhode Island	3.5
35	North Dakota	3.1		33	South Carolina	3.5
18	Ohio	7.0		35	Alabama	3.1
4	Oklahoma	16.5		35	North Dakota	3.1
44	Oregon	(1.5)		37	New York	2.9
23	Pennsylvania	5.9		38	Indiana	1.8
33	Rhode Island	3.5		38	Washington	1.8
33	South Carolina	3.5		40	Texas	(0.1)
10	South Dakota	10.7		41	Mississippi	(0.4)
46	Tennessee	(3.2)		42	Wisconsin	(0.8)
40	Texas	(0.1)		43	Michigan	(1.4)
7	Utah	11.3		44	Oregon	(1.5)
21	Vermont	6.0		45	Arizona	(2.0)
9	Virginia	10.8		46	Tennessee	(3.2)
38	Washington	1.8		47	Wyoming	(4.0)
11	West Virginia	9.4		48	Louisiana	(5.9)
42	Wisconsin	(0.8)		49	Missouri	(8.4)
47	Wyoming	(4.0)		50	New Hampshire	(9.6)

District of Columbia**   NA

Source: National Association of State Budget Officers
"2005 State Expenditure Report" (http://www.nasbo.org)
*Estimates for fiscal year 2006.
**Not available.

Medicaid Expenditures in 2005

National Total = $300,723,913,000*

RANK	STATE	EXPENDITURES	% of USA
26	Alabama	$3,837,474,000	1.3%
44	Alaska	983,489,000	0.3%
15	Arizona	5,725,920,000	1.9%
29	Arkansas	2,809,921,000	0.9%
2	California	33,662,911,000	11.2%
30	Colorado	2,796,730,000	0.9%
25	Connecticut	4,027,600,000	1.3%
45	Delaware	868,668,000	0.3%
5	Florida	13,218,246,000	4.4%
13	Georgia	7,333,266,000	2.4%
42	Hawaii	1,033,126,000	0.3%
43	Idaho	1,008,635,000	0.3%
7	Illinois	10,785,543,000	3.6%
19	Indiana	5,234,230,000	1.7%
32	Iowa	2,376,772,000	0.8%
36	Kansas	1,967,791,000	0.7%
23	Kentucky	4,253,083,000	1.4%
18	Louisiana	5,313,395,000	1.8%
34	Maine	2,242,389,000	0.7%
20	Maryland	5,136,302,000	1.7%
8	Massachusetts	9,556,864,000	3.2%
10	Michigan	8,656,267,000	2.9%
17	Minnesota	5,525,771,000	1.8%
27	Mississippi	3,342,615,000	1.1%
14	Missouri	6,528,988,000	2.2%
47	Montana	696,069,000	0.2%
38	Nebraska	1,377,176,000	0.5%
41	Nevada	1,184,065,000	0.4%
40	New Hampshire	1,244,583,000	0.4%
12	New Jersey	7,508,874,000	2.5%
33	New Mexico	2,363,670,000	0.8%
1	New York	42,752,347,000	14.2%
9	North Carolina	8,844,880,000	2.9%
49	North Dakota	508,465,000	0.2%
6	Ohio	11,572,449,000	3.8%
31	Oklahoma	2,712,780,000	0.9%
28	Oregon	2,810,668,000	0.9%
4	Pennsylvania	15,786,514,000	5.2%
37	Rhode Island	1,671,398,000	0.6%
24	South Carolina	4,068,509,000	1.4%
48	South Dakota	608,251,000	0.2%
11	Tennessee	7,557,404,000	2.5%
3	Texas	17,264,066,000	5.7%
39	Utah	1,341,242,000	0.4%
46	Vermont	859,484,000	0.3%
22	Virginia	4,425,081,000	1.5%
16	Washington	5,700,851,000	1.9%
35	West Virginia	2,161,356,000	0.7%
21	Wisconsin	4,751,657,000	1.6%
50	Wyoming	405,216,000	0.1%

RANK	STATE	EXPENDITURES	% of USA
1	New York	$42,752,347,000	14.2%
2	California	33,662,911,000	11.2%
3	Texas	17,264,066,000	5.7%
4	Pennsylvania	15,786,514,000	5.2%
5	Florida	13,218,246,000	4.4%
6	Ohio	11,572,449,000	3.8%
7	Illinois	10,785,543,000	3.6%
8	Massachusetts	9,556,864,000	3.2%
9	North Carolina	8,844,880,000	2.9%
10	Michigan	8,656,267,000	2.9%
11	Tennessee	7,557,404,000	2.5%
12	New Jersey	7,508,874,000	2.5%
13	Georgia	7,333,266,000	2.4%
14	Missouri	6,528,988,000	2.2%
15	Arizona	5,725,920,000	1.9%
16	Washington	5,700,851,000	1.9%
17	Minnesota	5,525,771,000	1.8%
18	Louisiana	5,313,395,000	1.8%
19	Indiana	5,234,230,000	1.7%
20	Maryland	5,136,302,000	1.7%
21	Wisconsin	4,751,657,000	1.6%
22	Virginia	4,425,081,000	1.5%
23	Kentucky	4,253,083,000	1.4%
24	South Carolina	4,068,509,000	1.4%
25	Connecticut	4,027,600,000	1.3%
26	Alabama	3,837,474,000	1.3%
27	Mississippi	3,342,615,000	1.1%
28	Oregon	2,810,668,000	0.9%
29	Arkansas	2,809,921,000	0.9%
30	Colorado	2,796,730,000	0.9%
31	Oklahoma	2,712,780,000	0.9%
32	Iowa	2,376,772,000	0.8%
33	New Mexico	2,363,670,000	0.8%
34	Maine	2,242,389,000	0.7%
35	West Virginia	2,161,356,000	0.7%
36	Kansas	1,967,791,000	0.7%
37	Rhode Island	1,671,398,000	0.6%
38	Nebraska	1,377,176,000	0.5%
39	Utah	1,341,242,000	0.4%
40	New Hampshire	1,244,583,000	0.4%
41	Nevada	1,184,065,000	0.4%
42	Hawaii	1,033,126,000	0.3%
43	Idaho	1,008,635,000	0.3%
44	Alaska	983,489,000	0.3%
45	Delaware	868,668,000	0.3%
46	Vermont	859,484,000	0.3%
47	Montana	696,069,000	0.2%
48	South Dakota	608,251,000	0.2%
49	North Dakota	508,465,000	0.2%
50	Wyoming	405,216,000	0.1%
	District of Columbia	1,254,160,000	0.4%

*Source: U.S. Department of Health and Human Services, Centers for Medicare and Medicaid Services
"2006 Data Compendium" (http://www.cms.hhs.gov/DataCompendium/18_2006_Data_Compendium.asp)*
*For fiscal year 2005. National total includes $1,066,702,000 in expenditures in U.S. territories. Net expenditures reported from Form CMS-64. Excludes ADM, Medicaid SCHIP expansions and CMS adjustments.

Per Capita Medicaid Expenditures in 2005

National Per Capita = $1,011*

ALPHA ORDER

RANK	STATE	PER CAPITA
31	Alabama	$844
5	Alaska	1,483
21	Arizona	962
19	Arkansas	1,012
24	California	931
47	Colorado	600
12	Connecticut	1,151
16	Delaware	1,032
44	Florida	744
34	Georgia	803
33	Hawaii	811
46	Idaho	706
30	Illinois	845
32	Indiana	835
35	Iowa	801
45	Kansas	716
18	Kentucky	1,019
11	Louisiana	1,179
2	Maine	1,701
25	Maryland	919
4	Massachusetts	1,486
29	Michigan	857
15	Minnesota	1,078
13	Mississippi	1,149
14	Missouri	1,126
43	Montana	745
39	Nebraska	783
50	Nevada	491
23	New Hampshire	952
27	New Jersey	863
9	New Mexico	1,227
1	New York	2,213
17	North Carolina	1,020
35	North Dakota	801
20	Ohio	1,009
41	Oklahoma	766
40	Oregon	772
7	Pennsylvania	1,273
3	Rhode Island	1,557
22	South Carolina	958
38	South Dakota	785
8	Tennessee	1,269
42	Texas	753
49	Utah	539
6	Vermont	1,381
48	Virginia	585
26	Washington	906
10	West Virginia	1,191
28	Wisconsin	860
37	Wyoming	796

RANK ORDER

RANK	STATE	PER CAPITA
1	New York	$2,213
2	Maine	1,701
3	Rhode Island	1,557
4	Massachusetts	1,486
5	Alaska	1,483
6	Vermont	1,381
7	Pennsylvania	1,273
8	Tennessee	1,269
9	New Mexico	1,227
10	West Virginia	1,191
11	Louisiana	1,179
12	Connecticut	1,151
13	Mississippi	1,149
14	Missouri	1,126
15	Minnesota	1,078
16	Delaware	1,032
17	North Carolina	1,020
18	Kentucky	1,019
19	Arkansas	1,012
20	Ohio	1,009
21	Arizona	962
22	South Carolina	958
23	New Hampshire	952
24	California	931
25	Maryland	919
26	Washington	906
27	New Jersey	863
28	Wisconsin	860
29	Michigan	857
30	Illinois	845
31	Alabama	844
32	Indiana	835
33	Hawaii	811
34	Georgia	803
35	Iowa	801
35	North Dakota	801
37	Wyoming	796
38	South Dakota	785
39	Nebraska	783
40	Oregon	772
41	Oklahoma	766
42	Texas	753
43	Montana	745
44	Florida	744
45	Kansas	716
46	Idaho	706
47	Colorado	600
48	Virginia	585
49	Utah	539
50	Nevada	491

District of Columbia 2,155

Source: MQ Press using data from U.S. Dept of Health & Human Services, Centers for Medicare and Medicaid Services "2006 Data Compendium" (http://www.cms.hhs.gov/DataCompendium/18_2006_Data_Compendium.asp)
*Figures for fiscal year 2005. National figure does not include expenditures or enrollees in U.S. territories. Net expenditures reported from Form CMS-64. Excludes ADM, Medicaid SCHIP expansions and CMS adjustments.

Medicaid Expenditures per Beneficiary in 2005

National Rate = $6,587 per Beneficiary*

ALPHA ORDER

RANK	STATE	PER BENEFICIARY
49	Alabama	$4,684
3	Alaska	9,979
38	Arizona	5,753
50	Arkansas	4,427
44	California	5,172
16	Colorado	7,187
4	Connecticut	9,838
32	Delaware	6,065
39	Florida	5,725
43	Georgia	5,194
45	Hawaii	5,087
34	Idaho	5,883
40	Illinois	5,675
29	Indiana	6,274
15	Iowa	7,262
19	Kansas	6,963
33	Kentucky	6,005
42	Louisiana	5,357
11	Maine	8,914
17	Maryland	7,163
7	Massachusetts	9,306
35	Michigan	5,877
5	Minnesota	9,595
41	Mississippi	5,475
13	Missouri	7,390
12	Montana	8,362
23	Nebraska	6,619
21	Nevada	6,818
1	New Hampshire	11,448
10	New Jersey	9,035
36	New Mexico	5,802
2	New York	10,207
18	North Carolina	7,073
6	North Dakota	9,362
22	Ohio	6,699
48	Oklahoma	4,743
20	Oregon	6,881
9	Pennsylvania	9,119
8	Rhode Island	9,192
46	South Carolina	4,886
47	South Dakota	4,794
31	Tennessee	6,185
30	Texas	6,232
27	Utah	6,488
24	Vermont	6,597
28	Virginia	6,343
25	Washington	6,563
14	West Virginia	7,357
37	Wisconsin	5,788
26	Wyoming	6,549

RANK ORDER

RANK	STATE	PER BENEFICIARY
1	New Hampshire	$11,448
2	New York	10,207
3	Alaska	9,979
4	Connecticut	9,838
5	Minnesota	9,595
6	North Dakota	9,362
7	Massachusetts	9,306
8	Rhode Island	9,192
9	Pennsylvania	9,119
10	New Jersey	9,035
11	Maine	8,914
12	Montana	8,362
13	Missouri	7,390
14	West Virginia	7,357
15	Iowa	7,262
16	Colorado	7,187
17	Maryland	7,163
18	North Carolina	7,073
19	Kansas	6,963
20	Oregon	6,881
21	Nevada	6,818
22	Ohio	6,699
23	Nebraska	6,619
24	Vermont	6,597
25	Washington	6,563
26	Wyoming	6,549
27	Utah	6,488
28	Virginia	6,343
29	Indiana	6,274
30	Texas	6,232
31	Tennessee	6,185
32	Delaware	6,065
33	Kentucky	6,005
34	Idaho	5,883
35	Michigan	5,877
36	New Mexico	5,802
37	Wisconsin	5,788
38	Arizona	5,753
39	Florida	5,725
40	Illinois	5,675
41	Mississippi	5,475
42	Louisiana	5,357
43	Georgia	5,194
44	California	5,172
45	Hawaii	5,087
46	South Carolina	4,886
47	South Dakota	4,794
48	Oklahoma	4,743
49	Alabama	4,684
50	Arkansas	4,427

| | District of Columbia | 8,818 |

Source: MQ Press using data from U.S. Dept of Health & Human Services, Centers for Medicare and Medicaid Services "2006 Data Compendium" (http://www.cms.hhs.gov/DataCompendium/18_2006_Data_Compendium.asp)
Figures for fiscal year 2005. National figure includes expenditures and enrollees in U.S. territories. Net expenditures reported from Form CMS-64. Excludes ADM, Medicaid SCHIP expansions and CMS adjustments.

Federal Medicaid Matching Fund Rate for 2007

National Average = 71.95% of States' Funds Matched by Federal Government*

ALPHA ORDER

RANK	STATE	RATE
11	Alabama	78.20
37	Alaska	65.75
13	Arizona	76.53
2	Arkansas	81.36
39	California	65.00
39	Colorado	65.00
39	Connecticut	65.00
39	Delaware	65.00
28	Florida	71.13
21	Georgia	73.38
30	Hawaii	70.29
5	Idaho	79.25
39	Illinois	65.00
19	Indiana	73.83
20	Iowa	73.39
25	Kansas	72.18
8	Kentucky	78.71
7	Louisiana	78.78
17	Maine	74.29
39	Maryland	65.00
39	Massachusetts	65.00
32	Michigan	69.47
39	Minnesota	65.00
1	Mississippi	83.12
22	Missouri	73.12
10	Montana	78.38
29	Nebraska	70.55
34	Nevada	67.75
39	New Hampshire	65.00
39	New Jersey	65.00
4	New Mexico	80.35
39	New York	65.00
15	North Carolina	75.16
14	North Dakota	75.30
26	Ohio	71.76
12	Oklahoma	77.70
23	Oregon	72.75
33	Pennsylvania	68.07
36	Rhode Island	66.65
9	South Carolina	78.68
18	South Dakota	74.04
16	Tennessee	74.56
24	Texas	72.55
6	Utah	79.10
27	Vermont	71.25
39	Virginia	65.00
38	Washington	65.08
3	West Virginia	80.97
31	Wisconsin	70.23
35	Wyoming	67.04

RANK ORDER

RANK	STATE	RATE
1	Mississippi	83.12
2	Arkansas	81.36
3	West Virginia	80.97
4	New Mexico	80.35
5	Idaho	79.25
6	Utah	79.10
7	Louisiana	78.78
8	Kentucky	78.71
9	South Carolina	78.68
10	Montana	78.38
11	Alabama	78.20
12	Oklahoma	77.70
13	Arizona	76.53
14	North Dakota	75.30
15	North Carolina	75.16
16	Tennessee	74.56
17	Maine	74.29
18	South Dakota	74.04
19	Indiana	73.83
20	Iowa	73.39
21	Georgia	73.38
22	Missouri	73.12
23	Oregon	72.75
24	Texas	72.55
25	Kansas	72.18
26	Ohio	71.76
27	Vermont	71.25
28	Florida	71.13
29	Nebraska	70.55
30	Hawaii	70.29
31	Wisconsin	70.23
32	Michigan	69.47
33	Pennsylvania	68.07
34	Nevada	67.75
35	Wyoming	67.04
36	Rhode Island	66.65
37	Alaska	65.75
38	Washington	65.08
39	California	65.00
39	Colorado	65.00
39	Connecticut	65.00
39	Delaware	65.00
39	Illinois	65.00
39	Maryland	65.00
39	Massachusetts	65.00
39	Minnesota	65.00
39	New Hampshire	65.00
39	New Jersey	65.00
39	New York	65.00
39	Virginia	65.00
	District of Columbia	79.00

Source: U.S. Department of Health and Human Services, Centers for Medicare and Medicaid Services
    "Enhanced Federal Medical Assistance Percentages" (http://aspe.os.dhhs.gov/health/fmap07.htm)
*For fiscal year 2007. These are "enhanced" matching rates established by the Children's Health Insurance
Program, signed into law in August 1997. Sixty-five percent is the minimum. National average is a simple average of
the 51 individual rates and is not weighted for population or funds.

State and Local Government Expenditures for Hospitals in 2004

National Total = $96,551,290,000*

ALPHA ORDER

RANK	STATE	EXPENDITURES	% of USA
7	Alabama	$3,497,716,000	3.6%
44	Alaska	96,435,000	0.1%
32	Arizona	660,279,000	0.7%
30	Arkansas	729,555,000	0.8%
1	California	13,749,224,000	14.2%
22	Colorado	1,450,407,000	1.5%
23	Connecticut	1,408,929,000	1.5%
47	Delaware	56,802,000	0.1%
4	Florida	5,230,882,000	5.4%
6	Georgia	3,503,953,000	3.6%
41	Hawaii	244,076,000	0.3%
36	Idaho	540,509,000	0.6%
15	Illinois	2,297,478,000	2.4%
13	Indiana	2,597,071,000	2.7%
20	Iowa	1,758,467,000	1.8%
33	Kansas	635,721,000	0.7%
27	Kentucky	967,492,000	1.0%
8	Louisiana	3,051,246,000	3.2%
42	Maine	116,832,000	0.1%
39	Maryland	405,108,000	0.4%
25	Massachusetts	1,136,044,000	1.2%
12	Michigan	2,611,002,000	2.7%
24	Minnesota	1,323,069,000	1.4%
18	Mississippi	2,040,983,000	2.1%
17	Missouri	2,050,113,000	2.1%
45	Montana	82,442,000	0.1%
35	Nebraska	544,390,000	0.6%
31	Nevada	664,843,000	0.7%
48	New Hampshire	50,196,000	0.1%
21	New Jersey	1,653,932,000	1.7%
34	New Mexico	575,025,000	0.6%
2	New York	9,817,622,000	10.2%
5	North Carolina	3,708,020,000	3.8%
49	North Dakota	44,063,000	0.0%
10	Ohio	2,816,266,000	2.9%
29	Oklahoma	841,098,000	0.9%
28	Oregon	893,412,000	0.9%
19	Pennsylvania	1,989,626,000	2.1%
43	Rhode Island	108,737,000	0.1%
11	South Carolina	2,635,877,000	2.7%
46	South Dakota	76,063,000	0.1%
14	Tennessee	2,484,812,000	2.6%
3	Texas	7,890,088,000	8.2%
37	Utah	533,144,000	0.6%
50	Vermont	14,621,000	0.0%
16	Virginia	2,194,282,000	2.3%
9	Washington	2,825,688,000	2.9%
40	West Virginia	283,023,000	0.3%
26	Wisconsin	980,842,000	1.0%
38	Wyoming	521,225,000	0.5%

RANK ORDER

RANK	STATE	EXPENDITURES	% of USA
1	California	$13,749,224,000	14.2%
2	New York	9,817,622,000	10.2%
3	Texas	7,890,088,000	8.2%
4	Florida	5,230,882,000	5.4%
5	North Carolina	3,708,020,000	3.8%
6	Georgia	3,503,953,000	3.6%
7	Alabama	3,497,716,000	3.6%
8	Louisiana	3,051,246,000	3.2%
9	Washington	2,825,688,000	2.9%
10	Ohio	2,816,266,000	2.9%
11	South Carolina	2,635,877,000	2.7%
12	Michigan	2,611,002,000	2.7%
13	Indiana	2,597,071,000	2.7%
14	Tennessee	2,484,812,000	2.6%
15	Illinois	2,297,478,000	2.4%
16	Virginia	2,194,282,000	2.3%
17	Missouri	2,050,113,000	2.1%
18	Mississippi	2,040,983,000	2.1%
19	Pennsylvania	1,989,626,000	2.1%
20	Iowa	1,758,467,000	1.8%
21	New Jersey	1,653,932,000	1.7%
22	Colorado	1,450,407,000	1.5%
23	Connecticut	1,408,929,000	1.5%
24	Minnesota	1,323,069,000	1.4%
25	Massachusetts	1,136,044,000	1.2%
26	Wisconsin	980,842,000	1.0%
27	Kentucky	967,492,000	1.0%
28	Oregon	893,412,000	0.9%
29	Oklahoma	841,098,000	0.9%
30	Arkansas	729,555,000	0.8%
31	Nevada	664,843,000	0.7%
32	Arizona	660,279,000	0.7%
33	Kansas	635,721,000	0.7%
34	New Mexico	575,025,000	0.6%
35	Nebraska	544,390,000	0.6%
36	Idaho	540,509,000	0.6%
37	Utah	533,144,000	0.6%
38	Wyoming	521,225,000	0.5%
39	Maryland	405,108,000	0.4%
40	West Virginia	283,023,000	0.3%
41	Hawaii	244,076,000	0.3%
42	Maine	116,832,000	0.1%
43	Rhode Island	108,737,000	0.1%
44	Alaska	96,435,000	0.1%
45	Montana	82,442,000	0.1%
46	South Dakota	76,063,000	0.1%
47	Delaware	56,802,000	0.1%
48	New Hampshire	50,196,000	0.1%
49	North Dakota	44,063,000	0.0%
50	Vermont	14,621,000	0.0%
	District of Columbia	162,560,000	0.2%

Source: U.S. Bureau of the Census, Governments Division
"State and Local Government Finances 2003-2004" (http://www.census.gov/govs/www/estimate04.html)
*Financing, construction, acquisition, maintenance or operation of hospital facilities, provision of hospital care and support of public or private hospitals.

Per Capita State and Local Government Expenditures for Hospitals in 2004

National Per Capita = $329*

ALPHA ORDER

RANK	STATE	PER CAPITA
2	Alabama	$774
40	Alaska	147
41	Arizona	115
24	Arkansas	266
15	California	384
18	Colorado	315
12	Connecticut	403
47	Delaware	69
21	Florida	301
13	Georgia	392
33	Hawaii	194
14	Idaho	388
35	Illinois	181
11	Indiana	417
6	Iowa	595
31	Kansas	232
30	Kentucky	234
4	Louisiana	679
44	Maine	89
46	Maryland	73
37	Massachusetts	177
26	Michigan	259
25	Minnesota	260
3	Mississippi	706
16	Missouri	356
44	Montana	89
19	Nebraska	312
23	Nevada	285
49	New Hampshire	39
34	New Jersey	191
20	New Mexico	303
7	New York	509
9	North Carolina	435
47	North Dakota	69
28	Ohio	246
29	Oklahoma	239
27	Oregon	249
38	Pennsylvania	161
42	Rhode Island	101
5	South Carolina	628
43	South Dakota	99
10	Tennessee	422
17	Texas	350
32	Utah	220
50	Vermont	24
22	Virginia	294
8	Washington	455
39	West Virginia	156
36	Wisconsin	178
1	Wyoming	1,031

RANK ORDER

RANK	STATE	PER CAPITA
1	Wyoming	$1,031
2	Alabama	774
3	Mississippi	706
4	Louisiana	679
5	South Carolina	628
6	Iowa	595
7	New York	509
8	Washington	455
9	North Carolina	435
10	Tennessee	422
11	Indiana	417
12	Connecticut	403
13	Georgia	392
14	Idaho	388
15	California	384
16	Missouri	356
17	Texas	350
18	Colorado	315
19	Nebraska	312
20	New Mexico	303
21	Florida	301
22	Virginia	294
23	Nevada	285
24	Arkansas	266
25	Minnesota	260
26	Michigan	259
27	Oregon	249
28	Ohio	246
29	Oklahoma	239
30	Kentucky	234
31	Kansas	232
32	Utah	220
33	Hawaii	194
34	New Jersey	191
35	Illinois	181
36	Wisconsin	178
37	Massachusetts	177
38	Pennsylvania	161
39	West Virginia	156
40	Alaska	147
41	Arizona	115
42	Rhode Island	101
43	South Dakota	99
44	Maine	89
44	Montana	89
46	Maryland	73
47	Delaware	69
47	North Dakota	69
49	New Hampshire	39
50	Vermont	24

District of Columbia 280

Source: Morgan Quitno Press using data from U.S. Bureau of the Census, Governments Division
 "State and Local Government Finances 2003-2004" (http://www.census.gov/govs/www/estimate04.html)
*Financing, construction, acquisition, maintenance or operation of hospital facilities, provision of hospital care and support of public or private hospitals.

Percent of State and Local Government Expenditures Used for Hospitals in 2004
National Percent = 5.1%*

RANK	STATE	PERCENT
1	Alabama	12.9
46	Alaska	1.1
40	Arizona	2.2
22	Arkansas	5.0
17	California	5.3
19	Colorado	5.1
15	Connecticut	5.6
48	Delaware	0.9
18	Florida	5.2
11	Georgia	7.0
34	Hawaii	2.8
10	Idaho	7.2
33	Illinois	2.9
9	Indiana	7.3
6	Iowa	9.6
28	Kansas	3.9
26	Kentucky	4.1
4	Louisiana	11.2
44	Maine	1.3
45	Maryland	1.2
39	Massachusetts	2.3
28	Michigan	3.9
32	Minnesota	3.6
2	Mississippi	11.8
12	Missouri	6.6
42	Montana	1.5
19	Nebraska	5.1
23	Nevada	4.9
49	New Hampshire	0.7
35	New Jersey	2.7
24	New Mexico	4.6
15	New York	5.6
8	North Carolina	7.6
46	North Dakota	1.1
30	Ohio	3.8
24	Oklahoma	4.6
27	Oregon	4.0
38	Pennsylvania	2.5
43	Rhode Island	1.4
5	South Carolina	10.3
41	South Dakota	1.8
7	Tennessee	7.9
14	Texas	6.4
30	Utah	3.8
50	Vermont	0.3
19	Virginia	5.1
12	Washington	6.6
35	West Virginia	2.7
35	Wisconsin	2.7
3	Wyoming	11.5

RANK	STATE	PERCENT
1	Alabama	12.9
2	Mississippi	11.8
3	Wyoming	11.5
4	Louisiana	11.2
5	South Carolina	10.3
6	Iowa	9.6
7	Tennessee	7.9
8	North Carolina	7.6
9	Indiana	7.3
10	Idaho	7.2
11	Georgia	7.0
12	Missouri	6.6
12	Washington	6.6
14	Texas	6.4
15	Connecticut	5.6
15	New York	5.6
17	California	5.3
18	Florida	5.2
19	Colorado	5.1
19	Nebraska	5.1
19	Virginia	5.1
22	Arkansas	5.0
23	Nevada	4.9
24	New Mexico	4.6
24	Oklahoma	4.6
26	Kentucky	4.1
27	Oregon	4.0
28	Kansas	3.9
28	Michigan	3.9
30	Ohio	3.8
30	Utah	3.8
32	Minnesota	3.6
33	Illinois	2.9
34	Hawaii	2.8
35	New Jersey	2.7
35	West Virginia	2.7
35	Wisconsin	2.7
38	Pennsylvania	2.5
39	Massachusetts	2.3
40	Arizona	2.2
41	South Dakota	1.8
42	Montana	1.5
43	Rhode Island	1.4
44	Maine	1.3
45	Maryland	1.2
46	Alaska	1.1
46	North Dakota	1.1
48	Delaware	0.9
49	New Hampshire	0.7
50	Vermont	0.3

District of Columbia	2.4

Source: Morgan Quitno Press using data from U.S. Bureau of the Census, Governments Division
"State and Local Government Finances 2003-2004" (http://www.census.gov/govs/www/estimate04.html)
As a percent of direct general expenditures. Financing, construction, acquisition, maintenance or operation of hospital facilities, provision of hospital care and support of public or private hospitals.

State and Local Government Expenditures for Health Programs in 2004

National Total = $63,124,983,000*

ALPHA ORDER

RANK	STATE	EXPENDITURES	% of USA
18	Alabama	$1,069,953,000	1.7%
46	Alaska	144,673,000	0.2%
12	Arizona	1,349,922,000	2.1%
34	Arkansas	345,383,000	0.5%
1	California	10,531,522,000	16.7%
19	Colorado	976,499,000	1.5%
35	Connecticut	342,936,000	0.5%
38	Delaware	291,692,000	0.5%
4	Florida	3,548,287,000	5.6%
11	Georgia	1,592,355,000	2.5%
32	Hawaii	429,591,000	0.7%
45	Idaho	156,619,000	0.2%
7	Illinois	3,101,551,000	4.9%
25	Indiana	727,338,000	1.2%
33	Iowa	372,775,000	0.6%
28	Kansas	472,836,000	0.7%
27	Kentucky	579,919,000	0.9%
26	Louisiana	615,328,000	1.0%
31	Maine	461,868,000	0.7%
13	Maryland	1,331,345,000	2.1%
22	Massachusetts	791,043,000	1.3%
2	Michigan	4,209,473,000	6.7%
23	Minnesota	765,374,000	1.2%
37	Mississippi	300,764,000	0.5%
20	Missouri	973,117,000	1.5%
41	Montana	272,181,000	0.4%
43	Nebraska	183,897,000	0.3%
36	Nevada	315,958,000	0.5%
47	New Hampshire	127,666,000	0.2%
17	New Jersey	1,156,552,000	1.8%
40	New Mexico	284,061,000	0.4%
3	New York	4,107,146,000	6.5%
9	North Carolina	2,243,408,000	3.6%
50	North Dakota	71,194,000	0.1%
5	Ohio	3,364,029,000	5.3%
30	Oklahoma	464,157,000	0.7%
24	Oregon	737,445,000	1.2%
6	Pennsylvania	3,275,115,000	5.2%
42	Rhode Island	212,494,000	0.3%
21	South Carolina	814,211,000	1.3%
48	South Dakota	111,758,000	0.2%
16	Tennessee	1,238,264,000	2.0%
8	Texas	2,411,108,000	3.8%
29	Utah	471,837,000	0.7%
49	Vermont	96,624,000	0.2%
14	Virginia	1,303,369,000	2.1%
10	Washington	1,928,177,000	3.1%
39	West Virginia	287,132,000	0.5%
15	Wisconsin	1,298,765,000	2.1%
44	Wyoming	179,211,000	0.3%

RANK ORDER

RANK	STATE	EXPENDITURES	% of USA
1	California	$10,531,522,000	16.7%
2	Michigan	4,209,473,000	6.7%
3	New York	4,107,146,000	6.5%
4	Florida	3,548,287,000	5.6%
5	Ohio	3,364,029,000	5.3%
6	Pennsylvania	3,275,115,000	5.2%
7	Illinois	3,101,551,000	4.9%
8	Texas	2,411,108,000	3.8%
9	North Carolina	2,243,408,000	3.6%
10	Washington	1,928,177,000	3.1%
11	Georgia	1,592,355,000	2.5%
12	Arizona	1,349,922,000	2.1%
13	Maryland	1,331,345,000	2.1%
14	Virginia	1,303,369,000	2.1%
15	Wisconsin	1,298,765,000	2.1%
16	Tennessee	1,238,264,000	2.0%
17	New Jersey	1,156,552,000	1.8%
18	Alabama	1,069,953,000	1.7%
19	Colorado	976,499,000	1.5%
20	Missouri	973,117,000	1.5%
21	South Carolina	814,211,000	1.3%
22	Massachusetts	791,043,000	1.3%
23	Minnesota	765,374,000	1.2%
24	Oregon	737,445,000	1.2%
25	Indiana	727,338,000	1.2%
26	Louisiana	615,328,000	1.0%
27	Kentucky	579,919,000	0.9%
28	Kansas	472,836,000	0.7%
29	Utah	471,837,000	0.7%
30	Oklahoma	464,157,000	0.7%
31	Maine	461,868,000	0.7%
32	Hawaii	429,591,000	0.7%
33	Iowa	372,775,000	0.6%
34	Arkansas	345,383,000	0.5%
35	Connecticut	342,936,000	0.5%
36	Nevada	315,958,000	0.5%
37	Mississippi	300,764,000	0.5%
38	Delaware	291,692,000	0.5%
39	West Virginia	287,132,000	0.5%
40	New Mexico	284,061,000	0.4%
41	Montana	272,181,000	0.4%
42	Rhode Island	212,494,000	0.3%
43	Nebraska	183,897,000	0.3%
44	Wyoming	179,211,000	0.3%
45	Idaho	156,619,000	0.2%
46	Alaska	144,673,000	0.2%
47	New Hampshire	127,666,000	0.2%
48	South Dakota	111,758,000	0.2%
49	Vermont	96,624,000	0.2%
50	North Dakota	71,194,000	0.1%
	District of Columbia	687,061,000	1.1%

Source: U.S. Bureau of the Census, Governments Division
"State and Local Government Finances 2003-2004" (http://www.census.gov/govs/www/estimate04.html)
*Includes outpatient health services other than hospital care, research and education, categorical health programs, treatment and immunization clinics, nursing and environmental health activities. Includes capital expenditures.

Per Capita State and Local Government Expenditures for Health Programs in 2004
National Per Capita = $215*

ALPHA ORDER

RANK	STATE	PER CAPITA
14	Alabama	$237
17	Alaska	220
16	Arizona	235
40	Arkansas	126
7	California	294
19	Colorado	212
49	Connecticut	98
3	Delaware	352
22	Florida	204
26	Georgia	178
5	Hawaii	341
44	Idaho	112
12	Illinois	244
43	Indiana	117
40	Iowa	126
28	Kansas	173
35	Kentucky	140
36	Louisiana	137
3	Maine	352
13	Maryland	240
42	Massachusetts	123
1	Michigan	417
32	Minnesota	150
48	Mississippi	104
29	Missouri	169
7	Montana	294
47	Nebraska	105
37	Nevada	135
49	New Hampshire	98
38	New Jersey	133
33	New Mexico	149
18	New York	213
11	North Carolina	263
44	North Dakota	112
7	Ohio	294
39	Oklahoma	132
21	Oregon	205
10	Pennsylvania	265
23	Rhode Island	197
25	South Carolina	194
34	South Dakota	145
20	Tennessee	210
46	Texas	107
24	Utah	195
31	Vermont	156
27	Virginia	174
6	Washington	311
30	West Virginia	159
15	Wisconsin	236
2	Wyoming	354

RANK ORDER

RANK	STATE	PER CAPITA
1	Michigan	$417
2	Wyoming	354
3	Delaware	352
3	Maine	352
5	Hawaii	341
6	Washington	311
7	California	294
7	Montana	294
7	Ohio	294
10	Pennsylvania	265
11	North Carolina	263
12	Illinois	244
13	Maryland	240
14	Alabama	237
15	Wisconsin	236
16	Arizona	235
17	Alaska	220
18	New York	213
19	Colorado	212
20	Tennessee	210
21	Oregon	205
22	Florida	204
23	Rhode Island	197
24	Utah	195
25	South Carolina	194
26	Georgia	178
27	Virginia	174
28	Kansas	173
29	Missouri	169
30	West Virginia	159
31	Vermont	156
32	Minnesota	150
33	New Mexico	149
34	South Dakota	145
35	Kentucky	140
36	Louisiana	137
37	Nevada	135
38	New Jersey	133
39	Oklahoma	132
40	Arkansas	126
40	Iowa	126
42	Massachusetts	123
43	Indiana	117
44	Idaho	112
44	North Dakota	112
46	Texas	107
47	Nebraska	105
48	Mississippi	104
49	Connecticut	98
49	New Hampshire	98
	District of Columbia	1,185

Source: Morgan Quitno Press using data from U.S. Bureau of the Census, Governments Division
"State and Local Government Finances 2003-2004" (http://www.census.gov/govs/www/estimate04.html)
*Includes outpatient health services other than hospital care, research and education, categorical health programs, treatment and immunization clinics, nursing and environmental health activities. Includes capital expenditures.

Percent of State and Local Government Expenditures
Used for Health Programs in 2004
National Percent = 3.3%*

ALPHA ORDER

RANK	STATE	PERCENT
13	Alabama	3.9
44	Alaska	1.7
7	Arizona	4.5
32	Arkansas	2.4
11	California	4.0
19	Colorado	3.4
50	Connecticut	1.4
5	Delaware	4.7
17	Florida	3.5
22	Georgia	3.2
2	Hawaii	5.0
38	Idaho	2.1
13	Illinois	3.9
40	Indiana	2.0
40	Iowa	2.0
26	Kansas	2.9
31	Kentucky	2.5
33	Louisiana	2.3
2	Maine	5.0
13	Maryland	3.9
49	Massachusetts	1.6
1	Michigan	6.2
38	Minnesota	2.1
44	Mississippi	1.7
24	Missouri	3.1
4	Montana	4.9
44	Nebraska	1.7
33	Nevada	2.3
44	New Hampshire	1.7
42	New Jersey	1.9
33	New Mexico	2.3
33	New York	2.3
6	North Carolina	4.6
44	North Dakota	1.7
7	Ohio	4.5
30	Oklahoma	2.6
21	Oregon	3.3
10	Pennsylvania	4.1
27	Rhode Island	2.8
22	South Carolina	3.2
28	South Dakota	2.7
13	Tennessee	3.9
42	Texas	1.9
19	Utah	3.4
37	Vermont	2.2
25	Virginia	3.0
7	Washington	4.5
28	West Virginia	2.7
17	Wisconsin	3.5
11	Wyoming	4.0

RANK ORDER

RANK	STATE	PERCENT
1	Michigan	6.2
2	Hawaii	5.0
2	Maine	5.0
4	Montana	4.9
5	Delaware	4.7
6	North Carolina	4.6
7	Arizona	4.5
7	Ohio	4.5
7	Washington	4.5
10	Pennsylvania	4.1
11	California	4.0
11	Wyoming	4.0
13	Alabama	3.9
13	Illinois	3.9
13	Maryland	3.9
13	Tennessee	3.9
17	Florida	3.5
17	Wisconsin	3.5
19	Colorado	3.4
19	Utah	3.4
21	Oregon	3.3
22	Georgia	3.2
22	South Carolina	3.2
24	Missouri	3.1
25	Virginia	3.0
26	Kansas	2.9
27	Rhode Island	2.8
28	South Dakota	2.7
28	West Virginia	2.7
30	Oklahoma	2.6
31	Kentucky	2.5
32	Arkansas	2.4
33	Louisiana	2.3
33	Nevada	2.3
33	New Mexico	2.3
33	New York	2.3
37	Vermont	2.2
38	Idaho	2.1
38	Minnesota	2.1
40	Indiana	2.0
40	Iowa	2.0
42	New Jersey	1.9
42	Texas	1.9
44	Alaska	1.7
44	Mississippi	1.7
44	Nebraska	1.7
44	New Hampshire	1.7
44	North Dakota	1.7
49	Massachusetts	1.6
50	Connecticut	1.4

District of Columbia — 10.2

Source: Morgan Quitno Press using data from U.S. Bureau of the Census, Governments Division
"State and Local Government Finances 2003-2004" (http://www.census.gov/govs/www/estimate04.html)
*As a percent of direct general expenditures. Includes outpatient health services other than hospital care, research and education, categorical health programs, treatment and immunization clinics, nursing and environmental health activities. Includes capital expenditures.

Estimated Tobacco Settlement Revenues in FY 2007

National Total = $6,985,000,000*

ALPHA ORDER

RANK	STATE	REVENUE	% of USA
25	Alabama	$94,300,000	1.4%
49	Alaska	19,900,000	0.3%
26	Arizona	86,000,000	1.2%
34	Arkansas	48,300,000	0.7%
1	California	745,000,000	10.7%
27	Colorado	80,000,000	1.1%
23	Connecticut	108,400,000	1.6%
45	Delaware	23,100,000	0.3%
4	Florida	393,600,000	5.6%
12	Georgia	143,300,000	2.1%
39	Hawaii	35,100,000	0.5%
47	Idaho	21,200,000	0.3%
7	Illinois	271,700,000	3.9%
22	Indiana	119,100,000	1.7%
32	Iowa	50,800,000	0.7%
33	Kansas	48,700,000	0.7%
24	Kentucky	102,800,000	1.5%
17	Louisiana	131,600,000	1.9%
35	Maine	44,900,000	0.6%
16	Maryland	131,900,000	1.9%
9	Massachusetts	235,700,000	3.4%
8	Michigan	254,000,000	3.6%
11	Minnesota	182,600,000	2.6%
18	Mississippi	121,700,000	1.7%
15	Missouri	132,800,000	1.9%
43	Montana	24,800,000	0.4%
41	Nebraska	34,700,000	0.5%
38	Nevada	35,600,000	0.5%
37	New Hampshire	38,900,000	0.6%
10	New Jersey	225,700,000	3.2%
40	New Mexico	34,800,000	0.5%
2	New York	744,900,000	10.7%
14	North Carolina	136,100,000	1.9%
46	North Dakota	21,400,000	0.3%
6	Ohio	294,000,000	4.2%
30	Oklahoma	60,500,000	0.9%
29	Oregon	67,000,000	1.0%
5	Pennsylvania	335,400,000	4.8%
36	Rhode Island	42,000,000	0.6%
28	South Carolina	68,700,000	1.0%
48	South Dakota	20,400,000	0.3%
13	Tennessee	142,500,000	2.0%
3	Texas	519,400,000	7.4%
42	Utah	26,000,000	0.4%
44	Vermont	24,000,000	0.3%
21	Virginia	119,300,000	1.7%
20	Washington	119,800,000	1.7%
31	West Virginia	51,700,000	0.7%
19	Wisconsin	120,900,000	1.7%
50	Wyoming	14,500,000	0.2%

RANK ORDER

RANK	STATE	REVENUE	% of USA
1	California	$745,000,000	10.7%
2	New York	744,900,000	10.7%
3	Texas	519,400,000	7.4%
4	Florida	393,600,000	5.6%
5	Pennsylvania	335,400,000	4.8%
6	Ohio	294,000,000	4.2%
7	Illinois	271,700,000	3.9%
8	Michigan	254,000,000	3.6%
9	Massachusetts	235,700,000	3.4%
10	New Jersey	225,700,000	3.2%
11	Minnesota	182,600,000	2.6%
12	Georgia	143,300,000	2.1%
13	Tennessee	142,500,000	2.0%
14	North Carolina	136,100,000	1.9%
15	Missouri	132,800,000	1.9%
16	Maryland	131,900,000	1.9%
17	Louisiana	131,600,000	1.9%
18	Mississippi	121,700,000	1.7%
19	Wisconsin	120,900,000	1.7%
20	Washington	119,800,000	1.7%
21	Virginia	119,300,000	1.7%
22	Indiana	119,100,000	1.7%
23	Connecticut	108,400,000	1.6%
24	Kentucky	102,800,000	1.5%
25	Alabama	94,300,000	1.4%
26	Arizona	86,000,000	1.2%
27	Colorado	80,000,000	1.1%
28	South Carolina	68,700,000	1.0%
29	Oregon	67,000,000	1.0%
30	Oklahoma	60,500,000	0.9%
31	West Virginia	51,700,000	0.7%
32	Iowa	50,800,000	0.7%
33	Kansas	48,700,000	0.7%
34	Arkansas	48,300,000	0.7%
35	Maine	44,900,000	0.6%
36	Rhode Island	42,000,000	0.6%
37	New Hampshire	38,900,000	0.6%
38	Nevada	35,600,000	0.5%
39	Hawaii	35,100,000	0.5%
40	New Mexico	34,800,000	0.5%
41	Nebraska	34,700,000	0.5%
42	Utah	26,000,000	0.4%
43	Montana	24,800,000	0.4%
44	Vermont	24,000,000	0.3%
45	Delaware	23,100,000	0.3%
46	North Dakota	21,400,000	0.3%
47	Idaho	21,200,000	0.3%
48	South Dakota	20,400,000	0.3%
49	Alaska	19,900,000	0.3%
50	Wyoming	14,500,000	0.2%
	District of Columbia	35,400,000	0.5%

Source: Campaign for Tobacco-Free Kids
"A Broken Promise to Our Children" (http://tobaccofreekids.org/reports/settlements/)
*For fiscal year 2007. Settlement originally reached in November 1998 and called for an estimated 25 years of payments.

Personal Health Care Expenditures in 2004

National Total = $1,560,242,000,000*

ALPHA ORDER

RANK	STATE	EXPENDITURES	% of USA
23	Alabama	$23,673,000,000	1.5%
47	Alaska	4,219,000,000	0.3%
21	Arizona	24,345,000,000	1.6%
33	Arkansas	12,988,000,000	0.8%
1	California	169,060,000,000	10.8%
25	Colorado	22,415,000,000	1.4%
26	Connecticut	21,973,000,000	1.4%
44	Delaware	5,266,000,000	0.3%
4	Florida	94,758,000,000	6.1%
12	Georgia	41,387,000,000	2.7%
42	Hawaii	6,330,000,000	0.4%
43	Idaho	5,758,000,000	0.4%
7	Illinois	65,167,000,000	4.2%
15	Indiana	32,957,000,000	2.1%
30	Iowa	15,235,000,000	1.0%
31	Kansas	14,110,000,000	0.9%
24	Kentucky	22,612,000,000	1.4%
22	Louisiana	23,799,000,000	1.5%
38	Maine	7,986,000,000	0.5%
20	Maryland	30,425,000,000	2.0%
10	Massachusetts	45,331,000,000	2.9%
8	Michigan	49,159,000,000	3.2%
19	Minnesota	31,091,000,000	2.0%
32	Mississippi	13,929,000,000	0.9%
16	Missouri	32,809,000,000	2.1%
45	Montana	4,572,000,000	0.3%
36	Nebraska	9,806,000,000	0.6%
34	Nevada	10,603,000,000	0.7%
40	New Hampshire	6,958,000,000	0.4%
9	New Jersey	49,064,000,000	3.1%
39	New Mexico	7,976,000,000	0.5%
2	New York	127,918,000,000	8.2%
11	North Carolina	44,541,000,000	2.9%
48	North Dakota	3,948,000,000	0.3%
6	Ohio	65,423,000,000	4.2%
29	Oklahoma	16,709,000,000	1.1%
28	Oregon	17,536,000,000	1.1%
5	Pennsylvania	74,660,000,000	4.8%
41	Rhode Island	6,867,000,000	0.4%
27	South Carolina	20,859,000,000	1.3%
46	South Dakota	4,392,000,000	0.3%
14	Tennessee	33,563,000,000	2.2%
3	Texas	106,774,000,000	6.8%
37	Utah	9,788,000,000	0.6%
49	Vermont	3,601,000,000	0.2%
13	Virginia	35,807,000,000	2.3%
17	Washington	32,253,000,000	2.1%
35	West Virginia	10,210,000,000	0.7%
18	Wisconsin	31,231,000,000	2.0%
50	Wyoming	2,301,000,000	0.1%

RANK ORDER

RANK	STATE	EXPENDITURES	% of USA
1	California	$169,060,000,000	10.8%
2	New York	127,918,000,000	8.2%
3	Texas	106,774,000,000	6.8%
4	Florida	94,758,000,000	6.1%
5	Pennsylvania	74,660,000,000	4.8%
6	Ohio	65,423,000,000	4.2%
7	Illinois	65,167,000,000	4.2%
8	Michigan	49,159,000,000	3.2%
9	New Jersey	49,064,000,000	3.1%
10	Massachusetts	45,331,000,000	2.9%
11	North Carolina	44,541,000,000	2.9%
12	Georgia	41,387,000,000	2.7%
13	Virginia	35,807,000,000	2.3%
14	Tennessee	33,563,000,000	2.2%
15	Indiana	32,957,000,000	2.1%
16	Missouri	32,809,000,000	2.1%
17	Washington	32,253,000,000	2.1%
18	Wisconsin	31,231,000,000	2.0%
19	Minnesota	31,091,000,000	2.0%
20	Maryland	30,425,000,000	2.0%
21	Arizona	24,345,000,000	1.6%
22	Louisiana	23,799,000,000	1.5%
23	Alabama	23,673,000,000	1.5%
24	Kentucky	22,612,000,000	1.4%
25	Colorado	22,415,000,000	1.4%
26	Connecticut	21,973,000,000	1.4%
27	South Carolina	20,859,000,000	1.3%
28	Oregon	17,536,000,000	1.1%
29	Oklahoma	16,709,000,000	1.1%
30	Iowa	15,235,000,000	1.0%
31	Kansas	14,110,000,000	0.9%
32	Mississippi	13,929,000,000	0.9%
33	Arkansas	12,988,000,000	0.8%
34	Nevada	10,603,000,000	0.7%
35	West Virginia	10,210,000,000	0.7%
36	Nebraska	9,806,000,000	0.6%
37	Utah	9,788,000,000	0.6%
38	Maine	7,986,000,000	0.5%
39	New Mexico	7,976,000,000	0.5%
40	New Hampshire	6,958,000,000	0.4%
41	Rhode Island	6,867,000,000	0.4%
42	Hawaii	6,330,000,000	0.4%
43	Idaho	5,758,000,000	0.4%
44	Delaware	5,266,000,000	0.3%
45	Montana	4,572,000,000	0.3%
46	South Dakota	4,392,000,000	0.3%
47	Alaska	4,219,000,000	0.3%
48	North Dakota	3,948,000,000	0.3%
49	Vermont	3,601,000,000	0.2%
50	Wyoming	2,301,000,000	0.1%
	District of Columbia	6,068,000,000	0.4%

Source: U.S. Department of Health and Human Services, Centers for Medicare and Medicaid Services
"State Health Care Expenditures" (http://www.cms.hhs.gov/NationalHealthExpendData/)
*By state of provider. Includes hospital care, physician services, dental services, home health care, drugs, vision products, nursing home care and other personal health care services and products.

Health Care Expenditures as a Percent of Gross State Product in 2004

National Percent = 13.4% of Total Gross State Product*

ALPHA ORDER

RANK ORDER

RANK	STATE	PERCENT		RANK	STATE	PERCENT
4	Alabama	17.1		1	West Virginia	20.5
36	Alaska	12.5		2	Maine	18.5
39	Arizona	12.2		3	Mississippi	18.3
10	Arkansas	16.2		4	Alabama	17.1
46	California	11.0		5	Kentucky	16.7
45	Colorado	11.2		5	North Dakota	16.7
44	Connecticut	11.7		7	Montana	16.5
49	Delaware	9.7		8	Rhode Island	16.4
12	Florida	15.9		9	Vermont	16.3
40	Georgia	12.1		10	Arkansas	16.2
35	Hawaii	12.6		11	Missouri	16.1
30	Idaho	13.3		12	Florida	15.9
38	Illinois	12.3		12	Pennsylvania	15.9
21	Indiana	14.5		14	Louisiana	15.7
30	Iowa	13.3		15	Ohio	15.6
24	Kansas	14.2		15	Oklahoma	15.6
5	Kentucky	16.7		17	Tennessee	15.5
14	Louisiana	15.7		18	South Carolina	15.4
2	Maine	18.5		19	South Dakota	14.9
28	Maryland	13.4		20	Wisconsin	14.8
23	Massachusetts	14.3		21	Indiana	14.5
33	Michigan	13.2		22	Nebraska	14.4
26	Minnesota	13.8		23	Massachusetts	14.3
3	Mississippi	18.3		24	Kansas	14.2
11	Missouri	16.1		24	New York	14.2
7	Montana	16.5		26	Minnesota	13.8
22	Nebraska	14.4		27	Oregon	13.7
48	Nevada	10.7		28	Maryland	13.4
28	New Hampshire	13.4		28	New Hampshire	13.4
43	New Jersey	11.8		30	Idaho	13.3
34	New Mexico	13.1		30	Iowa	13.3
24	New York	14.2		30	North Carolina	13.3
30	North Carolina	13.3		33	Michigan	13.2
5	North Dakota	16.7		34	New Mexico	13.1
15	Ohio	15.6		35	Hawaii	12.6
15	Oklahoma	15.6		36	Alaska	12.5
27	Oregon	13.7		37	Washington	12.4
12	Pennsylvania	15.9		38	Illinois	12.3
8	Rhode Island	16.4		39	Arizona	12.2
18	South Carolina	15.4		40	Georgia	12.1
19	South Dakota	14.9		40	Texas	12.1
17	Tennessee	15.5		42	Utah	11.9
40	Texas	12.1		43	New Jersey	11.8
42	Utah	11.9		44	Connecticut	11.7
9	Vermont	16.3		45	Colorado	11.2
46	Virginia	11.0		46	California	11.0
37	Washington	12.4		46	Virginia	11.0
1	West Virginia	20.5		48	Nevada	10.7
20	Wisconsin	14.8		49	Delaware	9.7
50	Wyoming	9.5		50	Wyoming	9.5

District of Columbia   8.1

*Source: U.S. Department of Health and Human Services, Centers for Medicare and Medicaid Services
"State Health Care Expenditures" (http://www.cms.hhs.gov/NationalHealthExpendData/)*
*By state of provider. Includes hospital care, physician services, dental services, home health care, drugs, vision products, nursing home care and other personal health care services and products.

Per Capita Personal Health Care Expenditures in 2004

National Per Capita = $5,313*

ALPHA ORDER

RANK	STATE	PER CAPITA
26	Alabama	$5,240
3	Alaska	6,423
47	Arizona	4,237
42	Arkansas	4,728
43	California	4,717
36	Colorado	4,874
6	Connecticut	6,289
5	Delaware	6,354
22	Florida	5,456
44	Georgia	4,632
32	Hawaii	5,027
49	Idaho	4,129
31	Illinois	5,126
24	Indiana	5,296
29	Iowa	5,158
30	Kansas	5,153
21	Kentucky	5,461
25	Louisiana	5,294
9	Maine	6,078
20	Maryland	5,479
1	Massachusetts	7,043
37	Michigan	4,870
8	Minnesota	6,103
38	Mississippi	4,815
13	Missouri	5,703
34	Montana	4,936
19	Nebraska	5,613
46	Nevada	4,546
23	New Hampshire	5,361
17	New Jersey	5,655
48	New Mexico	4,197
2	New York	6,631
27	North Carolina	5,221
7	North Dakota	6,209
12	Ohio	5,708
40	Oklahoma	4,743
35	Oregon	4,886
10	Pennsylvania	6,032
4	Rhode Island	6,365
33	South Carolina	4,973
13	South Dakota	5,703
13	Tennessee	5,703
41	Texas	4,742
50	Utah	4,042
11	Vermont	5,801
39	Virginia	4,792
28	Washington	5,197
18	West Virginia	5,638
16	Wisconsin	5,680
45	Wyoming	4,552

RANK ORDER

RANK	STATE	PER CAPITA
1	Massachusetts	$7,043
2	New York	6,631
3	Alaska	6,423
4	Rhode Island	6,365
5	Delaware	6,354
6	Connecticut	6,289
7	North Dakota	6,209
8	Minnesota	6,103
9	Maine	6,078
10	Pennsylvania	6,032
11	Vermont	5,801
12	Ohio	5,708
13	Missouri	5,703
13	South Dakota	5,703
13	Tennessee	5,703
16	Wisconsin	5,680
17	New Jersey	5,655
18	West Virginia	5,638
19	Nebraska	5,613
20	Maryland	5,479
21	Kentucky	5,461
22	Florida	5,456
23	New Hampshire	5,361
24	Indiana	5,296
25	Louisiana	5,294
26	Alabama	5,240
27	North Carolina	5,221
28	Washington	5,197
29	Iowa	5,158
30	Kansas	5,153
31	Illinois	5,126
32	Hawaii	5,027
33	South Carolina	4,973
34	Montana	4,936
35	Oregon	4,886
36	Colorado	4,874
37	Michigan	4,870
38	Mississippi	4,815
39	Virginia	4,792
40	Oklahoma	4,743
41	Texas	4,742
42	Arkansas	4,728
43	California	4,717
44	Georgia	4,632
45	Wyoming	4,552
46	Nevada	4,546
47	Arizona	4,237
48	New Mexico	4,197
49	Idaho	4,129
50	Utah	4,042

| | District of Columbia | 10,467 |

Source: MQ Press using data from U.S. Dept of Health & Human Services, Centers for Medicare and Medicaid Services "State Health Care Expenditures" (http://www.cms.hhs.gov/NationalHealthExpendData/)

*Estimates by state of provider. Per capita calculated using resident population. These figures may be skewed due to residents crossing state borders for care. Includes hospital care, physician services, dental services, home health care, drugs, vision products, nursing home care and other personal health care services and products.

Expenditures for Hospital Care in 2004

National Total = $570,756,000,000*

ALPHA ORDER

RANK	STATE	EXPENDITURES	% of USA
25	Alabama	$8,054,000,000	1.4%
48	Alaska	1,693,000,000	0.3%
22	Arizona	8,672,000,000	1.5%
32	Arkansas	5,013,000,000	0.9%
1	California	59,106,000,000	10.4%
26	Colorado	7,921,000,000	1.4%
27	Connecticut	6,771,000,000	1.2%
46	Delaware	1,821,000,000	0.3%
4	Florida	31,509,000,000	5.5%
12	Georgia	14,969,000,000	2.6%
42	Hawaii	2,491,000,000	0.4%
43	Idaho	2,080,000,000	0.4%
6	Illinois	24,819,000,000	4.3%
15	Indiana	12,524,000,000	2.2%
30	Iowa	5,856,000,000	1.0%
33	Kansas	4,833,000,000	0.8%
23	Kentucky	8,308,000,000	1.5%
21	Louisiana	9,528,000,000	1.7%
38	Maine	2,864,000,000	0.5%
19	Maryland	10,624,000,000	1.9%
9	Massachusetts	18,090,000,000	3.2%
8	Michigan	19,105,000,000	3.3%
20	Minnesota	10,601,000,000	1.9%
31	Mississippi	5,566,000,000	1.0%
13	Missouri	14,135,000,000	2.5%
45	Montana	1,865,000,000	0.3%
35	Nebraska	4,041,000,000	0.7%
37	Nevada	3,430,000,000	0.6%
41	New Hampshire	2,512,000,000	0.4%
11	New Jersey	16,282,000,000	2.9%
39	New Mexico	2,857,000,000	0.5%
2	New York	46,334,000,000	8.1%
10	North Carolina	16,407,000,000	2.9%
47	North Dakota	1,694,000,000	0.3%
7	Ohio	24,622,000,000	4.3%
28	Oklahoma	6,226,000,000	1.1%
29	Oregon	6,023,000,000	1.1%
5	Pennsylvania	27,325,000,000	4.8%
40	Rhode Island	2,613,000,000	0.5%
24	South Carolina	8,215,000,000	1.4%
44	South Dakota	1,921,000,000	0.3%
16	Tennessee	11,588,000,000	2.0%
3	Texas	40,859,000,000	7.2%
36	Utah	3,591,000,000	0.6%
49	Vermont	1,322,000,000	0.2%
14	Virginia	13,001,000,000	2.3%
18	Washington	11,158,000,000	2.0%
34	West Virginia	4,073,000,000	0.7%
17	Wisconsin	11,451,000,000	2.0%
50	Wyoming	899,000,000	0.2%

RANK ORDER

RANK	STATE	EXPENDITURES	% of USA
1	California	$59,106,000,000	10.4%
2	New York	46,334,000,000	8.1%
3	Texas	40,859,000,000	7.2%
4	Florida	31,509,000,000	5.5%
5	Pennsylvania	27,325,000,000	4.8%
6	Illinois	24,819,000,000	4.3%
7	Ohio	24,622,000,000	4.3%
8	Michigan	19,105,000,000	3.3%
9	Massachusetts	18,090,000,000	3.2%
10	North Carolina	16,407,000,000	2.9%
11	New Jersey	16,282,000,000	2.9%
12	Georgia	14,969,000,000	2.6%
13	Missouri	14,135,000,000	2.5%
14	Virginia	13,001,000,000	2.3%
15	Indiana	12,524,000,000	2.2%
16	Tennessee	11,588,000,000	2.0%
17	Wisconsin	11,451,000,000	2.0%
18	Washington	11,158,000,000	2.0%
19	Maryland	10,624,000,000	1.9%
20	Minnesota	10,601,000,000	1.9%
21	Louisiana	9,528,000,000	1.7%
22	Arizona	8,672,000,000	1.5%
23	Kentucky	8,308,000,000	1.5%
24	South Carolina	8,215,000,000	1.4%
25	Alabama	8,054,000,000	1.4%
26	Colorado	7,921,000,000	1.4%
27	Connecticut	6,771,000,000	1.2%
28	Oklahoma	6,226,000,000	1.1%
29	Oregon	6,023,000,000	1.1%
30	Iowa	5,856,000,000	1.0%
31	Mississippi	5,566,000,000	1.0%
32	Arkansas	5,013,000,000	0.9%
33	Kansas	4,833,000,000	0.8%
34	West Virginia	4,073,000,000	0.7%
35	Nebraska	4,041,000,000	0.7%
36	Utah	3,591,000,000	0.6%
37	Nevada	3,430,000,000	0.6%
38	Maine	2,864,000,000	0.5%
39	New Mexico	2,857,000,000	0.5%
40	Rhode Island	2,613,000,000	0.5%
41	New Hampshire	2,512,000,000	0.4%
42	Hawaii	2,491,000,000	0.4%
43	Idaho	2,080,000,000	0.4%
44	South Dakota	1,921,000,000	0.3%
45	Montana	1,865,000,000	0.3%
46	Delaware	1,821,000,000	0.3%
47	North Dakota	1,694,000,000	0.3%
48	Alaska	1,693,000,000	0.3%
49	Vermont	1,322,000,000	0.2%
50	Wyoming	899,000,000	0.2%
	District of Columbia	3,494,000,000	0.6%

Source: U.S. Department of Health and Human Services, Centers for Medicare and Medicaid Services
   "State Health Care Expenditures" (http://www.cms.hhs.gov/NationalHealthExpendData/)
By state of provider.

Percent of Total Personal Health Care Expenditures
Spent on Hospital Care in 2004
National Percent = 36.6%*

ALPHA ORDER

RANK ORDER

RANK	STATE	PERCENT	RANK	STATE	PERCENT
46	Alabama	34.0	1	South Dakota	43.7
6	Alaska	40.1	2	Missouri	43.1
36	Arizona	35.6	3	North Dakota	42.9
15	Arkansas	38.6	4	Nebraska	41.2
38	California	35.0	5	Montana	40.8
37	Colorado	35.3	6	Alaska	40.1
50	Connecticut	30.8	7	Louisiana	40.0
40	Delaware	34.6	7	Mississippi	40.0
47	Florida	33.3	9	Massachusetts	39.9
30	Georgia	36.2	9	West Virginia	39.9
11	Hawaii	39.4	11	Hawaii	39.4
32	Idaho	36.1	11	South Carolina	39.4
18	Illinois	38.1	13	Wyoming	39.1
20	Indiana	38.0	14	Michigan	38.9
16	Iowa	38.4	15	Arkansas	38.6
43	Kansas	34.3	16	Iowa	38.4
24	Kentucky	36.7	17	Texas	38.3
7	Louisiana	40.0	18	Illinois	38.1
34	Maine	35.9	18	Rhode Island	38.1
39	Maryland	34.9	20	Indiana	38.0
9	Massachusetts	39.9	21	Ohio	37.6
14	Michigan	38.9	22	Oklahoma	37.3
45	Minnesota	34.1	23	North Carolina	36.8
7	Mississippi	40.0	24	Kentucky	36.7
2	Missouri	43.1	24	Utah	36.7
5	Montana	40.8	24	Vermont	36.7
4	Nebraska	41.2	24	Wisconsin	36.7
49	Nevada	32.3	28	Pennsylvania	36.6
32	New Hampshire	36.1	29	Virginia	36.3
48	New Jersey	33.2	30	Georgia	36.2
35	New Mexico	35.8	30	New York	36.2
30	New York	36.2	32	Idaho	36.1
23	North Carolina	36.8	32	New Hampshire	36.1
3	North Dakota	42.9	34	Maine	35.9
21	Ohio	37.6	35	New Mexico	35.8
22	Oklahoma	37.3	36	Arizona	35.6
43	Oregon	34.3	37	Colorado	35.3
28	Pennsylvania	36.6	38	California	35.0
18	Rhode Island	38.1	39	Maryland	34.9
11	South Carolina	39.4	40	Delaware	34.6
1	South Dakota	43.7	40	Washington	34.6
42	Tennessee	34.5	42	Tennessee	34.5
17	Texas	38.3	43	Kansas	34.3
24	Utah	36.7	43	Oregon	34.3
24	Vermont	36.7	45	Minnesota	34.1
29	Virginia	36.3	46	Alabama	34.0
40	Washington	34.6	47	Florida	33.3
9	West Virginia	39.9	48	New Jersey	33.2
24	Wisconsin	36.7	49	Nevada	32.3
13	Wyoming	39.1	50	Connecticut	30.8

District of Columbia   57.6

Source: MQ Press using data from U.S. Dept of Health & Human Services, Centers for Medicare and Medicaid Services
"State Health Care Expenditures" (http://www.cms.hhs.gov/NationalHealthExpendData/)
*By state of provider.

Per Capita Expenditures for Hospital Care in 2004

National Per Capita = $1,944*

ALPHA ORDER

RANK	STATE	PER CAPITA
37	Alabama	$1,783
3	Alaska	2,578
46	Arizona	1,509
33	Arkansas	1,825
45	California	1,649
42	Colorado	1,723
26	Connecticut	1,938
11	Delaware	2,197
35	Florida	1,814
44	Georgia	1,675
22	Hawaii	1,978
48	Idaho	1,492
25	Illinois	1,952
19	Indiana	2,012
21	Iowa	1,983
40	Kansas	1,765
20	Kentucky	2,007
15	Louisiana	2,119
12	Maine	2,180
30	Maryland	1,913
1	Massachusetts	2,811
31	Michigan	1,893
17	Minnesota	2,081
28	Mississippi	1,924
5	Missouri	2,457
18	Montana	2,013
8	Nebraska	2,313
50	Nevada	1,471
27	New Hampshire	1,935
32	New Jersey	1,877
47	New Mexico	1,503
7	New York	2,402
29	North Carolina	1,923
2	North Dakota	2,664
13	Ohio	2,148
39	Oklahoma	1,767
43	Oregon	1,678
10	Pennsylvania	2,208
6	Rhode Island	2,422
24	South Carolina	1,958
4	South Dakota	2,494
23	Tennessee	1,969
34	Texas	1,815
49	Utah	1,483
14	Vermont	2,130
41	Virginia	1,740
36	Washington	1,798
9	West Virginia	2,249
16	Wisconsin	2,082
38	Wyoming	1,778

RANK ORDER

RANK	STATE	PER CAPITA
1	Massachusetts	$2,811
2	North Dakota	2,664
3	Alaska	2,578
4	South Dakota	2,494
5	Missouri	2,457
6	Rhode Island	2,422
7	New York	2,402
8	Nebraska	2,313
9	West Virginia	2,249
10	Pennsylvania	2,208
11	Delaware	2,197
12	Maine	2,180
13	Ohio	2,148
14	Vermont	2,130
15	Louisiana	2,119
16	Wisconsin	2,082
17	Minnesota	2,081
18	Montana	2,013
19	Indiana	2,012
20	Kentucky	2,007
21	Iowa	1,983
22	Hawaii	1,978
23	Tennessee	1,969
24	South Carolina	1,958
25	Illinois	1,952
26	Connecticut	1,938
27	New Hampshire	1,935
28	Mississippi	1,924
29	North Carolina	1,923
30	Maryland	1,913
31	Michigan	1,893
32	New Jersey	1,877
33	Arkansas	1,825
34	Texas	1,815
35	Florida	1,814
36	Washington	1,798
37	Alabama	1,783
38	Wyoming	1,778
39	Oklahoma	1,767
40	Kansas	1,765
41	Virginia	1,740
42	Colorado	1,723
43	Oregon	1,678
44	Georgia	1,675
45	California	1,649
46	Arizona	1,509
47	New Mexico	1,503
48	Idaho	1,492
49	Utah	1,483
50	Nevada	1,471

	District of Columbia	6,027

Source: MQ Press using data from U.S. Dept of Health & Human Services, Centers for Medicare and Medicaid Services "State Health Care Expenditures" (http://www.cms.hhs.gov/NationalHealthExpendData/)
*Estimates by state of provider. Per capita calculated using resident population. These figures may be skewed due to residents crossing state borders for care.

Expenditures for Physician and Clinical Services in 2004

National Total = $399,883,000,000*

ALPHA ORDER

RANK	STATE	EXPENDITURES	% of USA
23	Alabama	$6,567,000,000	1.6%
45	Alaska	1,205,000,000	0.3%
20	Arizona	7,333,000,000	1.8%
34	Arkansas	3,077,000,000	0.8%
1	California	50,552,000,000	12.6%
22	Colorado	6,757,000,000	1.7%
26	Connecticut	5,266,000,000	1.3%
42	Delaware	1,402,000,000	0.4%
4	Florida	26,370,000,000	6.6%
10	Georgia	11,090,000,000	2.8%
41	Hawaii	1,506,000,000	0.4%
43	Idaho	1,337,000,000	0.3%
6	Illinois	16,307,000,000	4.1%
18	Indiana	8,144,000,000	2.0%
31	Iowa	3,501,000,000	0.9%
30	Kansas	3,827,000,000	1.0%
25	Kentucky	5,763,000,000	1.4%
24	Louisiana	6,031,000,000	1.5%
39	Maine	1,750,000,000	0.4%
19	Maryland	8,017,000,000	2.0%
12	Massachusetts	10,086,000,000	2.5%
9	Michigan	11,202,000,000	2.8%
16	Minnesota	8,725,000,000	2.2%
33	Mississippi	3,113,000,000	0.8%
21	Missouri	7,043,000,000	1.8%
46	Montana	1,142,000,000	0.3%
37	Nebraska	2,319,000,000	0.6%
32	Nevada	3,383,000,000	0.8%
40	New Hampshire	1,687,000,000	0.4%
8	New Jersey	11,927,000,000	3.0%
38	New Mexico	1,919,000,000	0.5%
3	New York	26,728,000,000	6.7%
11	North Carolina	10,537,000,000	2.6%
49	North Dakota	832,000,000	0.2%
7	Ohio	15,367,000,000	3.8%
29	Oklahoma	4,192,000,000	1.0%
27	Oregon	5,132,000,000	1.3%
5	Pennsylvania	17,374,000,000	4.3%
44	Rhode Island	1,334,000,000	0.3%
28	South Carolina	5,127,000,000	1.3%
47	South Dakota	1,026,000,000	0.3%
13	Tennessee	9,560,000,000	2.4%
2	Texas	29,656,000,000	7.4%
35	Utah	2,446,000,000	0.6%
48	Vermont	846,000,000	0.2%
14	Virginia	9,457,000,000	2.4%
15	Washington	9,172,000,000	2.3%
36	West Virginia	2,324,000,000	0.6%
17	Wisconsin	8,638,000,000	2.2%
50	Wyoming	548,000,000	0.1%

RANK ORDER

RANK	STATE	EXPENDITURES	% of USA
1	California	$50,552,000,000	12.6%
2	Texas	29,656,000,000	7.4%
3	New York	26,728,000,000	6.7%
4	Florida	26,370,000,000	6.6%
5	Pennsylvania	17,374,000,000	4.3%
6	Illinois	16,307,000,000	4.1%
7	Ohio	15,367,000,000	3.8%
8	New Jersey	11,927,000,000	3.0%
9	Michigan	11,202,000,000	2.8%
10	Georgia	11,090,000,000	2.8%
11	North Carolina	10,537,000,000	2.6%
12	Massachusetts	10,086,000,000	2.5%
13	Tennessee	9,560,000,000	2.4%
14	Virginia	9,457,000,000	2.4%
15	Washington	9,172,000,000	2.3%
16	Minnesota	8,725,000,000	2.2%
17	Wisconsin	8,638,000,000	2.2%
18	Indiana	8,144,000,000	2.0%
19	Maryland	8,017,000,000	2.0%
20	Arizona	7,333,000,000	1.8%
21	Missouri	7,043,000,000	1.8%
22	Colorado	6,757,000,000	1.7%
23	Alabama	6,567,000,000	1.6%
24	Louisiana	6,031,000,000	1.5%
25	Kentucky	5,763,000,000	1.4%
26	Connecticut	5,266,000,000	1.3%
27	Oregon	5,132,000,000	1.3%
28	South Carolina	5,127,000,000	1.3%
29	Oklahoma	4,192,000,000	1.0%
30	Kansas	3,827,000,000	1.0%
31	Iowa	3,501,000,000	0.9%
32	Nevada	3,383,000,000	0.8%
33	Mississippi	3,113,000,000	0.8%
34	Arkansas	3,077,000,000	0.8%
35	Utah	2,446,000,000	0.6%
36	West Virginia	2,324,000,000	0.6%
37	Nebraska	2,319,000,000	0.6%
38	New Mexico	1,919,000,000	0.5%
39	Maine	1,750,000,000	0.4%
40	New Hampshire	1,687,000,000	0.4%
41	Hawaii	1,506,000,000	0.4%
42	Delaware	1,402,000,000	0.4%
43	Idaho	1,337,000,000	0.3%
44	Rhode Island	1,334,000,000	0.3%
45	Alaska	1,205,000,000	0.3%
46	Montana	1,142,000,000	0.3%
47	South Dakota	1,026,000,000	0.3%
48	Vermont	846,000,000	0.2%
49	North Dakota	832,000,000	0.2%
50	Wyoming	548,000,000	0.1%
	District of Columbia	1,241,000,000	0.3%

Source: U.S. Department of Health and Human Services, Centers for Medicare and Medicaid Services
"State Health Care Expenditures" (http://www.cms.hhs.gov/NationalHealthExpendData/)
*By state of provider. Includes private physician offices and clinics, independently billing laboratories and clinics run by U.S. Department of Veteran Affairs and the U.S. Indian Health Service.

Percent of Total Personal Health Care Expenditures
Spent on Physician and Clinical Services in 2004
National Percent = 25.6%*

ALPHA ORDER

RANK	STATE	PERCENT
12	Alabama	27.7
6	Alaska	28.6
2	Arizona	30.1
33	Arkansas	23.7
4	California	29.9
2	Colorado	30.1
30	Connecticut	24.0
16	Delaware	26.6
10	Florida	27.8
15	Georgia	26.8
31	Hawaii	23.8
40	Idaho	23.2
22	Illinois	25.0
25	Indiana	24.7
41	Iowa	23.0
14	Kansas	27.1
19	Kentucky	25.5
20	Louisiana	25.3
46	Maine	21.9
17	Maryland	26.4
45	Massachusetts	22.2
42	Michigan	22.8
9	Minnesota	28.1
44	Mississippi	22.3
47	Missouri	21.5
22	Montana	25.0
35	Nebraska	23.6
1	Nevada	31.9
28	New Hampshire	24.2
27	New Jersey	24.3
29	New Mexico	24.1
49	New York	20.9
33	North Carolina	23.7
48	North Dakota	21.1
36	Ohio	23.5
21	Oklahoma	25.1
5	Oregon	29.3
39	Pennsylvania	23.3
50	Rhode Island	19.4
26	South Carolina	24.6
38	South Dakota	23.4
7	Tennessee	28.5
10	Texas	27.8
22	Utah	25.0
36	Vermont	23.5
17	Virginia	26.4
8	Washington	28.4
42	West Virginia	22.8
12	Wisconsin	27.7
31	Wyoming	23.8

RANK ORDER

RANK	STATE	PERCENT
1	Nevada	31.9
2	Arizona	30.1
2	Colorado	30.1
4	California	29.9
5	Oregon	29.3
6	Alaska	28.6
7	Tennessee	28.5
8	Washington	28.4
9	Minnesota	28.1
10	Florida	27.8
10	Texas	27.8
12	Alabama	27.7
12	Wisconsin	27.7
14	Kansas	27.1
15	Georgia	26.8
16	Delaware	26.6
17	Maryland	26.4
17	Virginia	26.4
19	Kentucky	25.5
20	Louisiana	25.3
21	Oklahoma	25.1
22	Illinois	25.0
22	Montana	25.0
22	Utah	25.0
25	Indiana	24.7
26	South Carolina	24.6
27	New Jersey	24.3
28	New Hampshire	24.2
29	New Mexico	24.1
30	Connecticut	24.0
31	Hawaii	23.8
31	Wyoming	23.8
33	Arkansas	23.7
33	North Carolina	23.7
35	Nebraska	23.6
36	Ohio	23.5
36	Vermont	23.5
38	South Dakota	23.4
39	Pennsylvania	23.3
40	Idaho	23.2
41	Iowa	23.0
42	Michigan	22.8
42	West Virginia	22.8
44	Mississippi	22.3
45	Massachusetts	22.2
46	Maine	21.9
47	Missouri	21.5
48	North Dakota	21.1
49	New York	20.9
50	Rhode Island	19.4

| District of Columbia | 20.5 |

Source: MQ Press using data from U.S. Dept of Health & Human Services, Centers for Medicare and Medicaid Services "State Health Care Expenditures" (http://www.cms.hhs.gov/NationalHealthExpendData/)
By state of provider. Includes private physician offices and clinics, independently billing laboratories and clinics run by U.S. Department of Veteran Affairs and the U.S. Indian Health Service.

Per Capita Expenditures for Physician and Clinical Services in 2004

National Per Capita = $1,362*

RANK	STATE	PER CAPITA
11	Alabama	$1,454
1	Alaska	1,835
33	Arizona	1,276
44	Arkansas	1,120
15	California	1,410
10	Colorado	1,469
8	Connecticut	1,507
3	Delaware	1,692
7	Florida	1,518
35	Georgia	1,241
41	Hawaii	1,196
50	Idaho	959
31	Illinois	1,283
28	Indiana	1,309
43	Iowa	1,185
17	Kansas	1,398
18	Kentucky	1,392
22	Louisiana	1,342
24	Maine	1,332
13	Maryland	1,444
6	Massachusetts	1,567
45	Michigan	1,110
2	Minnesota	1,713
47	Mississippi	1,076
39	Missouri	1,224
38	Montana	1,233
26	Nebraska	1,327
12	Nevada	1,450
30	New Hampshire	1,300
20	New Jersey	1,375
48	New Mexico	1,010
19	New York	1,385
37	North Carolina	1,235
29	North Dakota	1,308
23	Ohio	1,341
42	Oklahoma	1,190
14	Oregon	1,430
16	Pennsylvania	1,404
36	Rhode Island	1,236
40	South Carolina	1,222
24	South Dakota	1,332
4	Tennessee	1,624
27	Texas	1,317
48	Utah	1,010
21	Vermont	1,363
34	Virginia	1,266
9	Washington	1,478
31	West Virginia	1,283
5	Wisconsin	1,571
46	Wyoming	1,084

RANK	STATE	PER CAPITA
1	Alaska	$1,835
2	Minnesota	1,713
3	Delaware	1,692
4	Tennessee	1,624
5	Wisconsin	1,571
6	Massachusetts	1,567
7	Florida	1,518
8	Connecticut	1,507
9	Washington	1,478
10	Colorado	1,469
11	Alabama	1,454
12	Nevada	1,450
13	Maryland	1,444
14	Oregon	1,430
15	California	1,410
16	Pennsylvania	1,404
17	Kansas	1,398
18	Kentucky	1,392
19	New York	1,385
20	New Jersey	1,375
21	Vermont	1,363
22	Louisiana	1,342
23	Ohio	1,341
24	Maine	1,332
24	South Dakota	1,332
26	Nebraska	1,327
27	Texas	1,317
28	Indiana	1,309
29	North Dakota	1,308
30	New Hampshire	1,300
31	Illinois	1,283
31	West Virginia	1,283
33	Arizona	1,276
34	Virginia	1,266
35	Georgia	1,241
36	Rhode Island	1,236
37	North Carolina	1,235
38	Montana	1,233
39	Missouri	1,224
40	South Carolina	1,222
41	Hawaii	1,196
42	Oklahoma	1,190
43	Iowa	1,185
44	Arkansas	1,120
45	Michigan	1,110
46	Wyoming	1,084
47	Mississippi	1,076
48	New Mexico	1,010
48	Utah	1,010
50	Idaho	959

| | District of Columbia | 2,141 |

Source: MQ Press using data from U.S. Dept of Health & Human Services, Centers for Medicare and Medicaid Services
"State Health Care Expenditures" (http://www.cms.hhs.gov/NationalHealthExpendData/)
*Estimates by state of provider. Per capita calculated using resident population. These figures may be skewed
due to residents crossing state borders for care. Includes private physician offices and clinics, independently
billing laboratories and clinics run by U.S. Department of Veteran Affairs and the U.S. Indian Health Service.

Expenditures for Dental Services in 2004

National Total = $81,532,000,000*

ALPHA ORDER

RANK ORDER

RANK	STATE	EXPENDITURES	% of USA	RANK	STATE	EXPENDITURES	% of USA
25	Alabama	$1,043,000,000	1.3%	1	California	$12,099,000,000	14.8%
45	Alaska	258,000,000	0.3%	2	New York	5,478,000,000	6.7%
20	Arizona	1,507,000,000	1.8%	3	Texas	4,881,000,000	6.0%
34	Arkansas	603,000,000	0.7%	4	Florida	4,103,000,000	5.0%
1	California	12,099,000,000	14.8%	5	Illinois	3,373,000,000	4.1%
19	Colorado	1,524,000,000	1.9%	6	Pennsylvania	3,256,000,000	4.0%
22	Connecticut	1,329,000,000	1.6%	7	Michigan	3,010,000,000	3.7%
44	Delaware	259,000,000	0.3%	8	Ohio	2,865,000,000	3.5%
4	Florida	4,103,000,000	5.0%	9	New Jersey	2,812,000,000	3.4%
11	Georgia	2,314,000,000	2.8%	10	Washington	2,561,000,000	3.1%
40	Hawaii	408,000,000	0.5%	11	Georgia	2,314,000,000	2.8%
37	Idaho	426,000,000	0.5%	12	Massachusetts	2,305,000,000	2.8%
5	Illinois	3,373,000,000	4.1%	13	North Carolina	2,221,000,000	2.7%
17	Indiana	1,616,000,000	2.0%	14	Virginia	2,053,000,000	2.5%
32	Iowa	696,000,000	0.9%	15	Wisconsin	1,774,000,000	2.2%
30	Kansas	716,000,000	0.9%	16	Minnesota	1,680,000,000	2.1%
29	Kentucky	822,000,000	1.0%	17	Indiana	1,616,000,000	2.0%
27	Louisiana	847,000,000	1.0%	18	Maryland	1,586,000,000	1.9%
41	Maine	351,000,000	0.4%	19	Colorado	1,524,000,000	1.9%
18	Maryland	1,586,000,000	1.9%	20	Arizona	1,507,000,000	1.8%
12	Massachusetts	2,305,000,000	2.8%	21	Tennessee	1,465,000,000	1.8%
7	Michigan	3,010,000,000	3.7%	22	Connecticut	1,329,000,000	1.6%
16	Minnesota	1,680,000,000	2.1%	23	Missouri	1,314,000,000	1.6%
35	Mississippi	520,000,000	0.6%	24	Oregon	1,273,000,000	1.6%
23	Missouri	1,314,000,000	1.6%	25	Alabama	1,043,000,000	1.3%
46	Montana	236,000,000	0.3%	26	South Carolina	947,000,000	1.2%
39	Nebraska	416,000,000	0.5%	27	Louisiana	847,000,000	1.0%
33	Nevada	638,000,000	0.8%	28	Oklahoma	823,000,000	1.0%
36	New Hampshire	480,000,000	0.6%	29	Kentucky	822,000,000	1.0%
9	New Jersey	2,812,000,000	3.4%	30	Kansas	716,000,000	0.9%
38	New Mexico	417,000,000	0.5%	31	Utah	711,000,000	0.9%
2	New York	5,478,000,000	6.7%	32	Iowa	696,000,000	0.9%
13	North Carolina	2,221,000,000	2.7%	33	Nevada	638,000,000	0.8%
49	North Dakota	183,000,000	0.2%	34	Arkansas	603,000,000	0.7%
8	Ohio	2,865,000,000	3.5%	35	Mississippi	520,000,000	0.6%
28	Oklahoma	823,000,000	1.0%	36	New Hampshire	480,000,000	0.6%
24	Oregon	1,273,000,000	1.6%	37	Idaho	426,000,000	0.5%
6	Pennsylvania	3,256,000,000	4.0%	38	New Mexico	417,000,000	0.5%
43	Rhode Island	292,000,000	0.4%	39	Nebraska	416,000,000	0.5%
26	South Carolina	947,000,000	1.2%	40	Hawaii	408,000,000	0.5%
47	South Dakota	206,000,000	0.3%	41	Maine	351,000,000	0.4%
21	Tennessee	1,465,000,000	1.8%	42	West Virginia	324,000,000	0.4%
3	Texas	4,881,000,000	6.0%	43	Rhode Island	292,000,000	0.4%
31	Utah	711,000,000	0.9%	44	Delaware	259,000,000	0.3%
48	Vermont	194,000,000	0.2%	45	Alaska	258,000,000	0.3%
14	Virginia	2,053,000,000	2.5%	46	Montana	236,000,000	0.3%
10	Washington	2,561,000,000	3.1%	47	South Dakota	206,000,000	0.3%
42	West Virginia	324,000,000	0.4%	48	Vermont	194,000,000	0.2%
15	Wisconsin	1,774,000,000	2.2%	49	North Dakota	183,000,000	0.2%
50	Wyoming	116,000,000	0.1%	50	Wyoming	116,000,000	0.1%
					District of Columbia	199,000,000	0.2%

Source: U.S. Department of Health and Human Services, Centers for Medicare and Medicaid Services "State Health Care Expenditures" (http://www.cms.hhs.gov/NationalHealthExpendData/)
By state of provider.

Percent of Total Personal Health Care Expenditures
Spent on Dental Services in 2004
National Percent = 5.2%*

ALPHA ORDER

RANK	STATE	PERCENT
37	Alabama	4.4
10	Alaska	6.1
9	Arizona	6.2
32	Arkansas	4.6
5	California	7.2
7	Colorado	6.8
12	Connecticut	6.0
28	Delaware	4.9
42	Florida	4.3
17	Georgia	5.6
8	Hawaii	6.4
2	Idaho	7.4
20	Illinois	5.2
28	Indiana	4.9
32	Iowa	4.6
24	Kansas	5.1
48	Kentucky	3.6
48	Louisiana	3.6
37	Maine	4.4
20	Maryland	5.2
24	Massachusetts	5.1
10	Michigan	6.1
18	Minnesota	5.4
47	Mississippi	3.7
46	Missouri	4.0
20	Montana	5.2
45	Nebraska	4.2
12	Nevada	6.0
6	New Hampshire	6.9
14	New Jersey	5.7
20	New Mexico	5.2
42	New York	4.3
26	North Carolina	5.0
32	North Dakota	4.6
37	Ohio	4.4
28	Oklahoma	4.9
3	Oregon	7.3
37	Pennsylvania	4.4
42	Rhode Island	4.3
36	South Carolina	4.5
31	South Dakota	4.7
37	Tennessee	4.4
32	Texas	4.6
3	Utah	7.3
18	Vermont	5.4
14	Virginia	5.7
1	Washington	7.9
50	West Virginia	3.2
14	Wisconsin	5.7
26	Wyoming	5.0

RANK ORDER

RANK	STATE	PERCENT
1	Washington	7.9
2	Idaho	7.4
3	Oregon	7.3
3	Utah	7.3
5	California	7.2
6	New Hampshire	6.9
7	Colorado	6.8
8	Hawaii	6.4
9	Arizona	6.2
10	Alaska	6.1
10	Michigan	6.1
12	Connecticut	6.0
12	Nevada	6.0
14	New Jersey	5.7
14	Virginia	5.7
14	Wisconsin	5.7
17	Georgia	5.6
18	Minnesota	5.4
18	Vermont	5.4
20	Illinois	5.2
20	Maryland	5.2
20	Montana	5.2
20	New Mexico	5.2
24	Kansas	5.1
24	Massachusetts	5.1
26	North Carolina	5.0
26	Wyoming	5.0
28	Delaware	4.9
28	Indiana	4.9
28	Oklahoma	4.9
31	South Dakota	4.7
32	Arkansas	4.6
32	Iowa	4.6
32	North Dakota	4.6
32	Texas	4.6
36	South Carolina	4.5
37	Alabama	4.4
37	Maine	4.4
37	Ohio	4.4
37	Pennsylvania	4.4
37	Tennessee	4.4
42	Florida	4.3
42	New York	4.3
42	Rhode Island	4.3
45	Nebraska	4.2
46	Missouri	4.0
47	Mississippi	3.7
48	Kentucky	3.6
48	Louisiana	3.6
50	West Virginia	3.2
	District of Columbia	3.3

Source: MQ Press using data from U.S. Dept of Health & Human Services, Centers for Medicare and Medicaid Services
"State Health Care Expenditures" (http://www.cms.hhs.gov/NationalHealthExpendData/)
*By state of provider.

Per Capita Expenditures for Dental Services in 2004

National Per Capita = $278*

ALPHA ORDER

RANK	STATE	PER CAPITA
40	Alabama	$231
2	Alaska	393
28	Arizona	262
44	Arkansas	220
7	California	338
8	Colorado	331
3	Connecticut	380
13	Delaware	313
37	Florida	236
32	Georgia	259
10	Hawaii	324
15	Idaho	305
26	Illinois	265
30	Indiana	260
37	Iowa	236
29	Kansas	261
47	Kentucky	199
48	Louisiana	188
24	Maine	267
19	Maryland	286
5	Massachusetts	358
16	Michigan	298
9	Minnesota	330
49	Mississippi	180
42	Missouri	228
33	Montana	255
36	Nebraska	238
22	Nevada	274
4	New Hampshire	370
10	New Jersey	324
45	New Mexico	219
20	New York	284
30	North Carolina	260
18	North Dakota	288
34	Ohio	250
39	Oklahoma	234
6	Oregon	355
27	Pennsylvania	263
23	Rhode Island	271
43	South Carolina	226
24	South Dakota	267
35	Tennessee	249
46	Texas	217
17	Utah	294
13	Vermont	313
21	Virginia	275
1	Washington	413
50	West Virginia	179
12	Wisconsin	323
41	Wyoming	229

RANK ORDER

RANK	STATE	PER CAPITA
1	Washington	$413
2	Alaska	393
3	Connecticut	380
4	New Hampshire	370
5	Massachusetts	358
6	Oregon	355
7	California	338
8	Colorado	331
9	Minnesota	330
10	Hawaii	324
10	New Jersey	324
12	Wisconsin	323
13	Delaware	313
13	Vermont	313
15	Idaho	305
16	Michigan	298
17	Utah	294
18	North Dakota	288
19	Maryland	286
20	New York	284
21	Virginia	275
22	Nevada	274
23	Rhode Island	271
24	Maine	267
24	South Dakota	267
26	Illinois	265
27	Pennsylvania	263
28	Arizona	262
29	Kansas	261
30	Indiana	260
30	North Carolina	260
32	Georgia	259
33	Montana	255
34	Ohio	250
35	Tennessee	249
36	Nebraska	238
37	Florida	236
37	Iowa	236
39	Oklahoma	234
40	Alabama	231
41	Wyoming	229
42	Missouri	228
43	South Carolina	226
44	Arkansas	220
45	New Mexico	219
46	Texas	217
47	Kentucky	199
48	Louisiana	188
49	Mississippi	180
50	West Virginia	179

| | District of Columbia | 343 |

Source: MQ Press using data from U.S. Dept of Health & Human Services, Centers for Medicare and Medicaid Services "State Health Care Expenditures" (http://www.cms.hhs.gov/NationalHealthExpendData/)

*Estimates by state of provider. Per capita calculated using resident population. These figures may be skewed due to residents crossing state borders for care.

Expenditures for Other Professional Health Care Services in 2004

National Total = $52,720,000,000*

ALPHA ORDER

RANK	STATE	EXPENDITURES	% of USA
27	Alabama	$670,000,000	1.3%
46	Alaska	166,000,000	0.3%
22	Arizona	922,000,000	1.7%
32	Arkansas	458,000,000	0.9%
1	California	6,250,000,000	11.9%
21	Colorado	969,000,000	1.8%
23	Connecticut	849,000,000	1.6%
43	Delaware	202,000,000	0.4%
2	Florida	3,602,000,000	6.8%
13	Georgia	1,267,000,000	2.4%
41	Hawaii	230,000,000	0.4%
40	Idaho	293,000,000	0.6%
6	Illinois	2,321,000,000	4.4%
19	Indiana	994,000,000	1.9%
29	Iowa	539,000,000	1.0%
31	Kansas	489,000,000	0.9%
24	Kentucky	800,000,000	1.5%
26	Louisiana	703,000,000	1.3%
39	Maine	303,000,000	0.6%
15	Maryland	1,070,000,000	2.0%
12	Massachusetts	1,313,000,000	2.5%
9	Michigan	1,859,000,000	3.5%
18	Minnesota	1,013,000,000	1.9%
35	Mississippi	339,000,000	0.6%
20	Missouri	977,000,000	1.9%
45	Montana	168,000,000	0.3%
38	Nebraska	305,000,000	0.6%
33	Nevada	381,000,000	0.7%
42	New Hampshire	223,000,000	0.4%
8	New Jersey	1,879,000,000	3.6%
37	New Mexico	313,000,000	0.6%
3	New York	3,522,000,000	6.7%
11	North Carolina	1,344,000,000	2.5%
49	North Dakota	113,000,000	0.2%
7	Ohio	2,292,000,000	4.3%
28	Oklahoma	544,000,000	1.0%
25	Oregon	717,000,000	1.4%
5	Pennsylvania	2,660,000,000	5.0%
44	Rhode Island	194,000,000	0.4%
30	South Carolina	512,000,000	1.0%
47	South Dakota	142,000,000	0.3%
16	Tennessee	1,066,000,000	2.0%
4	Texas	3,233,000,000	6.1%
34	Utah	343,000,000	0.7%
48	Vermont	131,000,000	0.2%
14	Virginia	1,107,000,000	2.1%
10	Washington	1,377,000,000	2.6%
36	West Virginia	338,000,000	0.6%
17	Wisconsin	1,018,000,000	1.9%
50	Wyoming	109,000,000	0.2%

RANK ORDER

RANK	STATE	EXPENDITURES	% of USA
1	California	$6,250,000,000	11.9%
2	Florida	3,602,000,000	6.8%
3	New York	3,522,000,000	6.7%
4	Texas	3,233,000,000	6.1%
5	Pennsylvania	2,660,000,000	5.0%
6	Illinois	2,321,000,000	4.4%
7	Ohio	2,292,000,000	4.3%
8	New Jersey	1,879,000,000	3.6%
9	Michigan	1,859,000,000	3.5%
10	Washington	1,377,000,000	2.6%
11	North Carolina	1,344,000,000	2.5%
12	Massachusetts	1,313,000,000	2.5%
13	Georgia	1,267,000,000	2.4%
14	Virginia	1,107,000,000	2.1%
15	Maryland	1,070,000,000	2.0%
16	Tennessee	1,066,000,000	2.0%
17	Wisconsin	1,018,000,000	1.9%
18	Minnesota	1,013,000,000	1.9%
19	Indiana	994,000,000	1.9%
20	Missouri	977,000,000	1.9%
21	Colorado	969,000,000	1.8%
22	Arizona	922,000,000	1.7%
23	Connecticut	849,000,000	1.6%
24	Kentucky	800,000,000	1.5%
25	Oregon	717,000,000	1.4%
26	Louisiana	703,000,000	1.3%
27	Alabama	670,000,000	1.3%
28	Oklahoma	544,000,000	1.0%
29	Iowa	539,000,000	1.0%
30	South Carolina	512,000,000	1.0%
31	Kansas	489,000,000	0.9%
32	Arkansas	458,000,000	0.9%
33	Nevada	381,000,000	0.7%
34	Utah	343,000,000	0.7%
35	Mississippi	339,000,000	0.6%
36	West Virginia	338,000,000	0.6%
37	New Mexico	313,000,000	0.6%
38	Nebraska	305,000,000	0.6%
39	Maine	303,000,000	0.6%
40	Idaho	293,000,000	0.6%
41	Hawaii	230,000,000	0.4%
42	New Hampshire	223,000,000	0.4%
43	Delaware	202,000,000	0.4%
44	Rhode Island	194,000,000	0.4%
45	Montana	168,000,000	0.3%
46	Alaska	166,000,000	0.3%
47	South Dakota	142,000,000	0.3%
48	Vermont	131,000,000	0.2%
49	North Dakota	113,000,000	0.2%
50	Wyoming	109,000,000	0.2%
	District of Columbia	92,000,000	0.2%

Source: U.S. Department of Health and Human Services, Centers for Medicare and Medicaid Services
"State Health Care Expenditures" (http://www.cms.hhs.gov/NationalHealthExpendData/)
*By state of provider. Includes services of licensed professionals such as chiropractors, optometrists, podiatrists and independently practicing nurses. Also includes Medicare ambulance services.

Percent of Total Personal Health Care Expenditures
Spent on Other Professional Health Care Services in 2004
National Percent = 3.4%*

ALPHA ORDER

RANK	STATE	PERCENT
46	Alabama	2.8
6	Alaska	3.9
9	Arizona	3.8
22	Arkansas	3.5
15	California	3.7
3	Colorado	4.3
6	Connecticut	3.9
9	Delaware	3.8
9	Florida	3.8
36	Georgia	3.1
17	Hawaii	3.6
1	Idaho	5.1
17	Illinois	3.6
39	Indiana	3.0
22	Iowa	3.5
22	Kansas	3.5
22	Kentucky	3.5
39	Louisiana	3.0
9	Maine	3.8
22	Maryland	3.5
44	Massachusetts	2.9
9	Michigan	3.8
29	Minnesota	3.3
50	Mississippi	2.4
39	Missouri	3.0
15	Montana	3.7
36	Nebraska	3.1
17	Nevada	3.6
33	New Hampshire	3.2
9	New Jersey	3.8
6	New Mexico	3.9
46	New York	2.8
39	North Carolina	3.0
44	North Dakota	2.9
22	Ohio	3.5
29	Oklahoma	3.3
5	Oregon	4.1
17	Pennsylvania	3.6
46	Rhode Island	2.8
49	South Carolina	2.5
33	South Dakota	3.2
33	Tennessee	3.2
39	Texas	3.0
22	Utah	3.5
17	Vermont	3.6
36	Virginia	3.1
3	Washington	4.3
29	West Virginia	3.3
29	Wisconsin	3.3
2	Wyoming	4.7

RANK ORDER

RANK	STATE	PERCENT
1	Idaho	5.1
2	Wyoming	4.7
3	Colorado	4.3
3	Washington	4.3
5	Oregon	4.1
6	Alaska	3.9
6	Connecticut	3.9
6	New Mexico	3.9
9	Arizona	3.8
9	Delaware	3.8
9	Florida	3.8
9	Maine	3.8
9	Michigan	3.8
9	New Jersey	3.8
15	California	3.7
15	Montana	3.7
17	Hawaii	3.6
17	Illinois	3.6
17	Nevada	3.6
17	Pennsylvania	3.6
17	Vermont	3.6
22	Arkansas	3.5
22	Iowa	3.5
22	Kansas	3.5
22	Kentucky	3.5
22	Maryland	3.5
22	Ohio	3.5
22	Utah	3.5
29	Minnesota	3.3
29	Oklahoma	3.3
29	West Virginia	3.3
29	Wisconsin	3.3
33	New Hampshire	3.2
33	South Dakota	3.2
33	Tennessee	3.2
36	Georgia	3.1
36	Nebraska	3.1
36	Virginia	3.1
39	Indiana	3.0
39	Louisiana	3.0
39	Missouri	3.0
39	North Carolina	3.0
39	Texas	3.0
44	Massachusetts	2.9
44	North Dakota	2.9
46	Alabama	2.8
46	New York	2.8
46	Rhode Island	2.8
49	South Carolina	2.5
50	Mississippi	2.4

District of Columbia   1.5

Source: MQ Press using data from U.S. Dept of Health & Human Services, Centers for Medicare and Medicaid Services "State Health Care Expenditures" (http://www.cms.hhs.gov/NationalHealthExpendData/)
By state of provider. Includes services of licensed professionals such as chiropractors, optometrists, podiatrists and independently practicing nurses. Also includes Medicare ambulance services.

Per Capita Expenditures for Other Professional Health Care Services in 2004

National Per Capita = $180*

<table>
<tr><td colspan="3">ALPHA ORDER</td><td colspan="3">RANK ORDER</td></tr>
<tr><td>RANK</td><td>STATE</td><td>PER CAPITA</td><td>RANK</td><td>STATE</td><td>PER CAPITA</td></tr>
<tr><td>44</td><td>Alabama</td><td>$148</td><td>1</td><td>Alaska</td><td>$253</td></tr>
<tr><td>1</td><td>Alaska</td><td>253</td><td>2</td><td>Delaware</td><td>244</td></tr>
<tr><td>39</td><td>Arizona</td><td>160</td><td>3</td><td>Connecticut</td><td>243</td></tr>
<tr><td>36</td><td>Arkansas</td><td>167</td><td>4</td><td>Maine</td><td>231</td></tr>
<tr><td>33</td><td>California</td><td>174</td><td>5</td><td>Washington</td><td>222</td></tr>
<tr><td>9</td><td>Colorado</td><td>211</td><td>6</td><td>New Jersey</td><td>217</td></tr>
<tr><td>3</td><td>Connecticut</td><td>243</td><td>7</td><td>Wyoming</td><td>216</td></tr>
<tr><td>2</td><td>Delaware</td><td>244</td><td>8</td><td>Pennsylvania</td><td>215</td></tr>
<tr><td>12</td><td>Florida</td><td>207</td><td>9</td><td>Colorado</td><td>211</td></tr>
<tr><td>47</td><td>Georgia</td><td>142</td><td>9</td><td>Vermont</td><td>211</td></tr>
<tr><td>23</td><td>Hawaii</td><td>183</td><td>11</td><td>Idaho</td><td>210</td></tr>
<tr><td>11</td><td>Idaho</td><td>210</td><td>12</td><td>Florida</td><td>207</td></tr>
<tr><td>23</td><td>Illinois</td><td>183</td><td>13</td><td>Massachusetts</td><td>204</td></tr>
<tr><td>39</td><td>Indiana</td><td>160</td><td>14</td><td>Ohio</td><td>200</td></tr>
<tr><td>26</td><td>Iowa</td><td>182</td><td>14</td><td>Oregon</td><td>200</td></tr>
<tr><td>30</td><td>Kansas</td><td>179</td><td>16</td><td>Minnesota</td><td>199</td></tr>
<tr><td>17</td><td>Kentucky</td><td>193</td><td>17</td><td>Kentucky</td><td>193</td></tr>
<tr><td>42</td><td>Louisiana</td><td>156</td><td>17</td><td>Maryland</td><td>193</td></tr>
<tr><td>4</td><td>Maine</td><td>231</td><td>19</td><td>West Virginia</td><td>187</td></tr>
<tr><td>17</td><td>Maryland</td><td>193</td><td>20</td><td>Wisconsin</td><td>185</td></tr>
<tr><td>13</td><td>Massachusetts</td><td>204</td><td>21</td><td>Michigan</td><td>184</td></tr>
<tr><td>21</td><td>Michigan</td><td>184</td><td>21</td><td>South Dakota</td><td>184</td></tr>
<tr><td>16</td><td>Minnesota</td><td>199</td><td>23</td><td>Hawaii</td><td>183</td></tr>
<tr><td>50</td><td>Mississippi</td><td>117</td><td>23</td><td>Illinois</td><td>183</td></tr>
<tr><td>35</td><td>Missouri</td><td>170</td><td>23</td><td>New York</td><td>183</td></tr>
<tr><td>27</td><td>Montana</td><td>181</td><td>26</td><td>Iowa</td><td>182</td></tr>
<tr><td>32</td><td>Nebraska</td><td>175</td><td>27</td><td>Montana</td><td>181</td></tr>
<tr><td>38</td><td>Nevada</td><td>163</td><td>27</td><td>Tennessee</td><td>181</td></tr>
<tr><td>34</td><td>New Hampshire</td><td>172</td><td>29</td><td>Rhode Island</td><td>180</td></tr>
<tr><td>6</td><td>New Jersey</td><td>217</td><td>30</td><td>Kansas</td><td>179</td></tr>
<tr><td>37</td><td>New Mexico</td><td>165</td><td>31</td><td>North Dakota</td><td>178</td></tr>
<tr><td>23</td><td>New York</td><td>183</td><td>32</td><td>Nebraska</td><td>175</td></tr>
<tr><td>41</td><td>North Carolina</td><td>158</td><td>33</td><td>California</td><td>174</td></tr>
<tr><td>31</td><td>North Dakota</td><td>178</td><td>34</td><td>New Hampshire</td><td>172</td></tr>
<tr><td>14</td><td>Ohio</td><td>200</td><td>35</td><td>Missouri</td><td>170</td></tr>
<tr><td>43</td><td>Oklahoma</td><td>154</td><td>36</td><td>Arkansas</td><td>167</td></tr>
<tr><td>14</td><td>Oregon</td><td>200</td><td>37</td><td>New Mexico</td><td>165</td></tr>
<tr><td>8</td><td>Pennsylvania</td><td>215</td><td>38</td><td>Nevada</td><td>163</td></tr>
<tr><td>29</td><td>Rhode Island</td><td>180</td><td>39</td><td>Arizona</td><td>160</td></tr>
<tr><td>49</td><td>South Carolina</td><td>122</td><td>39</td><td>Indiana</td><td>160</td></tr>
<tr><td>21</td><td>South Dakota</td><td>184</td><td>41</td><td>North Carolina</td><td>158</td></tr>
<tr><td>27</td><td>Tennessee</td><td>181</td><td>42</td><td>Louisiana</td><td>156</td></tr>
<tr><td>46</td><td>Texas</td><td>144</td><td>43</td><td>Oklahoma</td><td>154</td></tr>
<tr><td>47</td><td>Utah</td><td>142</td><td>44</td><td>Alabama</td><td>148</td></tr>
<tr><td>9</td><td>Vermont</td><td>211</td><td>44</td><td>Virginia</td><td>148</td></tr>
<tr><td>44</td><td>Virginia</td><td>148</td><td>46</td><td>Texas</td><td>144</td></tr>
<tr><td>5</td><td>Washington</td><td>222</td><td>47</td><td>Georgia</td><td>142</td></tr>
<tr><td>19</td><td>West Virginia</td><td>187</td><td>47</td><td>Utah</td><td>142</td></tr>
<tr><td>20</td><td>Wisconsin</td><td>185</td><td>49</td><td>South Carolina</td><td>122</td></tr>
<tr><td>7</td><td>Wyoming</td><td>216</td><td>50</td><td>Mississippi</td><td>117</td></tr>
<tr><td></td><td></td><td></td><td></td><td>District of Columbia</td><td>159</td></tr>
</table>

Source: MQ Press using data from U.S. Dept of Health & Human Services, Centers for Medicare and Medicaid Services
"State Health Care Expenditures" (http://www.cms.hhs.gov/NationalHealthExpendData/)
*Estimates by state of provider. Per capita calculated using resident population. These figures may be skewed
due to residents crossing state borders for care. Includes services of licensed professionals such as chiropractors,
optometrists, podiatrists and independently practicing nurses. Also includes Medicare ambulance services.

Expenditures for Nursing Home Care in 2004

National Total = $115,210,000,000*

ALPHA ORDER

RANK	STATE	EXPENDITURES	% of USA
25	Alabama	$1,459,000,000	1.3%
50	Alaska	73,000,000	0.1%
31	Arizona	1,055,000,000	0.9%
32	Arkansas	1,015,000,000	0.9%
2	California	8,451,000,000	7.3%
27	Colorado	1,192,000,000	1.0%
13	Connecticut	2,749,000,000	2.4%
41	Delaware	405,000,000	0.4%
5	Florida	6,532,000,000	5.7%
19	Georgia	2,278,000,000	2.0%
47	Hawaii	293,000,000	0.3%
44	Idaho	359,000,000	0.3%
7	Illinois	5,156,000,000	4.5%
12	Indiana	2,895,000,000	2.5%
22	Iowa	1,623,000,000	1.4%
29	Kansas	1,149,000,000	1.0%
24	Kentucky	1,512,000,000	1.3%
23	Louisiana	1,616,000,000	1.4%
37	Maine	625,000,000	0.5%
14	Maryland	2,549,000,000	2.2%
9	Massachusetts	4,190,000,000	3.6%
11	Michigan	3,146,000,000	2.7%
18	Minnesota	2,383,000,000	2.1%
30	Mississippi	1,084,000,000	0.9%
15	Missouri	2,484,000,000	2.2%
46	Montana	323,000,000	0.3%
34	Nebraska	873,000,000	0.8%
45	Nevada	328,000,000	0.3%
38	New Hampshire	542,000,000	0.5%
8	New Jersey	4,259,000,000	3.7%
43	New Mexico	366,000,000	0.3%
1	New York	13,259,000,000	11.5%
10	North Carolina	3,358,000,000	2.9%
42	North Dakota	395,000,000	0.3%
4	Ohio	6,870,000,000	6.0%
28	Oklahoma	1,160,000,000	1.0%
33	Oregon	905,000,000	0.8%
3	Pennsylvania	7,591,000,000	6.6%
36	Rhode Island	633,000,000	0.5%
26	South Carolina	1,215,000,000	1.1%
40	South Dakota	415,000,000	0.4%
20	Tennessee	2,225,000,000	1.9%
6	Texas	5,608,000,000	4.9%
39	Utah	432,000,000	0.4%
48	Vermont	239,000,000	0.2%
16	Virginia	2,445,000,000	2.1%
21	Washington	1,872,000,000	1.6%
35	West Virginia	684,000,000	0.6%
17	Wisconsin	2,428,000,000	2.1%
49	Wyoming	144,000,000	0.1%

RANK ORDER

RANK	STATE	EXPENDITURES	% of USA
1	New York	$13,259,000,000	11.5%
2	California	8,451,000,000	7.3%
3	Pennsylvania	7,591,000,000	6.6%
4	Ohio	6,870,000,000	6.0%
5	Florida	6,532,000,000	5.7%
6	Texas	5,608,000,000	4.9%
7	Illinois	5,156,000,000	4.5%
8	New Jersey	4,259,000,000	3.7%
9	Massachusetts	4,190,000,000	3.6%
10	North Carolina	3,358,000,000	2.9%
11	Michigan	3,146,000,000	2.7%
12	Indiana	2,895,000,000	2.5%
13	Connecticut	2,749,000,000	2.4%
14	Maryland	2,549,000,000	2.2%
15	Missouri	2,484,000,000	2.2%
16	Virginia	2,445,000,000	2.1%
17	Wisconsin	2,428,000,000	2.1%
18	Minnesota	2,383,000,000	2.1%
19	Georgia	2,278,000,000	2.0%
20	Tennessee	2,225,000,000	1.9%
21	Washington	1,872,000,000	1.6%
22	Iowa	1,623,000,000	1.4%
23	Louisiana	1,616,000,000	1.4%
24	Kentucky	1,512,000,000	1.3%
25	Alabama	1,459,000,000	1.3%
26	South Carolina	1,215,000,000	1.1%
27	Colorado	1,192,000,000	1.0%
28	Oklahoma	1,160,000,000	1.0%
29	Kansas	1,149,000,000	1.0%
30	Mississippi	1,084,000,000	0.9%
31	Arizona	1,055,000,000	0.9%
32	Arkansas	1,015,000,000	0.9%
33	Oregon	905,000,000	0.8%
34	Nebraska	873,000,000	0.8%
35	West Virginia	684,000,000	0.6%
36	Rhode Island	633,000,000	0.5%
37	Maine	625,000,000	0.5%
38	New Hampshire	542,000,000	0.5%
39	Utah	432,000,000	0.4%
40	South Dakota	415,000,000	0.4%
41	Delaware	405,000,000	0.4%
42	North Dakota	395,000,000	0.3%
43	New Mexico	366,000,000	0.3%
44	Idaho	359,000,000	0.3%
45	Nevada	328,000,000	0.3%
46	Montana	323,000,000	0.3%
47	Hawaii	293,000,000	0.3%
48	Vermont	239,000,000	0.2%
49	Wyoming	144,000,000	0.1%
50	Alaska	73,000,000	0.1%
	District of Columbia	369,000,000	0.3%

Source: U.S. Department of Health and Human Services, Centers for Medicare and Medicaid Services
"State Health Care Expenditures" (http://www.cms.hhs.gov/NationalHealthExpendData/)
By state of provider. Includes all freestanding nursing homes. Does not include nursing home services provided in long-term care units of hospitals.

Percent of Total Personal Health Care Expenditures
Spent on Nursing Home Care in 2004
National Percent = 7.4%*

ALPHA ORDER

RANK	STATE	PERCENT
36	Alabama	6.2
50	Alaska	1.7
48	Arizona	4.3
16	Arkansas	7.8
44	California	5.0
41	Colorado	5.3
1	Connecticut	12.5
21	Delaware	7.7
26	Florida	6.9
40	Georgia	5.5
45	Hawaii	4.6
36	Idaho	6.2
15	Illinois	7.9
11	Indiana	8.8
2	Iowa	10.7
14	Kansas	8.1
30	Kentucky	6.7
28	Louisiana	6.8
16	Maine	7.8
13	Maryland	8.4
8	Massachusetts	9.2
34	Michigan	6.4
21	Minnesota	7.7
16	Mississippi	7.8
23	Missouri	7.6
25	Montana	7.1
10	Nebraska	8.9
49	Nevada	3.1
16	New Hampshire	7.8
12	New Jersey	8.7
45	New Mexico	4.6
4	New York	10.4
24	North Carolina	7.5
6	North Dakota	10.0
3	Ohio	10.5
26	Oklahoma	6.9
43	Oregon	5.2
5	Pennsylvania	10.2
8	Rhode Island	9.2
38	South Carolina	5.8
7	South Dakota	9.4
32	Tennessee	6.6
41	Texas	5.3
47	Utah	4.4
32	Vermont	6.6
28	Virginia	6.8
38	Washington	5.8
30	West Virginia	6.7
16	Wisconsin	7.8
35	Wyoming	6.3

RANK ORDER

RANK	STATE	PERCENT
1	Connecticut	12.5
2	Iowa	10.7
3	Ohio	10.5
4	New York	10.4
5	Pennsylvania	10.2
6	North Dakota	10.0
7	South Dakota	9.4
8	Massachusetts	9.2
8	Rhode Island	9.2
10	Nebraska	8.9
11	Indiana	8.8
12	New Jersey	8.7
13	Maryland	8.4
14	Kansas	8.1
15	Illinois	7.9
16	Arkansas	7.8
16	Maine	7.8
16	Mississippi	7.8
16	New Hampshire	7.8
16	Wisconsin	7.8
21	Delaware	7.7
21	Minnesota	7.7
23	Missouri	7.6
24	North Carolina	7.5
25	Montana	7.1
26	Florida	6.9
26	Oklahoma	6.9
28	Louisiana	6.8
28	Virginia	6.8
30	Kentucky	6.7
30	West Virginia	6.7
32	Tennessee	6.6
32	Vermont	6.6
34	Michigan	6.4
35	Wyoming	6.3
36	Alabama	6.2
36	Idaho	6.2
38	South Carolina	5.8
38	Washington	5.8
40	Georgia	5.5
41	Colorado	5.3
41	Texas	5.3
43	Oregon	5.2
44	California	5.0
45	Hawaii	4.6
45	New Mexico	4.6
47	Utah	4.4
48	Arizona	4.3
49	Nevada	3.1
50	Alaska	1.7

| | District of Columbia | 6.1 |

Source: MQ Press using data from U.S. Dept of Health & Human Services, Centers for Medicare and Medicaid Services "State Health Care Expenditures" (http://www.cms.hhs.gov/NationalHealthExpendData/)
By state of provider. Includes all freestanding nursing homes. Does not include nursing home services provided in long-term care units of hospitals.

Per Capita Expenditures for Nursing Home Care in 2004

National Per Capita = $392*

ALPHA ORDER				RANK ORDER		
RANK	STATE	PER CAPITA		RANK	STATE	PER CAPITA
34	Alabama	$323		1	Connecticut	$787
50	Alaska	111		2	New York	687
47	Arizona	184		3	Massachusetts	651
28	Arkansas	370		4	North Dakota	621
44	California	236		5	Pennsylvania	613
39	Colorado	259		6	Ohio	599
1	Connecticut	787		7	Rhode Island	587
12	Delaware	489		8	Iowa	549
26	Florida	376		9	South Dakota	539
41	Georgia	255		10	Nebraska	500
45	Hawaii	233		11	New Jersey	491
40	Idaho	257		12	Delaware	489
21	Illinois	406		13	Maine	476
15	Indiana	465		14	Minnesota	468
8	Iowa	549		15	Indiana	465
19	Kansas	420		16	Maryland	459
29	Kentucky	365		17	Wisconsin	442
30	Louisiana	359		18	Missouri	432
13	Maine	476		19	Kansas	420
16	Maryland	459		20	New Hampshire	418
3	Massachusetts	651		21	Illinois	406
35	Michigan	312		22	North Carolina	394
14	Minnesota	468		23	Vermont	385
27	Mississippi	375		24	Tennessee	378
18	Missouri	432		24	West Virginia	378
31	Montana	349		26	Florida	376
10	Nebraska	500		27	Mississippi	375
49	Nevada	141		28	Arkansas	370
20	New Hampshire	418		29	Kentucky	365
11	New Jersey	491		30	Louisiana	359
46	New Mexico	193		31	Montana	349
2	New York	687		32	Oklahoma	329
22	North Carolina	394		33	Virginia	327
4	North Dakota	621		34	Alabama	323
6	Ohio	599		35	Michigan	312
32	Oklahoma	329		36	Washington	302
42	Oregon	252		37	South Carolina	290
5	Pennsylvania	613		38	Wyoming	285
7	Rhode Island	587		39	Colorado	259
37	South Carolina	$290		40	Idaho	257
9	South Dakota	539		41	Georgia	255
24	Tennessee	378		42	Oregon	252
43	Texas	249		43	Texas	249
48	Utah	178		44	California	236
23	Vermont	385		45	Hawaii	233
33	Virginia	327		46	New Mexico	193
36	Washington	302		47	Arizona	184
24	West Virginia	378		48	Utah	178
17	Wisconsin	442		49	Nevada	141
38	Wyoming	285		50	Alaska	111

District of Columbia   637

Source: MQ Press using data from U.S. Dept of Health & Human Services, Centers for Medicare and Medicaid Services
"State Health Care Expenditures" (http://www.cms.hhs.gov/NationalHealthExpendData/)
*Estimates by state of provider. Per capita calculated using resident population. These figures may be skewed
due to residents crossing state borders for care. Includes all freestanding nursing homes. Does not include nursing
home services provided in long-term care units of hospitals.

Expenditures for Prescription Drugs in 2004

National Total = $188,452,000,000*

ALPHA ORDER

RANK	STATE	EXPENDITURES	% of USA
18	Alabama	$3,646,000,000	1.9%
49	Alaska	345,000,000	0.2%
26	Arizona	2,736,000,000	1.5%
32	Arkansas	1,693,000,000	0.9%
1	California	17,070,000,000	9.1%
29	Colorado	1,834,000,000	1.0%
25	Connecticut	2,816,000,000	1.5%
44	Delaware	676,000,000	0.4%
3	Florida	12,692,000,000	6.7%
11	Georgia	5,612,000,000	3.0%
42	Hawaii	733,000,000	0.4%
43	Idaho	721,000,000	0.4%
6	Illinois	7,797,000,000	4.1%
15	Indiana	4,422,000,000	2.3%
30	Iowa	1,773,000,000	0.9%
31	Kansas	1,700,000,000	0.9%
19	Kentucky	3,527,000,000	1.9%
21	Louisiana	3,145,000,000	1.7%
39	Maine	952,000,000	0.5%
17	Maryland	3,813,000,000	2.0%
14	Massachusetts	4,767,000,000	2.5%
9	Michigan	6,709,000,000	3.6%
23	Minnesota	3,045,000,000	1.6%
28	Mississippi	1,957,000,000	1.0%
16	Missouri	3,846,000,000	2.0%
46	Montana	417,000,000	0.2%
37	Nebraska	1,136,000,000	0.6%
35	Nevada	1,223,000,000	0.6%
40	New Hampshire	804,000,000	0.4%
8	New Jersey	7,048,000,000	3.7%
41	New Mexico	774,000,000	0.4%
2	New York	15,678,000,000	8.3%
10	North Carolina	6,529,000,000	3.5%
45	North Dakota	456,000,000	0.2%
7	Ohio	7,673,000,000	4.1%
27	Oklahoma	2,154,000,000	1.1%
33	Oregon	1,499,000,000	0.8%
5	Pennsylvania	9,223,000,000	4.9%
38	Rhode Island	970,000,000	0.5%
24	South Carolina	2,983,000,000	1.6%
48	South Dakota	369,000,000	0.2%
12	Tennessee	5,060,000,000	2.7%
4	Texas	11,432,000,000	6.1%
36	Utah	1,162,000,000	0.6%
47	Vermont	394,000,000	0.2%
13	Virginia	4,932,000,000	2.6%
22	Washington	3,143,000,000	1.7%
34	West Virginia	1,467,000,000	0.8%
20	Wisconsin	3,337,000,000	1.8%
50	Wyoming	261,000,000	0.1%

RANK ORDER

RANK	STATE	EXPENDITURES	% of USA
1	California	$17,070,000,000	9.1%
2	New York	15,678,000,000	8.3%
3	Florida	12,692,000,000	6.7%
4	Texas	11,432,000,000	6.1%
5	Pennsylvania	9,223,000,000	4.9%
6	Illinois	7,797,000,000	4.1%
7	Ohio	7,673,000,000	4.1%
8	New Jersey	7,048,000,000	3.7%
9	Michigan	6,709,000,000	3.6%
10	North Carolina	6,529,000,000	3.5%
11	Georgia	5,612,000,000	3.0%
12	Tennessee	5,060,000,000	2.7%
13	Virginia	4,932,000,000	2.6%
14	Massachusetts	4,767,000,000	2.5%
15	Indiana	4,422,000,000	2.3%
16	Missouri	3,846,000,000	2.0%
17	Maryland	3,813,000,000	2.0%
18	Alabama	3,646,000,000	1.9%
19	Kentucky	3,527,000,000	1.9%
20	Wisconsin	3,337,000,000	1.8%
21	Louisiana	3,145,000,000	1.7%
22	Washington	3,143,000,000	1.7%
23	Minnesota	3,045,000,000	1.6%
24	South Carolina	2,983,000,000	1.6%
25	Connecticut	2,816,000,000	1.5%
26	Arizona	2,736,000,000	1.5%
27	Oklahoma	2,154,000,000	1.1%
28	Mississippi	1,957,000,000	1.0%
29	Colorado	1,834,000,000	1.0%
30	Iowa	1,773,000,000	0.9%
31	Kansas	1,700,000,000	0.9%
32	Arkansas	1,693,000,000	0.9%
33	Oregon	1,499,000,000	0.8%
34	West Virginia	1,467,000,000	0.8%
35	Nevada	1,223,000,000	0.6%
36	Utah	1,162,000,000	0.6%
37	Nebraska	1,136,000,000	0.6%
38	Rhode Island	970,000,000	0.5%
39	Maine	952,000,000	0.5%
40	New Hampshire	804,000,000	0.4%
41	New Mexico	774,000,000	0.4%
42	Hawaii	733,000,000	0.4%
43	Idaho	721,000,000	0.4%
44	Delaware	676,000,000	0.4%
45	North Dakota	456,000,000	0.2%
46	Montana	417,000,000	0.2%
47	Vermont	394,000,000	0.2%
48	South Dakota	369,000,000	0.2%
49	Alaska	345,000,000	0.2%
50	Wyoming	261,000,000	0.1%
	District of Columbia	301,000,000	0.2%

Source: U.S. Department of Health and Human Services, Centers for Medicare and Medicaid Services
   "State Health Care Expenditures" (http://www.cms.hhs.gov/NationalHealthExpendData/)
*Purchases in retail outlets. By state of outlet.

Percent of Total Personal Health Care Expenditures Spent
Spent on Prescription Drugs in 2004
National Percent = 12.1%*

ALPHA ORDER

RANK	STATE	PERCENT
2	Alabama	15.4
49	Alaska	8.2
37	Arizona	11.2
16	Arkansas	13.0
42	California	10.1
49	Colorado	8.2
18	Connecticut	12.8
18	Delaware	12.8
13	Florida	13.4
11	Georgia	13.6
30	Hawaii	11.6
20	Idaho	12.5
24	Illinois	12.0
13	Indiana	13.4
30	Iowa	11.6
24	Kansas	12.0
1	Kentucky	15.6
15	Louisiana	13.2
26	Maine	11.9
20	Maryland	12.5
41	Massachusetts	10.5
11	Michigan	13.6
43	Minnesota	9.8
9	Mississippi	14.0
28	Missouri	11.7
46	Montana	9.1
30	Nebraska	11.6
35	Nevada	11.5
30	New Hampshire	11.6
5	New Jersey	14.4
44	New Mexico	9.7
23	New York	12.3
4	North Carolina	14.7
30	North Dakota	11.6
28	Ohio	11.7
17	Oklahoma	12.9
47	Oregon	8.5
22	Pennsylvania	12.4
8	Rhode Island	14.1
7	South Carolina	14.3
48	South Dakota	8.4
3	Tennessee	15.1
39	Texas	10.7
26	Utah	11.9
38	Vermont	10.9
10	Virginia	13.8
44	Washington	9.7
5	West Virginia	14.4
39	Wisconsin	10.7
36	Wyoming	11.3

RANK ORDER

RANK	STATE	PERCENT
1	Kentucky	15.6
2	Alabama	15.4
3	Tennessee	15.1
4	North Carolina	14.7
5	New Jersey	14.4
5	West Virginia	14.4
7	South Carolina	14.3
8	Rhode Island	14.1
9	Mississippi	14.0
10	Virginia	13.8
11	Georgia	13.6
11	Michigan	13.6
13	Florida	13.4
13	Indiana	13.4
15	Louisiana	13.2
16	Arkansas	13.0
17	Oklahoma	12.9
18	Connecticut	12.8
18	Delaware	12.8
20	Idaho	12.5
20	Maryland	12.5
22	Pennsylvania	12.4
23	New York	12.3
24	Illinois	12.0
24	Kansas	12.0
26	Maine	11.9
26	Utah	11.9
28	Missouri	11.7
28	Ohio	11.7
30	Hawaii	11.6
30	Iowa	11.6
30	Nebraska	11.6
30	New Hampshire	11.6
30	North Dakota	11.6
35	Nevada	11.5
36	Wyoming	11.3
37	Arizona	11.2
38	Vermont	10.9
39	Texas	10.7
39	Wisconsin	10.7
41	Massachusetts	10.5
42	California	10.1
43	Minnesota	9.8
44	New Mexico	9.7
44	Washington	9.7
46	Montana	9.1
47	Oregon	8.5
48	South Dakota	8.4
49	Alaska	8.2
49	Colorado	8.2

| | District of Columbia | 5.0 |

Source: MQ Press using data from U.S. Dept of Health & Human Services, Centers for Medicare and Medicaid Services "State Health Care Expenditures" (http://www.cms.hhs.gov/NationalHealthExpendData/)
Purchases in retail outlets. By state of outlet.

Per Capita Expenditures for Prescription Drugs in 2004

National Per Capita = $642*

ALPHA ORDER

RANK	STATE	PER CAPITA
8	Alabama	$807
37	Alaska	525
45	Arizona	476
30	Arkansas	616
45	California	476
50	Colorado	399
9	Connecticut	806
4	Delaware	816
13	Florida	731
27	Georgia	628
36	Hawaii	582
39	Idaho	517
31	Illinois	613
16	Indiana	711
34	Iowa	600
28	Kansas	621
3	Kentucky	852
18	Louisiana	700
14	Maine	725
19	Maryland	687
12	Massachusetts	741
23	Michigan	665
35	Minnesota	598
20	Mississippi	677
21	Missouri	669
47	Montana	450
25	Nebraska	650
38	Nevada	524
29	New Hampshire	619
6	New Jersey	812
49	New Mexico	407
5	New York	813
10	North Carolina	765
15	North Dakota	717
21	Ohio	669
32	Oklahoma	611
48	Oregon	418
11	Pennsylvania	745
1	Rhode Island	899
16	South Carolina	711
44	South Dakota	479
2	Tennessee	860
41	Texas	508
43	Utah	480
26	Vermont	635
24	Virginia	660
42	Washington	506
7	West Virginia	810
33	Wisconsin	607
40	Wyoming	516

RANK ORDER

RANK	STATE	PER CAPITA
1	Rhode Island	$899
2	Tennessee	860
3	Kentucky	852
4	Delaware	816
5	New York	813
6	New Jersey	812
7	West Virginia	810
8	Alabama	807
9	Connecticut	806
10	North Carolina	765
11	Pennsylvania	745
12	Massachusetts	741
13	Florida	731
14	Maine	725
15	North Dakota	717
16	Indiana	711
16	South Carolina	711
18	Louisiana	700
19	Maryland	687
20	Mississippi	677
21	Missouri	669
21	Ohio	669
23	Michigan	665
24	Virginia	660
25	Nebraska	650
26	Vermont	635
27	Georgia	628
28	Kansas	621
29	New Hampshire	619
30	Arkansas	616
31	Illinois	613
32	Oklahoma	611
33	Wisconsin	607
34	Iowa	600
35	Minnesota	598
36	Hawaii	582
37	Alaska	525
38	Nevada	524
39	Idaho	517
40	Wyoming	516
41	Texas	508
42	Washington	506
43	Utah	480
44	South Dakota	479
45	Arizona	476
45	California	476
47	Montana	450
48	Oregon	418
49	New Mexico	407
50	Colorado	399

| | District of Columbia | 519 |

Source: MQ Press using data from U.S. Dept of Health & Human Services, Centers for Medicare and Medicaid Services "State Health Care Expenditures" (http://www.cms.hhs.gov/NationalHealthExpendData/)
*Estimates by state of outlet. Per capita calculated using resident population. These figures may be skewed due to residents crossing state borders for care. Purchases in retail outlets.

Projected National Health Care Expenditures in 2007

Total Health Care Expenditures = $2,325,700,000,000*

The 2004 health care expenditures broken down to the state level and shown on pages 301 to 321 were released in May of 2006 and are the most recent state health expenditure data available from the Centers for Medicare and Medicaid Services (CMS).

Given the high level of interest in health care finance data, we have assembled a table showing the most recent national level health care expenditure projections. We will continue to monitor CMS data releases and will include state expenditure updates in forthcoming editions.

	PROJECTED EXPENDITURES IN 2007	PROJECTED PERCENT CHANGE: 2006 TO 2007
Total Health Care Expenditures	$2,325,700,000,000	7.2
Per Capita Total Health Care Expenditures	$7,768	
Personal Health Care Expenditures	$1,928,700,000,000	7.0
Per Capita Personal Health Care Expenditures	$6,442	
Hospital Care Expenditures	$709,100,000,000	7.0
Per Capita Hospital Care Expenditures	$2,368	
Physician Services Expenditures	$496,500,000,000	7.2
Per Capita Physician Services Expenditures	$1,658	
Dental Services Expenditures	$101,300,000,000	7.4
Per Capita Dental Services Expenditures	$338	
Other Professional Services	$54,000,000,000	-9.5
Per Capita Other Professional Services	$180	
Home Health Care Expenditures	$57,300,000,000	7.9
Per Capita Home Health Care Expenditures	$191	
Prescription Drugs	$236,800,000,000	8.0
Per Capita Prescription Drugs	$791	
Nursing Home Care	$192,200,000,000	5.9
Per Capita Nursing Home Care	$642	
Other Personal Care Expenditures	$67,800,000,000	8.1
Per Capita Other Personal Care Expenditures	$226	

Source: U.S. Department of Health and Human Services, Centers for Medicare and Medicaid Services
    "National Health Care Expenditures Projections: 2005-2015"
    http://www.cms.hhs.gov/NationalHealthExpendData/downloads/proj2005.pdf
*Per Capita and percent change figures calculated by Morgan Quitno Press using 2006 Census population estimates. For definitions see the corresponding 2004 state tables in this chapter.

V. INCIDENCE OF DISEASE

323   Estimated New Cancer Cases in 2007
324   Estimated Rate of New Cancer Cases in 2007
325   Age-Adjusted Cancer Incidence Rates for Males in 2003
326   Age-Adjusted Cancer Incidence Rates for Females in 2003
327   Estimated New Cases of Bladder Cancer in 2007
328   Estimated Rate of New Bladder Cancer Cases in 2007
329   Estimated New Female Breast Cancer Cases in 2007
330   Age-Adjusted Incidence Rate of Female Breast Cancer Cases in 2003
331   Percent of Women 40 and Older Who Have Had a Mammogram in the Past Two Years: 2004
332   Estimated New Colon and Rectum Cancer Cases in 2007
333   Estimated Rate of New Colon and Rectum Cancer Cases in 2007
334   Percent of Adults Receiving Recent Sigmoidoscopy or Colonoscopy Exam: 2004
335   Estimated New Leukemia Cases in 2007
336   Estimated Rate of New Leukemia Cases in 2007
337   Estimated New Lung Cancer Cases in 2007
338   Estimated Rate of New Lung Cancer Cases in 2007
339   Estimated New Non-Hodgkin's Lymphoma Cases in 2007
340   Estimated Rate of New Non-Hodgkin's Lymphoma Cases in 2007
341   Estimated New Prostate Cancer Cases in 2007
342   Age-Adjusted Incidence Rate of Prostate Cancer Cases in 2003
343   Percent of Males Receiving Recent PSA Test for Prostate Cancer: 2004
344   Estimated New Skin Melanoma Cases in 2007
345   Estimated Rate of New Skin Melanoma Cases in 2007
346   Estimated New Cervical Cancer Cases in 2007
347   Estimated Rate of New Cervical Cancer Cases in 2007
348   Percent of Women 18 Years Old and Older Who Had a Pap Smear Within the Past Three Years: 2004
349   Estimated New Uterine Cancer Cases in 2007
350   Estimated Rate of New Uterine Cancer Cases in 2007
351   AIDS Cases Reported in 2005
352   AIDS Rate in 2005
353   AIDS Cases Reported Through December 2005
354   AIDS Cases in Children 12 Years and Younger Through December 2005
355   Chickenpox (Varicella) Cases Reported in 2006
356   Chickenpox (Varicella) Rate in 2006
357   E-Coli Cases Reported in 2006
358   E-Coli Rate in 2006
359   Hepatitis A and B Cases Reported in 2006
360   Hepatitis A and B Rate in 2006
361   Legionellosis Cases Reported in 2006
362   Legionellosis Rate in 2006
363   Lyme Disease Cases in 2006
364   Lyme Disease Rate in 2006
365   Malaria Cases Reported in 2006
366   Malaria Rate in 2006
367   Meningococcal Infections Reported in 2006
368   Meningococcal Infection Rate in 2006
369   Rabies (Animal) Cases Reported in 2006
370   Rabies (Animal) Rate in 2006
371   Rocky Mountain Spotted Fever Cases Reported in 2006
372   Rocky Mountain Spotted Fever Rate in 2006
373   Salmonellosis Cases Reported in 2006
374   Salmonellosis Rate in 2006
375   Shigellosis Cases Reported in 2006
376   Shigellosis Rate in 2006
377   West Nile Virus Disease Cases Reported in 2006
378   West Nile Disease Rate in 2006
379   Whooping Cough (Pertussis) Cases Reported in 2006
380   Whooping Cough (Pertussis) Rate in 2006
381   Percent of Children Aged 19 to 35 Months Immunized in 2005
382   Percent of Children Aged 19 to 35 Months Fully Immunized in 2005
383   Percent of Adults Aged 65 Years and Older Who Received Flu Shots in 2005

V. INCIDENCE OF DISEASE (Continued)

384 Percent of Adults Aged 65 Years and Older Who Have Had a Pneumonia Vaccine: 2005
385 Sexually Transmitted Diseases in 2005
386 Sexually Transmitted Disease Rate in 2005
387 Chlamydia Cases Reported in 2005
388 Chlamydia Rate in 2005
389 Gonorrhea Cases Reported in 2005
390 Gonorrhea Rate in 2005
391 Syphilis Cases Reported in 2005
392 Syphilis Rate in 2005
393 Percent of Adults Who Have Asthma: 2005
394 Percent of Children Who Have Asthma: 2005
395 Percent of Adults Who Have Been Told They Have Arthritis: 2005
396 Percent of Adults Who Have Been Told They Have Diabetes: 2005
397 Percent of Adults Reporting Serious Psychological Distress: 2004

Estimated New Cancer Cases in 2007

National Estimated Total = 1,444,920 New Cases*

ALPHA ORDER

RANK	STATE	CASES	% of USA
25	Alabama	20,590	1.4%
49	Alaska	2,500	0.2%
20	Arizona	26,270	1.8%
31	Arkansas	14,130	1.0%
1	California	151,250	10.5%
27	Colorado	19,190	1.3%
26	Connecticut	19,780	1.4%
45	Delaware	4,530	0.3%
2	Florida	106,560	7.4%
11	Georgia	35,440	2.5%
43	Hawaii	6,020	0.4%
42	Idaho	6,140	0.4%
6	Illinois	62,010	4.3%
15	Indiana	30,040	2.1%
30	Iowa	16,540	1.1%
32	Kansas	12,760	0.9%
22	Kentucky	22,850	1.6%
23	Louisiana	22,540	1.6%
37	Maine	8,340	0.6%
19	Maryland	26,390	1.8%
13	Massachusetts	34,920	2.4%
8	Michigan	54,410	3.8%
21	Minnesota	25,420	1.8%
33	Mississippi	12,470	0.9%
16	Missouri	29,930	2.1%
44	Montana	4,920	0.3%
36	Nebraska	8,720	0.6%
34	Nevada	11,030	0.8%
40	New Hampshire	7,140	0.5%
9	New Jersey	49,370	3.4%
38	New Mexico	8,030	0.6%
3	New York	100,960	7.0%
10	North Carolina	38,210	2.6%
48	North Dakota	3,340	0.2%
7	Ohio	59,220	4.1%
29	Oklahoma	17,170	1.2%
28	Oregon	18,630	1.3%
5	Pennsylvania	75,130	5.2%
41	Rhode Island	6,360	0.4%
24	South Carolina	21,370	1.5%
46	South Dakota	3,990	0.3%
17	Tennessee	28,440	2.0%
4	Texas	91,020	6.3%
39	Utah	7,660	0.5%
47	Vermont	3,500	0.2%
12	Virginia	35,090	2.4%
14	Washington	31,080	2.2%
35	West Virginia	10,490	0.7%
18	Wisconsin	28,130	1.9%
50	Wyoming	2,340	0.2%

RANK ORDER

RANK	STATE	CASES	% of USA
1	California	151,250	10.5%
2	Florida	106,560	7.4%
3	New York	100,960	7.0%
4	Texas	91,020	6.3%
5	Pennsylvania	75,130	5.2%
6	Illinois	62,010	4.3%
7	Ohio	59,220	4.1%
8	Michigan	54,410	3.8%
9	New Jersey	49,370	3.4%
10	North Carolina	38,210	2.6%
11	Georgia	35,440	2.5%
12	Virginia	35,090	2.4%
13	Massachusetts	34,920	2.4%
14	Washington	31,080	2.2%
15	Indiana	30,040	2.1%
16	Missouri	29,930	2.1%
17	Tennessee	28,440	2.0%
18	Wisconsin	28,130	1.9%
19	Maryland	26,390	1.8%
20	Arizona	26,270	1.8%
21	Minnesota	25,420	1.8%
22	Kentucky	22,850	1.6%
23	Louisiana	22,540	1.6%
24	South Carolina	21,370	1.5%
25	Alabama	20,590	1.4%
26	Connecticut	19,780	1.4%
27	Colorado	19,190	1.3%
28	Oregon	18,630	1.3%
29	Oklahoma	17,170	1.2%
30	Iowa	16,540	1.1%
31	Arkansas	14,130	1.0%
32	Kansas	12,760	0.9%
33	Mississippi	12,470	0.9%
34	Nevada	11,030	0.8%
35	West Virginia	10,490	0.7%
36	Nebraska	8,720	0.6%
37	Maine	8,340	0.6%
38	New Mexico	8,030	0.6%
39	Utah	7,660	0.5%
40	New Hampshire	7,140	0.5%
41	Rhode Island	6,360	0.4%
42	Idaho	6,140	0.4%
43	Hawaii	6,020	0.4%
44	Montana	4,920	0.3%
45	Delaware	4,530	0.3%
46	South Dakota	3,990	0.3%
47	Vermont	3,500	0.2%
48	North Dakota	3,340	0.2%
49	Alaska	2,500	0.2%
50	Wyoming	2,340	0.2%
	District of Columbia	2,540	0.2%

Source: American Cancer Society
   "Cancer Facts & Figures 2007" (Copyright 2007, American Cancer Society)
These estimates are offered as a rough guide and should not be regarded as definitive. They are calculated according to the distribution of estimated 2007 cancer deaths by state. Totals do not include basal and squamous cell skin cancers or in situ carcinomas except urinary bladder.

Estimated Rate of New Cancer Cases in 2007

National Estimated Rate = 482.6 New Cases per 100,000 Population*

ALPHA ORDER			RANK ORDER		
RANK	STATE	RATE	RANK	STATE	RATE
38	Alabama	447.7	1	Maine	631.1
49	Alaska	373.1	2	Pennsylvania	603.9
42	Arizona	426.0	3	Rhode Island	595.7
24	Arkansas	502.7	4	Florida	589.1
44	California	414.9	5	West Virginia	576.9
46	Colorado	403.7	6	New Jersey	565.9
7	Connecticut	564.4	7	Connecticut	564.4
14	Delaware	530.8	8	Vermont	561.0
4	Florida	589.1	9	Iowa	554.6
48	Georgia	378.5	10	Kentucky	543.3
34	Hawaii	468.3	11	New Hampshire	543.0
43	Idaho	418.7	12	Massachusetts	542.5
29	Illinois	483.2	13	Michigan	538.9
31	Indiana	475.8	14	Delaware	530.8
9	Iowa	554.6	15	Louisiana	525.7
35	Kansas	461.6	16	North Dakota	525.3
10	Kentucky	543.3	17	New York	522.9
15	Louisiana	525.7	18	Montana	520.8
1	Maine	631.1	19	Ohio	515.9
33	Maryland	469.9	20	Missouri	512.3
12	Massachusetts	542.5	21	South Dakota	510.3
13	Michigan	538.9	22	Wisconsin	506.3
27	Minnesota	492.0	23	Oregon	503.4
41	Mississippi	428.4	24	Arkansas	502.7
20	Missouri	512.3	25	South Carolina	494.5
18	Montana	520.8	26	Nebraska	493.1
26	Nebraska	493.1	27	Minnesota	492.0
39	Nevada	442.0	28	Washington	485.9
11	New Hampshire	543.0	29	Illinois	483.2
6	New Jersey	565.9	30	Oklahoma	479.7
45	New Mexico	410.8	31	Indiana	475.8
17	New York	522.9	32	Tennessee	471.0
40	North Carolina	431.4	33	Maryland	469.9
16	North Dakota	525.3	34	Hawaii	468.3
19	Ohio	515.9	35	Kansas	461.6
30	Oklahoma	479.7	36	Virginia	459.1
23	Oregon	503.4	37	Wyoming	454.4
2	Pennsylvania	603.9	38	Alabama	447.7
3	Rhode Island	595.7	39	Nevada	442.0
25	South Carolina	494.5	40	North Carolina	431.4
21	South Dakota	510.3	41	Mississippi	428.4
32	Tennessee	471.0	42	Arizona	426.0
47	Texas	387.2	43	Idaho	418.7
50	Utah	300.4	44	California	414.9
8	Vermont	561.0	45	New Mexico	410.8
36	Virginia	459.1	46	Colorado	403.7
28	Washington	485.9	47	Texas	387.2
5	West Virginia	576.9	48	Georgia	378.5
22	Wisconsin	506.3	49	Alaska	373.1
37	Wyoming	454.4	50	Utah	300.4
				District of Columbia	436.8

Source: Morgan Quitno Press using data from American Cancer Society
"Cancer Facts & Figures 2007" (Copyright 2007, American Cancer Society)
*These estimates are offered as a rough guide and should not be regarded as definitive. They are calculated according to the distribution of estimated 2007 cancer deaths by state. Totals do not include basal and squamous cell skin cancers or in situ carcinomas except urinary bladder. Rates calculated using 2006 Census resident population estimates.

Age-Adjusted Cancer Incidence Rates for Males in 2003

National Rate = 562.1 New Cases per 100,000 Male Population*

ALPHA ORDER

RANK	STATE	RATE
36	Alabama	526.5
25	Alaska	556.8
46	Arizona	462.4
31	Arkansas	544.1
38	California	520.9
41	Colorado	516.2
7	Connecticut	597.3
11	Delaware	586.8
20	Florida	562.2
17	Georgia	565.8
45	Hawaii	481.8
35	Idaho	530.0
13	Illinois	580.9
29	Indiana	545.7
24	Iowa	557.1
NA	Kansas**	NA
3	Kentucky	616.9
4	Louisiana	613.8
5	Maine	609.9
12	Maryland	581.6
9	Massachusetts	591.6
6	Michigan	608.6
22	Minnesota	559.4
NA	Mississippi**	NA
33	Missouri	537.4
23	Montana	558.8
27	Nebraska	551.0
32	Nevada	541.3
16	New Hampshire	571.7
2	New Jersey	623.9
44	New Mexico	485.0
18	New York	565.4
39	North Carolina	519.2
40	North Dakota	518.0
26	Ohio	551.9
28	Oklahoma	547.0
30	Oregon	545.4
8	Pennsylvania	594.4
1	Rhode Island	627.2
10	South Carolina	590.1
19	South Dakota	564.1
47	Tennessee	442.0
34	Texas	530.7
43	Utah	490.2
NA	Vermont**	NA
42	Virginia	510.5
15	Washington	573.7
14	West Virginia	574.6
21	Wisconsin	562.0
37	Wyoming	524.9

RANK ORDER

RANK	STATE	RATE
1	Rhode Island	627.2
2	New Jersey	623.9
3	Kentucky	616.9
4	Louisiana	613.8
5	Maine	609.9
6	Michigan	608.6
7	Connecticut	597.3
8	Pennsylvania	594.4
9	Massachusetts	591.6
10	South Carolina	590.1
11	Delaware	586.8
12	Maryland	581.6
13	Illinois	580.9
14	West Virginia	574.6
15	Washington	573.7
16	New Hampshire	571.7
17	Georgia	565.8
18	New York	565.4
19	South Dakota	564.1
20	Florida	562.2
21	Wisconsin	562.0
22	Minnesota	559.4
23	Montana	558.8
24	Iowa	557.1
25	Alaska	556.8
26	Ohio	551.9
27	Nebraska	551.0
28	Oklahoma	547.0
29	Indiana	545.7
30	Oregon	545.4
31	Arkansas	544.1
32	Nevada	541.3
33	Missouri	537.4
34	Texas	530.7
35	Idaho	530.0
36	Alabama	526.5
37	Wyoming	524.9
38	California	520.9
39	North Carolina	519.2
40	North Dakota	518.0
41	Colorado	516.2
42	Virginia	510.5
43	Utah	490.2
44	New Mexico	485.0
45	Hawaii	481.8
46	Arizona	462.4
47	Tennessee	442.0
NA	Kansas**	NA
NA	Mississippi**	NA
NA	Vermont**	NA

District of Columbia   635.6

Source: American Cancer Society
    "Cancer Facts & Figures 2007" (Copyright 2007, American Cancer Society)
*For 1999 to 2003. Age-adjusted to the 2000 U.S. standard population.
**Not available.

Age-Adjusted Cancer Incidence Rates for Females in 2003

National Rate = 415.3 New Cases per 100,000 Female Population*

ALPHA ORDER				RANK ORDER		
RANK	STATE	RATE		RANK	STATE	RATE
43	Alabama	365.2		1	Massachusetts	451.8
19	Alaska	421.2		2	New Jersey	448.7
44	Arizona	364.1		3	Rhode Island	448.6
38	Arkansas	377.1		4	Connecticut	448.3
31	California	398.5		5	Washington	448.0
29	Colorado	400.3		6	Maine	447.6
4	Connecticut	448.3		7	Kentucky	440.5
11	Delaware	433.4		8	New Hampshire	436.6
20	Florida	415.6		9	Oregon	436.5
34	Georgia	391.5		9	Pennsylvania	436.5
39	Hawaii	375.2		11	Delaware	433.4
32	Idaho	396.0		12	Michigan	429.9
15	Illinois	425.5		13	Maryland	428.3
21	Indiana	414.4		14	West Virginia	427.8
18	Iowa	424.2		15	Illinois	425.5
NA	Kansas**	NA		16	New York	424.8
7	Kentucky	440.5		17	Wisconsin	424.4
28	Louisiana	402.3		18	Iowa	424.2
6	Maine	447.6		19	Alaska	421.2
13	Maryland	428.3		20	Florida	415.6
1	Massachusetts	451.8		21	Indiana	414.4
12	Michigan	429.9		22	Nevada	414.2
25	Minnesota	412.3		23	Nebraska	413.4
NA	Mississippi**	NA		24	Ohio	412.6
27	Missouri	408.8		25	Minnesota	412.3
26	Montana	412.0		26	Montana	412.0
23	Nebraska	413.4		27	Missouri	408.8
22	Nevada	414.2		28	Louisiana	402.3
8	New Hampshire	436.6		29	Colorado	400.3
2	New Jersey	448.7		30	Oklahoma	399.6
45	New Mexico	357.3		31	California	398.5
16	New York	424.8		32	Idaho	396.0
40	North Carolina	372.6		33	South Dakota	395.7
42	North Dakota	366.9		34	Georgia	391.5
24	Ohio	412.6		35	Wyoming	390.3
30	Oklahoma	399.6		36	South Carolina	389.4
9	Oregon	436.5		37	Texas	383.4
9	Pennsylvania	436.5		38	Arkansas	377.1
3	Rhode Island	448.6		39	Hawaii	375.2
36	South Carolina	389.4		40	North Carolina	372.6
33	South Dakota	395.7		41	Virginia	367.6
46	Tennessee	351.2		42	North Dakota	366.9
37	Texas	383.4		43	Alabama	365.2
47	Utah	346.3		44	Arizona	364.1
NA	Vermont**	NA		45	New Mexico	357.3
41	Virginia	367.6		46	Tennessee	351.2
5	Washington	448.0		47	Utah	346.3
14	West Virginia	427.8		NA	Kansas**	NA
17	Wisconsin	424.4		NA	Mississippi**	NA
35	Wyoming	390.3		NA	Vermont**	NA
					District of Columbia	422.6

Source: American Cancer Society
"Cancer Facts & Figures 2007" (Copyright 2007, American Cancer Society)
For 1999 to 2003. Age-adjusted to the 2000 U.S. standard population.
**Not available.*

Estimated New Cases of Bladder Cancer in 2007

National Estimated Total = 67,160 New Cases*

ALPHA ORDER

RANK	STATE	CASES	% of USA
26	Alabama	850	1.3%
49	Alaska	110	0.2%
15	Arizona	1,360	2.0%
33	Arkansas	560	0.8%
1	California	6,590	9.8%
25	Colorado	880	1.3%
22	Connecticut	1,090	1.6%
44	Delaware	220	0.3%
2	Florida	5,460	8.1%
15	Georgia	1,360	2.0%
46	Hawaii	200	0.3%
42	Idaho	310	0.5%
7	Illinois	2,880	4.3%
13	Indiana	1,390	2.1%
29	Iowa	820	1.2%
31	Kansas	570	0.8%
23	Kentucky	970	1.4%
26	Louisiana	850	1.3%
36	Maine	470	0.7%
21	Maryland	1,150	1.7%
10	Massachusetts	1,950	2.9%
8	Michigan	2,700	4.0%
19	Minnesota	1,250	1.9%
35	Mississippi	480	0.7%
17	Missouri	1,350	2.0%
43	Montana	260	0.4%
37	Nebraska	430	0.6%
31	Nevada	570	0.8%
38	New Hampshire	390	0.6%
9	New Jersey	2,450	3.6%
40	New Mexico	350	0.5%
3	New York	4,980	7.4%
11	North Carolina	1,690	2.5%
46	North Dakota	200	0.3%
6	Ohio	2,940	4.4%
30	Oklahoma	710	1.1%
23	Oregon	970	1.4%
4	Pennsylvania	4,030	6.0%
39	Rhode Island	370	0.6%
28	South Carolina	840	1.3%
44	South Dakota	220	0.3%
20	Tennessee	1,230	1.8%
5	Texas	3,300	4.9%
41	Utah	340	0.5%
48	Vermont	170	0.3%
14	Virginia	1,380	2.1%
12	Washington	1,490	2.2%
34	West Virginia	500	0.7%
17	Wisconsin	1,350	2.0%
49	Wyoming	110	0.2%

RANK ORDER

RANK	STATE	CASES	% of USA
1	California	6,590	9.8%
2	Florida	5,460	8.1%
3	New York	4,980	7.4%
4	Pennsylvania	4,030	6.0%
5	Texas	3,300	4.9%
6	Ohio	2,940	4.4%
7	Illinois	2,880	4.3%
8	Michigan	2,700	4.0%
9	New Jersey	2,450	3.6%
10	Massachusetts	1,950	2.9%
11	North Carolina	1,690	2.5%
12	Washington	1,490	2.2%
13	Indiana	1,390	2.1%
14	Virginia	1,380	2.1%
15	Arizona	1,360	2.0%
15	Georgia	1,360	2.0%
17	Missouri	1,350	2.0%
17	Wisconsin	1,350	2.0%
19	Minnesota	1,250	1.9%
20	Tennessee	1,230	1.8%
21	Maryland	1,150	1.7%
22	Connecticut	1,090	1.6%
23	Kentucky	970	1.4%
23	Oregon	970	1.4%
25	Colorado	880	1.3%
26	Alabama	850	1.3%
26	Louisiana	850	1.3%
28	South Carolina	840	1.3%
29	Iowa	820	1.2%
30	Oklahoma	710	1.1%
31	Kansas	570	0.8%
31	Nevada	570	0.8%
33	Arkansas	560	0.8%
34	West Virginia	500	0.7%
35	Mississippi	480	0.7%
36	Maine	470	0.7%
37	Nebraska	430	0.6%
38	New Hampshire	390	0.6%
39	Rhode Island	370	0.6%
40	New Mexico	350	0.5%
41	Utah	340	0.5%
42	Idaho	310	0.5%
43	Montana	260	0.4%
44	Delaware	220	0.3%
44	South Dakota	220	0.3%
46	Hawaii	200	0.3%
46	North Dakota	200	0.3%
48	Vermont	170	0.3%
49	Alaska	110	0.2%
49	Wyoming	110	0.2%
	District of Columbia	90	0.1%

Source: American Cancer Society
   "Cancer Facts & Figures 2007" (Copyright 2007, American Cancer Society)
*These estimates are offered as a rough guide and should be interpreted with caution. They are calculated according to the distribution of estimated 2007 cancer deaths by state.

Estimated Rate of New Bladder Cancer Cases in 2007

National Estimated Rate = 22.4 New Cases per 100,000 Population*

ALPHA ORDER			RANK ORDER		
RANK	STATE	RATE	RANK	STATE	RATE
40	Alabama	18.5	1	Maine	35.6
46	Alaska	16.4	2	Rhode Island	34.7
28	Arizona	22.1	3	Pennsylvania	32.4
35	Arkansas	19.9	4	North Dakota	31.5
42	California	18.1	5	Connecticut	31.1
40	Colorado	18.5	6	Massachusetts	30.3
5	Connecticut	31.1	7	Florida	30.2
17	Delaware	25.8	8	New Hampshire	29.7
7	Florida	30.2	9	New Jersey	28.1
48	Georgia	14.5	9	South Dakota	28.1
47	Hawaii	15.6	11	Iowa	27.5
31	Idaho	21.1	11	Montana	27.5
27	Illinois	22.4	11	West Virginia	27.5
29	Indiana	22.0	14	Vermont	27.2
11	Iowa	27.5	15	Michigan	26.7
32	Kansas	20.6	16	Oregon	26.2
24	Kentucky	23.1	17	Delaware	25.8
36	Louisiana	19.8	17	New York	25.8
1	Maine	35.6	19	Ohio	25.6
33	Maryland	20.5	20	Nebraska	24.3
6	Massachusetts	30.3	20	Wisconsin	24.3
15	Michigan	26.7	22	Minnesota	24.2
22	Minnesota	24.2	23	Washington	23.3
45	Mississippi	16.5	24	Kentucky	23.1
24	Missouri	23.1	24	Missouri	23.1
11	Montana	27.5	26	Nevada	22.8
20	Nebraska	24.3	27	Illinois	22.4
26	Nevada	22.8	28	Arizona	22.1
8	New Hampshire	29.7	29	Indiana	22.0
9	New Jersey	28.1	30	Wyoming	21.4
44	New Mexico	17.9	31	Idaho	21.1
17	New York	25.8	32	Kansas	20.6
39	North Carolina	19.1	33	Maryland	20.5
4	North Dakota	31.5	34	Tennessee	20.4
19	Ohio	25.6	35	Arkansas	19.9
36	Oklahoma	19.8	36	Louisiana	19.8
16	Oregon	26.2	36	Oklahoma	19.8
3	Pennsylvania	32.4	38	South Carolina	19.4
2	Rhode Island	34.7	39	North Carolina	19.1
38	South Carolina	19.4	40	Alabama	18.5
9	South Dakota	28.1	40	Colorado	18.5
34	Tennessee	20.4	42	California	18.1
49	Texas	14.0	42	Virginia	18.1
50	Utah	13.3	44	New Mexico	17.9
14	Vermont	27.2	45	Mississippi	16.5
42	Virginia	18.1	46	Alaska	16.4
23	Washington	23.3	47	Hawaii	15.6
11	West Virginia	27.5	48	Georgia	14.5
20	Wisconsin	24.3	49	Texas	14.0
30	Wyoming	21.4	50	Utah	13.3
				District of Columbia	15.5

Source: Morgan Quitno Press using data from American Cancer Society
"Cancer Facts & Figures 2007" (Copyright 2007, American Cancer Society)
*These estimates are offered as a rough guide and should be interpreted with caution. They are calculated according to the distribution of estimated 2007 cancer deaths by state. Rates calculated using 2006 Census resident population estimates.

Estimated New Female Breast Cancer Cases in 2007

National Estimated Total = 178,480 New Cases*

ALPHA ORDER

RANK	STATE	CASES	% of USA
23	Alabama	2,750	1.5%
49	Alaska	340	0.2%
21	Arizona	3,220	1.8%
31	Arkansas	1,830	1.0%
1	California	19,790	11.1%
24	Colorado	2,660	1.5%
27	Connecticut	2,510	1.4%
45	Delaware	560	0.3%
4	Florida	11,710	6.6%
12	Georgia	4,520	2.5%
41	Hawaii	820	0.5%
42	Idaho	780	0.4%
6	Illinois	7,030	3.9%
17	Indiana	3,560	2.0%
30	Iowa	2,000	1.1%
32	Kansas	1,750	1.0%
26	Kentucky	2,590	1.5%
22	Louisiana	2,820	1.6%
38	Maine	980	0.5%
17	Maryland	3,560	2.0%
13	Massachusetts	4,260	2.4%
9	Michigan	5,900	3.3%
20	Minnesota	3,240	1.8%
33	Mississippi	1,620	0.9%
15	Missouri	3,730	2.1%
44	Montana	630	0.4%
36	Nebraska	1,160	0.6%
34	Nevada	1,180	0.7%
40	New Hampshire	890	0.5%
8	New Jersey	6,080	3.4%
37	New Mexico	1,080	0.6%
2	New York	12,580	7.0%
10	North Carolina	4,870	2.7%
47	North Dakota	440	0.2%
7	Ohio	6,710	3.8%
29	Oklahoma	2,200	1.2%
28	Oregon	2,460	1.4%
5	Pennsylvania	8,860	5.0%
43	Rhode Island	730	0.4%
25	South Carolina	2,600	1.5%
46	South Dakota	510	0.3%
16	Tennessee	3,690	2.1%
3	Texas	12,120	6.8%
39	Utah	920	0.5%
48	Vermont	420	0.2%
11	Virginia	4,570	2.6%
14	Washington	4,090	2.3%
34	West Virginia	1,180	0.7%
19	Wisconsin	3,340	1.9%
50	Wyoming	310	0.2%

RANK ORDER

RANK	STATE	CASES	% of USA
1	California	19,790	11.1%
2	New York	12,580	7.0%
3	Texas	12,120	6.8%
4	Florida	11,710	6.6%
5	Pennsylvania	8,860	5.0%
6	Illinois	7,030	3.9%
7	Ohio	6,710	3.8%
8	New Jersey	6,080	3.4%
9	Michigan	5,900	3.3%
10	North Carolina	4,870	2.7%
11	Virginia	4,570	2.6%
12	Georgia	4,520	2.5%
13	Massachusetts	4,260	2.4%
14	Washington	4,090	2.3%
15	Missouri	3,730	2.1%
16	Tennessee	3,690	2.1%
17	Indiana	3,560	2.0%
17	Maryland	3,560	2.0%
19	Wisconsin	3,340	1.9%
20	Minnesota	3,240	1.8%
21	Arizona	3,220	1.8%
22	Louisiana	2,820	1.6%
23	Alabama	2,750	1.5%
24	Colorado	2,660	1.5%
25	South Carolina	2,600	1.5%
26	Kentucky	2,590	1.5%
27	Connecticut	2,510	1.4%
28	Oregon	2,460	1.4%
29	Oklahoma	2,200	1.2%
30	Iowa	2,000	1.1%
31	Arkansas	1,830	1.0%
32	Kansas	1,750	1.0%
33	Mississippi	1,620	0.9%
34	Nevada	1,180	0.7%
34	West Virginia	1,180	0.7%
36	Nebraska	1,160	0.6%
37	New Mexico	1,080	0.6%
38	Maine	980	0.5%
39	Utah	920	0.5%
40	New Hampshire	890	0.5%
41	Hawaii	820	0.5%
42	Idaho	780	0.4%
43	Rhode Island	730	0.4%
44	Montana	630	0.4%
45	Delaware	560	0.3%
46	South Dakota	510	0.3%
47	North Dakota	440	0.2%
48	Vermont	420	0.2%
49	Alaska	340	0.2%
50	Wyoming	310	0.2%
	District of Columbia	320	0.2%

Source: American Cancer Society
"Cancer Facts & Figures 2007" (Copyright 2007, American Cancer Society)
*These estimates are offered as a rough guide and should be interpreted with caution. They are calculated according to the distribution of estimated 2007 cancer deaths by state.

Age-Adjusted Incidence Rate of Female Breast Cancer Cases in 2003

National Rate = 128.2 New Cases per 100,000 Female Population*

ALPHA ORDER

RANK	STATE	RATE
45	Alabama	115.3
7	Alaska	134.2
44	Arizona	116.7
39	Arkansas	121.0
15	California	129.8
7	Colorado	134.2
3	Connecticut	140.4
19	Delaware	128.8
35	Florida	123.0
32	Georgia	124.0
25	Hawaii	127.3
24	Idaho	128.2
16	Illinois	129.7
30	Indiana	124.8
20	Iowa	128.7
NA	Kansas**	NA
30	Kentucky	124.8
36	Louisiana	122.8
12	Maine	131.4
11	Maryland	131.9
4	Massachusetts	138.8
17	Michigan	129.4
5	Minnesota	135.9
NA	Mississippi**	NA
28	Missouri	125.4
22	Montana	128.4
12	Nebraska	131.4
40	Nevada	120.8
6	New Hampshire	135.2
9	New Jersey	133.9
46	New Mexico	115.0
26	New York	126.7
38	North Carolina	121.5
34	North Dakota	123.1
27	Ohio	126.6
23	Oklahoma	128.3
2	Oregon	142.6
17	Pennsylvania	129.4
14	Rhode Island	130.7
33	South Carolina	123.5
21	South Dakota	128.6
47	Tennessee	113.7
41	Texas	118.6
42	Utah	117.1
NA	Vermont**	NA
37	Virginia	122.2
1	Washington	146.7
43	West Virginia	116.9
9	Wisconsin	133.9
29	Wyoming	125.2

RANK ORDER

RANK	STATE	RATE
1	Washington	146.7
2	Oregon	142.6
3	Connecticut	140.4
4	Massachusetts	138.8
5	Minnesota	135.9
6	New Hampshire	135.2
7	Alaska	134.2
7	Colorado	134.2
9	New Jersey	133.9
9	Wisconsin	133.9
11	Maryland	131.9
12	Maine	131.4
12	Nebraska	131.4
14	Rhode Island	130.7
15	California	129.8
16	Illinois	129.7
17	Michigan	129.4
17	Pennsylvania	129.4
19	Delaware	128.8
20	Iowa	128.7
21	South Dakota	128.6
22	Montana	128.4
23	Oklahoma	128.3
24	Idaho	128.2
25	Hawaii	127.3
26	New York	126.7
27	Ohio	126.6
28	Missouri	125.4
29	Wyoming	125.2
30	Indiana	124.8
30	Kentucky	124.8
32	Georgia	124.0
33	South Carolina	123.5
34	North Dakota	123.1
35	Florida	123.0
36	Louisiana	122.8
37	Virginia	122.2
38	North Carolina	121.5
39	Arkansas	121.0
40	Nevada	120.8
41	Texas	118.6
42	Utah	117.1
43	West Virginia	116.9
44	Arizona	116.7
45	Alabama	115.3
46	New Mexico	115.0
47	Tennessee	113.7
NA	Kansas**	NA
NA	Mississippi**	NA
NA	Vermont**	NA
	District of Columbia	135.3

Source: American Cancer Society
"Cancer Facts & Figures 2007" (Copyright 2007, American Cancer Society)
*For 1999 to 2003. Age-adjusted to the 2000 U.S. standard population.
**Not available.

Percent of Women 40 and Older Who Have Had a Mammogram in the Past Two Years: 2004
National Median = 74.6% of Women*

RANK	STATE	PERCENT
18	Alabama	75.5
45	Alaska	67.0
18	Arizona	75.5
46	Arkansas	66.9
12	California	76.5
37	Colorado	71.2
5	Connecticut	81.1
1	Delaware	82.4
12	Florida	76.5
26	Georgia	74.5
NA	Hawaii**	NA
49	Idaho	63.8
14	Illinois	76.0
38	Indiana	69.2
23	Iowa	75.2
14	Kansas	76.0
18	Kentucky	75.5
27	Louisiana	74.2
4	Maine	81.8
8	Maryland	78.9
1	Massachusetts	82.4
8	Michigan	78.9
6	Minnesota	80.4
48	Mississippi	66.4
41	Missouri	68.9
35	Montana	71.8
16	Nebraska	75.9
38	Nevada	69.2
7	New Hampshire	80.1
24	New Jersey	74.9
40	New Mexico	69.0
18	New York	75.5
11	North Carolina	77.4
33	North Dakota	72.2
29	Ohio	73.5
44	Oklahoma	67.6
35	Oregon	71.8
30	Pennsylvania	73.4
1	Rhode Island	82.4
34	South Carolina	72.1
16	South Dakota	75.9
10	Tennessee	78.0
43	Texas	67.7
47	Utah	66.6
25	Vermont	74.7
28	Virginia	73.6
31	Washington	72.7
32	West Virginia	72.4
22	Wisconsin	75.4
42	Wyoming	68.1

RANK	STATE	PERCENT
1	Delaware	82.4
1	Massachusetts	82.4
1	Rhode Island	82.4
4	Maine	81.8
5	Connecticut	81.1
6	Minnesota	80.4
7	New Hampshire	80.1
8	Maryland	78.9
8	Michigan	78.9
10	Tennessee	78.0
11	North Carolina	77.4
12	California	76.5
12	Florida	76.5
14	Illinois	76.0
14	Kansas	76.0
16	Nebraska	75.9
16	South Dakota	75.9
18	Alabama	75.5
18	Arizona	75.5
18	Kentucky	75.5
18	New York	75.5
22	Wisconsin	75.4
23	Iowa	75.2
24	New Jersey	74.9
25	Vermont	74.7
26	Georgia	74.5
27	Louisiana	74.2
28	Virginia	73.6
29	Ohio	73.5
30	Pennsylvania	73.4
31	Washington	72.7
32	West Virginia	72.4
33	North Dakota	72.2
34	South Carolina	72.1
35	Montana	71.8
35	Oregon	71.8
37	Colorado	71.2
38	Indiana	69.2
38	Nevada	69.2
40	New Mexico	69.0
41	Missouri	68.9
42	Wyoming	68.1
43	Texas	67.7
44	Oklahoma	67.6
45	Alaska	67.0
46	Arkansas	66.9
47	Utah	66.6
48	Mississippi	66.4
49	Idaho	63.8
NA	Hawaii**	NA

District of Columbia	80.8

Source: U.S. Department of Health and Human Services, Centers for Disease Control and Prevention
"2004 Behavioral Risk Factor Surveillance Summary Prevalence Data" (http://apps.nccd.cdc.gov/brfss/)
Percent of women 40 years and older.
**Not available.*

Estimated New Colon and Rectum Cancer Cases in 2007

National Estimated Total = 153,760 New Cases*

<u>ALPHA ORDER</u>

RANK	STATE	CASES	% of USA
24	Alabama	2,350	1.5%
49	Alaska	270	0.2%
20	Arizona	2,750	1.8%
31	Arkansas	1,640	1.1%
1	California	15,000	9.8%
30	Colorado	1,790	1.2%
26	Connecticut	2,190	1.4%
45	Delaware	480	0.3%
2	Florida	11,420	7.4%
12	Georgia	3,690	2.4%
39	Hawaii	790	0.5%
43	Idaho	600	0.4%
6	Illinois	6,890	4.5%
14	Indiana	3,390	2.2%
27	Iowa	1,930	1.3%
33	Kansas	1,360	0.9%
22	Kentucky	2,570	1.7%
23	Louisiana	2,520	1.6%
37	Maine	880	0.6%
19	Maryland	2,870	1.9%
11	Massachusetts	3,850	2.5%
8	Michigan	5,570	3.6%
21	Minnesota	2,650	1.7%
32	Mississippi	1,440	0.9%
15	Missouri	3,380	2.2%
44	Montana	520	0.3%
36	Nebraska	920	0.6%
35	Nevada	1,120	0.7%
38	New Hampshire	800	0.5%
9	New Jersey	5,160	3.4%
39	New Mexico	790	0.5%
3	New York	10,710	7.0%
10	North Carolina	4,290	2.8%
47	North Dakota	410	0.3%
7	Ohio	6,410	4.2%
28	Oklahoma	1,880	1.2%
29	Oregon	1,830	1.2%
5	Pennsylvania	8,220	5.3%
42	Rhode Island	690	0.4%
25	South Carolina	2,230	1.5%
46	South Dakota	470	0.3%
16	Tennessee	3,100	2.0%
4	Texas	9,510	6.2%
41	Utah	740	0.5%
48	Vermont	390	0.3%
13	Virginia	3,530	2.3%
18	Washington	2,920	1.9%
34	West Virginia	1,210	0.8%
17	Wisconsin	3,090	2.0%
50	Wyoming	260	0.2%

<u>RANK ORDER</u>

RANK	STATE	CASES	% of USA
1	California	15,000	9.8%
2	Florida	11,420	7.4%
3	New York	10,710	7.0%
4	Texas	9,510	6.2%
5	Pennsylvania	8,220	5.3%
6	Illinois	6,890	4.5%
7	Ohio	6,410	4.2%
8	Michigan	5,570	3.6%
9	New Jersey	5,160	3.4%
10	North Carolina	4,290	2.8%
11	Massachusetts	3,850	2.5%
12	Georgia	3,690	2.4%
13	Virginia	3,530	2.3%
14	Indiana	3,390	2.2%
15	Missouri	3,380	2.2%
16	Tennessee	3,100	2.0%
17	Wisconsin	3,090	2.0%
18	Washington	2,920	1.9%
19	Maryland	2,870	1.9%
20	Arizona	2,750	1.8%
21	Minnesota	2,650	1.7%
22	Kentucky	2,570	1.7%
23	Louisiana	2,520	1.6%
24	Alabama	2,350	1.5%
25	South Carolina	2,230	1.5%
26	Connecticut	2,190	1.4%
27	Iowa	1,930	1.3%
28	Oklahoma	1,880	1.2%
29	Oregon	1,830	1.2%
30	Colorado	1,790	1.2%
31	Arkansas	1,640	1.1%
32	Mississippi	1,440	0.9%
33	Kansas	1,360	0.9%
34	West Virginia	1,210	0.8%
35	Nevada	1,120	0.7%
36	Nebraska	920	0.6%
37	Maine	880	0.6%
38	New Hampshire	800	0.5%
39	Hawaii	790	0.5%
39	New Mexico	790	0.5%
41	Utah	740	0.5%
42	Rhode Island	690	0.4%
43	Idaho	600	0.4%
44	Montana	520	0.3%
45	Delaware	480	0.3%
46	South Dakota	470	0.3%
47	North Dakota	410	0.3%
48	Vermont	390	0.3%
49	Alaska	270	0.2%
50	Wyoming	260	0.2%
	District of Columbia	270	0.2%

Source: American Cancer Society
"Cancer Facts & Figures 2007" (Copyright 2007, American Cancer Society)
These estimates are offered as a rough guide and should be interpreted with caution. They are calculated according to the distribution of estimated 2007 cancer deaths by state.

Estimated Rate of New Colon and Rectum Cancer Cases in 2007

National Estimated Rate = 51.4 New Cases per 100,000 Population*

ALPHA ORDER

RANK	STATE	RATE
32	Alabama	51.1
47	Alaska	40.3
42	Arizona	44.6
17	Arkansas	58.3
43	California	41.1
49	Colorado	37.7
8	Connecticut	62.5
19	Delaware	56.2
7	Florida	63.1
48	Georgia	39.4
10	Hawaii	61.5
44	Idaho	40.9
25	Illinois	53.7
25	Indiana	53.7
4	Iowa	64.7
37	Kansas	49.2
11	Kentucky	61.1
16	Louisiana	58.8
1	Maine	66.6
32	Maryland	51.1
14	Massachusetts	59.8
23	Michigan	55.2
30	Minnesota	51.3
35	Mississippi	49.5
18	Missouri	57.8
24	Montana	55.0
28	Nebraska	52.0
41	Nevada	44.9
12	New Hampshire	60.8
15	New Jersey	59.1
46	New Mexico	40.4
22	New York	55.5
38	North Carolina	48.4
6	North Dakota	64.5
20	Ohio	55.8
27	Oklahoma	52.5
36	Oregon	49.4
3	Pennsylvania	66.1
5	Rhode Island	64.6
29	South Carolina	51.6
13	South Dakota	60.1
30	Tennessee	51.3
45	Texas	40.5
50	Utah	29.0
8	Vermont	62.5
39	Virginia	46.2
40	Washington	45.7
2	West Virginia	66.5
21	Wisconsin	55.6
34	Wyoming	50.5

RANK ORDER

RANK	STATE	RATE
1	Maine	66.6
2	West Virginia	66.5
3	Pennsylvania	66.1
4	Iowa	64.7
5	Rhode Island	64.6
6	North Dakota	64.5
7	Florida	63.1
8	Connecticut	62.5
8	Vermont	62.5
10	Hawaii	61.5
11	Kentucky	61.1
12	New Hampshire	60.8
13	South Dakota	60.1
14	Massachusetts	59.8
15	New Jersey	59.1
16	Louisiana	58.8
17	Arkansas	58.3
18	Missouri	57.8
19	Delaware	56.2
20	Ohio	55.8
21	Wisconsin	55.6
22	New York	55.5
23	Michigan	55.2
24	Montana	55.0
25	Illinois	53.7
25	Indiana	53.7
27	Oklahoma	52.5
28	Nebraska	52.0
29	South Carolina	51.6
30	Minnesota	51.3
30	Tennessee	51.3
32	Alabama	51.1
32	Maryland	51.1
34	Wyoming	50.5
35	Mississippi	49.5
36	Oregon	49.4
37	Kansas	49.2
38	North Carolina	48.4
39	Virginia	46.2
40	Washington	45.7
41	Nevada	44.9
42	Arizona	44.6
43	California	41.1
44	Idaho	40.9
45	Texas	40.5
46	New Mexico	40.4
47	Alaska	40.3
48	Georgia	39.4
49	Colorado	37.7
50	Utah	29.0

District of Columbia 46.4

Source: Morgan Quitno Press using data from American Cancer Society
    "Cancer Facts & Figures 2007" (Copyright 2007, American Cancer Society)
*These estimates are offered as a rough guide and should be interpreted with caution. They are calculated
according to the distribution of estimated 2007 cancer deaths by state. Rates calculated using 2006 Census
resident population estimates.
population estimates.

Percent of Adults Receiving Recent Sigmoidoscopy or Colonoscopy Exam: 2004
National Median = 52.9% of Adults*

ALPHA ORDER

RANK ORDER

RANK	STATE	PERCENT	RANK	STATE	PERCENT
30	Alabama	50.9	1	Minnesota	66.2
31	Alaska	50.6	2	Connecticut	63.6
28	Arizona	52.0	3	Maryland	62.2
41	Arkansas	47.3	3	New Hampshire	62.2
23	California	53.8	5	Delaware	61.9
36	Colorado	50.0	6	Rhode Island	61.6
2	Connecticut	63.6	7	Massachusetts	61.2
5	Delaware	61.9	8	Michigan	60.4
16	Florida	56.1	9	Virginia	59.9
24	Georgia	53.7	10	Wisconsin	59.4
NA	Hawaii**	NA	11	Maine	59.1
41	Idaho	47.3	12	Vermont	58.8
38	Illinois	48.9	13	Washington	57.3
34	Indiana	50.5	14	New York	56.7
29	Iowa	51.6	15	New Jersey	56.6
37	Kansas	49.8	16	Florida	56.1
43	Kentucky	47.1	17	Utah	56.0
49	Louisiana	44.8	18	South Carolina	55.9
11	Maine	59.1	19	Oregon	54.8
3	Maryland	62.2	20	North Carolina	54.5
7	Massachusetts	61.2	21	North Dakota	53.9
8	Michigan	60.4	21	Pennsylvania	53.9
1	Minnesota	66.2	23	California	53.8
44	Mississippi	46.8	24	Georgia	53.7
26	Missouri	52.7	25	Ohio	53.1
27	Montana	52.5	26	Missouri	52.7
47	Nebraska	46.2	27	Montana	52.5
45	Nevada	46.7	28	Arizona	52.0
3	New Hampshire	62.2	29	Iowa	51.6
15	New Jersey	56.6	30	Alabama	50.9
31	New Mexico	50.6	31	Alaska	50.6
14	New York	56.7	31	New Mexico	50.6
20	North Carolina	54.5	31	Tennessee	50.6
21	North Dakota	53.9	34	Indiana	50.5
25	Ohio	53.1	35	South Dakota	50.2
46	Oklahoma	46.6	36	Colorado	50.0
19	Oregon	54.8	37	Kansas	49.8
21	Pennsylvania	53.9	38	Illinois	48.9
6	Rhode Island	61.6	39	Wyoming	48.4
18	South Carolina	55.9	40	Texas	48.3
35	South Dakota	50.2	41	Arkansas	47.3
31	Tennessee	50.6	41	Idaho	47.3
40	Texas	48.3	43	Kentucky	47.1
17	Utah	56.0	44	Mississippi	46.8
12	Vermont	58.8	45	Nevada	46.7
9	Virginia	59.9	46	Oklahoma	46.6
13	Washington	57.3	47	Nebraska	46.2
47	West Virginia	46.2	47	West Virginia	46.2
10	Wisconsin	59.4	49	Louisiana	44.8
39	Wyoming	48.4	NA	Hawaii**	NA

District of Columbia   63.1

Source: U.S. Department of Health and Human Services, Centers for Disease Control and Prevention
    "2004 Behavioral Risk Factor Surveillance Summary Prevalence Data" (http://apps.nccd.cdc.gov/brfss/)
*Persons 50 and older.
**Not available.

Estimated New Leukemia Cases in 2007

National Estimated Total = 44,240 New Cases*

ALPHA ORDER

RANK	STATE	CASES	% of USA
28	Alabama	550	1.2%
49	Alaska	70	0.2%
20	Arizona	740	1.7%
30	Arkansas	510	1.2%
1	California	4,610	10.4%
23	Colorado	670	1.5%
26	Connecticut	610	1.4%
46	Delaware	110	0.2%
2	Florida	3,360	7.6%
13	Georgia	960	2.2%
42	Hawaii	170	0.4%
40	Idaho	220	0.5%
6	Illinois	2,030	4.6%
16	Indiana	910	2.1%
25	Iowa	620	1.4%
32	Kansas	420	0.9%
21	Kentucky	680	1.5%
21	Louisiana	680	1.5%
39	Maine	250	0.6%
24	Maryland	630	1.4%
12	Massachusetts	1,010	2.3%
8	Michigan	1,680	3.8%
15	Minnesota	920	2.1%
33	Mississippi	340	0.8%
18	Missouri	890	2.0%
42	Montana	170	0.4%
38	Nebraska	290	0.7%
34	Nevada	330	0.7%
41	New Hampshire	190	0.4%
9	New Jersey	1,520	3.4%
35	New Mexico	310	0.7%
4	New York	3,080	7.0%
10	North Carolina	1,070	2.4%
46	North Dakota	110	0.2%
7	Ohio	1,710	3.9%
27	Oklahoma	570	1.3%
31	Oregon	500	1.1%
5	Pennsylvania	2,240	5.1%
42	Rhode Island	170	0.4%
28	South Carolina	550	1.2%
45	South Dakota	130	0.3%
19	Tennessee	800	1.8%
3	Texas	3,130	7.1%
36	Utah	300	0.7%
48	Vermont	80	0.2%
17	Virginia	900	2.0%
13	Washington	960	2.2%
36	West Virginia	300	0.7%
11	Wisconsin	1,040	2.4%
49	Wyoming	70	0.2%

RANK ORDER

RANK	STATE	CASES	% of USA
1	California	4,610	10.4%
2	Florida	3,360	7.6%
3	Texas	3,130	7.1%
4	New York	3,080	7.0%
5	Pennsylvania	2,240	5.1%
6	Illinois	2,030	4.6%
7	Ohio	1,710	3.9%
8	Michigan	1,680	3.8%
9	New Jersey	1,520	3.4%
10	North Carolina	1,070	2.4%
11	Wisconsin	1,040	2.4%
12	Massachusetts	1,010	2.3%
13	Georgia	960	2.2%
13	Washington	960	2.2%
15	Minnesota	920	2.1%
16	Indiana	910	2.1%
17	Virginia	900	2.0%
18	Missouri	890	2.0%
19	Tennessee	800	1.8%
20	Arizona	740	1.7%
21	Kentucky	680	1.5%
21	Louisiana	680	1.5%
23	Colorado	670	1.5%
24	Maryland	630	1.4%
25	Iowa	620	1.4%
26	Connecticut	610	1.4%
27	Oklahoma	570	1.3%
28	Alabama	550	1.2%
28	South Carolina	550	1.2%
30	Arkansas	510	1.2%
31	Oregon	500	1.1%
32	Kansas	420	0.9%
33	Mississippi	340	0.8%
34	Nevada	330	0.7%
35	New Mexico	310	0.7%
36	Utah	300	0.7%
36	West Virginia	300	0.7%
38	Nebraska	290	0.7%
39	Maine	250	0.6%
40	Idaho	220	0.5%
41	New Hampshire	190	0.4%
42	Hawaii	170	0.4%
42	Montana	170	0.4%
42	Rhode Island	170	0.4%
45	South Dakota	130	0.3%
46	Delaware	110	0.2%
46	North Dakota	110	0.2%
48	Vermont	80	0.2%
49	Alaska	70	0.2%
49	Wyoming	70	0.2%
	District of Columbia	60	0.1%

Source: American Cancer Society
"Cancer Facts & Figures 2007" (Copyright 2007, American Cancer Society)
*These estimates are offered as a rough guide and should be interpreted with caution. They are calculated according to the distribution of estimated 2007 cancer deaths by state.

Estimated Rate of New Leukemia Cases in 2007

National Estimated Rate = 14.8 New Cases per 100,000 Population*

<table>
<tr><td colspan="3">ALPHA ORDER</td><td colspan="3">RANK ORDER</td></tr>
<tr><td>RANK</td><td>STATE</td><td>RATE</td><td>RANK</td><td>STATE</td><td>RATE</td></tr>
<tr><td>43</td><td>Alabama</td><td>12.0</td><td>1</td><td>Iowa</td><td>20.8</td></tr>
<tr><td>49</td><td>Alaska</td><td>10.4</td><td>2</td><td>Maine</td><td>18.9</td></tr>
<tr><td>43</td><td>Arizona</td><td>12.0</td><td>3</td><td>Wisconsin</td><td>18.7</td></tr>
<tr><td>5</td><td>Arkansas</td><td>18.1</td><td>4</td><td>Florida</td><td>18.6</td></tr>
<tr><td>41</td><td>California</td><td>12.6</td><td>5</td><td>Arkansas</td><td>18.1</td></tr>
<tr><td>31</td><td>Colorado</td><td>14.1</td><td>6</td><td>Montana</td><td>18.0</td></tr>
<tr><td>9</td><td>Connecticut</td><td>17.4</td><td>6</td><td>Pennsylvania</td><td>18.0</td></tr>
<tr><td>38</td><td>Delaware</td><td>12.9</td><td>8</td><td>Minnesota</td><td>17.8</td></tr>
<tr><td>4</td><td>Florida</td><td>18.6</td><td>9</td><td>Connecticut</td><td>17.4</td></tr>
<tr><td>50</td><td>Georgia</td><td>10.3</td><td>9</td><td>New Jersey</td><td>17.4</td></tr>
<tr><td>35</td><td>Hawaii</td><td>13.2</td><td>11</td><td>North Dakota</td><td>17.3</td></tr>
<tr><td>26</td><td>Idaho</td><td>15.0</td><td>12</td><td>Michigan</td><td>16.6</td></tr>
<tr><td>22</td><td>Illinois</td><td>15.8</td><td>12</td><td>South Dakota</td><td>16.6</td></tr>
<tr><td>29</td><td>Indiana</td><td>14.4</td><td>14</td><td>West Virginia</td><td>16.5</td></tr>
<tr><td>1</td><td>Iowa</td><td>20.8</td><td>15</td><td>Nebraska</td><td>16.4</td></tr>
<tr><td>24</td><td>Kansas</td><td>15.2</td><td>16</td><td>Kentucky</td><td>16.2</td></tr>
<tr><td>16</td><td>Kentucky</td><td>16.2</td><td>17</td><td>New York</td><td>16.0</td></tr>
<tr><td>18</td><td>Louisiana</td><td>15.9</td><td>18</td><td>Louisiana</td><td>15.9</td></tr>
<tr><td>2</td><td>Maine</td><td>18.9</td><td>18</td><td>New Mexico</td><td>15.9</td></tr>
<tr><td>48</td><td>Maryland</td><td>11.2</td><td>18</td><td>Oklahoma</td><td>15.9</td></tr>
<tr><td>23</td><td>Massachusetts</td><td>15.7</td><td>18</td><td>Rhode Island</td><td>15.9</td></tr>
<tr><td>12</td><td>Michigan</td><td>16.6</td><td>22</td><td>Illinois</td><td>15.8</td></tr>
<tr><td>8</td><td>Minnesota</td><td>17.8</td><td>23</td><td>Massachusetts</td><td>15.7</td></tr>
<tr><td>47</td><td>Mississippi</td><td>11.7</td><td>24</td><td>Kansas</td><td>15.2</td></tr>
<tr><td>24</td><td>Missouri</td><td>15.2</td><td>24</td><td>Missouri</td><td>15.2</td></tr>
<tr><td>6</td><td>Montana</td><td>18.0</td><td>26</td><td>Idaho</td><td>15.0</td></tr>
<tr><td>15</td><td>Nebraska</td><td>16.4</td><td>26</td><td>Washington</td><td>15.0</td></tr>
<tr><td>35</td><td>Nevada</td><td>13.2</td><td>28</td><td>Ohio</td><td>14.9</td></tr>
<tr><td>29</td><td>New Hampshire</td><td>14.4</td><td>29</td><td>Indiana</td><td>14.4</td></tr>
<tr><td>9</td><td>New Jersey</td><td>17.4</td><td>29</td><td>New Hampshire</td><td>14.4</td></tr>
<tr><td>18</td><td>New Mexico</td><td>15.9</td><td>31</td><td>Colorado</td><td>14.1</td></tr>
<tr><td>17</td><td>New York</td><td>16.0</td><td>32</td><td>Wyoming</td><td>13.6</td></tr>
<tr><td>42</td><td>North Carolina</td><td>12.1</td><td>33</td><td>Oregon</td><td>13.5</td></tr>
<tr><td>11</td><td>North Dakota</td><td>17.3</td><td>34</td><td>Texas</td><td>13.3</td></tr>
<tr><td>28</td><td>Ohio</td><td>14.9</td><td>35</td><td>Hawaii</td><td>13.2</td></tr>
<tr><td>18</td><td>Oklahoma</td><td>15.9</td><td>35</td><td>Nevada</td><td>13.2</td></tr>
<tr><td>33</td><td>Oregon</td><td>13.5</td><td>35</td><td>Tennessee</td><td>13.2</td></tr>
<tr><td>6</td><td>Pennsylvania</td><td>18.0</td><td>38</td><td>Delaware</td><td>12.9</td></tr>
<tr><td>18</td><td>Rhode Island</td><td>15.9</td><td>39</td><td>Vermont</td><td>12.8</td></tr>
<tr><td>40</td><td>South Carolina</td><td>12.7</td><td>40</td><td>South Carolina</td><td>12.7</td></tr>
<tr><td>12</td><td>South Dakota</td><td>16.6</td><td>41</td><td>California</td><td>12.6</td></tr>
<tr><td>35</td><td>Tennessee</td><td>13.2</td><td>42</td><td>North Carolina</td><td>12.1</td></tr>
<tr><td>34</td><td>Texas</td><td>13.3</td><td>43</td><td>Alabama</td><td>12.0</td></tr>
<tr><td>45</td><td>Utah</td><td>11.8</td><td>43</td><td>Arizona</td><td>12.0</td></tr>
<tr><td>39</td><td>Vermont</td><td>12.8</td><td>45</td><td>Utah</td><td>11.8</td></tr>
<tr><td>45</td><td>Virginia</td><td>11.8</td><td>45</td><td>Virginia</td><td>11.8</td></tr>
<tr><td>26</td><td>Washington</td><td>15.0</td><td>47</td><td>Mississippi</td><td>11.7</td></tr>
<tr><td>14</td><td>West Virginia</td><td>16.5</td><td>48</td><td>Maryland</td><td>11.2</td></tr>
<tr><td>3</td><td>Wisconsin</td><td>18.7</td><td>49</td><td>Alaska</td><td>10.4</td></tr>
<tr><td>32</td><td>Wyoming</td><td>13.6</td><td>50</td><td>Georgia</td><td>10.3</td></tr>
<tr><td></td><td></td><td></td><td></td><td>District of Columbia</td><td>10.3</td></tr>
</table>

Source: Morgan Quitno Press using data from American Cancer Society
   "Cancer Facts & Figures 2007" (Copyright 2007, American Cancer Society)
*These estimates are offered as a rough guide and should be interpreted with caution. They are calculated according to the distribution of estimated 2007 cancer deaths by state. Rates calculated using 2006 Census resident population estimates.

Estimated New Lung Cancer Cases in 2007

National Estimated Total = 213,380 New Cases*

ALPHA ORDER

RANK	STATE	CASES	% of USA
21	Alabama	3,850	1.8%
49	Alaska	330	0.2%
22	Arizona	3,740	1.8%
29	Arkansas	2,420	1.1%
1	California	17,920	8.4%
33	Colorado	2,100	1.0%
27	Connecticut	2,720	1.3%
41	Delaware	770	0.4%
2	Florida	17,490	8.2%
11	Georgia	5,780	2.7%
43	Hawaii	690	0.3%
42	Idaho	760	0.4%
7	Illinois	9,550	4.5%
14	Indiana	5,210	2.4%
30	Iowa	2,290	1.1%
34	Kansas	1,870	0.9%
17	Kentucky	4,450	2.1%
23	Louisiana	3,510	1.6%
36	Maine	1,360	0.6%
18	Maryland	4,130	1.9%
16	Massachusetts	5,060	2.4%
8	Michigan	8,210	3.8%
26	Minnesota	3,160	1.5%
31	Mississippi	2,190	1.0%
13	Missouri	5,350	2.5%
43	Montana	690	0.3%
37	Nebraska	1,190	0.6%
35	Nevada	1,750	0.8%
38	New Hampshire	1,010	0.5%
9	New Jersey	6,310	3.0%
39	New Mexico	940	0.4%
4	New York	13,390	6.3%
10	North Carolina	6,290	2.9%
48	North Dakota	390	0.2%
6	Ohio	9,790	4.6%
25	Oklahoma	3,180	1.5%
28	Oregon	2,520	1.2%
5	Pennsylvania	10,500	4.9%
40	Rhode Island	920	0.4%
24	South Carolina	3,460	1.6%
46	South Dakota	490	0.2%
15	Tennessee	5,110	2.4%
3	Texas	13,520	6.3%
45	Utah	600	0.3%
47	Vermont	440	0.2%
12	Virginia	5,360	2.5%
19	Washington	3,970	1.9%
32	West Virginia	2,110	1.0%
20	Wisconsin	3,930	1.8%
50	Wyoming	290	0.1%

RANK ORDER

RANK	STATE	CASES	% of USA
1	California	17,920	8.4%
2	Florida	17,490	8.2%
3	Texas	13,520	6.3%
4	New York	13,390	6.3%
5	Pennsylvania	10,500	4.9%
6	Ohio	9,790	4.6%
7	Illinois	9,550	4.5%
8	Michigan	8,210	3.8%
9	New Jersey	6,310	3.0%
10	North Carolina	6,290	2.9%
11	Georgia	5,780	2.7%
12	Virginia	5,360	2.5%
13	Missouri	5,350	2.5%
14	Indiana	5,210	2.4%
15	Tennessee	5,110	2.4%
16	Massachusetts	5,060	2.4%
17	Kentucky	4,450	2.1%
18	Maryland	4,130	1.9%
19	Washington	3,970	1.9%
20	Wisconsin	3,930	1.8%
21	Alabama	3,850	1.8%
22	Arizona	3,740	1.8%
23	Louisiana	3,510	1.6%
24	South Carolina	3,460	1.6%
25	Oklahoma	3,180	1.5%
26	Minnesota	3,160	1.5%
27	Connecticut	2,720	1.3%
28	Oregon	2,520	1.2%
29	Arkansas	2,420	1.1%
30	Iowa	2,290	1.1%
31	Mississippi	2,190	1.0%
32	West Virginia	2,110	1.0%
33	Colorado	2,100	1.0%
34	Kansas	1,870	0.9%
35	Nevada	1,750	0.8%
36	Maine	1,360	0.6%
37	Nebraska	1,190	0.6%
38	New Hampshire	1,010	0.5%
39	New Mexico	940	0.4%
40	Rhode Island	920	0.4%
41	Delaware	770	0.4%
42	Idaho	760	0.4%
43	Hawaii	690	0.3%
43	Montana	690	0.3%
45	Utah	600	0.3%
46	South Dakota	490	0.2%
47	Vermont	440	0.2%
48	North Dakota	390	0.2%
49	Alaska	330	0.2%
50	Wyoming	290	0.1%
	District of Columbia	380	0.2%

Source: American Cancer Society
"Cancer Facts & Figures 2007" (Copyright 2007, American Cancer Society)
*These estimates are offered as a rough guide and should be interpreted with caution. They are calculated according to the distribution of estimated 2007 cancer deaths by state.

Estimated Rate of New Lung Cancer Cases in 2007

National Estimated Rate = 71.3 New Cases per 100,000 Population*

ALPHA ORDER				RANK ORDER		
RANK	STATE	RATE		RANK	STATE	RATE
13	Alabama	83.7		1	West Virginia	116.0
46	Alaska	49.2		2	Kentucky	105.8
41	Arizona	60.7		3	Maine	102.9
9	Arkansas	86.1		4	Florida	96.7
46	California	49.2		5	Missouri	91.6
49	Colorado	44.2		6	Delaware	90.2
19	Connecticut	77.6		7	Oklahoma	88.8
6	Delaware	90.2		8	Rhode Island	86.2
4	Florida	96.7		9	Arkansas	86.1
38	Georgia	61.7		10	Ohio	85.3
44	Hawaii	53.7		11	Tennessee	84.6
45	Idaho	51.8		12	Pennsylvania	84.4
23	Illinois	74.4		13	Alabama	83.7
14	Indiana	82.5		14	Indiana	82.5
20	Iowa	76.8		15	Louisiana	81.9
34	Kansas	67.7		16	Michigan	81.3
2	Kentucky	105.8		17	South Carolina	80.1
15	Louisiana	81.9		18	Massachusetts	78.6
3	Maine	102.9		19	Connecticut	77.6
24	Maryland	73.5		20	Iowa	76.8
18	Massachusetts	78.6		20	New Hampshire	76.8
16	Michigan	81.3		22	Mississippi	75.2
40	Minnesota	61.2		23	Illinois	74.4
22	Mississippi	75.2		24	Maryland	73.5
5	Missouri	91.6		25	Montana	73.0
25	Montana	73.0		26	New Jersey	72.3
35	Nebraska	67.3		27	North Carolina	71.0
30	Nevada	70.1		28	Wisconsin	70.7
20	New Hampshire	76.8		29	Vermont	70.5
26	New Jersey	72.3		30	Nevada	70.1
48	New Mexico	48.1		30	Virginia	70.1
32	New York	69.4		32	New York	69.4
27	North Carolina	71.0		33	Oregon	68.1
39	North Dakota	61.3		34	Kansas	67.7
10	Ohio	85.3		35	Nebraska	67.3
7	Oklahoma	88.8		36	South Dakota	62.7
33	Oregon	68.1		37	Washington	62.1
12	Pennsylvania	84.4		38	Georgia	61.7
8	Rhode Island	86.2		39	North Dakota	61.3
17	South Carolina	80.1		40	Minnesota	61.2
36	South Dakota	62.7		41	Arizona	60.7
11	Tennessee	84.6		42	Texas	57.5
42	Texas	57.5		43	Wyoming	56.3
50	Utah	23.5		44	Hawaii	53.7
29	Vermont	70.5		45	Idaho	51.8
30	Virginia	70.1		46	Alaska	49.2
37	Washington	62.1		46	California	49.2
1	West Virginia	116.0		48	New Mexico	48.1
28	Wisconsin	70.7		49	Colorado	44.2
43	Wyoming	56.3		50	Utah	23.5
				District of Columbia		65.3

Source: Morgan Quitno Press using data from American Cancer Society
        "Cancer Facts & Figures 2007" (Copyright 2007, American Cancer Society)
*These estimates are offered as a rough guide and should be interpreted with caution. They are calculated
according to the distribution of estimated 2007 cancer deaths by state. Rates calculated using 2006 Census
resident population estimates.

Estimated New Non-Hodgkin's Lymphoma Cases in 2007

National Estimated Total = 63,190 New Cases*

ALPHA ORDER

RANK	STATE	CASES	% of USA
27	Alabama	860	1.4%
49	Alaska	110	0.2%
21	Arizona	1,080	1.7%
31	Arkansas	600	0.9%
1	California	7,190	11.4%
25	Colorado	880	1.4%
26	Connecticut	870	1.4%
46	Delaware	170	0.3%
3	Florida	4,530	7.2%
14	Georgia	1,370	2.2%
43	Hawaii	250	0.4%
41	Idaho	280	0.4%
6	Illinois	2,670	4.2%
15	Indiana	1,310	2.1%
28	Iowa	800	1.3%
31	Kansas	600	0.9%
23	Kentucky	900	1.4%
22	Louisiana	920	1.5%
39	Maine	330	0.5%
20	Maryland	1,160	1.8%
11	Massachusetts	1,550	2.5%
8	Michigan	2,250	3.6%
19	Minnesota	1,170	1.9%
33	Mississippi	480	0.8%
17	Missouri	1,260	2.0%
44	Montana	220	0.3%
36	Nebraska	400	0.6%
35	Nevada	420	0.7%
40	New Hampshire	290	0.5%
9	New Jersey	2,200	3.5%
38	New Mexico	350	0.6%
2	New York	4,540	7.2%
10	North Carolina	1,610	2.5%
47	North Dakota	150	0.2%
7	Ohio	2,560	4.1%
30	Oklahoma	770	1.2%
24	Oregon	890	1.4%
5	Pennsylvania	3,330	5.3%
42	Rhode Island	260	0.4%
29	South Carolina	780	1.2%
45	South Dakota	180	0.3%
18	Tennessee	1,180	1.9%
4	Texas	4,140	6.6%
37	Utah	380	0.6%
48	Vermont	140	0.2%
13	Virginia	1,390	2.2%
12	Washington	1,500	2.4%
34	West Virginia	430	0.7%
16	Wisconsin	1,300	2.1%
49	Wyoming	110	0.2%

RANK ORDER

RANK	STATE	CASES	% of USA
1	California	7,190	11.4%
2	New York	4,540	7.2%
3	Florida	4,530	7.2%
4	Texas	4,140	6.6%
5	Pennsylvania	3,330	5.3%
6	Illinois	2,670	4.2%
7	Ohio	2,560	4.1%
8	Michigan	2,250	3.6%
9	New Jersey	2,200	3.5%
10	North Carolina	1,610	2.5%
11	Massachusetts	1,550	2.5%
12	Washington	1,500	2.4%
13	Virginia	1,390	2.2%
14	Georgia	1,370	2.2%
15	Indiana	1,310	2.1%
16	Wisconsin	1,300	2.1%
17	Missouri	1,260	2.0%
18	Tennessee	1,180	1.9%
19	Minnesota	1,170	1.9%
20	Maryland	1,160	1.8%
21	Arizona	1,080	1.7%
22	Louisiana	920	1.5%
23	Kentucky	900	1.4%
24	Oregon	890	1.4%
25	Colorado	880	1.4%
26	Connecticut	870	1.4%
27	Alabama	860	1.4%
28	Iowa	800	1.3%
29	South Carolina	780	1.2%
30	Oklahoma	770	1.2%
31	Arkansas	600	0.9%
31	Kansas	600	0.9%
33	Mississippi	480	0.8%
34	West Virginia	430	0.7%
35	Nevada	420	0.7%
36	Nebraska	400	0.6%
37	Utah	380	0.6%
38	New Mexico	350	0.6%
39	Maine	330	0.5%
40	New Hampshire	290	0.5%
41	Idaho	280	0.4%
42	Rhode Island	260	0.4%
43	Hawaii	250	0.4%
44	Montana	220	0.3%
45	South Dakota	180	0.3%
46	Delaware	170	0.3%
47	North Dakota	150	0.2%
48	Vermont	140	0.2%
49	Alaska	110	0.2%
49	Wyoming	110	0.2%
	District of Columbia	100	0.2%

Source: American Cancer Society
"Cancer Facts & Figures 2007" (Copyright 2007, American Cancer Society)
*These estimates are offered as a rough guide and should be interpreted with caution. They are calculated according to the distribution of estimated 2007 cancer deaths by state.

Estimated Rate of New Non-Hodgkin's Lymphoma Cases in 2007

National Estimated Rate = 21.1 New Cases per 100,000 Population*

ALPHA ORDER

RANK	STATE	RATE
38	Alabama	18.7
48	Alaska	16.4
45	Arizona	17.5
29	Arkansas	21.3
34	California	19.7
39	Colorado	18.5
6	Connecticut	24.8
33	Delaware	19.9
4	Florida	25.0
50	Georgia	14.6
36	Hawaii	19.4
37	Idaho	19.1
30	Illinois	20.8
31	Indiana	20.7
1	Iowa	26.8
23	Kansas	21.7
27	Kentucky	21.4
25	Louisiana	21.5
4	Maine	25.0
31	Maryland	20.7
8	Massachusetts	24.1
20	Michigan	22.3
17	Minnesota	22.6
47	Mississippi	16.5
24	Missouri	21.6
15	Montana	23.3
17	Nebraska	22.6
46	Nevada	16.8
22	New Hampshire	22.1
3	New Jersey	25.2
43	New Mexico	17.9
12	New York	23.5
40	North Carolina	18.2
10	North Dakota	23.6
20	Ohio	22.3
25	Oklahoma	21.5
9	Oregon	24.0
1	Pennsylvania	26.8
7	Rhode Island	24.4
42	South Carolina	18.1
16	South Dakota	23.0
35	Tennessee	19.5
44	Texas	17.6
49	Utah	14.9
19	Vermont	22.4
40	Virginia	18.2
12	Washington	23.5
10	West Virginia	23.6
14	Wisconsin	23.4
27	Wyoming	21.4

RANK ORDER

RANK	STATE	RATE
1	Iowa	26.8
1	Pennsylvania	26.8
3	New Jersey	25.2
4	Florida	25.0
4	Maine	25.0
6	Connecticut	24.8
7	Rhode Island	24.4
8	Massachusetts	24.1
9	Oregon	24.0
10	North Dakota	23.6
10	West Virginia	23.6
12	New York	23.5
12	Washington	23.5
14	Wisconsin	23.4
15	Montana	23.3
16	South Dakota	23.0
17	Minnesota	22.6
17	Nebraska	22.6
19	Vermont	22.4
20	Michigan	22.3
20	Ohio	22.3
22	New Hampshire	22.1
23	Kansas	21.7
24	Missouri	21.6
25	Louisiana	21.5
25	Oklahoma	21.5
27	Kentucky	21.4
27	Wyoming	21.4
29	Arkansas	21.3
30	Illinois	20.8
31	Indiana	20.7
31	Maryland	20.7
33	Delaware	19.9
34	California	19.7
35	Tennessee	19.5
36	Hawaii	19.4
37	Idaho	19.1
38	Alabama	18.7
39	Colorado	18.5
40	North Carolina	18.2
40	Virginia	18.2
42	South Carolina	18.1
43	New Mexico	17.9
44	Texas	17.6
45	Arizona	17.5
46	Nevada	16.8
47	Mississippi	16.5
48	Alaska	16.4
49	Utah	14.9
50	Georgia	14.6

District of Columbia   17.2

Source: Morgan Quitno Press using data from American Cancer Society
"Cancer Facts & Figures 2007" (Copyright 2007, American Cancer Society)
These estimates are offered as a rough guide and should be interpreted with caution. They are calculated according to the distribution of estimated 2007 cancer deaths by state. Rates calculated using 2006 Census resident population estimates.

Estimated New Prostate Cancer Cases in 2007

National Estimated Total = 218,890 New Cases*

ALPHA ORDER

RANK	STATE	CASES	% of USA
24	Alabama	3,010	1.4%
49	Alaska	420	0.2%
21	Arizona	3,400	1.6%
32	Arkansas	1,960	0.9%
1	California	24,590	11.2%
23	Colorado	3,160	1.4%
26	Connecticut	2,890	1.3%
44	Delaware	800	0.4%
3	Florida	15,710	7.2%
11	Georgia	5,850	2.7%
45	Hawaii	780	0.4%
40	Idaho	1,080	0.5%
9	Illinois	8,060	3.7%
19	Indiana	3,710	1.7%
30	Iowa	2,140	1.0%
35	Kansas	1,490	0.7%
27	Kentucky	2,880	1.3%
20	Louisiana	3,640	1.7%
39	Maine	1,210	0.6%
17	Maryland	4,690	2.1%
13	Massachusetts	5,180	2.4%
7	Michigan	8,200	3.7%
15	Minnesota	4,800	2.2%
31	Mississippi	2,010	0.9%
18	Missouri	3,910	1.8%
42	Montana	940	0.4%
38	Nebraska	1,260	0.6%
33	Nevada	1,550	0.7%
41	New Hampshire	1,050	0.5%
8	New Jersey	8,070	3.7%
37	New Mexico	1,410	0.6%
2	New York	15,770	7.2%
10	North Carolina	6,040	2.8%
48	North Dakota	520	0.2%
6	Ohio	8,260	3.8%
29	Oklahoma	2,510	1.1%
28	Oregon	2,870	1.3%
5	Pennsylvania	12,230	5.6%
43	Rhode Island	920	0.4%
22	South Carolina	3,380	1.5%
46	South Dakota	710	0.3%
25	Tennessee	3,000	1.4%
4	Texas	13,280	6.1%
34	Utah	1,510	0.7%
47	Vermont	550	0.3%
12	Virginia	5,330	2.4%
14	Washington	5,000	2.3%
36	West Virginia	1,430	0.7%
16	Wisconsin	4,770	2.2%
50	Wyoming	410	0.2%

RANK ORDER

RANK	STATE	CASES	% of USA
1	California	24,590	11.2%
2	New York	15,770	7.2%
3	Florida	15,710	7.2%
4	Texas	13,280	6.1%
5	Pennsylvania	12,230	5.6%
6	Ohio	8,260	3.8%
7	Michigan	8,200	3.7%
8	New Jersey	8,070	3.7%
9	Illinois	8,060	3.7%
10	North Carolina	6,040	2.8%
11	Georgia	5,850	2.7%
12	Virginia	5,330	2.4%
13	Massachusetts	5,180	2.4%
14	Washington	5,000	2.3%
15	Minnesota	4,800	2.2%
16	Wisconsin	4,770	2.2%
17	Maryland	4,690	2.1%
18	Missouri	3,910	1.8%
19	Indiana	3,710	1.7%
20	Louisiana	3,640	1.7%
21	Arizona	3,400	1.6%
22	South Carolina	3,380	1.5%
23	Colorado	3,160	1.4%
24	Alabama	3,010	1.4%
25	Tennessee	3,000	1.4%
26	Connecticut	2,890	1.3%
27	Kentucky	2,880	1.3%
28	Oregon	2,870	1.3%
29	Oklahoma	2,510	1.1%
30	Iowa	2,140	1.0%
31	Mississippi	2,010	0.9%
32	Arkansas	1,960	0.9%
33	Nevada	1,550	0.7%
34	Utah	1,510	0.7%
35	Kansas	1,490	0.7%
36	West Virginia	1,430	0.7%
37	New Mexico	1,410	0.6%
38	Nebraska	1,260	0.6%
39	Maine	1,210	0.6%
40	Idaho	1,080	0.5%
41	New Hampshire	1,050	0.5%
42	Montana	940	0.4%
43	Rhode Island	920	0.4%
44	Delaware	800	0.4%
45	Hawaii	780	0.4%
46	South Dakota	710	0.3%
47	Vermont	550	0.3%
48	North Dakota	520	0.2%
49	Alaska	420	0.2%
50	Wyoming	410	0.2%
	District of Columbia	540	0.2%

Source: American Cancer Society
   "Cancer Facts & Figures 2007" (Copyright 2007, American Cancer Society)
*These estimates are offered as a rough guide and should be interpreted with caution. They are calculated according to the distribution of estimated 2007 cancer deaths by state.

Age-Adjusted Incidence Rate of Prostate Cancer Cases in 2003

National Rate = 165.0 New Cases per 100,000 Male Population*

RANK	STATE	RATE
42	Alabama	140.4
22	Alaska	167.7
46	Arizona	118.2
32	Arkansas	154.2
30	California	158.3
27	Colorado	164.8
10	Connecticut	179.8
16	Delaware	176.1
35	Florida	152.7
23	Georgia	166.2
45	Hawaii	132.3
18	Idaho	171.9
25	Illinois	165.6
43	Indiana	138.6
32	Iowa	154.2
NA	Kansas**	NA
31	Kentucky	155.1
11	Louisiana	179.5
19	Maine	171.3
6	Maryland	185.2
12	Massachusetts	178.2
2	Michigan	199.1
4	Minnesota	188.6
NA	Mississippi**	NA
44	Missouri	136.8
7	Montana	183.6
24	Nebraska	165.7
38	Nevada	150.6
26	New Hampshire	165.3
1	New Jersey	200.3
37	New Mexico	152.2
21	New York	168.1
36	North Carolina	152.4
9	North Dakota	181.8
34	Ohio	154.1
39	Oklahoma	148.8
28	Oregon	164.1
17	Pennsylvania	172.3
13	Rhode Island	177.9
15	South Carolina	176.9
3	South Dakota	190.1
47	Tennessee	108.7
40	Texas	148.3
5	Utah	186.5
NA	Vermont**	NA
29	Virginia	161.4
14	Washington	177.1
41	West Virginia	148.2
20	Wisconsin	169.1
8	Wyoming	182.2

RANK	STATE	RATE
1	New Jersey	200.3
2	Michigan	199.1
3	South Dakota	190.1
4	Minnesota	188.6
5	Utah	186.5
6	Maryland	185.2
7	Montana	183.6
8	Wyoming	182.2
9	North Dakota	181.8
10	Connecticut	179.8
11	Louisiana	179.5
12	Massachusetts	178.2
13	Rhode Island	177.9
14	Washington	177.1
15	South Carolina	176.9
16	Delaware	176.1
17	Pennsylvania	172.3
18	Idaho	171.9
19	Maine	171.3
20	Wisconsin	169.1
21	New York	168.1
22	Alaska	167.7
23	Georgia	166.2
24	Nebraska	165.7
25	Illinois	165.6
26	New Hampshire	165.3
27	Colorado	164.8
28	Oregon	164.1
29	Virginia	161.4
30	California	158.3
31	Kentucky	155.1
32	Arkansas	154.2
32	Iowa	154.2
34	Ohio	154.1
35	Florida	152.7
36	North Carolina	152.4
37	New Mexico	152.2
38	Nevada	150.6
39	Oklahoma	148.8
40	Texas	148.3
41	West Virginia	148.2
42	Alabama	140.4
43	Indiana	138.6
44	Missouri	136.8
45	Hawaii	132.3
46	Arizona	118.2
47	Tennessee	108.7
NA	Kansas**	NA
NA	Mississippi**	NA
NA	Vermont**	NA

District of Columbia   227.1

Source: American Cancer Society
*   "Cancer Facts & Figures 2007" (Copyright 2007, American Cancer Society)*
For 1999 to 2003. Age-adjusted to the 2000 U.S. standard population.
***Not available.*

Percent of Males Receiving Recent PSA Test for Prostate Cancer: 2004

National Median = 52.0% of Men*

ALPHA ORDER			RANK ORDER		
RANK	**STATE**	**PERCENT**	**RANK**	**STATE**	**PERCENT**
20	Alabama	52.6	1	Wyoming	59.8
44	Alaska	45.5	2	Georgia	57.8
8	Arizona	54.3	3	Florida	57.5
36	Arkansas	48.1	4	North Carolina	55.3
25	California	51.5	5	Rhode Island	54.9
29	Colorado	49.9	6	South Carolina	54.5
21	Connecticut	52.5	7	Delaware	54.4
7	Delaware	54.4	8	Arizona	54.3
3	Florida	57.5	9	New Jersey	54.2
2	Georgia	57.8	10	Maryland	53.8
NA	Hawaii**	NA	10	Montana	53.8
38	Idaho	47.8	12	Michigan	53.7
30	Illinois	49.7	13	New York	53.5
34	Indiana	48.9	14	Kansas	53.4
23	Iowa	52.2	15	Louisiana	53.1
14	Kansas	53.4	15	Ohio	53.1
37	Kentucky	48.0	15	South Dakota	53.1
15	Louisiana	53.1	18	Mississippi	53.0
48	Maine	44.5	19	Virginia	52.9
10	Maryland	53.8	20	Alabama	52.6
26	Massachusetts	50.9	21	Connecticut	52.5
12	Michigan	53.7	22	West Virginia	52.3
47	Minnesota	44.8	23	Iowa	52.2
18	Mississippi	53.0	24	Tennessee	51.9
35	Missouri	48.5	25	California	51.5
10	Montana	53.8	26	Massachusetts	50.9
27	Nebraska	50.7	27	Nebraska	50.7
39	Nevada	47.7	28	Oklahoma	50.2
40	New Hampshire	47.5	29	Colorado	49.9
9	New Jersey	54.2	30	Illinois	49.7
33	New Mexico	49.0	31	Pennsylvania	49.4
13	New York	53.5	31	Texas	49.4
4	North Carolina	55.3	33	New Mexico	49.0
45	North Dakota	45.4	34	Indiana	48.9
15	Ohio	53.1	35	Missouri	48.5
28	Oklahoma	50.2	36	Arkansas	48.1
41	Oregon	47.0	37	Kentucky	48.0
31	Pennsylvania	49.4	38	Idaho	47.8
5	Rhode Island	54.9	39	Nevada	47.7
6	South Carolina	54.5	40	New Hampshire	47.5
15	South Dakota	53.1	41	Oregon	47.0
24	Tennessee	51.9	42	Utah	46.1
31	Texas	49.4	43	Wisconsin	45.9
42	Utah	46.1	44	Alaska	45.5
48	Vermont	44.5	45	North Dakota	45.4
19	Virginia	52.9	46	Washington	45.2
46	Washington	45.2	47	Minnesota	44.8
22	West Virginia	52.3	48	Maine	44.5
43	Wisconsin	45.9	48	Vermont	44.5
1	Wyoming	59.8	NA	Hawaii**	NA
				District of Columbia	57.8

Source: U.S. Department of Health and Human Services, Centers for Disease Control and Prevention
   "2004 Behavioral Risk Factor Surveillance Summary Prevalence Data" (http://apps.nccd.cdc.gov/brfss/)
*Men 40 and older receiving prostate-specific antigen (PSA) test within the past year.
**Not available.

Estimated New Skin Melanoma Cases in 2007

National Estimated Total = 59,940 New Cases*

ALPHA ORDER

RANK	STATE	CASES	% of USA
27	Alabama	740	1.2%
50	Alaska	80	0.1%
15	Arizona	1,300	2.2%
31	Arkansas	550	0.9%
1	California	6,860	11.4%
17	Colorado	1,210	2.0%
20	Connecticut	1,120	1.9%
44	Delaware	190	0.3%
2	Florida	4,380	7.3%
14	Georgia	1,460	2.4%
43	Hawaii	270	0.5%
39	Idaho	350	0.6%
9	Illinois	2,050	3.4%
16	Indiana	1,220	2.0%
29	Iowa	690	1.2%
33	Kansas	430	0.7%
22	Kentucky	1,050	1.8%
30	Louisiana	670	1.1%
35	Maine	410	0.7%
18	Maryland	1,150	1.9%
10	Massachusetts	1,820	3.0%
8	Michigan	2,080	3.5%
19	Minnesota	1,130	1.9%
41	Mississippi	320	0.5%
25	Missouri	870	1.5%
44	Montana	190	0.3%
40	Nebraska	340	0.6%
37	Nevada	390	0.7%
38	New Hampshire	370	0.6%
7	New Jersey	2,210	3.7%
34	New Mexico	420	0.7%
5	New York	3,070	5.1%
11	North Carolina	1,630	2.7%
48	North Dakota	120	0.2%
6	Ohio	2,390	4.0%
28	Oklahoma	720	1.2%
23	Oregon	990	1.7%
4	Pennsylvania	3,120	5.2%
42	Rhode Island	300	0.5%
25	South Carolina	870	1.5%
46	South Dakota	160	0.3%
24	Tennessee	980	1.6%
3	Texas	3,860	6.4%
32	Utah	500	0.8%
47	Vermont	150	0.3%
13	Virginia	1,510	2.5%
11	Washington	1,630	2.7%
35	West Virginia	410	0.7%
21	Wisconsin	1,070	1.8%
49	Wyoming	100	0.2%

RANK ORDER

RANK	STATE	CASES	% of USA
1	California	6,860	11.4%
2	Florida	4,380	7.3%
3	Texas	3,860	6.4%
4	Pennsylvania	3,120	5.2%
5	New York	3,070	5.1%
6	Ohio	2,390	4.0%
7	New Jersey	2,210	3.7%
8	Michigan	2,080	3.5%
9	Illinois	2,050	3.4%
10	Massachusetts	1,820	3.0%
11	North Carolina	1,630	2.7%
11	Washington	1,630	2.7%
13	Virginia	1,510	2.5%
14	Georgia	1,460	2.4%
15	Arizona	1,300	2.2%
16	Indiana	1,220	2.0%
17	Colorado	1,210	2.0%
18	Maryland	1,150	1.9%
19	Minnesota	1,130	1.9%
20	Connecticut	1,120	1.9%
21	Wisconsin	1,070	1.8%
22	Kentucky	1,050	1.8%
23	Oregon	990	1.7%
24	Tennessee	980	1.6%
25	Missouri	870	1.5%
25	South Carolina	870	1.5%
27	Alabama	740	1.2%
28	Oklahoma	720	1.2%
29	Iowa	690	1.2%
30	Louisiana	670	1.1%
31	Arkansas	550	0.9%
32	Utah	500	0.8%
33	Kansas	430	0.7%
34	New Mexico	420	0.7%
35	Maine	410	0.7%
35	West Virginia	410	0.7%
37	Nevada	390	0.7%
38	New Hampshire	370	0.6%
39	Idaho	350	0.6%
40	Nebraska	340	0.6%
41	Mississippi	320	0.5%
42	Rhode Island	300	0.5%
43	Hawaii	270	0.5%
44	Delaware	190	0.3%
44	Montana	190	0.3%
46	South Dakota	160	0.3%
47	Vermont	150	0.3%
48	North Dakota	120	0.2%
49	Wyoming	100	0.2%
50	Alaska	80	0.1%
	District of Columbia	60	0.1%

Source: American Cancer Society
   "Cancer Facts & Figures 2007" (Copyright 2007, American Cancer Society)
*These estimates are offered as a rough guide and should be interpreted with caution. They are calculated according to the distribution of estimated 2007 cancer deaths by state.

Estimated Rate of New Skin Melanoma Cases in 2007

National Estimated Rate = 20.0 New Cases per 100,000 Population*

ALPHA ORDER

RANK	STATE	CASES
41	Alabama	16.1
49	Alaska	11.9
20	Arizona	21.1
30	Arkansas	19.6
37	California	18.8
7	Colorado	25.5
1	Connecticut	32.0
17	Delaware	22.3
12	Florida	24.2
44	Georgia	15.6
21	Hawaii	21.0
14	Idaho	23.9
42	Illinois	16.0
33	Indiana	19.3
15	Iowa	23.1
44	Kansas	15.6
11	Kentucky	25.0
44	Louisiana	15.6
2	Maine	31.0
24	Maryland	20.5
3	Massachusetts	28.3
23	Michigan	20.6
18	Minnesota	21.9
50	Mississippi	11.0
48	Missouri	14.9
26	Montana	20.1
35	Nebraska	19.2
44	Nevada	15.6
4	New Hampshire	28.1
9	New Jersey	25.3
19	New Mexico	21.5
43	New York	15.9
38	North Carolina	18.4
36	North Dakota	18.9
22	Ohio	20.8
26	Oklahoma	20.1
6	Oregon	26.8
10	Pennsylvania	25.1
4	Rhode Island	28.1
26	South Carolina	20.1
24	South Dakota	20.5
40	Tennessee	16.2
39	Texas	16.4
30	Utah	19.6
13	Vermont	24.0
29	Virginia	19.8
7	Washington	25.5
16	West Virginia	22.5
33	Wisconsin	19.3
32	Wyoming	19.4

RANK ORDER

RANK	STATE	CASES
1	Connecticut	32.0
2	Maine	31.0
3	Massachusetts	28.3
4	New Hampshire	28.1
4	Rhode Island	28.1
6	Oregon	26.8
7	Colorado	25.5
7	Washington	25.5
9	New Jersey	25.3
10	Pennsylvania	25.1
11	Kentucky	25.0
12	Florida	24.2
13	Vermont	24.0
14	Idaho	23.9
15	Iowa	23.1
16	West Virginia	22.5
17	Delaware	22.3
18	Minnesota	21.9
19	New Mexico	21.5
20	Arizona	21.1
21	Hawaii	21.0
22	Ohio	20.8
23	Michigan	20.6
24	Maryland	20.5
24	South Dakota	20.5
26	Montana	20.1
26	Oklahoma	20.1
26	South Carolina	20.1
29	Virginia	19.8
30	Arkansas	19.6
30	Utah	19.6
32	Wyoming	19.4
33	Indiana	19.3
33	Wisconsin	19.3
35	Nebraska	19.2
36	North Dakota	18.9
37	California	18.8
38	North Carolina	18.4
39	Texas	16.4
40	Tennessee	16.2
41	Alabama	16.1
42	Illinois	16.0
43	New York	15.9
44	Georgia	15.6
44	Kansas	15.6
44	Louisiana	15.6
44	Nevada	15.6
48	Missouri	14.9
49	Alaska	11.9
50	Mississippi	11.0
	District of Columbia	10.3

Source: Morgan Quitno Press using data from American Cancer Society
"Cancer Facts & Figures 2007" (Copyright 2007, American Cancer Society)
*These estimates are offered as a rough guide and should be interpreted with caution. They are calculated according to the distribution of estimated 2007 cancer deaths by state. Rates calculated using 2006 Census resident population estimates.

Estimated New Cervical Cancer Cases in 2007

National Estimated Total = 11,150 New Cases*

ALPHA ORDER

RANK	STATE	CASES	% of USA
22	Alabama	170	1.5%
NA	Alaska**	NA	NA
18	Arizona	190	1.7%
28	Arkansas	130	1.2%
1	California	1,350	12.1%
25	Colorado	150	1.3%
31	Connecticut	100	0.9%
NA	Delaware**	NA	NA
3	Florida	850	7.6%
10	Georgia	330	3.0%
38	Hawaii	50	0.4%
NA	Idaho**	NA	NA
5	Illinois	530	4.8%
14	Indiana	240	2.2%
31	Iowa	100	0.9%
31	Kansas	100	0.9%
16	Kentucky	200	1.8%
16	Louisiana	200	1.8%
NA	Maine**	NA	NA
18	Maryland	190	1.7%
21	Massachusetts	180	1.6%
8	Michigan	370	3.3%
25	Minnesota	150	1.3%
29	Mississippi	120	1.1%
14	Missouri	240	2.2%
NA	Montana**	NA	NA
37	Nebraska	60	0.5%
34	Nevada	80	0.7%
NA	New Hampshire**	NA	NA
9	New Jersey	350	3.1%
36	New Mexico	70	0.6%
4	New York	790	7.1%
11	North Carolina	280	2.5%
NA	North Dakota**	NA	NA
7	Ohio	390	3.5%
24	Oklahoma	160	1.4%
30	Oregon	110	1.0%
6	Pennsylvania	420	3.8%
NA	Rhode Island**	NA	NA
18	South Carolina	190	1.7%
NA	South Dakota**	NA	NA
13	Tennessee	250	2.2%
2	Texas	940	8.4%
38	Utah	50	0.4%
NA	Vermont**	NA	NA
11	Virginia	280	2.5%
25	Washington	150	1.3%
34	West Virginia	80	0.7%
22	Wisconsin	170	1.5%
NA	Wyoming**	NA	NA

RANK ORDER

RANK	STATE	CASES	% of USA
1	California	1,350	12.1%
2	Texas	940	8.4%
3	Florida	850	7.6%
4	New York	790	7.1%
5	Illinois	530	4.8%
6	Pennsylvania	420	3.8%
7	Ohio	390	3.5%
8	Michigan	370	3.3%
9	New Jersey	350	3.1%
10	Georgia	330	3.0%
11	North Carolina	280	2.5%
11	Virginia	280	2.5%
13	Tennessee	250	2.2%
14	Indiana	240	2.2%
14	Missouri	240	2.2%
16	Kentucky	200	1.8%
16	Louisiana	200	1.8%
18	Arizona	190	1.7%
18	Maryland	190	1.7%
18	South Carolina	190	1.7%
21	Massachusetts	180	1.6%
22	Alabama	170	1.5%
22	Wisconsin	170	1.5%
24	Oklahoma	160	1.4%
25	Colorado	150	1.3%
25	Minnesota	150	1.3%
25	Washington	150	1.3%
28	Arkansas	130	1.2%
29	Mississippi	120	1.1%
30	Oregon	110	1.0%
31	Connecticut	100	0.9%
31	Iowa	100	0.9%
31	Kansas	100	0.9%
34	Nevada	80	0.7%
34	West Virginia	80	0.7%
36	New Mexico	70	0.6%
37	Nebraska	60	0.5%
38	Hawaii	50	0.4%
38	Utah	50	0.4%
NA	Alaska**	NA	NA
NA	Delaware**	NA	NA
NA	Idaho**	NA	NA
NA	Maine**	NA	NA
NA	Montana**	NA	NA
NA	New Hampshire**	NA	NA
NA	North Dakota**	NA	NA
NA	Rhode Island**	NA	NA
NA	South Dakota**	NA	NA
NA	Vermont**	NA	NA
NA	Wyoming**	NA	NA
	District of Columbia**	NA	NA

Source: American Cancer Society
"Cancer Facts & Figures 2007" (Copyright 2007, American Cancer Society)
*These estimates are offered as a rough guide and should be interpreted with caution. They are calculated according to the distribution of estimated 2007 cancer deaths by state.
**Not available.

Estimated Rate of New Cervical Cancer Cases in 2007

National Estimated Rate = 7.4 New Cases per 100,000 Female Population*

ALPHA ORDER

RANK	STATE	RATE
19	Alabama	7.2
NA	Alaska**	NA
31	Arizona	6.4
3	Arkansas	9.2
16	California	7.5
30	Colorado	6.5
36	Connecticut	5.5
NA	Delaware**	NA
1	Florida	9.4
19	Georgia	7.2
14	Hawaii	7.8
NA	Idaho**	NA
8	Illinois	8.2
16	Indiana	7.5
26	Iowa	6.6
19	Kansas	7.2
1	Kentucky	9.4
6	Louisiana	8.6
NA	Maine**	NA
26	Maryland	6.6
36	Massachusetts	5.5
19	Michigan	7.2
35	Minnesota	5.8
12	Mississippi	8.0
11	Missouri	8.1
NA	Montana**	NA
24	Nebraska	6.7
24	Nevada	6.7
NA	New Hampshire**	NA
14	New Jersey	7.8
23	New Mexico	7.1
12	New York	8.0
32	North Carolina	6.3
NA	North Dakota**	NA
26	Ohio	6.6
4	Oklahoma	8.9
34	Oregon	6.0
26	Pennsylvania	6.6
NA	Rhode Island**	NA
5	South Carolina	8.7
NA	South Dakota**	NA
8	Tennessee	8.2
8	Texas	8.2
39	Utah	4.1
NA	Vermont**	NA
18	Virginia	7.3
38	Washington	4.8
6	West Virginia	8.6
33	Wisconsin	6.1
NA	Wyoming**	NA

RANK ORDER

RANK	STATE	RATE
1	Florida	9.4
1	Kentucky	9.4
3	Arkansas	9.2
4	Oklahoma	8.9
5	South Carolina	8.7
6	Louisiana	8.6
6	West Virginia	8.6
8	Illinois	8.2
8	Tennessee	8.2
8	Texas	8.2
11	Missouri	8.1
12	Mississippi	8.0
12	New York	8.0
14	Hawaii	7.8
14	New Jersey	7.8
16	California	7.5
16	Indiana	7.5
18	Virginia	7.3
19	Alabama	7.2
19	Georgia	7.2
19	Kansas	7.2
19	Michigan	7.2
23	New Mexico	7.1
24	Nebraska	6.7
24	Nevada	6.7
26	Iowa	6.6
26	Maryland	6.6
26	Ohio	6.6
26	Pennsylvania	6.6
30	Colorado	6.5
31	Arizona	6.4
32	North Carolina	6.3
33	Wisconsin	6.1
34	Oregon	6.0
35	Minnesota	5.8
36	Connecticut	5.5
36	Massachusetts	5.5
38	Washington	4.8
39	Utah	4.1
NA	Alaska**	NA
NA	Delaware**	NA
NA	Idaho**	NA
NA	Maine**	NA
NA	Montana**	NA
NA	New Hampshire**	NA
NA	North Dakota**	NA
NA	Rhode Island**	NA
NA	South Dakota**	NA
NA	Vermont**	NA
NA	Wyoming**	NA
	District of Columbia**	NA

Source: Morgan Quitno Press using data from American Cancer Society
      "Cancer Facts & Figures 2007" (Copyright 2007, American Cancer Society)
*These estimates are offered as a rough guide and should be interpreted with caution. They are calculated according to the distribution of estimated 2007 cancer deaths by state. Rates calculated using 2005 Census female population estimates.
**Not available.

Percent of Women 18 Years Old and Older
Who Had a Pap Smear Within the Past Three Years: 2004
National Median = 85.9% of Women 18 Years and Older*

ALPHA ORDER

RANK	STATE	PERCENT
14	Alabama	87.4
5	Alaska	88.8
31	Arizona	85.1
47	Arkansas	81.7
34	California	84.7
8	Colorado	88.2
11	Connecticut	87.7
12	Delaware	87.6
40	Florida	84.0
9	Georgia	87.9
NA	Hawaii**	NA
48	Idaho	78.8
14	Illinois	87.4
45	Indiana	82.4
24	Iowa	86.0
22	Kansas	86.1
32	Kentucky	84.9
30	Louisiana	85.2
6	Maine	88.7
3	Maryland	88.9
2	Massachusetts	89.3
20	Michigan	86.5
10	Minnesota	87.8
37	Mississippi	84.5
33	Missouri	84.8
22	Montana	86.1
26	Nebraska	85.8
34	Nevada	84.7
1	New Hampshire	89.7
38	New Jersey	84.3
34	New Mexico	84.7
28	New York	85.4
7	North Carolina	88.3
42	North Dakota	83.2
21	Ohio	86.4
43	Oklahoma	82.9
41	Oregon	83.5
38	Pennsylvania	84.3
3	Rhode Island	88.9
19	South Carolina	87.1
18	South Dakota	87.2
16	Tennessee	87.3
46	Texas	82.1
49	Utah	78.2
12	Vermont	87.6
16	Virginia	87.3
28	Washington	85.4
44	West Virginia	82.5
27	Wisconsin	85.7
25	Wyoming	85.9

RANK ORDER

RANK	STATE	PERCENT
1	New Hampshire	89.7
2	Massachusetts	89.3
3	Maryland	88.9
3	Rhode Island	88.9
5	Alaska	88.8
6	Maine	88.7
7	North Carolina	88.3
8	Colorado	88.2
9	Georgia	87.9
10	Minnesota	87.8
11	Connecticut	87.7
12	Delaware	87.6
12	Vermont	87.6
14	Alabama	87.4
14	Illinois	87.4
16	Tennessee	87.3
16	Virginia	87.3
18	South Dakota	87.2
19	South Carolina	87.1
20	Michigan	86.5
21	Ohio	86.4
22	Kansas	86.1
22	Montana	86.1
24	Iowa	86.0
25	Wyoming	85.9
26	Nebraska	85.8
27	Wisconsin	85.7
28	New York	85.4
28	Washington	85.4
30	Louisiana	85.2
31	Arizona	85.1
32	Kentucky	84.9
33	Missouri	84.8
34	California	84.7
34	Nevada	84.7
34	New Mexico	84.7
37	Mississippi	84.5
38	New Jersey	84.3
38	Pennsylvania	84.3
40	Florida	84.0
41	Oregon	83.5
42	North Dakota	83.2
43	Oklahoma	82.9
44	West Virginia	82.5
45	Indiana	82.4
46	Texas	82.1
47	Arkansas	81.7
48	Idaho	78.8
49	Utah	78.2
NA	Hawaii**	NA

District of Columbia 88.4

Source: U.S. Department of Health and Human Services, Centers for Disease Control and Prevention
"2004 Behavioral Risk Factor Surveillance Summary Prevalence Data" (http://apps.nccd.cdc.gov/brfss/)
A Pap test is a test for cancer, especially of the female genital tract such as cancer of the cervix. Named after George Papanicolaou (1883-1962), American anatomist.
***Not available.*

Estimated New Uterine Cancer Cases in 2007

National Estimated Total = 39,080 New Cases*

ALPHA ORDER

RANK	STATE	CASES	% of USA
28	Alabama	460	1.2%
49	Alaska	60	0.2%
23	Arizona	550	1.4%
32	Arkansas	320	0.8%
1	California	3,870	9.9%
25	Colorado	490	1.3%
21	Connecticut	650	1.7%
44	Delaware	130	0.3%
3	Florida	2,490	6.4%
16	Georgia	810	2.1%
42	Hawaii	170	0.4%
43	Idaho	150	0.4%
7	Illinois	1,730	4.4%
13	Indiana	880	2.3%
24	Iowa	500	1.3%
31	Kansas	360	0.9%
22	Kentucky	560	1.4%
29	Louisiana	420	1.1%
34	Maine	270	0.7%
16	Maryland	810	2.1%
10	Massachusetts	1,110	2.8%
8	Michigan	1,610	4.1%
19	Minnesota	750	1.9%
36	Mississippi	230	0.6%
15	Missouri	830	2.1%
45	Montana	120	0.3%
35	Nebraska	260	0.7%
36	Nevada	230	0.6%
36	New Hampshire	230	0.6%
9	New Jersey	1,550	4.0%
40	New Mexico	200	0.5%
2	New York	3,240	8.3%
11	North Carolina	1,020	2.6%
48	North Dakota	100	0.3%
6	Ohio	1,800	4.6%
30	Oklahoma	400	1.0%
27	Oregon	470	1.2%
4	Pennsylvania	2,400	6.1%
41	Rhode Island	190	0.5%
26	South Carolina	480	1.2%
45	South Dakota	120	0.3%
20	Tennessee	660	1.7%
5	Texas	2,040	5.2%
39	Utah	220	0.6%
47	Vermont	110	0.3%
12	Virginia	970	2.5%
18	Washington	800	2.0%
33	West Virginia	310	0.8%
14	Wisconsin	860	2.2%
49	Wyoming	60	0.2%

RANK ORDER

RANK	STATE	CASES	% of USA
1	California	3,870	9.9%
2	New York	3,240	8.3%
3	Florida	2,490	6.4%
4	Pennsylvania	2,400	6.1%
5	Texas	2,040	5.2%
6	Ohio	1,800	4.6%
7	Illinois	1,730	4.4%
8	Michigan	1,610	4.1%
9	New Jersey	1,550	4.0%
10	Massachusetts	1,110	2.8%
11	North Carolina	1,020	2.6%
12	Virginia	970	2.5%
13	Indiana	880	2.3%
14	Wisconsin	860	2.2%
15	Missouri	830	2.1%
16	Georgia	810	2.1%
16	Maryland	810	2.1%
18	Washington	800	2.0%
19	Minnesota	750	1.9%
20	Tennessee	660	1.7%
21	Connecticut	650	1.7%
22	Kentucky	560	1.4%
23	Arizona	550	1.4%
24	Iowa	500	1.3%
25	Colorado	490	1.3%
26	South Carolina	480	1.2%
27	Oregon	470	1.2%
28	Alabama	460	1.2%
29	Louisiana	420	1.1%
30	Oklahoma	400	1.0%
31	Kansas	360	0.9%
32	Arkansas	320	0.8%
33	West Virginia	310	0.8%
34	Maine	270	0.7%
35	Nebraska	260	0.7%
36	Mississippi	230	0.6%
36	Nevada	230	0.6%
36	New Hampshire	230	0.6%
39	Utah	220	0.6%
40	New Mexico	200	0.5%
41	Rhode Island	190	0.5%
42	Hawaii	170	0.4%
43	Idaho	150	0.4%
44	Delaware	130	0.3%
45	Montana	120	0.3%
45	South Dakota	120	0.3%
47	Vermont	110	0.3%
48	North Dakota	100	0.3%
49	Alaska	60	0.2%
49	Wyoming	60	0.2%
	District of Columbia	70	0.2%

Source: American Cancer Society
   "Cancer Facts & Figures 2007" (Copyright 2007, American Cancer Society)
*These estimates are offered as a rough guide and should be interpreted with caution. They are calculated according to the distribution of estimated 2007 cancer deaths by state.

Estimated Rate of New Uterine Cancer Cases in 2007

National Estimated Rate = 26.0 New Cases per 100,000 Female Population*

ALPHA ORDER

RANK	STATE	RATE
42	Alabama	19.6
44	Alaska	18.7
45	Arizona	18.5
34	Arkansas	22.6
38	California	21.4
39	Colorado	21.2
3	Connecticut	36.0
17	Delaware	30.1
23	Florida	27.5
49	Georgia	17.7
24	Hawaii	26.6
40	Idaho	21.1
24	Illinois	26.6
22	Indiana	27.6
10	Iowa	33.2
27	Kansas	26.1
26	Kentucky	26.4
46	Louisiana	18.1
1	Maine	39.9
20	Maryland	28.1
8	Massachusetts	33.7
13	Michigan	31.3
19	Minnesota	29.0
50	Mississippi	15.3
21	Missouri	28.0
29	Montana	25.6
18	Nebraska	29.2
43	Nevada	19.4
6	New Hampshire	34.6
5	New Jersey	34.7
41	New Mexico	20.4
11	New York	32.6
33	North Carolina	23.1
12	North Dakota	31.4
16	Ohio	30.6
35	Oklahoma	22.3
28	Oregon	25.7
2	Pennsylvania	37.5
7	Rhode Island	34.2
36	South Carolina	22.0
15	South Dakota	30.7
37	Tennessee	21.7
48	Texas	17.8
47	Utah	17.9
4	Vermont	34.8
31	Virginia	25.2
30	Washington	25.4
9	West Virginia	33.4
14	Wisconsin	30.8
32	Wyoming	23.8

RANK ORDER

RANK	STATE	RATE
1	Maine	39.9
2	Pennsylvania	37.5
3	Connecticut	36.0
4	Vermont	34.8
5	New Jersey	34.7
6	New Hampshire	34.6
7	Rhode Island	34.2
8	Massachusetts	33.7
9	West Virginia	33.4
10	Iowa	33.2
11	New York	32.6
12	North Dakota	31.4
13	Michigan	31.3
14	Wisconsin	30.8
15	South Dakota	30.7
16	Ohio	30.6
17	Delaware	30.1
18	Nebraska	29.2
19	Minnesota	29.0
20	Maryland	28.1
21	Missouri	28.0
22	Indiana	27.6
23	Florida	27.5
24	Hawaii	26.6
24	Illinois	26.6
26	Kentucky	26.4
27	Kansas	26.1
28	Oregon	25.7
29	Montana	25.6
30	Washington	25.4
31	Virginia	25.2
32	Wyoming	23.8
33	North Carolina	23.1
34	Arkansas	22.6
35	Oklahoma	22.3
36	South Carolina	22.0
37	Tennessee	21.7
38	California	21.4
39	Colorado	21.2
40	Idaho	21.1
41	New Mexico	20.4
42	Alabama	19.6
43	Nevada	19.4
44	Alaska	18.7
45	Arizona	18.5
46	Louisiana	18.1
47	Utah	17.9
48	Texas	17.8
49	Georgia	17.7
50	Mississippi	15.3

District of Columbia   24.2

Source: Morgan Quitno Press using data from American Cancer Society
"Cancer Facts & Figures 2007" (Copyright 2007, American Cancer Society)
*These estimates are offered as a rough guide and should be interpreted with caution. They are calculated according to the distribution of estimated 2007 cancer deaths by state. Rates calculated using 2005 Census female population estimates.

AIDS Cases Reported in 2005

National Total = 40,733 New AIDS Cases*

RANK	STATE	CASES	% of USA
20	Alabama	518	1.3%
43	Alaska	26	0.1%
19	Arizona	642	1.6%
29	Arkansas	242	0.6%
3	California	4,088	10.0%
25	Colorado	359	0.9%
17	Connecticut	666	1.6%
32	Delaware	176	0.4%
2	Florida	4,960	12.2%
5	Georgia	2,333	5.7%
35	Hawaii	109	0.3%
44	Idaho	25	0.1%
6	Illinois	1,922	4.7%
22	Indiana	409	1.0%
37	Iowa	95	0.2%
36	Kansas	107	0.3%
28	Kentucky	257	0.6%
10	Louisiana	961	2.4%
45	Maine	21	0.1%
7	Maryland	1,595	3.9%
15	Massachusetts	692	1.7%
13	Michigan	822	2.0%
30	Minnesota	225	0.6%
23	Mississippi	387	1.0%
24	Missouri	386	0.9%
46	Montana	20	0.0%
41	Nebraska	53	0.1%
26	Nevada	296	0.7%
42	New Hampshire	34	0.1%
9	New Jersey	1,278	3.1%
33	New Mexico	136	0.3%
1	New York	6,299	15.5%
11	North Carolina	945	2.3%
48	North Dakota	10	0.0%
14	Ohio	784	1.9%
27	Oklahoma	282	0.7%
31	Oregon	220	0.5%
8	Pennsylvania	1,510	3.7%
38	Rhode Island	89	0.2%
16	South Carolina	668	1.6%
47	South Dakota	19	0.0%
12	Tennessee	841	2.1%
4	Texas	3,113	7.6%
40	Utah	65	0.2%
49	Vermont	6	0.0%
18	Virginia	646	1.6%
21	Washington	486	1.2%
39	West Virginia	74	0.2%
34	Wisconsin	123	0.3%
49	Wyoming	6	0.0%

RANK	STATE	CASES	% of USA
1	New York	6,299	15.5%
2	Florida	4,960	12.2%
3	California	4,088	10.0%
4	Texas	3,113	7.6%
5	Georgia	2,333	5.7%
6	Illinois	1,922	4.7%
7	Maryland	1,595	3.9%
8	Pennsylvania	1,510	3.7%
9	New Jersey	1,278	3.1%
10	Louisiana	961	2.4%
11	North Carolina	945	2.3%
12	Tennessee	841	2.1%
13	Michigan	822	2.0%
14	Ohio	784	1.9%
15	Massachusetts	692	1.7%
16	South Carolina	668	1.6%
17	Connecticut	666	1.6%
18	Virginia	646	1.6%
19	Arizona	642	1.6%
20	Alabama	518	1.3%
21	Washington	486	1.2%
22	Indiana	409	1.0%
23	Mississippi	387	1.0%
24	Missouri	386	0.9%
25	Colorado	359	0.9%
26	Nevada	296	0.7%
27	Oklahoma	282	0.7%
28	Kentucky	257	0.6%
29	Arkansas	242	0.6%
30	Minnesota	225	0.6%
31	Oregon	220	0.5%
32	Delaware	176	0.4%
33	New Mexico	136	0.3%
34	Wisconsin	123	0.3%
35	Hawaii	109	0.3%
36	Kansas	107	0.3%
37	Iowa	95	0.2%
38	Rhode Island	89	0.2%
39	West Virginia	74	0.2%
40	Utah	65	0.2%
41	Nebraska	53	0.1%
42	New Hampshire	34	0.1%
43	Alaska	26	0.1%
44	Idaho	25	0.1%
45	Maine	21	0.1%
46	Montana	20	0.0%
47	South Dakota	19	0.0%
48	North Dakota	10	0.0%
49	Vermont	6	0.0%
49	Wyoming	6	0.0%
	District of Columbia	707	1.7%

Source: U.S. Department of Health and Human Services, Centers for Disease Control and Prevention
        "HIV/AIDS Surveillance Report, 2005" (Vol. 17)
*Updated data. AIDS is Acquired Immunodeficiency Syndrome. It is a specific group of diseases or conditions
which are indicative of severe immunosuppression related to infection with the Human Immunodeficiency Virus
(HIV). National total does not include 1,033 new cases in Puerto Rico, 17 in the Virgin Islands and one in Guam.

AIDS Rate in 2005

National Rate = 13.7 New AIDS Cases Reported per 100,000 Population*

ALPHA ORDER

RANK	STATE	RATE
16	Alabama	11.4
37	Alaska	3.9
19	Arizona	10.8
21	Arkansas	8.7
17	California	11.3
27	Colorado	7.7
7	Connecticut	19.0
6	Delaware	20.9
3	Florida	27.9
4	Georgia	25.7
22	Hawaii	8.5
46	Idaho	1.7
9	Illinois	15.1
32	Indiana	6.5
39	Iowa	3.2
37	Kansas	3.9
33	Kentucky	6.2
5	Louisiana	21.2
47	Maine	1.6
2	Maryland	28.5
19	Massachusetts	10.8
25	Michigan	8.1
35	Minnesota	4.4
13	Mississippi	13.2
31	Missouri	6.7
45	Montana	2.1
40	Nebraska	3.0
14	Nevada	12.3
41	New Hampshire	2.6
10	New Jersey	14.7
29	New Mexico	7.1
1	New York	32.7
18	North Carolina	10.9
47	North Dakota	1.6
30	Ohio	6.8
26	Oklahoma	7.9
34	Oregon	6.0
15	Pennsylvania	12.1
24	Rhode Island	8.3
8	South Carolina	15.7
43	South Dakota	2.4
11	Tennessee	14.1
12	Texas	13.6
41	Utah	2.6
50	Vermont	1.0
22	Virginia	8.5
27	Washington	7.7
36	West Virginia	4.1
44	Wisconsin	2.2
49	Wyoming	1.2

RANK ORDER

RANK	STATE	RATE
1	New York	32.7
2	Maryland	28.5
3	Florida	27.9
4	Georgia	25.7
5	Louisiana	21.2
6	Delaware	20.9
7	Connecticut	19.0
8	South Carolina	15.7
9	Illinois	15.1
10	New Jersey	14.7
11	Tennessee	14.1
12	Texas	13.6
13	Mississippi	13.2
14	Nevada	12.3
15	Pennsylvania	12.1
16	Alabama	11.4
17	California	11.3
18	North Carolina	10.9
19	Arizona	10.8
19	Massachusetts	10.8
21	Arkansas	8.7
22	Hawaii	8.5
22	Virginia	8.5
24	Rhode Island	8.3
25	Michigan	8.1
26	Oklahoma	7.9
27	Colorado	7.7
27	Washington	7.7
29	New Mexico	7.1
30	Ohio	6.8
31	Missouri	6.7
32	Indiana	6.5
33	Kentucky	6.2
34	Oregon	6.0
35	Minnesota	4.4
36	West Virginia	4.1
37	Alaska	3.9
37	Kansas	3.9
39	Iowa	3.2
40	Nebraska	3.0
41	New Hampshire	2.6
41	Utah	2.6
43	South Dakota	2.4
44	Wisconsin	2.2
45	Montana	2.1
46	Idaho	1.7
47	Maine	1.6
47	North Dakota	1.6
49	Wyoming	1.2
50	Vermont	1.0

	District of Columbia	128.4

Source: U.S. Department of Health and Human Services, Centers for Disease Control and Prevention
      "HIV/AIDS Surveillance Report, 2005" (Vol. 17)
*Updated data. AIDS is Acquired Immunodeficiency Syndrome. It is a specific group of diseases or conditions
which are indicative of severe immunosuppression related to infection with the Human Immunodeficiency Virus
(HIV). National rate does not include cases or population in U.S. territories.

AIDS Cases Reported Through December 2005

National Total = 925,452 Reported AIDS Cases*

<table>
<tr><td colspan="4">ALPHA ORDER</td><td colspan="4">RANK ORDER</td></tr>
<tr><td>RANK</td><td>STATE</td><td>CASES</td><td>% of USA</td><td>RANK</td><td>STATE</td><td>CASES</td><td>% of USA</td></tr>
<tr><td>23</td><td>Alabama</td><td>8,252</td><td>0.9%</td><td>1</td><td>New York</td><td>172,377</td><td>18.6%</td></tr>
<tr><td>44</td><td>Alaska</td><td>621</td><td>0.1%</td><td>2</td><td>California</td><td>139,019</td><td>15.0%</td></tr>
<tr><td>21</td><td>Arizona</td><td>9,952</td><td>1.1%</td><td>3</td><td>Florida</td><td>100,809</td><td>10.9%</td></tr>
<tr><td>32</td><td>Arkansas</td><td>3,703</td><td>0.4%</td><td>4</td><td>Texas</td><td>67,227</td><td>7.3%</td></tr>
<tr><td>2</td><td>California</td><td>139,019</td><td>15.0%</td><td>5</td><td>New Jersey</td><td>48,431</td><td>5.2%</td></tr>
<tr><td>22</td><td>Colorado</td><td>8,480</td><td>0.9%</td><td>6</td><td>Illinois</td><td>32,595</td><td>3.5%</td></tr>
<tr><td>14</td><td>Connecticut</td><td>14,487</td><td>1.6%</td><td>7</td><td>Pennsylvania</td><td>31,977</td><td>3.5%</td></tr>
<tr><td>33</td><td>Delaware</td><td>3,458</td><td>0.4%</td><td>8</td><td>Georgia</td><td>30,405</td><td>3.3%</td></tr>
<tr><td>3</td><td>Florida</td><td>100,809</td><td>10.9%</td><td>9</td><td>Maryland</td><td>29,116</td><td>3.1%</td></tr>
<tr><td>8</td><td>Georgia</td><td>30,405</td><td>3.3%</td><td>10</td><td>Massachusetts</td><td>18,896</td><td>2.0%</td></tr>
<tr><td>34</td><td>Hawaii</td><td>2,857</td><td>0.3%</td><td>11</td><td>Louisiana</td><td>16,952</td><td>1.8%</td></tr>
<tr><td>45</td><td>Idaho</td><td>578</td><td>0.1%</td><td>12</td><td>Virginia</td><td>16,378</td><td>1.8%</td></tr>
<tr><td>6</td><td>Illinois</td><td>32,595</td><td>3.5%</td><td>13</td><td>North Carolina</td><td>14,915</td><td>1.6%</td></tr>
<tr><td>24</td><td>Indiana</td><td>7,963</td><td>0.9%</td><td>14</td><td>Connecticut</td><td>14,487</td><td>1.6%</td></tr>
<tr><td>39</td><td>Iowa</td><td>1,656</td><td>0.2%</td><td>15</td><td>Michigan</td><td>14,386</td><td>1.6%</td></tr>
<tr><td>35</td><td>Kansas</td><td>2,680</td><td>0.3%</td><td>16</td><td>Ohio</td><td>14,381</td><td>1.6%</td></tr>
<tr><td>30</td><td>Kentucky</td><td>4,453</td><td>0.5%</td><td>17</td><td>South Carolina</td><td>12,715</td><td>1.4%</td></tr>
<tr><td>11</td><td>Louisiana</td><td>16,952</td><td>1.8%</td><td>18</td><td>Tennessee</td><td>11,867</td><td>1.3%</td></tr>
<tr><td>42</td><td>Maine</td><td>1,053</td><td>0.1%</td><td>19</td><td>Washington</td><td>11,438</td><td>1.2%</td></tr>
<tr><td>9</td><td>Maryland</td><td>29,116</td><td>3.1%</td><td>20</td><td>Missouri</td><td>10,630</td><td>1.1%</td></tr>
<tr><td>10</td><td>Massachusetts</td><td>18,896</td><td>2.0%</td><td>21</td><td>Arizona</td><td>9,952</td><td>1.1%</td></tr>
<tr><td>15</td><td>Michigan</td><td>14,386</td><td>1.6%</td><td>22</td><td>Colorado</td><td>8,480</td><td>0.9%</td></tr>
<tr><td>29</td><td>Minnesota</td><td>4,632</td><td>0.5%</td><td>23</td><td>Alabama</td><td>8,252</td><td>0.9%</td></tr>
<tr><td>25</td><td>Mississippi</td><td>6,376</td><td>0.7%</td><td>24</td><td>Indiana</td><td>7,963</td><td>0.9%</td></tr>
<tr><td>20</td><td>Missouri</td><td>10,630</td><td>1.1%</td><td>25</td><td>Mississippi</td><td>6,376</td><td>0.7%</td></tr>
<tr><td>47</td><td>Montana</td><td>372</td><td>0.0%</td><td>26</td><td>Oregon</td><td>5,740</td><td>0.6%</td></tr>
<tr><td>41</td><td>Nebraska</td><td>1,377</td><td>0.1%</td><td>27</td><td>Nevada</td><td>5,481</td><td>0.6%</td></tr>
<tr><td>27</td><td>Nevada</td><td>5,481</td><td>0.6%</td><td>28</td><td>Oklahoma</td><td>4,651</td><td>0.5%</td></tr>
<tr><td>43</td><td>New Hampshire</td><td>1,032</td><td>0.1%</td><td>29</td><td>Minnesota</td><td>4,632</td><td>0.5%</td></tr>
<tr><td>5</td><td>New Jersey</td><td>48,431</td><td>5.2%</td><td>30</td><td>Kentucky</td><td>4,453</td><td>0.5%</td></tr>
<tr><td>36</td><td>New Mexico</td><td>2,526</td><td>0.3%</td><td>31</td><td>Wisconsin</td><td>4,332</td><td>0.5%</td></tr>
<tr><td>1</td><td>New York</td><td>172,377</td><td>18.6%</td><td>32</td><td>Arkansas</td><td>3,703</td><td>0.4%</td></tr>
<tr><td>13</td><td>North Carolina</td><td>14,915</td><td>1.6%</td><td>33</td><td>Delaware</td><td>3,458</td><td>0.4%</td></tr>
<tr><td>50</td><td>North Dakota</td><td>140</td><td>0.0%</td><td>34</td><td>Hawaii</td><td>2,857</td><td>0.3%</td></tr>
<tr><td>16</td><td>Ohio</td><td>14,381</td><td>1.6%</td><td>35</td><td>Kansas</td><td>2,680</td><td>0.3%</td></tr>
<tr><td>28</td><td>Oklahoma</td><td>4,651</td><td>0.5%</td><td>36</td><td>New Mexico</td><td>2,526</td><td>0.3%</td></tr>
<tr><td>26</td><td>Oregon</td><td>5,740</td><td>0.6%</td><td>37</td><td>Rhode Island</td><td>2,503</td><td>0.3%</td></tr>
<tr><td>7</td><td>Pennsylvania</td><td>31,977</td><td>3.5%</td><td>38</td><td>Utah</td><td>2,261</td><td>0.2%</td></tr>
<tr><td>37</td><td>Rhode Island</td><td>2,503</td><td>0.3%</td><td>39</td><td>Iowa</td><td>1,656</td><td>0.2%</td></tr>
<tr><td>17</td><td>South Carolina</td><td>12,715</td><td>1.4%</td><td>40</td><td>West Virginia</td><td>1,444</td><td>0.2%</td></tr>
<tr><td>48</td><td>South Dakota</td><td>244</td><td>0.0%</td><td>41</td><td>Nebraska</td><td>1,377</td><td>0.1%</td></tr>
<tr><td>18</td><td>Tennessee</td><td>11,867</td><td>1.3%</td><td>42</td><td>Maine</td><td>1,053</td><td>0.1%</td></tr>
<tr><td>4</td><td>Texas</td><td>67,227</td><td>7.3%</td><td>43</td><td>New Hampshire</td><td>1,032</td><td>0.1%</td></tr>
<tr><td>38</td><td>Utah</td><td>2,261</td><td>0.2%</td><td>44</td><td>Alaska</td><td>621</td><td>0.1%</td></tr>
<tr><td>46</td><td>Vermont</td><td>447</td><td>0.0%</td><td>45</td><td>Idaho</td><td>578</td><td>0.1%</td></tr>
<tr><td>12</td><td>Virginia</td><td>16,378</td><td>1.8%</td><td>46</td><td>Vermont</td><td>447</td><td>0.0%</td></tr>
<tr><td>19</td><td>Washington</td><td>11,438</td><td>1.2%</td><td>47</td><td>Montana</td><td>372</td><td>0.0%</td></tr>
<tr><td>40</td><td>West Virginia</td><td>1,444</td><td>0.2%</td><td>48</td><td>South Dakota</td><td>244</td><td>0.0%</td></tr>
<tr><td>31</td><td>Wisconsin</td><td>4,332</td><td>0.5%</td><td>49</td><td>Wyoming</td><td>225</td><td>0.0%</td></tr>
<tr><td>49</td><td>Wyoming</td><td>225</td><td>0.0%</td><td>50</td><td>North Dakota</td><td>140</td><td>0.0%</td></tr>
<tr><td></td><td></td><td></td><td></td><td></td><td>District of Columbia</td><td>16,962</td><td>1.8%</td></tr>
</table>

Source: U.S. Department of Health and Human Services, Centers for Disease Control and Prevention
"HIV/AIDS Surveillance Report, 2005" (Vol. 17)

*Cumulative through December 2005. AIDS is Acquired Immunodeficiency Syndrome. It is a specific group of diseases or conditions which are indicative of severe immunosuppression related to infection with the Human Immunodeficiency Virus (HIV). National total does not include 29,092 cases in Puerto Rico, 618 cases in the Virgin Islands and 75 cases in other U.S. territories.

AIDS Cases in Children 12 Years and Younger Through December 2005

National Total = 9,017 Juvenile AIDS Cases*

ALPHA ORDER

RANK	STATE	CASES	% of USA
18	Alabama	76	0.8%
44	Alaska	7	0.1%
23	Arizona	45	0.5%
24	Arkansas	36	0.4%
4	California	658	7.3%
27	Colorado	31	0.3%
11	Connecticut	183	2.0%
32	Delaware	25	0.3%
2	Florida	1,519	16.8%
9	Georgia	226	2.5%
36	Hawaii	17	0.2%
48	Idaho	2	0.0%
8	Illinois	281	3.1%
22	Indiana	55	0.6%
37	Iowa	14	0.2%
37	Kansas	14	0.2%
28	Kentucky	29	0.3%
14	Louisiana	131	1.5%
42	Maine	8	0.1%
7	Maryland	312	3.5%
10	Massachusetts	213	2.4%
16	Michigan	112	1.2%
30	Minnesota	27	0.3%
20	Mississippi	57	0.6%
19	Missouri	61	0.7%
47	Montana	3	0.0%
39	Nebraska	11	0.1%
28	Nevada	29	0.3%
41	New Hampshire	10	0.1%
3	New Jersey	772	8.6%
42	New Mexico	8	0.1%
1	New York	2,342	26.0%
15	North Carolina	118	1.3%
50	North Dakota	1	0.0%
13	Ohio	135	1.5%
32	Oklahoma	25	0.3%
35	Oregon	19	0.2%
6	Pennsylvania	358	4.0%
30	Rhode Island	27	0.3%
17	South Carolina	101	1.1%
46	South Dakota	5	0.1%
20	Tennessee	57	0.6%
5	Texas	391	4.3%
34	Utah	20	0.2%
45	Vermont	6	0.1%
12	Virginia	176	2.0%
25	Washington	34	0.4%
39	West Virginia	11	0.1%
26	Wisconsin	32	0.4%
48	Wyoming	2	0.0%

RANK ORDER

RANK	STATE	CASES	% of USA
1	New York	2,342	26.0%
2	Florida	1,519	16.8%
3	New Jersey	772	8.6%
4	California	658	7.3%
5	Texas	391	4.3%
6	Pennsylvania	358	4.0%
7	Maryland	312	3.5%
8	Illinois	281	3.1%
9	Georgia	226	2.5%
10	Massachusetts	213	2.4%
11	Connecticut	183	2.0%
12	Virginia	176	2.0%
13	Ohio	135	1.5%
14	Louisiana	131	1.5%
15	North Carolina	118	1.3%
16	Michigan	112	1.2%
17	South Carolina	101	1.1%
18	Alabama	76	0.8%
19	Missouri	61	0.7%
20	Mississippi	57	0.6%
20	Tennessee	57	0.6%
22	Indiana	55	0.6%
23	Arizona	45	0.5%
24	Arkansas	36	0.4%
25	Washington	34	0.4%
26	Wisconsin	32	0.4%
27	Colorado	31	0.3%
28	Kentucky	29	0.3%
28	Nevada	29	0.3%
30	Minnesota	27	0.3%
30	Rhode Island	27	0.3%
32	Delaware	25	0.3%
32	Oklahoma	25	0.3%
34	Utah	20	0.2%
35	Oregon	19	0.2%
36	Hawaii	17	0.2%
37	Iowa	14	0.2%
37	Kansas	14	0.2%
39	Nebraska	11	0.1%
39	West Virginia	11	0.1%
41	New Hampshire	10	0.1%
42	Maine	8	0.1%
42	New Mexico	8	0.1%
44	Alaska	7	0.1%
45	Vermont	6	0.1%
46	South Dakota	5	0.1%
47	Montana	3	0.0%
48	Idaho	2	0.0%
48	Wyoming	2	0.0%
50	North Dakota	1	0.0%
	District of Columbia	185	2.1%

Source: U.S. Department of Health and Human Services, Centers for Disease Control and Prevention
    "HIV/AIDS Surveillance Report, 2005" (Vol. 17)
*Cumulative through December 2005. AIDS is Acquired Immunodeficiency Syndrome. It is a specific group of diseases or conditions which are indicative of severe immunosuppression related to infection with the Human Immunodeficiency Virus (HIV). National total does not include 399 cases in Puerto Rico, 17 cases in the Virgin Islands and one case in Guam.

Chickenpox (Varicella) Cases Reported in 2006

National Total = 42,173 Cases*

ALPHA ORDER

RANK ORDER

RANK	STATE	CASES	% of USA		RANK	STATE	CASES	% of USA
18	Alabama	238	0.6%		1	Texas	10,079	23.9%
29	Alaska	0	0.0%		2	Ohio	8,761	20.8%
29	Arizona	0	0.0%		3	Michigan	5,070	12.0%
11	Arkansas	926	2.2%		4	Pennsylvania	5,061	12.0%
29	California	0	0.0%		5	Virginia	1,673	4.0%
7	Colorado	1,455	3.5%		6	West Virginia	1,469	3.5%
NA	Connecticut**	NA	NA		7	Colorado	1,455	3.5%
24	Delaware	66	0.2%		8	Missouri	1,399	3.3%
29	Florida	0	0.0%		9	South Carolina	1,123	2.7%
29	Georgia	0	0.0%		10	Utah	977	2.3%
NA	Hawaii**	NA	NA		11	Arkansas	926	2.2%
29	Idaho	0	0.0%		12	Wisconsin	774	1.8%
22	Illinois	68	0.2%		13	Vermont	742	1.8%
15	Indiana	475	1.1%		14	New Hampshire	483	1.1%
NA	Iowa**	NA	NA		15	Indiana	475	1.1%
16	Kansas	358	0.8%		16	Kansas	358	0.8%
NA	Kentucky**	NA	NA		17	New Mexico	356	0.8%
22	Louisiana	68	0.2%		18	Alabama	238	0.6%
19	Maine	151	0.4%		19	Maine	151	0.4%
29	Maryland	0	0.0%		20	South Dakota	115	0.3%
21	Massachusetts	94	0.2%		21	Massachusetts	94	0.2%
3	Michigan	5,070	12.0%		22	Illinois	68	0.2%
29	Minnesota	0	0.0%		22	Louisiana	68	0.2%
28	Mississippi	2	0.0%		24	Delaware	66	0.2%
8	Missouri	1,399	3.3%		25	Wyoming	64	0.2%
27	Montana	33	0.1%		26	North Dakota	45	0.1%
29	Nebraska	0	0.0%		27	Montana	33	0.1%
29	Nevada	0	0.0%		28	Mississippi	2	0.0%
14	New Hampshire	483	1.1%		29	Alaska	0	0.0%
29	New Jersey	0	0.0%		29	Arizona	0	0.0%
17	New Mexico	356	0.8%		29	California	0	0.0%
29	New York	0	0.0%		29	Florida	0	0.0%
29	North Carolina	0	0.0%		29	Georgia	0	0.0%
26	North Dakota	45	0.1%		29	Idaho	0	0.0%
2	Ohio	8,761	20.8%		29	Maryland	0	0.0%
29	Oklahoma	0	0.0%		29	Minnesota	0	0.0%
NA	Oregon**	NA	NA		29	Nebraska	0	0.0%
4	Pennsylvania	5,061	12.0%		29	Nevada	0	0.0%
29	Rhode Island	0	0.0%		29	New Jersey	0	0.0%
9	South Carolina	1,123	2.7%		29	New York	0	0.0%
20	South Dakota	115	0.3%		29	North Carolina	0	0.0%
NA	Tennessee**	NA	NA		29	Oklahoma	0	0.0%
1	Texas	10,079	23.9%		29	Rhode Island	0	0.0%
10	Utah	977	2.3%		NA	Connecticut**	NA	NA
13	Vermont	742	1.8%		NA	Hawaii**	NA	NA
5	Virginia	1,673	4.0%		NA	Iowa**	NA	NA
NA	Washington**	NA	NA		NA	Kentucky**	NA	NA
6	West Virginia	1,469	3.5%		NA	Oregon**	NA	NA
12	Wisconsin	774	1.8%		NA	Tennessee**	NA	NA
25	Wyoming	64	0.2%		NA	Washington**	NA	NA

| | District of Columbia | 48 | 0.1% |

Source: U.S. Department of Health and Human Services, National Center for Health Statistics
   "Morbidity and Mortality Weekly Report" (January 5, 2007, Vol. 55, Nos. 51 & 52)
*Provisional data. An illness with acute onset of generalized maculo-papulovesicular rash without other apparent cause.
**Not notifiable except Connecticut which is listed as unavailable.

Chickenpox (Varicella) Rate in 2006

National Rate = 14.1 Cases per 100,000 Population*

ALPHA ORDER

RANK	STATE	RATE
23	Alabama	5.2
29	Alaska	0.0
29	Arizona	0.0
9	Arkansas	32.9
29	California	0.0
10	Colorado	30.6
NA	Connecticut**	NA
20	Delaware	7.7
29	Florida	0.0
29	Georgia	0.0
NA	Hawaii**	NA
29	Idaho	0.0
27	Illinois	0.5
21	Indiana	7.5
NA	Iowa**	NA
17	Kansas	13.0
NA	Kentucky**	NA
25	Louisiana	1.6
19	Maine	11.4
29	Maryland	0.0
26	Massachusetts	1.5
4	Michigan	50.2
29	Minnesota	0.0
28	Mississippi	0.1
12	Missouri	23.9
24	Montana	3.5
29	Nebraska	0.0
29	Nevada	0.0
8	New Hampshire	36.7
29	New Jersey	0.0
14	New Mexico	18.2
29	New York	0.0
29	North Carolina	0.0
22	North Dakota	7.1
3	Ohio	76.3
29	Oklahoma	0.0
NA	Oregon**	NA
6	Pennsylvania	40.7
29	Rhode Island	0.0
11	South Carolina	26.0
15	South Dakota	14.7
NA	Tennessee**	NA
5	Texas	42.9
7	Utah	38.3
1	Vermont	118.9
13	Virginia	21.9
NA	Washington**	NA
2	West Virginia	80.8
16	Wisconsin	13.9
18	Wyoming	12.4

RANK ORDER

RANK	STATE	RATE
1	Vermont	118.9
2	West Virginia	80.8
3	Ohio	76.3
4	Michigan	50.2
5	Texas	42.9
6	Pennsylvania	40.7
7	Utah	38.3
8	New Hampshire	36.7
9	Arkansas	32.9
10	Colorado	30.6
11	South Carolina	26.0
12	Missouri	23.9
13	Virginia	21.9
14	New Mexico	18.2
15	South Dakota	14.7
16	Wisconsin	13.9
17	Kansas	13.0
18	Wyoming	12.4
19	Maine	11.4
20	Delaware	7.7
21	Indiana	7.5
22	North Dakota	7.1
23	Alabama	5.2
24	Montana	3.5
25	Louisiana	1.6
26	Massachusetts	1.5
27	Illinois	0.5
28	Mississippi	0.1
29	Alaska	0.0
29	Arizona	0.0
29	California	0.0
29	Florida	0.0
29	Georgia	0.0
29	Idaho	0.0
29	Maryland	0.0
29	Minnesota	0.0
29	Nebraska	0.0
29	Nevada	0.0
29	New Jersey	0.0
29	New York	0.0
29	North Carolina	0.0
29	Oklahoma	0.0
29	Rhode Island	0.0
NA	Connecticut**	NA
NA	Hawaii**	NA
NA	Iowa**	NA
NA	Kentucky**	NA
NA	Oregon**	NA
NA	Tennessee**	NA
NA	Washington**	NA

District of Columbia   8.3

*Source: Morgan Quitno Press using data from U.S. Dept. of Health & Human Serv's, National Center for Health Statistics
"Morbidity and Mortality Weekly Report" (January 5, 2007, Vol. 55, Nos. 51 & 52)*
*Provisional data. An illness with acute onset of generalized maculo-papulovesicular rash without other apparent cause.
**Not notifiable except Connecticut which is listed as unavailable.

E-Coli Cases Reported in 2006

National Total = 3,199 Cases*

ALPHA ORDER

RANK	STATE	CASES	% of USA
23	Alabama	49	1.5%
43	Alaska	0	0.0%
7	Arizona	129	4.0%
28	Arkansas	40	1.3%
43	California	0	0.0%
12	Colorado	102	3.2%
21	Connecticut	72	2.3%
35	Delaware	12	0.4%
11	Florida	106	3.3%
17	Georgia	84	2.6%
34	Hawaii	18	0.6%
18	Idaho	83	2.6%
18	Illinois	83	2.6%
16	Indiana	86	2.7%
5	Iowa	139	4.3%
29	Kansas	29	0.9%
14	Kentucky	101	3.2%
43	Louisiana	0	0.0%
26	Maine	45	1.4%
12	Maryland	102	3.2%
20	Massachusetts	82	2.6%
15	Michigan	93	2.9%
1	Minnesota	247	7.7%
43	Mississippi	0	0.0%
43	Missouri	0	0.0%
43	Montana	0	0.0%
22	Nebraska	55	1.7%
31	Nevada	25	0.8%
30	New Hampshire	27	0.8%
40	New Jersey	3	0.1%
39	New Mexico	4	0.1%
25	New York	47	1.5%
10	North Carolina	122	3.8%
43	North Dakota	0	0.0%
3	Ohio	196	6.1%
27	Oklahoma	43	1.3%
42	Oregon	1	0.0%
2	Pennsylvania	202	6.3%
38	Rhode Island	8	0.3%
37	South Carolina	10	0.3%
23	South Dakota	49	1.5%
32	Tennessee	24	0.8%
6	Texas	130	4.1%
9	Utah	123	3.8%
41	Vermont	2	0.1%
43	Virginia	0	0.0%
8	Washington	127	4.0%
35	West Virginia	12	0.4%
4	Wisconsin	182	5.7%
33	Wyoming	20	0.6%

RANK ORDER

RANK	STATE	CASES	% of USA
1	Minnesota	247	7.7%
2	Pennsylvania	202	6.3%
3	Ohio	196	6.1%
4	Wisconsin	182	5.7%
5	Iowa	139	4.3%
6	Texas	130	4.1%
7	Arizona	129	4.0%
8	Washington	127	4.0%
9	Utah	123	3.8%
10	North Carolina	122	3.8%
11	Florida	106	3.3%
12	Colorado	102	3.2%
12	Maryland	102	3.2%
14	Kentucky	101	3.2%
15	Michigan	93	2.9%
16	Indiana	86	2.7%
17	Georgia	84	2.6%
18	Idaho	83	2.6%
18	Illinois	83	2.6%
20	Massachusetts	82	2.6%
21	Connecticut	72	2.3%
22	Nebraska	55	1.7%
23	Alabama	49	1.5%
23	South Dakota	49	1.5%
25	New York	47	1.5%
26	Maine	45	1.4%
27	Oklahoma	43	1.3%
28	Arkansas	40	1.3%
29	Kansas	29	0.9%
30	New Hampshire	27	0.8%
31	Nevada	25	0.8%
32	Tennessee	24	0.8%
33	Wyoming	20	0.6%
34	Hawaii	18	0.6%
35	Delaware	12	0.4%
35	West Virginia	12	0.4%
37	South Carolina	10	0.3%
38	Rhode Island	8	0.3%
39	New Mexico	4	0.1%
40	New Jersey	3	0.1%
41	Vermont	2	0.1%
42	Oregon	1	0.0%
43	Alaska	0	0.0%
43	California	0	0.0%
43	Louisiana	0	0.0%
43	Mississippi	0	0.0%
43	Missouri	0	0.0%
43	Montana	0	0.0%
43	North Dakota	0	0.0%
43	Virginia	0	0.0%
	District of Columbia	3	0.1%

Source: U.S. Department of Health and Human Services, National Center for Health Statistics
        "Morbidity and Mortality Weekly Report" (January 5, 2007, Vol. 55, Nos. 51 & 52)
*Escherichia Coli is a common bacterium that normally inhabits the intestinal tracts of humans and animals but can cause infection in other parts of the body, especially the urinary tract. One strain, sometimes transmitted in hamburger meat, can cause serious infection resulting in sickness and death.

E-Coli Rate in 2006

National Rate = 1.1 Cases per 100,000 Population*

<table>
<tr><td colspan="3">ALPHA ORDER</td><td colspan="3">RANK ORDER</td></tr>
<tr><td>RANK</td><td>STATE</td><td>RATE</td><td>RANK</td><td>STATE</td><td>RATE</td></tr>
<tr><td>26</td><td>Alabama</td><td>1.1</td><td>1</td><td>South Dakota</td><td>6.3</td></tr>
<tr><td>41</td><td>Alaska</td><td>0.0</td><td>2</td><td>Idaho</td><td>5.7</td></tr>
<tr><td>11</td><td>Arizona</td><td>2.1</td><td>3</td><td>Minnesota</td><td>4.8</td></tr>
<tr><td>19</td><td>Arkansas</td><td>1.4</td><td>3</td><td>Utah</td><td>4.8</td></tr>
<tr><td>41</td><td>California</td><td>0.0</td><td>5</td><td>Iowa</td><td>4.7</td></tr>
<tr><td>11</td><td>Colorado</td><td>2.1</td><td>6</td><td>Wyoming</td><td>3.9</td></tr>
<tr><td>11</td><td>Connecticut</td><td>2.1</td><td>7</td><td>Maine</td><td>3.4</td></tr>
<tr><td>19</td><td>Delaware</td><td>1.4</td><td>8</td><td>Wisconsin</td><td>3.3</td></tr>
<tr><td>33</td><td>Florida</td><td>0.6</td><td>9</td><td>Nebraska</td><td>3.1</td></tr>
<tr><td>29</td><td>Georgia</td><td>0.9</td><td>10</td><td>Kentucky</td><td>2.4</td></tr>
<tr><td>19</td><td>Hawaii</td><td>1.4</td><td>11</td><td>Arizona</td><td>2.1</td></tr>
<tr><td>2</td><td>Idaho</td><td>5.7</td><td>11</td><td>Colorado</td><td>2.1</td></tr>
<tr><td>33</td><td>Illinois</td><td>0.6</td><td>11</td><td>Connecticut</td><td>2.1</td></tr>
<tr><td>19</td><td>Indiana</td><td>1.4</td><td>11</td><td>New Hampshire</td><td>2.1</td></tr>
<tr><td>5</td><td>Iowa</td><td>4.7</td><td>15</td><td>Washington</td><td>2.0</td></tr>
<tr><td>27</td><td>Kansas</td><td>1.0</td><td>16</td><td>Maryland</td><td>1.8</td></tr>
<tr><td>10</td><td>Kentucky</td><td>2.4</td><td>17</td><td>Ohio</td><td>1.7</td></tr>
<tr><td>41</td><td>Louisiana</td><td>0.0</td><td>18</td><td>Pennsylvania</td><td>1.6</td></tr>
<tr><td>7</td><td>Maine</td><td>3.4</td><td>19</td><td>Arkansas</td><td>1.4</td></tr>
<tr><td>16</td><td>Maryland</td><td>1.8</td><td>19</td><td>Delaware</td><td>1.4</td></tr>
<tr><td>24</td><td>Massachusetts</td><td>1.3</td><td>19</td><td>Hawaii</td><td>1.4</td></tr>
<tr><td>29</td><td>Michigan</td><td>0.9</td><td>19</td><td>Indiana</td><td>1.4</td></tr>
<tr><td>3</td><td>Minnesota</td><td>4.8</td><td>19</td><td>North Carolina</td><td>1.4</td></tr>
<tr><td>41</td><td>Mississippi</td><td>0.0</td><td>24</td><td>Massachusetts</td><td>1.3</td></tr>
<tr><td>41</td><td>Missouri</td><td>0.0</td><td>25</td><td>Oklahoma</td><td>1.2</td></tr>
<tr><td>41</td><td>Montana</td><td>0.0</td><td>26</td><td>Alabama</td><td>1.1</td></tr>
<tr><td>9</td><td>Nebraska</td><td>3.1</td><td>27</td><td>Kansas</td><td>1.0</td></tr>
<tr><td>27</td><td>Nevada</td><td>1.0</td><td>27</td><td>Nevada</td><td>1.0</td></tr>
<tr><td>11</td><td>New Hampshire</td><td>2.1</td><td>29</td><td>Georgia</td><td>0.9</td></tr>
<tr><td>41</td><td>New Jersey</td><td>0.0</td><td>29</td><td>Michigan</td><td>0.9</td></tr>
<tr><td>38</td><td>New Mexico</td><td>0.2</td><td>31</td><td>Rhode Island</td><td>0.7</td></tr>
<tr><td>38</td><td>New York</td><td>0.2</td><td>31</td><td>West Virginia</td><td>0.7</td></tr>
<tr><td>19</td><td>North Carolina</td><td>1.4</td><td>33</td><td>Florida</td><td>0.6</td></tr>
<tr><td>41</td><td>North Dakota</td><td>0.0</td><td>33</td><td>Illinois</td><td>0.6</td></tr>
<tr><td>17</td><td>Ohio</td><td>1.7</td><td>33</td><td>Texas</td><td>0.6</td></tr>
<tr><td>25</td><td>Oklahoma</td><td>1.2</td><td>36</td><td>Tennessee</td><td>0.4</td></tr>
<tr><td>41</td><td>Oregon</td><td>0.0</td><td>37</td><td>Vermont</td><td>0.3</td></tr>
<tr><td>18</td><td>Pennsylvania</td><td>1.6</td><td>38</td><td>New Mexico</td><td>0.2</td></tr>
<tr><td>31</td><td>Rhode Island</td><td>0.7</td><td>38</td><td>New York</td><td>0.2</td></tr>
<tr><td>38</td><td>South Carolina</td><td>0.2</td><td>38</td><td>South Carolina</td><td>0.2</td></tr>
<tr><td>1</td><td>South Dakota</td><td>6.3</td><td>41</td><td>Alaska</td><td>0.0</td></tr>
<tr><td>36</td><td>Tennessee</td><td>0.4</td><td>41</td><td>California</td><td>0.0</td></tr>
<tr><td>33</td><td>Texas</td><td>0.6</td><td>41</td><td>Louisiana</td><td>0.0</td></tr>
<tr><td>3</td><td>Utah</td><td>4.8</td><td>41</td><td>Mississippi</td><td>0.0</td></tr>
<tr><td>37</td><td>Vermont</td><td>0.3</td><td>41</td><td>Missouri</td><td>0.0</td></tr>
<tr><td>41</td><td>Virginia</td><td>0.0</td><td>41</td><td>Montana</td><td>0.0</td></tr>
<tr><td>15</td><td>Washington</td><td>2.0</td><td>41</td><td>New Jersey</td><td>0.0</td></tr>
<tr><td>31</td><td>West Virginia</td><td>0.7</td><td>41</td><td>North Dakota</td><td>0.0</td></tr>
<tr><td>8</td><td>Wisconsin</td><td>3.3</td><td>41</td><td>Oregon</td><td>0.0</td></tr>
<tr><td>6</td><td>Wyoming</td><td>3.9</td><td>41</td><td>Virginia</td><td>0.0</td></tr>
<tr><td></td><td></td><td></td><td></td><td>District of Columbia</td><td>0.5</td></tr>
</table>

Source: Morgan Quitno Press using data from U.S. Dept. of Health & Human Serv's, National Center for Health Statistics
"Morbidity and Mortality Weekly Report" (January 5, 2007, Vol. 55, Nos. 51 & 52)
*Escherichia Coli is a common bacterium that normally inhabits the intestinal tracts of humans and animals but can
cause infection in other parts of the body, especially the urinary tract. One strain, sometimes transmitted in
hamburger meat, can cause serious infection resulting in sickness and death.

Hepatitis A and B Cases Reported in 2006

National Total = 7,377 Cases*

ALPHA ORDER

RANK	STATE	CASES	% of USA
13	Alabama	167	2.3%
48	Alaska	9	0.1%
12	Arizona	177	2.4%
22	Arkansas	88	1.2%
1	California	1,330	18.0%
25	Colorado	73	1.0%
25	Connecticut	73	1.0%
29	Delaware	59	0.8%
3	Florida	644	8.7%
7	Georgia	244	3.3%
44	Hawaii	19	0.3%
43	Idaho	24	0.3%
18	Illinois	122	1.7%
23	Indiana	85	1.2%
41	Iowa	28	0.4%
38	Kansas	36	0.5%
21	Kentucky	101	1.4%
28	Louisiana	62	0.8%
40	Maine	29	0.4%
9	Maryland	211	2.9%
27	Massachusetts	65	0.9%
5	Michigan	258	3.5%
32	Minnesota	47	0.6%
32	Mississippi	47	0.6%
17	Missouri	128	1.7%
47	Montana	11	0.1%
37	Nebraska	39	0.5%
36	Nevada	41	0.6%
31	New Hampshire	50	0.7%
13	New Jersey	167	2.3%
39	New Mexico	35	0.5%
4	New York	364	4.9%
6	North Carolina	253	3.4%
50	North Dakota	0	0.0%
11	Ohio	178	2.4%
24	Oklahoma	82	1.1%
16	Oregon	130	1.8%
8	Pennsylvania	232	3.1%
42	Rhode Island	26	0.4%
19	South Carolina	107	1.5%
45	South Dakota	12	0.2%
10	Tennessee	204	2.8%
2	Texas	901	12.2%
34	Utah	46	0.6%
45	Vermont	12	0.2%
15	Virginia	132	1.8%
20	Washington	104	1.4%
30	West Virginia	58	0.8%
34	Wisconsin	46	0.6%
49	Wyoming	4	0.1%

RANK ORDER

RANK	STATE	CASES	% of USA
1	California	1,330	18.0%
2	Texas	901	12.2%
3	Florida	644	8.7%
4	New York	364	4.9%
5	Michigan	258	3.5%
6	North Carolina	253	3.4%
7	Georgia	244	3.3%
8	Pennsylvania	232	3.1%
9	Maryland	211	2.9%
10	Tennessee	204	2.8%
11	Ohio	178	2.4%
12	Arizona	177	2.4%
13	Alabama	167	2.3%
13	New Jersey	167	2.3%
15	Virginia	132	1.8%
16	Oregon	130	1.8%
17	Missouri	128	1.7%
18	Illinois	122	1.7%
19	South Carolina	107	1.5%
20	Washington	104	1.4%
21	Kentucky	101	1.4%
22	Arkansas	88	1.2%
23	Indiana	85	1.2%
24	Oklahoma	82	1.1%
25	Colorado	73	1.0%
25	Connecticut	73	1.0%
27	Massachusetts	65	0.9%
28	Louisiana	62	0.8%
29	Delaware	59	0.8%
30	West Virginia	58	0.8%
31	New Hampshire	50	0.7%
32	Minnesota	47	0.6%
32	Mississippi	47	0.6%
34	Utah	46	0.6%
34	Wisconsin	46	0.6%
36	Nevada	41	0.6%
37	Nebraska	39	0.5%
38	Kansas	36	0.5%
39	New Mexico	35	0.5%
40	Maine	29	0.4%
41	Iowa	28	0.4%
42	Rhode Island	26	0.4%
43	Idaho	24	0.3%
44	Hawaii	19	0.3%
45	South Dakota	12	0.2%
45	Vermont	12	0.2%
47	Montana	11	0.1%
48	Alaska	9	0.1%
49	Wyoming	4	0.1%
50	North Dakota	0	0.0%
	District of Columbia	17	0.2%

Source: U.S. Department of Health and Human Services, National Center for Health Statistics
"Morbidity and Mortality Weekly Report" (January 5, 2007, Vol. 55, Nos. 51 & 52)
*Provisional data. An inflammation of the liver.

Hepatitis A and B Rate in 2006

National Rate = 2.5 Cases per 100,000 Population*

ALPHA ORDER

RANK	STATE	RATE
5	Alabama	3.6
40	Alaska	1.3
12	Arizona	2.9
11	Arkansas	3.1
5	California	3.6
36	Colorado	1.5
23	Connecticut	2.1
1	Delaware	6.9
5	Florida	3.6
14	Georgia	2.6
36	Hawaii	1.5
31	Idaho	1.6
44	Illinois	1.0
40	Indiana	1.3
46	Iowa	0.9
40	Kansas	1.3
17	Kentucky	2.4
39	Louisiana	1.4
20	Maine	2.2
2	Maryland	3.8
44	Massachusetts	1.0
14	Michigan	2.6
46	Minnesota	0.9
31	Mississippi	1.6
20	Missouri	2.2
43	Montana	1.2
20	Nebraska	2.2
31	Nevada	1.6
2	New Hampshire	3.8
24	New Jersey	1.9
28	New Mexico	1.8
24	New York	1.9
12	North Carolina	2.9
50	North Dakota	0.0
31	Ohio	1.6
19	Oklahoma	2.3
8	Oregon	3.5
24	Pennsylvania	1.9
17	Rhode Island	2.4
16	South Carolina	2.5
36	South Dakota	1.5
9	Tennessee	3.4
2	Texas	3.8
28	Utah	1.8
24	Vermont	1.9
30	Virginia	1.7
31	Washington	1.6
10	West Virginia	3.2
48	Wisconsin	0.8
48	Wyoming	0.8

RANK ORDER

RANK	STATE	RATE
1	Delaware	6.9
2	Maryland	3.8
2	New Hampshire	3.8
2	Texas	3.8
5	Alabama	3.6
5	California	3.6
5	Florida	3.6
8	Oregon	3.5
9	Tennessee	3.4
10	West Virginia	3.2
11	Arkansas	3.1
12	Arizona	2.9
12	North Carolina	2.9
14	Georgia	2.6
14	Michigan	2.6
16	South Carolina	2.5
17	Kentucky	2.4
17	Rhode Island	2.4
19	Oklahoma	2.3
20	Maine	2.2
20	Missouri	2.2
20	Nebraska	2.2
23	Connecticut	2.1
24	New Jersey	1.9
24	New York	1.9
24	Pennsylvania	1.9
24	Vermont	1.9
28	New Mexico	1.8
28	Utah	1.8
30	Virginia	1.7
31	Idaho	1.6
31	Mississippi	1.6
31	Nevada	1.6
31	Ohio	1.6
31	Washington	1.6
36	Colorado	1.5
36	Hawaii	1.5
36	South Dakota	1.5
39	Louisiana	1.4
40	Alaska	1.3
40	Indiana	1.3
40	Kansas	1.3
43	Montana	1.2
44	Illinois	1.0
44	Massachusetts	1.0
46	Iowa	0.9
46	Minnesota	0.9
48	Wisconsin	0.8
48	Wyoming	0.8
50	North Dakota	0.0

District of Columbia   2.9

Source: Morgan Quitno Press using data from U.S. Dept. of Health & Human Serv's, National Center for Health Statistics
"Morbidity and Mortality Weekly Report" (January 5, 2007, Vol. 55, Nos. 51 & 52)
*Provisional data. An inflammation of the liver.

Legionellosis Cases Reported in 2006

National Total = 2,409 Cases*

ALPHA ORDER

RANK	STATE	CASES	% of USA
27	Alabama	15	0.6%
45	Alaska	0	0.0%
16	Arizona	39	1.6%
42	Arkansas	3	0.1%
8	California	84	3.5%
23	Colorado	22	0.9%
10	Connecticut	56	2.3%
28	Delaware	12	0.5%
4	Florida	171	7.1%
18	Georgia	29	1.2%
45	Hawaii	0	0.0%
29	Idaho	11	0.5%
25	Illinois	21	0.9%
17	Indiana	36	1.5%
30	Iowa	10	0.4%
36	Kansas	6	0.2%
13	Kentucky	44	1.8%
41	Louisiana	4	0.2%
30	Maine	10	0.4%
6	Maryland	100	4.2%
20	Massachusetts	27	1.1%
5	Michigan	150	6.2%
21	Minnesota	25	1.0%
42	Mississippi	3	0.1%
23	Missouri	22	0.9%
36	Montana	6	0.2%
32	Nebraska	9	0.4%
33	Nevada	8	0.3%
44	New Hampshire	1	0.0%
7	New Jersey	96	4.0%
38	New Mexico	5	0.2%
1	New York	463	19.2%
15	North Carolina	40	1.7%
45	North Dakota	0	0.0%
3	Ohio	230	9.5%
35	Oklahoma	7	0.3%
NA	Oregon**	NA	NA
2	Pennsylvania	323	13.4%
22	Rhode Island	23	1.0%
38	South Carolina	5	0.2%
38	South Dakota	5	0.2%
12	Tennessee	45	1.9%
11	Texas	47	2.0%
18	Utah	29	1.2%
33	Vermont	8	0.3%
9	Virginia	68	2.8%
45	Washington	0	0.0%
26	West Virginia	16	0.7%
14	Wisconsin	42	1.7%
45	Wyoming	0	0.0%

RANK ORDER

RANK	STATE	CASES	% of USA
1	New York	463	19.2%
2	Pennsylvania	323	13.4%
3	Ohio	230	9.5%
4	Florida	171	7.1%
5	Michigan	150	6.2%
6	Maryland	100	4.2%
7	New Jersey	96	4.0%
8	California	84	3.5%
9	Virginia	68	2.8%
10	Connecticut	56	2.3%
11	Texas	47	2.0%
12	Tennessee	45	1.9%
13	Kentucky	44	1.8%
14	Wisconsin	42	1.7%
15	North Carolina	40	1.7%
16	Arizona	39	1.6%
17	Indiana	36	1.5%
18	Georgia	29	1.2%
18	Utah	29	1.2%
20	Massachusetts	27	1.1%
21	Minnesota	25	1.0%
22	Rhode Island	23	1.0%
23	Colorado	22	0.9%
23	Missouri	22	0.9%
25	Illinois	21	0.9%
26	West Virginia	16	0.7%
27	Alabama	15	0.6%
28	Delaware	12	0.5%
29	Idaho	11	0.5%
30	Iowa	10	0.4%
30	Maine	10	0.4%
32	Nebraska	9	0.4%
33	Nevada	8	0.3%
33	Vermont	8	0.3%
35	Oklahoma	7	0.3%
36	Kansas	6	0.2%
36	Montana	6	0.2%
38	New Mexico	5	0.2%
38	South Carolina	5	0.2%
38	South Dakota	5	0.2%
41	Louisiana	4	0.2%
42	Arkansas	3	0.1%
42	Mississippi	3	0.1%
44	New Hampshire	1	0.0%
45	Alaska	0	0.0%
45	Hawaii	0	0.0%
45	North Dakota	0	0.0%
45	Washington	0	0.0%
45	Wyoming	0	0.0%
NA	Oregon**	NA	NA

| | District of Columbia | 33 | 1.4% |

Source: U.S. Department of Health and Human Services, National Center for Health Statistics
"Morbidity and Mortality Weekly Report" (January 5, 2007, Vol. 55, Nos. 51 & 52)
*Provisional data. A pneumonia-like disease (Legionnaire's Disease).
**Not notifiable.

Legionellosis Rate in 2006

National Rate = 0.8 Cases per 100,000 Population*

ALPHA ORDER

RANK	STATE	RATE
30	Alabama	0.3
45	Alaska	0.0
20	Arizona	0.6
40	Arkansas	0.1
35	California	0.2
24	Colorado	0.5
6	Connecticut	1.6
8	Delaware	1.4
13	Florida	0.9
30	Georgia	0.3
45	Hawaii	0.0
16	Idaho	0.8
35	Illinois	0.2
20	Indiana	0.6
30	Iowa	0.3
35	Kansas	0.2
12	Kentucky	1.0
40	Louisiana	0.1
16	Maine	0.8
5	Maryland	1.8
28	Massachusetts	0.4
7	Michigan	1.5
24	Minnesota	0.5
40	Mississippi	0.1
28	Missouri	0.4
20	Montana	0.6
24	Nebraska	0.5
30	Nevada	0.3
40	New Hampshire	0.1
10	New Jersey	1.1
30	New Mexico	0.3
2	New York	2.4
24	North Carolina	0.5
45	North Dakota	0.0
4	Ohio	2.0
35	Oklahoma	0.2
NA	Oregon**	NA
1	Pennsylvania	2.6
3	Rhode Island	2.2
40	South Carolina	0.1
20	South Dakota	0.6
19	Tennessee	0.7
35	Texas	0.2
10	Utah	1.1
9	Vermont	1.3
13	Virginia	0.9
45	Washington	0.0
13	West Virginia	0.9
16	Wisconsin	0.8
45	Wyoming	0.0

RANK ORDER

RANK	STATE	RATE
1	Pennsylvania	2.6
2	New York	2.4
3	Rhode Island	2.2
4	Ohio	2.0
5	Maryland	1.8
6	Connecticut	1.6
7	Michigan	1.5
8	Delaware	1.4
9	Vermont	1.3
10	New Jersey	1.1
10	Utah	1.1
12	Kentucky	1.0
13	Florida	0.9
13	Virginia	0.9
13	West Virginia	0.9
16	Idaho	0.8
16	Maine	0.8
16	Wisconsin	0.8
19	Tennessee	0.7
20	Arizona	0.6
20	Indiana	0.6
20	Montana	0.6
20	South Dakota	0.6
24	Colorado	0.5
24	Minnesota	0.5
24	Nebraska	0.5
24	North Carolina	0.5
28	Massachusetts	0.4
28	Missouri	0.4
30	Alabama	0.3
30	Georgia	0.3
30	Iowa	0.3
30	Nevada	0.3
30	New Mexico	0.3
35	California	0.2
35	Illinois	0.2
35	Kansas	0.2
35	Oklahoma	0.2
35	Texas	0.2
40	Arkansas	0.1
40	Louisiana	0.1
40	Mississippi	0.1
40	New Hampshire	0.1
40	South Carolina	0.1
45	Alaska	0.0
45	Hawaii	0.0
45	North Dakota	0.0
45	Washington	0.0
45	Wyoming	0.0
NA	Oregon**	NA

District of Columbia 5.7

Source: Morgan Quitno Press using data from U.S. Dept. of Health & Human Serv's, National Center for Health Statistics
"Morbidity and Mortality Weekly Report" (January 5, 2007, Vol. 55, Nos. 51 & 52)
*Provisional data. A pneumonia-like disease (Legionnaire's Disease).
**Not notifiable.

362

Lyme Disease Cases in 2006

National Total = 17,002 Cases*

ALPHA ORDER

RANK	STATE	CASES	% of USA
24	Alabama	16	0.1%
36	Alaska	3	0.0%
31	Arizona	7	0.0%
44	Arkansas	0	0.0%
13	California	169	1.0%
40	Colorado	1	0.0%
4	Connecticut	1,694	10.0%
9	Delaware	466	2.7%
16	Florida	60	0.4%
30	Georgia	8	0.0%
NA	Hawaii**	NA	NA
31	Idaho	7	0.0%
44	Illinois	0	0.0%
21	Indiana	21	0.1%
15	Iowa	87	0.5%
35	Kansas	5	0.0%
31	Kentucky	7	0.0%
44	Louisiana	0	0.0%
11	Maine	287	1.7%
6	Maryland	967	5.7%
19	Massachusetts	33	0.2%
17	Michigan	58	0.3%
7	Minnesota	729	4.3%
40	Mississippi	1	0.0%
27	Missouri	13	0.1%
44	Montana	0	0.0%
29	Nebraska	11	0.1%
36	Nevada	3	0.0%
8	New Hampshire	567	3.3%
3	New Jersey	1,918	11.3%
36	New Mexico	3	0.0%
1	New York	4,217	24.8%
20	North Carolina	30	0.2%
44	North Dakota	0	0.0%
18	Ohio	42	0.2%
44	Oklahoma	0	0.0%
25	Oregon	15	0.1%
2	Pennsylvania	3,399	20.0%
12	Rhode Island	235	1.4%
23	South Carolina	18	0.1%
40	South Dakota	1	0.0%
28	Tennessee	12	0.1%
22	Texas	20	0.1%
34	Utah	6	0.0%
14	Vermont	104	0.6%
10	Virginia	317	1.9%
36	Washington	3	0.0%
26	West Virginia	14	0.1%
5	Wisconsin	1,368	8.0%
40	Wyoming	1	0.0%

RANK ORDER

RANK	STATE	CASES	% of USA
1	New York	4,217	24.8%
2	Pennsylvania	3,399	20.0%
3	New Jersey	1,918	11.3%
4	Connecticut	1,694	10.0%
5	Wisconsin	1,368	8.0%
6	Maryland	967	5.7%
7	Minnesota	729	4.3%
8	New Hampshire	567	3.3%
9	Delaware	466	2.7%
10	Virginia	317	1.9%
11	Maine	287	1.7%
12	Rhode Island	235	1.4%
13	California	169	1.0%
14	Vermont	104	0.6%
15	Iowa	87	0.5%
16	Florida	60	0.4%
17	Michigan	58	0.3%
18	Ohio	42	0.2%
19	Massachusetts	33	0.2%
20	North Carolina	30	0.2%
21	Indiana	21	0.1%
22	Texas	20	0.1%
23	South Carolina	18	0.1%
24	Alabama	16	0.1%
25	Oregon	15	0.1%
26	West Virginia	14	0.1%
27	Missouri	13	0.1%
28	Tennessee	12	0.1%
29	Nebraska	11	0.1%
30	Georgia	8	0.0%
31	Arizona	7	0.0%
31	Idaho	7	0.0%
31	Kentucky	7	0.0%
34	Utah	6	0.0%
35	Kansas	5	0.0%
36	Alaska	3	0.0%
36	Nevada	3	0.0%
36	New Mexico	3	0.0%
36	Washington	3	0.0%
40	Colorado	1	0.0%
40	Mississippi	1	0.0%
40	South Dakota	1	0.0%
40	Wyoming	1	0.0%
44	Arkansas	0	0.0%
44	Illinois	0	0.0%
44	Louisiana	0	0.0%
44	Montana	0	0.0%
44	North Dakota	0	0.0%
44	Oklahoma	0	0.0%
NA	Hawaii**	NA	NA
	District of Columbia	59	0.3%

Source: U.S. Department of Health and Human Services, National Center for Health Statistics
   "Morbidity and Mortality Weekly Report" (January 5, 2007, Vol. 55, Nos. 51 & 52)
Provisional data. Caused by ticks-lesions, followed by arthritis of large joints, myalgia, malaise and neurologic
and cardiac manifestations. Named after Old Lyme, CT, where the disease was first reported.
***Not notifiable.*

Lyme Disease Rate in 2006

National Rate = 5.7 Cases per 100,000 Population*

RANK	STATE	RATE
25	Alabama	0.3
21	Alaska	0.4
36	Arizona	0.1
41	Arkansas	0.0
18	California	0.5
41	Colorado	0.0
2	Connecticut	48.3
1	Delaware	54.6
25	Florida	0.3
36	Georgia	0.1
NA	Hawaii**	NA
18	Idaho	0.5
41	Illinois	0.0
25	Indiana	0.3
14	Iowa	2.9
29	Kansas	0.2
29	Kentucky	0.2
41	Louisiana	0.0
9	Maine	21.7
10	Maryland	17.2
18	Massachusetts	0.5
16	Michigan	0.6
12	Minnesota	14.1
41	Mississippi	0.0
29	Missouri	0.2
41	Montana	0.0
16	Nebraska	0.6
36	Nevada	0.1
3	New Hampshire	43.1
6	New Jersey	22.0
29	New Mexico	0.2
8	New York	21.8
25	North Carolina	0.3
41	North Dakota	0.0
21	Ohio	0.4
41	Oklahoma	0.0
21	Oregon	0.4
4	Pennsylvania	27.3
6	Rhode Island	22.0
21	South Carolina	0.4
36	South Dakota	0.1
29	Tennessee	0.2
36	Texas	0.1
29	Utah	0.2
11	Vermont	16.7
13	Virginia	4.1
41	Washington	0.0
15	West Virginia	0.8
5	Wisconsin	24.6
29	Wyoming	0.2

RANK	STATE	RATE
1	Delaware	54.6
2	Connecticut	48.3
3	New Hampshire	43.1
4	Pennsylvania	27.3
5	Wisconsin	24.6
6	New Jersey	22.0
6	Rhode Island	22.0
8	New York	21.8
9	Maine	21.7
10	Maryland	17.2
11	Vermont	16.7
12	Minnesota	14.1
13	Virginia	4.1
14	Iowa	2.9
15	West Virginia	0.8
16	Michigan	0.6
16	Nebraska	0.6
18	California	0.5
18	Idaho	0.5
18	Massachusetts	0.5
21	Alaska	0.4
21	Ohio	0.4
21	Oregon	0.4
21	South Carolina	0.4
25	Alabama	0.3
25	Florida	0.3
25	Indiana	0.3
25	North Carolina	0.3
29	Kansas	0.2
29	Kentucky	0.2
29	Missouri	0.2
29	New Mexico	0.2
29	Tennessee	0.2
29	Utah	0.2
29	Wyoming	0.2
36	Arizona	0.1
36	Georgia	0.1
36	Nevada	0.1
36	South Dakota	0.1
36	Texas	0.1
41	Arkansas	0.0
41	Colorado	0.0
41	Illinois	0.0
41	Louisiana	0.0
41	Mississippi	0.0
41	Montana	0.0
41	North Dakota	0.0
41	Oklahoma	0.0
41	Washington	0.0
NA	Hawaii**	NA

	District of Columbia	10.1

Source: Morgan Quitno Press using data from U.S. Dept. of Health & Human Serv's, National Center for Health Statistics "Morbidity and Mortality Weekly Report" (January 5, 2007, Vol. 55, Nos. 51 & 52)
*Provisional data. Caused by ticks-lesions, followed by arthritis of large joints, myalgia, malaise and neurologic and cardiac manifestations. Named after Old Lyme, CT, where the disease was first reported.
**Not notifiable.

Malaria Cases Reported in 2006

National Total = 1,257 Cases*

ALPHA ORDER

RANK ORDER

RANK	STATE	CASES	% of USA
23	Alabama	11	0.9%
15	Alaska	23	1.8%
15	Arizona	23	1.8%
41	Arkansas	3	0.2%
2	California	154	12.3%
20	Colorado	17	1.4%
23	Connecticut	11	0.9%
33	Delaware	5	0.4%
6	Florida	63	5.0%
3	Georgia	83	6.6%
28	Hawaii	8	0.6%
46	Idaho	1	0.1%
7	Illinois	62	4.9%
23	Indiana	11	0.9%
43	Iowa	2	0.2%
28	Kansas	8	0.6%
36	Kentucky	4	0.3%
33	Louisiana	5	0.4%
36	Maine	4	0.3%
4	Maryland	70	5.6%
18	Massachusetts	19	1.5%
17	Michigan	21	1.7%
10	Minnesota	39	3.1%
36	Mississippi	4	0.3%
31	Missouri	6	0.5%
43	Montana	2	0.2%
33	Nebraska	5	0.4%
36	Nevada	4	0.3%
26	New Hampshire	10	0.8%
14	New Jersey	28	2.2%
36	New Mexico	4	0.3%
1	New York	201	16.0%
12	North Carolina	31	2.5%
46	North Dakota	1	0.1%
13	Ohio	29	2.3%
30	Oklahoma	7	0.6%
22	Oregon	12	1.0%
9	Pennsylvania	47	3.7%
41	Rhode Island	3	0.2%
26	South Carolina	10	0.8%
46	South Dakota	1	0.1%
31	Tennessee	6	0.5%
5	Texas	69	5.5%
20	Utah	17	1.4%
46	Vermont	1	0.1%
8	Virginia	54	4.3%
11	Washington	33	2.6%
43	West Virginia	2	0.2%
19	Wisconsin	18	1.4%
50	Wyoming	0	0.0%

RANK	STATE	CASES	% of USA
1	New York	201	16.0%
2	California	154	12.3%
3	Georgia	83	6.6%
4	Maryland	70	5.6%
5	Texas	69	5.5%
6	Florida	63	5.0%
7	Illinois	62	4.9%
8	Virginia	54	4.3%
9	Pennsylvania	47	3.7%
10	Minnesota	39	3.1%
11	Washington	33	2.6%
12	North Carolina	31	2.5%
13	Ohio	29	2.3%
14	New Jersey	28	2.2%
15	Alaska	23	1.8%
15	Arizona	23	1.8%
17	Michigan	21	1.7%
18	Massachusetts	19	1.5%
19	Wisconsin	18	1.4%
20	Colorado	17	1.4%
20	Utah	17	1.4%
22	Oregon	12	1.0%
23	Alabama	11	0.9%
23	Connecticut	11	0.9%
23	Indiana	11	0.9%
26	New Hampshire	10	0.8%
26	South Carolina	10	0.8%
28	Hawaii	8	0.6%
28	Kansas	8	0.6%
30	Oklahoma	7	0.6%
31	Missouri	6	0.5%
31	Tennessee	6	0.5%
33	Delaware	5	0.4%
33	Louisiana	5	0.4%
33	Nebraska	5	0.4%
36	Kentucky	4	0.3%
36	Maine	4	0.3%
36	Mississippi	4	0.3%
36	Nevada	4	0.3%
36	New Mexico	4	0.3%
41	Arkansas	3	0.2%
41	Rhode Island	3	0.2%
43	Iowa	2	0.2%
43	Montana	2	0.2%
43	West Virginia	2	0.2%
46	Idaho	1	0.1%
46	North Dakota	1	0.1%
46	South Dakota	1	0.1%
46	Vermont	1	0.1%
50	Wyoming	0	0.0%
	District of Columbia	5	0.4%

Source: U.S. Department of Health and Human Services, National Center for Health Statistics
     "Morbidity and Mortality Weekly Report" (January 5, 2007, Vol. 55, Nos. 51 & 52)
*Provisional data. Infectious disease usually transmitted by bites of infected mosquitoes. Symptoms include high fever, shaking chills, sweating and anemia.

Malaria Rate in 2006

National Rate = 0.4 Cases per 100,000 Population*

ALPHA ORDER

RANK	STATE	RATE
30	Alabama	0.2
1	Alaska	3.4
13	Arizona	0.4
40	Arkansas	0.1
13	California	0.4
13	Colorado	0.4
18	Connecticut	0.3
9	Delaware	0.6
18	Florida	0.3
4	Georgia	0.9
9	Hawaii	0.6
40	Idaho	0.1
11	Illinois	0.5
30	Indiana	0.2
40	Iowa	0.1
18	Kansas	0.3
40	Kentucky	0.1
40	Louisiana	0.1
18	Maine	0.3
2	Maryland	1.2
18	Massachusetts	0.3
30	Michigan	0.2
5	Minnesota	0.8
40	Mississippi	0.1
40	Missouri	0.1
30	Montana	0.2
18	Nebraska	0.3
30	Nevada	0.2
5	New Hampshire	0.8
18	New Jersey	0.3
30	New Mexico	0.2
3	New York	1.0
13	North Carolina	0.4
30	North Dakota	0.2
18	Ohio	0.3
30	Oklahoma	0.2
18	Oregon	0.3
13	Pennsylvania	0.4
18	Rhode Island	0.3
30	South Carolina	0.2
40	South Dakota	0.1
40	Tennessee	0.1
18	Texas	0.3
7	Utah	0.7
30	Vermont	0.2
7	Virginia	0.7
11	Washington	0.5
40	West Virginia	0.1
18	Wisconsin	0.3
50	Wyoming	0.0

RANK ORDER

RANK	STATE	RATE
1	Alaska	3.4
2	Maryland	1.2
3	New York	1.0
4	Georgia	0.9
5	Minnesota	0.8
5	New Hampshire	0.8
7	Utah	0.7
7	Virginia	0.7
9	Delaware	0.6
9	Hawaii	0.6
11	Illinois	0.5
11	Washington	0.5
13	Arizona	0.4
13	California	0.4
13	Colorado	0.4
13	North Carolina	0.4
13	Pennsylvania	0.4
18	Connecticut	0.3
18	Florida	0.3
18	Kansas	0.3
18	Maine	0.3
18	Massachusetts	0.3
18	Nebraska	0.3
18	New Jersey	0.3
18	Ohio	0.3
18	Oregon	0.3
18	Rhode Island	0.3
18	Texas	0.3
18	Wisconsin	0.3
30	Alabama	0.2
30	Indiana	0.2
30	Michigan	0.2
30	Montana	0.2
30	Nevada	0.2
30	New Mexico	0.2
30	North Dakota	0.2
30	Oklahoma	0.2
30	South Carolina	0.2
30	Vermont	0.2
40	Arkansas	0.1
40	Idaho	0.1
40	Iowa	0.1
40	Kentucky	0.1
40	Louisiana	0.1
40	Mississippi	0.1
40	Missouri	0.1
40	South Dakota	0.1
40	Tennessee	0.1
40	West Virginia	0.1
50	Wyoming	0.0

District of Columbia — 0.9

Source: Morgan Quitno Press using data from U.S. Dept. of Health & Human Serv's, National Center for Health Statistics
"Morbidity and Mortality Weekly Report" (January 5, 2007, Vol. 55, Nos. 51 & 52)
*Provisional data. Infectious disease usually transmitted by bites of infected mosquitoes. Symptoms include high fever, shaking chills, sweating and anemia.

Meningococcal Infections Reported in 2006

National Total = 1,063 Cases*

RANK	STATE	CASES	% of USA
26	Alabama	11	1.0%
45	Alaska	3	0.3%
18	Arizona	17	1.6%
29	Arkansas	10	0.9%
1	California	176	16.6%
16	Colorado	20	1.9%
29	Connecticut	10	0.9%
35	Delaware	6	0.6%
3	Florida	80	7.5%
19	Georgia	16	1.5%
29	Hawaii	10	0.9%
42	Idaho	4	0.4%
17	Illinois	18	1.7%
12	Indiana	23	2.2%
13	Iowa	22	2.1%
45	Kansas	3	0.3%
26	Kentucky	11	1.0%
34	Louisiana	7	0.7%
33	Maine	8	0.8%
22	Maryland	15	1.4%
22	Massachusetts	15	1.4%
13	Michigan	22	2.1%
19	Minnesota	16	1.5%
40	Mississippi	5	0.5%
24	Missouri	14	1.3%
40	Montana	5	0.5%
35	Nebraska	6	0.6%
42	Nevada	4	0.4%
35	New Hampshire	6	0.6%
19	New Jersey	16	1.5%
35	New Mexico	6	0.6%
2	New York	96	9.0%
8	North Carolina	32	3.0%
50	North Dakota	1	0.1%
6	Ohio	43	4.0%
26	Oklahoma	11	1.0%
4	Oregon	64	6.0%
5	Pennsylvania	51	4.8%
49	Rhode Island	2	0.2%
10	South Carolina	24	2.3%
45	South Dakota	3	0.3%
10	Tennessee	24	2.3%
9	Texas	30	2.8%
35	Utah	6	0.6%
45	Vermont	3	0.3%
15	Virginia	21	2.0%
7	Washington	38	3.6%
32	West Virginia	9	0.8%
24	Wisconsin	14	1.3%
42	Wyoming	4	0.4%

RANK	STATE	CASES	% of USA
1	California	176	16.6%
2	New York	96	9.0%
3	Florida	80	7.5%
4	Oregon	64	6.0%
5	Pennsylvania	51	4.8%
6	Ohio	43	4.0%
7	Washington	38	3.6%
8	North Carolina	32	3.0%
9	Texas	30	2.8%
10	South Carolina	24	2.3%
10	Tennessee	24	2.3%
12	Indiana	23	2.2%
13	Iowa	22	2.1%
13	Michigan	22	2.1%
15	Virginia	21	2.0%
16	Colorado	20	1.9%
17	Illinois	18	1.7%
18	Arizona	17	1.6%
19	Georgia	16	1.5%
19	Minnesota	16	1.5%
19	New Jersey	16	1.5%
22	Maryland	15	1.4%
22	Massachusetts	15	1.4%
24	Missouri	14	1.3%
24	Wisconsin	14	1.3%
26	Alabama	11	1.0%
26	Kentucky	11	1.0%
26	Oklahoma	11	1.0%
29	Arkansas	10	0.9%
29	Connecticut	10	0.9%
29	Hawaii	10	0.9%
32	West Virginia	9	0.8%
33	Maine	8	0.8%
34	Louisiana	7	0.7%
35	Delaware	6	0.6%
35	Nebraska	6	0.6%
35	New Hampshire	6	0.6%
35	New Mexico	6	0.6%
35	Utah	6	0.6%
40	Mississippi	5	0.5%
40	Montana	5	0.5%
42	Idaho	4	0.4%
42	Nevada	4	0.4%
42	Wyoming	4	0.4%
45	Alaska	3	0.3%
45	Kansas	3	0.3%
45	South Dakota	3	0.3%
45	Vermont	3	0.3%
49	Rhode Island	2	0.2%
50	North Dakota	1	0.1%
	District of Columbia	2	0.2%

Source: U.S. Department of Health and Human Services, National Center for Health Statistics
"Morbidity and Mortality Weekly Report" (January 5, 2007, Vol. 55, Nos. 51 & 52)
*Provisional data. A bacterium (Neisseria meningitidis) that causes cerebrospinal meningitis.

Meningococcal Infection Rate in 2006

National Rate = 0.4 Cases per 100,000 Population*

<u>ALPHA ORDER</u>

RANK	STATE	RATE
36	Alabama	0.2
15	Alaska	0.4
25	Arizona	0.3
15	Arkansas	0.4
9	California	0.5
15	Colorado	0.4
25	Connecticut	0.3
4	Delaware	0.7
15	Florida	0.4
36	Georgia	0.2
2	Hawaii	0.8
25	Idaho	0.3
48	Illinois	0.1
15	Indiana	0.4
4	Iowa	0.7
48	Kansas	0.1
25	Kentucky	0.3
36	Louisiana	0.2
6	Maine	0.6
25	Maryland	0.3
36	Massachusetts	0.2
36	Michigan	0.2
25	Minnesota	0.3
36	Mississippi	0.2
36	Missouri	0.2
9	Montana	0.5
25	Nebraska	0.3
36	Nevada	0.2
9	New Hampshire	0.5
36	New Jersey	0.2
25	New Mexico	0.3
9	New York	0.5
15	North Carolina	0.4
36	North Dakota	0.2
15	Ohio	0.4
25	Oklahoma	0.3
1	Oregon	1.7
15	Pennsylvania	0.4
36	Rhode Island	0.2
6	South Carolina	0.6
15	South Dakota	0.4
15	Tennessee	0.4
48	Texas	0.1
36	Utah	0.2
9	Vermont	0.5
25	Virginia	0.3
6	Washington	0.6
9	West Virginia	0.5
25	Wisconsin	0.3
2	Wyoming	0.8

<u>RANK ORDER</u>

RANK	STATE	RATE
1	Oregon	1.7
2	Hawaii	0.8
2	Wyoming	0.8
4	Delaware	0.7
4	Iowa	0.7
6	Maine	0.6
6	South Carolina	0.6
6	Washington	0.6
9	California	0.5
9	Montana	0.5
9	New Hampshire	0.5
9	New York	0.5
9	Vermont	0.5
9	West Virginia	0.5
15	Alaska	0.4
15	Arkansas	0.4
15	Colorado	0.4
15	Florida	0.4
15	Indiana	0.4
15	North Carolina	0.4
15	Ohio	0.4
15	Pennsylvania	0.4
15	South Dakota	0.4
15	Tennessee	0.4
25	Arizona	0.3
25	Connecticut	0.3
25	Idaho	0.3
25	Kentucky	0.3
25	Maryland	0.3
25	Minnesota	0.3
25	Nebraska	0.3
25	New Mexico	0.3
25	Oklahoma	0.3
25	Virginia	0.3
25	Wisconsin	0.3
36	Alabama	0.2
36	Georgia	0.2
36	Louisiana	0.2
36	Massachusetts	0.2
36	Michigan	0.2
36	Mississippi	0.2
36	Missouri	0.2
36	Nevada	0.2
36	New Jersey	0.2
36	North Dakota	0.2
36	Rhode Island	0.2
36	Utah	0.2
48	Illinois	0.1
48	Kansas	0.1
48	Texas	0.1

District of Columbia   0.3

*Source: Morgan Quitno Press using data from U.S. Dept. of Health & Human Serv's, National Center for Health Statistics
"Morbidity and Mortality Weekly Report" (January 5, 2007, Vol. 55, Nos. 51 & 52)*
Provisional data. A bacterium (Neisseria meningitidis) that causes cerebrospinal meningitis.

Rabies (Animal) Cases Reported in 2006

National Total = 6,110 Cases*

ALPHA ORDER

RANK	STATE	CASES	% of USA
17	Alabama	84	1.4%
35	Alaska	17	0.3%
14	Arizona	137	2.2%
29	Arkansas	32	0.5%
12	California	170	2.8%
43	Colorado	0	0.0%
8	Connecticut	206	3.4%
43	Delaware	0	0.0%
11	Florida	176	2.9%
7	Georgia	253	4.1%
43	Hawaii	0	0.0%
31	Idaho	25	0.4%
26	Illinois	46	0.8%
37	Indiana	11	0.2%
23	Iowa	57	0.9%
18	Kansas	82	1.3%
30	Kentucky	28	0.5%
43	Louisiana	0	0.0%
15	Maine	123	2.0%
6	Maryland	318	5.2%
9	Massachusetts	178	2.9%
25	Michigan	47	0.8%
27	Minnesota	40	0.7%
41	Mississippi	4	0.1%
20	Missouri	67	1.1%
36	Montana	14	0.2%
43	Nebraska	0	0.0%
42	Nevada	2	0.0%
24	New Hampshire	55	0.9%
NA	New Jersey**	NA	NA
39	New Mexico	10	0.2%
3	New York	586	9.6%
4	North Carolina	512	8.4%
33	North Dakota	24	0.4%
22	Ohio	58	0.9%
21	Oklahoma	66	1.1%
31	Oregon	25	0.4%
1	Pennsylvania	1,000	16.4%
33	Rhode Island	24	0.4%
10	South Carolina	177	2.9%
28	South Dakota	36	0.6%
13	Tennessee	138	2.3%
5	Texas	471	7.7%
37	Utah	11	0.2%
19	Vermont	73	1.2%
2	Virginia	601	9.8%
NA	Washington**	NA	NA
16	West Virginia	118	1.9%
NA	Wisconsin**	NA	NA
40	Wyoming	8	0.1%

RANK ORDER

RANK	STATE	CASES	% of USA
1	Pennsylvania	1,000	16.4%
2	Virginia	601	9.8%
3	New York	586	9.6%
4	North Carolina	512	8.4%
5	Texas	471	7.7%
6	Maryland	318	5.2%
7	Georgia	253	4.1%
8	Connecticut	206	3.4%
9	Massachusetts	178	2.9%
10	South Carolina	177	2.9%
11	Florida	176	2.9%
12	California	170	2.8%
13	Tennessee	138	2.3%
14	Arizona	137	2.2%
15	Maine	123	2.0%
16	West Virginia	118	1.9%
17	Alabama	84	1.4%
18	Kansas	82	1.3%
19	Vermont	73	1.2%
20	Missouri	67	1.1%
21	Oklahoma	66	1.1%
22	Ohio	58	0.9%
23	Iowa	57	0.9%
24	New Hampshire	55	0.9%
25	Michigan	47	0.8%
26	Illinois	46	0.8%
27	Minnesota	40	0.7%
28	South Dakota	36	0.6%
29	Arkansas	32	0.5%
30	Kentucky	28	0.5%
31	Idaho	25	0.4%
31	Oregon	25	0.4%
33	North Dakota	24	0.4%
33	Rhode Island	24	0.4%
35	Alaska	17	0.3%
36	Montana	14	0.2%
37	Indiana	11	0.2%
37	Utah	11	0.2%
39	New Mexico	10	0.2%
40	Wyoming	8	0.1%
41	Mississippi	4	0.1%
42	Nevada	2	0.0%
43	Colorado	0	0.0%
43	Delaware	0	0.0%
43	Hawaii	0	0.0%
43	Louisiana	0	0.0%
43	Nebraska	0	0.0%
NA	New Jersey**	NA	NA
NA	Washington**	NA	NA
NA	Wisconsin**	NA	NA
	District of Columbia	0	0.0%

Source: U.S. Department of Health and Human Services, National Center for Health Statistics
    "Morbidity and Mortality Weekly Report" (January 5, 2007, Vol. 55, Nos. 51 & 52)
*Provisional data. An acute, infectious, often fatal viral disease of most warm-blooded animals, especially wolves, cats, and dogs, that attacks the central nervous system and is transmitted by the bite of infected animals.
**Not available.

Rabies (Animal) Rate in 2006

National Rate = 2.0 Cases per 100,000 Human Population*

ALPHA ORDER				RANK ORDER		
RANK	STATE	RATE		RANK	STATE	RATE
23	Alabama	1.8		1	Vermont	11.7
17	Alaska	2.5		2	Maine	9.3
19	Arizona	2.2		3	Pennsylvania	8.0
28	Arkansas	1.1		4	Virginia	7.9
34	California	0.5		5	West Virginia	6.5
43	Colorado	0.0		6	Connecticut	5.9
6	Connecticut	5.9		7	North Carolina	5.8
43	Delaware	0.0		8	Maryland	5.7
30	Florida	1.0		9	South Dakota	4.6
16	Georgia	2.7		10	New Hampshire	4.2
43	Hawaii	0.0		11	South Carolina	4.1
25	Idaho	1.7		12	North Dakota	3.8
38	Illinois	0.4		13	Kansas	3.0
40	Indiana	0.2		13	New York	3.0
22	Iowa	1.9		15	Massachusetts	2.8
13	Kansas	3.0		16	Georgia	2.7
32	Kentucky	0.7		17	Alaska	2.5
43	Louisiana	0.0		18	Tennessee	2.3
2	Maine	9.3		19	Arizona	2.2
8	Maryland	5.7		19	Rhode Island	2.2
15	Massachusetts	2.8		21	Texas	2.0
34	Michigan	0.5		22	Iowa	1.9
31	Minnesota	0.8		23	Alabama	1.8
41	Mississippi	0.1		23	Oklahoma	1.8
28	Missouri	1.1		25	Idaho	1.7
27	Montana	1.5		26	Wyoming	1.6
43	Nebraska	0.0		27	Montana	1.5
41	Nevada	0.1		28	Arkansas	1.1
10	New Hampshire	4.2		28	Missouri	1.1
NA	New Jersey**	NA		30	Florida	1.0
34	New Mexico	0.5		31	Minnesota	0.8
13	New York	3.0		32	Kentucky	0.7
7	North Carolina	5.8		32	Oregon	0.7
12	North Dakota	3.8		34	California	0.5
34	Ohio	0.5		34	Michigan	0.5
23	Oklahoma	1.8		34	New Mexico	0.5
32	Oregon	0.7		34	Ohio	0.5
3	Pennsylvania	8.0		38	Illinois	0.4
19	Rhode Island	2.2		38	Utah	0.4
11	South Carolina	4.1		40	Indiana	0.2
9	South Dakota	4.6		41	Mississippi	0.1
18	Tennessee	2.3		41	Nevada	0.1
21	Texas	2.0		43	Colorado	0.0
38	Utah	0.4		43	Delaware	0.0
1	Vermont	11.7		43	Hawaii	0.0
4	Virginia	7.9		43	Louisiana	0.0
NA	Washington**	NA		43	Nebraska	0.0
5	West Virginia	6.5		NA	New Jersey**	NA
NA	Wisconsin**	NA		NA	Washington**	NA
26	Wyoming	1.6		NA	Wisconsin**	NA

District of Columbia 0.0

Source: Morgan Quitno Press using data from U.S. Dept. of Health & Human Serv's, National Center for Health Statistics
"Morbidity and Mortality Weekly Report" (January 5, 2007, Vol. 55, Nos. 51 & 52)
*Provisional data. An acute, infectious, often fatal viral disease of most warm-blooded animals, especially wolves,
cats, and dogs, that attacks the central nervous system and is transmitted by the bite of infected animals.
**Not available.

Rocky Mountain Spotted Fever Cases Reported in 2006

National Total = 2,092 Cases*

ALPHA ORDER

RANK	STATE	CASES	% of USA
4	Alabama	136	6.5%
43	Alaska	0	0.0%
19	Arizona	10	0.5%
7	Arkansas	51	2.4%
25	California	5	0.2%
35	Colorado	2	0.1%
43	Connecticut	0	0.0%
17	Delaware	21	1.0%
13	Florida	28	1.3%
8	Georgia	50	2.4%
43	Hawaii	0	0.0%
18	Idaho	14	0.7%
25	Illinois	5	0.2%
21	Indiana	7	0.3%
25	Iowa	5	0.2%
38	Kansas	1	0.0%
32	Kentucky	3	0.1%
25	Louisiana	5	0.2%
NA	Maine**	NA	NA
6	Maryland	80	3.8%
38	Massachusetts	1	0.0%
25	Michigan	5	0.2%
25	Minnesota	5	0.2%
31	Mississippi	4	0.2%
3	Missouri	170	8.1%
35	Montana	2	0.1%
15	Nebraska	25	1.2%
32	Nevada	3	0.1%
38	New Hampshire	1	0.0%
21	New Jersey	7	0.3%
20	New Mexico	9	0.4%
12	New York	29	1.4%
1	North Carolina	842	40.2%
43	North Dakota	0	0.0%
14	Ohio	26	1.2%
10	Oklahoma	38	1.8%
35	Oregon	2	0.1%
8	Pennsylvania	50	2.4%
38	Rhode Island	1	0.0%
11	South Carolina	36	1.7%
43	South Dakota	0	0.0%
2	Tennessee	257	12.3%
15	Texas	25	1.2%
24	Utah	6	0.3%
43	Vermont	0	0.0%
5	Virginia	113	5.4%
NA	Washington**	NA	NA
32	West Virginia	3	0.1%
38	Wisconsin	1	0.0%
21	Wyoming	7	0.3%

RANK ORDER

RANK	STATE	CASES	% of USA
1	North Carolina	842	40.2%
2	Tennessee	257	12.3%
3	Missouri	170	8.1%
4	Alabama	136	6.5%
5	Virginia	113	5.4%
6	Maryland	80	3.8%
7	Arkansas	51	2.4%
8	Georgia	50	2.4%
8	Pennsylvania	50	2.4%
10	Oklahoma	38	1.8%
11	South Carolina	36	1.7%
12	New York	29	1.4%
13	Florida	28	1.3%
14	Ohio	26	1.2%
15	Nebraska	25	1.2%
15	Texas	25	1.2%
17	Delaware	21	1.0%
18	Idaho	14	0.7%
19	Arizona	10	0.5%
20	New Mexico	9	0.4%
21	Indiana	7	0.3%
21	New Jersey	7	0.3%
21	Wyoming	7	0.3%
24	Utah	6	0.3%
25	California	5	0.2%
25	Illinois	5	0.2%
25	Iowa	5	0.2%
25	Louisiana	5	0.2%
25	Michigan	5	0.2%
25	Minnesota	5	0.2%
31	Mississippi	4	0.2%
32	Kentucky	3	0.1%
32	Nevada	3	0.1%
32	West Virginia	3	0.1%
35	Colorado	2	0.1%
35	Montana	2	0.1%
35	Oregon	2	0.1%
38	Kansas	1	0.0%
38	Massachusetts	1	0.0%
38	New Hampshire	1	0.0%
38	Rhode Island	1	0.0%
38	Wisconsin	1	0.0%
43	Alaska	0	0.0%
43	Connecticut	0	0.0%
43	Hawaii	0	0.0%
43	North Dakota	0	0.0%
43	South Dakota	0	0.0%
43	Vermont	0	0.0%
NA	Maine**	NA	NA
NA	Washington**	NA	NA
	District of Columbia	1	0.0%

Source: U.S. Department of Health and Human Services, National Center for Health Statistics
"Morbidity and Mortality Weekly Report" (January 5, 2007, Vol. 55, Nos. 51 & 52)
Provisional data. An illness caused by Rickettsia rickettsii, a bacterial pathogen transmitted to humans through contact with ticks. Characterized by acute onset of fever, and may be accompanied by headache, malaise, myalgia, nausea/vomiting, or neurologic signs. A rash is often present on the palms and soles.
**Not available.*

Rocky Mountain Spotted Fever Rate in 2006

National Rate = 0.7 Cases per 100,000 Population*

ALPHA ORDER

RANK	STATE	RATE
3	Alabama	3.0
36	Alaska	0.0
17	Arizona	0.2
6	Arkansas	1.8
36	California	0.0
36	Colorado	0.0
36	Connecticut	0.0
5	Delaware	2.5
17	Florida	0.2
14	Georgia	0.5
36	Hawaii	0.0
12	Idaho	1.0
36	Illinois	0.0
25	Indiana	0.1
17	Iowa	0.2
36	Kansas	0.0
25	Kentucky	0.1
25	Louisiana	0.1
NA	Maine**	NA
8	Maryland	1.4
36	Massachusetts	0.0
36	Michigan	0.0
25	Minnesota	0.1
25	Mississippi	0.1
4	Missouri	2.9
17	Montana	0.2
8	Nebraska	1.4
25	Nevada	0.1
25	New Hampshire	0.1
25	New Jersey	0.1
14	New Mexico	0.5
17	New York	0.2
1	North Carolina	9.5
36	North Dakota	0.0
17	Ohio	0.2
11	Oklahoma	1.1
25	Oregon	0.1
16	Pennsylvania	0.4
25	Rhode Island	0.1
13	South Carolina	0.8
36	South Dakota	0.0
2	Tennessee	4.3
25	Texas	0.1
17	Utah	0.2
36	Vermont	0.0
7	Virginia	1.5
NA	Washington**	NA
17	West Virginia	0.2
36	Wisconsin	0.0
8	Wyoming	1.4

RANK ORDER

RANK	STATE	RATE
1	North Carolina	9.5
2	Tennessee	4.3
3	Alabama	3.0
4	Missouri	2.9
5	Delaware	2.5
6	Arkansas	1.8
7	Virginia	1.5
8	Maryland	1.4
8	Nebraska	1.4
8	Wyoming	1.4
11	Oklahoma	1.1
12	Idaho	1.0
13	South Carolina	0.8
14	Georgia	0.5
14	New Mexico	0.5
16	Pennsylvania	0.4
17	Arizona	0.2
17	Florida	0.2
17	Iowa	0.2
17	Montana	0.2
17	New York	0.2
17	Ohio	0.2
17	Utah	0.2
17	West Virginia	0.2
25	Indiana	0.1
25	Kentucky	0.1
25	Louisiana	0.1
25	Minnesota	0.1
25	Mississippi	0.1
25	Nevada	0.1
25	New Hampshire	0.1
25	New Jersey	0.1
25	Oregon	0.1
25	Rhode Island	0.1
25	Texas	0.1
36	Alaska	0.0
36	California	0.0
36	Colorado	0.0
36	Connecticut	0.0
36	Hawaii	0.0
36	Illinois	0.0
36	Kansas	0.0
36	Massachusetts	0.0
36	Michigan	0.0
36	North Dakota	0.0
36	South Dakota	0.0
36	Vermont	0.0
36	Wisconsin	0.0
NA	Maine**	NA
NA	Washington**	NA

District of Columbia 0.2

Source: Morgan Quitno Press using data from U.S. Dept. of Health & Human Serv's, National Center for Health Statistics "Morbidity and Mortality Weekly Report" (January 5, 2007, Vol. 55, Nos. 51 & 52)
Provisional data. An illness caused by Rickettsia rickettsii, a bacterial pathogen transmitted to humans through contact with ticks. Characterized by acute onset of fever, and may be accompanied by headache, malaise, myalgia, nausea/vomiting, or neurologic signs. A rash is often present on the palms and soles.
**Not available.*

Salmonellosis Cases Reported in 2006

National Total = 41,924 Cases*

<u>ALPHA ORDER</u>

RANK	STATE	CASES	% of USA
8	Alabama	1,387	3.3%
48	Alaska	76	0.2%
15	Arizona	900	2.1%
14	Arkansas	924	2.2%
2	California	4,550	10.9%
26	Colorado	606	1.4%
29	Connecticut	479	1.1%
41	Delaware	144	0.3%
1	Florida	4,929	11.8%
5	Georgia	1,777	4.2%
35	Hawaii	262	0.6%
40	Idaho	175	0.4%
10	Illinois	1,163	2.8%
16	Indiana	828	2.0%
31	Iowa	442	1.1%
33	Kansas	367	0.9%
30	Kentucky	448	1.1%
17	Louisiana	825	2.0%
45	Maine	120	0.3%
24	Maryland	728	1.7%
21	Massachusetts	782	1.9%
13	Michigan	972	2.3%
25	Minnesota	704	1.7%
22	Mississippi	757	1.8%
23	Missouri	754	1.8%
44	Montana	129	0.3%
38	Nebraska	197	0.5%
39	Nevada	186	0.4%
37	New Hampshire	217	0.5%
19	New Jersey	803	1.9%
36	New Mexico	242	0.6%
3	New York	2,530	6.0%
6	North Carolina	1,691	4.0%
50	North Dakota	28	0.1%
9	Ohio	1,291	3.1%
28	Oklahoma	501	1.2%
32	Oregon	418	1.0%
7	Pennsylvania	1,664	4.0%
46	Rhode Island	95	0.2%
12	South Carolina	1,011	2.4%
43	South Dakota	133	0.3%
20	Tennessee	793	1.9%
4	Texas	1,944	4.6%
34	Utah	284	0.7%
47	Vermont	81	0.2%
11	Virginia	1,022	2.4%
27	Washington	510	1.2%
42	West Virginia	140	0.3%
18	Wisconsin	807	1.9%
49	Wyoming	46	0.1%

<u>RANK ORDER</u>

RANK	STATE	CASES	% of USA
1	Florida	4,929	11.8%
2	California	4,550	10.9%
3	New York	2,530	6.0%
4	Texas	1,944	4.6%
5	Georgia	1,777	4.2%
6	North Carolina	1,691	4.0%
7	Pennsylvania	1,664	4.0%
8	Alabama	1,387	3.3%
9	Ohio	1,291	3.1%
10	Illinois	1,163	2.8%
11	Virginia	1,022	2.4%
12	South Carolina	1,011	2.4%
13	Michigan	972	2.3%
14	Arkansas	924	2.2%
15	Arizona	900	2.1%
16	Indiana	828	2.0%
17	Louisiana	825	2.0%
18	Wisconsin	807	1.9%
19	New Jersey	803	1.9%
20	Tennessee	793	1.9%
21	Massachusetts	782	1.9%
22	Mississippi	757	1.8%
23	Missouri	754	1.8%
24	Maryland	728	1.7%
25	Minnesota	704	1.7%
26	Colorado	606	1.4%
27	Washington	510	1.2%
28	Oklahoma	501	1.2%
29	Connecticut	479	1.1%
30	Kentucky	448	1.1%
31	Iowa	442	1.1%
32	Oregon	418	1.0%
33	Kansas	367	0.9%
34	Utah	284	0.7%
35	Hawaii	262	0.6%
36	New Mexico	242	0.6%
37	New Hampshire	217	0.5%
38	Nebraska	197	0.5%
39	Nevada	186	0.4%
40	Idaho	175	0.4%
41	Delaware	144	0.3%
42	West Virginia	140	0.3%
43	South Dakota	133	0.3%
44	Montana	129	0.3%
45	Maine	120	0.3%
46	Rhode Island	95	0.2%
47	Vermont	81	0.2%
48	Alaska	76	0.2%
49	Wyoming	46	0.1%
50	North Dakota	28	0.1%
	District of Columbia	62	0.1%

Source: U.S. Department of Health and Human Services, National Center for Health Statistics
   "Morbidity and Mortality Weekly Report" (January 5, 2007, Vol. 55, Nos. 51 & 52)
Provisional data. Any disease caused by a salmonella infection, which may be manifested as food poisoning with acute gastroenteritis, vomiting and diarrhea.

Salmonellosis Rate in 2006

National Rate = 14.0 Cases per 100,000 Population*

ALPHA ORDER

RANK	STATE	RATE	RANK	STATE	RATE
2	Alabama	30.2	1	Arkansas	32.9
34	Alaska	11.3	2	Alabama	30.2
14	Arizona	14.6	3	Florida	27.2
1	Arkansas	32.9	4	Mississippi	26.0
30	California	12.5	5	South Carolina	23.4
29	Colorado	12.7	6	Hawaii	20.4
17	Connecticut	13.7	7	Louisiana	19.2
11	Delaware	16.9	8	North Carolina	19.1
3	Florida	27.2	9	Georgia	19.0
9	Georgia	19.0	10	South Dakota	17.0
6	Hawaii	20.4	11	Delaware	16.9
33	Idaho	11.9	12	New Hampshire	16.5
42	Illinois	9.1	13	Iowa	14.8
23	Indiana	13.1	14	Arizona	14.6
13	Iowa	14.8	15	Wisconsin	14.5
22	Kansas	13.3	16	Oklahoma	14.0
39	Kentucky	10.7	17	Connecticut	13.7
7	Louisiana	19.2	17	Montana	13.7
42	Maine	9.1	19	Minnesota	13.6
26	Maryland	13.0	20	Pennsylvania	13.4
32	Massachusetts	12.1	20	Virginia	13.4
40	Michigan	9.6	22	Kansas	13.3
19	Minnesota	13.6	23	Indiana	13.1
4	Mississippi	26.0	23	New York	13.1
28	Missouri	12.9	23	Tennessee	13.1
17	Montana	13.7	26	Maryland	13.0
37	Nebraska	11.1	26	Vermont	13.0
49	Nevada	7.5	28	Missouri	12.9
12	New Hampshire	16.5	29	Colorado	12.7
41	New Jersey	9.2	30	California	12.5
31	New Mexico	12.4	31	New Mexico	12.4
23	New York	13.1	32	Massachusetts	12.1
8	North Carolina	19.1	33	Idaho	11.9
50	North Dakota	4.4	34	Alaska	11.3
36	Ohio	11.2	34	Oregon	11.3
16	Oklahoma	14.0	36	Ohio	11.2
34	Oregon	11.3	37	Nebraska	11.1
20	Pennsylvania	13.4	37	Utah	11.1
44	Rhode Island	8.9	39	Kentucky	10.7
5	South Carolina	23.4	40	Michigan	9.6
10	South Dakota	17.0	41	New Jersey	9.2
23	Tennessee	13.1	42	Illinois	9.1
46	Texas	8.3	42	Maine	9.1
37	Utah	11.1	44	Rhode Island	8.9
26	Vermont	13.0	44	Wyoming	8.9
20	Virginia	13.4	46	Texas	8.3
47	Washington	8.0	47	Washington	8.0
48	West Virginia	7.7	48	West Virginia	7.7
15	Wisconsin	14.5	49	Nevada	7.5
44	Wyoming	8.9	50	North Dakota	4.4

District of Columbia   10.7

Source: Morgan Quitno Press using data from U.S. Dept. of Health & Human Serv's, National Center for Health Statistics "Morbidity and Mortality Weekly Report" (January 5, 2007, Vol. 55, Nos. 51 & 52)

Provisional data. Any disease caused by a salmonella infection, which may be manifested as food poisoning with acute gastroenteritis, vomiting and diarrhea.

Shigellosis Cases Reported in 2006

National Total = 13,660 Cases*

ALPHA ORDER

RANK	STATE	CASES	% of USA
7	Alabama	490	3.6%
47	Alaska	9	0.1%
5	Arizona	742	5.4%
29	Arkansas	125	0.9%
1	California	1,716	12.6%
13	Colorado	235	1.7%
40	Connecticut	64	0.5%
46	Delaware	11	0.1%
2	Florida	1,646	12.0%
4	Georgia	1,286	9.4%
42	Hawaii	44	0.3%
43	Idaho	15	0.1%
10	Illinois	376	2.8%
18	Indiana	165	1.2%
30	Iowa	121	0.9%
24	Kansas	139	1.0%
14	Kentucky	234	1.7%
22	Louisiana	143	1.0%
48	Maine	6	0.0%
26	Maryland	128	0.9%
26	Massachusetts	128	0.9%
21	Michigan	148	1.1%
11	Minnesota	243	1.8%
32	Mississippi	111	0.8%
6	Missouri	654	4.8%
40	Montana	64	0.5%
28	Nebraska	127	0.9%
34	Nevada	107	0.8%
45	New Hampshire	12	0.1%
12	New Jersey	242	1.8%
17	New Mexico	168	1.2%
8	New York	483	3.5%
19	North Carolina	160	1.2%
35	North Dakota	103	0.8%
15	Ohio	197	1.4%
25	Oklahoma	135	1.0%
31	Oregon	120	0.9%
36	Pennsylvania	88	0.6%
43	Rhode Island	15	0.1%
39	South Carolina	73	0.5%
9	South Dakota	380	2.8%
16	Tennessee	173	1.3%
3	Texas	1,433	10.5%
38	Utah	82	0.6%
48	Vermont	6	0.0%
32	Virginia	111	0.8%
20	Washington	150	1.1%
48	West Virginia	6	0.0%
22	Wisconsin	143	1.0%
37	Wyoming	86	0.6%

RANK ORDER

RANK	STATE	CASES	% of USA
1	California	1,716	12.6%
2	Florida	1,646	12.0%
3	Texas	1,433	10.5%
4	Georgia	1,286	9.4%
5	Arizona	742	5.4%
6	Missouri	654	4.8%
7	Alabama	490	3.6%
8	New York	483	3.5%
9	South Dakota	380	2.8%
10	Illinois	376	2.8%
11	Minnesota	243	1.8%
12	New Jersey	242	1.8%
13	Colorado	235	1.7%
14	Kentucky	234	1.7%
15	Ohio	197	1.4%
16	Tennessee	173	1.3%
17	New Mexico	168	1.2%
18	Indiana	165	1.2%
19	North Carolina	160	1.2%
20	Washington	150	1.1%
21	Michigan	148	1.1%
22	Louisiana	143	1.0%
22	Wisconsin	143	1.0%
24	Kansas	139	1.0%
25	Oklahoma	135	1.0%
26	Maryland	128	0.9%
26	Massachusetts	128	0.9%
28	Nebraska	127	0.9%
29	Arkansas	125	0.9%
30	Iowa	121	0.9%
31	Oregon	120	0.9%
32	Mississippi	111	0.8%
32	Virginia	111	0.8%
34	Nevada	107	0.8%
35	North Dakota	103	0.8%
36	Pennsylvania	88	0.6%
37	Wyoming	86	0.6%
38	Utah	82	0.6%
39	South Carolina	73	0.5%
40	Connecticut	64	0.5%
40	Montana	64	0.5%
42	Hawaii	44	0.3%
43	Idaho	15	0.1%
43	Rhode Island	15	0.1%
45	New Hampshire	12	0.1%
46	Delaware	11	0.1%
47	Alaska	9	0.1%
48	Maine	6	0.0%
48	Vermont	6	0.0%
48	West Virginia	6	0.0%
	District of Columbia	17	0.1%

Source: U.S. Department of Health and Human Services, National Center for Health Statistics
   "Morbidity and Mortality Weekly Report" (January 5, 2007, Vol. 55, Nos. 51 & 52)
*Provisional data. Dysentery caused by any of various species of shigellae, occurring most frequently in areas where poor sanitation and malnutrition are prevalent and commonly affecting children and infants.

Shigellosis Rate in 2006

National Rate = 4.6 Cases per 100,000 Population*

ALPHA ORDER

RANK	STATE	RATE
7	Alabama	10.7
43	Alaska	1.3
5	Arizona	12.0
18	Arkansas	4.4
16	California	4.7
15	Colorado	4.9
36	Connecticut	1.8
43	Delaware	1.3
8	Florida	9.1
4	Georgia	13.7
23	Hawaii	3.4
45	Idaho	1.0
27	Illinois	2.9
30	Indiana	2.6
20	Iowa	4.1
14	Kansas	5.0
13	Kentucky	5.6
24	Louisiana	3.3
49	Maine	0.5
33	Maryland	2.3
35	Massachusetts	2.0
40	Michigan	1.5
16	Minnesota	4.7
21	Mississippi	3.8
6	Missouri	11.2
11	Montana	6.8
10	Nebraska	7.2
19	Nevada	4.3
47	New Hampshire	0.9
29	New Jersey	2.8
9	New Mexico	8.6
32	New York	2.5
36	North Carolina	1.8
3	North Dakota	16.2
38	Ohio	1.7
21	Oklahoma	3.8
25	Oregon	3.2
48	Pennsylvania	0.7
42	Rhode Island	1.4
38	South Carolina	1.7
1	South Dakota	48.6
27	Tennessee	2.9
12	Texas	6.1
25	Utah	3.2
45	Vermont	1.0
40	Virginia	1.5
33	Washington	2.3
50	West Virginia	0.3
30	Wisconsin	2.6
2	Wyoming	16.7

RANK ORDER

RANK	STATE	RATE
1	South Dakota	48.6
2	Wyoming	16.7
3	North Dakota	16.2
4	Georgia	13.7
5	Arizona	12.0
6	Missouri	11.2
7	Alabama	10.7
8	Florida	9.1
9	New Mexico	8.6
10	Nebraska	7.2
11	Montana	6.8
12	Texas	6.1
13	Kentucky	5.6
14	Kansas	5.0
15	Colorado	4.9
16	California	4.7
16	Minnesota	4.7
18	Arkansas	4.4
19	Nevada	4.3
20	Iowa	4.1
21	Mississippi	3.8
21	Oklahoma	3.8
23	Hawaii	3.4
24	Louisiana	3.3
25	Oregon	3.2
25	Utah	3.2
27	Illinois	2.9
27	Tennessee	2.9
29	New Jersey	2.8
30	Indiana	2.6
30	Wisconsin	2.6
32	New York	2.5
33	Maryland	2.3
33	Washington	2.3
35	Massachusetts	2.0
36	Connecticut	1.8
36	North Carolina	1.8
38	Ohio	1.7
38	South Carolina	1.7
40	Michigan	1.5
40	Virginia	1.5
42	Rhode Island	1.4
43	Alaska	1.3
43	Delaware	1.3
45	Idaho	1.0
45	Vermont	1.0
47	New Hampshire	0.9
48	Pennsylvania	0.7
49	Maine	0.5
50	West Virginia	0.3

| | District of Columbia | 2.9 |

Source: Morgan Quitno Press using data from U.S. Dept. of Health & Human Serv's, National Center for Health Statistics "Morbidity and Mortality Weekly Report" (January 5, 2007, Vol. 55, Nos. 51 & 52)

*Provisional data. Dysentery caused by any of various species of shigellae, occurring most frequently in areas where poor sanitation and malnutrition are prevalent and commonly affecting children and infants.

West Nile Virus Disease Cases Reported in 2006

National Total = 4,103 Cases*

ALPHA ORDER

RANK	STATE	CASES	% of USA
34	Alabama	7	0.2%
43	Alaska	0	0.0%
13	Arizona	97	2.4%
25	Arkansas	28	0.7%
4	California	272	6.6%
2	Colorado	333	8.1%
30	Connecticut	9	0.2%
43	Delaware	0	0.0%
38	Florida	3	0.1%
32	Georgia	8	0.2%
43	Hawaii	0	0.0%
1	Idaho	961	23.4%
6	Illinois	210	5.1%
14	Indiana	81	2.0%
22	Iowa	36	0.9%
24	Kansas	30	0.7%
35	Kentucky	6	0.1%
8	Louisiana	172	4.2%
43	Maine	0	0.0%
29	Maryland	10	0.2%
38	Massachusetts	3	0.1%
19	Michigan	52	1.3%
16	Minnesota	65	1.6%
7	Mississippi	181	4.4%
18	Missouri	61	1.5%
23	Montana	34	0.8%
5	Nebraska	264	6.4%
11	Nevada	123	3.0%
43	New Hampshire	0	0.0%
36	New Jersey	5	0.1%
32	New Mexico	8	0.2%
26	New York	23	0.6%
41	North Carolina	1	0.0%
10	North Dakota	137	3.3%
20	Ohio	47	1.1%
20	Oklahoma	47	1.1%
15	Oregon	69	1.7%
30	Pennsylvania	9	0.2%
43	Rhode Island	0	0.0%
36	South Carolina	5	0.1%
12	South Dakota	113	2.8%
28	Tennessee	18	0.4%
3	Texas	327	8.0%
9	Utah	158	3.9%
43	Vermont	0	0.0%
43	Virginia	0	0.0%
38	Washington	3	0.1%
41	West Virginia	1	0.0%
27	Wisconsin	20	0.5%
16	Wyoming	65	1.6%

RANK ORDER

RANK	STATE	CASES	% of USA
1	Idaho	961	23.4%
2	Colorado	333	8.1%
3	Texas	327	8.0%
4	California	272	6.6%
5	Nebraska	264	6.4%
6	Illinois	210	5.1%
7	Mississippi	181	4.4%
8	Louisiana	172	4.2%
9	Utah	158	3.9%
10	North Dakota	137	3.3%
11	Nevada	123	3.0%
12	South Dakota	113	2.8%
13	Arizona	97	2.4%
14	Indiana	81	2.0%
15	Oregon	69	1.7%
16	Minnesota	65	1.6%
16	Wyoming	65	1.6%
18	Missouri	61	1.5%
19	Michigan	52	1.3%
20	Ohio	47	1.1%
20	Oklahoma	47	1.1%
22	Iowa	36	0.9%
23	Montana	34	0.8%
24	Kansas	30	0.7%
25	Arkansas	28	0.7%
26	New York	23	0.6%
27	Wisconsin	20	0.5%
28	Tennessee	18	0.4%
29	Maryland	10	0.2%
30	Connecticut	9	0.2%
30	Pennsylvania	9	0.2%
32	Georgia	8	0.2%
32	New Mexico	8	0.2%
34	Alabama	7	0.2%
35	Kentucky	6	0.1%
36	New Jersey	5	0.1%
36	South Carolina	5	0.1%
38	Florida	3	0.1%
38	Massachusetts	3	0.1%
38	Washington	3	0.1%
41	North Carolina	1	0.0%
41	West Virginia	1	0.0%
43	Alaska	0	0.0%
43	Delaware	0	0.0%
43	Hawaii	0	0.0%
43	Maine	0	0.0%
43	New Hampshire	0	0.0%
43	Rhode Island	0	0.0%
43	Vermont	0	0.0%
43	Virginia	0	0.0%
	District of Columbia	1	0.0%

Source: U.S. Department of Health and Human Services, National Center for Health Statistics "Morbidity and Mortality Weekly Report" (January 5, 2007, Vol. 55, Nos. 51 & 52)
Provisional data. A flavivirus typically carried by mosquitoes.

West Nile Disease Rate in 2006

National Rate = 1.4 Cases per 100,000 Population

ALPHA ORDER

RANK	STATE	RATE
30	Alabama	0.2
39	Alaska	0.0
13	Arizona	1.6
21	Arkansas	1.0
23	California	0.7
6	Colorado	7.0
28	Connecticut	0.3
39	Delaware	0.0
39	Florida	0.0
32	Georgia	0.1
39	Hawaii	0.0
1	Idaho	65.5
13	Illinois	1.6
16	Indiana	1.3
19	Iowa	1.2
20	Kansas	1.1
32	Kentucky	0.1
10	Louisiana	4.0
39	Maine	0.0
30	Maryland	0.2
39	Massachusetts	0.0
24	Michigan	0.5
16	Minnesota	1.3
7	Mississippi	6.2
21	Missouri	1.0
11	Montana	3.6
3	Nebraska	14.9
9	Nevada	4.9
39	New Hampshire	0.0
32	New Jersey	0.1
25	New Mexico	0.4
32	New York	0.1
39	North Carolina	0.0
2	North Dakota	21.5
25	Ohio	0.4
16	Oklahoma	1.3
12	Oregon	1.9
32	Pennsylvania	0.1
39	Rhode Island	0.0
32	South Carolina	0.1
4	South Dakota	14.5
28	Tennessee	0.3
15	Texas	1.4
7	Utah	6.2
39	Vermont	0.0
39	Virginia	0.0
39	Washington	0.0
32	West Virginia	0.1
25	Wisconsin	0.4
5	Wyoming	12.6

RANK ORDER

RANK	STATE	RATE
1	Idaho	65.5
2	North Dakota	21.5
3	Nebraska	14.9
4	South Dakota	14.5
5	Wyoming	12.6
6	Colorado	7.0
7	Mississippi	6.2
7	Utah	6.2
9	Nevada	4.9
10	Louisiana	4.0
11	Montana	3.6
12	Oregon	1.9
13	Arizona	1.6
13	Illinois	1.6
15	Texas	1.4
16	Indiana	1.3
16	Minnesota	1.3
16	Oklahoma	1.3
19	Iowa	1.2
20	Kansas	1.1
21	Arkansas	1.0
21	Missouri	1.0
23	California	0.7
24	Michigan	0.5
25	New Mexico	0.4
25	Ohio	0.4
25	Wisconsin	0.4
28	Connecticut	0.3
28	Tennessee	0.3
30	Alabama	0.2
30	Maryland	0.2
32	Georgia	0.1
32	Kentucky	0.1
32	New Jersey	0.1
32	New York	0.1
32	Pennsylvania	0.1
32	South Carolina	0.1
32	West Virginia	0.1
39	Alaska	0.0
39	Delaware	0.0
39	Florida	0.0
39	Hawaii	0.0
39	Maine	0.0
39	Massachusetts	0.0
39	New Hampshire	0.0
39	North Carolina	0.0
39	Rhode Island	0.0
39	Vermont	0.0
39	Virginia	0.0
39	Washington	0.0
	District of Columbia	0.2

Source: Morgan Quitno Press using data from U.S. Dept. of Health & Human Serv's, National Center for Health Statistics
    "Morbidity and Mortality Weekly Report" (January 5, 2007, Vol. 55, Nos. 51 & 52)
*Provisional data. A flavivirus typically carried by mosquitoes.

Whooping Cough (Pertussis) Cases Reported in 2006

National Total = 13,144 Cases*

ALPHA ORDER

RANK	STATE	CASES	% of USA
24	Alabama	165	1.3%
41	Alaska	65	0.5%
10	Arizona	476	3.6%
38	Arkansas	75	0.6%
1	California	1,335	10.2%
5	Colorado	718	5.5%
34	Connecticut	91	0.7%
50	Delaware	3	0.0%
18	Florida	230	1.7%
47	Georgia	25	0.2%
36	Hawaii	80	0.6%
35	Idaho	86	0.7%
11	Illinois	453	3.4%
17	Indiana	231	1.8%
15	Iowa	274	2.1%
13	Kansas	320	2.4%
42	Kentucky	55	0.4%
49	Louisiana	13	0.1%
30	Maine	112	0.9%
27	Maryland	128	1.0%
9	Massachusetts	594	4.5%
8	Michigan	617	4.7%
25	Minnesota	164	1.2%
44	Mississippi	42	0.3%
14	Missouri	301	2.3%
31	Montana	109	0.8%
33	Nebraska	97	0.7%
40	Nevada	66	0.5%
20	New Hampshire	190	1.4%
21	New Jersey	185	1.4%
27	New Mexico	128	1.0%
2	New York	1,056	8.0%
16	North Carolina	237	1.8%
46	North Dakota	26	0.2%
7	Ohio	631	4.8%
45	Oklahoma	28	0.2%
32	Oregon	105	0.8%
6	Pennsylvania	672	5.1%
39	Rhode Island	70	0.5%
22	South Carolina	173	1.3%
48	South Dakota	20	0.2%
26	Tennessee	162	1.2%
4	Texas	736	5.6%
3	Utah	861	6.6%
29	Vermont	117	0.9%
19	Virginia	202	1.5%
12	Washington	321	2.4%
43	West Virginia	47	0.4%
23	Wisconsin	168	1.3%
37	Wyoming	78	0.6%

RANK ORDER

RANK	STATE	CASES	% of USA
1	California	1,335	10.2%
2	New York	1,056	8.0%
3	Utah	861	6.6%
4	Texas	736	5.6%
5	Colorado	718	5.5%
6	Pennsylvania	672	5.1%
7	Ohio	631	4.8%
8	Michigan	617	4.7%
9	Massachusetts	594	4.5%
10	Arizona	476	3.6%
11	Illinois	453	3.4%
12	Washington	321	2.4%
13	Kansas	320	2.4%
14	Missouri	301	2.3%
15	Iowa	274	2.1%
16	North Carolina	237	1.8%
17	Indiana	231	1.8%
18	Florida	230	1.7%
19	Virginia	202	1.5%
20	New Hampshire	190	1.4%
21	New Jersey	185	1.4%
22	South Carolina	173	1.3%
23	Wisconsin	168	1.3%
24	Alabama	165	1.3%
25	Minnesota	164	1.2%
26	Tennessee	162	1.2%
27	Maryland	128	1.0%
27	New Mexico	128	1.0%
29	Vermont	117	0.9%
30	Maine	112	0.9%
31	Montana	109	0.8%
32	Oregon	105	0.8%
33	Nebraska	97	0.7%
34	Connecticut	91	0.7%
35	Idaho	86	0.7%
36	Hawaii	80	0.6%
37	Wyoming	78	0.6%
38	Arkansas	75	0.6%
39	Rhode Island	70	0.5%
40	Nevada	66	0.5%
41	Alaska	65	0.5%
42	Kentucky	55	0.4%
43	West Virginia	47	0.4%
44	Mississippi	42	0.3%
45	Oklahoma	28	0.2%
46	North Dakota	26	0.2%
47	Georgia	25	0.2%
48	South Dakota	20	0.2%
49	Louisiana	13	0.1%
50	Delaware	3	0.0%
	District of Columbia	6	0.0%

*Source: U.S. Department of Health and Human Services, National Center for Health Statistics
"Morbidity and Mortality Weekly Report" (January 5, 2007, Vol. 55, Nos. 51 & 52)*
Provisional data. Acute, highly contagious infection of respiratory tract.

Whooping Cough (Pertussis) Rate in 2006

National Rate = 4.4 Cases per 100,000 Population*

ALPHA ORDER

RANK	STATE	RATE
28	Alabama	3.6
8	Alaska	9.7
12	Arizona	7.7
34	Arkansas	2.7
26	California	3.7
3	Colorado	15.1
37	Connecticut	2.6
48	Delaware	0.4
45	Florida	1.3
49	Georgia	0.3
15	Hawaii	6.2
17	Idaho	5.9
29	Illinois	3.5
26	Indiana	3.7
9	Iowa	9.2
6	Kansas	11.6
45	Kentucky	1.3
49	Louisiana	0.3
11	Maine	8.5
42	Maryland	2.3
9	Massachusetts	9.2
16	Michigan	6.1
30	Minnesota	3.2
44	Mississippi	1.4
22	Missouri	5.2
7	Montana	11.5
18	Nebraska	5.5
37	Nevada	2.6
5	New Hampshire	14.4
43	New Jersey	2.1
14	New Mexico	6.5
18	New York	5.5
34	North Carolina	2.7
24	North Dakota	4.1
18	Ohio	5.5
47	Oklahoma	0.8
33	Oregon	2.8
21	Pennsylvania	5.4
13	Rhode Island	6.6
25	South Carolina	4.0
37	South Dakota	2.6
34	Tennessee	2.7
31	Texas	3.1
1	Utah	33.8
2	Vermont	18.8
37	Virginia	2.6
23	Washington	5.0
37	West Virginia	2.6
32	Wisconsin	3.0
3	Wyoming	15.1

RANK ORDER

RANK	STATE	RATE
1	Utah	33.8
2	Vermont	18.8
3	Colorado	15.1
3	Wyoming	15.1
5	New Hampshire	14.4
6	Kansas	11.6
7	Montana	11.5
8	Alaska	9.7
9	Iowa	9.2
9	Massachusetts	9.2
11	Maine	8.5
12	Arizona	7.7
13	Rhode Island	6.6
14	New Mexico	6.5
15	Hawaii	6.2
16	Michigan	6.1
17	Idaho	5.9
18	Nebraska	5.5
18	New York	5.5
18	Ohio	5.5
21	Pennsylvania	5.4
22	Missouri	5.2
23	Washington	5.0
24	North Dakota	4.1
25	South Carolina	4.0
26	California	3.7
26	Indiana	3.7
28	Alabama	3.6
29	Illinois	3.5
30	Minnesota	3.2
31	Texas	3.1
32	Wisconsin	3.0
33	Oregon	2.8
34	Arkansas	2.7
34	North Carolina	2.7
34	Tennessee	2.7
37	Connecticut	2.6
37	Nevada	2.6
37	South Dakota	2.6
37	Virginia	2.6
37	West Virginia	2.6
42	Maryland	2.3
43	New Jersey	2.1
44	Mississippi	1.4
45	Florida	1.3
45	Kentucky	1.3
47	Oklahoma	0.8
48	Delaware	0.4
49	Georgia	0.3
49	Louisiana	0.3

District of Columbia	1.0

Source: Morgan Quitno Press using data from U.S. Dept. of Health & Human Serv's, National Center for Health Statistics
"Morbidity and Mortality Weekly Report" (January 5, 2007, Vol. 55, Nos. 51 & 52)
*Provisional data. Acute, highly contagious infection of respiratory tract.

Percent of Children Aged 19 to 35 Months Immunized in 2005

National Percent = 82.4%*

<table>
<tr><td colspan="3">ALPHA ORDER</td><td colspan="3">RANK ORDER</td></tr>
<tr><td>RANK</td><td>STATE</td><td>PERCENT</td><td>RANK</td><td>STATE</td><td>PERCENT</td></tr>
<tr><td>13</td><td>Alabama</td><td>85.1</td><td>1</td><td>Massachusetts</td><td>95.4</td></tr>
<tr><td>44</td><td>Alaska</td><td>77.7</td><td>2</td><td>Nebraska</td><td>89.8</td></tr>
<tr><td>33</td><td>Arizona</td><td>81.0</td><td>3</td><td>Connecticut</td><td>89.4</td></tr>
<tr><td>50</td><td>Arkansas</td><td>69.3</td><td>4</td><td>North Carolina</td><td>89.1</td></tr>
<tr><td>37</td><td>California</td><td>79.9</td><td>5</td><td>South Dakota</td><td>88.1</td></tr>
<tr><td>19</td><td>Colorado</td><td>84.4</td><td>6</td><td>Maine</td><td>88.0</td></tr>
<tr><td>3</td><td>Connecticut</td><td>89.4</td><td>7</td><td>Delaware</td><td>86.7</td></tr>
<tr><td>7</td><td>Delaware</td><td>86.7</td><td>8</td><td>North Dakota</td><td>86.3</td></tr>
<tr><td>30</td><td>Florida</td><td>81.2</td><td>9</td><td>Kansas</td><td>86.2</td></tr>
<tr><td>10</td><td>Georgia</td><td>85.9</td><td>10</td><td>Georgia</td><td>85.9</td></tr>
<tr><td>32</td><td>Hawaii</td><td>81.1</td><td>11</td><td>Virginia</td><td>85.8</td></tr>
<tr><td>39</td><td>Idaho</td><td>79.3</td><td>12</td><td>Minnesota</td><td>85.5</td></tr>
<tr><td>18</td><td>Illinois</td><td>84.8</td><td>13</td><td>Alabama</td><td>85.1</td></tr>
<tr><td>40</td><td>Indiana</td><td>78.5</td><td>14</td><td>New Hampshire</td><td>85.0</td></tr>
<tr><td>17</td><td>Iowa</td><td>84.9</td><td>14</td><td>Ohio</td><td>85.0</td></tr>
<tr><td>9</td><td>Kansas</td><td>86.2</td><td>14</td><td>Wisconsin</td><td>85.0</td></tr>
<tr><td>29</td><td>Kentucky</td><td>82.9</td><td>17</td><td>Iowa</td><td>84.9</td></tr>
<tr><td>45</td><td>Louisiana</td><td>77.1</td><td>18</td><td>Illinois</td><td>84.8</td></tr>
<tr><td>6</td><td>Maine</td><td>88.0</td><td>19</td><td>Colorado</td><td>84.4</td></tr>
<tr><td>22</td><td>Maryland</td><td>84.2</td><td>19</td><td>Mississippi</td><td>84.4</td></tr>
<tr><td>1</td><td>Massachusetts</td><td>95.4</td><td>21</td><td>Rhode Island</td><td>84.3</td></tr>
<tr><td>22</td><td>Michigan</td><td>84.2</td><td>22</td><td>Maryland</td><td>84.2</td></tr>
<tr><td>12</td><td>Minnesota</td><td>85.5</td><td>22</td><td>Michigan</td><td>84.2</td></tr>
<tr><td>19</td><td>Mississippi</td><td>84.4</td><td>24</td><td>Tennessee</td><td>83.8</td></tr>
<tr><td>34</td><td>Missouri</td><td>80.9</td><td>25</td><td>New York</td><td>83.7</td></tr>
<tr><td>28</td><td>Montana</td><td>83.1</td><td>26</td><td>Pennsylvania</td><td>83.4</td></tr>
<tr><td>2</td><td>Nebraska</td><td>89.8</td><td>26</td><td>Vermont</td><td>83.4</td></tr>
<tr><td>49</td><td>Nevada</td><td>71.1</td><td>28</td><td>Montana</td><td>83.1</td></tr>
<tr><td>14</td><td>New Hampshire</td><td>85.0</td><td>29</td><td>Kentucky</td><td>82.9</td></tr>
<tr><td>40</td><td>New Jersey</td><td>78.5</td><td>30</td><td>Florida</td><td>81.2</td></tr>
<tr><td>38</td><td>New Mexico</td><td>79.6</td><td>30</td><td>Washington</td><td>81.2</td></tr>
<tr><td>25</td><td>New York</td><td>83.7</td><td>32</td><td>Hawaii</td><td>81.1</td></tr>
<tr><td>4</td><td>North Carolina</td><td>89.1</td><td>33</td><td>Arizona</td><td>81.0</td></tr>
<tr><td>8</td><td>North Dakota</td><td>86.3</td><td>34</td><td>Missouri</td><td>80.9</td></tr>
<tr><td>14</td><td>Ohio</td><td>85.0</td><td>35</td><td>Texas</td><td>80.8</td></tr>
<tr><td>46</td><td>Oklahoma</td><td>76.9</td><td>36</td><td>Wyoming</td><td>80.5</td></tr>
<tr><td>48</td><td>Oregon</td><td>75.3</td><td>37</td><td>California</td><td>79.9</td></tr>
<tr><td>26</td><td>Pennsylvania</td><td>83.4</td><td>38</td><td>New Mexico</td><td>79.6</td></tr>
<tr><td>21</td><td>Rhode Island</td><td>84.3</td><td>39</td><td>Idaho</td><td>79.3</td></tr>
<tr><td>40</td><td>South Carolina</td><td>78.5</td><td>40</td><td>Indiana</td><td>78.5</td></tr>
<tr><td>5</td><td>South Dakota</td><td>88.1</td><td>40</td><td>New Jersey</td><td>78.5</td></tr>
<tr><td>24</td><td>Tennessee</td><td>83.8</td><td>40</td><td>South Carolina</td><td>78.5</td></tr>
<tr><td>35</td><td>Texas</td><td>80.8</td><td>43</td><td>West Virginia</td><td>78.2</td></tr>
<tr><td>47</td><td>Utah</td><td>75.7</td><td>44</td><td>Alaska</td><td>77.7</td></tr>
<tr><td>26</td><td>Vermont</td><td>83.4</td><td>45</td><td>Louisiana</td><td>77.1</td></tr>
<tr><td>11</td><td>Virginia</td><td>85.8</td><td>46</td><td>Oklahoma</td><td>76.9</td></tr>
<tr><td>30</td><td>Washington</td><td>81.2</td><td>47</td><td>Utah</td><td>75.7</td></tr>
<tr><td>43</td><td>West Virginia</td><td>78.2</td><td>48</td><td>Oregon</td><td>75.3</td></tr>
<tr><td>14</td><td>Wisconsin</td><td>85.0</td><td>49</td><td>Nevada</td><td>71.1</td></tr>
<tr><td>36</td><td>Wyoming</td><td>80.5</td><td>50</td><td>Arkansas</td><td>69.3</td></tr>
<tr><td></td><td></td><td></td><td></td><td>District of Columbia</td><td>78.0</td></tr>
</table>

Source: U.S. Department of Health and Human Services, Centers for Disease Control and Prevention
"State Vaccination Coverage Levels" (Morbidity and Mortality Weekly Report, Vol. 55, No. 36, Sept 15, 2006)
*This table is consistent with previous tables showing "fully" immunized children. Figures here are for the 4:3:1:3 series. Children received four doses of DTP/DT/DTaP (Diphtheria, Tetanus, Pertussis (Whooping Cough), Acellular Pertussis), three doses of OPV (Oral Poliovirus Vaccine), one dose of MCV (Measles-Containing Vaccine) and three doses of Hib (Haemophilus influenzae type b). Hepatitis B and Varicella vaccines are not included in this series.

Percent of Children Aged 19 to 35 Months Fully Immunized in 2005

National Percent = 76.1%*

ALPHA ORDER			RANK ORDER		
RANK	STATE	PERCENT	RANK	STATE	PERCENT
4	Alabama	81.7	1	Massachusetts	90.7
41	Alaska	68.1	2	Nebraska	83.9
29	Arizona	74.9	3	Georgia	82.4
48	Arkansas	64.2	4	Alabama	81.7
33	California	74.0	4	Virginia	81.7
15	Colorado	78.6	6	Delaware	81.6
8	Connecticut	81.5	6	North Carolina	81.6
6	Delaware	81.6	8	Connecticut	81.5
17	Florida	78.2	9	Michigan	80.6
3	Georgia	82.4	10	Rhode Island	80.1
20	Hawaii	77.5	11	Tennessee	80.0
40	Idaho	68.4	12	South Dakota	79.5
25	Illinois	76.7	13	Mississippi	79.1
39	Indiana	69.9	14	North Dakota	78.7
26	Iowa	75.9	15	Colorado	78.6
37	Kansas	72.0	15	Maryland	78.6
38	Kentucky	71.1	17	Florida	78.2
32	Louisiana	74.1	18	Minnesota	78.1
27	Maine	75.8	19	Ohio	77.7
15	Maryland	78.6	20	Hawaii	77.5
1	Massachusetts	90.7	21	Pennsylvania	77.3
9	Michigan	80.6	22	New Hampshire	77.1
18	Minnesota	78.1	22	Wisconsin	77.1
13	Mississippi	79.1	24	Texas	76.8
34	Missouri	73.1	25	Illinois	76.7
46	Montana	65.4	26	Iowa	75.9
2	Nebraska	83.9	27	Maine	75.8
49	Nevada	63.2	28	South Carolina	75.6
22	New Hampshire	77.1	29	Arizona	74.9
35	New Jersey	72.4	30	New Mexico	74.6
30	New Mexico	74.6	31	New York	74.4
31	New York	74.4	32	Louisiana	74.1
6	North Carolina	81.6	33	California	74.0
14	North Dakota	78.7	34	Missouri	73.1
19	Ohio	77.7	35	New Jersey	72.4
36	Oklahoma	72.3	36	Oklahoma	72.3
47	Oregon	65.3	37	Kansas	72.0
21	Pennsylvania	77.3	38	Kentucky	71.1
10	Rhode Island	80.1	39	Indiana	69.9
28	South Carolina	75.6	40	Idaho	68.4
12	South Dakota	79.5	41	Alaska	68.1
11	Tennessee	80.0	41	Utah	68.1
24	Texas	76.8	43	West Virginia	67.5
41	Utah	68.1	44	Wyoming	66.9
50	Vermont	62.9	45	Washington	66.3
4	Virginia	81.7	46	Montana	65.4
45	Washington	66.3	47	Oregon	65.3
43	West Virginia	67.5	48	Arkansas	64.2
22	Wisconsin	77.1	49	Nevada	63.2
44	Wyoming	66.9	50	Vermont	62.9
				District of Columbia	72.1

Source: U.S. Department of Health and Human Services, Centers for Disease Control and Prevention
"State Vaccination Coverage Levels" (Morbidity and Mortality Weekly Report, Vol. 55, No. 36, Sept 15, 2006)
*Fully immunized (4:3:1:3:3:1 series) children received four doses of DTP/DT/DTaP (Diphtheria, Tetanus, Pertussis (Whooping Cough), Acellular Pertussis), three doses of OPV (Oral Poliovirus Vaccine), one dose of MCV (Measles-Containing Vaccine), three doses of Hib (Haemophilus influenzae type b), three doses of Hepatitis B vaccine and one dose of Varicella (chickenpox) vaccine. This differs from previous "fully" immunized tables.

Percent of Adults Aged 65 Years and Older Who Received Flu Shots in 2005

National Median = 65.7%*

ALPHA ORDER

RANK ORDER

RANK	STATE	PERCENT		RANK	STATE	PERCENT
44	Alabama	60.8		1	Minnesota	78.1
42	Alaska	61.1		2	South Dakota	76.3
34	Arizona	62.5		3	Colorado	74.2
28	Arkansas	65.2		4	Oklahoma	73.2
24	California	65.9		5	Wyoming	72.9
3	Colorado	74.2		6	Nebraska	72.6
10	Connecticut	71.1		7	Hawaii	72.1
26	Delaware	65.7		8	Wisconsin	71.8
49	Florida	55.6		9	Iowa	71.7
44	Georgia	60.8		10	Connecticut	71.1
7	Hawaii	72.1		11	New Hampshire	70.2
31	Idaho	63.9		12	North Dakota	70.1
48	Illinois	55.9		13	Massachusetts	69.8
30	Indiana	64.0		14	Utah	69.6
9	Iowa	71.7		15	Montana	69.5
24	Kansas	65.9		16	Oregon	68.9
35	Kentucky	62.4		17	New Mexico	68.0
35	Louisiana	62.4		18	Washington	67.8
19	Maine	67.7		19	Maine	67.7
46	Maryland	59.3		20	Rhode Island	67.2
13	Massachusetts	69.8		21	Michigan	67.1
21	Michigan	67.1		22	Virginia	66.8
1	Minnesota	78.1		23	Vermont	66.3
41	Mississippi	61.5		24	California	65.9
38	Missouri	61.7		24	Kansas	65.9
15	Montana	69.5		26	Delaware	65.7
6	Nebraska	72.6		27	North Carolina	65.5
50	Nevada	53.0		28	Arkansas	65.2
11	New Hampshire	70.2		29	Ohio	64.7
33	New Jersey	63.4		30	Indiana	64.0
17	New Mexico	68.0		31	Idaho	63.9
37	New York	61.8		32	West Virginia	63.6
27	North Carolina	65.5		33	New Jersey	63.4
12	North Dakota	70.1		34	Arizona	62.5
29	Ohio	64.7		35	Kentucky	62.4
4	Oklahoma	73.2		35	Louisiana	62.4
16	Oregon	68.9		37	New York	61.8
46	Pennsylvania	59.3		38	Missouri	61.7
20	Rhode Island	67.2		39	Tennessee	61.6
43	South Carolina	60.9		39	Texas	61.6
2	South Dakota	76.3		41	Mississippi	61.5
39	Tennessee	61.6		42	Alaska	61.1
39	Texas	61.6		43	South Carolina	60.9
14	Utah	69.6		44	Alabama	60.8
23	Vermont	66.3		44	Georgia	60.8
22	Virginia	66.8		46	Maryland	59.3
18	Washington	67.8		46	Pennsylvania	59.3
32	West Virginia	63.6		48	Illinois	55.9
8	Wisconsin	71.8		49	Florida	55.6
5	Wyoming	72.9		50	Nevada	53.0

District of Columbia 54.7

Source: U.S. Department of Health and Human Services, Centers for Disease Control and Prevention
"2005 Behavioral Risk Factor Surveillance Summary Prevalence Data" (http://apps.nccd.cdc.gov/brfss/)
*Percent of adults 65 years old and older who reported receiving influenza vaccine during the preceding 12 months.

Percent of Adults Aged 65 Years and Older
Who Have Had a Pneumonia Vaccine: 2005
National Median = 65.9%*

ALPHA ORDER

RANK	STATE	PERCENT
44	Alabama	61.9
48	Alaska	61.1
30	Arizona	65.4
49	Arkansas	57.4
47	California	61.3
8	Colorado	70.2
12	Connecticut	69.3
25	Delaware	65.9
40	Florida	62.4
39	Georgia	62.5
25	Hawaii	65.9
45	Idaho	61.6
50	Illinois	57.0
31	Indiana	65.3
13	Iowa	69.1
18	Kansas	66.8
38	Kentucky	62.9
3	Louisiana	71.4
35	Maine	64.4
42	Maryland	62.0
32	Massachusetts	64.8
23	Michigan	66.2
6	Minnesota	71.1
27	Mississippi	65.7
32	Missouri	64.8
9	Montana	69.9
15	Nebraska	67.9
10	Nevada	69.8
10	New Hampshire	69.8
36	New Jersey	64.0
34	New Mexico	64.7
42	New York	62.0
23	North Carolina	66.2
1	North Dakota	71.7
46	Ohio	61.5
6	Oklahoma	71.1
3	Oregon	71.4
16	Pennsylvania	67.2
2	Rhode Island	71.5
29	South Carolina	65.6
22	South Dakota	66.3
37	Tennessee	63.8
41	Texas	62.2
21	Utah	66.4
19	Vermont	66.7
20	Virginia	66.5
17	Washington	66.9
14	West Virginia	68.2
27	Wisconsin	65.7
5	Wyoming	71.2

RANK ORDER

RANK	STATE	PERCENT
1	North Dakota	71.7
2	Rhode Island	71.5
3	Louisiana	71.4
3	Oregon	71.4
5	Wyoming	71.2
6	Minnesota	71.1
6	Oklahoma	71.1
8	Colorado	70.2
9	Montana	69.9
10	Nevada	69.8
10	New Hampshire	69.8
12	Connecticut	69.3
13	Iowa	69.1
14	West Virginia	68.2
15	Nebraska	67.9
16	Pennsylvania	67.2
17	Washington	66.9
18	Kansas	66.8
19	Vermont	66.7
20	Virginia	66.5
21	Utah	66.4
22	South Dakota	66.3
23	Michigan	66.2
23	North Carolina	66.2
25	Delaware	65.9
25	Hawaii	65.9
27	Mississippi	65.7
27	Wisconsin	65.7
29	South Carolina	65.6
30	Arizona	65.4
31	Indiana	65.3
32	Massachusetts	64.8
32	Missouri	64.8
34	New Mexico	64.7
35	Maine	64.4
36	New Jersey	64.0
37	Tennessee	63.8
38	Kentucky	62.9
39	Georgia	62.5
40	Florida	62.4
41	Texas	62.2
42	Maryland	62.0
42	New York	62.0
44	Alabama	61.9
45	Idaho	61.6
46	Ohio	61.5
47	California	61.3
48	Alaska	61.1
49	Arkansas	57.4
50	Illinois	57.0
	District of Columbia	51.6

Source: U.S. Department of Health and Human Services, Centers for Disease Control and Prevention
"2005 Behavioral Risk Factor Surveillance Summary Prevalence Data" (http://apps.nccd.cdc.gov/brfss/)
*Percent of adults 65 years old and older who reported ever receiving a pneumonia vaccine.

Sexually Transmitted Diseases in 2005

National Total = 1,324,779 Cases*

ALPHA ORDER

RANK	STATE	CASES	% of USA
18	Alabama	26,684	2.0%
39	Alaska	4,964	0.4%
19	Arizona	26,391	2.0%
29	Arkansas	13,035	1.0%
1	California	166,640	12.6%
24	Colorado	18,702	1.4%
28	Connecticut	13,847	1.0%
40	Delaware	4,316	0.3%
6	Florida	64,322	4.9%
8	Georgia	50,067	3.8%
36	Hawaii	6,524	0.5%
44	Idaho	2,938	0.2%
4	Illinois	71,103	5.4%
15	Indiana	28,219	2.1%
35	Iowa	9,005	0.7%
34	Kansas	10,043	0.8%
30	Kentucky	11,338	0.9%
16	Louisiana	27,081	2.0%
46	Maine	2,397	0.2%
21	Maryland	25,639	1.9%
26	Massachusetts	17,074	1.3%
7	Michigan	56,519	4.3%
27	Minnesota	15,741	1.2%
14	Mississippi	28,488	2.2%
11	Missouri	31,973	2.4%
45	Montana	2,565	0.2%
37	Nebraska	6,260	0.5%
32	Nevada	10,310	0.8%
47	New Hampshire	2,035	0.2%
22	New Jersey	25,007	1.9%
33	New Mexico	10,064	0.8%
3	New York	82,389	6.2%
10	North Carolina	46,534	3.5%
48	North Dakota	1,796	0.1%
5	Ohio	65,003	4.9%
25	Oklahoma	18,679	1.4%
31	Oregon	10,621	0.8%
9	Pennsylvania	48,682	3.7%
41	Rhode Island	3,731	0.3%
17	South Carolina	26,941	2.0%
43	South Dakota	3,054	0.2%
12	Tennessee	31,906	2.4%
2	Texas	98,844	7.5%
38	Utah	5,339	0.4%
50	Vermont	1,018	0.1%
13	Virginia	31,157	2.4%
23	Washington	22,507	1.7%
42	West Virginia	3,717	0.3%
20	Wisconsin	26,371	2.0%
49	Wyoming	1,261	0.1%

RANK ORDER

RANK	STATE	CASES	% of USA
1	California	166,640	12.6%
2	Texas	98,844	7.5%
3	New York	82,389	6.2%
4	Illinois	71,103	5.4%
5	Ohio	65,003	4.9%
6	Florida	64,322	4.9%
7	Michigan	56,519	4.3%
8	Georgia	50,067	3.8%
9	Pennsylvania	48,682	3.7%
10	North Carolina	46,534	3.5%
11	Missouri	31,973	2.4%
12	Tennessee	31,906	2.4%
13	Virginia	31,157	2.4%
14	Mississippi	28,488	2.2%
15	Indiana	28,219	2.1%
16	Louisiana	27,081	2.0%
17	South Carolina	26,941	2.0%
18	Alabama	26,684	2.0%
19	Arizona	26,391	2.0%
20	Wisconsin	26,371	2.0%
21	Maryland	25,639	1.9%
22	New Jersey	25,007	1.9%
23	Washington	22,507	1.7%
24	Colorado	18,702	1.4%
25	Oklahoma	18,679	1.4%
26	Massachusetts	17,074	1.3%
27	Minnesota	15,741	1.2%
28	Connecticut	13,847	1.0%
29	Arkansas	13,035	1.0%
30	Kentucky	11,338	0.9%
31	Oregon	10,621	0.8%
32	Nevada	10,310	0.8%
33	New Mexico	10,064	0.8%
34	Kansas	10,043	0.8%
35	Iowa	9,005	0.7%
36	Hawaii	6,524	0.5%
37	Nebraska	6,260	0.5%
38	Utah	5,339	0.4%
39	Alaska	4,964	0.4%
40	Delaware	4,316	0.3%
41	Rhode Island	3,731	0.3%
42	West Virginia	3,717	0.3%
43	South Dakota	3,054	0.2%
44	Idaho	2,938	0.2%
45	Montana	2,565	0.2%
46	Maine	2,397	0.2%
47	New Hampshire	2,035	0.2%
48	North Dakota	1,796	0.1%
49	Wyoming	1,261	0.1%
50	Vermont	1,018	0.1%
	District of Columbia	5,938	0.4%

Source: Morgan Quitno Press using data from U.S. Dept. of Health and Human Services, Nat'l Center for Health Statistics
"Sexually Transmitted Disease Surveillance 2005" (http://www.cdc.gov/std/stats/TOC2005.htm)
*Includes chancroid, chlamydia, gonorrhea and primary and secondary syphilis.

Sexually Transmitted Disease Rate in 2005

National Rate = 451.1 Cases per 100,000 Population*

ALPHA ORDER

RANK	STATE	RATE
5	Alabama	589.0
2	Alaska	757.3
21	Arizona	459.4
18	Arkansas	473.6
19	California	464.3
27	Colorado	406.5
29	Connecticut	395.3
15	Delaware	519.8
31	Florida	369.8
7	Georgia	567.0
16	Hawaii	516.7
46	Idaho	210.8
8	Illinois	559.3
22	Indiana	452.4
37	Iowa	304.8
32	Kansas	367.1
42	Kentucky	273.5
4	Louisiana	599.8
48	Maine	182.0
20	Maryland	461.3
43	Massachusetts	266.0
9	Michigan	558.9
36	Minnesota	308.7
1	Mississippi	981.3
10	Missouri	555.6
41	Montana	276.7
34	Nebraska	358.3
23	Nevada	441.7
50	New Hampshire	156.5
39	New Jersey	287.5
14	New Mexico	528.7
25	New York	428.5
11	North Carolina	544.9
40	North Dakota	283.2
6	Ohio	567.2
13	Oklahoma	530.1
38	Oregon	295.5
30	Pennsylvania	392.4
35	Rhode Island	345.2
3	South Carolina	641.7
28	South Dakota	396.2
12	Tennessee	540.7
24	Texas	439.5
45	Utah	223.4
49	Vermont	163.9
26	Virginia	417.7
33	Washington	362.9
47	West Virginia	204.8
17	Wisconsin	478.6
44	Wyoming	249.0

RANK ORDER

RANK	STATE	RATE
1	Mississippi	981.3
2	Alaska	757.3
3	South Carolina	641.7
4	Louisiana	599.8
5	Alabama	589.0
6	Ohio	567.2
7	Georgia	567.0
8	Illinois	559.3
9	Michigan	558.9
10	Missouri	555.6
11	North Carolina	544.9
12	Tennessee	540.7
13	Oklahoma	530.1
14	New Mexico	528.7
15	Delaware	519.8
16	Hawaii	516.7
17	Wisconsin	478.6
18	Arkansas	473.6
19	California	464.3
20	Maryland	461.3
21	Arizona	459.4
22	Indiana	452.4
23	Nevada	441.7
24	Texas	439.5
25	New York	428.5
26	Virginia	417.7
27	Colorado	406.5
28	South Dakota	396.2
29	Connecticut	395.3
30	Pennsylvania	392.4
31	Florida	369.8
32	Kansas	367.1
33	Washington	362.9
34	Nebraska	358.3
35	Rhode Island	345.2
36	Minnesota	308.7
37	Iowa	304.8
38	Oregon	295.5
39	New Jersey	287.5
40	North Dakota	283.2
41	Montana	276.7
42	Kentucky	273.5
43	Massachusetts	266.0
44	Wyoming	249.0
45	Utah	223.4
46	Idaho	210.8
47	West Virginia	204.8
48	Maine	182.0
49	Vermont	163.9
50	New Hampshire	156.5

District of Columbia 1,020.2

Source: Morgan Quitno Press using data from U.S. Dept. of Health and Human Services, Nat'l Center for Health Statistics "Sexually Transmitted Disease Surveillance 2005" (http://www.cdc.gov/std/stats/TOC2005.htm)
Includes chancroid, chlamydia, gonorrhea and primary and secondary syphilis.

Chlamydia Cases Reported in 2005

National Total = 976,445 Cases*

ALPHA ORDER

RANK	STATE	CASES	% of USA
23	Alabama	17,109	1.8%
39	Alaska	4,355	0.4%
15	Arizona	21,264	2.2%
30	Arkansas	8,507	0.9%
1	California	130,716	13.4%
24	Colorado	15,432	1.6%
28	Connecticut	11,039	1.1%
40	Delaware	3,392	0.3%
6	Florida	43,372	4.4%
9	Georgia	33,562	3.4%
36	Hawaii	5,489	0.6%
43	Idaho	2,799	0.3%
4	Illinois	50,559	5.2%
17	Indiana	20,063	2.1%
34	Iowa	7,390	0.8%
33	Kansas	7,419	0.8%
32	Kentucky	8,351	0.9%
22	Louisiana	17,227	1.8%
46	Maine	2,254	0.2%
21	Maryland	18,291	1.9%
25	Massachusetts	14,411	1.5%
7	Michigan	38,730	4.0%
27	Minnesota	12,189	1.2%
14	Mississippi	21,268	2.2%
13	Missouri	22,371	2.3%
45	Montana	2,400	0.2%
37	Nebraska	5,098	0.5%
35	Nevada	7,321	0.7%
47	New Hampshire	1,842	0.2%
18	New Jersey	19,152	2.0%
31	New Mexico	8,456	0.9%
3	New York	63,966	6.6%
10	North Carolina	31,183	3.2%
48	North Dakota	1,667	0.2%
5	Ohio	43,806	4.5%
26	Oklahoma	13,407	1.4%
29	Oregon	9,018	0.9%
8	Pennsylvania	37,261	3.8%
41	Rhode Island	3,269	0.3%
20	South Carolina	18,296	1.9%
44	South Dakota	2,701	0.3%
11	Tennessee	23,084	2.4%
2	Texas	71,860	7.4%
38	Utah	4,602	0.5%
50	Vermont	957	0.1%
12	Virginia	22,668	2.3%
19	Washington	18,616	1.9%
42	West Virginia	2,944	0.3%
16	Wisconsin	20,461	2.1%
49	Wyoming	1,173	0.1%

RANK ORDER

RANK	STATE	CASES	% of USA
1	California	130,716	13.4%
2	Texas	71,860	7.4%
3	New York	63,966	6.6%
4	Illinois	50,559	5.2%
5	Ohio	43,806	4.5%
6	Florida	43,372	4.4%
7	Michigan	38,730	4.0%
8	Pennsylvania	37,261	3.8%
9	Georgia	33,562	3.4%
10	North Carolina	31,183	3.2%
11	Tennessee	23,084	2.4%
12	Virginia	22,668	2.3%
13	Missouri	22,371	2.3%
14	Mississippi	21,268	2.2%
15	Arizona	21,264	2.2%
16	Wisconsin	20,461	2.1%
17	Indiana	20,063	2.1%
18	New Jersey	19,152	2.0%
19	Washington	18,616	1.9%
20	South Carolina	18,296	1.9%
21	Maryland	18,291	1.9%
22	Louisiana	17,227	1.8%
23	Alabama	17,109	1.8%
24	Colorado	15,432	1.6%
25	Massachusetts	14,411	1.5%
26	Oklahoma	13,407	1.4%
27	Minnesota	12,189	1.2%
28	Connecticut	11,039	1.1%
29	Oregon	9,018	0.9%
30	Arkansas	8,507	0.9%
31	New Mexico	8,456	0.9%
32	Kentucky	8,351	0.9%
33	Kansas	7,419	0.8%
34	Iowa	7,390	0.8%
35	Nevada	7,321	0.7%
36	Hawaii	5,489	0.6%
37	Nebraska	5,098	0.5%
38	Utah	4,602	0.5%
39	Alaska	4,355	0.4%
40	Delaware	3,392	0.3%
41	Rhode Island	3,269	0.3%
42	West Virginia	2,944	0.3%
43	Idaho	2,799	0.3%
44	South Dakota	2,701	0.3%
45	Montana	2,400	0.2%
46	Maine	2,254	0.2%
47	New Hampshire	1,842	0.2%
48	North Dakota	1,667	0.2%
49	Wyoming	1,173	0.1%
50	Vermont	957	0.1%
	District of Columbia	3,678	0.4%

Source: U.S. Department of Health and Human Services, National Center for Health Statistics
"Sexually Transmitted Disease Surveillance 2005" (http://www.cdc.gov/std/stats/TOC2005.htm)
*Any of several common, often asymptomatic, sexually transmitted diseases caused by the microorganism Chlamydia trachomatis, including nonspecific urethritis in men.

Chlamydia Rate in 2005

National Rate = 332.5 Cases per 100,000 Population*

RANK	STATE	RATE
15	Alabama	377.7
2	Alaska	664.4
17	Arizona	370.2
28	Arkansas	309.1
19	California	364.2
21	Colorado	335.4
26	Connecticut	315.1
6	Delaware	408.5
39	Florida	249.3
14	Georgia	380.1
5	Hawaii	434.7
45	Idaho	200.9
7	Illinois	397.7
24	Indiana	321.6
38	Iowa	250.1
34	Kansas	271.2
44	Kentucky	201.4
12	Louisiana	381.5
47	Maine	171.1
23	Maryland	329.1
42	Massachusetts	224.6
10	Michigan	383.0
40	Minnesota	239.0
1	Mississippi	732.6
9	Missouri	388.7
36	Montana	258.9
33	Nebraska	291.8
27	Nevada	313.6
50	New Hampshire	141.7
43	New Jersey	220.2
3	New Mexico	444.3
22	New York	332.7
18	North Carolina	365.1
35	North Dakota	262.8
11	Ohio	382.3
13	Oklahoma	380.5
37	Oregon	250.9
31	Pennsylvania	300.3
30	Rhode Island	302.5
4	South Carolina	435.8
20	South Dakota	350.4
8	Tennessee	391.2
25	Texas	319.5
46	Utah	192.6
49	Vermont	154.0
29	Virginia	303.9
32	Washington	300.1
48	West Virginia	162.2
16	Wisconsin	371.4
41	Wyoming	231.6

RANK	STATE	RATE
1	Mississippi	732.6
2	Alaska	664.4
3	New Mexico	444.3
4	South Carolina	435.8
5	Hawaii	434.7
6	Delaware	408.5
7	Illinois	397.7
8	Tennessee	391.2
9	Missouri	388.7
10	Michigan	383.0
11	Ohio	382.3
12	Louisiana	381.5
13	Oklahoma	380.5
14	Georgia	380.1
15	Alabama	377.7
16	Wisconsin	371.4
17	Arizona	370.2
18	North Carolina	365.1
19	California	364.2
20	South Dakota	350.4
21	Colorado	335.4
22	New York	332.7
23	Maryland	329.1
24	Indiana	321.6
25	Texas	319.5
26	Connecticut	315.1
27	Nevada	313.6
28	Arkansas	309.1
29	Virginia	303.9
30	Rhode Island	302.5
31	Pennsylvania	300.3
32	Washington	300.1
33	Nebraska	291.8
34	Kansas	271.2
35	North Dakota	262.8
36	Montana	258.9
37	Oregon	250.9
38	Iowa	250.1
39	Florida	249.3
40	Minnesota	239.0
41	Wyoming	231.6
42	Massachusetts	224.6
43	New Jersey	220.2
44	Kentucky	201.4
45	Idaho	200.9
46	Utah	192.6
47	Maine	171.1
48	West Virginia	162.2
49	Vermont	154.0
50	New Hampshire	141.7

District of Columbia 631.9

Source: U.S. Department of Health and Human Services, National Center for Health Statistics "Sexually Transmitted Disease Surveillance 2005" (http://www.cdc.gov/std/stats/TOC2005.htm)
*Any of several common, often asymptomatic, sexually transmitted diseases caused by the microorganism Chlamydia trachomatis, including nonspecific urethritis in men.

Gonorrhea Cases Reported in 2005

National Total = 339,593 Cases*

ALPHA ORDER

RANK	STATE	CASES	% of USA
13	Alabama	9,406	2.8%
41	Alaska	600	0.2%
23	Arizona	4,951	1.5%
24	Arkansas	4,476	1.3%
1	California	34,338	10.1%
27	Colorado	3,224	0.9%
30	Connecticut	2,750	0.8%
38	Delaware	913	0.3%
4	Florida	20,225	6.0%
8	Georgia	15,860	4.7%
37	Hawaii	1,024	0.3%
48	Idaho	119	0.0%
5	Illinois	20,019	5.9%
17	Indiana	8,094	2.4%
33	Iowa	1,606	0.5%
31	Kansas	2,605	0.8%
28	Kentucky	2,935	0.9%
11	Louisiana	9,572	2.8%
46	Maine	142	0.0%
19	Maryland	7,035	2.1%
32	Massachusetts	2,537	0.7%
7	Michigan	17,684	5.2%
26	Minnesota	3,482	1.0%
18	Mississippi	7,171	2.1%
12	Missouri	9,455	2.8%
45	Montana	158	0.0%
36	Nebraska	1,158	0.3%
29	Nevada	2,880	0.8%
44	New Hampshire	177	0.1%
21	New Jersey	5,722	1.7%
35	New Mexico	1,552	0.5%
6	New York	17,717	5.2%
9	North Carolina	15,072	4.4%
47	North Dakota	128	0.0%
3	Ohio	20,985	6.2%
22	Oklahoma	5,228	1.5%
34	Oregon	1,562	0.5%
10	Pennsylvania	11,222	3.3%
42	Rhode Island	438	0.1%
15	South Carolina	8,561	2.5%
43	South Dakota	351	0.1%
14	Tennessee	8,605	2.5%
2	Texas	26,110	7.7%
40	Utah	727	0.2%
50	Vermont	60	0.0%
16	Virginia	8,346	2.5%
25	Washington	3,739	1.1%
39	West Virginia	770	0.2%
20	Wisconsin	5,869	1.7%
49	Wyoming	87	0.0%

RANK ORDER

RANK	STATE	CASES	% of USA
1	California	34,338	10.1%
2	Texas	26,110	7.7%
3	Ohio	20,985	6.2%
4	Florida	20,225	6.0%
5	Illinois	20,019	5.9%
6	New York	17,717	5.2%
7	Michigan	17,684	5.2%
8	Georgia	15,860	4.7%
9	North Carolina	15,072	4.4%
10	Pennsylvania	11,222	3.3%
11	Louisiana	9,572	2.8%
12	Missouri	9,455	2.8%
13	Alabama	9,406	2.8%
14	Tennessee	8,605	2.5%
15	South Carolina	8,561	2.5%
16	Virginia	8,346	2.5%
17	Indiana	8,094	2.4%
18	Mississippi	7,171	2.1%
19	Maryland	7,035	2.1%
20	Wisconsin	5,869	1.7%
21	New Jersey	5,722	1.7%
22	Oklahoma	5,228	1.5%
23	Arizona	4,951	1.5%
24	Arkansas	4,476	1.3%
25	Washington	3,739	1.1%
26	Minnesota	3,482	1.0%
27	Colorado	3,224	0.9%
28	Kentucky	2,935	0.9%
29	Nevada	2,880	0.8%
30	Connecticut	2,750	0.8%
31	Kansas	2,605	0.8%
32	Massachusetts	2,537	0.7%
33	Iowa	1,606	0.5%
34	Oregon	1,562	0.5%
35	New Mexico	1,552	0.5%
36	Nebraska	1,158	0.3%
37	Hawaii	1,024	0.3%
38	Delaware	913	0.3%
39	West Virginia	770	0.2%
40	Utah	727	0.2%
41	Alaska	600	0.2%
42	Rhode Island	438	0.1%
43	South Dakota	351	0.1%
44	New Hampshire	177	0.1%
45	Montana	158	0.0%
46	Maine	142	0.0%
47	North Dakota	128	0.0%
48	Idaho	119	0.0%
49	Wyoming	87	0.0%
50	Vermont	60	0.0%
	District of Columbia	2,146	0.6%

Source: U.S. Department of Health and Human Services, National Center for Health Statistics
   "Sexually Transmitted Disease Surveillance 2005" (http://www.cdc.gov/std/stats/TOC2005.htm)
*Gonorrhea is a sexually transmitted disease caused by gonococcal bacteria that affects the mucous membrane chiefly of the genital and urinary tracts and is characterized by an acute purulent discharge and painful or difficult urination, though women often have no symptoms.

Gonorrhea Rate in 2005

National Rate = 115.6 Cases per 100,000 Population*

ALPHA ORDER				RANK ORDER		
RANK	STATE	RATE		RANK	STATE	RATE
3	Alabama	207.6		1	Mississippi	247.0
25	Alaska	91.5		2	Louisiana	212.0
27	Arizona	86.2		3	Alabama	207.6
10	Arkansas	162.6		4	South Carolina	203.9
22	California	95.7		5	Ohio	183.1
32	Colorado	70.1		6	Georgia	179.6
30	Connecticut	78.5		7	North Carolina	176.5
20	Delaware	110.0		8	Michigan	174.9
17	Florida	116.3		9	Missouri	164.3
6	Georgia	179.6		10	Arkansas	162.6
29	Hawaii	81.1		11	Illinois	157.5
50	Idaho	8.5		12	Oklahoma	148.4
11	Illinois	157.5		13	Tennessee	145.8
14	Indiana	129.8		14	Indiana	129.8
37	Iowa	54.4		15	Maryland	126.6
23	Kansas	95.2		16	Nevada	123.4
31	Kentucky	70.8		17	Florida	116.3
2	Louisiana	212.0		18	Texas	116.1
48	Maine	10.8		19	Virginia	111.9
15	Maryland	126.6		20	Delaware	110.0
42	Massachusetts	39.5		21	Wisconsin	106.5
8	Michigan	174.9		22	California	95.7
33	Minnesota	68.3		23	Kansas	95.2
1	Mississippi	247.0		24	New York	92.1
9	Missouri	164.3		25	Alaska	91.5
46	Montana	17.0		26	Pennsylvania	90.5
34	Nebraska	66.3		27	Arizona	86.2
16	Nevada	123.4		28	New Mexico	81.5
47	New Hampshire	13.6		29	Hawaii	81.1
35	New Jersey	65.8		30	Connecticut	78.5
28	New Mexico	81.5		31	Kentucky	70.8
24	New York	92.1		32	Colorado	70.1
7	North Carolina	176.5		33	Minnesota	68.3
44	North Dakota	20.2		34	Nebraska	66.3
5	Ohio	183.1		35	New Jersey	65.8
12	Oklahoma	148.4		36	Washington	60.3
39	Oregon	43.5		37	Iowa	54.4
26	Pennsylvania	90.5		38	South Dakota	45.5
41	Rhode Island	40.5		39	Oregon	43.5
4	South Carolina	203.9		40	West Virginia	42.4
38	South Dakota	45.5		41	Rhode Island	40.5
13	Tennessee	145.8		42	Massachusetts	39.5
18	Texas	116.1		43	Utah	30.4
43	Utah	30.4		44	North Dakota	20.2
49	Vermont	9.7		45	Wyoming	17.2
19	Virginia	111.9		46	Montana	17.0
36	Washington	60.3		47	New Hampshire	13.6
40	West Virginia	42.4		48	Maine	10.8
21	Wisconsin	106.5		49	Vermont	9.7
45	Wyoming	17.2		50	Idaho	8.5
				District of Columbia		368.7

Source: U.S. Department of Health and Human Services, National Center for Health Statistics
   "Sexually Transmitted Disease Surveillance 2005" (http://www.cdc.gov/std/stats/TOC2005.htm)
*Gonorrhea is a sexually transmitted disease caused by gonococcal bacteria that affects the mucous membrane chiefly of the genital and urinary tracts and is characterized by an acute purulent discharge and painful or difficult urination, though women often have no symptoms.

Syphilis Cases Reported in 2005

National Total = 8,724 Cases*

ALPHA ORDER

RANK	STATE	CASES	% of USA
14	Alabama	169	2.0%
41	Alaska	9	0.1%
13	Arizona	175	2.1%
27	Arkansas	52	0.6%
1	California	1,585	19.2%
30	Colorado	46	0.6%
25	Connecticut	58	0.7%
38	Delaware	11	0.1%
3	Florida	724	8.8%
5	Georgia	645	7.8%
38	Hawaii	11	0.1%
35	Idaho	20	0.2%
6	Illinois	525	6.3%
24	Indiana	62	0.7%
41	Iowa	9	0.1%
36	Kansas	19	0.2%
27	Kentucky	52	0.6%
8	Louisiana	278	3.4%
47	Maine	1	0.0%
7	Maryland	313	3.8%
19	Massachusetts	125	1.5%
21	Michigan	105	1.3%
23	Minnesota	70	0.8%
29	Mississippi	49	0.6%
16	Missouri	147	1.8%
43	Montana	7	0.1%
44	Nebraska	4	0.0%
20	Nevada	109	1.3%
37	New Hampshire	16	0.2%
18	New Jersey	133	1.6%
26	New Mexico	56	0.7%
4	New York	705	8.5%
9	North Carolina	274	3.3%
47	North Dakota	1	0.0%
11	Ohio	211	2.6%
31	Oklahoma	44	0.5%
32	Oregon	41	0.5%
12	Pennsylvania	199	2.4%
34	Rhode Island	24	0.3%
22	South Carolina	84	1.0%
46	South Dakota	2	0.0%
10	Tennessee	217	2.6%
2	Texas	873	10.6%
40	Utah	10	0.1%
47	Vermont	1	0.0%
17	Virginia	143	1.7%
15	Washington	152	1.8%
45	West Virginia	3	0.0%
32	Wisconsin	41	0.5%
50	Wyoming	0	0.0%

RANK ORDER

RANK	STATE	CASES	% of USA
1	California	1,585	19.2%
2	Texas	873	10.6%
3	Florida	724	8.8%
4	New York	705	8.5%
5	Georgia	645	7.8%
6	Illinois	525	6.3%
7	Maryland	313	3.8%
8	Louisiana	278	3.4%
9	North Carolina	274	3.3%
10	Tennessee	217	2.6%
11	Ohio	211	2.6%
12	Pennsylvania	199	2.4%
13	Arizona	175	2.1%
14	Alabama	169	2.0%
15	Washington	152	1.8%
16	Missouri	147	1.8%
17	Virginia	143	1.7%
18	New Jersey	133	1.6%
19	Massachusetts	125	1.5%
20	Nevada	109	1.3%
21	Michigan	105	1.3%
22	South Carolina	84	1.0%
23	Minnesota	70	0.8%
24	Indiana	62	0.7%
25	Connecticut	58	0.7%
26	New Mexico	56	0.7%
27	Arkansas	52	0.6%
27	Kentucky	52	0.6%
29	Mississippi	49	0.6%
30	Colorado	46	0.6%
31	Oklahoma	44	0.5%
32	Oregon	41	0.5%
32	Wisconsin	41	0.5%
34	Rhode Island	24	0.3%
35	Idaho	20	0.2%
36	Kansas	19	0.2%
37	New Hampshire	16	0.2%
38	Delaware	11	0.1%
38	Hawaii	11	0.1%
40	Utah	10	0.1%
41	Alaska	9	0.1%
41	Iowa	9	0.1%
43	Montana	7	0.1%
44	Nebraska	4	0.0%
45	West Virginia	3	0.0%
46	South Dakota	2	0.0%
47	Maine	1	0.0%
47	North Dakota	1	0.0%
47	Vermont	1	0.0%
50	Wyoming	0	0.0%
	District of Columbia	114	1.4%

Source: U.S. Department of Health and Human Services, National Center for Health Statistics
"Sexually Transmitted Disease Surveillance 2005" (http://www.cdc.gov/std/stats/TOC2005.htm)
*Includes only primary and secondary cases. Does not include 24,554 cases in other stages. A chronic infectious disease caused by a spirochete (Treponema pallidum), either transmitted by direct contact, usually in sexual intercourse, or passed from mother to child in utero, and progressing through three stages characterized respectively by local formation of chancres, ulcerous skin eruptions, and systemic infection leading to general paresis.

Syphilis Rate in 2005

National Rate = 3.0 Cases per 100,000 Population*

ALPHA ORDER

RANK	STATE	RATE
9	Alabama	3.7
27	Alaska	1.4
13	Arizona	3.0
19	Arkansas	1.9
5	California	4.4
35	Colorado	1.0
23	Connecticut	1.7
30	Delaware	1.3
6	Florida	4.2
1	Georgia	7.3
38	Hawaii	0.9
27	Idaho	1.4
7	Illinois	4.1
35	Indiana	1.0
43	Iowa	0.3
40	Kansas	0.7
30	Kentucky	1.3
2	Louisiana	6.2
49	Maine	0.1
3	Maryland	5.6
19	Massachusetts	1.9
35	Michigan	1.0
27	Minnesota	1.4
23	Mississippi	1.7
15	Missouri	2.6
39	Montana	0.8
45	Nebraska	0.2
4	Nevada	4.7
32	New Hampshire	1.2
26	New Jersey	1.5
14	New Mexico	2.9
9	New York	3.7
12	North Carolina	3.2
45	North Dakota	0.2
22	Ohio	1.8
32	Oklahoma	1.2
34	Oregon	1.1
25	Pennsylvania	1.6
17	Rhode Island	2.2
18	South Carolina	2.0
43	South Dakota	0.3
9	Tennessee	3.7
8	Texas	3.9
42	Utah	0.4
45	Vermont	0.2
19	Virginia	1.9
16	Washington	2.5
45	West Virginia	0.2
40	Wisconsin	0.7
50	Wyoming	0.0

RANK ORDER

RANK	STATE	RATE
1	Georgia	7.3
2	Louisiana	6.2
3	Maryland	5.6
4	Nevada	4.7
5	California	4.4
6	Florida	4.2
7	Illinois	4.1
8	Texas	3.9
9	Alabama	3.7
9	New York	3.7
9	Tennessee	3.7
12	North Carolina	3.2
13	Arizona	3.0
14	New Mexico	2.9
15	Missouri	2.6
16	Washington	2.5
17	Rhode Island	2.2
18	South Carolina	2.0
19	Arkansas	1.9
19	Massachusetts	1.9
19	Virginia	1.9
22	Ohio	1.8
23	Connecticut	1.7
23	Mississippi	1.7
25	Pennsylvania	1.6
26	New Jersey	1.5
27	Alaska	1.4
27	Idaho	1.4
27	Minnesota	1.4
30	Delaware	1.3
30	Kentucky	1.3
32	New Hampshire	1.2
32	Oklahoma	1.2
34	Oregon	1.1
35	Colorado	1.0
35	Indiana	1.0
35	Michigan	1.0
38	Hawaii	0.9
39	Montana	0.8
40	Kansas	0.7
40	Wisconsin	0.7
42	Utah	0.4
43	Iowa	0.3
43	South Dakota	0.3
45	Nebraska	0.2
45	North Dakota	0.2
45	Vermont	0.2
45	West Virginia	0.2
49	Maine	0.1
50	Wyoming	0.0

| | District of Columbia | 19.6 |

Source: U.S. Department of Health and Human Services, National Center for Health Statistics
"Sexually Transmitted Disease Surveillance 2005" (http://www.cdc.gov/std/stats/TOC2005.htm)
*Includes only primary and secondary cases. Does not include 24,554 cases in other stages. A chronic infectious disease caused by a spirochete (Treponema pallidum), either transmitted by direct contact, usually in sexual intercourse, or passed from mother to child in utero, and progressing through three stages characterized respectively by local formation of chancres, ulcerous skin eruptions, and systemic infection leading to general paresis.

Percent of Adults Who Have Asthma: 2005

National Median = 8.0% of Adults*

ALPHA ORDER

RANK	STATE	PERCENT
41	Alabama	7.1
27	Alaska	7.8
33	Arizona	7.4
30	Arkansas	7.5
38	California	7.2
20	Colorado	8.2
23	Connecticut	8.0
16	Delaware	8.5
45	Florida	6.8
34	Georgia	7.3
30	Hawaii	7.5
34	Idaho	7.3
43	Illinois	7.0
20	Indiana	8.2
38	Iowa	7.2
44	Kansas	6.9
14	Kentucky	8.8
50	Louisiana	5.9
3	Maine	10.2
19	Maryland	8.3
6	Massachusetts	9.6
11	Michigan	9.1
18	Minnesota	8.4
38	Mississippi	7.2
12	Missouri	9.0
26	Montana	7.9
47	Nebraska	6.7
41	Nevada	7.1
2	New Hampshire	10.3
30	New Jersey	7.5
13	New Mexico	8.9
7	New York	9.3
49	North Carolina	6.5
34	North Dakota	7.3
23	Ohio	8.0
16	Oklahoma	8.5
4	Oregon	10.1
22	Pennsylvania	8.1
1	Rhode Island	10.7
48	South Carolina	6.6
34	South Dakota	7.3
29	Tennessee	7.7
45	Texas	6.8
23	Utah	8.0
5	Vermont	9.8
15	Virginia	8.7
8	Washington	9.2
8	West Virginia	9.2
8	Wisconsin	9.2
27	Wyoming	7.8

RANK ORDER

RANK	STATE	PERCENT
1	Rhode Island	10.7
2	New Hampshire	10.3
3	Maine	10.2
4	Oregon	10.1
5	Vermont	9.8
6	Massachusetts	9.6
7	New York	9.3
8	Washington	9.2
8	West Virginia	9.2
8	Wisconsin	9.2
11	Michigan	9.1
12	Missouri	9.0
13	New Mexico	8.9
14	Kentucky	8.8
15	Virginia	8.7
16	Delaware	8.5
16	Oklahoma	8.5
18	Minnesota	8.4
19	Maryland	8.3
20	Colorado	8.2
20	Indiana	8.2
22	Pennsylvania	8.1
23	Connecticut	8.0
23	Ohio	8.0
23	Utah	8.0
26	Montana	7.9
27	Alaska	7.8
27	Wyoming	7.8
29	Tennessee	7.7
30	Arkansas	7.5
30	Hawaii	7.5
30	New Jersey	7.5
33	Arizona	7.4
34	Georgia	7.3
34	Idaho	7.3
34	North Dakota	7.3
34	South Dakota	7.3
38	California	7.2
38	Iowa	7.2
38	Mississippi	7.2
41	Alabama	7.1
41	Nevada	7.1
43	Illinois	7.0
44	Kansas	6.9
45	Florida	6.8
45	Texas	6.8
47	Nebraska	6.7
48	South Carolina	6.6
49	North Carolina	6.5
50	Louisiana	5.9

| | District of Columbia | 9.2 |

Source: U.S. Department of Health and Human Services, Centers for Disease Control and Prevention
"2005 Behavioral Risk Factor Surveillance Summary Prevalence Data" (http://apps.nccd.cdc.gov/brfss/)
*Percent of adults who answered yes to the questions "Have you ever been told by a doctor, nurse or other health professional that you had asthma?" and "Do you still have asthma?"

Percent of Children Who Have Asthma: 2005

National Percent = 8.6% of Children*

ALPHA ORDER

RANK	STATE	PERCENT
17	Alabama	8.7
NA	Alaska**	NA
34	Arizona	7.7
23	Arkansas	8.5
38	California	7.1
23	Colorado	8.5
9	Connecticut	9.9
14	Delaware	8.8
13	Florida	8.9
31	Georgia	7.9
2	Hawaii	10.9
NA	Idaho**	NA
12	Illinois	9.0
25	Indiana	8.4
38	Iowa	7.1
14	Kansas	8.8
6	Kentucky	10.4
27	Louisiana	8.3
NA	Maine**	NA
3	Maryland	10.8
1	Massachusetts	12.1
11	Michigan	9.4
33	Minnesota	7.8
25	Mississippi	8.4
20	Missouri	8.6
NA	Montana**	NA
17	Nebraska	8.7
40	Nevada	4.4
35	New Hampshire	7.5
14	New Jersey	8.8
20	New Mexico	8.6
7	New York	10.2
28	North Carolina	8.1
NA	North Dakota**	NA
7	Ohio	10.2
3	Oklahoma	10.8
28	Oregon	8.1
9	Pennsylvania	9.9
5	Rhode Island	10.5
28	South Carolina	8.1
NA	South Dakota**	NA
37	Tennessee	7.3
31	Texas	7.9
40	Utah	4.4
NA	Vermont**	NA
17	Virginia	8.7
36	Washington	7.4
NA	West Virginia**	NA
20	Wisconsin	8.6
NA	Wyoming**	NA

RANK ORDER

RANK	STATE	PERCENT
1	Massachusetts	12.1
2	Hawaii	10.9
3	Maryland	10.8
3	Oklahoma	10.8
5	Rhode Island	10.5
6	Kentucky	10.4
7	New York	10.2
7	Ohio	10.2
9	Connecticut	9.9
9	Pennsylvania	9.9
11	Michigan	9.4
12	Illinois	9.0
13	Florida	8.9
14	Delaware	8.8
14	Kansas	8.8
14	New Jersey	8.8
17	Alabama	8.7
17	Nebraska	8.7
17	Virginia	8.7
20	Missouri	8.6
20	New Mexico	8.6
20	Wisconsin	8.6
23	Arkansas	8.5
23	Colorado	8.5
25	Indiana	8.4
25	Mississippi	8.4
27	Louisiana	8.3
28	North Carolina	8.1
28	Oregon	8.1
28	South Carolina	8.1
31	Georgia	7.9
31	Texas	7.9
33	Minnesota	7.8
34	Arizona	7.7
35	New Hampshire	7.5
36	Washington	7.4
37	Tennessee	7.3
38	California	7.1
38	Iowa	7.1
40	Nevada	4.4
40	Utah	4.4
NA	Alaska**	NA
NA	Idaho**	NA
NA	Maine**	NA
NA	Montana**	NA
NA	North Dakota**	NA
NA	South Dakota**	NA
NA	Vermont**	NA
NA	West Virginia**	NA
NA	Wyoming**	NA

District of Columbia   10.3

Source: U.S. Department of Health and Human Services, National Center for Health Statistics
"The State of Childhood Asthma, United States, 1980-2005" (Advance Data No. 381, December 12, 2006)
*Annual average for period 2001-2005. Figures reflect prevalence among children 0-17 years of age.
**Insufficient sample size for reliable data.

Percent of Adults Who Have Been Told They Have Arthritis: 2005

National Median = 27.0%*

<table>
<tr><td colspan="3">ALPHA ORDER</td><td colspan="3">RANK ORDER</td></tr>
<tr><td>RANK</td><td>STATE</td><td>PERCENT</td><td>RANK</td><td>STATE</td><td>PERCENT</td></tr>
<tr><td>2</td><td>Alabama</td><td>32.9</td><td>1</td><td>West Virginia</td><td>34.9</td></tr>
<tr><td>46</td><td>Alaska</td><td>23.2</td><td>2</td><td>Alabama</td><td>32.9</td></tr>
<tr><td>32</td><td>Arizona</td><td>26.1</td><td>3</td><td>Mississippi</td><td>32.1</td></tr>
<tr><td>8</td><td>Arkansas</td><td>30.7</td><td>3</td><td>Missouri</td><td>32.1</td></tr>
<tr><td>48</td><td>California</td><td>22.3</td><td>5</td><td>Pennsylvania</td><td>31.7</td></tr>
<tr><td>45</td><td>Colorado</td><td>23.3</td><td>6</td><td>Michigan</td><td>30.8</td></tr>
<tr><td>38</td><td>Connecticut</td><td>25.5</td><td>6</td><td>South Carolina</td><td>30.8</td></tr>
<tr><td>14</td><td>Delaware</td><td>29.2</td><td>8</td><td>Arkansas</td><td>30.7</td></tr>
<tr><td>21</td><td>Florida</td><td>27.4</td><td>9</td><td>Maine</td><td>30.5</td></tr>
<tr><td>37</td><td>Georgia</td><td>25.8</td><td>10</td><td>Oklahoma</td><td>30.3</td></tr>
<tr><td>50</td><td>Hawaii</td><td>22.1</td><td>11</td><td>Ohio</td><td>30.1</td></tr>
<tr><td>38</td><td>Idaho</td><td>25.5</td><td>12</td><td>Tennessee</td><td>29.7</td></tr>
<tr><td>42</td><td>Illinois</td><td>24.8</td><td>13</td><td>Indiana</td><td>29.3</td></tr>
<tr><td>13</td><td>Indiana</td><td>29.3</td><td>14</td><td>Delaware</td><td>29.2</td></tr>
<tr><td>21</td><td>Iowa</td><td>27.4</td><td>15</td><td>Kentucky</td><td>28.8</td></tr>
<tr><td>27</td><td>Kansas</td><td>26.9</td><td>16</td><td>Rhode Island</td><td>28.2</td></tr>
<tr><td>15</td><td>Kentucky</td><td>28.8</td><td>17</td><td>South Dakota</td><td>27.9</td></tr>
<tr><td>29</td><td>Louisiana</td><td>26.7</td><td>18</td><td>Wisconsin</td><td>27.7</td></tr>
<tr><td>9</td><td>Maine</td><td>30.5</td><td>19</td><td>Virginia</td><td>27.6</td></tr>
<tr><td>20</td><td>Maryland</td><td>27.5</td><td>20</td><td>Maryland</td><td>27.5</td></tr>
<tr><td>36</td><td>Massachusetts</td><td>25.9</td><td>21</td><td>Florida</td><td>27.4</td></tr>
<tr><td>6</td><td>Michigan</td><td>30.8</td><td>21</td><td>Iowa</td><td>27.4</td></tr>
<tr><td>38</td><td>Minnesota</td><td>25.5</td><td>21</td><td>Vermont</td><td>27.4</td></tr>
<tr><td>3</td><td>Mississippi</td><td>32.1</td><td>21</td><td>Wyoming</td><td>27.4</td></tr>
<tr><td>3</td><td>Missouri</td><td>32.1</td><td>25</td><td>North Carolina</td><td>27.3</td></tr>
<tr><td>30</td><td>Montana</td><td>26.4</td><td>26</td><td>Oregon</td><td>27.0</td></tr>
<tr><td>32</td><td>Nebraska</td><td>26.1</td><td>27</td><td>Kansas</td><td>26.9</td></tr>
<tr><td>41</td><td>Nevada</td><td>25.1</td><td>27</td><td>New Hampshire</td><td>26.9</td></tr>
<tr><td>27</td><td>New Hampshire</td><td>26.9</td><td>29</td><td>Louisiana</td><td>26.7</td></tr>
<tr><td>43</td><td>New Jersey</td><td>24.4</td><td>30</td><td>Montana</td><td>26.4</td></tr>
<tr><td>43</td><td>New Mexico</td><td>24.4</td><td>31</td><td>Washington</td><td>26.2</td></tr>
<tr><td>32</td><td>New York</td><td>26.1</td><td>32</td><td>Arizona</td><td>26.1</td></tr>
<tr><td>25</td><td>North Carolina</td><td>27.3</td><td>32</td><td>Nebraska</td><td>26.1</td></tr>
<tr><td>35</td><td>North Dakota</td><td>26.0</td><td>32</td><td>New York</td><td>26.1</td></tr>
<tr><td>11</td><td>Ohio</td><td>30.1</td><td>35</td><td>North Dakota</td><td>26.0</td></tr>
<tr><td>10</td><td>Oklahoma</td><td>30.3</td><td>36</td><td>Massachusetts</td><td>25.9</td></tr>
<tr><td>26</td><td>Oregon</td><td>27.0</td><td>37</td><td>Georgia</td><td>25.8</td></tr>
<tr><td>5</td><td>Pennsylvania</td><td>31.7</td><td>38</td><td>Connecticut</td><td>25.5</td></tr>
<tr><td>16</td><td>Rhode Island</td><td>28.2</td><td>38</td><td>Idaho</td><td>25.5</td></tr>
<tr><td>6</td><td>South Carolina</td><td>30.8</td><td>38</td><td>Minnesota</td><td>25.5</td></tr>
<tr><td>17</td><td>South Dakota</td><td>27.9</td><td>41</td><td>Nevada</td><td>25.1</td></tr>
<tr><td>12</td><td>Tennessee</td><td>29.7</td><td>42</td><td>Illinois</td><td>24.8</td></tr>
<tr><td>48</td><td>Texas</td><td>22.3</td><td>43</td><td>New Jersey</td><td>24.4</td></tr>
<tr><td>47</td><td>Utah</td><td>22.7</td><td>43</td><td>New Mexico</td><td>24.4</td></tr>
<tr><td>21</td><td>Vermont</td><td>27.4</td><td>45</td><td>Colorado</td><td>23.3</td></tr>
<tr><td>19</td><td>Virginia</td><td>27.6</td><td>46</td><td>Alaska</td><td>23.2</td></tr>
<tr><td>31</td><td>Washington</td><td>26.2</td><td>47</td><td>Utah</td><td>22.7</td></tr>
<tr><td>1</td><td>West Virginia</td><td>34.9</td><td>48</td><td>California</td><td>22.3</td></tr>
<tr><td>18</td><td>Wisconsin</td><td>27.7</td><td>48</td><td>Texas</td><td>22.3</td></tr>
<tr><td>21</td><td>Wyoming</td><td>27.4</td><td>50</td><td>Hawaii</td><td>22.1</td></tr>
<tr><td></td><td></td><td></td><td></td><td>District of Columbia</td><td>22.4</td></tr>
</table>

Source: U.S. Department of Health and Human Services, Centers for Disease Control and Prevention
   "2005 Behavioral Risk Factor Surveillance Summary Prevalence Data" (http://apps.nccd.cdc.gov/brfss/)
*Of population 18 years old and older.

Percent of Adults Who Have Been Told They Have Diabetes: 2005

National Median = 7.3% of Adults*

ALPHA ORDER

RANK	STATE	PERCENT
3	Alabama	9.8
50	Alaska	4.4
23	Arizona	7.5
14	Arkansas	8.1
29	California	7.1
49	Colorado	4.8
38	Connecticut	6.5
10	Delaware	8.6
9	Florida	8.8
12	Georgia	8.3
25	Hawaii	7.3
33	Idaho	6.8
18	Illinois	7.9
12	Indiana	8.3
33	Iowa	6.8
31	Kansas	6.9
7	Kentucky	8.9
5	Louisiana	9.2
23	Maine	7.5
28	Maryland	7.2
41	Massachusetts	6.4
14	Michigan	8.1
46	Minnesota	5.8
3	Mississippi	9.8
20	Missouri	7.7
47	Montana	5.7
25	Nebraska	7.3
29	Nevada	7.1
38	New Hampshire	6.5
20	New Jersey	7.7
25	New Mexico	7.3
14	New York	8.1
11	North Carolina	8.5
35	North Dakota	6.7
20	Ohio	7.7
7	Oklahoma	8.9
35	Oregon	6.7
14	Pennsylvania	8.1
41	Rhode Island	6.4
2	South Carolina	10.3
41	South Dakota	6.4
6	Tennessee	9.1
18	Texas	7.9
48	Utah	5.5
45	Vermont	6.0
31	Virginia	6.9
44	Washington	6.3
1	West Virginia	10.4
37	Wisconsin	6.6
38	Wyoming	6.5

RANK ORDER

RANK	STATE	PERCENT
1	West Virginia	10.4
2	South Carolina	10.3
3	Alabama	9.8
3	Mississippi	9.8
5	Louisiana	9.2
6	Tennessee	9.1
7	Kentucky	8.9
7	Oklahoma	8.9
9	Florida	8.8
10	Delaware	8.6
11	North Carolina	8.5
12	Georgia	8.3
12	Indiana	8.3
14	Arkansas	8.1
14	Michigan	8.1
14	New York	8.1
14	Pennsylvania	8.1
18	Illinois	7.9
18	Texas	7.9
20	Missouri	7.7
20	New Jersey	7.7
20	Ohio	7.7
23	Arizona	7.5
23	Maine	7.5
25	Hawaii	7.3
25	Nebraska	7.3
25	New Mexico	7.3
28	Maryland	7.2
29	California	7.1
29	Nevada	7.1
31	Kansas	6.9
31	Virginia	6.9
33	Idaho	6.8
33	Iowa	6.8
35	North Dakota	6.7
35	Oregon	6.7
37	Wisconsin	6.6
38	Connecticut	6.5
38	New Hampshire	6.5
38	Wyoming	6.5
41	Massachusetts	6.4
41	Rhode Island	6.4
41	South Dakota	6.4
44	Washington	6.3
45	Vermont	6.0
46	Minnesota	5.8
47	Montana	5.7
48	Utah	5.5
49	Colorado	4.8
50	Alaska	4.4

	District of Columbia	7.1

*Source: U.S. Department of Health and Human Services, Centers for Disease Control and Prevention
"2005 Behavioral Risk Factor Surveillance Summary Prevalence Data" (http://apps.nccd.cdc.gov/brfss/)
Of population 18 years old and older. Does not include pregnancy-related diabetes.

Percent of Adults Reporting Serious Psychological Distress: 2004

National Percent = 9.6% of Population*

ALPHA ORDER

RANK	STATE	PERCENT
40	Alabama	8.8
40	Alaska	8.8
6	Arizona	11.3
22	Arkansas	9.9
32	California	9.3
17	Colorado	10.1
35	Connecticut	9.0
23	Delaware	9.8
35	Florida	9.0
10	Georgia	10.8
50	Hawaii	7.1
11	Idaho	10.7
38	Illinois	8.9
14	Indiana	10.3
30	Iowa	9.4
27	Kansas	9.7
4	Kentucky	11.7
23	Louisiana	9.8
12	Maine	10.5
44	Maryland	8.7
40	Massachusetts	8.8
34	Michigan	9.2
44	Minnesota	8.7
28	Mississippi	9.6
5	Missouri	11.5
35	Montana	9.0
47	Nebraska	8.6
14	Nevada	10.3
30	New Hampshire	9.4
32	New Jersey	9.3
12	New Mexico	10.5
29	New York	9.5
20	North Carolina	10.0
23	North Dakota	9.8
17	Ohio	10.1
8	Oklahoma	10.9
20	Oregon	10.0
48	Pennsylvania	8.5
2	Rhode Island	12.2
17	South Carolina	10.1
49	South Dakota	8.3
14	Tennessee	10.3
23	Texas	9.8
3	Utah	12.0
38	Vermont	8.9
40	Virginia	8.8
8	Washington	10.9
1	West Virginia	12.7
44	Wisconsin	8.7
7	Wyoming	11.1

RANK ORDER

RANK	STATE	PERCENT
1	West Virginia	12.7
2	Rhode Island	12.2
3	Utah	12.0
4	Kentucky	11.7
5	Missouri	11.5
6	Arizona	11.3
7	Wyoming	11.1
8	Oklahoma	10.9
8	Washington	10.9
10	Georgia	10.8
11	Idaho	10.7
12	Maine	10.5
12	New Mexico	10.5
14	Indiana	10.3
14	Nevada	10.3
14	Tennessee	10.3
17	Colorado	10.1
17	Ohio	10.1
17	South Carolina	10.1
20	North Carolina	10.0
20	Oregon	10.0
22	Arkansas	9.9
23	Delaware	9.8
23	Louisiana	9.8
23	North Dakota	9.8
23	Texas	9.8
27	Kansas	9.7
28	Mississippi	9.6
29	New York	9.5
30	Iowa	9.4
30	New Hampshire	9.4
32	California	9.3
32	New Jersey	9.3
34	Michigan	9.2
35	Connecticut	9.0
35	Florida	9.0
35	Montana	9.0
38	Illinois	8.9
38	Vermont	8.9
40	Alabama	8.8
40	Alaska	8.8
40	Massachusetts	8.8
40	Virginia	8.8
44	Maryland	8.7
44	Minnesota	8.7
44	Wisconsin	8.7
47	Nebraska	8.6
48	Pennsylvania	8.5
49	South Dakota	8.3
50	Hawaii	7.1

District of Columbia 9.8

Source: U.S. Department of Health and Human Services, Substance Abuse and Mental Health Services Administration "2003-2004 National Surveys on Drug Use and Health" (September 2005)
Population 18 years and older. Serious psychological distress was previously referred to as serious mental illness. It is defined as having a diagnosable mental, behavioral or emotional disorder that resulted in functional impairment that substantially interfered with or limited one or more major life activities.

VI. PROVIDERS

398   Health Care Practitioners and Technicians in 2005
399   Rate of Health Care Practitioners and Technicians in 2005
400   Average Annual Wages of Health Care Practitioners and Technicians in 2005
401   Physicians in 2005
402   Rate of Physicians in 2005
403   Percent of Physicians Who Are Female: 2005
404   Percent of Physicians Under 35 Years Old in 2005
405   Percent of Physicians 65 Years Old and Older in 2005
406   Physicians in Patient Care in 2005
407   Rate of Physicians in Patient Care in 2005
408   Physicians in Primary Care in 2005
409   Rate of Physicians in Primary Care in 2005
410   Percent of Physicians in Primary Care in 2005
411   Percent of Population Lacking Access to Primary Care in 2006
412   Physicians in General/Family Practice in 2005
413   Rate of Physicians in General/Family Practice in 2005
414   Average Annual Wages of Family and General Practitioners in 2005
415   Percent of Physicians Who Are Specialists in 2005
416   Physicians in Medical Specialties in 2005
417   Rate of Nonfederal Physicians in Medical Specialties in 2005
418   Physicians in Internal Medicine in 2005
419   Rate of Physicians in Internal Medicine in 2005
420   Physicians in Pediatrics in 2005
421   Rate of Physicians in Pediatrics in 2005
422   Physicians in Surgical Specialties in 2005
423   Rate of Physicians in Surgical Specialties in 2005
424   Average Annual Wages of Surgeons in 2005
425   Physicians in General Surgery in 2005
426   Rate of Physicians in General Surgery in 2005
427   Physicians in Obstetrics and Gynecology in 2005
428   Rate of Physicians in Obstetrics and Gynecology in 2005
429   Physicians in Ophthalmology in 2005
430   Rate of Physicians in Ophthalmology in 2005
431   Physicians in Orthopedic Surgery in 2005
432   Rate of Physicians in Orthopedic Surgery in 2005
433   Physicians in Plastic Surgery in 2005
434   Rate of Physicians in Plastic Surgery in 2005
435   Physicians in Other Specialties in 2005
436   Rate of Physicians in Other Specialties in 2005
437   Physicians in Anesthesiology in 2005
438   Rate of Physicians in Anesthesiology in 2005
439   Physicians in Psychiatry in 2005
440   Rate of Physicians in Psychiatry in 2005
441   Percent of Population Lacking Access to Mental Health Care in 2006
442   International Medical School Graduates in 2005
443   International Medical School Graduates as a Percent of Physicians in 2005
444   Osteopathic Physicians in 2006
445   Rate of Osteopathic Physicians in 2006
446   Podiatrists in 2005
447   Rate of Podiatrists in 2005
448   Average Annual Wages of Podiatrists in 2005
449   Doctors of Chiropractic in 2005
450   Rate of Doctors of Chiropractic in 2005
451   Average Annual Wages of Chiropractors in 2005
452   Physician Assistants in Clinical Practice in 2007
453   Rate of Physician Assistants in Clinical Practice in 2007
454   Average Annual Wages of Physician Assistants in 2005
455   Registered Nurses in 2005
456   Rate of Registered Nurses in 2005
457   Average Annual Wages of Registered Nurses in 2005
458   Licensed Practical and Licensed Vocational Nurses in 2005

VI. PROVIDERS (continued)

459   Rate of Licensed Practical and Licensed Vocational Nurses in 2005
460   Average Annual Wages of Licensed Practical and Licensed Vocational Nurses in 2005
461   Physical Therapists in 2005
462   Rate of Physical Therapists in 2005
463   Average Annual Wages of Physical Therapists in 2005
464   Dentists in 2004
465   Rate of Dentists in 2004
466   Average Annual Wages of Dentists in 2005
467   Percent of Population Lacking Access to Dental Care in 2006
468   Pharmacists in 2005
469   Rate of Pharmacists in 2005
470   Average Annual Wages of Pharmacists in 2005
471   Optometrists in 2005
472   Rate of Optometrists in 2005
473   Average Annual Wages of Optometrists in 2005
474   Emergency Medical Technicians and Paramedics in 2005
475   Rate of Emergency Medical Technicians and Paramedics in 2005
476   Average Annual Wages of Emergency Medical Technicians and Paramedics in 2005
477   Employment in Health Care Support Industries in 2005
478   Rate of Employees in Health Care Support Industries in 2005
479   Average Annual Wages of Employees in Health Care Support Industries in 2005

Health Care Practitioners and Technicians in 2005

National Total = 6,435,620 Practitioners and Technicians*

ALPHA ORDER

RANK	STATE	PRACTITIONERS	% of USA
22	Alabama	102,960	1.6%
49	Alaska	12,590	0.2%
24	Arizona	97,960	1.5%
33	Arkansas	61,990	1.0%
1	California	582,750	9.1%
25	Colorado	92,790	1.4%
27	Connecticut	87,360	1.4%
45	Delaware	20,850	0.3%
4	Florida	386,000	6.0%
12	Georgia	175,500	2.7%
43	Hawaii	22,720	0.4%
42	Idaho	26,480	0.4%
6	Illinois	292,500	4.5%
15	Indiana	149,210	2.3%
29	Iowa	70,830	1.1%
31	Kansas	65,610	1.0%
23	Kentucky	98,340	1.5%
21	Louisiana	108,490	1.7%
39	Maine	33,160	0.5%
19	Maryland	127,530	2.0%
10	Massachusetts	190,450	3.0%
8	Michigan	225,230	3.5%
17	Minnesota	136,270	2.1%
32	Mississippi	64,760	1.0%
13	Missouri	153,460	2.4%
46	Montana	20,720	0.3%
35	Nebraska	47,630	0.7%
38	Nevada	37,990	0.6%
40	New Hampshire	30,440	0.5%
9	New Jersey	193,960	3.0%
37	New Mexico	38,060	0.6%
3	New York	430,650	6.7%
11	North Carolina	187,030	2.9%
47	North Dakota	18,010	0.3%
7	Ohio	290,140	4.5%
28	Oklahoma	80,450	1.3%
30	Oregon	69,520	1.1%
5	Pennsylvania	329,350	5.1%
41	Rhode Island	28,140	0.4%
26	South Carolina	88,030	1.4%
44	South Dakota	21,780	0.3%
16	Tennessee	148,880	2.3%
2	Texas	435,490	6.8%
34	Utah	47,710	0.7%
48	Vermont	14,940	0.2%
14	Virginia	153,280	2.4%
20	Washington	123,940	1.9%
36	West Virginia	44,900	0.7%
18	Wisconsin	131,710	2.0%
50	Wyoming	10,280	0.2%

RANK ORDER

RANK	STATE	PRACTITIONERS	% of USA
1	California	582,750	9.1%
2	Texas	435,490	6.8%
3	New York	430,650	6.7%
4	Florida	386,000	6.0%
5	Pennsylvania	329,350	5.1%
6	Illinois	292,500	4.5%
7	Ohio	290,140	4.5%
8	Michigan	225,230	3.5%
9	New Jersey	193,960	3.0%
10	Massachusetts	190,450	3.0%
11	North Carolina	187,030	2.9%
12	Georgia	175,500	2.7%
13	Missouri	153,460	2.4%
14	Virginia	153,280	2.4%
15	Indiana	149,210	2.3%
16	Tennessee	148,880	2.3%
17	Minnesota	136,270	2.1%
18	Wisconsin	131,710	2.0%
19	Maryland	127,530	2.0%
20	Washington	123,940	1.9%
21	Louisiana	108,490	1.7%
22	Alabama	102,960	1.6%
23	Kentucky	98,340	1.5%
24	Arizona	97,960	1.5%
25	Colorado	92,790	1.4%
26	South Carolina	88,030	1.4%
27	Connecticut	87,360	1.4%
28	Oklahoma	80,450	1.3%
29	Iowa	70,830	1.1%
30	Oregon	69,520	1.1%
31	Kansas	65,610	1.0%
32	Mississippi	64,760	1.0%
33	Arkansas	61,990	1.0%
34	Utah	47,710	0.7%
35	Nebraska	47,630	0.7%
36	West Virginia	44,900	0.7%
37	New Mexico	38,060	0.6%
38	Nevada	37,990	0.6%
39	Maine	33,160	0.5%
40	New Hampshire	30,440	0.5%
41	Rhode Island	28,140	0.4%
42	Idaho	26,480	0.4%
43	Hawaii	22,720	0.4%
44	South Dakota	21,780	0.3%
45	Delaware	20,850	0.3%
46	Montana	20,720	0.3%
47	North Dakota	18,010	0.3%
48	Vermont	14,940	0.2%
49	Alaska	12,590	0.2%
50	Wyoming	10,280	0.2%
	District of Columbia	26,930	0.4%

Source: U.S. Department of Labor, Bureau of Labor Statistics
"Occupational Employment and Wages, 2005" (http://www.bls.gov/oes/)
Does not include self-employed. Includes various doctors, dentists, nurses, therapists, optometrists, paramedics and technicians. Does not include assistants and aides listed under health care support occupations.
Veterinarians and veterinarian technicians have been subtracted from the totals.

Rate of Health Care Practitioners and Technicians in 2005

National Rate = 2,170 Practitioners and Technicians per 100,000 Population*

ALPHA ORDER

RANK ORDER

RANK	STATE	RATE		RANK	STATE	RATE
26	Alabama	2,264		1	Massachusetts	2,960
45	Alaska	1,898		2	North Dakota	2,838
48	Arizona	1,646		3	South Dakota	2,811
27	Arkansas	2,233		4	Nebraska	2,709
49	California	1,612		5	Minnesota	2,658
38	Colorado	1,990		6	Pennsylvania	2,655
12	Connecticut	2,496		7	Missouri	2,647
13	Delaware	2,477		8	Rhode Island	2,621
33	Florida	2,172		9	Ohio	2,529
41	Georgia	1,922		10	Maine	2,516
47	Hawaii	1,784		11	Tennessee	2,500
46	Idaho	1,853		12	Connecticut	2,496
23	Illinois	2,291		13	Delaware	2,477
20	Indiana	2,381		14	West Virginia	2,475
17	Iowa	2,388		15	Louisiana	2,407
18	Kansas	2,387		16	Vermont	2,400
21	Kentucky	2,357		17	Iowa	2,388
15	Louisiana	2,407		18	Kansas	2,387
10	Maine	2,516		19	Wisconsin	2,383
24	Maryland	2,282		20	Indiana	2,381
1	Massachusetts	2,960		21	Kentucky	2,357
28	Michigan	2,230		22	New Hampshire	2,329
5	Minnesota	2,658		23	Illinois	2,291
31	Mississippi	2,227		24	Maryland	2,282
7	Missouri	2,647		25	Oklahoma	2,270
32	Montana	2,217		26	Alabama	2,264
4	Nebraska	2,709		27	Arkansas	2,233
50	Nevada	1,575		28	Michigan	2,230
22	New Hampshire	2,329		28	New York	2,230
30	New Jersey	2,229		30	New Jersey	2,229
39	New Mexico	1,976		31	Mississippi	2,227
28	New York	2,230		32	Montana	2,217
34	North Carolina	2,157		33	Florida	2,172
2	North Dakota	2,838		34	North Carolina	2,157
9	Ohio	2,529		35	South Carolina	2,073
25	Oklahoma	2,270		36	Virginia	2,026
43	Oregon	1,910		37	Wyoming	2,020
6	Pennsylvania	2,655		38	Colorado	1,990
8	Rhode Island	2,621		39	New Mexico	1,976
35	South Carolina	2,073		40	Washington	1,970
3	South Dakota	2,811		41	Georgia	1,922
11	Tennessee	2,500		42	Utah	1,916
44	Texas	1,899		43	Oregon	1,910
42	Utah	1,916		44	Texas	1,899
16	Vermont	2,400		45	Alaska	1,898
36	Virginia	2,026		46	Idaho	1,853
40	Washington	1,970		47	Hawaii	1,784
14	West Virginia	2,475		48	Arizona	1,646
19	Wisconsin	2,383		49	California	1,612
37	Wyoming	2,020		50	Nevada	1,575

District of Columbia   4,627

Source: Morgan Quitno Press using data from U.S. Department of Labor, Bureau of Labor Statistics
   "Occupational Employment and Wages, 2005" (http://www.bls.gov/oes/)
*Does not include self-employed. Includes various doctors, dentists, nurses, therapists, optometrists, paramedics
and technicians. Does not include assistants and aides listed under health care support occupations.
Veterinarians and veterinarian technicians have been subtracted from the totals.

Average Annual Wages of Health Care Practitioners and Technicians in 2005

National Average = $59,170*

ALPHA ORDER

RANK	STATE	WAGES
46	Alabama	$49,580
4	Alaska	66,850
18	Arizona	59,820
48	Arkansas	48,490
1	California	69,690
17	Colorado	60,570
6	Connecticut	65,970
14	Delaware	61,920
24	Florida	57,670
29	Georgia	55,530
12	Hawaii	63,510
30	Idaho	55,370
35	Illinois	53,340
37	Indiana	52,710
42	Iowa	50,890
40	Kansas	51,610
43	Kentucky	50,820
44	Louisiana	50,180
19	Maine	59,670
3	Maryland	67,620
9	Massachusetts	64,440
13	Michigan	62,530
11	Minnesota	63,520
47	Mississippi	49,170
38	Missouri	52,660
45	Montana	49,860
34	Nebraska	53,500
7	Nevada	65,830
16	New Hampshire	60,900
2	New Jersey	69,270
27	New Mexico	56,430
8	New York	65,780
28	North Carolina	56,410
49	North Dakota	48,240
20	Ohio	58,830
50	Oklahoma	47,970
5	Oregon	66,060
32	Pennsylvania	55,240
15	Rhode Island	61,650
33	South Carolina	54,850
41	South Dakota	51,420
39	Tennessee	51,850
26	Texas	56,540
25	Utah	56,750
23	Vermont	58,400
21	Virginia	58,680
10	Washington	64,210
36	West Virginia	53,160
22	Wisconsin	58,650
30	Wyoming	55,370

RANK ORDER

RANK	STATE	WAGES
1	California	$69,690
2	New Jersey	69,270
3	Maryland	67,620
4	Alaska	66,850
5	Oregon	66,060
6	Connecticut	65,970
7	Nevada	65,830
8	New York	65,780
9	Massachusetts	64,440
10	Washington	64,210
11	Minnesota	63,520
12	Hawaii	63,510
13	Michigan	62,530
14	Delaware	61,920
15	Rhode Island	61,650
16	New Hampshire	60,900
17	Colorado	60,570
18	Arizona	59,820
19	Maine	59,670
20	Ohio	58,830
21	Virginia	58,680
22	Wisconsin	58,650
23	Vermont	58,400
24	Florida	57,670
25	Utah	56,750
26	Texas	56,540
27	New Mexico	56,430
28	North Carolina	56,410
29	Georgia	55,530
30	Idaho	55,370
30	Wyoming	55,370
32	Pennsylvania	55,240
33	South Carolina	54,850
34	Nebraska	53,500
35	Illinois	53,340
36	West Virginia	53,160
37	Indiana	52,710
38	Missouri	52,660
39	Tennessee	51,850
40	Kansas	51,610
41	South Dakota	51,420
42	Iowa	50,890
43	Kentucky	50,820
44	Louisiana	50,180
45	Montana	49,860
46	Alabama	49,580
47	Mississippi	49,170
48	Arkansas	48,490
49	North Dakota	48,240
50	Oklahoma	47,970

District of Columbia   65,250

Source: U.S. Department of Labor, Bureau of Labor Statistics
"Occupational Employment and Wages, 2005" (http://www.bls.gov/oes/)
*Does not include self-employed. Includes various doctors, dentists, nurses, therapists, optometrists, paramedics and technicians. Does not include assistants and aides listed under health care support occupations.

Physicians in 2005

National Total = 889,195 Physicians*

RANK	STATE	PHYSICIANS	% of USA
27	Alabama	10,809	1.2%
49	Alaska	1,643	0.2%
21	Arizona	14,699	1.7%
32	Arkansas	6,315	0.7%
1	California	108,053	12.2%
23	Colorado	13,816	1.6%
22	Connecticut	14,234	1.6%
46	Delaware	2,372	0.3%
4	Florida	52,324	5.9%
14	Georgia	22,222	2.5%
39	Hawaii	4,528	0.5%
43	Idaho	2,825	0.3%
6	Illinois	38,513	4.3%
20	Indiana	14,977	1.7%
31	Iowa	6,319	0.7%
29	Kansas	6,978	0.8%
28	Kentucky	10,646	1.2%
24	Louisiana	12,650	1.4%
41	Maine	4,095	0.5%
11	Maryland	25,498	2.9%
8	Massachusetts	31,908	3.6%
10	Michigan	27,316	3.1%
17	Minnesota	16,373	1.8%
33	Mississippi	5,872	0.7%
19	Missouri	15,322	1.7%
45	Montana	2,496	0.3%
37	Nebraska	4,727	0.5%
36	Nevada	5,196	0.6%
42	New Hampshire	4,003	0.5%
9	New Jersey	29,786	3.3%
35	New Mexico	5,292	0.6%
2	New York	82,301	9.3%
12	North Carolina	24,698	2.8%
48	North Dakota	1,712	0.2%
7	Ohio	33,618	3.8%
30	Oklahoma	6,950	0.8%
25	Oregon	11,301	1.3%
5	Pennsylvania	41,358	4.7%
40	Rhode Island	4,259	0.5%
26	South Carolina	10,992	1.2%
47	South Dakota	1,936	0.2%
16	Tennessee	17,349	2.0%
3	Texas	53,571	6.0%
34	Utah	5,857	0.7%
44	Vermont	2,624	0.3%
13	Virginia	23,049	2.6%
15	Washington	19,349	2.2%
38	West Virginia	4,681	0.5%
18	Wisconsin	15,855	1.8%
50	Wyoming	1,113	0.1%

RANK	STATE	PHYSICIANS	% of USA
1	California	108,053	12.2%
2	New York	82,301	9.3%
3	Texas	53,571	6.0%
4	Florida	52,324	5.9%
5	Pennsylvania	41,358	4.7%
6	Illinois	38,513	4.3%
7	Ohio	33,618	3.8%
8	Massachusetts	31,908	3.6%
9	New Jersey	29,786	3.3%
10	Michigan	27,316	3.1%
11	Maryland	25,498	2.9%
12	North Carolina	24,698	2.8%
13	Virginia	23,049	2.6%
14	Georgia	22,222	2.5%
15	Washington	19,349	2.2%
16	Tennessee	17,349	2.0%
17	Minnesota	16,373	1.8%
18	Wisconsin	15,855	1.8%
19	Missouri	15,322	1.7%
20	Indiana	14,977	1.7%
21	Arizona	14,699	1.7%
22	Connecticut	14,234	1.6%
23	Colorado	13,816	1.6%
24	Louisiana	12,650	1.4%
25	Oregon	11,301	1.3%
26	South Carolina	10,992	1.2%
27	Alabama	10,809	1.2%
28	Kentucky	10,646	1.2%
29	Kansas	6,978	0.8%
30	Oklahoma	6,950	0.8%
31	Iowa	6,319	0.7%
32	Arkansas	6,315	0.7%
33	Mississippi	5,872	0.7%
34	Utah	5,857	0.7%
35	New Mexico	5,292	0.6%
36	Nevada	5,196	0.6%
37	Nebraska	4,727	0.5%
38	West Virginia	4,681	0.5%
39	Hawaii	4,528	0.5%
40	Rhode Island	4,259	0.5%
41	Maine	4,095	0.5%
42	New Hampshire	4,003	0.5%
43	Idaho	2,825	0.3%
44	Vermont	2,624	0.3%
45	Montana	2,496	0.3%
46	Delaware	2,372	0.3%
47	South Dakota	1,936	0.2%
48	North Dakota	1,712	0.2%
49	Alaska	1,643	0.2%
50	Wyoming	1,113	0.1%
	District of Columbia	4,815	0.5%

Source: American Medical Association (Chicago, Illinois)
   "Physician Characteristics and Distribution in the U.S." (2007 Edition)
*As of December 31, 2005. Total does not include 12,858 physicians in the U.S. territories and possessions, at APO's and FPO's and whose addresses are unknown.

Rate of Physicians in 2005

National Rate = 300 Physicians per 100,000 Population*

ALPHA ORDER

RANK	STATE	RATE
41	Alabama	238
37	Alaska	248
38	Arizona	247
44	Arkansas	228
17	California	299
18	Colorado	296
5	Connecticut	407
24	Delaware	282
19	Florida	294
39	Georgia	243
7	Hawaii	356
49	Idaho	198
16	Illinois	302
40	Indiana	239
47	Iowa	213
35	Kansas	254
34	Kentucky	255
25	Louisiana	281
11	Maine	311
2	Maryland	456
1	Massachusetts	496
27	Michigan	270
10	Minnesota	319
48	Mississippi	202
31	Missouri	264
30	Montana	267
29	Nebraska	269
46	Nevada	215
14	New Hampshire	306
8	New Jersey	342
26	New Mexico	275
3	New York	426
23	North Carolina	285
27	North Dakota	270
20	Ohio	293
50	Oklahoma	196
11	Oregon	311
9	Pennsylvania	333
6	Rhode Island	397
32	South Carolina	259
36	South Dakota	250
21	Tennessee	291
43	Texas	234
42	Utah	235
4	Vermont	422
15	Virginia	305
13	Washington	308
33	West Virginia	258
22	Wisconsin	287
45	Wyoming	219

RANK ORDER

RANK	STATE	RATE
1	Massachusetts	496
2	Maryland	456
3	New York	426
4	Vermont	422
5	Connecticut	407
6	Rhode Island	397
7	Hawaii	356
8	New Jersey	342
9	Pennsylvania	333
10	Minnesota	319
11	Maine	311
11	Oregon	311
13	Washington	308
14	New Hampshire	306
15	Virginia	305
16	Illinois	302
17	California	299
18	Colorado	296
19	Florida	294
20	Ohio	293
21	Tennessee	291
22	Wisconsin	287
23	North Carolina	285
24	Delaware	282
25	Louisiana	281
26	New Mexico	275
27	Michigan	270
27	North Dakota	270
29	Nebraska	269
30	Montana	267
31	Missouri	264
32	South Carolina	259
33	West Virginia	258
34	Kentucky	255
35	Kansas	254
36	South Dakota	250
37	Alaska	248
38	Arizona	247
39	Georgia	243
40	Indiana	239
41	Alabama	238
42	Utah	235
43	Texas	234
44	Arkansas	228
45	Wyoming	219
46	Nevada	215
47	Iowa	213
48	Mississippi	202
49	Idaho	198
50	Oklahoma	196

District of Columbia   827

Source: Morgan Quitno Press using data from American Medical Association (Chicago, Illinois)
"Physician Characteristics and Distribution in the U.S." (2007 Edition)
As of December 31, 2005. National rate does not include physicians in the U.S. territories and possessions, at APO's and FPO's and whose addresses are unknown.

Percent of Physicians Who Are Female: 2005

National Percent = 27.1% of Physicians*

ALPHA ORDER

RANK	STATE	PERCENT
40	Alabama	21.4
8	Alaska	29.7
29	Arizona	24.7
42	Arkansas	21.0
16	California	27.5
13	Colorado	28.3
11	Connecticut	28.4
10	Delaware	29.2
42	Florida	21.0
25	Georgia	26.0
21	Hawaii	26.3
50	Idaho	18.1
4	Illinois	31.2
31	Indiana	24.2
35	Iowa	22.3
30	Kansas	24.5
32	Kentucky	24.1
34	Louisiana	23.7
25	Maine	26.0
2	Maryland	31.8
1	Massachusetts	33.3
11	Michigan	28.4
15	Minnesota	27.7
48	Mississippi	19.5
21	Missouri	26.3
45	Montana	20.1
33	Nebraska	23.9
38	Nevada	22.0
27	New Hampshire	25.7
5	New Jersey	30.7
7	New Mexico	30.3
3	New York	31.3
23	North Carolina	26.1
45	North Dakota	20.1
19	Ohio	27.2
40	Oklahoma	21.4
20	Oregon	26.8
18	Pennsylvania	27.4
5	Rhode Island	30.7
37	South Carolina	22.2
44	South Dakota	20.8
35	Tennessee	22.3
23	Texas	26.1
47	Utah	19.7
9	Vermont	29.6
14	Virginia	28.2
16	Washington	27.5
39	West Virginia	21.9
28	Wisconsin	25.6
49	Wyoming	18.4

RANK ORDER

RANK	STATE	PERCENT
1	Massachusetts	33.3
2	Maryland	31.8
3	New York	31.3
4	Illinois	31.2
5	New Jersey	30.7
5	Rhode Island	30.7
7	New Mexico	30.3
8	Alaska	29.7
9	Vermont	29.6
10	Delaware	29.2
11	Connecticut	28.4
11	Michigan	28.4
13	Colorado	28.3
14	Virginia	28.2
15	Minnesota	27.7
16	California	27.5
16	Washington	27.5
18	Pennsylvania	27.4
19	Ohio	27.2
20	Oregon	26.8
21	Hawaii	26.3
21	Missouri	26.3
23	North Carolina	26.1
23	Texas	26.1
25	Georgia	26.0
25	Maine	26.0
27	New Hampshire	25.7
28	Wisconsin	25.6
29	Arizona	24.7
30	Kansas	24.5
31	Indiana	24.2
32	Kentucky	24.1
33	Nebraska	23.9
34	Louisiana	23.7
35	Iowa	22.3
35	Tennessee	22.3
37	South Carolina	22.2
38	Nevada	22.0
39	West Virginia	21.9
40	Alabama	21.4
40	Oklahoma	21.4
42	Arkansas	21.0
42	Florida	21.0
44	South Dakota	20.8
45	Montana	20.1
45	North Dakota	20.1
47	Utah	19.7
48	Mississippi	19.5
49	Wyoming	18.4
50	Idaho	18.1

	District of Columbia	35.1

Source: Morgan Quitno Press using data from American Medical Association (Chicago, Illinois)
    "Physician Characteristics and Distribution in the U.S." (2007 Edition)
*As of December 31, 2005. National percent does not include physicians in the U.S. territories and possessions, at APO's and FPO's and whose addresses are unknown.

Percent of Physicians Under 35 Years Old in 2005

National Percent = 15.6% of Physicians*

ALPHA ORDER				RANK ORDER		
RANK	STATE	PERCENT		RANK	STATE	PERCENT
19	Alabama	15.5		1	Illinois	20.5
47	Alaska	8.7		2	Rhode Island	20.0
38	Arizona	11.6		3	Massachusetts	19.7
25	Arkansas	14.7		4	Missouri	19.3
31	California	13.5		5	New York	19.2
34	Colorado	12.8		6	Ohio	19.1
17	Connecticut	15.6		7	Michigan	18.7
20	Delaware	15.4		8	Louisiana	17.7
45	Florida	9.4		9	Nebraska	17.6
26	Georgia	14.5		10	Pennsylvania	17.4
37	Hawaii	12.1		11	Minnesota	16.9
48	Idaho	7.0		12	Texas	16.7
1	Illinois	20.5		13	North Carolina	16.4
26	Indiana	14.5		14	Iowa	16.0
14	Iowa	16.0		15	West Virginia	15.8
28	Kansas	14.4		16	South Carolina	15.7
22	Kentucky	15.3		17	Connecticut	15.6
8	Louisiana	17.7		17	Maryland	15.6
46	Maine	9.1		19	Alabama	15.5
17	Maryland	15.6		20	Delaware	15.4
3	Massachusetts	19.7		20	Virginia	15.4
7	Michigan	18.7		22	Kentucky	15.3
11	Minnesota	16.9		23	Utah	15.0
34	Mississippi	12.8		24	Tennessee	14.8
4	Missouri	19.3		25	Arkansas	14.7
50	Montana	4.4		26	Georgia	14.5
9	Nebraska	17.6		26	Indiana	14.5
43	Nevada	10.0		28	Kansas	14.4
42	New Hampshire	10.2		29	Vermont	14.0
31	New Jersey	13.5		29	Wisconsin	14.0
36	New Mexico	12.2		31	California	13.5
5	New York	19.2		31	New Jersey	13.5
13	North Carolina	16.4		33	Oklahoma	13.4
40	North Dakota	11.0		34	Colorado	12.8
6	Ohio	19.1		34	Mississippi	12.8
33	Oklahoma	13.4		36	New Mexico	12.2
40	Oregon	11.0		37	Hawaii	12.1
10	Pennsylvania	17.4		38	Arizona	11.6
2	Rhode Island	20.0		39	Washington	11.5
16	South Carolina	15.7		40	North Dakota	11.0
44	South Dakota	9.9		40	Oregon	11.0
24	Tennessee	14.8		42	New Hampshire	10.2
12	Texas	16.7		43	Nevada	10.0
23	Utah	15.0		44	South Dakota	9.9
29	Vermont	14.0		45	Florida	9.4
20	Virginia	15.4		46	Maine	9.1
39	Washington	11.5		47	Alaska	8.7
15	West Virginia	15.8		48	Idaho	7.0
29	Wisconsin	14.0		49	Wyoming	6.4
49	Wyoming	6.4		50	Montana	4.4

District of Columbia   23.5

Source: Morgan Quitno Press using data from American Medical Association (Chicago, Illinois)
   "Physician Characteristics and Distribution in the U.S." (2007 Edition)
*As of December 31, 2005. National percent does not include physicians in the U.S. territories and possessions, at APO's and FPO's and whose addresses are unknown.

Percent of Physicians 65 Years Old and Older in 2005

National Percent = 18.8% of Physicians*

ALPHA ORDER

RANK	STATE	PERCENT
47	Alabama	15.8
50	Alaska	13.8
6	Arizona	21.4
31	Arkansas	17.3
3	California	22.2
26	Colorado	18.1
18	Connecticut	19.2
10	Delaware	20.4
1	Florida	26.0
44	Georgia	16.0
11	Hawaii	20.0
9	Idaho	20.6
39	Illinois	16.2
36	Indiana	16.3
29	Iowa	17.5
15	Kansas	19.5
44	Kentucky	16.0
31	Louisiana	17.3
4	Maine	22.1
23	Maryland	18.5
36	Massachusetts	16.3
28	Michigan	17.7
48	Minnesota	15.7
22	Mississippi	18.6
48	Missouri	15.7
2	Montana	22.8
39	Nebraska	16.2
8	Nevada	20.7
7	New Hampshire	20.8
20	New Jersey	18.8
26	New Mexico	18.1
17	New York	19.3
42	North Carolina	16.1
34	North Dakota	16.8
31	Ohio	17.3
13	Oklahoma	19.9
13	Oregon	19.9
21	Pennsylvania	18.7
25	Rhode Island	18.2
29	South Carolina	17.5
39	South Dakota	16.2
44	Tennessee	16.0
42	Texas	16.1
36	Utah	16.3
11	Vermont	20.0
23	Virginia	18.5
15	Washington	19.5
19	West Virginia	18.9
35	Wisconsin	16.7
5	Wyoming	21.9

RANK ORDER

RANK	STATE	PERCENT
1	Florida	26.0
2	Montana	22.8
3	California	22.2
4	Maine	22.1
5	Wyoming	21.9
6	Arizona	21.4
7	New Hampshire	20.8
8	Nevada	20.7
9	Idaho	20.6
10	Delaware	20.4
11	Hawaii	20.0
11	Vermont	20.0
13	Oklahoma	19.9
13	Oregon	19.9
15	Kansas	19.5
15	Washington	19.5
17	New York	19.3
18	Connecticut	19.2
19	West Virginia	18.9
20	New Jersey	18.8
21	Pennsylvania	18.7
22	Mississippi	18.6
23	Maryland	18.5
23	Virginia	18.5
25	Rhode Island	18.2
26	Colorado	18.1
26	New Mexico	18.1
28	Michigan	17.7
29	Iowa	17.5
29	South Carolina	17.5
31	Arkansas	17.3
31	Louisiana	17.3
31	Ohio	17.3
34	North Dakota	16.8
35	Wisconsin	16.7
36	Indiana	16.3
36	Massachusetts	16.3
36	Utah	16.3
39	Illinois	16.2
39	Nebraska	16.2
39	South Dakota	16.2
42	North Carolina	16.1
42	Texas	16.1
44	Georgia	16.0
44	Kentucky	16.0
44	Tennessee	16.0
47	Alabama	15.8
48	Minnesota	15.7
48	Missouri	15.7
50	Alaska	13.8

District of Columbia	19.4

Source: Morgan Quitno Press using data from American Medical Association (Chicago, Illinois)
    "Physician Characteristics and Distribution in the U.S." (2007 Edition)
As of December 31, 2005. National percent does not include physicians in the U.S. territories and possessions, at APO's and FPO's and whose addresses are unknown.

Physicians in Patient Care in 2005

National Total = 707,927 Physicians*

ALPHA ORDER

RANK	STATE	PHYSICIANS	% of USA
26	Alabama	9,020	1.3%
49	Alaska	1,417	0.2%
21	Arizona	11,385	1.6%
31	Arkansas	5,247	0.7%
1	California	84,424	11.9%
23	Colorado	10,995	1.6%
22	Connecticut	11,161	1.6%
46	Delaware	1,891	0.3%
4	Florida	39,848	5.6%
14	Georgia	18,227	2.6%
39	Hawaii	3,601	0.5%
43	Idaho	2,321	0.3%
6	Illinois	31,172	4.4%
20	Indiana	12,450	1.8%
32	Iowa	4,920	0.7%
29	Kansas	5,591	0.8%
27	Kentucky	8,833	1.2%
24	Louisiana	10,509	1.5%
41	Maine	3,214	0.5%
12	Maryland	19,280	2.7%
8	Massachusetts	24,567	3.5%
10	Michigan	21,808	3.1%
17	Minnesota	13,177	1.9%
33	Mississippi	4,815	0.7%
19	Missouri	12,486	1.8%
45	Montana	1,983	0.3%
37	Nebraska	3,840	0.5%
35	Nevada	4,241	0.6%
42	New Hampshire	3,154	0.4%
9	New Jersey	24,099	3.4%
36	New Mexico	4,151	0.6%
2	New York	65,260	9.2%
11	North Carolina	19,785	2.8%
48	North Dakota	1,422	0.2%
7	Ohio	26,868	3.8%
30	Oklahoma	5,590	0.8%
28	Oregon	8,816	1.2%
5	Pennsylvania	32,052	4.5%
40	Rhode Island	3,444	0.5%
25	South Carolina	9,074	1.3%
47	South Dakota	1,597	0.2%
16	Tennessee	14,367	2.0%
3	Texas	44,311	6.3%
34	Utah	4,722	0.7%
44	Vermont	2,000	0.3%
13	Virginia	18,503	2.6%
15	Washington	15,016	2.1%
38	West Virginia	3,793	0.5%
18	Wisconsin	12,951	1.8%
50	Wyoming	900	0.1%

RANK ORDER

RANK	STATE	PHYSICIANS	% of USA
1	California	84,424	11.9%
2	New York	65,260	9.2%
3	Texas	44,311	6.3%
4	Florida	39,848	5.6%
5	Pennsylvania	32,052	4.5%
6	Illinois	31,172	4.4%
7	Ohio	26,868	3.8%
8	Massachusetts	24,567	3.5%
9	New Jersey	24,099	3.4%
10	Michigan	21,808	3.1%
11	North Carolina	19,785	2.8%
12	Maryland	19,280	2.7%
13	Virginia	18,503	2.6%
14	Georgia	18,227	2.6%
15	Washington	15,016	2.1%
16	Tennessee	14,367	2.0%
17	Minnesota	13,177	1.9%
18	Wisconsin	12,951	1.8%
19	Missouri	12,486	1.8%
20	Indiana	12,450	1.8%
21	Arizona	11,385	1.6%
22	Connecticut	11,161	1.6%
23	Colorado	10,995	1.6%
24	Louisiana	10,509	1.5%
25	South Carolina	9,074	1.3%
26	Alabama	9,020	1.3%
27	Kentucky	8,833	1.2%
28	Oregon	8,816	1.2%
29	Kansas	5,591	0.8%
30	Oklahoma	5,590	0.8%
31	Arkansas	5,247	0.7%
32	Iowa	4,920	0.7%
33	Mississippi	4,815	0.7%
34	Utah	4,722	0.7%
35	Nevada	4,241	0.6%
36	New Mexico	4,151	0.6%
37	Nebraska	3,840	0.5%
38	West Virginia	3,793	0.5%
39	Hawaii	3,601	0.5%
40	Rhode Island	3,444	0.5%
41	Maine	3,214	0.5%
42	New Hampshire	3,154	0.4%
43	Idaho	2,321	0.3%
44	Vermont	2,000	0.3%
45	Montana	1,983	0.3%
46	Delaware	1,891	0.3%
47	South Dakota	1,597	0.2%
48	North Dakota	1,422	0.2%
49	Alaska	1,417	0.2%
50	Wyoming	900	0.1%
	District of Columbia	3,629	0.5%

Source: American Medical Association (Chicago, Illinois)
   "Physician Characteristics and Distribution in the U.S." (2007 Edition)
*As of December 31, 2005. Total does not include 10,546 physicians in U.S. territories and possessions.

Rate of Physicians in Patient Care in 2005

National Rate = 239 Physicians per 100,000 Population*

ALPHA ORDER

RANK	STATE	RATE
40	Alabama	198
31	Alaska	214
42	Arizona	191
44	Arkansas	189
19	California	234
18	Colorado	236
6	Connecticut	319
24	Delaware	225
25	Florida	224
38	Georgia	200
7	Hawaii	283
49	Idaho	162
12	Illinois	244
39	Indiana	199
47	Iowa	166
37	Kansas	203
33	Kentucky	212
22	Louisiana	233
12	Maine	244
2	Maryland	345
1	Massachusetts	382
28	Michigan	216
10	Minnesota	257
47	Mississippi	166
30	Missouri	215
33	Montana	212
27	Nebraska	218
46	Nevada	176
15	New Hampshire	241
8	New Jersey	277
28	New Mexico	216
3	New York	338
23	North Carolina	228
25	North Dakota	224
19	Ohio	234
50	Oklahoma	158
14	Oregon	242
9	Pennsylvania	258
4	Rhode Island	321
31	South Carolina	214
36	South Dakota	206
15	Tennessee	241
41	Texas	193
43	Utah	190
4	Vermont	321
11	Virginia	245
17	Washington	239
35	West Virginia	209
19	Wisconsin	234
45	Wyoming	177

RANK ORDER

RANK	STATE	RATE
1	Massachusetts	382
2	Maryland	345
3	New York	338
4	Rhode Island	321
4	Vermont	321
6	Connecticut	319
7	Hawaii	283
8	New Jersey	277
9	Pennsylvania	258
10	Minnesota	257
11	Virginia	245
12	Illinois	244
12	Maine	244
14	Oregon	242
15	New Hampshire	241
15	Tennessee	241
17	Washington	239
18	Colorado	236
19	California	234
19	Ohio	234
19	Wisconsin	234
22	Louisiana	233
23	North Carolina	228
24	Delaware	225
25	Florida	224
25	North Dakota	224
27	Nebraska	218
28	Michigan	216
28	New Mexico	216
30	Missouri	215
31	Alaska	214
31	South Carolina	214
33	Kentucky	212
33	Montana	212
35	West Virginia	209
36	South Dakota	206
37	Kansas	203
38	Georgia	200
39	Indiana	199
40	Alabama	198
41	Texas	193
42	Arizona	191
43	Utah	190
44	Arkansas	189
45	Wyoming	177
46	Nevada	176
47	Iowa	166
47	Mississippi	166
49	Idaho	162
50	Oklahoma	158

District of Columbia 623

Source: Morgan Quitno Press using data from American Medical Association (Chicago, Illinois)
    "Physician Characteristics and Distribution in the U.S." (2007 Edition)
*As of December 31, 2005. National rate does not include physicians in the U.S. territories and possessions.

Physicians In Primary Care In 2005

National Total = 294,597 Physicians*

ALPHA ORDER

RANK	STATE	PHYSICIANS	% of USA
26	Alabama	3,862	1.3%
48	Alaska	701	0.2%
21	Arizona	4,632	1.6%
31	Arkansas	2,279	0.8%
1	California	35,924	12.2%
22	Colorado	4,581	1.6%
23	Connecticut	4,472	1.5%
46	Delaware	739	0.3%
4	Florida	15,487	5.3%
12	Georgia	7,993	2.7%
39	Hawaii	1,615	0.5%
43	Idaho	1,014	0.3%
5	Illinois	13,713	4.7%
19	Indiana	5,244	1.8%
32	Iowa	2,081	0.7%
30	Kansas	2,399	0.8%
28	Kentucky	3,614	1.2%
24	Louisiana	4,220	1.4%
40	Maine	1,407	0.5%
14	Maryland	7,742	2.6%
9	Massachusetts	9,417	3.2%
10	Michigan	9,380	3.2%
17	Minnesota	5,857	2.0%
33	Mississippi	2,011	0.7%
20	Missouri	4,916	1.7%
45	Montana	861	0.3%
37	Nebraska	1,736	0.6%
36	Nevada	1,786	0.6%
42	New Hampshire	1,343	0.5%
8	New Jersey	10,034	3.4%
35	New Mexico	1,878	0.6%
2	New York	26,675	9.1%
11	North Carolina	8,180	2.8%
49	North Dakota	670	0.2%
7	Ohio	11,081	3.8%
29	Oklahoma	2,409	0.8%
27	Oregon	3,843	1.3%
6	Pennsylvania	12,492	4.2%
40	Rhode Island	1,407	0.5%
25	South Carolina	3,882	1.3%
47	South Dakota	721	0.2%
16	Tennessee	5,941	2.0%
3	Texas	18,023	6.1%
34	Utah	1,906	0.6%
44	Vermont	890	0.3%
13	Virginia	7,909	2.7%
15	Washington	6,571	2.2%
38	West Virginia	1,618	0.5%
18	Wisconsin	5,582	1.9%
50	Wyoming	433	0.1%

RANK ORDER

RANK	STATE	PHYSICIANS	% of USA
1	California	35,924	12.2%
2	New York	26,675	9.1%
3	Texas	18,023	6.1%
4	Florida	15,487	5.3%
5	Illinois	13,713	4.7%
6	Pennsylvania	12,492	4.2%
7	Ohio	11,081	3.8%
8	New Jersey	10,034	3.4%
9	Massachusetts	9,417	3.2%
10	Michigan	9,380	3.2%
11	North Carolina	8,180	2.8%
12	Georgia	7,993	2.7%
13	Virginia	7,909	2.7%
14	Maryland	7,742	2.6%
15	Washington	6,571	2.2%
16	Tennessee	5,941	2.0%
17	Minnesota	5,857	2.0%
18	Wisconsin	5,582	1.9%
19	Indiana	5,244	1.8%
20	Missouri	4,916	1.7%
21	Arizona	4,632	1.6%
22	Colorado	4,581	1.6%
23	Connecticut	4,472	1.5%
24	Louisiana	4,220	1.4%
25	South Carolina	3,882	1.3%
26	Alabama	3,862	1.3%
27	Oregon	3,843	1.3%
28	Kentucky	3,614	1.2%
29	Oklahoma	2,409	0.8%
30	Kansas	2,399	0.8%
31	Arkansas	2,279	0.8%
32	Iowa	2,081	0.7%
33	Mississippi	2,011	0.7%
34	Utah	1,906	0.6%
35	New Mexico	1,878	0.6%
36	Nevada	1,786	0.6%
37	Nebraska	1,736	0.6%
38	West Virginia	1,618	0.5%
39	Hawaii	1,615	0.5%
40	Maine	1,407	0.5%
40	Rhode Island	1,407	0.5%
42	New Hampshire	1,343	0.5%
43	Idaho	1,014	0.3%
44	Vermont	890	0.3%
45	Montana	861	0.3%
46	Delaware	739	0.3%
47	South Dakota	721	0.2%
48	Alaska	701	0.2%
49	North Dakota	670	0.2%
50	Wyoming	433	0.1%
	District of Columbia	1,426	0.5%

Source: American Medical Association (Chicago, Illinois)
"Physician Characteristics and Distribution in the U.S." (2007 Edition)
As of December 31, 2005. National total does not include 5,425 physicians in U.S. territories and possessions.
Primary Care Specialties include Family Practice, General Practice, Internal Medicine, Obstetrics/Gynecology and Pediatrics excluding subspecialties within each category.

Rate of Physicians in Primary Care in 2005

National Rate = 99 Physicians per 100,000 Population*

ALPHA ORDER

RANK	STATE	RATE
38	Alabama	85
12	Alaska	106
44	Arizona	78
42	Arkansas	82
21	California	99
23	Colorado	98
6	Connecticut	128
33	Delaware	88
35	Florida	87
33	Georgia	88
7	Hawaii	127
47	Idaho	71
10	Illinois	107
41	Indiana	84
48	Iowa	70
35	Kansas	87
35	Kentucky	87
26	Louisiana	94
10	Maine	107
3	Maryland	139
1	Massachusetts	146
28	Michigan	93
9	Minnesota	114
49	Mississippi	69
38	Missouri	85
30	Montana	92
21	Nebraska	99
46	Nevada	74
17	New Hampshire	103
8	New Jersey	115
23	New Mexico	98
4	New York	138
26	North Carolina	94
12	North Dakota	106
25	Ohio	97
50	Oklahoma	68
12	Oregon	106
18	Pennsylvania	101
5	Rhode Island	131
31	South Carolina	91
28	South Dakota	93
20	Tennessee	100
43	Texas	79
45	Utah	77
2	Vermont	143
15	Virginia	105
16	Washington	104
32	West Virginia	89
18	Wisconsin	101
38	Wyoming	85

RANK ORDER

RANK	STATE	RATE
1	Massachusetts	146
2	Vermont	143
3	Maryland	139
4	New York	138
5	Rhode Island	131
6	Connecticut	128
7	Hawaii	127
8	New Jersey	115
9	Minnesota	114
10	Illinois	107
10	Maine	107
12	Alaska	106
12	North Dakota	106
12	Oregon	106
15	Virginia	105
16	Washington	104
17	New Hampshire	103
18	Pennsylvania	101
18	Wisconsin	101
20	Tennessee	100
21	California	99
21	Nebraska	99
23	Colorado	98
23	New Mexico	98
25	Ohio	97
26	Louisiana	94
26	North Carolina	94
28	Michigan	93
28	South Dakota	93
30	Montana	92
31	South Carolina	91
32	West Virginia	89
33	Delaware	88
33	Georgia	88
35	Florida	87
35	Kansas	87
35	Kentucky	87
38	Alabama	85
38	Missouri	85
38	Wyoming	85
41	Indiana	84
42	Arkansas	82
43	Texas	79
44	Arizona	78
45	Utah	77
46	Nevada	74
47	Idaho	71
48	Iowa	70
49	Mississippi	69
50	Oklahoma	68
	District of Columbia	245

Source: Morgan Quitno Press using data from American Medical Association (Chicago, Illinois)
"Physician Characteristics and Distribution in the U.S." (2007 Edition)
*As of December 31, 2005. National rate does not include physicians in U.S. territories and possessions. Primary Care Specialties include Family Practice, General Practice, Internal Medicine, Obstetrics/Gynecology and Pediatrics excluding subspecialties within each category.

Percent of Physicians in Primary Care in 2005

National Percent = 33.1% of Physicians*

ALPHA ORDER				RANK ORDER		
RANK	STATE	PERCENT		RANK	STATE	PERCENT
10	Alabama	35.7		1	Alaska	42.7
1	Alaska	42.7		2	North Dakota	39.1
44	Arizona	31.5		3	Wyoming	38.9
6	Arkansas	36.1		4	South Dakota	37.2
35	California	33.2		5	Nebraska	36.7
35	Colorado	33.2		6	Arkansas	36.1
45	Connecticut	31.4		7	Georgia	36.0
46	Delaware	31.2		8	Idaho	35.9
49	Florida	29.6		9	Minnesota	35.8
7	Georgia	36.0		10	Alabama	35.7
10	Hawaii	35.7		10	Hawaii	35.7
8	Idaho	35.9		12	Illinois	35.6
12	Illinois	35.6		13	New Mexico	35.5
16	Indiana	35.0		14	South Carolina	35.3
40	Iowa	32.9		15	Wisconsin	35.2
20	Kansas	34.4		16	Indiana	35.0
29	Kentucky	33.9		17	Oklahoma	34.7
34	Louisiana	33.4		18	West Virginia	34.6
20	Maine	34.4		19	Montana	34.5
47	Maryland	30.4		20	Kansas	34.4
50	Massachusetts	29.5		20	Maine	34.4
23	Michigan	34.3		20	Nevada	34.4
9	Minnesota	35.8		23	Michigan	34.3
25	Mississippi	34.2		23	Virginia	34.3
43	Missouri	32.1		25	Mississippi	34.2
19	Montana	34.5		25	Tennessee	34.2
5	Nebraska	36.7		27	Oregon	34.0
20	Nevada	34.4		27	Washington	34.0
33	New Hampshire	33.5		29	Kentucky	33.9
31	New Jersey	33.7		29	Vermont	33.9
13	New Mexico	35.5		31	New Jersey	33.7
42	New York	32.4		32	Texas	33.6
37	North Carolina	33.1		33	New Hampshire	33.5
2	North Dakota	39.1		34	Louisiana	33.4
38	Ohio	33.0		35	California	33.2
17	Oklahoma	34.7		35	Colorado	33.2
27	Oregon	34.0		37	North Carolina	33.1
48	Pennsylvania	30.2		38	Ohio	33.0
38	Rhode Island	33.0		38	Rhode Island	33.0
14	South Carolina	35.3		40	Iowa	32.9
4	South Dakota	37.2		41	Utah	32.5
25	Tennessee	34.2		42	New York	32.4
32	Texas	33.6		43	Missouri	32.1
41	Utah	32.5		44	Arizona	31.5
29	Vermont	33.9		45	Connecticut	31.4
23	Virginia	34.3		46	Delaware	31.2
27	Washington	34.0		47	Maryland	30.4
18	West Virginia	34.6		48	Pennsylvania	30.2
15	Wisconsin	35.2		49	Florida	29.6
3	Wyoming	38.9		50	Massachusetts	29.5
					District of Columbia	29.6

Source: Morgan Quitno Press using data from American Medical Association (Chicago, Illinois)
"Physician Characteristics and Distribution in the U.S." (2007 Edition)
*As of December 31, 2005. National percent does not include physicians in U.S. territories and possessions.
Primary Care Specialties include Family Practice, General Practice, Internal Medicine, Obstetrics/Gynecology and
Pediatrics excluding subspecialties within each category.

Percent of Population Lacking Access to Primary Care in 2006

National Percent = 11.3% of Population*

ALPHA ORDER

RANK	STATE	PERCENT
5	Alabama	23.7
16	Alaska	13.4
17	Arizona	13.0
30	Arkansas	9.4
28	California	9.8
29	Colorado	9.6
35	Connecticut	8.8
17	Delaware	13.0
11	Florida	15.7
15	Georgia	14.0
48	Hawaii	3.6
10	Idaho	18.0
20	Illinois	12.6
36	Indiana	8.2
30	Iowa	9.4
32	Kansas	9.2
23	Kentucky	11.2
1	Louisiana	35.7
40	Maine	6.6
46	Maryland	5.1
47	Massachusetts	4.9
25	Michigan	10.8
44	Minnesota	5.7
2	Mississippi	30.0
9	Missouri	19.7
8	Montana	19.9
45	Nebraska	5.6
13	Nevada	14.8
42	New Hampshire	5.9
50	New Jersey	2.2
3	New Mexico	28.5
24	New York	11.0
38	North Carolina	7.0
6	North Dakota	21.8
39	Ohio	6.9
12	Oklahoma	15.2
41	Oregon	6.4
42	Pennsylvania	5.9
37	Rhode Island	7.9
14	South Carolina	14.6
4	South Dakota	24.7
22	Tennessee	12.0
19	Texas	12.8
20	Utah	12.6
49	Vermont	2.7
34	Virginia	9.0
33	Washington	9.1
26	West Virginia	10.6
27	Wisconsin	10.5
7	Wyoming	20.8

RANK ORDER

RANK	STATE	PERCENT
1	Louisiana	35.7
2	Mississippi	30.0
3	New Mexico	28.5
4	South Dakota	24.7
5	Alabama	23.7
6	North Dakota	21.8
7	Wyoming	20.8
8	Montana	19.9
9	Missouri	19.7
10	Idaho	18.0
11	Florida	15.7
12	Oklahoma	15.2
13	Nevada	14.8
14	South Carolina	14.6
15	Georgia	14.0
16	Alaska	13.4
17	Arizona	13.0
17	Delaware	13.0
19	Texas	12.8
20	Illinois	12.6
20	Utah	12.6
22	Tennessee	12.0
23	Kentucky	11.2
24	New York	11.0
25	Michigan	10.8
26	West Virginia	10.6
27	Wisconsin	10.5
28	California	9.8
29	Colorado	9.6
30	Arkansas	9.4
30	Iowa	9.4
32	Kansas	9.2
33	Washington	9.1
34	Virginia	9.0
35	Connecticut	8.8
36	Indiana	8.2
37	Rhode Island	7.9
38	North Carolina	7.0
39	Ohio	6.9
40	Maine	6.6
41	Oregon	6.4
42	New Hampshire	5.9
42	Pennsylvania	5.9
44	Minnesota	5.7
45	Nebraska	5.6
46	Maryland	5.1
47	Massachusetts	4.9
48	Hawaii	3.6
49	Vermont	2.7
50	New Jersey	2.2

District of Columbia   26.0

Source: Morgan Quitno Press using data from U.S. Dept. of Health and Human Services, Div. of Shortage Designation
"Selected Statistics on Health Professional Shortage Areas" (as of September 30, 2006)
*Percent of population considered under-served by primary medical practitioners (Family & General Practice doctors, Internists, Ob/Gyns and Pediatricians). An under-served population does not have primary medical care within reasonable economic and geographic bounds.

Physicians in General/Family Practice in 2005

National Total = 90,316 Physicians*

ALPHA ORDER

RANK	STATE	PHYSICIANS	% of USA
26	Alabama	1,316	1.5%
44	Alaska	399	0.4%
20	Arizona	1,518	1.7%
28	Arkansas	1,225	1.4%
1	California	10,778	11.9%
17	Colorado	1,788	2.0%
37	Connecticut	610	0.7%
50	Delaware	235	0.3%
3	Florida	4,895	5.4%
15	Georgia	2,341	2.6%
43	Hawaii	417	0.5%
39	Idaho	570	0.6%
4	Illinois	3,843	4.3%
13	Indiana	2,411	2.7%
29	Iowa	1,142	1.3%
30	Kansas	1,115	1.2%
24	Kentucky	1,348	1.5%
25	Louisiana	1,321	1.5%
38	Maine	593	0.7%
22	Maryland	1,377	1.5%
27	Massachusetts	1,298	1.4%
11	Michigan	2,776	3.1%
10	Minnesota	2,817	3.1%
33	Mississippi	798	0.9%
21	Missouri	1,385	1.5%
42	Montana	439	0.5%
32	Nebraska	877	1.0%
40	Nevada	562	0.6%
41	New Hampshire	476	0.5%
18	New Jersey	1,580	1.7%
34	New Mexico	784	0.9%
5	New York	3,841	4.3%
9	North Carolina	2,837	3.1%
46	North Dakota	367	0.4%
7	Ohio	3,485	3.9%
31	Oklahoma	1,049	1.2%
23	Oregon	1,365	1.5%
6	Pennsylvania	3,742	4.1%
49	Rhode Island	237	0.3%
19	South Carolina	1,568	1.7%
45	South Dakota	380	0.4%
16	Tennessee	1,931	2.1%
2	Texas	6,341	7.0%
35	Utah	714	0.8%
47	Vermont	319	0.4%
12	Virginia	2,634	2.9%
8	Washington	2,923	3.2%
36	West Virginia	676	0.7%
14	Wisconsin	2,410	2.7%
48	Wyoming	245	0.3%

RANK ORDER

RANK	STATE	PHYSICIANS	% of USA
1	California	10,778	11.9%
2	Texas	6,341	7.0%
3	Florida	4,895	5.4%
4	Illinois	3,843	4.3%
5	New York	3,841	4.3%
6	Pennsylvania	3,742	4.1%
7	Ohio	3,485	3.9%
8	Washington	2,923	3.2%
9	North Carolina	2,837	3.1%
10	Minnesota	2,817	3.1%
11	Michigan	2,776	3.1%
12	Virginia	2,634	2.9%
13	Indiana	2,411	2.7%
14	Wisconsin	2,410	2.7%
15	Georgia	2,341	2.6%
16	Tennessee	1,931	2.1%
17	Colorado	1,788	2.0%
18	New Jersey	1,580	1.7%
19	South Carolina	1,568	1.7%
20	Arizona	1,518	1.7%
21	Missouri	1,385	1.5%
22	Maryland	1,377	1.5%
23	Oregon	1,365	1.5%
24	Kentucky	1,348	1.5%
25	Louisiana	1,321	1.5%
26	Alabama	1,316	1.5%
27	Massachusetts	1,298	1.4%
28	Arkansas	1,225	1.4%
29	Iowa	1,142	1.3%
30	Kansas	1,115	1.2%
31	Oklahoma	1,049	1.2%
32	Nebraska	877	1.0%
33	Mississippi	798	0.9%
34	New Mexico	784	0.9%
35	Utah	714	0.8%
36	West Virginia	676	0.7%
37	Connecticut	610	0.7%
38	Maine	593	0.7%
39	Idaho	570	0.6%
40	Nevada	562	0.6%
41	New Hampshire	476	0.5%
42	Montana	439	0.5%
43	Hawaii	417	0.5%
44	Alaska	399	0.4%
45	South Dakota	380	0.4%
46	North Dakota	367	0.4%
47	Vermont	319	0.4%
48	Wyoming	245	0.3%
49	Rhode Island	237	0.3%
50	Delaware	235	0.3%
	District of Columbia	218	0.2%

Source: American Medical Association (Chicago, Illinois)
  "Physician Characteristics and Distribution in the U.S." (2007 Edition)
As of December 31, 2005. Total does not include 2,434 physicians in U.S. territories and possessions.
Internists, Ob/Gyns and Pediatricians).

Rate of Physicians in General/Family Practice in 2005

National Rate = 30 Physicians per 100,000 Population*

ALPHA ORDER

RANK	STATE	RATE
33	Alabama	29
1	Alaska	60
42	Arizona	25
11	Arkansas	44
28	California	30
17	Colorado	38
50	Connecticut	17
36	Delaware	28
36	Florida	28
41	Georgia	26
24	Hawaii	33
15	Idaho	40
28	Illinois	30
17	Indiana	38
16	Iowa	39
13	Kansas	41
26	Kentucky	32
33	Louisiana	29
10	Maine	45
42	Maryland	25
47	Massachusetts	20
39	Michigan	27
3	Minnesota	55
39	Mississippi	27
44	Missouri	24
8	Montana	47
5	Nebraska	50
45	Nevada	23
22	New Hampshire	36
49	New Jersey	18
13	New Mexico	41
47	New York	20
24	North Carolina	33
2	North Dakota	58
28	Ohio	30
28	Oklahoma	30
17	Oregon	38
28	Pennsylvania	30
46	Rhode Island	22
20	South Carolina	37
6	South Dakota	49
26	Tennessee	32
36	Texas	28
33	Utah	29
4	Vermont	51
23	Virginia	35
9	Washington	46
20	West Virginia	37
11	Wisconsin	44
7	Wyoming	48

RANK ORDER

RANK	STATE	RATE
1	Alaska	60
2	North Dakota	58
3	Minnesota	55
4	Vermont	51
5	Nebraska	50
6	South Dakota	49
7	Wyoming	48
8	Montana	47
9	Washington	46
10	Maine	45
11	Arkansas	44
11	Wisconsin	44
13	Kansas	41
13	New Mexico	41
15	Idaho	40
16	Iowa	39
17	Colorado	38
17	Indiana	38
17	Oregon	38
20	South Carolina	37
20	West Virginia	37
22	New Hampshire	36
23	Virginia	35
24	Hawaii	33
24	North Carolina	33
26	Kentucky	32
26	Tennessee	32
28	California	30
28	Illinois	30
28	Ohio	30
28	Oklahoma	30
28	Pennsylvania	30
33	Alabama	29
33	Louisiana	29
33	Utah	29
36	Delaware	28
36	Florida	28
36	Texas	28
39	Michigan	27
39	Mississippi	27
41	Georgia	26
42	Arizona	25
42	Maryland	25
44	Missouri	24
45	Nevada	23
46	Rhode Island	22
47	Massachusetts	20
47	New York	20
49	New Jersey	18
50	Connecticut	17
	District of Columbia	37

Source: Morgan Quitno Press using data from American Medical Association (Chicago, Illinois)
"Physician Characteristics and Distribution in the U.S." (2007 Edition)
*As of December 31, 2005. National rate does not include physicians in U.S. territories and possessions.

Average Annual Wages of Family and General Practitioners in 2005

National Average = $140,370*

ALPHA ORDER				RANK ORDER		
RANK	STATE	WAGES		RANK	STATE	WAGES
22	Alabama	$148,540		1	Kansas	$174,570
10	Alaska	155,360		2	Maryland	165,210
23	Arizona	148,170		3	Louisiana	164,100
4	Arkansas	160,980		4	Arkansas	160,980
37	California	133,420		5	Wisconsin	160,250
45	Colorado	126,830		6	Nevada	158,820
13	Connecticut	153,810		7	North Dakota	158,650
38	Delaware	133,110		8	Mississippi	158,470
15	Florida	152,320		9	Nebraska	155,830
28	Georgia	142,970		10	Alaska	155,360
36	Hawaii	134,190		11	New Mexico	155,050
17	Idaho	151,870		12	West Virginia	154,780
41	Illinois	130,580		13	Connecticut	153,810
29	Indiana	142,320		14	Ohio	152,480
33	Iowa	139,040		15	Florida	152,320
1	Kansas	174,570		16	Utah	151,900
27	Kentucky	144,290		17	Idaho	151,870
3	Louisiana	164,100		17	Missouri	151,870
39	Maine	132,890		19	Massachusetts	151,740
2	Maryland	165,210		20	Wyoming	151,710
19	Massachusetts	151,740		21	North Carolina	149,070
32	Michigan	139,550		22	Alabama	148,540
24	Minnesota	147,750		23	Arizona	148,170
8	Mississippi	158,470		24	Minnesota	147,750
17	Missouri	151,870		25	New Hampshire	146,900
47	Montana	121,550		26	New York	144,500
9	Nebraska	155,830		27	Kentucky	144,290
6	Nevada	158,820		28	Georgia	142,970
25	New Hampshire	146,900		29	Indiana	142,320
44	New Jersey	128,090		30	South Dakota	141,420
11	New Mexico	155,050		31	Rhode Island	141,250
26	New York	144,500		32	Michigan	139,550
21	North Carolina	149,070		33	Iowa	139,040
7	North Dakota	158,650		34	Oklahoma	135,450
14	Ohio	152,480		35	Washington	135,250
34	Oklahoma	135,450		36	Hawaii	134,190
NA	Oregon**	NA		37	California	133,420
42	Pennsylvania	130,150		38	Delaware	133,110
31	Rhode Island	141,250		39	Maine	132,890
NA	South Carolina**	NA		39	Vermont	132,890
30	South Dakota	141,420		41	Illinois	130,580
48	Tennessee	78,220		42	Pennsylvania	130,150
46	Texas	125,880		43	Virginia	129,780
16	Utah	151,900		44	New Jersey	128,090
39	Vermont	132,890		45	Colorado	126,830
43	Virginia	129,780		46	Texas	125,880
35	Washington	135,250		47	Montana	121,550
12	West Virginia	154,780		48	Tennessee	78,220
5	Wisconsin	160,250		NA	Oregon**	NA
20	Wyoming	151,710		NA	South Carolina**	NA

District of Columbia   89,990

Source: U.S. Department of Labor, Bureau of Labor Statistics
    "Occupational Employment and Wages, 2005" (http://www.bls.gov/oes/)
*Does not include self-employed.
**Not available.

Percent of Physicians Who Are Specialists in 2005

National Percent = 74.3% of Physicians*

ALPHA ORDER

RANK	STATE	PERCENT
14	Alabama	75.0
44	Alaska	66.2
28	Arizona	71.3
42	Arkansas	67.2
24	California	73.1
26	Colorado	71.7
2	Connecticut	80.5
17	Delaware	74.1
33	Florida	70.3
9	Georgia	76.3
12	Hawaii	75.1
49	Idaho	64.6
11	Illinois	75.4
29	Indiana	71.1
47	Iowa	64.7
39	Kansas	68.0
18	Kentucky	73.9
8	Louisiana	76.4
37	Maine	69.0
6	Maryland	79.9
5	Massachusetts	80.1
15	Michigan	74.3
39	Minnesota	68.0
26	Mississippi	71.7
7	Missouri	77.3
47	Montana	64.7
43	Nebraska	67.1
21	Nevada	73.5
30	New Hampshire	70.8
1	New Jersey	80.7
38	New Mexico	68.8
4	New York	80.2
20	North Carolina	73.6
46	North Dakota	65.2
19	Ohio	73.7
36	Oklahoma	69.2
33	Oregon	70.3
16	Pennsylvania	74.2
3	Rhode Island	80.3
25	South Carolina	72.0
45	South Dakota	65.7
10	Tennessee	75.9
12	Texas	75.1
22	Utah	73.4
35	Vermont	69.9
23	Virginia	73.3
41	Washington	67.9
31	West Virginia	70.7
31	Wisconsin	70.7
50	Wyoming	62.1

RANK ORDER

RANK	STATE	PERCENT
1	New Jersey	80.7
2	Connecticut	80.5
3	Rhode Island	80.3
4	New York	80.2
5	Massachusetts	80.1
6	Maryland	79.9
7	Missouri	77.3
8	Louisiana	76.4
9	Georgia	76.3
10	Tennessee	75.9
11	Illinois	75.4
12	Hawaii	75.1
12	Texas	75.1
14	Alabama	75.0
15	Michigan	74.3
16	Pennsylvania	74.2
17	Delaware	74.1
18	Kentucky	73.9
19	Ohio	73.7
20	North Carolina	73.6
21	Nevada	73.5
22	Utah	73.4
23	Virginia	73.3
24	California	73.1
25	South Carolina	72.0
26	Colorado	71.7
26	Mississippi	71.7
28	Arizona	71.3
29	Indiana	71.1
30	New Hampshire	70.8
31	West Virginia	70.7
31	Wisconsin	70.7
33	Florida	70.3
33	Oregon	70.3
35	Vermont	69.9
36	Oklahoma	69.2
37	Maine	69.0
38	New Mexico	68.8
39	Kansas	68.0
39	Minnesota	68.0
41	Washington	67.9
42	Arkansas	67.2
43	Nebraska	67.1
44	Alaska	66.2
45	South Dakota	65.7
46	North Dakota	65.2
47	Iowa	64.7
47	Montana	64.7
49	Idaho	64.6
50	Wyoming	62.1

District of Columbia	81.2

Source: Morgan Quitno Press using data from American Medical Association (Chicago, Illinois)
    "Physician Characteristics and Distribution in the U.S." (2007 Edition)
*As of December 31, 2005. National percent does not include physicians in U.S. territories and possessions.
Includes physicians in medical, surgical and other specialties.

Physicians in Medical Specialties in 2005

National Total = 283,774 Physicians*

ALPHA ORDER

RANK	STATE	PHYSICIANS	% of USA
25	Alabama	3,422	1.2%
49	Alaska	345	0.1%
21	Arizona	4,302	1.5%
31	Arkansas	1,655	0.6%
1	California	33,418	11.8%
24	Colorado	3,865	1.4%
16	Connecticut	5,344	1.9%
43	Delaware	748	0.3%
4	Florida	15,829	5.6%
13	Georgia	7,102	2.5%
38	Hawaii	1,431	0.5%
45	Idaho	601	0.2%
6	Illinois	13,108	4.6%
22	Indiana	4,187	1.5%
36	Iowa	1,493	0.5%
30	Kansas	1,795	0.6%
26	Kentucky	3,149	1.1%
23	Louisiana	4,010	1.4%
42	Maine	1,084	0.4%
10	Maryland	9,258	3.3%
7	Massachusetts	12,027	4.2%
11	Michigan	8,837	3.1%
19	Minnesota	4,739	1.7%
34	Mississippi	1,630	0.6%
17	Missouri	5,210	1.8%
46	Montana	557	0.2%
40	Nebraska	1,232	0.4%
35	Nevada	1,586	0.6%
41	New Hampshire	1,153	0.4%
8	New Jersey	11,592	4.1%
37	New Mexico	1,481	0.5%
2	New York	30,942	10.9%
12	North Carolina	7,599	2.7%
48	North Dakota	430	0.2%
9	Ohio	10,758	3.8%
29	Oklahoma	1,912	0.7%
27	Oregon	3,145	1.1%
5	Pennsylvania	13,192	4.6%
32	Rhode Island	1,654	0.6%
28	South Carolina	3,084	1.1%
47	South Dakota	482	0.2%
15	Tennessee	5,690	2.0%
3	Texas	16,361	5.8%
33	Utah	1,648	0.6%
43	Vermont	748	0.3%
14	Virginia	6,964	2.5%
17	Washington	5,210	1.8%
39	West Virginia	1,315	0.5%
20	Wisconsin	4,487	1.6%
50	Wyoming	209	0.1%

RANK ORDER

RANK	STATE	PHYSICIANS	% of USA
1	California	33,418	11.8%
2	New York	30,942	10.9%
3	Texas	16,361	5.8%
4	Florida	15,829	5.6%
5	Pennsylvania	13,192	4.6%
6	Illinois	13,108	4.6%
7	Massachusetts	12,027	4.2%
8	New Jersey	11,592	4.1%
9	Ohio	10,758	3.8%
10	Maryland	9,258	3.3%
11	Michigan	8,837	3.1%
12	North Carolina	7,599	2.7%
13	Georgia	7,102	2.5%
14	Virginia	6,964	2.5%
15	Tennessee	5,690	2.0%
16	Connecticut	5,344	1.9%
17	Missouri	5,210	1.8%
17	Washington	5,210	1.8%
19	Minnesota	4,739	1.7%
20	Wisconsin	4,487	1.6%
21	Arizona	4,302	1.5%
22	Indiana	4,187	1.5%
23	Louisiana	4,010	1.4%
24	Colorado	3,865	1.4%
25	Alabama	3,422	1.2%
26	Kentucky	3,149	1.1%
27	Oregon	3,145	1.1%
28	South Carolina	3,084	1.1%
29	Oklahoma	1,912	0.7%
30	Kansas	1,795	0.6%
31	Arkansas	1,655	0.6%
32	Rhode Island	1,654	0.6%
33	Utah	1,648	0.6%
34	Mississippi	1,630	0.6%
35	Nevada	1,586	0.6%
36	Iowa	1,493	0.5%
37	New Mexico	1,481	0.5%
38	Hawaii	1,431	0.5%
39	West Virginia	1,315	0.5%
40	Nebraska	1,232	0.4%
41	New Hampshire	1,153	0.4%
42	Maine	1,084	0.4%
43	Delaware	748	0.3%
43	Vermont	748	0.3%
45	Idaho	601	0.2%
46	Montana	557	0.2%
47	South Dakota	482	0.2%
48	North Dakota	430	0.2%
49	Alaska	345	0.1%
50	Wyoming	209	0.1%
	District of Columbia	1,754	0.6%

Source: American Medical Association (Chicago, Illinois)
"Physician Characteristics and Distribution in the U.S." (2007 Edition)
As of December 31, 2005. Total does not include 3,503 physicians in U.S. territories and possessions. Medical Specialties are Allergy/Immunology, Cardiovascular Diseases, Dermatology, Gastroenterology, Internal Medicine, Pediatrics, Pediatric Cardiology and Pulmonary Diseases.

Rate of Nonfederal Physicians in Medical Specialties in 2005

National Rate = 96 Physicians per 100,000 Population*

RANK	STATE	RATE		RANK	STATE	RATE
30	Alabama	75		1	Massachusetts	187
47	Alaska	52		2	Maryland	166
33	Arizona	72		3	New York	160
43	Arkansas	60		4	Rhode Island	154
13	California	92		5	Connecticut	153
24	Colorado	83		6	New Jersey	133
5	Connecticut	153		7	Vermont	120
17	Delaware	89		8	Hawaii	112
17	Florida	89		9	Pennsylvania	106
28	Georgia	78		10	Illinois	103
8	Hawaii	112		11	Tennessee	96
49	Idaho	42		12	Ohio	94
10	Illinois	103		13	California	92
38	Indiana	67		13	Minnesota	92
48	Iowa	50		13	Virginia	92
41	Kansas	65		16	Missouri	90
30	Kentucky	75		17	Delaware	89
17	Louisiana	89		17	Florida	89
26	Maine	82		17	Louisiana	89
2	Maryland	166		20	New Hampshire	88
1	Massachusetts	187		20	North Carolina	88
22	Michigan	87		22	Michigan	87
13	Minnesota	92		23	Oregon	86
45	Mississippi	56		24	Colorado	83
16	Missouri	90		24	Washington	83
43	Montana	60		26	Maine	82
36	Nebraska	70		27	Wisconsin	81
39	Nevada	66		28	Georgia	78
20	New Hampshire	88		29	New Mexico	77
6	New Jersey	133		30	Alabama	75
29	New Mexico	77		30	Kentucky	75
3	New York	160		32	South Carolina	73
20	North Carolina	88		33	Arizona	72
37	North Dakota	68		33	West Virginia	72
12	Ohio	94		35	Texas	71
46	Oklahoma	54		36	Nebraska	70
23	Oregon	86		37	North Dakota	68
9	Pennsylvania	106		38	Indiana	67
4	Rhode Island	154		39	Nevada	66
32	South Carolina	73		39	Utah	66
42	South Dakota	62		41	Kansas	65
11	Tennessee	96		42	South Dakota	62
35	Texas	71		43	Arkansas	60
39	Utah	66		43	Montana	60
7	Vermont	120		45	Mississippi	56
13	Virginia	92		46	Oklahoma	54
24	Washington	83		47	Alaska	52
33	West Virginia	72		48	Iowa	50
27	Wisconsin	81		49	Idaho	42
50	Wyoming	41		50	Wyoming	41

District of Columbia 301

Source: Morgan Quitno Press using data from American Medical Association (Chicago, Illinois)
    "Physician Characteristics and Distribution in the U.S." (2007 Edition)
*As of December 31, 2005. National rate does not include physicians in U.S. territories and possessions. Medical Specialties are Allergy/Immunology, Cardiovascular Diseases, Dermatology, Gastroenterology, Internal Medicine, Pediatrics, Pediatric Cardiology and Pulmonary Diseases.

Physicians in Internal Medicine in 2005

National Total = 152,294 Physicians*

ALPHA ORDER

RANK	STATE	PHYSICIANS	% of USA
26	Alabama	1,845	1.2%
49	Alaska	162	0.1%
21	Arizona	2,228	1.5%
36	Arkansas	772	0.5%
1	California	17,853	11.7%
23	Colorado	1,997	1.3%
15	Connecticut	3,131	2.1%
44	Delaware	352	0.2%
4	Florida	7,947	5.2%
13	Georgia	3,767	2.5%
35	Hawaii	807	0.5%
45	Idaho	305	0.2%
5	Illinois	7,513	4.9%
22	Indiana	2,111	1.4%
39	Iowa	703	0.5%
32	Kansas	908	0.6%
27	Kentucky	1,574	1.0%
24	Louisiana	1,985	1.3%
42	Maine	587	0.4%
10	Maryland	5,163	3.4%
7	Massachusetts	7,018	4.6%
11	Michigan	4,996	3.3%
19	Minnesota	2,545	1.7%
33	Mississippi	833	0.5%
18	Missouri	2,772	1.8%
46	Montana	302	0.2%
40	Nebraska	637	0.4%
31	Nevada	909	0.6%
41	New Hampshire	623	0.4%
8	New Jersey	6,208	4.1%
34	New Mexico	820	0.5%
2	New York	17,741	11.6%
12	North Carolina	3,909	2.6%
48	North Dakota	267	0.2%
9	Ohio	5,485	3.6%
29	Oklahoma	995	0.7%
25	Oregon	1,874	1.2%
6	Pennsylvania	7,220	4.7%
30	Rhode Island	916	0.6%
28	South Carolina	1,541	1.0%
47	South Dakota	279	0.2%
16	Tennessee	2,951	1.9%
3	Texas	7,960	5.2%
37	Utah	724	0.5%
43	Vermont	422	0.3%
14	Virginia	3,629	2.4%
17	Washington	2,788	1.8%
38	West Virginia	709	0.5%
20	Wisconsin	2,424	1.6%
50	Wyoming	116	0.1%

RANK ORDER

RANK	STATE	PHYSICIANS	% of USA
1	California	17,853	11.7%
2	New York	17,741	11.6%
3	Texas	7,960	5.2%
4	Florida	7,947	5.2%
5	Illinois	7,513	4.9%
6	Pennsylvania	7,220	4.7%
7	Massachusetts	7,018	4.6%
8	New Jersey	6,208	4.1%
9	Ohio	5,485	3.6%
10	Maryland	5,163	3.4%
11	Michigan	4,996	3.3%
12	North Carolina	3,909	2.6%
13	Georgia	3,767	2.5%
14	Virginia	3,629	2.4%
15	Connecticut	3,131	2.1%
16	Tennessee	2,951	1.9%
17	Washington	2,788	1.8%
18	Missouri	2,772	1.8%
19	Minnesota	2,545	1.7%
20	Wisconsin	2,424	1.6%
21	Arizona	2,228	1.5%
22	Indiana	2,111	1.4%
23	Colorado	1,997	1.3%
24	Louisiana	1,985	1.3%
25	Oregon	1,874	1.2%
26	Alabama	1,845	1.2%
27	Kentucky	1,574	1.0%
28	South Carolina	1,541	1.0%
29	Oklahoma	995	0.7%
30	Rhode Island	916	0.6%
31	Nevada	909	0.6%
32	Kansas	908	0.6%
33	Mississippi	833	0.5%
34	New Mexico	820	0.5%
35	Hawaii	807	0.5%
36	Arkansas	772	0.5%
37	Utah	724	0.5%
38	West Virginia	709	0.5%
39	Iowa	703	0.5%
40	Nebraska	637	0.4%
41	New Hampshire	623	0.4%
42	Maine	587	0.4%
43	Vermont	422	0.3%
44	Delaware	352	0.2%
45	Idaho	305	0.2%
46	Montana	302	0.2%
47	South Dakota	279	0.2%
48	North Dakota	267	0.2%
49	Alaska	162	0.1%
50	Wyoming	116	0.1%
	District of Columbia	971	0.6%

Source: American Medical Association (Chicago, Illinois)
"Physician Characteristics and Distribution in the U.S." (2007 Edition)
As of December 31, 2005. Total does not include 1,708 physicians in U.S. territories and possessions. Internal Medicine includes Diabetes, Endocrinology, Geriatrics, Hematology, Infectious Diseases, Nephrology, Nutrition, Medical Oncology and Rheumatology.

Rate of Physicians in Internal Medicine in 2005

National Rate = 51 Physicians per 100,000 Population*

ALPHA ORDER

RANK	STATE	RATE
30	Alabama	41
47	Alaska	24
35	Arizona	37
45	Arkansas	28
14	California	49
26	Colorado	43
4	Connecticut	89
28	Delaware	42
20	Florida	45
30	Georgia	41
8	Hawaii	63
50	Idaho	21
9	Illinois	59
40	Indiana	34
47	Iowa	24
41	Kansas	33
33	Kentucky	38
23	Louisiana	44
20	Maine	45
2	Maryland	92
1	Massachusetts	109
14	Michigan	49
12	Minnesota	50
43	Mississippi	29
16	Missouri	48
42	Montana	32
36	Nebraska	36
33	Nevada	38
16	New Hampshire	48
6	New Jersey	71
26	New Mexico	43
2	New York	92
20	North Carolina	45
28	North Dakota	42
16	Ohio	48
45	Oklahoma	28
11	Oregon	51
10	Pennsylvania	58
5	Rhode Island	85
36	South Carolina	36
36	South Dakota	36
12	Tennessee	50
39	Texas	35
43	Utah	29
7	Vermont	68
16	Virginia	48
23	Washington	44
32	West Virginia	39
23	Wisconsin	44
49	Wyoming	23

RANK ORDER

RANK	STATE	RATE
1	Massachusetts	109
2	Maryland	92
2	New York	92
4	Connecticut	89
5	Rhode Island	85
6	New Jersey	71
7	Vermont	68
8	Hawaii	63
9	Illinois	59
10	Pennsylvania	58
11	Oregon	51
12	Minnesota	50
12	Tennessee	50
14	California	49
14	Michigan	49
16	Missouri	48
16	New Hampshire	48
16	Ohio	48
16	Virginia	48
20	Florida	45
20	Maine	45
20	North Carolina	45
23	Louisiana	44
23	Washington	44
23	Wisconsin	44
26	Colorado	43
26	New Mexico	43
28	Delaware	42
28	North Dakota	42
30	Alabama	41
30	Georgia	41
32	West Virginia	39
33	Kentucky	38
33	Nevada	38
35	Arizona	37
36	Nebraska	36
36	South Carolina	36
36	South Dakota	36
39	Texas	35
40	Indiana	34
41	Kansas	33
42	Montana	32
43	Mississippi	29
43	Utah	29
45	Arkansas	28
45	Oklahoma	28
47	Alaska	24
47	Iowa	24
49	Wyoming	23
50	Idaho	21

District of Columbia 167

Source: Morgan Quitno Press using data from American Medical Association (Chicago, Illinois)
"Physician Characteristics and Distribution in the U.S." (2007 Edition)
*As of December 31, 2005. National rate does not include physicians in U.S. territories and possessions. Internal Medicine includes Diabetes, Endocrinology, Geriatrics, Hematology, Infectious Diseases, Nephrology, Nutrition, Medical Oncology and Rheumatology.

Physicians in Pediatrics in 2005

National Total = 71,079 Physicians*

ALPHA ORDER

RANK	STATE	PHYSICIANS	% of USA
27	Alabama	817	1.1%
46	Alaska	122	0.2%
23	Arizona	1,074	1.5%
30	Arkansas	473	0.7%
1	California	8,617	12.1%
24	Colorado	996	1.4%
18	Connecticut	1,119	1.6%
43	Delaware	243	0.3%
4	Florida	3,775	5.3%
13	Georgia	1,895	2.7%
33	Hawaii	404	0.6%
45	Idaho	128	0.2%
5	Illinois	3,076	4.3%
20	Indiana	1,103	1.6%
37	Iowa	364	0.5%
31	Kansas	470	0.7%
25	Kentucky	861	1.2%
22	Louisiana	1,091	1.5%
42	Maine	268	0.4%
10	Maryland	2,307	3.2%
9	Massachusetts	2,677	3.8%
11	Michigan	2,180	3.1%
19	Minnesota	1,112	1.6%
35	Mississippi	394	0.6%
17	Missouri	1,281	1.8%
47	Montana	115	0.2%
39	Nebraska	313	0.4%
38	Nevada	345	0.5%
41	New Hampshire	285	0.4%
7	New Jersey	2,993	4.2%
36	New Mexico	371	0.5%
2	New York	7,422	10.4%
12	North Carolina	1,960	2.8%
49	North Dakota	84	0.1%
6	Ohio	3,032	4.3%
32	Oklahoma	460	0.6%
28	Oregon	682	1.0%
8	Pennsylvania	2,896	4.1%
34	Rhode Island	396	0.6%
26	South Carolina	830	1.2%
48	South Dakota	92	0.1%
15	Tennessee	1,493	2.1%
3	Texas	4,631	6.5%
29	Utah	540	0.8%
44	Vermont	191	0.3%
14	Virginia	1,886	2.7%
16	Washington	1,309	1.8%
40	West Virginia	310	0.4%
21	Wisconsin	1,101	1.5%
50	Wyoming	49	0.1%

RANK ORDER

RANK	STATE	PHYSICIANS	% of USA
1	California	8,617	12.1%
2	New York	7,422	10.4%
3	Texas	4,631	6.5%
4	Florida	3,775	5.3%
5	Illinois	3,076	4.3%
6	Ohio	3,032	4.3%
7	New Jersey	2,993	4.2%
8	Pennsylvania	2,896	4.1%
9	Massachusetts	2,677	3.8%
10	Maryland	2,307	3.2%
11	Michigan	2,180	3.1%
12	North Carolina	1,960	2.8%
13	Georgia	1,895	2.7%
14	Virginia	1,886	2.7%
15	Tennessee	1,493	2.1%
16	Washington	1,309	1.8%
17	Missouri	1,281	1.8%
18	Connecticut	1,119	1.6%
19	Minnesota	1,112	1.6%
20	Indiana	1,103	1.6%
21	Wisconsin	1,101	1.5%
22	Louisiana	1,091	1.5%
23	Arizona	1,074	1.5%
24	Colorado	996	1.4%
25	Kentucky	861	1.2%
26	South Carolina	830	1.2%
27	Alabama	817	1.1%
28	Oregon	682	1.0%
29	Utah	540	0.8%
30	Arkansas	473	0.7%
31	Kansas	470	0.7%
32	Oklahoma	460	0.6%
33	Hawaii	404	0.6%
34	Rhode Island	396	0.6%
35	Mississippi	394	0.6%
36	New Mexico	371	0.5%
37	Iowa	364	0.5%
38	Nevada	345	0.5%
39	Nebraska	313	0.4%
40	West Virginia	310	0.4%
41	New Hampshire	285	0.4%
42	Maine	268	0.4%
43	Delaware	243	0.3%
44	Vermont	191	0.3%
45	Idaho	128	0.2%
46	Alaska	122	0.2%
47	Montana	115	0.2%
48	South Dakota	92	0.1%
49	North Dakota	84	0.1%
50	Wyoming	49	0.1%
	District of Columbia	446	0.6%

Source: American Medical Association (Chicago, Illinois)
"Physician Characteristics and Distribution in the U.S." (2007 Edition)
*As of December 31, 2005. Total does not include 1,209 physicians in U.S. territories and possessions. Pediatrics includes Adolescent Medicine, Neonatal-Perinatal, Pediatric Allergy, Pediatric Endocrinology, Pediatric Pulmonology, Pediatric Hematology-Oncology and Pediatric Nephrology.

Rate of Physicians in Pediatrics in 2005

National Rate = 97 Physicians per 100,000 Population 17 Years and Younger*

ALPHA ORDER | | | RANK ORDER | |

RANK	STATE	RATE	RANK	STATE	RATE
33	Alabama	75	1	Massachusetts	184
41	Alaska	65	2	Maryland	164
40	Arizona	68	3	New York	163
37	Arkansas	70	4	Rhode Island	161
22	California	89	5	Vermont	144
27	Colorado	84	6	New Jersey	138
8	Connecticut	134	7	Hawaii	135
9	Delaware	124	8	Connecticut	134
18	Florida	93	9	Delaware	124
30	Georgia	80	10	Ohio	110
7	Hawaii	135	11	Tennessee	107
50	Idaho	34	12	Pennsylvania	103
15	Illinois	95	12	Virginia	103
39	Indiana	69	14	Maine	97
45	Iowa	54	15	Illinois	95
37	Kansas	70	15	Louisiana	95
23	Kentucky	88	17	New Hampshire	94
15	Louisiana	95	18	Florida	93
14	Maine	97	18	Missouri	93
2	Maryland	164	20	North Carolina	92
1	Massachusetts	184	21	Minnesota	90
25	Michigan	86	22	California	89
21	Minnesota	90	23	Kentucky	88
47	Mississippi	53	23	Washington	88
18	Missouri	93	25	Michigan	86
43	Montana	56	26	Wisconsin	85
34	Nebraska	73	27	Colorado	84
43	Nevada	56	28	South Carolina	81
17	New Hampshire	94	28	West Virginia	81
6	New Jersey	138	30	Georgia	80
32	New Mexico	76	30	Oregon	80
3	New York	163	32	New Mexico	76
20	North Carolina	92	33	Alabama	75
42	North Dakota	62	34	Nebraska	73
10	Ohio	110	34	Texas	73
45	Oklahoma	54	34	Utah	73
30	Oregon	80	37	Arkansas	70
12	Pennsylvania	103	37	Kansas	70
4	Rhode Island	161	39	Indiana	69
28	South Carolina	81	40	Arizona	68
48	South Dakota	49	41	Alaska	65
11	Tennessee	107	42	North Dakota	62
34	Texas	73	43	Montana	56
34	Utah	73	43	Nevada	56
5	Vermont	144	45	Iowa	54
12	Virginia	103	45	Oklahoma	54
23	Washington	88	47	Mississippi	53
28	West Virginia	81	48	South Dakota	49
26	Wisconsin	85	49	Wyoming	43
49	Wyoming	43	50	Idaho	34
				District of Columbia	395

Source: Morgan Quitno Press using data from American Medical Association (Chicago, Illinois)
    "Physician Characteristics and Distribution in the U.S." (2007 Edition)

As of December 31, 2005. National rate does not include physicians in U.S. territories and possessions. Pediatrics includes Adolescent Medicine, Neonatal-Perinatal, Pediatric Allergy, Pediatric Endocrinology, Pediatric Pulmonology, Pediatric Hematology-Oncology and Pediatric Nephrology.

Physicians in Surgical Specialties in 2005

National Total = 160,897 Physicians*

ALPHA ORDER

RANK	STATE	PHYSICIANS	% of USA
25	Alabama	2,276	1.4%
48	Alaska	338	0.2%
22	Arizona	2,536	1.6%
33	Arkansas	1,161	0.7%
1	California	18,829	11.7%
23	Colorado	2,523	1.6%
24	Connecticut	2,508	1.6%
45	Delaware	445	0.3%
4	Florida	9,284	5.8%
12	Georgia	4,515	2.8%
39	Hawaii	811	0.5%
43	Idaho	599	0.4%
6	Illinois	6,614	4.1%
20	Indiana	2,732	1.7%
32	Iowa	1,172	0.7%
30	Kansas	1,298	0.8%
27	Kentucky	2,087	1.3%
19	Louisiana	2,766	1.7%
42	Maine	717	0.4%
13	Maryland	4,315	2.7%
10	Massachusetts	4,748	3.0%
9	Michigan	4,929	3.1%
21	Minnesota	2,684	1.7%
31	Mississippi	1,286	0.8%
17	Missouri	2,932	1.8%
44	Montana	496	0.3%
37	Nebraska	904	0.6%
35	Nevada	938	0.6%
41	New Hampshire	732	0.5%
8	New Jersey	5,409	3.4%
38	New Mexico	840	0.5%
2	New York	14,193	8.8%
11	North Carolina	4,718	2.9%
49	North Dakota	302	0.2%
7	Ohio	6,117	3.8%
29	Oklahoma	1,329	0.8%
28	Oregon	2,025	1.3%
5	Pennsylvania	7,286	4.5%
40	Rhode Island	746	0.5%
26	South Carolina	2,249	1.4%
47	South Dakota	388	0.2%
15	Tennessee	3,544	2.2%
3	Texas	10,701	6.7%
34	Utah	1,144	0.7%
46	Vermont	430	0.3%
14	Virginia	4,283	2.7%
16	Washington	3,191	2.0%
36	West Virginia	917	0.6%
18	Wisconsin	2,801	1.7%
50	Wyoming	232	0.1%

RANK ORDER

RANK	STATE	PHYSICIANS	% of USA
1	California	18,829	11.7%
2	New York	14,193	8.8%
3	Texas	10,701	6.7%
4	Florida	9,284	5.8%
5	Pennsylvania	7,286	4.5%
6	Illinois	6,614	4.1%
7	Ohio	6,117	3.8%
8	New Jersey	5,409	3.4%
9	Michigan	4,929	3.1%
10	Massachusetts	4,748	3.0%
11	North Carolina	4,718	2.9%
12	Georgia	4,515	2.8%
13	Maryland	4,315	2.7%
14	Virginia	4,283	2.7%
15	Tennessee	3,544	2.2%
16	Washington	3,191	2.0%
17	Missouri	2,932	1.8%
18	Wisconsin	2,801	1.7%
19	Louisiana	2,766	1.7%
20	Indiana	2,732	1.7%
21	Minnesota	2,684	1.7%
22	Arizona	2,536	1.6%
23	Colorado	2,523	1.6%
24	Connecticut	2,508	1.6%
25	Alabama	2,276	1.4%
26	South Carolina	2,249	1.4%
27	Kentucky	2,087	1.3%
28	Oregon	2,025	1.3%
29	Oklahoma	1,329	0.8%
30	Kansas	1,298	0.8%
31	Mississippi	1,286	0.8%
32	Iowa	1,172	0.7%
33	Arkansas	1,161	0.7%
34	Utah	1,144	0.7%
35	Nevada	938	0.6%
36	West Virginia	917	0.6%
37	Nebraska	904	0.6%
38	New Mexico	840	0.5%
39	Hawaii	811	0.5%
40	Rhode Island	746	0.5%
41	New Hampshire	732	0.5%
42	Maine	717	0.4%
43	Idaho	599	0.4%
44	Montana	496	0.3%
45	Delaware	445	0.3%
46	Vermont	430	0.3%
47	South Dakota	388	0.2%
48	Alaska	338	0.2%
49	North Dakota	302	0.2%
50	Wyoming	232	0.1%
	District of Columbia	877	0.5%

Source: American Medical Association (Chicago, Illinois)
"Physician Characteristics and Distribution in the U.S." (2007 Edition)
As of December 31, 2005. Total does not include 1,812 physicians in U.S. territories and possessions. Surgical Specialties include Colon and Rectal, General, Neurological, Obstetrics & Gynecology, Ophthalmology, Orthopedic, Otolaryngology, Plastic, Thoracic and Urological Surgeries.

Rate of Physicians in Surgical Specialties in 2005

National Rate = 54 Physicians per 100,000 Population*

ALPHA ORDER

RANK	STATE	RATE
32	Alabama	50
26	Alaska	51
45	Arizona	43
46	Arkansas	42
22	California	52
15	Colorado	54
4	Connecticut	72
18	Delaware	53
22	Florida	52
35	Georgia	49
7	Hawaii	64
46	Idaho	42
22	Illinois	52
42	Indiana	44
48	Iowa	40
38	Kansas	47
32	Kentucky	50
9	Louisiana	61
15	Maine	54
1	Maryland	77
2	Massachusetts	74
35	Michigan	49
22	Minnesota	52
42	Mississippi	44
26	Missouri	51
18	Montana	53
26	Nebraska	51
49	Nevada	39
13	New Hampshire	56
8	New Jersey	62
42	New Mexico	44
3	New York	73
15	North Carolina	54
37	North Dakota	48
18	Ohio	53
50	Oklahoma	38
13	Oregon	56
11	Pennsylvania	59
5	Rhode Island	69
18	South Carolina	53
32	South Dakota	50
10	Tennessee	60
38	Texas	47
40	Utah	46
5	Vermont	69
12	Virginia	57
26	Washington	51
26	West Virginia	51
26	Wisconsin	51
40	Wyoming	46

RANK ORDER

RANK	STATE	RATE
1	Maryland	77
2	Massachusetts	74
3	New York	73
4	Connecticut	72
5	Rhode Island	69
5	Vermont	69
7	Hawaii	64
8	New Jersey	62
9	Louisiana	61
10	Tennessee	60
11	Pennsylvania	59
12	Virginia	57
13	New Hampshire	56
13	Oregon	56
15	Colorado	54
15	Maine	54
15	North Carolina	54
18	Delaware	53
18	Montana	53
18	Ohio	53
18	South Carolina	53
22	California	52
22	Florida	52
22	Illinois	52
22	Minnesota	52
26	Alaska	51
26	Missouri	51
26	Nebraska	51
26	Washington	51
26	West Virginia	51
26	Wisconsin	51
32	Alabama	50
32	Kentucky	50
32	South Dakota	50
35	Georgia	49
35	Michigan	49
37	North Dakota	48
38	Kansas	47
38	Texas	47
40	Utah	46
40	Wyoming	46
42	Indiana	44
42	Mississippi	44
42	New Mexico	44
45	Arizona	43
46	Arkansas	42
46	Idaho	42
48	Iowa	40
49	Nevada	39
50	Oklahoma	38

District of Columbia — 151

Source: Morgan Quitno Press using data from American Medical Association (Chicago, Illinois)
"Physician Characteristics and Distribution in the U.S." (2007 Edition)
*As of December 31, 2005. National rate does not include physicians in U.S. territories and possessions. Surgical Specialties include Colon and Rectal, General, Neurological, Obstetrics & Gynecology, Ophthalmology, Orthopedic, Otolaryngology, Plastic, Thoracic and Urological Surgeries.

Average Annual Wages of Surgeons in 2005

National Average = $177,690*

ALPHA ORDER

RANK	STATE	WAGES
37	Alabama	$176,010
NA	Alaska**	NA
40	Arizona	172,710
32	Arkansas	180,120
45	California	158,980
35	Colorado	176,400
41	Connecticut	171,470
42	Delaware	170,190
38	Florida	172,900
25	Georgia	183,810
NA	Hawaii**	NA
21	Idaho	185,380
43	Illinois	162,660
7	Indiana	191,580
33	Iowa	179,960
4	Kansas	193,400
12	Kentucky	188,500
34	Louisiana	178,960
5	Maine	192,670
23	Maryland	184,600
36	Massachusetts	176,340
24	Michigan	184,160
11	Minnesota	189,290
13	Mississippi	187,550
17	Missouri	186,190
8	Montana	190,530
22	Nebraska	184,800
9	Nevada	189,860
3	New Hampshire	193,520
2	New Jersey	193,540
31	New Mexico	180,680
39	New York	172,870
26	North Carolina	183,770
46	North Dakota	143,210
14	Ohio	187,540
1	Oklahoma	194,520
NA	Oregon**	NA
44	Pennsylvania	161,920
6	Rhode Island	192,250
10	South Carolina	189,670
29	South Dakota	181,990
30	Tennessee	181,570
28	Texas	182,310
19	Utah	186,080
NA	Vermont**	NA
16	Virginia	186,850
20	Washington	185,780
27	West Virginia	182,930
15	Wisconsin	187,000
18	Wyoming	186,110

RANK ORDER

RANK	STATE	WAGES
1	Oklahoma	$194,520
2	New Jersey	193,540
3	New Hampshire	193,520
4	Kansas	193,400
5	Maine	192,670
6	Rhode Island	192,250
7	Indiana	191,580
8	Montana	190,530
9	Nevada	189,860
10	South Carolina	189,670
11	Minnesota	189,290
12	Kentucky	188,500
13	Mississippi	187,550
14	Ohio	187,540
15	Wisconsin	187,000
16	Virginia	186,850
17	Missouri	186,190
18	Wyoming	186,110
19	Utah	186,080
20	Washington	185,780
21	Idaho	185,380
22	Nebraska	184,800
23	Maryland	184,600
24	Michigan	184,160
25	Georgia	183,810
26	North Carolina	183,770
27	West Virginia	182,930
28	Texas	182,310
29	South Dakota	181,990
30	Tennessee	181,570
31	New Mexico	180,680
32	Arkansas	180,120
33	Iowa	179,960
34	Louisiana	178,960
35	Colorado	176,400
36	Massachusetts	176,340
37	Alabama	176,010
38	Florida	172,900
39	New York	172,870
40	Arizona	172,710
41	Connecticut	171,470
42	Delaware	170,190
43	Illinois	162,660
44	Pennsylvania	161,920
45	California	158,980
46	North Dakota	143,210
NA	Alaska**	NA
NA	Hawaii**	NA
NA	Oregon**	NA
NA	Vermont**	NA

District of Columbia   136,150

Source: U.S. Department of Labor, Bureau of Labor Statistics
 "Occupational Employment and Wages, 2005" (http://www.bls.gov/oes/)
*Does not include self-employed.
**Not available.

Physicians in General Surgery in 2005

National Total = 37,384 Physicians*

ALPHA ORDER

RANK ORDER

RANK	STATE	PHYSICIANS	% of USA	RANK	STATE	PHYSICIANS	% of USA
26	Alabama	539	1.4%	1	California	4,098	11.0%
49	Alaska	72	0.2%	2	New York	3,428	9.2%
21	Arizona	588	1.6%	3	Texas	2,351	6.3%
33	Arkansas	263	0.7%	4	Pennsylvania	1,900	5.1%
1	California	4,098	11.0%	5	Florida	1,877	5.0%
23	Colorado	557	1.5%	6	Illinois	1,553	4.2%
24	Connecticut	556	1.5%	7	Ohio	1,540	4.1%
45	Delaware	113	0.3%	8	Michigan	1,266	3.4%
5	Florida	1,877	5.0%	9	Massachusetts	1,247	3.3%
12	Georgia	1,029	2.8%	10	New Jersey	1,237	3.3%
40	Hawaii	175	0.5%	11	North Carolina	1,080	2.9%
43	Idaho	137	0.4%	12	Georgia	1,029	2.8%
6	Illinois	1,553	4.2%	13	Maryland	962	2.6%
22	Indiana	586	1.6%	14	Virginia	946	2.5%
31	Iowa	300	0.8%	15	Tennessee	876	2.3%
29	Kansas	317	0.8%	16	Washington	715	1.9%
27	Kentucky	533	1.4%	17	Missouri	658	1.8%
19	Louisiana	634	1.7%	18	Wisconsin	644	1.7%
39	Maine	197	0.5%	19	Louisiana	634	1.7%
13	Maryland	962	2.6%	20	Minnesota	612	1.6%
9	Massachusetts	1,247	3.3%	21	Arizona	588	1.6%
8	Michigan	1,266	3.4%	22	Indiana	586	1.6%
20	Minnesota	612	1.6%	23	Colorado	557	1.5%
32	Mississippi	283	0.8%	24	Connecticut	556	1.5%
17	Missouri	658	1.8%	25	South Carolina	548	1.5%
47	Montana	104	0.3%	26	Alabama	539	1.4%
35	Nebraska	246	0.7%	27	Kentucky	533	1.4%
37	Nevada	209	0.6%	28	Oregon	475	1.3%
40	New Hampshire	175	0.5%	29	Kansas	317	0.8%
10	New Jersey	1,237	3.3%	30	Oklahoma	306	0.8%
38	New Mexico	207	0.6%	31	Iowa	300	0.8%
2	New York	3,428	9.2%	32	Mississippi	283	0.8%
11	North Carolina	1,080	2.9%	33	Arkansas	263	0.7%
48	North Dakota	82	0.2%	34	West Virginia	256	0.7%
7	Ohio	1,540	4.1%	35	Nebraska	246	0.7%
30	Oklahoma	306	0.8%	36	Utah	218	0.6%
28	Oregon	475	1.3%	37	Nevada	209	0.6%
4	Pennsylvania	1,900	5.1%	38	New Mexico	207	0.6%
40	Rhode Island	175	0.5%	39	Maine	197	0.5%
25	South Carolina	548	1.5%	40	Hawaii	175	0.5%
46	South Dakota	105	0.3%	40	New Hampshire	175	0.5%
15	Tennessee	876	2.3%	40	Rhode Island	175	0.5%
3	Texas	2,351	6.3%	43	Idaho	137	0.4%
36	Utah	218	0.6%	44	Vermont	120	0.3%
44	Vermont	120	0.3%	45	Delaware	113	0.3%
14	Virginia	946	2.5%	46	South Dakota	105	0.3%
16	Washington	715	1.9%	47	Montana	104	0.3%
34	West Virginia	256	0.7%	48	North Dakota	82	0.2%
18	Wisconsin	644	1.7%	49	Alaska	72	0.2%
50	Wyoming	50	0.1%	50	Wyoming	50	0.1%
					District of Columbia	239	0.6%

Source: American Medical Association (Chicago, Illinois)
"Physician Characteristics and Distribution in the U.S." (2007 Edition)
*As of December 31, 2005. Total does not include 473 physicians in U.S. territories and possessions. General Surgery includes Abdominal, Cardiovascular, Hand, Head and Neck, Pediatric, Traumatic and Vascular Surgeries.

Rate of Physicians in General Surgery in 2005

National Rate = 13 Physicians per 100,000 Population*

ALPHA ORDER

RANK	STATE	RATE
25	Alabama	12
32	Alaska	11
40	Arizona	10
46	Arkansas	9
32	California	11
25	Colorado	12
5	Connecticut	16
16	Delaware	13
32	Florida	11
32	Georgia	11
10	Hawaii	14
40	Idaho	10
25	Illinois	12
46	Indiana	9
40	Iowa	10
25	Kansas	12
16	Kentucky	13
10	Louisiana	14
7	Maine	15
4	Maryland	17
1	Massachusetts	19
16	Michigan	13
25	Minnesota	12
40	Mississippi	10
32	Missouri	11
32	Montana	11
10	Nebraska	14
46	Nevada	9
16	New Hampshire	13
10	New Jersey	14
32	New Mexico	11
3	New York	18
25	North Carolina	12
16	North Dakota	13
16	Ohio	13
46	Oklahoma	9
16	Oregon	13
7	Pennsylvania	15
5	Rhode Island	16
16	South Carolina	13
10	South Dakota	14
7	Tennessee	15
40	Texas	10
46	Utah	9
1	Vermont	19
16	Virginia	13
32	Washington	11
10	West Virginia	14
25	Wisconsin	12
40	Wyoming	10

RANK ORDER

RANK	STATE	RATE
1	Massachusetts	19
1	Vermont	19
3	New York	18
4	Maryland	17
5	Connecticut	16
5	Rhode Island	16
7	Maine	15
7	Pennsylvania	15
7	Tennessee	15
10	Hawaii	14
10	Louisiana	14
10	Nebraska	14
10	New Jersey	14
10	South Dakota	14
10	West Virginia	14
16	Delaware	13
16	Kentucky	13
16	Michigan	13
16	New Hampshire	13
16	North Dakota	13
16	Ohio	13
16	Oregon	13
16	South Carolina	13
16	Virginia	13
25	Alabama	12
25	Colorado	12
25	Illinois	12
25	Kansas	12
25	Minnesota	12
25	North Carolina	12
25	Wisconsin	12
32	Alaska	11
32	California	11
32	Florida	11
32	Georgia	11
32	Missouri	11
32	Montana	11
32	New Mexico	11
32	Washington	11
40	Arizona	10
40	Idaho	10
40	Iowa	10
40	Mississippi	10
40	Texas	10
40	Wyoming	10
46	Arkansas	9
46	Indiana	9
46	Nevada	9
46	Oklahoma	9
46	Utah	9
	District of Columbia	41

Source: Morgan Quitno Press using data from American Medical Association (Chicago, Illinois)
"Physician Characteristics and Distribution in the U.S." (2007 Edition)
*As of December 31, 2005. National rate does not include physicians in U.S. territories and possessions. General Surgery includes Abdominal, Cardiovascular, Hand, Head and Neck, Pediatric, Traumatic and Vascular Surgeries.

Physicians in Obstetrics and Gynecology in 2005

National Total = 41,955 Physicians*

ALPHA ORDER

RANK	STATE	PHYSICIANS	% of USA
26	Alabama	573	1.4%
47	Alaska	83	0.2%
21	Arizona	682	1.6%
33	Arkansas	269	0.6%
1	California	4,971	11.8%
22	Colorado	657	1.6%
19	Connecticut	709	1.7%
46	Delaware	110	0.3%
4	Florida	2,246	5.4%
9	Georgia	1,403	3.3%
35	Hawaii	253	0.6%
43	Idaho	139	0.3%
5	Illinois	1,883	4.5%
20	Indiana	707	1.7%
36	Iowa	218	0.5%
31	Kansas	298	0.7%
27	Kentucky	516	1.2%
18	Louisiana	717	1.7%
42	Maine	165	0.4%
14	Maryland	1,157	2.8%
13	Massachusetts	1,159	2.8%
10	Michigan	1,366	3.3%
24	Minnesota	602	1.4%
29	Mississippi	334	0.8%
17	Missouri	722	1.7%
44	Montana	111	0.3%
41	Nebraska	192	0.5%
34	Nevada	267	0.6%
40	New Hampshire	201	0.5%
7	New Jersey	1,556	3.7%
37	New Mexico	213	0.5%
2	New York	3,833	9.1%
11	North Carolina	1,303	3.1%
50	North Dakota	52	0.1%
8	Ohio	1,552	3.7%
30	Oklahoma	321	0.8%
27	Oregon	516	1.2%
6	Pennsylvania	1,693	4.0%
39	Rhode Island	202	0.5%
25	South Carolina	590	1.4%
48	South Dakota	73	0.2%
15	Tennessee	886	2.1%
3	Texas	2,971	7.1%
32	Utah	286	0.7%
44	Vermont	111	0.3%
12	Virginia	1,206	2.9%
16	Washington	763	1.8%
38	West Virginia	208	0.5%
23	Wisconsin	626	1.5%
49	Wyoming	55	0.1%

RANK ORDER

RANK	STATE	PHYSICIANS	% of USA
1	California	4,971	11.8%
2	New York	3,833	9.1%
3	Texas	2,971	7.1%
4	Florida	2,246	5.4%
5	Illinois	1,883	4.5%
6	Pennsylvania	1,693	4.0%
7	New Jersey	1,556	3.7%
8	Ohio	1,552	3.7%
9	Georgia	1,403	3.3%
10	Michigan	1,366	3.3%
11	North Carolina	1,303	3.1%
12	Virginia	1,206	2.9%
13	Massachusetts	1,159	2.8%
14	Maryland	1,157	2.8%
15	Tennessee	886	2.1%
16	Washington	763	1.8%
17	Missouri	722	1.7%
18	Louisiana	717	1.7%
19	Connecticut	709	1.7%
20	Indiana	707	1.7%
21	Arizona	682	1.6%
22	Colorado	657	1.6%
23	Wisconsin	626	1.5%
24	Minnesota	602	1.4%
25	South Carolina	590	1.4%
26	Alabama	573	1.4%
27	Kentucky	516	1.2%
27	Oregon	516	1.2%
29	Mississippi	334	0.8%
30	Oklahoma	321	0.8%
31	Kansas	298	0.7%
32	Utah	286	0.7%
33	Arkansas	269	0.6%
34	Nevada	267	0.6%
35	Hawaii	253	0.6%
36	Iowa	218	0.5%
37	New Mexico	213	0.5%
38	West Virginia	208	0.5%
39	Rhode Island	202	0.5%
40	New Hampshire	201	0.5%
41	Nebraska	192	0.5%
42	Maine	165	0.4%
43	Idaho	139	0.3%
44	Montana	111	0.3%
44	Vermont	111	0.3%
46	Delaware	110	0.3%
47	Alaska	83	0.2%
48	South Dakota	73	0.2%
49	Wyoming	55	0.1%
50	North Dakota	52	0.1%
	District of Columbia	229	0.5%

Source: American Medical Association (Chicago, Illinois)
   "Physician Characteristics and Distribution in the U.S." (2007 Edition)
*As of December 31, 2005. Total does not include 645 physicians in U.S. territories and possessions. Obstetrics and Gynecology includes Gynecology and Oncology, Maternal and Fetal Medicine and Reproductive Endocrinology.

Rate of Physicians in Obstetrics and Gynecology in 2005

National Rate = 28 Physicians per 100,000 Female Population*

ALPHA ORDER

RANK	STATE	RATE
27	Alabama	24
21	Alaska	26
33	Arizona	23
46	Arkansas	19
18	California	27
16	Colorado	28
3	Connecticut	39
25	Delaware	25
25	Florida	25
9	Georgia	31
1	Hawaii	40
45	Idaho	20
14	Illinois	29
37	Indiana	22
50	Iowa	14
37	Kansas	22
27	Kentucky	24
9	Louisiana	31
27	Maine	24
1	Maryland	40
6	Massachusetts	35
18	Michigan	27
33	Minnesota	23
37	Mississippi	22
27	Missouri	24
27	Montana	24
37	Nebraska	22
33	Nevada	23
12	New Hampshire	30
6	New Jersey	35
37	New Mexico	22
3	New York	39
12	North Carolina	30
49	North Dakota	16
21	Ohio	26
48	Oklahoma	18
16	Oregon	28
21	Pennsylvania	26
5	Rhode Island	36
18	South Carolina	27
46	South Dakota	19
14	Tennessee	29
21	Texas	26
33	Utah	23
6	Vermont	35
9	Virginia	31
27	Washington	24
37	West Virginia	22
37	Wisconsin	22
37	Wyoming	22

RANK ORDER

RANK	STATE	RATE
1	Hawaii	40
1	Maryland	40
3	Connecticut	39
3	New York	39
5	Rhode Island	36
6	Massachusetts	35
6	New Jersey	35
6	Vermont	35
9	Georgia	31
9	Louisiana	31
9	Virginia	31
12	New Hampshire	30
12	North Carolina	30
14	Illinois	29
14	Tennessee	29
16	Colorado	28
16	Oregon	28
18	California	27
18	Michigan	27
18	South Carolina	27
21	Alaska	26
21	Ohio	26
21	Pennsylvania	26
21	Texas	26
25	Delaware	25
25	Florida	25
27	Alabama	24
27	Kentucky	24
27	Maine	24
27	Missouri	24
27	Montana	24
27	Washington	24
33	Arizona	23
33	Minnesota	23
33	Nevada	23
33	Utah	23
37	Indiana	22
37	Kansas	22
37	Mississippi	22
37	Nebraska	22
37	New Mexico	22
37	West Virginia	22
37	Wisconsin	22
37	Wyoming	22
45	Idaho	20
46	Arkansas	19
46	South Dakota	19
48	Oklahoma	18
49	North Dakota	16
50	Iowa	14

| | District of Columbia | 79 |

Source: Morgan Quitno Press using data from American Medical Association (Chicago, Illinois)
"Physician Characteristics and Distribution in the U.S." (2007 Edition)

*As of December 31, 2005. National rate does not include physicians in U.S. territories and possessions. Obstetrics and Gynecology includes Gynecology and Oncology, Maternal and Fetal Medicine and Reproductive Endocrinology.

Physicians in Ophthalmology in 2005

National Total = 18,674 Physicians*

ALPHA ORDER

RANK	STATE	PHYSICIANS	% of USA
27	Alabama	225	1.2%
49	Alaska	32	0.2%
22	Arizona	295	1.6%
33	Arkansas	137	0.7%
1	California	2,330	12.5%
24	Colorado	280	1.5%
19	Connecticut	316	1.7%
46	Delaware	42	0.2%
3	Florida	1,241	6.6%
14	Georgia	438	2.3%
36	Hawaii	99	0.5%
43	Idaho	56	0.3%
6	Illinois	750	4.0%
23	Indiana	292	1.6%
29	Iowa	162	0.9%
30	Kansas	159	0.9%
28	Kentucky	197	1.1%
21	Louisiana	304	1.6%
41	Maine	81	0.4%
9	Maryland	574	3.1%
11	Massachusetts	537	2.9%
10	Michigan	567	3.0%
19	Minnesota	316	1.7%
31	Mississippi	146	0.8%
18	Missouri	331	1.8%
44	Montana	53	0.3%
38	Nebraska	96	0.5%
37	Nevada	98	0.5%
42	New Hampshire	73	0.4%
7	New Jersey	650	3.5%
39	New Mexico	87	0.5%
2	New York	1,834	9.8%
13	North Carolina	473	2.5%
48	North Dakota	38	0.2%
8	Ohio	645	3.5%
32	Oklahoma	140	0.7%
26	Oregon	227	1.2%
5	Pennsylvania	888	4.8%
40	Rhode Island	82	0.4%
25	South Carolina	248	1.3%
47	South Dakota	41	0.2%
15	Tennessee	371	2.0%
4	Texas	1,131	6.1%
34	Utah	131	0.7%
45	Vermont	45	0.2%
12	Virginia	479	2.6%
16	Washington	369	2.0%
35	West Virginia	100	0.5%
17	Wisconsin	347	1.9%
50	Wyoming	19	0.1%

RANK ORDER

RANK	STATE	PHYSICIANS	% of USA
1	California	2,330	12.5%
2	New York	1,834	9.8%
3	Florida	1,241	6.6%
4	Texas	1,131	6.1%
5	Pennsylvania	888	4.8%
6	Illinois	750	4.0%
7	New Jersey	650	3.5%
8	Ohio	645	3.5%
9	Maryland	574	3.1%
10	Michigan	567	3.0%
11	Massachusetts	537	2.9%
12	Virginia	479	2.6%
13	North Carolina	473	2.5%
14	Georgia	438	2.3%
15	Tennessee	371	2.0%
16	Washington	369	2.0%
17	Wisconsin	347	1.9%
18	Missouri	331	1.8%
19	Connecticut	316	1.7%
19	Minnesota	316	1.7%
21	Louisiana	304	1.6%
22	Arizona	295	1.6%
23	Indiana	292	1.6%
24	Colorado	280	1.5%
25	South Carolina	248	1.3%
26	Oregon	227	1.2%
27	Alabama	225	1.2%
28	Kentucky	197	1.1%
29	Iowa	162	0.9%
30	Kansas	159	0.9%
31	Mississippi	146	0.8%
32	Oklahoma	140	0.7%
33	Arkansas	137	0.7%
34	Utah	131	0.7%
35	West Virginia	100	0.5%
36	Hawaii	99	0.5%
37	Nevada	98	0.5%
38	Nebraska	96	0.5%
39	New Mexico	87	0.5%
40	Rhode Island	82	0.4%
41	Maine	81	0.4%
42	New Hampshire	73	0.4%
43	Idaho	56	0.3%
44	Montana	53	0.3%
45	Vermont	45	0.2%
46	Delaware	42	0.2%
47	South Dakota	41	0.2%
48	North Dakota	38	0.2%
49	Alaska	32	0.2%
50	Wyoming	19	0.1%
	District of Columbia	102	0.5%

Source: American Medical Association (Chicago, Illinois)
   "Physician Characteristics and Distribution in the U.S." (2007 Edition)
*As of December 31, 2005. Total does not include 196 physicians in U.S. territories and possessions.
Ophthalmology is the branch of medicine dealing with the anatomy, functions and diseases of the eye.

Rate of Physicians in Ophthalmology in 2005

National Rate = 6 Physicians per 100,000 Population*

ALPHA ORDER				RANK ORDER		
RANK	STATE	RATE		RANK	STATE	RATE
31	Alabama	5		1	Maryland	10
31	Alaska	5		2	Connecticut	9
31	Arizona	5		2	New York	9
31	Arkansas	5		4	Hawaii	8
12	California	6		4	Massachusetts	8
12	Colorado	6		4	Rhode Island	8
2	Connecticut	9		7	Florida	7
31	Delaware	5		7	Louisiana	7
7	Florida	7		7	New Jersey	7
31	Georgia	5		7	Pennsylvania	7
4	Hawaii	8		7	Vermont	7
47	Idaho	4		12	California	6
12	Illinois	6		12	Colorado	6
31	Indiana	5		12	Illinois	6
31	Iowa	5		12	Kansas	6
12	Kansas	6		12	Maine	6
31	Kentucky	5		12	Michigan	6
7	Louisiana	7		12	Minnesota	6
12	Maine	6		12	Missouri	6
1	Maryland	10		12	Montana	6
4	Massachusetts	8		12	New Hampshire	6
12	Michigan	6		12	North Dakota	6
12	Minnesota	6		12	Ohio	6
31	Mississippi	5		12	Oregon	6
12	Missouri	6		12	South Carolina	6
12	Montana	6		12	Tennessee	6
31	Nebraska	5		12	Virginia	6
47	Nevada	4		12	Washington	6
12	New Hampshire	6		12	West Virginia	6
7	New Jersey	7		12	Wisconsin	6
31	New Mexico	5		31	Alabama	5
2	New York	9		31	Alaska	5
31	North Carolina	5		31	Arizona	5
12	North Dakota	6		31	Arkansas	5
12	Ohio	6		31	Delaware	5
47	Oklahoma	4		31	Georgia	5
12	Oregon	6		31	Indiana	5
7	Pennsylvania	7		31	Iowa	5
4	Rhode Island	8		31	Kentucky	5
12	South Carolina	6		31	Mississippi	5
31	South Dakota	5		31	Nebraska	5
12	Tennessee	6		31	New Mexico	5
31	Texas	5		31	North Carolina	5
31	Utah	5		31	South Dakota	5
7	Vermont	7		31	Texas	5
12	Virginia	6		31	Utah	5
12	Washington	6		47	Idaho	4
12	West Virginia	6		47	Nevada	4
12	Wisconsin	6		47	Oklahoma	4
47	Wyoming	4		47	Wyoming	4

District of Columbia   18

Source: Morgan Quitno Press using data from American Medical Association (Chicago, Illinois)
"Physician Characteristics and Distribution in the U.S." (2007 Edition)
As of December 31, 2005. National rate does not include physicians in U.S. territories and possessions.
Ophthalmology is the branch of medicine dealing with the anatomy, functions and diseases of the eye.

Physicians in Orthopedic Surgery in 2005

National Total = 23,969 Physicians*

ALPHA ORDER

RANK	STATE	PHYSICIANS	% of USA
26	Alabama	349	1.5%
47	Alaska	74	0.3%
25	Arizona	361	1.5%
33	Arkansas	189	0.8%
1	California	2,869	12.0%
19	Colorado	449	1.9%
23	Connecticut	366	1.5%
48	Delaware	72	0.3%
4	Florida	1,315	5.5%
14	Georgia	619	2.6%
43	Hawaii	115	0.5%
38	Idaho	133	0.6%
6	Illinois	921	3.8%
19	Indiana	449	1.9%
31	Iowa	198	0.8%
30	Kansas	217	0.9%
28	Kentucky	307	1.3%
22	Louisiana	398	1.7%
39	Maine	130	0.5%
12	Maryland	625	2.6%
8	Massachusetts	747	3.1%
13	Michigan	622	2.6%
17	Minnesota	493	2.1%
34	Mississippi	184	0.8%
21	Missouri	436	1.8%
44	Montana	110	0.5%
35	Nebraska	164	0.7%
37	Nevada	138	0.6%
39	New Hampshire	130	0.5%
9	New Jersey	733	3.1%
36	New Mexico	146	0.6%
2	New York	1,826	7.6%
10	North Carolina	707	2.9%
50	North Dakota	50	0.2%
7	Ohio	861	3.6%
29	Oklahoma	222	0.9%
27	Oregon	328	1.4%
5	Pennsylvania	1,052	4.4%
42	Rhode Island	116	0.5%
24	South Carolina	362	1.5%
45	South Dakota	77	0.3%
16	Tennessee	533	2.2%
3	Texas	1,553	6.5%
32	Utah	192	0.8%
46	Vermont	75	0.3%
11	Virginia	639	2.7%
15	Washington	543	2.3%
41	West Virginia	117	0.5%
18	Wisconsin	489	2.0%
49	Wyoming	63	0.3%

RANK ORDER

RANK	STATE	PHYSICIANS	% of USA
1	California	2,869	12.0%
2	New York	1,826	7.6%
3	Texas	1,553	6.5%
4	Florida	1,315	5.5%
5	Pennsylvania	1,052	4.4%
6	Illinois	921	3.8%
7	Ohio	861	3.6%
8	Massachusetts	747	3.1%
9	New Jersey	733	3.1%
10	North Carolina	707	2.9%
11	Virginia	639	2.7%
12	Maryland	625	2.6%
13	Michigan	622	2.6%
14	Georgia	619	2.6%
15	Washington	543	2.3%
16	Tennessee	533	2.2%
17	Minnesota	493	2.1%
18	Wisconsin	489	2.0%
19	Colorado	449	1.9%
19	Indiana	449	1.9%
21	Missouri	436	1.8%
22	Louisiana	398	1.7%
23	Connecticut	366	1.5%
24	South Carolina	362	1.5%
25	Arizona	361	1.5%
26	Alabama	349	1.5%
27	Oregon	328	1.4%
28	Kentucky	307	1.3%
29	Oklahoma	222	0.9%
30	Kansas	217	0.9%
31	Iowa	198	0.8%
32	Utah	192	0.8%
33	Arkansas	189	0.8%
34	Mississippi	184	0.8%
35	Nebraska	164	0.7%
36	New Mexico	146	0.6%
37	Nevada	138	0.6%
38	Idaho	133	0.6%
39	Maine	130	0.5%
39	New Hampshire	130	0.5%
41	West Virginia	117	0.5%
42	Rhode Island	116	0.5%
43	Hawaii	115	0.5%
44	Montana	110	0.5%
45	South Dakota	77	0.3%
46	Vermont	75	0.3%
47	Alaska	74	0.3%
48	Delaware	72	0.3%
49	Wyoming	63	0.3%
50	North Dakota	50	0.2%
	District of Columbia	105	0.4%

Source: American Medical Association (Chicago, Illinois)
"Physician Characteristics and Distribution in the U.S." (2007 Edition)
As of December 31, 2005. Total does not include 171 physicians in U.S. territories and possessions.
Orthopedics is the branch of medicine dealing with the skeletal system.

Rate of Physicians in Orthopedic Surgery in 2005

National Rate = 8 Physicians per 100,000 Population*

ALPHA ORDER

RANK	STATE	RATE
25	Alabama	8
5	Alaska	11
45	Arizona	6
37	Arkansas	7
25	California	8
8	Colorado	10
8	Connecticut	10
14	Delaware	9
37	Florida	7
37	Georgia	7
14	Hawaii	9
14	Idaho	9
37	Illinois	7
37	Indiana	7
37	Iowa	7
25	Kansas	8
37	Kentucky	7
14	Louisiana	9
8	Maine	10
5	Maryland	11
1	Massachusetts	12
45	Michigan	6
8	Minnesota	10
45	Mississippi	6
25	Missouri	8
1	Montana	12
14	Nebraska	9
45	Nevada	6
8	New Hampshire	10
25	New Jersey	8
25	New Mexico	8
14	New York	9
25	North Carolina	8
25	North Dakota	8
25	Ohio	8
45	Oklahoma	6
14	Oregon	9
25	Pennsylvania	8
5	Rhode Island	11
14	South Carolina	9
8	South Dakota	10
14	Tennessee	9
37	Texas	7
25	Utah	8
1	Vermont	12
25	Virginia	8
14	Washington	9
45	West Virginia	6
14	Wisconsin	9
1	Wyoming	12

RANK ORDER

RANK	STATE	RATE
1	Massachusetts	12
1	Montana	12
1	Vermont	12
1	Wyoming	12
5	Alaska	11
5	Maryland	11
5	Rhode Island	11
8	Colorado	10
8	Connecticut	10
8	Maine	10
8	Minnesota	10
8	New Hampshire	10
8	South Dakota	10
14	Delaware	9
14	Hawaii	9
14	Idaho	9
14	Louisiana	9
14	Nebraska	9
14	New York	9
14	Oregon	9
14	South Carolina	9
14	Tennessee	9
14	Washington	9
14	Wisconsin	9
25	Alabama	8
25	California	8
25	Kansas	8
25	Missouri	8
25	New Jersey	8
25	New Mexico	8
25	North Carolina	8
25	North Dakota	8
25	Ohio	8
25	Pennsylvania	8
25	Utah	8
25	Virginia	8
37	Arkansas	7
37	Florida	7
37	Georgia	7
37	Illinois	7
37	Indiana	7
37	Iowa	7
37	Kentucky	7
37	Texas	7
45	Arizona	6
45	Michigan	6
45	Mississippi	6
45	Nevada	6
45	Oklahoma	6
45	West Virginia	6

	District of Columbia	18

Source: Morgan Quitno Press using data from American Medical Association (Chicago, Illinois) "Physician Characteristics and Distribution in the U.S." (2007 Edition)

*As of December 31, 2005. National rate does not include physicians in U.S. territories and possessions.
Orthopedics is the branch of medicine dealing with the skeletal system.

Physicians in Plastic Surgery in 2005

National Total = 6,980 Physicians*

ALPHA ORDER

RANK	STATE	PHYSICIANS	% of USA
26	Alabama	80	1.1%
48	Alaska	8	0.1%
18	Arizona	127	1.8%
34	Arkansas	35	0.5%
1	California	1,062	15.2%
19	Colorado	106	1.5%
22	Connecticut	94	1.3%
41	Delaware	22	0.3%
3	Florida	563	8.1%
12	Georgia	183	2.6%
34	Hawaii	35	0.5%
43	Idaho	19	0.3%
6	Illinois	244	3.5%
20	Indiana	95	1.4%
39	Iowa	29	0.4%
30	Kansas	61	0.9%
20	Kentucky	95	1.4%
25	Louisiana	87	1.2%
45	Maine	14	0.2%
13	Maryland	175	2.5%
10	Massachusetts	189	2.7%
9	Michigan	203	2.9%
24	Minnesota	93	1.3%
32	Mississippi	43	0.6%
16	Missouri	145	2.1%
44	Montana	15	0.2%
40	Nebraska	26	0.4%
31	Nevada	45	0.6%
42	New Hampshire	21	0.3%
7	New Jersey	229	3.3%
37	New Mexico	31	0.4%
2	New York	649	9.3%
11	North Carolina	185	2.7%
46	North Dakota	12	0.2%
8	Ohio	206	3.0%
33	Oklahoma	40	0.6%
29	Oregon	69	1.0%
5	Pennsylvania	273	3.9%
38	Rhode Island	30	0.4%
27	South Carolina	79	1.1%
47	South Dakota	11	0.2%
15	Tennessee	148	2.1%
4	Texas	546	7.8%
28	Utah	77	1.1%
48	Vermont	8	0.1%
13	Virginia	175	2.5%
17	Washington	129	1.8%
36	West Virginia	32	0.5%
22	Wisconsin	94	1.3%
50	Wyoming	3	0.0%

RANK ORDER

RANK	STATE	PHYSICIANS	% of USA
1	California	1,062	15.2%
2	New York	649	9.3%
3	Florida	563	8.1%
4	Texas	546	7.8%
5	Pennsylvania	273	3.9%
6	Illinois	244	3.5%
7	New Jersey	229	3.3%
8	Ohio	206	3.0%
9	Michigan	203	2.9%
10	Massachusetts	189	2.7%
11	North Carolina	185	2.7%
12	Georgia	183	2.6%
13	Maryland	175	2.5%
13	Virginia	175	2.5%
15	Tennessee	148	2.1%
16	Missouri	145	2.1%
17	Washington	129	1.8%
18	Arizona	127	1.8%
19	Colorado	106	1.5%
20	Indiana	95	1.4%
20	Kentucky	95	1.4%
22	Connecticut	94	1.3%
22	Wisconsin	94	1.3%
24	Minnesota	93	1.3%
25	Louisiana	87	1.2%
26	Alabama	80	1.1%
27	South Carolina	79	1.1%
28	Utah	77	1.1%
29	Oregon	69	1.0%
30	Kansas	61	0.9%
31	Nevada	45	0.6%
32	Mississippi	43	0.6%
33	Oklahoma	40	0.6%
34	Arkansas	35	0.5%
34	Hawaii	35	0.5%
36	West Virginia	32	0.5%
37	New Mexico	31	0.4%
38	Rhode Island	30	0.4%
39	Iowa	29	0.4%
40	Nebraska	26	0.4%
41	Delaware	22	0.3%
42	New Hampshire	21	0.3%
43	Idaho	19	0.3%
44	Montana	15	0.2%
45	Maine	14	0.2%
46	North Dakota	12	0.2%
47	South Dakota	11	0.2%
48	Alaska	8	0.1%
48	Vermont	8	0.1%
50	Wyoming	3	0.0%
	District of Columbia	40	0.6%

Source: American Medical Association (Chicago, Illinois)
   "Physician Characteristics and Distribution in the U.S." (2007 Edition)
*As of December 31, 2005. Total does not include 41 physicians in U.S. territories and possessions.

Rate of Physicians in Plastic Surgery in 2005

National Rate = 2 Physicians per 100,000 Population*

ALPHA ORDER

RANK	STATE	RATE
13	Alabama	2
40	Alaska	1
13	Arizona	2
40	Arkansas	1
1	California	3
13	Colorado	2
1	Connecticut	3
1	Delaware	3
1	Florida	3
13	Georgia	2
1	Hawaii	3
40	Idaho	1
13	Illinois	2
13	Indiana	2
40	Iowa	1
13	Kansas	2
13	Kentucky	2
13	Louisiana	2
40	Maine	1
1	Maryland	3
1	Massachusetts	3
13	Michigan	2
13	Minnesota	2
40	Mississippi	1
1	Missouri	3
13	Montana	2
40	Nebraska	1
13	Nevada	2
13	New Hampshire	2
1	New Jersey	3
13	New Mexico	2
1	New York	3
13	North Carolina	2
13	North Dakota	2
13	Ohio	2
40	Oklahoma	1
13	Oregon	2
13	Pennsylvania	2
1	Rhode Island	3
13	South Carolina	2
40	South Dakota	1
13	Tennessee	2
13	Texas	2
1	Utah	3
40	Vermont	1
13	Virginia	2
13	Washington	2
13	West Virginia	2
13	Wisconsin	2
40	Wyoming	1

RANK ORDER

RANK	STATE	RATE
1	California	3
1	Connecticut	3
1	Delaware	3
1	Florida	3
1	Hawaii	3
1	Maryland	3
1	Massachusetts	3
1	Missouri	3
1	New Jersey	3
1	New York	3
1	Rhode Island	3
1	Utah	3
13	Alabama	2
13	Arizona	2
13	Colorado	2
13	Georgia	2
13	Illinois	2
13	Indiana	2
13	Kansas	2
13	Kentucky	2
13	Louisiana	2
13	Michigan	2
13	Minnesota	2
13	Montana	2
13	Nevada	2
13	New Hampshire	2
13	New Mexico	2
13	North Carolina	2
13	North Dakota	2
13	Ohio	2
13	Oregon	2
13	Pennsylvania	2
13	South Carolina	2
13	Tennessee	2
13	Texas	2
13	Virginia	2
13	Washington	2
13	West Virginia	2
13	Wisconsin	2
40	Alaska	1
40	Arkansas	1
40	Idaho	1
40	Iowa	1
40	Maine	1
40	Mississippi	1
40	Nebraska	1
40	Oklahoma	1
40	South Dakota	1
40	Vermont	1
40	Wyoming	1

District of Columbia 7

Source: Morgan Quitno Press using data from American Medical Association (Chicago, Illinois)
"Physician Characteristics and Distribution in the U.S." (2007 Edition)
*As of December 31, 2005. National rate does not include physicians in U.S. territories and possessions.

Physicians in Other Specialties in 2005

National Total = 216,438 Physicians*

ALPHA ORDER

RANK	STATE	PHYSICIANS	% of USA
28	Alabama	2,409	1.1%
47	Alaska	404	0.2%
21	Arizona	3,638	1.7%
32	Arkansas	1,426	0.7%
1	California	26,696	12.3%
23	Colorado	3,520	1.6%
22	Connecticut	3,613	1.7%
45	Delaware	564	0.3%
4	Florida	11,673	5.4%
14	Georgia	5,331	2.5%
37	Hawaii	1,157	0.5%
44	Idaho	624	0.3%
6	Illinois	9,333	4.3%
18	Indiana	3,727	1.7%
33	Iowa	1,421	0.7%
29	Kansas	1,655	0.8%
26	Kentucky	2,629	1.2%
24	Louisiana	2,892	1.3%
40	Maine	1,024	0.5%
10	Maryland	6,789	3.1%
7	Massachusetts	8,777	4.1%
11	Michigan	6,530	3.0%
20	Minnesota	3,704	1.7%
36	Mississippi	1,293	0.6%
19	Missouri	3,709	1.7%
46	Montana	561	0.3%
39	Nebraska	1,035	0.5%
35	Nevada	1,297	0.6%
42	New Hampshire	950	0.4%
9	New Jersey	7,031	3.2%
34	New Mexico	1,320	0.6%
2	New York	20,838	9.6%
12	North Carolina	5,852	2.7%
49	North Dakota	385	0.2%
8	Ohio	7,896	3.6%
30	Oklahoma	1,571	0.7%
25	Oregon	2,772	1.3%
5	Pennsylvania	10,205	4.7%
41	Rhode Island	1,018	0.5%
27	South Carolina	2,585	1.2%
48	South Dakota	401	0.2%
17	Tennessee	3,926	1.8%
3	Texas	13,162	6.1%
31	Utah	1,508	0.7%
43	Vermont	657	0.3%
13	Virginia	5,652	2.6%
15	Washington	4,744	2.2%
38	West Virginia	1,079	0.5%
16	Wisconsin	3,928	1.8%
50	Wyoming	250	0.1%

RANK ORDER

RANK	STATE	PHYSICIANS	% of USA
1	California	26,696	12.3%
2	New York	20,838	9.6%
3	Texas	13,162	6.1%
4	Florida	11,673	5.4%
5	Pennsylvania	10,205	4.7%
6	Illinois	9,333	4.3%
7	Massachusetts	8,777	4.1%
8	Ohio	7,896	3.6%
9	New Jersey	7,031	3.2%
10	Maryland	6,789	3.1%
11	Michigan	6,530	3.0%
12	North Carolina	5,852	2.7%
13	Virginia	5,652	2.6%
14	Georgia	5,331	2.5%
15	Washington	4,744	2.2%
16	Wisconsin	3,928	1.8%
17	Tennessee	3,926	1.8%
18	Indiana	3,727	1.7%
19	Missouri	3,709	1.7%
20	Minnesota	3,704	1.7%
21	Arizona	3,638	1.7%
22	Connecticut	3,613	1.7%
23	Colorado	3,520	1.6%
24	Louisiana	2,892	1.3%
25	Oregon	2,772	1.3%
26	Kentucky	2,629	1.2%
27	South Carolina	2,585	1.2%
28	Alabama	2,409	1.1%
29	Kansas	1,655	0.8%
30	Oklahoma	1,571	0.7%
31	Utah	1,508	0.7%
32	Arkansas	1,426	0.7%
33	Iowa	1,421	0.7%
34	New Mexico	1,320	0.6%
35	Nevada	1,297	0.6%
36	Mississippi	1,293	0.6%
37	Hawaii	1,157	0.5%
38	West Virginia	1,079	0.5%
39	Nebraska	1,035	0.5%
40	Maine	1,024	0.5%
41	Rhode Island	1,018	0.5%
42	New Hampshire	950	0.4%
43	Vermont	657	0.3%
44	Idaho	624	0.3%
45	Delaware	564	0.3%
46	Montana	561	0.3%
47	Alaska	404	0.2%
48	South Dakota	401	0.2%
49	North Dakota	385	0.2%
50	Wyoming	250	0.1%
	District of Columbia	1,277	0.6%

Source: American Medical Association (Chicago, Illinois)
    "Physician Characteristics and Distribution in the U.S." (2007 Edition)
*As of December 31, 2005. Total does not include 3,264 physicians in U.S. territories and possessions. Other Specialties include Aerospace Medicine, Anesthesiology, Child Psychiatry, Diagnostic Radiology, Emergency Medicine, Forensic Pathology, Nuclear Medicine, Occupational Medicine, Neurology, Psychiatry, Public Health, Anatomic/Clinical Pathology, Radiology, Radiation Oncology and other specialties.

Rate of Physicians in Other Specialties in 2005

National Rate = 73 Physicians per 100,000 Population*

ALPHA ORDER

RANK	STATE	RATE
43	Alabama	53
30	Alaska	61
30	Arizona	61
45	Arkansas	51
15	California	74
12	Colorado	75
5	Connecticut	103
22	Delaware	67
24	Florida	66
40	Georgia	58
7	Hawaii	91
48	Idaho	44
16	Illinois	73
37	Indiana	59
47	Iowa	48
35	Kansas	60
29	Kentucky	63
27	Louisiana	64
10	Maine	78
2	Maryland	121
1	Massachusetts	136
26	Michigan	65
18	Minnesota	72
48	Mississippi	44
27	Missouri	64
35	Montana	60
37	Nebraska	59
42	Nevada	54
16	New Hampshire	73
9	New Jersey	81
20	New Mexico	69
3	New York	108
22	North Carolina	67
30	North Dakota	61
20	Ohio	69
48	Oklahoma	44
11	Oregon	76
8	Pennsylvania	82
6	Rhode Island	95
30	South Carolina	61
44	South Dakota	52
24	Tennessee	66
41	Texas	57
30	Utah	61
4	Vermont	106
12	Virginia	75
12	Washington	75
37	West Virginia	59
19	Wisconsin	71
46	Wyoming	49

RANK ORDER

RANK	STATE	RATE
1	Massachusetts	136
2	Maryland	121
3	New York	108
4	Vermont	106
5	Connecticut	103
6	Rhode Island	95
7	Hawaii	91
8	Pennsylvania	82
9	New Jersey	81
10	Maine	78
11	Oregon	76
12	Colorado	75
12	Virginia	75
12	Washington	75
15	California	74
16	Illinois	73
16	New Hampshire	73
18	Minnesota	72
19	Wisconsin	71
20	New Mexico	69
20	Ohio	69
22	Delaware	67
22	North Carolina	67
24	Florida	66
24	Tennessee	66
26	Michigan	65
27	Louisiana	64
27	Missouri	64
29	Kentucky	63
30	Alaska	61
30	Arizona	61
30	North Dakota	61
30	South Carolina	61
30	Utah	61
35	Kansas	60
35	Montana	60
37	Indiana	59
37	Nebraska	59
37	West Virginia	59
40	Georgia	58
41	Texas	57
42	Nevada	54
43	Alabama	53
44	South Dakota	52
45	Arkansas	51
46	Wyoming	49
47	Iowa	48
48	Idaho	44
48	Mississippi	44
48	Oklahoma	44

District of Columbia 219

*Source: Morgan Quitno Press using data from American Medical Association (Chicago, Illinois)
"Physician Characteristics and Distribution in the U.S." (2007 Edition)*
As of December 31, 2005. National rate does not include physicians in U.S. territories and possessions. Other Specialties include Aerospace Medicine, Anesthesiology, Child Psychiatry, Diagnostic Radiology, Emergency Medicine, Forensic Pathology, Nuclear Medicine, Occupational Medicine, Neurology, Psychiatry, Public Health, Anatomic/Clinical Pathology, Radiology, Radiation Oncology and other specialties.

Physicians in Anesthesiology in 2005

National Total = 40,246 Physicians*

ALPHA ORDER

RANK	STATE	PHYSICIANS	% of USA
27	Alabama	473	1.2%
47	Alaska	78	0.2%
17	Arizona	834	2.1%
34	Arkansas	284	0.7%
1	California	4,939	12.3%
20	Colorado	701	1.7%
25	Connecticut	519	1.3%
46	Delaware	88	0.2%
4	Florida	2,549	6.3%
16	Georgia	903	2.2%
41	Hawaii	157	0.4%
44	Idaho	107	0.3%
5	Illinois	1,850	4.6%
15	Indiana	912	2.3%
33	Iowa	318	0.8%
32	Kansas	329	0.8%
23	Kentucky	563	1.4%
26	Louisiana	511	1.3%
39	Maine	171	0.4%
10	Maryland	1,044	2.6%
9	Massachusetts	1,391	3.5%
13	Michigan	955	2.4%
22	Minnesota	570	1.4%
35	Mississippi	250	0.6%
21	Missouri	675	1.7%
42	Montana	117	0.3%
36	Nebraska	220	0.5%
31	Nevada	346	0.9%
38	New Hampshire	178	0.4%
8	New Jersey	1,486	3.7%
37	New Mexico	214	0.5%
2	New York	3,399	8.4%
12	North Carolina	963	2.4%
48	North Dakota	64	0.2%
7	Ohio	1,504	3.7%
30	Oklahoma	353	0.9%
24	Oregon	549	1.4%
6	Pennsylvania	1,646	4.1%
42	Rhode Island	117	0.3%
28	South Carolina	460	1.1%
49	South Dakota	61	0.2%
19	Tennessee	769	1.9%
3	Texas	3,066	7.6%
29	Utah	354	0.9%
45	Vermont	106	0.3%
11	Virginia	966	2.4%
14	Washington	949	2.4%
39	West Virginia	171	0.4%
18	Wisconsin	830	2.1%
50	Wyoming	52	0.1%

RANK ORDER

RANK	STATE	PHYSICIANS	% of USA
1	California	4,939	12.3%
2	New York	3,399	8.4%
3	Texas	3,066	7.6%
4	Florida	2,549	6.3%
5	Illinois	1,850	4.6%
6	Pennsylvania	1,646	4.1%
7	Ohio	1,504	3.7%
8	New Jersey	1,486	3.7%
9	Massachusetts	1,391	3.5%
10	Maryland	1,044	2.6%
11	Virginia	966	2.4%
12	North Carolina	963	2.4%
13	Michigan	955	2.4%
14	Washington	949	2.4%
15	Indiana	912	2.3%
16	Georgia	903	2.2%
17	Arizona	834	2.1%
18	Wisconsin	830	2.1%
19	Tennessee	769	1.9%
20	Colorado	701	1.7%
21	Missouri	675	1.7%
22	Minnesota	570	1.4%
23	Kentucky	563	1.4%
24	Oregon	549	1.4%
25	Connecticut	519	1.3%
26	Louisiana	511	1.3%
27	Alabama	473	1.2%
28	South Carolina	460	1.1%
29	Utah	354	0.9%
30	Oklahoma	353	0.9%
31	Nevada	346	0.9%
32	Kansas	329	0.8%
33	Iowa	318	0.8%
34	Arkansas	284	0.7%
35	Mississippi	250	0.6%
36	Nebraska	220	0.5%
37	New Mexico	214	0.5%
38	New Hampshire	178	0.4%
39	Maine	171	0.4%
39	West Virginia	171	0.4%
41	Hawaii	157	0.4%
42	Montana	117	0.3%
42	Rhode Island	117	0.3%
44	Idaho	107	0.3%
45	Vermont	106	0.3%
46	Delaware	88	0.2%
47	Alaska	78	0.2%
48	North Dakota	64	0.2%
49	South Dakota	61	0.2%
50	Wyoming	52	0.1%
	District of Columbia	135	0.3%

Source: American Medical Association (Chicago, Illinois)
   "Physician Characteristics and Distribution in the U.S." (2007 Edition)
*As of December 31, 2005. Total does not include 248 physicians in U.S. territories and possessions.

Rate of Physicians in Anesthesiology in 2005

National Rate = 14 Physicians per 100,000 Population*

ALPHA ORDER

RANK	STATE	RATE
39	Alabama	10
28	Alaska	12
12	Arizona	14
39	Arkansas	10
12	California	14
6	Colorado	15
6	Connecticut	15
39	Delaware	10
12	Florida	14
39	Georgia	10
28	Hawaii	12
50	Idaho	7
12	Illinois	14
6	Indiana	15
32	Iowa	11
28	Kansas	12
19	Kentucky	13
32	Louisiana	11
19	Maine	13
2	Maryland	19
1	Massachusetts	22
46	Michigan	9
32	Minnesota	11
46	Mississippi	9
28	Missouri	12
19	Montana	13
19	Nebraska	13
12	Nevada	14
12	New Hampshire	14
4	New Jersey	17
32	New Mexico	11
3	New York	18
32	North Carolina	11
39	North Dakota	10
19	Ohio	13
39	Oklahoma	10
6	Oregon	15
19	Pennsylvania	13
32	Rhode Island	11
32	South Carolina	11
49	South Dakota	8
19	Tennessee	13
19	Texas	13
12	Utah	14
4	Vermont	17
19	Virginia	13
6	Washington	15
46	West Virginia	9
6	Wisconsin	15
39	Wyoming	10

RANK ORDER

RANK	STATE	RATE
1	Massachusetts	22
2	Maryland	19
3	New York	18
4	New Jersey	17
4	Vermont	17
6	Colorado	15
6	Connecticut	15
6	Indiana	15
6	Oregon	15
6	Washington	15
6	Wisconsin	15
12	Arizona	14
12	California	14
12	Florida	14
12	Illinois	14
12	Nevada	14
12	New Hampshire	14
12	Utah	14
19	Kentucky	13
19	Maine	13
19	Montana	13
19	Nebraska	13
19	Ohio	13
19	Pennsylvania	13
19	Tennessee	13
19	Texas	13
19	Virginia	13
28	Alaska	12
28	Hawaii	12
28	Kansas	12
28	Missouri	12
32	Iowa	11
32	Louisiana	11
32	Minnesota	11
32	New Mexico	11
32	North Carolina	11
32	Rhode Island	11
32	South Carolina	11
39	Alabama	10
39	Arkansas	10
39	Delaware	10
39	Georgia	10
39	North Dakota	10
39	Oklahoma	10
39	Wyoming	10
46	Michigan	9
46	Mississippi	9
46	West Virginia	9
49	South Dakota	8
50	Idaho	7

| | District of Columbia | 23 |

Source: Morgan Quitno Press using data from American Medical Association (Chicago, Illinois)
"Physician Characteristics and Distribution in the U.S." (2007 Edition)
*As of December 31, 2005. National rate does not include physicians in U.S. territories and possessions.

Physicians in Psychiatry in 2005

National Total = 41,101 Physicians*

ALPHA ORDER

RANK ORDER

RANK	STATE	PHYSICIANS	% of USA
28	Alabama	348	0.8%
46	Alaska	82	0.2%
21	Arizona	582	1.4%
35	Arkansas	222	0.5%
2	California	5,674	13.8%
18	Colorado	606	1.5%
14	Connecticut	962	2.3%
44	Delaware	100	0.2%
6	Florida	1,759	4.3%
15	Georgia	898	2.2%
32	Hawaii	258	0.6%
46	Idaho	82	0.2%
7	Illinois	1,586	3.9%
25	Indiana	479	1.2%
37	Iowa	199	0.5%
29	Kansas	295	0.7%
27	Kentucky	403	1.0%
23	Louisiana	487	1.2%
34	Maine	232	0.6%
9	Maryland	1,410	3.4%
3	Massachusetts	2,187	5.3%
12	Michigan	1,081	2.6%
22	Minnesota	552	1.3%
36	Mississippi	214	0.5%
19	Missouri	596	1.5%
45	Montana	84	0.2%
41	Nebraska	172	0.4%
40	Nevada	173	0.4%
39	New Hampshire	185	0.5%
8	New Jersey	1,446	3.5%
31	New Mexico	276	0.7%
1	New York	5,695	13.9%
13	North Carolina	1,061	2.6%
48	North Dakota	74	0.2%
10	Ohio	1,214	3.0%
30	Oklahoma	281	0.7%
26	Oregon	472	1.1%
4	Pennsylvania	2,016	4.9%
33	Rhode Island	252	0.6%
24	South Carolina	482	1.2%
49	South Dakota	68	0.2%
20	Tennessee	594	1.4%
5	Texas	1,862	4.5%
38	Utah	196	0.5%
43	Vermont	162	0.4%
11	Virginia	1,088	2.6%
16	Washington	791	1.9%
42	West Virginia	166	0.4%
17	Wisconsin	610	1.5%
50	Wyoming	37	0.1%

RANK	STATE	PHYSICIANS	% of USA
1	New York	5,695	13.9%
2	California	5,674	13.8%
3	Massachusetts	2,187	5.3%
4	Pennsylvania	2,016	4.9%
5	Texas	1,862	4.5%
6	Florida	1,759	4.3%
7	Illinois	1,586	3.9%
8	New Jersey	1,446	3.5%
9	Maryland	1,410	3.4%
10	Ohio	1,214	3.0%
11	Virginia	1,088	2.6%
12	Michigan	1,081	2.6%
13	North Carolina	1,061	2.6%
14	Connecticut	962	2.3%
15	Georgia	898	2.2%
16	Washington	791	1.9%
17	Wisconsin	610	1.5%
18	Colorado	606	1.5%
19	Missouri	596	1.5%
20	Tennessee	594	1.4%
21	Arizona	582	1.4%
22	Minnesota	552	1.3%
23	Louisiana	487	1.2%
24	South Carolina	482	1.2%
25	Indiana	479	1.2%
26	Oregon	472	1.1%
27	Kentucky	403	1.0%
28	Alabama	348	0.8%
29	Kansas	295	0.7%
30	Oklahoma	281	0.7%
31	New Mexico	276	0.7%
32	Hawaii	258	0.6%
33	Rhode Island	252	0.6%
34	Maine	232	0.6%
35	Arkansas	222	0.5%
36	Mississippi	214	0.5%
37	Iowa	199	0.5%
38	Utah	196	0.5%
39	New Hampshire	185	0.5%
40	Nevada	173	0.4%
41	Nebraska	172	0.4%
42	West Virginia	166	0.4%
43	Vermont	162	0.4%
44	Delaware	100	0.2%
45	Montana	84	0.2%
46	Alaska	82	0.2%
46	Idaho	82	0.2%
48	North Dakota	74	0.2%
49	South Dakota	68	0.2%
50	Wyoming	37	0.1%
	District of Columbia	350	0.9%

Source: American Medical Association (Chicago, Illinois)
   "Physician Characteristics and Distribution in the U.S." (2007 Edition)
*As of December 31, 2005. Total does not include 497 physicians in U.S. territories and possessions. Psychiatry includes psychoanalysis.

Rate of Physicians in Psychiatry in 2005

National Rate = 14 Physicians per 100,000 Population*

ALPHA ORDER

RANK	STATE	RATE
40	Alabama	8
18	Alaska	12
30	Arizona	10
40	Arkansas	8
10	California	16
15	Colorado	13
3	Connecticut	27
18	Delaware	12
30	Florida	10
30	Georgia	10
7	Hawaii	20
50	Idaho	6
18	Illinois	12
40	Indiana	8
46	Iowa	7
23	Kansas	11
30	Kentucky	10
23	Louisiana	11
8	Maine	18
5	Maryland	25
1	Massachusetts	34
23	Michigan	11
23	Minnesota	11
46	Mississippi	7
30	Missouri	10
37	Montana	9
30	Nebraska	10
46	Nevada	7
12	New Hampshire	14
9	New Jersey	17
12	New Mexico	14
2	New York	29
18	North Carolina	12
18	North Dakota	12
23	Ohio	11
40	Oklahoma	8
15	Oregon	13
10	Pennsylvania	16
6	Rhode Island	23
23	South Carolina	11
37	South Dakota	9
30	Tennessee	10
40	Texas	8
40	Utah	8
4	Vermont	26
12	Virginia	14
15	Washington	13
37	West Virginia	9
23	Wisconsin	11
46	Wyoming	7

RANK ORDER

RANK	STATE	RATE
1	Massachusetts	34
2	New York	29
3	Connecticut	27
4	Vermont	26
5	Maryland	25
6	Rhode Island	23
7	Hawaii	20
8	Maine	18
9	New Jersey	17
10	California	16
10	Pennsylvania	16
12	New Hampshire	14
12	New Mexico	14
12	Virginia	14
15	Colorado	13
15	Oregon	13
15	Washington	13
18	Alaska	12
18	Delaware	12
18	Illinois	12
18	North Carolina	12
18	North Dakota	12
23	Kansas	11
23	Louisiana	11
23	Michigan	11
23	Minnesota	11
23	Ohio	11
23	South Carolina	11
23	Wisconsin	11
30	Arizona	10
30	Florida	10
30	Georgia	10
30	Kentucky	10
30	Missouri	10
30	Nebraska	10
30	Tennessee	10
37	Montana	9
37	South Dakota	9
37	West Virginia	9
40	Alabama	8
40	Arkansas	8
40	Indiana	8
40	Oklahoma	8
40	Texas	8
40	Utah	8
46	Iowa	7
46	Mississippi	7
46	Nevada	7
46	Wyoming	7
50	Idaho	6

District of Columbia 60

Source: Morgan Quitno Press using data from American Medical Association (Chicago, Illinois)
"Physician Characteristics and Distribution in the U.S." (2007 Edition)
*As of December 31, 2005. National rate does not include physicians in U.S. territories and possessions.
Psychiatry includes psychoanalysis.

Percent of Population Lacking Access to Mental Health Care in 2006

National Percent = 17.1% of Population*

ALPHA ORDER

RANK	STATE	PERCENT
3	Alabama	48.8
19	Alaska	30.7
38	Arizona	9.3
8	Arkansas	42.1
40	California	7.9
37	Colorado	9.5
48	Connecticut	1.6
50	Delaware	0.0
41	Florida	7.8
23	Georgia	24.0
39	Hawaii	8.0
2	Idaho	62.1
29	Illinois	17.0
33	Indiana	13.9
14	Iowa	34.8
13	Kansas	34.9
9	Kentucky	41.9
4	Louisiana	46.2
32	Maine	14.2
45	Maryland	4.5
49	Massachusetts	0.7
31	Michigan	14.9
26	Minnesota	18.7
10	Mississippi	40.4
20	Missouri	27.3
11	Montana	40.0
7	Nebraska	43.8
42	Nevada	7.2
46	New Hampshire	4.4
47	New Jersey	4.3
5	New Mexico	46.1
43	New York	6.4
44	North Carolina	5.8
14	North Dakota	34.8
35	Ohio	11.0
12	Oklahoma	35.4
26	Oregon	18.7
36	Pennsylvania	9.9
25	Rhode Island	21.7
16	South Carolina	34.6
6	South Dakota	44.9
17	Tennessee	33.3
21	Texas	25.9
18	Utah	32.6
34	Vermont	12.4
30	Virginia	15.0
28	Washington	17.2
22	West Virginia	24.9
24	Wisconsin	21.8
1	Wyoming	76.6

RANK ORDER

RANK	STATE	PERCENT
1	Wyoming	76.6
2	Idaho	62.1
3	Alabama	48.8
4	Louisiana	46.2
5	New Mexico	46.1
6	South Dakota	44.9
7	Nebraska	43.8
8	Arkansas	42.1
9	Kentucky	41.9
10	Mississippi	40.4
11	Montana	40.0
12	Oklahoma	35.4
13	Kansas	34.9
14	Iowa	34.8
14	North Dakota	34.8
16	South Carolina	34.6
17	Tennessee	33.3
18	Utah	32.6
19	Alaska	30.7
20	Missouri	27.3
21	Texas	25.9
22	West Virginia	24.9
23	Georgia	24.0
24	Wisconsin	21.8
25	Rhode Island	21.7
26	Minnesota	18.7
26	Oregon	18.7
28	Washington	17.2
29	Illinois	17.0
30	Virginia	15.0
31	Michigan	14.9
32	Maine	14.2
33	Indiana	13.9
34	Vermont	12.4
35	Ohio	11.0
36	Pennsylvania	9.9
37	Colorado	9.5
38	Arizona	9.3
39	Hawaii	8.0
40	California	7.9
41	Florida	7.8
42	Nevada	7.2
43	New York	6.4
44	North Carolina	5.8
45	Maryland	4.5
46	New Hampshire	4.4
47	New Jersey	4.3
48	Connecticut	1.6
49	Massachusetts	0.7
50	Delaware	0.0

District of Columbia   13.5

Source: Morgan Quitno Press using data from U.S. Dept. of Health and Human Services, Div. of Shortage Designation
"Selected Statistics on Health Professional Shortage Areas" (as of September 30, 2006)
*Percent of population considered under-served by mental health practitioners. An under-served population does not have primary medical care within reasonable economic and geographic bounds.

International Medical School Graduates in 2005

National Total = 222,435 Nonfederal Physicians*

ALPHA ORDER

RANK	STATE	PHYSICIANS	% of USA
25	Alabama	1,708	0.8%
48	Alaska	113	0.1%
18	Arizona	3,032	1.4%
35	Arkansas	965	0.4%
2	California	24,510	11.0%
33	Colorado	990	0.4%
14	Connecticut	4,104	1.8%
38	Delaware	728	0.3%
3	Florida	18,861	8.5%
13	Georgia	4,226	1.9%
39	Hawaii	679	0.3%
50	Idaho	94	0.0%
5	Illinois	13,101	5.9%
16	Indiana	3,081	1.4%
31	Iowa	1,186	0.5%
29	Kansas	1,273	0.6%
23	Kentucky	2,245	1.0%
24	Louisiana	2,237	1.0%
41	Maine	567	0.3%
10	Maryland	6,929	3.1%
11	Massachusetts	6,807	3.1%
9	Michigan	9,227	4.1%
21	Minnesota	2,370	1.1%
37	Mississippi	754	0.3%
15	Missouri	3,382	1.5%
47	Montana	117	0.1%
40	Nebraska	641	0.3%
27	Nevada	1,497	0.7%
42	New Hampshire	545	0.2%
4	New Jersey	13,339	6.0%
36	New Mexico	884	0.4%
1	New York	34,455	15.5%
17	North Carolina	3,061	1.4%
44	North Dakota	440	0.2%
8	Ohio	9,672	4.3%
30	Oklahoma	1,271	0.6%
34	Oregon	971	0.4%
7	Pennsylvania	10,528	4.7%
32	Rhode Island	1,158	0.5%
28	South Carolina	1,378	0.6%
45	South Dakota	268	0.1%
20	Tennessee	2,827	1.3%
6	Texas	12,729	5.7%
43	Utah	474	0.2%
46	Vermont	232	0.1%
12	Virginia	4,786	2.2%
22	Washington	2,303	1.0%
25	West Virginia	1,708	0.8%
19	Wisconsin	2,872	1.3%
49	Wyoming	103	0.0%

RANK ORDER

RANK	STATE	PHYSICIANS	% of USA
1	New York	34,455	15.5%
2	California	24,510	11.0%
3	Florida	18,861	8.5%
4	New Jersey	13,339	6.0%
5	Illinois	13,101	5.9%
6	Texas	12,729	5.7%
7	Pennsylvania	10,528	4.7%
8	Ohio	9,672	4.3%
9	Michigan	9,227	4.1%
10	Maryland	6,929	3.1%
11	Massachusetts	6,807	3.1%
12	Virginia	4,786	2.2%
13	Georgia	4,226	1.9%
14	Connecticut	4,104	1.8%
15	Missouri	3,382	1.5%
16	Indiana	3,081	1.4%
17	North Carolina	3,061	1.4%
18	Arizona	3,032	1.4%
19	Wisconsin	2,872	1.3%
20	Tennessee	2,827	1.3%
21	Minnesota	2,370	1.1%
22	Washington	2,303	1.0%
23	Kentucky	2,245	1.0%
24	Louisiana	2,237	1.0%
25	Alabama	1,708	0.8%
25	West Virginia	1,708	0.8%
27	Nevada	1,497	0.7%
28	South Carolina	1,378	0.6%
29	Kansas	1,273	0.6%
30	Oklahoma	1,271	0.6%
31	Iowa	1,186	0.5%
32	Rhode Island	1,158	0.5%
33	Colorado	990	0.4%
34	Oregon	971	0.4%
35	Arkansas	965	0.4%
36	New Mexico	884	0.4%
37	Mississippi	754	0.3%
38	Delaware	728	0.3%
39	Hawaii	679	0.3%
40	Nebraska	641	0.3%
41	Maine	567	0.3%
42	New Hampshire	545	0.2%
43	Utah	474	0.2%
44	North Dakota	440	0.2%
45	South Dakota	268	0.1%
46	Vermont	232	0.1%
47	Montana	117	0.1%
48	Alaska	113	0.1%
49	Wyoming	103	0.0%
50	Idaho	94	0.0%
	District of Columbia	1,007	0.5%

Source: American Medical Association (Chicago, Illinois)
 "Physician Characteristics and Distribution in the U.S." (2007 Edition)
As of December 31, 2005. Total does not include 6,230 physicians in U.S. territories and possessions.

International Medical School Graduates as a Percent of Physicians in 2005

National Percent = 25.0% of Physicians*

ALPHA ORDER

RANK	STATE	PERCENT
31	Alabama	15.8
48	Alaska	6.9
21	Arizona	20.6
32	Arkansas	15.3
16	California	22.7
47	Colorado	7.2
8	Connecticut	28.8
7	Delaware	30.7
4	Florida	36.0
23	Georgia	19.0
33	Hawaii	15.0
50	Idaho	3.3
5	Illinois	34.0
21	Indiana	20.6
24	Iowa	18.8
26	Kansas	18.2
19	Kentucky	21.1
28	Louisiana	17.7
35	Maine	13.8
11	Maryland	27.2
18	Massachusetts	21.3
6	Michigan	33.8
34	Minnesota	14.5
39	Mississippi	12.8
17	Missouri	22.1
49	Montana	4.7
37	Nebraska	13.6
8	Nevada	28.8
37	New Hampshire	13.6
1	New Jersey	44.8
29	New Mexico	16.7
2	New York	41.9
41	North Carolina	12.4
13	North Dakota	25.7
8	Ohio	28.8
25	Oklahoma	18.3
45	Oregon	8.6
14	Pennsylvania	25.5
11	Rhode Island	27.2
40	South Carolina	12.5
35	South Dakota	13.8
30	Tennessee	16.3
15	Texas	23.8
46	Utah	8.1
44	Vermont	8.8
20	Virginia	20.8
42	Washington	11.9
3	West Virginia	36.5
27	Wisconsin	18.1
43	Wyoming	9.3

RANK ORDER

RANK	STATE	PERCENT
1	New Jersey	44.8
2	New York	41.9
3	West Virginia	36.5
4	Florida	36.0
5	Illinois	34.0
6	Michigan	33.8
7	Delaware	30.7
8	Connecticut	28.8
8	Nevada	28.8
8	Ohio	28.8
11	Maryland	27.2
11	Rhode Island	27.2
13	North Dakota	25.7
14	Pennsylvania	25.5
15	Texas	23.8
16	California	22.7
17	Missouri	22.1
18	Massachusetts	21.3
19	Kentucky	21.1
20	Virginia	20.8
21	Arizona	20.6
21	Indiana	20.6
23	Georgia	19.0
24	Iowa	18.8
25	Oklahoma	18.3
26	Kansas	18.2
27	Wisconsin	18.1
28	Louisiana	17.7
29	New Mexico	16.7
30	Tennessee	16.3
31	Alabama	15.8
32	Arkansas	15.3
33	Hawaii	15.0
34	Minnesota	14.5
35	Maine	13.8
35	South Dakota	13.8
37	Nebraska	13.6
37	New Hampshire	13.6
39	Mississippi	12.8
40	South Carolina	12.5
41	North Carolina	12.4
42	Washington	11.9
43	Wyoming	9.3
44	Vermont	8.8
45	Oregon	8.6
46	Utah	8.1
47	Colorado	7.2
48	Alaska	6.9
49	Montana	4.7
50	Idaho	3.3

District of Columbia   20.9

Source: Morgan Quitno Press using data from American Medical Association (Chicago, Illinois)
    "Physician Characteristics and Distribution in the U.S." (2007 Edition)
*As of December 31, 2005. National rate does not include physicians in the U.S. territories and possessions.

Osteopathic Physicians in 2006

National Total = 52,599 Osteopathic Physicians*

ALPHA ORDER

RANK	STATE	OSTEOPATHS	% of USA
43	Alabama	134	0.3%
32	Alaska	358	0.7%
36	Arizona	230	0.4%
12	Arkansas	1,467	2.8%
6	California	3,484	6.6%
14	Colorado	850	1.6%
31	Connecticut	382	0.7%
47	Delaware	58	0.1%
5	Florida	3,512	6.7%
17	Georgia	719	1.4%
41	Hawaii	177	0.3%
13	Idaho	1,055	2.0%
39	Illinois	192	0.4%
9	Indiana	2,288	4.3%
16	Iowa	758	1.4%
23	Kansas	610	1.2%
29	Kentucky	393	0.7%
45	Louisiana	108	0.2%
24	Maine	604	1.1%
21	Maryland	617	1.2%
25	Massachusetts	581	1.1%
2	Michigan	4,811	9.1%
29	Minnesota	393	0.7%
10	Mississippi	1,804	3.4%
34	Missouri	294	0.6%
44	Montana	111	0.2%
20	Nebraska	623	1.2%
49	Nevada	56	0.1%
42	New Hampshire	139	0.3%
40	New Jersey	191	0.4%
8	New Mexico	2,876	5.5%
37	New York	206	0.4%
28	North Carolina	408	0.8%
4	North Dakota	3,541	6.7%
3	Ohio	3,629	6.9%
11	Oklahoma	1,470	2.8%
26	Oregon	506	1.0%
1	Pennsylvania	5,422	10.3%
38	Rhode Island	199	0.4%
33	South Carolina	346	0.7%
46	South Dakota	91	0.2%
27	Tennessee	487	0.9%
7	Texas	3,127	5.9%
35	Utah	240	0.5%
15	Vermont	780	1.5%
50	Virginia	54	0.1%
18	Washington	687	1.3%
19	West Virginia	634	1.2%
22	Wisconsin	615	1.2%
48	Wyoming	57	0.1%

RANK ORDER

RANK	STATE	OSTEOPATHS	% of USA
1	Pennsylvania	5,422	10.3%
2	Michigan	4,811	9.1%
3	Ohio	3,629	6.9%
4	North Dakota	3,541	6.7%
5	Florida	3,512	6.7%
6	California	3,484	6.6%
7	Texas	3,127	5.9%
8	New Mexico	2,876	5.5%
9	Indiana	2,288	4.3%
10	Mississippi	1,804	3.4%
11	Oklahoma	1,470	2.8%
12	Arkansas	1,467	2.8%
13	Idaho	1,055	2.0%
14	Colorado	850	1.6%
15	Vermont	780	1.5%
16	Iowa	758	1.4%
17	Georgia	719	1.4%
18	Washington	687	1.3%
19	West Virginia	634	1.2%
20	Nebraska	623	1.2%
21	Maryland	617	1.2%
22	Wisconsin	615	1.2%
23	Kansas	610	1.2%
24	Maine	604	1.1%
25	Massachusetts	581	1.1%
26	Oregon	506	1.0%
27	Tennessee	487	0.9%
28	North Carolina	408	0.8%
29	Kentucky	393	0.7%
29	Minnesota	393	0.7%
31	Connecticut	382	0.7%
32	Alaska	358	0.7%
33	South Carolina	346	0.7%
34	Missouri	294	0.6%
35	Utah	240	0.5%
36	Arizona	230	0.4%
37	New York	206	0.4%
38	Rhode Island	199	0.4%
39	Illinois	192	0.4%
40	New Jersey	191	0.4%
41	Hawaii	177	0.3%
42	New Hampshire	139	0.3%
43	Alabama	134	0.3%
44	Montana	111	0.2%
45	Louisiana	108	0.2%
46	South Dakota	91	0.2%
47	Delaware	58	0.1%
48	Wyoming	57	0.1%
49	Nevada	56	0.1%
50	Virginia	54	0.1%
	District of Columbia	225	0.4%

Source: American Osteopathic Association
    "Fact Sheet 2006" (http://www.do-online.osteotech.org/pdf/ost_factsheet.pdf)
*Active osteopaths under age 65 as of June 1, 2006. National total does not include 228 osteopaths not shown by state. Osteopaths practice a system of medicine based on the theory that disturbances in the musculoskeletal system affect other body parts, causing many disorders that can be corrected by various manipulative techniques in conjunction with conventional medical, surgical, pharmacological, and other therapeutic procedures.

Rate of Osteopathic Physicians in 2006

National Rate = 18 Osteopaths per 100,000 Population*

ALPHA ORDER

RANK	STATE	RATE
44	Alabama	3
6	Alaska	53
43	Arizona	4
7	Arkansas	52
32	California	10
20	Colorado	18
26	Connecticut	11
40	Delaware	7
18	Florida	19
36	Georgia	8
21	Hawaii	14
4	Idaho	72
48	Illinois	1
12	Indiana	36
16	Iowa	25
17	Kansas	22
33	Kentucky	9
44	Louisiana	3
9	Maine	46
26	Maryland	11
33	Massachusetts	9
8	Michigan	48
36	Minnesota	8
5	Mississippi	62
41	Missouri	5
24	Montana	12
13	Nebraska	35
46	Nevada	2
26	New Hampshire	11
46	New Jersey	2
2	New Mexico	147
48	New York	1
41	North Carolina	5
1	North Dakota	557
15	Ohio	32
11	Oklahoma	41
21	Oregon	14
10	Pennsylvania	44
18	Rhode Island	19
36	South Carolina	8
24	South Dakota	12
36	Tennessee	8
23	Texas	13
33	Utah	9
3	Vermont	125
48	Virginia	1
26	Washington	11
13	West Virginia	35
26	Wisconsin	11
26	Wyoming	11

RANK ORDER

RANK	STATE	RATE
1	North Dakota	557
2	New Mexico	147
3	Vermont	125
4	Idaho	72
5	Mississippi	62
6	Alaska	53
7	Arkansas	52
8	Michigan	48
9	Maine	46
10	Pennsylvania	44
11	Oklahoma	41
12	Indiana	36
13	Nebraska	35
13	West Virginia	35
15	Ohio	32
16	Iowa	25
17	Kansas	22
18	Florida	19
18	Rhode Island	19
20	Colorado	18
21	Hawaii	14
21	Oregon	14
23	Texas	13
24	Montana	12
24	South Dakota	12
26	Connecticut	11
26	Maryland	11
26	New Hampshire	11
26	Washington	11
26	Wisconsin	11
26	Wyoming	11
32	California	10
33	Kentucky	9
33	Massachusetts	9
33	Utah	9
36	Georgia	8
36	Minnesota	8
36	South Carolina	8
36	Tennessee	8
40	Delaware	7
41	Missouri	5
41	North Carolina	5
43	Arizona	4
44	Alabama	3
44	Louisiana	3
46	Nevada	2
46	New Jersey	2
48	Illinois	1
48	New York	1
48	Virginia	1

| | District of Columbia | 39 |

Source: Morgan Quitno Press using data from American Osteopathic Association
    "Fact Sheet 2006" (http://www.do-online.osteotech.org/pdf/ost_factsheet.pdf)
*Active osteopaths under age 65 as of June 1, 2006. National rate does not include osteopaths not shown by
state. Osteopaths practice a system of medicine based on the theory that disturbances in the musculoskeletal
system affect other body parts, causing many disorders that can be corrected by various manipulative techniques in
conjunction with conventional medical, surgical, pharmacological, and other therapeutic procedures.

Podiatrists in 2005

National Total = 8,290 Podiatrists*

ALPHA ORDER

RANK	STATE	PODIATRISTS	% of USA
25	Alabama	70	0.8%
NA	Alaska**	NA	NA
10	Arizona	260	3.1%
NA	Arkansas**	NA	NA
2	California	730	8.8%
19	Colorado	120	1.4%
15	Connecticut	160	1.9%
25	Delaware	70	0.8%
2	Florida	730	8.8%
20	Georgia	110	1.3%
NA	Hawaii**	NA	NA
33	Idaho	30	0.4%
9	Illinois	280	3.4%
21	Indiana	100	1.2%
25	Iowa	70	0.8%
33	Kansas	30	0.4%
30	Kentucky	40	0.5%
33	Louisiana	30	0.4%
30	Maine	40	0.5%
11	Maryland	240	2.9%
21	Massachusetts	100	1.2%
7	Michigan	350	4.2%
15	Minnesota	160	1.9%
NA	Mississippi**	NA	NA
18	Missouri	140	1.7%
29	Montana	50	0.6%
25	Nebraska	70	0.8%
30	Nevada	40	0.5%
33	New Hampshire	30	0.4%
7	New Jersey	350	4.2%
NA	New Mexico**	NA	NA
1	New York	860	10.4%
14	North Carolina	170	2.1%
NA	North Dakota**	NA	NA
4	Ohio	600	7.2%
NA	Oklahoma**	NA	NA
NA	Oregon**	NA	NA
5	Pennsylvania	540	6.5%
NA	Rhode Island**	NA	NA
23	South Carolina	90	1.1%
NA	South Dakota**	NA	NA
24	Tennessee	80	1.0%
6	Texas	410	4.9%
NA	Utah**	NA	NA
NA	Vermont**	NA	NA
17	Virginia	150	1.8%
13	Washington	180	2.2%
NA	West Virginia**	NA	NA
12	Wisconsin	210	2.5%
NA	Wyoming**	NA	NA

RANK ORDER

RANK	STATE	PODIATRISTS	% of USA
1	New York	860	10.4%
2	California	730	8.8%
2	Florida	730	8.8%
4	Ohio	600	7.2%
5	Pennsylvania	540	6.5%
6	Texas	410	4.9%
7	Michigan	350	4.2%
7	New Jersey	350	4.2%
9	Illinois	280	3.4%
10	Arizona	260	3.1%
11	Maryland	240	2.9%
12	Wisconsin	210	2.5%
13	Washington	180	2.2%
14	North Carolina	170	2.1%
15	Connecticut	160	1.9%
15	Minnesota	160	1.9%
17	Virginia	150	1.8%
18	Missouri	140	1.7%
19	Colorado	120	1.4%
20	Georgia	110	1.3%
21	Indiana	100	1.2%
21	Massachusetts	100	1.2%
23	South Carolina	90	1.1%
24	Tennessee	80	1.0%
25	Alabama	70	0.8%
25	Delaware	70	0.8%
25	Iowa	70	0.8%
25	Nebraska	70	0.8%
29	Montana	50	0.6%
30	Kentucky	40	0.5%
30	Maine	40	0.5%
30	Nevada	40	0.5%
33	Idaho	30	0.4%
33	Kansas	30	0.4%
33	Louisiana	30	0.4%
33	New Hampshire	30	0.4%
NA	Alaska**	NA	NA
NA	Arkansas**	NA	NA
NA	Hawaii**	NA	NA
NA	Mississippi**	NA	NA
NA	New Mexico**	NA	NA
NA	North Dakota**	NA	NA
NA	Oklahoma**	NA	NA
NA	Oregon**	NA	NA
NA	Rhode Island**	NA	NA
NA	South Dakota**	NA	NA
NA	Utah**	NA	NA
NA	Vermont**	NA	NA
NA	West Virginia**	NA	NA
NA	Wyoming**	NA	NA
	District of Columbia**	NA	NA

Source: U.S. Department of Labor, Bureau of Labor Statistics
    "Occupational Employment and Wages, 2005" (http://www.bls.gov/oes/)
*Does not include self-employed.
**Not available.

Rate of Podiatrists in 2005

National Rate = 3 Podiatrists per 100,000 Population*

ALPHA ORDER

RANK	STATE	RATE
18	Alabama	2
NA	Alaska**	NA
5	Arizona	4
NA	Arkansas**	NA
18	California	2
13	Colorado	3
2	Connecticut	5
1	Delaware	8
5	Florida	4
32	Georgia	1
NA	Hawaii**	NA
18	Idaho	2
18	Illinois	2
18	Indiana	2
18	Iowa	2
32	Kansas	1
32	Kentucky	1
32	Louisiana	1
13	Maine	3
5	Maryland	4
18	Massachusetts	2
13	Michigan	3
13	Minnesota	3
NA	Mississippi**	NA
18	Missouri	2
2	Montana	5
5	Nebraska	4
18	Nevada	2
18	New Hampshire	2
5	New Jersey	4
NA	New Mexico**	NA
5	New York	4
18	North Carolina	2
NA	North Dakota**	NA
2	Ohio	5
NA	Oklahoma**	NA
NA	Oregon**	NA
5	Pennsylvania	4
NA	Rhode Island**	NA
18	South Carolina	2
NA	South Dakota**	NA
32	Tennessee	1
18	Texas	2
NA	Utah**	NA
NA	Vermont**	NA
18	Virginia	2
13	Washington	3
NA	West Virginia**	NA
5	Wisconsin	4
NA	Wyoming**	NA

RANK ORDER

RANK	STATE	RATE
1	Delaware	8
2	Connecticut	5
2	Montana	5
2	Ohio	5
5	Arizona	4
5	Florida	4
5	Maryland	4
5	Nebraska	4
5	New Jersey	4
5	New York	4
5	Pennsylvania	4
5	Wisconsin	4
13	Colorado	3
13	Maine	3
13	Michigan	3
13	Minnesota	3
13	Washington	3
18	Alabama	2
18	California	2
18	Idaho	2
18	Illinois	2
18	Indiana	2
18	Iowa	2
18	Massachusetts	2
18	Missouri	2
18	Nevada	2
18	New Hampshire	2
18	North Carolina	2
18	South Carolina	2
18	Texas	2
18	Virginia	2
32	Georgia	1
32	Kansas	1
32	Kentucky	1
32	Louisiana	1
32	Tennessee	1
NA	Alaska**	NA
NA	Arkansas**	NA
NA	Hawaii**	NA
NA	Mississippi**	NA
NA	New Mexico**	NA
NA	North Dakota**	NA
NA	Oklahoma**	NA
NA	Oregon**	NA
NA	Rhode Island**	NA
NA	South Dakota**	NA
NA	Utah**	NA
NA	Vermont**	NA
NA	West Virginia**	NA
NA	Wyoming**	NA
	District of Columbia**	NA

Source: Morgan Quitno Press using data from U.S. Department of Labor, Bureau of Labor Statistics
"Occupational Employment and Wages, 2005" (http://www.bls.gov/oes/)
*Does not include self-employed.
**Not available.

Average Annual Wages of Podiatrists in 2005

National Average = $111,250*

ALPHA ORDER

RANK	STATE	WAGES
17	Alabama	$117,210
NA	Alaska**	NA
34	Arizona	89,860
NA	Arkansas**	NA
32	California	92,160
16	Colorado	122,330
10	Connecticut	127,420
24	Delaware	109,390
19	Florida	115,480
7	Georgia	134,360
36	Hawaii	79,560
37	Idaho	62,000
18	Illinois	117,180
14	Indiana	124,220
26	Iowa	105,580
30	Kansas	95,820
1	Kentucky	176,110
33	Louisiana	90,260
35	Maine	87,830
15	Maryland	124,210
27	Massachusetts	104,210
12	Michigan	125,870
11	Minnesota	125,930
NA	Mississippi**	NA
4	Missouri	148,560
31	Montana	92,640
9	Nebraska	132,070
5	Nevada	137,720
8	New Hampshire	132,470
21	New Jersey	112,250
38	New Mexico	58,220
25	New York	108,540
3	North Carolina	158,840
NA	North Dakota**	NA
28	Ohio	103,490
2	Oklahoma	175,100
NA	Oregon**	NA
20	Pennsylvania	113,030
NA	Rhode Island**	NA
13	South Carolina	124,630
NA	South Dakota**	NA
22	Tennessee	111,270
29	Texas	100,880
39	Utah	54,280
NA	Vermont**	NA
6	Virginia	137,120
NA	Washington**	NA
NA	West Virginia**	NA
23	Wisconsin	110,540
NA	Wyoming**	NA

RANK ORDER

RANK	STATE	WAGES
1	Kentucky	$176,110
2	Oklahoma	175,100
3	North Carolina	158,840
4	Missouri	148,560
5	Nevada	137,720
6	Virginia	137,120
7	Georgia	134,360
8	New Hampshire	132,470
9	Nebraska	132,070
10	Connecticut	127,420
11	Minnesota	125,930
12	Michigan	125,870
13	South Carolina	124,630
14	Indiana	124,220
15	Maryland	124,210
16	Colorado	122,330
17	Alabama	117,210
18	Illinois	117,180
19	Florida	115,480
20	Pennsylvania	113,030
21	New Jersey	112,250
22	Tennessee	111,270
23	Wisconsin	110,540
24	Delaware	109,390
25	New York	108,540
26	Iowa	105,580
27	Massachusetts	104,210
28	Ohio	103,490
29	Texas	100,880
30	Kansas	95,820
31	Montana	92,640
32	California	92,160
33	Louisiana	90,260
34	Arizona	89,860
35	Maine	87,830
36	Hawaii	79,560
37	Idaho	62,000
38	New Mexico	58,220
39	Utah	54,280
NA	Alaska**	NA
NA	Arkansas**	NA
NA	Mississippi**	NA
NA	North Dakota**	NA
NA	Oregon**	NA
NA	Rhode Island**	NA
NA	South Dakota**	NA
NA	Vermont**	NA
NA	Washington**	NA
NA	West Virginia**	NA
NA	Wyoming**	NA
	District of Columbia**	NA

Source: U.S. Department of Labor, Bureau of Labor Statistics
   "Occupational Employment and Wages, 2005" (http://www.bls.gov/oes/)
*Does not include self-employed.
**Not available.

Doctors of Chiropractic in 2005

National Total = 86,932 Chiropractors*

ALPHA ORDER

RANK	STATE	CHIROPRACTORS	% of USA
30	Alabama	776	0.9%
49	Alaska	216	0.2%
10	Arizona	2,561	2.9%
35	Arkansas	580	0.7%
1	California	13,763	15.8%
12	Colorado	2,304	2.7%
26	Connecticut	984	1.1%
45	Delaware	285	0.3%
3	Florida	4,791	5.5%
8	Georgia	3,037	3.5%
32	Hawaii	624	0.7%
37	Idaho	459	0.5%
6	Illinois	3,541	4.1%
25	Indiana	1,086	1.2%
20	Iowa	1,460	1.7%
27	Kansas	832	1.0%
23	Kentucky	1,127	1.3%
34	Louisiana	581	0.7%
40	Maine	356	0.4%
31	Maryland	711	0.8%
17	Massachusetts	1,937	2.2%
9	Michigan	2,929	3.4%
11	Minnesota	2,318	2.7%
42	Mississippi	332	0.4%
16	Missouri	2,067	2.4%
41	Montana	350	0.4%
38	Nebraska	447	0.5%
33	Nevada	595	0.7%
39	New Hampshire	424	0.5%
7	New Jersey	3,218	3.7%
36	New Mexico	579	0.7%
2	New York	6,245	7.2%
18	North Carolina	1,755	2.0%
47	North Dakota	270	0.3%
15	Ohio	2,161	2.5%
29	Oklahoma	779	0.9%
22	Oregon	1,217	1.4%
5	Pennsylvania	4,000	4.6%
46	Rhode Island	272	0.3%
21	South Carolina	1,435	1.7%
44	South Dakota	306	0.4%
24	Tennessee	1,099	1.3%
4	Texas	4,392	5.1%
28	Utah	809	0.9%
48	Vermont	247	0.3%
19	Virginia	1,604	1.8%
14	Washington	2,194	2.5%
43	West Virginia	326	0.4%
13	Wisconsin	2,274	2.6%
50	Wyoming	203	0.2%

RANK ORDER

RANK	STATE	CHIROPRACTORS	% of USA
1	California	13,763	15.8%
2	New York	6,245	7.2%
3	Florida	4,791	5.5%
4	Texas	4,392	5.1%
5	Pennsylvania	4,000	4.6%
6	Illinois	3,541	4.1%
7	New Jersey	3,218	3.7%
8	Georgia	3,037	3.5%
9	Michigan	2,929	3.4%
10	Arizona	2,561	2.9%
11	Minnesota	2,318	2.7%
12	Colorado	2,304	2.7%
13	Wisconsin	2,274	2.6%
14	Washington	2,194	2.5%
15	Ohio	2,161	2.5%
16	Missouri	2,067	2.4%
17	Massachusetts	1,937	2.2%
18	North Carolina	1,755	2.0%
19	Virginia	1,604	1.8%
20	Iowa	1,460	1.7%
21	South Carolina	1,435	1.7%
22	Oregon	1,217	1.4%
23	Kentucky	1,127	1.3%
24	Tennessee	1,099	1.3%
25	Indiana	1,086	1.2%
26	Connecticut	984	1.1%
27	Kansas	832	1.0%
28	Utah	809	0.9%
29	Oklahoma	779	0.9%
30	Alabama	776	0.9%
31	Maryland	711	0.8%
32	Hawaii	624	0.7%
33	Nevada	595	0.7%
34	Louisiana	581	0.7%
35	Arkansas	580	0.7%
36	New Mexico	579	0.7%
37	Idaho	459	0.5%
38	Nebraska	447	0.5%
39	New Hampshire	424	0.5%
40	Maine	356	0.4%
41	Montana	350	0.4%
42	Mississippi	332	0.4%
43	West Virginia	326	0.4%
44	South Dakota	306	0.4%
45	Delaware	285	0.3%
46	Rhode Island	272	0.3%
47	North Dakota	270	0.3%
48	Vermont	247	0.3%
49	Alaska	216	0.2%
50	Wyoming	203	0.2%
	District of Columbia	74	0.1%

*Source: Federation of Chiropractic Licensing Boards
"Official Directory" (http://www.fclb.org/directory/index.htm)*

As of December 2005. Licensed active doctors. There is some duplication as some doctors are licensed in more than one state.

Rate of Doctors of Chiropractic in 2005

National Rate = 29 Chiropractors per 100,000 Population*

ALPHA ORDER

RANK	STATE	RATE
46	Alabama	17
18	Alaska	33
5	Arizona	43
39	Arkansas	21
11	California	38
1	Colorado	49
30	Connecticut	28
16	Delaware	34
32	Florida	27
18	Georgia	33
1	Hawaii	49
21	Idaho	32
30	Illinois	28
46	Indiana	17
1	Iowa	49
26	Kansas	30
32	Kentucky	27
48	Louisiana	13
32	Maine	27
48	Maryland	13
26	Massachusetts	30
29	Michigan	29
4	Minnesota	45
50	Mississippi	11
14	Missouri	36
12	Montana	37
35	Nebraska	25
35	Nevada	25
21	New Hampshire	32
12	New Jersey	37
26	New Mexico	30
21	New York	32
41	North Carolina	20
5	North Dakota	43
42	Ohio	19
38	Oklahoma	22
18	Oregon	33
21	Pennsylvania	32
35	Rhode Island	25
16	South Carolina	34
10	South Dakota	39
44	Tennessee	18
42	Texas	19
21	Utah	32
8	Vermont	40
39	Virginia	21
15	Washington	35
44	West Virginia	18
7	Wisconsin	41
8	Wyoming	40

RANK ORDER

RANK	STATE	RATE
1	Colorado	49
1	Hawaii	49
1	Iowa	49
4	Minnesota	45
5	Arizona	43
5	North Dakota	43
7	Wisconsin	41
8	Vermont	40
8	Wyoming	40
10	South Dakota	39
11	California	38
12	Montana	37
12	New Jersey	37
14	Missouri	36
15	Washington	35
16	Delaware	34
16	South Carolina	34
18	Alaska	33
18	Georgia	33
18	Oregon	33
21	Idaho	32
21	New Hampshire	32
21	New York	32
21	Pennsylvania	32
21	Utah	32
26	Kansas	30
26	Massachusetts	30
26	New Mexico	30
29	Michigan	29
30	Connecticut	28
30	Illinois	28
32	Florida	27
32	Kentucky	27
32	Maine	27
35	Nebraska	25
35	Nevada	25
35	Rhode Island	25
38	Oklahoma	22
39	Arkansas	21
39	Virginia	21
41	North Carolina	20
42	Ohio	19
42	Texas	19
44	Tennessee	18
44	West Virginia	18
46	Alabama	17
46	Indiana	17
48	Louisiana	13
48	Maryland	13
50	Mississippi	11

District of Columbia 13

Source: Morgan Quitno Press using data from Federation of Chiropractic Licensing Boards "Official Directory" (http://www.fclb.org/directory/index.htm)

*As of December 2005. Licensed active doctors. There is some duplication as some doctors are licensed in more than one state.

Average Annual Wages of Chiropractors in 2005

National Average = $82,060*

ALPHA ORDER

RANK	STATE	WAGES
21	Alabama	$90,760
1	Alaska	131,130
18	Arizona	94,740
9	Arkansas	103,790
34	California	73,120
8	Colorado	103,800
15	Connecticut	97,040
2	Delaware	122,690
37	Florida	70,190
47	Georgia	56,420
40	Hawaii	67,230
NA	Idaho**	NA
25	Illinois	86,660
24	Indiana	87,080
32	Iowa	74,830
27	Kansas	83,560
13	Kentucky	98,990
19	Louisiana	94,330
44	Maine	62,240
10	Maryland	102,710
28	Massachusetts	79,120
20	Michigan	92,460
36	Minnesota	71,420
45	Mississippi	59,490
43	Missouri	63,070
35	Montana	71,650
39	Nebraska	67,260
3	Nevada	114,300
5	New Hampshire	107,450
23	New Jersey	87,680
41	New Mexico	66,420
29	New York	77,740
4	North Carolina	110,000
46	North Dakota	58,520
14	Ohio	97,630
11	Oklahoma	101,250
NA	Oregon**	NA
42	Pennsylvania	65,200
31	Rhode Island	75,720
6	South Carolina	105,940
17	South Dakota	96,280
22	Tennessee	89,940
33	Texas	73,700
38	Utah	69,800
NA	Vermont**	NA
26	Virginia	83,990
16	Washington	96,980
12	West Virginia	99,110
7	Wisconsin	104,230
30	Wyoming	77,640

RANK ORDER

RANK	STATE	WAGES
1	Alaska	$131,130
2	Delaware	122,690
3	Nevada	114,300
4	North Carolina	110,000
5	New Hampshire	107,450
6	South Carolina	105,940
7	Wisconsin	104,230
8	Colorado	103,800
9	Arkansas	103,790
10	Maryland	102,710
11	Oklahoma	101,250
12	West Virginia	99,110
13	Kentucky	98,990
14	Ohio	97,630
15	Connecticut	97,040
16	Washington	96,980
17	South Dakota	96,280
18	Arizona	94,740
19	Louisiana	94,330
20	Michigan	92,460
21	Alabama	90,760
22	Tennessee	89,940
23	New Jersey	87,680
24	Indiana	87,080
25	Illinois	86,660
26	Virginia	83,990
27	Kansas	83,560
28	Massachusetts	79,120
29	New York	77,740
30	Wyoming	77,640
31	Rhode Island	75,720
32	Iowa	74,830
33	Texas	73,700
34	California	73,120
35	Montana	71,650
36	Minnesota	71,420
37	Florida	70,190
38	Utah	69,800
39	Nebraska	67,260
40	Hawaii	67,230
41	New Mexico	66,420
42	Pennsylvania	65,200
43	Missouri	63,070
44	Maine	62,240
45	Mississippi	59,490
46	North Dakota	58,520
47	Georgia	56,420
NA	Idaho**	NA
NA	Oregon**	NA
NA	Vermont**	NA
	District of Columbia**	NA

Source: U.S. Department of Labor, Bureau of Labor Statistics
      "Occupational Employment and Wages, 2005" (http://www.bls.gov/oes/)
*Does not include self-employed.
**Not available.

Physician Assistants in Clinical Practice in 2007

National Total = 63,285 Physician Assistants*

ALPHA ORDER

RANK	STATE	PAs	% of USA
40	Alabama	334	0.5%
42	Alaska	321	0.5%
15	Arizona	1,412	2.2%
49	Arkansas	99	0.2%
2	California	6,148	9.7%
13	Colorado	1,500	2.4%
18	Connecticut	1,197	1.9%
46	Delaware	182	0.3%
4	Florida	3,843	6.1%
8	Georgia	2,129	3.4%
48	Hawaii	142	0.2%
36	Idaho	423	0.7%
12	Illinois	1,685	2.7%
31	Indiana	534	0.8%
26	Iowa	672	1.1%
24	Kansas	710	1.1%
23	Kentucky	718	1.1%
35	Louisiana	431	0.7%
33	Maine	482	0.8%
11	Maryland	1,702	2.7%
14	Massachusetts	1,447	2.3%
7	Michigan	2,688	4.2%
20	Minnesota	990	1.6%
50	Mississippi	58	0.1%
32	Missouri	518	0.8%
41	Montana	328	0.5%
28	Nebraska	643	1.0%
37	Nevada	394	0.6%
39	New Hampshire	358	0.6%
19	New Jersey	1,164	1.8%
34	New Mexico	453	0.7%
1	New York	7,057	11.2%
6	North Carolina	3,059	4.8%
43	North Dakota	211	0.3%
10	Ohio	1,715	2.7%
21	Oklahoma	916	1.4%
25	Oregon	696	1.1%
5	Pennsylvania	3,788	6.0%
44	Rhode Island	208	0.3%
29	South Carolina	620	1.0%
38	South Dakota	367	0.6%
22	Tennessee	846	1.3%
3	Texas	3,920	6.2%
30	Utah	569	0.9%
45	Vermont	194	0.3%
17	Virginia	1,333	2.1%
9	Washington	1,749	2.8%
27	West Virginia	654	1.0%
16	Wisconsin	1,349	2.1%
47	Wyoming	169	0.3%

RANK ORDER

RANK	STATE	PAs	% of USA
1	New York	7,057	11.2%
2	California	6,148	9.7%
3	Texas	3,920	6.2%
4	Florida	3,843	6.1%
5	Pennsylvania	3,788	6.0%
6	North Carolina	3,059	4.8%
7	Michigan	2,688	4.2%
8	Georgia	2,129	3.4%
9	Washington	1,749	2.8%
10	Ohio	1,715	2.7%
11	Maryland	1,702	2.7%
12	Illinois	1,685	2.7%
13	Colorado	1,500	2.4%
14	Massachusetts	1,447	2.3%
15	Arizona	1,412	2.2%
16	Wisconsin	1,349	2.1%
17	Virginia	1,333	2.1%
18	Connecticut	1,197	1.9%
19	New Jersey	1,164	1.8%
20	Minnesota	990	1.6%
21	Oklahoma	916	1.4%
22	Tennessee	846	1.3%
23	Kentucky	718	1.1%
24	Kansas	710	1.1%
25	Oregon	696	1.1%
26	Iowa	672	1.1%
27	West Virginia	654	1.0%
28	Nebraska	643	1.0%
29	South Carolina	620	1.0%
30	Utah	569	0.9%
31	Indiana	534	0.8%
32	Missouri	518	0.8%
33	Maine	482	0.8%
34	New Mexico	453	0.7%
35	Louisiana	431	0.7%
36	Idaho	423	0.7%
37	Nevada	394	0.6%
38	South Dakota	367	0.6%
39	New Hampshire	358	0.6%
40	Alabama	334	0.5%
41	Montana	328	0.5%
42	Alaska	321	0.5%
43	North Dakota	211	0.3%
44	Rhode Island	208	0.3%
45	Vermont	194	0.3%
46	Delaware	182	0.3%
47	Wyoming	169	0.3%
48	Hawaii	142	0.2%
49	Arkansas	99	0.2%
50	Mississippi	58	0.1%
	District of Columbia	160	0.3%

Source: The American Academy of Physician Assistants
"Projected Number of People in Clinical Practice as PAs as of January 1, 2007"
(http://www.aapa.org/research/06number-clinpractice06.pdf)
*Projected. National total does not include 329 physician assistants who work outside the United States or whose location is unknown.

Rate of Physician Assistants in Clinical Practice in 2007

National Rate = 21 PAs per 100,000 Population*

ALPHA ORDER

RANK	STATE	RATE
48	Alabama	7
1	Alaska	48
23	Arizona	23
49	Arkansas	4
34	California	17
12	Colorado	32
9	Connecticut	34
29	Delaware	21
29	Florida	21
23	Georgia	23
44	Hawaii	11
16	Idaho	29
42	Illinois	13
47	Indiana	8
23	Iowa	23
20	Kansas	26
34	Kentucky	17
45	Louisiana	10
4	Maine	36
14	Maryland	30
27	Massachusetts	22
17	Michigan	27
31	Minnesota	19
50	Mississippi	2
46	Missouri	9
7	Montana	35
4	Nebraska	36
38	Nevada	16
17	New Hampshire	27
42	New Jersey	13
23	New Mexico	23
3	New York	37
7	North Carolina	35
10	North Dakota	33
39	Ohio	15
20	Oklahoma	26
31	Oregon	19
14	Pennsylvania	30
31	Rhode Island	19
40	South Carolina	14
2	South Dakota	47
40	Tennessee	14
34	Texas	17
27	Utah	22
13	Vermont	31
34	Virginia	17
17	Washington	27
4	West Virginia	36
22	Wisconsin	24
10	Wyoming	33

RANK ORDER

RANK	STATE	RATE
1	Alaska	48
2	South Dakota	47
3	New York	37
4	Maine	36
4	Nebraska	36
4	West Virginia	36
7	Montana	35
7	North Carolina	35
9	Connecticut	34
10	North Dakota	33
10	Wyoming	33
12	Colorado	32
13	Vermont	31
14	Maryland	30
14	Pennsylvania	30
16	Idaho	29
17	Michigan	27
17	New Hampshire	27
17	Washington	27
20	Kansas	26
20	Oklahoma	26
22	Wisconsin	24
23	Arizona	23
23	Georgia	23
23	Iowa	23
23	New Mexico	23
27	Massachusetts	22
27	Utah	22
29	Delaware	21
29	Florida	21
31	Minnesota	19
31	Oregon	19
31	Rhode Island	19
34	California	17
34	Kentucky	17
34	Texas	17
34	Virginia	17
38	Nevada	16
39	Ohio	15
40	South Carolina	14
40	Tennessee	14
42	Illinois	13
42	New Jersey	13
44	Hawaii	11
45	Louisiana	10
46	Missouri	9
47	Indiana	8
48	Alabama	7
49	Arkansas	4
50	Mississippi	2

District of Columbia	28

Source: Morgan Quitno Press using data from The American Academy of Physician Assistants
"Projected Number of People in Clinical Practice as PAs as of January 1, 2007"
(http://www.aapa.org/research/06number-clinpractice06.pdf)
*Projected. Rates calculated using 2006 Census population figures.

Average Annual Wages of Physician Assistants in 2005

National Average = $71,070*

ALPHA ORDER

RANK	STATE	WAGES
46	Alabama	$51,540
1	Alaska	87,480
33	Arizona	64,530
40	Arkansas	58,370
5	California	78,870
29	Colorado	69,490
4	Connecticut	80,270
25	Delaware	71,210
7	Florida	78,390
38	Georgia	61,030
45	Hawaii	53,880
34	Idaho	62,710
44	Illinois	56,730
37	Indiana	62,150
27	Iowa	70,760
18	Kansas	72,860
28	Kentucky	69,590
47	Louisiana	50,840
9	Maine	77,490
2	Maryland	83,450
21	Massachusetts	72,040
22	Michigan	71,790
12	Minnesota	75,630
49	Mississippi	45,330
35	Missouri	62,540
32	Montana	65,470
11	Nebraska	76,510
43	Nevada	56,890
16	New Hampshire	73,390
19	New Jersey	72,810
48	New Mexico	46,170
14	New York	73,510
20	North Carolina	72,070
36	North Dakota	62,190
17	Ohio	73,360
13	Oklahoma	74,970
15	Oregon	73,440
41	Pennsylvania	57,770
23	Rhode Island	71,560
39	South Carolina	59,630
24	South Dakota	71,450
31	Tennessee	65,690
3	Texas	82,040
8	Utah	78,230
6	Vermont	78,850
30	Virginia	66,820
10	Washington	76,890
26	West Virginia	71,120
NA	Wisconsin**	NA
42	Wyoming	57,710

RANK ORDER

RANK	STATE	WAGES
1	Alaska	$87,480
2	Maryland	83,450
3	Texas	82,040
4	Connecticut	80,270
5	California	78,870
6	Vermont	78,850
7	Florida	78,390
8	Utah	78,230
9	Maine	77,490
10	Washington	76,890
11	Nebraska	76,510
12	Minnesota	75,630
13	Oklahoma	74,970
14	New York	73,510
15	Oregon	73,440
16	New Hampshire	73,390
17	Ohio	73,360
18	Kansas	72,860
19	New Jersey	72,810
20	North Carolina	72,070
21	Massachusetts	72,040
22	Michigan	71,790
23	Rhode Island	71,560
24	South Dakota	71,450
25	Delaware	71,210
26	West Virginia	71,120
27	Iowa	70,760
28	Kentucky	69,590
29	Colorado	69,490
30	Virginia	66,820
31	Tennessee	65,690
32	Montana	65,470
33	Arizona	64,530
34	Idaho	62,710
35	Missouri	62,540
36	North Dakota	62,190
37	Indiana	62,150
38	Georgia	61,030
39	South Carolina	59,630
40	Arkansas	58,370
41	Pennsylvania	57,770
42	Wyoming	57,710
43	Nevada	56,890
44	Illinois	56,730
45	Hawaii	53,880
46	Alabama	51,540
47	Louisiana	50,840
48	New Mexico	46,170
49	Mississippi	45,330
NA	Wisconsin**	NA
	District of Columbia	60,300

Source: U.S. Department of Labor, Bureau of Labor Statistics
"Occupational Employment and Wages, 2005" (http://www.bls.gov/oes/)
*Does not include self-employed.
**Not available.

Registered Nurses in 2005

National Total = 2,368,070 Registered Nurses*

ALPHA ORDER

RANK	STATE	NURSES	% of USA
23	Alabama	37,270	1.6%
49	Alaska	5,050	0.2%
27	Arizona	31,010	1.3%
33	Arkansas	20,250	0.9%
1	California	226,350	9.6%
25	Colorado	33,050	1.4%
24	Connecticut	34,120	1.4%
45	Delaware	7,710	0.3%
4	Florida	138,760	5.9%
12	Georgia	59,720	2.5%
43	Hawaii	9,240	0.4%
42	Idaho	9,390	0.4%
7	Illinois	102,510	4.3%
15	Indiana	52,330	2.2%
28	Iowa	29,940	1.3%
31	Kansas	25,330	1.1%
22	Kentucky	37,720	1.6%
21	Louisiana	39,510	1.7%
38	Maine	13,330	0.6%
18	Maryland	49,010	2.1%
10	Massachusetts	76,870	3.2%
8	Michigan	81,370	3.4%
17	Minnesota	49,390	2.1%
30	Mississippi	25,970	1.1%
14	Missouri	53,440	2.3%
46	Montana	7,490	0.3%
34	Nebraska	16,460	0.7%
37	Nevada	13,980	0.6%
39	New Hampshire	12,210	0.5%
9	New Jersey	80,940	3.4%
40	New Mexico	11,170	0.5%
2	New York	164,370	6.9%
11	North Carolina	72,130	3.0%
47	North Dakota	6,740	0.3%
6	Ohio	106,600	4.5%
32	Oklahoma	24,670	1.0%
29	Oregon	27,970	1.2%
5	Pennsylvania	123,650	5.2%
41	Rhode Island	10,620	0.4%
26	South Carolina	31,160	1.3%
44	South Dakota	9,040	0.4%
16	Tennessee	52,090	2.2%
3	Texas	149,950	6.3%
36	Utah	15,550	0.7%
48	Vermont	5,560	0.2%
13	Virginia	53,850	2.3%
19	Washington	47,930	2.0%
35	West Virginia	15,640	0.7%
20	Wisconsin	47,380	2.0%
50	Wyoming	3,940	0.2%

RANK ORDER

RANK	STATE	NURSES	% of USA
1	California	226,350	9.6%
2	New York	164,370	6.9%
3	Texas	149,950	6.3%
4	Florida	138,760	5.9%
5	Pennsylvania	123,650	5.2%
6	Ohio	106,600	4.5%
7	Illinois	102,510	4.3%
8	Michigan	81,370	3.4%
9	New Jersey	80,940	3.4%
10	Massachusetts	76,870	3.2%
11	North Carolina	72,130	3.0%
12	Georgia	59,720	2.5%
13	Virginia	53,850	2.3%
14	Missouri	53,440	2.3%
15	Indiana	52,330	2.2%
16	Tennessee	52,090	2.2%
17	Minnesota	49,390	2.1%
18	Maryland	49,010	2.1%
19	Washington	47,930	2.0%
20	Wisconsin	47,380	2.0%
21	Louisiana	39,510	1.7%
22	Kentucky	37,720	1.6%
23	Alabama	37,270	1.6%
24	Connecticut	34,120	1.4%
25	Colorado	33,050	1.4%
26	South Carolina	31,160	1.3%
27	Arizona	31,010	1.3%
28	Iowa	29,940	1.3%
29	Oregon	27,970	1.2%
30	Mississippi	25,970	1.1%
31	Kansas	25,330	1.1%
32	Oklahoma	24,670	1.0%
33	Arkansas	20,250	0.9%
34	Nebraska	16,460	0.7%
35	West Virginia	15,640	0.7%
36	Utah	15,550	0.7%
37	Nevada	13,980	0.6%
38	Maine	13,330	0.6%
39	New Hampshire	12,210	0.5%
40	New Mexico	11,170	0.5%
41	Rhode Island	10,620	0.4%
42	Idaho	9,390	0.4%
43	Hawaii	9,240	0.4%
44	South Dakota	9,040	0.4%
45	Delaware	7,710	0.3%
46	Montana	7,490	0.3%
47	North Dakota	6,740	0.3%
48	Vermont	5,560	0.2%
49	Alaska	5,050	0.2%
50	Wyoming	3,940	0.2%
	District of Columbia	8,340	0.4%

Source: U.S. Department of Labor, Bureau of Labor Statistics
    "Occupational Employment and Wages, 2005" (http://www.bls.gov/oes/)
*Does not include self-employed.

Rate of Registered Nurses in 2005

National Rate = 799 Nurses per 100,000 Population*

ALPHA ORDER				RANK ORDER		
RANK	STATE	RATE		RANK	STATE	RATE
28	Alabama	819		1	Massachusetts	1,195
36	Alaska	761		2	South Dakota	1,167
50	Arizona	521		3	North Dakota	1,062
38	Arkansas	730		4	Maine	1,011
46	California	626		5	Iowa	1,010
41	Colorado	709		6	Pennsylvania	997
8	Connecticut	975		7	Rhode Island	989
16	Delaware	916		8	Connecticut	975
32	Florida	781		9	Minnesota	963
44	Georgia	654		10	Nebraska	936
39	Hawaii	726		11	New Hampshire	934
43	Idaho	657		12	New Jersey	930
30	Illinois	803		13	Ohio	929
26	Indiana	835		14	Kansas	922
5	Iowa	1,010		14	Missouri	922
14	Kansas	922		16	Delaware	916
17	Kentucky	904		17	Kentucky	904
20	Louisiana	877		18	Mississippi	893
4	Maine	1,011		18	Vermont	893
20	Maryland	877		20	Louisiana	877
1	Massachusetts	1,195		20	Maryland	877
29	Michigan	806		22	Tennessee	875
9	Minnesota	963		23	West Virginia	862
18	Mississippi	893		24	Wisconsin	857
14	Missouri	922		25	New York	851
31	Montana	801		26	Indiana	835
10	Nebraska	936		27	North Carolina	832
48	Nevada	580		28	Alabama	819
11	New Hampshire	934		29	Michigan	806
12	New Jersey	930		30	Illinois	803
48	New Mexico	580		31	Montana	801
25	New York	851		32	Florida	781
27	North Carolina	832		33	Wyoming	774
3	North Dakota	1,062		34	Oregon	769
13	Ohio	929		35	Washington	762
42	Oklahoma	696		36	Alaska	761
34	Oregon	769		37	South Carolina	734
6	Pennsylvania	997		38	Arkansas	730
7	Rhode Island	989		39	Hawaii	726
37	South Carolina	734		40	Virginia	712
2	South Dakota	1,167		41	Colorado	709
22	Tennessee	875		42	Oklahoma	696
44	Texas	654		43	Idaho	657
47	Utah	624		44	Georgia	654
18	Vermont	893		44	Texas	654
40	Virginia	712		46	California	626
35	Washington	762		47	Utah	624
23	West Virginia	862		48	Nevada	580
24	Wisconsin	857		48	New Mexico	580
33	Wyoming	774		50	Arizona	521
					District of Columbia	1,433

Source: Morgan Quitno Press using data from U.S. Department of Labor, Bureau of Labor Statistics
   "Occupational Employment and Wages, 2005" (http://www.bls.gov/oes/)
*Does not include self-employed.

Average Annual Wages of Registered Nurses in 2005

National Average = $56,880*

ALPHA ORDER				RANK ORDER		
RANK	**STATE**	**WAGES**		**RANK**	**STATE**	**WAGES**
40	Alabama	$48,840		1	California	$70,430
9	Alaska	60,820		2	Maryland	67,330
17	Arizona	56,280		3	Massachusetts	66,250
41	Arkansas	48,620		4	Hawaii	65,490
1	California	70,430		5	New Jersey	63,070
16	Colorado	56,340		6	New York	63,010
8	Connecticut	61,990		7	Washington	62,220
14	Delaware	58,260		8	Connecticut	61,990
25	Florida	53,190		9	Alaska	60,820
29	Georgia	52,430		10	Minnesota	60,500
4	Hawaii	65,490		11	Oregon	60,270
39	Idaho	49,460		12	Nevada	59,660
23	Illinois	53,470		13	Rhode Island	58,400
37	Indiana	50,020		14	Delaware	58,260
50	Iowa	45,330		15	Michigan	57,190
49	Kansas	46,990		16	Colorado	56,340
35	Kentucky	50,370		17	Arizona	56,280
33	Louisiana	50,950		18	Wisconsin	55,060
27	Maine	52,840		19	Texas	54,810
2	Maryland	67,330		20	Virginia	54,480
3	Massachusetts	66,250		21	New Mexico	54,380
15	Michigan	57,190		22	Pennsylvania	54,040
10	Minnesota	60,500		23	Illinois	53,470
42	Mississippi	48,460		24	New Hampshire	53,340
34	Missouri	50,650		25	Florida	53,190
42	Montana	48,460		26	Ohio	53,150
38	Nebraska	50,000		27	Maine	52,840
12	Nevada	59,660		28	Utah	52,490
24	New Hampshire	53,340		29	Georgia	52,430
5	New Jersey	63,070		30	South Carolina	52,060
21	New Mexico	54,380		31	North Carolina	51,970
6	New York	63,010		32	Tennessee	51,250
31	North Carolina	51,970		33	Louisiana	50,950
46	North Dakota	48,110		34	Missouri	50,650
26	Ohio	53,150		35	Kentucky	50,370
48	Oklahoma	47,200		36	Vermont	50,060
11	Oregon	60,270		37	Indiana	50,020
22	Pennsylvania	54,040		38	Nebraska	50,000
13	Rhode Island	58,400		39	Idaho	49,460
30	South Carolina	52,060		40	Alabama	48,840
47	South Dakota	47,500		41	Arkansas	48,620
32	Tennessee	51,250		42	Mississippi	48,460
19	Texas	54,810		42	Montana	48,460
28	Utah	52,490		44	West Virginia	48,340
36	Vermont	50,060		45	Wyoming	48,210
20	Virginia	54,480		46	North Dakota	48,110
7	Washington	62,220		47	South Dakota	47,500
44	West Virginia	48,340		48	Oklahoma	47,200
18	Wisconsin	55,060		49	Kansas	46,990
45	Wyoming	48,210		50	Iowa	45,330
					District of Columbia	59,130

Source: U.S. Department of Labor, Bureau of Labor Statistics
   "Occupational Employment and Wages, 2005" (http://www.bls.gov/oes/)
*Does not include self-employed.

Licensed Practical and Licensed Vocational Nurses in 2005

National Total = 710,020 LPN/LVNs*

ALPHA ORDER

RANK	STATE	NURSES	% of USA
19	Alabama	14,290	2.0%
50	Alaska	520	0.1%
28	Arizona	8,800	1.2%
21	Arkansas	12,340	1.7%
2	California	52,480	7.4%
30	Colorado	7,120	1.0%
29	Connecticut	8,320	1.2%
47	Delaware	1,750	0.2%
4	Florida	48,920	6.9%
8	Georgia	23,510	3.3%
44	Hawaii	1,970	0.3%
36	Idaho	3,100	0.4%
7	Illinois	23,710	3.3%
12	Indiana	18,300	2.6%
33	Iowa	6,610	0.9%
31	Kansas	7,070	1.0%
22	Kentucky	11,820	1.7%
10	Louisiana	19,380	2.7%
46	Maine	1,900	0.3%
27	Maryland	9,010	1.3%
17	Massachusetts	16,710	2.4%
15	Michigan	17,850	2.5%
13	Minnesota	18,190	2.6%
26	Mississippi	9,950	1.4%
16	Missouri	17,570	2.5%
39	Montana	2,790	0.4%
34	Nebraska	5,920	0.8%
41	Nevada	2,700	0.4%
42	New Hampshire	2,330	0.3%
14	New Jersey	17,870	2.5%
35	New Mexico	4,610	0.6%
3	New York	50,060	7.1%
18	North Carolina	15,990	2.3%
40	North Dakota	2,770	0.4%
5	Ohio	37,160	5.2%
20	Oklahoma	13,770	1.9%
38	Oregon	2,850	0.4%
6	Pennsylvania	35,390	5.0%
45	Rhode Island	1,930	0.3%
23	South Carolina	10,680	1.5%
43	South Dakota	2,010	0.3%
9	Tennessee	21,550	3.0%
1	Texas	65,170	9.2%
37	Utah	2,940	0.4%
48	Vermont	1,490	0.2%
11	Virginia	19,190	2.7%
25	Washington	10,090	1.4%
32	West Virginia	6,650	0.9%
24	Wisconsin	10,280	1.4%
49	Wyoming	730	0.1%

RANK ORDER

RANK	STATE	NURSES	% of USA
1	Texas	65,170	9.2%
2	California	52,480	7.4%
3	New York	50,060	7.1%
4	Florida	48,920	6.9%
5	Ohio	37,160	5.2%
6	Pennsylvania	35,390	5.0%
7	Illinois	23,710	3.3%
8	Georgia	23,510	3.3%
9	Tennessee	21,550	3.0%
10	Louisiana	19,380	2.7%
11	Virginia	19,190	2.7%
12	Indiana	18,300	2.6%
13	Minnesota	18,190	2.6%
14	New Jersey	17,870	2.5%
15	Michigan	17,850	2.5%
16	Missouri	17,570	2.5%
17	Massachusetts	16,710	2.4%
18	North Carolina	15,990	2.3%
19	Alabama	14,290	2.0%
20	Oklahoma	13,770	1.9%
21	Arkansas	12,340	1.7%
22	Kentucky	11,820	1.7%
23	South Carolina	10,680	1.5%
24	Wisconsin	10,280	1.4%
25	Washington	10,090	1.4%
26	Mississippi	9,950	1.4%
27	Maryland	9,010	1.3%
28	Arizona	8,800	1.2%
29	Connecticut	8,320	1.2%
30	Colorado	7,120	1.0%
31	Kansas	7,070	1.0%
32	West Virginia	6,650	0.9%
33	Iowa	6,610	0.9%
34	Nebraska	5,920	0.8%
35	New Mexico	4,610	0.6%
36	Idaho	3,100	0.4%
37	Utah	2,940	0.4%
38	Oregon	2,850	0.4%
39	Montana	2,790	0.4%
40	North Dakota	2,770	0.4%
41	Nevada	2,700	0.4%
42	New Hampshire	2,330	0.3%
43	South Dakota	2,010	0.3%
44	Hawaii	1,970	0.3%
45	Rhode Island	1,930	0.3%
46	Maine	1,900	0.3%
47	Delaware	1,750	0.2%
48	Vermont	1,490	0.2%
49	Wyoming	730	0.1%
50	Alaska	520	0.1%
	District of Columbia	1,900	0.3%

Source: U.S. Department of Labor, Bureau of Labor Statistics
"Occupational Employment and Wages, 2005" (http://www.bls.gov/oes/)
*Does not include self-employed.

Rate of Licensed Practical and Licensed Vocational Nurses in 2005

National Rate = 239 LPN/LVNs per 100,000 Population*

ALPHA ORDER

RANK	STATE	RATE
11	Alabama	314
49	Alaska	78
43	Arizona	148
1	Arkansas	445
44	California	145
42	Colorado	153
28	Connecticut	238
31	Delaware	208
18	Florida	275
22	Georgia	257
41	Hawaii	155
30	Idaho	217
33	Illinois	186
14	Indiana	292
29	Iowa	223
22	Kansas	257
17	Kentucky	283
3	Louisiana	430
45	Maine	144
39	Maryland	161
19	Massachusetts	260
38	Michigan	177
7	Minnesota	355
8	Mississippi	342
12	Missouri	303
13	Montana	298
9	Nebraska	337
48	Nevada	112
37	New Hampshire	178
32	New Jersey	205
26	New Mexico	239
20	New York	259
35	North Carolina	184
2	North Dakota	436
10	Ohio	324
4	Oklahoma	389
49	Oregon	78
15	Pennsylvania	285
36	Rhode Island	180
25	South Carolina	251
20	South Dakota	259
6	Tennessee	362
16	Texas	284
47	Utah	118
26	Vermont	239
24	Virginia	254
40	Washington	160
5	West Virginia	367
33	Wisconsin	186
46	Wyoming	143

RANK ORDER

RANK	STATE	RATE
1	Arkansas	445
2	North Dakota	436
3	Louisiana	430
4	Oklahoma	389
5	West Virginia	367
6	Tennessee	362
7	Minnesota	355
8	Mississippi	342
9	Nebraska	337
10	Ohio	324
11	Alabama	314
12	Missouri	303
13	Montana	298
14	Indiana	292
15	Pennsylvania	285
16	Texas	284
17	Kentucky	283
18	Florida	275
19	Massachusetts	260
20	New York	259
20	South Dakota	259
22	Georgia	257
22	Kansas	257
24	Virginia	254
25	South Carolina	251
26	New Mexico	239
26	Vermont	239
28	Connecticut	238
29	Iowa	223
30	Idaho	217
31	Delaware	208
32	New Jersey	205
33	Illinois	186
33	Wisconsin	186
35	North Carolina	184
36	Rhode Island	180
37	New Hampshire	178
38	Michigan	177
39	Maryland	161
40	Washington	160
41	Hawaii	155
42	Colorado	153
43	Arizona	148
44	California	145
45	Maine	144
46	Wyoming	143
47	Utah	118
48	Nevada	112
49	Alaska	78
49	Oregon	78

District of Columbia	326

Source: Morgan Quitno Press using data from U.S. Department of Labor, Bureau of Labor Statistics
"Occupational Employment and Wages, 2005" (http://www.bls.gov/oes/)
*Does not include self-employed.

Average Annual Wages of Licensed Practical and Licensed Vocational Nurses in 2005
National Average = $36,210*

ALPHA ORDER

RANK	STATE	WAGES
49	Alabama	$28,920
8	Alaska	40,990
13	Arizona	38,620
45	Arkansas	30,000
6	California	43,080
18	Colorado	37,550
1	Connecticut	49,240
7	Delaware	42,660
22	Florida	35,930
39	Georgia	31,600
19	Hawaii	37,520
34	Idaho	32,950
23	Illinois	35,470
30	Indiana	34,520
36	Iowa	32,330
37	Kansas	32,240
35	Kentucky	32,930
43	Louisiana	30,870
31	Maine	33,750
5	Maryland	44,440
3	Massachusetts	45,780
16	Michigan	37,700
24	Minnesota	35,180
50	Mississippi	28,140
41	Missouri	31,380
46	Montana	29,920
38	Nebraska	32,230
11	Nevada	39,280
12	New Hampshire	38,630
2	New Jersey	45,960
13	New Mexico	38,620
17	New York	37,610
25	North Carolina	34,940
44	North Dakota	30,620
21	Ohio	36,390
42	Oklahoma	31,020
10	Oregon	39,630
15	Pennsylvania	37,990
4	Rhode Island	44,470
26	South Carolina	34,920
47	South Dakota	29,140
40	Tennessee	31,530
29	Texas	34,700
32	Utah	33,730
28	Vermont	34,760
27	Virginia	34,780
9	Washington	39,880
48	West Virginia	28,950
20	Wisconsin	36,840
33	Wyoming	32,960

RANK ORDER

RANK	STATE	WAGES
1	Connecticut	$49,240
2	New Jersey	45,960
3	Massachusetts	45,780
4	Rhode Island	44,470
5	Maryland	44,440
6	California	43,080
7	Delaware	42,660
8	Alaska	40,990
9	Washington	39,880
10	Oregon	39,630
11	Nevada	39,280
12	New Hampshire	38,630
13	Arizona	38,620
13	New Mexico	38,620
15	Pennsylvania	37,990
16	Michigan	37,700
17	New York	37,610
18	Colorado	37,550
19	Hawaii	37,520
20	Wisconsin	36,840
21	Ohio	36,390
22	Florida	35,930
23	Illinois	35,470
24	Minnesota	35,180
25	North Carolina	34,940
26	South Carolina	34,920
27	Virginia	34,780
28	Vermont	34,760
29	Texas	34,700
30	Indiana	34,520
31	Maine	33,750
32	Utah	33,730
33	Wyoming	32,960
34	Idaho	32,950
35	Kentucky	32,930
36	Iowa	32,330
37	Kansas	32,240
38	Nebraska	32,230
39	Georgia	31,600
40	Tennessee	31,530
41	Missouri	31,380
42	Oklahoma	31,020
43	Louisiana	30,870
44	North Dakota	30,620
45	Arkansas	30,000
46	Montana	29,920
47	South Dakota	29,140
48	West Virginia	28,950
49	Alabama	28,920
50	Mississippi	28,140

District of Columbia   47,160

Source: U.S. Department of Labor, Bureau of Labor Statistics
   "Occupational Employment and Wages, 2005" (http://www.bls.gov/oes/)
*Does not include self-employed.

Physical Therapists in 2005

National Total = 151,280 Physical Therapists*

<u>ALPHA ORDER</u>

RANK	STATE	THERAPISTS	% of USA
27	Alabama	1,730	1.1%
49	Alaska	300	0.2%
23	Arizona	2,520	1.7%
33	Arkansas	1,110	0.7%
1	California	13,350	8.8%
15	Colorado	3,430	2.3%
22	Connecticut	2,850	1.9%
47	Delaware	420	0.3%
3	Florida	9,380	6.2%
21	Georgia	2,930	1.9%
46	Hawaii	470	0.3%
42	Idaho	640	0.4%
6	Illinois	6,450	4.3%
13	Indiana	3,530	2.3%
30	Iowa	1,430	0.9%
32	Kansas	1,190	0.8%
25	Kentucky	1,940	1.3%
24	Louisiana	2,110	1.4%
37	Maine	920	0.6%
20	Maryland	3,030	2.0%
9	Massachusetts	5,500	3.6%
10	Michigan	5,170	3.4%
14	Minnesota	3,500	2.3%
31	Mississippi	1,210	0.8%
17	Missouri	3,330	2.2%
42	Montana	640	0.4%
38	Nebraska	910	0.6%
36	Nevada	960	0.6%
39	New Hampshire	860	0.6%
8	New Jersey	5,580	3.7%
41	New Mexico	720	0.5%
2	New York	12,390	8.2%
11	North Carolina	3,780	2.5%
48	North Dakota	350	0.2%
7	Ohio	5,600	3.7%
28	Oklahoma	1,670	1.1%
29	Oregon	1,640	1.1%
5	Pennsylvania	8,810	5.8%
40	Rhode Island	760	0.5%
26	South Carolina	1,850	1.2%
45	South Dakota	510	0.3%
16	Tennessee	3,350	2.2%
4	Texas	9,130	6.0%
35	Utah	1,010	0.7%
44	Vermont	560	0.4%
18	Virginia	3,310	2.2%
19	Washington	3,090	2.0%
34	West Virginia	1,080	0.7%
12	Wisconsin	3,680	2.4%
50	Wyoming	260	0.2%

<u>RANK ORDER</u>

RANK	STATE	THERAPISTS	% of USA
1	California	13,350	8.8%
2	New York	12,390	8.2%
3	Florida	9,380	6.2%
4	Texas	9,130	6.0%
5	Pennsylvania	8,810	5.8%
6	Illinois	6,450	4.3%
7	Ohio	5,600	3.7%
8	New Jersey	5,580	3.7%
9	Massachusetts	5,500	3.6%
10	Michigan	5,170	3.4%
11	North Carolina	3,780	2.5%
12	Wisconsin	3,680	2.4%
13	Indiana	3,530	2.3%
14	Minnesota	3,500	2.3%
15	Colorado	3,430	2.3%
16	Tennessee	3,350	2.2%
17	Missouri	3,330	2.2%
18	Virginia	3,310	2.2%
19	Washington	3,090	2.0%
20	Maryland	3,030	2.0%
21	Georgia	2,930	1.9%
22	Connecticut	2,850	1.9%
23	Arizona	2,520	1.7%
24	Louisiana	2,110	1.4%
25	Kentucky	1,940	1.3%
26	South Carolina	1,850	1.2%
27	Alabama	1,730	1.1%
28	Oklahoma	1,670	1.1%
29	Oregon	1,640	1.1%
30	Iowa	1,430	0.9%
31	Mississippi	1,210	0.8%
32	Kansas	1,190	0.8%
33	Arkansas	1,110	0.7%
34	West Virginia	1,080	0.7%
35	Utah	1,010	0.7%
36	Nevada	960	0.6%
37	Maine	920	0.6%
38	Nebraska	910	0.6%
39	New Hampshire	860	0.6%
40	Rhode Island	760	0.5%
41	New Mexico	720	0.5%
42	Idaho	640	0.4%
42	Montana	640	0.4%
44	Vermont	560	0.4%
45	South Dakota	510	0.3%
46	Hawaii	470	0.3%
47	Delaware	420	0.3%
48	North Dakota	350	0.2%
49	Alaska	300	0.2%
50	Wyoming	260	0.2%
	District of Columbia	340	0.2%

Source: U.S. Department of Labor, Bureau of Labor Statistics
   "Occupational Employment and Wages, 2005" (http://www.bls.gov/oes/)
Does not include self-employed.

Rate of Physical Therapists in 2005

National Rate = 51 Physical Therapists per 100,000 Population*

ALPHA ORDER			RANK ORDER		
RANK	STATE	RATE	RANK	STATE	RATE
46	Alabama	38	1	Vermont	90
33	Alaska	45	2	Massachusetts	85
40	Arizona	42	3	Connecticut	81
43	Arkansas	40	4	Colorado	74
47	California	37	5	Pennsylvania	71
4	Colorado	74	5	Rhode Island	71
3	Connecticut	81	7	Maine	70
26	Delaware	50	8	Minnesota	68
21	Florida	53	8	Montana	68
50	Georgia	32	10	Wisconsin	67
47	Hawaii	37	11	New Hampshire	66
33	Idaho	45	11	South Dakota	66
23	Illinois	51	13	New Jersey	64
17	Indiana	56	13	New York	64
29	Iowa	48	15	West Virginia	60
39	Kansas	43	16	Missouri	57
32	Kentucky	46	17	Indiana	56
30	Louisiana	47	17	Tennessee	56
7	Maine	70	19	North Dakota	55
20	Maryland	54	20	Maryland	54
2	Massachusetts	85	21	Florida	53
23	Michigan	51	22	Nebraska	52
8	Minnesota	68	23	Illinois	51
40	Mississippi	42	23	Michigan	51
16	Missouri	57	23	Wyoming	51
8	Montana	68	26	Delaware	50
22	Nebraska	52	27	Ohio	49
43	Nevada	40	27	Washington	49
11	New Hampshire	66	29	Iowa	48
13	New Jersey	64	30	Louisiana	47
47	New Mexico	37	30	Oklahoma	47
13	New York	64	32	Kentucky	46
36	North Carolina	44	33	Alaska	45
19	North Dakota	55	33	Idaho	45
27	Ohio	49	33	Oregon	45
30	Oklahoma	47	36	North Carolina	44
33	Oregon	45	36	South Carolina	44
5	Pennsylvania	71	36	Virginia	44
5	Rhode Island	71	39	Kansas	43
36	South Carolina	44	40	Arizona	42
11	South Dakota	66	40	Mississippi	42
17	Tennessee	56	42	Utah	41
43	Texas	40	43	Arkansas	40
42	Utah	41	43	Nevada	40
1	Vermont	90	43	Texas	40
36	Virginia	44	46	Alabama	38
27	Washington	49	47	California	37
15	West Virginia	60	47	Hawaii	37
10	Wisconsin	67	47	New Mexico	37
23	Wyoming	51	50	Georgia	32
				District of Columbia	58

Source: Morgan Quitno Press using data from U.S. Department of Labor, Bureau of Labor Statistics
"Occupational Employment and Wages, 2005" (http://www.bls.gov/oes/)
*Does not include self-employed.

Average Annual Wages of Physical Therapists in 2005

National Average = $65,350*

ALPHA ORDER				RANK ORDER		
RANK	STATE	WAGES		RANK	STATE	WAGES
34	Alabama	$61,700		1	New Jersey	$72,780
2	Alaska	72,360		2	Alaska	72,360
29	Arizona	62,790		3	California	70,960
20	Arkansas	63,830		4	Louisiana	70,740
3	California	70,960		5	Texas	70,590
44	Colorado	57,780		6	Nevada	69,890
7	Connecticut	69,850		7	Connecticut	69,850
27	Delaware	63,120		8	Idaho	69,440
17	Florida	64,920		9	New York	69,160
26	Georgia	63,250		10	West Virginia	67,350
40	Hawaii	60,270		11	Michigan	66,120
8	Idaho	69,440		12	Virginia	65,960
21	Illinois	63,810		13	Maryland	65,250
35	Indiana	61,400		13	Pennsylvania	65,250
41	Iowa	58,930		15	Tennessee	65,240
39	Kansas	60,330		16	Ohio	64,940
24	Kentucky	63,280		17	Florida	64,920
4	Louisiana	70,740		18	Washington	64,190
36	Maine	60,970		19	Mississippi	64,070
13	Maryland	65,250		20	Arkansas	63,830
33	Massachusetts	61,820		21	Illinois	63,810
11	Michigan	66,120		22	Oklahoma	63,740
48	Minnesota	56,520		23	North Carolina	63,450
19	Mississippi	64,070		24	Kentucky	63,280
43	Missouri	58,420		25	Utah	63,260
46	Montana	57,690		26	Georgia	63,250
31	Nebraska	62,160		27	Delaware	63,120
6	Nevada	69,890		28	Oregon	62,970
42	New Hampshire	58,730		29	Arizona	62,790
1	New Jersey	72,780		30	Wisconsin	62,580
47	New Mexico	57,480		31	Nebraska	62,160
9	New York	69,160		32	South Carolina	61,870
23	North Carolina	63,450		33	Massachusetts	61,820
50	North Dakota	54,710		34	Alabama	61,700
16	Ohio	64,940		35	Indiana	61,400
22	Oklahoma	63,740		36	Maine	60,970
28	Oregon	62,970		37	Wyoming	60,910
13	Pennsylvania	65,250		38	Rhode Island	60,610
38	Rhode Island	60,610		39	Kansas	60,330
32	South Carolina	61,870		40	Hawaii	60,270
45	South Dakota	57,770		41	Iowa	58,930
15	Tennessee	65,240		42	New Hampshire	58,730
5	Texas	70,590		43	Missouri	58,420
25	Utah	63,260		44	Colorado	57,780
49	Vermont	55,450		45	South Dakota	57,770
12	Virginia	65,960		46	Montana	57,690
18	Washington	64,190		47	New Mexico	57,480
10	West Virginia	67,350		48	Minnesota	56,520
30	Wisconsin	62,580		49	Vermont	55,450
37	Wyoming	60,910		50	North Dakota	54,710
					District of Columbia	65,720

Source: U.S. Department of Labor, Bureau of Labor Statistics
   "Occupational Employment and Wages, 2005" (http://www.bls.gov/oes/)
*Does not include self-employed.

Dentists in 2004

National Total = 175,705 Dentists*

ALPHA ORDER

RANK	STATE	DENTISTS	% of USA
27	Alabama	1,951	1.1%
45	Alaska	472	0.3%
22	Arizona	2,770	1.6%
33	Arkansas	1,150	0.7%
1	California	26,339	15.0%
19	Colorado	3,000	1.7%
23	Connecticut	2,645	1.5%
46	Delaware	381	0.2%
4	Florida	9,167	5.2%
14	Georgia	3,916	2.2%
36	Hawaii	1,039	0.6%
40	Idaho	790	0.4%
5	Illinois	8,166	4.6%
20	Indiana	2,978	1.7%
31	Iowa	1,556	0.9%
32	Kansas	1,394	0.8%
25	Kentucky	2,293	1.3%
26	Louisiana	2,099	1.2%
42	Maine	639	0.4%
13	Maryland	4,124	2.3%
10	Massachusetts	5,298	3.0%
8	Michigan	6,108	3.5%
17	Minnesota	3,067	1.7%
34	Mississippi	1,149	0.7%
21	Missouri	2,813	1.6%
44	Montana	522	0.3%
35	Nebraska	1,100	0.6%
37	Nevada	1,007	0.6%
41	New Hampshire	773	0.4%
7	New Jersey	6,829	3.9%
38	New Mexico	856	0.5%
2	New York	15,206	8.7%
15	North Carolina	3,788	2.2%
49	North Dakota	314	0.2%
9	Ohio	6,041	3.4%
29	Oklahoma	1,722	1.0%
24	Oregon	2,406	1.4%
6	Pennsylvania	7,929	4.5%
43	Rhode Island	572	0.3%
28	South Carolina	1,944	1.1%
47	South Dakota	373	0.2%
18	Tennessee	3,041	1.7%
3	Texas	10,352	5.9%
30	Utah	1,571	0.9%
48	Vermont	363	0.2%
11	Virginia	4,327	2.5%
12	Washington	4,321	2.5%
39	West Virginia	827	0.5%
16	Wisconsin	3,195	1.8%
50	Wyoming	270	0.2%

RANK ORDER

RANK	STATE	DENTISTS	% of USA
1	California	26,339	15.0%
2	New York	15,206	8.7%
3	Texas	10,352	5.9%
4	Florida	9,167	5.2%
5	Illinois	8,166	4.6%
6	Pennsylvania	7,929	4.5%
7	New Jersey	6,829	3.9%
8	Michigan	6,108	3.5%
9	Ohio	6,041	3.4%
10	Massachusetts	5,298	3.0%
11	Virginia	4,327	2.5%
12	Washington	4,321	2.5%
13	Maryland	4,124	2.3%
14	Georgia	3,916	2.2%
15	North Carolina	3,788	2.2%
16	Wisconsin	3,195	1.8%
17	Minnesota	3,067	1.7%
18	Tennessee	3,041	1.7%
19	Colorado	3,000	1.7%
20	Indiana	2,978	1.7%
21	Missouri	2,813	1.6%
22	Arizona	2,770	1.6%
23	Connecticut	2,645	1.5%
24	Oregon	2,406	1.4%
25	Kentucky	2,293	1.3%
26	Louisiana	2,099	1.2%
27	Alabama	1,951	1.1%
28	South Carolina	1,944	1.1%
29	Oklahoma	1,722	1.0%
30	Utah	1,571	0.9%
31	Iowa	1,556	0.9%
32	Kansas	1,394	0.8%
33	Arkansas	1,150	0.7%
34	Mississippi	1,149	0.7%
35	Nebraska	1,100	0.6%
36	Hawaii	1,039	0.6%
37	Nevada	1,007	0.6%
38	New Mexico	856	0.5%
39	West Virginia	827	0.5%
40	Idaho	790	0.4%
41	New Hampshire	773	0.4%
42	Maine	639	0.4%
43	Rhode Island	572	0.3%
44	Montana	522	0.3%
45	Alaska	472	0.3%
46	Delaware	381	0.2%
47	South Dakota	373	0.2%
48	Vermont	363	0.2%
49	North Dakota	314	0.2%
50	Wyoming	270	0.2%
	District of Columbia	652	0.4%

Source: American Dental Association
"Distribution of Dentists, by Region and State, 2004"
*Professionally active dentists. Total includes 100 dentists for whom state is not known. Total does not include
2,168 dentists in territories nor dentists in the Armed Forces stationed overseas.

Rate of Dentists in 2004

National Rate = 60 Dentists per 100,000 Population*

ALPHA ORDER

RANK	STATE	RATE
47	Alabama	43
8	Alaska	72
36	Arizona	48
49	Arkansas	42
7	California	73
11	Colorado	65
5	Connecticut	76
40	Delaware	46
25	Florida	53
45	Georgia	44
1	Hawaii	83
22	Idaho	57
13	Illinois	64
36	Indiana	48
25	Iowa	53
31	Kansas	51
24	Kentucky	55
39	Louisiana	47
32	Maine	49
6	Maryland	74
2	Massachusetts	82
16	Michigan	61
17	Minnesota	60
50	Mississippi	40
32	Missouri	49
23	Montana	56
15	Nebraska	63
47	Nevada	43
17	New Hampshire	60
3	New Jersey	79
44	New Mexico	45
3	New York	79
45	North Carolina	44
32	North Dakota	49
25	Ohio	53
32	Oklahoma	49
10	Oregon	67
13	Pennsylvania	64
25	Rhode Island	53
40	South Carolina	46
36	South Dakota	48
30	Tennessee	52
40	Texas	46
11	Utah	65
19	Vermont	58
19	Virginia	58
9	Washington	70
40	West Virginia	46
19	Wisconsin	58
25	Wyoming	53

RANK ORDER

RANK	STATE	RATE
1	Hawaii	83
2	Massachusetts	82
3	New Jersey	79
3	New York	79
5	Connecticut	76
6	Maryland	74
7	California	73
8	Alaska	72
9	Washington	70
10	Oregon	67
11	Colorado	65
11	Utah	65
13	Illinois	64
13	Pennsylvania	64
15	Nebraska	63
16	Michigan	61
17	Minnesota	60
17	New Hampshire	60
19	Vermont	58
19	Virginia	58
19	Wisconsin	58
22	Idaho	57
23	Montana	56
24	Kentucky	55
25	Florida	53
25	Iowa	53
25	Ohio	53
25	Rhode Island	53
25	Wyoming	53
30	Tennessee	52
31	Kansas	51
32	Maine	49
32	Missouri	49
32	North Dakota	49
32	Oklahoma	49
36	Arizona	48
36	Indiana	48
36	South Dakota	48
39	Louisiana	47
40	Delaware	46
40	South Carolina	46
40	Texas	46
40	West Virginia	46
44	New Mexico	45
45	Georgia	44
45	North Carolina	44
47	Alabama	43
47	Nevada	43
49	Arkansas	42
50	Mississippi	40

District of Columbia   112

Source: Morgan Quitno Press using data from American Dental Association
    "Distribution of Dentists, by Region and State, 2004"
Professionally active dentists. National rate includes dentists for whom state is not known. National rate does not include dentists in territories nor dentists in the Armed Forces stationed overseas.

Average Annual Wages of Dentists in 2005

National Average = $133,680*

RANK	STATE	WAGES
35	Alabama	$125,620
NA	Alaska**	NA
33	Arizona	129,820
45	Arkansas	88,780
26	California	136,510
9	Colorado	147,300
2	Connecticut	166,570
6	Delaware	154,590
32	Florida	131,220
12	Georgia	145,440
7	Hawaii	152,880
39	Idaho	117,220
42	Illinois	103,470
23	Indiana	137,390
24	Iowa	137,230
38	Kansas	117,980
43	Kentucky	103,360
44	Louisiana	98,890
1	Maine	182,840
36	Maryland	122,940
29	Massachusetts	134,080
16	Michigan	141,240
15	Minnesota	142,470
17	Mississippi	140,310
14	Missouri	144,380
46	Montana	82,010
31	Nebraska	132,920
28	Nevada	135,370
4	New Hampshire	157,180
34	New Jersey	128,330
18	New Mexico	139,570
30	New York	133,580
3	North Carolina	164,440
NA	North Dakota**	NA
5	Ohio	154,630
40	Oklahoma	114,610
NA	Oregon**	NA
41	Pennsylvania	111,630
10	Rhode Island	146,740
37	South Carolina	122,160
8	South Dakota	147,570
27	Tennessee	135,850
21	Texas	139,140
25	Utah	136,530
20	Vermont	139,290
13	Virginia	144,720
19	Washington	139,350
22	West Virginia	138,040
11	Wisconsin	146,000
NA	Wyoming**	NA

RANK	STATE	WAGES
1	Maine	$182,840
2	Connecticut	166,570
3	North Carolina	164,440
4	New Hampshire	157,180
5	Ohio	154,630
6	Delaware	154,590
7	Hawaii	152,880
8	South Dakota	147,570
9	Colorado	147,300
10	Rhode Island	146,740
11	Wisconsin	146,000
12	Georgia	145,440
13	Virginia	144,720
14	Missouri	144,380
15	Minnesota	142,470
16	Michigan	141,240
17	Mississippi	140,310
18	New Mexico	139,570
19	Washington	139,350
20	Vermont	139,290
21	Texas	139,140
22	West Virginia	138,040
23	Indiana	137,390
24	Iowa	137,230
25	Utah	136,530
26	California	136,510
27	Tennessee	135,850
28	Nevada	135,370
29	Massachusetts	134,080
30	New York	133,580
31	Nebraska	132,920
32	Florida	131,220
33	Arizona	129,820
34	New Jersey	128,330
35	Alabama	125,620
36	Maryland	122,940
37	South Carolina	122,160
38	Kansas	117,980
39	Idaho	117,220
40	Oklahoma	114,610
41	Pennsylvania	111,630
42	Illinois	103,470
43	Kentucky	103,360
44	Louisiana	98,890
45	Arkansas	88,780
46	Montana	82,010
NA	Alaska**	NA
NA	North Dakota**	NA
NA	Oregon**	NA
NA	Wyoming**	NA
	District of Columbia**	NA

Source: U.S. Department of Labor, Bureau of Labor Statistics
"Occupational Employment and Wages, 2005" (http://www.bls.gov/oes/)
General dentists. Does not include self-employed.
**Not available.*

Percent of Population Lacking Access to Dental Care in 2006

National Percent = 9.3% of Population*

ALPHA ORDER

RANK	STATE	PERCENT
2	Alabama	26.9
17	Alaska	12.4
30	Arizona	7.4
41	Arkansas	4.4
46	California	3.4
41	Colorado	4.4
36	Connecticut	6.4
11	Delaware	17.8
14	Florida	15.2
27	Georgia	8.7
33	Hawaii	6.9
8	Idaho	18.6
26	Illinois	9.0
43	Indiana	4.0
33	Iowa	6.9
12	Kansas	17.5
45	Kentucky	3.6
1	Louisiana	28.7
4	Maine	21.2
37	Maryland	5.5
39	Massachusetts	4.9
22	Michigan	10.0
47	Minnesota	3.3
9	Mississippi	18.3
10	Missouri	18.0
5	Montana	21.0
49	Nebraska	1.6
15	Nevada	14.6
44	New Hampshire	3.9
50	New Jersey	1.1
3	New Mexico	26.4
38	New York	5.1
18	North Carolina	11.9
30	North Dakota	7.4
35	Ohio	6.7
40	Oklahoma	4.8
16	Oregon	13.0
28	Pennsylvania	8.4
23	Rhode Island	9.8
5	South Carolina	21.0
21	South Dakota	11.1
7	Tennessee	19.5
20	Texas	11.3
13	Utah	16.3
47	Vermont	3.3
25	Virginia	9.3
29	Washington	7.7
32	West Virginia	7.2
24	Wisconsin	9.5
19	Wyoming	11.5

RANK ORDER

RANK	STATE	PERCENT
1	Louisiana	28.7
2	Alabama	26.9
3	New Mexico	26.4
4	Maine	21.2
5	Montana	21.0
5	South Carolina	21.0
7	Tennessee	19.5
8	Idaho	18.6
9	Mississippi	18.3
10	Missouri	18.0
11	Delaware	17.8
12	Kansas	17.5
13	Utah	16.3
14	Florida	15.2
15	Nevada	14.6
16	Oregon	13.0
17	Alaska	12.4
18	North Carolina	11.9
19	Wyoming	11.5
20	Texas	11.3
21	South Dakota	11.1
22	Michigan	10.0
23	Rhode Island	9.8
24	Wisconsin	9.5
25	Virginia	9.3
26	Illinois	9.0
27	Georgia	8.7
28	Pennsylvania	8.4
29	Washington	7.7
30	Arizona	7.4
30	North Dakota	7.4
32	West Virginia	7.2
33	Hawaii	6.9
33	Iowa	6.9
35	Ohio	6.7
36	Connecticut	6.4
37	Maryland	5.5
38	New York	5.1
39	Massachusetts	4.9
40	Oklahoma	4.8
41	Arkansas	4.4
41	Colorado	4.4
43	Indiana	4.0
44	New Hampshire	3.9
45	Kentucky	3.6
46	California	3.4
47	Minnesota	3.3
47	Vermont	3.3
49	Nebraska	1.6
50	New Jersey	1.1

District of Columbia	10.2	

Source: Morgan Quitno Press using data from U.S. Dept. of Health and Human Services, Div. of Shortage Designation
"Selected Statistics on Health Professional Shortage Areas" (as of September 30, 2006)
*Percent of population considered under-served by dental practitioners. An under-served population does not have
primary medical care within reasonable economic and geographic bounds.

Pharmacists in 2005

National Total = 229,740 Pharmacists*

ALPHA ORDER

RANK	STATE	PHARMACISTS	% of USA
20	Alabama	4,300	1.9%
50	Alaska	360	0.2%
22	Arizona	4,110	1.8%
31	Arkansas	2,330	1.0%
1	California	23,360	10.2%
25	Colorado	3,540	1.5%
30	Connecticut	2,350	1.0%
47	Delaware	560	0.2%
3	Florida	15,130	6.6%
10	Georgia	6,710	2.9%
39	Hawaii	1,040	0.5%
42	Idaho	920	0.4%
7	Illinois	9,340	4.1%
14	Indiana	5,330	2.3%
29	Iowa	2,550	1.1%
32	Kansas	2,300	1.0%
26	Kentucky	3,470	1.5%
23	Louisiana	3,950	1.7%
39	Maine	1,040	0.5%
19	Maryland	4,390	1.9%
13	Massachusetts	5,370	2.3%
8	Michigan	8,110	3.5%
21	Minnesota	4,140	1.8%
33	Mississippi	2,280	1.0%
18	Missouri	4,700	2.0%
42	Montana	920	0.4%
36	Nebraska	1,810	0.8%
35	Nevada	1,900	0.8%
41	New Hampshire	990	0.4%
9	New Jersey	7,400	3.2%
38	New Mexico	1,290	0.6%
4	New York	13,400	5.8%
11	North Carolina	6,480	2.8%
46	North Dakota	630	0.3%
6	Ohio	9,350	4.1%
27	Oklahoma	2,940	1.3%
28	Oregon	2,930	1.3%
5	Pennsylvania	11,510	5.0%
45	Rhode Island	760	0.3%
24	South Carolina	3,570	1.6%
44	South Dakota	780	0.3%
12	Tennessee	5,430	2.4%
2	Texas	15,840	6.9%
34	Utah	1,920	0.8%
49	Vermont	400	0.2%
15	Virginia	5,290	2.3%
17	Washington	4,870	2.1%
37	West Virginia	1,670	0.7%
16	Wisconsin	4,930	2.1%
48	Wyoming	470	0.2%

RANK ORDER

RANK	STATE	PHARMACISTS	% of USA
1	California	23,360	10.2%
2	Texas	15,840	6.9%
3	Florida	15,130	6.6%
4	New York	13,400	5.8%
5	Pennsylvania	11,510	5.0%
6	Ohio	9,350	4.1%
7	Illinois	9,340	4.1%
8	Michigan	8,110	3.5%
9	New Jersey	7,400	3.2%
10	Georgia	6,710	2.9%
11	North Carolina	6,480	2.8%
12	Tennessee	5,430	2.4%
13	Massachusetts	5,370	2.3%
14	Indiana	5,330	2.3%
15	Virginia	5,290	2.3%
16	Wisconsin	4,930	2.1%
17	Washington	4,870	2.1%
18	Missouri	4,700	2.0%
19	Maryland	4,390	1.9%
20	Alabama	4,300	1.9%
21	Minnesota	4,140	1.8%
22	Arizona	4,110	1.8%
23	Louisiana	3,950	1.7%
24	South Carolina	3,570	1.6%
25	Colorado	3,540	1.5%
26	Kentucky	3,470	1.5%
27	Oklahoma	2,940	1.3%
28	Oregon	2,930	1.3%
29	Iowa	2,550	1.1%
30	Connecticut	2,350	1.0%
31	Arkansas	2,330	1.0%
32	Kansas	2,300	1.0%
33	Mississippi	2,280	1.0%
34	Utah	1,920	0.8%
35	Nevada	1,900	0.8%
36	Nebraska	1,810	0.8%
37	West Virginia	1,670	0.7%
38	New Mexico	1,290	0.6%
39	Hawaii	1,040	0.5%
39	Maine	1,040	0.5%
41	New Hampshire	990	0.4%
42	Idaho	920	0.4%
42	Montana	920	0.4%
44	South Dakota	780	0.3%
45	Rhode Island	760	0.3%
46	North Dakota	630	0.3%
47	Delaware	560	0.2%
48	Wyoming	470	0.2%
49	Vermont	400	0.2%
50	Alaska	360	0.2%
	District of Columbia	540	0.2%

Source: U.S. Department of Labor, Bureau of Labor Statistics
"Occupational Employment and Wages, 2005" (http://www.bls.gov/oes/)
*Does not include self-employed.

Rate of Pharmacists in 2005

National Rate = 77 Pharmacists per 100,000 Population*

ALPHA ORDER				RANK ORDER		
RANK	STATE	RATE		RANK	STATE	RATE
5	Alabama	95		1	Nebraska	103
50	Alaska	54		2	South Dakota	101
41	Arizona	69		3	North Dakota	99
16	Arkansas	84		4	Montana	98
47	California	65		5	Alabama	95
34	Colorado	76		6	Pennsylvania	93
44	Connecticut	67		7	West Virginia	92
44	Delaware	67		7	Wyoming	92
13	Florida	85		9	Tennessee	91
37	Georgia	73		10	Wisconsin	89
22	Hawaii	82		11	Louisiana	88
48	Idaho	64		12	Iowa	86
37	Illinois	73		13	Florida	85
13	Indiana	85		13	Indiana	85
12	Iowa	86		13	New Jersey	85
16	Kansas	84		16	Arkansas	84
19	Kentucky	83		16	Kansas	84
11	Louisiana	88		16	South Carolina	84
28	Maine	79		19	Kentucky	83
28	Maryland	79		19	Massachusetts	83
19	Massachusetts	83		19	Oklahoma	83
27	Michigan	80		22	Hawaii	82
24	Minnesota	81		22	Ohio	82
31	Mississippi	78		24	Minnesota	81
24	Missouri	81		24	Missouri	81
4	Montana	98		24	Oregon	81
1	Nebraska	103		27	Michigan	80
28	Nevada	79		28	Maine	79
34	New Hampshire	76		28	Maryland	79
13	New Jersey	85		28	Nevada	79
44	New Mexico	67		31	Mississippi	78
41	New York	69		32	Utah	77
36	North Carolina	75		32	Washington	77
3	North Dakota	99		34	Colorado	76
22	Ohio	82		34	New Hampshire	76
19	Oklahoma	83		36	North Carolina	75
24	Oregon	81		37	Georgia	73
6	Pennsylvania	93		37	Illinois	73
39	Rhode Island	71		39	Rhode Island	71
16	South Carolina	84		40	Virginia	70
2	South Dakota	101		41	Arizona	69
9	Tennessee	91		41	New York	69
41	Texas	69		41	Texas	69
32	Utah	77		44	Connecticut	67
48	Vermont	64		44	Delaware	67
40	Virginia	70		44	New Mexico	67
32	Washington	77		47	California	65
7	West Virginia	92		48	Idaho	64
10	Wisconsin	89		48	Vermont	64
7	Wyoming	92		50	Alaska	54
					District of Columbia	93

Source: Morgan Quitno Press using data from U.S. Department of Labor, Bureau of Labor Statistics
   "Occupational Employment and Wages, 2005" (http://www.bls.gov/oes/)
*Does not include self-employed.

Average Annual Wages of Pharmacists in 2005

National Average = $88,650*

ALPHA ORDER

ALPHA ORDER

RANK	STATE	WAGES		RANK	STATE	WAGES
35	Alabama	$84,640		1	California	$99,630
2	Alaska	97,650		2	Alaska	97,650
23	Arizona	87,940		3	Maine	97,010
31	Arkansas	85,800		4	Vermont	95,000
1	California	99,630		5	Minnesota	94,470
18	Colorado	88,860		6	Nevada	93,660
17	Connecticut	88,950		7	Tennessee	92,590
20	Delaware	88,220		8	Wisconsin	91,420
16	Florida	88,990		9	Texas	91,250
26	Georgia	87,690		10	Kentucky	90,920
28	Hawaii	87,290		11	New York	90,490
37	Idaho	83,620		12	Michigan	90,280
22	Illinois	88,120		13	West Virginia	90,040
38	Indiana	83,220		14	North Carolina	89,500
41	Iowa	81,930		15	South Carolina	89,270
49	Kansas	77,050		16	Florida	88,990
10	Kentucky	90,920		17	Connecticut	88,950
36	Louisiana	83,650		18	Colorado	88,860
3	Maine	97,010		19	Utah	88,850
34	Maryland	85,350		20	Delaware	88,220
47	Massachusetts	79,520		21	Oregon	88,160
12	Michigan	90,280		22	Illinois	88,120
5	Minnesota	94,470		23	Arizona	87,940
39	Mississippi	82,440		24	Virginia	87,760
27	Missouri	87,650		25	New Hampshire	87,750
48	Montana	78,780		26	Georgia	87,690
46	Nebraska	79,930		27	Missouri	87,650
6	Nevada	93,660		28	Hawaii	87,290
25	New Hampshire	87,750		29	New Jersey	87,070
29	New Jersey	87,070		30	Ohio	87,010
42	New Mexico	81,390		31	Arkansas	85,800
11	New York	90,490		32	Rhode Island	85,630
14	North Carolina	89,500		33	Washington	85,480
50	North Dakota	75,300		34	Maryland	85,350
30	Ohio	87,010		35	Alabama	84,640
45	Oklahoma	80,050		36	Louisiana	83,650
21	Oregon	88,160		37	Idaho	83,620
43	Pennsylvania	81,250		38	Indiana	83,220
32	Rhode Island	85,630		39	Mississippi	82,440
15	South Carolina	89,270		40	Wyoming	82,030
44	South Dakota	81,170		41	Iowa	81,930
7	Tennessee	92,590		42	New Mexico	81,390
9	Texas	91,250		43	Pennsylvania	81,250
19	Utah	88,850		44	South Dakota	81,170
4	Vermont	95,000		45	Oklahoma	80,050
24	Virginia	87,760		46	Nebraska	79,930
33	Washington	85,480		47	Massachusetts	79,520
13	West Virginia	90,040		48	Montana	78,780
8	Wisconsin	91,420		49	Kansas	77,050
40	Wyoming	82,030		50	North Dakota	75,300
					District of Columbia	70,660

RANK ORDER

Source: U.S. Department of Labor, Bureau of Labor Statistics
   "Occupational Employment and Wages, 2005" (http://www.bls.gov/oes/)
Does not include self-employed.

Optometrists in 2005

National Total = 23,720 Optometrists*

ALPHA ORDER

ALPHA ORDER

RANK	STATE	OPTOMETRISTS	% of USA
23	Alabama	390	1.6%
45	Alaska	70	0.3%
20	Arizona	420	1.8%
25	Arkansas	330	1.4%
1	California	2,550	10.8%
21	Colorado	410	1.7%
30	Connecticut	240	1.0%
43	Delaware	90	0.4%
8	Florida	990	4.2%
15	Georgia	500	2.1%
43	Hawaii	90	0.4%
39	Idaho	120	0.5%
2	Illinois	1,440	6.1%
11	Indiana	630	2.7%
27	Iowa	320	1.3%
28	Kansas	310	1.3%
29	Kentucky	250	1.1%
33	Louisiana	180	0.8%
45	Maine	70	0.3%
21	Maryland	410	1.7%
14	Massachusetts	510	2.2%
4	Michigan	1,290	5.4%
10	Minnesota	740	3.1%
35	Mississippi	160	0.7%
13	Missouri	580	2.4%
45	Montana	70	0.3%
30	Nebraska	240	1.0%
38	Nevada	140	0.6%
34	New Hampshire	170	0.7%
9	New Jersey	790	3.3%
32	New Mexico	190	0.8%
3	New York	1,300	5.5%
12	North Carolina	600	2.5%
36	North Dakota	150	0.6%
6	Ohio	1,080	4.6%
24	Oklahoma	360	1.5%
25	Oregon	330	1.4%
7	Pennsylvania	1,050	4.4%
NA	Rhode Island**	NA	NA
39	South Carolina	120	0.5%
41	South Dakota	100	0.4%
16	Tennessee	490	2.1%
5	Texas	1,250	5.3%
NA	Utah**	NA	NA
48	Vermont	50	0.2%
16	Virginia	490	2.1%
18	Washington	440	1.9%
36	West Virginia	150	0.6%
19	Wisconsin	430	1.8%
41	Wyoming	100	0.4%

RANK ORDER

RANK	STATE	OPTOMETRISTS	% of USA
1	California	2,550	10.8%
2	Illinois	1,440	6.1%
3	New York	1,300	5.5%
4	Michigan	1,290	5.4%
5	Texas	1,250	5.3%
6	Ohio	1,080	4.6%
7	Pennsylvania	1,050	4.4%
8	Florida	990	4.2%
9	New Jersey	790	3.3%
10	Minnesota	740	3.1%
11	Indiana	630	2.7%
12	North Carolina	600	2.5%
13	Missouri	580	2.4%
14	Massachusetts	510	2.2%
15	Georgia	500	2.1%
16	Tennessee	490	2.1%
16	Virginia	490	2.1%
18	Washington	440	1.9%
19	Wisconsin	430	1.8%
20	Arizona	420	1.8%
21	Colorado	410	1.7%
21	Maryland	410	1.7%
23	Alabama	390	1.6%
24	Oklahoma	360	1.5%
25	Arkansas	330	1.4%
25	Oregon	330	1.4%
27	Iowa	320	1.3%
28	Kansas	310	1.3%
29	Kentucky	250	1.1%
30	Connecticut	240	1.0%
30	Nebraska	240	1.0%
32	New Mexico	190	0.8%
33	Louisiana	180	0.8%
34	New Hampshire	170	0.7%
35	Mississippi	160	0.7%
36	North Dakota	150	0.6%
36	West Virginia	150	0.6%
38	Nevada	140	0.6%
39	Idaho	120	0.5%
39	South Carolina	120	0.5%
41	South Dakota	100	0.4%
41	Wyoming	100	0.4%
43	Delaware	90	0.4%
43	Hawaii	90	0.4%
45	Alaska	70	0.3%
45	Maine	70	0.3%
45	Montana	70	0.3%
48	Vermont	50	0.2%
NA	Rhode Island**	NA	NA
NA	Utah**	NA	NA
	District of Columbia	130	0.5%

Source: U.S. Department of Labor, Bureau of Labor Statistics
   "Occupational Employment and Wages, 2005" (http://www.bls.gov/oes/)
*Does not include self-employed.
**Not available.

Rate of Optometrists in 2005

National Rate = 8 Optometrists per 100,000 Population*

ALPHA ORDER

RANK	STATE	RATE
18	Alabama	9
9	Alaska	11
30	Arizona	7
8	Arkansas	12
30	California	7
18	Colorado	9
30	Connecticut	7
9	Delaware	11
39	Florida	6
44	Georgia	5
30	Hawaii	7
23	Idaho	8
9	Illinois	11
14	Indiana	10
9	Iowa	11
9	Kansas	11
39	Kentucky	6
47	Louisiana	4
44	Maine	5
30	Maryland	7
23	Massachusetts	8
5	Michigan	13
3	Minnesota	14
39	Mississippi	6
14	Missouri	10
30	Montana	7
3	Nebraska	14
39	Nevada	6
5	New Hampshire	13
18	New Jersey	9
14	New Mexico	10
30	New York	7
30	North Carolina	7
1	North Dakota	24
18	Ohio	9
14	Oklahoma	10
18	Oregon	9
23	Pennsylvania	8
NA	Rhode Island**	NA
48	South Carolina	3
5	South Dakota	13
23	Tennessee	8
44	Texas	5
NA	Utah**	NA
23	Vermont	8
39	Virginia	6
30	Washington	7
23	West Virginia	8
23	Wisconsin	8
2	Wyoming	20

RANK ORDER

RANK	STATE	RATE
1	North Dakota	24
2	Wyoming	20
3	Minnesota	14
3	Nebraska	14
5	Michigan	13
5	New Hampshire	13
5	South Dakota	13
8	Arkansas	12
9	Alaska	11
9	Delaware	11
9	Illinois	11
9	Iowa	11
9	Kansas	11
14	Indiana	10
14	Missouri	10
14	New Mexico	10
14	Oklahoma	10
18	Alabama	9
18	Colorado	9
18	New Jersey	9
18	Ohio	9
18	Oregon	9
23	Idaho	8
23	Massachusetts	8
23	Pennsylvania	8
23	Tennessee	8
23	Vermont	8
23	West Virginia	8
23	Wisconsin	8
30	Arizona	7
30	California	7
30	Connecticut	7
30	Hawaii	7
30	Maryland	7
30	Montana	7
30	New York	7
30	North Carolina	7
30	Washington	7
39	Florida	6
39	Kentucky	6
39	Mississippi	6
39	Nevada	6
39	Virginia	6
44	Georgia	5
44	Maine	5
44	Texas	5
47	Louisiana	4
48	South Carolina	3
NA	Rhode Island**	NA
NA	Utah**	NA
	District of Columbia	22

Source: Morgan Quitno Press using data from U.S. Department of Labor, Bureau of Labor Statistics
    "Occupational Employment and Wages, 2005" (http://www.bls.gov/oes/)
*Does not include self-employed.
**Not available.

Average Annual Wages of Optometrists in 2005

National Average = $95,500*

	ALPHA ORDER			RANK ORDER	
RANK	STATE	WAGES	RANK	STATE	WAGES
42	Alabama	$80,180	1	Alaska	$148,000
1	Alaska	148,000	2	New Hampshire	129,350
39	Arizona	84,030	3	Delaware	125,290
4	Arkansas	120,930	4	Arkansas	120,930
32	California	89,950	5	Georgia	118,560
48	Colorado	64,630	6	North Carolina	118,380
13	Connecticut	108,140	7	Minnesota	117,380
3	Delaware	125,290	8	Ohio	115,990
18	Florida	103,470	9	Maine	114,980
5	Georgia	118,560	10	Washington	114,800
35	Hawaii	88,130	11	South Dakota	114,080
49	Idaho	60,400	12	New York	113,420
37	Illinois	86,530	13	Connecticut	108,140
43	Indiana	79,880	14	Nebraska	107,390
24	Iowa	96,230	15	Vermont	107,220
25	Kansas	94,520	16	Virginia	105,400
36	Kentucky	87,970	17	Oklahoma	104,830
30	Louisiana	92,910	18	Florida	103,470
9	Maine	114,980	19	New Jersey	102,120
34	Maryland	89,300	20	Mississippi	97,840
47	Massachusetts	71,450	21	Nevada	97,300
23	Michigan	96,380	22	North Dakota	97,220
7	Minnesota	117,380	23	Michigan	96,380
20	Mississippi	97,840	24	Iowa	96,230
45	Missouri	75,140	25	Kansas	94,520
31	Montana	90,210	26	Wisconsin	94,480
14	Nebraska	107,390	27	Wyoming	94,450
21	Nevada	97,300	28	West Virginia	94,270
2	New Hampshire	129,350	29	New Mexico	94,080
19	New Jersey	102,120	30	Louisiana	92,910
29	New Mexico	94,080	31	Montana	90,210
12	New York	113,420	32	California	89,950
6	North Carolina	118,380	33	Tennessee	89,600
22	North Dakota	97,220	34	Maryland	89,300
8	Ohio	115,990	35	Hawaii	88,130
17	Oklahoma	104,830	36	Kentucky	87,970
38	Oregon	84,440	37	Illinois	86,530
40	Pennsylvania	81,210	38	Oregon	84,440
NA	Rhode Island**	NA	39	Arizona	84,030
44	South Carolina	78,180	40	Pennsylvania	81,210
11	South Dakota	114,080	41	Texas	80,640
33	Tennessee	89,600	42	Alabama	80,180
41	Texas	80,640	43	Indiana	79,880
46	Utah	75,130	44	South Carolina	78,180
15	Vermont	107,220	45	Missouri	75,140
16	Virginia	105,400	46	Utah	75,130
10	Washington	114,800	47	Massachusetts	71,450
28	West Virginia	94,270	48	Colorado	64,630
26	Wisconsin	94,480	49	Idaho	60,400
27	Wyoming	94,450	NA	Rhode Island**	NA
				District of Columbia	67,380

Source: U.S. Department of Labor, Bureau of Labor Statistics
    "Occupational Employment and Wages, 2005" (http://www.bls.gov/oes/)
*Does not include self-employed.
**Not available.

Emergency Medical Technicians and Paramedics in 2005

National Total = 196,880 Technicians and Paramedics*

ALPHA ORDER

RANK ORDER

RANK	STATE	PARAMEDICS	% of USA		RANK	STATE	PARAMEDICS	% of USA
24	Alabama	2,850	1.4%		1	Texas	13,040	6.6%
50	Alaska	220	0.1%		2	Illinois	12,540	6.4%
27	Arizona	2,630	1.3%		3	California	11,970	6.1%
30	Arkansas	2,190	1.1%		4	Pennsylvania	11,690	5.9%
3	California	11,970	6.1%		5	Ohio	11,310	5.7%
23	Colorado	2,970	1.5%		6	New York	10,520	5.3%
28	Connecticut	2,470	1.3%		7	Florida	7,650	3.9%
42	Delaware	600	0.3%		8	Georgia	7,230	3.7%
7	Florida	7,650	3.9%		9	Wisconsin	7,140	3.6%
8	Georgia	7,230	3.7%		10	North Carolina	6,790	3.4%
44	Hawaii	570	0.3%		11	Missouri	6,700	3.4%
46	Idaho	550	0.3%		12	Michigan	6,670	3.4%
2	Illinois	12,540	6.4%		13	Tennessee	5,630	2.9%
15	Indiana	4,890	2.5%		14	Massachusetts	5,090	2.6%
31	Iowa	2,130	1.1%		15	Indiana	4,890	2.5%
29	Kansas	2,400	1.2%		16	New Jersey	4,700	2.4%
19	Kentucky	4,140	2.1%		17	Oklahoma	4,370	2.2%
25	Louisiana	2,800	1.4%		18	Maryland	4,320	2.2%
34	Maine	1,410	0.7%		19	Kentucky	4,140	2.1%
18	Maryland	4,320	2.2%		20	Minnesota	3,990	2.0%
14	Massachusetts	5,090	2.6%		21	South Carolina	3,790	1.9%
12	Michigan	6,670	3.4%		22	Virginia	3,050	1.5%
20	Minnesota	3,990	2.0%		23	Colorado	2,970	1.5%
35	Mississippi	1,370	0.7%		24	Alabama	2,850	1.4%
11	Missouri	6,700	3.4%		25	Louisiana	2,800	1.4%
43	Montana	580	0.3%		26	Washington	2,740	1.4%
47	Nebraska	480	0.2%		27	Arizona	2,630	1.3%
38	Nevada	890	0.5%		28	Connecticut	2,470	1.3%
39	New Hampshire	880	0.4%		29	Kansas	2,400	1.2%
16	New Jersey	4,700	2.4%		30	Arkansas	2,190	1.1%
37	New Mexico	950	0.5%		31	Iowa	2,130	1.1%
6	New York	10,520	5.3%		32	Utah	1,560	0.8%
10	North Carolina	6,790	3.4%		33	West Virginia	1,490	0.8%
44	North Dakota	570	0.3%		34	Maine	1,410	0.7%
5	Ohio	11,310	5.7%		35	Mississippi	1,370	0.7%
17	Oklahoma	4,370	2.2%		36	Oregon	1,120	0.6%
36	Oregon	1,120	0.6%		37	New Mexico	950	0.5%
4	Pennsylvania	11,690	5.9%		38	Nevada	890	0.5%
39	Rhode Island	880	0.4%		39	New Hampshire	880	0.4%
21	South Carolina	3,790	1.9%		39	Rhode Island	880	0.4%
41	South Dakota	770	0.4%		41	South Dakota	770	0.4%
13	Tennessee	5,630	2.9%		42	Delaware	600	0.3%
1	Texas	13,040	6.6%		43	Montana	580	0.3%
32	Utah	1,560	0.8%		44	Hawaii	570	0.3%
48	Vermont	370	0.2%		44	North Dakota	570	0.3%
22	Virginia	3,050	1.5%		46	Idaho	550	0.3%
26	Washington	2,740	1.4%		47	Nebraska	480	0.2%
33	West Virginia	1,490	0.8%		48	Vermont	370	0.2%
9	Wisconsin	7,140	3.6%		49	Wyoming	360	0.2%
49	Wyoming	360	0.2%		50	Alaska	220	0.1%

	District of Columbia	890	0.5%

Source: U.S. Department of Labor, Bureau of Labor Statistics
   "Occupational Employment and Wages, 2005" (http://www.bls.gov/oes/)
*Does not include self-employed.

Rate of Emergency Medical Technicians and Paramedics in 2005

National Rate = 66 Technicians and Paramedics per 100,000 Population*

ALPHA ORDER

RANK	STATE	RATE
30	Alabama	63
47	Alaska	33
41	Arizona	44
16	Arkansas	79
47	California	33
29	Colorado	64
24	Connecticut	71
24	Delaware	71
43	Florida	43
16	Georgia	79
40	Hawaii	45
45	Idaho	38
8	Illinois	98
19	Indiana	78
23	Iowa	72
13	Kansas	87
5	Kentucky	99
32	Louisiana	62
4	Maine	107
22	Maryland	77
16	Massachusetts	79
28	Michigan	66
19	Minnesota	78
39	Mississippi	47
3	Missouri	116
32	Montana	62
50	Nebraska	27
46	Nevada	37
27	New Hampshire	67
36	New Jersey	54
38	New Mexico	49
36	New York	54
19	North Carolina	78
11	North Dakota	90
5	Ohio	99
2	Oklahoma	123
49	Oregon	31
10	Pennsylvania	94
14	Rhode Island	82
12	South Carolina	89
5	South Dakota	99
9	Tennessee	95
35	Texas	57
30	Utah	63
34	Vermont	59
44	Virginia	40
41	Washington	44
14	West Virginia	82
1	Wisconsin	129
24	Wyoming	71

RANK ORDER

RANK	STATE	RATE
1	Wisconsin	129
2	Oklahoma	123
3	Missouri	116
4	Maine	107
5	Kentucky	99
5	Ohio	99
5	South Dakota	99
8	Illinois	98
9	Tennessee	95
10	Pennsylvania	94
11	North Dakota	90
12	South Carolina	89
13	Kansas	87
14	Rhode Island	82
14	West Virginia	82
16	Arkansas	79
16	Georgia	79
16	Massachusetts	79
19	Indiana	78
19	Minnesota	78
19	North Carolina	78
22	Maryland	77
23	Iowa	72
24	Connecticut	71
24	Delaware	71
24	Wyoming	71
27	New Hampshire	67
28	Michigan	66
29	Colorado	64
30	Alabama	63
30	Utah	63
32	Louisiana	62
32	Montana	62
34	Vermont	59
35	Texas	57
36	New Jersey	54
36	New York	54
38	New Mexico	49
39	Mississippi	47
40	Hawaii	45
41	Arizona	44
41	Washington	44
43	Florida	43
44	Virginia	40
45	Idaho	38
46	Nevada	37
47	Alaska	33
47	California	33
49	Oregon	31
50	Nebraska	27

District of Columbia 153

Source: Morgan Quitno Press using data from U.S. Department of Labor, Bureau of Labor Statistics
"Occupational Employment and Wages, 2005" (http://www.bls.gov/oes/)
*Does not include self-employed.

Average Annual Wages of
Emergency Medical Technicians and Paramedics in 2005
National Average = $28,440*

ALPHA ORDER

RANK	STATE	WAGES		RANK	STATE	WAGES
46	Alabama	$22,280		1	Alaska	$45,750
1	Alaska	45,750		2	Washington	38,650
38	Arizona	25,530		3	Maryland	38,340
42	Arkansas	23,940		4	Nevada	37,980
19	California	29,020		5	Hawaii	36,580
11	Colorado	33,500		6	Massachusetts	36,160
9	Connecticut	33,710		7	New York	35,440
8	Delaware	34,400		8	Delaware	34,400
21	Florida	28,460		9	Connecticut	33,710
22	Georgia	28,050		10	Rhode Island	33,530
5	Hawaii	36,580		11	Colorado	33,500
16	Idaho	29,860		12	Oregon	33,250
17	Illinois	29,820		13	New Jersey	32,110
27	Indiana	26,950		14	Minnesota	30,620
37	Iowa	25,640		15	New Hampshire	30,080
47	Kansas	21,310		16	Idaho	29,860
44	Kentucky	23,610		17	Illinois	29,820
40	Louisiana	25,040		18	New Mexico	29,170
39	Maine	25,470		19	California	29,020
3	Maryland	38,340		20	Missouri	28,570
6	Massachusetts	36,160		21	Florida	28,460
23	Michigan	27,920		22	Georgia	28,050
14	Minnesota	30,620		23	Michigan	27,920
43	Mississippi	23,700		24	North Carolina	27,760
20	Missouri	28,570		25	Ohio	27,700
48	Montana	21,030		26	South Carolina	27,140
32	Nebraska	26,080		27	Indiana	26,950
4	Nevada	37,980		28	North Dakota	26,860
15	New Hampshire	30,080		29	Vermont	26,490
13	New Jersey	32,110		30	Virginia	26,430
18	New Mexico	29,170		31	Wyoming	26,400
7	New York	35,440		32	Nebraska	26,080
24	North Carolina	27,760		33	Tennessee	25,940
28	North Dakota	26,860		33	Texas	25,940
25	Ohio	27,700		35	Utah	25,850
50	Oklahoma	20,340		36	Pennsylvania	25,680
12	Oregon	33,250		37	Iowa	25,640
36	Pennsylvania	25,680		38	Arizona	25,530
10	Rhode Island	33,530		39	Maine	25,470
26	South Carolina	27,140		40	Louisiana	25,040
45	South Dakota	23,010		41	Wisconsin	24,380
33	Tennessee	25,940		42	Arkansas	23,940
33	Texas	25,940		43	Mississippi	23,700
35	Utah	25,850		44	Kentucky	23,610
29	Vermont	26,490		45	South Dakota	23,010
30	Virginia	26,430		46	Alabama	22,280
2	Washington	38,650		47	Kansas	21,310
49	West Virginia	20,930		48	Montana	21,030
41	Wisconsin	24,380		49	West Virginia	20,930
31	Wyoming	26,400		50	Oklahoma	20,340
					District of Columbia	40,730

Source: U.S. Department of Labor, Bureau of Labor Statistics
"Occupational Employment and Wages, 2005" (http://www.bls.gov/oes/)
*Does not include self-employed.

Employment in Health Care Support Industries in 2005

National Total = 3,363,800 Aides and Assistants*

ALPHA ORDER

RANK ORDER

RANK	STATE	EMPLOYEES	% of USA		RANK	STATE	EMPLOYEES	% of USA
25	Alabama	45,630	1.4%		1	California	311,570	9.3%
50	Alaska	6,180	0.2%		2	New York	292,270	8.7%
22	Arizona	51,380	1.5%		3	Texas	225,560	6.7%
33	Arkansas	29,990	0.9%		4	Florida	189,610	5.6%
1	California	311,570	9.3%		5	Ohio	167,780	5.0%
30	Colorado	39,850	1.2%		6	Pennsylvania	164,510	4.9%
23	Connecticut	50,000	1.5%		7	Illinois	130,200	3.9%
47	Delaware	9,290	0.3%		8	Michigan	123,780	3.7%
4	Florida	189,610	5.6%		9	North Carolina	117,390	3.5%
12	Georgia	79,660	2.4%		10	New Jersey	104,740	3.1%
43	Hawaii	13,340	0.4%		11	Massachusetts	90,160	2.7%
41	Idaho	16,230	0.5%		12	Georgia	79,660	2.4%
7	Illinois	130,200	3.9%		13	Wisconsin	78,550	2.3%
18	Indiana	64,340	1.9%		14	Minnesota	72,770	2.2%
27	Iowa	43,960	1.3%		15	Missouri	71,990	2.1%
29	Kansas	41,250	1.2%		16	Virginia	68,400	2.0%
24	Kentucky	49,440	1.5%		17	Washington	64,540	1.9%
21	Louisiana	53,380	1.6%		18	Indiana	64,340	1.9%
38	Maine	19,050	0.6%		19	Tennessee	62,570	1.9%
20	Maryland	59,090	1.8%		20	Maryland	59,090	1.8%
11	Massachusetts	90,160	2.7%		21	Louisiana	53,380	1.6%
8	Michigan	123,780	3.7%		22	Arizona	51,380	1.5%
14	Minnesota	72,770	2.2%		23	Connecticut	50,000	1.5%
32	Mississippi	30,600	0.9%		24	Kentucky	49,440	1.5%
15	Missouri	71,990	2.1%		25	Alabama	45,630	1.4%
44	Montana	11,300	0.3%		26	Oklahoma	45,540	1.4%
35	Nebraska	24,260	0.7%		27	Iowa	43,960	1.3%
39	Nevada	18,090	0.5%		28	South Carolina	43,700	1.3%
42	New Hampshire	14,410	0.4%		29	Kansas	41,250	1.2%
10	New Jersey	104,740	3.1%		30	Colorado	39,850	1.2%
37	New Mexico	19,490	0.6%		31	Oregon	38,280	1.1%
2	New York	292,270	8.7%		32	Mississippi	30,600	0.9%
9	North Carolina	117,390	3.5%		33	Arkansas	29,990	0.9%
45	North Dakota	11,070	0.3%		34	Utah	24,500	0.7%
5	Ohio	167,780	5.0%		35	Nebraska	24,260	0.7%
26	Oklahoma	45,540	1.4%		36	West Virginia	23,730	0.7%
31	Oregon	38,280	1.1%		37	New Mexico	19,490	0.6%
6	Pennsylvania	164,510	4.9%		38	Maine	19,050	0.6%
40	Rhode Island	17,010	0.5%		39	Nevada	18,090	0.5%
28	South Carolina	43,700	1.3%		40	Rhode Island	17,010	0.5%
46	South Dakota	10,300	0.3%		41	Idaho	16,230	0.5%
19	Tennessee	62,570	1.9%		42	New Hampshire	14,410	0.4%
3	Texas	225,560	6.7%		43	Hawaii	13,340	0.4%
34	Utah	24,500	0.7%		44	Montana	11,300	0.3%
48	Vermont	8,740	0.3%		45	North Dakota	11,070	0.3%
16	Virginia	68,400	2.0%		46	South Dakota	10,300	0.3%
17	Washington	64,540	1.9%		47	Delaware	9,290	0.3%
36	West Virginia	23,730	0.7%		48	Vermont	8,740	0.3%
13	Wisconsin	78,550	2.3%		49	Wyoming	6,430	0.2%
49	Wyoming	6,430	0.2%		50	Alaska	6,180	0.2%
						District of Columbia	7,910	0.2%

Source: U.S. Department of Labor, Bureau of Labor Statistics
   "Occupational Employment and Wages, 2005" (http://www.bls.gov/oes/)
*Does not include self-employed. Includes various health care assistants and aides not included in the category of health care practitioners and technicians. Among the included occupations are home health aides, nursing aides, psychiatric aides, dental assistants and pharmacy aides.

Rate of Employees in Health Care Support Industries in 2005

National Rate = 1,134 Aides and Assistants per 100,000 Population*

ALPHA ORDER

RANK	STATE	RATE
41	Alabama	1,003
44	Alaska	932
47	Arizona	863
29	Arkansas	1,080
48	California	862
49	Colorado	855
8	Connecticut	1,428
27	Delaware	1,104
30	Florida	1,067
46	Georgia	872
35	Hawaii	1,048
26	Idaho	1,135
39	Illinois	1,020
37	Indiana	1,027
5	Iowa	1,482
4	Kansas	1,501
24	Kentucky	1,185
25	Louisiana	1,184
7	Maine	1,445
31	Maryland	1,057
12	Massachusetts	1,401
21	Michigan	1,225
10	Minnesota	1,419
32	Mississippi	1,052
20	Missouri	1,242
22	Montana	1,209
13	Nebraska	1,380
50	Nevada	750
28	New Hampshire	1,103
23	New Jersey	1,203
40	New Mexico	1,012
3	New York	1,513
14	North Carolina	1,354
1	North Dakota	1,744
6	Ohio	1,463
18	Oklahoma	1,285
32	Oregon	1,052
16	Pennsylvania	1,326
2	Rhode Island	1,584
36	South Carolina	1,029
15	South Dakota	1,329
34	Tennessee	1,051
42	Texas	984
42	Utah	984
11	Vermont	1,404
45	Virginia	904
38	Washington	1,026
17	West Virginia	1,308
9	Wisconsin	1,421
19	Wyoming	1,264

RANK ORDER

RANK	STATE	RATE
1	North Dakota	1,744
2	Rhode Island	1,584
3	New York	1,513
4	Kansas	1,501
5	Iowa	1,482
6	Ohio	1,463
7	Maine	1,445
8	Connecticut	1,428
9	Wisconsin	1,421
10	Minnesota	1,419
11	Vermont	1,404
12	Massachusetts	1,401
13	Nebraska	1,380
14	North Carolina	1,354
15	South Dakota	1,329
16	Pennsylvania	1,326
17	West Virginia	1,308
18	Oklahoma	1,285
19	Wyoming	1,264
20	Missouri	1,242
21	Michigan	1,225
22	Montana	1,209
23	New Jersey	1,203
24	Kentucky	1,185
25	Louisiana	1,184
26	Idaho	1,135
27	Delaware	1,104
28	New Hampshire	1,103
29	Arkansas	1,080
30	Florida	1,067
31	Maryland	1,057
32	Mississippi	1,052
32	Oregon	1,052
34	Tennessee	1,051
35	Hawaii	1,048
36	South Carolina	1,029
37	Indiana	1,027
38	Washington	1,026
39	Illinois	1,020
40	New Mexico	1,012
41	Alabama	1,003
42	Texas	984
42	Utah	984
44	Alaska	932
45	Virginia	904
46	Georgia	872
47	Arizona	863
48	California	862
49	Colorado	855
50	Nevada	750

District of Columbia   1,359

Source: Morgan Quitno Press using data from U.S. Department of Labor, Bureau of Labor Statistics
    "Occupational Employment and Wages, 2005" (http://www.bls.gov/oes/)
*Does not include self-employed. Includes various health care assistants and aides not included in the category of health care practitioners and technicians. Among the included occupations are home health aides, nursing aides, psychiatric aides, dental assistants and pharmacy aides.

Average Annual Wages of Employees in Health Care Support Industries in 2005

National Average = $23,850*

ALPHA ORDER

RANK	STATE	WAGES
47	Alabama	$19,410
1	Alaska	30,410
19	Arizona	23,960
46	Arkansas	19,540
5	California	27,030
8	Colorado	26,670
2	Connecticut	28,420
14	Delaware	25,740
27	Florida	22,900
36	Georgia	21,850
6	Hawaii	26,860
35	Idaho	21,880
20	Illinois	23,890
21	Indiana	23,590
29	Iowa	22,510
37	Kansas	21,830
34	Kentucky	21,980
50	Louisiana	18,360
25	Maine	23,080
12	Maryland	26,000
3	Massachusetts	27,940
15	Michigan	25,450
13	Minnesota	25,760
49	Mississippi	18,430
39	Missouri	21,500
43	Montana	20,560
28	Nebraska	22,620
7	Nevada	26,780
9	New Hampshire	26,550
11	New Jersey	26,100
32	New Mexico	22,030
16	New York	25,420
38	North Carolina	21,530
40	North Dakota	21,260
23	Ohio	23,390
43	Oklahoma	20,560
17	Oregon	25,410
21	Pennsylvania	23,590
10	Rhode Island	26,400
41	South Carolina	21,230
42	South Dakota	21,110
31	Tennessee	22,440
45	Texas	20,450
33	Utah	22,000
26	Vermont	23,060
24	Virginia	23,280
4	Washington	27,460
48	West Virginia	19,200
18	Wisconsin	24,520
30	Wyoming	22,470

RANK ORDER

RANK	STATE	WAGES
1	Alaska	$30,410
2	Connecticut	28,420
3	Massachusetts	27,940
4	Washington	27,460
5	California	27,030
6	Hawaii	26,860
7	Nevada	26,780
8	Colorado	26,670
9	New Hampshire	26,550
10	Rhode Island	26,400
11	New Jersey	26,100
12	Maryland	26,000
13	Minnesota	25,760
14	Delaware	25,740
15	Michigan	25,450
16	New York	25,420
17	Oregon	25,410
18	Wisconsin	24,520
19	Arizona	23,960
20	Illinois	23,890
21	Indiana	23,590
21	Pennsylvania	23,590
23	Ohio	23,390
24	Virginia	23,280
25	Maine	23,080
26	Vermont	23,060
27	Florida	22,900
28	Nebraska	22,620
29	Iowa	22,510
30	Wyoming	22,470
31	Tennessee	22,440
32	New Mexico	22,030
33	Utah	22,000
34	Kentucky	21,980
35	Idaho	21,880
36	Georgia	21,850
37	Kansas	21,830
38	North Carolina	21,530
39	Missouri	21,500
40	North Dakota	21,260
41	South Carolina	21,230
42	South Dakota	21,110
43	Montana	20,560
43	Oklahoma	20,560
45	Texas	20,450
46	Arkansas	19,540
47	Alabama	19,410
48	West Virginia	19,200
49	Mississippi	18,430
50	Louisiana	18,360

| | District of Columbia | 26,930 |

Source: U.S. Department of Labor, Bureau of Labor Statistics
    "Occupational Employment and Wages, 2005" (http://www.bls.gov/oes/)
*Does not include self-employed. Includes various health care assistants and aides not included in the category of health care practitioners and technicians. Among the included occupations are home health aides, nursing aides, psychiatric aides, dental assistants and pharmacy aides.

VII. PHYSICAL FITNESS

480   Users of Exercise Equipment in 2005
481   Participants in Golf in 2005
482   Participants in Running/Jogging in 2005
483   Participants in Swimming in 2005
484   Participants in Tennis in 2005
485   Alcohol Consumption in 2004
486   Adult Per Capita Alcohol Consumption in 2004
487   Apparent Beer Consumption in 2004
488   Adult Per Capita Beer Consumption in 2004
489   Wine Consumption in 2004
490   Adult Per Capita Wine Consumption in 2004
491   Distilled Spirits Consumption in 2004
492   Adult Per Capita Distilled Spirits Consumption in 2004
493   Percent of Adults Who Do Not Drink Alcohol: 2005
494   Percent of Adults Who Are Binge Drinkers: 2005
495   Percent of Adults Who Smoke: 2005
496   Percent of Men Who Smoke: 2005
497   Percent of Women Who Smoke: 2005
498   Percent of Adults Who are Former Smokers: 2005
499   Percent of Adults Who Have Never Smoked: 2005
500   Percent of Population Who are Illicit Drug Users: 2004
501   Percent of Adults Overweight: 2005
502   Percent of Adults Obese: 2005
503   Percent of Adults Overweight or Obese: 2005
504   Percent of Adults Who Do Not Exercise: 2005
505   Percent of Adults Who Exercise Vigorously: 2005
506   Percent of Adults Who are Disabled: 2005
507   Percent of Adults with High Blood Pressure: 2005
508   Percent of Adults with High Cholesterol: 2005
509   Percent of Adults Who Have Visited a Dentist or Dental Clinic: 2004
510   Percent of Adults 65 Years Old and Older Who Have Lost All Their Natural Teeth: 2004
511   Percent of Adults Who Average Five or More Servings of Fruits and Vegetables Each Day: 2005
512   Percent of Adults Rating Their Health as Fair or Poor in 2005
513   Safety Belt Usage Rate in 2006

Users of Exercise Equipment in 2005

National Total = 54,248,000 Users

RANK	STATE	USERS	% of USA
28	Alabama	616,000	1.1%
NA	Alaska*	NA	NA
24	Arizona	816,000	1.5%
31	Arkansas	453,000	0.8%
1	California	5,029,000	9.3%
12	Colorado	1,644,000	3.0%
20	Connecticut	962,000	1.8%
45	Delaware	117,000	0.2%
4	Florida	3,567,000	6.6%
11	Georgia	1,674,000	3.1%
NA	Hawaii*	NA	NA
35	Idaho	324,000	0.6%
5	Illinois	2,920,000	5.4%
17	Indiana	1,126,000	2.1%
32	Iowa	406,000	0.7%
36	Kansas	319,000	0.6%
21	Kentucky	897,000	1.7%
22	Louisiana	876,000	1.6%
43	Maine	196,000	0.4%
15	Maryland	1,279,000	2.4%
18	Massachusetts	1,081,000	2.0%
9	Michigan	1,908,000	3.5%
19	Minnesota	986,000	1.8%
33	Mississippi	347,000	0.6%
25	Missouri	758,000	1.4%
44	Montana	171,000	0.3%
38	Nebraska	271,000	0.5%
34	Nevada	326,000	0.6%
40	New Hampshire	232,000	0.4%
8	New Jersey	2,055,000	3.8%
48	New Mexico	73,000	0.1%
2	New York	3,953,000	7.3%
14	North Carolina	1,335,000	2.5%
42	North Dakota	199,000	0.4%
7	Ohio	2,244,000	4.1%
30	Oklahoma	478,000	0.9%
27	Oregon	713,000	1.3%
6	Pennsylvania	2,702,000	5.0%
37	Rhode Island	278,000	0.5%
26	South Carolina	719,000	1.3%
47	South Dakota	104,000	0.2%
23	Tennessee	843,000	1.6%
3	Texas	3,630,000	6.7%
29	Utah	591,000	1.1%
41	Vermont	211,000	0.4%
13	Virginia	1,513,000	2.8%
10	Washington	1,749,000	3.2%
39	West Virginia	251,000	0.5%
16	Wisconsin	1,195,000	2.2%
46	Wyoming	111,000	0.2%

RANK	STATE	USERS	% of USA
1	California	5,029,000	9.3%
2	New York	3,953,000	7.3%
3	Texas	3,630,000	6.7%
4	Florida	3,567,000	6.6%
5	Illinois	2,920,000	5.4%
6	Pennsylvania	2,702,000	5.0%
7	Ohio	2,244,000	4.1%
8	New Jersey	2,055,000	3.8%
9	Michigan	1,908,000	3.5%
10	Washington	1,749,000	3.2%
11	Georgia	1,674,000	3.1%
12	Colorado	1,644,000	3.0%
13	Virginia	1,513,000	2.8%
14	North Carolina	1,335,000	2.5%
15	Maryland	1,279,000	2.4%
16	Wisconsin	1,195,000	2.2%
17	Indiana	1,126,000	2.1%
18	Massachusetts	1,081,000	2.0%
19	Minnesota	986,000	1.8%
20	Connecticut	962,000	1.8%
21	Kentucky	897,000	1.7%
22	Louisiana	876,000	1.6%
23	Tennessee	843,000	1.6%
24	Arizona	816,000	1.5%
25	Missouri	758,000	1.4%
26	South Carolina	719,000	1.3%
27	Oregon	713,000	1.3%
28	Alabama	616,000	1.1%
29	Utah	591,000	1.1%
30	Oklahoma	478,000	0.9%
31	Arkansas	453,000	0.8%
32	Iowa	406,000	0.7%
33	Mississippi	347,000	0.6%
34	Nevada	326,000	0.6%
35	Idaho	324,000	0.6%
36	Kansas	319,000	0.6%
37	Rhode Island	278,000	0.5%
38	Nebraska	271,000	0.5%
39	West Virginia	251,000	0.5%
40	New Hampshire	232,000	0.4%
41	Vermont	211,000	0.4%
42	North Dakota	199,000	0.4%
43	Maine	196,000	0.4%
44	Montana	171,000	0.3%
45	Delaware	117,000	0.2%
46	Wyoming	111,000	0.2%
47	South Dakota	104,000	0.2%
48	New Mexico	73,000	0.1%
NA	Alaska*	NA	NA
NA	Hawaii*	NA	NA
	District of Columbia*	NA	NA

Source: The National Sporting Goods Association
"NSGA Sports Participation Survey, January-December 2005 (Copyright 2006, reprinted with permission)
Not available.

Participants in Golf in 2005

National Total = 24,669,000 Golfers

ALPHA ORDER

RANK	STATE	GOLFERS	% of USA
27	Alabama	247,000	1.0%
NA	Alaska*	NA	NA
23	Arizona	351,000	1.4%
38	Arkansas	120,000	0.5%
1	California	3,104,000	12.6%
13	Colorado	660,000	2.7%
29	Connecticut	223,000	0.9%
45	Delaware	41,000	0.2%
3	Florida	1,468,000	6.0%
15	Georgia	551,000	2.2%
NA	Hawaii*	NA	NA
39	Idaho	110,000	0.4%
6	Illinois	1,383,000	5.6%
20	Indiana	453,000	1.8%
22	Iowa	367,000	1.5%
33	Kansas	172,000	0.7%
24	Kentucky	307,000	1.2%
30	Louisiana	200,000	0.8%
47	Maine	7,000	0.0%
26	Maryland	262,000	1.1%
14	Massachusetts	582,000	2.4%
7	Michigan	1,086,000	4.4%
12	Minnesota	697,000	2.8%
32	Mississippi	179,000	0.7%
21	Missouri	426,000	1.7%
42	Montana	83,000	0.3%
37	Nebraska	127,000	0.5%
17	Nevada	498,000	2.0%
41	New Hampshire	92,000	0.4%
18	New Jersey	485,000	2.0%
40	New Mexico	107,000	0.4%
5	New York	1,429,000	5.8%
8	North Carolina	996,000	4.0%
43	North Dakota	73,000	0.3%
9	Ohio	948,000	3.8%
31	Oklahoma	191,000	0.8%
25	Oregon	284,000	1.2%
4	Pennsylvania	1,437,000	5.8%
44	Rhode Island	58,000	0.2%
27	South Carolina	247,000	1.0%
36	South Dakota	138,000	0.6%
19	Tennessee	468,000	1.9%
2	Texas	1,477,000	6.0%
34	Utah	156,000	0.6%
48	Vermont	0	0.0%
15	Virginia	551,000	2.2%
11	Washington	787,000	3.2%
35	West Virginia	145,000	0.6%
10	Wisconsin	856,000	3.5%
46	Wyoming	40,000	0.2%

RANK ORDER

RANK	STATE	GOLFERS	% of USA
1	California	3,104,000	12.6%
2	Texas	1,477,000	6.0%
3	Florida	1,468,000	6.0%
4	Pennsylvania	1,437,000	5.8%
5	New York	1,429,000	5.8%
6	Illinois	1,383,000	5.6%
7	Michigan	1,086,000	4.4%
8	North Carolina	996,000	4.0%
9	Ohio	948,000	3.8%
10	Wisconsin	856,000	3.5%
11	Washington	787,000	3.2%
12	Minnesota	697,000	2.8%
13	Colorado	660,000	2.7%
14	Massachusetts	582,000	2.4%
15	Georgia	551,000	2.2%
15	Virginia	551,000	2.2%
17	Nevada	498,000	2.0%
18	New Jersey	485,000	2.0%
19	Tennessee	468,000	1.9%
20	Indiana	453,000	1.8%
21	Missouri	426,000	1.7%
22	Iowa	367,000	1.5%
23	Arizona	351,000	1.4%
24	Kentucky	307,000	1.2%
25	Oregon	284,000	1.2%
26	Maryland	262,000	1.1%
27	Alabama	247,000	1.0%
27	South Carolina	247,000	1.0%
29	Connecticut	223,000	0.9%
30	Louisiana	200,000	0.8%
31	Oklahoma	191,000	0.8%
32	Mississippi	179,000	0.7%
33	Kansas	172,000	0.7%
34	Utah	156,000	0.6%
35	West Virginia	145,000	0.6%
36	South Dakota	138,000	0.6%
37	Nebraska	127,000	0.5%
38	Arkansas	120,000	0.5%
39	Idaho	110,000	0.4%
40	New Mexico	107,000	0.4%
41	New Hampshire	92,000	0.4%
42	Montana	83,000	0.3%
43	North Dakota	73,000	0.3%
44	Rhode Island	58,000	0.2%
45	Delaware	41,000	0.2%
46	Wyoming	40,000	0.2%
47	Maine	7,000	0.0%
48	Vermont	0	0.0%
NA	Alaska*	NA	NA
NA	Hawaii*	NA	NA
	District of Columbia*	NA	NA

Source: The National Sporting Goods Association
"NSGA Sports Participation Survey, January-December 2005 (Copyright 2006, reprinted with permission)
Not available.

Participants in Running/Jogging in 2005

National Total = 29,220,000 Runners/Joggers

ALPHA ORDER

RANK	STATE	RUNNERS	% of USA
21	Alabama	501,000	1.7%
NA	Alaska*	NA	NA
23	Arizona	488,000	1.7%
31	Arkansas	252,000	0.9%
1	California	3,964,000	13.6%
13	Colorado	836,000	2.9%
38	Connecticut	142,000	0.5%
35	Delaware	155,000	0.5%
3	Florida	1,800,000	6.2%
10	Georgia	957,000	3.3%
NA	Hawaii*	NA	NA
33	Idaho	228,000	0.8%
5	Illinois	1,419,000	4.9%
18	Indiana	613,000	2.1%
27	Iowa	374,000	1.3%
34	Kansas	226,000	0.8%
19	Kentucky	596,000	2.0%
28	Louisiana	321,000	1.1%
46	Maine	58,000	0.2%
20	Maryland	538,000	1.8%
16	Massachusetts	691,000	2.4%
11	Michigan	910,000	3.1%
17	Minnesota	636,000	2.2%
45	Mississippi	87,000	0.3%
24	Missouri	436,000	1.5%
43	Montana	92,000	0.3%
41	Nebraska	105,000	0.4%
26	Nevada	378,000	1.3%
42	New Hampshire	100,000	0.3%
12	New Jersey	857,000	2.9%
47	New Mexico	50,000	0.2%
2	New York	1,812,000	6.2%
9	North Carolina	960,000	3.3%
40	North Dakota	106,000	0.4%
8	Ohio	980,000	3.4%
29	Oklahoma	305,000	1.0%
30	Oregon	291,000	1.0%
6	Pennsylvania	1,237,000	4.2%
35	Rhode Island	155,000	0.5%
32	South Carolina	229,000	0.8%
44	South Dakota	88,000	0.3%
25	Tennessee	387,000	1.3%
4	Texas	1,488,000	5.1%
22	Utah	499,000	1.7%
39	Vermont	137,000	0.5%
7	Virginia	1,032,000	3.5%
15	Washington	732,000	2.5%
37	West Virginia	153,000	0.5%
14	Wisconsin	788,000	2.7%
48	Wyoming	31,000	0.1%

RANK ORDER

RANK	STATE	RUNNERS	% of USA
1	California	3,964,000	13.6%
2	New York	1,812,000	6.2%
3	Florida	1,800,000	6.2%
4	Texas	1,488,000	5.1%
5	Illinois	1,419,000	4.9%
6	Pennsylvania	1,237,000	4.2%
7	Virginia	1,032,000	3.5%
8	Ohio	980,000	3.4%
9	North Carolina	960,000	3.3%
10	Georgia	957,000	3.3%
11	Michigan	910,000	3.1%
12	New Jersey	857,000	2.9%
13	Colorado	836,000	2.9%
14	Wisconsin	788,000	2.7%
15	Washington	732,000	2.5%
16	Massachusetts	691,000	2.4%
17	Minnesota	636,000	2.2%
18	Indiana	613,000	2.1%
19	Kentucky	596,000	2.0%
20	Maryland	538,000	1.8%
21	Alabama	501,000	1.7%
22	Utah	499,000	1.7%
23	Arizona	488,000	1.7%
24	Missouri	436,000	1.5%
25	Tennessee	387,000	1.3%
26	Nevada	378,000	1.3%
27	Iowa	374,000	1.3%
28	Louisiana	321,000	1.1%
29	Oklahoma	305,000	1.0%
30	Oregon	291,000	1.0%
31	Arkansas	252,000	0.9%
32	South Carolina	229,000	0.8%
33	Idaho	228,000	0.8%
34	Kansas	226,000	0.8%
35	Delaware	155,000	0.5%
35	Rhode Island	155,000	0.5%
37	West Virginia	153,000	0.5%
38	Connecticut	142,000	0.5%
39	Vermont	137,000	0.5%
40	North Dakota	106,000	0.4%
41	Nebraska	105,000	0.4%
42	New Hampshire	100,000	0.3%
43	Montana	92,000	0.3%
44	South Dakota	88,000	0.3%
45	Mississippi	87,000	0.3%
46	Maine	58,000	0.2%
47	New Mexico	50,000	0.2%
48	Wyoming	31,000	0.1%
NA	Alaska*	NA	NA
NA	Hawaii*	NA	NA
	District of Columbia*	NA	NA

Source: The National Sporting Goods Association
"NSGA Sports Participation Survey, January-December 2005 (Copyright 2006, reprinted with permission)
Not available.

Participants in Swimming in 2005

National Total = 57,972,000 Swimmers

ALPHA ORDER

ALPHA ORDER

RANK	STATE	SWIMMERS	% of USA
21	Alabama	1,048,000	1.8%
NA	Alaska*	NA	NA
18	Arizona	1,247,000	2.2%
34	Arkansas	430,000	0.7%
1	California	5,918,000	10.2%
22	Colorado	943,000	1.6%
28	Connecticut	665,000	1.1%
42	Delaware	209,000	0.4%
2	Florida	4,125,000	7.1%
9	Georgia	2,066,000	3.6%
NA	Hawaii*	NA	NA
38	Idaho	300,000	0.5%
6	Illinois	2,732,000	4.7%
16	Indiana	1,278,000	2.2%
32	Iowa	482,000	0.8%
41	Kansas	227,000	0.4%
19	Kentucky	1,163,000	2.0%
25	Louisiana	732,000	1.3%
39	Maine	292,000	0.5%
26	Maryland	727,000	1.3%
14	Massachusetts	1,651,000	2.8%
10	Michigan	2,065,000	3.6%
23	Minnesota	922,000	1.6%
27	Mississippi	706,000	1.2%
11	Missouri	1,807,000	3.1%
47	Montana	83,000	0.1%
44	Nebraska	135,000	0.2%
33	Nevada	466,000	0.8%
36	New Hampshire	356,000	0.6%
7	New Jersey	2,159,000	3.7%
43	New Mexico	168,000	0.3%
3	New York	3,782,000	6.5%
15	North Carolina	1,429,000	2.5%
45	North Dakota	119,000	0.2%
8	Ohio	2,086,000	3.6%
29	Oklahoma	612,000	1.1%
30	Oregon	570,000	1.0%
4	Pennsylvania	3,213,000	5.5%
40	Rhode Island	282,000	0.5%
24	South Carolina	822,000	1.4%
48	South Dakota	25,000	0.0%
12	Tennessee	1,697,000	2.9%
5	Texas	2,855,000	4.9%
31	Utah	519,000	0.9%
37	Vermont	340,000	0.6%
13	Virginia	1,686,000	2.9%
17	Washington	1,249,000	2.2%
35	West Virginia	387,000	0.7%
20	Wisconsin	1,102,000	1.9%
46	Wyoming	95,000	0.2%

RANK ORDER

RANK	STATE	SWIMMERS	% of USA
1	California	5,918,000	10.2%
2	Florida	4,125,000	7.1%
3	New York	3,782,000	6.5%
4	Pennsylvania	3,213,000	5.5%
5	Texas	2,855,000	4.9%
6	Illinois	2,732,000	4.7%
7	New Jersey	2,159,000	3.7%
8	Ohio	2,086,000	3.6%
9	Georgia	2,066,000	3.6%
10	Michigan	2,065,000	3.6%
11	Missouri	1,807,000	3.1%
12	Tennessee	1,697,000	2.9%
13	Virginia	1,686,000	2.9%
14	Massachusetts	1,651,000	2.8%
15	North Carolina	1,429,000	2.5%
16	Indiana	1,278,000	2.2%
17	Washington	1,249,000	2.2%
18	Arizona	1,247,000	2.2%
19	Kentucky	1,163,000	2.0%
20	Wisconsin	1,102,000	1.9%
21	Alabama	1,048,000	1.8%
22	Colorado	943,000	1.6%
23	Minnesota	922,000	1.6%
24	South Carolina	822,000	1.4%
25	Louisiana	732,000	1.3%
26	Maryland	727,000	1.3%
27	Mississippi	706,000	1.2%
28	Connecticut	665,000	1.1%
29	Oklahoma	612,000	1.1%
30	Oregon	570,000	1.0%
31	Utah	519,000	0.9%
32	Iowa	482,000	0.8%
33	Nevada	466,000	0.8%
34	Arkansas	430,000	0.7%
35	West Virginia	387,000	0.7%
36	New Hampshire	356,000	0.6%
37	Vermont	340,000	0.6%
38	Idaho	300,000	0.5%
39	Maine	292,000	0.5%
40	Rhode Island	282,000	0.5%
41	Kansas	227,000	0.4%
42	Delaware	209,000	0.4%
43	New Mexico	168,000	0.3%
44	Nebraska	135,000	0.2%
45	North Dakota	119,000	0.2%
46	Wyoming	95,000	0.2%
47	Montana	83,000	0.1%
48	South Dakota	25,000	0.0%
NA	Alaska*	NA	NA
NA	Hawaii*	NA	NA
	District of Columbia*	NA	NA

Source: The National Sporting Goods Association
    "NSGA Sports Participation Survey, January-December 2005 (Copyright 2006, reprinted with permission)
*Not available.

Participants in Tennis in 2005

National Total = 11,120,000 Tennis Players

RANK	STATE	PLAYERS	% of USA
18	Alabama	231,000	2.1%
NA	Alaska*	NA	NA
20	Arizona	229,000	2.1%
33	Arkansas	67,000	0.6%
1	California	1,403,000	12.6%
7	Colorado	388,000	3.5%
31	Connecticut	95,000	0.9%
45	Delaware	16,000	0.1%
2	Florida	1,237,000	11.1%
5	Georgia	437,000	3.9%
NA	Hawaii*	NA	NA
29	Idaho	122,000	1.1%
9	Illinois	349,000	3.1%
28	Indiana	129,000	1.2%
42	Iowa	25,000	0.2%
34	Kansas	48,000	0.4%
13	Kentucky	310,000	2.8%
16	Louisiana	251,000	2.3%
41	Maine	26,000	0.2%
27	Maryland	145,000	1.3%
24	Massachusetts	186,000	1.7%
25	Michigan	173,000	1.6%
8	Minnesota	356,000	3.2%
23	Mississippi	199,000	1.8%
15	Missouri	256,000	2.3%
37	Montana	42,000	0.4%
44	Nebraska	19,000	0.2%
NA	Nevada*	NA	NA
40	New Hampshire	29,000	0.3%
6	New Jersey	414,000	3.7%
NA	New Mexico*	NA	NA
3	New York	767,000	6.9%
19	North Carolina	230,000	2.1%
43	North Dakota	21,000	0.2%
11	Ohio	345,000	3.1%
17	Oklahoma	234,000	2.1%
32	Oregon	79,000	0.7%
4	Pennsylvania	445,000	4.0%
39	Rhode Island	35,000	0.3%
21	South Carolina	227,000	2.0%
35	South Dakota	45,000	0.4%
26	Tennessee	154,000	1.4%
14	Texas	285,000	2.6%
30	Utah	107,000	1.0%
38	Vermont	41,000	0.4%
12	Virginia	317,000	2.9%
22	Washington	217,000	2.0%
36	West Virginia	43,000	0.4%
10	Wisconsin	346,000	3.1%
NA	Wyoming*	NA	NA

RANK	STATE	PLAYERS	% of USA
1	California	1,403,000	12.6%
2	Florida	1,237,000	11.1%
3	New York	767,000	6.9%
4	Pennsylvania	445,000	4.0%
5	Georgia	437,000	3.9%
6	New Jersey	414,000	3.7%
7	Colorado	388,000	3.5%
8	Minnesota	356,000	3.2%
9	Illinois	349,000	3.1%
10	Wisconsin	346,000	3.1%
11	Ohio	345,000	3.1%
12	Virginia	317,000	2.9%
13	Kentucky	310,000	2.8%
14	Texas	285,000	2.6%
15	Missouri	256,000	2.3%
16	Louisiana	251,000	2.3%
17	Oklahoma	234,000	2.1%
18	Alabama	231,000	2.1%
19	North Carolina	230,000	2.1%
20	Arizona	229,000	2.1%
21	South Carolina	227,000	2.0%
22	Washington	217,000	2.0%
23	Mississippi	199,000	1.8%
24	Massachusetts	186,000	1.7%
25	Michigan	173,000	1.6%
26	Tennessee	154,000	1.4%
27	Maryland	145,000	1.3%
28	Indiana	129,000	1.2%
29	Idaho	122,000	1.1%
30	Utah	107,000	1.0%
31	Connecticut	95,000	0.9%
32	Oregon	79,000	0.7%
33	Arkansas	67,000	0.6%
34	Kansas	48,000	0.4%
35	South Dakota	45,000	0.4%
36	West Virginia	43,000	0.4%
37	Montana	42,000	0.4%
38	Vermont	41,000	0.4%
39	Rhode Island	35,000	0.3%
40	New Hampshire	29,000	0.3%
41	Maine	26,000	0.2%
42	Iowa	25,000	0.2%
43	North Dakota	21,000	0.2%
44	Nebraska	19,000	0.2%
45	Delaware	16,000	0.1%
NA	Alaska*	NA	NA
NA	Hawaii*	NA	NA
NA	Nevada*	NA	NA
NA	New Mexico*	NA	NA
NA	Wyoming*	NA	NA
	District of Columbia*	NA	NA

Source: The National Sporting Goods Association
"NSGA Sports Participation Survey, January-December 2005 (Copyright 2006, reprinted with permission)
Not available.

Alcohol Consumption in 2004

National Total = 529,812,000 Gallons*

RANK	STATE	GALLONS	% of USA
26	Alabama	7,016,000	1.3%
47	Alaska	1,405,000	0.3%
16	Arizona	10,978,000	2.1%
35	Arkansas	4,021,000	0.8%
1	California	63,613,000	12.0%
20	Colorado	9,902,000	1.9%
28	Connecticut	6,398,000	1.2%
43	Delaware	2,219,000	0.4%
3	Florida	38,725,000	7.3%
10	Georgia	14,649,000	2.8%
41	Hawaii	2,638,000	0.5%
39	Idaho	2,662,000	0.5%
6	Illinois	22,502,000	4.2%
19	Indiana	10,068,000	1.9%
30	Iowa	5,094,000	1.0%
34	Kansas	4,083,000	0.8%
29	Kentucky	6,116,000	1.2%
23	Louisiana	8,614,000	1.6%
38	Maine	2,667,000	0.5%
21	Maryland	9,660,000	1.8%
12	Massachusetts	13,335,000	2.5%
8	Michigan	17,539,000	3.3%
18	Minnesota	10,271,000	1.9%
31	Mississippi	4,953,000	0.9%
17	Missouri	10,743,000	2.0%
45	Montana	2,027,000	0.4%
37	Nebraska	3,203,000	0.6%
27	Nevada	6,794,000	1.3%
33	New Hampshire	4,360,000	0.8%
9	New Jersey	16,091,000	3.0%
36	New Mexico	3,590,000	0.7%
4	New York	30,743,000	5.8%
11	North Carolina	13,587,000	2.6%
48	North Dakota	1,328,000	0.3%
7	Ohio	18,243,000	3.4%
32	Oklahoma	4,366,000	0.8%
25	Oregon	7,121,000	1.3%
5	Pennsylvania	22,769,000	4.3%
44	Rhode Island	2,147,000	0.4%
24	South Carolina	8,311,000	1.6%
46	South Dakota	1,521,000	0.3%
22	Tennessee	9,273,000	1.8%
2	Texas	38,788,000	7.3%
42	Utah	2,349,000	0.4%
49	Vermont	1,317,000	0.2%
14	Virginia	12,512,000	2.4%
15	Washington	11,155,000	2.1%
40	West Virginia	2,655,000	0.5%
13	Wisconsin	12,795,000	2.4%
50	Wyoming	1,065,000	0.2%

RANK	STATE	GALLONS	% of USA
1	California	63,613,000	12.0%
2	Texas	38,788,000	7.3%
3	Florida	38,725,000	7.3%
4	New York	30,743,000	5.8%
5	Pennsylvania	22,769,000	4.3%
6	Illinois	22,502,000	4.2%
7	Ohio	18,243,000	3.4%
8	Michigan	17,539,000	3.3%
9	New Jersey	16,091,000	3.0%
10	Georgia	14,649,000	2.8%
11	North Carolina	13,587,000	2.6%
12	Massachusetts	13,335,000	2.5%
13	Wisconsin	12,795,000	2.4%
14	Virginia	12,512,000	2.4%
15	Washington	11,155,000	2.1%
16	Arizona	10,978,000	2.1%
17	Missouri	10,743,000	2.0%
18	Minnesota	10,271,000	1.9%
19	Indiana	10,068,000	1.9%
20	Colorado	9,902,000	1.9%
21	Maryland	9,660,000	1.8%
22	Tennessee	9,273,000	1.8%
23	Louisiana	8,614,000	1.6%
24	South Carolina	8,311,000	1.6%
25	Oregon	7,121,000	1.3%
26	Alabama	7,016,000	1.3%
27	Nevada	6,794,000	1.3%
28	Connecticut	6,398,000	1.2%
29	Kentucky	6,116,000	1.2%
30	Iowa	5,094,000	1.0%
31	Mississippi	4,953,000	0.9%
32	Oklahoma	4,366,000	0.8%
33	New Hampshire	4,360,000	0.8%
34	Kansas	4,083,000	0.8%
35	Arkansas	4,021,000	0.8%
36	New Mexico	3,590,000	0.7%
37	Nebraska	3,203,000	0.6%
38	Maine	2,667,000	0.5%
39	Idaho	2,662,000	0.5%
40	West Virginia	2,655,000	0.5%
41	Hawaii	2,638,000	0.5%
42	Utah	2,349,000	0.4%
43	Delaware	2,219,000	0.4%
44	Rhode Island	2,147,000	0.4%
45	Montana	2,027,000	0.4%
46	South Dakota	1,521,000	0.3%
47	Alaska	1,405,000	0.3%
48	North Dakota	1,328,000	0.3%
49	Vermont	1,317,000	0.2%
50	Wyoming	1,065,000	0.2%
	District of Columbia	1,827,000	0.3%

Source: U.S. Department of Health and Human Services, National Institute on Alcohol Abuse and Alcoholism
"Volume Beverage and Ethanol Consumption for States" (http://www.niaaa.nih.gov/Resources/)
*This is apparent consumption of actual alcohol, not entire volume of an alcoholic beverage (e.g. wine is roughly 11% absolute alcohol content). Apparent consumption is based on several sources which together approximate sales but do not actually measure consumption. Accordingly, figures for some states may be skewed by purchases by nonresidents.

Adult Per Capita Alcohol Consumption in 2004

National Per Capita = 2.5 Gallons Consumed per Adult 21 Years and Older*

ALPHA ORDER

RANK	STATE	PER CAPITA
40	Alabama	2.2
4	Alaska	3.2
13	Arizona	2.8
45	Arkansas	2.1
24	California	2.6
6	Colorado	3.1
29	Connecticut	2.5
3	Delaware	3.7
7	Florida	3.0
36	Georgia	2.4
9	Hawaii	2.9
13	Idaho	2.8
29	Illinois	2.5
38	Indiana	2.3
36	Iowa	2.4
45	Kansas	2.1
47	Kentucky	2.0
19	Louisiana	2.7
19	Maine	2.7
29	Maryland	2.5
13	Massachusetts	2.8
29	Michigan	2.5
13	Minnesota	2.8
29	Mississippi	2.5
24	Missouri	2.6
7	Montana	3.0
24	Nebraska	2.6
2	Nevada	4.1
1	New Hampshire	4.6
24	New Jersey	2.6
19	New Mexico	2.7
40	New York	2.2
40	North Carolina	2.2
9	North Dakota	2.9
40	Ohio	2.2
49	Oklahoma	1.7
19	Oregon	2.7
29	Pennsylvania	2.5
19	Rhode Island	2.7
13	South Carolina	2.8
13	South Dakota	2.8
40	Tennessee	2.2
24	Texas	2.6
50	Utah	1.5
9	Vermont	2.9
38	Virginia	2.3
29	Washington	2.5
47	West Virginia	2.0
4	Wisconsin	3.2
9	Wyoming	2.9

RANK ORDER

RANK	STATE	PER CAPITA
1	New Hampshire	4.6
2	Nevada	4.1
3	Delaware	3.7
4	Alaska	3.2
4	Wisconsin	3.2
6	Colorado	3.1
7	Florida	3.0
7	Montana	3.0
9	Hawaii	2.9
9	North Dakota	2.9
9	Vermont	2.9
9	Wyoming	2.9
13	Arizona	2.8
13	Idaho	2.8
13	Massachusetts	2.8
13	Minnesota	2.8
13	South Carolina	2.8
13	South Dakota	2.8
19	Louisiana	2.7
19	Maine	2.7
19	New Mexico	2.7
19	Oregon	2.7
19	Rhode Island	2.7
24	California	2.6
24	Missouri	2.6
24	Nebraska	2.6
24	New Jersey	2.6
24	Texas	2.6
29	Connecticut	2.5
29	Illinois	2.5
29	Maryland	2.5
29	Michigan	2.5
29	Mississippi	2.5
29	Pennsylvania	2.5
29	Washington	2.5
36	Georgia	2.4
36	Iowa	2.4
38	Indiana	2.3
38	Virginia	2.3
40	Alabama	2.2
40	New York	2.2
40	North Carolina	2.2
40	Ohio	2.2
40	Tennessee	2.2
45	Arkansas	2.1
45	Kansas	2.1
47	Kentucky	2.0
47	West Virginia	2.0
49	Oklahoma	1.7
50	Utah	1.5

District of Columbia 4.3

Source: Morgan Quitno Press using data from U.S. Dept. of HHS, National Institute on Alcohol Abuse and Alcoholism "Volume Beverage and Ethanol Consumption for States" (http://www.niaaa.nih.gov/Resources/)

This is apparent consumption of actual alcohol, not entire volume of an alcoholic beverage (e.g. wine is roughly 11% absolute alcohol content). Apparent consumption is based on several sources which together approximate sales but do not actually measure consumption. Accordingly, figures for some states may be skewed by purchases by nonresidents.

Apparent Beer Consumption in 2004

National Total = 6,383,382,000 Gallons of Beer Consumed*

ALPHA ORDER

RANK	STATE	GALLONS	% of USA
25	Alabama	97,065,000	1.5%
49	Alaska	15,120,000	0.2%
14	Arizona	139,618,000	2.2%
34	Arkansas	53,100,000	0.8%
1	California	667,800,000	10.5%
23	Colorado	106,906,000	1.7%
32	Connecticut	58,571,000	0.9%
45	Delaware	21,345,000	0.3%
3	Florida	429,372,000	6.7%
9	Georgia	183,825,000	2.9%
39	Hawaii	31,815,000	0.5%
42	Idaho	27,680,000	0.4%
6	Illinois	277,570,000	4.3%
18	Indiana	126,581,000	2.0%
28	Iowa	74,058,000	1.2%
33	Kansas	55,629,000	0.9%
26	Kentucky	80,329,000	1.3%
21	Louisiana	111,945,000	1.8%
40	Maine	30,600,000	0.5%
24	Maryland	102,721,000	1.6%
17	Massachusetts	129,649,000	2.0%
8	Michigan	208,418,000	3.3%
20	Minnesota	113,509,000	1.8%
30	Mississippi	71,618,000	1.1%
15	Missouri	138,277,000	2.2%
43	Montana	26,483,000	0.4%
36	Nebraska	44,841,000	0.7%
29	Nevada	72,456,000	1.1%
38	New Hampshire	40,791,000	0.6%
13	New Jersey	149,233,000	2.3%
35	New Mexico	49,163,000	0.8%
5	New York	320,758,000	5.0%
10	North Carolina	178,539,000	2.8%
47	North Dakota	17,661,000	0.3%
7	Ohio	274,950,000	4.3%
31	Oklahoma	59,656,000	0.9%
27	Oregon	79,689,000	1.2%
4	Pennsylvania	328,330,000	5.1%
44	Rhode Island	22,193,000	0.3%
22	South Carolina	109,305,000	1.7%
46	South Dakota	20,835,000	0.3%
16	Tennessee	130,035,000	2.0%
2	Texas	565,038,000	8.9%
41	Utah	30,375,000	0.5%
48	Vermont	15,368,000	0.2%
11	Virginia	154,389,000	2.4%
19	Washington	117,675,000	1.8%
37	West Virginia	42,228,000	0.7%
12	Wisconsin	152,572,000	2.4%
50	Wyoming	13,080,000	0.2%

RANK ORDER

RANK	STATE	GALLONS	% of USA
1	California	667,800,000	10.5%
2	Texas	565,038,000	8.9%
3	Florida	429,372,000	6.7%
4	Pennsylvania	328,330,000	5.1%
5	New York	320,758,000	5.0%
6	Illinois	277,570,000	4.3%
7	Ohio	274,950,000	4.3%
8	Michigan	208,418,000	3.3%
9	Georgia	183,825,000	2.9%
10	North Carolina	178,539,000	2.8%
11	Virginia	154,389,000	2.4%
12	Wisconsin	152,572,000	2.4%
13	New Jersey	149,233,000	2.3%
14	Arizona	139,618,000	2.2%
15	Missouri	138,277,000	2.2%
16	Tennessee	130,035,000	2.0%
17	Massachusetts	129,649,000	2.0%
18	Indiana	126,581,000	2.0%
19	Washington	117,675,000	1.8%
20	Minnesota	113,509,000	1.8%
21	Louisiana	111,945,000	1.8%
22	South Carolina	109,305,000	1.7%
23	Colorado	106,906,000	1.7%
24	Maryland	102,721,000	1.6%
25	Alabama	97,065,000	1.5%
26	Kentucky	80,329,000	1.3%
27	Oregon	79,689,000	1.2%
28	Iowa	74,058,000	1.2%
29	Nevada	72,456,000	1.1%
30	Mississippi	71,618,000	1.1%
31	Oklahoma	59,656,000	0.9%
32	Connecticut	58,571,000	0.9%
33	Kansas	55,629,000	0.9%
34	Arkansas	53,100,000	0.8%
35	New Mexico	49,163,000	0.8%
36	Nebraska	44,841,000	0.7%
37	West Virginia	42,228,000	0.7%
38	New Hampshire	40,791,000	0.6%
39	Hawaii	31,815,000	0.5%
40	Maine	30,600,000	0.5%
41	Utah	30,375,000	0.5%
42	Idaho	27,680,000	0.4%
43	Montana	26,483,000	0.4%
44	Rhode Island	22,193,000	0.3%
45	Delaware	21,345,000	0.3%
46	South Dakota	20,835,000	0.3%
47	North Dakota	17,661,000	0.3%
48	Vermont	15,368,000	0.2%
49	Alaska	15,120,000	0.2%
50	Wyoming	13,080,000	0.2%
	District of Columbia	14,625,000	0.2%

Source: U.S. Department of Health and Human Services, National Institute on Alcohol Abuse and Alcoholism
"Volume Beverage and Ethanol Consumption for States" (http://www.niaaa.nih.gov/Resources/)
*This is apparent consumption and is based on several sources which together approximate sales but do not
actually measure consumption. Reported state volumes reflect only in-state purchases. Accordingly, figures for
some states may be skewed by purchases by nonresidents.

Adult Per Capita Beer Consumption in 2004

National Per Capita = 30.7 Gallons Consumed per Adult 21 Years and Older*

ALPHA ORDER

RANK	STATE	PER CAPITA
31	Alabama	30.0
18	Alaska	34.9
16	Arizona	35.3
41	Arkansas	27.2
42	California	27.0
24	Colorado	33.0
48	Connecticut	23.2
14	Delaware	35.5
20	Florida	33.8
32	Georgia	29.6
17	Hawaii	35.0
35	Idaho	29.0
28	Illinois	31.0
35	Indiana	29.0
19	Iowa	34.6
37	Kansas	28.9
43	Kentucky	26.9
13	Louisiana	35.7
25	Maine	31.3
45	Maryland	26.1
40	Massachusetts	27.6
34	Michigan	29.2
25	Minnesota	31.3
14	Mississippi	35.5
21	Missouri	33.6
3	Montana	39.3
10	Nebraska	36.4
1	Nevada	44.1
2	New Hampshire	43.4
46	New Jersey	24.1
7	New Mexico	37.3
49	New York	23.0
33	North Carolina	29.3
6	North Dakota	38.0
21	Ohio	33.6
47	Oklahoma	23.8
29	Oregon	30.7
11	Pennsylvania	36.3
39	Rhode Island	28.0
9	South Carolina	36.5
5	South Dakota	38.5
30	Tennessee	30.5
8	Texas	37.2
50	Utah	19.6
23	Vermont	33.5
38	Virginia	28.8
44	Washington	26.5
27	West Virginia	31.1
4	Wisconsin	38.7
12	Wyoming	36.0

RANK ORDER

RANK	STATE	PER CAPITA
1	Nevada	44.1
2	New Hampshire	43.4
3	Montana	39.3
4	Wisconsin	38.7
5	South Dakota	38.5
6	North Dakota	38.0
7	New Mexico	37.3
8	Texas	37.2
9	South Carolina	36.5
10	Nebraska	36.4
11	Pennsylvania	36.3
12	Wyoming	36.0
13	Louisiana	35.7
14	Delaware	35.5
14	Mississippi	35.5
16	Arizona	35.3
17	Hawaii	35.0
18	Alaska	34.9
19	Iowa	34.6
20	Florida	33.8
21	Missouri	33.6
21	Ohio	33.6
23	Vermont	33.5
24	Colorado	33.0
25	Maine	31.3
25	Minnesota	31.3
27	West Virginia	31.1
28	Illinois	31.0
29	Oregon	30.7
30	Tennessee	30.5
31	Alabama	30.0
32	Georgia	29.6
33	North Carolina	29.3
34	Michigan	29.2
35	Idaho	29.0
35	Indiana	29.0
37	Kansas	28.9
38	Virginia	28.8
39	Rhode Island	28.0
40	Massachusetts	27.6
41	Arkansas	27.2
42	California	27.0
43	Kentucky	26.9
44	Washington	26.5
45	Maryland	26.1
46	New Jersey	24.1
47	Oklahoma	23.8
48	Connecticut	23.2
49	New York	23.0
50	Utah	19.6
	District of Columbia	34.2

Source: Morgan Quitno Press using data from U.S. Dept. of HHS, National Institute on Alcohol Abuse and Alcoholism
"Volume Beverage and Ethanol Consumption for States" (http://www.niaaa.nih.gov/Resources/)
*This is apparent consumption and is based on several sources which together approximate sales but do not actually measure consumption. Reported state volumes reflect only in-state purchases. Accordingly, figures for some states may be skewed by purchases by nonresidents.

Wine Consumption in 2004

National Total = 637,769,000 Gallons of Wine Consumed*

<table>
<tr><td colspan="4">ALPHA ORDER</td><td colspan="4">RANK ORDER</td></tr>
<tr><th>RANK</th><th>STATE</th><th>GALLONS</th><th>% of USA</th><th>RANK</th><th>STATE</th><th>GALLONS</th><th>% of USA</th></tr>
<tr><td>30</td><td>Alabama</td><td>5,643,000</td><td>0.9%</td><td>1</td><td>California</td><td>113,210,000</td><td>17.8%</td></tr>
<tr><td>46</td><td>Alaska</td><td>1,781,000</td><td>0.3%</td><td>2</td><td>Florida</td><td>51,330,000</td><td>8.0%</td></tr>
<tr><td>16</td><td>Arizona</td><td>11,721,000</td><td>1.8%</td><td>3</td><td>New York</td><td>50,632,000</td><td>7.9%</td></tr>
<tr><td>40</td><td>Arkansas</td><td>2,631,000</td><td>0.4%</td><td>4</td><td>Texas</td><td>32,569,000</td><td>5.1%</td></tr>
<tr><td>1</td><td>California</td><td>113,210,000</td><td>17.8%</td><td>5</td><td>New Jersey</td><td>28,074,000</td><td>4.4%</td></tr>
<tr><td>15</td><td>Colorado</td><td>12,401,000</td><td>1.9%</td><td>6</td><td>Illinois</td><td>24,903,000</td><td>3.9%</td></tr>
<tr><td>17</td><td>Connecticut</td><td>11,717,000</td><td>1.8%</td><td>7</td><td>Massachusetts</td><td>23,778,000</td><td>3.7%</td></tr>
<tr><td>35</td><td>Delaware</td><td>3,011,000</td><td>0.5%</td><td>8</td><td>Pennsylvania</td><td>18,988,000</td><td>3.0%</td></tr>
<tr><td>2</td><td>Florida</td><td>51,330,000</td><td>8.0%</td><td>9</td><td>Washington</td><td>18,259,000</td><td>2.9%</td></tr>
<tr><td>14</td><td>Georgia</td><td>14,492,000</td><td>2.3%</td><td>10</td><td>Michigan</td><td>17,850,000</td><td>2.8%</td></tr>
<tr><td>32</td><td>Hawaii</td><td>3,906,000</td><td>0.6%</td><td>11</td><td>Virginia</td><td>17,580,000</td><td>2.8%</td></tr>
<tr><td>28</td><td>Idaho</td><td>6,128,000</td><td>1.0%</td><td>12</td><td>Ohio</td><td>15,630,000</td><td>2.5%</td></tr>
<tr><td>6</td><td>Illinois</td><td>24,903,000</td><td>3.9%</td><td>13</td><td>North Carolina</td><td>14,641,000</td><td>2.3%</td></tr>
<tr><td>24</td><td>Indiana</td><td>8,536,000</td><td>1.3%</td><td>14</td><td>Georgia</td><td>14,492,000</td><td>2.3%</td></tr>
<tr><td>37</td><td>Iowa</td><td>2,959,000</td><td>0.5%</td><td>15</td><td>Colorado</td><td>12,401,000</td><td>1.9%</td></tr>
<tr><td>39</td><td>Kansas</td><td>2,700,000</td><td>0.4%</td><td>16</td><td>Arizona</td><td>11,721,000</td><td>1.8%</td></tr>
<tr><td>31</td><td>Kentucky</td><td>4,494,000</td><td>0.7%</td><td>17</td><td>Connecticut</td><td>11,717,000</td><td>1.8%</td></tr>
<tr><td>25</td><td>Louisiana</td><td>7,220,000</td><td>1.1%</td><td>18</td><td>Maryland</td><td>11,422,000</td><td>1.8%</td></tr>
<tr><td>33</td><td>Maine</td><td>3,510,000</td><td>0.6%</td><td>19</td><td>Oregon</td><td>11,133,000</td><td>1.7%</td></tr>
<tr><td>18</td><td>Maryland</td><td>11,422,000</td><td>1.8%</td><td>20</td><td>Wisconsin</td><td>10,439,000</td><td>1.6%</td></tr>
<tr><td>7</td><td>Massachusetts</td><td>23,778,000</td><td>3.7%</td><td>21</td><td>Minnesota</td><td>10,041,000</td><td>1.6%</td></tr>
<tr><td>10</td><td>Michigan</td><td>17,850,000</td><td>2.8%</td><td>22</td><td>Missouri</td><td>9,579,000</td><td>1.5%</td></tr>
<tr><td>21</td><td>Minnesota</td><td>10,041,000</td><td>1.6%</td><td>23</td><td>Nevada</td><td>9,190,000</td><td>1.4%</td></tr>
<tr><td>42</td><td>Mississippi</td><td>2,152,000</td><td>0.3%</td><td>24</td><td>Indiana</td><td>8,536,000</td><td>1.3%</td></tr>
<tr><td>22</td><td>Missouri</td><td>9,579,000</td><td>1.5%</td><td>25</td><td>Louisiana</td><td>7,220,000</td><td>1.1%</td></tr>
<tr><td>45</td><td>Montana</td><td>2,042,000</td><td>0.3%</td><td>26</td><td>Tennessee</td><td>6,730,000</td><td>1.1%</td></tr>
<tr><td>43</td><td>Nebraska</td><td>2,134,000</td><td>0.3%</td><td>27</td><td>South Carolina</td><td>6,258,000</td><td>1.0%</td></tr>
<tr><td>23</td><td>Nevada</td><td>9,190,000</td><td>1.4%</td><td>28</td><td>Idaho</td><td>6,128,000</td><td>1.0%</td></tr>
<tr><td>29</td><td>New Hampshire</td><td>5,852,000</td><td>0.9%</td><td>29</td><td>New Hampshire</td><td>5,852,000</td><td>0.9%</td></tr>
<tr><td>5</td><td>New Jersey</td><td>28,074,000</td><td>4.4%</td><td>30</td><td>Alabama</td><td>5,643,000</td><td>0.9%</td></tr>
<tr><td>38</td><td>New Mexico</td><td>2,915,000</td><td>0.5%</td><td>31</td><td>Kentucky</td><td>4,494,000</td><td>0.7%</td></tr>
<tr><td>3</td><td>New York</td><td>50,632,000</td><td>7.9%</td><td>32</td><td>Hawaii</td><td>3,906,000</td><td>0.6%</td></tr>
<tr><td>13</td><td>North Carolina</td><td>14,641,000</td><td>2.3%</td><td>33</td><td>Maine</td><td>3,510,000</td><td>0.6%</td></tr>
<tr><td>49</td><td>North Dakota</td><td>727,000</td><td>0.1%</td><td>34</td><td>Rhode Island</td><td>3,419,000</td><td>0.5%</td></tr>
<tr><td>12</td><td>Ohio</td><td>15,630,000</td><td>2.5%</td><td>35</td><td>Delaware</td><td>3,011,000</td><td>0.5%</td></tr>
<tr><td>36</td><td>Oklahoma</td><td>2,963,000</td><td>0.5%</td><td>36</td><td>Oklahoma</td><td>2,963,000</td><td>0.5%</td></tr>
<tr><td>19</td><td>Oregon</td><td>11,133,000</td><td>1.7%</td><td>37</td><td>Iowa</td><td>2,959,000</td><td>0.5%</td></tr>
<tr><td>8</td><td>Pennsylvania</td><td>18,988,000</td><td>3.0%</td><td>38</td><td>New Mexico</td><td>2,915,000</td><td>0.5%</td></tr>
<tr><td>34</td><td>Rhode Island</td><td>3,419,000</td><td>0.5%</td><td>39</td><td>Kansas</td><td>2,700,000</td><td>0.4%</td></tr>
<tr><td>27</td><td>South Carolina</td><td>6,258,000</td><td>1.0%</td><td>40</td><td>Arkansas</td><td>2,631,000</td><td>0.4%</td></tr>
<tr><td>48</td><td>South Dakota</td><td>856,000</td><td>0.1%</td><td>41</td><td>Vermont</td><td>2,196,000</td><td>0.3%</td></tr>
<tr><td>26</td><td>Tennessee</td><td>6,730,000</td><td>1.1%</td><td>42</td><td>Mississippi</td><td>2,152,000</td><td>0.3%</td></tr>
<tr><td>4</td><td>Texas</td><td>32,569,000</td><td>5.1%</td><td>43</td><td>Nebraska</td><td>2,134,000</td><td>0.3%</td></tr>
<tr><td>44</td><td>Utah</td><td>2,094,000</td><td>0.3%</td><td>44</td><td>Utah</td><td>2,094,000</td><td>0.3%</td></tr>
<tr><td>41</td><td>Vermont</td><td>2,196,000</td><td>0.3%</td><td>45</td><td>Montana</td><td>2,042,000</td><td>0.3%</td></tr>
<tr><td>11</td><td>Virginia</td><td>17,580,000</td><td>2.8%</td><td>46</td><td>Alaska</td><td>1,781,000</td><td>0.3%</td></tr>
<tr><td>9</td><td>Washington</td><td>18,259,000</td><td>2.9%</td><td>47</td><td>West Virginia</td><td>1,214,000</td><td>0.2%</td></tr>
<tr><td>47</td><td>West Virginia</td><td>1,214,000</td><td>0.2%</td><td>48</td><td>South Dakota</td><td>856,000</td><td>0.1%</td></tr>
<tr><td>20</td><td>Wisconsin</td><td>10,439,000</td><td>1.6%</td><td>49</td><td>North Dakota</td><td>727,000</td><td>0.1%</td></tr>
<tr><td>50</td><td>Wyoming</td><td>724,000</td><td>0.1%</td><td>50</td><td>Wyoming</td><td>724,000</td><td>0.1%</td></tr>
<tr><td></td><td></td><td></td><td></td><td></td><td>District of Columbia</td><td>3,395,000</td><td>0.5%</td></tr>
</table>

Source: U.S. Department of Health and Human Services, National Institute on Alcohol Abuse and Alcoholism
"Volume Beverage and Ethanol Consumption for States" (http://www.niaaa.nih.gov/Resources/)
This is apparent consumption and is based on several sources which together approximate sales but do not actually measure consumption. Reported state volumes reflect only in-state purchases. Accordingly, figures for some states may be skewed by purchases by nonresidents.

Adult Per Capita Wine Consumption in 2004

National Per Capita = 3.1 Gallons Consumed per Adult 21 Years and Older

ALPHA ORDER

RANK ORDER

RANK	STATE	PER CAPITA	RANK	STATE	PER CAPITA
38	Alabama	1.7	1	Idaho	6.4
13	Alaska	4.1	2	New Hampshire	6.2
20	Arizona	3.0	3	Nevada	5.6
46	Arkansas	1.3	4	Massachusetts	5.1
7	California	4.6	5	Delaware	5.0
16	Colorado	3.8	6	Vermont	4.8
7	Connecticut	4.6	7	California	4.6
5	Delaware	5.0	7	Connecticut	4.6
15	Florida	4.0	9	New Jersey	4.5
28	Georgia	2.3	10	Hawaii	4.3
10	Hawaii	4.3	10	Oregon	4.3
1	Idaho	6.4	10	Rhode Island	4.3
23	Illinois	2.8	13	Alaska	4.1
35	Indiana	2.0	13	Washington	4.1
44	Iowa	1.4	15	Florida	4.0
44	Kansas	1.4	16	Colorado	3.8
43	Kentucky	1.5	17	Maine	3.6
28	Louisiana	2.3	17	New York	3.6
17	Maine	3.6	19	Virginia	3.3
22	Maryland	2.9	20	Arizona	3.0
4	Massachusetts	5.1	20	Montana	3.0
26	Michigan	2.5	22	Maryland	2.9
23	Minnesota	2.8	23	Illinois	2.8
49	Mississippi	1.1	23	Minnesota	2.8
28	Missouri	2.3	25	Wisconsin	2.6
20	Montana	3.0	26	Michigan	2.5
38	Nebraska	1.7	27	North Carolina	2.4
3	Nevada	5.6	28	Georgia	2.3
2	New Hampshire	6.2	28	Louisiana	2.3
9	New Jersey	4.5	28	Missouri	2.3
31	New Mexico	2.2	31	New Mexico	2.2
17	New York	3.6	32	Pennsylvania	2.1
27	North Carolina	2.4	32	South Carolina	2.1
40	North Dakota	1.6	32	Texas	2.1
37	Ohio	1.9	35	Indiana	2.0
48	Oklahoma	1.2	35	Wyoming	2.0
10	Oregon	4.3	37	Ohio	1.9
32	Pennsylvania	2.1	38	Alabama	1.7
10	Rhode Island	4.3	38	Nebraska	1.7
32	South Carolina	2.1	40	North Dakota	1.6
40	South Dakota	1.6	40	South Dakota	1.6
40	Tennessee	1.6	40	Tennessee	1.6
32	Texas	2.1	43	Kentucky	1.5
46	Utah	1.3	44	Iowa	1.4
6	Vermont	4.8	44	Kansas	1.4
19	Virginia	3.3	46	Arkansas	1.3
13	Washington	4.1	46	Utah	1.3
50	West Virginia	0.9	48	Oklahoma	1.2
25	Wisconsin	2.6	49	Mississippi	1.1
35	Wyoming	2.0	50	West Virginia	0.9

District of Columbia 7.9

Source: Morgan Quitno Press using data from U.S. Dept. of HHS, National Institute on Alcohol Abuse and Alcoholism "Volume Beverage and Ethanol Consumption for States" (http://www.niaaa.nih.gov/Resources/)
*This is apparent consumption and is based on several sources which together approximate sales but do not actually measure consumption. Reported state volumes reflect only in-state purchases. Accordingly, figures for some states may be skewed by purchases by nonresidents.

Distilled Spirits Consumption in 2004

National Total = 389,994,000 Gallons of Distilled Spirits Consumed*

ALPHA ORDER

RANK ORDER

RANK	STATE	GALLONS	% of USA
29	Alabama	4,673,000	1.2%
46	Alaska	1,203,000	0.3%
21	Arizona	7,746,000	2.0%
34	Arkansas	3,144,000	0.8%
1	California	46,126,000	11.8%
17	Colorado	8,496,000	2.2%
26	Connecticut	5,476,000	1.4%
38	Delaware	2,117,000	0.5%
2	Florida	31,099,000	8.0%
10	Georgia	10,968,000	2.8%
42	Hawaii	1,710,000	0.4%
43	Idaho	1,524,000	0.4%
5	Illinois	16,541,000	4.2%
20	Indiana	7,958,000	2.0%
32	Iowa	3,357,000	0.9%
35	Kansas	2,996,000	0.8%
28	Kentucky	4,675,000	1.2%
22	Louisiana	6,436,000	1.7%
39	Maine	2,036,000	0.5%
15	Maryland	8,673,000	2.2%
11	Massachusetts	10,787,000	2.8%
6	Michigan	14,253,000	3.7%
12	Minnesota	9,410,000	2.4%
31	Mississippi	3,535,000	0.9%
19	Missouri	7,994,000	2.0%
45	Montana	1,392,000	0.4%
37	Nebraska	2,214,000	0.6%
25	Nevada	5,714,000	1.5%
30	New Hampshire	4,305,000	1.1%
7	New Jersey	14,000,000	3.6%
36	New Mexico	2,436,000	0.6%
3	New York	23,788,000	6.1%
14	North Carolina	8,915,000	2.3%
48	North Dakota	1,069,000	0.3%
13	Ohio	9,378,000	2.4%
33	Oklahoma	3,162,000	0.8%
27	Oregon	5,107,000	1.3%
8	Pennsylvania	13,491,000	3.5%
41	Rhode Island	1,722,000	0.4%
23	South Carolina	6,290,000	1.6%
47	South Dakota	1,151,000	0.3%
24	Tennessee	6,211,000	1.6%
4	Texas	22,288,000	5.7%
40	Utah	1,733,000	0.4%
50	Vermont	833,000	0.2%
18	Virginia	8,020,000	2.1%
16	Washington	8,526,000	2.2%
44	West Virginia	1,455,000	0.4%
9	Wisconsin	11,151,000	2.9%
49	Wyoming	932,000	0.2%

RANK	STATE	GALLONS	% of USA
1	California	46,126,000	11.8%
2	Florida	31,099,000	8.0%
3	New York	23,788,000	6.1%
4	Texas	22,288,000	5.7%
5	Illinois	16,541,000	4.2%
6	Michigan	14,253,000	3.7%
7	New Jersey	14,000,000	3.6%
8	Pennsylvania	13,491,000	3.5%
9	Wisconsin	11,151,000	2.9%
10	Georgia	10,968,000	2.8%
11	Massachusetts	10,787,000	2.8%
12	Minnesota	9,410,000	2.4%
13	Ohio	9,378,000	2.4%
14	North Carolina	8,915,000	2.3%
15	Maryland	8,673,000	2.2%
16	Washington	8,526,000	2.2%
17	Colorado	8,496,000	2.2%
18	Virginia	8,020,000	2.1%
19	Missouri	7,994,000	2.0%
20	Indiana	7,958,000	2.0%
21	Arizona	7,746,000	2.0%
22	Louisiana	6,436,000	1.7%
23	South Carolina	6,290,000	1.6%
24	Tennessee	6,211,000	1.6%
25	Nevada	5,714,000	1.5%
26	Connecticut	5,476,000	1.4%
27	Oregon	5,107,000	1.3%
28	Kentucky	4,675,000	1.2%
29	Alabama	4,673,000	1.2%
30	New Hampshire	4,305,000	1.1%
31	Mississippi	3,535,000	0.9%
32	Iowa	3,357,000	0.9%
33	Oklahoma	3,162,000	0.8%
34	Arkansas	3,144,000	0.8%
35	Kansas	2,996,000	0.8%
36	New Mexico	2,436,000	0.6%
37	Nebraska	2,214,000	0.6%
38	Delaware	2,117,000	0.5%
39	Maine	2,036,000	0.5%
40	Utah	1,733,000	0.4%
41	Rhode Island	1,722,000	0.4%
42	Hawaii	1,710,000	0.4%
43	Idaho	1,524,000	0.4%
44	West Virginia	1,455,000	0.4%
45	Montana	1,392,000	0.4%
46	Alaska	1,203,000	0.3%
47	South Dakota	1,151,000	0.3%
48	North Dakota	1,069,000	0.3%
49	Wyoming	932,000	0.2%
50	Vermont	833,000	0.2%
	District of Columbia	1,778,000	0.5%

Source: U.S. Department of Health and Human Services, National Institute on Alcohol Abuse and Alcoholism "Volume Beverage and Ethanol Consumption for States" (http://www.niaaa.nlh.gov/Resources/)
This is apparent consumption and is based on several sources which together approximate sales but do not actually measure consumption. Reported state volumes reflect only in-state purchases. Accordingly, figures for some states may be skewed by purchases by nonresidents.

Adult Per Capita Distilled Spirits Consumption in 2004

National Per Capita = 1.9 Gallons Consumed per Adult 21 Years and Older*

ALPHA ORDER

RANK	STATE	PER CAPITA
46	Alabama	1.4
4	Alaska	2.8
21	Arizona	2.0
36	Arkansas	1.6
24	California	1.9
6	Colorado	2.6
13	Connecticut	2.2
2	Delaware	3.5
9	Florida	2.4
28	Georgia	1.8
24	Hawaii	1.9
36	Idaho	1.6
28	Illinois	1.8
28	Indiana	1.8
36	Iowa	1.6
36	Kansas	1.6
36	Kentucky	1.6
16	Louisiana	2.1
16	Maine	2.1
13	Maryland	2.2
10	Massachusetts	2.3
21	Michigan	2.0
6	Minnesota	2.6
28	Mississippi	1.8
24	Missouri	1.9
16	Montana	2.1
28	Nebraska	1.8
2	Nevada	3.5
1	New Hampshire	4.6
10	New Jersey	2.3
28	New Mexico	1.8
35	New York	1.7
41	North Carolina	1.5
10	North Dakota	2.3
48	Ohio	1.1
47	Oklahoma	1.3
21	Oregon	2.0
41	Pennsylvania	1.5
13	Rhode Island	2.2
16	South Carolina	2.1
16	South Dakota	2.1
41	Tennessee	1.5
41	Texas	1.5
48	Utah	1.1
28	Vermont	1.8
41	Virginia	1.5
24	Washington	1.9
48	West Virginia	1.1
4	Wisconsin	2.8
6	Wyoming	2.6

RANK ORDER

RANK	STATE	PER CAPITA
1	New Hampshire	4.6
2	Delaware	3.5
2	Nevada	3.5
4	Alaska	2.8
4	Wisconsin	2.8
6	Colorado	2.6
6	Minnesota	2.6
6	Wyoming	2.6
9	Florida	2.4
10	Massachusetts	2.3
10	New Jersey	2.3
10	North Dakota	2.3
13	Connecticut	2.2
13	Maryland	2.2
13	Rhode Island	2.2
16	Louisiana	2.1
16	Maine	2.1
16	Montana	2.1
16	South Carolina	2.1
16	South Dakota	2.1
21	Arizona	2.0
21	Michigan	2.0
21	Oregon	2.0
24	California	1.9
24	Hawaii	1.9
24	Missouri	1.9
24	Washington	1.9
28	Georgia	1.8
28	Illinois	1.8
28	Indiana	1.8
28	Mississippi	1.8
28	Nebraska	1.8
28	New Mexico	1.8
28	Vermont	1.8
35	New York	1.7
36	Arkansas	1.6
36	Idaho	1.6
36	Iowa	1.6
36	Kansas	1.6
36	Kentucky	1.6
41	North Carolina	1.5
41	Pennsylvania	1.5
41	Tennessee	1.5
41	Texas	1.5
41	Virginia	1.5
46	Alabama	1.4
47	Oklahoma	1.3
48	Ohio	1.1
48	Utah	1.1
48	West Virginia	1.1

District of Columbia 4.2

Source: Morgan Quitno Press using data from U.S. Dept. of HHS, National Institute on Alcohol Abuse and Alcoholism
"Volume Beverage and Ethanol Consumption for States" (http://www.niaaa.nih.gov/Resources/)
*This is apparent consumption and is based on several sources which together approximate sales but do not
actually measure consumption. Reported state volumes reflect only in-state purchases. Accordingly, figures for
some states may be skewed by purchases by nonresidents.

Percent of Adults Who Do Not Drink Alcohol: 2005

National Median = 43.8% of Adults*

RANK	STATE	PERCENT
6	Alabama	60.8
39	Alaska	40.4
30	Arizona	42.9
7	Arkansas	60.7
26	California	43.8
44	Colorado	37.8
49	Connecticut	32.7
29	Delaware	43.0
25	Florida	44.4
12	Georgia	53.7
17	Hawaii	48.6
14	Idaho	52.2
27	Illinois	43.6
16	Indiana	49.9
24	Iowa	44.5
11	Kansas	53.8
4	Kentucky	65.1
10	Louisiana	56.5
34	Maine	42.0
33	Maryland	42.1
48	Massachusetts	35.0
28	Michigan	43.2
47	Minnesota	35.3
5	Mississippi	62.5
18	Missouri	48.2
36	Montana	41.4
32	Nebraska	42.7
41	Nevada	40.3
46	New Hampshire	35.6
38	New Jersey	40.6
18	New Mexico	48.2
30	New York	42.9
9	North Carolina	57.1
39	North Dakota	40.4
22	Ohio	45.0
8	Oklahoma	57.7
35	Oregon	41.7
23	Pennsylvania	44.7
43	Rhode Island	38.4
13	South Carolina	53.5
36	South Dakota	41.4
3	Tennessee	65.3
15	Texas	50.1
1	Utah	72.7
45	Vermont	35.7
20	Virginia	45.3
42	Washington	39.3
2	West Virginia	68.0
50	Wisconsin	32.1
21	Wyoming	45.1

RANK	STATE	PERCENT
1	Utah	72.7
2	West Virginia	68.0
3	Tennessee	65.3
4	Kentucky	65.1
5	Mississippi	62.5
6	Alabama	60.8
7	Arkansas	60.7
8	Oklahoma	57.7
9	North Carolina	57.1
10	Louisiana	56.5
11	Kansas	53.8
12	Georgia	53.7
13	South Carolina	53.5
14	Idaho	52.2
15	Texas	50.1
16	Indiana	49.9
17	Hawaii	48.6
18	Missouri	48.2
18	New Mexico	48.2
20	Virginia	45.3
21	Wyoming	45.1
22	Ohio	45.0
23	Pennsylvania	44.7
24	Iowa	44.5
25	Florida	44.4
26	California	43.8
27	Illinois	43.6
28	Michigan	43.2
29	Delaware	43.0
30	Arizona	42.9
30	New York	42.9
32	Nebraska	42.7
33	Maryland	42.1
34	Maine	42.0
35	Oregon	41.7
36	Montana	41.4
36	South Dakota	41.4
38	New Jersey	40.6
39	Alaska	40.4
39	North Dakota	40.4
41	Nevada	40.3
42	Washington	39.3
43	Rhode Island	38.4
44	Colorado	37.8
45	Vermont	35.7
46	New Hampshire	35.6
47	Minnesota	35.3
48	Massachusetts	35.0
49	Connecticut	32.7
50	Wisconsin	32.1
	District of Columbia	38.4

*Source: U.S. Department of Health and Human Services, Centers for Disease Control and Prevention
"2005 Behavioral Risk Factor Surveillance Summary Prevalence Data" (http://apps.nccd.cdc.gov/brfss/)*
Persons 18 and older reporting not having at least one drink of alcohol in the past 30 days.

Percent of Adults Who Are Binge Drinkers: 2005

National Median = 14.4% of Adults*

ALPHA ORDER

RANK ORDER

RANK	STATE	PERCENT		RANK	STATE	PERCENT
44	Alabama	10.4		1	Wisconsin	22.1
7	Alaska	17.5		2	North Dakota	18.9
24	Arizona	14.5		3	Minnesota	18.7
44	Arkansas	10.4		4	Iowa	18.6
29	California	14.0		5	South Dakota	18.0
13	Colorado	16.2		6	Nevada	17.6
20	Connecticut	14.8		7	Alaska	17.5
17	Delaware	15.6		8	Nebraska	17.3
28	Florida	14.1		9	Illinois	16.8
40	Georgia	12.1		9	Montana	16.8
12	Hawaii	16.5		11	Michigan	16.6
34	Idaho	13.3		12	Hawaii	16.5
9	Illinois	16.8		13	Colorado	16.2
26	Indiana	14.3		14	Pennsylvania	16.0
4	Iowa	18.6		15	Vermont	15.8
38	Kansas	12.4		16	Massachusetts	15.7
44	Kentucky	10.4		17	Delaware	15.6
29	Louisiana	14.0		18	Ohio	15.2
29	Maine	14.0		19	Rhode Island	15.1
41	Maryland	11.9		20	Connecticut	14.8
16	Massachusetts	15.7		21	Missouri	14.7
11	Michigan	16.6		21	New Hampshire	14.7
3	Minnesota	18.7		21	New York	14.7
47	Mississippi	9.8		24	Arizona	14.5
21	Missouri	14.7		25	Wyoming	14.4
9	Montana	16.8		26	Indiana	14.3
8	Nebraska	17.3		26	Texas	14.3
6	Nevada	17.6		28	Florida	14.1
21	New Hampshire	14.7		29	California	14.0
35	New Jersey	13.2		29	Louisiana	14.0
42	New Mexico	10.6		29	Maine	14.0
21	New York	14.7		32	Oregon	13.9
43	North Carolina	10.5		33	Washington	13.8
2	North Dakota	18.9		34	Idaho	13.3
18	Ohio	15.2		35	New Jersey	13.2
37	Oklahoma	12.6		36	South Carolina	12.8
32	Oregon	13.9		37	Oklahoma	12.6
14	Pennsylvania	16.0		38	Kansas	12.4
19	Rhode Island	15.1		39	Virginia	12.2
36	South Carolina	12.8		40	Georgia	12.1
5	South Dakota	18.0		41	Maryland	11.9
49	Tennessee	8.6		42	New Mexico	10.6
26	Texas	14.3		43	North Carolina	10.5
50	Utah	8.3		44	Alabama	10.4
15	Vermont	15.8		44	Arkansas	10.4
39	Virginia	12.2		44	Kentucky	10.4
33	Washington	13.8		47	Mississippi	9.8
48	West Virginia	9.1		48	West Virginia	9.1
1	Wisconsin	22.1		49	Tennessee	8.6
25	Wyoming	14.4		50	Utah	8.3

District of Columbia   16.8

Source: U.S. Department of Health and Human Services, Centers for Disease Control and Prevention
"2005 Behavioral Risk Factor Surveillance Summary Prevalence Data" (http://apps.nccd.cdc.gov/brfss/)
*Persons 18 and older reporting consumption of five or more alcoholic drinks on one or more occasions during the previous month.

Percent of Adults Who Smoke: 2005

National Median = 20.6% of Adults*

<table>
<tr><td colspan="3">ALPHA ORDER</td><td colspan="3">RANK ORDER</td></tr>
<tr><td>RANK</td><td>STATE</td><td>PERCENT</td><td>RANK</td><td>STATE</td><td>PERCENT</td></tr>
<tr><td>7</td><td>Alabama</td><td>24.8</td><td>1</td><td>Kentucky</td><td>28.7</td></tr>
<tr><td>6</td><td>Alaska</td><td>24.9</td><td>2</td><td>Indiana</td><td>27.3</td></tr>
<tr><td>30</td><td>Arizona</td><td>20.2</td><td>3</td><td>Tennessee</td><td>26.7</td></tr>
<tr><td>10</td><td>Arkansas</td><td>23.5</td><td>3</td><td>West Virginia</td><td>26.7</td></tr>
<tr><td>49</td><td>California</td><td>15.2</td><td>5</td><td>Oklahoma</td><td>25.1</td></tr>
<tr><td>35</td><td>Colorado</td><td>19.8</td><td>6</td><td>Alaska</td><td>24.9</td></tr>
<tr><td>48</td><td>Connecticut</td><td>16.5</td><td>7</td><td>Alabama</td><td>24.8</td></tr>
<tr><td>25</td><td>Delaware</td><td>20.6</td><td>8</td><td>Mississippi</td><td>23.6</td></tr>
<tr><td>19</td><td>Florida</td><td>21.7</td><td>8</td><td>Pennsylvania</td><td>23.6</td></tr>
<tr><td>17</td><td>Georgia</td><td>22.1</td><td>10</td><td>Arkansas</td><td>23.5</td></tr>
<tr><td>47</td><td>Hawaii</td><td>17.0</td><td>11</td><td>Missouri</td><td>23.4</td></tr>
<tr><td>44</td><td>Idaho</td><td>17.9</td><td>12</td><td>Nevada</td><td>23.1</td></tr>
<tr><td>34</td><td>Illinois</td><td>19.9</td><td>13</td><td>Louisiana</td><td>22.6</td></tr>
<tr><td>2</td><td>Indiana</td><td>27.3</td><td>13</td><td>North Carolina</td><td>22.6</td></tr>
<tr><td>28</td><td>Iowa</td><td>20.4</td><td>15</td><td>South Carolina</td><td>22.5</td></tr>
<tr><td>45</td><td>Kansas</td><td>17.8</td><td>16</td><td>Ohio</td><td>22.3</td></tr>
<tr><td>1</td><td>Kentucky</td><td>28.7</td><td>17</td><td>Georgia</td><td>22.1</td></tr>
<tr><td>13</td><td>Louisiana</td><td>22.6</td><td>18</td><td>Michigan</td><td>22.0</td></tr>
<tr><td>23</td><td>Maine</td><td>20.8</td><td>19</td><td>Florida</td><td>21.7</td></tr>
<tr><td>40</td><td>Maryland</td><td>18.9</td><td>20</td><td>New Mexico</td><td>21.5</td></tr>
<tr><td>42</td><td>Massachusetts</td><td>18.1</td><td>21</td><td>Nebraska</td><td>21.3</td></tr>
<tr><td>18</td><td>Michigan</td><td>22.0</td><td>21</td><td>Wyoming</td><td>21.3</td></tr>
<tr><td>32</td><td>Minnesota</td><td>20.0</td><td>23</td><td>Maine</td><td>20.8</td></tr>
<tr><td>8</td><td>Mississippi</td><td>23.6</td><td>24</td><td>Wisconsin</td><td>20.7</td></tr>
<tr><td>11</td><td>Missouri</td><td>23.4</td><td>25</td><td>Delaware</td><td>20.6</td></tr>
<tr><td>39</td><td>Montana</td><td>19.2</td><td>25</td><td>Virginia</td><td>20.6</td></tr>
<tr><td>21</td><td>Nebraska</td><td>21.3</td><td>27</td><td>New York</td><td>20.5</td></tr>
<tr><td>12</td><td>Nevada</td><td>23.1</td><td>28</td><td>Iowa</td><td>20.4</td></tr>
<tr><td>28</td><td>New Hampshire</td><td>20.4</td><td>28</td><td>New Hampshire</td><td>20.4</td></tr>
<tr><td>43</td><td>New Jersey</td><td>18.0</td><td>30</td><td>Arizona</td><td>20.2</td></tr>
<tr><td>20</td><td>New Mexico</td><td>21.5</td><td>31</td><td>North Dakota</td><td>20.1</td></tr>
<tr><td>27</td><td>New York</td><td>20.5</td><td>32</td><td>Minnesota</td><td>20.0</td></tr>
<tr><td>13</td><td>North Carolina</td><td>22.6</td><td>32</td><td>Texas</td><td>20.0</td></tr>
<tr><td>31</td><td>North Dakota</td><td>20.1</td><td>34</td><td>Illinois</td><td>19.9</td></tr>
<tr><td>16</td><td>Ohio</td><td>22.3</td><td>35</td><td>Colorado</td><td>19.8</td></tr>
<tr><td>5</td><td>Oklahoma</td><td>25.1</td><td>35</td><td>Rhode Island</td><td>19.8</td></tr>
<tr><td>41</td><td>Oregon</td><td>18.5</td><td>35</td><td>South Dakota</td><td>19.8</td></tr>
<tr><td>8</td><td>Pennsylvania</td><td>23.6</td><td>38</td><td>Vermont</td><td>19.3</td></tr>
<tr><td>35</td><td>Rhode Island</td><td>19.8</td><td>39</td><td>Montana</td><td>19.2</td></tr>
<tr><td>15</td><td>South Carolina</td><td>22.5</td><td>40</td><td>Maryland</td><td>18.9</td></tr>
<tr><td>35</td><td>South Dakota</td><td>19.8</td><td>41</td><td>Oregon</td><td>18.5</td></tr>
<tr><td>3</td><td>Tennessee</td><td>26.7</td><td>42</td><td>Massachusetts</td><td>18.1</td></tr>
<tr><td>32</td><td>Texas</td><td>20.0</td><td>43</td><td>New Jersey</td><td>18.0</td></tr>
<tr><td>50</td><td>Utah</td><td>11.5</td><td>44</td><td>Idaho</td><td>17.9</td></tr>
<tr><td>38</td><td>Vermont</td><td>19.3</td><td>45</td><td>Kansas</td><td>17.8</td></tr>
<tr><td>25</td><td>Virginia</td><td>20.6</td><td>46</td><td>Washington</td><td>17.6</td></tr>
<tr><td>46</td><td>Washington</td><td>17.6</td><td>47</td><td>Hawaii</td><td>17.0</td></tr>
<tr><td>3</td><td>West Virginia</td><td>26.7</td><td>48</td><td>Connecticut</td><td>16.5</td></tr>
<tr><td>24</td><td>Wisconsin</td><td>20.7</td><td>49</td><td>California</td><td>15.2</td></tr>
<tr><td>21</td><td>Wyoming</td><td>21.3</td><td>50</td><td>Utah</td><td>11.5</td></tr>
<tr><td></td><td></td><td></td><td></td><td>District of Columbia</td><td>20.0</td></tr>
</table>

Source: U.S. Department of Health and Human Services, Centers for Disease Control and Prevention
"2005 Behavioral Risk Factor Surveillance Summary Prevalence Data" (http://apps.nccd.cdc.gov/brfss/)
*Persons 18 and older who have smoked more than 100 cigarettes during their lifetime and who currently smoke everyday or some days.

Percent of Men Who Smoke: 2005

National Median = 22.1% of Men*

ALPHA ORDER

RANK ORDER

RANK	STATE	PERCENT		RANK	STATE	PERCENT
3	Alabama	29.6		1	Kentucky	30.5
5	Alaska	27.8		2	Indiana	29.7
26	Arizona	21.9		3	Alabama	29.6
11	Arkansas	25.2		4	Tennessee	29.2
45	California	19.1		5	Alaska	27.8
29	Colorado	21.6		6	West Virginia	27.4
49	Connecticut	17.0		7	Oklahoma	26.5
23	Delaware	22.5		8	Mississippi	25.8
16	Florida	24.7		9	North Carolina	25.6
13	Georgia	25.1		10	South Carolina	25.3
44	Hawaii	19.2		11	Arkansas	25.2
39	Idaho	19.6		11	Nevada	25.2
33	Illinois	21.1		13	Georgia	25.1
2	Indiana	29.7		14	Pennsylvania	25.0
28	Iowa	21.8		15	Missouri	24.9
47	Kansas	18.9		16	Florida	24.7
1	Kentucky	30.5		17	Louisiana	24.6
17	Louisiana	24.6		18	New Mexico	24.4
24	Maine	22.2		19	Michigan	24.0
40	Maryland	19.5		20	Nebraska	23.4
48	Massachusetts	18.2		21	Texas	23.3
19	Michigan	24.0		22	New York	23.0
34	Minnesota	21.0		23	Delaware	22.5
8	Mississippi	25.8		24	Maine	22.2
15	Missouri	24.9		25	Wisconsin	22.1
43	Montana	19.3		26	Arizona	21.9
20	Nebraska	23.4		26	Ohio	21.9
11	Nevada	25.2		28	Iowa	21.8
38	New Hampshire	20.3		29	Colorado	21.6
41	New Jersey	19.4		29	North Dakota	21.6
18	New Mexico	24.4		29	Vermont	21.6
22	New York	23.0		29	Virginia	21.6
9	North Carolina	25.6		33	Illinois	21.1
29	North Dakota	21.6		34	Minnesota	21.0
26	Ohio	21.9		35	Oregon	20.6
7	Oklahoma	26.5		36	Wyoming	20.5
35	Oregon	20.6		37	South Dakota	20.4
14	Pennsylvania	25.0		38	New Hampshire	20.3
41	Rhode Island	19.4		39	Idaho	19.6
10	South Carolina	25.3		40	Maryland	19.5
37	South Dakota	20.4		41	New Jersey	19.4
4	Tennessee	29.2		41	Rhode Island	19.4
21	Texas	23.3		43	Montana	19.3
50	Utah	13.7		44	Hawaii	19.2
29	Vermont	21.6		45	California	19.1
29	Virginia	21.6		45	Washington	19.1
45	Washington	19.1		47	Kansas	18.9
6	West Virginia	27.4		48	Massachusetts	18.2
25	Wisconsin	22.1		49	Connecticut	17.0
36	Wyoming	20.5		50	Utah	13.7

	District of Columbia	23.0

Source: U.S. Department of Health and Human Services, Centers for Disease Control and Prevention
  "2005 Behavioral Risk Factor Surveillance System" (http://apps.nccd.cdc.gov/brfss/)
*Males age 18 and older who have smoked more than 100 cigarettes during their lifetime and who currently smoke everyday or some days.

Percent of Women Who Smoke: 2005

National Median = 19.2% of Women*

ALPHA ORDER				RANK ORDER		
RANK	STATE	PERCENT		RANK	STATE	PERCENT
16	Alabama	20.4		1	Kentucky	26.9
10	Alaska	21.9		2	West Virginia	26.0
35	Arizona	18.6		3	Indiana	25.0
10	Arkansas	21.9		4	Tennessee	24.4
49	California	11.3		5	Oklahoma	23.8
38	Colorado	18.0		6	Ohio	22.8
46	Connecticut	16.2		7	Pennsylvania	22.4
30	Delaware	19.0		8	Wyoming	22.2
31	Florida	18.8		9	Missouri	22.1
24	Georgia	19.3		10	Alaska	21.9
48	Hawaii	14.9		10	Arkansas	21.9
45	Idaho	16.3		12	Mississippi	21.7
31	Illinois	18.8		13	Nevada	20.9
3	Indiana	25.0		14	Louisiana	20.6
28	Iowa	19.1		15	New Hampshire	20.5
42	Kansas	16.8		16	Alabama	20.4
1	Kentucky	26.9		17	Michigan	20.1
14	Louisiana	20.6		17	Rhode Island	20.1
22	Maine	19.5		19	South Carolina	20.0
36	Maryland	18.3		20	North Carolina	19.8
39	Massachusetts	17.9		21	Virginia	19.7
17	Michigan	20.1		22	Maine	19.5
28	Minnesota	19.1		23	Wisconsin	19.4
12	Mississippi	21.7		24	Georgia	19.3
9	Missouri	22.1		25	Montana	19.2
25	Montana	19.2		25	Nebraska	19.2
25	Nebraska	19.2		25	South Dakota	19.2
13	Nevada	20.9		28	Iowa	19.1
15	New Hampshire	20.5		28	Minnesota	19.1
43	New Jersey	16.7		30	Delaware	19.0
31	New Mexico	18.8		31	Florida	18.8
37	New York	18.1		31	Illinois	18.8
20	North Carolina	19.8		31	New Mexico	18.8
34	North Dakota	18.7		34	North Dakota	18.7
6	Ohio	22.8		35	Arizona	18.6
5	Oklahoma	23.8		36	Maryland	18.3
44	Oregon	16.5		37	New York	18.1
7	Pennsylvania	22.4		38	Colorado	18.0
17	Rhode Island	20.1		39	Massachusetts	17.9
19	South Carolina	20.0		40	Vermont	17.0
25	South Dakota	19.2		41	Texas	16.9
4	Tennessee	24.4		42	Kansas	16.8
41	Texas	16.9		43	New Jersey	16.7
50	Utah	9.3		44	Oregon	16.5
40	Vermont	17.0		45	Idaho	16.3
21	Virginia	19.7		46	Connecticut	16.2
47	Washington	16.0		47	Washington	16.0
2	West Virginia	26.0		48	Hawaii	14.9
23	Wisconsin	19.4		49	California	11.3
8	Wyoming	22.2		50	Utah	9.3
					District of Columbia	17.5

Source: U.S. Department of Health and Human Services, Centers for Disease Control and Prevention
   "2005 Behavioral Risk Factor Surveillance System" (http://apps.nccd.cdc.gov/brfss/)
*Females age 18 and older who have smoked more than 100 cigarettes during their lifetime and who currently smoke everyday or some days.

Percent of Adults Who are Former Smokers: 2005

National Median = 24.8% of Adults*

ALPHA ORDER

RANK	STATE	PERCENT
48	Alabama	20.9
37	Alaska	23.8
19	Arizona	25.5
24	Arkansas	24.9
39	California	23.3
25	Colorado	24.8
4	Connecticut	29.4
11	Delaware	27.2
12	Florida	26.7
45	Georgia	21.9
14	Hawaii	26.2
42	Idaho	22.7
33	Illinois	24.0
40	Indiana	22.9
25	Iowa	24.8
27	Kansas	24.4
33	Kentucky	24.0
46	Louisiana	21.0
2	Maine	30.1
40	Maryland	22.9
8	Massachusetts	27.5
16	Michigan	26.0
6	Minnesota	28.7
48	Mississippi	20.9
31	Missouri	24.2
7	Montana	28.5
42	Nebraska	22.7
33	Nevada	24.0
3	New Hampshire	29.5
19	New Jersey	25.5
27	New Mexico	24.4
18	New York	25.6
38	North Carolina	23.6
19	North Dakota	25.5
17	Ohio	25.8
33	Oklahoma	24.0
9	Oregon	27.4
22	Pennsylvania	25.4
5	Rhode Island	28.8
27	South Carolina	24.4
22	South Dakota	25.4
44	Tennessee	22.0
46	Texas	21.0
50	Utah	16.0
1	Vermont	30.8
32	Virginia	24.1
10	Washington	27.3
30	West Virginia	24.3
15	Wisconsin	26.1
12	Wyoming	26.7

RANK ORDER

RANK	STATE	PERCENT
1	Vermont	30.8
2	Maine	30.1
3	New Hampshire	29.5
4	Connecticut	29.4
5	Rhode Island	28.8
6	Minnesota	28.7
7	Montana	28.5
8	Massachusetts	27.5
9	Oregon	27.4
10	Washington	27.3
11	Delaware	27.2
12	Florida	26.7
12	Wyoming	26.7
14	Hawaii	26.2
15	Wisconsin	26.1
16	Michigan	26.0
17	Ohio	25.8
18	New York	25.6
19	Arizona	25.5
19	New Jersey	25.5
19	North Dakota	25.5
22	Pennsylvania	25.4
22	South Dakota	25.4
24	Arkansas	24.9
25	Colorado	24.8
25	Iowa	24.8
27	Kansas	24.4
27	New Mexico	24.4
27	South Carolina	24.4
30	West Virginia	24.3
31	Missouri	24.2
32	Virginia	24.1
33	Illinois	24.0
33	Kentucky	24.0
33	Nevada	24.0
33	Oklahoma	24.0
37	Alaska	23.8
38	North Carolina	23.6
39	California	23.3
40	Indiana	22.9
40	Maryland	22.9
42	Idaho	22.7
42	Nebraska	22.7
44	Tennessee	22.0
45	Georgia	21.9
46	Louisiana	21.0
46	Texas	21.0
48	Alabama	20.9
48	Mississippi	20.9
50	Utah	16.0

| | District of Columbia | 21.5 |

Source: U.S. Department of Health and Human Services, Centers for Disease Control and Prevention
"2005 Behavioral Risk Factor Surveillance Summary Prevalence Data" (http://apps.nccd.cdc.gov/brfss/)
*Persons 18 and older who have smoked more than 100 cigarettes during their lifetime and who currently do not smoke.

Percent of Adults Who Have Never Smoked: 2005

National Median = 54.0% of Adults*

ALPHA ORDER

RANK	STATE	PERCENT
21	Alabama	54.3
41	Alaska	51.2
21	Arizona	54.3
37	Arkansas	51.6
2	California	61.5
14	Colorado	55.4
23	Connecticut	54.1
33	Delaware	52.1
37	Florida	51.6
12	Georgia	56.0
7	Hawaii	56.8
3	Idaho	59.3
10	Illinois	56.1
47	Indiana	49.8
17	Iowa	54.8
6	Kansas	57.8
50	Kentucky	47.3
8	Louisiana	56.5
48	Maine	49.1
5	Maryland	58.3
19	Massachusetts	54.5
34	Michigan	52.0
41	Minnesota	51.2
13	Mississippi	55.5
31	Missouri	52.4
32	Montana	52.3
10	Nebraska	56.1
30	Nevada	52.9
45	New Hampshire	50.1
8	New Jersey	56.5
23	New Mexico	54.1
25	New York	54.0
27	North Carolina	53.8
20	North Dakota	54.4
35	Ohio	51.9
44	Oklahoma	50.9
25	Oregon	54.0
43	Pennsylvania	51.0
39	Rhode Island	51.4
29	South Carolina	53.1
17	South Dakota	54.8
40	Tennessee	51.3
4	Texas	59.0
1	Utah	72.5
46	Vermont	50.0
15	Virginia	55.2
16	Washington	55.1
49	West Virginia	49.0
28	Wisconsin	53.2
35	Wyoming	51.9

RANK ORDER

RANK	STATE	PERCENT
1	Utah	72.5
2	California	61.5
3	Idaho	59.3
4	Texas	59.0
5	Maryland	58.3
6	Kansas	57.8
7	Hawaii	56.8
8	Louisiana	56.5
8	New Jersey	56.5
10	Illinois	56.1
10	Nebraska	56.1
12	Georgia	56.0
13	Mississippi	55.5
14	Colorado	55.4
15	Virginia	55.2
16	Washington	55.1
17	Iowa	54.8
17	South Dakota	54.8
19	Massachusetts	54.5
20	North Dakota	54.4
21	Alabama	54.3
21	Arizona	54.3
23	Connecticut	54.1
23	New Mexico	54.1
25	New York	54.0
25	Oregon	54.0
27	North Carolina	53.8
28	Wisconsin	53.2
29	South Carolina	53.1
30	Nevada	52.9
31	Missouri	52.4
32	Montana	52.3
33	Delaware	52.1
34	Michigan	52.0
35	Ohio	51.9
35	Wyoming	51.9
37	Arkansas	51.6
37	Florida	51.6
39	Rhode Island	51.4
40	Tennessee	51.3
41	Alaska	51.2
41	Minnesota	51.2
43	Pennsylvania	51.0
44	Oklahoma	50.9
45	New Hampshire	50.1
46	Vermont	50.0
47	Indiana	49.8
48	Maine	49.1
49	West Virginia	49.0
50	Kentucky	47.3

District of Columbia — 58.5

Source: U.S. Department of Health and Human Services, Centers for Disease Control and Prevention
  "2005 Behavioral Risk Factor Surveillance Summary Prevalence Data" (http://apps.nccd.cdc.gov/brfss/)
*Persons 18 and older who have not smoked more than 100 cigarettes during their lifetime.

Percent of Population Who are Illicit Drug Users: 2004

National Percent = 8.1% of Population*

ALPHA ORDER

RANK	STATE	PERCENT
42	Alabama	6.9
1	Alaska	11.8
20	Arizona	8.3
32	Arkansas	7.5
13	California	8.9
5	Colorado	10.2
17	Connecticut	8.5
15	Delaware	8.6
26	Florida	7.8
22	Georgia	8.0
22	Hawaii	8.0
42	Idaho	6.9
31	Illinois	7.6
34	Indiana	7.4
49	Iowa	6.5
48	Kansas	6.7
15	Kentucky	8.6
29	Louisiana	7.7
10	Maine	9.3
39	Maryland	7.0
5	Massachusetts	10.2
12	Michigan	9.0
34	Minnesota	7.4
50	Mississippi	5.8
21	Missouri	8.1
8	Montana	9.7
42	Nebraska	6.9
14	Nevada	8.7
7	New Hampshire	9.9
42	New Jersey	6.9
2	New Mexico	11.3
11	New York	9.1
38	North Carolina	7.2
32	North Dakota	7.5
24	Ohio	7.9
19	Oklahoma	8.4
9	Oregon	9.5
26	Pennsylvania	7.8
3	Rhode Island	10.8
29	South Carolina	7.7
39	South Dakota	7.0
47	Tennessee	6.8
39	Texas	7.0
42	Utah	6.9
4	Vermont	10.4
37	Virginia	7.3
17	Washington	8.5
34	West Virginia	7.4
26	Wisconsin	7.8
24	Wyoming	7.9

RANK ORDER

RANK	STATE	PERCENT
1	Alaska	11.8
2	New Mexico	11.3
3	Rhode Island	10.8
4	Vermont	10.4
5	Colorado	10.2
5	Massachusetts	10.2
7	New Hampshire	9.9
8	Montana	9.7
9	Oregon	9.5
10	Maine	9.3
11	New York	9.1
12	Michigan	9.0
13	California	8.9
14	Nevada	8.7
15	Delaware	8.6
15	Kentucky	8.6
17	Connecticut	8.5
17	Washington	8.5
19	Oklahoma	8.4
20	Arizona	8.3
21	Missouri	8.1
22	Georgia	8.0
22	Hawaii	8.0
24	Ohio	7.9
24	Wyoming	7.9
26	Florida	7.8
26	Pennsylvania	7.8
26	Wisconsin	7.8
29	Louisiana	7.7
29	South Carolina	7.7
31	Illinois	7.6
32	Arkansas	7.5
32	North Dakota	7.5
34	Indiana	7.4
34	Minnesota	7.4
34	West Virginia	7.4
37	Virginia	7.3
38	North Carolina	7.2
39	Maryland	7.0
39	South Dakota	7.0
39	Texas	7.0
42	Alabama	6.9
42	Idaho	6.9
42	Nebraska	6.9
42	New Jersey	6.9
42	Utah	6.9
47	Tennessee	6.8
48	Kansas	6.7
49	Iowa	6.5
50	Mississippi	5.8

| | District of Columbia | 9.6 |

Source: U.S. Department of Health and Human Services, Substance Abuse and Mental Health Services Administration "2003-2004 National Survey on Drug Use and Health" (March 2006, http://www.oas.samhsa.gov/statesList.htm)
*Population 12 years and older who used any illicit drug at least once within month of survey.

Percent of Adults Overweight: 2005

National Median = 36.7% of Adults*

ALPHA ORDER

RANK	STATE	PERCENT
40	Alabama	35.6
22	Alaska	36.8
44	Arizona	35.1
25	Arkansas	36.7
7	California	37.9
25	Colorado	36.7
5	Connecticut	38.1
1	Delaware	39.4
7	Florida	37.9
30	Georgia	36.4
50	Hawaii	33.3
22	Idaho	36.8
39	Illinois	35.7
44	Indiana	35.1
15	Iowa	37.1
20	Kansas	36.9
32	Kentucky	36.3
49	Louisiana	33.8
20	Maine	36.9
25	Maryland	36.7
43	Massachusetts	35.4
32	Michigan	36.3
13	Minnesota	37.2
30	Mississippi	36.4
19	Missouri	37.0
34	Montana	36.2
13	Nebraska	37.2
9	Nevada	37.6
22	New Hampshire	36.8
15	New Jersey	37.1
3	New Mexico	38.6
9	New York	37.6
25	North Carolina	36.7
2	North Dakota	38.8
5	Ohio	38.1
35	Oklahoma	36.1
38	Oregon	35.9
29	Pennsylvania	36.6
4	Rhode Island	38.2
42	South Carolina	35.5
12	South Dakota	37.3
47	Tennessee	34.9
15	Texas	37.1
46	Utah	35.0
40	Vermont	35.6
35	Virginia	36.1
35	Washington	36.1
48	West Virginia	34.8
15	Wisconsin	37.1
11	Wyoming	37.4

RANK ORDER

RANK	STATE	PERCENT
1	Delaware	39.4
2	North Dakota	38.8
3	New Mexico	38.6
4	Rhode Island	38.2
5	Connecticut	38.1
5	Ohio	38.1
7	California	37.9
7	Florida	37.9
9	Nevada	37.6
9	New York	37.6
11	Wyoming	37.4
12	South Dakota	37.3
13	Minnesota	37.2
13	Nebraska	37.2
15	Iowa	37.1
15	New Jersey	37.1
15	Texas	37.1
15	Wisconsin	37.1
19	Missouri	37.0
20	Kansas	36.9
20	Maine	36.9
22	Alaska	36.8
22	Idaho	36.8
22	New Hampshire	36.8
25	Arkansas	36.7
25	Colorado	36.7
25	Maryland	36.7
25	North Carolina	36.7
29	Pennsylvania	36.6
30	Georgia	36.4
30	Mississippi	36.4
32	Kentucky	36.3
32	Michigan	36.3
34	Montana	36.2
35	Oklahoma	36.1
35	Virginia	36.1
35	Washington	36.1
38	Oregon	35.9
39	Illinois	35.7
40	Alabama	35.6
40	Vermont	35.6
42	South Carolina	35.5
43	Massachusetts	35.4
44	Arizona	35.1
44	Indiana	35.1
46	Utah	35.0
47	Tennessee	34.9
48	West Virginia	34.8
49	Louisiana	33.8
50	Hawaii	33.3
	District of Columbia	33.3

*Source: U.S. Department of Health and Human Services, Centers for Disease Control and Prevention
"2005 Behavioral Risk Factor Surveillance Summary Prevalence Data" (http://apps.nccd.cdc.gov/brfss/)*
*Persons 18 and older. Does not include obese adults. Overweight is defined as a Body Mass Index (BMI) of 25.0
to 29.9 regardless of sex. BMI is a ratio of height to weight. As an example, a person 5' 8" and weighing 171
pounds has a BMI of 26. See http://www.cdc.gov/nccdphp/dnpa/bmi/bmi-adult.htm.

Percent of Adults Obese: 2005

National Median = 24.4% of Adults*

ALPHA ORDER

RANK	STATE	PERCENT
5	Alabama	28.9
8	Alaska	27.4
44	Arizona	21.1
7	Arkansas	28.0
36	California	22.7
50	Colorado	17.8
48	Connecticut	20.1
32	Delaware	23.5
35	Florida	22.8
14	Georgia	26.5
49	Hawaii	19.7
24	Idaho	24.5
22	Illinois	25.1
10	Indiana	27.2
19	Iowa	25.4
29	Kansas	23.9
6	Kentucky	28.6
2	Louisiana	30.8
36	Maine	22.7
25	Maryland	24.4
46	Massachusetts	20.7
15	Michigan	26.2
31	Minnesota	23.7
1	Mississippi	30.9
12	Missouri	26.9
41	Montana	21.3
16	Nebraska	26.0
42	Nevada	21.2
34	New Hampshire	23.1
39	New Jersey	22.1
40	New Mexico	21.7
38	New York	22.2
17	North Carolina	25.9
19	North Dakota	25.4
27	Ohio	24.3
13	Oklahoma	26.8
30	Oregon	23.8
21	Pennsylvania	25.3
45	Rhode Island	21.0
4	South Carolina	29.1
18	South Dakota	25.5
8	Tennessee	27.4
11	Texas	27.0
42	Utah	21.2
47	Vermont	20.2
22	Virginia	25.1
33	Washington	23.3
3	West Virginia	30.6
25	Wisconsin	24.4
28	Wyoming	24.2

RANK ORDER

RANK	STATE	PERCENT
1	Mississippi	30.9
2	Louisiana	30.8
3	West Virginia	30.6
4	South Carolina	29.1
5	Alabama	28.9
6	Kentucky	28.6
7	Arkansas	28.0
8	Alaska	27.4
8	Tennessee	27.4
10	Indiana	27.2
11	Texas	27.0
12	Missouri	26.9
13	Oklahoma	26.8
14	Georgia	26.5
15	Michigan	26.2
16	Nebraska	26.0
17	North Carolina	25.9
18	South Dakota	25.5
19	Iowa	25.4
19	North Dakota	25.4
21	Pennsylvania	25.3
22	Illinois	25.1
22	Virginia	25.1
24	Idaho	24.5
25	Maryland	24.4
25	Wisconsin	24.4
27	Ohio	24.3
28	Wyoming	24.2
29	Kansas	23.9
30	Oregon	23.8
31	Minnesota	23.7
32	Delaware	23.5
33	Washington	23.3
34	New Hampshire	23.1
35	Florida	22.8
36	California	22.7
36	Maine	22.7
38	New York	22.2
39	New Jersey	22.1
40	New Mexico	21.7
41	Montana	21.3
42	Nevada	21.2
42	Utah	21.2
44	Arizona	21.1
45	Rhode Island	21.0
46	Massachusetts	20.7
47	Vermont	20.2
48	Connecticut	20.1
49	Hawaii	19.7
50	Colorado	17.8
	District of Columbia	21.7

Source: U.S. Department of Health and Human Services, Centers for Disease Control and Prevention
"2005 Behavioral Risk Factor Surveillance Summary Prevalence Data" (http://apps.nccd.cdc.gov/brfss/)
*Persons 18 and older.   Obese is defined as a Body Mass Index (BMI) of 30.0 or more regardless of sex. BMI is a ratio of height to weight. As an example, a person 5' 8" and weighing 197 pounds has a BMI of 30.
See http://www.cdc.gov/nccdphp/dnpa/bmi/bmi-adult.htm.

Percent of Adults Overweight or Obese: 2005

National Median = 61.1% of Adults*

ALPHA ORDER

RANK	STATE	PERCENT
7	Alabama	64.5
8	Alaska	64.2
45	Arizona	56.2
4	Arkansas	64.7
33	California	60.6
49	Colorado	54.5
43	Connecticut	58.2
13	Delaware	62.9
32	Florida	60.7
13	Georgia	62.9
50	Hawaii	53.0
26	Idaho	61.3
30	Illinois	60.8
21	Indiana	62.3
18	Iowa	62.5
30	Kansas	60.8
3	Kentucky	64.9
5	Louisiana	64.6
38	Maine	59.6
28	Maryland	61.1
47	Massachusetts	56.1
18	Michigan	62.5
29	Minnesota	60.9
1	Mississippi	67.3
11	Missouri	63.9
44	Montana	57.5
12	Nebraska	63.2
42	Nevada	58.8
35	New Hampshire	59.9
40	New Jersey	59.2
34	New Mexico	60.3
36	New York	59.8
17	North Carolina	62.6
8	North Dakota	64.2
20	Ohio	62.4
13	Oklahoma	62.9
37	Oregon	59.7
23	Pennsylvania	61.9
40	Rhode Island	59.2
5	South Carolina	64.6
16	South Dakota	62.8
21	Tennessee	62.3
10	Texas	64.1
45	Utah	56.2
48	Vermont	55.8
27	Virginia	61.2
39	Washington	59.4
2	West Virginia	65.4
25	Wisconsin	61.5
24	Wyoming	61.6

RANK ORDER

RANK	STATE	PERCENT
1	Mississippi	67.3
2	West Virginia	65.4
3	Kentucky	64.9
4	Arkansas	64.7
5	Louisiana	64.6
5	South Carolina	64.6
7	Alabama	64.5
8	Alaska	64.2
8	North Dakota	64.2
10	Texas	64.1
11	Missouri	63.9
12	Nebraska	63.2
13	Delaware	62.9
13	Georgia	62.9
13	Oklahoma	62.9
16	South Dakota	62.8
17	North Carolina	62.6
18	Iowa	62.5
18	Michigan	62.5
20	Ohio	62.4
21	Indiana	62.3
21	Tennessee	62.3
23	Pennsylvania	61.9
24	Wyoming	61.6
25	Wisconsin	61.5
26	Idaho	61.3
27	Virginia	61.2
28	Maryland	61.1
29	Minnesota	60.9
30	Illinois	60.8
30	Kansas	60.8
32	Florida	60.7
33	California	60.6
34	New Mexico	60.3
35	New Hampshire	59.9
36	New York	59.8
37	Oregon	59.7
38	Maine	59.6
39	Washington	59.4
40	New Jersey	59.2
40	Rhode Island	59.2
42	Nevada	58.8
43	Connecticut	58.2
44	Montana	57.5
45	Arizona	56.2
45	Utah	56.2
47	Massachusetts	56.1
48	Vermont	55.8
49	Colorado	54.5
50	Hawaii	53.0

District of Columbia — 55.0

Source: Morgan Quitno Press using data from US Dept of Health & Human Serv's, Centers for Disease Control-Prevention "2005 Behavioral Risk Factor Surveillance Summary Prevalence Data" (http://apps.nccd.cdc.gov/brfss/)
*Persons 18 and older. Overweight is defined as a Body Mass Index (BMI) of 25.0 to 29.9 regardless of sex. Obese is a BMI of 30.0 or greater. BMI is a ratio of height to weight. As an example, a person 5' 8" and weighing 165 pounds has a BMI of 25. The same height at 197 pounds has a BMI of 30. See http://www.cdc.gov/nccdphp/dnpa/bmi/bmi-adult.htm.

Percent of Adults Who Do Not Exercise: 2005

National Median = 23.8% of Adults*

ALPHA ORDER RANK ORDER

RANK	STATE	PERCENT		RANK	STATE	PERCENT
7	Alabama	29.7		1	Louisiana	33.4
40	Alaska	21.4		2	Tennessee	33.1
32	Arizona	22.6		3	Mississippi	32.4
5	Arkansas	30.6		4	Kentucky	31.5
25	California	23.9		5	Arkansas	30.6
49	Colorado	17.3		5	Oklahoma	30.6
42	Connecticut	21.2		7	Alabama	29.7
27	Delaware	23.3		8	New Jersey	29.2
13	Florida	26.9		9	West Virginia	28.5
11	Georgia	27.2		10	Texas	27.4
43	Hawaii	19.5		11	Georgia	27.2
38	Idaho	21.6		12	New York	27.1
19	Illinois	25.6		13	Florida	26.9
13	Indiana	26.9		13	Indiana	26.9
23	Iowa	24.7		15	Nevada	26.8
24	Kansas	24.4		16	South Carolina	26.3
4	Kentucky	31.5		17	Rhode Island	25.9
1	Louisiana	33.4		18	Pennsylvania	25.8
36	Maine	22.3		19	Illinois	25.6
31	Maryland	22.9		19	North Carolina	25.6
27	Massachusetts	23.3		19	Ohio	25.6
33	Michigan	22.5		22	Missouri	25.4
50	Minnesota	16.2		23	Iowa	24.7
3	Mississippi	32.4		24	Kansas	24.4
22	Missouri	25.4		25	California	23.9
35	Montana	22.4		26	Nebraska	23.8
26	Nebraska	23.8		27	Delaware	23.3
15	Nevada	26.8		27	Massachusetts	23.3
38	New Hampshire	21.6		27	New Mexico	23.3
8	New Jersey	29.2		30	North Dakota	23.1
27	New Mexico	23.3		31	Maryland	22.9
12	New York	27.1		32	Arizona	22.6
19	North Carolina	25.6		33	Michigan	22.5
30	North Dakota	23.1		33	South Dakota	22.5
19	Ohio	25.6		35	Montana	22.4
5	Oklahoma	30.6		36	Maine	22.3
46	Oregon	18.6		37	Wyoming	22.0
18	Pennsylvania	25.8		38	Idaho	21.6
17	Rhode Island	25.9		38	New Hampshire	21.6
16	South Carolina	26.3		40	Alaska	21.4
33	South Dakota	22.5		41	Virginia	21.3
2	Tennessee	33.1		42	Connecticut	21.2
10	Texas	27.4		43	Hawaii	19.5
47	Utah	18.5		44	Vermont	19.2
44	Vermont	19.2		45	Wisconsin	18.7
41	Virginia	21.3		46	Oregon	18.6
48	Washington	17.4		47	Utah	18.5
9	West Virginia	28.5		48	Washington	17.4
45	Wisconsin	18.7		49	Colorado	17.3
37	Wyoming	22.0		50	Minnesota	16.2

District of Columbia 22.5

Source: U.S. Department of Health and Human Services, Centers for Disease Control and Prevention
"2005 Behavioral Risk Factor Surveillance Summary Prevalence Data" (http://apps.nccd.cdc.gov/brfss/)
Persons 18 and older who, in the previous month, did not participate in any physical activities.

Percent of Adults Who Exercise Vigorously: 2005

National Median = 27.5% of Adults*

ALPHA ORDER

RANK	STATE	PERCENT
47	Alabama	20.3
2	Alaska	35.9
22	Arizona	28.9
36	Arkansas	24.8
1	California	36.2
9	Colorado	32.6
12	Connecticut	31.0
35	Delaware	24.9
38	Florida	24.6
40	Georgia	23.7
17	Hawaii	30.2
11	Idaho	31.1
30	Illinois	25.7
29	Indiana	27.1
42	Iowa	22.9
34	Kansas	25.0
50	Kentucky	16.8
46	Louisiana	20.7
13	Maine	30.8
20	Maryland	29.6
19	Massachusetts	29.7
24	Michigan	28.1
23	Minnesota	28.3
45	Mississippi	20.9
32	Missouri	25.3
4	Montana	33.1
37	Nebraska	24.7
9	Nevada	32.6
7	New Hampshire	32.9
31	New Jersey	25.5
21	New Mexico	29.0
27	New York	27.3
44	North Carolina	22.2
25	North Dakota	27.5
28	Ohio	27.2
43	Oklahoma	22.5
14	Oregon	30.7
26	Pennsylvania	27.4
18	Rhode Island	29.9
38	South Carolina	24.6
41	South Dakota	23.5
49	Tennessee	17.4
32	Texas	25.3
3	Utah	34.3
4	Vermont	33.1
16	Virginia	30.4
15	Washington	30.6
48	West Virginia	17.6
8	Wisconsin	32.8
4	Wyoming	33.1

RANK ORDER

RANK	STATE	PERCENT
1	California	36.2
2	Alaska	35.9
3	Utah	34.3
4	Montana	33.1
4	Vermont	33.1
4	Wyoming	33.1
7	New Hampshire	32.9
8	Wisconsin	32.8
9	Colorado	32.6
9	Nevada	32.6
11	Idaho	31.1
12	Connecticut	31.0
13	Maine	30.8
14	Oregon	30.7
15	Washington	30.6
16	Virginia	30.4
17	Hawaii	30.2
18	Rhode Island	29.9
19	Massachusetts	29.7
20	Maryland	29.6
21	New Mexico	29.0
22	Arizona	28.9
23	Minnesota	28.3
24	Michigan	28.1
25	North Dakota	27.5
26	Pennsylvania	27.4
27	New York	27.3
28	Ohio	27.2
29	Indiana	27.1
30	Illinois	25.7
31	New Jersey	25.5
32	Missouri	25.3
32	Texas	25.3
34	Kansas	25.0
35	Delaware	24.9
36	Arkansas	24.8
37	Nebraska	24.7
38	Florida	24.6
38	South Carolina	24.6
40	Georgia	23.7
41	South Dakota	23.5
42	Iowa	22.9
43	Oklahoma	22.5
44	North Carolina	22.2
45	Mississippi	20.9
46	Louisiana	20.7
47	Alabama	20.3
48	West Virginia	17.6
49	Tennessee	17.4
50	Kentucky	16.8
	District of Columbia	31.5

Source: U.S. Department of Health and Human Services, Centers for Disease Control and Prevention
    "2005 Behavioral Risk Factor Surveillance Summary Prevalence Data" (http://apps.nccd.cdc.gov/brfss/)
*Persons 18 and older.   Activity that caused large increases in breathing or heart rate at least 20 minutes three or more times per week (such as running, aerobics or heavy yard work).

Percent of Adults Who are Disabled: 2005

National Median = 18.6%*

ALPHA ORDER

RANK	STATE	PERCENT
3	Alabama	22.4
17	Alaska	19.3
16	Arizona	19.4
8	Arkansas	21.0
33	California	17.5
44	Colorado	16.2
46	Connecticut	15.2
36	Delaware	17.2
23	Florida	19.0
23	Georgia	19.0
49	Hawaii	14.7
10	Idaho	20.5
50	Illinois	13.9
36	Indiana	17.2
40	Iowa	16.9
29	Kansas	18.2
2	Kentucky	22.6
26	Louisiana	18.6
15	Maine	19.5
45	Maryland	15.7
42	Massachusetts	16.8
14	Michigan	19.8
10	Minnesota	20.5
6	Mississippi	22.1
9	Missouri	20.9
10	Montana	20.5
34	Nebraska	17.3
17	Nevada	19.3
34	New Hampshire	17.3
47	New Jersey	15.1
17	New Mexico	19.3
36	New York	17.2
30	North Carolina	17.8
48	North Dakota	14.8
30	Ohio	17.8
5	Oklahoma	22.2
3	Oregon	22.4
27	Pennsylvania	18.4
40	Rhode Island	16.9
20	South Carolina	19.2
23	South Dakota	19.0
13	Tennessee	20.1
42	Texas	16.8
20	Utah	19.2
20	Vermont	19.2
32	Virginia	17.6
7	Washington	21.8
1	West Virginia	27.4
36	Wisconsin	17.2
27	Wyoming	18.4

RANK ORDER

RANK	STATE	PERCENT
1	West Virginia	27.4
2	Kentucky	22.6
3	Alabama	22.4
3	Oregon	22.4
5	Oklahoma	22.2
6	Mississippi	22.1
7	Washington	21.8
8	Arkansas	21.0
9	Missouri	20.9
10	Idaho	20.5
10	Minnesota	20.5
10	Montana	20.5
13	Tennessee	20.1
14	Michigan	19.8
15	Maine	19.5
16	Arizona	19.4
17	Alaska	19.3
17	Nevada	19.3
17	New Mexico	19.3
20	South Carolina	19.2
20	Utah	19.2
20	Vermont	19.2
23	Florida	19.0
23	Georgia	19.0
23	South Dakota	19.0
26	Louisiana	18.6
27	Pennsylvania	18.4
27	Wyoming	18.4
29	Kansas	18.2
30	North Carolina	17.8
30	Ohio	17.8
32	Virginia	17.6
33	California	17.5
34	Nebraska	17.3
34	New Hampshire	17.3
36	Delaware	17.2
36	Indiana	17.2
36	New York	17.2
36	Wisconsin	17.2
40	Iowa	16.9
40	Rhode Island	16.9
42	Massachusetts	16.8
42	Texas	16.8
44	Colorado	16.2
45	Maryland	15.7
46	Connecticut	15.2
47	New Jersey	15.1
48	North Dakota	14.8
49	Hawaii	14.7
50	Illinois	13.9

District of Columbia	13.7

Source: U.S. Department of Health and Human Services, Centers for Disease Control and Prevention
"2005 Behavioral Risk Factor Surveillance Summary Prevalence Data" (http://apps.nccd.cdc.gov/brfss/)
*Persons 18 and older. Adults who are limited in any activities because of physical, mental or emotional problems.

Percent of Adults with High Blood Pressure: 2005

National Median = 25.5% of Adults*

ALPHA ORDER

RANK	STATE	PERCENT
4	Alabama	31.2
48	Alaska	21.5
46	Arizona	22.3
9	Arkansas	29.0
22	California	25.7
49	Colorado	20.1
38	Connecticut	23.8
11	Delaware	28.0
13	Florida	27.7
18	Georgia	26.5
33	Hawaii	24.2
40	Idaho	23.6
24	Illinois	25.5
20	Indiana	26.2
30	Iowa	24.5
33	Kansas	24.2
10	Kentucky	28.2
7	Louisiana	29.4
23	Maine	25.6
21	Maryland	26.0
29	Massachusetts	24.8
12	Michigan	27.8
47	Minnesota	21.9
1	Mississippi	33.3
14	Missouri	27.3
37	Montana	24.0
30	Nebraska	24.5
35	Nevada	24.1
42	New Hampshire	23.3
26	New Jersey	25.4
45	New Mexico	22.8
24	New York	25.5
8	North Carolina	29.2
42	North Dakota	23.3
16	Ohio	27.0
6	Oklahoma	29.8
40	Oregon	23.6
15	Pennsylvania	27.2
19	Rhode Island	26.3
2	South Carolina	31.4
27	South Dakota	25.1
5	Tennessee	30.2
32	Texas	24.3
50	Utah	18.4
39	Vermont	23.7
17	Virginia	26.8
35	Washington	24.1
2	West Virginia	31.4
28	Wisconsin	25.0
42	Wyoming	23.3

RANK ORDER

RANK	STATE	PERCENT
1	Mississippi	33.3
2	South Carolina	31.4
2	West Virginia	31.4
4	Alabama	31.2
5	Tennessee	30.2
6	Oklahoma	29.8
7	Louisiana	29.4
8	North Carolina	29.2
9	Arkansas	29.0
10	Kentucky	28.2
11	Delaware	28.0
12	Michigan	27.8
13	Florida	27.7
14	Missouri	27.3
15	Pennsylvania	27.2
16	Ohio	27.0
17	Virginia	26.8
18	Georgia	26.5
19	Rhode Island	26.3
20	Indiana	26.2
21	Maryland	26.0
22	California	25.7
23	Maine	25.6
24	Illinois	25.5
24	New York	25.5
26	New Jersey	25.4
27	South Dakota	25.1
28	Wisconsin	25.0
29	Massachusetts	24.8
30	Iowa	24.5
30	Nebraska	24.5
32	Texas	24.3
33	Hawaii	24.2
33	Kansas	24.2
35	Nevada	24.1
35	Washington	24.1
37	Montana	24.0
38	Connecticut	23.8
39	Vermont	23.7
40	Idaho	23.6
40	Oregon	23.6
42	New Hampshire	23.3
42	North Dakota	23.3
42	Wyoming	23.3
45	New Mexico	22.8
46	Arizona	22.3
47	Minnesota	21.9
48	Alaska	21.5
49	Colorado	20.1
50	Utah	18.4
	District of Columbia	27.1

Source: U.S. Department of Health and Human Services, Centers for Disease Control and Prevention
   "2005 Behavioral Risk Factor Surveillance Summary Prevalence Data" (http://apps.nccd.cdc.gov/brfss/)
*Persons 18 and older who have been told by a doctor, nurse or other health professional that they have high blood pressure.

Percent of Adults with High Cholesterol: 2005

National Median = 35.6% of Adults*

ALPHA ORDER

RANK	STATE	PERCENT
7	Alabama	38.3
46	Alaska	32.8
37	Arizona	33.8
12	Arkansas	37.5
30	California	35.2
44	Colorado	33.1
37	Connecticut	33.8
4	Delaware	38.9
2	Florida	39.7
48	Georgia	32.3
33	Hawaii	34.6
19	Idaho	36.3
21	Illinois	36.2
9	Indiana	38.0
26	Iowa	35.6
40	Kansas	33.4
8	Kentucky	38.1
50	Louisiana	30.3
21	Maine	36.2
43	Maryland	33.2
25	Massachusetts	35.7
4	Michigan	38.9
47	Minnesota	32.6
11	Mississippi	37.6
6	Missouri	38.7
40	Montana	33.4
30	Nebraska	35.2
3	Nevada	39.2
29	New Hampshire	35.3
17	New Jersey	36.7
49	New Mexico	30.6
27	New York	35.5
19	North Carolina	36.3
32	North Dakota	35.0
13	Ohio	37.2
10	Oklahoma	37.8
24	Oregon	35.8
16	Pennsylvania	37.0
33	Rhode Island	34.6
13	South Carolina	37.2
35	South Dakota	34.0
45	Tennessee	32.9
35	Texas	34.0
42	Utah	33.3
39	Vermont	33.7
15	Virginia	37.1
17	Washington	36.7
1	West Virginia	39.9
27	Wisconsin	35.5
23	Wyoming	35.9

RANK ORDER

RANK	STATE	PERCENT
1	West Virginia	39.9
2	Florida	39.7
3	Nevada	39.2
4	Delaware	38.9
4	Michigan	38.9
6	Missouri	38.7
7	Alabama	38.3
8	Kentucky	38.1
9	Indiana	38.0
10	Oklahoma	37.8
11	Mississippi	37.6
12	Arkansas	37.5
13	Ohio	37.2
13	South Carolina	37.2
15	Virginia	37.1
16	Pennsylvania	37.0
17	New Jersey	36.7
17	Washington	36.7
19	Idaho	36.3
19	North Carolina	36.3
21	Illinois	36.2
21	Maine	36.2
23	Wyoming	35.9
24	Oregon	35.8
25	Massachusetts	35.7
26	Iowa	35.6
27	New York	35.5
27	Wisconsin	35.5
29	New Hampshire	35.3
30	California	35.2
30	Nebraska	35.2
32	North Dakota	35.0
33	Hawaii	34.6
33	Rhode Island	34.6
35	South Dakota	34.0
35	Texas	34.0
37	Arizona	33.8
37	Connecticut	33.8
39	Vermont	33.7
40	Kansas	33.4
40	Montana	33.4
42	Utah	33.3
43	Maryland	33.2
44	Colorado	33.1
45	Tennessee	32.9
46	Alaska	32.8
47	Minnesota	32.6
48	Georgia	32.3
49	New Mexico	30.6
50	Louisiana	30.3

District of Columbia	31.5

Source: U.S. Department of Health and Human Services, Centers for Disease Control and Prevention
"2005 Behavioral Risk Factor Surveillance Summary Prevalence Data" (http://apps.nccd.cdc.gov/brfss/)
*Persons 18 and older who have had their cholesterol checked and have been told that they have high blood cholesterol.

Percent of Adults Who Have Visited a Dentist or Dental Clinic: 2004

National Median = 70.2%*

ALPHA ORDER

RANK	STATE	PERCENT
31	Alabama	69.2
27	Alaska	69.6
33	Arizona	68.5
48	Arkansas	60.8
25	California	70.4
18	Colorado	72.2
1	Connecticut	80.6
7	Delaware	77.1
35	Florida	68.2
37	Georgia	68.1
NA	Hawaii**	NA
40	Idaho	67.7
16	Illinois	72.6
41	Indiana	66.5
12	Iowa	75.0
13	Kansas	74.5
23	Kentucky	71.2
35	Louisiana	68.2
28	Maine	69.5
9	Maryland	75.8
3	Massachusetts	79.4
8	Michigan	76.8
2	Minnesota	79.7
49	Mississippi	59.4
44	Missouri	63.9
42	Montana	65.8
11	Nebraska	75.2
43	Nevada	64.4
5	New Hampshire	77.5
10	New Jersey	75.7
39	New Mexico	67.9
21	New York	71.7
30	North Carolina	69.4
28	North Dakota	69.5
19	Ohio	72.1
46	Oklahoma	61.3
33	Oregon	68.5
26	Pennsylvania	69.8
4	Rhode Island	78.5
32	South Carolina	68.6
20	South Dakota	72.0
22	Tennessee	71.5
47	Texas	61.2
17	Utah	72.3
14	Vermont	74.2
15	Virginia	73.5
24	Washington	71.0
45	West Virginia	62.5
5	Wisconsin	77.5
37	Wyoming	68.1

RANK ORDER

RANK	STATE	PERCENT
1	Connecticut	80.6
2	Minnesota	79.7
3	Massachusetts	79.4
4	Rhode Island	78.5
5	New Hampshire	77.5
5	Wisconsin	77.5
7	Delaware	77.1
8	Michigan	76.8
9	Maryland	75.8
10	New Jersey	75.7
11	Nebraska	75.2
12	Iowa	75.0
13	Kansas	74.5
14	Vermont	74.2
15	Virginia	73.5
16	Illinois	72.6
17	Utah	72.3
18	Colorado	72.2
19	Ohio	72.1
20	South Dakota	72.0
21	New York	71.7
22	Tennessee	71.5
23	Kentucky	71.2
24	Washington	71.0
25	California	70.4
26	Pennsylvania	69.8
27	Alaska	69.6
28	Maine	69.5
28	North Dakota	69.5
30	North Carolina	69.4
31	Alabama	69.2
32	South Carolina	68.6
33	Arizona	68.5
33	Oregon	68.5
35	Florida	68.2
35	Louisiana	68.2
37	Georgia	68.1
37	Wyoming	68.1
39	New Mexico	67.9
40	Idaho	67.7
41	Indiana	66.5
42	Montana	65.8
43	Nevada	64.4
44	Missouri	63.9
45	West Virginia	62.5
46	Oklahoma	61.3
47	Texas	61.2
48	Arkansas	60.8
49	Mississippi	59.4
NA	Hawaii**	NA

District of Columbia		72.1

Source: U.S. Department of Health and Human Services, Centers for Disease Control and Prevention
"2004 Behavioral Risk Factor Surveillance Summary Prevalence Data" (http://apps.nccd.cdc.gov/brfss/)
*Persons 18 and older who have visited a dentist within the past year for any reason.
**Not available.

Percent of Adults 65 Years Old and Older
Who Have Lost All Their Natural Teeth: 2004
National Median = 21.2%*

ALPHA ORDER

RANK	STATE	PERCENT
4	Alabama	31.9
20	Alaska	23.0
45	Arizona	14.9
15	Arkansas	24.6
47	California	13.7
35	Colorado	18.0
49	Connecticut	12.4
26	Delaware	21.1
32	Florida	18.7
9	Georgia	28.2
NA	Hawaii**	NA
21	Idaho	22.4
32	Illinois	18.7
11	Indiana	27.3
18	Iowa	23.2
10	Kansas	27.8
2	Kentucky	38.1
5	Louisiana	31.3
16	Maine	24.2
41	Maryland	16.6
43	Massachusetts	16.4
37	Michigan	17.1
46	Minnesota	14.3
7	Mississippi	29.5
13	Missouri	25.2
29	Montana	19.6
19	Nebraska	23.1
42	Nevada	16.5
27	New Hampshire	21.0
38	New Jersey	16.9
22	New Mexico	21.8
39	New York	16.8
8	North Carolina	28.3
14	North Dakota	24.9
28	Ohio	20.4
6	Oklahoma	31.1
36	Oregon	17.7
17	Pennsylvania	23.7
34	Rhode Island	18.4
22	South Carolina	21.8
12	South Dakota	26.1
3	Tennessee	32.2
39	Texas	16.8
48	Utah	13.5
25	Vermont	21.2
31	Virginia	19.3
44	Washington	16.1
1	West Virginia	42.8
29	Wisconsin	19.6
22	Wyoming	21.8

RANK ORDER

RANK	STATE	PERCENT
1	West Virginia	42.8
2	Kentucky	38.1
3	Tennessee	32.2
4	Alabama	31.9
5	Louisiana	31.3
6	Oklahoma	31.1
7	Mississippi	29.5
8	North Carolina	28.3
9	Georgia	28.2
10	Kansas	27.8
11	Indiana	27.3
12	South Dakota	26.1
13	Missouri	25.2
14	North Dakota	24.9
15	Arkansas	24.6
16	Maine	24.2
17	Pennsylvania	23.7
18	Iowa	23.2
19	Nebraska	23.1
20	Alaska	23.0
21	Idaho	22.4
22	New Mexico	21.8
22	South Carolina	21.8
22	Wyoming	21.8
25	Vermont	21.2
26	Delaware	21.1
27	New Hampshire	21.0
28	Ohio	20.4
29	Montana	19.6
29	Wisconsin	19.6
31	Virginia	19.3
32	Florida	18.7
32	Illinois	18.7
34	Rhode Island	18.4
35	Colorado	18.0
36	Oregon	17.7
37	Michigan	17.1
38	New Jersey	16.9
39	New York	16.8
39	Texas	16.8
41	Maryland	16.6
42	Nevada	16.5
43	Massachusetts	16.4
44	Washington	16.1
45	Arizona	14.9
46	Minnesota	14.3
47	California	13.7
48	Utah	13.5
49	Connecticut	12.4
NA	Hawaii**	NA
	District of Columbia	19.3

Source: U.S. Department of Health and Human Services, Centers for Disease Control and Prevention
   "2004 Behavioral Risk Factor Surveillance Summary Prevalence Data" (http://apps.nccd.cdc.gov/brfss/)
Those who have had all their natural teeth extracted.
**Not available.*

Percent of Adults Who Average Five or More Servings of Fruits and Vegetables Each Day: 2005
National Median = 23.2%*

ALPHA ORDER

RANK	STATE	PERCENT
44	Alabama	20.1
16	Alaska	24.8
23	Arizona	23.7
40	Arkansas	21.0
3	California	28.9
18	Colorado	24.5
7	Connecticut	27.4
38	Delaware	21.3
10	Florida	26.2
24	Georgia	23.2
18	Hawaii	24.5
24	Idaho	23.2
21	Illinois	24.0
34	Indiana	22.0
47	Iowa	19.5
46	Kansas	19.9
48	Kentucky	16.8
42	Louisiana	20.2
4	Maine	28.7
4	Maryland	28.7
6	Massachusetts	28.6
26	Michigan	22.8
18	Minnesota	24.5
49	Mississippi	16.5
27	Missouri	22.6
17	Montana	24.7
42	Nebraska	20.2
30	Nevada	22.5
2	New Hampshire	29.1
13	New Jersey	25.9
37	New Mexico	21.5
12	New York	26.0
30	North Carolina	22.5
35	North Dakota	21.8
27	Ohio	22.6
50	Oklahoma	15.7
13	Oregon	25.9
22	Pennsylvania	23.9
8	Rhode Island	26.8
39	South Carolina	21.2
41	South Dakota	20.5
9	Tennessee	26.5
27	Texas	22.6
33	Utah	22.1
1	Vermont	30.8
10	Virginia	26.2
15	Washington	25.2
45	West Virginia	20.0
32	Wisconsin	22.2
35	Wyoming	21.8

RANK ORDER

RANK	STATE	PERCENT
1	Vermont	30.8
2	New Hampshire	29.1
3	California	28.9
4	Maine	28.7
4	Maryland	28.7
6	Massachusetts	28.6
7	Connecticut	27.4
8	Rhode Island	26.8
9	Tennessee	26.5
10	Florida	26.2
10	Virginia	26.2
12	New York	26.0
13	New Jersey	25.9
13	Oregon	25.9
15	Washington	25.2
16	Alaska	24.8
17	Montana	24.7
18	Colorado	24.5
18	Hawaii	24.5
18	Minnesota	24.5
21	Illinois	24.0
22	Pennsylvania	23.9
23	Arizona	23.7
24	Georgia	23.2
24	Idaho	23.2
26	Michigan	22.8
27	Missouri	22.6
27	Ohio	22.6
27	Texas	22.6
30	Nevada	22.5
30	North Carolina	22.5
32	Wisconsin	22.2
33	Utah	22.1
34	Indiana	22.0
35	North Dakota	21.8
35	Wyoming	21.8
37	New Mexico	21.5
38	Delaware	21.3
39	South Carolina	21.2
40	Arkansas	21.0
41	South Dakota	20.5
42	Louisiana	20.2
42	Nebraska	20.2
44	Alabama	20.1
45	West Virginia	20.0
46	Kansas	19.9
47	Iowa	19.5
48	Kentucky	16.8
49	Mississippi	16.5
50	Oklahoma	15.7

	District of Columbia	32.3

Source: U.S. Department of Health and Human Services, Centers for Disease Control and Prevention
"2005 Behavioral Risk Factor Surveillance Summary Prevalence Data" (http://apps.nccd.cdc.gov/brfss/)
*Persons 18 and older.

Percent of Adults Rating Their Health as Fair or Poor in 2005

National Median = 14.8% of Adults*

ALPHA ORDER

RANK	STATE	PERCENT
6	Alabama	21.0
40	Alaska	12.8
23	Arizona	15.5
4	Arkansas	21.6
13	California	17.6
42	Colorado	12.7
43	Connecticut	12.2
37	Delaware	13.0
12	Florida	17.7
18	Georgia	16.7
30	Hawaii	13.6
25	Idaho	14.9
22	Illinois	15.7
18	Indiana	16.7
43	Iowa	12.2
36	Kansas	13.1
2	Kentucky	23.7
5	Louisiana	21.2
27	Maine	14.7
47	Maryland	11.9
34	Massachusetts	13.2
24	Michigan	15.1
49	Minnesota	11.3
3	Mississippi	23.6
13	Missouri	17.6
29	Montana	14.4
32	Nebraska	13.3
15	Nevada	17.2
50	New Hampshire	11.1
20	New Jersey	16.6
11	New Mexico	17.9
17	New York	16.9
10	North Carolina	18.6
46	North Dakota	12.0
26	Ohio	14.8
9	Oklahoma	18.7
21	Oregon	16.1
28	Pennsylvania	14.6
34	Rhode Island	13.2
15	South Carolina	17.2
40	South Dakota	12.8
8	Tennessee	19.5
7	Texas	19.8
37	Utah	13.0
48	Vermont	11.5
32	Virginia	13.3
31	Washington	13.4
1	West Virginia	24.7
45	Wisconsin	12.1
37	Wyoming	13.0

RANK ORDER

RANK	STATE	PERCENT
1	West Virginia	24.7
2	Kentucky	23.7
3	Mississippi	23.6
4	Arkansas	21.6
5	Louisiana	21.2
6	Alabama	21.0
7	Texas	19.8
8	Tennessee	19.5
9	Oklahoma	18.7
10	North Carolina	18.6
11	New Mexico	17.9
12	Florida	17.7
13	California	17.6
13	Missouri	17.6
15	Nevada	17.2
15	South Carolina	17.2
17	New York	16.9
18	Georgia	16.7
18	Indiana	16.7
20	New Jersey	16.6
21	Oregon	16.1
22	Illinois	15.7
23	Arizona	15.5
24	Michigan	15.1
25	Idaho	14.9
26	Ohio	14.8
27	Maine	14.7
28	Pennsylvania	14.6
29	Montana	14.4
30	Hawaii	13.6
31	Washington	13.4
32	Nebraska	13.3
32	Virginia	13.3
34	Massachusetts	13.2
34	Rhode Island	13.2
36	Kansas	13.1
37	Delaware	13.0
37	Utah	13.0
37	Wyoming	13.0
40	Alaska	12.8
40	South Dakota	12.8
42	Colorado	12.7
43	Connecticut	12.2
43	Iowa	12.2
45	Wisconsin	12.1
46	North Dakota	12.0
47	Maryland	11.9
48	Vermont	11.5
49	Minnesota	11.3
50	New Hampshire	11.1

District of Columbia	12.5

Source: U.S. Department of Health and Human Services, Centers for Disease Control and Prevention
"2005 Behavioral Risk Factor Surveillance Summary Prevalence Data" (http://apps.nccd.cdc.gov/brfss/)
*Persons 18 and older.

Safety Belt Usage Rate in 2006

National Rate = 81.0% Use Safety Belts*

ALPHA ORDER				RANK ORDER		
RANK	STATE	PERCENT		RANK	STATE	PERCENT
20	Alabama	82.9		1	Washington	96.3
18	Alaska	83.2		2	Michigan	94.3
NA	Arizona**	NA		3	Oregon	94.1
38	Arkansas	69.3		4	California	93.4
4	California	93.4		5	Hawaii	92.5
23	Colorado	80.3		6	Texas	90.4
16	Connecticut	83.5		7	New Jersey	90.0
13	Delaware	86.1		8	Iowa	89.6
NA	Florida**	NA		8	New Mexico	89.6
NA	Georgia**	NA		10	Utah	88.6
5	Hawaii	92.5		11	North Carolina	88.5
24	Idaho	79.8		12	Illinois	87.8
12	Illinois	87.8		13	Delaware	86.1
14	Indiana	84.3		14	Indiana	84.3
8	Iowa	89.6		15	Oklahoma	83.7
35	Kansas	73.5		16	Connecticut	83.5
39	Kentucky	67.2		17	Minnesota	83.3
33	Louisiana	74.8		18	Alaska	83.2
29	Maine	77.2		19	New York	83.0
NA	Maryland**	NA		20	Alabama	82.9
40	Massachusetts	66.9		21	Vermont	82.4
2	Michigan	94.3		22	Ohio	81.7
17	Minnesota	83.3		23	Colorado	80.3
34	Mississippi	73.6		24	Idaho	79.8
32	Missouri	75.2		25	Montana	79.0
25	Montana	79.0		25	North Dakota	79.0
30	Nebraska	76.0		27	Virginia	78.7
NA	Nevada**	NA		28	Tennessee	78.6
NA	New Hampshire**	NA		29	Maine	77.2
7	New Jersey	90.0		30	Nebraska	76.0
8	New Mexico	89.6		31	Wisconsin	75.4
19	New York	83.0		32	Missouri	75.2
11	North Carolina	88.5		33	Louisiana	74.8
25	North Dakota	79.0		34	Mississippi	73.6
22	Ohio	81.7		35	Kansas	73.5
15	Oklahoma	83.7		36	South Carolina	72.5
3	Oregon	94.1		37	South Dakota	71.3
NA	Pennsylvania**	NA		38	Arkansas	69.3
NA	Rhode Island**	NA		39	Kentucky	67.2
36	South Carolina	72.5		40	Massachusetts	66.9
37	South Dakota	71.3		41	Wyoming	63.5
28	Tennessee	78.6		NA	Arizona**	NA
6	Texas	90.4		NA	Florida**	NA
10	Utah	88.6		NA	Georgia**	NA
21	Vermont	82.4		NA	Maryland**	NA
27	Virginia	78.7		NA	Nevada**	NA
1	Washington	96.3		NA	New Hampshire**	NA
NA	West Virginia**	NA		NA	Pennsylvania**	NA
31	Wisconsin	75.4		NA	Rhode Island**	NA
41	Wyoming	63.5		NA	West Virginia**	NA
					District of Columbia	85.4

Source: U.S. Department of Transportation, National Highway Traffic Safety Administration
   "Safety Belt Use in 2006" (http://www-nrd.nhtsa.dot.gov/pdf/nrd-30/NCSA/RNotes/2007/810690.pdf)
*National estimate is from the National Occupant Protection Use Survey (NOPUS) using a different methodology.
**Not available.

VIII. APPENDIX

Population Charts

A-1   Population in 2006
A-2   Population in 2005
A-3   Male Population in 2005
A-4   Female Population in 2005

Population in 2006

National Total = 299,398,484*

ALPHA ORDER

RANK ORDER

RANK	STATE	POPULATION	% of USA
23	Alabama	4,599,030	1.5%
47	Alaska	670,053	0.2%
16	Arizona	6,166,318	2.1%
32	Arkansas	2,810,872	0.9%
1	California	36,457,549	12.2%
22	Colorado	4,753,377	1.6%
29	Connecticut	3,504,809	1.2%
45	Delaware	853,476	0.3%
4	Florida	18,089,888	6.0%
9	Georgia	9,363,941	3.1%
42	Hawaii	1,285,498	0.4%
39	Idaho	1,466,465	0.5%
5	Illinois	12,831,970	4.3%
15	Indiana	6,313,520	2.1%
30	Iowa	2,982,085	1.0%
33	Kansas	2,764,075	0.9%
26	Kentucky	4,206,074	1.4%
25	Louisiana	4,287,768	1.4%
40	Maine	1,321,574	0.4%
19	Maryland	5,615,727	1.9%
13	Massachusetts	6,437,193	2.2%
8	Michigan	10,095,643	3.4%
21	Minnesota	5,167,101	1.7%
31	Mississippi	2,910,540	1.0%
18	Missouri	5,842,713	2.0%
44	Montana	944,632	0.3%
38	Nebraska	1,768,331	0.6%
35	Nevada	2,495,529	0.8%
41	New Hampshire	1,314,895	0.4%
11	New Jersey	8,724,560	2.9%
36	New Mexico	1,954,599	0.7%
3	New York	19,306,183	6.4%
10	North Carolina	8,856,505	3.0%
48	North Dakota	635,867	0.2%
7	Ohio	11,478,006	3.8%
28	Oklahoma	3,579,212	1.2%
27	Oregon	3,700,758	1.2%
6	Pennsylvania	12,440,621	4.2%
43	Rhode Island	1,067,610	0.4%
24	South Carolina	4,321,249	1.4%
46	South Dakota	781,919	0.3%
17	Tennessee	6,038,803	2.0%
2	Texas	23,507,783	7.9%
34	Utah	2,550,063	0.9%
49	Vermont	623,908	0.2%
12	Virginia	7,642,884	2.6%
14	Washington	6,395,798	2.1%
37	West Virginia	1,818,470	0.6%
20	Wisconsin	5,556,506	1.9%
50	Wyoming	515,004	0.2%

RANK	STATE	POPULATION	% of USA
1	California	36,457,549	12.2%
2	Texas	23,507,783	7.9%
3	New York	19,306,183	6.4%
4	Florida	18,089,888	6.0%
5	Illinois	12,831,970	4.3%
6	Pennsylvania	12,440,621	4.2%
7	Ohio	11,478,006	3.8%
8	Michigan	10,095,643	3.4%
9	Georgia	9,363,941	3.1%
10	North Carolina	8,856,505	3.0%
11	New Jersey	8,724,560	2.9%
12	Virginia	7,642,884	2.6%
13	Massachusetts	6,437,193	2.2%
14	Washington	6,395,798	2.1%
15	Indiana	6,313,520	2.1%
16	Arizona	6,166,318	2.1%
17	Tennessee	6,038,803	2.0%
18	Missouri	5,842,713	2.0%
19	Maryland	5,615,727	1.9%
20	Wisconsin	5,556,506	1.9%
21	Minnesota	5,167,101	1.7%
22	Colorado	4,753,377	1.6%
23	Alabama	4,599,030	1.5%
24	South Carolina	4,321,249	1.4%
25	Louisiana	4,287,768	1.4%
26	Kentucky	4,206,074	1.4%
27	Oregon	3,700,758	1.2%
28	Oklahoma	3,579,212	1.2%
29	Connecticut	3,504,809	1.2%
30	Iowa	2,982,085	1.0%
31	Mississippi	2,910,540	1.0%
32	Arkansas	2,810,872	0.9%
33	Kansas	2,764,075	0.9%
34	Utah	2,550,063	0.9%
35	Nevada	2,495,529	0.8%
36	New Mexico	1,954,599	0.7%
37	West Virginia	1,818,470	0.6%
38	Nebraska	1,768,331	0.6%
39	Idaho	1,466,465	0.5%
40	Maine	1,321,574	0.4%
41	New Hampshire	1,314,895	0.4%
42	Hawaii	1,285,498	0.4%
43	Rhode Island	1,067,610	0.4%
44	Montana	944,632	0.3%
45	Delaware	853,476	0.3%
46	South Dakota	781,919	0.3%
47	Alaska	670,053	0.2%
48	North Dakota	635,867	0.2%
49	Vermont	623,908	0.2%
50	Wyoming	515,004	0.2%
	District of Columbia	581,530	0.2%

Source: U.S. Bureau of the Census
    "Population Estimates" (December 22, 2006, http://www.census.gov/popest/estimates.php)
*Resident population.

Population in 2005

National Total = 296,507,061*

ALPHA ORDER

RANK	STATE	POPULATION	% of USA
23	Alabama	4,548,327	1.5%
47	Alaska	663,253	0.2%
17	Arizona	5,953,007	2.0%
32	Arkansas	2,775,708	0.9%
1	California	36,154,147	12.2%
22	Colorado	4,663,295	1.6%
29	Connecticut	3,500,701	1.2%
45	Delaware	841,741	0.3%
4	Florida	17,768,191	6.0%
9	Georgia	9,132,553	3.1%
42	Hawaii	1,273,278	0.4%
39	Idaho	1,429,367	0.5%
5	Illinois	12,765,427	4.3%
15	Indiana	6,266,019	2.1%
30	Iowa	2,965,524	1.0%
33	Kansas	2,748,172	0.9%
26	Kentucky	4,172,608	1.4%
24	Louisiana	4,507,331	1.5%
40	Maine	1,318,220	0.4%
19	Maryland	5,589,599	1.9%
13	Massachusetts	6,433,367	2.2%
8	Michigan	10,100,833	3.4%
21	Minnesota	5,126,739	1.7%
31	Mississippi	2,908,496	1.0%
18	Missouri	5,797,703	2.0%
44	Montana	934,737	0.3%
38	Nebraska	1,758,163	0.6%
35	Nevada	2,412,301	0.8%
41	New Hampshire	1,306,819	0.4%
10	New Jersey	8,703,150	2.9%
36	New Mexico	1,925,985	0.6%
3	New York	19,315,721	6.5%
11	North Carolina	8,672,459	2.9%
48	North Dakota	634,605	0.2%
7	Ohio	11,470,685	3.9%
28	Oklahoma	3,543,442	1.2%
27	Oregon	3,638,871	1.2%
6	Pennsylvania	12,405,348	4.2%
43	Rhode Island	1,073,579	0.4%
25	South Carolina	4,246,933	1.4%
46	South Dakota	774,883	0.3%
16	Tennessee	5,955,745	2.0%
2	Texas	22,928,508	7.7%
34	Utah	2,490,334	0.8%
49	Vermont	622,387	0.2%
12	Virginia	7,564,327	2.6%
14	Washington	6,291,899	2.1%
37	West Virginia	1,814,083	0.6%
20	Wisconsin	5,527,644	1.9%
50	Wyoming	508,798	0.2%

RANK ORDER

RANK	STATE	POPULATION	% of USA
1	California	36,154,147	12.2%
2	Texas	22,928,508	7.7%
3	New York	19,315,721	6.5%
4	Florida	17,768,191	6.0%
5	Illinois	12,765,427	4.3%
6	Pennsylvania	12,405,348	4.2%
7	Ohio	11,470,685	3.9%
8	Michigan	10,100,833	3.4%
9	Georgia	9,132,553	3.1%
10	New Jersey	8,703,150	2.9%
11	North Carolina	8,672,459	2.9%
12	Virginia	7,564,327	2.6%
13	Massachusetts	6,433,367	2.2%
14	Washington	6,291,899	2.1%
15	Indiana	6,266,019	2.1%
16	Tennessee	5,955,745	2.0%
17	Arizona	5,953,007	2.0%
18	Missouri	5,797,703	2.0%
19	Maryland	5,589,599	1.9%
20	Wisconsin	5,527,644	1.9%
21	Minnesota	5,126,739	1.7%
22	Colorado	4,663,295	1.6%
23	Alabama	4,548,327	1.5%
24	Louisiana	4,507,331	1.5%
25	South Carolina	4,246,933	1.4%
26	Kentucky	4,172,608	1.4%
27	Oregon	3,638,871	1.2%
28	Oklahoma	3,543,442	1.2%
29	Connecticut	3,500,701	1.2%
30	Iowa	2,965,524	1.0%
31	Mississippi	2,908,496	1.0%
32	Arkansas	2,775,708	0.9%
33	Kansas	2,748,172	0.9%
34	Utah	2,490,334	0.8%
35	Nevada	2,412,301	0.8%
36	New Mexico	1,925,985	0.6%
37	West Virginia	1,814,083	0.6%
38	Nebraska	1,758,163	0.6%
39	Idaho	1,429,367	0.5%
40	Maine	1,318,220	0.4%
41	New Hampshire	1,306,819	0.4%
42	Hawaii	1,273,278	0.4%
43	Rhode Island	1,073,579	0.4%
44	Montana	934,737	0.3%
45	Delaware	841,741	0.3%
46	South Dakota	774,883	0.3%
47	Alaska	663,253	0.2%
48	North Dakota	634,605	0.2%
49	Vermont	622,387	0.2%
50	Wyoming	508,798	0.2%
	District of Columbia	582,049	0.2%

Source: U.S. Bureau of the Census
"Population Estimates" (December 22, 2006, http://www.census.gov/popest/estimates.php)
Resident population. Revised estimates.

Male Population in 2005

National Total = 145,999,746 Males

ALPHA ORDER

RANK	STATE	MALES	% of USA
23	Alabama	2,211,662	1.5%
47	Alaska	343,182	0.2%
16	Arizona	2,973,074	2.0%
33	Arkansas	1,362,963	0.9%
1	California	18,045,453	12.4%
22	Colorado	2,355,606	1.6%
29	Connecticut	1,705,031	1.2%
45	Delaware	411,306	0.3%
4	Florida	8,724,726	6.0%
9	Georgia	4,487,546	3.1%
42	Hawaii	635,720	0.4%
39	Idaho	716,877	0.5%
5	Illinois	6,271,000	4.3%
15	Indiana	3,088,305	2.1%
30	Iowa	1,460,749	1.0%
32	Kansas	1,363,613	0.9%
26	Kentucky	2,050,124	1.4%
24	Louisiana	2,199,721	1.5%
41	Maine	645,593	0.4%
20	Maryland	2,713,312	1.9%
14	Massachusetts	3,101,020	2.1%
8	Michigan	4,975,717	3.4%
21	Minnesota	2,548,392	1.7%
31	Mississippi	1,418,613	1.0%
18	Missouri	2,836,099	1.9%
44	Montana	466,908	0.3%
38	Nebraska	869,754	0.6%
35	Nevada	1,229,376	0.8%
40	New Hampshire	645,711	0.4%
11	New Jersey	4,248,897	2.9%
36	New Mexico	948,404	0.6%
3	New York	9,327,052	6.4%
10	North Carolina	4,271,569	2.9%
48	North Dakota	317,772	0.2%
7	Ohio	5,587,607	3.8%
28	Oklahoma	1,753,274	1.2%
27	Oregon	1,810,911	1.2%
6	Pennsylvania	6,030,173	4.1%
43	Rhode Island	519,847	0.4%
25	South Carolina	2,074,231	1.4%
46	South Dakota	385,620	0.3%
17	Tennessee	2,920,666	2.0%
2	Texas	11,388,179	7.8%
34	Utah	1,240,211	0.8%
49	Vermont	306,876	0.2%
12	Virginia	3,723,365	2.6%
13	Washington	3,138,979	2.1%
37	West Virginia	889,241	0.6%
19	Wisconsin	2,741,855	1.9%
50	Wyoming	256,726	0.2%

RANK ORDER

RANK	STATE	MALES	% of USA
1	California	18,045,453	12.4%
2	Texas	11,388,179	7.8%
3	New York	9,327,052	6.4%
4	Florida	8,724,726	6.0%
5	Illinois	6,271,000	4.3%
6	Pennsylvania	6,030,173	4.1%
7	Ohio	5,587,607	3.8%
8	Michigan	4,975,717	3.4%
9	Georgia	4,487,546	3.1%
10	North Carolina	4,271,569	2.9%
11	New Jersey	4,248,897	2.9%
12	Virginia	3,723,365	2.6%
13	Washington	3,138,979	2.1%
14	Massachusetts	3,101,020	2.1%
15	Indiana	3,088,305	2.1%
16	Arizona	2,973,074	2.0%
17	Tennessee	2,920,666	2.0%
18	Missouri	2,836,099	1.9%
19	Wisconsin	2,741,855	1.9%
20	Maryland	2,713,312	1.9%
21	Minnesota	2,548,392	1.7%
22	Colorado	2,355,606	1.6%
23	Alabama	2,211,662	1.5%
24	Louisiana	2,199,721	1.5%
25	South Carolina	2,074,231	1.4%
26	Kentucky	2,050,124	1.4%
27	Oregon	1,810,911	1.2%
28	Oklahoma	1,753,274	1.2%
29	Connecticut	1,705,031	1.2%
30	Iowa	1,460,749	1.0%
31	Mississippi	1,418,613	1.0%
32	Kansas	1,363,613	0.9%
33	Arkansas	1,362,963	0.9%
34	Utah	1,240,211	0.8%
35	Nevada	1,229,376	0.8%
36	New Mexico	948,404	0.6%
37	West Virginia	889,241	0.6%
38	Nebraska	869,754	0.6%
39	Idaho	716,877	0.5%
40	New Hampshire	645,711	0.4%
41	Maine	645,593	0.4%
42	Hawaii	635,720	0.4%
43	Rhode Island	519,847	0.4%
44	Montana	466,908	0.3%
45	Delaware	411,306	0.3%
46	South Dakota	385,620	0.3%
47	Alaska	343,182	0.2%
48	North Dakota	317,772	0.2%
49	Vermont	306,876	0.2%
50	Wyoming	256,726	0.2%
	District of Columbia	261,138	0.2%

Source: Morgan Quitno Press using data from U.S. Bureau of the Census
"SC-EST2005-AGESEX_RES - State Characteristic Estimates"
(http://www.census.gov/popest/datasets.html)

Female Population in 2005

National Total = 150,410,658 Females

<table>
<tr><td colspan="4">ALPHA ORDER</td><td colspan="4">RANK ORDER</td></tr>
<tr><td>RANK</td><td>STATE</td><td>FEMALES</td><td>% of USA</td><td>RANK</td><td>STATE</td><td>FEMALES</td><td>% of USA</td></tr>
<tr><td>22</td><td>Alabama</td><td>2,346,146</td><td>1.6%</td><td>1</td><td>California</td><td>18,086,694</td><td>12.0%</td></tr>
<tr><td>47</td><td>Alaska</td><td>320,479</td><td>0.2%</td><td>2</td><td>Texas</td><td>11,471,789</td><td>7.6%</td></tr>
<tr><td>17</td><td>Arizona</td><td>2,966,218</td><td>2.0%</td><td>3</td><td>New York</td><td>9,927,578</td><td>6.6%</td></tr>
<tr><td>32</td><td>Arkansas</td><td>1,416,191</td><td>0.9%</td><td>4</td><td>Florida</td><td>9,065,138</td><td>6.0%</td></tr>
<tr><td>1</td><td>California</td><td>18,086,694</td><td>12.0%</td><td>5</td><td>Illinois</td><td>6,492,371</td><td>4.3%</td></tr>
<tr><td>24</td><td>Colorado</td><td>2,309,571</td><td>1.5%</td><td>6</td><td>Pennsylvania</td><td>6,399,443</td><td>4.3%</td></tr>
<tr><td>28</td><td>Connecticut</td><td>1,805,266</td><td>1.2%</td><td>7</td><td>Ohio</td><td>5,876,435</td><td>3.9%</td></tr>
<tr><td>45</td><td>Delaware</td><td>432,218</td><td>0.3%</td><td>8</td><td>Michigan</td><td>5,145,143</td><td>3.4%</td></tr>
<tr><td>4</td><td>Florida</td><td>9,065,138</td><td>6.0%</td><td>9</td><td>Georgia</td><td>4,585,030</td><td>3.0%</td></tr>
<tr><td>9</td><td>Georgia</td><td>4,585,030</td><td>3.0%</td><td>10</td><td>New Jersey</td><td>4,469,028</td><td>3.0%</td></tr>
<tr><td>42</td><td>Hawaii</td><td>639,474</td><td>0.4%</td><td>11</td><td>North Carolina</td><td>4,411,673</td><td>2.9%</td></tr>
<tr><td>39</td><td>Idaho</td><td>712,219</td><td>0.5%</td><td>12</td><td>Virginia</td><td>3,844,100</td><td>2.6%</td></tr>
<tr><td>5</td><td>Illinois</td><td>6,492,371</td><td>4.3%</td><td>13</td><td>Massachusetts</td><td>3,297,723</td><td>2.2%</td></tr>
<tr><td>14</td><td>Indiana</td><td>3,183,668</td><td>2.1%</td><td>14</td><td>Indiana</td><td>3,183,668</td><td>2.1%</td></tr>
<tr><td>30</td><td>Iowa</td><td>1,505,585</td><td>1.0%</td><td>15</td><td>Washington</td><td>3,148,780</td><td>2.1%</td></tr>
<tr><td>33</td><td>Kansas</td><td>1,381,074</td><td>0.9%</td><td>16</td><td>Tennessee</td><td>3,042,293</td><td>2.0%</td></tr>
<tr><td>26</td><td>Kentucky</td><td>2,123,281</td><td>1.4%</td><td>17</td><td>Arizona</td><td>2,966,218</td><td>2.0%</td></tr>
<tr><td>23</td><td>Louisiana</td><td>2,323,907</td><td>1.5%</td><td>18</td><td>Missouri</td><td>2,964,211</td><td>2.0%</td></tr>
<tr><td>40</td><td>Maine</td><td>675,912</td><td>0.4%</td><td>19</td><td>Maryland</td><td>2,887,076</td><td>1.9%</td></tr>
<tr><td>19</td><td>Maryland</td><td>2,887,076</td><td>1.9%</td><td>20</td><td>Wisconsin</td><td>2,794,346</td><td>1.9%</td></tr>
<tr><td>13</td><td>Massachusetts</td><td>3,297,723</td><td>2.2%</td><td>21</td><td>Minnesota</td><td>2,584,407</td><td>1.7%</td></tr>
<tr><td>8</td><td>Michigan</td><td>5,145,143</td><td>3.4%</td><td>22</td><td>Alabama</td><td>2,346,146</td><td>1.6%</td></tr>
<tr><td>21</td><td>Minnesota</td><td>2,584,407</td><td>1.7%</td><td>23</td><td>Louisiana</td><td>2,323,907</td><td>1.5%</td></tr>
<tr><td>31</td><td>Mississippi</td><td>1,502,475</td><td>1.0%</td><td>24</td><td>Colorado</td><td>2,309,571</td><td>1.5%</td></tr>
<tr><td>18</td><td>Missouri</td><td>2,964,211</td><td>2.0%</td><td>25</td><td>South Carolina</td><td>2,180,852</td><td>1.4%</td></tr>
<tr><td>44</td><td>Montana</td><td>468,762</td><td>0.3%</td><td>26</td><td>Kentucky</td><td>2,123,281</td><td>1.4%</td></tr>
<tr><td>38</td><td>Nebraska</td><td>889,033</td><td>0.6%</td><td>27</td><td>Oregon</td><td>1,830,145</td><td>1.2%</td></tr>
<tr><td>35</td><td>Nevada</td><td>1,185,431</td><td>0.8%</td><td>28</td><td>Connecticut</td><td>1,805,266</td><td>1.2%</td></tr>
<tr><td>41</td><td>New Hampshire</td><td>664,229</td><td>0.4%</td><td>29</td><td>Oklahoma</td><td>1,794,610</td><td>1.2%</td></tr>
<tr><td>10</td><td>New Jersey</td><td>4,469,028</td><td>3.0%</td><td>30</td><td>Iowa</td><td>1,505,585</td><td>1.0%</td></tr>
<tr><td>36</td><td>New Mexico</td><td>979,980</td><td>0.7%</td><td>31</td><td>Mississippi</td><td>1,502,475</td><td>1.0%</td></tr>
<tr><td>3</td><td>New York</td><td>9,927,578</td><td>6.6%</td><td>32</td><td>Arkansas</td><td>1,416,191</td><td>0.9%</td></tr>
<tr><td>11</td><td>North Carolina</td><td>4,411,673</td><td>2.9%</td><td>33</td><td>Kansas</td><td>1,381,074</td><td>0.9%</td></tr>
<tr><td>48</td><td>North Dakota</td><td>318,905</td><td>0.2%</td><td>34</td><td>Utah</td><td>1,229,374</td><td>0.8%</td></tr>
<tr><td>7</td><td>Ohio</td><td>5,876,435</td><td>3.9%</td><td>35</td><td>Nevada</td><td>1,185,431</td><td>0.8%</td></tr>
<tr><td>29</td><td>Oklahoma</td><td>1,794,610</td><td>1.2%</td><td>36</td><td>New Mexico</td><td>979,980</td><td>0.7%</td></tr>
<tr><td>27</td><td>Oregon</td><td>1,830,145</td><td>1.2%</td><td>37</td><td>West Virginia</td><td>927,615</td><td>0.6%</td></tr>
<tr><td>6</td><td>Pennsylvania</td><td>6,399,443</td><td>4.3%</td><td>38</td><td>Nebraska</td><td>889,033</td><td>0.6%</td></tr>
<tr><td>43</td><td>Rhode Island</td><td>556,342</td><td>0.4%</td><td>39</td><td>Idaho</td><td>712,219</td><td>0.5%</td></tr>
<tr><td>25</td><td>South Carolina</td><td>2,180,852</td><td>1.4%</td><td>40</td><td>Maine</td><td>675,912</td><td>0.4%</td></tr>
<tr><td>46</td><td>South Dakota</td><td>390,313</td><td>0.3%</td><td>41</td><td>New Hampshire</td><td>664,229</td><td>0.4%</td></tr>
<tr><td>16</td><td>Tennessee</td><td>3,042,293</td><td>2.0%</td><td>42</td><td>Hawaii</td><td>639,474</td><td>0.4%</td></tr>
<tr><td>2</td><td>Texas</td><td>11,471,789</td><td>7.6%</td><td>43</td><td>Rhode Island</td><td>556,342</td><td>0.4%</td></tr>
<tr><td>34</td><td>Utah</td><td>1,229,374</td><td>0.8%</td><td>44</td><td>Montana</td><td>468,762</td><td>0.3%</td></tr>
<tr><td>49</td><td>Vermont</td><td>316,174</td><td>0.2%</td><td>45</td><td>Delaware</td><td>432,218</td><td>0.3%</td></tr>
<tr><td>12</td><td>Virginia</td><td>3,844,100</td><td>2.6%</td><td>46</td><td>South Dakota</td><td>390,313</td><td>0.3%</td></tr>
<tr><td>15</td><td>Washington</td><td>3,148,780</td><td>2.1%</td><td>47</td><td>Alaska</td><td>320,479</td><td>0.2%</td></tr>
<tr><td>37</td><td>West Virginia</td><td>927,615</td><td>0.6%</td><td>48</td><td>North Dakota</td><td>318,905</td><td>0.2%</td></tr>
<tr><td>20</td><td>Wisconsin</td><td>2,794,346</td><td>1.9%</td><td>49</td><td>Vermont</td><td>316,174</td><td>0.2%</td></tr>
<tr><td>50</td><td>Wyoming</td><td>252,568</td><td>0.2%</td><td>50</td><td>Wyoming</td><td>252,568</td><td>0.2%</td></tr>
<tr><td></td><td></td><td></td><td></td><td></td><td>District of Columbia</td><td>289,383</td><td>0.2%</td></tr>
</table>

Source: Morgan Quitno Press using data from U.S. Bureau of the Census
  "SC-EST2005-AGESEX_RES - State Characteristic Estimates"
  (http://www.census.gov/popest/datasets.html)

IX. SOURCES

American Academy of Physicians Assistants
950 North Washington Street
Alexandria, VA 22314-1552
703-836-2272
www.aapa.org

American Cancer Society, Inc.
1599 Clifton Road, NE.
Atlanta, GA   30329-4251
800-227-2345
www.cancer.org

American Dental Association
211 E. Chicago Ave.
Chicago, IL   60611-2678
312-440-2500
www.ada.org

American Hospital Association
One North Franklin
Chicago, IL   60606-3421
312-422-3000
www.aha.org

American Medical Association
515 North State Street
Chicago, IL   60610
800-621-8335
www.ama-assn.org

American Osteopathic Association
142 East Ontario Street
Chicago, IL   60611
800-621-1773
www.osteopathic.org

Bureau of Labor Statistics
2 Massachusetts Ave., NE
Washington, DC 20212-0001
202-691-6170
www.bls.gov/iif/

Census Bureau
4700 Silver Hill Road
Washington, DC   20233-0001
301-457-2800
www.census.gov

Centers for Disease Control and Prevention
1600 Clifton Road, NE.
Atlanta, GA   30333
800-311-3435
www.cdc.gov

Centers for Medicare and Medicaid Services
7500 Security Boulevard
Baltimore, MD   21244-1850
877-267-2323
www.cms.hhs.gov

Federation of Chiropractic Licensing Boards
5401 W 10th Street, Ste 101
Greeley, CO   80634-4400
970-356-3500
www.fclb.org

Health Resources and Services Admin
Division of Practitioner Data Banks
5600 Fishers Lane
Rockville MD 20857
800-767-6732
Www.hrsa.gov

HealthLeaders/InterStudy
210 12th Avenue South
Nashville TN 37203
888-293-9675
www.hmodata.com

Medical Expenditure Panel Survey
Agency for Healthcare Research and Quality
540 Gaither Road
Rockville MD 20850
301-427-1364
www.meps.ahrq.gov

National Association of State Budget Officers
444 N Capitol Street, NW
Washington DC 20001-1551
202-624-5382
www.nasbo.org

National Center for Health Statistics
U.S. Department of Health and Human Services
3311 Toledo Road
Hyattsville, MD   20782
866-441-NCHS (6247)
www.cdc.gov/nchs/

**National Institute on Alcohol Abuse
and Alcoholism**
National Institutes of Health
5635 Fishers Lane, MSC 9304
Bethesda, MD 20892-9304
301-443-9970
www.niaaa.nih.gov/

National Highway Traffic Safety Admin.
400 Seventh Street, SW
Washington, DC 20590
888-327-4236
www.nhtsa.dot.gov

National Sporting Goods Association
1601 Feehanville Drive, Ste 300
Mt. Prospect, IL   60056
847-296-6742
www.nsga.org

Smoking and Health Office
Centers for Disease Control and Prevention
4770 Buford Hwy, NE., Mail Stop K-50
Atlanta, GA   30341-3717
770-488-5703
www.cdc.gov/tobacco/

Substance Abuse and Mental Health Services Admin.
1 Choke Cherry Road, Room 8-1036
Rockville MD 20857
240-276-2130
www.samhsa.gov

X. INDEX

Abortion
  by age of woman 77-81
  by stage of gestation 82-85
  first time, percent 71
  numbers of 66
  rate of 69
  ratio of 68
  to out-of-state residents 70
  to teenagers 77-81
Accidents, deaths by 169-171
Admissions to community hospitals 202
AIDS
  cases 351-354
  children cases 354
  deaths 112-114
Alcohol consumption 486, 487
Alcohol-induced deaths 184-186
Anesthesiologists 438, 439
Alzheimer's Disease, deaths by 139-141
Assisted reproductive technology
  births from 54-57
  multiple births from 57
  procedures 53
Asthma, percent of adults with 396
Beds, hospital
  average number per hospital 201
  children's hospital 214
  community hospital 199-201
  nursing home 227, 228
  psychiatric hospital 218
  rehabilitation hospital 216
Beer consumption 488, 489
Binge drinkers 495
Births
  by age of mother 32-46
  by assisted reproductive technology 54-57
  by method of delivery 47-52
  by race of mother 7-11, 15-18, 23-26, 37-42
  Hispanic 11, 12, 19, 20, 27, 28
  low birthweight 12-19
  number of 1, 4
  rates 2, 5
  to teenagers 33-44
  to unmarried women 21-28
  to young teens 43,44
Bladder cancer, cases 327, 328
Blood pressure, percent with high 507
Brain cancer, deaths by 119, 120
Breast cancer
  cases 329, 330
  deaths 121, 122
Cancer
  bladder cases 327, 328
  brain deaths 119, 120
  breast (female) 121, 122, 329, 330
  cases, total and by cause 323-350
  cervical cases 346, 347
  colon and rectum 123, 124, 332, 333

Cancer (continued)
  deaths by 115-138, 157-159
  leukemia 125, 126, 335, 336
  liver deaths 127, 128
  lung 129, 130, 337, 338
  lymphoma 131, 132, 339, 340
  ovarian deaths 137, 138
  pancreatic deaths 133, 134
  prostate 135, 136, 341, 342
  skin melanoma cases 344, 345
  uterine cases 349, 350
Cerebrovascular disease, deaths by 142-144
Cervical cancer cases 346, 347
Cesarean births 49-51
Children's hospitals 213, 214
Children's insurance 248, 256-262
Chiropractors 450, 451
Chlamydia cases 390, 391
Cholesterol, percent with high 508
Chronic liver disease, deaths by 145-147
Chronic lower respiratory disease, deaths by
  148-150
Colon and rectum cancer
  cases 332, 333
  deaths 123, 124
Community hospitals
  beds in 199, 200
  number of 189
  per square miles 191
  rate of 190
Community mental health centers 220
Deaths
  by cause 112-188
  infant 95-105
  neonatal 106-111
  numbers of 86, 88, 92
  occupational 187, 188
  rates 87, 89-91, 93, 94
Dentists
  access to 468
  number of 465
  rate of 466
  visits to 509
Diabetes mellitus
  deaths by 151-153
  percent of adults with 397
Distilled spirits, consumption of 492, 493
Doctors (see physicians)
Drinkers, binge 495
Drug plan, Medicare 277, 278
Drugs
  expenditures for 316-318
  use of illicit 501
Emergency medical technicians 475-477
Emergency outpatient visits 208
Expenditures, personal health care 307-309
Employment, health industries 399, 400, 478, 479
Exercise 505, 506

X. INDEX (continued)

Exercise equipment, use of 481
Fatalities, occupational 187, 188
Fertility, rate of 6
Finance, health care 233-322
Firearm injury, deaths from 175-177
For-profit hospitals 197
General surgeons 426, 427
General/family practice physicians 413, 414
Golf, participants in 482
Gonorrhea, cases and rates 392, 393
Government health insurance 254, 260
Government health expenditures 300-305
Graduates of international medical schools
 443, 444
Gynecologists and obstetricians 428, 429
Health insurance (see insurance)
Health Maintenance Organizations (HMOs)
 269-273
Health practitioners
 employment 399, 400
 wages of 401
Health programs, government expenditures for
 303-305
Health care support industries
 employment 478, 479
 wages 480
Heart disease, deaths by 154-156
Hepatitis, cases and rates 359-362
HMOs 269-273
Home health agencies 223
Homicide, deaths by 178-180
Hospices 224, 225
Hospital
 admissions 202
 average stay in 205
 beds 199-201
 community 189-209
 expenditures for care in 310-312
 for profit 197
 government expenditures for 300-302
 in rural areas 194, 195
 in urban areas 192, 193
 non-government not-for-profit 196
 number of 189
 occupancy rate 206
 psychiatric 217, 218
 state and local government-owned 198
Immunizations 385, 386
Infant deaths 95-105
Influenza and pneumonia, deaths by 163-165
Injury, deaths by 166-168
Inpatient days, community hospitals 203
Insurance
 children's health 248, 256-260
 coverage 237-261
 employment-based 234-242, 252, 258
 government 254, 260
 Medicaid 262, 288-299

Insurance (continued)
 Medicare 274-287
 military health 255, 261
 premiums 237-242
 private health 234-236, 251, 257
Internal medicine physicians 419, 420
International medical school graduates 443, 444
Investor-owned hospitals 197
Jogging/running, participants in 483
Kidney disease, deaths from 160-162
Legionellosis, cases and rates 363, 364
Leukemia 125, 126, 335, 336
Licensed practical and vocational nurses 459-461
Liquor, consumption of 492, 493
Liver cancer, deaths 127, 128
Liver disease, deaths by 145-147
Low birth weight births 13-20
Lung cancer
 cases 337, 338
 deaths 129, 130
Lyme disease, cases and rates 365, 366
Malaria, cases and rates 367, 369
Malignant neoplasms (cancers) deaths 157-159
Malpractice, medical payments 233
Managed health care 269-273, 281, 282, 290, 291
Mammograms, prevalence of 331
Medicaid
 children covered by 262
 enrollees 288-291
 expenditures 292-294
 facilities 210-228
 federal match 299
Medicare
 enrollees 274-276
 facilities 210-228
 managed care enrollees 281, 282
 payments 285-287
 physicians 283, 284
 prescription drug plan 277, 278
Melanoma (skin cancer) cases 344, 345
Meningitis, cases and rates 369, 370
Mental health
 access to 442
 community centers 220
 percent with serious mental illness 398
Military health insurance 255, 261
Mortality 86-188
Mothers, teenage 32-44
Motor vehicle accidents, deaths by 172-174
Natality 1-65
Neonatal deaths
 by race 108-111
 number of 106, 108, 110
 rate of 107, 109, 111
Nephritis, deaths by 160-162
Nondrinkers 494
Non-government not-for-profit hospitals 196
Nurses 456-461

X. INDEX (continued)

Nephritis, deaths by 157-159
Nondrinkers 493
Non-government not-for-profit hospitals 193
Nurses 455-460
Nursing homes
 beds 224, 225
 expenditures for care 316-318
 numbers of 223
 occupancy rate 226
 resident rate 227
 population 228
Nutrition, fruits and vegetables intake 511
Obese adults 502, 503
Obstetricians and gynecologists 427, 428
Occupancy rates, hospital 203
Occupational fatalities 184, 185
Operations, surgical 206
Ophthalmologists 429, 430
Optometrists 471-473
Osteopathic physicians 444, 445
Outpatient visits 204
Ovarian cancer deaths 134, 135
Overweight or obese
 percent of adults 501-503
Pap smears, frequency of 348
Paramedics 474-476
Pediatric physicians 420, 421
Pertussis, cases and rates 379, 380
Pharmacists 468-470
Physical therapists 461-463
Physical therapy facilities 218
Physician assistants 452-454
Physicians
 expenditures for services 307-309
 Chiropractic 449-451
 M.D. by age 404, 405
 M.D. by sex 403
 M.D. by specialty 415-440
 M.D. in patient care 406, 407
 M.D. in primary care 408-410
 Medicare participation 278
 Osteopathic 444, 445
 Podiatric 446-448
Plastic surgeons 433, 434
Pneumonia and influenza, deaths by 160-162
Pneumonia vaccinations 384
Podiatrists 446-448
Population, of states A1-A4
Pregnancy rate
 overall 29
 teenage 30, 31
Premiums, average for health insurance 234, 237
Prenatal care 58-65
Prescription drug plan, Medicare 274, 275
Prescription drugs, expenditures for 319-321
Primary care
 access to 411
 physicians in 408-410

Private health insurance 231-233, 248, 254
Prostate cancer
 cases 341, 342
 deaths 132, 133
Providers, health care 398-479
PSA test, percent receiving 343
Psychiatric hospitals 214, 215
Psychiatrists 439, 440
Rabies (animal), cases and rates 369, 370
Rectum and colon cancer
 cases 332, 333
 deaths 120, 121
Rehabilitation hospitals 212, 213
Respiratory diseases, deaths from 145-147
Registered nurses 455-457
Running/jogging, participants 482
Rural health clinics 219
Salmonellosis, cases and rates 373, 374
SCHIP 260-265
Sexually transmitted diseases 385-392
Seatbelt use 513
Shigellosis, cases and rates 375, 376
Skin melanoma cases 344, 345
Smokers
 by sex 496, 497
 former 498
 never have smoked 499
 percent of adult population 495
Specialists, medical 415-440
Sports participation 480-484
State and local government expenditures for health
 297-299
State and local government expenditures for
 hospitals 294-296
State and local government-owned hospitals 195
Suicide, deaths by 178-180
Surgeons 422-434
Surgery centers 216
Surgical operations 206
Swimming, participants 483
Syphilis, cases and rates 391, 392
Teenage births
 by race 37-42
 number of 32
 rate of 33, 36
 to young teens 43, 44
Tennis, participants 484
Tobacco settlement, state funds from 300
Tooth loss 510
Uninsured 240-245
Unmarried women, births to 21-28
Vaccinations 381-384
Vaginal births 47, 48
West Nile Disease, cases and rates 377, 378
Whooping cough, cases and rates 379, 380
Wine consumption 489, 490
Young teens, births to 43, 44

Births and Reproductive Health

Deaths

Facilities

Finance

Incidence of Disease

Providers

Physical Fitness

CHAPTER INDEX

HOW TO USE THIS INDEX

Place left thumb on the outer edge of this page. To locate the desired entry, fold back the remaining page edges and align the index edge mark with the appropriate page edge mark.

Other books by Morgan Quitno Press:

- *State Trends*
- *State Rankings*
- *Crime State Rankings*
- *City Crime Rankings*
- *Education State Rankings*

Call toll free: 1-800-457-0742 or visit us at www.statestats.com